Transnational Litigation in Comparative Perspective

Transnational Litigation in Comparative Perspective

THEORY AND APPLICATION

STEPHEN C. MCCAFFREY
University of Pacific McGeorge School of Law

THOMAS O. MAIN
University of Pacific McGeorge School of Law

New York Oxford
OXFORD UNIVERSITY PRESS
2010

Oxford University Press, Inc., publishes works that further Oxford University's objective of excellence in research, scholarship, and education.

Oxford New York
Auckland Cape Town Dar es Salaam Hong Kong Karachi
Kuala Lumpur Madrid Melbourne Mexico City Nairobi
New Delhi Shanghai Taipei Toronto

With offices in
Argentina Austria Brazil Chile Czech Republic France Greece
Guatemala Hungary Italy Japan Poland Portugal Singapore
South Korea Switzerland Thailand Turkey Ukraine Vietnam

Published by Oxford University Press, Inc.
198 Madison Avenue, New York, New York 10016
http://www.oup.com

Oxford is a registered trademark of Oxford University Press.

ISBN 978-0-19-530904-1

Printing number: 9 8 7 6 5 4 3 2 1
Printed in the United States of America
on acid-free paper

We dedicate this book to our students,
whose perspective, curiosity, and insight remind us
that we are students, too.

CONTENTS

ACKNOWLEDGMENTS

The authors are thankful to all those who helped make this work possible. The expertise and contributions of our international librarians Paul Howard, Jack Schroeder, and James Wirrell are incorporated throughout this book. We have also enjoyed the thoughtful insights and benefitted from the tireless efforts of R.K. Van Every in our faculty support office. Generations of research assistants and students have also made excellent suggestions and important contributions.

In addition, Steve wishes to thank Hans-Henrik Lidgard and Finn Martensen, with whom he taught an earlier version of these materials for a number of years. And he is grateful, as always, for the steadfast support of his wife, Susan. Thom wishes to thank his mentor, Steve Subrin, for his ongoing inspiration, wisdom, and guidance. And he thanks his best friend, Paula, for all that she does, says, and is.

Finally, we thank the judges, professors, and practitioners whose scholarship we have included in this book. Certain specific acknowledgements follow.

ALI/UNIDROIT Principles of Transnational Civil Procedure, copyright 2006 by The American Law Institute for the entire work, and copyright 2006 by UNIDROIT for the Principles only. Reprinted with permission. All rights reserved.

Anderson & Okuda, Translation of Japan's Private International Law: Act on the General Rules of Application of Laws [Ho no Tekyo ni Kansuru Tsusokuho], Law No. 10 of 1898 (as newly titled and amended 21 June 2006), 8 Asian-Pac. L. & Pol'y J. 138 (2006). Reprinted with permission of Asian-Pacific Law and Policy Journal.

Borchers, Comparing Personal Jurisdiction in the United States and the European Community: Lessons for American Reform, 40 Am. J. Comp. L. 121 (1992). Reprinted with permission of American Journal of Comparative Law and Patrick J. Borchers.

Brand & Jablonski, Forum Non Conveniens: History, Global Practice and Future Under the Hague Convention on Choice of Court Agreements (2007). Reprinted with permission of Center for International Legal Education, University of Pittsburgh School of Law.

Currie, Methods and Objectives in the Conflict of Laws, 1959 Duke L.J. 171. Reprinted with permission of Duke Law Journal.

Ehrenzweig, The Lex Fori—Basic Rule in the Conflict of Laws, 58 Mich. L. Rev. 637 (1960). Reprinted from Michigan Law Review, March 1960, Vol. 58, No. 5. Copyright 1960 by The Michigan Law Review Association.

Jingzhou, Enforcing Judgments in the People's Republic of China, International Execution Against Judgment Debtors (2007). Reprinted with permission of Jingzhou Tao.

Fox, The Law of State Immunity (2d ed. 2008). Reprinted with permission of Hazel Fox.

Herrmann, Drawing a Contrast: Interim Measures of Protection, 9 Vindobona J. of Intl. Comml. L. & Arb. 49 (2005). Reprinted with permission of The Vindobona Journal and Anne Herrmann.

Hill, A Policy Analysis of the American Law of Foreign State Immunity, 50 Fordham L. Rev. 155 (1981). Reprinted with permission of the Fordham Law Review.

Juenger, The Recognition Problem, 36 Am. J. Comp. L. 1 (1988). Reprinted with permission of the American Journal of Comparative Law.

Lauterpacht, Aspects of the Administration of International Justice (1991). Reprinted with permission of Elihu Lauterpacht.

McCaffrey, The U.S. Legal System: A Practice Handbook (1983). Reprinted with permission of Wolters Kluwer Law & Business.

Oxman, Direct Discovery and Other Means of Obtaining Evidence Abroad, 37 U. Mia. L. Rev. 733 (1983). Reprinted with permission of Bernard H. Oxman.

Paulsson, Rediscovering the New York Convention: Further Reflections on Chromalloy, Mealey's Int'l Arbitration Reports No. 4 p. 20. Reprinted with permission of Jan Paulsson.

Reed, Recognition and Enforcement of Foreign Judgments (1938). Reprinted by permission of the publishers from Recognition and Enforcement of Foreign Judgments by Horace Emerson Read, pp. 62–63, 112–117, Cambridge, Mass.: Harvard University Press, Copyright ©1938 by the President and Fellows of Harvard College, Copyright © renewed 1966 by Horace Emerson Read.

Restatement (3d) of Foreign Relations Law of the United States. Copyright 1987 by The American Law Institute. Reprinted with permission. All rights reserved.

Schack, Transnational Service of Process: A Call for Uniform and Mandatory Rules, Unif. L. Rev. / Rev. dr. unif. (2001), 827–839. Reprinted with permission of Uniform Law Review.

Smit, International Res Judicata and Collateral Estoppel, 9 UCLA L. Rev. 44 (1962). Repritned with permission of Hans Smit.

Stuerner, Transnational Civil Procedure: Discovery and Sanctions Against Non-Compliance, Unif. L. Rev. / Rev. dr. unif. (2001), 871–886. Reprinted with permission of Uniform Law Review.

Suarez-Mendez, The Agent for Service of Process in Mexico, 35 Int'l Law News 14 (Winter 2006). Reprinted with permission of the American Bar Association.

Subrin, Discovery in Global Perspective: Are We Nuts?, 52 DePaul L. Rev. 299 (2002). Reprinted with permission of DePaul Law Review and Stephen N. Subrin.

Symeonides, Choice of Law in the American Courts in 2007: Twenty-First Annual Survey, 56 Am. J. Comp. L. 243 (2008). Reprinted with permission of American Journal of Comparative Law and Symeon Symeonides.

Twitchell, Why We Keep Doing Business With Doing-Business Jurisdiction, 2001 U. Chi. Legal F. 171. Reprinted with permission of University of Chicago Law School.

Valente, The Man Without a Country Resides at Charles de Gaulle, Wall Street Journal, Oct. 7, 1994. Reprinted with permission of Dow Jones & Company, Inc.

Von Mehren, Recognition and Enforcement of Foreign Judgments, 167 Recueil des Cours 20 (1981). Reprinted with permission of the Academie de Droit International.

Wang & Yao, Notice Service, International Encyclopaedia of Laws (2001). Reprinted with permission of Kluwer Law International.

Weintraub, Choice of Law for Quantification of Damages, 42 Tex. Int'l L.J. 331 (2007). Reprinted with permission of University of Texas at Austin and Russell J. Weintraub.

Zekoll, A Landmark Decision by the German Federal Court of Justice, 30 Colum. J. Transnat'l L. 641 (1992). Reprinted with permission of the Columbia Journal of Transnational Law.

Transnational Litigation in Comparative Perspective

CHAPTER 1

Introduction and Overview

Litigation in domestic courts that has some connection with another country or countries is hardly a new phenomenon, but it is one that is increasing in frequency. Everything from people and diseases to goods and communications are now in constant motion around the globe at a speed, and in quantities, that would not have been imaginable even several decades ago. At the same time, concerns about immigration are leading to calls to build walls and seal borders in some developed countries; international borders are in other ways becoming ever more porous—even almost irrelevant, for some purposes, such as communication via the Internet.

All of this leads to a growing potential for transnational litigation. The term "transnational" is convenient for many of the same reasons cited by Philip C. Jessup, Judge of the International Court of Justice (ICJ) from 1961 to 1970. Jessup famously explored the concept of "transnational law" in a series of lectures at the Yale Law School in 1956. He defined the expression to include: "all law which regulates actions or events that transcend national frontiers. Both public and private international law are included, as are other rules which do not wholly fit into such standard categories.... Transnational situations, then, may involve individuals, corporations, states, organizations of states, or other groups." Philip C. Jessup, Transnational Law 2, 3 (1956). "[T]he term 'international' is misleading since it suggests that one is concerned only with the relations of one nation (or state) to other nations (or states)." Id. at 1. ("State" is the term used in the field of public international law to refer to a nation or country.)

The concept of transnational law recognizes that norms governing state and nonstate actors cannot realistically be conceptualized as being confined in hermetically sealed containers called public and private international law, because humans in their daily interactions often do not observe such boundaries. In this spirit, we use the term "transnational litigation" in its broad sense to refer to disputes before judicial or arbitral tribunals having elements involving more than one country. The disputes may involve only private actors or both state and nonstate actors. We exclude from the scope of the term, and thus from the coverage of this book, disputes between states. Such cases belong to the field of public international law and would be resolved through diplomatic channels, or—with the consent of the states involved—before the ICJ or an arbitral tribunal. A few words about these and other international tribunals may help to distinguish them from the kinds of fora—whether judicial or arbitral—typically involved in transnational litigation.

International tribunals, as that expression is used here, are institutions that are generally established by treaties. They may deal with disputes between states only, between private parties and states, or even between individuals and the international community. Thus there are various kinds of international tribunals. Let us first consider those that hear disputes between states. The one that has already been mentioned, the International Court of Justice (ICJ or World Court), was established by the United Nations Charter, a treaty, as the "principal judicial organ of the United Nations." United Nations Charter, Article 92. The ICJ functions in accordance with its Statute—or constitution—also a treaty, that "forms an integral part of the . . . Charter." Id. As with other international tribunals that hear disputes between states, the jurisdiction of the ICJ is consensual. This means that states may generally decide for themselves whether they wish to submit a dispute to a neutral third party (or even whether they may have violated international law in the first instance). Thus the ICJ adjudicates cases that states bring to it, by mutual consent. That consent may be expressed in a treaty provision ("Any dispute arising out of this agreement may be submitted by either party to the International Court of Justice for resolution"), in a declaration generally accepting the ICJ's jurisdiction in any case brought by another state that has accepted the same obligation, or in a special agreement accepting the Court's jurisdiction in a particular case. In addition, states have established tribunals or dispute resolution processes to adjudicate disputes between themselves in such sectors as the Law of the Sea (the International Tribunal for the Law of the Sea, or ITLOS) and international trade. The latter field has benefited from the development of a particularly effective dispute resolution mechanism—the "Dispute Settlement Body"—under the World Trade Organization (WTO) treaty, with the power to order measures for the enforcement of its judgments.

Turning to international tribunals that have jurisdiction over individuals, those that may come first to mind are international criminal tribunals. The International Criminal Court (ICC) was established by its own Statute in 1998. The ICC tries individuals for crimes under international law including genocide, crimes against humanity, war crimes and the crime of aggression. It may thus be said to represent the interests of the international community. There are also ad hoc international criminal tribunals that have been set up—sometimes by U.N. Security Council resolution—to deal with situations such as those in the former Yugoslavia, Rwanda, and Cambodia. But all international tribunals with jurisdiction to hear disputes involving private parties are not criminal courts. A well-known institution, for example, is the International Center for the Settlement of Investment Disputes (ICSID), an arm of the World Bank established by the 1965 Convention on the Settlement of Investment Disputes between States and Nationals of Other States. ICSID provides facilities for conciliation and arbitration of international investment disputes between private parties and countries in which they have invested.

While the focus of the book is on transnational dispute resolution, perhaps its chief purpose is to sensitize the student and lawyer to issues that may arise in any relationship between different actors that has one or more transnational aspects. Thus the most important lessons that one should take away from the study of these materials may be those involving planning—including everything from planning at the stage of advising a client on the formulation of a standard-form contract to planning when the client walks into your office to announce that a serious dispute has arisen with a business or other counterpart, and that attempts to resolve it through negotiation have failed.

As its title indicates, this book deals principally with litigation. However, its fundamental purpose is to investigate and illuminate how transnational disputes are resolved in different legal systems. The materials are therefore not confined to litigation but consider also the resolution of transnational disputes through arbitration. Rather than devoting a separate chapter to this form of dispute resolution, the book covers arbitration pervasively, in chapters relating to specific issues. Still, understand that we cannot give arbitration the attention that it would receive in a separate course devoted to that subject; fortunately, many law schools offer that course.

An effort has been made to present subjects in the order in which they would generally arise in transnational litigation or arbitration. However, the nature of litigation (and arbitration) is such that many of the subjects are in fact interrelated, so that the lawyer will be thinking about, and perhaps acting upon, more than one issue at the same time. This is perhaps not a terribly efficient way of studying transnational litigation, however; while recognizing that the order of coverage may be somewhat artificial, your editors believe that it is sufficiently characteristic of transnational dispute resolution in general to be used to good advantage for the purpose of exploring the field.

We begin with interim measures of relief. That a transnational litigator considers this matter first may seem counterintuitive and audaciously optimistic. The plaintiff lawyer's concern is that years from now when the litigation is over, their victory will be pyrrhic unless the defendant is able to satisfy or perform the relief ordered by the court. So that lawyer ascertains where the prospective defendant has assets against which a judgment or arbitral award could be enforced, and tries to protect those assets from day one so that they do not become unavailable during the litigation. Chapter 2 explores the tension between the various interests that are at stake at this early stage in litigation and surveys the approach of several states.

In Chapters 3 through 5, we consider where the suit should be filed. Obviously this question is lurking also in Chapter 2 because the availability of interim measures varies by jurisdiction; but we focus here on a different cluster of issues. Specifically, in Chapter 3, we consider personal jurisdiction over foreign defendants. A survey of state practices in this regard shows considerable variation both as to the bases for establishing personal jurisdiction and as to the process for approaching that question. Then, in Chapter 4 we consider the related doctrine of forum non conveniens, and contemplate why some states give their courts discretion to decline to hear cases even when they have jurisdiction. And in Chapter 5 we consider the transactional lawyers' effort to avoid most of these questions by including forum selection clauses in their contract document.

The next two chapters regard unique questions that arise when the defendant is a foreign state or state entity, or when foreign state regulation is involved in the case. Most states recognize the immunity of fellow sovereigns, and in Chapter 6 we survey some of the exceptions to immunity that states have carved out of their once-absolute doctrines. Chapter 7, in turn, focuses on the Act of State doctrine. This doctrine precludes parties from challenging the validity of certain acts of a foreign sovereign—whether or not that sovereign is actually a party to the case.

All legal systems require that the defendant be given timely notice of plaintiff's action. This is accomplished through service of process on the defendant, and is the focus of Chapter 8. As you will see, special problems can arise when the defendant is located in a country other than that of the forum, especially because who may serve process, and how it is served, can vary considerably in different legal systems. Analogous issues arise in the context of gathering evidence abroad, where the contrasts between the approaches followed in different legal systems may be even sharper. In particular, United States-style "discovery" is virtually unknown elsewhere, creating the potential for a clash of legal orders and possibly leading to the nonenforceability of a judgment, unless the lawyer proceeds carefully. Those issues are explored in Chapter 9.

Once jurisdiction has been established and process has been served, it will be necessary to determine the law governing the issues raised by the case. This process or field, which is the focus of Chapter 10, goes by several names, including choice of law, conflict of laws, and private international law. In some systems, it is for the parties to raise the issue that a law other than that of the forum should apply; in other systems this is done by the court. In either case, lawyers in transnational litigation or arbitration must have an appreciation of the possibility that the law of another state will apply and the ability to use rules of choice of law to their clients' advantage insofar as possible.

Finally, once a judgment or arbitral award has been obtained, it must be enforced. The enforcement of foreign judgments and foreign arbitral awards are tackled in Chapters 11 and 12, respectively. As with other issues in the field of transnational litigation, states follow different approaches with regard to the recognition and enforcement of foreign judgments. Looking ahead to the enforcement stage at the earliest phases of litigation planning may in fact alter the strategy to be pursued. For example, in addition to the possible need to obtain protective measures as noted earlier, if the state in which defendant's assets are located does not enforce foreign country judgments in the absence of a treaty obligation to do so, it may be preferable to bring suit there rather than in the state that otherwise appeared optimal. Although there is no global treaty in force on enforcement of judgments, there is such an agreement on arbitral awards (the 1958 New York Convention on the Recognition and Enforcement of Foreign Arbitral Awards). This, of course, does not prevent award-enforcement issues from arising, however.

We conclude with a few words about our general approach to this course. First, understand that the challenges of transnational litigation that we will explore are universal to all states. Second, they are challenges because each topic is the product of some tension among competing norms, values, and interests, without an obvious single right answer. A principal goal of this book is to make sure that you understand the challenges that each state must confront—and to appreciate that states usually have some range of options.

Each chapter in this casebook begins with a hypothetical problem that introduces a fundamental issue of transnational litigation and offers a factual skeleton for understanding the theoretical tensions that frame the challenge. Consider the hypotheticals deliberately and thoughtfully; try to identify and understand your intuitive response to the questions presented. Then use the materials in the remainder of the chapter to confront or verify that preliminary response.

This book undertakes a comparative approach to ensure that you appreciate the many dimensions of the challenge and the diverse range of possible solutions. Rather than focusing on the doctrine in any single jurisdiction, we want you to have the tools to understand (and to question) the approach of all legal systems. To be sure, there is a price for this approach: we are unable to mine the depths of the doctrinal minutiae of any single jurisdiction. (This text is no substitute for a treatise.) Yet we are confident that once you are in practice—whatever the jurisdiction and however the law might then have evolved between now and then—you will be able to frame the right research questions, to recognize an answer when you find it, and to benefit your clients with advocacy that draws upon a more nuanced appreciation of policy choices and alternatives.

CHAPTER 2

Protective Measures

A. Introduction

A prime concern in transnational litigation is the time delays and uncertainties that are involved in every step of the procedure: serving foreign defendants may take time; the competence of the forum may be challenged on various grounds; the process of gathering evidence could be elaborate; the process of executing a judgment may be cumbersome. Indeed, every chapter in this book reveals the complexity and time-consuming nature of transnational litigation. Accordingly, it is wise to anticipate that such litigation may take even longer than traditional domestic litigation, which itself can be subject to substantial time delays.

It is therefore important for the lawyer to consider at an early stage of the procedure whether there are reasons to believe that the final enforcement of the judgment may be disturbed or prevented because of events that may occur during the litigation. In other words, there is a risk that, even if a favorable judgment is obtained, it will be unenforceable or meaningless because the judgment debtor has taken steps to remove assets or otherwise obstruct enforcement. In such cases, interim measures of relief, or protective measures, if available, may help to ensure enforceability of a judgment (or arbitral award). Interim measures of relief could be in rem orders taken against property or in personam orders directed at individuals. In rem is a technical term used to designate proceedings or actions instituted against particular property (the res). Such proceedings or actions are distinguished from those against individuals or legal entities, which are said to be in personam. Examples of provisional measures include: attaching, seizing, or arresting an asset; requiring the deposit of property; entering a record in a public registry; making an order to prohibit some activity, service, or other conduct; making an order to require some activity, service, or other conduct; and voiding or suspending acts or agreements.

One common concern leading to a request for preliminary relief is that defendant will not have the funds to satisfy a final judgment. In some jurisdictions a plaintiff may obtain some security to minimize this risk. Consider the following hypothetical.

The Problem: A Heavy Toll*

The Government of Mexico initiated a program to modernize its highways. Rather than fund the project with public money, the Government elicited private financing by allowing the builders and operators to charge tolls. Grupo Mexicano de Desarrollo, S.A. ("GMD"), a Mexican corporation, was hired to build the roads. GMD is a large construction company that is engaged in a broad range of public works and infrastructure projects in Mexico and throughout Latin America, including bridges, tunnels, dams, and airports.

With some of the highways completed and others still under construction, the Mexican economy suffered a severe downturn, and toll road traffic and revenues fell far below anticipated levels. To raise the money it needed to continue construction, GMD issued $250 million of unsecured notes. The largest purchaser of these notes was Alliance Bond Fund ("the Fund"), an investment fund in New York.

Within a couple of years of the bond offering, GMD was in serious financial trouble and stopped making the interest payments that were due on the notes. In addition to the notes, GMD owed more than $450 million to other creditors, including the Mexican government, Mexican banks, trade creditors, and former employees.

Sympathetic to the plight of GMD (and still desiring a modern intercity highway network), the Government of Mexico promised $300 million worth of government-backed notes ("Government Notes") to GMD. With this promise, GMD undertook to restructure its debt, reduce its costs, and seek additional equity contributions in order to improve its financial situation. GMD assigned its right to $20 million of the Government Notes to a Mexican trust that would fund the cost of severance packages for terminated employees. GMD also pledged $130 million of the Government Notes to satisfy tax liabilities. GMD further announced that it was nearing an agreement with several Mexican banks to reduce its $250 million bank debt. In addition, GMD was negotiating with the Fund to restructure that debt, but those efforts failed to produce an agreement.

Before GMD could pledge any more of the Government Notes to the Mexican banks or any other creditor, the Fund exercised its contractual right to demand immediate payment on the notes, filed a lawsuit in the Southern District of New York seeking damages, and requested a preliminary injunction. The requested injunction would enjoin GMD from using the proceeds of the Government Notes. GMD has no defense on the merits of the breach of contract claim. GMD has no

---

* This hypothetical is based on *Grupo Mexicano de Desarrollo S.A. v. Alliance Bond Fund*, 527 U.S. 308 (1999).

assets or operations in the United States, but it consented to personal jurisdiction in New York as part of the financing arrangement with the Fund.

Should a trial court have authority to prohibit GMD from using the Government Notes? You may assume that distribution of the Government Notes would irreparably harm the Fund because any final judgment is ultimately likely to be uncollectible.

B. Doctrinal Justifications

Interim measures of relief, also called protective, conservatory or provisional measures, provide a plaintiff with an immediate if temporary protection of rights or property pending a decision on the merits. Such measures may seem indispensable to plaintiffs if a judgment is later to have any practical significance. Yet measures interfering with a defendant's use of assets can also create enormous settlement leverage and unjust coercion, resulting in hardships for defendants. Thus, the measures available in a particular jurisdiction typically strike some balance between the interests of plaintiffs and putative creditors, on one hand, and defendants and putative debtors, on the other.

Before considering the significance of having the creditors and debtors located in different countries, it is worthwhile to contemplate the choices that every legal system must make about ordering protective measures even in the purely domestic context. Consider, for example, a lawsuit filed by plaintiff P against defendant D.

One threshold matter concerns the types of preliminary relief that the court can award P. Can the court require D to make an interim payment to P or post a bond in P's favor? Can the court require D to perform certain acts during the pendency of the litigation or can it only preserve the status quo? Can the court seize assets that belong to D and give them to P?

Next, consider whether the available types of preliminary relief should vary depending on the substance and/or size of the lawsuit. Will judges have broad discretion to tailor the relief to the unique circumstances presented or does the potential for misuse of such authority warrant doctrinal certainty and predictability?

Of course a legal system that offers any preliminary relief to plaintiffs must be concerned also with abuse of that process by plaintiffs. Indeed, plaintiffs can enjoy significant practical and tactical advantages by interfering with defendant's conduct or assets by simply initiating a lawsuit and requesting preliminary relief. Accordingly, plaintiffs must demonstrate their entitlement to provisional relief. And the core indicia of entitlement common to most legal systems are (1) the likelihood that plaintiff will ultimately prevail; and (2) the need for preliminary relief.

If a court were certain that P would ultimately prevail, it would make sense, in most cases, to require D to provide the relief to which P was entitled as soon as possible. (Why delay justice to P, and why allow D to evade its responsibility?) But the ability to predict whether P will ultimately prevail is, of course, highly speculative. After all, the many stages of litigation—pleadings, motions, gathering evidence, trials, and the like—serve some purpose in the search for truth.

A second factor at the core of this inquiry for most systems is the genuineness of the need for preliminary relief. There is less (or maybe even no) need for preliminary relief if P can be awarded final relief, in the event she ultimately prevails, that will fully remedy the wrong she has suffered. If P wins a money judgment that includes a generous award of prejudgment interest, we might imagine that she will, with final relief, be made whole. But conversely, there may be a compelling need for preliminary relief if the court will be unable to remedy the wrong with final relief even if P ultimately wins. For example, the demolition of an historical monument, the destruction of an ecosystem, the inability to compete in an election, or the denial of access to an elementary school may be the consequences of wrongs that simply cannot be undone with damage judgments and interest payments.

These two core factors are manifest in the jurisprudence of all legal sytems through a variety of elements, doctrines, and measures, that we collapse here into a handful of markers. Appreciate how each of these markers introduces a continuum of approaches—a range of options that makes it easier or harder for plaintiffs to obtain preliminary relief. Also, understand that it is the combination of these markers that the system must calibrate effectively; dialing one of the markers "up" might, in turn, allow another marker to be dialed "down."

Plaintiff must demonstrate some possibility of success on the merits	Plaintiff must offer prima facie evidence of wrongdoing
Proceedings may occur ex parte and with little or no judicial involvement	Defendants must have notice and opportunity to be heard before a judge
At later stage, court may order sanctions upon proof that plaintiff acted in bad faith by requesting preliminary relief	At preliminary stage, plaintiff required to post a bond ($2x) to secure damages that might be caused by imposing the precautionary measure
Plaintiff to demonstrate that they may suffer from delay in relief	Court must find irreparable injury absent the requested provisional remedy
With regard to selecting the form of the relief, court's concern is maximum protection for plaintiff's interest	Preference for measures that are least burdensome to defendant who, after all, is not an adjudicated wrongdoer
Court inclined to grant preliminary relief to ensure the integrity and legitimacy of a final judgment	With respect for other branches and systems, court relucant to use awesome power of equity prior to full adjudication

One additional question that arises in the context of transnational litigation is whether the court can (and should) grant preliminary relief that is extraterritorial. For example, the bank account that would be the subject of a freeze order may be in another jurisdiction. Or an order requiring the defendant to perform certain acts may involve defendant's overseas operations. Or the alleged infringement that would be enjoined may be occurring, in whole or in part, in another jurisdiction. We begin to explore some of these issues in the following excerpt.

Sir Nicholas Browne-Wilkinson, The New Technologies

25 Israel L. Rev. 145, 145–151 (1991)

In this paper I want to address certain practical problems which I encounter in my daily work as a trial judge.

I sit in the Chancery Division of the High Court in London. Over the years the work of that Division has changed fundamentally. It no longer consists of endless disputes about the construction and administration of trusts and wills, the descendants of Jarndyce v. Jarndyce in Dickens' Bleak House. Instead, there is a mix of work, financial, property, intellectual property and company litigation. A surprising, and unacceptable, amount of such work now involves dishonest conduct of one kind or another. But although the nature of the work has changed, in general the jurisdiction of the court has not. As with the courts of all countries, the order of the English High Court is effective only within the local area of national sovereignty, England and Wales, and over people operating within that area. Just as it did over 600 years ago, the jurisdiction of the High Courts stops running at Dover and Lands End.

Whilst concepts of judicial jurisdiction have stood still, the world has not. Aircraft enable people to be out of the jurisdiction in 20 minutes. Satellite communications mean that information and news is instantly available worldwide. The Fax enables written instructions to be given and received across the world virtually instantaneously. Electronic transfers of funds can be made at the touch of a button. Whilst lawyers are still trying to understand the problem and find a judge to make the necessary order, the snatched child is on its way to the United States of America, confidential information is being published in Australia, the fruits of financial fraud have been transferred to a numbered account of Switzerland, bearer shares transferred from an English company to a Panamanian or Dutch Antilles company.

The growing internationalism of the world community is reflected in the work of the court. I estimate that well over half the work I do now involves international considerations: Jarndyce v. Jarndyce has become Jarndyce (International Holdings) SA v. Jarndyce (UK) Limited. Thus in May 1991 I did not deal with a single case which was purely internal and domestic to the United Kingdom. There was a dispute between the London based former flight attendants of Pan Am on the one hand and their new American employers and American Trades Unions on the other; a dispute between the Nissan Motor Company and its United Kingdom distributors; a problem arising from the fraudulent investment of funds by a London finance house through its Gibraltar subsidiary. Simultaneously, in the Chancery Division alone, there were being heard disputes relating to the worldwide rights in the name "Apple," claims by an Arab bank against an allegedly dishonest former employee and similar claims by two other foreign banks against foreign employees....

Where are such deals made? What is their proper law? Which countries' courts will have jurisdiction over them? These are problems of a new kind presenting great challenges to courts sitting in their territorial jurisdiction. However, they will in due course no doubt be solved by the development of the existing rules of Private International Law. The courts of each country will, ex post facto, decide which courts have jurisdiction and what system of law to apply. In solving problems of this kind, problems of substantive law, the court will be able to adjudicate at comparative leisure on what has happened in the past. Although speed of resolution is of course desirable, it is not essential. There will be time for the process of trial and judicial consideration to take place. The speed and methodology of the new technological systems raise new problems for adjudication: they do not dictate the speed and methodology of the judicial solution to those problems.

The field of interim relief is quite different. In that field, the speed at which modern technology works is in my view threatening the roots of justice itself. In many cases, unless there is some court which can by interlocutory order hold the status quo before it is changed, eventual justice becomes impossible....

[T]he same technology which has provided the impetus towards multi-national corporations has provided an equally strong impetus towards international fraud on a very large scale. In such cases, the fruits of the crime are usually concealed in a network of companies incorporated in many different jurisdictions: one enterprising French lawyer has even written a textbook on how to achieve this. A typical structure has the following features. At the top of the pile there will be a Liechtenstein Anstalt. The beneficial ownership of an Anstalt is not known and cannot be discovered under Liechtenstein law. Moreover its beneficial ownership can be changed at will by "the Founder." The assets of the Anstalt consist of cash (which is deposited in numbered accounts in Switzerland) and bearer shares controlling companies incorporated in havens all over the world, say Panama. The Panamanian companies in turn will hold shares either directly or indirectly through chains of subsidiaries in the companies directly implicated in the fraud.

Such a structure presents almost insuperable difficulties to those seeking to recover the proceeds of the fraud. First they do not know, and they have no means of discovering, the structure lying behind the only entity of which they know, the company that committed the fraud. Second, even if they discover the structure, the fruits of the fraud may be vested in any one of the companies in the chain, those companies being incorporated in many different jurisdictions. In what court should proceedings be brought? Which court, if any, can give an effective remedy? Third, if proceedings are threatened in any one jurisdiction against any one of the companies, the assets of that company can be transferred out of the jurisdiction of that court instantaneously by electronic transfers of funds. Alternatively, faxed directions can be given to transfer the bearer shares which control the company. The assets have flown the jurisdiction before the court can do anything. Fourth, if those defrauded do discover the existence of the Anstalt at the top of the pile, they have to sue it in Liechtenstein. Although Liechtenstein ostensibly conforms to the normal rules of international law by enforcing the judgments of foreign courts of competent jurisdiction, it attaches an important proviso: the judgment of the foreign court will only be enforced if the defendant does not object!...

Given the territorial limits of each court's jurisdiction, the unraveling of the beneficial ownership and the recovery of the funds representing the fruits of the fraud require the intervention of the local courts where each of the companies or individuals are incorporated or resident or where the assets are to be found. The ability of the fraudster to switch the local situation of assets or bearer shares virtually instantaneously means that the fraudster can keep one jump ahead of the courts of any one jurisdiction by switching the funds to another jurisdiction.

Eric S. Rein, International Fraud: Freeze, Seize, and Retrieve

116 Banking L.J. 144 (1999)

As technology evolves at exponential rates, it becomes easier to transfer funds faster using means undetectable in attempts to fraudulently conceal assets.... International fraud is a successful and thriving business. The popularity of electronic fund transfers authorized by telephone, computer or facsimile has caused the movement of money to occur more rapidly. The widespread use of nominee companies and offshore accounts, the increased sophistication of legitimate financial transactions, and the reluctance of bankers and other professionals from inquiring into the financial affairs have contributed to the ease and speed with which substantial funds can be transferred from country to country, while concealing the source and identity of those who control the transactions....

Very sophisticated techniques have been utilized to conceal assets. For instance, a fraudster transfers funds to a cooperative business associate who has an international business. The business associate disguises those funds as a legitimate-seeming payment to one of his companies. The business associate then transfers the funds by wire transfer to an offshore account, commingled with funds for the purchase of legitimate imports. Those imports' value are then inflated to conceal the transfers. Assets have now been hidden. A successful recovery of those assets requires a focused, but rapid, effort to identify, seize and freeze the assets.

In the problem that opened this chapter, the New York federal district court has personal jurisdiction over the Mexican defendant, but the defendant's pertinent assets—the Government Notes—are located in Mexico. The facts and procedural history presented in this Problem track very closely *Grupo Mexicano de Desarrollo, S.A. v. Alliance Bond Fund,* a case that appeared before the United States Supreme Court in 1999. The materials in this section exploring the doctrinal justifications for interim protective measures include two amicus briefs that were filed in that case, beginning with one in support of the Fund. (For purposes of appreciating the procedural posture of this case, we note that the federal trial court granted the preliminary injunction, and the U.S. Court of Appeals for the Second Circuit affirmed.)

United States Supreme Court Amicus Brief: The Securities Indus. Assoc. and the Emerging Markets Traders Assoc. in Support of Respondents

Grupo Mexicano de Desarrollo, S.A. v. Alliance Bond Fund, Inc.

Feb. 16, 1999; 1999 WL 73810 at *3–*10

The rule ... that a federal court in an action at law for money damages lacks power to enjoin a defendant's dissipation of assets would, if adopted, do serious harm to global capital markets and to United States investors in those markets....

The importance of international capital transactions in which foreign entities raise capital in the United States securities markets is enormous. In 1997, non-United States issuers registered over $100 billion in securities for public offering in the United States. More than 1,000 companies from 55 countries had SEC reporting obligations in the United States by the end of 1997, the last year for which statistics are available.

But foreign registrants represent only a small portion of foreign equity trading. In 1997, the value of global equity trading hit $19.5 trillion, a 43% increase over the record $13.6 trillion traded in 1996; markets in the United States accounted for 52.4% of that trading. Moreover, gross sales of foreign bonds by foreigners to U.S. residents exceeded $1.999 trillion and gross sales of foreign stocks and bonds together exceeded $2.295 trillion. Over $15.6 billion in Mexican bonds alone were sold to residents of the United States in 1997. Between 1994 and 1997, United States residents increased their net purchases (purchases minus sales) of foreign bonds by 422%.

The growth in international capital transactions has brought and continues to bring enormous benefits to United States investors and to people all over the world. For investors in this country, of course, this trend has given rise to greater opportunities for diversification and higher yields than are available through instruments sold exclusively by United States issuers. From the foreign issuers' perspective, in many countries, including those lately emerged or still emerging from conditions of dire poverty, capital for development is now available on an unprecedented scale. The home countries of issuers that are now benefiting from access to the United States' capital markets include Colombia, Malaysia, Lebanon, Liberia, Zaire and Syria.... The list of emerging market countries whose nationals have sold securities in 1997 alone includes: Argentina, Bahamas, Bermuda, Bosnia, Brazil, British West Indies, Bulgaria, Chile, Colombia, Croatia, Czech Republic, Ecuador, Egypt, Ghana, Guatemala, Herzegovina, Hungary, Indonesia, Israel, Jamaica, Lebanon, Liberia, Malaysia, Mexico, Montenegro, Morocco, Netherlands Antilles, Palestine, Panama, People's Republic of China, Peru, Philippines, Poland, Romania, Russia, Serbia, Singapore, Slovenia, Syria, Thailand, Trinidad and Tobago, Turkey, Uruguay, Venezuela, and Zaire.... It is surely in the interests of both the United States and the developing world to foster the growth of these markets by assuring that participants in them have the benefit of modern and effective legal remedies.

Today's international capital markets are extraordinarily "efficient" in two senses of the term. First, they are efficient in the speed at which transactions can be accomplished. Literally billions of dollars can be moved from one country to another almost instantaneously, by computer transmission. The markets are also "efficient" in their assessment of information relevant to risk. Cf. Basic Inc. v. Levinson, 485 U.S. 224, 246–47 & n. 24 (1988) (recognizing that "[r]ecent empirical studies have tended to confirm Congress' premise that the market price of shares traded on well developed markets reflects all publicly available information"). Investors calculate their risks with great precision, and insist on a return on investment that compensates them for that risk. This means that anything that needlessly increases investors' risks increases the cost of raising money in the United States capital markets and makes it that much more difficult for those markets to perform their function.

The power of courts in the United States to grant injunctive relief against the dissipation of assets, wherever located, is an important underpinning of the legal regime in which international capital markets operate.... [If courts lack that authority, the risk of default and dissipation] is palpable and must be factored into every transaction.

When a foreign issuer does default and then dissipates its assets, petitioners concede that attachment and similar remedies will generally be useless, since the debtor's assets will be located in foreign countries, or can be moved to foreign countries in a matter of seconds. And when the debtor and its assets are outside the country, the United States bankruptcy laws are not effective to prevent discrimination among creditors, as they are in disputes with United States parties on both sides.

Even sophisticated investors cannot adequately protect themselves through contract. After all, here respondents were induced to invest through promises by the issuer to submit to the personal jurisdiction of the United States courts and to treat the United States investors on a pari passu basis with its unsecured home country creditors. Yet such contractual provisions would prove completely unavailing against any financially beleaguered foreign issuer which, out of dishonesty or by virtue of local political and economic pressures, decides systematically to favor local creditors. When the problem of discrimination in favor of the debtor's home-country creditors arises, it can be dealt with effectively only by [enjoining the defendant]. If the court were [not empowered to issue such relief], some investors will conclude that overseas investment is imprudent, and many will demand a higher rate of return to compensate for the increased risk of uncollectibility. This will foreseeably curtail—and in some cases altogether deny—access to the United States capital markets by foreign issuers on reasonable economic terms....

"We live in a time of rapidly growing commercial and financial sophistication and it behooves the courts to adapt their practices to meet the current wiles of those defendants who are prepared to devote as much energy to making themselves immune to the court orders as to resist the making of such orders on the merits of their case." Derby & Co. v. Weldon, [1989] 1 All Eng. Rep. 1002, 1007 (C.A.)....

United States Supreme Court Amicus Brief: The Dominican Republic in Support of Petitioners

Grupo Mexicano de Desarrollo, S.A. v. Alliance Bond Fund, Inc.

Jan. 14, 1999; 1999 WL 23655 at *3–*16

Introduction

[T]his Court has traditionally recognized that comity and the concerns underlying it must be taken into account when United States courts decide disputes that involve foreign nations, foreign persons or foreign property. In deference to these concerns, this Court has determined in a variety of contexts that, even where judicial power may exist in the abstract, its exercise should be limited in order to avoid affronts to other nations that also have an interest in a party to, or the subject matter of, a dispute with transnational connections....

The effects of [an extraterritorial freeze] cannot be minimized. [Vesting courts with such authority] allows any creditor who can obtain personal jurisdiction in the United States over a foreign debtor—whether under a debt instrument or otherwise—single-handedly to prevent that debtor from either voluntarily restructuring its indebtedness to its local creditors or acting consistently with the legal priorities and obligations imposed upon it by local law with respect to the repayment of its local debts. [This] threatens to entangle United States courts in the reorganization of financially troubled foreign corporations even when... they have no property in the United States and therefore cannot be the subject of either plenary or ancillary proceedings under the United States Bankruptcy Code.

Since the Mexican debt crisis of 1982, numerous countries throughout the world have been required to restructure both their public sector and private sector debt in order to deal with their own economic problems and the fluctuations of the global economy. [Granting courts the authority to impose an extraterritorial freeze] would decisively alter the balance among the parties to such restructurings, by allowing any dissatisfied creditor not merely to obtain a judgment for money due to it, but for all intents and purposes to execute upon that judgment through the use of extraterritorial injunctions directed at the debtor's foreign assets, in derogation of the rights of creditors who do not have the benefit of a United States court order. Nor would the [authority] be limited to private sector foreign debtors, for its reasoning could be employed against sovereign debtors as well....

Every Nation Enjoys the Right to Exercise Sovereign Power Within its Territorial Boundaries

This Court has always approached extraterritorial extensions of the powers of the United States with caution. This caution is founded on both considerations of prudence and principles of sovereignty embedded in the law of nations, which has always been considered to be a part of the jurisprudence of the United States. See The Paquete Habana, 175 U.S. 677, 700 (1900). Under the classic view of sovereignty, each nation has the exclusive authority to exercise governmental power within its territorial borders:

> The jurisdiction of the nation within its own territory is necessarily exclusive and absolute; it is susceptible of no limitation, not imposed by itself. Any restriction upon it, deriving validity from an external source, would imply a diminution of its sovereignty, to the extent of the restriction, and an investment of that sovereignty, to the same extent, in that power which would impose such restriction. All exceptions, therefore, to the full and complete power of a nation, within its own territories, must be traced up to the consent of the nation itself.

The Schooner Exch. v. McFaddon, 11 U.S. [7 Cranch] 116, 135 (1812) (Marshall, C.J.); see also Hilton v. Guyot, 159 U.S. 113, 163 (1895) ("No law has any effect, of its own force, beyond the limits of the sovereignty from which its authority is derived."). There can be no doubt here that the property over which the Second Circuit effectively exercised dominion, albeit in the procedural form of an injunction directed in personam at the property's foreign owner, was subject to the sovereign power of Mexico, not to the power of the United States.

Exercising Judicial Remedies Extraterritorially Implicates Principles of Foreign Sovereign and International Comity

The extraterritorial exercise of sovereign power—whether legislative or judicial—threatens to infringe on the sovereign power of another nation, thereby ultimately undermining the sovereignty of all states, including the extraterritorial actor. This Court has therefore moved with circumspection and care in dealing with situations in which the exercise of the power of the United States may result in such infringement. In construing the exercise of the legislative power embodied in Acts of Congress, the Court has held, for example, that legislation prescribing standards of conduct is always to be construed not to regulate beyond the territorial boundaries of the United States unless a contrary legislative intent appears. Steele v. Bulova Watch Co., 344 U.S.280, 282, 285 (1952). This judicial presumption derives from this Court's desire to protect against "unintended clashes between [U.S.] laws and those of other nations which could result in international discord." EEOC v. Arabian Am. Oil Co., 499 U.S. 244, 248 (1991).

Likewise, the Court has consistently ruled that exercise of the judicial power of the United States should be informed by a respect for the laws and interests of other sovereigns. As the Court long ago recognized:

> The extent to which the law of one nation, as put in force within its territory, whether by executive order, by legislative act, or by judicial decree, shall be allowed to operate within the dominion of another nation, depends upon what our greatest jurists have been content to call "the comity of nations."
>
> Hilton, 159 U.S. at 163

The principle of international comity refers to the "spirit of cooperation in which a domestic tribunal approaches the resolution of cases touching the laws and interests of other sovereign states." Société Nationale Industrielle Aérospatiale v. United States District Court, 482 U.S. 522, 544 n. 27 (1987).

> Comity is not just a vague political concern favoring international cooperation when it is in our interest to do so. Rather it is a principle under which judicial decisions reflect the systemic value of reciprocal tolerance and goodwill.
>
> Id. at 555 (Blackmun, J., dissenting)

The controlling considerations are the interacting interests of the United States and of foreign countries, and in assessing them we must move with the circumspection appropriate when this Court is adjudicating issues inevitably entangled in the conduct of our international relations. Romero v. International Terminal Operating Co., 358 U.S. 354, 383 (1959). This Court has admonished the lower federal courts to "demonstrate due respect for any special problem confronted by the foreign litigant on account of its nationality or the location of its operations, and for any sovereign interest expressed by a foreign state." Société Nationale, 482 U.S. at 546.

This sensitivity to the sovereign interests of other nations is reflected in a variety of constraints that this Court has recognized on the exercise of judicial power: the doctrines of sovereign immunity, ... act of state, choice-of-law rules, and comity all reflect the self-interest of the United States in respecting, at the overlap of territorial boundaries, the relevant interests of foreign nations. In light of these self-imposed constraints, the Court has developed an entire body of case law for the purpose of guiding the legitimate exercise of judicial power where the potential for conflict with another sovereign exists. See, e.g., The Bremen v. Zapata Off-Shore Co., 407 U.S. 1, 15 (1972) (deferring to competence of foreign court selected by parties to adjudicate claim); Romero, 358 U.S. 354 (declining to impose Jones Act liability on foreign ship where vessel merely passed through U.S. territorial waters); Mitsubishi Motors Corp. v. Soler Chrysler-Plymouth, Inc., 473 U.S. 614 (1985) (deferring to competence of arbitral tribunal); Piper Aircraft Co. v. Reyno, 454 U.S. 235 (1981) (deferring to competence of foreign courts to resolve transnational claims).[4] ...

Exercising Judicial Control Over Extraterritorial Assets in the Context of a Financially Troubled Foreign Company Threatens to Conflict with Local Authority and Reorganization Regimes

The effect of the district court's order was first to freeze—and later to order the transfer of—the petitioners' principal assets in Mexico, thereby making their property unavailable to pay claims of petitioners' other creditors, including tax claims

---

[4] These constraints are, of course, in addition to those required by constitutional principles of federalism in the interaction of United States courts with the sovereignty of the states and state judiciaries.

by the Mexican government, severance claims of Mexican employees and claims of Mexican bank creditors, that in the aggregate were considerably greater than the claim held by respondents. The record reflects that petitioners were in financial distress and were seeking to negotiate the restructuring of their debt to Mexican and foreign creditors alike. The record also reflects that petitioners' five largest creditors, the Mexican government, Mexican banks, Mexican financial institutions, trade creditors and terminated employees, held obligations with a value six times greater than those held by the group of United States creditors whose interests the district court's order was designed to protect. Id.

Many nations, including Mexico and a number of other countries in Latin America, do not have a statutory framework like Chapter 11 of the Bankruptcy Code for reorganizing financially troubled companies under judicial supervision rather than liquidating them.[5] Instead, companies in these countries that need to restructure their debts must typically conduct private negotiations with all interested parties to arrive at a consensual solution. Litigation remains a possibility in these countries for enforcing creditor rights, but the practical impediments to realizing on the debtor's limited assets in most cases channel creditor choice toward either negotiation with the debtor or forcing liquidation proceedings. Such negotiations are of course informed by the statutory priorities mandated by the debtor-creditor laws and insolvency laws of the debtor's sovereign, which would be applied if liquidation occurred.

These priorities, and more generally, the debtor-creditor regimes of which they are a part, reflect the policies of the nation where the debtor and its property are located. With their preference for voluntary debt restructurings negotiated between a debtor and its creditors, whether domestic or foreign, they are entitled to the same respect, as regards property within that nation's territory, that the United States would expect United States bankruptcy policies and priorities to be accorded by foreign sovereigns with respect to property in this country.

The Second Circuit's extraterritorial freeze decision is the antithesis of this kind of respect for the operation of foreign legal regimes within the territories of foreign states. By preventing payment of foreign debts to foreign creditors out of the debtor's foreign property, it disregards the debt priority schemes of foreign law. More generally, it subverts the reorganization regimes of foreign countries with respect to assets within their jurisdiction. If a United States court can exercise the power to freeze all assets of a foreign company, based solely on its submission to personal jurisdiction with respect to a particular credit agreement, the court effectively freezes the restructuring process for all creditors, irrespective of their priority or status. The Court of Appeals' decision permits United States creditors to hold

---

[5] *E.g.,* The Dominican Republic, Guatemala, Uruguay, and Chile. Mexico, for example, has a provision for suspension of payments (suspension de pagos) as part of its bankruptcy law, see Mexican Bankruptcy Law Arts. 408–411, but it is seldom used because a suspension request must be accompanied by a completed restructuring agreement and is otherwise subject to significant practical restrictions.

the reorganization process of a foreign company hostage, even when, as here, most of its creditors (and all of its priority creditors) are foreign and no resolution of its debts would be possible in any United States proceeding.[6]...

As a general principle of Mexican law, as is the case in many countries,[7] before a company is declared bankrupt by a judicial authority,[8] it is free to manage its assets and to pay any of its bona fide creditors to the exclusion of others. There is no suggestion in the record that any of petitioners' Mexican creditors were not bona fide, and the petitioners were therefore entirely within their rights in paying the legitimate claims of these creditors. Indeed, under New York law as well, which governed the notes held by respondents, it is completely permissible for a debtor, outside of bankruptcy, to pay one bona fide creditor rather than another. The only body of law that would proscribe an insolvent debtor's paying one creditor in preference to another would be the United States Bankruptcy Code (and only to the extent of providing, in certain circumstances, for the debtor in possession or bankruptcy trustee to recover preferential payments for the benefit of all of its unsecured creditors, see 11 U.S.C. § 547), but petitioners neither were nor could have been the subject of any case or proceeding under the Bankruptcy Code.

Not only were any payments that may have preferred certain bona fide creditors over others permitted under the laws of Mexico and most other countries, including the United States, but the "priority of creditors" that the Court of Appeals decried was required, to a significant extent, by Mexican law. Section XXIII of Article 123 of the Mexican Constitution expressly creates a super-priority in favor of workers and employees for salaries due during the year preceding bankruptcy. In addition, the Mexican fiscal code establishes a priority in favor of tax liabilities. C.F.F. Art. 149.[9] These types of legislative priorities in allocating the limited assets

---

6 Because, as in this case, litigation over loan agreements will typically not support federal question jurisdiction, the only creditors who could sue a private foreign debtor in federal court and obtain the kind of preliminary relief granted here are United States citizens, as the joinder of any alien creditors as plaintiffs would defeat diversity jursdiction. 28 U.S.C. § 1332(a)(2). Inasmuch as foreign debtors are likely to have at least as many foreign creditors as United States creditors, no United States district court will have before it all the creditors necessary to effect a complete resolution of the debtor's obligations, even if it were otherwise appropriate for a district court to act in effect as an insolvency tribunal for a foreign debtor that could not be the subject of United States bankruptcy proceedings.

7 *E.g.*, Argentina: Civil Code Arts. 31, 35, 52, 53, Bankruptcy Law Arts. 16, 107; Chile: Civil Code Art. 1446, Bankruptcy Law Arts. 64, 72; Mexico: Civil Code Art. 1798, Bankruptcy Law Arts. 83, 408–411; Peru: Civil Code Arts. 3, 76; Legislative Decree 845, arts. 19, 118.

8 In the case of Mexico, a company's freedom to manage its assets will also be restricted once it has filed for suspension of payments.

9 In this respect, Mexico is no different from most other countries of Central and South America that have a priority structure established by law. *See, e.g.*, Dominican Republic: Civil Code Arts. 2092–2113, Code of Commerce Arts. 546–548; Guatemala: Code of Civil and Merchant Procedure Arts. 379–397, Code of Commerce Arts. 233, 682, 872; Peru: Civil Code Arts. 1118–1131, 1055–1090, Legislative Decree 845 of Sept. 21, 1996 Art. 24; Uruguay: Civil Code Arts. 2368–2371, Code of Commerce Arts. 1732–1760; Argentina: Civil Code Arts. 3875–3938, Bankrutpcy Law Arts. 239–250; Chile: Civil Code Arts. 2465–2491. Nor is it unlike the priority system prescribed in the United States. *Cf.* United States Bankruptcy Code § 507.

of financially distressed debtors are fundamental aspects of Mexican debtor-creditor, as they are under the legal systems of most nations.

The fact that the Court of Appeals viewed as an "improper... priority" a Mexican debtor's decision to follow Mexican law and pay Mexican taxes and Mexican employees ahead of United States lenders speaks volumes for its parochial vision and failure to extend comity to another nation's legal regime over property in the foreign state's territory. One can readily imagine how the United States would view a foreign court's decision that a United States national's payment of federal and state income taxes "improperly" created a "priority" at the expense of foreign creditors, so as to justify the foreign court in enjoining further use of the debtor's United States property for such "improper" purposes. Yet the Second Circuit gave no though whatever, it seems, to the comity implications of its disdainful characterization of a Mexican debtor's compliance with its obligations to pay taxes to its own sovereign in Mexico, pay wages and severance to its employees and pay the other legitimate claims of its local creditors out of its local property.

Finally, and perversely, the lower court's injunctive "remedy" sequestering the debtor's foreign property simply reversed the "preference" posited by the Court of Appeals, by preferring United States creditors over non–United States creditors with respect to property located outside the United States and otherwise available to satisfy foreign creditors' claims. The freeze of petitioners' assets effectively prevented satisfaction of the claims of Mexican creditors until the claims of the United States creditors were decided. When the district court then took the next step and ordered the assets to be transferred to the United States creditors, it effectively converted the unsecured United States creditors into fully secured creditors....

In the last analysis, comity requires self-restraint. In a world of independent sovereigns, each with its own laws over persons and property within its territory, self-restraint is essential to preventing collisions between nations and allowing the international legal system to function in a way that accommodates the interests of all of its legitimate actors.... Considerations of international comity make it inappropriate for United States courts to issue orders that, in effect if not in name, exercise jurisdiction over property outside the United States belonging to non-United States defendants when the defendants have done no more than pay their bona fide debts to their local governmental and private sector creditors in accordance with local law.

Comments and Questions

1. Should it matter whether GMD is deceitfully trying to transfer their assets to the detriment of the Fund or is, instead, simply unable presently to meet its financial obligations to GMD? Unless your answer is unqualifiedly negative, who should have the burden to prove exactly what?

2. Should it matter whether the Mexican courts have, in fact, asserted jurisdiction over litigation matters involving GMD and any of its creditors? If yes, what if

that litigation had not been filed, but was imminent?—or foreseeable?—or possible? If no, what deference or respect is owed the Mexican courts and legal system?

3. Could the contractual terms of the Government Notes (between Mexico and GMD) have any bearing on the outcome of this litigation?

4. If you feel that the court should have the capacity to enjoin GMD's use of the Government Notes, would you also vest the New York court with authority to enjoin GMD from using or disposing of assets completely unrelated to this project that are located in, say, Brazil?

C. National Practice

The national practice of courts with regard to interim protective measure has many more similarities than differences. Almost all common law and civil law jurisdictions offer some measure of protection for plaintiffs that also appreciates the competing interests of defendants. With regard to transnational litigation, differences among jurisdictions tend to center around their position on the following issues: (i) whether the targeted assets or mandate reaches outside the territory; and (ii) whether interim protective measures are available to support foreign litigation. You should envision a continuum of approaches as to each. For example, regarding the former, an extraterritorial reach could be available only for certain types of claims or be limited to particular assets and/or mandates. Regarding the latter, measures may be granted only upon request of the foreign court or upon a showing of exceptional circumstances.

1. United Kingdom

The British may offer plaintiffs the most protective interim measures of any system in the world. The English Court of Appeal itself has recognized its innovation as "one of the most imaginative, important, and, on the whole, most beneficial of modern times."*

a. The Mareva Injunction

Prior to the development of the Mareva injunction in 1975, creditors possessed few or no legal rights over the property of their debtors prior to entry of a final judgment. After a judgment had been entered, legal and equitable remedies such as a damages award, attachment, or lien could be enforced upon a debtor's property. But creditors feared, of course, that debtors would dissipate or destroy any such property during the course of litigation and would be "judgment proof." Yet for centuries the courts offered no relief:

> I know of no case where, because it was highly probable that if the action were brought to a hearing the plaintiff could establish that the debt was due from the

* *Deutsche Schachtbau- und Tiefbohrgesellschaft v. R'as al Kaimah National Oil Co.* [1987] 3 W.L.R. 1023, 1036 (C.A.).

> defendant, the defendant has been ordered to give security until that [debt] has been established by the judgment or decree.... [Such an order] would be introducing an entirely new and wrong principle, even though we might think that, having regard to the circumstances of the case, it would be highly just to make the order.

Lister v. Stubbs [1890] 45 Ch.D. 1, 13–14 (C.A.). "The only remedy for an unsecured creditor is to obtain his judgment and take out execution." Mills v. Northern Railway of Buenos Ares Co. [1870] 5 Ch. App. 621, HL.

This precedent was radically altered in 1975 by Lord Denning, one of the English Court of Appeal's most controversial and popular judges. In Nippon Yusen Kaisha v. Karagerorgis, [1975] 1 W.L.R. 1093 (Eng. C.A.), John and George Karageorgis chartered three ships from Nippon Yusen Kaisha, a Japanese shipowner, but then failed to pay for the charters. The shipowner filed suit and sought an injunction restraining the defendants from removing their assets from the jurisdiction. The High Court refused, but on appeal Lord Denning granted the plaintiff's request:

> We are told that an injunction of this kind has never been done before. It has never been the practice of the English Courts to seize assets of a defendant in advance of judgment, or to restrain the disposal of them.... It seems to me that the time has come when we should revise our practice.

Lord Denning cited no case authority for his ruling and did not distinguish Lister v. Stubbs. Instead, he held the freezing injunction authorized by § 45 of the Judicature Acts of 1925 allowing the High Court to grant a mandamus or injunction or appoint a receiver by an interlocutory order in "all cases where it appears to the Court to be just or convenient to do so." One month after Nippon Yusen Kaisha, Lord Denning issued his seminal opinion in Mareva Compania Naviera.

Mareva Compania Naviera S.A. v. Int'l Bulkcarriers S.A.

I All ER 213 [1980]

The plaintiffs, Mareva Compania Naviera S.A. ("the shipowners"), issued a writ on 20th June 1975 claiming against the defendants, International Bulcarriers S.A. ("the charterers"), unpaid hire and damages for repudiation of a charterparty. On an ex parte application Donaldson J granted an injunction until 17.00 hours on 23rd June restraining the charterers from removing or disposing out of the jurisdiction moneys standing to the credit of the charterers' account at a London Bank. The shipowners appealed against Donaldson J's refusal to extend the injunction beyond 17.00 hours on 23rd June....

Lord Denning MR

...The plaintiffs are shipowners who owned the vessel Mareva. They let it to the defendants on a time charter for a trip out to the Far East and back. The vessel was to be put at the disposal of the charterers at Rotterdam. Hire was payable half monthly in advance and the rate was (US)$3,850 a day from the time of delivery. The vessel was duly delivered to the charterers on 12th May 1975. The charterers sub-chartered it. They let it on a voyage charter to the President of India. Freight was payable under that voyage charter: 90% was to be paid against the documents and the 10% later.

Under the voyage charter the vessel was loaded at Bordeaux on 29th May 1975 with a cargo of fertiliser consigned to India. The Indian High Commission, in accordance with the obligations under the voyage charter, paid 90% of the freight. But paid it to a Bank in London. It was paid out to the Bank of Bilbao in London to the credit of the charterers. The total sum which the Indian High Commission paid into the Bank was £174,000. Out of that the charterers paid to the shipowners, the plaintiffs, the first two instalments of the half monthly hire. They paid those instalments by credit transferred to the shipowners. The third was due on 12th June 1975, but the charterers failed to pay it. They could easily have done it, of course, by making a credit transfer in favour of the shipowners. But they did not do it. Telexes passed which make it quite plain that the charterers were unable to pay. They said they were not able to fulfil any part of their obligations under the charter, and they had no alternative but to stop trading. Their efforts to obtain further financial support had been fruitless.

Whereupon the shipowners treated the charterers' conduct as a repudiation of the charter. They issued a writ on 20th June. They claimed the unpaid hire, which comes to (US)$ 30,800, and damages for the repudiation. The total will be very large. They have served the writ on agents here, and they have applied for an injunction to restrain the disposal of those moneys which are now in the Bank. They rely on the recent case of Nippon Yusen Kaisha v. Karageorgis.[2] . . . Donaldson J felt that he was bound by Lister & Co. v. Stubbs[[3]] and that he had no power to grant an injunction. But, in deference to the recent case, he did grant an injunction, but only until 17.00 hours today (23rd June 1975), on the understanding that by that time this court would be able to reconsider the position.

Now counsel for the shipowners has been very helpful. He has drawn our attention not only to Lister and Co v. Stubbs but also to § 45 of the Supreme Court of Judicature (Consolidation) Act 1925, which repeats § 25(8) of the Judicature Act 1873. It says:

> A mandamus or an injunction may be granted or a receiver appointed by an interlocutory Order of the Court in all cases in which it shall appear to the Court to be just or convenient. . . .

In Beddow v. Beddow[6] Jessel MR gave a very wide interpretation to that section. He said: "I have unlimited power to grant an injunction in any case where it would be right or just to do so. . . ."

There is only one qualification to be made. The court will not grant an injunction to protect a person who has no legal or equitable right whatever. That appears

---

[2] [1975] 3 All ER 282, [1975] 1 WLR 1093.

[3] (1890) 45 Ch D 1, [1886–90] All ER Rep 797.

[6] (1878) 9 Ch D 89 at 93.

from North London Railway Co. v. Great Northern Railway Co.[7] But, subject to that qualification, the statute gives a wide general power to the courts. It is well summarised in Halsbury's Laws of England:[8]

> . . . now, therefore, whenever a right, which can be asserted either at law or in equity, does exist, then whatever the previous practice may have been, the Court is enabled by virtue of this provision, in a proper case, to grant an injunction to protect that right.

In my opinion that principle applies to a creditor who has a right to be paid the debt owing to him, even before he has established his right by getting judgement for it. If it appears that the debt is due and owing, and there is a danger that the debtor may dispose of his assets so as to defeat it before judgment, the court has jurisdiction in a proper case to grant an interlocutory judgment so as to prevent him disposing of those assets. It seems to me that this is a proper case for the exercise of this jurisdiction. There is money in a Bank in London which stands in the name of those charterers. The charterers have control of it. They may at any time dispose of it or remove it out of this country. If they do so, the shipowners may never get their charter hire. The ship is now on the high seas. It has passed Cape Town on its way to India. It will complete the voyage and the cargo will be discharged. And the shipowners may not get their charter hire at all. In face of this danger, I think this court ought to grant an injunction to restrain the charterers from disposing of those moneys now in the Bank in London until the trial or judgment in this action. If the charterers have any grievance about it when they hear of it, they can apply to discharge it. But meanwhile the shipowners should be protected. It is only just and right that this court should grant an injunction. I would therefore continue the injunction.

Roskill LJ

I agree that this injunction should be extended until judgment in the action or until further order. The application to this court is made ex parte, and is necessitated by the fact that the learned judge, Donaldson J. understandingly in the circumstances, refused to extend the jurisdiction beyond 17.00 hours this afternoon (23rd June 1975). Though the admirable argument to which we have listened puts the case very fairly both for and against continuing the injunction, the fact remains that, we have only heard argument from one side and I do not think it would be right to express any opinion as to what the result would be were this matter hereafter to be argued fully. But, as at present advised, it seems reasonably clear, first, that this court has jurisdiction to continue this injunction, and secondly, that the difficult question is whether on the present facts this court ought at this stage to continue it until judgment or further order. Donaldson J. in his judgment of which we have a full note, has asked a number of other questions of this court which at

---

[7] (1883) 11 QBD 30.

[8] 21 Halsbury's Laws (3rd ed.) 348, para 729; see now 24 Halsbury's Laws (4th ed.) para 918.

present it would be wrong for us to seek to answer. If the charterers were represented, it would no doubt be said on their behalf that the decision of this court in Lister & Co. v. Stubbs precludes this court, not as a matter of jurisdiction but as a matter of practice, from granting this injunction.

Indeed it is right to say that, as far as my own experience in the Commercial Court is concerned, an injunction in this form has in the past from time to time been applied for but has been consistently refused. This court should not, therefore, on an ex parte interlocutory application be too ready to disturb the practice of the past save for good reasons. But on the facts of this case, there are three good reasons for granting this injunction. First, this ship was on time charter from the plaintiffs to the defendants on the New York Produce form, which provided, a little unusually, for a daily rate of hire payable half-monthly in advance and only the first two half-monthly instalments have been paid; secondly, there there has been what would seem to be a plain and unexcused default in the payment of the third half-monthly instalment, and indeed a repudiation of the time charter by the charterers; thirdly, that third instalment fell due when the ship was under voyage charter from the time charterers to the President of India as voyage charterer.

On the evidence the charterers have already received £174,000 from the voyage charterers. Yet they have sent a telex to the shipowners in London on 17th June stating that their efforts to raise further financial support have been fruitless and that they have no alternative but to stop trading. If therefore this court does not interfere by injunction, it is apparent that the shipowners will suffer a grave injustice which this court has the power to help avoid; the injustice being that the ship will have to continue on her voyage to India and perhaps, as is not unknown in Indian ports, wait a long time there for discharge without remuneration while the charterers will be able to dissipate that £174,000.

In my judgment it would be wrong to tolerate this if it can be avoided. If it is necessary to find a reason for distinguishing this case from Lister & Co v. Stubbs, I would venture to suggest that it is at least arguable that the court should interfere to protect the shipowners' rights which arise under cl 18 of the time charter. The relevant part reads: "That the Owners shall have a lien upon all cargoes, and all sub-freights for any amounts due under this Charter, including General Average contributions."

There is or may be a legal or perhaps equitable right which the shipowners may be entitled to have protected by the court. The full extent and nature of that right has long been a controversial matter which may have to be resolved hereafter and I therefore say no more about it.

For those narrow reasons I should continue this injunction until judgment or further order. It is open to the charterers to apply to discharge the injunction or to apply for a stay under the arbitration clause at any time if they are so advised. I agree with the order proposed by Lord Denning MR.

Ormrod LJ

I agree. In my judgment the charterers here have a very strong case on the merits. We have not heard any argument from the other side because it is an ex parte application. In these circumstances I would reserve my own views until I have heard argument from the other side if any such argument is put forward. But, in the absence of any such argument, in my view the injunction should be continued.

Appeal allowed. Injunction continued.

Comments and Questions

1. British courts emphasize that a cautious approach is appropriate before what has been called one of the court's "nuclear weapons" is deployed, particularly if an order is sought and obtained without notice to the person made subject to the order. Case law has developed three threshold requirements that a successful applicant must establish in order to obtain a Mareva order:

First, an application must have a "good arguable case" on the merits of the underlying action. "English courts have resisted the temptation to explain the concept in percentage terms because most Mareva applications are ex parte and prospects of success cannot be quantified. In essence, 'good arguable case' means that on the material before the court the plaintiff appears to have real prospects of success." David Capper, The Need for a Mareva Injunctions Reconsidered, 73 Fordham L. Rev. 2161, 2163 (2005). However, the standard does not require a preponderance of evidence nor even a quantum of evidence that would satisfy summary judgment. Mr. Justice Lloyd, in Ninemia Maritime Corporation v. Trave Schiffahrtsgesellschaft M.B.H.und Co. K.G., [1983] 2 Lloyd's Rep. 600, 605 (Eng. C.A.), described the relatively minimal standard as one where the applicant's claim must be "more than barely capable of serious argument." See Jeffrey L. Wilson, Three if By Equity: Mareva Orders & The New British Invasion, 19 St. John's J. Legal Comment. 673, 703 (2005).

Second, there must be a real risk that any judgment the plaintiff obtains in the proceedings will go unsatisfied. That the defendant is a foreigner will not alone satisfy this standard. Even the removal of assets from the jurisdiction may be insufficient proof. Rather, the court should require "solid evidence... of the likelihood of dissipation." Thune Investments Ltd v. Tomlinson [2003] EWCA Civ 1272, July 29 2003. Each case will of course turn on its own facts, but relevant factors could include:

(a) the nature of the assets which are to be the subject of the proposed order, and the ease or difficulty with which they could be disposed of or dissipated;
(b) the nature and financial standing of the defendant's business, and the length of time for which he has carried it on;
(c) the domicile or residence of the defendant; and
(d) the defendant's behavior in response to the claim.

Gee, Mareva Injunctions and Anton Piller Relief 195–198 (4th ed. 1998). The defendant's dishonesty may assist, but again may not be enough in itself. As Peter

Gibson LJ said in Thune, supra: "It is appropriate in each case for the court to scrutinize with care whether what is alleged to have been the dishonesty of the person against whom the order is sought in itself really justifies the inference that that person has assets which he is likely to dissipate unless restricted."

Third, it must be just and convenient in all the circumstances of the case to grant the relief sought. To this end, the plaintiff's application

> must show the utmost good faith and disclose his case fully and fairly. He must, for the protection and information of the defendant, summarize his case and the evidence in support of it by an affidavit or affidavits sworn before or immediately after the application. He must identify the crucial points for and against the application, and not rely on general statements and the mere exhibiting of numerous documents. He must investigate the nature of the cause of action asserted and the facts relied on before applying and identify any likely defences. He must disclose all facts which reasonably could or would be taken into account by the Judge in deciding whether to grant the application. It is no excuse for the applicant to say that he was not aware of the importance of matters he has omitted to state. If the duty of full and fair disclosure is not observed the Court may discharge the injunction even if after full enquiry the view is taken that the order made was just and convenient and would probably have been made even if there had been full disclosure...
>
> Siporex Trade S. A. v. Comdel Commodities Ltd [1986] 2 Lloyd's Rep. 428, 437.

Further, the prospective judgment creditor may also be required to post an undertaking for damages (i.e., a bond) if the claim should fail.

2. As use of the Mareva injunction increased, it finally became codified in 1981. Section 37(1) of the Supreme Court Act 1981, states that "The High Court may by order (whether interlocutory or final) grant an injunction or appoint a receiver in all cases in which it appears to the court to be just and convenient to do so." Specific power to grant a Mareva injunction is provided in Section 37(3) of the Act:

> The power of the High Court under subsection (1) to grant an interlocutory injunction restraining a party to any proceedings from removing from the jurisdiction of the High Court, or otherwise dealing with, assets located within that jurisdiction shall be exercisable in cases where that party is, as well as in cases where he is not, domiciled, resident or present within that jurisdiction.

3. Until 1989, Mareva injunctions had restrained defendants from dealing with assets that were located only in England. In a sequence of cases creating the so-called worldwide Mareva, the courts reasoned that, because the Mareva injunction operates in personam on the conscience of the defendant, there is no reason to restrict the scope of the injunction to assets within England. Provided the defendant is personally subject to the jurisdiction of the English court, Mareva injunctions can effect a worldwide pre-judgment freezing order. Derby & Co. Ltd. and Others v. Welden, 1990 Ch. 48

(C.A. 1988). The injunction is not limited to commercial cases. Barcley-Johnson v. Yuill [1980] 3 All E.R. 190.

4. The consequences of granting or denying a request for a Mareva injunction can be profound. Is vesting the authority to make this determination within the broad exercise of judicial discretion, then, uniquely appropriate or perilously unsuitable?

5. There are important practical considerations when a Mareva operates on a worldwide basis. In Babanaft Int'l Co. S.A. v. Bassatne, [1990] 1 Ch. 13 (Eng. C.A. 1988), the Mareva injunction was issued on the worldwide assets of the defendant, and the plaintiff's solicitors notified nearly 50 banks and other entities in various countries of the terms of the injunction against the defendant's assets. In holding that an unqualified injunction freezing assets outside the court's jurisdiction could amount to an "exorbitant assertion of extraterritorial jurisdiction," the court refined the injunction with a proviso that the order would not affect third parties "unless and to the extent that it is enforced by the Courts of the States in which any of the defendants' assets are located." Id. at 37. Further refinements to the so-called Babanaft Proviso have added additional safeguards, but English courts continue to issue worldwide asset restraints. Indeed, in one case, where the steps taken by the defendants to render their assets judgment proof were, even by the standards of these cases, exceptionally convoluted and complicated, the court appointed by way of Mareva relief, a receiver of the worldwide assets of the defendants. See Derby & Co. Ltd. v. Weldon (Nos. 3 & 4), 1990 Ch. 65 (C.A. 1988).

6. The Mareva order only "freezes" a defendant's assets so that they cannot be dissipated or destroyed prior to entry of a judgment. To effectuate the spirit and letter of the Mareva order, English courts utilize three ancillary enforcement orders:

(1) Disclosure orders. These orders require defendants to disclose all of their worldwide assets.
(2) Norwich orders. These orders require third parties, usually banks, to provide "full information" about the assets of named defendants.
(3) Anton Piller orders. These orders, discussed in the next section, authorize plaintiff's attorneys to search the defendant's premises and seize items and documents that might constitute evidence.

b. The Anton Piller Order

In several situations there has been a need to allow a plaintiff to enter the premises of a defendant in order to obtain evidence or prevent evidence from being destroyed. The situation frequently occurs in cases involving industrial property rights, where there may be a risk that the defendant may sell off or otherwise dispose of the products that are (or include) the subject of the dispute. The British have created a specific instrument to deal with this situation. Basically, the system used is an order to prevent a defendant from concealing or destroying evidence in the form of documents or other property. It is granted in an ex parte procedure.

In the Anton Pillar case, the Court of Appeal issued an order to permit the plaintiff to enter the premises of the defendant in order to inspect, remove or make copies of documents.

Anton Piller K.G. v. Manuf. Processes Ltd.
[1975 A. No. 6292]; [1976] 2 W.L.R. 162

Interlocutory appeal from Brightman J

On November 26, 1975, on the ex parte motion of the plaintiffs, Anton Piller KG (a limited partnership), Brightman J., on the plaintiffs' undertaking (1) forthwith to issue a writ of summons in their intended action against the defendants, Manufacturing Processes Ltd. ("M.P.L."), Bernard Preston Wallace and Alfred Henry Stephen Baker, and (2) to abide by any order of the court as to damages sustained by the defendants by reason of any order to be made, ordered that the defendants be restrained until December 2, 1975, or further order, from (i) infringing the plaintiffs' copyrights in original circuit board drawings and photographs therefrom for their equipment, (ii) publicising or using other than for the plaintiffs' benefit any confidential information or documents supplied to them by the plaintiffs, (iii) manufacturing or helping others to manufacture copies of the plaintiffs' equipment, (iv) disposing of or destroying (a) infringements of such copyrights (b) documents or articles relating to the design, manufacture or supply of the plaintiffs' equipment.

Brightman J. declined to order the further relief set out in a schedule:

> That the defendants...do permit such persons not exceeding two as may be duly authorised by the plaintiffs and members or employees not exceeding two of the plaintiffs' solicitors to enter forthwith the premises known as...or such parts thereof as shall be occupied or used by the defendants at any hour between 8...in the forenoon and 9...in the evening for the purpose of (a) inspecting all documents or articles relating to the design, manufacture, sale or supply of copies of the plaintiffs' equipment...(b) removing into the plaintiffs' solicitors' custody (i) all original documents relating to the manufacture, operation or maintenance of the plaintiffs' equipment which...had been supplied by the plaintiffs to the defendants (ii) all documents or articles relating to the design, manufacture, sale or supply of copies of the plaintiffs' equipment....

The plaintiffs, who had been willing to undertake that the documents or articles removed would not be used by them save for the purposes of the action without leave of the court, issued a writ against the defendants claiming injunctions, delivery up of all infringing copies of copyright material and inquiries as to damages.

The plaintiffs appealed ex parte by leave of the judge against the refusal to grant the relief set out in the schedule. The appeal was heard in chambers on December 2.

So far as is known there have been seven ex parte applications to the courts for "permit" orders for inspection, five of which have been granted. In the case of an order made by Goff J. on October 28, 1974, Pall Europe Ltd. v. Microfiltrex Ltd.

(unreported) [1974 P. No. 4640] solicitors were present and incriminating material was found.

The courts have recognised that it is a very severe form of order that is sought. Yet every day of the week orders are made severely restricting a defendant's business activities, his property or his actions. In many cases an injunction would be enough but there are cases where matter may be destroyed. There is matter here which might well be made unavailable in the action by destruction or other disposition.

R.S.C., Ord. 29, r. 2 deals with the "Detention, preservation, etc., of subject matter of cause or matter." By Ord. 29, r. 2 (5) an application for an order under the rule has to be made by "summons or by notice."

It is under the inherent jurisdiction of the court that power is found to make the order sought. The Court of Chancery has such power, e.g., to prevent property from being removed from the jurisdiction.

As to the power to "permit" inspection, see United Company of Merchants of England, Trading to the East Indies v. Kynaston (1821) 3 Bli.(O.S.) 153, per Lord Redesdale at pp. 163–164. Lord Redesdale said at p. 166 that Earl of Lonsdale v. Curwen, (1799) 3 Bli.(O.S.) 168 (note) was directly in point and that "the order was made before the decree, and upon a question where the rights of the parties were uncertain." This is an equitable, discretionary, remedy. Anwyl v. Owens (1853) 22 L.J.Ch. 995 where "the object of the application" was to "preserve property during litigation" is entirely consistent with the Kynaston decision and with the present application made to preserve property during the trial. For an example of an ex parte application for an order for inspection of premises made in an emergency, see Hennessy v. Rohmann, Osborne & Co. [1877] W.N. 14, where the application was made under the then Ord. 52, r. 3, and Malins V.-C. said that "the circumstances... warranted him in making an immediate order for inspection of the premises, "although he did not act under that rule. The court has inherent power to dispense with notice. See also Morris v. Howell (1888) 22 L.R.Ir. 77. In Fowler v. Lewy (1875) 1 Char.Cham.Cas. 14 Quain J. said that he could not make an order for inspection ex parte.

This application falls within the words of Templeman J. in E.M.I. Ltd. v. Pandit [1975] 1 W.L.R. 302, 307–308 but Templeman J. went too far in imposing stringency on plaintiffs. The plaintiffs in the present case want to preserve property so that it cannot be used to their prejudice and in order to prevent the defendants destroying it. Enormous damage may be done to the plaintiffs. Brightman J. recognised "the strong prima facie evidence" of what the defendants are doing. It is virtually impossible to establish that the defendant is a proven rogue on an ex parte application. That standard is too high. Brightman J.'s judgment was too restrictive.

The defendants did not appear and were not represented.

At the conclusion of the hearing in chambers the court made an order ex parte substantially in the form of the schedule to the order of Brightman J. The order was directed to be drawn up on December 2 and served and the court said that the reasons for the order would be delivered on December 8.

Cur. adv. vult.

Lord Denning MR

During the last 18 months the judges of the Chancery Division have been making orders of a kind not known before. They have some resemblance to search warrants. Under these orders, the plaintiff and his solicitors are authorised to enter the defendant's premises so as to inspect papers, provided the defendant gives permission.

Now this is the important point: The court orders the defendant to give them permission. The judges have been making these orders on ex parte applications without prior notice to the defendant. None of the cases have been reported except the one before Templeman J. on December 3, 1974, E.M.I. Ltd. v. Pandit [1975] 1 W.L.R. 302. But in the present case Brightman J. refused to make such an order.

On appeal to us, Mr. Laddie appears for the plaintiffs. He has appeared in most of these cases, and can claim the credit—or the responsibility—for them. He represented to us that in this case it was in the interests of justice that the application should not be made public at the time it was made. So we heard it in camera. It was last Tuesday. After hearing his submissions, we made the order. We now come to give our reasons in public. But at the outset I must state the facts, for it is obvious that such an order can only be justified in the most exceptional circumstances.

Anton Piller KG ("Pillers"), the plaintiffs, are German manufacturers of high repute. They make electric motors and generators. They play an important part in the big new computer industry. They supply equipment for it. They have recently designed a frequency converter specially for supplying the computers of International Business Machines.

Since 1972 Pillers have had, as their agents in the United Kingdom, a company here called Manufacturing Processes Ltd. ("M.P.L."), which is run by Mr. A. H. S. Baker and Mr. B. P. Wallace, their two directors. These agents are dealers who get machines from Pillers in Germany and sell them to customers in England. Pillers supply M.P.L. with much confidential information about the machines, including a manual showing how they work, and drawings which are the subject of copyright.

Very recently Pillers have found out—so they say—that these English agents, M.P.L., have been in secret communication with other German companies called Ferrostaal and Lechmotoren. The object of these communications is that M.P.L. should supply these other German companies with drawings and materials and other confidential information so that they can manufacture power units like Pillers. Pillers got to know of these communications through two "defectors," if I may call them so. One was the commercial manager of M.P.L., Mr. Brian Firth; the other was the sales manager, Mr. William Raymond Knight. These two were so upset by what was going on in M.P.L. that on their own initiative, without any approach by Pillers whatever, on October 2, 1975, one or both flew to Germany. They told Pillers what they knew about the arrangements with Ferrostaal and Lechmotoren. They disclosed also that M.P.L. was negotiating with Canadian and United States firms. In making these disclosures, both Mr. Firth and Mr. Knight were putting themselves in a perilous position, but Pillers assured them that they would safeguard their future employment.

The disclosures—coming from defectors—might have been considered untrustworthy. But they were supported by documents which emanated from both Ferrostaal and Lechmotoren. They showed that M.P.L. was in regular communication with those German companies. They were sending them drawings and arranging for inspection of the Piller machine, for the express purpose that the Lechmotoren company might manufacture a prototype machine copied from Pillers. One of the most telling communications was a telex from a representative of Ferrostaal to Mr. Wallace saying:

> It is the opinion of Mr. S. (of Lechmotoren) that the best way to find a final solution for the... prototype is to send Mr. Beck (also of Lechmotoren) to you as soon as the... latest design of P. (Piller) has arrived in your factory. In this case it is guaranteed that the Lech prototype will have exactly the same features as the P-type. We hope you will agree to this proposal and we ask you to let us have your telex in order to arrange Mr. Beck's visit accordingly.

On getting this information, Pillers were extremely worried. They were about to produce a fine new frequency converter called the "Silent Block." They feared that M.P.L., in co-operation with the German manufacturers, would make a copy of their "Silent Block" and ruin their market. They determined to apply to the court for an injunction to restrain M.P.L. and their directors, the defendants, from infringing their copyright or using confidential information or making copies of their machines. But they were fearful that if the defendants were given notice of this application, they would take steps to destroy documents or send them to Germany or elsewhere, so that there would be none in existence by the time that discovery was had in the action.

So, on Wednesday, November 26, 1975, Pillers' solicitors prepared a draft writ of summons and, with an affidavit, they went before Brightman J. and asked, first, for an interim injunction to restrain infringement, etc., and, secondly, for an order that they might be permitted to enter the defendants' premises so as to inspect the documents of the plaintiffs and remove them, or copies of them. Brightman J. granted an interim injunction, but refused to order inspection or removal of the documents. He said:

> There is strong prima facie evidence that the defendant company is now engaged in seeking to copy the plaintiffs' components for its own financial profit to the great detriment of the plaintiffs and in breach of the plaintiffs' rights.

He realised that the defendants might suppress evidence or misuse documentary material, but he thought that that was a risk which must be accepted in civil matters save in extreme cases. "Otherwise," he said,

> it seems to me that an order on the lines sought might become an instrument of oppression, particularly in a case where a plaintiff of big standing and deep pocket is ranged against a small man who is alleged on the evidence of one side only to have infringed the plaintiffs' rights.

Let me say at once that no court in this land has any power to issue a search warrant to enter a man's house so as to see if there are papers or documents there which are of an incriminating nature, whether libels or infringements of copyright or anything else of the kind. No constable or bailiff can knock at the door and demand entry so as to inspect papers or documents. The householder can shut the door in his face and say "Get out." That was established in the leading case of Entick v. Carrington (1765) 2 Wils.K.B. 275. None of us would wish to whittle down that principle in the slightest. But the order sought in this case is not a search warrant. It does not authorise the plaintiffs' solicitors or anyone else to enter the defendants' premises against their will. It does not authorise the breaking down of any doors, nor the slipping in by a back door, nor getting in by an open door or window. It only authorises entry and inspection by the permission of the defendants. The plaintiffs must get the defendants' permission. But it does do this: It brings pressure on the defendants to give permission. It does more. It actually orders them to give permission—with, I suppose, the result that if they do not give permission, they are guilty of contempt of court.

This may seem to be a search warrant in disguise. But it was fully considered in the House of Lords 150 years ago and held to be legitimate. The case is United Company of Merchants of England, Trading to the East Indies v. Kynaston (1821) 3 Bli.(O.S.) 153. Lord Redesdale said, at pp. 163–164:

> The arguments urged for the appellants at the Bar are founded upon the supposition, that the court has directed a forcible inspection. This is an erroneous view of the case. The order is to permit; and if the East India Company should refuse to permit inspection, they will be guilty of a contempt of the court.... It is an order operating on the person requiring the defendants to permit inspection, not giving authority of force, or to break open the doors of their warehouse.

That case was not, however, concerned with papers or things. It was only as to the value of a warehouse; and that could not be obtained without an inspection. But the distinction drawn by Lord Redesdale affords ground for thinking that there is jurisdiction to make an order that the defendant "do permit" when it is necessary in the interests of justice.

Accepting such to be the case, the question is in what circumstances ought such an order be made. If the defendant is given notice beforehand and is able to argue the pros and cons, it is warranted by that case in the House of Lords and by R.S.C., Ord. 29, r. 2 (1) and (5). But it is a far stronger thing to make such an order ex parte without giving him notice. This is not covered by the Rules of the Supreme Court and must be based on the inherent jurisdiction of the court. There are one or two old precedents which give some colour for it, Hennessy v. Rohmann, Osborne & Co. [1877] W.N. 14, and Morris v. Howell (1888) 22 L.R.Ir. 77, an Irish case. But they do not go very far. So it falls to us to consider it on principle. It seems to me that such an order can be made by a judge ex parte, but it should only be made where it is essential that the plaintiff should have inspection so that justice can be done between the parties: and when, if the defendant were forewarned, there is a grave danger that vital evidence will be destroyed, that papers will be burnt or lost or hidden, or taken beyond the jurisdiction, and so the ends of justice be defeated: and when the inspection would do no real harm to the defendant or his case.

Nevertheless, in the enforcement of this order, the plaintiffs must act with due circumspection. On the service of it, the plaintiffs should be attended by their solicitor, who is an officer of the court. They should give the defendants an opportunity of considering it and of consulting their own solicitor. If the defendants wish to apply to discharge the order as having been improperly obtained, they must be allowed to do so. If the defendants refuse permission to enter or to inspect, the plaintiffs must not force their way in. They must accept the refusal, and bring it to the notice of the court afterwards, if need be on an application to commit.

You might think that with all these safeguards against abuse, it would be of little use to make such an order. But it can be effective in this way: It serves to tell the defendants that, on the evidence put before it, the court is of opinion that they ought to permit inspection—nay, it orders them to permit—and that they refuse at their peril. It puts them in peril not only of proceedings for contempt, but also of adverse inferences being drawn against them; so much so that their own solicitor may often advise them to comply. We are told that in two at least of the cases such an order has been effective. We are prepared, therefore, to sanction its continuance, but only in an extreme case where there is grave danger of property being smuggled away or of vital evidence being destroyed.

On the evidence in this case, we decided last Tuesday that there was sufficient justification to make an order. We did it on the precedent framed by Templeman J. It contains an undertaking in damages which is to be supported (as the plaintiffs are overseas) by a bond for £10,000. It gives an interim injunction to restraint the infringement of copyright and breach of confidential information, etc. It orders that the defendants do permit one or two of the plaintiffs and one or two of their solicitors to enter the defendants' premises for the purpose of inspecting documents, files or things, and removing those which belong to the plaintiffs. This was, of course, only an interim order pending the return of the summons. It is to be heard, we believe, tomorrow by the judge.

ORMROD LJ

I agree with all that Lord Denning M.R. has said. The proposed order is at the extremity of this court's powers. Such orders, therefore, will rarely be made, and only when there is no alternative way of ensuring that justice is done to the applicant.

There are three essential pre-conditions for the making of such an order, in my judgment. First, there must be an extremely strong prima facie case. Secondly, the damage, potential or actual, must be very serious for the applicant. Thirdly, there must be clear evidence that the defendants have in their possession incriminating documents or things, and that there is a real possibility that they may destroy such material before any application inter partes can be made.

The form of the order makes it plain that the court is not ordering or granting anything equivalent to a search warrant. The order is an order on the defendant in personam to permit inspection. It is therefore open to him to refuse to comply with such an order, but at his peril either of further proceedings for contempt of court—in which case, of course, the court will have the widest discretion as to how to deal with it, and if it turns out that the order was made improperly in the first place, the contempt will be dealt with accordingly—but more important, of course, the refusal to comply may be the most damning evidence against the defendant at the subsequent trial. Great responsibility clearly rests on the solicitors for the applicant to ensure that the carrying out of such an order is meticulously carefully done with the fullest respect for the defendant's rights, as Lord Denning M.R. has said, of applying to the court, should he feel it necessary to do so, before permitting the inspection.

In the circumstances of the present case, all those conditions to my mind are satisfied, and this order is essential in the interests of justice. I agree, therefore, that the appeal should be allowed.

Shaw LJ

I agree with both judgments. The overriding consideration in the exercise of this salutary jurisdiction is that it is to be resorted to only in circumstances where the normal processes of the law would be rendered nugatory if some immediate and effective measure was not available. When such an order is made, the party who has procured the court to make it must act with prudence and caution in pursuance of it.

Comments and Questions

1. Are you alarmed by this case? Do you accept that these orders are not thinly-disguised search warrants?

2. As is clear from the Anton Piller judgment, the plaintiff has to show a strong prima facie case. The threatened harm must be serious. The order should not be used for the purpose of a fishing expedition. On the contrary, the plaintiff has to establish that the defendant is in possession of the relevant documents and that there is a real possibility that he may destroy them. In addition, as in the Mareva injunction, the petitioner typically must post a bond.

3. During the execution of the order, the petitioner, assisted by his lawyer, is not to enter the defendant's premises without permission from the defendant. If the defendant refuses to answer questions or denies access to his premises, no force can be used. The defendant is rather acting in contempt of the court. A defendant is not even allowed to refuse answering questions based on the grounds that it may incriminate him without being in contempt of court. However, evidence obtained in civil matters is not admissible in criminal proceedings.

4. If you represented the defendant in the Anton Piller case, what course of action would you advise (once the order became known to you)?

c. Support of Foreign Proceedings

The following case illustrates a worldwide Mareva injunction that is "worldwide" in three different respects: First, notice that the injunction restrains the defendants from reaching the assets no matter where they are located. Second, the Anton Piller diclosure order reaches worldwide. Third, and most importantly for this section, the underlying proceedings on the substance of the matter are being conducted in France.

Republic of Haiti v. Duvalier

[1989] 2 W.L.R. 261 (C.A.); [1990] 1 A.B. 202

Cur. adv. vult.

STAUGHTON LJ
Jean-Claude Duvalier, the first defendant in these proceedings, was the President of the Republic of Haiti from 1971 until 7 February 1986. The second defendant is his wife, Michele Bennett Duvalier; and the sixth defendant his mother. She is the widow of Francois Duvalier, who was the President from 1957 until his death in 1971. Those three members of the family are the appellants in this court. All are now resident in France.

The Republic of Haiti started proceedings in the Tribunal de Grande Instance at Grasse in July 1986; five of its agencies were later added as co-plaintiffs. Those proceedings were against various members of the Duvalier family, including Jean-Claude Duvalier, his wife and mother, and their associates. It is said that they were responsible for embezzling sums totalling U.S.$120 million from the republic during the presidency of Jean-Claude Duvalier, that is between 1971 and 1986. Indeed it is suggested that this is only the tip of the iceberg, and that very much larger sums were involved.

The defendants in the French action altogether deny liability. They observe that it has been a tradition in Haiti for over 180 years for a new government to take legal proceedings against those who were in charge under the previous regime. One is reminded of the Roman historian who noticed that it was the practice of the later emperors to bring to justice the murderers of the previous emperor but one. But this appeal is scarcely concerned with the merits of the substantive claims made in France. It is acknowledged that the republic's evidence demonstrates a prima facie case, or even a good arguable case. Mr. Strauss, for the republic, goes further; he submits that there is a very strong case, to which the defendants have offered no substantive or detailed answer, either in the French proceedings or in the courts of this country. Unless it is essential to do so, I do not feel that I should make any comment at this stage upon the strength of the republic's case. It is enough that on the affidavit evidence there is a case to answer, or a good arguable case, such as would justify the use of interim protective measures in an English domestic case, and would also justify service out of the jurisdiction if that is permitted by the Rules of the Supreme Court.

What is more striking, and less usual, is the evidence, that the members of the Duvalier family have been attempting to conceal their assets, or place them beyond the reach of courts of law. It is unnecessary to set out this evidence in detail, since the conclusion from it is admitted. In the affidavit of Professor Vaisse, a French lawyer acting for the Duvalier family, there is this passage:

> 9. The plaintiffs have drawn attention to the fact that assets in the control of the defendants have, when threatened with legal attachment proceedings, been removed from the jurisdictions concerned. It is my understanding that this has occurred. This does not reflect any doubts that the defendants have about the merits of their position. They are simply aware that there is a worldwide campaign being conducted against them by the Haitian Government supported by the United States Government to persecute them by seizing their assets wherever they can be found. This campaign is assisted by the international press which provokes prejudice against them wherever they go and they have merely sought to frustrate this campaign which I submit is a normal reaction in the circumstances....

If those be the true facts, one would suppose that the Duvalier family would welcome an early trial of the case against them by a just court in a country which has, by international law, jurisdiction to try it.

It is, however, necessary to enlarge upon that admission by referring to some features of the evidence which are striking. First, the republic's evidence exhibits extracts from a book with the title "Les Banques Suisses et L'Argent" written by a French lawyer, Maitre J.-C. Carteron. This is said to treat the concealment of funds within the Swiss banking system. It points to the advantage of using a fiduciary as the legal owner of the assets to be concealed, rather than the beneficial owner himself, and the added advantage to choosing a lawyer as the fiduciary. "Le secret de sa profession"—(translated "his professional secrecy")—"protégera totalement l'identité du client." There is evidence that Maitre Carteron, between 1984 and 6 February 1986 (which was when the Duvalier family left Haiti), received approximately $500,000 in Switzerland from Haitian Government funds. There is also evidence of 13 telexes or telephone calls from the Ministry of Finance or the National Palace in Haiti to Maitre Carteron's number in Geneva, the last telephone call being on 6 February 1986. Furthermore, there is evidence that the Duvalier family made use of the idea, whether or not derived from Maitre Carteron's book, of employing a professional lawyer as intermediary. Some documents have been disclosed pursuant to an order of Knox J. (which I shall refer to later) by Turner & Co., an English firm of solicitors in which Paul Turner and John Stephen Matlin are partners. Amongst other things, Turner & Co. were asked to identify bank accounts:

> from which or to which any moneys which belongs to any of the first to tenth defendants (whether directly or indirectly) or which are reasonably apparent or believed by Turner & Co. to be moneys in which one or more of the first to tenth defendants is or are beneficially interested or otherwise held by a nominee or trustee, have been transferred.

The answer listed 17 accounts, at 11 different banks, in seven different countries. Eleven of the accounts were in the name of Turner & Co. or the partners of the firm.

A second striking feature emerges from documents which the republic has obtained by proceedings in Jersey. These tend to show that Mr. Matlin arranged for the deposit with the Hongkong and Shanghai Banking Corporation (C.I.) Ltd., via their correspondent in Toronto and for the credit of "Messrs. Turner & Co. No. 2 Clients' Account" of Canadian treasury bills worth in excess of Can.$40 million. Turner & Co., in answer to the order for disclosure of the first to tenth defendants' assets, wrote: "Canadian Government treasury bills have been held by us on occasion. They have all been encashed."

I should also refer to the evidence which tends to show, as Professor Vaisse admits, that assets threatened with attachment have been removed from the jurisdictions concerned. I can summarise that evidence by saying that it leads to one of three possible conclusions: (1) the Duvalier family or their advisers have somehow obtained advance notice of the republic's efforts at attachment; or (2) assets are moved so regularly and so frequently that it is no coincidence if some have been moved just before attachment took effect; or (3) it is coincidence.

It should be emphasized as to all this evidence that no wrongdoing on the part of Turner & Co. or its partners is alleged on behalf of the republic. Furthermore, Mr. Matlin has said in an affidavit that he has never heard of Maitre Carteron, or read his book; nor was he even aware of it until it was referred to in the republic's evidence. He says that he is not aware of any elaborate and co-ordinated scheme to conceal funds.

The English proceedings

On 3 June 1988 the Republic of Haiti and the five other plaintiffs in the French action made an ex parte application to Knox J. sitting as a vacation judge of the Commercial Court. In the writ issued that day they were named as plaintiffs, and the first to tenth defendants were members of the Duvalier family and their associates. None of those defendants had an address within the jurisdiction. The eleventh defendants were Barclays Bank Plc. of Lombard Street, London, E.C.3. The order made by Knox J. can be summarised as follows, so far as is material: (1) the plaintiffs undertook to notify the defendants of the terms of the order by 4 p.m. on 6 June, and to notify Mr. Matlin forthwith; (2) the first to tenth defendants were restrained from dealing with assets which represented the proceeds of the payments which are complained of in the French action; (3) the first to tenth defendants were restrained from removing from the jurisdiction or dealing with their assets within the jurisdiction save in so far as they exceed $120 million in value; (4) the first to tenth defendants were ordered, acting by Messrs. Turner and Matlin, to disclose to the plaintiff's solicitors by 10 a.m. on 6 June information known to Mr. Turner or Mr. Matlin as to the nature, location and value of those defendants' assets; (5) the defendants were ordered, in particular by Messrs. Turner and

Matlin, not to disclose the making of the order for the time being; (6) there was leave to serve out of the jurisdiction and substituted service.

Notice that not only was the order made in the absence of the defendants and without their knowledge; it was also not to be communicated to them until after their solicitors had complied with that part of it relating to disclosure of information. In those respects it was in line with current English practice. Whilst there may not be much point in making an order that a defendant himself disclose documents or provide information ex parte, since he will have to know of the order before he complies with it, the situation is different where information or documents are sought from some third party or even the solicitors as in this case, or when there is to be a compulsory search by an Anton Piller order. That is why particular caution is needed in making such orders.

On 6 June 1988 the solicitors applied to Knox J. to vary or discharge his order. He declined to do so. The time limits for compliance with the order and notification of it to the defendants were extended. On 7 June the solicitors appealed to this court. Their appeal was heard in camera, and did not feature in the cause list. It would seem from the judgment of Lord Donaldson of Lymington M.R. that the principal points argued were: (i) whether the relief sought was within section 25 of the Civil Jurisdiction and Judgments Act 1982; (ii) whether an English court should make an order for the disclosure of information about assets abroad, except in connection with a tracing claim; (iii) whether the plaintiffs' affidavits were sufficient in point of form; and (iv) whether the solicitors could rely on legal professional privilege.

The Court of Appeal rejected the solicitors' argument on all four grounds. I need say nothing about their reasons on grounds (i) and (iii), since those arguments were not repeated before us; nor need I consider ground (iv), since a further claim for legal professional privilege is, by agreement, to be remitted to a Commercial judge. Mr. Strauss accepts that the affidavit on its face appears to assert a valid claim for privilege in respect of a limited class of information. As to ground (ii), the Master of the Rolls said in terms that he was not happy to accept the suggested limitation on the disclosure of information about assets abroad, viz. that it should only be ordered in connection with a tracing claim. But he found on the evidence before the court that the French action was in the nature of a tracing claim. The appeal was allowed only to the extent that the time limits were again varied. In all other respects it was dismissed.

On 7 and 8 June 1988 Phillips J. made three orders permitting the republic to use certain information provided by Turner & Co. for the purpose of legal proceedings in some other jurisdictions. This was necessary because the republic had given an undertaking to Knox J., although not recorded in his order, that it would not use the information disclosed pursuant to his order without the leave of the court. Counsel instructed by Turner & Co. on behalf of the defendants appeared before Phillips J.; it does not seem that the defendants themselves were aware by then that the order of Knox J. had been made. That again would be in line with English practice and common sense, since the intention was to obtain Mareva orders abroad, or information as to the new location of assets by order of foreign courts.

Thereafter the defendants were informed of the English proceedings. They were served with a summons on behalf of the republic seeking disclosure of further information and documents relating to the assets of the first to tenth defendants. That was met by a summons on behalf of the first, second and sixth defendants to set aside proceedings under R.S.C., Ord. 12, r.8, in effect for want of jurisdiction. Those applications came before Leggatt J. inter partes but in chambers. On 22 June 1988 he made the order from which this appeal is brought. By that order Leggatt J., so far as is material for present purposes, (1) dismissed the application to set aside the English proceedings under Ord. 12, r. 8; (2) upheld the order of Knox J. which restrained the first to tenth defendants from dealing with assets, wherever they might be, which represented the proceeds of the payments complained of in the French action; (3) upheld the order of Knox J. which restrained the first to tenth defendants from removing from the jurisdiction or dealing with their assets within the jurisdiction, up to a limit of $120 million; (4) ordered that the first to tenth defendants acting by Messrs. Turner and Matlin do within 24 hours permit inspection of documents, and disclose information, relating to their assets wherever they may be....

Service without leave

The crucial feature of this case is that the republic does not seek any substantive relief in England. It seeks only information, as to where the assets of the Duvalier family are, and a temporary restraint on dealing with those assets. It is said that these remedies are sought in aid of the French action; and so in a sense they are. But whether further proceedings will be confined to France, and to the tribunal of Grasse, is at the very least doubtful. To the extent that the information already disclosed, and to be disclosed under the order of Leggatt J., reveals assets in other jurisdictions, there may well be other proceedings of an interim nature and possibly also seeking substantive relief.

Until the Civil Jurisdiction and Judgments Act 1982 came into force, an English court would not have entertained a claim of this limited nature. The republic would not have had a cause of action: see Siskina (Owners of cargo lately ladeen on board) v. Distos Compania Naviera S.A. [1979] A.C. 210. There Lord Diplock said, at p. 256:

> A right to obtain an interlocutory injunction is not a cause of action. It cannot stand on its own....the High Court has no power to grant an interlocutory injunction except in protection or assertion of some legal or equitable right which it has jurisdiction to enforce by final judgment....

That conclusion is now superseded by section 25(1) of the Civil Jurisdiction and Judgments Act 1982:

> The High Court in England and Wales or Northern Ireland shall have power to grant interim relief where—(a) proceedings have been or are to be commenced in a contracting state other than the United Kingdom..."

Restraint on dealing with assets which are out of the jurisdiction

In the light of recent authority, Mr. Gee conceded that the court has power to restrain a defendant who is not resident here from dealing with his assets which are out of the jurisdiction. He desires only to keep the point open in case this dispute goes further. Nevertheless I consider that, as the issue goes to the jurisdiction of this court and is of considerable general importance, we ought to examine it. In doing so it is necessary to travel over some ground which is also relevant to discretion.

It may be that the powers of the court are wider, and certainly discretion is more readily exercised, if a plaintiff's claim is what is called a tracing claim. For my part, I think that the true distinction lies between a proprietary claim on the one hand, and a claim which seeks only a money judgment on the other. A proprietary claim is one by which the plaintiff seeks the return of chattels or land which are his property, or claims that a specified debt is owed by a third party to him and not to the defendant.

Thus far there is no difficulty. A plaintiff who seeks to enforce a claim of that kind will more readily be afforded interim remedies, in order to preserve the asset which he is seeking to recover, than one who merely seeks a judgment for debt or damages. But if the asset has been converted into some other form of property the question of tracing arises. If the defendant stole the plaintiff's peas, sold them and bought beans with the proceeds, the plaintiff claims that the beans are his property. Or if the defendant misappropriated the plaintiff's credit balance with the X bank, and established a credit with the Y bank from the proceeds, the plaintiff claims that the debt due from the Y bank is his property. In that last case, if the proceedings are brought by the plaintiff against the defendant only, the relief claimed can be no more than a declaration, and an injunction against interference with the plaintiff's property. Ultimately the right must be enforced against the debtor—in my example, the Y bank.

With that introduction I turn to consider whether the claim which the republic seeks to enforce in France is a proprietary claim. New evidence has emerged since this dispute was last before the Court of Appeal, when the proceedings were ex parte so far as the defendants were concerned. In form the claim in the French action is for damages in tort. But process is available there to attach specific assets held by the defendants, which would result in the republic having priority over other creditors. The republic has in fact made use of that process in respect of two assets—a flat in Paris and a chateau in France. It has not yet sought any proprietary remedy in respect of other assets of the Duvalier family in the French proceedings because it does not know what or where those assets are. The very object of the English proceedings is to find out. When they are discovered, I do not doubt that the republic will seek to assert any proprietary remedy that may be available, whether in France or some other jurisdiction.

In that state of affairs I would not go so far as to say that the action in France, in aid of which these proceedings are said to be brought, is itself a proprietary or tracing claim. It does not presently assert ownership of any of the assets expected to be revealed by orders in the English proceedings. But I am confident that ownership will be asserted when and where the assets are found. This is then something of a hybrid situation; and one should perhaps consider it on the basis that interim relief is sought in aid of a monetary claim only, without any claim to ownership of the Duvaliers' assets.

The law on this topic has developed in recent years; and in particular a distinction has emerged between pre-judgment and post-judgment restraint. Our courts are more willing to restrain a defendant from dealing with his assets after, than before, judgment has been given against him. (In passing, I would say that an injunction granted after judgment should normally, in my view, be of limited duration; the plaintiff should be encouraged to proceed with proper methods of execution; perpetual injunctions restraining a defendant from dealing with his assets until the crack of doom are undesirable.) This, of course, is a pre-judgment case.

The decision of this court in Ashtiani v. Kashi [1987] Q.B. 888 was concerned with a Mareva injunction, pre-judgment, over assets within the jurisdiction, coupled with an order for disclosure of assets worldwide. The injunction was discharged. Both Dillon L.J. and Neill L.J. considered that a Mareva injunction should be limited to assets within the jurisdiction, if there is no proprietary or tracing claim. But I think that they regarded this limitation as arising from settled practice, rather than from any restriction on the powers of the court. There are indications in both judgments to that effect. Nicholls L.J. agreed with both judgments.

The problem was extensively reviewed by this court in Babanaft International Co. S.A. v. Bassatne [1990] Ch. 13. That was a post-judgment case, and what was said as to injunctions before judgment was obiter. The court upheld a worldwide injunction on dealing with assets, subject to a proviso which I shall consider later. There were some features in the Babanaft case that are similar to those in the present case. The judgment was against two individuals, whom Kerr L.J. described as "unusually peripatetic in their lifestyle and elusive in the way they do business and hold assets," for $15 million. He said, at p. 22G:

> All "their" assets appear to be held in the names of a large network of companies incorporated in many countries in which they or members of their families hold bearer shares.

The judge below had found that they would be likely to take any step open to them to frustrate the execution of the judgment. I do not attempt to summarize the reasoning of Kerr L.J. He concluded, at p. 28A-B:

> I therefore proceed on the basis that in appropriate cases, though these may well be rare, there is nothing to preclude our courts from granting Mareva type injunctions against defendants which extend to their assets outside the jurisdiction.

Neill L.J. said, at p. 39A-C:

> I was a party to the decision in Ashtiani v. Kashi and I remain of the opinion that it accurately reflected the way in which the jurisdiction to grant Mareva injunctions

> had been exercised and developed in England... I am satisfied, however, that the court has jurisdiction to grant a Mareva injunction over foreign assets, and that in this developing branch of the law the decision in Ashtiani... may require further consideration in a future case.

Nicholls L.J. declined to express any opinion on the pre-judgment position.

For my part, if the point had not been conceded before us, I would have agreed with the view expressed by Kerr L.J., for the reasons given in his judgment, that there is jurisdiction to grant a Mareva injunction, pending trial, over assets worldwide; and that cases where it will be appropriate to grant such an injunction will be rare—if not very rare indeed.

Discretion

This arises in two ways. First, the judge had to consider whether it was just and convenient to grant an injunction, in terms of section 37(1) of the Supreme Court Act 1981. Secondly, he ought to have refused interim relief under section 25(2) of the Civil Jurisdiction and Judgments Act 1982 if the fact that the court had no jurisdiction apart from that section made it "inexpedient" to grant relief. Mr. Gee advanced different arguments on discretion in relation to the order restraining dealings with assets abroad on the one hand, and the order for disclosure of information on the other.

As to the first of those orders, he observes that the English courts have no jurisdiction on the merits, none of the first to tenth defendants are resident here, there is no judgment against them, the assets concerned are mainly, if not wholly, outside the jurisdiction, and the proper court to make such orders is either the French court at Grasse or the court(s) having jurisdiction where the assets are located.

I can see considerable force in that last point. It is supported by the judgment of the European Court in Denilauler v. S.n.c. Couchet Frères [1980] E.C.R. 1553, 1570, where it was said:

> The courts of the place or, in any event, of the contracting state, where the assets subject to the measures sought are located, are those best able to assess the circumstances which may lead to the grant or refusal of the measures sought....

But the republic, when it launched the English proceedings, did not know where the assets were located. One of its objects was to find out. The proceedings were started here because it was here that the information was available. There is a case to be made for any injunction over assets abroad to be of limited duration. This would preserve the republic's position until there had been a reasonable opportunity, after discovering where the assets were, to apply for some interim relief in the jurisdiction(s) where the assets were. But although the question of a time limit was raised by the court in the course of the argument, no application was made that one should be imposed.

Mr. Gee also argued that it was wrong in principle to order persons not resident in this country as to what they should or should not do out of the jurisdiction, and relied on the judgment of Hoffmann J. in Mackinnon v. Donaldson, Lufkin and Jenrette Securities Corporation [1986] Ch. 482. That case was actually concerned with an order against a bank, which was not a party to the action. There have been many cases where parties out of jurisdiction have been subjected to an injunction as to their conduct abroad, for example, as to commencing or continuing proceedings there, or bringing children back to this country: see In re Liddell's Settlement Trusts [1936] Ch. 365, 374, where Romer L.J. said:

> The moment a person is properly served under... Order XI that person, so far as the jurisdiction of this court is concerned, is precisely in same position as a person who is in this country.

Mr. Gee argues that even though substantive relief may be granted in such cases, interim relief should not be. I can see no ground for drawing that distinction.

It is beyond question that the injunction granted by Knox J. and upheld by Leggatt J. was a most unusual measure, such as should very rarely be granted. But this case is most unusual. It is not the nature or strength of the republic's cause of action which puts it in that category. What to my mind is determinative is the plain and admitted intention of the defendants to move their assets out of the reach of the courts of law, coupled with the resources they have obtained and the skill they have hitherto shown in doing that, and the vast amount of money involved. This case demands international co-operation between all nations. As the judge said, if ever there was a case for the exercise of the court's powers, this must be it. Or to quote Kerr L.J. in the Babanaft case, at p. 33D-E:

> some situations... cry out—as a matter of justice to the plaintiffs—for disclosure orders and Mareva type injunctions covering foreign assets of defendants even before judgment.

and I think that this is such a case. If the Duvalier family have a defence to the substantive claim, and feel that they are being persecuted, then their remedy, as I have said, is to co-operate in securing an early trial of the dispute. It is not to secrete their assets where even the most just decision in the world cannot reach them.

As to discretion in connection with the information order, Mr. Gee's objection is as to the use which the republic may make of the information obtained. It gave an undertaking to Knox J., as I have said, not to use the information without leave of the court; and it has three times applied for and obtained that leave. But it is said that the court would have no sanction which could be imposed if the republic were to break that undertaking in the future. This was not taken into account by the judge; but he can scarcely be blamed for that, as the point was not raised before him. Kerr L.J. in the Babanaft case did not agree that, as a general rule, such an undertaking should be required. But Neill L.J. and Nicholls L.J. differed from Kerr L.J. on that point; and Nicholls L.J. said that normally the court will need to be satisfied that it has a sufficient degree of control over the plaintiff to secure compliance with the undertaking.

It is difficult to see how, as a matter of law, the court could ensure that it had that degree of control over the Republic of Haiti, short of requiring a bank guarantee in a very large sum which could be called on in the event that the undertaking was broken. But I doubt if the court should make such a demand on a foreign sovereign state, or assume that it would be at all likely to break an undertaking given to the court. The republic has complied scrupulously with its undertaking in the past; and if it were to come about that the undertaking were broken in the future, I would expect that foreign court, particularly those in the European Community, would take that into account in exercising any discretion they may have in proceedings between the republic and the Duvalier family. I do not consider that, in this case, the discretion to order disclosure of information ought to have been exercised against the republic because it is not in law subject to the control of the English courts....

Comments and Questions

1. Since the underlying litigation is before the French court, why not simply leave to that court system all questions regarding preliminary relief? Let us consider three possible scenarios regarding the French court and the relief that the Republic requested here of the English court: (i) the French court did not have the authority to do so; (ii) the French court had the authority but declined to exercise it; or (iii) the French court had the authority but was not asked to exercise it. Under which of these scenarios should the English court complement the foreign litigation by providing provisional relief?

2. If the French court could not or would not issue the preliminary relief the plaintiffs seek, wouldn't this suggest that the Republic of Haiti made a poor choice in choosing the French forum? If the Republic of Haiti could not have chosen England as a forum for the underlying litigation, how can an award of preliminary relief from the English courts be appropriate? Why allow forum shopping solely for the purpose of obtaining preliminary relief?

3. Is the interim relief ordered in this case an application of procedural law or of substantive law? Why is the defendant subject to the mandate of that law?

4. Does the court draw a distinction between restraining a defendant from dealing with his assets for fear that he would hide them in order to defeat his creditors and restraining him to ensure that his assets are protected from commercial risks or spending decisions that might reduce their value as a potential source for satisfying a judgment? Is that right?

2. United States

In the United States system there are two basic methods for a prospective judgment creditor to obtain protection pending final judgment. First, attachments or garnishment orders may put certain of the defendant's property into legal custody. Second, injunctions may restrain the defendant from doing certain acts. Importantly, this latter category generally does not include a Mareva-style injunction.

Attachments and garnishments provide the protection most commonly available to prospective judgment creditors. An attachment order authorizes the sheriff to physically seize certain of the defendant's tangible property. In most jurisdictions, a pre-judgment attachment would issue only if the plaintiff offered sworn testimony that a debt was due and unpaid, and also that the defendant was moving out of state or was secretly disposing of its property. Under some attachment statutes, the sheriff would have the statutory authority to sell the defendant's property if the seized property was depreciating quickly or was otherwise expensive to keep or maintain. Attachments can be of limited use because (1) many state attachment statutes are limited to contract or certain other specified types of claims; and (2) prejudgment attachment usually requires in-rem jurisdiction, which means that the asset to be attached must be located within the jurisdiction.

Much like attachment orders, garnishment orders can give a prospective judgment creditor certain control over the defendant's property. But unlike attachments, garnishments can reach tangible or intangible personal property of the debtor while that property is in the hands of a third party (e.g., the debtor's bank). A garnishment order directs the sheriff to seize tangible property, and to attach constructively the rest of the defendant's property. But garnishment orders, too, are usually limited to contract claims (or exclude tort claims from their scope) and cannot reach property held by a garnishee outside the state.

Injunctions are equitable remedies that operate in personam. Injunctions—whether labeled a temporary restraining order or a preliminary injunction—can require the defendant to perform or refrain from performing particular acts. However, in the case that formed the basis of the hypothetical that opened this chapter, the Supreme Court held that a federal court has no authority to grant a pre-judgment injunction to prevent defendants from dissipating their assets in a case where a plaintiff has made only legal claims. Thus, the classic Mareva scenario was explicitly foreclosed by the Supreme Court of the United States in 1999 in *Grupo Mexicano de Desarrollo v. Alliance Bond Fund*, 527 U.S. 308 (1999). Indeed, the United States is the only major common law jurisdiction where the Mareva injunction has not flourished.

Justice Scalia's opinion in Group Mexicano concluded that federal courts were constrained with regard to available equitable remedies by the Judiciary Act of 1789 which limited equitable remedies to those which were "being administered by the English Court of Chancery at the time of the separation of the two countries." In reaching the decision of the Court to reverse the grant of such a preliminary remedy by the United States District Court for the Southern District of New York and affirmed by the Second Circuit, Justice Scalia noted that federal equity courts had typically rejected this form of relief. He reiterated the rule (as exemplified in England by *Lister v. Stubbs* and in numerous American cases) that "a general creditor (one without a judgment) has no cognizable interest, either at law or in equity, in the property of his debtor, and therefore could not interfere with the debtor's use of that property." Justice Ginsburg's dissent posited that the increasing complexity of international transactions required an invocation of the "grand aims of equity," conferring an expansive power in the federal courts to craft new remedies to deal with new problems. Justice Scalia, in response, did not dispute the inherent flexibility of equitable remedies to deal with emerging problems, but he did take issue with allowing that flexibility to extend beyond the "broad boundaries of traditional equitable relief." Further, he observed that the scenario of debtors seeking to avoid payment of their debts and creditors seeking prompt repayment was certainly not a new problem, let alone one which required "wrenching departure from past practice."

Having decided it was beyond the power of the federal courts to issue a Mareva-style injunction, the Court did not need to reach a conclusion as to whether it would be an advisable remedy to adopt. Nevertheless, the Court continued, and that portion of the opinion is reprinted below.

Grupo Mexicano de Desarrollo v. Alliance Bond Fund

527 U.S. 308, 327–331 (1999)

Justice Scalia delivered the opinion of the Court:

As further support for the proposition that the relief accorded here was unknown to traditional equity practice, it is instructive that the English Court of Chancery, from which the First Congress borrowed in conferring equitable powers on the federal courts, did not provide an injunctive remedy such as this until 1975. In that year, the Court of Appeal decided Mareva Compania Naviera S.A. v. International Bulkcarriers S.A., 2 Lloyd's Rep. 509. Mareva, although acknowledging that the prior case of Lister & Co. v. Stubbs, [1890] 45 Ch. D. 1 (C. A.), said that a court has no power to protect a creditor before he gets judgment, relied on a statute giving courts the authority to grant an interlocutory injunction "'in all cases in which it shall appear to the court to be just or convenient,'" 2 Lloyd's Rep., at 510 (quoting Judicature Act of 1925, Law Reports 1925(2), 15 & 16 Geo. V, ch. 49, § 45). It held (in the words of Lord Denning) that "[i]f it appears that the debt is due and owing—and there is a danger that the debtor may dispose of his assets so as to defeat it before judgment—the Court has jurisdiction in a proper case to grant an interlocutory judgment so as to prevent him [sic] disposing of those assets." 2 Lloyd's Rep., at 510. The Mareva injunction has now been confirmed by statute. See Supreme Court Act of 1981, § 37, 11 Halsbury's Statutes 966, 1001 (1991 reissue).

Commentators have emphasized that the adoption of Mareva injunctions was a dramatic departure from prior practice.

> Before 1975 the courts would not grant an injunction to restrain a defendant from disposing of his assets pendente lite merely because the plaintiff feared that by the time he obtained judgment the defendant would have no assets against which execution could be levied. Applications for such injunctions were consistently refused in the English Commercial Court as elsewhere. They were thought to be so clearly beyond the powers of the court as to be "wholly unarguable"

Hetherington, Introduction to the Mareva Injunction, in Mareva Injunctions 1, n. 1 (M. Hetherington ed. 1983). See also Wasserman, Equity Renewed: Preliminary Injunctions to Secure Potential Money Judgments, 67 Wash. L. Rev. 257, 337 (1992) (stating that Mareva "revolutionized English practice"). The Mareva injunction has been recognized as a powerful tool for general creditors; indeed, it has been called the "nuclear weapo[n] of the law." R. Ough & W. Flenley, The Mareva Injunction and Anton Piller Order: Practice and Precedents xi (2d ed.1993).

The parties debate whether Mareva was based on statutory authority or on inherent equitable power. See Brief for Petitioners 17, n. 8; Brief for Respondents 35–36. Regardless of the answer to this question, it is indisputable that the English courts of equity did not actually exercise this power until 1975, and that federal courts in this country have traditionally applied the principle that courts of equity will not, as a general matter, interfere with the debtor's disposition of his property at the instance of a nonjudgment creditor. We think it incompatible with our traditionally cautious approach to equitable powers, which leaves any substantial expansion of past practice to Congress, to decree the elimination of this significant protection for debtors.

The parties and amici discuss various arguments for and against creating the preliminary injunctive remedy at issue in this case. The United States suggests that the factors supporting such a remedy include

> simplicity and uniformity of procedure; preservation of the court's ability to render a judgment that will prove enforceable; prevention of inequitable conduct on the part of defendants; avoiding disparities between defendants that have assets within the jurisdiction (which would be subject to pre-judgment attachment 'at law') and those that do not; avoiding the necessity for plaintiffs to locate a forum in which the defendant has substantial assets; and, in an age of easy global mobility of capital, preserving the attractiveness of the United States as a center for financial transactions."
>
> Brief for United States as Amicus Curiae 16.

But there are weighty considerations on the other side as well, the most significant of which is the historical principle that before judgment (or its equivalent) an unsecured creditor has no rights at law or in equity in the property of his debtor. As one treatise writer explained:

> A rule of procedure which allowed any prowling creditor, before his claim was definitely established by judgment, and without reference to the character of his demand, to file a bill to discover assets, or to impeach transfers, or interfere with the business affairs of the alleged debtor, would manifestly be susceptible of the grossest abuse. A more powerful weapon of oppression could not be placed at the disposal of unscrupulous litigants.
>
> Wait, Fraudulent Conveyances § 73, at 110–111.

The requirement that the creditor obtain a prior judgment is a fundamental protection in debtor-creditor law—rendered all the more important in our federal system by the debtor's right to a jury trial on the legal claim. There are other factors which likewise give us pause: The remedy sought here could render Fed. R. Civ. P. 64, which authorizes use of state prejudgment remedies, a virtual irrelevance. Why go through the trouble of complying with local attachment and garnishment statutes when this all-purpose prejudgment injunction is available? More importantly, by adding, through judicial fiat, a new and powerful weapon to the creditor's arsenal, the new rule could radically alter the balance between debtor's and creditor's rights which has been developed over centuries through many laws—including those relating to bankruptcy, fraudulent conveyances, and preferences. Because any rational creditor would want to protect his investment, such a remedy might induce creditors to engage in a "race to the courthouse" in cases involving insolvent or near-insolvent debtors, which might prove financially fatal to the struggling debtor. (In this case, we might observe, the respondents did not represent all of the holders of the Notes; they were an active few who sought to benefit at the expense of the other noteholders as well as GMD's other creditors.) It is significant that, in England, use of the Mareva injunction has expanded rapidly. "Since 1975, the English courts have awarded Mareva injunctions to freeze assets in an ever-increasing set of circumstances both within and beyond the commercial setting to an ever-expanding number of plaintiffs." Wasserman, supra, at 339. As early as 1984, one observer stated that "[t]here are now a steady flow of such applications to our Courts which have been estimated to exceed one thousand per month." Shenton, Attachments and Other Interim Court Remedies in Support of Arbitration, 1984 Int'l Bus. Law. 101, 104.

We do not decide which side has the better of these arguments. We set them forth only to demonstrate that resolving them in this forum is incompatible with the democratic and self-deprecating judgment we have long since made: that the equitable powers conferred by the Judiciary Act of 1789 did not include the power to create remedies previously unknown to equity jurisprudence. Even when sitting as a court in equity, we have no authority to craft a "nuclear weapon" of the law like the one advocated here. Joseph Story made the point many years ago:

> If, indeed, a Court of Equity in England did possess the unbounded jurisdiction, which has been thus generally ascribed to it, of correcting, controlling, moderating, and even superceding the law, and of enforcing all the rights, as well as charities, arising from natural law and justice, and of freeing itself from all regard to former rules and precedents, it would be the most gigantic in its sway, and the most formidable instrument of arbitrary power, that could well be devised. It would literally place the whole rights and property of the community under the arbitrary will of the Judge, acting, if you please, arbitrio boni judicis, and it may be, ex aequo et bono, according to his own notions and conscience; but still acting with a despotic and sovereign authority. A Court of Chancery might then well deserve the spirited rebuke of Seldon; "For law we have a measure, and know what to trust to—Equity is according to the conscience of him, that is Chancellor; and as that is larger, or narrower, so is Equity. Tis all one, as if they should make the standard for the measure the Chancellor's foot. What an uncertain measure would this be? One

> Chancellor has a long foot; another a short foot; a third an indifferent foot. It is the same thing with the Chancellor's conscience."
>
> 1 Commentaries on Equity Jurisprudence § 19, at 21

The debate concerning this formidable power over debtors should be conducted and resolved where such issues belong in our democracy: in the Congress.

Because such a remedy was historically unavailable from a court of equity, we hold that the District Court had no authority to issue a preliminary injunction preventing petitioners from disposing of their assets pending adjudication of respondents' contract claim for money damages. We reverse the judgment of the Second Circuit and remand the case for further proceedings consistent with this opinion.

[We have omitted Justice Ginsburg's opinion concurring in part and dissenting in part, in which Justices Stevens, Souter, and Breyer joined.]

Comments and Questions

1. Do you agree with the Court's decision? Without a protective order, what are the chances plaintiff will be able to recover any money judgment it receives? Does the Court's decision tip the balance too far in favor of debtors? Should Congress change the law? Is there a middle ground?

2. The Grupo Mexicano decision holds that the traditional equitable authority of a federal court does not authorize a Mareva-style remedy in cases seeking money damages. Through federal or state legislation, however, "the whole Mareva procedure can serve as an inspiration for what any American court might do in similar circumstances." David D. Siegel, News, N.Y.L.J., Sept. 2, 2003, at s3. See also Jeffrey T. Kirshner & Ronald J. Silverman, Mareva Orders: Fact or Fiction in the United States, Am. Bankr. Inst. J., Nov. 2002, at 24 (suggesting that Mareva-style injunctions should be used domestically); Rhonda Wasserman, Equity Renewed: Preliminary Injunctions to Secure Potential Money Judgments, 67 Wash. L. Rev. 257, 348 (1992) (advocating for adoption of Mareva-style injunctions in United States). Understand that, pursuant to Fed. R. Civ. P. 64, state legislation authorizing Mareva injunctions could also be utilized by federal courts located within that state.

3. Few states, however, have actually expanded the equitable power of their courts through legislation. Moreover, courts of the State of New York, for example, has specifically endorsed the Grupo Mexicano decision.

> Justice Scalia, in Grupo Mexicano, 527 U.S. at 328-329, and others (see, e.g., Sibley and Smith, Taking a Lesson From English Courts on Restricting the Movement of Assets, NYLJ, Nov. 16, 1998, at 1, col 1) have cogently described the profound effects that the availability of world-wide Mareva preliminary injunctions would have on world-wide commerce. That is, the widespread use of this remedy would drastically unbalance existing creditors' and debtors' rights under the present Federal and State statutory and decisional schemes, and substantially interfere

> with the sovereignty and debtor/creditor/bankruptcy laws of, and the rights of interested domiciliaries in, foreign countries. At the very least, the availability of such a powerful, discretionary provisional remedy, even when that discretion is exercised by courts with caution and restraint, would introduce uncertainty in results...
>
> Credit Agricole Indosuez v. Rossiykiy Kredit Bank,
> 94 N.Y.2d 541, 550–551 (2000)

4. In addition to attachments, garnishments, and (permissible) injunctions, states often provide for a range of other specialized remedies. Replevin is an action by an owner or another person (usually a secured creditor) with an interest in property that is located within the jurisdiction to recover possession of that property. Sequestration is a form of (or substitute for) attachment. Arrest is a prejudgment seizure that usually refers to ships. And a receivership may be used in the process of transferring an asset into the legal custody and control of the court.

3. European Union

In addition to the Mareva injunction in common law member states of the European Union, interim protective measures have long been available in the civil law countries. Operating under various names such as arrest (Germany), saisie conservatoire (France), or sequestro (Italy), these devices are often available ex parte, may require the plaintiff to post a bond, and impose greater or lesser thresholds of proof of entitlement to justify the immediate if provisional relief. And like the Mareva jurisprudence but unlike U.S. practice, it is common in these jurisdictions that the protective measures are available regardless of the forum that has jurisdiction on the merits. Schlosser describes one remarkable example:

> [W]hen the Iranian revolution broke out, the new government publicly announced its decision to discontinue repayment of debts. It also ordered its nationals and corporate entities to do likewise, whereupon American and English banks obtained in a German court the garnishment of the Iranians' German bank accounts. The seizure of the 190 million German marks was of particular value to the banks because, unlike Mareva injunctions and American freezing injunctions, the attachment gave security to them. The German courts, however, did not have jurisdiction as to the merits of the case due to arbitration clauses included in the respective agreements.
>
> Peter F. Schlosser, Coordinated Transnational Interaction in Civil Litigation and Arbitration, 12 Mich. J. Int'l L. 150, 154 (1990).
> (In the United States, Iranian assets were frozen pursuant to an executive order. See Dames & Moore v. Regan, 453 U.S. 654 (1981).)

The Brussels Regulation, legislation that binds the member states of the E.U. (and to which we will give considerable attention in the next chapter), does not contain substantive rules regarding interim protective measures, but it does acknowledge the practical importance of such interim measures for litigants. Article 31 reads:

> Application may be made to the courts of a Member State for such provisional, including protective, measures as may be available under the law of that State, even if, under this Regulation, the courts of another Member State have jurisdiction as to the substance of the matter.

Article 47 further specifies that during the time provided for an appeal of an enforcement decision "no measures of enforcement may be taken other than protective measures against the property of the party against whom enforcement is sought." Again the specific procedure is left to national law. Importantly, Article 31 provides litigants with the option of submitting separate applications in distinct jurisdictions. All Member States have an obligation to assist pending litigation in another Member State.

D. Interim Measures in Support of Arbitration

As we discuss throughout this volume, arbitration can be a favorable alternative for the resolution of many disputes. Arbitration can be simpler, cheaper, and quicker; its procedures can be tailored to fit the dispute; and the matter may be resolved privately and confidentially. However, there are also drawbacks to arbitration, and the unavailability or ineffectiveness of interim measures was once a shortcoming.

Whether in an arbitration proceeding or in traditional litigation, the parties have the same concerns about interim relief: plaintiffs want to minimize the risk of obtaining hollow judgments, but we hesitate to require defendants to conform to court orders until plaintiffs have proven their case. The arbitrator stands in a very different position than a judge, however. Judges are part of the state infrastructure, and can enforce their orders through their contempt power. By contrast, arbitrators are private citizens often affiliated with private institutions possessing far less coercive power over the parties. Arbitrators thus have no inherent authority to enforce orders requiring or prohibiting the performance of a particular act. Arbitrators can exert some coercive power by suggesting that an adverse factual inference may be drawn against a party that fails to obey, but this can be an empty threat.

Two sources have developed to authorize interim measures in support of arbitration. First, courts have acted as adjuncts to the arbitral proceedings for the limited purpose of ordering and enforcing preliminary relief. Compare this type of assistance to that furnished by one court to complement another court (a la *Republic of Haiti v. Duvalier*, supra). Are the circumstances substantially similar or fundamentally different? If a court is to provide provisional relief to complement an arbitral proceeding, should it apply its own standards for preliminary relief or simply "take orders" from the arbitrator? Of course any independent inquiry by the court can undermine the value of arbitration as a simpler, cheaper, and quicker alternative. Predictably, then, a second source of authority developed: some legislatures have empowered arbitrators to order certain forms of relief.

Anne Herrmann, Drawing a Contrast: Interim Measures of Protection

9 Vindobona J. of Intl. Comml. L. & Arb. 49, 50–64 (2005)

For many years in a number of jurisdictions arbitral tribunals did not have the power to order interim measures, or at least such powers were limited, as historically this was a power vested in the courts only. However, over the last years there has been an increasing activity by legislatures with the aim of improving the legal framework for arbitral proceedings on both domestic and international levels. Since the adoption of the UNCITRAL Model Law on International Commercial Arbitration (hereafter "UNCITRAL Model Law") on 21 June 1985 by the United Nations Commission on International Trade Law (UNCITRAL) many countries have enacted new arbitration laws that often bring the grant of interim measures within the powers of arbitral tribunals. This essay deals with the power of arbitral tribunals subject to the laws of the United States of America and Germany to grant interim measures in arbitral proceedings.

When comparing the approach of the United States and German laws concerning interim measures in the arbitral setting, the following three issues will be discussed: (i) the arbitral tribunal's authority to order interim measures of protection, (ii) the relationship between court-ordered interim relief and arbitration, and (iii) the enforcement of provisional measures ordered by arbitral tribunals....

United States of America

[The United States enacted the Federal Arbitration Act (FAA) on 12 February 1925 through the enactment of Chapter II of Title Nine of the United States Code. The Uniform Arbitration Act (UAA) is a model law that is in some form the basis of arbitration law in 49 states.]

[B]oth the FAA and the UAA are silent on the arbitral tribunal's powers to order interim relief. However, U.S. courts have held that, although the FAA and the UAA do not expressly confer on arbitral tribunals the power to grant such measures, they have the inherent power to grant provisional remedies, as long as this is not in contradiction with the arbitration agreement of the parties. The Ninth Circuit reasoned that "temporary equitable relief in arbitral proceedings can be indispensable to preserve assets or enforce performance which, if not preserved or enforced, may render a final award meaningless."[17] The Second Circuit pronounced that "New York law gives arbitral tribunals significant power to fashion remedies that they assume will do justice between the parties. An arbitral tribunal's paramount duty is to reach an equitable result... under New York law, arbitral tribunals have power

---

[17] Pacific Reins. Mgmt. Corp. v. Ohio Reins. Corp., 935 F.2d 1019 (9th Cir. 1991).

to fashion relief that a court might not properly grant"[18] Another Federal Court stated that "if an arbitral award of equitable relief based upon a finding of irreparable harm is to have any meaning at all, the parties must be capable of enforcing or vacating it at the time it is made."[19] Only few lower courts have held that an arbitral tribunal lacks power under the FAA to order interim measures where the parties have not expressly conferred such power to it. One court stated:

> Having reviewed the Agreement in the light of its language, its context, and the parties' apparent intent, and in terms of the question of the arbitrator's authority to fashion relief, we conclude that the arbitrator's award of a six million dollar cash surety bond does not draw its essence therefrom and that it is in manifest disregard thereof and must be set aside.[21]

There seems to be no U.S. authority that the FAA forbids arbitral tribunals from granting interim relief when the arbitration agreement of the parties expressly provides for it. This seems to be consistent with the FAA's basic rule that arbitration agreements are enforceable.

Hence, the arbitration agreement can be a source from which arbitral tribunals derive their power to grant injunctive relief; an arbitral tribunal will have such powers to grant interim measures as were conferred to it by the agreement of the parties. While an ad hoc arbitration agreement, which is drawn after a dispute has arisen and when the parties usually have a clearer idea of the matters in dispute may well confer special powers upon the arbitral tribunals, the standard arbitration clause that is typically contained in the commercial contract between the parties does not usually grant any special powers to the arbitral tribunals other than those contained in the rules that the parties may submit to in their agreement to arbitrate, e.g. rules of international arbitration institutions or the lex loci arbitri, the law of the seat of the arbitration. However, if the parties do not make reference to a set of rules it is unlikely that the clause itself would grant the power to the arbitral tribunal.

[The United States is also a party to the Convention on the Recognition and Enforcement of Foreign Arbitral Awards (the "New York Convention"). We will examine this convention in a later chapter since, as its title suggests, it pertains to the enforcement of awards. There is an argument, however, that the New York Convention is relevant even in the context of interim relief measures, since Article II(3) provides that "[t]he court of a Contracting State, when seized of an action in a matter in respect of which the parties have made an agreement within the meaning of this article, shall, at the request of one of the parties, refer the parties to arbitration, unless it finds that the said agreement is null and void, inoperative or incapable of being performed." The question, then, is whether the mandate that the courts "shall refer the parties to arbitration," includes some authority to order interim measures.]

---

[18] Sperry Intl. Trade, Inc. v. Govt. of Israel, 689 F.2d 301 (2nd Cir. 1982).

[19] Compania Chilena de Navegacion Interoceanica, S.A. v. Norton, Lilly & Co., 652 F. Supp. 1512, 1517 (S.D.N.Y. 1987).

[21] Swift Indus., Inc. v. Botany Indus., Inc., 466 F.2d 1125, 1134 (3rd Cir. 1972).

In McCreary Tire & Rubber Co. v. CEAT,[27] the Court of Appeals for the Third Circuit held that Art. II (3) of the New York Convention... divests national courts of jurisdiction to order attachment in aid of arbitration, or to do anything else other than to compel arbitration. [Other courts, however,] have concluded that the New York Convention does not address the question of provisional relief in aid of arbitration. In Carolina Power & Light Co. v. Uranex[30] a federal district court pronounced that coercive remedies available only from the courts could often facilitate the arbitral proceedings instead of disparaging them. The court held that resort to courts for interim measures is not necessarily inconsistent with the general reference of the substance of the claim to arbitration.

Ultimately, however, the question of whether an attachment order can be obtained in the United States before the award has been made remains uncertain and depends on the place where the measure is sought, as the Supreme Court has yet to resolve this conflict. Even if the approach were followed that the New York Convention does not forbid court-ordered provisional measures, national law may still do so. The FAA has governed the federal policy on commercial disputes brought before arbitral tribunals since 1926. One intention of Congress when enacting the FAA was to avoid the delay and expense of litigation and to support the practical justice in the arbitration of disputes. While not yet addressed by the Supreme Court, the question of the judiciary's power to grant provisional relief pending arbitration has been decided by lower courts. Some courts have concluded that §§ 3 and 4 of the FAA deny them the jurisdiction to order provisional measures in aid of arbitration.

In Merrill Lynch, Pierce, Fenner & Smith, Inc. v. Bradley[36] the Fourth Circuit held that "9 U.S.C. § 3 does not preclude a district court from granting one party a preliminary injunction to preserve the status quo pending arbitration."

> Where a dispute is subject to mandatory arbitration under the Federal Arbitration Act, a district court has the discretion to grant a preliminary injunction to preserve the status quo pending the arbitration of the parties' dispute if the enjoined conduct would render that process a "hollow formality."

The Court rested its decision on the fact that no clear mandate or language within the FAA abrogated courts' equitable powers, and on the reasoning that Congress could not have intended to contest the courts' power to grant equitable remedies of interim relief without an "evaluation of the statute's effects."... [But other courts have] held that absent an agreement by the parties permitting the courts to order interim measures the "unmistakably clear congressional purpose" was to bar the courts from granting injunctive relief.[43]...

---

[27] McCreary Tire & Rubber Co. v. CEAT, 501 F.2d 1032 (3rd Cir. 1974).

[30] Carolina Power & Light Company v. Uranex, 451 F. Supp. 1044 (N.D. Cal. 1977).

[36] Merrill Lynch, Pierce, Fenner & Smith, Inc. v. Kenneth Dale Bradley, Samuel L. Collins, 756 F.2d 1048 (4th Cir. 1985).

[43] Merrill Lynch, Pierce, Fenner & Smith, Inc. v. Hovey, 726 F.2d 1286 (8th Cir. 1984).

Germany

The new German law on arbitration came into effect on 1 January 1998. The Tenth Book of the Code of Civil Procedure (hereafter "ZPO") which had contained the German arbitration law ever since the ZPO came into force in 1879 was fully replaced by a new text which is based on the 1985 UNCITRAL Model Law on International Commercial Arbitration. Additionally, in 1992 the institutional framework for national and international arbitration in Germany was reorganised by concentrating existing former institutions at the Federal level within the German Institute for Arbitration (Deutsche Institution für Schiedsgerichtsbarkeit).

In § 1025(1) the new law adopted the "territoriality principle" as opposed to the "procedural theory" that had governed the old law. Pursuant to the "territoriality principle" the German law of arbitration will govern the proceedings whenever Germany is the seat of the arbitration. However, Germany was never a nation that was particularly popular as a place of international commercial arbitration, even though it has traditionally played a major role in European and world-wide commerce. The reasons why international businessmen avoided Germany as a situs for their arbitration proceedings probably included a lack of familiarity with the German language, but mainly with the German law in general, and the fact that the German arbitration law as it was before 1998 was not up to date with modern developments in the practice and the law of international arbitration. Therefore, one major motivation for modeling the new arbitration law after the UNCITRAL Model Law was to make Germany more attractive internationally as a forum for arbitration, as the adoption of the UNCITRAL Model Law signals that Germany encourages international standards for international law and practice, making the country attractive to any international party that is familiar with the UNCITRAL Model Law, which has been widely adopted....

Germany adopted the New York Convention in 1961, complementing the already existing statutory rules of the ZPO, namely § 1044, providing for the recognition and enforceability of foreign arbitration awards. However, the Convention does not address the question of whether and when an arbitral tribunal may order provisional relief.

Before the reform of the ZPO, the arbitral tribunal's authority to order interim measures was one of the classic topics of discussion in the field of arbitration. While strong voices in the literature pleaded for an exclusive competence of the arbitral tribunal to order interim measures, the courts and other parts of the literature declared that only courts had the power to order provisional relief. By enacting the new legislation, the legislature put an end to the debate and declared that provisional relief can be obtained from arbitral tribunals. It is § 1041 (1) ZPO that deals with the arbitral tribunal's competence to order interim measures of protection. The new approach is based on Art. 17 UNCITRAL Model Law, with minor changes in the wording. Section 1041 (1) provides arbitral tribunals with a broad power to order interim relief. The arbitral tribunal's power is not limited to certain measures and depends on the arbitral tribunal's evaluation of whether the measure is necessary and appropriate in the particular circumstances. This is not so in court proceedings, where the judge has to order the interim measure if the prerequisites set out in the law are met.

The arbitral tribunal's authority to order interim relief is made subject to a contrary agreement by the parties, § 1041 (1). If in their agreement to arbitrate the parties refer to arbitration rules of an institution and those rules do not allow for arbitrator-ordered interim relief, then that is regarded as a "contrary agreement" under § 1041(1).

By interpretation of § 1041 (2) it can be concluded that the arbitral tribunal is not limited to ordering provisional measures that fit the German enforcement system, because the provision states that the court may re-design an order of an arbitral tribunal if that is necessary for the purpose of enforcement of the measure. If the arbitral tribunal was limited to orders traditionally known to German law there would be no need for a judge to re-fashion the orders. Therefore, § 1041 (2) gains importance in the case where an arbitral tribunal orders a provisional measure not common to the German law, such as the English law concept of worldwide Mareva injunction.

Based on Art. 9 UNCITRAL Model Law, § 1033 provides for the courts' parallel competence to order interim measures either before or during arbitral proceedings. This is important in practice in view of the fact that interim measures by the arbitral tribunal itself, though possible according to § 1041 of the ZPO, are not always available or enforceable. Although based on Art. 9 UNCITRAL Model Law, § 1033 differs in that it states that the courts can only take interim measures of protection relating to the issue in dispute in the arbitration proceedings. This limits the scope of the support that the parties are entitled to get from the courts. Section 1032 provides that if an action that is subject to arbitration is brought before a court the judge shall refer the parties to arbitration, unless the respondent fails to raise an objection prior to the beginning of the oral hearing on the substance of the dispute. The jurisdiction of the courts granted by § 1033 however cannot be abrogated by the parties. While some authors emphasize the declaratory character of the norm others emphasize that § 1033 vests the courts with original jurisdiction to order provisional measures. If the first view that § 1033 is merely of a declaratory character is followed, then the courts' jurisdiction must be established under the provisions of the ZPO generally dealing with the competence of courts to order interim measures of protection.

Section 1025(2) states that an application for any interim measure of protection pursuant to § 1033 can be filed at a German court even if the seat of the arbitration, determined pursuant to § 1043, is outside of Germany or has not yet been determined. In that case the rules of international civil procedural law determine the court's jurisdiction. In summary, the situation is that when there is an arbitration agreement, it is up to the parties to decide where they want to apply to for interim measures.

***

In 2006, the UNCITRAL Model Law was amended to include much more detail about interim measures and preliminary orders. Excerpts from the model follow.

Additional excerpts from this model, including sections that are cross-referenced below, appear in Chapter 7.

UNCITRAL Model Law on International Commercial Arbitration

24 I.L.M. 1302 (1985), as amended (2006)

Chapter II. Arbitration Agreement

Article 9. Arbitration agreement and interim measures by court

It is not incompatible with an arbitration agreement for a party to request, before or during arbitral proceedings, from a court an interim measure of protection and for a court to grant such measure....

Chapter IV. Jurisdiction of Arbitral Tribunal

Article 16. Competence of arbitral tribunal to rule on its jurisdiction

(1) The arbitral tribunal may rule on its own jurisdiction, including any objections with respect to the existence or validity of the arbitration agreement. For that purpose, an arbitration clause which forms part of a contract shall be treated as an agreement independent of the other terms of the contract. A decision by the arbitral tribunal that the contract is null and void shall not entail ipso jure the invalidity of the arbitration clause.

(2) A plea that the arbitral tribunal does not have jurisdiction shall be raised not later than the submission of the statement of defence. A party is not precluded from raising such a plea by the fact that he has appointed, or participated in the appointment of, an arbitrator. A plea that the arbitral tribunal is exceeding the scope of its authority shall be raised as soon as the matter alleged to be beyond the scope of its authority is raised during the arbitral proceedings. The arbitral tribunal may, in either case, admit a later plea if it considers the delay justified.

(3) The arbitral tribunal may rule on a plea referred to in paragraph (2) of this article either as a preliminary question or in an award on the merits. If the arbitral tribunal rules as a preliminary question that it has jurisdiction, any party may request, within thirty days after having received notice of that ruling, the court specified in article 6 to decide the matter, which decision shall be subject to no appeal; while such a request is pending, the arbitral tribunal may continue the arbitral proceedings and make an award.

Chapter IV A. Interim Measures and Preliminary Orders

Section 1. Interim measures

Article 17. Power of arbitral tribunal to order interim measures

(1) Unless otherwise agreed by the parties, the arbitral tribunal may, at the request of a party, grant interim measures.

(2) An interim measure is any temporary measure, whether in the form of an award or in another form, by which, at any time prior to the issuance of the award by which the dispute is finally decided, the arbitral tribunal orders a party to:

(a) Maintain or restore the status quo pending determination of the dispute;

(b) Take action that would prevent, or refrain from taking action that is likely to cause, current or imminent harm or prejudice to the arbitral process itself;

(c) Provide a means of preserving assets out of which a subsequent award may be satisfied; or

(d) Preserve evidence that may be relevant and material to the resolution of the dispute.

Article 17 A. Conditions for granting interim measures

(1) The party requesting an interim measure under article 17(2)(a), (b) and (c) shall satisfy the arbitral tribunal that:

(a) Harm not adequately reparable by an award of damages is likely to result if the measure is not ordered, and such harm substantially outweighs the harm that is likely to result to the party against whom the measure is directed if the measure is granted; and

(b) There is a reasonable possibility that the requesting party will succeed on the merits of the claim. The determination on this possibility shall not affect the discretion of the arbitral tribunal in making any subsequent determination.

(2) With regard to a request for an interim measure under article 17(2)(d), the requirements in paragraphs (1)(a) and (b) of this article shall apply only to the extent the arbitral tribunal considers appropriate.

Section 2. Preliminary orders

Article 17 B. Applications for preliminary orders and conditions for granting preliminary orders

(1) Unless otherwise agreed by the parties, a party may, without notice to any other party, make a request for an interim measure together with an application for a preliminary order directing a party not to frustrate the purpose of the interim measure requested.

(2) The arbitral tribunal may grant a preliminary order provided it considers that prior disclosure of the request for the interim measure to the party against whom it is directed risks frustrating the purpose of the measure.

(3) The conditions defined under article 17A apply to any preliminary order, provided that the harm to be assessed under article 17A(1)(a), is the harm likely to result from the order being granted or not.

Article 17 C. Specific regime for preliminary orders

(1) Immediately after the arbitral tribunal has made a determination in respect of an application for a preliminary order, the arbitral tribunal shall give notice to all parties of the request for the interim measure, the application for the preliminary

order, the preliminary order, if any, and all other communications, including by indicating the content of oral communication, between any party and the arbitral tribunal in relation thereto.

(2) At the same time, the arbitral tribunal shall give an opportunity to any party against whom a preliminary order is directed to present its case at the earliest practicable time.

(3) The arbitral tribunal shall decide promptly on any objection to the preliminary order.

(4) A preliminary order shall expire after twenty days from the date on which it was issued by the arbitral tribunal. However, the arbitral tribunal may issue an interim measure adopting or modifying the preliminary order, after the party against whom the preliminary order is directed has been given notice and an opportunity to present its case.

(5) A preliminary order shall be binding on the parties but shall not be subject to enforcement by a court. Such a preliminary order does not constitute an award.

Section 3. Provisions applicable to interim measures and preliminary orders

Article 17 D. Modification, suspension, termination

The arbitral tribunal may modify, suspend, or terminate an interim measure or a preliminary order it has granted, upon application of any party or, in exceptional circumstances and upon prior notice to the parties, on the arbitral tribunal's own initiative.

Article 17 E. Provision of security

(1) The arbitral tribunal may require the party requesting an interim measure to provide appropriate security in connection with the measure.

(2) The arbitral tribunal shall require the party applying for a preliminary order to provide security in connection with the order unless the arbitral tribunal considers it inappropriate or unnecessary to do so.

Article 17 F. Disclosure

(1) The arbitral tribnal may require any party promptly to disclose any material change in the circumstances on the basis of which the measure was requested or granted.

(2) The party applying for a preliminary order shall disclose to the arbitral tribunal all circumstances that are likely to be relevant to the arbitral tribunal's determination whether to grant or maintain the order, and such obligation shall continue until the party against whom the order has been requested has had an opportunity to present its case. Thereafter, paragraph (1) of this article shall apply.

Article 17 G. Costs and damages

The party requesting an interim measure or applying for a preliminary order shall be liable for any costs and damages caused by the measure or the order to any party if the arbitral tribunal later determines that, in the circumstances, the measure or the order should not have been granted. The arbitral tribunal may award such costs and damages at any point during the proceedings.

Section 4. Recognition and enforcement of interim measures

Article 17 H. Recognition and enforcement

(1) An interim measure issued by an arbitral tribunal shall be recognized as binding and, unless otherwise provided by the arbitral tribunal, enforced upon application to the competent court, irrespective of the country in which it was issued, subject to the provisions of article 17 I.

(2) The party who is seeking or has obtained recognition or enforcement of an interim measure shall promptly inform the court of any termination, suspension or modification of that interim measure.

(3) The court of the State where recognition or enforcement is sought may, if it considers it proper, order the requesting party to provide appropriate security if the arbitral tribunal has not already made a determination with respect to security or where such a decision is necessary to protect the rights of third parties.

Article 17 I. Grounds for refusing recognition or enforcement***

(1) Recognition or enforcement of an interim measure may be refused only:

- (a) At the request of the party against whom it is invoked if the court is satisfied that:
  - (i) Such refusal is warranted on the grounds set forth in article 36(1)(a)(i), (ii), (iii) or (iv); or
  - (ii) The arbitral tribunal's decision with respect to the provision of security in connection with the interim measure issued by the arbitral tribunal has not been complied with; or
  - (iii) The interim measure has been terminated or suspended by the arbitral tribunal or, where so empowered, by the court of the State in which the arbitration takes place or under the law of which that interim measure was granted; or
- (b) If the court finds that:
  - (i) The interim measure is incompatible with the powers conferred upon the court unless the court decides to reformulate the interim measure to the extent necessary to adapt it to its own powers and procedures for the purposes of enforcing that interim measure and without modifying its substance; or
  - (ii) Any of the grounds set forth in article 36(1)(b)(i) or (ii), apply to the recognition and enforcement of the interim measure.

(2) Any determination made by the court on any ground in paragraph (1) of this article shall be effective only for the purposes of the application to recognize and enforce the interim measure. The court where recognition or enforcement is sought shall not, in making that determination, undertake a review of the substance of the interim measure.

*** The conditions set forth in article 17 I are intended to limit the number of circumstances in which the court may refuse to enforce an interim measure. It would not be contrary to the level of harmonization sought to be achieved by these model provisions if a State were to adopt fewer circumstances in which enforcement may be refused.

Section 5. Court-ordered interim measures

Article 17 J. Court-ordered interim measures

A court shall have the same power of issuing an interim measure in relation to arbitration proceedings, irrespective of whether their place is in the territory of this State, as it has in relation to proceedings in courts. The court shall exercise such power in accordance with its own procedures in consideration of the specific features of international arbitration.

Comments and Questions

1. Does the awesome power of equity belong in the hands of arbitrators? (Why) Does it belong in the hands of judges?

2. Do the courts of the country of the seat of arbitration have some obligation to facilitate a meaningful arbitral proceeding? Are formal and nonformal modes of dispute resolution competitors or complements?

3. The excerpt from Anne Herrman, who is a lawyer in Paris, references at note 30 Carolina Power & Light Company v. Uranex, 451 F. Supp. 1044 (N.D. Cal. 1977). This case deserves further attention.

In 1973 Carolina Power & Light Company ("CP&L"), a North Carolina public utility company, contracted with defendant Uranex for the delivery of uranium concentrates to CP&L during the period 1977 to 1986. Uranex is a French groupement d'interet economique that markets uranium internationally. After the price of uranium fuel rose dramatically, Uranex either would not or could not deliver at the contract price. Pursuant to a clause in their contract, CP&L and Uranex took their dispute to arbitration in New York.

With the arbitration underway, CP&L proceeded ex parte in a California federal court to attach an $85 million debt owed to Uranex by Homestake Mining Company, a California company. The debt had no relationship to the CP&L-Uranex litigation except as a potential source for CP&L to satisfy any judgment that it might obtain. And but for the attachment, the funds would have been transferred to Uranex (in France). Other than being owed money by the California corporation, Uranex had absolutely no connection with nor assets in California.

Should the California court issue an attachment to secure any monetary award that CP&L might obtain in the New York arbitral proceeding?

4. Hermman argues that the uncertainty that persists under U.S. law (vis-à-vis Germany) is problematic or at least undesirable. Does the fact that the U.S. has not amended the FAA suggest that the regime works well and to the satisfaction of the U.S. on the domestic level?

5. From a policy perspective, should the United States adopt the UNCITRAL Model Law, or amend the FAA based on the UNCITRAL Model Law? To be sure, the international competition for arbitral business has led other governments, such as Germany, to enact new or revised international arbitration statutes. In whose

interest is it to offer an environment that is popular as a seat of international arbitral proceedings?

E. Antisuit Injunctions

Parallel litigation is a recurring theme in this course. Whenever a dispute has some transnational character, the courts of all jurisdictions involved might legitimately—and simultaneously—undertake to resolve the dispute. But in which state(s) should the litigation take place? One multilateral solution to this dilemma is for the states to adopt a "first in time" approach, to wit: the country where the action was first filed has exclusive jurisdiction. This approach, which generally describes contemporary European practice, avoids the prospect of irreconcilable judgments and delivers much certainty. But it also creates a "race to the courthouse" that encourages parties to initiate formal litigation at the earliest stages of a dispute. Moreover, it is a crude solution to a nuanced problem: where the litigation was first filed offers little insight into the question where a case should proceed.

Yet allowing parallel proceedings is also an inelegant solution. Allowing two cases to proceed in tandem is, at best, duplicative and will often lead to inconsistent judgments. Moreover, given the practice regarding the recognition and enforcement of foreign judgments (which we will study later), the party who first receives a favorable judgment will be in an advantageous position. Accordingly, this is but a different race—a "race to judgment." And the parties' incentive will be to expedite their own proceeding and to prolong the other.

An injunction restraining a party from continuing with proceedings commenced by that party in another forum is a particular form of interim remedy that is peculiar to Anglo-American common law systems. A court might issue such an order to protect its own jurisdiction over the case; or the court might issue the order to facilitate an arbitral proceeding underway in the forum state. These orders, commonly called anti-suit injunctions, are especially controversial because they directly interfere with proceedings in another jurisdiction. Although the injunction is directed to the parties (rather than to the other court), the purpose and effect of the injunction is to prevent the other forum from exercising jurisdiction. Accordingly, common law courts are reluctant to grant an antisuit injunction simply to avoid parallel litigation or to prevent a race to judgment.

Gau Shan Co., Ltd. v. Bankers Trust Co.

956 F.2d 1349 (6th Cir. 1992)

Ryan, Circuit Judge

I

[Gau Shan Co., Ltd. ("Gau Shan") is a Hong Kong corporation that markets cotton to the People's Republic of China. Julien Company ("Julien") is a Tennessee corporation that uses Bankers Trust Company ("Bankers Trust"), another American corporation, as its primary source of financing its cotton sales. Gau Shan sought assurances that Bankers Trust would provide the funds necessary for Julien to release cotton that Gau Shan wished to purchase from Julien and sell to the People's Republic of China. In response to this request for assurances, Andrew Halle, a vice president of Bankers Trust, assured Gau Shan that he "would work something out." Based on these assurances, Gau Shan agreed to sell 15,000 metric tons of cotton to China and contracted with Julien as a source of supply.

Halle learned afterward that Julien had an overdue debt owed to LOR, Incorporated ("LOR") that was unrelated to the contracts with Gau Shan. Because Julien did not have the funds to pay the overdue debt, Halle suggested that Julien pay the overdue debt with money that Bankers Trust would prepay to Julien for the cotton Julien agreed to sell to Gau Shan. Halle then called Gau Shan in Hong Kong and told them "that Bankers Trust could not advance the necessary money to Julien unless Gau Shan signed a $20 million promissory note payable to Bankers Trust." Under protest, Gau Shan signed the note.

Bankers Trust deposited $20 million in Julien's account and then wired the entire $20 million out of Julien's account to LOR's account in another bank in satisfaction of the unrelated overdue debt. Halle anticipated that LOR, upon satisfaction of the debt, would release some certificated cotton that Julien was selling to yet another party. This unrelated sale was to produce funds that could be used to purchase the cotton that Julien contracted to supply to Gau Shan. Things did not go entirely according to plan, however, and "because of some problems with the release of the certificated cotton, Julien shipped to China only about 24% of the cotton it had agreed to ship on Gau Shan's behalf." This resulted in Gau Shan only fulfilling part of its contractual obligation to the People's Republic of China.

Bankers Trust demanded payment on Gau Shan's note advising Gau Shan that if payment was not made by February 26, 1990, it would file suit in Hong Kong for collection on the note. Rather than paying the note, however, Gau Shan filed suit in the United States District Court for the Western District of Tennessee on February 23, 1990, asking for rescission of the note, alleging that it was induced to sign it by Halle's fraud.

On February 23, the district court issued a temporary restraining order, followed at a later date by a preliminary injunction enjoining Bankers Trust from initiating a suit in Hong Kong regarding the note against Gau Shan. The district court determined at the hearing for the preliminary injunction that:

> Gau Shan would be irreparably harmed if Bankers Trust sued Gau Shan in Hong Kong or if Bankers Trust exercised its rights under Hong Kong law to appoint a receiver for Gau Shan pursuant to Hong Kong judicial procedure or under a deed of charge governed by Hong Kong law.

The district court also determined "that Gau Shan had demonstrated a strong likelihood that it could succeed on the merits of its underlying fraud claims." The district court concluded that:

> [T]he dictates of international comity did not preclude the issuance of an injunction here.... [B]ecause parallel proceedings duplicate the parties and issues, the

> federal courts' important public policy of a just, speedy and inexpensive determination…would be evaded should Bankers Trust be permitted to sue Gau Shan in Hong Kong.

Bankers Trust appealed the district court's order

II

The underlying issue is whether, in issuing its preliminary injunction, the district court "improperly applie[d] the law or use[d] an erroneous legal standard" by misinterpreting applicable principles of international comity.

A. International Comity

It is well settled that American courts have the "power to control the conduct of persons subject to their jurisdiction to the extent of forbidding them from suing in foreign jurisdictions." Laker Airways Ltd. v. Sabena, Belgian World Airlines, 731 F.2d 909, 926 (D.C. Cir. 1984) (footnote omitted). However, "parallel proceedings on the same in personam claim should ordinarily be allowed to proceed simultaneously, at least until a judgment is reached in one [jurisdiction] which can be pled as res judicata in the other." Id. at 926–27 (footnote omitted). For this reason, injunctions "restraining litigants from proceeding in courts of independent countries are rarely issued." Id. at 927 (footnote omitted).

The circuits are split concerning the proper standards to be applied, in the context of considerations of international comity, in determining whether a foreign antisuit injunction should be issued. The Ninth and Fifth Circuits hold that a duplication of the parties and issues, alone, is generally sufficient to justify the issuance of such an injunction. See, e.g., Seattle Totems Hockey Club, Inc. v. National Hockey League, 652 F.2d 852, 856 (9th Cir. 1981), cert. denied, 457 U.S. 1105 (1982); In re Unterweser Reederei, GmbH, 428 F.2d 888, 896 (5th Cir. 1970), rev'd on other grounds, 407 U.S. 1 (1972). These courts rely primarily upon considerations of vexatiousness or oppressiveness in a race to judgment in the foreign forum as sufficient grounds for an injunction. But, the Second and D.C. Circuits have held that the standard for granting a foreign antisuit injunction is whether the injunction is necessary to protect the forum court's jurisdiction or to prevent evasion of the forum court's important public policies. See, e.g., Sea Containers Ltd. v. Stena AB, 890 F.2d 1205, 1214 (D.C. Cir. 1989); China Trade & Dev. Corp. v. M.V. Choong Yong, 837 F.2d 33, 36 (2d Cir. 1987); Laker Airways, 731 F.2d at 927, 937. This circuit has not addressed the question.

1. Fifth and Ninth Circuits' View

In Seattle Totems, the Ninth Circuit affirmed the issuance of an antisuit injunction against the defendants in an antitrust suit brought against the National Hockey League (NHL) which had sought to file a suit involving the same breach of contract claim in Canadian courts. 652 F.2d at 856. The NHL, plaintiffs in the Canadian action, admitted that under Fed. R. Civ. P. 13(a) their contract claim would constitute a compulsory counterclaim in the antitrust lawsuit pending in the United States court. Id. at 853. However, Canadian law did not require that the defendant raise its compulsory counterclaim. Id. at 854. The Ninth Circuit found that the district court properly invoked Rule 13(a) to govern the pending litigation rather than Canadian law and held that the injunction against the Canadian suit was proper. Id. at 853–54.

The court in Seattle Totems stated that "foreign litigation may be enjoined when it would (1) frustrate a policy of the forum issuing the injunction; (2) be vexatious or oppressive; (3) threaten the issuing courts [sic] in rem or quasi in rem jurisdiction, or (4) where the proceedings prejudice other equitable considerations." Id. at 855. The court held that the lower court did not abuse its discretion by enjoining the prosecution of the contract claim in Canada in view of relevant factors, including "the convenience to the parties and witnesses, the interests of the court in promoting the efficient administration of justice and the potential prejudice to one party or another." Id. at 856.

The court in Seattle Totems cited as authority the Fifth Circuit case of In re Unterweser Reederei, 428 F.2d 888, 896 (5th Cir. 1970), wherein the Fifth Circuit affirmed the lower court's decision enjoining one of the parties from prosecuting in English courts a claim which had been pled as a counterclaim in the pending district court action. The Fifth Circuit stated that, "allowing simultaneous prosecution of the same action in a foreign forum thousands of miles away would result in 'inequitable hardship' and 'tend to frustrate and delay the speedy and efficient determination of the cause.'" Id. at 896 (footnote omitted).

Thus, the Fifth and Ninth Circuits hold that a duplication of the parties and issues, alone, is sufficient to justify a foreign antisuit injunction.

2. Second and D.C. Circuits' View

In Laker Airways, American and other non-British defendants were enjoined from seeking relief in English courts as an attempt to escape United States antitrust laws for their conduct in the United States. 731 F.2d at 956. The D.C. Circuit upheld the trial court's injunction, finding that the antitrust laws were clearly applicable to the conduct which was the subject of the claims. The court held that "a preliminary injunction [was] imperative to preserve the court's jurisdiction." Id.

Similarly, the Second Circuit adopted the Laker Airways analysis in deciding to reverse the lower court's decision to issue an injunction. China Trade, 837 F.2d at 35. The Second Circuit held that a foreign antisuit injunction was not justified because the Korean litigation did not threaten the district court's jurisdiction or threaten any important public policies. Id. at 37.

Thus, the Second and D.C. Circuits hold that the only proper grounds to grant a foreign antisuit injunction are: (1) to protect the forum's jurisdiction, or (2) to prevent evasion of the forum's important public policies. These circuits hold that a duplication of the parties and issues, alone, is not sufficient to justify a foreign antisuit injunction. China Trade, 837 F.2d at 36; Laker Airways, 731 F.2d at 928.

The district court in this case, in concluding that the dictates of international comity did not preclude the issuance of an injunction here, did not adopt the approaches of either the Fifth and Ninth Circuits or the Second and D.C. Circuits.

Instead, the court used elements from each and found that because parallel proceedings duplicate the parties and issues, the federal courts' important public policy of a just, speedy and inexpensive determination of every action under Fed. R. Civ. P. 1 and 13 would be evaded should Bankers Trust be permitted to sue Gau Shan in Hong Kong. Gau Shan agrees and argues that these and other factors favor litigation of Bankers Trust's collection claim in Tennessee.

Bankers Trust responds that this court should adopt the analysis of the Second and D.C. Circuits that a foreign antisuit injunction should issue only when the foreign proceeding (1) threatens the jurisdiction of the United States court, or (2) evades strong public policies of the United States. Bankers Trust contends there is no threat to this court's jurisdiction because the Hong Kong suit would not affect this suit. It also contends that a suit in Hong Kong would not evade any important public policies of the United States. We agree.

III

Comity dictates that foreign antisuit injunctions be issued sparingly and only in the rarest of cases. Laker Airways, 731 F.2d at 927. The days of American hegemony over international economic affairs have long since passed. The United States cannot today impose its economic will on the rest of the world and expect meek compliance, if indeed it ever could. The modern era is one of world economic interdependence, and economic interdependence requires cooperation and comity between nations. In an increasingly international market, commercial transactions involving players from multiple nations have become commonplace. Every one of these transactions presents the possibility of concurrent jurisdiction in the courts of the nations of the parties involved concerning any dispute arising in the transaction. This case is an example. Here, we have the possibility of concurrent jurisdiction in Hong Kong and the United States. Gau Shan asks this court to disregard the principles of international comity and affirm the issuance of an antisuit injunction which effectively denies the Hong Kong court jurisdiction over a matter otherwise properly before it, and reserves to a United States court exclusive jurisdiction over a dispute involving parties from different nations. Before taking such a drastic step, this court must consider carefully the implications of such action under principles of international comity.

Although an antisuit injunction does not directly interfere in a foreign court's jurisdiction, it "effectively restrict[s] the foreign court's ability to exercise its jurisdiction." Laker Airways, 731 F.2d at 927. In this case, for example, the injunction restricts the Hong Kong court's ability to exercise its jurisdiction by enjoining Bankers Trust from bringing suit in Hong Kong. In a case in which parties to an international transaction file separate suits in different forums, the availability of antisuit injunctions presents the possibility that no relief will be granted. If both the foreign court and the United States court issue injunctions preventing their respective nationals from prosecuting a suit in the foreign forum, both actions will be paralyzed and neither party will be able to obtain any relief. The more readily courts resort to this extraordinary device, the more frequently this sort of undesirable stalemate will occur.

The inappropriate use of antisuit injunctions can have unintended, widespread effects. International commerce depends in no small part on the ability of merchants to predict the likely consequences of their conduct in overseas markets. Predictability depends in turn on an atmosphere of cooperation and reciprocity between nations. The issuance of antisuit injunctions threatens predictability by making cooperation and reciprocity between courts of different nations less likely.

In this regard, antisuit injunctions are even more destructive of international comity than, for example, refusals to enforce foreign judgments. At least in the latter context foreign courts are given the opportunity to exercise their jurisdiction. Antisuit injunctions, on the other hand, deny foreign courts the right to exercise their proper jurisdiction. Such action conveys the message, intended or not, that the issuing court has so little confidence in the foreign court's ability to adjudicate a given dispute fairly and efficiently that it is unwilling even to allow the possibility. Foreign courts can be expected to reciprocate such disrespect. Reciprocity and cooperation can only suffer as a result. Accordingly, foreign antisuit injunctions should be issued only in the most extreme cases.

The district court concluded that these concerns of international comity are outweighed in this case by the threat that concurrent litigation in Hong Kong would pose to the policy of the federal courts "to secure the just, speedy, and inexpensive determination of every action." Fed. R. Civ. P. 1. According to the district court, the issuance of an antisuit injunction in this case was justified in order to prevent "vexatious" litigation in Hong Kong that would delay and complicate the litigation already pending in its court. We cannot agree. We conclude that the district court's reasoning, in deciding that this case did not violate the dictates of international comity, is more properly the analysis to be used when considering a motion for dismissal of a case on forum non conveniens grounds rather than a motion for a foreign antisuit injunction. The policies of avoiding hardships to the parties and promoting the economies of consolidated litigation "do not outweigh the important principles of comity that compel deference and mutual respect for concurrent foreign proceedings. Thus, the better rule is that duplication of parties and issues alone is not sufficient to justify issuance of an antisuit injunction." Laker Airways, 731 F.2d at 928 (footnotes omitted). See also China Trade, 837 F.2d at 36.

Factors such as "vexatiousness" or "oppressiveness" and a "race to judgment" are "likely to be present whenever parallel actions are proceeding concurrently." China Trade, 837 F.2d at 36. An antisuit injunction based upon these factors would tend to debilitate the policy that permits parallel actions to continue and that disfavors antisuit injunctions. Id. We think the reasoning of the Second and D.C. Circuits, identifying the proper criteria for issuance of antisuit injunctions, more satisfactorily accommodates the important principles of international comity a federal court should take into account. Therefore, we shall consider only two factors in determining whether Bankers Trust should be enjoined from proceeding in its Hong Kong action: (1) whether this court's jurisdiction is threatened by the Hong Kong action, and (2) whether this court's important public policies are being evaded by the Hong Kong action.

IV

A. Protecting Jurisdiction

"Courts have a duty to protect their legitimately conferred jurisdiction to the extent necessary to provide full justice to litigants." Laker Airways, 731 F.2d at 927. Therefore, "when the action of a litigant in another forum threatens to paralyze the jurisdiction of the court, the court may consider the effectiveness and propriety of issuing an injunction against the litigant's participation in the foreign proceedings." Id.

Such threats to a court's jurisdiction, however, are quite unusual. Our review of the case law reveals only two scenarios that have been held to threaten a court's jurisdiction. First, it has long been recognized that concurrent proceedings pose an inherent threat to a court's jurisdiction where the basis for that jurisdiction is in rem or quasi in rem. See China Trade, 837 F.2d at 36. Where jurisdiction is based on the presence of property within the court's jurisdictional boundaries, a concurrent proceeding in a foreign jurisdiction poses the danger that the foreign court will order the transfer of the property out of the jurisdictional boundaries of the first court, thus depriving it of jurisdiction over the matter. This concern, of course, is not present in this in personam proceeding.

Second, "[e]ven in in personam proceedings, if a foreign court is not merely proceeding in parallel but is attempting to carve out exclusive jurisdiction over the action, an injunction may also be necessary to protect the enjoining court's jurisdiction." China Trade, 837 F.2d at 36. This is the type of threat to jurisdiction that prompted the court in Laker Airways to issue an antisuit injunction. Laker Airways, 731 F.2d at 915. The Laker Airways court concluded:

> Ordinarily antisuit injunctions are not properly invoked to preempt parallel proceedings on the same in personam claim in foreign tribunals. However, KLM and Sabena do not qualify under this general rule because the foreign action they seek to [enjoin] is interdictory and not parallel. It was instituted by the foreign defendants for the sole purpose of terminating the United States claim.

Id. Indeed, in Laker Airways, the British Court of Appeals actually enjoined Laker from pursuing its claims against British defendants in a United States court under United States law. Id. Such a direct interference with the jurisdiction of the United States court justified the defensive issuance of an antisuit injunction against the remaining defendants in the Laker case. Id.

Although there are many factors which favor this case being heard in the United States, and in particular Tennessee, we find nothing to indicate that the federal court's jurisdiction is threatened. Gau Shan offers no reason why this court should conclude that the Hong Kong courts would enter an antisuit injunction in this case. Moreover, Bankers Trust has stipulated that it would not seek such relief in the Hong Kong courts. Gau Shan argues that the district court's jurisdiction is threatened because, under Hong Kong law, Bankers Trust would be allowed to appoint a receiver of its choice for Gau Shan without court approval pursuant to a "Deed of Charge." The bank-appointed receiver would have the power to discharge Gau Shan's employees and to abandon any proceedings concerning Gau Shan's assets. Gau Shan contends that such an appointment could result in a dismissal of this lawsuit without ever reaching the merits of the controversy.

Although we agree with the trial court that this Deed of Charge, which is unknown in this country, is contrary to the laws of the United States, we do not find that our jurisdiction is threatened. The possibility that a holding of a Hong Kong court might permit Bankers Trust to gain control of Gau Shan is not a threat to the jurisdiction of the United States courts; rather, it is merely a threat to Gau Shan's interest in prosecuting its lawsuit. In Sea Containers Ltd. v. Stena AB, 890 F.2d 1205, 1212–13 (D.C. Cir. 1989), the court noted this distinction and concluded that its jurisdiction was not threatened by the possibility that a ruling of a foreign court might eventually result in the voluntary dismissal of the claim before the United States court. We agree. Moreover, Bankers Trust has represented to the district court and to this court that it will not exercise any of its receivership rights under Hong Kong law should it be permitted to proceed with its suit in Hong Kong. Therefore, we find that this court's jurisdiction is not threatened.

B. Important Public Policies

An antisuit injunction may be appropriate when a party seeks to evade the forum's important policies by litigating before a foreign court. "While an injunction may be appropriate when a party attempts to evade compliance with a statute of the forum that effectuates important public policies, an injunction is not appropriate merely to prevent a party from seeking 'slight advantages in the substantive or procedural law to be applied in a foreign court.'" China Trade, 837 F.2d at 37 (quoting Laker Airways, 731 F.2d at 931 n. 73).

Gau Shan argues that the United States has a significant public policy, as stated in Fed. R. Civ. P. 1, of providing "the just, speedy, and inexpensive determination of every action." Moreover, Gau Shan argues, citing Seattle Totems, that under Fed. R. Civ. P. 13(a) Bankers Trust should be barred from instituting its Hong Kong action because it is required under the compulsory counterclaim rule to bring, in this litigation, the claim it wishes to prosecute in the Hong Kong suit. Gau Shan states that the purpose of requiring a defendant's claim to be brought as a counterclaim in a pending action is "to prevent multiplicity of actions and to achieve resolution in a single lawsuit of all disputes arising out of common matters." Seattle Totems, 652 F.2d at 854 (quoting Southern Construction Co. v. Pickard, 371 U.S. 57, 60 (1962)).

However, as noted earlier, this is an argument for dismissing a case on forum non conveniens grounds rather than one for enjoining a party from bringing a suit in a foreign forum. Principles of international comity require that foreign antisuit injunctions should be issued only in the most compelling circumstances and that absent such circumstances parallel proceedings should be permitted. If we were to hold that duplication of parties and issues is a sufficient basis for the issuance of a foreign antisuit injunction, parallel proceedings would never be permitted because by definition such proceedings involve the same claim and therefore the same parties and issues.

Gau Shan also argues that the district court did not abuse its discretion in granting the antisuit injunction because Bankers Trust's purpose in filing a Hong Kong action would be to avoid the regulatory effect of Tennessee's statute which provides treble damages for procurement of breach of contract. See Tenn. Code Ann. § 47-50-109. Gau Shan notes that Tennessee law will control its tort claims and asserts that this remedy is designed to effectuate important public policies of the state. Hong Kong law does not provide a comparable remedy. Gau Shan suggests that the public policy behind Tennessee's remedy might be evaded if the Hong Kong action reaches judgment first and is asserted as res judicata in the Tennessee action. Gau Shan concludes that the antisuit injunction was therefore justified because it prevented the possible evasion of these important policies.

We recognize that Tennessee's procurement of breach statute serves the public policy of the state. However, so does every other statute on the Tennessee books. If any advantage in law was sufficient to justify application of the public policy exception, antisuit injunctions would become common and international comity a consideration of secondary importance. Procedural or substantive advantages offered by the forum law do not, of themselves, provide grounds for an antisuit injunction.

Although there is very little case law on the magnitude of the importance of public policy considerations to the decision whether to permit an antisuit injunction, some guidance is offered by cases that analyze public policy concerns as a factor in the decision whether to enforce a foreign judgment. In that context, courts rarely resort to public policy as a basis for refusing to enforce a foreign judgment. See Tahan v. Hodgson, 662 F.2d 862, 866–67 (D.C. Cir. 1981). Indeed, the D.C. Circuit enforced a foreign judgment where it found that the judgment was not "so 'repugnant to fundamental notions of what is decent and just' that American public policy requires nonenforcement" of the judgment. Id. at 866. To the extent there is a parallel, we think the unavailability of a treble damages remedy in Hong Kong is not so "repugnant to fundamental notions of what is decent and just" as to permit the issuance of an antisuit injunction.

We also note that Gau Shan points only to the public policy of the State of Tennessee. It does not point to any national public policy. When weighed against the concerns of international comity, the public policies of a state deserve less weight than the public policies of the nation. Indeed, although evasion of an important national policy might outweigh certain principles of international comity, we question whether the public policy of one state could ever outweigh those principles. In any case, we find that the public policy asserted by Gau Shan does not outweigh those principles here.

We therefore hold that only the evasion of the most compelling public policies of the forum will support the issuance of an antisuit injunction and conclude that the public policy that informs Tennessee's treble damages remedy for procurement of breach of contract does not rise to that level.

The apparent reason an American litigant chooses to file suit in a foreign jurisdiction is, of course, relevant to the question whether important public policies are offended. Bankers Trust stated that its reason for suing in Hong Kong was because Gau Shan is a Hong Kong corporation and its assets are located there. We find nothing in the record to the contrary. Certainly the federal court may not penalize Bankers Trust for making a strategic decision to sue in Hong Kong. We are not persuaded that Bankers Trust is attempting to evade any important public policy of this forum.

Gau Shan also argues that the cases demonstrate that whenever both the controlling law and the citizenship of the party being enjoined are within the United States, foreign antisuit injunctions have always been sustained. While that may be how the few decided cases sort out, no court has based its decision on this fact and, as nearly as we can tell, its presence in these cases is merely coincidental. Indeed, the Laker Airways court considered and rejected this very argument in the context of the defendants' contention in that case that the court should defer to the British injunction on the ground that the British court was enjoining its own national. Laker Airways, 731 F.2d at 935–36. Noting that "[t]erritoriality, not nationality, is the customary and preferred base of jurisdiction," the court concluded that whatever interests sovereign nations have in controlling the actions of their nationals, they have equal if not greater interests in seeing that their public policies are vindicated in their courts. Id. at 935. Moreover, the court noted, rules based on nationality tend to promote nationalism and discrimination at the expense of international comity. Id. at 936. We agree with the reasoning of the Laker Airways court and therefore reject Gau Shan's argument in this respect.

Thus, we find that the lower court erred in finding that international comity did not bar the issuance of a preliminary injunction. This court's jurisdiction is not threatened nor are important public policies being evaded. We hold therefore that international comity precludes the issuance of an antisuit injunction in this case.

V

For all of the foregoing reasons, we conclude that the district court abused its discretion in issuing a preliminary injunction enjoining Bankers Trust from proceeding in the Hong Kong courts. The cause is remanded to the district court which is directed to enter an order dissolving the temporary injunction and to conduct such further proceedings as are consistent herewith.

Comments and Questions

1. Are you convinced by the court's reasoning? Or was the court simply aiding a local party?

2. Does the Grupo Mexicano decision of the Supreme Court shed any light on how the Supreme Court would resolve this uncertainty about the availability of (or standard for) anti-suit injunctions?

3. Remember that antisuit injunctions are unique to the common law tradition. English precedent curbs the discretionary standard for issuing antisuit injunctions to two basic categories: (1) situations in which England is the "natural forum" and foreign litigation would be "vexatious or oppressive" and (2) cases in which the foreign action constitutes a breach of a forum selection clause or arbitration agreement.

4. Antisuit injunctions (and interim measures of relief generally) introduce issues that surface repeatedly throughout this book. When a dispute crosses national borders the interests and/or court systems of many countries may be implicated. The tensions introduced in this chapter will be explored further in the context of jurisdiction, parallel proceedings, forum non conveniens, lis pendens, stays, conflict of laws, the extraterritorial application of laws, and elsewhere in this text.

Concluding Comments and Questions

Return to the problem that opened this chapter and revisit the question presented. How should national systems strike the balance between ensuring meaningful litigation in their own courts, on one hand, and avoiding interference with other systems, on the other?

F. Bibliography of Additional Resources

Barton Legum (ed.), International Litigation Strategies and Practice (Am. Bar Ass'n 2005)

Campbell McLachlan, Continuing Controversy Over Provisional Measures in International Disputes, 7 Int'l L. Forum Du Droit Int'l 5 (2005)

David Capper, The Need for Mareva Injunctions Reconsidered, 73 Fordham L. Rev. 2161 (2005)

Dennis Campbell & Dharmendra Popat, Strategies for Effective Management of Crossborder Recognition and Enforcement of American Money Judgments, 56 Am. Jur. Trials 529 (1995 & Supp. 2007)

George A. Bermann, Provisional Relief in Transnational Litigation, 35 Colum. J. Transnat'l L. 553 (1997)

J.G. Merrills, Interim Measures of Protection in the Recent Jurisprudence of the International Court of Justice, 44 Int'l & Comp. L.Q. 90 (1995)

Jarrod Wong, The Issuance of Interim Measures in International Disputes: A Proposal Requiring a Reasonable Possibility of Success on the Underlying Merits, 33 Ga. J. Int'l & Comp. L. 605 (2004)

Kate Brown, The Availability of Court-Ordered Interim and Conservatory Measures in Aid of International Arbitration in the United States of America and France—A Comparative Essay, 8 Int'l Trade & Bus. L. Ann. 135 (2005)

Panagiota Kelali, Provisional Relief in Transnational Litigation in the Internet Era, 24 J. MARSHALL J. COMPUTER & INFO. L. 263 (2006)

Panagiota Kelali, Provisional Relief in Transnational Litigation in the Internet Era: What is in the U.S.'s Best Interest?, 24 J. MARSHALL J. of COMPUTER & INFO. L. 263 (2006)

Peter Westberg, Interim Measures and Civil Litigation, 31 SUFFOLK TRANSNAT'L L. REV. 13 (2007)

Richard H. Kreindler & Judith L. Holdsworth (eds.), TRANSNATIONAL LITIGATION: A PRACTITIONER'S GUIDE (Oceana 1997 & Supp. 2007)

Richard H. Kreindler, TRANSNATIONAL LITIGATION: A BASIC PRIMER (Oceana 1998).

Robin Cheryl Miller, Annotation, Propriety of Federal Court Injunction Against Suit in Foreign Country, 78 A.L.R. FED. 831 (1986)

Samuel P. Baumgartner, Is Transnational Litigation Different?, 25 U. PA. J. INT'L ECON. L. 1297 (2004)

Steven R. Swanson, Antisuit Injunctions in Support of International Arbitration, 81 TUL. L. REV. 395 (2006)

Theodore Eisenberg (ed.), DEBTOR-CREDITOR LAW (Matthew Bender 1982)

Tim Taylor & Nigel Cooper, EUROPEAN LITIGATION HANDBOOK (Sweet & Maxwell 1995)

Ved P. Nanda & David K. Pansius, LITIGATION OF INTERNATIONAL DISPUTES IN U.S. COURTS (Thomson West 2d ed. 2005 & Supp. 2007)

Wendy A. Kennett, ENFORCEMENT OF JUDGMENTS IN EUROPE (Oxford Univ. Press 2000)

CHAPTER 3

Personal Jurisdiction

A. Introduction

This chapter is concerned with "jurisdiction to adjudicate," an expression that refers to the authority of a state to subject persons and things to its judicial process. When a person or thing is in another country, one must address the extent to which that makes a difference—that is, to what extent is a national court able to reach beyond its country's sovereign boundaries to adjudicate the dispute. Limitations on the exercise of authority over persons or things abroad may derive from several sources. They might be self-imposed by courts in the spirit of cooperation among sovereign nations sensitive to over-reaching. Or they could be imposed by a constitutional mandate. Or legislatures could have the authority and will to limit the scope of the judiciary's jurisdiction to adjudicate. Or limitations may be imposed by public international law. We will see examples of many of these forms of limitations in this chapter.

The term "jurisdiction" can refer to the authority of the court to adjudicate a foreign defendant's rights and obligations. The legitimacy of the exercise of that authority often requires some assessment of the relationship between the forum state, on the one hand, and the plaintiff and/or the defendant and/or the underlying dispute, on the other hand. But "jurisdiction" can also refer to the territory of the court. Property that is located within the territory of the court may be subject to the court's jurisdiction or adjudicatory authority, regardless of whether the owner of the property, or the lawsuit, has any connection with the forum state.

The Problem: Don't Take it Personally*

In the December 30, 1996, issue of *Forbes,* the magazine published an article titled "Godfather of the Kremlin?" that portrayed Boris Berezovsky as a Mafia boss who had his rivals murdered. Mr. Berezovsky was a businessman in Russia who became a billionaire during the presidency of Boris Yeltsin. He was active in the privatization of the Russian economy, using his political connections to acquire stakes in state companies including the state airline, oil properties, and media enterprises. The magazine article declared that "Berezovsky stands tall as one of the most powerful men in Russia. Behind him lies a trail of corpses, uncollectible debts and competitors terrified for their lives." One of the picture's captions reads: "These guys are criminals on an outrageous scale. It's as if Lucky Luciano were chairman of the board of Chrysler."

The publisher of *Forbes* is Forbes, Inc., a New York corporation with its principal place of business in New York City. *Forbes* is a long-established magazine that is written, edited, produced, and published in the United States. The total circulation of the magazine is approximately 750,000 copies, 99 percent of which are sold in the United States and Canada. The editor of the magazine at the time of publication was James Michaels. The article was written primarily by Paul Klebnikov, but with other contributing authors. Mr. Michaels, Mr. Klebnikov, and the other individuals are all U.S. citizens who live in New York.

Mr. Berezovsky wants to file a libel suit against *Forbes,* Michaels, and the authors. For a variety of reasons, the plaintiff prefers to file in England, rather than in Russia or the United States. The English circulation of the magazine comprised some 2,000 copies. It was (and is) also published worldwide on the internet.

(1) Should the English courts have jurisdiction to adjudicate this matter?
(2) For purposes of the personal jurisdiction analysis, does it matter whether Mr. Berezovsky has any contacts with England? If his children attended Cambridge University? If he maintained a vacation home there? If he intended to retire there?
(3) For purposes of the personal jurisdiction analysis, should it matter whether Forbes has an employee stationed in the United Kingdom? Does it matter whether that employee is a journalist, someone selling advertisements, a corporate officer, or an information technology provider? What if the journalist is not really an employee, but a freelance reporter? What if the salesperson just started working two weeks ago? What if the information technology provider works solely on matters involving the company's email servers?
(4) For purposes of the personal jurisdiction analysis, if you represented the plaintiff and had the opportunity to pose ten interrogatories to the individual defendants, what would you ask them?
(5) If there is jurisdiction over Forbes in England, could British courts conclude that it necessarily follows that there is jurisdiction over the individual defendants?

* This hypothetical is based on *Berezovsky v. Michaels,* [2000] 1 W.L.R. 1004 (H.L.).

B. Jurisdictional Bases

There are a number of contacts that could be relevant in the calculus of determining whether a court has jurisdiction to adjudicate. In this section we introduce a number of them. With each factor, consider whether that type of contact is truly relevant to the issue of whether the court has jurisdiction to adjudicate. If it is relevant, consider two more questions: First, is this factor dispositive of the issue? Some contacts may alone be sufficient to establish personal jurisdiction, while others might simply be a component of a multivariate analysis. Second, ask whether this factor is a prerequisite to the exercise of jurisdiction. You might feel strongly that the absence of a particular contact should divest the court of jurisdiction to hear the case.

In the following subsections we provide a brief overview of the principal bases of personal jurisdiction. Understand that each is but one in a menu of options for a country—or you—to consider appropriate.

1. Domicile

Probably the least controversial of all bases for the exercise of jurisdiction is that the defendant is domiciled in the forum state. An individual's domicile is usually defined as the state where one was last both present and intending to remain indefinitely. Legal persons are domiciled in the state in which they are organized.

Domicile is a proper basis for exercising jurisdiction, the thinking goes, because the duty to submit to the court's authority is incident to the privilege of being affiliated with that state, whether through the close factual connection provided by domicile or through the legal connection resulting from incorporation. That every state may rightfully exercise jurisdiction over its citizens can be traced to Roman law.

But what if an individual defendant is temporarily absent from the state of his domicile? Many jurisdictions would nevertheless find such a defendant amenable to suit there. And what if a defendant resides in the forum state, but is not domiciled there? Residence can be, but is seldom enough, by itself, to confer jurisdiction.

2. Physical Presence

Some systems have held that any defendant who is served with process in the forum state is subject to its adjudicative authority. This approach too is firmly grounded in ancient tradition, though chiefly in the common law. It has long been thought a party that is within a territory may justly be subjected to its process and bound by any judgment rendered against it. And so long as an individual defendant is present and is also domiciled or resides there, the exercise of jurisdiction on this basis is uncontroversial.

But of course a defendant may be served while he is temporarily in the state. Does presence in the state, even for an instant, gives the state judicial jurisdiction over an individual? Someone could be changing planes at an airport or even simply flying over the airspace of the forum state. Such applications are often referred to as "tag" jurisdiction. Some jurisdictions undertake to quantify the quantum or nature of the "presence" that will or won't suffice. Can a prospective defendant be tricked into coming into a state for purposes of service of process—maybe the lure of a prize, or a call for help? Could he be dragged, kicking and screaming, into the state for those purposes? What if the defendant is in the state as a result of some court order in an unrelated action? What if the defendant is in the state solely for the purpose of doing charity work for two weeks—or is visiting his children for the day? Must the presence be intentional and/or voluntary? More fundamentally, why should serving a person with court papers while she is in the court's territory ever be enough, by itself, to create jurisdiction?

Physical presence is also a difficult concept to apply to entities such as corporations and other organizations. These entities are, of course, legal fictions that are not actually present anywhere. States thus can take the position that physical presence is applicable only as to individuals. Or states can undertake to define exactly which manifestations of the entity make it amenable to service—its buildings, employees, customers, products, advertisements, agents, affiliates, partners, and so forth.

3. Consent

A third possible basis for the exercise of the court's jurisdiction is the defendant's consent. Consent may be expressed by words or by conduct, and could be either intentional or inadvertent. Consent can be used to establish jurisdiction in a particular forum, and also to oust all other fora of jurisdiction.

Generally speaking, states recognize authority to adjudicate the rights of a defendant who has entered into a contract submitting itself to the jurisdiction of a state by contract—even if that defendant would not otherwise be amenable to a suit in that state. This approach allows the parties to freely negotiate this important term, thereby effecting an efficient allocation of the burden and expense, promoting certainty and predictability, and reducing the overall costs of doing business. As with any contractual term, however, a state must ascertain its tolerance for fraud, undue influence, or overweening bargaining power in this context. The decision whether to enforce a consent clause that is embedded in a consumer contract, for example, requires a system to choose between tremendous efficiency gains and fidelity to a meaningful jurisprudence of consent; or, put another way, a choice between higher prices for all consumers and forum choices for a few consumers.

Consent to jurisdiction may also be established by voluntarily participating as a party in the action. A system may perceive any objection to the court's jurisdiction as an individual right rather than an issue about the legitimacy of the court's authority. And where it is an individual right, it follows that that interest could be waived by the individual. Thus by appearing in the court, the authority to adjudicate that defendant's rights may be (unless defendant makes a special appearance) established by consent. This approach is simple enough when the defendant is purposefully consenting. But countries that adopt this reasoning must then address a related issue: the inadvertent waiver of the right. Is a defendant voluntarily participating as a party if he appears to contest that the court has personal jurisdiction? If he challenges personal jurisdiction and also challenges some form of interim relief imposed against him?

4. Doing Business

Some defendants may have no physical presence in a state (e.g., no residence, real estate, employees, offices), yet enjoy the benefits of doing business there. Especially in the ever expanding global Internet economy, out-of-state defendants may provide considerable amounts of goods or services to customers inside the forum state. And some jurisdictions consider such activity a sufficient basis for establishing jurisdiction over that defendant. A defendant who reaps the benefits of doing business within the forum state, the thinking goes, should also be subject to the state's process and bound by any judgment rendered against it.

Doing business in the forum state could, in theory, be a basis for exercising jurisdiction even if the business done within the state has no connection to the pending litigation. Or a jurisdiction might adopt doing business as a basis for exercising jurisdiction but require some nexus between that business and the litigation. Another threshold question is whether the relevant timeframe is the moment of the incident giving rise to the lawsuit, the date the lawsuit was filed, or some other time. What if defendant was doing a substantial amount of business but discontinued that business one year prior to the events giving rise to the lawsuit? Or what if defendant started doing business in the jurisdiction after the events giving rise to the lawsuit, but before the lawsuit was filed? What if the business commenced after the lawsuit was filed? Answers to these questions reflect interesting assumptions about how a system views its authority to adjudicate disputes.

Of course "doing business" also raises a host of interpretive questions that systems must confront if they pursue this course. Exactly how much "business" triggers the obligation to appear before that state's courts? Does marketing or advertising constitute business, or is it just sales? How many sales? Does it include the sale of services or just goods? Does doing business include activity such as fund-raising by a non-profit inside the forum state? Some internet sellers may sell products that can be delivered electronically to buyers; are these sellers doing business in a forum state even if they are unaware that they are doing so?

Of course a system could recognize doing business as a basis for the exercise of jurisdiction and adopt definitive rules to ensure predictability or at least to avoid chaos. What are the strengths and weaknesses of rigid rules, on one hand, and flexible standards, on the other?

5. Acts

A state may claim jurisdiction to adjudicate because the defendant has done some particular act in the state. This basis differs from doing business jurisdiction in that (1) typically the plaintiff's cause of action must arise out of that defendant's act; and (2) the act could be a single isolated event within the forum state. Thus a foreigner who enters the forum state, commits a tort, and then leaves would in most systems be subject to personal jurisdiction in an action relating to that tort even if he has no property in the forum state and has done no business there. The rationale is that a person who engages in an act that is proscribed by a state may justly be called before that state's courts to answer for it. A state has an interest in all acts undertaken within its territory, in enforcing its laws, and in providing a meaningful remedy to its citizens and residents.

But of course the situs of an act is often debatable. For example, does a defamatory act occur where it is uttered and/or where it is heard? Does a manufacturing defect occur in the state of manufacture and/or where the defective product is sold by an intermediary and/or in the state of injury? If a sequence of acts scattered across months and states constitutes a fraud, where did the fraud occur? A state could insist that even the most remote connection will suffice, but what is the downside to such an aggressive approach? Consider these hypotheticals in the context of the internet where the defendant may not even have known that she was acting "in" the forum state.

6. Effects

A complement or extension of acting within the jurisdiction is causing some effect in the forum state even without entering the forum state. One who lobs a rock across a border and through a window is similarly situated to the person who breaks the window from within the state. The state's interest in these cases is substantially the same.

Applied broadly, an effects test could provide adjudicative jurisdiction over virtually any defendant who is sued by a resident plaintiff. Because of medical expenses, lost wages, and so forth, the effect of an injury can be realized wherever the plaintiff is or happens to move next (regardless of where the tort occurred). Or, in a contract case, the consequences of a breach could cause an effect upon a contracting party in any of a number of places entirely unforeseeable to the breaching party. Accordingly, jurisdictions that recognize an effects test may limit its scope to intentional torts or even intentional torts where defendant had the specific intention of causing effects in the forum state.

7. Ownership or Possession of Property

Some states have held that defendants who own or possess property that is located in the forum state are also subject to jurisdiction therein. Jurisdiction over property—or, more accurately, over the defendant's interest in the property—has traditionally been divided into two categories in the common law. True "in rem" proceedings seek to determine the interests of everyone, "all the world," in a particular thing—regardless of whether a particular individual is named in the suit. Common examples of this kind of action are admiralty, eminent domain, forfeiture, and probate. Exercise of jurisdiction over property in these cases is relatively uncontroversial.

The second category, "quasi-in-rem" jurisdiction, involves suits against named individuals, and claims that may be related or unrelated to the property. For example, in a slip-and-fall action precipitated by a dimly lit stairway, the injured plaintiff might sue the owner of the property, who could be a foreigner. The slip-and-fall action against the defendant is related to the property, but it is not an in rem action because the case would not be about determining title to the property. Some states would find jurisdiction based upon the defendant's ownership of property within the forum. Of course if a particular state recognized all of the jurisdictional bases outlined in these pages, this plaintiff could also point to doing-business, acts, and effects.

Often called "umbrella rules," the latter form of quasi in rem jurisdiction permits jurisdiction over an individual who leaves a piece of property such as an umbrella in the forum country. When exercising authority on this basis, courts view the property as a proxy for the defendant. Some jurisdictions have adopted a moderated use of this technique by limiting the amount of any judgment obtained against the defendant to the value of the property.

8. Plaintiff's Connection

All of the above bases for exercising personal jurisdiction are focused on the defendant's connection to the forum state. The interest in providing plaintiff with a forum for redress is, of course, reason to aggressively pursue each of those bases. But to go one step further: it is certainly possible that a system could orient its jurisprudence regarding the jurisdiction to adjudicate around the plaintiff's connection to the forum state. Indeed, a state might simply provide a forum for any plaintiff who was a national, or even a resident.

C. Illustrations of National Practice

1. United States

Patrick J. Borchers, Personal Jurisdiction in the United States

Comparing Personal Jurisdiction in the United States and the European Community: Lessons for American Reform, 40 Am. J. Comp. L. 121, 127–132 (1992)

Personal jurisdiction in the United States is an issue of constitutional law. This was not always so. Early on, the Supreme Court considered jurisdictional precepts to be a matter of common law, deduced from international law.[12] The only constitutional provision of any significance was the full faith and credit clause, and its implementing statute, which the court held required states to give conclusive effect to the judgments of their sister states. The Supreme Court, however, countenanced an exception to the principle of unquestioning judgment recognition for judgments rendered in violation of the common-law, international, rules of

[12] *See, e.g.*, D'Arcy v. Ketchum, 52 U.S. (11 How.) 165 (1851).

jurisdiction. Thus the Supreme Court claimed the right only to announce indirect[17] rules of jurisdiction.

The metamorphosis of the Supreme Court's role from indirect to direct regulator of jurisdiction began with *Pennoyer v. Neff.*[18] In Pennoyer the Court restated the traditional international rules of jurisdiction. These rules allowed for in rem jurisdiction based upon the attachment of property within the forum state prior to the commencement of the action. In personam jurisdiction could only be based upon personal service of process upon the defendant while in the forum state, the defendant's consent to jurisdiction, or the defendant's voluntary appearance. Thus, absent the defendant voluntarily assenting to the jurisdiction of the court, personal jurisdiction required a symbolic assertion of sovereignty. For in rem actions it was the seizure of property, for in personam actions it was the "seizure" of the person through personal service while in the forum state....

[T]he Pennoyer court invoked the due process clause of the fourteenth amendment, and most have understood the Court to have assumed the power to regulate jurisdiction directly.... [Thus,] by the early twentieth century the Court had interpreted the due process clause of the fourteenth amendment to require that state courts assert jurisdiction only upon one of the traditionally recognized bases. [T]hese bases were both grossly overinclusive and underinclusive. They were overinclusive because they allowed a state to take jurisdiction based upon the mere fortuity that the defendant had been served while passing through the state or the plaintiff had located some of defendant's property within the state and had it attached. They were underinclusive because if the plaintiff had the misfortune to select a defendant who could not be served within the state and owned no property within its borders, jurisdiction was an impossibility, no matter how rational and sensible the plaitniff's choice of forum might be. Corporate defendants were especially slippery because of the Court's holding that serving process on one of the corporate officers within the state was not a basis for jurisdiction over the corporation, thus making it impossible to "tag" a corporation.

The Court moved haltingly to mitigate this unacceptable state of affairs. Its primary vehicle was to expand the notion of "consent" Thus, for instance, the Court held that drivers of automobiles and sellers of insurance policies within a state had implicitly "consented" to the jurisdiction of those states. Somewhat later, the Court held that domicile was an acceptable basis for personal jurisdiction.

The Court's most important announcement, since its ascension to the role of direct regulator of jurisdiction, came in *International Shoe Co. v. Washington.*[30]

[17] "Indirect rules of jurisdiction" is the civilian term for rules that operate only when judgment recognition is sought. When a judgment is presented for recognition, the court must first examine it to determine whether the judgment-rendering court had jurisdiction. When a litigant opposed recognition in the judgment-recognizing court, this is often termed a "collateral attack" on jurisdiction. Indirect rules give rise only to collateral attacks. By contrast, direct rules of jurisdiction operate on the judgment-rendering court, allowing the litigant to directly attack the court's jurisdiction prior to entry of a judgment.

[18] 95 U.S. 714 (1878).

[30] 326 U.S. 310 (1945).

In International Shoe, the Court added a new basis for personal jurisdiction, holding that a showing of "minimum contacts" between the defendant and the forum was sufficient to satisfy the due process clause. "Minimum contacts," the Court suggested, might take one of two forms. First, even "single or occasional acts" within the forum might be enough to satisfy the Constitution if those acts are related to the theory of the action. Second, even unrelated acts might satisfy the Constitution if done in a "systematic and continuous" fashion.

Since International Shoe the Supreme Court has decided a substantial number of cases, attempting to explain the phrase "minimum contacts." [But] the Court's explanation of the theoretical foundation of the minimum contacts test has vacillated. International Shoe by dismissing the importance of the symbolic assertion of sovereignty, undercut Pennoyer's "turf" theory of [jurisdiction]. Thus, International Shoe appeared to endorse the position that personal jurisdiction is a matter of individual entitlement, rather than a mechanism for resolving the competing claims of sovereigns. Over the course of the next forty-six years, however, the Court revived,[38] then dismissed,[39] then revived,[40] then dismissed,[41] then revived,[42] a "sovereignty" factor in the jurisdictional calculus. This uneven conceptualization has made for erratic navigation.

In *Shaffer v. Heitner,*[43] the Court revisited the traditional basis of jurisdiction via attachment of the defendant's property. Purporting to overturn Pennoyer's "turf" theory, the Court reasoned that the presence of the defendant's property was no longer an automatic guarantee of jurisdiciotn. To exercise jurisdiction, the Court held that it was necessary to establish the existence of "minimum contacts" between the defendant and the forum state. Therefore, the Court concluded, "all assertions of state-court jurisdiction must be evaluated according to the standards set forth in International Shoe and its progeny."

The demise of attachment as a basis for jurisdiction, coupled with the Court's "all assertions" dictum, led most commentators to conclude that the other Pennoyer-era basis, personal service within the forum, was also constitutionally infirm. However, in *Burnham v. Superior Court,*[48] a plurality of the Court led by Justice Scalia resuscitated Pennoyer and the "turf" theory, holding that tag jurisdiction's historical pedigree was such that it could not violate the Constitution. The concurring justices rejected Scalia's historical thesis, but reasoned alternatively that a three-day visit amounts to minimum contacts with the forum. As a practical matter, therefore, tag jurisdiction is alive and well in the United States and Pennoyer endures.

---

[38] Hanson v. Denckla, 357 U.S. 235, 251 (1958).

[39] Shaffer v. Heitner, 433 U.S. 186, 204 n.20 (1977).

[40] World-Wide Volkswagen Corp. v. Woodson, 444 U.S. 286, 294 (1980).

[41] Insurance Corp. of Ireland, Ltd. v. Compagnie des Bauzites de Guinee, 456 U.S. 694, 702 n.10 (1982).

[42] Burnham v. Superior Court, 110 S. Ct. 2105 (1990); Asahi Metal Indus. Co. v. Superior Court, 480 U.S. 102, 113–14 (1987).

[43] 433 U.S. 186 (1977).

[48] 110 S. Ct. 2105 (1990).

Comments and Questions

1. This survey of the evolution of the American law of jurisdiction to adjudicate should not be concluded without making brief mention of statutory developments that have paralleled those in the case law reviewed above. Statutes are relevant because the courts cannot reach someone outside the jurisdiction unless the exercise of jurisdiction is authorized by statute and the exercise is constitutional. The statutory authorizations are typically called "long-arm statutes." A typical long-arm statute would authorize a court to exercise personal jurisdiction over a person, who acts directly or by an agent, as to a cause of action that arises from the person's

- transacting any business in this state;
- contracting to supply services or things in this state;
- causing tortious injury by an act or omission in this state;
- causing tortious injury in this state by an act or omission outside this state if he regularly does or solicits business, or engages in any other persistent course of conduct, or derives substantial revenue from goods used or consumed or services rendered, in this state;
- having an interest in, using, or possessing real property in this state; or
- contracting to insure any person, property, or risk located within this state at the time of contracting.

2. If the exercise is statutorily authorized, then the follow-up inquiry must determine whether such an exercise is consistent with due process. Some jurisdictions have combined the steps by adopting a long-arm statute that permits exercise of judicial jurisdiction to the fullest extent permitted by the Constitution.

3. The jurisdictional analysis is the same whether the case is filed in state or federal court, except that Fed. R. Civ. P. 4(k) gives the federal courts greater reach under certain limited circumstances requiring, among other prerequisites, a claim under federal law. In most tort and contract cases, however, plaintiffs are seeking relief under state law.

Asahi Metal Industrial Co. v. Superior Court

480 U.S. 102 (1987)

Justice O'Connor announced the judgment of the Court and delivered the unanimous opinion of the Court with respect to Part I, the opinion of the Court with respect to Part II-B, in which The Chief Justice, Justice Brennan, Justice White, Justice Marshall, Justice Blackmun, Justice Powell, and Justice Stevens join, and an opinion with respect to Parts II-A and III, in which The Chief Justice, Justice Powell, and Justice Scalia join.

This case presents the question whether the mere awareness on the part of a foreign defendant that the components it manufactured, sold, and delivered outside the United States would reach the forum state in the stream of commerce constitutes "minimum contacts" between the defendant and the forum state such that the exercise of jurisdiction "does not offend 'traditional notions of fair play and substantial justice.'" International Shoe Co. v. Washington, 326 U.S. 310, 316 (1945), quoting Milliken v. Meyer, 311 U.S. 457, 463 (1940).

I

On September 23, 1978, on Interstate Highway 80 in Solano County, California, Gary Zurcher lost control of his Honda motorcycle and collided with a tractor. Zurcher was severely injured, and his passenger and wife, Ruth Ann Moreno, was killed. In September 1979, Zurcher filed a product liability action in the Superior Court of the State of California in and for the County of Solano. Zurcher alleged that the 1978 accident was caused by a sudden loss of air and an explosion in the rear tire of the motorcycle, and alleged that the motorcycle tire, tube, and sealant were defective. Zurcher's complaint named, inter alia, Cheng Shin Rubber Industrial Co., Ltd. (Cheng Shin), the Taiwanese manufacturer of the tube. Cheng Shin in turn filed a cross-complaint seeking indemnification from its codefendants and from petitioner Asahi Metal Industry Co., Ltd. (Asahi), the manufacturer of the tube's valve assembly. Zurcher's claims against Cheng Shin and the other defendants were eventually settled and dismissed, leaving only Cheng Shin's indemnity action against Asahi.

California's long-arm statute authorizes the exercise of jurisdiction "on any basis not inconsistent with the Constitution of this state or of the United States." Cal. Code Civ.Proc.Ann § 410.10 (West 1973). Asahi moved to quash Cheng Shin's service of summons arguing the State could not exert jurisdiction over it consistent with the Due Process Clause of the Fourteenth Amendment.

In relation to the motion, the following information was submitted by Asahi and Cheng Shin. Asahi is a Japanese corporation. It manufactures tire valve assemblies in Japan and sells the assemblies to Cheng Shin, and to several other tire manufacturers, for use as components in finished tire tubes. Asahi's sales to Cheng Shin took place in Taiwan. The shipments from Asahi to Cheng Shin were sent from Japan to Taiwan. Cheng Shin bought and incorporated into its tire tubes 150,000 Asahi valve assemblies in 1978; 500,000 in 1979; 500,000 in 1980; 100,000 in 1981; and 100,000 in 1982. Sales to Cheng Shin accounted for 1.24 percent of Asahi's income in 1981 and 0.44 percent in 1982. Cheng Shin alleged that approximately 20 percent of its sales in the United States are in California. Cheng Shin purchases valve assemblies from other suppliers as well, and sells finished tubes throughout the world.

In 1983 an attorney for Cheng Shin conducted an informal examination of the valve stems of the tire tubes sold in one cyclery in Solano County. The attorney declared that of the approximately 115 tire tubes in the store, 97 were purportedly manufactured in Japan or Taiwan, and of those 97, 21 valve stems were marked with the circled letter "A", apparently Asahi's trademark. Of the 21 Asahi valve stems, 12 were incorporated into Cheng Shin tire tubes. The store contained 41 other Cheng Shin tubes that incorporated the valve assemblies of other manufacturers. Declaration of Kenneth B. An affidavit of a manager of Cheng Shin whose duties included the purchasing of component parts stated: "'In discussions with Asahi regarding the purchase of valve stem assemblies the fact that my Company sells tubes throughout the world and specifically the United States has been discussed. I am informed and believe that Asahi was fully aware that valve stem assemblies sold to my Company and to others would end up throughout the United States and in California.'" 39 Cal.3d 35, 48, n. 4 (1985). An affidavit of the president of Asahi, on the other hand, declared that Asahi "'has never contemplated that its limited sales of tire valves to Cheng Shin in Taiwan would subject it to lawsuits in California.'" The record does not include any contract between Cheng Shin and Asahi.

Primarily on the basis of the above information, the Superior Court denied the motion to quash summons, stating that "Asahi obviously does business on an international scale. It is not unreasonable that they defend claims of defect in their product on an international scale."

The Court of Appeal of the State of California issued a peremptory writ of mandate commanding the Superior Court to quash service of summons. The court concluded that "it would be unreasonable to require Asahi to respond in California solely on the basis of ultimately realized foreseeability that the product into which its component was embodied would be sold all over the world including California."

The Supreme Court of the State of California reversed and discharged the writ issued by the Court of Appeal. The court observed that "Asahi has no offices, property or agents in California. It solicits no business in California and has made no direct sales [in California]." Moreover, "Asahi did not design or control the system of distribution that carried its valve assemblies into California." Nevertheless, the court found the exercise of jurisdiction over Asahi to be consistent with the Due Process Clause. It concluded that Asahi knew that some of the valve assemblies sold to Cheng Shin would be incorporated into tire tubes sold in California, and that Asahi benefited indirectly from the sale in California of products incorporating its components. The court considered Asahi's intentional act of placing its components into the stream of commerce—that is, by delivering the components to Cheng Shin in Taiwan—coupled with Asahi's awareness that some of the components would eventually find their way into California, sufficient to form the basis for state court jurisdiction under the Due Process Clause.

We granted certiorari, and now reverse.

II

A

The Due Process Clause of the Fourteenth Amendment limits the power of a state court to exert personal jurisdiction over a nonresident defendant. "[T]he constitutional touchstone" of the determination whether an exercise of personal jurisdiction comports with due process "remains whether the defendant purposefully established 'minimum contacts' in the forum State." Burger King Corp. v. Rudzewicz, 471 U.S. 462, 474 (1985), quoting International Shoe Co. v. Washington, 326 U.S. 310, 316. Most recently we have reaffirmed the oft-quoted reasoning of Hanson v. Denckla, 357 U.S. 235, 253 (1958), that minimum contacts must have a basis in "some act by which the defendant purposefully avails itself of the privilege of conducting activities within the forum State, thus invoking the benefits and protections of its laws." Burger King, 471 U.S., at 475. "Jurisdiction is proper... where the contacts proximately result from actions by the defendant himself that create a 'substantial connection' with the forum State." Ibid., quoting McGee v. International Life Insurance Co., 355 U.S. 220, 223 (1957) (emphasis in original).

Applying the principle that minimum contacts must be based on an act of the defendant, the Court in World-Wide Volkswagen Corp. v. Woodson, 444 U.S. 286 (1980), rejected the assertion that a consumer's unilateral act of bringing the defendant's product into the forum State was a sufficient constitutional basis for personal jurisdiction over the defendant. It had been argued in World-Wide Volkswagen that because an automobile retailer and its wholesale distributor sold a product mobile by design and purpose, they could foresee being haled into court in the distant States into which their customers might drive. The Court rejected this concept of foreseeability as an insufficient basis for jurisdiction under the Due Process Clause. Id., at 295–296. The Court disclaimed, however, the idea that "foreseeability is wholly irrelevant" to personal jurisdiction, concluding that "[t]he forum State does not exceed its powers under the Due Process Clause if it asserts personal jurisdiction over a corporation that delivers its products into the stream of commerce with the expectation that they will be purchased by consumers in the forum State." Id., 297–298 (citation omitted). The Court reasoned:

> When a corporation "purposefully avails itself of the privilege of conducting activities within the forum State," Hanson v. Denckla, 357 U.S. [235,] 253 (1958)], it has clear notice that it is subject to suit there, and can act to alleviate the risk of burdensome litigation by procuring insurance, passing the expected costs on to customers, or, if the risks are too great, severing its connection with the State. Hence if the sale of a product of a manufacturer or distributor... is not simply an isolated occurrence, but arises from the efforts of the manufacturer or distributor to serve, directly or indirectly, the market for its product in other States, it is not unreasonable to subject it to suit in one of those States if its allegedly defective merchandise has there been the source of injury to its owners or to others. Id., at 297.

In World-Wide Volkswagen itself, the state court sought to base jurisdiction not on any act of the defendant, but on the foreseeable unilateral actions of the consumer. Since World-Wide Volkswagen, lower courts have been confronted with cases in which the defendant acted by placing a product in the stream of commerce, and the stream eventually swept defendant's product into the forum State, but the defendant did nothing else to purposefully avail itself of the market in the forum state. Some courts have understood the Due Process Clause, as interpreted in World-Wide Volkswagen, to allow an exercise of personal jurisdiction to be based on no more than the defendant's act of placing the product in the stream of commerce. Other courts have understood the Due Process Clause and the above-quoted language in World-Wide Volkswagen to require the action of the defendant to be more purposefully directed at the forum State than the mere act of placing a product in the stream of commerce.

The reasoning of the Supreme Court of California in the present case illustrates the former interpretation of World-Wide Volkswagen. The Supreme Court of California held that, because the stream of commerce eventually brought some valves Asahi sold Cheng Shin into California, Asahi's awareness that its valves would be sold in California was sufficient to permit California to exercise jurisdiction over Asahi consistent with the requirements of the Due Process Clause. The Supreme Court of California's position was consistent with those courts that have held that mere foreseeability or awareness was a constitutionally sufficient basis for personal jurisdiction if the defendant's product made its way into the forum State while still in the stream of commerce.

Other courts, however, have understood the Due Process Clause to require something more than that the defendant was aware of its product's entry into the forum State through the stream of commerce in order for the state to exert jurisdiction over the defendant. In the present case, for example, the State Court of Appeal did not read the Due Process Clause, as interpreted by World-Wide Volkswagen, to allow "mere foreseeability that the product will enter the forum state [to] be enough by itself to establish jurisdiction over the distributor and retailer." In Humble v. Toyota Motor Co., Ltd., 727 F.2d 709 (8th Cir. 1984), an injured car passenger brought suit against Arakawa Auto Body Company, a Japanese corporation that manufactured car seats for Toyota. Arakawa did no business in the United States; it had no office, affiliate, subsidiary, or agent in the United States; it manufactured its component parts outside the United States and delivered them to Toyota Motor Company in Japan. The Court of Appeals, adopting the reasoning of the District Court in that case, noted that although it "does not doubt that Arakawa could have foreseen that its product would find its way into the United States," it would be "manifestly unjust" to require Arakawa to defend itself in the United States. Id., at 710–711, quoting 578 F. Supp. 530, 533 (N.D. Ia. 1982).

We now find this latter position to be consonant with the requirements of due process. The "substantial connection," Burger King, 471 U.S., at 475; McGee, 355 U.S., at 223, between the defendant and the forum State necessary for a finding of minimum contacts must come about by an action of the defendant purposefully directed toward the forum State. Burger King, supra, 471 U.S., at 476; Keeton v. Hustler Magazine, Inc., 465 U.S. 770, 774 (1984). The placement of a product into the stream of commerce, without more, is not an act of the defendant purposefully directed toward the forum State. Additional conduct of the defendant may indicate an intent or purpose to serve the market in the forum State, for example, designing the product for the market in the forum State, advertising in the forum State, establishing channels for providing regular advice to customers in the forum State, or marketing the product through a distributor who has agreed to serve as the sales agent in the forum State. But a defendant's awareness that the stream of commerce may or will sweep the product into the forum State does not convert the mere act of placing the product into the stream into an act purposefully directed toward the forum State.

Assuming, arguendo, that respondents have established Asahi's awareness that some of the valves sold to Cheng Shin would be incorporated into tire tubes sold in California, respondents have not demonstrated any action by Asahi to purposefully avail itself of the California market. Asahi does not do business in California. It has no office, agents, employees, or property in California. It does not advertise or otherwise solicit business in California. It did not create, control, or employ the distribution system that brought its valves to California. There is no evidence that Asahi designed its product in anticipation of sales in California. On the basis of these facts, the exertion of personal jurisdiction over Asahi by the Superior Court of California† exceeds the limits of Due Process.

B

The strictures of the Due Process Clause forbid a state court from exercising personal jurisdiction over Asahi under circumstances that would offend "traditional notions of fair play and substantial justice." International Shoe Co. v. Washington, 326 U.S., at 316, quoting Milliken v. Meyer, 311 U.S., at 463.

We have previously explained that the determination of the reasonableness of the exercise of jurisdiction in each case will depend on an evaluation of several factors. A court must consider the burden on the defendant, the interests of the forum state, and the plaintiff's interest in obtaining relief. It must also weigh in its determination "the interstate judicial system's interest in obtaining the most efficient resolution of controversies; and the shared interest of the several States in furthering fundamental substantive social policies." World-Wide Volkswagen, 444 U.S., at 292 (citations omitted).

A consideration of these factors in the present case clearly reveals the unreasonableness of the assertion of jurisdiction over Asahi, even apart from the question of the placement of goods in the stream of commerce.

Certainly the burden on the defendant in this case is severe. Asahi has been commanded by the Supreme Court of California not only to traverse the distance between Asahi's headquarters in Japan and the Superior Court of California in and for the County of Solano, but also to submit its dispute with Cheng Shin to a foreign nation's judicial system. The unique burdens placed upon one who must defend oneself in a foreign legal system should have significant weight in assessing the reasonableness of stretching the long arm of personal jurisdiction over national borders.

When minimum contacts have been established, often the interests of the plaintiff and the forum in the exercise of jurisdiction will justify even the serious

† We have no occasion here to determine whether Congress could, consistent with the Due Process Clause of the Fifth Amendment, authorize federal court personal jurisdiction over alien defendants based on the aggregate of *national* contacts, rather than on the contacts between the defendant and the State in which the federal court sits....

burdens placed on the alien defendant. In the present case, however, the interests of the plaintiff and the forum in California's assertion of jurisdiction over Asahi are slight. All that remains is a claim for indemnification asserted by Cheng Shin, a Taiwanese corporation, against Asahi. The transaction on which the indemnification claims is based took place in Taiwan; Asahi's components were shipped from Japan to Taiwan. Cheng Shin has not demonstrated that it is more convenient for it to litigate its indemnification claim against Asahi in California rather than in Taiwan or Japan.

Because the plaintiff is not a California resident, California's legitimate interests in the dispute have considerably diminished. The Supreme Court of California argued that the State had an interest in "protecting its consumers by ensuring that foreign manufacturers comply with the state's safety standards." 39 Cal.3d, at 49. The State Supreme Court's definition of California's interest, however, was overly broad. The dispute between Cheng Shin and Asahi is primarily about indemnification rather than safety standards. Moreover, it is not at all clear at this point that California law should govern the question whether a Japanese corporation should indemnify a Taiwanese corporation on the basis of a sale made in Taiwan and a shipment of goods from Japan to Taiwan. Phillips Petroleum v. Shutts, 472 U.S. 797 (1985); Allstate Insurance Co. v. Hague, 449 U.S. 302, 312–313 (1981). The possibility of being haled into a California court as a result of an accident involving Asahi's components undoubtedly creates an additional deterrent to the manufacture of unsafe components; however, similar pressures will be placed on Asahi by the purchasers of its components as long as those who use Asahi components in their final products, and sell those products in California, are subject to the application of California tort law.

World-Wide Volkswagen also admonished courts to take into consideration the interests of the "several States," in addition to the forum state, in the efficient judicial resolution of the dispute and the advancement of substantive policies. In the present case, this advice calls for a court to consider the procedural and substantive policies of other nations whose interests are affected by the assertion of jurisdiction by the California court. The procedural and substantive interests of other nations in a state court's assertion of jurisdiction over an alien defendant will differ from case to case. In every case, however, those interests, as well as the Federal interest in its foreign relations policies, will be best served by a careful inquiry into the reasonableness of the assertion of jurisdiction in the particular case, and an unwillingness to find the serious burdens on an alien defendant outweighed by minimal interests on the part of the plaintiff or the forum State. "Great care and reserve should be exercised when extending our notions of personal jurisdiction into the international field." United States v. First National City Bank, 379 U.S. 378, 404 (1965) (Harlan, J., dissenting).

Considering the international context, the heavy burden on the alien defendant, and the slight interests of the plaintiff and the forum State, the exercise of personal jurisdiction by a California court over Asahi in this instance would be unreasonable and unfair.

III

Because the facts of this case do not establish minimum contacts such that the exercise of personal jurisdiction is consistent with fair play and substantial justice, the judgment of Supreme Court of California is reversed, and the case is remanded for further proceedings not inconsistent with this opinion.

JUSTICE BRENNAN, with whom JUSTICE WHITE, JUSTICE MARSHALL, and JUSTICE BLACKMUN join, concurring in part and in the judgment.

I do not agree with the plurality's interpretation of the stream-of-commerce theory, nor with its conclusion that Asahi did not "purposely avail itself of the California market." I do agree, however, with the Court's conclusion in Part II-B that the exercise of personal jurisdiction over Asahi in this case would not comport with "fair play and substantial justice," International Shoe Co. v. Washington, 326 U.S. 310, 320 (1945). This is one of those rare cases in which "minimum requirements inherent in the concept of 'fair play and substantial justice'... defeat the reasonableness of jurisdiction even [though] the defendant has purposefully engaged in forum activities." Burger King Corp. v. Rudzewicz, 471 U.S. 462, 477–478 (1985). I therefore join Parts I and II-B of the Court's opinion, and write separately to explain my disagreement with Part II-A.

The plurality states that "defendant's awareness that the stream of commerce may or will sweep the product into the forum State does not convert the mere act of placing the product into the stream into an act purposefully directed toward the forum State." The plurality would therefore require a plaintiff to show "[a]dditional conduct" directed toward the forum before finding the exercise of jurisdiction over the defendant to be consistent with the Due Process Clause. Ibid. I see no need for such a showing, however. The stream of commerce refers not to unpredictable currents or eddies, but to the regular and anticipated flow of products from manufacture to distribution to retail sale. As long as a participant in this process is aware that the final product is being marketed in the forum State, the possibility of a lawsuit there cannot come as a surprise. Nor will the litigation present a burden for which there is no corresponding benefit. A defendant who has placed goods in the stream of commerce benefits economically from the retail sale of the final product in the forum State, and indirectly benefits from the State's laws that regulate and facilitate commercial activity. These benefits accrue regardless of whether that participant directly conducts business in the forum State, or engages in additional conduct directed toward that State. Accordingly, most courts and commentators have found that jurisdiction premised on the placement of a product into the stream of commerce is consistent with the Due Process Clause, and have not required a showing of additional conduct. [citing authorities]

The plurality's endorsement of what appears to be the minority view among Federal Courts of Appeals represents a marked retreat from its analysis in World-Wide Volkswagen v. Woodson, 444 U.S. 286 (1980). In that case, "respondents [sought] to base jurisdiction on one, isolated occurrence and whatever inferences can be drawn therefrom: the fortuitous circumstance that a single

Audi automobile, sold in New York to New York residents, happened to suffer an accident while passing through Oklahoma." Id., at 295. The Court held that the possibility of an accident in Oklahoma, while to some extent foreseeable in light of the inherent mobility of the automobile, was not enough to establish minimum contacts between the forum State and the retailer or distributor. Id., at 295–296. The Court then carefully explained:

> this is not to say, of course, that foreseeability is wholly irrelevant. But the foreseeability that is critical to due process analysis is not the mere likelihood that a product will find its way into the forum State. Rather, it is that the defendant's conduct and connection with the forum State are such that he should reasonably anticipate being haled into Court there. (Id., at 297.)

The Court reasoned that when a corporation may reasonably anticipate litigation in a particular forum, it cannot claim that such litigation is unjust or unfair, because it "can act to alleviate the risk of burdensome litigation by procuring insurance, passing the expected costs on to consumers, or, if the risks are too great, severing its connection with the State." Ibid.

To illustrate the point, the Court contrasted the foreseeability of litigation in a State to which a consumer fortuitously transports a defendant's product (insufficient contacts) with the foreseeability of litigation in a State where the defendant's product was regularly sold (sufficient contacts). The Court stated:

> Hence if the sale of a product of a manufacturer or distributor such as Audi or Volkswagen is not simply an isolated occurrence, but arises from the efforts of the manufacturer or distributor to serve, directly or indirectly, the market for its product in other States, it is not unreasonable to subject it to suit in one of those States if its allegedly defective merchandise has there been the source of injury to its owner or to others. The forum State does not exceed its powers under the Due Process clause if it asserts personal jurisdiction over a corporation that delivers its products into the stream of commerce with the expectation that they will be purchased by consumers in the forum State." (Id., at 297–298 (emphasis added).)

The Court concluded its illustration by referring to Gray v. American Radiator & Standard Sanitary Corp., 22 Ill.2d 432 (1961), a well-known stream-of-commerce case in which the Illinois Supreme Court applied the theory to assert jurisdiction over a component-parts manufacturer that sold no components directly in Illinois, but did sell them to a manufacturer who incorporated them into a final product that was sold in Illinois. Ibid.

The Court in World-Wide Volkswagen thus took great care to distinguish "between a case involving goods which reach a distant State through a chain of distribution and a case involving goods which reach the same State because a consumer...took them there." 444 U.S., at 306–307 (Brennan, J., dissenting). The California Supreme Court took note of this distinction, and correctly concluded that our holding in World-Wide Volkswagen preserved the stream-of-commerce theory.

In this case the facts found by the California Supreme Court support its finding of minimum contacts. The Court found that "[a]lthough Asahi did not design or control the system of distribution that carried its valve assemblies into California, Asahi was aware of the distribution system's operation, and it knew that it would benefit economically from the sale in California of products incorporating its components."[4] Accordingly, I cannot join the plurality's determination that Asahi's regular and extensive sales of component parts to a manufacturer it knew was making regular sales of the final product in California is insufficient to establish minimum contacts with California.

JUSTICE STEVENS, with whom JUSTICE WHITE and JUSTICE BLACKMUN join, concurring in part and concurring in the judgment.

The judgment of the Supreme Court of California should be reversed for the reasons stated in Part II-B of the Court's opinion. While I join Parts I and II-B, I do not join Part II-A for two reasons. First it is not necessary to the Court's decision. An examination of minimum contacts is not always necessary to determine whether a state court's assertion of personal jurisdiction is constitutional. See Burger King Corp. v. Rudzewicz, 471 U.S. 462, 476–478 (1985). Part II-B establishes, after considering the factors set forth in World-Wide Volkswagen Corp. v. Woodson, 444 U.S. 286, 292 (1980), that California's exercise of jurisdiction over Asahi in this case would be "unreasonable and unfair." This finding alone requires reversal; this case fits within the rule that "minimum requirements inherent in the concept of 'fair play and substantial justice' may defeat the reasonableness of jurisdiction even if the defendant has purposefully engaged in forum activities." Burger King, 471 U.S., at 477–478 (quoting International Shoe Co. v. Washington, 326 U.S. 310, 320 (1945)). Accordingly, I see no reason in this case for the Court to articulate "purposeful direction" or any other test as the nexus between an act of a defendant and the forum State that is necessary to establish minimum contacts.

Second, even assuming that the test ought to be formulated here, Part II-A misapplies it to the facts of this case. The Court seems to assume that an unwavering line can be drawn between "mere awareness" that a component will find its way into the forum State and "purposeful availment" of the forum's market. Over the course of its dealings with Cheng Shin, Asahi has arguably engaged in a higher quantum of conduct than "[t]he placement of a product into the stream of commerce, without more . . ." Ibid. Whether or not this conduct rises to the level of purposeful availment requires a constitutional determination that is affected by the volume, the value, and the hazardous character of the components. In most circumstances I would be inclined to conclude that a regular course of

---

[4] Moreover, the Court found that at least 18 percent of the tubes sold in a particular California motorcycle supply shop contained Asahi valve assemblies, and that Asahi had on ongoing business relationship with Cheng Shin involving average annual sales of hundreds of thousands of valve assemblies.

dealing that results in deliveries of over 100,000 units annually over a period of several years would constitute "purposeful availment" even though the item delivered to the forum State was a standard product marketed throughout the world.

Comments and Questions

1. Justice O'Connor delivered the unanimous opinion of the Court with respect to Part I of her opinion. Upon behalf of how many members of the Court did she speak with regard to the other Parts?

2. The Court did not give clear direction for the lower courts who faced similar cases after Asahi. Consider, for example, Felix v. Bomoro KG, 241 Cal.Rptr. 670 (2d Dist. Ct. App. 1987). This suit was filed against the West German manufacturer of a door latch assembly for the 1965 Volkswagen Squareback. Plaintiff alleged that the assembly was defectively designed, resulting in her being thrown from the vehicle during an accident that occurred in California. After being served with the complaint, defendant appeared specially and moved to quash service on the ground that it lacked the requisite minimum contacts with California to justify the state's assertion of personal jurisdiction over it. In support of the motion, defendant stated that it had no property, offices, employees, agents, or bank accounts in California, that it did not purchase or sell goods in the state and that it neither solicited business nor advertised in California. Defendant further stated that the vehicle in question was manufactured in West Germany, and that it had been informed by Volkswagen, the vehicle's manufacturer, that the type of vehicle involved was to be marketed and sold only in Europe and not in the United States. The district court dismissed for lack of personal jurisdiction and the plaintiffs appealed.

The court concluded that "the strictures of the due process clause forbid a court from exercising personal jurisdiction over a foreign corporation that merely places its products in the stream of commerce even though it may foresee that those products will ultimately wind their way into the forum state." Rather, "a foreign corporation must knowingly avail itself of the benefits accruing from its activities within the forum before jurisdiction will attach." In the view of the court, "it would be manifestly unjust to require Bomoro to defend itself against Felix's suit in this state.... The only possible contacts that Bomoro could be said to have with California are by way of the fact that Volkswagen sells automobiles here, containing parts designed and manufactured in Germany by defendant. The vehicles themselves, however, are manufactured in Europe and the component parts are designed by Bomoro according to Volkswagen's specifications....

"Although defendant...could have foreseen that its product would find its way into the United States and California[,]...Felix...has failed to present any facts which establish a substantial connection between Bomoro and this state. Defendant has not advertised, solicited any business, or otherwise sought to serve any particular market in this state.... We think it clear that the extent to which Bomoro could reasonably anticipate being involved in litigation in California was minimal at best....

"The appropriate test is not knowledge or awareness of the ultimate destination of the product, but whether the manufacturer has purposefully engaged in forum activities so it can reasonably expect to be haled into court there, and, even then, the minimum requirements of 'fair play and substantial justice' may defeat jurisdiction. The contracts in this case are simply too fortuit[ous] and tenuous to warrant the exercise of personal jurisdiction over Bomoro."

Is this ruling consistent with Asahi? Is it also true that if the district court had found personal jurisdiction, that this would have constituted reversible error?

3. Consider this hypothetical: a Texas resident brings an action in federal court in Texas against the Japanese manufacturer of a lighter that malfunctioned, burning her seriously. The defendant is incorporated in Japan and has its principal place of business there. The lighter in question was manufactured, assembled, sold and delivered to the Scripto Corp. ("Scripto") in Japan. Defendant sells three to four million of the lighters to Scripto per year. Scripto, the exclusive distributor of these lighters in the United States, markets them in many American states. The defendant was aware that at least one Scripto customer had national retail outlets. Do Texas courts have personal jurisdiction over the Japanese corporation? See Oswalt v. Tokai-Seiki K.K., 616 F.2d 191 (5th Cir. 1980).

If you represented these plaintiffs and could add only one of the following facts to the above account, which would be most helpful to you: (1) Texas is the fourth largest market in the United States for cigarette lighters; (2) corporate officers of the defendant corporation were in the State of Texas recently to discuss a possible joint venture regarding ballpoint pens with a Texas corporation; (3) defendant complies with a law of the State of Texas that requires (as do twenty other states) that cigarette lighters be manufactured with at least 25 percent recyclable material.

4. Consider another application of Asahi. Plaintiff filed a suit in Colorado against a French tire manufacturer to recover for injuries sustained in one-car accident in Colorado when one of the defendant's tires allegedly failed. Defendant was incorporated in France and all its manufacturing facilities are located there. Defendant sells tires to Sears and Michelin New York (a N.Y. corporation), f.o.b. its plant in France, for eventual resale in the United States. Thus, defendant relinquishes title to and control over these tires upon sale. The tire in question was one of four new Michelin tires purchased from a German retailer by an American serviceman who installed it on his automobile. This vehicle was subsequently shipped to the U.S. and was eventually transferred to a Colorado car dealership, from which plaintiffs purchased it. The Colorado court exercised jurisdiction over defendant because the defendant indirectly sought to serve a

nationwide market, including Colorado, and therefore purposely availed itself of the Colorado market. See Le Manufacture Française des Pneumatiques Michelin v. District Court, 620 P.2d 1040 (Colorado 1980). But this case was decided before Asahi. Would Asahi require a different result?

5. One issue that arises frequently, although not exclusively, in transnational litigation is the attribution of contacts of an agent or affiliate. For example, the foreign parent of a domestic corporation might be the more attractive defendant. (This could happen where the domestic corporation is defunct, inadequately insured, or otherwise judgment-proof. Or, in employment cases, for example, a worker's compensation scheme might preclude suit against the employer-subsidiary but not the parent.) But if the foreign corporation has no presence or contacts in the forum state other than this subsidiary, can the court assert personal jurisdiction? (Of course a related question is whether that foreign corporation could be substantively liable for the acts of its subsidiary, but the plaintiff's lawyer will worry about that later. Indeed, if the plaintiff's lawyer can establish personal jurisdiction, she may be able to negotiate a settlement rather quickly from a foreign defendant who may be a reluctant litigant.) But generally, before the separate corporate identity of one corporation will be disregarded and treated as the alter ego of another, it must be shown that the affiliate is so controlled and its affairs so conducted by the other that it is a mere instrumentality. In fact, a court may even require a showing that the observance of the fiction of separate existence would, under the circumstances, sanction a fraud or promote injustice. See Hollister v. Colopast A/S, 16 U.S.P.Q.2d 1718, 1990 WL 141423 (N.d. Ill. 1990); Telcordia Tech., Inc. v. Alcatel S.A. and Alcatel USA, Inc. 2005 WL 1268061 (D. Del. 2005).

Graduate Management Admissions Council v. Raju

241 F. Supp.2d 589 (E.D.Va. 2003)

Ellis, District Judge.

This copyright and trademark action against a citizen of India grows out of defendant's use of a foreign Internet website with an infringing domain name to sell plaintiff's copyrighted materials throughout the world including the United States. Defendant has defaulted and plaintiff has demonstrated a right to copyright and trademark relief provided there is personal jurisdiction over defendant. Thus, explored and resolved here is the question whether there is personal jurisdiction over a citizen of India who registers and operates a foreign website selling plaintiff's test preparation materials in apparent violation of United States copyright and trademark laws, where (i) the copyright and trademark holder is located in Virginia, (ii) the website contains a purported testimonial from a Virginia citizen, (iii) infringing materials were sold and delivered to two individuals in Virginia, and (iv) the website contains ordering information for United States citizens.

I

Plaintiff Graduate Management Admission Council ("GMAC") is a non-profit Virginia corporation located in McLean, Virginia. GMAC develops and owns all rights to the Graduate Management Admission Test ("GMAT"), which is used to assess the qualifications of applicants to approximately 1700 graduate business management programs in the United States and elsewhere. The GMAT forms and the questions created by GMAC are original, copyrightable materials, and GMAC enjoys exclusive rights to copy, distribute, display, publish, and prepare derivative works. GMAC routinely registers all of its test forms and questions with the Register of Copyrights. In addition, GMAC has registered "GMAT" as a trademark with the United States Patent and Trademark Office.

Defendant Narasimha Raju ("Raju") is a citizen of India. Raju registered the domain names <gmatplus.com> and <gmatplus.net> in April and May of 2000. According to the record, the original registrar for these domain names was wespe.de, located in Germany. The record further reflects that Raju subsequently changed the registrar for <gmatplus.com> to Domain People, Inc., and the registrar for <gmatplus.net> first to Enom, Inc., and then to 123Register.com.[2] The registry for both of these domain names, as for all ".com" and ".net" domain names, is VeriSign Global Registry Services, located in Herndon, Virginia.

Using these domain names, Raju operates a website under the name of "GMATplus" which sells GMAT questions for test preparation purposes. The site purports to sell, for as much as $199, seven books containing "100% actual questions, which were never published in any GMAT books and material."[4] Significantly, the promotional text on the website claims that 74% of recent test takers scoring above 700 on the GMAT were from India, China, Korea, Japan, and Taiwan, even though only 22% of all test takers come from those five countries. The GMATplus website attributes this disproportionate success to the fact that "most of [these high scorers from these countries] have access to 100 percent of unpublished previous questions in these countries." According to GMAC, Raju sold and delivered infringing materials to individuals located in Virginia on at least two known occasions.[5]

The GMATplus website facilitates the ordering of materials through a two step process, combining a money transfer arranged through a third party with online ordering through a provided email address. Potential customers are directed first to contact Western Union or MoneyGram to set up a payment to Narasimha Raju in Hyderabad, India, and then to send an email to "gmatplus @yahoo.com"

---

[2] Although the location of these registrars is not specified in the complaint, the public record shows that wespe.de is located in Germany, Domain People, Inc. is located in Canada, Enom, Inc. is located in Washington state, and 123Register.com is located in California.

[4] Because GMAC does not publish most questions used on prior exams, but rather reuses them, Raju's alleged publication of GMAT questions not only violates GMAC's copyrights, it also undermines the integrity of the test.

[5] These materials did not contain secure, unpublished questions, but did include material copyrighted by GMAC.

containing the customer's name, address, and telephone number and the money transfer reference number provided by Western Union or MoneyGram. The provided email address is only to be used for "shipping and payment" purposes, not for general questions about the products. The ordering information appears to facilitate worldwide orders, but places specific emphasis on the United States and Canada. The site provides the toll free numbers for Western Union or MoneyGram to be used "in the U.S. or Canada," while those located "in other countries" are provided hyperlinks to Western Union's and MoneyGram's websites so that they can find the office nearest to them. The site promises delivery to "most parts of the world (including the US) within 3–5 working days." No countries or markets other than the United States and Canada are mentioned by name on the ordering page. Furthermore, of the six testimonials that appear on the website, three are purportedly from the customers in the United States, including one in Virginia, with the other three coming from customers in Singapore, Australia, and France.

On April 24, 2002, GMAC filed a five count complaint against Raju alleging (i) copyright infringement, in violation of 17 U.S.C. § 501(a), (ii) trademark infringement, in violation of 15 U.S.C. § § 1114(1) and 1117(a), (iii) trademark dilution, in violation of 15 U.S.C. § 1125(c), (iv) cyberpiracy, in violation of 15 U.S.C. § 1125(d), and (v) unfair competition in violation of 15 U.S.C. § 1125(a). By Order dated September 9, 2002, it was noted that the defendant was properly served, pursuant to Rule 4(f)(C)(ii), Fed.R.Civ.P., and that the defendant appeared to be in default for failing to respond to the complaint. Accordingly, that Order directed a magistrate judge to prepare a report and recommendation concerning (i) whether personal jurisdiction existed over the defendant, (ii) whether default should be entered against the defendant, and (iii) if so, the appropriate relief to be awarded the plaintiff.

In a Report and Recommendation dated October 11, 2002, the magistrate judge recommended a finding of no personal jurisdiction over Raju. On October 25, 2002, GMAC responded by filing an objection to the Report, contesting that recommendation. Accordingly, the matter is now ripe for a determination of whether there is personal jurisdiction over Raju based on the facts alleged in the record.

II

A

The determination of in personam jurisdiction involves a two-step inquiry. A court must first determine whether the facts of the case fall within the reach of Virginia's long-arm statute. Second, a court must determine "whether the long-arm statute's reach in the case exceeds its constitutional grasp," by considering whether the exercise of personal jurisdiction is consistent with "traditional notions of fair play and substantial justice" under the Due Process clause.

1. Virginia long-arm statute

The conduct alleged by GMAC clearly places Raju within the reach of the Virginia long-arm statute. The Virginia long-arm statute provides for personal jurisdiction over a person "causing tortious injury in this Commonwealth by an act or omission outside this Commonwealth if he regularly does or solicits business, or engages in any other persistent course of conduct, or derives substantial revenue from goods used or consumed or services rendered, in this Commonwealth." Va. Code § 8.01–328.1(A)(4). Raju's actions in operating his website and selling the GMATplus materials caused tortious injury to GMAC in Virginia through his alleged actions in violation of federal trademark and copyright law. Moreover, it is well established that soliciting business through a website accessible by Virginians satisfies the remaining requirement of the long-arm statute, namely that the person "does or solicits business, or engages in any other persistent course of conduct" in Virginia. Thus, the magistrate judge properly concluded that the requirements of the Virginia long-arm statute were met.

2. Due Process analysis

The second prong of the personal jurisdictional inquiry requires a consideration of the constitutionality of personal jurisdiction under the Due Process clause. Under the well-established International Shoe formulation, the exercise of personal jurisdiction over a defendant requires that the defendant "have certain minimum contacts with [the forum] such that the maintenance of a suit does not offend 'traditional notions of fair play and substantial justice.'" See Int'l Shoe Co. v. Washington, 326 U.S. 310, 316 91945); see also ALS Scan, 293 F.3d at 710–12 (discussing the modern development of personal jurisdiction doctrine). Personal jurisdiction can be established under either general or specific jurisdiction. See Helicopteros Nacionales de Colombia S.A. v. Hall, 466 U.S. 408, 414 (1984). Where, as here, the defendant's contacts with the forum are also the basis for the suit, specific jurisdiction is appropriate. In determining whether specific jurisdiction exists, courts must consider "(1) the extent to which the defendant 'purposefully avail[ed]' itself of the privilege of conducting activities in the State; (2) whether the plaintiff's claims arise out of those activities directed at the State; and (3) whether the exercise of personal jurisdiction would be constitutionally 'reasonable.'" Id.[9]

As the Fourth Circuit noted in ALS Scan, Inc. v. Digital Service Consultants, 293 F.3d 707, 710 (4th Cir. 2002), this due process analysis must take account of the modern reality of widespread Internet electronic communications. See ALS, 293 F.3d at 713. Accordingly, the Fourth Circuit recently adopted the Zippo "sliding-scale" approach for determining whether Internet activity can serve as a basis for personal jurisdiction. See ALS, 293 F.3d at 713–14 (discussing Zippo Manuf. Co. v. Zippo Dot Com, Inc., 952 F. Supp. 1119 (W.D. Pa. 1997)).

Under the now-familiar Zippo test, the likelihood that personal jurisdiction can be constitutionally exercised is determined by focusing on "the nature and the quality of commercial activity that an entity conducts over the Internet." Id. at 713. Passive websites, that do "little more" than make information available to

---

[9] General jurisdiction, which is necessary when the contacts with the forum are not the basis for the suit, is analyzed under the more demanding "continuous and systematic" standard.

users in other jurisdictions, cannot support personal jurisdiction everywhere that information is accessed. Id. at 714. At the other end of the spectrum are situations where a defendant "clearly does business over the Internet," for example through the "knowing and repeated transmission of files over the Internet," which clearly do support personal jurisdiction. Id. In between is the "middle ground" of "interactive Web sites" which are not passive, because they allow a user to exchange information with the host computer, but also do not constitute "clearly do[ing] business over the Internet." Id. To determine whether an "interactive" website is grounds for personal jurisdiction, a court must consider the "level of interactivity and the commercial nature of the exchange of information that occurs on the Web site." Id.

In this regard, the Fourth Circuit "adopt[ed] and adapt[ed] the Zippo model" as follows:

> [A] State may, consistent with due process, exercise judicial power over a person outside of the State when that person (1) directs electronic activity into the State, (2) with the manifested intent of engaging in business or other interactions within the State, and (3) that activity creates, in a person within the State, a potential cause of action cognizable in the State's courts.

ALS, 293 F.3d at 714. A comparison of this formulation to the original Zippo test indicates that the ALS test emphasizes that requirement of purposeful targeting of a particular forum, not just the level of interactivity. Under the ALS test, the defendant must direct activity into the forum state, with the intent to engage in business within the state. As the ALS panel makes clear, personal jurisdiction requires "purposeful availment," that is "purposeful conduct directed at the State." Id. at 712–13 (emphasis in original).

In this case, GMAC asserts that the following contacts support a finding of personal jurisdiction based on Raju's contacts with Virginia: First, Raju's site is not merely passive; through it, he solicited orders of his infringing materials from Virginia residents. Second, Raju specifically targeted Virginia residents, by listing a testimonial from a Virginia customer and by selling and shipping materials to at least two Virginia residents. Third, Raju's activities were targeted at and infringed the rights of GMAC, a Virginia corporation. Fourth, colleges and universities in Virginia rely on the GMAT. Finally, Raju registered the allegedly infringing domain name with Network Solutions, Inc. ("NSI"), a Virginia company which served as the registry for all ".com" and ".net" domain names.

These contacts, evaluated in light of the three part ALS test, point ultimately to the absence of personal jurisdiction. See ALS, 293 F.3d at 714. Although some parts of the test are met, it is doubtful whether Raju can be said to have "direct[ed] electronic activity into the state" with the "intent of engaging in business... within the State," as required by the first and second elements of the ALS test. Id. First, mere registration of the domain name with a company located in Virginia does not support personal jurisdiction in this state. Second, the potential indirect injury suffered by the colleges and universities which rely on GMAT scores in their admissions process is too indirect and too diffuse to support a finding that the defendant specifically targeted Virginia. Significantly, over 1700 programs worldwide use the GMAT to evaluate candidates, thus there is no basis to conclude that Raju was knowingly targeting Virginia institutions. Third, based on the circumstances of this case, the shipment of materials to two Virginia customers is not a sufficient basis for personal jurisdiction, although the question is close....

Finally, GMAC also relies on the fact that the tortious conduct was targeted at GMAC, which is located in Virginia. In some circumstances, the location of the plaintiff, as the "focal point... of the harm suffered" can form the basis for personal jurisdiction. Calder v. Jones, 465 U.S. 783 (1984). The ALS test accommodates the Calder approach to finding jurisdiction based on the location of the harm caused by the tortious conduct. See Young, 315 F.3d at 262–63; ALS, 293 F.3d at 714. However, the Calder approach does not obviate the requirement to show purposeful availment, it is rather an alternate method of proving that the defendant directed his activities at the forum.... Here, there is no indication that Raju purposefully directed his tortious activity at Virginia. Indeed, Raju's GMATplus site consistently refers to "ETS" as the entity that administers the GMAT and publishes test questions. Thus, there is no indication that Raju should "reasonably anticipate being hauled into court" in Virginia based on GMAC's location there, when there is no showing that he was even aware of GMAC, let alone GMAC's location in Virginia.

In sum, the magistrate judge correctly concluded that there is no basis for personal jurisdiction in Virginia under Rule 4(k)(1)(A) based on the contacts with Virginia asserted by GMAC.

B

Although not raised by GMAC in its complaint or in its brief in opposition to the Report and Recommendation, there is an alternate basis for personal jurisdiction in this case under Rule 4(k)(2), Fed.R.Civ.P. This Rule provides for personal jurisdiction through nationwide service of process over any defendant provided (i) exercise of jurisdiction is consistent with the Constitution and the laws of the United States, (ii) the claim arises under federal law, and (iii) the defendant is not subject to the jurisdiction of the courts of general jurisdiction of any state. See Rule 4(k)(2), Fed. R. Civ. P. Rule 4(k)(2) was added in 1993 to deal with a gap in federal personal jurisdiction law in situations where a defendant does not reside in the United States, and lacks contacts with a single state sufficient to justify personal jurisdiction, but has enough contacts with the United States as a whole to satisfy the due process requirements. Precisely this situation is presented here.

1. Due Process analysis

The first element of the Rule 4(k)(2) analysis requires the same minimum contacts due process analysis as is conducted under Rule 4(k)(1)(A), with the significant difference that the relevant forum is the United States as a whole, not an individual State.

In considering Raju's contacts with the United States in this case, the ALS test for determining personal jurisdiction based on electronic activities, must be adapted for the purpose of national contacts analysis. Substituting the United States as the relevant forum, the test requires a showing in this case (i) that Raju directed his electronic activity into the United States, (ii) that he did so with the manifest intent of engaging in business or other interactions within the United States, and (iii) that his activity creates a potential cause of action in a person within the United States that is cognizable in the United States' courts. See ALS, 293 F.3d at 714.

Raju's alleged activity plainly creates a potential cause of action in a person within the United States which is cognizable in federal courts, satisfying the third element of the ALS test. GMAC is a Virginia non-profit corporation and thus a "person" within the United States. GMAC's causes of action are based on federal law, and thus are clearly cognizable in federal courts. It is also clear that Raju's intent is to "engag[e] in business," namely the business of selling his GMAT test preparation materials to buyers for a substantial fee. Thus, the second element of the ALS test is fulfilled in part. All that remains is a showing that Raju "directed his electronic activity" into the United States, with the intent of engaging in business "within the United States," as required by the first and second elements of the ALS test.

The record clearly indicates that Raju directed his activity at the United States market and specifically targeted United States customers. The intended market for business conducted through a website can be determined by considering the apparent focus of the website as a whole.... The relevant question is whether the website is "designed to attract or serve a [United States] audience." Id.

There is ample evidence that Raju targeted the United States market. First, and most significantly, the GMATplus site provides specific ordering information for United States customers. The ordering information page directs customers who "live in the United States or Canada" to contact Western Union or MoneyGram, and provides the toll free numbers for use by those customers. Other customers are directed simply to "contact [their] local MoneyGram office" or use a hyperlink to MoneyGram to find the nearest local office. No other countries apart from the United States and Canada are mentioned by name on the ordering information page. Thus, ordering information for customers in the United States (and Canada) is provided first and with more specificity than for customers from other countries. Second, the ordering information page informs customers that materials will "reach most parts of the world (including the US) within 3–5 working days." Third, the prices for the products are listed in dollars, presumably United States dollars. Fourth, three of the six testimonials are purportedly from United States citizens. Fifth, the promotional text on the site suggests that Raju's materials will allow American citizens and others to catch up with test takers from "India, China, Korea, Japan, and Taiwan," who purportedly score better on the test as a group than "their American or European counterparts...because most of them have access to 100 percent of unpublished previous questions in these countries." Finally, Raju confirmed his apparent intent to serve United States customers by shipping his materials to the two Virginia residents mentioned in the record.

In sum, it is quite clear upon review of the GMATplus website and the record as a whole that while Raju may have aimed his website at the entire, worldwide market of GMAT test takers, he specifically directed his electronic activity at the United States market and did in fact ship materials in the United States. Thus, GMAT has shown under the ALS test that Raju "direct[ed] his electronic activity into [the United States] with the manifested intent of engaging in business... within [the United States]," satisfying the remaining elements of the ALS test. It follows that the exercise of personal jurisdiction based on nationwide contacts under 4(k)(2) comports with constitutional due process requirements in this case.

2. Remaining issues under Rule 4(k)(2)

The second element of Rule 4(k)(2)—that the claim arise under federal law—is readily shown. See Rule 4(k)(2), Fed. R. Civ. P. GMAC's five claims, for copyright infringement, trademark infringement, dilution, cyberpiracy, and unfair competition, all arise under and are expressly predicated on federal statutes.

The final element of Rule 4(k)(2) requires a showing that the defendant is not subject to the jurisdiction of the courts of general jurisdiction of any state. See Rule 4(k)(2), Fed. R. Civ. P. Federal courts have struggled in determining how fairly to assign the burden of making this showing, since it apparently places a burden on plaintiffs, who bear the burden of establishing personal jurisdiction, to "prove a negative," namely that the defendant is not subject to personal jurisdiction, in all fifty states. See, e.g. Swiss American Bank, 191 F.3d at 40–42 (applying a burden-shifting approach modeled on the McDonnell Douglas approach); ISI Int'l, Inc. v. Borden Ladner Gevais, LLP, 256 F.3d 548, 552 (7th Cir. 2001) (applying a more pragmatic approach, whereby the defendant must name a suitable forum state or concede that jurisdiction is not available in any state). Yet, on this record, it is readily apparent that personal jurisdiction is unavailable in any state. There are no specific contacts with any state other than Virginia, and the Virginia contacts are not sufficient to support jurisdiction in Virginia. Moreover, plaintiffs have no access to evidence that might provide more detail on Raju's possible contacts with other states; the defendant is in default and has neither appeared nor been subject to discovery. Accordingly, the proper conclusion on this record is that there is no personal jurisdiction over Raju in any district.

A final matter that must be addressed before finding jurisdiction under Rule 4(k)(2) in this case is the fact that GMAC has not asserted 4(k)(2) as a basis for jurisdiction. This omission is not decisive, for it is clear that "[f]ederal courts are entitled to apply the proper body of law, whether the parties name it or not." ISI Int'l, 256 F.3d at 551–52 (citing Kamen v. Kemper Financial Services, Inc., 500 U.S. 90 (1991), and finding jurisdiction under Rule 4(k)(2) though the parties did not raise Rule 4(k)(2) at the district court or appellate level). GMAC has consistently argued that jurisdiction would be proper in the Virginia courts, which is in apparent contradiction with a claim of personal jurisdiction under Rule 4(k)(2). Yet, personal jurisdiction claims may be properly analyzed in the alternative under 4(k)(1)(A) and 4(k)(2). See Dee-K Enterprises, 982 F. Supp. at 1144 n. 10 (holding that

Rule 4(k)(2) provides an alternative basis for jurisdiction to the extent that plaintiffs allegations do not support jurisdiction under the Virginia long-arm statute). Thus, neither GMAC's failure to assert jurisdiction under 4(k)(2), nor its assertion of jurisdiction under Rule 4(k)(1)(A) operate to change the conclusion that there is jurisdiction here under Rule 4(k)(2)'s nationwide contacts analysis.

In sum, the record shows that there is no personal jurisdiction over Raju in any state court, that GMAC's claims arise under federal law, and that Raju's contacts with the United States are sufficient to permit the exercise of personal jurisdiction in this matter without violating due process. In other words, while the record clearly shows that Raju directed his activities at the United States market, in apparent violation of GMAC's rights, he did not sufficiently direct his activities at any given state to justify a finding of personal jurisdiction in any state court. Rule 4(k)(2) was enacted precisely to fill this gap in personal jurisdiction under Rule 4(k)(1)(A). Accordingly, there is personal jurisdiction over Raju under Rule 4(k)(2). To find otherwise would not only frustrate GMAC's attempts in this case to vindicate its rights under United States law, by requiring GMAC to turn to foreign courts to vindicate those rights against a likely elusive defendant, it would also provide a blueprint whereby other individuals bent on violating United States trademark and copyright laws could do so without risking suit in a United States court.

III

In conclusion, there is personal jurisdiction here over Raju under Rule 4(k)(2), Fed. R. Civ. P. It is also apparent on the record that Raju is in default. Accordingly, the magistrate judge is directed in an accompanying order to take whatever steps deemed necessary to determine the appropriate relief to be awarded GMAC in this matter.

The Clerk is directed to send a copy of this Memorandum Opinion to all counsel of record.

Comments and Questions

1. Do you agree that the court lacked jurisdiction under the Virginia long-arm statute? Wasn't it foreseeable that harm would be caused to GMAT in that state? If so, or if it had been foreseeable, is that not enough to support personal jurisdiction? Why or why not?

2. Do you agree that while Raju was not subject to jurisdiction under Virginia's long-arm statute, he had nationwide contacts sufficient to satisfy Fed. R. Civ. P. 4(k)(2)?

3. As discussed earlier, another method for establishing personal jurisdiction over a defendant is transitory or "tag" jurisdiction.

> Among the most firmly established principles of personal jurisdiction in American tradition is that the courts of a State have jurisdiction over nonresidents who are physically present in the State. The view developed early that each State had the

> power to hale before its courts any individual who could be found within its borders, and that once having acquired jurisdiction over such a person by properly serving him with process, the State could retain jurisdiction to enter judgment against him, no matter how fleeting his visit. That view had antecedents in English common-law practice, which sometimes allowed "transitory" actions, arising out of events outside the country, to be maintained against seemingly nonresident defendants who were present in England. Justice Story believed the principle, which he traced to Roman origins, to be firmly grounded in English tradition: "[B]y the common law[,] personal actions, being transitory, may be brought in any place, where the party defendant may be found," for "every nation may...rightfully exercise jurisdiction over all persons within its domains." J. Story, Commentaries on the Conflict of Laws §§ 554, 543 (1846). See also id., §§ 530-538; Picquet v. Swan, supra, at 611-612 (Story, J.) ("Where a party is within a territory, he may justly be subjected to its process, and bound personally by the judgment pronounced, on such process, against him"). This American jurisdictional practice is, moreover, not merely old; it is continuing.... We do not know of a single state or federal statute, or a single judicial decision resting upon state law, that has abandoned in-state service as a basis of jurisdiction....
>
> [J]urisdiction based on physical presence alone constitutes due process because it is one of the continuing traditions of our legal system that define the due process standard of [minimum contacts and] "traditional notions of fair play and substantial justice." That standard was developed by analogy to "physical presence," and it would be perverse to say it could now be turned against that touchstone of jurisdiction.

Burnham v. Superior Court of California, 495 U.S. 604, 610–620 (1990). That said, some commentators believe that courts could use customary international law to invalidate tag jurisdiction over foreign defendants. See Restatement (Third) of Foreign Relations Law, § 421(2)(a) & cmt. e & reporter's note 5.

4. As first mentioned in the excerpt by Professor Borchers, supra, a corporate defendant that has a systematic and continuous presence in the forum may also be subject to personal jurisdiction under a theory of general jurisdiction. A subset of this category is often referred to as "doing business" jurisdiction, as discussed above, and parties frequently fight about exactly what constitutes "systematic" and "continuous" in this highly fact-specific inquiry.

Mary Twitchell, Doing-Business Jurisdiction

Why We Keep Doing Business With Doing-Business Jurisdiction
2001 U. Chi. Legal F. 171, 194–203

Why do we persist in subjecting defendants to such a loose, unpredictable, poorly defined, and poorly defended standard? Several reasons are self-evident. First, it is a traditional practice going back to very early cases. Second, as long as we use a weak standard, the test is fairly easy to administer because courts need only assess a single variable, the continuity and systematic nature—and, less frequently, the substantiality—of the defendant's contacts. Finally, given the variety of business activities that can occur in a forum and our uncertainties about the constitutional underpinnings of the doctrine, devising a more definitive standard is just too hard. Courts and legislatures discovered early on that it is hard to define "doing business" with any precision....

Moreover, doing-business jurisdiction generally does little harm. Most defendants are domestic and will have to defend somewhere in the United States anyway. Furthermore, if most cases are somewhat related to the defendant's contacts, then perhaps nothing more than continuous and systematic contacts is needed for a result that is generally reasonable, even if not fully supported by current constitutional theory....

But we cannot blithely accept this status quo. If we are to continue to ground personal jurisdiction on the Constitution... we need a persuasive theoretical basis for doing-business jurisdiction that either justifies its extreme breadth or limits its boundaries, and our decisions should fairly reflect whatever principle we adopt. These results should also be reasonably predictable, giving defendants notice of which commercial activities will expose them to a forum's plenary power.

We may never reach these goals, but circumstances may force us to try, primarily because of the pressure put on us by foreign defendants appalled to find that general jurisdiction exposure is the price of doing regular business in U.S. markets. Although general jurisdiction may be unfair in many cases, it is especially unfair when exercised over foreign business enterprises for several related reasons.

1. *Lowered foreseeability*. Citizens of countries that do not allow general activities-based jurisdiction over defendants where they are doing-business—that is, citizens of almost every country in the world[99]—may not expect or foresee it, and will perceive it as extraordinarily unfair. This problem is compounded by the lack of a uniform national rule clearly describing the extent to which nondomestic entities may be exposed to such jurisdiction.

2. *Unpredictability*. This factor presents a problem for both domestic and foreign defendants. Even if a corporation is aware of the existence of doing-business jurisdiction, the case law is so unsettled that few companies can predict when and to what extent they may be subject to such jurisdiction. Results can vary both state by state and case by case. Given this uncertainty and the expense of litigating jurisdiction, especially for smaller enterprises that may not have regular experience with litigating in the United States, businesses may choose not to assert a defense at all, or may choose not to appeal a negative ruling at the trial level...

---

[99] *But see* Linda J. Silberman, *Can the Hague Judgments Project Be Saved?: A Perspective from the United States,* in John J. Barcelo, III and Kevin M. Clermont, eds. A Global Law of Jurisdiction and Judgments: Lessons from the Hague (Kluwer Intl 2001) (noting that England and Japan also permit form of "doing business" jurisdiction over unrelated claims in some circumstances).

3. *More significant exposure.* For an American defendant, being subjected to doing-business jurisdiction means, at worst, having to defend in an additional American state. A change of law may be a significant risk, but otherwise the system is very much the same. A foreign defendant, on the other hand, is subject to jurisdiction in what is often a dramatically different judicial system a long distance from home. Unless it has been engaged in substantial commercial activities here for a long time, it is likely to be unfamiliar with our litigation system and will by definition be seen as an "outsider." . . .

Because of the heightened fairness problems present when general jurisdiction is exercised over foreign corporations, it would seem to follow that if we are going to curtail general doing-business jurisdiction anywhere, it should be here. And yet there is a paradox: the fairness problems may be greater, but the needs of domestic plaintiffs also increase.

For Americans suing Americans, if general jurisdiction is refused, there is always an alternate forum within the same system, the defendant's home. When suing a foreign enterprise, unless the suit fits into our unsettled but potentially narrow definition of specific jurisdiction, there will be no domestic jurisdiction at all. Doing-business jurisdiction gives U.S. courts the power to decide claims arising elsewhere, and jurisdiction over additional defendants in a dispute that may originally be based on specific jurisdiction. It also enhances the possibility that a defendant will not fight an expensive personal jurisdiction battle at either the trial or appellate level.

4. *Systemic differences.* Systemic differences also cause problems of a different sort. Plaintiffs obtain greater advantages in U.S. courts such as jury trials, contingent fees for their lawyers, broader discovery rules, and broader substantive laws. It is difficult for potential tort defendants from foreign countries to contract around this problem.

5. *Can foreign corporations ever be "insiders"?* It is hard to know what we should do in this difficult situation in which our national interests conflict with the interests of other countries. [Perhaps] general jurisdiction should only be exercised over defendants with enough ties to the forum, and enough clout within the forum, so that the costs of subjecting them to plenary forum power on any cause of action are not externalized. Otherwise, the political theory supporting general doing-business jurisdiction fails.

It is probably no accident that true outsiders—that is, foreign commercial actors rather than domestic defendants—have raised the first significant challenge to this form of jurisdiction. Anyone who wonders why the domestic defense bar does not jump on the bandwagon might consider this fact: of those reported cases finding general jurisdiction over defendants, a significant number of them were commercial suits brought by American business entities, not consumer suits brought by individuals. Like other domestic plaintiffs, American business enterprises benefit from the role that our broad doing-business rule plays in our overall jurisdictional structure.

6. *The risks of using doing-business jurisdiction to decide internet cases.* Another problem . . . is the risk that American states may inappropriately use their general

jurisdiction powers to reach defendants using the internet for commercial activities. Unlike the specific jurisdiction question, a state can decide that it has doing-business jurisdiction without any consideration of its regulatory authority over the claim presented. Because the standard is so ill-defined, a court can focus merely on the presence of "continuous and systematic" contacts, find "general" jurisdiction, and compel the defendant to respond to the state's regulatory authority. In sum, the mere existence of this overbroad general jurisdiction power can undercut whatever carefully-designed standard we might develop for determining when specific jurisdiction exists over global commercial activity that causes some effect within a particular nation.... Without any of the checks supplied by the considerations that play a role in determining that specific jurisdiction exists, serious regulatory over-reaching can result.

The current Hague proposal[111] would resolve many of the problems foreign defendants face by disallowing all forms of general doing-business jurisdiction in transnational cases. This would reduce the legitimate concerns of foreign defendants, but it would leave Americans without access to local fora for some cases that have traditionally, and perhaps properly, been decided here. No matter how generously the proposal's language permitting jurisdiction is read... under the current proposal plaintiffs would not be able to sue foreign defendants in the United States on claims having no relationship to the defendant's domestic activities. This result is, of course, viewed by many other nations as a reasonable limit on what is perceived as an exorbitant exercise of jurisdiction, but we are probably not ready to go that far in curtailing this jurisdiction....

Comments and Questions

1. Why should a court ever assert jurisdiction over a defendant if the plaintiff's claim has no relationship to the defendant's activities in the forum state?

2. Professor Twitchell was correct in predicting the demise of the proposed Hague Convention. Salvaged from the wreckage of a decade of negotiations was a more modest undertaking, a Convention on Choice of Court Agreements, which was concluded in 2005. See http://www.hcch.net. The Convention includes provisions that require courts in member states to assume jurisdiction (or to deny it, as the case may be) pursuant to certain forum selection agreements in commercial cases as well as provisions that require other states to enforce resulting judgments. The regime makes qualifying forum selection clauses more likely to be honored and more likely to lead to judgments that would be recognized and enforced elsewhere. Only Mexico has ratified this treaty; but others are expected to follow eventually. We will consider forum selection clauses more fully in Chapter 5.

---

[111] Hague Conference on Private International Law, Preliminary Draft Convention on Jurisdiction and Foreign Judgments in Civil and Commerical Matters (adopted Oct. 30, 1999).

2. European Union

Patrick J. Borchers, Personal Jurisdiction in Europe

Comparing Personal Jurisdiction in the United States and he European Community: Lessons for American Reform 40 Am. J. Comp. L. 121, 123–127 (1992)

The development of jurisdictional precepts in Europe has been longer and smoother [than in the United States]. For our purposes, however, the relevant history is quite recent. In 1960, a committee of legal experts and representatives from the Member States of the European Community was established pursuant to Article 220 of the Treaty of Rome to "enter into negotiations with each other with a view to securing for the benefit of their nationals... the simplification of formalities governing the reciprocal recognition and enforcement of judgments of courts or tribunals and of arbitral awards."[52] Although several different approaches to fulfilling this mandate were considered, the chosen approach was to negotiate a multilateral accord to supersede existing bilateral recognition conventions.

As farsighted as the multilateral approach seems in retrospect, equally farsighted was the decision to employ direct as well as indirect restraints on jurisdiction. This decision was a substantial break from prior bilateral conventions which controlled jurisdiction only indirectly, i.e., at the judgment recognition stage. The use of dual restraints allowed the Convention's drafters to address the twin vices of jurisdiction among Member States: exorbitant national jurisdictional rules, and extremely narrow judgment recognition practices resulting in a sort of law of the jungle in transnational enforcement.

One of the fundamental principles of the Convention is the use of the domiciliary nexus as a basis for directly regulating jurisdiction. A defendant domiciled in a Member State may only be sued in the European Community where the Convention allows for jurisdiction, and conversely, when the Convention provides for jurisdiction, a court has no authority to decline jurisdiction.... The Convention's principal rule of direct jurisdiction, subject to many variations discussed below, is that defendants are to be sued in the courts of their State of domicile.[59] The Convention also countenances a sort of ancillary jurisdiction, provid[ing] that multiple defendants

[52] Treaty Establishing the European Economic Community (Treaty of Rome), March 25, 1957, art. 220, 298 U.N.T.S. 11 (entered into force January 1, 1958); *see* Jenard, "Report on the Convention on jurisdiction and the enforcement of judgments in civil and commercial matters," 1979 O.J. Eur. Comm. (No. C 59) 1, 3 reprinted in A. Dashwood, R. Hacon & R. White, A Guide to the Civil Jurisdiction and Judgements Convention 329 (1987).

[59] Brussels Convention on Jurisdiction and the Enforcement of Judgments in Civil and Commercial Matters, September 27, 1968, amended by Luxembourg Convention of the Accession to the 1968 Convention of Denmark, the Republic of Ireland, and the United Kingdom, October 9, 1978, 1978 O.J. Eur. Comm. (No. L 304) 77 reprinted in 18 I.L.M. 8, 21 (1979) (entered into force between the original six Member States and Denmark on November 1, 1986, between these countries and the United Kingdom on November 1, 1987, and between these countries and Ireland on June 1, 1988) (hereafter cited as Brussels Convention). Domicile was chosen over nationality to avoid discrimination on the basis of nationality.

may be sued in a Contracting State where any one of them is domiciled, [allowing] a court seised of an original proceeding to hear any third-party proceedings, [and allowing] jurisdiction for a counterclaim arising out of the same facts as the original claim.

As a general proposition, these direct rules are applicable only to disputes between persons domiciled in different States. The Convention is also generally inapplicable to defendants domiciled outside the European Community. Thus as to "outsider" defendants—including, of course, the United States domiciliaries—the national rules of jurisdiction, including the famous exorbitant bases, still apply.

The second fundamental principle is that judgments ordinarily should be recognized without reexamination by the recognizing court. In this respect the drafters emulated the full faith and credit principle that governs recognition between United States courts.*

One aspect of the judgment recognition rules is of special importance to outsiders. The principle of largely unquestioning judgment recognition includes judgments against persons not domiciled in the Community, and thus not protected by the Convention, even if the judgment is entered on an admittedly exorbitant jurisdictional basis. Thus, for instance, a French court could enter a judgment against a United States domiciliary with jurisdiction taken solely on the basis that the plaintiff is French, and other European Community courts would be duty-bound to recognize this decree. This is a far broader effect than such a judgment would have enjoyed prior to the Convention. Although…the Convention allows countries outside the Community to enter into bilateral agreements with Member States to avoid the recognition of judgments based on exorbitant grounds of jurisdiction, [t]he only serious effort in this direction thus far has been negotiations between the United States and the United Kingdom, which ultimately broke down because of the British insurers' wariness of large American jury verdicts.

Perhaps the most important and dramatic feature of the Convention is the role given to the European Court of Justice. The Convention's drafters feared that national courts, if left to their own devices, might inevitably drift back to pre-existing national practices, thus resulting in widely divergent interpretations of the Convention. The solution was a 1971 Protocol giving appellate jurisdiction from specified national appellate tribunals to the Court of Justice in matters of interpretation of the Convention.[73]

The Convention's influence has also spread to the European Free Trade Association, a group of countries including Austria, Finland, Iceland, Norway, Sweden and Switzerland. Although the possibility of extending the Brussels

---

* Eds. Note: One important distinction is that the recognizing court generally cannot examine whether the rendering court had jurisdiction.

[73] Protocol on the Interpretation of the 1968 convention by the European court, June 3, 1971, amended by Convention on the Accession to the 1968 Convention of Denmark, the Republic of Ireland, and the United Kingdom, October 9, 1978, 1978 O.J. Eur. Comm. (No. L 304) 97 reprinted in 18 I.L.M. 8, 36 (1979).

convention to the EFTA countries was considered, ultimately a convention parallel to the Brussels Convention was adopted at a conference in Lugano and opened for signature. The Lugano Convention, when completely in force, will extend the benefits of the Brussels Convention to practically all of Western Europe.

[Since Professor Borchers wrote this article, the Brussels and Lugano Conventions were incorporated with some changes into the Council Regulation on Jurisdiction and the Recognition and Enforcement of Judgments in Civil and Commercial Matters which came into effect on March 1, 2002 (the "Brussels Regulation" or "Brussels I Regulation") and is binding on all Member States except Denmark, which is bound by the Brussels Convention instead. Excerpts from the Brussels Regulation follow.]

Council Regulation (EC) No 44/2001 of 22 December 2000 on Jurisdiction and the Recognition and Enforcement of Judgments in Civil and Commercial Matters

Whereas:

(11) The rules of jurisdiction must be highly predictable and founded on the principle that jurisdiction is generally based on the defendant's domicile and jurisdiction must always be available on this ground save in a few well-defined situations in which the subject-matter of the litigation or the autonomy of the parties warrants a different linking factor. The domicile of a legal person must be defined autonomously so as to make the common rules more transparent and avoid conflicts of jurisdiction....

(13) In relation to insurance, consumer contracts and employment, the weaker party should be protected by rules of jurisdiction more favourable to his interests than the general rules provide for.

(14) The autonomy of the parties to a contract, other than an insurance, consumer or employment contract, where only limited autonomy to determine the courts having jurisdiction is allowed, must be respected subject to the exclusive grounds of jurisdiction laid down in this Regulation....

Chapter I: Scope

Article 1

1. This Regulation shall apply in civil and commercial matters whatever the nature of the court or tribunal. It shall not extend, in particular, to revenue, customs or administrative matters.
2. The Regulation shall not apply to:
   (a) the status or legal capacity of natural persons, rights in property arising out of a matrimonial relationship, wills and succession;
   (b) bankruptcy, proceedings relating to the winding-up of insolvent companies or other legal persons, judicial arrangements, compositions and analogous proceedings;

(c) social security;
(d) arbitration.

3. In this Regulation, the term 'Member State' shall mean Member States with the exception of Denmark.

Chapter II: Jurisdiction

Section 1: General provisions

Article 2

1. Subject to this Regulation, persons domiciled in a Member State shall, whatever their nationality, be sued in the courts of that Member State.
2. Persons who are not nationals of the Member State in which they are domiciled shall be governed by the rules of jurisdiction applicable to nationals of that State.

Article 3

1. Persons domiciled in a Member State may be sued in the courts of another Member State only by virtue of the rules set out in Sections 2 to 7 of this Chapter.
2. In particular the rules of national jurisdiction set out in Annex I shall not be applicable as against them.

Article 4

1. If the defendant is not domiciled in a Member State, the jurisdiction of the courts of each Member State shall, subject to Articles 22 and 23, be determined by the law of that Member State.
2. As against such a defendant, any person domiciled in a Member State may, whatever his nationality, avail himself in that State of the rules of jurisdiction there in force, and in particular those specified in Annex I, in the same way as the nationals of that State.

Section 2: Special jurisdiction

Article 5

A person domiciled in a Member State may, in another Member State, be sued:

1. (a) in matters relating to a contract, in the courts for the place of performance of the obligation in question;
   (b) for the purpose of this provision and unless otherwise agreed, the place of performance of the obligation in question shall be:
   — in the case of the sale of goods, the place in a Member State where, under the contract, the goods were delivered or should have been delivered,
   — in the case of the provision of services, the place in a Member State where, under the contract, the services were provided or should have been provided,
   (c) if subparagraph (b) does not apply then subparagraph (a) applies;
2. in matters relating to maintenance, in the courts for the place where the maintenance creditor is domiciled or habitually resident or, if the matter is ancillary

to proceedings concerning the status of a person, in the court which, according to its own law, has jurisdiction to entertain those proceedings, unless that jurisdiction is based solely on the nationality of one of the parties;

3. in matters relating to tort, delict or quasi-delict, in the courts for the place where the harmful event occurred or may occur;
4. as regards a civil claim for damages or restitution which is based on an act giving rise to criminal proceedings, in the court seised of those proceedings, to the extent that that court has jurisdiction under its own law to entertain civil proceedings;
5. as regards a dispute arising out of the operations of a branch, agency or other establishment, in the courts for the place in which the branch, agency or other establishment is situated;
6. as settlor, trustee or beneficiary of a trust created by the operation of a statute, or by a written instrument, or created orally and evidenced in writing, in the courts of the Member State in which the trust is domiciled;
7. as regards a dispute concerning the payment of remuneration claimed in respect of the salvage of a cargo or freight, in the court under the authority of which the cargo or freight in question:
   (a) has been arrested to secure such payment, or
   (b) could have been so arrested, but bail or other security has been given; provided that this provision shall apply only if it is claimed that the defendant has an interest in the cargo or freight or had such an interest at the time of salvage.

Article 6

A person domiciled in a Member State may also be sued:

1. where he is one of a number of defendants, in the courts for the place where any one of them is domiciled, provided the claims are so closely connected that it is expedient to hear and determine them together to avoid the risk of irreconcilable judgments resulting from separate proceedings;
2. as a third party in an action on a warranty or guarantee or in any other third party proceedings, in the court seised of the original proceedings, unless these were instituted solely with the object of removing him from the jurisdiction of the court which would be competent in his case;
3. on a counter-claim arising from the same contract or facts on which the original claim was based, in the court in which the original claim is pending;
4. in matters relating to a contract, if the action may be combined with an action against the same defendant in matters relating to rights in rem in immovable property, in the court of the Member State in which the property is situated....

Section 3: Jurisdiction in matters relating to insurance

Article 8

In matters relating to insurance, jurisdiction shall be determined by this Section, without prejudice to Article 4 and point 5 of Article 5.

Article 9

1. An insurer domiciled in a Member State may be sued:
   (a) in the courts of the Member State where he is domiciled, or
   (b) in another Member State, in the case of actions brought by the policyholder, the insured or a beneficiary, in the courts for the place where the plaintiff is domiciled,
   (c) if he is a co-insurer, in the courts of a Member State in which proceedings are brought against the leading insurer.
2. An insurer who is not domiciled in a Member State but has a branch, agency or other establishment in one of the Member States shall, in disputes arising out of the operations of the branch, agency or establishment, be deemed to be domiciled in that Member State.

Article 10

In respect of liability insurance or insurance of immovable property, the insurer may in addition be sued in the courts for the place where the harmful event occurred. The same applies if movable and immovable property are covered by the same insurance policy and both are adversely affected by the same contingency.

Article 11

1. In respect of liability insurance, the insurer may also, if the law of the court permits it, be joined in proceedings which the injured party has brought against the insured....

Article 12

1. ...[A]n insurer may bring proceedings only in the courts of the Member State in which the defendant is domiciled, irrespective of whether he is the policyholder, the insured or a beneficiary....

Article 13

The provisions of this Section may be departed from only by an agreement:
1. which is entered into after the dispute has arisen, or
2. which allows the policyholder, the insured or a beneficiary to bring proceedings in courts other than those indicated in this Section,...

Section 4: Jurisdiction over consumer contracts

Article 15

1. In matters relating to a contract concluded by a person, the consumer, for a purpose which can be regarded as being outside his trade or profession, jurisdiction shall be determined by this Section, without prejudice to Article 4 and point 5 of Article 5, if:
   (a) it is a contract for the sale of goods on instalment credit terms; or
   (b) it is a contract for a loan repayable by instalments, or for any other form of credit, made to finance the sale of goods; or
   (c) in all other cases, the contract has been concluded with a person who pursues commercial or professional activities in the Member State of

the consumer's domicile or, by any means, directs such activities to that Member State or to several States including that Member State, and the contract falls within the scope of such activities.

2. Where a consumer enters into a contract with a party who is not domiciled in a Member State but has a branch, agency or other establishment in one of the Member States, that party shall, in disputes arising out of the operations of the branch, agency or establishment, be deemed to be domiciled in that State.
3. This Section shall not apply to a contract of transport other than a contract which, for an inclusive price, provides for a combination of travel and accommodation.

Article 16

1. A consumer may bring proceedings against the other party to a contract either in the courts of the Member State in which that party is domiciled or in the courts for the place where the consumer is domiciled.
2. Proceedings may be brought against a consumer by the other party to the contract only in the courts of the Member State in which the consumer is domiciled....

Article 17

The provisions of this Section may be departed from only by an agreement:

1. which is entered into after the dispute has arisen; or
2. which allows the consumer to bring proceedings in courts other than those indicated in this Section; or
3. which is entered into by the consumer and the other party to the contract, both of whom are at the time of conclusion of the contract domiciled or habitually resident in the same Member State, and which confers jurisdiction on the courts of that Member State, provided that such an agreement is not contrary to the law of that Member State.

Section 5: Jurisdiction over individual contracts of employment

Article 18

1. In matters relating to individual contracts of employment, jurisdiction shall be determined by this Section, without prejudice to Article 4 and point 5 of Article 5.
2. Where an employee enters into an individual contract of employment with an employer who is not domiciled in a Member State but has a branch, agency or other establishment in one of the Member States, the employer shall, in disputes arising out of the operations of the branch, agency or establishment, be deemed to be domiciled in that Member State.

Article 19

An employer domiciled in a Member State may be sued:

1. in the courts of the Member State where he is domiciled; or
2. in another Member State:

(a) in the courts for the place where the employee habitually carries out his work or in the courts for the last place where he did so, or
(b) if the employee does not or did not habitually carry out his work in any one country, in the courts for the place where the business which engaged the employee is or was situated.

Article 20

1. An employer may bring proceedings only in the courts of the Member State in which the employee is domiciled.
2. The provisions of this Section shall not affect the right to bring a counter-claim in the court in which, in accordance with this Section, the original claim is pending.

Article 21

The provisions of this Section may be departed from only by an agreement on jurisdiction:

1. which is entered into after the dispute has arisen; or
2. which allows the employee to bring proceedings in courts other than those indicated in this Section.

Section 6: Exclusive jurisdiction

Article 22

The following courts shall have exclusive jurisdiction, regardless of domicile:

1. in proceedings which have as their object rights in rem in immovable property or tenancies of immovable property, the courts of the Member State in which the property is situated....

2. in proceedings which have as their object the validity of the constitution, the nullity or the dissolution of companies or other legal persons or associations of natural or legal persons, or of the validity of the decisions of their organs, the courts of the Member State in which the company, legal person or association has its seat. In order to determine that seat, the court shall apply its rules of private international law;...

4. in proceedings concerned with the registration or validity of patents, trade marks, designs, or other similar rights required to be deposited or registered, the courts of the Member State in which the deposit or registration has been applied for, has taken place or is under the terms of a Community instrument or an international convention deemed to have taken place.

Without prejudice to the jurisdiction of the European Patent Office under the Convention on the Grant of European Patents, signed at Munich on 5 October 1973, the courts of each Member State shall have exclusive jurisdiction, regardless of domicile, in proceedings concerned with the registration or validity of any European patent granted for that State;

5. in proceedings concerned with the enforcement of judgments, the courts of the Member State in which the judgment has been or is to be enforced.

Section 7: Prorogation of jurisdiction

Article 23

1. If the parties, one or more of whom is domiciled in a Member State, have agreed that a court or the courts of a Member State are to have jurisdiction to settle any disputes which have arisen or which may arise in connection with a particular legal relationship, that court or those courts shall have jurisdiction. Such jurisdiction shall be exclusive unless the parties have agreed otherwise. Such an agreement conferring jurisdiction shall be either:
   (a) in writing or evidenced in writing; or
   (b) in a form which accords with practices which the parties have established between themselves; or
   (c) in international trade or commerce, in a form which accords with a usage of which the parties are or ought to have been aware and which in such trade or commerce is widely known to, and regularly observed by, parties to contracts of the type involved in the particular trade or commerce concerned.
2. Any communication by electronic means which provides a durable record of the agreement shall be equivalent to 'writing'.
3. Where such an agreement is concluded by parties, none of whom is domiciled in a Member State, the courts of other Member States shall have no jurisdiction over their disputes unless the court or courts chosen have declined jurisdiction. . . .

Article 24

Apart from jurisdiction derived from other provisions of this Regulation, a court of a Member State before which a defendant enters an appearance shall have jurisdiction. This rule shall not apply where appearance was entered to contest the jurisdiction, or where another court has exclusive jurisdiction by virtue of Article 22.

Section 9: Lis pendens—related actions

Article 27

1. Where proceedings involving the same cause of action and between the same parties are brought in the courts of different Member States, any court other than the court first seised shall of its own motion stay its proceedings until such time as the jurisdiction of the court first seised is established.
2. Where the jurisdiction of the court first seised is established, any court other than the court first seised shall decline jurisdiction in favour of that court.

Article 28

1. Where related actions are pending in the courts of different Member States, any court other than the court first seised may stay its proceedings.
2. Where these actions are pending at first instance, any court other than the court first seised may also, on the application of one of the parties, decline

jurisdiction if the court first seised has jurisdiction over the actions in question and its law permits the consolidation thereof.

3. For the purposes of this Article, actions are deemed to be related where they are so closely connected that it is expedient to hear and determine them together to avoid the risk of irreconcilable judgments resulting from separate proceedings....

Chapter V: General Provisions

Article 59

1. In order to determine whether a party is domiciled in the Member State whose courts are seised of a matter, the court shall apply its internal law.
2. If a party is not domiciled in the Member State whose courts are seised of the matter, then, in order to determine whether the party is domiciled in another Member State, the court shall apply the law of that Member State.

Article 60

1. For the purposes of this Regulation, a company or other legal person or association of natural or legal persons is domiciled at the place where it has its:
   (a) statutory seat, or
   (b) central administration, or
   (c) principal place of business....

Comments and Questions

1. Let us focus more carefully on certain provisions of the Regulation. As Professor Borchers emphasized, the starting point for analyzing personal jurisdiction under this regime is domicile. Reread Article 2. Then, notice that Article 3 provides that "persons domiciled in a Member State may be sued in the courts of another Member State only by virtue of the rules set out in Sections 2 to 7 of this Chapter." (Emphasis added.) Accordingly if a defendant is being sued anywhere other than their own domicile it must be because of some basis that is additional, or an exception to the general rule.

In order to determine what is understood by "domicile" the courts of the country in question will apply their internal law. See Article 59. And if the defendant is a company or some other entity that is not a natural person, the seat of that company (or other entity) forms the basis for determining where the domicile is. And again, in order to determine what is to be viewed as the seat, the court in the country in question will apply its own rules on private international law. See Article 60. The combination of Articles 59 and 60 means that the determination of domicile is not made based on a common-E.U. rule but rather on the basis of the national laws of the country in question.

2. Consider the following situation. Where is "Alfred" domiciled?

> ROISSY, France—Merhan Karimi Nasseri arrived here at Charles de Gaulle Airport in November 1988 with a one-way ticket to London. Six years later, he is still waiting to take off.

In the so-called Europe without frontiers, Mr. Nasseri lives in the Terminal One transit area, a legal twilight zone. It's a bizarre chapter in immigration annals. "Officially, he is a man who does not exist," says Philippe Bargain, the airport medical director.

Mr. Nasseri, who is known as Alfred, claims British citizenship. But Britain won't let him into the country. French authorities insist Mr. Nasseri has been staying in France without proper authorization, but they can't deport him because he doesn't hold a valid passport. In the space for "nationality," his French identification card says: "To be determined."

"Deport him to where?" asks Christian Bourguet, a noted French immigration attorney who voluntarily took on Mr. Nasseri's case pro bono. "A court cannot order someone deported to an undetermined country. Impossible."

So, Mr. Nasseri lives at CHARLES DE GAULLE, wearing the same navy-blue corduroy trousers and blue nylon jacket he had on when he got there six years ago with one suitcase, two shirts, a spare pair of shoes, a deck of playing cards and the equivalent of $500 in French francs.

A taciturn man with hollow cheeks, deep eyes and Chaplinesque moustache, Mr. Nasseri says, "I cannot let myself think, 'How did all these years go by?' My situation didn't oblige me to do something else."

Mr. Nasseri's strange predicament dates back to wartime Persia. According to papers filed with a French court, Mr. Nasseri was born in 1945 in Masjed Soleiman, a section of current-day Iran which then was under the jurisdiction of the British government—hence his claim of British citizenship.

His father was an Iranian physician working for the Anglo-Iranian Oil Co., a precursor of British Petroleum PLC. Records at a Brussels social-service agency show Mr. Nasseri was in England from 1974 to 1975. He returned to Iran and eventually was imprisoned for anti-Shah activities. In 1977, Mr. Nasseri says authorities in Teheran revoked his regular Iranian passport and issued papers permitting him to travel from Iran but never return. That year, he sought political refugee status in Britain. He was refused.

Over the next four years, Mr. Nasseri applied on separate occasions for refugee status in Germany, France, Italy and Yugoslavia. All refused him. Finally, in October 1986, the office of the U.N. High Commissioner for Refugees in Brussels accepted his request for political asylum from Iran, status which permitted him to travel to and apply for a resident's visa in any of the Geneva Convention countries. But Mr. Nasseri says he lost his refugee certificate in a Paris train station sometime in August 1988.

In November of that year, he bought a ticket on British Airways to London's Heathrow Airport. He had with him copies of his report to the French police about losing his refugee papers. Although this wasn't normal policy, airline officials allowed him to board the flight to London. At Heathrow, though, British immigration officers refused to let him in. They ordered him back to his point of departure, Charles de Gaulle.

He has lived in that airport ever since, through numerous hearings and appeals to decide his status. A victory of sorts came in 1992 when the U.N. Commissioner's office in Brussels confirmed that Mr. Nasseri "still benefits from his original status as refugee." A French tribunal then agreed to give Mr. Nasseri a 15-day travel permit to go sort out his papers in Brussels. Theoretically, his lawyer says, with new documentation, Mr. Nasseri should be free to travel anywhere in the Geneva Convention countries—including Great Britain. But Mr. Nasseri has his suspicions: When he previously tried to cross the Belgian frontier, he was turned back because his papers weren't in order.

So he stays at the airport, standing firm. He says he won't budge from Charles de Gaulle until he gets a British visa—which seems unlikely. "He's not our responsibility. He's an Iranian," says a consular officer at the British Embassy in Brussels.

The British Home Office in London, which handles immigration matters, is equally discouraging. Mr. Nasseri's claim to British citizenship, based on his birth in Soleiman, "does not seem to affect nationality in this case," a Home Office spokeswoman says.

Mr. Nasseri isn't buying any of this. He says it is his lifelong dream to go to Britain to take a degree in business administration. "Then I would like to work in government," he says. "Such a hope always keeps me fresh."

Some would say Mr. Nasseri's single-mindedness borders on obsession. The airport medical director, whose specialty is psychiatry, says Mr. Nasseri isn't insane. "Of course, there is some pathology there: the pathology of a man who would spend six years in an airport," says Dr. Bargain.

Meanwhile, he keeps an eye on Mr. Nasseri, and Mr. Nasseri survives on the kindness of strangers. His perch: a plastic bench across from the airport Burger King. This particular morning, an Aer Lingus ticket agent gives him two meal tickets to an airport restaurant. An Irish passenger in transit offers tea bags and powdered soup left over from her travels.

He showers in passenger facilities, shaves with a Remington electric razor Dr. Bargain gave him. From flight attendants, he receives a constant supply of toothpaste, mouthwash and after-shave left over from first-class passenger travel kits. Airport workers call Mr. Nasseri the mascot of Charles de Gaulle. He calls the help they give him "solidarity for my cause." He receives no government assistance.

Mr. Nasseri records the events of each day in a loose-leaf paper diary. Entry for Tuesday, Aug. 30, 1994: "Met Marcel. War veteran. Has been all over the world. Canadian Merchant Military. Injured by Germans... Now lives in Canada. He says living in Canada is better than USA. I say I think so."

He falls asleep under bright fluorescent lights at about 11:30, after the last flights have taken off for the day. The only sound likely to disturb him is the whine of the floor-polishing machines.

The days are tedious, but Mr. Nasseri says he doesn't get depressed. "I keep busy. I listen to music," he says, indicating a cassette player Dr. Bargain gave him. "I have always the same mood."

> He concedes his lack of social life. "But it is not possible to have any connections at this time," he says. "I do talk with some flight attendants. But I cannot bother anybody. The gendarmes would be on me in a minute."
>
> His honesty is legendary. Twice in the last year, he has turned in lost wallets full of cash. "Alfred is not a street person, a beggar. He has done his studies. He has a dignity about him," says Jacques Ausina, a French producer who hopes to make a documentary on Mr. Nasseri.
>
> Mr. Nasseri also has impressed travelers passing through France. He has cards and notes from all over the world, some addressed simply, "Alfred, Boutique Level, Charles de Gaulle Airport, France."
>
> Wrote one woman from Dorchester, England: "I have thought about you as I go about doing the day-to-day things we all take for granted here in England. There has been a prayer for you every night in our house, and will continue to be until your situation is resolved."...
>
> Judith Valente, The Man Without a Country Resides at Charles de Gaulle, Wall St. Journal, October 7, 1994.

Tom Hanks made "Alfred" famous in the 2004 movie, "The Terminal."

3. A person domiciled in a contracting state may also be sued in other states than the state where he or she is domiciled, providing another contracting state has special jurisdiction. These rules are found in Articles 5 and 6, and must be examined carefully in light of the factual circumstances presented in each case. Rules leading to special jurisdiction in states other than the state of the defendant's domicile can be based on various grounds.

For example, a contract can form the basis for special jurisdiction if the place of performance of the contract is another state. See Article 5.1. Another important example, from Article 5.3, allows jurisdiction in tort cases in the state where the harmful event occurred. This means that if a person domiciled in Country X commits a tortious act in Country Y (both being member states of the EU) then the courts of both countries would have jurisdiction over the defendant, and the plaintiff can choose in which country she wants to file her suit.

In cases involving multiple defendants, Article 6.1 becomes extremely important. This Article states that a defendant domiciled in a contracting state may also be sued in the courts of any contracting state where any defendant in the case is domiciled. This means that if a plaintiff brings suit against three defendants, each of whom is domiciled in a different EU country, then the plaintiff may choose to bring suit in any of those three countries. This rule is an alternative to the special jurisdiction rules in Article 5. And this can, in the case of the three defendant lawsuit just hypothesized, lead to even more possible jurisdictions. If, for example, the three defendants had entered into a contract to be performed in a fourth state, then the plaintiff would have the possibility of bring suit in any of the four states. Is this approach fair to the defendant(s) not domiciled in the plaintiff's chosen forum?

4. The Regulation provides special rules for cases involving insurance matters, consumer contracts, and employment disputes. See Articles 8–14; 15–17; and 18–21, respectively. Why do these plaintiffs enjoy particularized jurisdiction rules? Are these three the only categories of plaintiffs that deserve preferential treatment?

5. Once the possible jurisdictions according to Article 2 and the rules on special jurisdiction have been determined, it is always necessary to determine whether the result reached is in conflict with the rules on exclusive jurisdiction found in Article 22. The exclusive jurisdiction rules override the results reached under the general and/or special jurisdiction rules. Article 22 lists five different situations that can lead to exclusive jurisdiction. The first and foremost rule is found in Article 22.1 dealing with matters pertaining to real property.

6. It is important to note that the rules on general jurisdiction in Article 2 and the rules on special jurisdiction apply only to cases where the defendant is domiciled in one of the contracting states. (Note that the trigger is domicile, not nationality.) If the defendant is not domiciled in another contracting state, then the courts of each contracting state use their own internal laws to determine the question of jurisdiction. Why does Article 4 openly discriminate against outsiders? What interests does different treatment serve? (Is this approach necessary? Prudent?) This rule is very important because the local laws of these countries may have exorbitant—or excessive—rules of jurisdiction. Annex I to the Regulation, which is referenced in Article 3(2), provides a list of each country's exorbitant grounds. We will return to a discussion of Annex I shortly.

7. The Regulation contemplates the possibility that the parties to a lawsuit will enter into choice of forum agreements. These agreements can be established either in conjunction with the formation of a contract or much later, after a dispute has arisen. These rules, found in Article 23, fall into two groups. First, the Article deals with situations where one or more of the parties to the choice of forum agreement are domiciled in a member state. And in this situation, the courts of the chosen country shall have exclusive jurisdiction, provided the agreement entered into fulfills the requirements set out in Article 23 for such agreements to be binding. (How formal are those requirements?)

Second, the Article deals with the situation where none of the parties that have established the choice of forum agreement is domiciled in a member state. In this situation, the courts of other member states have no jurisdiction over the parties' dispute unless the court or the courts chosen have declined jurisdiction. Thus the courts of a member state are always bound by the parties' choice of forum agreement provided at least one of the parties is an EU domiciliary and the agreement is in a form that fulfills the requirements of Article 23. Where none of the parties are domiciled in an EU country, the court chosen may decline jurisdiction. Such determination will be taken on the basis of that country's internal laws.

Notice that vulnerable groups are again protected. Thus strict limitations on the use of forum selection clauses in the context of insurance, consumer contracts, and employment cases are set forth in Articles 13, 17 and 21, respectively.

8. In summary, then, the Regulation framework contemplates the following nine steps of inquiry:

(1) Scope. Does Article 1 exclude the fact situation?
(2) Member Status. Is the defendant domiciled in a Member State? See Article 4.
(3) Domicile. Is there general jurisdiction in the forum because the defendant is domiciled there? See Articles 2 & 59–61.
(4) Special Jurisdiction. Is there jurisdiction in the forum pursuant to the special rules of Article 5?
(5) Additional Parties or Claims. Are there additional parties or claims over which there is jurisdiction pursuant to Article 6?
(6) Special Rules. Are special rules implicated because this is an insurance, consumer contract or employment matter? See Articles 8–14; 15–17; and 18–21, respectively.
(7) Exclusive Jurisdiction. Is jurisdiction invalidated by the exclusive jurisdiction of another court? See Article 22.
(8) Prorogation. Is there a forum selection clause that invalidates the jurisdiction of this court? See Articles 23 & 24.
(9) Lis pendens. Is the same cause of action pending in the court of another Member State? See Articles 27–30.

9. What are the advantages and disadvantages of codifying the permissible bases for personal jurisdiction rather than applying general principles on a case-by-case basis? Can codes remove ambiguity and complexity?

10. The following hypotheticals will allow you to develop familiarity with the mechanics of the Brussels Regulation.

a. Hassan Shenavai is an architect who lives and works along the river Alsenz in Rockenhausen, Germany. Mr. Shenavai claims that he and Klaus Kreischer had an oral agreement whereby Mr. Shenavai would draw architectural plans for three holiday homes that Mr. Kreischer was planning to build in Germany. Mr. Kreischer is domiciled in the Netherlands. Mr. Shenavai completed the drawings and demands payment; Mr. Kreischer denies that there was a contract and, thus, denies any debt. Does the Amstergericht [Local Court] Rockenhausen have jurisdiction over Mr. Kreischer? What additional facts do you need? See Shenavai v. Kreischer, (Case No. 266/85), [1987] ECR 239, 241–45.

b. Johann Gruber is a farmer who owns a farm building in Upper Austria close to the German border. The building is constructed around a square; he lives in twelve rooms (about one half) of the building and uses the other half to house 200 pigs. Bay Wa AG is a German company that sells building materials and garden supplies in Germany and Austria. Wishing to replace the roof tiles of his building, Gruber examined a Bay Wa advertisement in an Austrian newspaper. Gruber telephoned the nearest Bay Wa, which was across the border in Pocking,

Germany, to ask them about the tiles he had seen advertised. When the Pocking store did not have that particular tile for sale, Gruber asked many questions about the different types of available tiles, and ultimately committed to a particular style. Bay Wa faxed confirmation of the purchase to his home; and Gruber picked up the tiles in Pocking. After installing the tiles, Gruber found significant variations in color and quality, and thus wants to sue for breach of warranty. Does the Landesgericht Steyr (Austria) have jurisdiction over Bay Wa? Do you need any additional facts? See Gruber v. Bay Wa AG, (Case No. 464/01), [2005] ECR 439.

c. What if the facts of *Asahi Metal Industry Co. v. Superior Court,* supra, arose within the framework of the Brussels Regulation? For this purpose imagine that Cheng Shin is a company from the Netherlands, that Asahi is from Spain, and that the accident happened in Italy. If Zurcher is a Californian can he file suit in Italy and obtain jurisdiction over both Cheng Shin and Asahi? Now imagine that Zurcher is an Italian who files in Italy, but names Cheng Shin as the sole defendant; will the Italian court have jurisdiction over Asahi if Cheng Shin has a (third party) claim against it?

11. We might also imagine that the defendants in any of the above hypotheticals are domiciled somewhere outside the EU. In other words, Mr. Shenavai's customer might be a New Yorker; Bay Wa could have been a Chinese seller; and so forth. As we have already seen, the Regulation does not apply to these defendants; instead, the national law of the forum state determines the scope of the court's jurisdiction to adjudicate. And in most of these countries, codes with an approach much like the form of the Regulation enumerate the permissible grounds for exercising jurisdiction.

In contract cases, for example, codes in the European countries provide that the national courts may exercise territorial authority over the case provided that the forum state was the:

- place of formation (e.g., Italy); and/or
- place of payment (e.g., Luxembourg); and/or
- place of past performance (e.g., Germany); and/or
- place of anticipated future performance (e.g., Belgium).

And consistent with the tradition of the civil law, a distinct set of codes would enumerate the bases for jurisdiction for other substantive areas. In tort cases, for example, the forum may have jurisdiction if the forum state was the:

- place of allegedly wrongful conduct (e.g., France); and/or
- place of harm (e.g., Austria).

Under this approach, satisfaction of the factual condition establishes adjudicatory jurisdiction.

The provisions in these codes may of course expand even to very tenuous bases for the exercise of jurisdiction to adjudicate. Although it is often repeated that the European approach to personal jurisdiction is much more restrained than the American approach, that statement is imprecise, if not also false. Even under the Brussels Regulation we have seen how the exercise of Special Jurisdiction (and particularly Articles 6) could reach defendants that would be unreachable under similar conditions in the United States. The national law of many of these countries is even more aggressive. Article 3(2) of the Regulation emphasizes that certain rules of national jurisdiction will not be applicable in litigation involving persons domiciled in Member States. That Article refers to Annex I, which in turn lists these exorbitant bases of jurisdiction. In the following table the left-hand column reprints the text of Annex I, while the right-hand column includes our explanation of the enumerated bases.

Rules of Jurisdiction Referred to in Article 3(2) and Article 4(2)

Annex I to the Brussels Regulation

—in Belgium: Article 15 of the Civil Code (Code civil/Burgerlijk Wetboek) and Article 638 of the Judicial Code (Code judiciaire/Gerechtelijk Wetboek)	Nonresident Belgian citizens and domiciliaries are required to appear for obligations incurred in a foreign country with an alien.
—in Germany: Article 23 of the Code of Civil Procedure (Zivilprozessordnung)	Umbrella provision confers unlimited personal jurisdiction over any defendant with assets in forum, regardless of their value.
—in Greece, Article 40 of the Code of Civil Procedure (Kodikas Politikis Dikonomias)	Another umbrella provision.
—in France, Articles 14 and 15 of the Civil Code (Code civil)	French courts have exclusive jurisdiction over actions against French nationals. And French nationals may sue aliens in French courts.
—in Ireland: the rules which enable jurisdiction to be founded on the document instituting the proceedings having been served on the defendant during his temporary presence in Ireland	This is called "tag" or "transient" jurisdiction in the United States.
—in Italy: Articles 3 and 4 of Act 218 of 31 May 1995	Corporations can be sued if they have a legal representative in the forum.
—in Luxembourg: Articles 14 and 15 of the Civil Code (Code civil)	These rules are much like the French.
—in the Netherlands: Articles 126(3) and 127 of the Code of Civil Procedure (Wetboek van Burgerlijke Rechtsvordering)	These rules are also much like the French, but somewhat more limited.

—in Austria: Article 99 of the Court Jurisdiction Act (Jurisdiktionsnorm)	Another umbrella provision.
—in Portugal: Articles 65 and 65A of the Code of Civil Procedure (Código de Processo Civil) and Article 11 of the Code of Labour Procedure (Código de Processo de Trabalho)	Jurisdiction when, if situation were reversed, plaintiff could be sued by defendant in his national courts. Court also has exclusive jurisdiction over labor and employment cases involving nationals.
—in Finland: the second, third and fourth sentences of the first paragraph of Section 1 of Chapter 10 of the Code of Judicial Procedure (oikeudenkäymiskaari/rättegångsbalken)	Tag jurisdiction, jurisdiction over nonresident citizens, and an umbrella provision.
—in Sweden: the first sentence of the first paragraph of Section 3 of Chapter 10 of the Code of Judicial Procedure (rättegångsbalken)	Another umbrella provision.
—in the United Kingdom: rules which enable jurisdiction to be founded on: (a) the document instituting the proceedings having been served on the defendant during his temporary presence in the United Kingdom; or (b) the presence within the United Kingdom of property belonging to the defendant; or (c) the seizure by the plaintiff of property situated in the United Kingdom.	More tag jurisdiction accompanied by another umbrella provision.

One of the most famous, or at least memorable, exercises of exorbitant jurisdiction involved the French skier Jean-Claude Killy, who won the triple crown of alpine skiing with gold medals in the slalom, giant slalom, and downhill events at the 1968 Olympics. An Austrian court asserted personal jurisdiction over Killy in a paternity suit based on an undergarment that Killy left in a hotel room there. David D. Siegel then memorialized this event in verse:

PACK UP YOUR TROUBLES—CAREFULLY

Why the gasping? Why so waxen?
What's the matter, Anglo-Saxon?
Don't you like our theoretical advance?
Don't you find cerebral pleasure
In the comprehensive measure
Of the things our law can do with someone's pants?
If our courts in sober session
Happen into the possession
Of a pair of drawers whose occupant fled fast,
We indulge the helpful fiction
That we've also jurisdiction

Over him whose fleeting form they covered last.
It is really a refinement
That we discharge this assignment
Only after he who owns the shorts has gone.
We would deem it much too bold of
Any sheriff to take hold of
Someone's garment while the poor chap has it on.
Take advantage of this power.
Should your marriage, say, go sour,
You could sue your wife in any land you please:
In advance, while things are peaceful,
Just come tour with a valise full
Of her petticoats and female B.V.D.'s.
If you're threatened by our action
You may find some satisfaction
In advice we urge that tourists keep in mind:
No amusement will you lack here;
Just be sure that when you pack here
You have not left any underwear behind.

David D. Siegel, In *Vagrant Verse*, 76
CASE & COMMENT 56, 62–63, Sept.-Oct. (1971)

What is the policy rational for such a jurisdictional provision?

3. Egypt

The Code of Civil Procedure in Egypt devotes a set of articles to cases involving territorial jurisdiction, and undertakes an approach typical of the European codes already discussed. Generally speaking, the court asserts jurisdiction over Egyptian citizens, regardless of their current domicile or residence. And it asserts jurisdiction over Egyptian domiciliaries and residents, regardless of their current citizenship. The most common exception to that general rule involves property actions where the property is located elsewhere.

Article 30 of the Code enumerates the cases in which the Egyptian courts have jurisdiction for claims raised against a foreign defendant who has neither a domicile nor a residence in Egypt. Among the most common are the following:

1. If the foreigner has an elected domicile in Egypt for the execution of a legal act.
2. If the case concerns property located in Egypt or an obligation undertaken, executed or requiring performance in Egypt, or if it concerns a bankruptcy registered in Egypt.
3. If one of the defendants has a domicile or a residence in Egypt.

The courts will also take jurisdiction if the defendant consents—whether expressly or tacitly.

4. Kenya*

The Kenyan courts will exercise jurisdiction over foreigners when the cause of action arises either wholly or in part in Kenya. Indeed, in contrast with systems that recognize jurisdictional bases premised on status (e.g., domicile) or unrelated conduct (e.g., doing business or presence), the Kenyan analysis focuses almost exclusively on the situs of conduct regarding the cause of action. For example, Kenyan courts will assert jurisdiction over a breach of contract claim only if the contract was executed in Kenya or if the obligation was to be performed in Kenya. Yet they may not exercise jurisdiction—even over a Kenyan national in a suit initiated by a Kenayn national—if the actions complained of were transacted and completed elsewhere.

5. China*

In China jurisdiction is authorized by the Civil Procedure Law of the People's Republic of China (CPL), as interpreted by the Supreme People's Court's Opinion on the Application of the Civil Procedure Law of the People's Republic of China. China generally follows Civil Law principles in exercising civil jurisdiction. Chapter two, sub-chapter two of the CPL, entitled "Territorial Jurisdiction" provides that a Chinese court may generally exercise jurisdiction over defendants who are domiciled or who reside in China. And in status cases, Chinese courts will have jurisdiction if the plaintiff is domiciled or resides in the forum. In all other situations, there must be some connection between the dispute and the forum to establish jurisdiction.

Provisions typical of code (i.e., Civil Law) states detail the circumstances under which jurisdiction can be established. Contract disputes can be brought in the forum if: the defendant is domiciled or resides there; the contract was to be performed there; the contract was executed there; or the subject of the contract is located there. Tort actions can only be brought if the defendant is domiciled there or the tortious action was committed there.

Comments and Questions

1. As a way of concluding this part of the chapter, we reprint below Principle 2 from the Principles of Transnational Civil Procedure. An effort to harmonize procedural law at an international level was undertaken jointly by the American Law Institute (ALI) and the International Institute for the Unification of Private Law (UNIDROIT). The project was especially ambitious given the fundamental differences between the common law and civil law systems (although EU countries had to deal with this issue as well). Although the scope of their work is

---

* This text relies heavily on Justus Momanyi Bwonwonga, Kenya, in INTERNATIONAL ENCYCLOPAEDIA OF LAWS 39 (Kluwer 2000).

* This text relies heavily on Arthur Anyuan Yuan, *Enforcing and Collecting Money Judgments in China From a U.S. Judgment Creditor's Perspective,* 36 Geo. Wash. Int'l L. Rev. 757,768 (2004).

limited to transnational commercial disputes, the Principles of Transnational Civil Procedure thus might fairly be characterized as reflecting an emerging international consensus.

Transnational Civil Procedure Principles (with commentary)

Cambridge Univ. Press (2006)

Jurisdiction Over Parties

2.1 Jurisdiction over a party may be exercised:
- 2.1.1 By consent of the parties to submit the dispute to the tribunal;
- 2.1.2 When there is a substantial connection between the forum state and the party or the transaction or occurrence in dispute. A substantial connection exists when a significant part of the transaction or occurrence occurred in the forum state, when an individual defendant is a habitual resident of the forum state or a jural entity has received its charter of organization or has its principal place of business therein, or when property to which the dispute relates is located in the forum state.

2.2 Jurisdiction may also be exercised, when no other forum is reasonably available, on the basis of:
- 2.2.1 Presence or nationality of the defendant in the forum state; or
- 2.2.2 Presence in the forum state of the defendnat's property, whether or not the dispute relates to the property, but the court's authority should be limited to the property or its value.

2.3 A court may grant provisional measures with respect to a person or to property in the territory of the forum state, even if the court does not have jurisdiction over the controversy.

2.4 Exercise of jurisdiction must ordinarily be declined when the parties have previously agreed that some other tribunal has exclusive jurisdiction.

2.5 Jurisdiction may be declined or the proceeding suspended when the court is manifestly inappropriate relative to another more appropriate court that could exercise jurisdiction.

2.6 The court should decline jurisdiction or suspend the proceeding, when the dispute is previously pending in another court competent to exercise jurisdiction, unless it appears that the dispute will not be fairly, effectively, and expeditiously resolved in that forum.

Comments and Questions

1. Does the methodology of Principle 2 more closely resemble a civil law or common law approach? How about the content?

2. Would expansion of the scope of the Transnational Principles to include non-commercial disputes require any revision of them?

3. The concepts recognized in Principles 2.5 and 2.6 are explored in Chapter 4.

Concluding Comments and Questions

1. Revisit the problem that opened this chapter and your answers to the questions posed there. Have your answers changed?

2. After studying the comparative materials in this Chapter, would you say that national approaches are substantially similar or that they are fundamentally dissimilar? To the extent that the approaches differ, what accounts for the variation—culture, tradition, different normative preferences?

D. Bibliography of Additional Resources

Adam Samuel, JURISDICTIONAL PROBLEMS IN INTERNATIONAL COMMERCIAL ARBITRATION: A STUDY OF BELGIAN, DUTCH, ENGLISH, FRENCH, SWEDISH, SWISS, U.S., AND WEST GERMAN LAW (Schulthess Polygraphischer Verlag 1989)

Austin L. Parrish, Sovereignty, Not Due Process: Personal Jurisdiction Over Nonresident Alien Defendants, 41 WAKE FOREST L. REV. 1 (2006)

Barton Legum (ed.), INTERNATIONAL LITIGATION STRATEGIES AND PRACTICE (Am. Bar Ass'n 2005)

4 A & 4B Charles Alan Wright & Arthur R. Miller, FEDERAL PRACTICE AND PROCEDURE §§ 1061--1075 (Thomson West 3d ed. 2002)

David Epstein, Jeffrey L. Snyder & Chrales S. Baldwin, INTERNATIONAL LITIGATION: A GUIDE TO JURISDICTION, PRACTICE, AND STRATEGY (Martinus Nijhoff 3d ed. 1998 & Supp. 2007).

Debra L. Basset, U.S. Class Actions Go Global: Transnational Class Actions and Personal Jurisdiction, 72 FORDHAM L. REV. 41 (2003)

Debra L. Bassett, Implied Consent to Personal Jurisdiction in Transnational Class Litigation, 2004 MICH. ST. L. REV. 619 (2004)

Emil Petrossian, In Pursuit of the Perfect Forum: Transnational Forum Shopping in the United States and England, 40 LOY. L.A. L. REV. 1257 (2006)

James Wm. Moore, MOORE'S FEDERAL PRACTICE (Matthew Bender 3d ed. 1997 & Supp. 2007).

Mary Keyes, JURISDICTION IN INTERNATIONAL LITIGATION (Federation 2005)

Patrick Capps, Stratos Konstadinidis, and Malcolm Evans, (eds.), ASSERTING JURISDICTION: INTERNATIONAL AND EUROPEAN LEGAL PERSPECTIVES (Hart 2003)

Richard H. Kreindler & Judith L. Holdsworth (eds.), TRANSNATIONAL LITIGATION: A PRACTITIONER'S GUIDE (Oceana 1997 & Supp. 2007)

Richard H. Kreindler, TRANSNATIONAL LITIGATION: A BASIC PRIMER (Oceana 1998)

Stephen J. Newman, Proof of Personal Jurisdiction in the Internet Age, 59 AM. JUR. PROOF OF FACTS 3d 1 (2000 & Supp. 2007)

Tim Taylor & Nigel Cooper, EUROPEAN LITIGATION HANDBOOK (Sweet & Maxwell 1995)

Ved P. Nanda & David K. Pansius, LITIGATION OF INTERNATIONAL DISPUTES IN U.S. COURTS (Thomson West 2d ed. 2005 & Supp. 2007)

CHAPTER 4

Forum Non Conveniens

A. Introduction

In most common law countries, the doctrine of forum non conveniens is an important part of the court's determination regarding the exercise of its jurisdiction. A plaintiff in a given case may be able to persuade the court that it would not violate due process for the court to exercise personal jurisdiction over the defendant, yet the defendant can get the case dismissed nevertheless by persuading the court that there is a more appropriate forum for the litigation. Over time, this doctrinal analysis has evolved from a more rigid form applicable only in exceptional cases where the suit is vexatious or oppressive to a much more fluid form that requires a balancing of various interests and factors. Forum non conveniens is not a component of the analysis to determine jurisdiction, but rather part of the court's decision whether to exercise its jurisdiction to adjudicate.

Yet the civil law systems generally have no such mechanism. As you read the materials in this chapter, consider why the civil law systems have not pursued a similar course. Is this because the discretionary decline of jurisdiction is a bad idea? Is it unnecessary in the civil law countries because the jurisdictional rules achieve the same result?

The Problem: A Shell Game?*

Royal Dutch is a holding company incorporated and headquartered in the Netherlands. Shell Transport is a holding company incorporated and headquartered in England. These two companies jointly control and operate the Royal

* This hypothetical is based on *Wiwa v. Royal Dutch Shell Petroleum Co.*, 226 F.3d 88 (2d Cir. 2000). Much of the factual detail is drawn from papers published by the Center for Constitutional Rights. *See* http://ccrjustice.org/ourcases/current-cases/wiwa-v.-royal-dutch-petroleum,-wiwa-v.-anderson-and-wiwa-v.-shell-petroleum-d.

Dutch/Shell Group, a global conglomerate of affiliated but formally independent oil and gas companies. Among the network of affiliates is Shell Petroleum Nigeria, a wholly owned Nigerian subsidiary that engages in extensive oil exploration and development activity in the Ogoni region of Nigeria.

A group of Nigerian émigrés to the United States have filed a lawsuit in a U.S. federal district court in New York City against Royal Dutch, Shell Transport, and various affiliates, alleging that the defendants participated in grave human rights abuses by the Nigerian government, including summary execution, crimes against humanity, torture, inhumane treatment, arbitrary arrest, and wrongful death. The claims were brought under the federal Alien Tort Claims, Torture Victim Protection, and Racketeer Influenced and Corrupt Organizations acts.

Royal Dutch/Shell began using land in the Ogoni area of Nigeria for oil production in 1958. Pollution resulting from the oil production has contaminated the local water supply and agricultural land upon which the region's economy is based. Also, Royal Dutch/Shell for decades worked with the Nigerian military regime to suppress any and all demonstrations that were carried out in opposition to the oil company's activities. The oil company and its Nigerian subsidiary provided monetary and logistical support to the Nigerian police and bribed witnesses to produce false testimonies.

In 1995, the company and its subsidiary colluded with the Nigerian government to bring about the arrest and execution of the Ogoni 9. The Ogoni 9 was a group of activists that were hanged on November 10, 1995, after a "trial" before a special military tribunal based on fabricated charges. One of the nine, Ken Saro-Wiwa, was an internationally renowned writer and activist and was the leader of the Movement for the Survival of the Ogoni People (MOSOP). He is represented in this case by Ken Wiwa, Mr. Saro-Wiwa's son and the executor of his estate. Mr. Saro-Wiwa was outspoken in condemning Shell for polluting and destroying the Ogoni ecosystem, and he led the struggle for the autonomy of the Ogoni people and for an equitable distribution of Nigeria's oil riches. Human rights groups and political leaders around the world condemned both the executions and the lack of due process that was accorded to the victims in connection with the so-called trial.

Other incidents of torture and detention include that of Owens Wiwa, who was detained for more than a year under false charges to prevent him from protesting. During his detention he was beaten repeatedly. Michael Vizor, a member of MOSOP's youth wing, was beaten by police in front of his children when he would not confess to a false charge. He also had 400,000 Naira [the equivalent of approximately (U.S.) $18,000] in cash and documents stolen from his house during his arrest. He was further tortured and denied medical assistance during his wrongful detention. Another plaintiff, Uebari N-nah, was shot and killed in October 1993 near a Shell flow station at Korokoro, Rivers State, Nigeria.

Other plaintiffs were attacked by troops summoned by Royal Dutch/Shell during a peaceful demonstration against Shell and the Nigerian military regime for bulldozing farmland in Bira Gokana for a pipeline contracted by Willbros West Africa, Inc. Karalolo Kogbara was shot by Nigerian troops while she was speaking out against the bulldozing of her crops. Plaintiff Michael Tema Vizor was arrested, beaten, and detained for four days without charge for participating in the same protest.

The complaint contains no allegations regarding acts by these defendants in the United States. Nevertheless, defendants maintain offices in New York City, and thus have sufficient presence for the court to exercise personal jurisdiction over all of them.

(1) Why would plaintiffs file this action in the United States?

(2) Does this litigation belong in a U.S. court? Do you think there is a single appropriate situs for litigation of this sort, or could (perhaps even should) multiple jurisdictions examine the underlying conduct?

(3) If you represent Shell Transport and/or Royal Dutch you have a choice: will you argue to the New York court that this case belongs in the United States, England, the Netherlands, and/or Nigeria?

(4) If you are a judge who is vested with the discretionary authority to dismiss this case so that it may be litigated in a more appropriate forum, what specific information would you demand to make such a determination? Which party should have the burden to prove exactly what?

(5) If you were a member of the legislature who drafted the Alien Tort Claims Act, Torture Victim Protection Act, or Racketeer Influenced and Corrupt Organizations Act, should you include statutory language making claims under those acts more or less vulnerable to forum non conveniens dismissals?

***

It may be important to emphasize early in this chapter the significance of a forum non conveniens dismissal. Informal surveys show that claims dismissed on forum non conveniens have generally not been tried elsewhere. "A survey of more than fifty personal injury actions dismissed under forum non conveniens doctrine [showed that] only one case was actually tried in a foreign court."[*] Another survey sought responses from the plaintiffs' lawyers in the 180 reported transnational cases that the federal courts dismissed on forum non conveniens grounds from 1947 to 1984; with a response rate of nearly fifty percent, not one case resulted in a plaintiff's win in the foreign court.[**] Most of the cases were instead abandoned or settled for little. Often, "only an outright dismissal with prejudice could be more 'outcome determinative' than a [forum non conveniens] dismissal to a distant forum in a foreign land."[†]

[*] Dante Figueroa, *Are There Ways Out of the Current Forum Non Conveniens Impasse Between the United States and Latin America?*, 1 Bus. L. Brief (Am. U.) 42, 45 (2005) (quoting Himly Ismail, *Forum Non Conveniens, United States Multinational Corporations, and Personal Injuries in the Third World: Your Place or Mine?*, 11 B.C. Third World L.J. 249, 250 n.7 (1991)).

[**] David W. Robertson, *Forum Non Conveniens in America and England: "A Rather Fantastic Fiction,"* 103 Law Q. Rev. 398, 418-420 (1987).

[†] *In re Air Crash Disaster near New Orleans, La. On July 9, 1982*, 821 F.2d 1147, 1156 (5th Cir. 1987) (en banc), vacated on other grounds sub nom. *Pan Am World Airways, Inc. v. Lopez*, 490 U.S. 1032 (1989), on remand, 883 F.2d 17 (5th Cir. 1989).

B. Common Law Origins and Framework

Ronald A. Brand & Scott R. Jablonski, Forum Non Conveniens in Common Law Systems

Forum Non Conveniens: History, Global Practice, and Future Under the Hague Convention on Choice of Court Agreements 1–100 (Oxford 2007)

Differences in legal systems can make consideration of the forum non conveniens doctrine a rather complex concept. First,... even in common law systems where the doctrine is a part of the procedural law, its application varies from country to country. One variation is the extent to which the doctrine is incorporated into basic jurisdictional analysis. In England and Canada, for example, the doctrine is applicable to basic jurisdictional analysis. Thus, there are times when a forum non conveniens analysis comes into play even before the initial determination of jurisdiction is complete. This is sometimes referred to as a forum conveniens analysis....

[Another] factor making complete understanding of the doctrine of forum non conveniens difficult is that it is only one part of a package of issues arising from concerns with parallel litigation in multiple judicial systems. Forum non conveniens applies when there are courts in at least two judicial systems with jurisdiction to hear the case. While civil law legal systems tend to prefer a lis alibi pendens approach to this problem, doing so encourages a race to the courthouse. The loser of the race is destined to have its filing rejected by a court that will defer to the court first seised. Another part of the package of procedural issues in parallel litigation is the anti-suit injunction (and even the anti-anti-suit injunction). Forum non conveniens is thus only one part of the parallel litigation puzzle....

I. Scotland

The term "forum non conveniens" was not used in the early seventeenth century Scottish decisions that are credited with originating the doctrine. Those courts assumed the authority, in the "interests of justice," to decline to hear a case even when jurisdiction was otherwise proper. While this discretionary authority originated as a part of the determination of jurisdiction and went by the name "forum non competens," by the mid-nineteenth century it had evolved into a separate analysis, considered to be a question on the merits to be addressed after jurisdiction was established. In the 1865 case of Longworth v. Hope,[5] Scotland's Court of Session acknowledged the power to stay proceedings in the interest of justice, but also emphasized the narrow scope of such power. The Court, in finding that Scotland was the more appropriate forum in which to entertain a libel action, stressed that deference should be given to a plaintiff's choice of forum, even while conceding that England was a more appropriate forum for assessing damages in the particular case. Later in the nineteenth century, courts in Scotland explicitly

[5] 3 M. 1049, 1052-55 (Sess. Cas. 1865) (Scot.).

replaced the term "forum non competens" with the phrase "forum non conveniens" to better reflect the nature of the plea.

Some thirty years after Longworth, the Court of Session reaffirmed the limited scope of a forum non conveniens dismissal in Sim v. Robinow,[8] stating that "the Court has never refused to exercise its jurisdiction upon the ground of a mere balance of convenience and inconvenience." The Sim Court added that "the plea can never be sustained unless the court is satisfied that there is some other tribunal, having competent jurisdiction, in which the case may be tried more suitably for the interests of all the parties and for the ends of justice."...

In 1926, the House of Lords in La Société du Gaz de Paris v. La Société Anonyme de Navigation "Les Armateurs Français," considered the Scottish doctrine, finding the existence of a more appropriate forum to be the core of the forum non conveniens analysis. The Law Lords applied a balancing test to hold that France was the more appropriate forum and that a stay in Scotland was appropriate.... The defendant raising the plea carried the general burden of proof, but did not have to prove that trial in Scotland would be an abuse of process or would be oppressive or vexatious to him....

II. England

[In Logan v. Bank of Scotland,[23] the] court adopted something similar to the forum non conveniens test used in Scotland, enumerating the various factors to be weighted in the analysis and even claiming to use a test similar to that applied by the Scottish courts, but at the same time noting that those courts were more prone to grant a stay on grounds of inconvenience rather than the more difficult-to-prove test of vexation to the defendant. The English court also stressed the fact that the plaintiff in Logan would not be put at a juridical disadvantage as a result of the stay in England....

The 1973 House of Lords decision in The Atlantic Star[37] began a movement toward relaxing the defendant's burden in a forum non conveniens analysis under English law. Dutch barge owners brought suit against the Dutch owners of a container ship for damages resulting from the container ship's collision with the barge at sea. The defendant argued that the case had absolutely no connection with England other than the container ship's occasional stops in English ports. Lord Reid's opinion... indicated a clear movement from a strict traditional test to a more liberal modern standard:

> I think that a key to the solution of the problem may be found in a liberal interpretation of what is oppressive on the part of the plaintiff. The position of the defendant must be put in the scales. In the end it must be left to the discretion of the court in each case where a stay is sought, and the question would be whether the

---

[8] 19 R. 665, 667-68 (Sess. Cas. 1892) (Scot.).

[23] 1 K.B. 141 (C.A.).

[37] [1974] A.C. 436 (H.L.) (appeal taken from Eng.).

> defendants have clearly shown that to allow the case to proceed in England would in a reasonable sense be oppressive looking to all the circumstances including the personal position of the defendant.

Lord Wilberforce provided a list of the factors that weighed in favor of granting the defendant's motion. The factors included that similar proceedings arising out of the collision had already been instituted in Belgium; that witnesses were in Belgium; that Belgian law applied to the action; and that none of the parties was English or had any connection with England other than occasional port stops....

The next milestone in English forum non conveniens law was the 1978 case of MacShannon v. Rockware Glass Ltd.[47]... In MacShannon, Scottish plaintiffs sued English defendants in England because the plaintiffs expected higher damages there, and because there would have been a longer delay in Scottish courts. The Court of Appeal used the case to further refine the test for granting a forum non conveniens stay, moving closer to the Scottish doctrine:

> In order to justify a stay two conditions must be satisfied, one positive and the other negative: (a) the defendant must satisfy the court that there is another forum to whose jurisdiction he is amenable in which justice can be done between the parties at substantially less inconvenience and expense, and (b) the stay must not deprive the plaintiff of a legitimate personal or juridical advantage which would be available to him if he invoked the jurisdiction of the English court.

While acknowledging the importance of a plaintiff's choice of forum, the MacShannon Court held that the plaintiff's advantage in proceeding in England "must be real," and that the plaintiff's genuine belief that he has an advantage is alone not enough. Rather, "the advantage relied upon as a ground for diverting the action from its natural forum must be shown objectively and on the balance of probability to exist." The Court moved from the traditional rule, which placed upon the defendant the burden of proving that the plaintiff would not suffer injustice as the result of dismissal, and instead shifted the burden to the plaintiff to demonstrate that a stay or dismissal would create an injustice....

Current application of the doctrine of forum non conveniens in England is defined by Spiliada Maritime Corp. v. Cansulex Ltd.,[81] decided in 1986 by the House of Lords. Liberian plaintiffs brought an action in England against Canadian defendants. The Canadian defendants were already defendants in England in a related action (on a separate, but similar, claim) brought by English plaintiffs. Although the issue before the court was whether to grant leave to serve process ex juris on the defendants, the Law Lords determined that the test for granting such leave is essentially the same as the forum non conveniens test for grating a stay of the proceedings. Thus, in approving the granting of the Liberian plaintiffs' request for leave to allow service ex juris, the House of Lords expressly acknowledged the doctrine of forum non conveniens as English law, authorizing service

[47] A.C. 795 (H.L.).
[81] [1987] A.C. 460 (H.L.).

and the trial court's retention of the case. Lord Goff of Chiveley summarized the modern English test, focusing on these elements:

1) "[A] stay will only be granted... where the court is satisfied that there is some other forum, having competent jurisdiction, which is the appropriate forum for the trial of the action."
2) "In general the burden of proof rests on the defendant to persuade the court to exercise its discretion to grant a stay."
3) If jurisdiction is a matter of right in England, as opposed to jurisdiction ex juris in which the plaintiff must request leave to serve the defendant outside the jurisdiction, then "the burden resting on the defendant is not just to show that England is not the natural or appropriate forum for the trial, but to establish that there is another available forum which is clearly or distinctly more appropriate than the English forum.... [I]f, in any case, the connection of the defendant with the English forum is a fragile one (for example, if he is served with proceedings during a short visit to this country), it should be all the easier for him to prove that there is another clearly more appropriate forum for the trial overseas."
4) While not every case presents a "'natural forum'...'with which the action had the most real and substantial connection,"' the court must look at connecting factors including (1) the availability of witnesses, (2) the law governing the relevant transaction, and (3) the places where the parties reside or carry on business.
5) If there is no other available forum "which is clearly more appropriate for the trial of the action," the court will refuse a stay.
6) If "there is some other available forum which prima facie is clearly more appropriate for the trial of the action," the court ordinarily will grant a stay. At this point, however, the burden of proof shifts to the plaintiff, who may prove "circumstances by reason of which justice requires that a stay should nevertheless not be granted." Moreover, "[t]he court should [not] be deterred from grating a stay... simply because the plaintiff will be deprived of such an advantage, provided that the court is satisfied that substantial justice will be done in the available appropriate forum."...

III. The United States

Modern forum non conveniens doctrine in the United is anchored in three Supreme Court decisions: two in 1947 (Gulf Oil Corp. v. Gilbert[39] and Koster v. Lumbermens Mutual Casualty Co.[40]) and one in 1981 (Piper Aircraft Co. v. Reyno[41]). [Gilbert and Koster recognized the authority of a court to dismiss on grounds of forum non conveniens, but emphasized that the discretion was to be used judiciously. While the plaintiff should not be able to "vex," "harass," or "oppress" the defendant by

---

[39] 330 U.S. 501.

[40] 330 U.S. 518.

[41] 454 U.S. 235.

selecting an inconvenient forum, the plaintiff's choice of forum "should rarely be disturbed."

Both Gilbert and Koster involved domestic situations where the alternative forum was another venue in the United States. One year after the Court's Gilbert and Koster decisions,] a major legislative development narrowed the scope of the doctrine in the federal courts when Congress enacted section 1404(a) of Title 28 of the U.S. Code—a venue provision that transformed the way in which federal courts handle problems of forum shopping and docket congestion. Section 1404(a) provides that "[f]or the convenience of parties and witnesses, in the interest of justice, a district court may transfer any civil action to any other district or division where it might have been brought." This provision had a significant effect on both the role and scope of forum non conveniens in diversity cases, virtually eliminating dismissals based on forum non conveniens in federal courts where all parties to the suit are from the United States. Under section 1404(a), a transfer is both easier to obtain (its requirements are more liberal than the test for granting a dismissal based on forum non conveniens) and more available (while only the defendant may request dismissal based on forum non conveniens, either party may move for a transfer of venue under section 1404(a)) than dismissal on grounds of forum non conveniens.

The 1981 Supreme Court decision in Piper Aircraft Co v. Reyno served to refine further the modern U.S. doctrine of forum non conveniens. [This opinion is excerpted later in this chapter.]

IV. Canada

In Canada, the doctrine of forum non conveniens developed first in the common law provinces and later in Québec....

[The common law provinces largely track the English model. One distinction that sets Canadian law apart from its cousins in other common law jurisdictions is that the test for establishing jurisdiction and the test for deciding whether or not to exercise that jurisdiction are the same. Considerations applied to motions to dismiss based on forum non conveniens grounds are therefore also taken in account in determining jurisdiction in the first instance (jurisdiction simpliciter), and the analysis in each instance appears to be the same.]

Québec, unlike the other Canadian provinces, is a civil law jurisdiction drawing upon French legal traditions. It would thus be expected not to have adopted the doctrine of forum non conveniens. Recent changes in the Québec Civil Code defy this expectation, however.... Article 3135 explicitly adopts a forum non conveniens analysis:

> Even though a Québec authority has jurisdiction to hear a dispute, it may exceptionally and on an application by a party, decline jurisdiction if it considers that the authorities of another country are in a better position to decide.[134]

[134] Art. 3135 Civ. Code Que. (2001) (Can.).

Contrary to the blending of forum non conveniens and jurisdiction issues in other Canadian provinces, this provision requires that a Québec court first decide whether it has jurisdiction before it entertains a motion for dismissal on grounds that there is another, more appropriate forum.

Québec Civil Code Article 3137 on lis alibi pendens illustrates a second codification of a court's discretionary power to decline jurisdiction when a parallel action is pending in a foreign court:

> On application of a party, a Québec authority may stay its ruling on an action brought before it if another action, between the same parties, based on the same facts and having the same object is pending before a foreign authority, provided that the latter action can result in a decision which may be recognized in Québec, or if such a decision has already been rendered by a foreign authority.

This discretionary authority to defer to a foreign court provides a middle ground between the traditional, strict civil law approach to lis alibi pendens and common law discretion based upon forum non conveniens principles....

The codification of forum non conveniens in Québec law has not escaped criticism. By its very nature, the doctrine is a discretionary tool for courts, and therefore inconsistent with traditional civil law expectations of predictability based on legislative rules. This tension has been noted by civil law scholars in Québec.[53].... At this point, however, the Québec experiment with concepts of forum non conveniens is in place, and provides important comparative opportunities.

V. Australia

The Australian High Court first clearly adopted forum non conveniens principles in its 1908 decision in Maritime Insurance Co. Ltd. v. Geelong Harbor Trust Commissioners,[1] where it followed the "vexation and oppression" test of the House of Lords in Logan v. Bank of Scotland.[2] This meant that relief from suit in an Australian court would be granted if "the exercise of the jurisdiction would [subject the defendant to] injustice."[3] As in Canada, the United States, and the United Kingdom, more recent cases have revisited this strict traditional test. However, while the other three countries have moved to a more liberal "most appropriate forum" standard, Australia has remained closer to the original test, moving forward from a strict vexation and oppression test, but clinging to an analysis focusing primarily on whether the Australian forum is clearly inappropriate. This test acknowledges the developments in the House of Lords' opinion in Spiliada, but nonetheless results in a unique approach....

---

[53] Jeffrey Talpis & Shelley L. Kath, *The exceptional as commonplace in Québec forum non conveniens law: Cambior, a case in point*, 34 Revue Juridique Themis 761, 796-797 (2000)....

[1] 6 C.L.R. 194 (1908).

[2] [1906] 1 K.B. 141 (C.A.)....

[3] 6 C.L.R. 194, 198 (1908), quoting *Logan v. Bank of Scotland* [1906] 1 K.B. 141, 150.

> First, a plaintiff who has regularly invoked the jurisdiction of a court has a prima facie right to insist upon its exercise. Secondly, the traditional power to stay proceedings which have been regularly commenced, on inappropriate forum grounds, is to be exercised in accordance with the general principle empowering a court to dismiss or stay proceedings which are oppressive, vexatious or an abuse of process and the rationale for the exercise of the power to stay is the avoidance of injustice between the parties in the particular case. Thirdly, the mere fact that the balance of convenience favours another jurisdiction or that some other jurisdiction would provide a more appropriate forum does not justify the dismissal of the action or the grant of a stay. Finally, the jurisdiction to grant a stay or dismiss the action is to be exercised "with great care" or "extreme caution."
>
> [Voth v. Manildra Flour Mills Pty. Ltd., 171 C.L.R. 538 (1990).] . . .

The High Court has declined to liberalize the Australian doctrine further so as to bring it closer to that in other common law jurisdictions. In Dow Jones & Co. Inc. v. Gutnick, [210 C.L.R. 575, [2002] H.C.A. 56, 194 A.L.R. 433 (2002)], a well-known Australian businessman with substantial financial ties to the United States filed a claim in the Supreme Court of Victoria for damages resulting from the defendant's allegedly defamatory remarks about the plaintiff and his business activities. These statements were found in an article in Barron's Magazine, published by Dow Jones. Gutnick based his claim on both the internet publication of the article in question and the paper editions containing the article sold in Victoria. Dow Jones moved for dismissal on several grounds, including that Victoria was a clearly inappropriate forum.

The Supreme Court of Victoria refused to grant a stay in favor of the New Jersey [U.S.] forum, based largely on its own Rule 7.05(2)(b), which allows a stay if Victoria "is not a convenient forum for the trial of the proceeding." The defendant agued that the wording of the Rule indicates that the test for granting a stay in Victoria is less stringent than the "clearly inappropriate forum" test announced in Voth and, instead, leans more toward the Spiliada approach. The lower court, however, considered the language of Rule 7.05(b)(2) to do "no more or less than, in an English-literal form, convey the meaning and substance of the concept of forum non conveniens considered by the High Court in [Voth]." Victoria was found to be "both the appropriate and convenient forum" for the case.

On appeal, both the Victoria Court of Appeal and the High Court affirmed the trial court. The High Court found that determining where the allegedly defamatory publication was published would also "determine[] . . . whether proceedings in the Supreme Court of Victoria should, as Dow Jones contended, be stayed on the ground that the Court was a clearly inappropriate forum for the determination of the action." As to the test for forum non conveniens, the High Court firmly endorsed the "clearly inappropriate forum" test set forth in Voth:

> [I]t is now established that an Australian court will decline, on the ground of forum non conveniens, to exercise jurisdiction which has been regularly invoked by a plaintiff, whether by personal service or under relevant long-arm jurisdiction

provisions, only when it is shown that the forum whose jurisdiction is invoked by the plaintiff is clearly inappropriate.

Upon finding that Victoria was the forum where the alleged tort occurred, the High Court ruled that Victoria law applied to the substantive issues at bar, and affirmed the lower court's decision to deny a stay.

In his concurrence, Justice Kirby reiterated his preference for adopting a forum non conveniens doctrine in Australia more aligned with the modern English doctrine, but conceded that:

> [A]lthough the formulation by the House of Lords has found favour in most Commonwealth jurisdictions, and is more harmonious with the rules of public international law respectful of comity between nations and their courts, I must accept that this Court has adopted an approach more defensive of the exercise of properly invoked jurisdiction by Australian courts.

Comments and Questions

1. One distinction between Australia and the other common law countries is the preference for a "clearly inappropriate forum" test as opposed to what can generally be called the "more appropriate forum" test. How significant is this distinction?

2. Does a strict approach to forum non conveniens dismissals advance or undermine principles regarding the separation of powers between the legislative and judicial branches of a government?

3. Does a strict approach to forum non conveniens dismissals advance or undermine comity between and among jurisdictions?

4. Articulate why the existence of related proceedings filed elsewhere should militate in favor of granting a forum non conveniens dismissal. Then articulate why the existence of related proceedings elsewhere could be a significant reason to deny such a motion.

1. American Cases

In 1981, the Supreme Court further defined the modern doctrine of forum non conveniens in U.S. courts. That case follows.

Piper Aircraft Co. v. Reyno

454 U.S. 235 (1981)

JUSTICE MARSHALL delivered the opinion of the Court.

These cases arise out of an air crash that took place in Scotland. Respondent, acting as representative of the estates of several Scottish citizens killed in the accident, brought wrongful-death actions against petitioners that were ultimately transferred to the United States District Court for the Middle District of Pennsylvania. Petitioners moved to dismiss on the ground of forum non conveniens. After noting that an alternative forum existed in Scotland, the District Court granted their motions. The United States Court of Appeals for the Third Circuit reversed. The Court of Appeals based its decision, at least in part, on the ground that dismissal is automatically barred where the law of the alternative forum is less favorable to the plaintiff than the law of the forum chosen by the plaintiff. Because we conclude that the possibility of an unfavorable change in law should not, by itself, bar dismissal, and because we conclude that the District Court did not otherwise abuse its discretion, we reverse.

I

A

In July 1976, a small commercial aircraft crashed in the Scottish highlands during the course of a charter flight from Blackpool to Perth. The pilot and five passengers were killed instantly. The decedents were all Scottish subjects and residents, as are their heirs and next of kin. There were no eyewitnesses to the accident. At the time of the crash the plane was subject to Scottish air traffic control.

The aircraft, a twin-engine Piper Aztec, was manufactured in Pennsylvania by petitioner Piper Aircraft Co. (Piper). The propellers were manufactured in Ohio by petitioner Hartzell Propeller, Inc. (Hartzell). At the time of the crash the aircraft was registered in Great Britain and was owned and maintained by Air Navigation and Trading Co., Ltd. (Air Navigation). It was operated by McDonald Aviation, Ltd. (McDonald), a Scottish air taxi service. Both Air Navigation and McDonald were organized in the United Kingdom. The wreckage of the plane is now in a hangar in Farnsborough, England.

The British Department of Trade investigated the accident shortly after it occurred. A preliminary report found that the plane crashed after developing a spin, and suggested that mechanical failure in the plane or the propeller was responsible. At Hartzell's request, this report was reviewed by a three-member Review Board, which held a 9-day adversary hearing attended by all interested parties. The Review Board found no evidence of defective equipment and indicated that pilot error may have contributed to the accident. The pilot, who had obtained his commercial pilot's license only three months earlier, was flying over high ground at an altitude considerably lower than the minimum height required by his company's operations manual.

In July 1977, a California probate court appointed respondent Gaynell Reyno administratrix of the estates of the five passengers. Reyno is not related to and does not know any of the decedents or their survivors; she was a legal secretary to the attorney who filed this lawsuit. Several days after her appointment, Reyno commenced separate wrongful-death actions against Piper and Hartzell in the Superior Court of California, claiming negligence and strict liability. Air Navigation, McDonald, and the estate of the pilot are not parties to this litigation. The survivors of the five passengers whose estates are represented by Reyno filed a separate action in the United Kingdom against Air Navigation, McDonald, and the pilot's estate. Reyno candidly admits that the action against Piper and Hartzell was filed in the United States because its laws regarding liability, capacity to sue, and damages are more favorable to her position than are those of Scotland. Scottish law does not recognize strict liability in tort. Moreover, it permits wrongful-death actions only when brought by a decedent's relatives. The relatives may sue only for "loss of support and society."

On petitioners' motion, the suit was removed to the United States District Court for the Central District of California. Piper then moved for transfer to the United States District Court for the Middle District of Pennsylvania, pursuant to 28 U. S. C. § 1404(a).[4] Hartzell moved to dismiss for lack of personal jurisdiction, or in the alternative, to transfer.[5] In December 1977, the District Court quashed service on Hartzell and transferred the case to the Middle District of Pennsylvania. Respondent then properly served process on Hartzell.

B

In May 1978, after the suit had been transferred, both Hartzell and Piper moved to dismiss the action on the ground of forum non conveniens. The District Court granted these motions in October 1979. It relied on the balancing test set forth by this Court in Gulf Oil Corp. v. Gilbert, 330 U.S. 501 (1947), and its companion case, Koster v. Lumbermens Mut. Cas. Co., 330 U.S. 518 (1947). In those decisions, the Court stated that a plaintiff's choice of forum should rarely be disturbed. However, when an alternative forum has jurisdiction to hear the case, and when trial in the chosen forum would "establish...oppressiveness and vexation to a defendant...out of all proportion to plaintiff's convenience," or when the "chosen forum [is] inappropriate because of considerations affecting the court's own administrative and legal problems," the court may, in the exercise of its sound discretion, dismiss the case. Koster, supra, at 524. To guide trial court discretion, the Court provided a list of "private interest factors" affecting the convenience of the litigants, and a list of "public interest factors" affecting the convenience of the forum. Gilbert, supra, at 508–509.[6]

---

[4] Section 1404(a) provides: "For the convenience of parties and witnesses, in the interest of justice, a district court may transfer any civil action to any other district or division where it might have been brought."

[5] The District Court concluded that it could not assert personal jurisdiction over Hartzell consistent with due process. However, it decided not to dismiss Hartzell because the corporation would be amenable to process in Pennsylvania.

[6] The factors pertaining to the private interests of the litigants included the "relative ease of access to sources of proof; availability of compulsory process for attendance of unwilling, and the cost of obtaining attendance of willing, witnesses; possibility of view of premises, if view would be appropriate to the action; and all other practical problems that make trial of a case easy, expeditious and inexpensive." Gilbert, 330 U.S., at 508. The public factors bearing on the question included the administrative difficulties flowing from court congestion; the "local interest in having localized controversies decided at home"; the interest in having the trial of a diversity case in a forum that is at home with the law that must govern the action; the avoidance of unnecessary problems in conflict of laws, or in the application of foreign law; and the unfairness of burdening citizens in an unrelated forum with jury duty. Id., at 509.

After describing our decisions in Gilbert and Koster, the District Court analyzed the facts of these cases. It began by observing that an alternative forum existed in Scotland; Piper and Hartzell had agreed to submit to the jurisdiction of the Scottish courts and to waive any statute of limitations defense that might be available. It then stated that plaintiff's choice of forum was entitled to little weight. The court recognized that a plaintiff's choice ordinarily deserves substantial deference. It noted, however, that Reyno "is a representative of foreign citizens and residents seeking a forum in the United States because of the more liberal rules concerning products liability law," and that "the courts have been less solicitous when the plaintiff is not an American citizen or resident, and particularly when the foreign citizens seek to benefit from the more liberal tort rules provided for the protection of citizens and residents of the United States."

The District Court next examined several factors relating to the private interests of the litigants, and determined that these factors strongly pointed towards Scotland as the appropriate forum. Although evidence concerning the design, manufacture, and testing of the plane and propeller is located in the United States, the connections with Scotland are otherwise "overwhelming." The real parties in interest are citizens of Scotland, as were all the decedents. Witnesses who could testify regarding the maintenance of the aircraft, the training of the pilot, and the investigation of the accident—all essential to the defense—are in Great Britain. Moreover, all witnesses to damages are located in Scotland. Trial would be aided by familiarity with Scottish topography, and by easy access to the wreckage.

The District Court reasoned that because crucial witnesses and evidence were beyond the reach of compulsory process, and because the defendants would not be able to implead potential Scottish third-party defendants, it would be "unfair to make Piper and Hartzell proceed to trial in this forum." The survivors had brought separate actions in Scotland against the pilot, McDonald, and Air Navigation. "[It] would be fairer to all parties and less costly if the entire case was presented to one jury with available testimony from all relevant witnesses." Although the court recognized that if trial were held in the United States, Piper and Hartzell could file indemnity or contribution actions against the Scottish defendants, it believed that there was a significant risk of inconsistent verdicts.[7]

The District Court concluded that the relevant public interests also pointed strongly towards dismissal. The court determined that Pennsylvania law would apply to Piper and Scottish law to Hartzell if the case were tried in the Middle District of Pennsylvania.[8] As a result, "trial in this forum would be hopelessly complex and confusing for a jury." In addition, the court noted that it was unfamiliar with Scottish law and thus would have to rely upon experts from that country. The

[7] The District Court explained that inconsistent verdicts might result if petitioners were held liable on the basis of strict liability here, and then required to prove negligence in an indemnity action in Scotland. Moreover, even if the same standard of liability applied, there was a danger that different juries would find different facts and produce inconsistent results.

[8] Under *Klaxon v. Stentor Electric Mfg. Co.*, 313 U.S. 487 (1941), a court ordinarily must apply the choice-of-law rules of the State in which it sits. However, where a case is transferred pursuant to 28 U. S. C. § 1404(a), it must apply the choice-of-law rules of the State from which the case was transferred.

court also found that the trial would be enormously costly and time-consuming; that it would be unfair to burden citizens with jury duty when the Middle District of Pennsylvania has little connection with the controversy; and that Scotland has a substantial interest in the outcome of the litigation.

In opposing the motions to dismiss, respondent contended that dismissal would be unfair because Scottish law was less favorable. The District Court explicitly rejected this claim. It reasoned that the possibility that dismissal might lead to an unfavorable change in the law did not deserve significant weight; any deficiency in the foreign law was a "matter to be dealt with in the foreign forum."

C

On appeal, the United States Court of Appeals for the Third Circuit reversed and remanded for trial. The decision to reverse appears to be based on two alternative grounds. First, the Court held that the District Court abused its discretion in conducting the Gilbert analysis. Second, the Court held that dismissal is never appropriate where the law of the alternative forum is less favorable to the plaintiff....

We granted certiorari in these cases to consider the questions they raise concerning the proper application of the doctrine of forum non conveniens.

II

The Court of Appeals erred in holding that plaintiffs may defeat a motion to dismiss on the ground of forum non conveniens merely by showing that the substantive law that would be applied in the alternative forum is less favorable to the plaintiffs than that of the present forum. The possibility of a change in substantive law should ordinarily not be given conclusive or even substantial weight in the forum non conveniens inquiry.

We expressly rejected the position adopted by the Court of Appeals in our decision in Canada Malting Co. v. Paterson Steamships, Ltd., 285 U.S. 413 (1932). That case arose out of a collision between two vessels in American waters. The Canadian owners of cargo lost in the accident sued the Canadian owners of one of the vessels in Federal District Court. The cargo owners chose an American court in large part because the relevant American liability rules were more favorable than the Canadian rules. The District Court dismissed on grounds of forum non conveniens. The plaintiffs argued that dismissal was inappropriate because Canadian laws were less favorable to them. This Court nonetheless affirmed:

> We have no occasion to enquire by what law the rights of the parties are governed, as we are of the opinion that, under any view of that question, it lay within the

---

Van Dusen v. Barrack, 376 U.S. 612 (1946). Relying on these two cases, the District Court concluded that California choice-of-law rules would apply to Piper, and Pennsylvania choice-of-law rules would apply to Hartzell. It further concluded that California applied a "governmental interests" analysis in resolving choice-of-law problems, and that Pennsylvania employed a "significant contacts" analysis. The court used the "governmental interests" analysis to determine that Pennsylvania liability rules would apply to Piper, and the "significant contacts" analysis to determine that Scottish liability rules would apply to Hartzell.

> discretion of the District Court to decline to assume jurisdiction over the controversy.... "[The] court will not take cognizance of the case if justice would be as well done by remitting the parties to their home forum." Id., at 419–420.

The Court further stated that "[there] was no basis for the contention that the District Court abused its discretion." 285 U.S., at 423.

It is true that Canada Malting was decided before Gilbert, and that the doctrine of forum non conveniens was not fully crystallized until our decision in that case. However, Gilbert in no way affects the validity of Canada Malting. Indeed, by holding that the central focus of the forum non conveniens inquiry is convenience, Gilbert implicitly recognized that dismissal may not be barred solely because of the possibility of an unfavorable change in law. Under Gilbert, dismissal will ordinarily be appropriate where trial in the plaintiff's chosen forum imposes a heavy burden on the defendant or the court, and where the plaintiff is unable to offer any specific reasons of convenience supporting his choice. If substantial weight were given to the possibility of an unfavorable change in law, however, dismissal might be barred even where trial in the chosen forum was plainly inconvenient.

The Court of Appeals' decision is inconsistent with this Court's earlier forum non conveniens decisions in another respect. Those decisions have repeatedly emphasized the need to retain flexibility. In Gilbert, the Court refused to identify specific circumstances "which will justify or require either grant or denial of remedy." 330 U.S., at 508. Similarly, in Koster, the Court rejected the contention that where a trial would involve inquiry into the internal affairs of a foreign corporation, dismissal was always appropriate. "That is one, but only one, factor which may show convenience." 330 U.S., at 527. And in Williams v. Green Bay & Western R. Co., 326 U.S. 549, 557 (1946), we stated that we would not lay down a rigid rule to govern discretion, and that "[each] case turns on its facts." If central emphasis were placed on any one factor, the forum non conveniens doctrine would lose much of the very flexibility that makes it so valuable.

In fact, if conclusive or substantial weight were given to the possibility of a change in law, the forum non conveniens doctrine would become virtually useless. Jurisdiction and venue requirements are often easily satisfied. As a result, many plaintiffs are able to choose from among several forums. Ordinarily, these plaintiffs will select that forum whose choice-of-law rules are most advantageous. Thus, if the possibility of an unfavorable change in substantive law is given substantial weight in the forum non conveniens inquiry, dismissal would rarely be proper....

The Court of Appeals' approach is not only inconsistent with the purpose of the forum non conveniens doctrine, but also poses substantial practical problems. If the possibility of a change in law were given substantial weight, deciding motions to dismiss on the ground of forum non conveniens would become quite difficult. Choice-of-law analysis would become extremely important, and the courts would frequently be required to interpret the law of foreign jurisdictions. First, the trial court would have to determine what law would apply if the case were tried in the chosen forum, and what law would apply if the case were tried in the alternative forum. It would then have to compare the rights, remedies, and procedures available under the law that would be applied in each forum. Dismissal would be appropriate only if the court concluded that the law applied by the alternative forum is as favorable to the plaintiff as that of the chosen forum. The doctrine of forum non conveniens, however, is designed in part to help courts avoid conducting complex exercises in comparative law. As we stated in Gilbert, the public interest factors point towards dismissal where the court would be required to "untangle problems in conflict of laws, and in law foreign to itself." 330 U.S., at 509.

Upholding the decision of the Court of Appeals would result in other practical problems. At least where the foreign plaintiff named an American manufacturer as defendant, a court could not dismiss the case on grounds of forum non conveniens where dismissal might lead to an unfavorable change in law. The American courts, which are already extremely attractive to foreign plaintiffs, would become even more attractive. The flow of litigation into the United States would increase and further congest already crowded courts.

The Court of Appeals based its decision, at least in part, on an analogy between dismissals on grounds of forum non conveniens and transfers between federal courts pursuant to § 1404(a). In Van Dusen v. Barrack, 376 U.S. 612 (1964), this Court ruled that a § 1404(a) transfer should not result in a change in the applicable law. Relying on dictum in an earlier Third Circuit opinion interpreting Van Dusen, the court below held that that principle is also applicable to a dismissal on forum non conveniens grounds. 630 F.2d, at 164, and n. 51 (citing DeMateos v. Texaco, Inc., 562 F.2d, at 899). However, § 1404(a) transfers are different than dismissals on the ground of forum non conveniens.

Congress enacted § 1404(a) to permit change of venue between federal courts. Although the statute was drafted in accordance with the doctrine of forum non conveniens... it was intended to be a revision rather than a codification of the common law. District courts were given more discretion to transfer under § 1404(a) than they had to dismiss on grounds of forum non conveniens.

The reasoning employed in Van Dusen v. Barrack is simply inapplicable to dismissals on grounds of forum non conveniens. That case did not discuss the common-law doctrine. Rather, it focused on "the construction and application" of § 1404(a). Emphasizing the remedial purpose of the statute, Barrack concluded that Congress could not have intended a transfer to be accompanied by a change in law. The statute was designed as a "federal housekeeping measure," allowing easy change of venue within a unified federal system. The Court feared that if a change in venue were accompanied by a change in law, forum-shopping parties would take unfair advantage of the relaxed standards for transfer. The rule was necessary to ensure the just and efficient operation of the statute.

We do not hold that the possibility of an unfavorable change in law should never be a relevant consideration in a forum non conveniens inquiry. Of course, if the remedy provided by the alternative forum is so clearly inadequate or unsatisfactory that it is no remedy at all, the unfavorable change in law may be given substantial weight; the district court may conclude that dismissal would not be in the interests of justice.[22] In these cases, however, the remedies that would be provided by the Scottish courts do not fall within this category. Although the relatives of the decedents may not be able to rely on a strict liability theory, and although their potential damages award may be smaller, there is no danger that they will be deprived of any remedy or treated unfairly.

III

The Court of Appeals also erred in rejecting the District Court's Gilbert analysis. The Court of Appeals stated that more weight should have been given to the plaintiff's choice of forum, and criticized the District Court's analysis of the private and public interests. However, the District Court's decision regarding the deference due plaintiff's choice of forum was appropriate. Furthermore, we do not believe that the District Court abused its discretion in weighing the private and public interests.

A

The District Court acknowledged that there is ordinarily a strong presumption in favor of the plaintiff's choice of forum, which may be overcome only when the private and public interest factors clearly point towards trial in the alternative forum. It held, however, that the presumption applies with less force when the plaintiff or real parties in interest are foreign.

The District Court's distinction between resident or citizen plaintiffs and foreign plaintiffs is fully justified. In Koster, the Court indicated that a plaintiff's choice of forum is entitled to greater deference when the plaintiff has chosen the home forum. 330 U.S., at 524.[23] When the home forum has been chosen, it is reasonable to assume that this choice is convenient. When the plaintiff is foreign, however, this assumption is much less reasonable. Because the central purpose of

---

[22] At the outset of any forum non conveniens inquiry, the court must determine whether there exists an alternative forum. Ordinarily, this requirement will be satisfied when the defendant is "amenable to process" in the other jurisdiction. *Gilbert*, 330 U.S., at 506-507. In rare circumstances, however, where the remedy offered by the other forum is clearly unsatisfactory, the other forum may not be an adequate alternative, and the initial requirement may not be satisfied. Thus, for example, dismissal would not be appropriate where the alternative forum does not permit litigation of the subject matter of the dispute. *Cf. Phoenix Canada Oil Co. Ltd. v. Texaco, Inc.*, 78 F.R.D. 445 (Del. 1978) (court refuses to dismiss, where alternative forum is Ecuador, it is unclear whether Ecuadorean tribunal will hear the case, and there is no generally codified Ecuadorean legal remedy for the unjust enrichment and tort claims asserted).

[23] In *Koster*, we stated that "[in] any balancing of conveniences, a real showing of convenience by a plaintiff who has sued in his home forum will normally outweigh the inconvenience the defendant may have shown." 330 U.S., at 524. . . . As the District Court correctly noted in its opinion, 479 F. Supp., at 731; see also n. 10, supra, the lower federal courts have routinely given less weight to a foreign plaintiff's choice of forum. [citing cases] A citizen's forum choice should not be given dispositive weight, however. . . . Citizens or residents deserve somewhat more deference than foreign plaintiffs, but dismissal should not be automatically barred when a plaintiff has filed suit in his home forum. As always, if the balance of conveniences suggests that trial in the chosen forum would be unnecessarily burdensome for the defendant or the court, dismissal is proper.

any forum non conveniens inquiry is to ensure that the trial is convenient, a foreign plaintiff's choice deserves less deference.[24]

B

The forum non conveniens determination is committed to the sound discretion of the trial court. It may be reversed only when there has been a clear abuse of discretion; where the court has considered all relevant public and private interest factors, and where its balancing of these factors is reasonable, its decision deserves substantial deference....

(1)

In analyzing the private interest factors, the District Court stated that the connections with Scotland are "overwhelming." This characterization may be somewhat exaggerated. Particularly with respect to the question of relative ease of access to sources of proof, the private interests point in both directions. As respondent emphasizes, records concerning the design, manufacture, and testing of the propeller and plane are located in the United States. She would have greater access to sources of proof relevant to her strict liability and negligence theories if trial were held here.[25] However, the District Court did not act unreasonably in concluding that fewer evidentiary problems would be posed if the trial were held in Scotland. A large proportion of the relevant evidence is located in Great Britain.

The Court of Appeals found that the problems of proof could not be given any weight because Piper and Hartzell failed to describe with specificity the evidence they would not be able to obtain if trial were held in the United States. It suggested that defendants seeking forum non conveniens dismissal must submit affidavits identifying the witnesses they would call and the testimony these witnesses would provide if the trial were held in the alternative forum. Such detail is not necessary. Piper and Hartzell have moved for dismissal precisely because many crucial witnesses are located beyond the reach of compulsory process, and thus are difficult to identify or interview. Requiring extensive investigation would defeat the purpose of their motion. Of course, defendants must provide enough information to enable the District Court to balance the parties' interests. Our examination of the record convinces us that sufficient information was provided here. Both Piper and Hartzell submitted affidavits describing the evidentiary problems they would face if the trial were held in the United States.[27]

---

[24] Respondent argues that since plaintiffs will ordinarily file suit in the jurisdiction that offers the most favorable law, establishing a strong presumption in favor of both home and foreign plaintiffs will ensure that defendants will always be held to the highest possible standard of accountability for their purported wrongdoing. However, the deference accorded a plaintiff's choice of forum has never been intended to guarantee that the plaintiff will be able to select the law that will govern the case.

[25] In the future, where similar problems are presented, district courts might dismiss subject to the condition that defendant corporations agree to provide the records relevant to the plaintiff's claims.

[27] The affidavit provided to the District Court by Piper states that it would call the following witnesses: the relatives of the decedents; the owners and employees of McDonald; the persons responsible for the training and licensing of the pilot; the persons responsible for servicing and maintaining the aircraft; and two or three of its own employees involved in the design and manufacture of the aircraft.

The District Court correctly concluded that the problems posed by the inability to implead potential third-party defendants clearly supported holding the trial in Scotland. Joinder of the pilot's estate, Air Navigation, and McDonald is crucial to the presentation of petitioners' defense. If Piper and Hartzell can show that the accident was caused not by a design defect, but rather by the negligence of the pilot, the plane's owners, or the charter company, they will be relieved of all liability. It is true, of course, that if Hartzell and Piper were found liable after a trial in the United States, they could institute an action for indemnity or contribution against these parties in Scotland. It would be far more convenient, however, to resolve all claims in one trial. The Court of Appeals rejected this argument. Forcing petitioners to rely on actions for indemnity or contributions would be "burdensome" but not "unfair." Finding that trial in the plaintiff's chosen forum would be burdensome, however, is sufficient to support dismissal on grounds of forum non conveniens.

(2)

The District Court's review of the factors relating to the public interest was also reasonable. On the basis of its choice-of-law analysis, it concluded that if the case were tried in the Middle District of Pennsylvania, Pennsylvania law would apply to Piper and Scottish law to Hartzell. It stated that a trial involving two sets of laws would be confusing to the jury. It also noted its own lack of familiarity with Scottish law. Consideration of these problems was clearly appropriate under Gilbert; in that case we explicitly held that the need to apply foreign law pointed towards dismissal. The Court of Appeals found that the District Court's choice-of-law analysis was incorrect, and that American law would apply to both Hartzell and Piper. Thus, lack of familiarity with foreign law would not be a problem. Even if the Court of Appeals' conclusion is correct, however, all other public interest factors favored trial in Scotland.

Scotland has a very strong interest in this litigation. The accident occurred in its airspace. All of the decedents were Scottish. Apart from Piper and Hartzell, all potential plaintiffs and defendants are either Scottish or English. As we stated in Gilbert, there is "a local interest in having localized controversies decided at home." Respondent argues that American citizens have an interest in ensuring that American manufacturers are deterred from producing defective products, and that additional deterrence might be obtained if Piper and Hartzell were tried in the United States, where they could be sued on the basis of both negligence and strict liability. However, the incremental deterrence that would be gained if this trial were held in an American court is likely to be insignificant. The American interest in this accident is simply not sufficient to justify the enormous commitment of judicial time and resources that would inevitably be required if the case were to be tried here. . . .

[The opinions of Justice Stevens, dissenting (joined by Justice Brennan), and Justice White, concurring in part and dissenting in part, are omitted. Neither Justice Powell nor Justice O'Connor took part in the decision.]

Comments and Questions

1. Conceptually, the issue of forum non conveniens arises after the court determines that it has jurisdiction. How does the forum non conveniens inquiry differ from the "fair play and substantial justice" inquiry that is part of the personal jurisdictional analysis? Why not simply combine these inquiries (as in the common law provinces of Canada)?

2. What makes an alternate forum adequate if not the outcome of the litigation? Is it the general reputation of the country? Whether the procedural system looks sufficiently similar to one's own? Or is a forum adequate provided plaintiff may recover something.

3. Would it have been an abuse of discretion for the court in *Piper* to deny a forum non conveniens motion?

4. Is the question whether these foreign plaintiffs should recover under Pennsylvania law a question about the substantive law of Pennsylvania or about the procedural common law of forum non conveniens?

5. The doctrine of forum non conveniens gives courts discretion to decline to hear a case. Criminal prosecutors are thought to have broad prosecutorial discretion to decide which cases to pursue and when. Should a similar authority be vested with judges? Is the exercise of forum non conveniens in Piper sanctioning a form of discrimination against foreign plaintiffs; or is that characterization terribly unfair?

In re Union Carbide Corp. Gas Plant Disaster

809 F.2d 195 (2nd Cir.), cert. denied 484 U.S. 871 (1987)

[On the night of December 2–3, 1984, the most tragic industrial disaster in history occurred in the city of Bhopal, state of Madhya Pradesh, Union of India. Located there was a chemical plant owned and operated by Union Carbide India Limited ("UCIL"). The plant, situated in the northern sector of the city, had numerous hutments adjacent to it on its southern side which were occupied by impoverished squatters. UCIL manufactured the pesticides Sevin and Temik at the Bhopal plant at the request of, and with the approval of, the Government of India.... UCIL was incorporated under Indian law in 1934. 50.9% of its stock is owned by the defendant, Union Carbide Corporation, a New York corporation.... Methyl isocyanate (MIC), a highly toxic gas, is an ingredient in the production of both Sevin and Temik. On the night of the tragedy MIC leaked from the plant in substantial quantities for reasons not yet determined.

The prevailing winds on the early morning of December 3, 1984, were from northwest to southeast. They blew the deadly gas into the overpopulated hutments adjacent to the plant and into the most densely occupied parts of the city. The results were horrendous. Estimates of deaths directly attributable to the leak range as high as 2,100. No one is sure exactly how many perished. Over 200,000 people suffered injuries—some serious and permanent—some mild and temporary. Livestock were killed and crops damaged. Businesses were interrupted.

On December 7, 1984, the first lawsuit was filed by American lawyers in the United States on behalf of thousands of Indians.... Since then 144 additional actions have been commenced in federal courts in the United States. The actions have all been joined and assigned by the Judicial Panel on Multidistrict Litigation to the Southern District of New York....

The Indian Government on March 29, 1985, enacted legislation, the Bhopal Gas Leak Disaster (Processing of Claims) Act (21 of 1985) ("Bhopal Act"), providing that the Government of India has the exclusive right to represent Indian plaintiffs in India and elsewhere in connection with the tragedy. Pursuant to the Bhopal Act, the Union of India, on April 8, 1985, filed a complaint with this Court setting forth claims for relief similar to those in the consolidated complaint of June 28, 1985.

On September 24, 1985, pursuant to the Bhopal Act, the Central Government of India framed a "scheme" for the Registration and Processing of Claims arising out of the disaster. According to the Union of India's counsel, over 487,000 claims have been filed in India pursuant to the "scheme."

There presently are 145 actions filed in the United States District Court for the Southern District of New York under the Judicial Panel for Multidistrict Litigation's order of February 6, 1985, involving approximately 200,000 plaintiffs. (This fact summary is taken from the District Court opinion, 634 F. Supp. 842 (1986).]

MANSFIELD, CIRCUIT JUDGE

After hearing argument on January 3, 1986, the district court, on May 12, 1986, 634 F.Supp. 842, in a thoroughly reasoned 63-page opinion granted the motion, dismissing the lawsuits before it on condition that UCC [Union Carbide Corp., U.S.]:

(1) consent to the jurisdiction of the courts of India and continue to waive defenses based on the statute of limitations,
(2) agree to satisfy any judgment rendered by an Indian court against it and upheld on appeal, provided the judgment and affirmance "comport with the minimal requirements of due process," and
(3) be subject to discovery under the Federal Rules of Civil Procedure of the United States.

On June 12, 1986, UCC accepted these conditions subject to its right to appeal them; and on June 24, 1986, the district court entered its order of dismissal. In September 1986 the UOI [Union of India], acting pursuant to its authority under the Bhopal Act, brought suit on behalf of all claimants against UCC and UCIL [Union Carbide India, Ltd.] in the District Court of Bhopal, where many individual suits by victims of the disaster were then pending.

In its opinion dismissing the actions the district court analyzed the forum non conveniens issues, applying the standards and weighing the factors suggested by the Supreme Court in Gulf Oil Corp. v. Gilbert, 330 U.S. 501 (1947), and

Piper Aircraft Co. v. Reyno, 454 U.S. 235. At the outset Judge Keenan concluded, in accordance with the Court's expressed views in Piper that, since the plaintiffs were not residents of the United States but of a foreign country, their choice of the United States as a forum would not be given the deference to which it would be entitled if this country were their home. See Piper, 454 U.S. at 256. Following the dictates of Piper, the district court declined to compare the advantages and disadvantages to the respective parties of American versus Indian Laws or to determine the impact upon plaintiffs' claims of the laws of India, where UCC had acknowledged that it would make itself amenable to process, except to ascertain whether India provided an adequate alternative forum, as distinguished from no remedy at all. Judge Keenan reviewed thoroughly the affidavits of experts on India's law and legal system, which described in detail its procedural and substantive aspects, and concluded that, despite some of the Indian system's disadvantages, it afforded an adequate alternative forum for the enforcement of plaintiffs' claims.

The Indian judiciary was found by the court to be a developed, independent and progressive one, which has demonstrated its capability of circumventing long delays and backlogs prevalent in the Indian Courts' handling of ordinary cases by devising special expediting procedures in extraordinary cases, such as by directing its High Court to hear them on a daily basis, appointing special tribunals to handle them, and assigning daily hearing duties to a single judge. He found that Indian courts have competently dealt with complex technological issues. Since the Bhopal Act provides that the case may be treated speedily, effectively and to the best advantage of the claimants, and since the Union of India represents the claimants, the prosecution of the claims is expected to be adequately staffed by the Attorney General or Solicitor General of India.

The tort law of India, which is derived from common law and British precedent, was found to be suitable for resolution of legal issues arising in cases involving highly complex technology. Moreover, Indian courts would be in a superior position to construe and apply applicable Indian laws and standards than would courts of the United States. Third parties may be interpleaded under Order 1, Rule 10(2) of the Indian Code of Civil Procedure, and defendants may seek contribution from third parties. The absence in India of a class action procedure comparable to that in federal courts here was found not to deprive the plaintiffs of a remedy, in view of existing Indian legal authorization for "representative" suits under Order 1, Rule 8 of the Indian Code of Civil Procedure, which would permit an Indian court to create representative classes. Judge Keenan further found that the absence of juries and contingent fee arrangements in India would not deprive the claimants of an adequate remedy.

In two areas bearing upon the adequacy of the Indian forum the district court decided to impose somewhat unusual conditions on the transfer of the American cases to India. One condition dealt with pre-trial discovery. Indian courts, following the British pattern, permit parties to have pre-trial discovery of each other through written interrogatories, liberal inspection of documents and requests for admissions. Non-party witnesses can be interviewed and summoned to appear at trial or to produce documents. See India Code Civ. Proc., Order 16, Rule 6. Witnesses unable to appear at trial are sometimes permitted to give evidence by means of affidavits. See id. Order 19. Discovery in India, however, as in Britain, is limited to evidence that may be admitted at trial. Litigants are not permitted to engage in wide-ranging discovery of the type authorized by Fed. R. Civ. P. 26(b), which allows inquiry into any unprivileged matter that could reasonably lead to the discovery of admissible evidence.

Judge Keenan, concluding that the Indian system might limit the victims' access to sources of proof, directed that dismissal of the actions on grounds of form non conveniens must be conditioned on UCC's consent to discovery of it in accordance with the Federal Rules of Civil Procedure after the cases were transferred to India. He added, "While the Court feels that it would be fair to bind the plaintiffs to American discovery rules, too, it has no authority to do so."

Another condition imposed by the district court upon dismissal on grounds of forum non conveniens dealt with the enforceability in the United States of any judgment rendered by an Indian court in the cases. Judge Keenan, expressing the view that an Indian judgment might possibly not be enforceable in the United States, provided in his order that UCC must "agree to satisfy any judgment rendered by an Indian court, and if applicable, upheld by an appellate court in that country, where such judgment and affirmance comport with the minimal requirements of due process."

As the district court found, the record shows that the private interests of the respective parties weigh heavily in favor of dismissal on grounds of forum non conveniens. The many witnesses and sources of proof are almost entirely located in India, where the accident occurred, and could not be compelled to appear for trial in the United States. The Bhopal plant at the time of the accident was operated by some 193 Indian nationals, including the managers of seven operating units employed by the Agricultural Products Division of UCIL, who reported to Indian Works Managers in Bhopal. The plant was maintained by seven functional departments employing over 200 more Indian nationals. UCIL kept at the plant daily, weekly and monthly records of plant operations and records of maintenance as well as records of the plant's Quality Control, Purchasing and Store branches, all operated by Indian employees. The great majority of documents bearing on the design, safety, start-up and operation of the plant, as well as the safety training of the plant's employees, is located in India.[2] Proof to be offered at trial would be derived from interviews of these witnesses in India and study of the records located there to determine whether the accident was caused by negligence on the part of the management or employees in the operation of the plant, by fault in its

---

[2] At oral argument UOI's counsel stated that UCC refused UOI's offer to furnish copies of some of the documents to UCC in the United States. The district court, on the other hand, found that following the disaster India's Central Bureau of Investigation seized, among other documents, daily, weekly and monthly records of the Bhopal plant operations. UCC states that of the 78,000 pages of documents seized, some 36,000 are plant operation records, of which 1,700 pages relate to plant maintenance in 1983 and 1984.

design, or by sabotage. In short, India has greater ease of access to the proof than does the United States.

The plaintiffs seeks to prove that the accident was caused by negligence on the part of UCC in originally contributing to the design of the plant and its provision for storage of excessive amounts of the gas at the plant. As Judge Keenan found, however, UCC's participation was limited and its involvement in plant operations terminated long before the accident. Under 1973 agreements negotiated at arm's-length with UCIL, UCC did provide a summary "process design package" for construction of the plant and the services of some of its technicians to monitor the progress of UCIL in detailing the design and erecting the plant. However, the UOI controlled the terms of the agreements and precluded UCC from exercising any authority to "detail design, erect and commission the plant," which was done independently over the period from 1972 to 1980 by UCIL process design engineers who supervised, among many others, some 55 to 60 Indian engineers employed by the Bombay engineering firm of Humphreys and Glasgow. The preliminary process design information furnished by UCC could not have been used to construct the plant. Construction required the detailed process design and engineering data prepared by hundreds of Indian engineers, process designers and sub-contractors. During the ten years spent constructing the plant, its design and configuration underwent many changes.

The vital parts of the Bhopal plant, including its storage tank, monitoring instrumentation, and vent gas scrubber, were manufactured by Indians in India. Although some 40 UCIL employees were given some safety training at UCC's plant in West Virginia, they represented a small fraction of the Bhopal plant's employees. The vast majority of plant employees were selected and trained by UCIL in Bhopal. The manual for start-up of the Bhopal plant was prepared by Indians employed by UCIL.

In short, the plant has been constructed and managed by Indians in India. No Americans were employed at the plant at the time of the accident. In the five years from 1980 to 1984, although more than 1,000 Indians were employed at the plant, only one American was employed there and he left in 1982. No Americans visited the plant for more than one year prior to the accident, and during the 5-year period before the accident the communications between the plant and the United States were almost non-existent.

The vast majority of material witnesses and documentary proof bearing on causation of and liability for the accident is located in India, not the United States, and would be more accessible to an Indian court than to a United States court. The records are almost entirely in Hindi or other Indian languages, understandable to an Indian court without translation. The witnesses for the most part do not speak English but Indian languages understood by an Indian court but not by an American court. These witnesses could be required to appear in an Indian court but not in a court of the United States. Although witnesses in the United States could not be subpoenaed to appear in India, they are comparatively few in number and most are employed by UCC which, as a party, would produce them in India, with lower overall transportation costs than if the parties were to attempt to bring hundreds of Indian witnesses to the United States. Lastly, Judge Keenan properly concluded that an Indian court would be in a better position to direct and supervise a viewing of the Bhopal plant, which was sealed after the accident. Such a viewing could be of help to a court in determining liability issues.

After a thorough review, the district court concluded that the public interest concerns, like the private ones, also weigh heavily in favor of India as the situs for trial and disposition of the cases. The accident and all relevant events occurred in India. The victims, over 200,000 in number, are citizens of India and located there. The witnesses are almost entirely Indian citizens. The Union of India has a greater interest than does the United States in facilitating the trial and adjudication of the victims' claims. Despite the contentions of plaintiffs and amici that it would be in the public interest to avoid a "double standard" by requiring an American parent corporation (UCC) to submit to the jurisdiction of American courts, India has a stronger countervailing interest in adjudicating the claims in its courts according to its standards rather than having American values and standards of care imposed upon it. India's interest is increased by the fact that it has for years treated UCIL as an Indian national, subjecting it to intensive regulations and governmental supervision of the construction, development and operation of the Bhopal plant, its emissions, water and air pollution, and safety precautions. Numerous Indian government officials have regularly conducted on-site inspections of the plant and approved its machinery and equipment, including its facilities for storage of the lethal methyl isocyanate gas that escaped and caused the disaster giving rise to the claims. Thus India has considered the plant to be an Indian one and the disaster to be an Indian problem. It therefore has a deep interest in ensuring compliance with its safety standards. Moreover, plaintiffs have conceded that in view of India's strong interest and its greater contacts with the plant, its operations, its employees, and the victims of the accident, the law of India, as the place where the tort occurred, will undoubtedly govern. In contrast, the American interests are relatively minor. Indeed, a long trial of the 145 cases here would unduly burden an already overburdened court, involving both jury hardship and heavy expense. It would face the court with numerous practical difficulties, including the almost impossible task of attempting to understand extensive relevant Indian regulations published in a foreign language and the slow process of receiving testimony of scores of witnesses through interpreters.

Having made the foregoing findings, Judge Keenan dismissed the actions against UCC on grounds of forum non conveniens upon the conditions indicated above, after obtaining UCC's consent to those conditions subject to its right to appeal the order. After the plaintiffs filed their notice of appeal, UCC and the Union of India filed cross appeals.

Upon these appeals, the plaintiffs continue to oppose the dismissal. The Union of India, however, has changed its position and now supports the district court's order. UCC, as it did in the district court, opposes as unfair the condition that it submit to discovery pursuant to the Federal Rules of Civil Procedure without reciprocally obligating the plaintiffs and Union of India to be subject to discovery on the same basis so that both sides might be treated equally, giving each the same access to the facts in the others' possession.

Upon argument of the appeal, UCC also took the position that the district court's order requiring it to satisfy any Indian court judgment was unfair unless some method were provided, such as continued availability of the district court as a forum, to ensure that any denial of due process by the Indian courts could be remedied promptly by the federal court here rather than delay resolution of the issue until termination of the Indian court proceedings and appeal, which might take several years. UCC's argument in this respect was based on the sudden issuance by the Indian court in Bhopal of a temporary order freezing all of UCC's assets, which could have caused it irreparable injury if it had been continued indefinitely,[3] and by the conflict of interest posed by the UOI's position in the Indian courts where, since the UOI would appear both as a plaintiff and a defendant, it might as a plaintiff voluntarily dismiss its claims against itself as a defendant or, as a co-defendant with UCC, be tempted to shed all blame upon UCC even though the UOI had in fact been responsible for supervision, regulation and safety of UCIL's Bhopal plant.

Discussion

The standard to be applied in reviewing the district court's forum non conveniens dismissal was clearly expressed by the Supreme Court in Piper Aircraft Co. v. Reyno, supra, 454 U.S. at 257, as follows:

> The forum non conveniens determination is committed to the sound discretion of the trial court. It may be reversed only when there has been a clear abuse of discretion; where the court has considered all relevant public and private interest factors, and where its balancing of these factors is reasonable, its decision deserves substantial deference.

Having reviewed Judge Keenan's detailed decision, in which he thoroughly considered the comparative adequacy of the forums and the public and private interests involved, we are satisfied that there was no abuse of discretion in his granting dismissal of the action. On the contrary, it might reasonably be concluded that it would have been an abuse of discretion to deny a forum non conveniens dismissal. Practically all relevant factors demonstrate that transfer of the cases to India for trial and adjudication is both fair and just to the parties.

Plaintiffs' principal contentions in favor of retention of the cases by the district court are that deference to the plaintiffs' choice of forum has been inadequate, that the Indian courts are insufficiently equipped for the task, that UCC has its principal place of business here, that the most probative evidence regarding negligence and causation is to be found here, that federal courts are much better equipped through experience and procedures to handle such complex actions efficiently

---

[3] The Indian court's temporary restraining order has since been dissolved upon UCC's agreement to maintain sufficient assets to satisfy a judgment rendered against it in India.

than are Indian courts, and that a transfer of the cases to India will jeopardize a $350 million settlement being negotiated by plaintiffs' counsel. All of these arguments, however, must be rejected.

Little or no deference can be paid to the plaintiff's choice of a United States forum when all but a few of the 200,000 plaintiffs are Indian citizens located in India who, according to the UOI, have revoked the authorizations of American counsel to represent them here and have substituted the UOI, which now prefers Indian courts. The finding of our district court, after exhaustive analysis of the evidence, that the Indian courts provide a reasonably adequate alternative forum cannot be labelled clearly erroneous or an abuse of discretion.

The emphasis placed by plaintiffs on UCC's having its domicile here, where personal jurisdiction over it exists, is robbed of significance by its consent to Indian jurisdiction. Plaintiffs' contention that the most crucial and probative evidence is located in the United States is simply not in accord with the record or the district court's findings. Although basic design programs were prepared in the United States and some assistance furnished to UCIL at the outset of the 10-year period during which the Bhopal plant was constructed, the proof bearing on the issues to be tried is almost entirely located in India. This includes the principal witnesses and documents bearing on the development and construction of the plant, the detailed designs, the implementation of plans, the operation and regulation of the plant, its safety precautions, the facts with respect to the accident itself, and the deaths and injuries attributable to the accident.

Although the plaintiffs' American counsel may at one time have been close to reaching a $350 million settlement of the cases, no such settlement was ever finalized. No draft joint stipulation in writing or settlement agreement appears to have been prepared, much less approved by the parties. No petition for certification of a settlement class under Fed.R.Civ.P.23 has ever been presented. Most important, the UOI, which is itself a plaintiff and states that it now represents the Indian plaintiffs formerly represented by American counsel, is firmly opposed to the $350 million "settlement" as inadequate. Under these circumstances, to order a Rule 23 "fairness" hearing would be futile. The district court's denial of the American counsels' motion for such a hearing must accordingly be affirmed.

The conditions imposed by the district court upon its forum non conveniens dismissal stand on a different footing.... The first condition, that UCC consent to the Indian court's personal jurisdiction over it and waive the statue of limitations as a defense, are not unusual and have been imposed in numerous cases where the foreign court would not provide an adequate alternative in the absence of such a condition. See, e.g. Schertenleib, supra, 589 F.2d at 1166; Bailey v. Dolphin Int'l, Inc., 697 F.2d 1268, 1280 (5th Cir.1983). The remaining conditions, however, pose problems.

In requiring that UCC consent to enforceability of an Indian judgment against it, the district court proceeded at least in part on the erroneous assumption that, absent such a requirement, the plaintiffs, if they should succeed in obtaining an Indian judgment against UCC, might not be able to enforce it against UCC in the

United States. The law, however, is to the contrary. Under New York law, which governs actions brought in New York to enforce foreign judgments, a foreign-country judgment that is final, conclusive and enforceable where rendered must be recognized and will be enforced as "conclusive between the parties to the extent that it grants or denies recovery of a sum of money" except that it is not deemed to be conclusive if:

1. The judgment was rendered under a system which does not provide impartial tribunals or procedures compatible with the requirements of due process of law;
2. the foreign court did not have personal jurisdiction over the defendant.

Art. 53, Recognition of Foreign Country Money Judgments, 7B N.Y.Civ.Prac.L. & R. §§ 5301–09 (McKinney 1978). Although § 5304 further provides that under certain specified conditions a foreign country judgment need not be recognized, none of these conditions would apply to the present cases except for the possibility of failure to provide UCC with sufficient notice of proceedings or the existence of fraud in obtaining the judgment, which do not presently exist but conceivably could occur in the future.

UCC contends that Indian courts, while providing an adequate alternative forum, do not observe due process standards that would be required as a matter of course in this country. As evidence of this apprehension it points to the haste with which the Indian court in Bhopal issued a temporary order freezing its assets throughout the world and the possibility of serious prejudice to it if the UOI is permitted to have the double and conflicting status of both plaintiff and co-defendant in the Indian court proceedings. It argues that we should protect it against such denial of due process by authorizing Judge Keenan to retain the authority after forum non conveniens dismissal of the cases here, to monitor the Indian court proceedings and be available on call to rectify in some undefined way any abuses of UCC's right to due process as they might occur in India.

UCC's proposed remedy is not only impractical but evidences an abysmal ignorance of basic jurisdictional principles, so much so that it borders on the frivolous. The district court's jurisdiction is limited to proceedings before it in this country. Once it dismisses those proceedings on grounds of forum non conveniens it ceases to have any further jurisdiction over the matter unless and until a proceeding may some day be brought to enforce here a final and conclusive Indian money judgment. Nor could we, even if we attempted to retain some sort of supervisory jurisdiction, impose our due process requirements upon Indian courts, which are governed by their laws, not ours. The concept of shared jurisdictions is both illusory and unrealistic. The parties cannot simultaneously submit to both jurisdictions the resolution of the pre-trial and trial issues when there is only one consolidated case pending in one court. Any denial by the Indian courts of due process can be raised by UCC as a defense to the plaintiffs' later attempt to enforce a resulting judgment against UCC in this country.

We are concerned, however, that as it is written the district court's requirement that UCC consent to the enforcement of a final Indian judgment, which was imposed on the erroneous assumption that such a judgment might not otherwise be enforceable in the United States, may create misunderstandings and problems of construction. Although the order's provision that the judgment "comport with the minimal requirements of due process" (emphasis supplied) probably is intended to refer to "due process" as used in the New York Foreign Country Money Judgments Law and others like it, there is the risk that it may also be interpreted as providing for a lesser standard than we would otherwise require. Since the court's condition with respect to enforceability of any final Indian judgment is predicated on an erroneous legal assumption and its "due process" language is ambiguous, and since the district court's purpose is fully served by New York's statute providing for recognition of foreign-country money judgments, it was error to impose this condition upon the parties.

We also believe that the district court erred in requiring UCC to consent (which UCC did under protest and subject to its right of appeal) to broad discovery of it by the plaintiffs under the Federal Rules of Civil Procedure when UCC is confined to the more limited discovery authorized under Indian law. We recognize that under some circumstances, such as when a moving defendant unconditionally consents thereto or no undiscovered evidence of consequence is believed to be under the control of a plaintiff or co-defendant, it may be appropriate to condition a forum non conveniens dismissal on the moving defendant's submission to discovery under the Federal Rules without requiring reciprocal discovery of it by the plaintiff. See, e.g., Piper Aircraft v. Reyno, supra, 454 U.S. at 257 n. 25 (suggesting that district courts can condition dismissal upon a defendant's agreeing to provide all relevant records); Ali v. Offshore Co., 753 F.2d 1327, 1334 n. 16 (5th Cir. 1985) (same); Boskoff v. Transportes Aereos Portugueses, 17 Av. Cas. (CCH) 18,613, at 18,616 (N.D.Ill.1983) (accepting defendant's voluntary commitment to provide discovery in foreign forum according to Federal Rules). Basic justice dictates that both sides be treated equally, with each having equal access to the evidence in the possession or under the control of the other. Application of this fundamental principle in the present case is especially appropriate since the UOI, as the sovereign government of India, is expected to be a party to the Indian litigation, possibly on both sides.

For these reasons we direct that the condition with respect to the discovery of UCC under the Federal Rules of Civil Procedure be deleted without prejudice to the right of the parties to have reciprocal discovery of each other on equal terms under the Federal Rules, subject to such approval as may be required of the Indian court in which the case will be pending. If, for instance, Indian authorities will permit mutual discovery pursuant to the Federal Rules, the district court's order, as modified in accordance with this opinion, should not be construed to bar such procedure. In the absence of such a court-sanctioned agreement, however, the parties will be limited by the applicable discovery rules of the Indian court in which the claims will be pending.

As so modified the district court's order is affirmed.

Comments and Questions

1. One would have hoped that, especially given the international notoriety the Bhopal disaster received, by now the victims would have been compensated and the site cleaned up. Unfortunately, this is not the case:

a. the site of the plant has not been cleaned up, so its toxins continue to pollute the environment and the water;
b. twenty-two thousand people have died either in the immediate aftermath of the the toxic release or in the years since;
c. one hundred thousand survivors suffer chronic and serious health problems because of their exposure to the toxic release;
d. no one has been held to be responsible for what happened in Bhopal; and
e. as of September 2004, only about $140 million of the $470 million settlement paid by Union Carbide Corporation had been paid to actual victims.

Devalene Cooper, Thinking About Justice "Outside of the Box": Could Restorative Justice Practices Create Justice for Victims of International Disasters?, 42 New Eng. L. Rev. 693 (2008). See also Amnesty International, Clouds of Injustice: Bhopal Disaster 20 Years On (2004), available at http://www.amnesty.org/en/library/info/ASA20/015/2004. How could this be? Can you think of other ways relief might have been brought to the victims? See, e.g., Stephen McCaffrey, Accidents Do Happen: Hazardous Technology and International Tort Litigation, 1 Transnat'l L. 41 (1988).

William Gladstone, the nineteenth century British politician, is often quoted for the expression "Justice delayed, is justice denied." Was it the New York court's responsibility to ensure justice for the victims of this accident?

2. In Bhopal, the Indian government supported the forum non conveniens dismissal. But consider situations in which the foreign government would support the efforts of their citizens to sue American defendants in American courts. (After all, you might say, these multinational corporations are engaged in destructive practices that are injuring people and destroying the environment; why not hold them accountable in U.S. courts?)

> [S]ome Latin American countries have augmented their jurisdictional rules with "blocking statutes." These statutes deny native courts jurisdiction over claims first brought in the United States, thus blocking the effects of forum non conveniens by rendering the Latin American court an unacceptable forum. Latin American countries hope to force U.S. courts, which have far more resources than their Latin counterparts to handle mass torts, to assert and retain jurisdiction over the case. Costa Rica, Guatemala, Ecuador, the Dominican Republica, and Nicaragua have all drafted or enacted blocking statutes.

M. Ryan Casey & Barrett Ristroph, Boomerang Litigation: How Convenient is Forum Non Conveniens in Transnational Litigation?, 4 B.Y.U. Int'l L. & Mgmt. Rev. 21, 27 (2007) (citing all code provisions).

> More recent proposals for addressing the forum non conveniens dilemma in Latin America suggest including in Latin American statutes provisions that would declare evidence gathered in the U.S. proceeding to be admissible in the Latin American proceeding and/or provisions that would alter the burden of proof by having the U.S. defendant prove that it acted with due diligence in negligence cases, or by proving an act of God as being the only excuse in a case of strict liability....

[I]n addition to those statutes enacted in Latin American jurisdictions, the Latin American Parliament has promulgated a Model Law on International Jurisdiction Applicable to Tort Liability. That model law, like those laws promulgated in Ecuador and Guatemala, if adopted by a Latin American country, would block access to that country's courts after a forum non conveniens dismissal. That model law also provides for the application of damages and pecuniary sanctions in accordance with the relevant standards and amounts of the pertinent foreign law.

E. E. Daschbach, Where There's a Will, There's a Way: The Cause for a Cure and Remedial Prescriptions for Forum Non Conveniens as Applied in Latin American Plaintiffs' Actions Against U.S. Multinationals, 13 L. & Bus. Rev. Am. 11, 57–58 (2007).

How would you expect a U.S. court to receive a plaintiff's argument that the alternative forum is inadequate because there is a statute in that country denying those courts of jurisdiction when the case has first been filed elsewhere?

3. The Bhopal case illustrates another aspect of judicial discretion: conditional dismissals. Conditions imposed in the context of forum non conveniens dismissals include: (i) a requirement that defendants consent to personal jurisdiction in the foreign forum; (ii) waiver of any statute of limitations defense; (iii) consent to broad discovery; (iv) an agreement to satisfy any foreign judgment. Does the authority to grant or to deny a motion to dismiss on grounds of forum non conveniens include that authority to grant the motion on the condition that the movant accept certain conditions? Does the greater include this lesser?

2. English Cases

We next turn to a contemporary look at the English doctrine. The Lubbe case that follows arises out of asbestos mining in South Africa, where there existed a great deal of asbestos-related disease caused by exposure to asbestos fibers. More than half of former asbestos mineworkers in the Northern Cape Area suffer from lung diseases caused by asbestos, and as many as one in twelve of the general population in certain mining areas suffer merely by virtue of their proximity to the mines. The principal disease is asbestosis—a debilitating and often fatal condition. Some of the mines are owned and operated by a British-based company: Cape Asbestos Plc. ("Cape"). Cape withdrew from South Africa and paid compensation to its British workers who had suffered lung disease, but refused to pay compensation to around 3,000 South African workers and residents who claimed to have suffered asbestosis. See David Wilkinson Environment and Law 61 (Routledge 2002). After failing to receive compensation from the company, approximately 3,000 plaintiffs filed an action in the High Court in London. Cape invoked the doctrine of forum non conveniens.

Lubbe and Others v. Cape PLC

House of Lords [2000] 2 Lloyd's Rep. 383

Lord Bingham of Cornhill

My Lords, the central issue between the plaintiffs and the defendant in these interlocutory appeals is whether proceedings brought by the plaintiffs against the defendant should be tried in this country or in South Africa....

As reformulated during the first Court of Appeal hearing the main issue raised by the plaintiffs' claim was put in this way:

> Whether a parent company which is proved to exercise de facto control over the operations of a (foreign) subsidiary and which knows, through its directors, that those operations involve risks to the health of workers employed by the subsidiary and/or persons in the vicinity of its factory or other business premises, owes a duty of care to those workers and/or other persons in relation to the control which it exercises over and the advice which it gives to the subsidiary company.

The first of the writs in these proceedings was issued by Mrs. Lubbe and four other plaintiffs on Feb. 14, 1997 (and when she died the action was continued by Mr. Lubbe as her personal representative). The defendant promptly applied to stay the proceedings on the ground of forum non conveniens. This application came before Mr. Michel Kallipetis, Q.C. sitting as a Deputy Judge of the Queen's Bench Division, who acceded to it. He sought to apply the principles authoritatively laid down by this House in Spiliada Maritime Corporation v. Cansulex Ltd., [1987] 1 Lloyd's Rep. 1; [1987] A.C. 460, and for reasons given in a lengthy and careful judgment dated Jan. 12, 1998 he concluded that everything pointed towards South Africa as the natural forum for the trial of the action and that there was no pressing circumstance which would justify him in deciding that the interests of justice required a trial in this country instead of the natural forum in South Africa.

The plaintiffs appealed and [the Court of Appeal held that the High Court failed to give weight to the fact that the claim of negligence was made against the parent defendant as opposed to the subsidiaries in South Africa, and because the only reason the defendant could be sued in South Africa was because of its agreement to such a condition in a prior court hearing.] Taking those matters into account, the Court of Appeal held that the defendant did not show that South Africa was clearly and distinctly the more appropriate forum....

After the refusal of leave by your Lordships in December, 1998, writs were issued by all the remaining plaintiffs in these proceedings. It is unnecessary to summarize the detailed procedural steps which followed. It is enough to note that the defendant applied to stay all the actions, including the Lubbe action, on grounds of forum non conveniens and abuse of process, and directions were given to consolidate the various proceedings (without prejudice to the position of the Lubbe plaintiffs) into a group action.

The defendant's summons to stay came before Mr. Justice Buckley who heard detailed submissions and considered copious documentary material.... He concluded that South Africa was clearly and distinctly the more appropriate forum for trial of this group action and that there were no sufficient reasons for nevertheless refusing a stay. In reaching this last opinion he considered and discounted a number of objections raised by the plaintiffs, including the alleged unavailability of legal aid in South Africa. Of that submission he said:

> In all the circumstances, I cannot find that legal aid would not be granted, if applied for in South Africa. I readily accept there may be difficulties and some delay but that, at least in part, must flow from the claimants' decision not to apply for legal aid in South Africa and to issue proceedings here, when, as [the plaintiffs' solicitor] well knew, the defendant would contest jurisdiction.

The Judge accordingly ordered a stay of proceedings. He considered an argument advanced by the defendant that the proceedings were an abuse. The basis of this argument was that the solicitors representing the Lubbe plaintiffs had misled the first Court of Appeal and the House of Lords by failing to disclose their intention, if jurisdiction in England was established in the Lubbe case, to launch a multi-plaintiff group action, and also that the bringing of a group action was oppressive and an abuse. The Judge expressed criticism of the solicitors representing the Lubbe plaintiffs but stopped short of finding abuse of the process. The Judge also considered an argument, advanced by the defendant, suggesting that there were public interest grounds for concluding that the proceedings should be tried in South Africa: the Judge reached his decision independently of this argument, but considered that it reinforced his decision. He gave both sides leave to appeal.

Thus the matter came before the Court of Appeal again, and in judgments given on Nov. 29, 1999 ([2000] 1 Lloyd's Rep. 139) the appeals were dismissed. Lord Justice Pill described the factors pointing towards South Africa as the more appropriate forum as "overwhelming." The action had the most real and substantial connection with South Africa and considerations of expense and convenience pointed strongly in that direction. The public interest considerations supported that conclusion. He was not persuaded by the argument that the South African High Court would be unable to handle these actions, and with reference to legal representation he said:

> I have already referred to the high repute in which the South African Courts are held. There is also in South Africa a legal profession with high standards and a tradition of public service, though I do not suggest that lawyers in South Africa, any more than those anywhere else, can be expected to act on a large scale without prospects of remuneration. While I would not be prepared to apply the second stage of the Spiliada test, so as to permit English litigation, even in the absence of

> evidence that legal representation will be available, I am unable to conclude that in the circumstances it would not become available for claims in South African Courts. Moreover, given the accessibility to the wealth of scientific, technical and medical evidence available in this context, I am confident that it could be made available in a South African Court, to the extent required to achieve a proper consideration of the plaintiffs' cases. The action would by no means be novel or speculative.

Lord Justice Pill was not prepared to strike out the proceedings as an abuse of process. He recorded that the plaintiffs had not pursued their contention that art. 2 of the Brussels Convention deprived the English Court of any discretion to stay an action brought against a defendant domiciled here, since they did not wish the proceedings to be delayed while a reference was made to the European Court of Justice. He considered that the bringing of the multi-plaintiff group action entitled the Court of Appeal to reconsider the decision of the first Court of Appeal in the Lubbe action and to reach a different conclusion. He dismissed the appeal....

The applicable principles

Where a plaintiff sues a defendant as of right in the English Court and the defendant applies to stay the proceedings on grounds of forum non conveniens, the principles to be applied by the English Court in deciding that application in any case not governed by art. 2 of the Brussels Convention are not in doubt. They derive from the judgment of Lord Kinnear in Sim v. Robinow, (1892) 19 R. 665 at p. 668 where he said:

> ...the plea can never be sustained unless the court is satisfied that there is some other tribunal having competent jurisdiction, in which the case may be tried more suitably for the interests of all the parties and for the ends of justice.

Thus it is the interest of all the parties, not those of the plaintiff only or the defendant only, and the ends of justice as judged by the Court on all the facts of the case before it, which must control the decision of the Court. In Spiliada it was stated (at p. 10; p. 476):

> ...The basic principle is that a stay will only be granted on the ground of forum non conveniens where the Court is satisfied that there is some other available forum, having competent jurisdiction, which is the appropriate forum for the trial of the action, i.e. in which the case may be tried more suitably for the interests of all the parties and the ends of justice.

In applying this principle the Court's first task is to consider whether the defendant who seeks a stay is able to discharge the burden resting upon him now just to show that England is not the natural or appropriate forum for the trial but to establish that there is another available forum which is clearly or distinctly more appropriate than the English forum. In this way, proper regard is had to the fact that jurisdiction has been founded in England as of right. At this first stage of the inquiry the Court will consider what factors there are which point in the direction of another forum. If the Court concludes at that stage that there is no other available forum which is clearly more appropriate for the trial of the action, that is likely to be the end of the matter. But if the Court concludes at that stage that there is some other available forum which prima facie is more appropriate for the trial of the action it will ordinarily grant a stay unless the plaintiff can show that there are circumstances by reason of which justice requires that a stay should nevertheless not be granted. In this second stage the Court will concentrate its attention not only on factors connecting the proceedings with the foreign or the English forum but on whether the plaintiff will obtain justice in the foreign jurisdiction. The plaintiff will not ordinarily discharge the burden lying upon him by showing that he will enjoy procedural advantages, or a higher scale of damages or more generous rules of limitation if he sues in England; generally speaking, the plaintiff must take a foreign forum as he finds it, even if it is in some respects less advantageous to him than the English forum. It is only if the plaintiff can establish that substantial justice will not be done in the appropriate forum that a stay will be refused.

This is not an easy condition for a plaintiff to satisfy, and it is not necessarily enough to show that legal aid is available in this country but not in the more appropriate foreign forum. Lord Goff of Chieveley said in Connelly v. R.T.Z. Corporation Plc, [1998] A.C. 854 at 873:

> I therefore start from the position that, at least as a general rule, the court will not refuse to grant a stay simply because the plaintiff has shown that no financial assistance, for example in the form of legal aid, will be available to him in the appropriate forum, whereas such financial assistance will be available to him in England. Many smaller jurisdictions cannot afford a system of legal aid. Suppose that the plaintiff has been injured in a motor accident in such a country, and succeeds in establishing English jurisdiction on the defendant by service on him in this country where the plaintiff is eligible for legal aid, I cannot think that the absence of legal aid in the appropriate jurisdiction would in itself justify the refusal of a stay on the ground of forum non conveniens. In this connection it should not be forgotten that financial assistance for litigation is not necessarily regarded as essential, even in sophisticated legal systems. It was not widely available in this country until 1949; and even since that date it has been only available for persons with limited means. People above that limit may well lack the means to litigate, which provides one reason for the recent legalisation of conditional fee agreements.

Even so, the availability of financial assistance in this country, coupled with its non-availability in the appropriate forum, may exceptionally be a relevant factor in this context. The question, however, remains whether the plaintiff can establish that substantial justice will not in the particular circumstances of the case be done if the plaintiff has to proceed in the appropriate forum where no financial assistance is available.

In Connelly a majority of the House held that the case before it was such an exceptional case. The nature and complexity of the case were such that it could not be tried at all without the benefit of legal representation and expert scientific assistance, available in this country but not in the more appropriate forum, Namibia. That being so, the majority of the House concluded that the Namibian forum was not one in which the case could be tried more suitably for the interests of all the parties and for the ends of justice.

The present cases

The issues in the present cases fall into two segments. The first segment concerns the responsibility of the defendant as a parent company for ensuring the observance of proper standards of health and safety by its overseas subsidiaries. Resolution of this issue will be likely to involve an inquiry into what part the defendant played in controlling the operations of the group, what its directors and employees knew or ought to have known, what action was taken and not taken, whether the defendant owed a duty of care to employees of group companies overseas and whether, if so, that duty was broken. Much of the evidence material to this inquiry would, in the ordinary way, be documentary and much of it would be found in the offices of the parent company, including minutes of meetings, reports by directors and employees on visits overseas and correspondence.

The second segment of the cases involves the personal injury issues relevant to each individual: diagnosis, prognosis, causation (including the contribution made to a plaintiff's condition by any sources of contamination for which the defendant was not responsible) and special damage. Investigation of these issues would necessarily involve the evidence and medical examination of each plaintiff and an inquiry into the conditions in which that plaintiff worked or lived and the period for which he did so. Where the claim is made on behalf of a deceased person, the inquiry would be essentially the same, although probably more difficult.

In his review of the Lubbe case, which was alone before him, Mr. Kallipetis considered that the convenience of trying the personal injury issues in South Africa outweighed any benefit there might be in trying the parent company responsibility issue here. That was in my opinion a tenable though not an inevitable conclusion on the case as then presented. The two reasons given by the first Court of Appeal for disturbing that exercise of judgment are not to my mind convincing. Mr. Kallipetis' judgment does not suggest that he overlooked the way in which the plaintiffs put their case, although he did not express it very clearly (perhaps because the pleading was not very clear). The first Court of Appeal thought it undermined the defendant's application for a stay that the South African forum only became available as a result of the defendant's undertaking to submit, but for reasons given by my noble and learned friend Lord Hope of Craighead (with which I fully agree) this was not a factor which should have weighed in the balance either way. I would not accept the argument advanced by the plaintiffs on this point. I question whether the first Court of Appeal was justified in disturbing Mr. Kallipetis' conclusion and substituting its own. But its own assessment of the balance between the parent company responsibility issue and the personal injury issues is not shown to be unreasonable or wrong. On the case as then presented there was room for the view that South Africa was not shown to be a clearly more appropriate forum. This is a field in which differing conclusions can be reached by different tribunals without either being susceptible to legal challenge. The jurisdiction to stay is liable to be perverted if parties litigate the issue at different levels of the judicial hierarchy in the hope of persuading a higher Court to strike a different balance in the factors pointing for and against a foreign forum.

The emergence of over 3000 new plaintiffs following the decision of the first Court of Appeal had an obvious and significant effect on the balance of the proceedings. While the parent company responsibility issue remained very much what it had always been, the personal injury issues assumed very much greater significance. To investigate, prepare and resolve these issues, in relation to each of the plaintiffs, would plainly involve a careful, detailed and cumbersome factual inquiry and, at least potentially, a very large body of expert evidence. In this changed situation Mr. Justice Buckley, applying the first stage of the Spiliada test, regarded South Africa as clearly the more appropriate forum for trial of the group action and the second Court of Appeal agreed. Both Courts were in my view plainly correct. The enhanced significance of the personal injury issues tipped the balance very clearly in favour of South Africa at the first stage of the Spiliada exercise, and no effective criticism has been made of that conclusion. The brunt of the plaintiffs' argument on these appeals to the House has been directed not against the decisions of Mr. Justice Buckley and the second Court of Appeal on the first stage of the Spiliada test but against their conclusion that the plaintiffs had not shown that substantial justice would not be done in the more appropriate South African forum.

Funding

The plaintiffs submitted that legal aid in South Africa had been withdrawn for personal injury claims, that there was no reasonable likelihood of any lawyer or group of lawyers being able or willing to fund proceedings of this weight and complexity under the contingency fee arrangements permitted in South Africa since April, 1999 and that there was no other available source of funding open to the plaintiffs. These were, they argued, proceedings which could not be effectively prosecuted without legal representation and adequate funding. To stay proceedings in England, where legal representation and adequate funding are available, in favour of the South African forum where they are not would accordingly deny the plaintiffs any realistic prospect of pursuing their claims to trial.

The defendant roundly challenged these assertions. Reliance was placed on the facts that the plaintiffs had not applied for legal aid in South Africa before its withdrawal and had made no determined effort to obtain funding in South Africa. Even if legal aid was no longer available in South Africa, contingency fee agreements were now permissible and it was unrealistic to suppose that South African Counsel and attorneys would be any less ready to act than English Counsel and solicitors if the claims were judged to have a reasonable prospect of success. If contingency fee arrangements could not be made in South Africa because South African Counsel and attorneys did not judge the claims to have a reasonable prospect of success, that did not involve a denial of justice to the plaintiffs. In any event there were other potential sources of assistance available to the plaintiffs in South Africa.

The material placed before the House (and the lower Courts) relevant to these issues is very extensive and cannot conveniently be summarized. The following conclusions are in my opinion to be drawn from it:

(1) The proceedings as now constituted can only be handled efficiently, cost-effectively and expeditiously on a group basis. It is impossible at this stage to predict with accuracy what procedural directions might on that basis be given in future (although the directions could only relate to the conduct of proceedings in England). Obvious possibilities include the trial of a preliminary issue on the parent company responsibility question and the trial of selected lead cases to test the outcome in different factual situations. It would be very highly desirable, if possible, to avoid determination of these claims on a plaintiff by plaintiff basis.

(2) The plaintiffs' claims raise a serious legal issue concerning the duty of the defendant as a parent company, and it would be necessary to decide whether that duty was governed by English or South African law. If a duty were held to exist, there would be a serious factual issue whether the defendant was in breach of it. If the plaintiffs were successful on these questions, the personal injury issues would have, even in the context of a group action, to be investigated, prepared and quantified. This would be a heavy and difficult task. It could only be done by, or under the supervision of, professional lawyers. It would call for high quality expert advice and evidence, certainly on medical and industrial issues, very possibly on other issues also. I see no reason to question the judgment of a South African attorney instructed by the defendant who swore:

> The magnitude and complexity of both the factual and legal issues will require the application in South Africa of considerable financial resources and manpower, if there is to be any reasonable prospect of addressing the plaintiffs' allegations meaningfully.

It is significant that Professor Unterhalter, an independent expert approached by the defendant, observed:

> Detailed expert evidence would be required on a number of aspects of the matter. Without agreement between the parties as to how the issues might be limited. I would venture no opinion as to the length and magnitude of this litigation, save to say that it is likely to be drawn out and complex, and would almost certainly come before the Supreme Court of Appeal in due course.

(3) A possibility must exist that the proceedings may culminate in settlement. The plaintiffs confidently predict such an outcome if they succeed on the parent company responsibility issue. But the defendant has given no indication that the claims will not be fully contested. In the Spiliada case Mr. Justice Staughton thought

it right to decide the stay application on the assumption that there would be a trial, and it would seem to me wrong in principle to reject a submission that justice will not be done in a foreign forum on the basis of a speculative assumption that, if a stay is granted, proceedings in the foreign forum will culminate in a just settlement without the need for a trial.

(4) In a letter dated Sept. 20, 1999 to Leigh, Day and Co. representing some of the plaintiffs, the Legal Aid Board of South Africa wrote:

> It will however be of interest to you to note that on 13 September 1999 the Legal Aid Board resolved, because of the financial crisis faced by it, as per the attached letter to the Minister of Justice, to exclude from the operation of the legal aid scheme operated by the South African Legal Aid Board with effect from 1 November 1999 funding in respect of personal injury claims and all other claims sounding in money.

Other material before the House makes plain that before this decision the Legal Aid Board had experienced a period of extreme financial stringency. Despite suggestions to the contrary there is no convincing evidence to suggest that legal aid might be made available in South Africa to fund this potentially protracted and expensive litigation. Written submissions on behalf of the Republic of South Africa contain no hint that public funds might, exceptionally, be made available to fund it.

(5) The South African Contingency Fees Act (No. 66 of 1997) sanctioned a new regime similar (although not identical) to that governing conditional fees in this country. It enables Counsel and attorneys to undertake work for plaintiffs on the basis that if the claim is successful they will receive a fee in excess of that ordinarily chargeable, and that they receive nothing if the claim fails. This regime does not apply to the fees of expert witnesses, who may not be engaged on the basis that they are paid only if the plaintiff by whom they are called is successful. The defendant referred to an affidavit sworn by very experienced South African Counsel who deposed:

> In my view, if a firm of attorneys with a reasonable infrastructure is of the view that the claims of the present Plaintiffs are good, this would mean that the firm would be able to earn very substantial sums of money by way of fees. At the same time, one should not lose sight of the fact that this case is likely to have a very high profile and that the Plaintiffs' attorney/s would be accorded a great deal of positive publicity in the media. This would be a further inducement to take on a case of this nature. There is every reason to believe that there would be no shortage of firms of attorneys who would be desirous of taking on such a case if they believed that it had good prospects of success.

Accordingly, if there are attorneys in South Africa who are as positive about the prospects of success as [the plaintiffs' solicitor] is (as conveyed in his affidavit), I feel sure that there will be no lack of attorneys in South Africa prepared to represent these plaintiffs under Contingency Fee arrangements.

This very general assertion of belief by a member of the Bar was flatly contradicted by a number of other equally distinguished Counsel who provided sworn statements to the plaintiffs, and Counsel for the defendant indicated that he placed no reliance on it. More significantly, it received no support from any practising attorney, and it would be attorneys who would be required, if these proceedings were undertaken for the plaintiffs on a contingency fee basis, to finance the investigation of the claims, the obtaining and calling of evidence and the conduct of the trial during a period which would inevitably last for months and, very much more probably, years. The clear, strong and unchallenged view of the attorneys who provided statements to the plaintiffs was that no firm of South African attorneys with expertise in this field had the means or would undertake the risk of conducting these proceedings on a contingency fee basis. The defendant suggested that financial support and professional assistance might be given to the plaintiffs by the Legal Resources Centre, but this suggestion was authoritatively contradicted. In a recent affidavit the possibility was raised that assistance might be forthcoming from the European Union Foundation for Human Rights in South Africa, but the evidence did not support the possibility of assistance on the scale necessary to fund this litigation.

(6) If these proceedings were stayed in favour of the more appropriate forum in South Africa the probability is that the plaintiffs would have no means of obtaining the professional representation and the expert evidence which would be essential if these claims were to be justly decided. This would amount to a denial of justice. In the special and unusual circumstances of these proceedings, lack of the means, in South Africa, to prosecute these claims to a conclusion provides a compelling ground, at the second stage of the Spiliada test, for refusing to stay the proceedings here.

(7) The conclusions on the funding issue reached by the second Court of Appeal did not in my opinion take account of the evidence, which did not permit the finding which the Court made.

The plaintiffs, as a ground for challenging the appropriateness of the South African forum, relied on the absence of established procedures in South Africa for handling group actions such as the present. They compared that situation with the procedural situation here, where the conduct of group actions is governed by a recently-developed but now tried and established framework of rules, practice directions and subordinate legislation. I do not regard this objection, standing alone, as compelling. It involves the kind of procedural comparison which the English Court should be careful to eschew (Spiliada, p. 14; p. 482: Connelly, p. 872), and the evidence is clear that South African Courts have inherent jurisdiction to adopt procedures appropriate to the cases they are called upon to handle. There is force in the observations of Lord Justice Pill ([2000] 1 Lloyd's Rep. 139 at p. 162):

> I am entirely unpersuaded by arguments that the South African High Court would be unable to handle these actions efficiently either on the ground that there are

> territorial divisions within South Africa or because there is at present no procedure expressly providing for group actions. It is common ground that the law potentially to be applied is the same throughout South Africa.

In England, there has been a vast amount of litigation by victims of asbestos dust without resort to group actions. Whether by a form of group action or otherwise, I have no doubt that the High Court of South Africa will be able to devise and adopt suitable procedures for the efficient dispatch of business such as this. None of the evidence or submissions on behalf of the plaintiffs suggests any significant obstacle to that efficient dispatch by the Court of cases before it.

I do, however, think that the absence, as yet, of developed procedures for handling group actions in South Africa reinforces the submissions made by the plaintiffs on the funding issue. It is one thing to embark on and fund a heavy group action where the procedures governing the conduct of the proceedings are known to and understood by experienced Judges and practitioners. It may be quite another where the exercise is novel and untried. There must then be an increased likelihood of interlocutory decisions which are contentious, with the likelihood of appeals and delay. It cannot be assumed that all Judges will respond to this new procedural challenge in the same innovative spirit. The exercise of jurisdiction by the South African High Court through separate territorial divisions, while not a potent obstacle in itself, could contribute to delay, uncertainty and cost. The procedural novelty of these proceedings, if pursued in South Africa, must in my view act as a further disincentive to any person or body considering whether or not to finance the proceedings.

Third parties

Both before Mr. Justice Buckley and the second Court of Appeal it was contended by the defendant and accepted as a factor pointing towards the appropriateness of the South African forum that the defendant, if sued there, could make and enforce claims against third parties who could be shown to have contributed to the plaintiffs' condition, whereas it might be difficult to join such parties and enforce judgments if the actions were pursued here.... The Courts below were in my judgment right to treat the third party consideration as one strengthening the appropriateness of the South African forum, but I am persuaded by the plaintiffs' response that the refusal of a stay will not expose the defendant to a significant risk of prejudice so long as any new claimants are admitted to the group only upon their binding themselves by the undertaking of the present plaintiffs....

Public interest

Both the plaintiffs and the defendant placed reliance on public interest considerations as strengthening their contentions that these proceedings should be tried in the forum for which they respectively contended. I agree with my noble and learned friend Lord Hope of Craighead, for the reasons which he gives, that public interest considerations not related to the private interests of the parties and the ends of justice have no bearing on the decision which the Court has to make. Where a catastrophe has occurred in a particular place, the facts that numerous victims live in that place, that the relevant evidence is to be found there and that site inspections are most conveniently and inexpensively carried out there will provide factors connecting any ensuing litigation with the Court exercising jurisdiction in that place....

Article 2 of the Brussels Convention

The House received and heard erudite argument on the applicability of art. 2 of the Brussels Convention to a case such as the present. The plaintiffs submitted that the Court was precluded by art. 2 from granting a stay. The defendant argued that the jurisdiction of the Court to grant a stay in favour of a forum in a non-Contracting State was unaffected by art. 2. The correctness of the Court of Appeal decision in In re Harrods (Buenos Aires) Ltd., [1992] Ch. 72 was an issue. Both parties argued that the answer for which they respectively contended was clearly correct. If it was not, the plaintiffs invited the House to seek a ruling from the European Court of Justice, a course which the defendant resisted.

For reasons already given, I am unwilling to stay the plaintiffs' proceedings in this country. It is accordingly unnecessary to decide whether the effect of art. 2 is to deprive the English Court of jurisdiction to grant a stay in a case such as this. Had it been necessary to resolve that question, I would have thought it necessary to seek a ruling on the applicability on art. 2 from the European Court of Justice, since I do not consider the answer to that question to be clear.

Conclusion

I would dismiss the defendant's appeal against the decision of the first Court of Appeal. I would allow the plaintiffs' appeal against the decision of the second Court of Appeal and remove the stay which that Court upheld. The defendant must bear the costs of both appeals, and also the costs of proceedings before Mr. Justice Buckley and the second Court of Appeal.

Lord Hope of Craighead:
My Lords, I have had the advantage of reading in draft the speech of my noble and learned friend Lord Bingham of Cornhill. I agree with it, and for the reasons which he has given I too would allow the claimants' appeals and dismiss the appeal by the defendant....

Public interest

In my opinion the principles on which the doctrine of forum non conveniens rest leave no room for considerations of public interest or public policy which cannot be related to the private interests of any of the parties or the ends of justice in the case which is before the Court.

I would...decline to follow those Judges in the United States who would decide issues as to where a case ought to be tried on broad grounds of public policy: see Union Carbide Corporation Gas Plant Disaster at Bhopal, (1986) 634 F. Supp. 842 and Piper Aircraft Co. v. Reyno, (1981) 454 U.S. 235. I respectfully agree with Deane, J.'s observation in Oceanic Sun Line Special Shipping Co. Inc. v. Fay, [1988] 165 C.L.R. 197 at p. 255 that the Court is not equipped to conduct the kind of inquiry and assessment of the international as well as the domestic implications that would be needed if it were to follow that approach. However tempting it may be to give effect to concerns about the expense and inconvenience to the administration of justice of litigating actions such as these in this country on the one hand or in South Africa on the other, the argument must be resolved upon an examination of their effect upon the interests of the parties who are before the Court and securing the ends of justice in their case. I would hold that considerations of policy which cannot be dealt with in this way should be left out of account in the application to the case of the Spiliada principles.

Comments and Questions

1. What factors should be relevant in determining the adequacy of the alternative forum? Would it be useful to categorize some considerations as relevant and others irrelevant? Useful to whom?

2. Consider the relevance and significance if the alternative forum lacks one or more of these: (i) pretrial discovery; (ii) the right to cross-examine witnesses; (iii) jury trials; (iv) a class action device; (v) legal aid; (vi) contingency fee arrangements; or (vii) appeals.

3. Must the alternative forum have life-tenured judges or, at least, an "independent judiciary"; exactly what must the judge conclude? What if the judiciary is dominated by the political branches of the government? (What are the indicia of such a phenomenon?) A corrupt judiciary is surely an inadequate forum, but exactly what evidence of corruption would support such a finding? (How many judges must be convicted? Investigated? How recently? If there is a demonstrated problem with corruption in one region, are all of the courts in that country suspect?)

4. Should a court look at the ability of plaintiff to pay the filing fees in the alternative forum? In Latin America, for example, litigation can be cost-prohibitive where plaintiffs must post a bond in order to secure the eventual payment of court costs and attorneys fees. See, e.g., Código Proceal Civil Cod. Proc. Civ. Art. 33 (Braz.).

5. Should they consider judicial workloads and delays?

6. Lord Bingham's opinion recognizes the impending collision between the intersection of the English doctrine of forum non conveniens and the Brussels Regulation, but he is able to avoid resolving it here. The problem is that the Brussels Regulation makes no provision for the doctrine of forum non conveniens. Accordingly, whether an English judge has discretion to invoke its common

law doctrine depends on whether the case falls inside or outside the scope of the Regulation.

7. The European Court of Justice (ECJ) recently held that in order for the Brussels Regulation to apply there must be some international element to the transaction. And in a case involving an English plaintiff pursuing claims against English and Jamaican defendants (regarding personal injuries that occurred in Jamaica), the ECJ held that the international element need not derive from the involvement of multiple member states. Rather, "[t]he involvement of a Contracting State and a non-Contracting State...would also make the legal relationship at issue international in nature." Accordingly, "the Brussels Convention precludes a court of a Contracting State from declining the jurisdiction conferred on it by...that convention on the ground that a court of a non-Contracting State would be a more appropriate forum for the trial of the action even if the jurisdiction of no other Contracting State is in issue or the proceedings have no connecting factors to any other Contracting State." Owusu v. Jackson (Case No. 281/02), [2005] 2 W.L.R. 942, ECJ. As a practical matter, then, the common law powers of the English courts have been greatly restricted by the European Court of Justice.

C. Civil Law Alternatives

This is a short unit because the civil law countries long ago rejected the notion of forum non conveniens dismissals. Still, invoking a theme that echoes throughout this text, the following materials suggest that, in fact, differences between the common law and civil law countries are often overstated.

Ronald A. Brand & Scott R. Jablonski, Related Doctrines in Civil Law Systems

Forum Non Conveniens: History, Global Practice, and Future Under the Hague Convention on Choice of Court Agreements 121–128 (Oxford 2007)

The concept of forum non conveniens is generally inconsistent with civil law systems in which there is a belief in the predictability of comprehensive procedural codes created by the legislature and the absence of all but minimal discretion in the role of the judge. Thus, it normally is thought in such systems that when an action has been filed and jurisdiction exists, that jurisdiction must be exercised. This is tempered by the jurisdiction-defeating rule of lis alibi pendens, which requires a court to defer to another court first seised of the same case. [See Brussels Regulation art. 27.] The result is a clear choice for a race to the courthouse (first-seised wins the jurisdictional competition), rather than the corresponding race to judgment in common law legal systems that tend to allow parallel litigation combined with the discretion to decline jurisdiction where it is deemed appropriate to do so. A brief review of several examples serves to highlight the more rigid civil law approach to issues of declining jurisdiction, as well as the limited possibilities for exception.

Germany

No express provision of German law allows for a forum non conveniens doctrine, and German law of jurisdiction is distinguished by strict, clearly defined, statutory rules which generally do not give discretion to the judge. Nonetheless, some German courts have declined jurisdiction in cases using reasoning is some ways similar to common law forum non conveniens decisions. In 1961, the Oberlandesgericht Nurnberg declined jurisdiction where a less expensive trial was available in an alternative forum.[6] Similarly, a court in Hamburg required a "sufficient domestic element" as a prerequisite to upholding a choice of court clause selecting that court in a contractual agreement, choosing instead to treat the clause as a mere presumption of the forum's appropriateness.[7] A Frankfurt court even went so far as to refer explicitly to the forum non conveniens doctrine in declining jurisdiction in a non-contentious matter with perpetuatio fori jurisdiction (a child custody matter).[8]

Article 101(1) of the German Federal Constitution, designed to prevent manipulations in determining the judge in a particular case, states that "[n]o one may be removed from the jurisdiction of his lawful judge." Thus, it has been said that "an integration of the forum non conveniens doctrine would only be permissible if the specific legal judge could be determined with sufficient degree of certainty." Some have gone so far as to argue that dismissals based on forum non conveniens would violate the right of a person to have recourse to a court of law (Justizgewährungsanspruch), which is derived from the principle that a state is to be governed by the rule of law (Rechtsstaatsprinzip). This is consistent with a rigid view of jurisdiction favored by many in Germany:

> [T]he majority view favors legal certainty against the individual flexibility offered by the forum non conveniens doctrine. The majority bases its opinion on the patent rigidity of German procedural law, which acknowledges few and exclusive exceptions. The legislature intends to provide little discretion at the jurisdictional level.[12]
>
> Legal certainty requires clear and foreseeable jurisdictional rules. Adopting the doctrine of forum non conveniens into the German system, which rests on

---

[6] Oberlandesgericht Nurnberg, IPRspr. 1960/61 No. 207; 1961 AWD 18.

[7] Landgericht Hamburg, Recht der Internationalen Wirtschaft [RIW], 22 (1976) 228.

[8] Oberlandesgericht Frankfurt, Praxis des Internationalen Privat-und-Verfahrens-Rechts [IPRax], 3 (1983) 294....

[12] Alexander Reus, *Judicial Discretion: A Comparative View of the Doctrine of Forum Non Conveniens in the United States, the United Kingdom, and Germany,* 16 Loy. L.A. Int'l L. & Comp. L.J. 455, 503 (1994).

statutorily standardized jurisdictional interests, would be paramount to breaking that system.[13]

It has been suggested that the procedural requirement of a "legitimate interest to take legal action" (Rechtsschutzbedürfnis) might be an indirect route to a concept of forum non conveniens, if it could be shown that a German judgment would not be enforced abroad and would therefore demonstrate a lack of legitimate interest. But this approach has been generally rejected, and the desire for legal certainly plays such an important role in Germany that courts have upheld and retained jurisdiction even when it is clear that the plaintiff has manipulated the rules of jurisdiction.

Japan

Japan also takes a rather rigid civil law approach to jurisdictional issues. Still, a 1986 case applied the doctrine of "special circumstances" to reach a result very similar to that found in common law forum non conveniens cases. In Sei Mukoda [et al. v. Boeing Co.], the family of a victim of a Taiwanese airline accident in Taiwan sued two U.S. companies (Boeing and United Airlines). The Tokyo District Court held that "if a venue for local territorial competence provided in the Code of Civil Procedure (CCP) is located in Japan, it would accord with the principle of justice and reason to sustain the jurisdiction of the Japanese court, unless we find some special circumstances." The court went on to state, that "[s]uch special circumstances exist where, in light of the concrete facts of the case concerned, sustaining the Japanese court's jurisdiction would result in contradicting the ideas of promoting impartiality between the parties and fair and prompt administration of justice." Finding that it would be difficult to secure a fair trial in Japan, since crucial evidence in Taiwan would not be available due to a lack of diplomatic relations, the court focused on four factors to determine the fairness of continuing the proceedings in Japan:

(1) whether Taiwanese courts should dismiss on account of lack of international jurisdiction;
(2) whether the plaintiffs had enough money to bring an action in Taiwan;
(3) whether a Taiwanese court should not dismiss the claim on account of prescription; and
(4) whether the plaintiffs could enforce the judgment they might obtain in Taiwan.

The court ultimately dismissed the case on the grounds that special circumstances made the assertion of jurisdiction by a Japanese court unreasonable.

In one aspect, the Japanese doctrine of special circumstances and the common law doctrine of forum non conveniens in the United Kingdom, Canada, and

---

[13] Haimo Schack, *Germany*, in Declining Jurisdiction in Private International Law 189, 194 (James J. Fawcett ed., 1995).

Australia look rather similar. The court in Japan considered only private interest factors in the application of its doctrine of special circumstances. These private factors include the "relative ease of access to source of proof, availability of compulsory process for attendance of unwilling witnesses, the cost of obtaining attendance thereof, the enforceability of a judgment, and other relative advantages and obstacles to a fair, proper and prompt trial."

Another aspect of the special circumstances doctrine in Japan sets it apart from the common law doctrine of forum non conveniens: Japanese courts cannot stay a case or dismiss with conditions: "[T]here are only two choices for Japanese courts, either sustain jurisdiction or dismiss the case completely." Finally, it appears that a Japanese court may dismiss a case even where it has not first determined that another more appropriate forum exists.

The Brussels Regulation

Current European continental civil law practice is perhaps best demonstrated by the provisions of the Brussels Regulation,... [which] provides a comprehensive approach to jurisdiction and the recognition and enforcement of judgments. In doing so, it makes no provision for the doctrine of forum non conveniens, thereby operating to prohibit the application of the doctrine within the European Union system. Instead, the Brussels Regulation establishes... a strict rule of lis pendens is Article 27. This lis pendens rule reads as follows:

1. Where proceedings involving the same cause of action and between the same parties are brought in the courts of different Member States, any court other than the court first seised shall of its own motion stay its proceedings until such time as the jurisdiction of the court first seised is established.
2. Where the jurisdiction of the court first seised is established, any court other than the court first seised shall decline jurisdiction in favour of that court.

With this rule, the Brussels system creates a strict race to the courthouse. The first court seised captures jurisdiction, and an action filed in the court of a second Member State must be stayed, and ultimately dismissed, in favor of the first action. The importance of Article 27 was emphasized most recently in the Gasser case,[36] where the court gave precedence to the lis pendens concept over recognition of a purported choice of court agreement between the parties to the action. When an action was first instituted in Italy by one party, and then a second action was begun in Austria under a choice of court agreement by the other party, the European Court of Justice held that [the Brussels Regulation] requires that "a court second seised whose jurisdiction has been claimed under an agreement conferring jurisdiction must nevertheless stay proceedings until the court first seised has declared that it has no jurisdiction," even where "the duration of the proceedings before the courts of the Contracting State in which the court first seised is established

[36] Case C-116/02, *Erich Gasser GmbH v. MISAT Srl.*, [2003] E.C.R. I-14693 (9 Dec. 2003).

is excessively long."[37] Italian courts are notoriously slow in moving cases to conclusion, resulting in the "Italian torpedo" tactic of filing first in Italy to prevent a natural plaintiff from brining a successful action elsewhere. Granting priority to a rule of lis pendens serves to exacerbate this problem by preventing either parallel litigation or the resolution of the case in an expeditious manner in the natural forum.

Comments and Questions

1. Is it unethical to deploy the Italian torpedo tactic? Are you a zealous advocate for your client if you don't?

2. Professor Brand's account of the German and Japanese analogues to forum non conveniens teaches an important lesson about comparative study. Understand that every procedural system is a complex and dynamic amalgam with interconnected rules and doctrines—and worse (or, better, depending on your perspective), even an accurate picture of the procedural system can be distorted by tradition, culture, language, and other forces that may be unknown to the observer.

Concluding Comments and Questions

1. The ECJ (and other systems that reject the doctrine of forum non conveniens) emphasizes the importance of the principle of certainty. Are common law systems that recognize the doctrine of forum non conveniens less committed to the principle of certainty? What principles are advanced by the doctrine of forum non conveniens? Are these principles more compelling than the principle of certainty?
2. Return to the problem that opened this chapter. If the New York court has jurisdiction to hear the case, the defendant has been properly served, and U.S. federal law (reflecting American public policy) provides a substantive cause of action for recovery, why should such a case be dismissed? Are cases involving human rights abuses more or less suitable for forum non conveniens dismissals?

D. Bibliography of Additional Resources

Alexander Reus, Judicial Discretion: A Comparative View of the Doctrine of Forum Non Conveniens in the United States, the United Kingdom, and Germany, 16 LOY. L.A. INT'L & COMP. L.J. 455 (1994)

Barton Legum (ed.), INTERNATIONAL LITIGATION STRATEGIES AND PRACTICE (Am. Bar Ass'n 2005)

4A & 4B Charles Alan Wright & Arthur R. Miller, FEDERAL PRACTICE AND PROCEDURE §§ 1061–1075 (Thomson West 3d ed. 2002)

[37] Id.

Dante Figueroa, Conflicts of Jurisdiction Between the United States and Latin America in the Context of Forum Non Conveniens Dismissal, 37 U. Miami Inter-Am. L. Rev. 119 (2005)

David Epstein, Jeffrey L. Snyder & Chrales S. Baldwin, International Litigation: A Guide to Jurisdiction, Practice, and Strategy (Martinus Nijhoff 3d ed. 1998 & Supp. 2007).

E. E. Daschbach, Where There's a Will, There's a Way: The Cause for a Cure and Remedial Prescriptions for Forum Non Conveniens as Applied in Latin American Plaintiffs' Actions Against U.S. Multinationals, 13 L. & Bus. Rev. Am. 11 (2007)

Elizabeth T. Lear, National Interests, Foreign Injuries, and Federal Forum Non Conveniens, 41 U.C. Davis L. Rev. 559 (2007)

James Wm. Moore, Moore's Federal Practice (Matthew Bender 3d ed. 1997 & Supp. 2007)

Julius Jurianto, Forum Non Conveniens: Another Look at Conditional Dismissals, 83 U. Det. Mercy L. Rev. 369 (2005)

Linda J. Silberman, Developments in Jurisdiction and Forum Non Conveniens in International Litigation: Thoughts on Reform and a Proposal for a Uniform Standard, 28 Tex. Int'l L.J. 501 (1993)

M. Ryan Casey & Barrett Ristroph, Boomerang Litigation: How Convenient is Forum Non Conveniens in Transnational Litigation?, 4 B.Y.U. Int'l L. & Mgmt. Rev. 21 (2007)

Michael M. Karayanni, Forum Non Conveniens in the Modern Age: A Comparative and Methodological Analysis of Anglo-American Law (Transnational 2004)

Richard H. Kreindler & Judith L. Holdsworth (eds.), Transnational Litigation: A Practitioner's Guide (Oceana 1997 & Supp. 2007)

Richard H. Kreindler, Transnational Litigation: A Basic Primer (Oceana 1998)

Ronald A. Brand & Scott R. Jablonski, Forum Non Conveniens: History, Global Practice, and Future Under the Hague Convnetion on Choice of Court Agreements (Oxford 2007)

Stückelberg, Lis Pendens and Forum Non Conveniens at the Hague Conference, 26 Brook. J. Int'l L. 949 (2001)

Tim Taylor & Nigel Cooper, European Litigation Handbook (Sweet & Maxwell 1995)

Ved P. Nanda & David K. Pansius, Litigation of International Disputes in U.S. Courts (Thomson West 2d ed. 2005 & Supp. 2007)

Walter W. Heiser, Forum Non Conveniens and Choice of Law: The Impact of Applying Foreign Law in Transnational Tort Actions, 51 Wayne L. Rev. 1161 (2005)

CHAPTER 5

Forum Selection Clauses

A. Introduction

One of the lawyer's chief responsibilities is to anticipate and, to the extent possible, help the client to avoid problems. A forum selection clause can be an essential element of such planning. A forum selection clause is a provision in a contract providing for disputes to be brought before a specified court, in language such as "all disputes arising out of or related to this agreement shall be resolved in the High Court of Justice in London," or "...in the Superior Court of the County of San Francisco," or the courts of some other country. These clauses can also select an arbitral forum. For example, the parties might agree that "Any controversy or claim arising out of or relating to this contract shall be settled by arbitration administered by the American Arbitration Association."

Forum selection clauses can have two consequences: First, the clause can constitute consent by each party to the contract to be sued at the chosen forum. And, second, the clause can deprive courts that would otherwise have jurisdiction over the parties and the controversy of jurisdiction to hear the case. When a contracting party agrees to a forum selection clause designating either an optional or exclusive site for litigation (or arbitration), the clause may be labeled a prorogation clause if a contracting party then sues in the designated forum. When a contracting party sues in a forum other than that agreed upon by contract, the forum selection clause may be called a derogation clause, that is, one undermining the forum's jurisdiction. These terms can be tricky, so it is important to read for context. Some lawyers use the terms "prorogation" and "derogation" to distinguish between exclusive and nonexclusive clauses; in other words, a nonexclusive clause might establish jurisdiction in State X (prorogation) without necessarily negating jurisdiction elsewhere, while an exclusive clause establishes jurisdiction in State X to the exclusion (derogation) of all others.

The Problem: Have It Your Way

Burger King Corporation is a Florida corporation whose principal offices are in Miami. It is one of the world's largest restaurant organizations, with over 11,100 outlets in 65 countries. Almost 90 percent of its restaurants are owned and operated by independent franchisees through a franchise operation that the company styles the "Burger King System"—"a comprehensive restaurant format and operating system for the sale of uniform and quality food products." Burger King licenses its franchisees to use its trademarks and service marks for a period of twenty years and leases standardized restaurant facilities to them for the same term. In addition, franchisees acquire a variety of proprietary information concerning the "standards, specifications, procedures and methods for operating a Burger King Restaurant." They also receive market research and advertising assistance; ongoing training in restaurant management; and accounting, cost-control, and inventory-control guidance. By permitting franchisees to tap into Burger King's established national reputation and to benefit from proven procedures for dispensing standardized fare, this system enables them to go into the restaurant business with significantly lowered barriers to entry.

In exchange for these benefits, franchisees pay Burger King an initial $50,000 franchise fee and commit themselves to payment of monthly royalties, advertising and sales promotion fees, and rent computed in part from monthly gross sales. Franchisees also agree to submit to the national organization's exacting regulation of virtually every conceivable aspect of their operations.

Rae Pierce, a young but rather sophisticated businesswoman from Las Vegas, filed an application for a franchise with Burger King's southwest regional office in Tempe, Arizona. Her application proposed three possible locations, all on the northern edge of Las Vegas. Her application was was forwarded to Burger King's Miami headquarters; successful negotiations followed, and her restaurant opened on the north side of Las Vegas about three years ago.

The restaurant was very profitable for the first two years of its operation, but is now merely breaking even. Pierce is an entrepreneur who would like to transform the restaurant into something unique—adding menu items featuring local produce, converting some of the parking lot into a grassy picnic space, installing solar panels to conserve energy, and other innovations. Although the franchise agreement is not entirely clear on these points, Burger King has resisted all of the proposed changes because they might undermine the uniformity of their brand.

Pierce has hired the firm where you are employed, a large regional law firm with offices in Las Vegas, Nevada; Tucson, Arizona; Los Angeles, California; and San Diego, California. Assume that another associate's careful review of the franchise agreement and applicable law (which is that of Florida) suggests that you have a fairly strong argument with regard to most of your client's proposed changes. The partner in charge of this case is considering two possible courses of action: (1) seek a declaratory judgment which could clarify the rights and obligations of the parties under the franchise agreement; or (2) advise our client to proceed with the changes, and prepare to deal with the lawsuit if and when Burger King files it.

The franchise agreement likely contains a forum selection clause. Consider how each of the following possible clauses would affect your strategy and could affect the outcome of the case.

(1) "All disputes arising out of or in connection with this agreement and the relationship created hereby shall be litigated only in the courts of Miami, Florida."

(2) "Any controversy or claim arising out of or relating to this contract, or the breach thereof, must be litigated in the courts of the State of Rhode Island."

(3) "It is agreed by and between the parties that all disputes and matters whatsoever arising under, in connection with or incident to the agreement shall be litigated in and before the High Court of Justice in London England, to the exclusion of the courts of any other state or country."

(4) "Any controversy or claim arising out or relating to this contract shall be determined exclusively by an arbitral proceeding before the Florida Arbitration Association in Miami, Florida."

(5) "The parties hereby consent to submit to the Centre for Effective Dispute Resolution in the United Kingdom any disputes relating to or arising out of this Agreement for settlement by arbitration."

(6) "Any dispute in connection with this agreement shall be finally settled by arbitration in accordance with the American Aribration Association, but without prejudice to any of the parties' procedural rights under the Federal Rules of Civil Procedure."

B. Choice of Court Agreements

Forum selection can be a significant, even dispositive factor in determining the outcome of the case. The procedural law of the forum will be applied—thereby determining the availability vel non of juries, discovery, experts, pretrial motions, appeals, and the like. The forum will apply its own rules to determine the applicable substantive law; that substantive law, in turn, will define, among other parameters, the available causes of action, elements, and defenses. And, of course, each forum has its own character, culture, language, traditions, and accessibility that may make it more or less favorable for your client. Put bluntly, the consequences are enormous. One question, then, for any legal system is the extent to which the court should respect the parties' autonomous decision to resolve this issue by including a forum selection or choice of court clause in the terms of their agreement. We begin with two countries representative of the common law system.

1. Common Law Perspective

In the following case, two companies on opposite sides of the Atlantic Ocean entered into an agreement. One of the parties, Zapata, is an oil conglomerate in Houston, Texas. Zapata had an oil-drilling rig (the Chaparral) in the Gulf of Mexico that they wanted moved to the Adriatic Sea. Unterweser Reederei Gmbh, a German a towing and tugboat service company, agreed to perform the task. The contract for towage included a forum selection clause providing for adjudication in London.

A few days into the voyage, while still in the Gulf of Mexico, a severe storm damaged the rig. Zapata instructed Unterweser to tow the rig to Tampa, Florida, for inspection and repair. Zapata blamed Unterweser for much of the damage and filed a lawsuit in Florida seeking compensation. While that case was pending, Unterweser initiated an action in the English courts, pursuant to the forum-selection clause. Opinions from both countries follow.

Unterweser Reederei G.m.b.H. v. Zapata Offshore Company

U.K. Court of Appeal.

[1968] 2 Lloyd's L.Rep. 158

Lord Justice Willmer:

This is an application for leave to appeal from an order made by Mr. Justice Karminski on July 4, 1968, whereby he dismissed the defendants' application to set aside an order of the learned Registrar giving leave to serve a writ out of the jurisdiction. In order to deal with the application, it has been necessary to go into all the circumstances of the case, and in substance to hear the appeal. The question at issue between the parties arises out of a marine casualty which took place in January, 1968. The plaintiffs are well-known towage contractors and owners of a tug called the Bremen. The defendants are a company incorporated in the United States of America who carry on business inter alia in the operation of oil rigs.

In November, 1967, the plaintiffs and the defendants entered into a contract in writing for the towage of an oil rig called the Chaparral belonging to the defendants from a place called Venice in Louisiana to Ravenna in Italy by the tug Bremen. We have been referred to a number of the clauses in the contract, only one of which need be mentioned now. The concluding provision of the contract was:

> Any dispute arising must be treated before the London Court of Justice.

The towage from Venice began on Jan. 4, 1968. By Jan. 9, when the tow was still within the Gulf of Mexico, disaster overtook it, and it was necessary to take refuge in the port of Tampa in Florida. Each party blamed the other for the disaster which occurred, and each has asserted a claim for damages. The plaintiff tug-owners say that the defendants were at fault in that the oil rig being towed was not in a seaworthy condition. The defendants on their part say that the tug was not seaworthy to undertake the voyage, and also that it was negligently operated. There are all the elements present for an interesting battle to ascertain whose fault it was. The defendants got their blow in first, because immediately upon arrival of the tug and tow at Tampa they instituted proceedings in Admiralty in the United States District Court at Tampa, and in the course of those proceedings the tug was arrested. The release of the tug was eventually obtained upon security being furnished satisfactory to the defendants in the sum of U.S. $3,500,000.

On Feb. 21, 1968, the plaintiffs issued the writ in the present action and sought leave to serve that writ out of the jurisdiction on the American owners of the oil rig. Leave to serve the writ out of the jurisdiction was obtained from the learned Registrar, and it was that matter which came before the learned Judge. The grounds upon which the plaintiffs sought leave to serve the writ out of the jurisdiction were, first, that the contract was one which "by its terms, or by implication, was governed by English law", and secondly, that the contract contained an express term to the effect that the High Court should have jurisdiction.

In the meantime, however, the present plaintiffs had taken steps to defend themselves in the proceedings which were being carried on in Tampa. Those proceedings involved taking depositions from a number of witnesses, and in that operation both the present plaintiffs and the present defendants took part. Depositions appear to have been taken from a considerable number of witnesses. But from an early date the plaintiffs took exception to the jurisdiction of the Court at Tampa, and instituted proceedings to set aside or stay the American action. Those proceedings came before the United States District Court in Tampa on Apr. 29, 1968, when judgment was reserved. Up to date, so far as we have been informed, no judgment has yet been delivered, and it is not, therefore, known whether the action instituted by the defendants in America will be set aside or stayed. At present, however, assuming that leave to serve this writ out of the jurisdiction stands, there is a situation when proceedings are on foot in both countries. The position is further complicated by the fact that, just before the matter came before Mr. Justice Karminski at the beginning of this month, the plaintiffs launched proceedings for exoneration or limitation of their liability in the United States of America.* It is to be pointed out that that is a course which they had to take, if the American proceedings were allowed to continue, within six months of the institution of those proceedings. Time was running out against them, and they were, therefore, forced to institute those proceedings at the beginning of this month in order to preserve their rights.

The learned Judge knew of the institution of those proceedings but he did not actually know (although I have no doubt that he had good reason to suspect) that, immediately following the institution of those proceedings, an order would be made by the American Court which, among other things, enjoined the defendants against prosecuting any claim of theirs against the plaintiffs pending the determination of the plaintiffs' limitation proceedings. That, it has been said, would effectively prevent the defendants, if they were so minded, from putting forward a counterclaim in any proceedings in this country. That is a matter much relied upon by the defendants as showing that, as a matter of convenience, and in order to avoid duplication of proceedings, leave ought not to be granted to serve this writ out of the jurisdiction.

* [Eds.' Note: The Limitation of Liability Act was enacted in the mid-1800s to encourage shipbuilding and ownership. Absent any proof of personal fault on the part of the owner of the vessel, the owner's liability was capped at the value of the vessel. To take advantage of this provision, however, an action must be initiated within six months.]

Reliance is also placed upon the fact that, under American procedure, it appears that a party sued as a defendant there (as are the present plaintiffs) who has a counterclaim against the plaintiff in that country, is compelled to assert that counterclaim within a certain limit of time, or he will be for all time barred. That is another reason why it is suggested on behalf of the defendants that, as a matter of convenience, proceedings ought not to be allowed to continue in this country, since it is said that it will be necessary for the present plaintiffs to assert their claim by way of counterclaim in the United States.

The law on the subject, I think, is not open to doubt, and I do not think that it is really necessary to cite the authorities to which we have been referred. It is always open to parties to stipulate (as they did in this case) that a particular Court shall have jurisdiction over any dispute arising out of their contract. Here the parties chose to stipulate that disputes were to be referred to the "London Court", which I take as meaning the High Court in this country. Prima facie it is the policy of the Court to hold parties to the bargain into which they have entered. Prima facie it is to be presumed, therefore, that the plaintiffs should have leave to prosecute their proceedings in this country, and in pursuance of that to serve their writ out of the jurisdiction. But that is not an inflexible rule, as was shown, for instance, by the case of The Fehmarn, [1957] 1 Lloyd's Rep. 511; (C.a.) [1957] 2 Lloyd's Rep. 551, in which I was myself concerned, and which came to this Court. That was a case in which the Court in its discretion declined to give effect to a stipulation made by the parties in their contract conferring jurisdiction on a foreign Court.

I approach the matter, therefore, in this way, that the Court has a discretion, but it is a discretion which, in the ordinary way and in the absence of strong reason to the contrary, will be exercised in favour of holding parties to their bargain. The question is whether sufficient circumstances have been shown to exist in this case to make it desirable, on the grounds of balance of convenience, that proceedings should not take place in this country, the stipulated forum, but that the parties should be left to fight out their battles in the United States of America.

The learned Judge in his discretion came to the conclusion that it was proper to grant leave to serve the writ out of the jurisdiction so that the action might proceed in this country. We in this Court should not interfere with the Judge's exercise of his discretion unless it is shown that he acted on some wrong principle, or misapprehended the facts, or unless it is shown that his exercise of his discretion was plainly wrong.

It is said that the situation has to some extent altered since the time when the learned Judge had the matter before him, by reason particularly of the plaintiffs' institution of exoneration and limitation proceedings in the United States to which I have referred. That is the only new factor which has arisen since the time when the learned Judge delivered his judgment.

I am unable to see that the Judge acted on any wrong principle. I do not think that the new facts said to have been brought to light really alter the complexion of the case to any material extent, nor am I prepared to say that the learned Judge's exercise of his discretion is shown to have been plainly wrong.

I should record the fact that in an affidavit put in on behalf of the plaintiffs today, the offer is made (and Mr. Lloyd on behalf of the plaintiffs has renewed it in the course of the argument) to waive the provisions of the restraining order which has been obtained by the plaintiffs in the United States so as to relieve the defendants of any difficulty which they might otherwise have in putting forward a counterclaim in this country if they want to. I should also record the fact that an offer has been made on behalf of the plaintiffs (which still holds good) to hold the security which has been furnished in America as available to cover any counterclaim which may be brought in this country. I refer to those two circumstances because I think that they are in their turn relevant to the question whether it is right to allow these plaintiffs to pursue their action in this country in accordance with their contractual bargain. I think that it is, and that the learned Judge reached the right conclusion.

In the circumstances I think that the appropriate order for us to make is that the defendants be granted leave to appeal, but that the appeal be dismissed.

Lord Justice Diplock:
I agree, and add very little.

It has long been recognized that the jurisdiction of the High Court to give leave for service of a writ, or notice of a writ, out of the jurisdiction under Order 11, r. 1, is one which should be exercised with caution, because there are circumstances set out in that rule in which service outside the jurisdiction is authorized which are in conflict with the ordinary rules of comity, that is to say, the Courts in this country assert a jurisdiction in themselves wider than that which they recognize in the Courts of other countries. That need for caution has been frequently expressed. It was expressed by Lord Justice Farwell 50 years ago in The Hagen, [1908] P. 189, at p. 201, and has been re-asserted fairly recently by this Court in 1967 in Mackender and Others v. Feldia A.G. and Others, [1967] 2 Q.B. 590; [1966] 2 Lloyd's Rep. 449.

Those observations should be read in relation to an application for service out of the jurisdiction under r. 1. Rule 2, which is a separate rule and applies to this case, authorizes service out of the jurisdiction where the contract contains a term to the effect that the High Court has jurisdiction to hear and determine any action in respect to the contract. This does not raise any question of conflict with ordinary comity because, so far as I know, it is the policy of the Courts of most countries, if it be reasonable at any rate to do so, to see that parties keep their word; and having had the privilege of reading a memorandum brief which has been accepted in the Federal District Court at Tampa on behalf of the plaintiffs in this action, it looks to me as if there is some ground at any rate for saying that the Federal Courts and State Courts in the United States take the same view.

When it comes to a case under Order 11, r. 2, as distinct from a case under Order 11, r. 1, I say again in this case, as I said in Mackender (sup., at pp. 604 and 459 of the respective reports):

> ...Where parties have agreed to submit all their disputes under a contract to the exclusive jurisdiction of a foreign court, I myself should require very strong reasons to induce me to permit one of them to go back on his word....

We should, I think, apply the same principle whether the forum of contractual choice is England or of some other country. The question arises more frequently before us where the forum of contractual choice is some other country, as in Mackender's Case, sup., where the choice was Belgium. In the present case the choice of the parties was the English Court, and as I say I should myself require strong grounds for saying that one of the parties should not keep his word.

There is, of course, undoubtedly a discretion on the part of the Court in this case to refuse to allow service of the writ outside the jurisdiction, despite the contractual term in the contract. The learned Judge from whom this appeal is brought recognized that he had a discretion. So far as I can see he applied his mind to all the relevant matters; and, even if I myself might have come to some other conclusion, I do not think that any ground has been put forward which would justify the Court in interfering with his discretion. Having said that, let me say, as must have been apparent during the course of this hearing, I agree entirely with his decision. I should have done the same myself.

Lord Justice Widgery:
I agree with both judgments. The parties here have quite deliberately chosen that their dispute shall be decided in the Courts of this country, and it would need strong grounds in my view to deprive either party who sought to take advantage of that course from receiving the advantage which he expects from it. I also would put my decision on the footing that there is no reason here to suppose that the learned Judge exercised his discretion improperly. But, like my Lord, I feel that had I had to decide the matter myself, I should have reached precisely the same conclusion. I also would dismiss this appeal.

The Bremen et al. v. Zapata Off-Shore Company

407 U.S. 1 (1972)

Chief Justice Burger delivered the opinion of the Court:
We granted certiorari to review a judgment of the United States Court of Appeals for the Fifth Circuit declining to enforce a forum-selection clause governing disputes arising under an international towage contract between petitioners and respondent. The circuits have differed in their approach to such clauses. For the reasons stated hereafter, we vacate the judgment of the Court of Appeals.

In November 1967, respondent Zapata, a Houston-based American corporation, contracted with petitioner Unterweser, a German corporation, to tow Zapata's ocean-going, self-elevating drilling rig Chaparral from Louisiana to a point off Ravenna, Italy, in the Adriatic Sea, where Zapata had agreed to drill certain wells.

Zapata had solicited bids for the towage, and several companies including Unterweser had responded. Unterweser was the low bidder and Zapata requested it to submit a contract, which it did. The contract submitted by Unterweser contained the following provision, which is at issue in this case:

Any dispute arising must be treated before the London Court of Justice.

In addition the contract contained two clauses purporting to exculpate Unterweser from liability for damages to the towed barge.[2]

After reviewing the contract and making several changes, but without any alteration in the forum-selection or exculpatory clauses, a Zapata vice president executed the contract and forwarded it to Unterweser in Germany, where Unterweser accepted the changes, and the contract became effective.

On January 5, 1968, Unterweser's deep sea tug Bremen departed Venice, Louisiana, with the Chaparral in tow bound for Italy. On January 9, while the flotilla was in international waters in the middle of the Gulf of Mexico, a severe storm arose. The sharp roll of the Chaparral in Gulf waters caused its elevator legs, which had been raised for the voyage, to break off and fall into the sea, seriously damaging the Chaparral. In this emergency situation Zapata instructed the Bremen to tow its damaged rig to Tampa, Florida, the nearest port of refuge.

On January 12, Zapata, ignoring its contract promise to litigate "any dispute arising" in the English courts, commenced a suit in admiralty in the United States District Court at Tampa, seeking $3,500,000 damages against Unterweser in personam and the Bremen in rem, alleging negligent towage and breach of contract.[3] Unterweser responded by invoking the forum clause of the towage contract, and moved to dismiss for lack of jurisdiction or on forum non conveniens grounds, or in the alternative to stay the action pending submission of the dispute to the "London Court of Justice." Shortly thereafter, in February, before the District Court had ruled on its motion to stay or dismiss the United States action, Unterweser commenced an action against Zapata seeking damages for breach of the towage contract in the High Court of Justice in London, as the contract provided. Zapata appeared in that court to contest jurisdiction, but its challenge was rejected, the English courts holding that the contractual forum provision conferred jurisdiction.[4]

---

[2] The General Towage Conditions of the contract included the following:

"1.... (Unterweser and its) masters and crews are not responsible for defaults and/or errors in the navigation of the tow.

"2....

"b) Damages suffered by the towed object are in any case for account of its Owners."

In addition, the contract provided that any insurance of the Chaparral was to be "for account of" Zapata. Unterweser's initial telegraphic bid had also offered to "arrange insurance covering towage risk for rig if desired." As Zapata had chosen to be self-insured on all its rigs, the loss in this case was not compensated by insurance.

[3] The Bremen was arrested by a United States marshal acting pursuant to Zapata's complaint immediately upon her arrival in Tampa. The tug was subsequently released when Unterweser furnished security in the amount of $3,500,000.

[4] Zapata appeared specially and moved to set aside service of process outside the country. Justice Karminski of the High Court of Justice denied the motion on the ground the contractual choice-of-forum provision conferred jurisdiction and would be enforced, absent a factual showing it would not be "fair and right" to do so. He did not believe Zapata had made such a showing, and held that it should be required to "stick to (its) bargain." App. 206, 211, 213. The Court of Appeal dismissed an appeal on the ground that Justice Karminski had properly applied the English rule. [The Court quotes from Lord Justice Willmer's opinion.]

In the meantime, Unterweser was faced with a dilemma in the pending action in the United States court at Tampa. The six-month period for filing action to limit its liability to Zapata and other potential claimants was about to expire,[5] but the United States District Court in Tampa had not yet ruled on Unterweser's motion to dismiss or stay Zapata's action. On July 2, 1968, confronted with difficult alternatives, Unterweser filed an action to limit its liability in the District Court in Tampa. That court entered the customary injunction against proceedings outside the limitation court, and Zapata refiled its initial claim in the limitation action.[6]

It was only at this juncture, on July 29, after the six-month period for filing the limitation action had run, that the District Court denied Unterweser's January motion to dismiss or stay Zapata's initial action. In denying the motion, that court relied on the prior decision of the Court of Appeals in Carbon Black Export, Inc. v. The Monrosa, 254 F.2d 297 (5th Cir. 1958), cert. dismissed, 359 U.S. 180 (1959). In that case the Court of Appeals had held a forum-selection clause unenforceable, reiterating the traditional view of many American courts that "agreements in advance of controversy whose object is to oust the jurisdiction of the courts are contrary to public policy and will not be enforced." 254 F.2d, at 300–301.[7] Apparently concluding that it was bound by the Carbon Black case, the District Court gave the forum-selection clause little, if any, weight. Instead, the court treated the motion to dismiss under normal forum non conveniens doctrine applicable in the absence of such a clause, citing Gulf Oil Corp. v. Gilbert, 330 U.S. 501 (1947). Under that doctrine "unless the balance is strongly in favor of the defendant, the plaintiff's choice of forum should rarely be disturbed." Id. at 508. The District Court concluded: "the balance of conveniences here is not strongly in favor of (Unterweser) and (Zapata's) choice of forum should not be disturbed."

Thereafter, on January 21, 1969, the District Court denied another motion by Unterweser to stay the limitation action pending determination of the controversy in the High Court of Justice in London and granted Zapata's motion to restrain Unterweser from litigating further in the London court. The District Judge ruled that, having taken jurisdiction in the limitation proceeding, he had jurisdiction to determine all matters relating to the controversy. He ruled that Unterweser should

---

5 46 U.S.C. §§ 183, 185. *See generally* G. Gilmore & C. Black, Admiralty § 10–15 (1957).

6 In its limitation complaint, Unterweser stated it "reserve[d] all rights" under its previous motion to dismiss or stay Zapata's action, and reasserted that the High Court of Justice was the proper forum for determining the entire controversy, including its own right to limited liability, in accord with the contractual forum clause. Unterweser later counterclaimed, setting forth the same contractual cause of action as in its English action and a further cause of action for salvage arising out of the Bremen's services following the casualty. In its counterclaim, Unterweser again asserted that the High Court of Justice in London was the proper forum for determining all aspects of the controversy, including its counterclaim.

7 The *Carbon Black* court went on to say that it was, in any event, unnecessary for it to reject the more liberal position taken in *Wm. H. Muller & co. v. Swedish American Line Ltd.*, 224 F.2d 806 (2nd Cir.), *cert. denied,* 350 U.S. 903 (1955), because the case before it had a greater nexus with the United States than that in *Muller.*

be required to "do equity" by refraining from also litigating the controversy in the London court, not only for the reasons he had previously stated for denying Unterweser's first motion to stay Zapata's action, but also because Unterweser had invoked the United States court's jurisdiction to obtain the benefit of thc Limitation Act.

On appeal, a divided panel of the Court of Appeals affirmed, and on rehearing en banc the panel opinion was adopted, with six of the 14 en banc judges dissenting. As had the District Court, the majority rested on the Carbon Black decision, concluding that "at the very least" that case stood for the proposition that a forum-selection clause "will not be enforced unless the selected state would provide a more convenient forum than the state in which suit is brought." From that premise the Court of Appeals proceeded to conclude that, apart from the forum-selection clause, the District Court did not abuse its discretion in refusing to decline jurisdiction on the basis of forum non conveniens. It noted that (1) the flotilla never "escaped the Fifth Circuit's mare nostrum, and the casualty occurred in close proximity to the district court"; (2) a considerable number of potential witnesses, including Zapata crewmen, resided in the Gulf Coast area; (3) preparation for the voyage and inspection and repair work had been performed in the Gulf area; (4) the testimony of the Bremen crew was available by way of deposition; (5) England had no interest in or contact with the controversy other than the forum-selection clause. The Court of Appeals majority further noted that Zapata was a United States citizen and "[t]he discretion of the district court to remand the case to a foreign forum was consequently limited"—especially since it appeared likely that the English courts would enforce the exculpatory clauses.[8] In the Court of Appeals' view, enforcement of such clauses would be contrary to public policy in American courts under Bisso v. Inland Waterways Corp., 349 U.S. 85 (1955), and Dixilyn Drilling Corp. v. Crewscent Towing & Salvage Co., 372 U.S. 697 (1963). Therefore, "[t]he district court was entitled to consider that remanding Zapata to a foreign forum, with no practical contact with the controversy, could raise a bar to recovery by a United States citizen which its own convenient courts would not countenance."[9]

We hold, with the six dissenting members of the Court of Appeals, that far too little weight and effect were given to the forum clause in resolving this controversy. For at least two decades we have witnessed an expansion of overseas

---

[8] The record contains an undisputed affidavit of a British solicitor stating an opinion that the exculpatory clauses of the contract would be held "*prima facie* valid and enforceable" against Zapata in any action maintained in England in which Zapata alleged that defaults or errors in Unterweser's tow caused the casualty and damage to the Chaparral. In addition, it is not disputed that while the limitation fund in the District Court in Tampa amounts to $1,390,000, the limitation fund in England would be only slightly in excess of $80,000 under English law.

[9] The Court of Appeals also indicated in passing that even if it took the view that choice-of-forum clauses were enforceable unless "unreasonable" it was "doubtful" that enforcement would be proper here because the exculpatory clauses would deny Zapata relief to which it was "entitled" and because England was "seriously inconvenient" for trial of the action.

commercial activities by business enterprises based in the United States. The barrier of distance that once tended to confine a business concern to a modest territory no longer does so. Here we see an American company with special expertise contracting with a foreign company to tow a complex machine thousands of miles across seas and oceans. The expansion of American business and industry will hardly be encouraged if, notwithstanding solemn contracts, we insist on a parochial concept that all disputes must be resolved under our laws and in our courts. Absent a contract forum, the considerations relied on by the Court of Appeals would be persuasive reasons for holding an American forum convenient in the traditional sense, but in an era of expanding world trade and commerce, the absolute aspects of the doctrine of the Carbon Black case have little place and would be a heavy hand indeed on the future development of international commercial dealings by Americans. We cannot have trade and commerce in world markets and international waters exclusively on our terms, governed by our laws, and resolved in our courts.

Forum-selection clauses have historically not been favored by American courts. Many courts, federal and state, have declined to enforce such clauses on the ground that they were "contrary to public policy," or that their effect was to "oust the jurisdiction" of the court. Although this view apparently still has considerable acceptance, other courts are tending to adopt a more hospitable attitude toward forum-selection clauses. This view, advanced in the well-reasoned dissenting opinion in the instant case, is that such clauses are prima facie valid and should be enforced unless enforcement is shown by the resisting party to be "unreasonable" under the circumstances. We believe this is the correct doctrine to be followed by federal district courts sitting in admiralty. It is merely the other side of the proposition recognized by this Court in National Equipment Rental, Ltd. v. Szukhent, 375 U.S. 311 (1964), holding that in federal courts a party may validly consent to be sued in a jurisdiction where he cannot be found for service of process through contractual designation of an "agent" for receipt of process in that jurisdiction. In so holding, the Court stated:

> [I]t is settled...that parties to a contract may agree in advance to submit to the jurisdiction of a given court to permit notice to be served by the opposing party, or even to waive notice altogether. Id., at 315–316.

This approach is substantially that followed in other common-law countries including England. It is the view advanced by noted scholars and that adopted by the Restatement of the Conflict of Laws.[13] It accords with ancient concepts of freedom of contract and reflects an appreciation of the expanding horizons of American contractors who seek business in all parts of the world. Not surprisingly,

---

[13] Restatement (Second) of the Conflict of Laws § 80 (1971); Reese, *The Contractual Forum: Situation in the United States*, 13 Am. J. Comp. Law 187 (1964); A. Ehrenzweig, Conflict of Laws § 41 (1962). *See also* Model Choice of Forum Act (National Conference of Commissioners on Uniform State Laws 1968).

foreign businessmen prefer, as do we, to have disputes resolved in their own courts, but if that choice is not available, then in a neutral forum with expertise in the subject matter. Plainly, the courts of England meet the standards of neutrality and long experience in admiralty litigation. The choice of that forum was made in an arm's-length negotiation by experienced and sophisticated businessmen, and absent some compelling and countervailing reason it should be honored by the parties and enforced by the courts.

The argument that such clauses are improper because they tend to "oust" a court of jurisdiction is hardly more than a vestigial legal fiction. It appears to rest at core on historical judicial resistance to any attempt to reduce the power and business of a particular court and has little place in an era when all courts are overloaded and when businesses once essentially local now operate in world markets. It reflects something of a provincial attitude regarding the fairness of other tribunals. No one seriously contends in this case that the forum selection clause "ousted" the District Court of jurisdiction over Zapata's action. The threshold question is whether that court should have exercised its jurisdiction to do more than give effect to the legitimate expectations of the parties, manifested in their freely negotiated agreement, by specifically enforcing the forum clause.

There are compelling reasons why a freely negotiated private international agreement, unaffected by fraud, undue influence, or overweening bargaining power,[14] such as that involved here, should be given full effect. In this case, for example, we are concerned with a far from routine transaction between companies of two different nations contemplating the tow of an extremely costly piece of equipment from Louisiana across the Gulf of Mexico and the Atlantic Ocean, through the Mediterranean Sea to its final destination in the Adriatic Sea. In the course of its voyage, it was to traverse the waters of many jurisdictions. The Chaparral could have been damaged at any point along the route, and there were countless possible ports of refuge. That the accident occurred in the Gulf of Mexico and the barge was towed to Tampa in an emergency were mere fortuities. It cannot be doubted for a moment that the parties sought to provide for a neutral forum for the resolution of any disputes arising during the tow. Manifestly much uncertainty and possibly great inconvenience to both parties could arise if a suit could be maintained in any jurisdiction in which an accident might occur or if jurisdiction were left to any place where the Bremen or Unterweser might happen

[14] The record here refutes any notion of overweening bargaining power. Judge Wisdom, dissenting, in the Court of Appeals noted: "Zapata has neither presented evidence of nor alleged fraud or undue bargaining power in the agreement. Unterweser was only one of several companies bidding on the project. No evidence contradicts its Managing Director's affidavit that it specified English courts 'in an effort to meet Zapata Off-Shore Company half way.' Zapata's Vice President has declared by affidavit that no specific negotiations concerning the forum clause took place. But this was not simply a form contract with boilerplate language that Zapata had no power to alter. The towing of an oil rig across the Atlantic was a new business. Zapata did make alterations to the contract submitted by Unterweser. The forum clause could hardly be ignored. It is the final sentence of the agreement, immediately preceding the date and the parties' signatures. . . ." 428 F.2d 888, 907.

to be found.[15] The elimination of all such uncertainties by agreeing in advance on a forum acceptable to both parties is an indispensable element in international trade, commerce, and contracting. There is strong evidence that the forum clause was a vital part of the agreement,[16] and it would be unrealistic to think that the parties did not conduct their negotiations, including fixing the monetary terms, with the consequences of the forum clause figuring prominently in their calculations. Under these circumstances, as Justice Karminski reasoned in sustaining jurisdiction over Zapata in the High Court of Justice, "[t]he force of an agreement for litigation in this country, freely entered into between two competent parties, seems to me to be very powerful."

Thus, in the light of present-day commercial realities and expanding international trade we conclude that the forum clause should control absent a strong showing that it should be set aside. Although their opinions are not altogether explicit, it seems reasonably clear that the District Court and the Court of Appeals placed the burden on Unterweser to show that London would be a more convenient forum than Tampa, although the contract expressly resolved that issue. The correct approach would have been to enforce the forum clause specifically unless Zapata could clearly show that enforcement would be unreasonable and unjust, or that the clause was invalid for such reasons as fraud or overreaching. Accordingly, the case must be remanded for reconsideration.

---

[15] At the very least, the clause was an effort to eliminate all uncertainty as to the nature, location, and outlook of the forum in which these companies of differing nationalities might find themselves. Moreover, while the contract here did not specifically provide that the substantive law of England should be applied, it is the general rule in English courts that the parties are assumed, absent contrary indication, to have designated the forum with the view that it should apply its own law. *See, e.g., Tzortzis v. Monark Line A/B,* (1968) 1 W.L.R. 406 (CA); *see generally* 1 T. Carver, Carriage by Sea 496–497 (12th ed. 1971); G. Cheshire, Private International Law 193 (7th ed. 1965); A. Dicey & J. Morris, The Conflict of Laws 705, 1046 (8th ed. 1967); Collins, *Arbitration Clauses and Forum Selecting Clauses in the Conflict of Laws: Some Recent Developments in England,* 2 J. Mar. L. & Comm. 363, 365–370 and n. 7 (1971). It is therefore reasonable to conclude that the forum clause was also an effort to obtain certainty as to the applicable substantive law.

The record contains an affidavit of a Managing Director of Unterweser stating that Unterweser considered the choice-of-forum provision to be of "overriding importance" to the transaction. He stated that Unterweser towage contracts ordinarily provide for exclusive German jurisdiction and application of German law, but that "[I]n this instance, in an effort to meet (Zapata) half way, (Unterweser) proposed the London Court of Justice. Had this provision not been accepted by (Zapata), (Unterweser) would not have entered into the towage contract. . . ." He also stated that the parties intended, by designating the London forum, that English law would be applied. A responsive affidavit by Hoyt Taylor, a vice president of Zapata, denied that there were any discussions between Zapata and Unterweser concerning the forum clause or the question of the applicable law.

[16] *See* nn. 14–15, *supra.* Zapata has denied specifically discussing the forum clause with Unterweser, but, as Judge Wisdom pointed out, Zapata made numerous changes in the contract without altering the forum clause, which could hardly have escaped its attention. Zapata is clearly not unsophisticated in such matters. The contract of its wholly owned subsidiary with an Italian corporation covering the contemplated drilling operations in the Adriatic Sea provided that all disputes were to be settled by arbitration in London under English law, and contained broad exculpatory clauses. App. 306–311.

We note, however, that there is nothing in the record presently before us that would support a refusal to enforce the forum clause. The Court of Appeals suggested that enforcement would be contrary to the public policy of the forum under Bisso v. Inland Waterways Corp., 349 U.S. 85 (1955), because of the prospect that the English courts would enforce the clauses of the towage contract purporting to exculpate Unterweser from liability for damages to the Chaparral. A contractual choice-of-forum clause should be held unenforceable if enforcement would contravene a strong public policy of the forum in which suit is brought, whether declared by statute or by judicial decision. See, e.g., Boyd v. Grand Trunk W.R. Co., 338 U.S. 263 (1949). It is clear, however, that whatever the proper scope of the policy expressed in Bisso, it does not reach this case. Bisso rested on considerations with respect to the towage business strictly in American waters, and those considerations are not controlling in an international commercial agreement. Speaking for the dissenting judges in the Court of Appeals, Judge Wisdom pointed out:

> [W]e should be careful not to overemphasize the strength of the [Bisso] policy.... [T]wo concerns underlie the rejection of exculpatory agreements: that they may be produced by overweening bargaining power; and that they do not sufficiently discourage negligence....Here the conduct in question is that of a foreign party occurring in international waters outside our jurisdiction. The evidence disputes any notion of overreaching in the contractual agreement. And for all we know, the uncertainties and dangers in the new field of transoceanic towage of oil rigs were so great that the tower was unwilling to take financial responsibility for the risks, and the parties thus allocated responsibility for the voyage to the tow. It is equally possible that the contract price took this factor into account. I conclude that we should not invalidate the forum selection clause here unless we are firmly convinced that we would thereby significantly encourage negligent conduct within the boundaries of the United States. 428 F.2d, at 907–908. (Footnotes omitted.)

Courts have also suggested that a forum clause, even though it is freely bargained for and contravenes no important public policy of the forum, may nevertheless be "unreasonable" and unenforceable if the chosen forum is seriously inconvenient for the trial of the action. Of course, where it can be said with reasonable assurance that at the time they entered the contract, the parties to a freely negotiated private international commercial agreement contemplated the claimed inconvenience, it is difficult to see why any such claim of inconvenience should be heard to render the forum clause unenforceable. We are not here dealing with an agreement between two Americans to resolve their essentially local disputes in a remote alien forum. In such a case, the serious inconvenience of the contractual forum to one or both of the parties might carry greater weight in determining the reasonableness of the forum clause. The remoteness of the forum might suggest that the agreement was an adhesive one, or that the parties did not have the particular controversy in mind when they made their agreement; yet even there the party claiming should bear a heavy burden of proof.[18] Similarly, selection of a remote forum to apply differing foreign law to an essentially American controversy might contravene an important public policy of the forum. For example, so long as Bisso governs American courts with respect to the towage business in American waters, it would quite arguably be improper to permit an American tower to avoid that policy by providing a foreign forum for resolution of his disputes with an American towee.

This case, however, involves a freely negotiated international commercial transaction between a German and an American corporation for towage of a vessel from the Gulf of Mexico to the Adriatic Sea. As noted, selection of a London forum was clearly a reasonable effort to bring vital certainty to this international transaction and to provide a neutral forum experienced and capable in the resolution of admiralty litigation. Whatever "inconvenience" Zapata would suffer by being forced to litigate in the contractual forum as it agreed to do was clearly foreseeable at the time of contracting. In such circumstances it should be incumbent on the party seeking to escape his contract to show that trial in the contractual forum will be so gravely difficult and inconvenient that he will for all practical purposes be deprived of his day in court. Absent that, there is no basis for concluding that it would be unfair, unjust, or unreasonable to hold that party to his bargain.

In the course of its ruling on Unterweser's second motion to stay the proceedings in Tampa, the District Court did make a conclusory finding that the balance of convenience was "strongly" in favor of litigation in Tampa. However, as previously noted, in making that finding the court erroneously placed the burden of proof on Unterweser to show that the balance of convenience was strongly in its favor.[19] Moreover, the finding falls far short of a conclusion that Zapata would be effectively deprived of its day in court should it be forced to litigate in London.

---

[18] *See, e.g.*, Model Choice of Forum Act § 3(3), *supra*, n. 13, comment: "On rare occasions, the state of the forum may be a substantially more convenient place for the trial of a particular controversy than the chosen state. If so, the present clause would permit the action to proceed. This result will presumably be in accord with the desires of the parties. It can be assumed that they did not have the particular controversy in mind when they made the choice-of-forum agreement since they would not consciously have agreed to have the action brought in an inconvenient place."

[19] Applying the proper burden of proof, Justice Karminski in the High Court of Justice at London made the following findings, which appear to have substantial support in the record:

> [Zapata] pointed out that in this case the balance of convenience so far as witnesses were concerned pointed in the direction of having the case heard and tried in the United States District Court at Tampa in Florida because the probability is that most, but not necessarily all, of the witnesses will be American. The answer, as it seems to me, is that a substantial minority at least of witnesses are likely to be German. The tug was a German vessel and was, as far as I know, manned by a German crew. . . . Where they all are now or are likely to be when this matter is litigated I do not know, because the experience of the Admiralty Court here strongly points out that maritime witnesses in the course of their duties move about freely. The homes of the German crew presumably are in Germany. There is probably a balance of numbers in favour of the Americans, but not, as I am inclined to think, a very heavy balance. App. 212.

It should also be noted that if the exculpatory clause is enforced in the English courts, many of Zapata's witnesses on the questions of negligence and damage may be completely unnecessary.

Indeed, it cannot even be assumed that it would be placed to the expense of transporting its witnesses to London. It is not unusual for important issues in international admiralty cases to be dealt with by deposition. Both the District Court and the Court of Appeals majority appeared satisfied that Unterweser could receive a fair hearing in Tampa by using deposition testimony of its witnesses from distant places, and there is no reason to conclude that Zapata could not use deposition testimony to equal advantage if forced to litigate in London as it bound itself to do. Nevertheless, to allow Zapata opportunity to carry its heavy burden of showing not only that the balance of convenience is strongly in favor of trial in Tampa (that is, that it will be far more inconvenient for Zapata to litigate in London than it will be for Unterweser to litigate in Tampa), but also that a London trial will be so manifestly and gravely inconvenient to Zapata that it will be effectively deprived of a meaningful day in court, we remand for further proceedings.

Zapata's remaining contentions do not require extended treatment. It is clear that Unterweser's action in filing its limitation complaint in the District Court in Tampa was, so far as Zapata was concerned, solely a defensive measure made necessary as a response to Zapata's breach of the forum clause of the contract. When the six-month statutory period for filing an action to limit its liability had almost run without the District Court's having ruled on Unterweser's initial motion to dismiss or stay Zapata's action pursuant to the forum clause, Unterweser had no other prudent alternative but to protect itself by filing for limitation of its liability. Its action in so doing was a direct consequence of Zapata's failure to abide by the forum clause of the towage contract. There is no basis on which to conclude that this purely necessary defensive action by Unterweser should preclude it from relying on the forum clause it bargained for.

For the first time in this litigation, Zapata has suggested to this Court that the forum clause should not be construed to provide for an exclusive forum or to include in rem actions. However, the language of the clause is clearly mandatory and all-encompassing; the language of the clause in the Carbon Black case was far different.

The judgment of the Court of Appeals is vacated and the case is remanded for further proceedings consistent with this opinion.

Mr. Justice White, concurring:
I concur in the opinion and judgment of the Court except insofar as the opinion comments on the issues which are remanded to the District Court. In my view these issues are best left for consideration by the District Court in the first instance.

Mr. Justice Douglas, dissenting:
Petitioner Unterweser contracted with respondent to tow respondent's drilling barge from Louisiana to Italy. The towage contract contained a "forum selection clause" providing that any dispute must be litigated before the High Court of Justice in London, England. While the barge was being towed in the Gulf of Mexico a casualty was suffered. The tow made for Tampa Bay, the nearest port, where respondent brought suit for damages in the District Court.

Petitioners sued respondent in the High Court of Justice in London, which denied respondent's motion to dismiss.

Petitioners, having previously moved the District Court to dismiss, filed a complaint in that court seeking exoneration or limitation of liability as provided in 46 U.S.C. § 185. Respondent filed its claim in the limitation proceedings, asserting the same cause of action as in its original action. Petitioners then filed objections to respondent's claim and counterclaimed against respondent, alleging the same claims embodied in its English action, plus an additional salvage claim.

Respondent moved for an injunction against petitioners' litigating further in the English case and the District Court granted the injunction pending determination of the limitation action. Petitioners moved to stay their own limitation proceeding pending a resolution of the suit in the English court. That motion was denied.

That was the posture of the case as it reached the Court of Appeals, petitioners appealing from the last two orders. The Court of Appeals affirmed.

Chief Justice Taft in Hartford Accident & Indemnity Co. of Hartford v. Southern Pacific, 273 U.S. 207, 214 in discussing the Limitation of Liability Act said that "the great object of the statute was to encourage shipbuilding and to induce the investment of money in this branch of industry by limiting the venture of those who build the ship to the loss of the ship itself or her freight then pending, in cases of damage or wrong happening, without the privity or knowledge of the ship owner, and by the fault or neglect of the master or other persons on board; that the origin of this proceeding for limitation of liability is to be found in the general maritime law differing from the English maritime law; and that such a proceeding is entirely within the constitutional grant of power to Congress to establish courts of admiralty and maritime jurisdiction."

Chief Justice Taft went on to describe how the owner of a vessel who, in case the vessel is found at fault, may limit his liability to the value of the vessel and may bring all claimants "into concourse in the proceeding by monition" and they may be enjoined from suing the owner and the vessel on such claims in any other court. Id. at 215.

Chief Justice Taft concluded: "[T]his Court has by its rules and decisions given the statute a very broad and equitable construction for the purpose of carrying out its purpose, and for facilitating a settlement of the whole controversy over such losses as are comprehended within it, and that all the ease with which rights can be adjusted in equity is intended to be given to the proceeding. It is the administration of equity in an admiralty court.... The proceeding partakes in a way of the features of a bill to enjoin a multiplicity of suits, a bill in the nature of an interpleader, and a creditor's bill. It looks to a complete and just disposition of a many cornered controversy, and is applicable to proceedings in rem against the ship, as well as to proceedings in personam against the owner; the limitation extending to the owner's property as well as to his person." Id. at 215–216.

The Limitation Court is a court of equity and traditionally an equity court may enjoin litigation in another court where equitable considerations indicate that the other litigation might prejudice the proceedings in the Limitation Court. Petitioners' petition for limitation subjects them to the full equitable powers of the Limitation Court.

Respondent is a citizen of this country. Moreover, if it were remitted to the English court, its substantive rights would be adversely affected. Exculpatory provisions in the towage control provide (1) that petitioners, the masters and the crews "are not responsible for defaults and/or errors in the navigation of the tow" and (2) that "[d]amages suffered by the towed object are in any case for account of its Owners."

Under our decision in Dixilyn Drilling Corp. v. Crescent Towing & Salvage Co., 372 U.S. 697, 698, "a contract which exempts the tower from liability for its own negligence" is not enforceable, though there is evidence in the present record that it is enforceable in England. That policy was first announced in Bisso v. Inland Waterways Corp., 349 U.S. 85; and followed in Boston Metals Co. v. The Winding Gulf, 349 U.S. 122; Dixilyn, supra; Gray v. Johansson, 287 F.2d 852 (5th Cir.); California Co. v. Jumonville, 327 F.2d 988 (5th Cir.); American S.S. Co. v. Great Lakes Towing Co., 333 F.2d 426 (7th Cir.); D. R. Kincaid, Ltd. v. Trans-Pacific Towing, Inc., 367 F.2d 857 (9th Cir.); A. L. Mechling Barge Lines, Inc. v. Derby Co., 399 F.2d 304 (5th Cir.). Cf. United States v. Seckinger, 397 U.S. 203. Although the casualty occurred on the high seas, the Bisso doctrine is nonetheless applicable. The Scotland, 105 U.S. 24; The Belgenland, 114 U.S. 355; The Gylfe v. The Trujillo, 209 F.2d 386 (2nd Cir.).

Moreover, the casualty occurred close to the District Court, a number of potential witnesses, including respondent's crewmen, reside in that area, and the inspection and repair work were done there. The testimony of the tower's crewmen, residing in Germany, is already available by way of depositions taken in the proceedings.

All in all, the District Court judge exercised his discretion wisely in enjoining petitioners from pursuing the litigation in England.* I would affirm the judgment below.

---

* It is said that because these parties specifically agreed to litigate their disputes before the London Court of Justice, the District Court, absent "unreasonable" circumstances, should have honored that choice by declining to exercise its jurisdiction. The forum-selection clause, however, is part and parcel of the exculpatory provision in the towing agreement which, as mentioned in the text, is not enforceable in American courts. For only by avoiding litigation in the United States could petitioners hope to evade the *Bisso* doctrine.

Judges in this country have traditionally been hostile to attempts to circumvent the public policy against exculpatory agreements. For example, clauses specifying that the law of a foreign place (which favors such releases) should control have regularly been ignored. Thus, in *The Kensington,* 183 U.S. 263, 276, the Court held void an exemption from liability despite the fact that the contract provided that it should be construed under Belgian law which was more tolerant. And *see E. Gerli & Co. v. Cunard S.S. Co.,* 48 F.2d 115, 117 (2nd Cir); *Oceanic Stream Nav. Co. v. Corcoran,* 9 F.2d 724, 731 (2nd Cir.); *In re Lea Fabrics, Inc.,* 226 F. Supp. 232, 237 (D.C.N.J.); *F. A. Straus & Co. v. Canadian P.R. Co.,* 254 N.Y. 407; *Siegelman v. Cunard White Star,* 221 F.2d 189, 199 (2nd Cir.) (Frank, J., dissenting). 6A A. Corbin on Contracts § 1446 (1962).

Comments and Questions

1. How can it be said that Zapata will have its "day in court" if Unterweser's exculpatory clause is given effect by the English court, as it most likely would be?

2. It is important to realize that the Court does not say that all forum selection clauses must be enforced. Rather, the Court remands the case to give Zapata an opportunity to "clearly show" or "to carry its heavy burden of showing" that enforcement of the clause would be "unreasonable and unjust," or "so manifestly and gravely inconvenient to Zapata that it will be effectively deprived of a meaningful day in court." In the actual case, Zapata made no such effort. (Why not?) Can you think of situations when enforcement of a forum selection clause would be so unjust that a party could meet the heavy burden? See, e.g., McDonnell Douglas Corp. v. Islamic Republic of Iran, 758 F.2d 341 (8th Cir. 1985) (permitting American plaintiffs to sue in the United States, notwithstanding forum selection clauses choosing Iranian courts).

3. Prior to The Bremen forum selection clauses were viewed with tremendous skepticism because they could oust a court of its natural jurisdiction. Why was this view no longer compelling? Does a court (or a judicial system) have any interest in the resolution of a dispute between two private parties? (Did the Florida courts in The Bremen?) Does the public have any interest in the resolution of such a dispute? (Did Floridians in The Bremen?)

4. How significant in The Bremen is the fact that the clause was negotiated between sophisticated businesses? Selection of a forum is one of the elements in the price or the allocation of risk and—the thinking goes—courts should hold parties to their bargain. But what if there was no actual negotiation? Or what does The Bremen indicate about the enforceability of a forum selection clause contained in a form contract between two merchants? Generally speaking, in the United States, these contractual provisions will be enforced whether or not the clause was actually bargained for.

5. What about a form contract between a merchant and a consumer? In Carnival Cruise Lines, Inc. v. Shute, 499 U.S. 585 (1991), Mr. and Mrs. Shute, residents of a suburb of Seattle, Washington, purchased tickets through a local travel agency for a cruise from Los Angeles to Mexico and back. Mrs. Shute was injured

---

The instant stratagem of specifying a foreign forum is essentially the same as invoking a foreign law of construction except that the present circumvention also requires the American party to travel across an ocean to seek relief. Unless we are prepared to overrule *Bisso* we should not countenance devices designed solely for the purpose of evading its prohibition.

It is argued, however, that one of the rationales of the *Bisso* doctrine, "to protect those in need of goods or services from being overreached by others who have power to drive hard bargains" (349 U.S., at 91), does not apply here because these parties may have been of equal bargaining stature. Yet we have often adopted prophylactic rules rather than attempt to sort the core cases from the marginal ones. In any event, the other objective of the *Bisso* doctrine, to "discourage negligence by making wrongdoers pay damages" (*Ibid.*) applies here and in every case regardless of the relative bargaining strengths of the parties.

on the boat and, after returning home, sued Carnival in Washington. But buried in the boilerplate language of the passenger ticket was a clause identifying Florida as the exclusive forum for the resolution of all disputes. Relying on The Bremen, the U.S. Supreme Court enforced the clause. Justice Blackmun, writing for a seven-member majority, held that the forum selection clause was permissible for several reasons:

> First, a cruise line has a special interest in limiting the fora in which it potentially could be subject to suit.... [Second], a clause establishing ex ante the forum for dispute resolution has the salutary effect of dispelling any confusion about where suits arising from the contract must be brought and defended, sparing litigants the time and expense of pretrial motions to determine the correct forum, and conserving judicial resources that otherwise would be devoted to deciding those motions.... Finally, it stands to reason that passengers who purchase tickets containing a forum clause like that at issue in this case benefit in the form of reduced fares reflecting the savings that the cruise line enjoys by limiting the fora in which it may be sued.

The Court emphasized "that forum-selection clauses contained in form passage contracts are subject to judicial scrutiny for fundamental fairness." But absent any finding in the district court of "bad-faith motive" or "fraud or overreaching," the Shutes failed to satisfy the "heavy burden of proof required to set aside the clause." Put another way, Florida was not the "remote alien forum" that was hypothesized in The Bremen.

How could this have happened? Are you outraged? Or is this the logical result of The Bremen? How far would you expect the court to stretch Shute? If a Japanese company had offered the Mexican cruise, and the ticket contained a forum selection clause that pointed to Tokyo, would the court enforce it in a suit by Mrs. Shute?

6. In another case involving the same forum-selection clause as in Shute, 238 passengers sued Carnival to recover damages for personal injuries suffered during a heavy storm. The California courts refused to enforce the clause but the United States Supreme Court reversed and remanded for reconsideration in light of Shute. Carnival Cruise Lines, Inc. v. Superior Court, 499 U.S. 972 (1991). On remand, the California appellate court held that:

> the forum-selection clause is unenforceable as to any particular plaintiff if the court determines that such plaintiff did not have sufficient notice of the forum-selection clause prior to entering into the contract for passage. Absent such notice, the requisite mutual consent to that contractual term is lacking and no valid contract with respect to such clause thus exists.

Carnival Cruise Lines, Inc. v. Superior Court, 234 Cal.App. 3d 1019 (2nd Dist. 1991). The court remanded to the trial court for determination of the issue of notice. If you represented Carnival Cruise Lines, what would you advise them to do in light of this decision?

7. Courts have upheld cruise-ticket forum-selection clauses in situations that make Carnival Cruise Lines look mundane. See, e.g., Hodes v. S.N.C. Achille Lauro, 858 F.2d 905 (3rd Cir. 1988), where the court required plaintiffs to go to Naples to sue, in accordance with a clause in the ticket that also selected Italian law. In that case, which arose out of the terrorist hijacking of the *Achille Lauro,* the plaintiffs alleged that they did not actually receive their tickets until "immediately before boarding the ship" in Genoa, Italy; no one discussed the terms of the ticket with them. The court summarized thus: "Finding that the clause satisfies the 'reasonable communicativeness' test..., and that its enforcement would not violate the principles the Supreme Court set forth in The Bremen..., we hold the foreign forum selection clause should be enforced and thus reverse the decision of the lower court." Id. Is this holding required by The Bremen? Is it consistent with that case? It may be contrasted with Calzavara v. Biehl & Co., 181 S.2d 809 (La.App. 1966), denying effect to a clause selecting an Italian forum. The clause was contained in a ticket for transportation from New Orleans to Italy; Louisiana was the place of the plaintiff's residence and the state of defendant's incorporation.

2. Civil Law Perspective

This is a short unit because the civil law countries have long held the liberal view of party autonomy more recently embraced in the United States. We see in the Brussels Regulation, for example, a typical approach regarding the enforcement of forum selection clauses.

Council Regulation (EC) No 44/2001 of 22 December 2000 on Jurisdiction and the Recognition and Enforcement of Judgments in Civil and Commercial Matters

Article 23

1. If the parties, one or more of whom is domiciled in a Member State, have agreed that a court or the courts of a Member State are to have jurisdiction to settle any disputes which have arisen or which may arise in connection with a particular legal relationship, that court or those courts shall have jurisdiction. Such jurisdiction shall be exclusive unless the parties have agreed otherwise. Such an agreement conferring jurisdiction shall be either:
   (a) in writing or evidenced in writing; or
   (b) in a form which accords with practices which the parties have established between themselves; or
   (c) in international trade or commerce, in a form which accords with a usage of which the parties are or ought to have been aware and which in such trade or commerce is widely known to, and regularly observed by,

parties to contracts of the type involved in the particular trade or commerce concerned.

2. Any communication by electronic means which provides a durable record of the agreement shall be equivalent to 'writing'.
3. Where such an agreement is concluded by parties, none of whom is domiciled in a Member State, the courts of other Member States shall have no jurisdiction over their disputes unless the court or courts chosen have declined jurisdiction....

Comments and Questions

1. Because the Brussels Regulation does not recognize a doctrine of forum non conveniens, the establishment of jurisdiction pursuant to Article 23 is conclusive.

2. Notice that Article 23 includes a default rule that a forum selection clause is exclusive. This is an important distinction from American jurisprudence. Is such a presumption useful? Logical?

3. Remember from our introduction of the Brussels Regulation in the personal jurisdiction chapter that there are special rules for cases involving insurance matters, consumer contracts, and employment disputes. See Articles 8–14; 15–17; and 18–21, respectively. In these categories of cases, agreements to litigate elsewhere are enforceable only when (1) they are entered into after the dispute has arisen; (2) they allow the protected party additional forum options; or (3) the clause selects a forum that is the habitual residence of both parties. As demonstrated by the discussion introducing Carnival Cruise Lines above, U.S. law provides no categorical limitations on the enforcement of forum selection clauses for consumer contracts.

4. The following hypothetical will allow you to develop familiarity with the mechanics of the Brussels Regulation.

> After the conclusion of negotiations conducted by one of its employees at the offices in Como, Italy, of the Company Industrie Tessili Italiana Como ("Tessili") and after receipt of several samples, Dunlop AG, whose registered office is in Hanau, Germany, sent an order for 310 women's ski suits. Printed on Dunlop's letter were its conditions of purchase, including the following clause: "Jurisdiction. The court in Hanau am Main shall have jurisdiction to deal with disputes arising from this contract." Tessili completed the ski suits within six weeks and sent them to Dunlop through a shipping company. Tessili's shipment included an invoice with various conditions of sale, including the following clause: "The court in Como shall have jurisdiction in any dispute which may arise and the purchaser waives his right to have the dispute decided by any other court." A few months later, Dunlop found defects in the ski suits and filed a breach of warranty claim against Tessili in Hanau. Does the Landgericht Hanau (Regional Court) have jurisdiction over Tessili? What additional facts do you need? See Industrie Tessili Italiana Como v. Dunlop AG, (Case No. 12/76), [1976] ECR 1473.

5. In 2005, the member states of the Hague Conference on Private International Law concluded a Convention on Choice of Court Agreements. See http://www.hcch.net. To ensure even greater certainty that a forum selection clause will be recognized, the Convention requires both that "[t]he court or courts of a Contracting State designated in an exclusive choice of court agreement shall have jurisdiction to decide a dispute to which the agreement applies" and also that "[i]f the parties have entered into an exclusive choice of court agreement, any court in a Contracting State other than that of the chosen court shall suspend or dismiss the proceedings." Convention on Choice of Court Agreements, June 30, 2005, Hague Conference on Private International Law, arts. 5 & 7 (2005). Later in this course we will revisit the Choice of Court Convention to discuss how the convention would provide much greater certainty that any judgment issued by the court selected by the parties would be enforced elsewhere.

As of this writing (November 2008), only Mexico has ratified this treaty. However, the U.S. Secretary of State has authorized signature, and the Commission of the European Union has recommended that the European Union join as well. Thus the treaty may find traction.

C. Arbitration Clauses

An arbitration is the product of a private contract. An arbitration clause entrusts the controversy to a private decision maker rather than a forum selection clause which would confer that power on some state's courts.

It has long been understood—in the United States at least since the passage in 1925 of what is now chapter 1 of the Federal Arbitration Act (the "FAA")—that validly concluded agreements to arbitrate are enforceable. In fact, the FAA, in combination with a network of state and foreign arbitration acts, and the New York Arbitration Convention,* provides for a rather seamless enforcement of arbitration clauses—and, importantly, arbitration awards. Although we have already seen that forum selection clauses are very likely to be enforced, there is no analogous legislative mandate; indeed, there are no federal statutes and (except for the budding Choice of Court Convention) no treaties. Consider why there would be more enthusiasm for arbitral proceedings than for formal court proceedings. (Or is that an unfair characterization of this phenomenon?)

A persistent question facing all court systems is which issues, if any, are not arbitrable. Although a system might be willing to allow private parties in a commercial contract dispute to resolve that matter in some private forum, the arbitration of public law issues are (even) more problematic. American

* We will discuss the New York Convention on the Recognition and Enforcement of Foreign Arbitral Awards of 1958 (the "New York Convention"), 21 U.S.T. 2518, T.I.A.S. No. 6997, 330 U.N.T.S. 38, at length in Chapter 12

jurisprudence on the question of arbitrability begins with the seminal case, Wilko v. Swan, 346 U.S. 427 (1953). In Wilko a customer of a brokerage firm brought an action against partners of the firm under the Securities Act of 1933, to recover damages as a result of factual misrepresentations made by the broker. A contract between the parties included an arbitration clause. The Court found:

> Two policies, not easily reconcilable, are involved in this case. Congress has afforded participants in transactions subject to its legislative power an opportunity generally to secure prompt, economical and adequate solutions of controversies through arbitration.... On the other hand, it has enacted the Securities Act [of 1933] to protect the rights of investors and has forbidden a waiver of any of those rights. Recognizing the advantages that prior agreements for arbitration may provide for the solution of commercial controversies, we decide that the intention of Congress concerning the sale of securities is better carried out by holding invalid such an agreement for arbitration of issues arising under the Act.

346 U.S. at 438. The following case is substantially similar, except that it is a transnational matter rather than wholly domestic.

Scherk v. Alberto-Culver Co.

417 U.S. 506 (1974)

Mr. Justice Stewart delivered the opinion of the Court:

Alberto-Culver Co., the respondent, is an American company incorporated in Delaware with its principal office in Illinois. It manufactures and distributes toiletries and hair products in this country and abroad. During the 1960's Alberto-Culver decided to expand its overseas operations, and as part of this program it approached the petitioner Fritz Scherk, a German citizen residing at the time of trial in Switzerland. Scherk was the owner of three interrelated business entities, organized under the laws of Germany and Liechtenstein, that were engaged in the manufacture of toiletries and the licensing of trademarks for such toiletries. An initial contact with Scherk was made by a representative of Alberto-Culver in Germany in June 1967, and negotiations followed at further meetings in both Europe and the United States during 1967 and 1968. In February 1969 a contract was signed in Vienna, Austria, which provided for the transfer of the ownership of Scherk's enterprises to Alberto-Culver, along with all rights held by these enterprises to trademarks in cosmetic goods. The contract contained a number of express warranties whereby Scherk guaranteed the sole and unencumbered ownership of these trademarks. In addition, the contract contained an arbitration clause providing that "any controversy or claim [that] shall arise out of this agreement or the breach thereof" would be referred to arbitration before the International Chamber of Commerce in Paris, France, and that "[t]he laws of the

State of Illinois, U.S.A. shall apply to and govern this agreement, its interpretation and performance."[1]

The closing of the transaction took place in Geneva, Switzerland, in June 1969. Nearly one year later Alberto-Culver allegedly discovered that the trademark rights purchased under the contract were subject to substantial encumbrances that threatened to give others superior rights to the trademarks and to restrict or preclude Alberto-Culver's use of them. Alberto-Culver thereupon tendered back to Scherk the property that had been transferred to it and offered to rescind the contract. Upon Scherk's refusal, Alberto-Culver commenced this action for damages and other relief in a Federal District Court in Illinois, contending that Scherk's fraudulent representations concerning the status of the trademark rights constituted violations of § 10(b) of the Securities Exchange Act of 1934, 48 Stat. 891, 15 U.S.C. § 78j(b), and Rule 10b-5 promulgated thereunder, 17 CFR § 240.10b-5.

In response, Scherk filed a motion to dismiss the action for want of personal and subject-matter jurisdiction as well as on the basis of forum non conveniens, or, alternatively, to stay the action pending arbitration in Paris pursuant to the agreement of the parties. Alberto-Culver, in turn, opposed this motion and sought a preliminary injunction restraining the prosecution of arbitration proceedings. On December 2, 1971, the District Court denied Scherk's motion to dismiss, and, on January 14, 1972, it granted a preliminary order enjoining Scherk from proceeding with arbitration. In taking these actions the court relied entirely on this Court's decision in Wilko v. Swan, 346 U.S. 427, which held that an agreement to arbitrate could not preclude a buyer of a security from seeking a judicial remedy under the Securities Act of 1933, in view of the language of § 14 of that Act, barring "[a]ny condition, stipulation, or provision binding any person acquiring any security to waive compliance with any provision of this subchapter...." 48 Stat. 84, 15 U.S.C. § 77n. The Court of Appeals for the Seventh Circuit, with one judge dissenting, affirmed, upon what it considered the controlling authority of the Wilko decision. 484 F.2d 611. Because of the importance of the question presented we granted Scherk's petition for a writ of certiorari.

---

[1] The arbitration clause relating to the transfer of one of Scherk's business entities, similar to the clauses covering the other two, reads in its entirety as follows: "The parties agree that if any controversy or claim shall arise out of this agreement or the breach thereof and either party shall request that the matter shall be settled by arbitration, the matter shall be settled exclusively by arbitration in accordance with the rules then obtaining of the International Chamber of Commerce, Paris, France, by a single arbitrator, if the parties shall agree upon one, or by one arbitrator appointed by each party and a third arbitrator appointed by the other arbitrators. In case of any failure of a party to make an appointment referred to above within four weeks after notice of the controversy, such appointment shall be made by said Chamber. All arbitration proceedings shall be held in Paris, France, and each party agrees to comply in all respects with any award made in any such proceeding and to the entry of a judgment in any jurisdiction upon any award rendered in such proceeding. The laws of the State of Illinois, U.S.A. shall apply to and govern this agreement, its interpretation and performance."

I

The United States Arbitration Act, now 9 U.S.C. § 1 et seq., reversing centuries of judicial hostility to arbitration agreements,[4] was designed to allow parties to avoid "the costliness and delays of litigation," and to place arbitration agreements "upon the same footing as other contracts. . . ." H.R. Rep. No.96, 68th Cong., 1st Sess., 1, 2 (1924); see also S. Rep. No.536, 68th Cong., 1st Sess. (1924). Accordingly the Act provides that an arbitration agreement such as is here involved "shall be valid, irrevocable, and enforceable, save upon such grounds as exist at law or in equity for the revocation of any contract." 9 U.S.C. § 2. The Act also provides in § 3 for a stay of proceedings in a case where a court is satisfied that the issue before it is arbitrable under the agreement, and § 4 of the Act directs a federal court to order parties to proceed to arbitration if there has been a "failure, neglect, or refusal" of any party to honor an agreement to arbitrate.

In Wilko v. Swan, supra, this Court acknowledged that the Act reflects a legislative recognition of the "desirability of arbitration as an alternative to the complications of litigation," 346 U.S., at 431, but nonetheless declined to apply the Act's provisions. . . .

The Court found that "[t]wo policies, not easily reconcilable, are involved in this case." 346 U.S., at 438. On the one hand, the Arbitration Act stressed "the need for avoiding the delay and expense of litigation," id., and directed that such agreements be "valid, irrevocable, and enforceable" in federal courts. On the other hand, the Securities Act of 1933 was "[d]esigned to protect investors" and to require "issuers, underwriters, and dealers to make full and fair disclosure of the character of securities sold in interstate and foreign commerce and to prevent fraud in their sale," by creating "a special right to recover for misrepresentation. . . ." 346 U.S., at 431 (footnote omitted). In particular, the Court noted that § 14 of the Securities Act, 15 U.S.C. § 77n, provides:

> Any condition, stipulation, or provision binding any person acquiring any security to waive compliance with any provision of this subchapter or of the rules and regulations of the Commission shall be void.

The Court ruled that an agreement to arbitrate "is a 'stipulation,' and (that) the right to select the judicial forum is the kind of 'provision' that cannot be waived under § 14 of the Securities Act." 346 U.S., at 434–435. Thus, Wilko's advance agreement to arbitrate any disputes subsequently arising out of his contract to purchase the securities was unenforceable under the terms of § 14 of the Securities Act of 1933.

Alberto-Culver, relying on this precedent, contends that the District Court and Court of Appeals were correct in holding that its agreement to arbitrate

---

[4] English courts traditionally considered irrevocable arbitration agreements as 'ousting' the courts of jurisdiction, and refused to enforce such agreements for this reason. This view was adopted by American courts as part of the common law up to the time of the adoption of the Arbitration Act. See H.R. Rep.No. 96, 68th Cong., 1st Sess., 1, 2 (1924); Sturges & Murphy, *Some Confusing Matters Relating to Arbitration under the United States Arbitration Act*, 17 Law & Contemp. Prob. 580.

disputes arising under the contract with Scherk is similarly unenforceable in view of its contentions that Scherk's conduct constituted violations of the Securities Exchange Act of 1934 and rules promulgated thereunder. For the reasons that follow, we reject this contention and hold that the provisions of the Arbitration Act cannot be ignored in this case.

At the outset, a colorable argument could be made that even the semantic reasoning of the Wilko opinion does not control the case before us. Wilko concerned a suit brought under § 12(2) of the Securities Act of 1933, which provides a defrauded purchaser with the "special right" of a private remedy for civil liability, 346 U.S., at 431. There is no statutory counterpart of § 12(2) in the Securities Exchange Act of 1934, and neither § 10(b) of that Act nor Rule 10b-5 speaks of a private remedy to redress violations of the kind alleged here. While federal case law has established that § 10(b) and Rule 10b-5 create an implied private cause of action, see 6 L. Loss, Securities Regulation 3869–3873 (1969) and cases cited therein; cf. J.I. Case Co. v. Borak, 377 U.S. 426, the Act itself does not establish the "special right" that the Court in Wilko found significant. Furthermore, while both the Securities Act of 1933 and the Securities Exchange Act of 1934 contain sections barring waiver of compliance with any "provision" of the respective Acts, certain of the "provisions" of the 1933 Act that the Court held could not be waived by Wilko's agreement to arbitrate find no counterpart in the 1934 Act. In particular, the Court in Wilko noted that the jurisdictional provision of the 1933 Act, 15 U.S.C. § 77v, allowed a plaintiff to bring suit "in any court of competent jurisdiction-federal or state-and removal from a state court is prohibited." 346 U.S., at 431. The analogous provision of the 1934 Act, by contrast, provides for suit only in the federal district courts that have "exclusive jurisdiction," 15 U.S.C. § 78aa, thus significantly restricting the plaintiff's choice of forum.

Accepting the premise, however, that the operative portions of the language of the 1933 Act relied upon in Wilko are contained in the Securities Exchange Act of 1934, the respondent's reliance on Wilko in this case ignores the significant and, we find, crucial differences between the agreement involved in Wilko and the one signed by the parties here. Alberto-Culver's contract to purchase the business entities belonging to Scherk was a truly international agreement. Alberto-Culver is an American corporation with its principal place of business and the vast bulk of its activity in this country, while Scherk is a citizen of Germany whose companies were organized under the laws of Germany and Liechtenstein. The negotiations leading to the signing of the contract in Austria and to the closing in Switzerland took place in the United States, England, and Germany, and involved consultations with legal and trademark experts from each of those countries and from Liechtenstein. Finally, and most significantly, the subject matter of the contract concerned the sale of business enterprises organized under the laws of and primarily situated in European countries, whose activities were largely, if not entirely, directed to European markets.

Such a contract involves considerations and policies significantly different from those found controlling in Wilko. In Wilko, quite apart from the arbitration provision, there was no question but that the laws of the United States generally, and the federal securities laws in particular, would govern disputes arising out of the stock-purchase agreement. The parties, the negotiations, and the subject matter of the contract were all situated in this country, and no credible claim could have been entertained that any international conflict-of-laws problems would arise. In this case, by contrast, in the absence of the arbitration provision considerable uncertainty existed at the time of the agreement, and still exists, concerning the law applicable to the resolution of disputes arising out of the contract.[9]

Such uncertainty will almost inevitably exist with respect to any contract touching two or more countries, each with its own substantive laws and conflict-of-laws rules. A contractual provision specifying in advance the forum in which disputes shall be litigated and the law to be applied is, therefore, an almost indispensable precondition to achievement of the orderliness and predictability essential to any international business transaction. Furthermore, such a provision obviates the danger that a dispute under the agreement might be submitted to a forum hostile to the interests of one of the parties or unfamiliar with the problem area involved.

A parochial refusal by the courts of one country to enforce an international arbitration agreement would not only frustrate these purposes, but would invite unseemly and mutually destructive jockeying by the parties to secure tactical litigation advantages. In the present case, for example, it is not inconceivable that if Scherk had anticipated that Alberto-Culver would be able in this country to enjoin resort to arbitration he might have sought an order in France or some other country enjoining Alberto-Culver from proceeding with its litigation in the United States. Whatever recognition the courts of this country might ultimately have granted to the order of the foreign court, the dicey atmosphere of such a legal no-man's-land would surely damage the fabric of international commerce and trade, and imperil the willingness and ability of businessmen to enter into international commercial agreements.

The exception to the clear provisions of the Arbitration Act carved out by Wilko is simply inapposite to a case such as the one before us. In Wilko the Court reasoned that "[w]hen the security buyer, prior to any violation of the Securities Act, waives his right to sue in courts, he gives up more than would a participant in other business transactions. The security buyer has a wider choice of courts and venue. He thus surrenders one of the advantages the Act gives him. . . ." 346 U.S., at 435. In the context of an international contract, however, these advantages become chimerical since, as indicated above, an opposing party may by speedy resort to a foreign court block or hinder access to the American court of the purchaser's choice.

---

9 Together with his motion for a stay pending arbitration, Scherk moved that the complaint be dismissed because the federal securities laws do not apply to this international transaction, *cf. Leasco Data Processing Equipment Corp v. Maxwell*, 468 F.2d 1326 (2nd Cir. 1972). Since only the order granting the injunction was appealed, this contention was not considered by the Court of Appeals and is not before this Court.

Two Terms ago in The Bremen v. Zapata Off-Shore Co., 407 U.S. 1, we rejected the doctrine that a forum-selection clause of a contract, although voluntarily adopted by the parties, will not be respected in a suit brought in the United States "unless the selected state would provide a more convenient forum than the state in which suit is brought." Id., at 7. Rather, we concluded that a "forum clause should control absent a strong showing that it should be set aside." Id., at 15. We noted that "much uncertainty and possibly great inconvenience to both parties could arise if a suit could be maintained in any jurisdiction in which an accident might occur or if jurisdiction were left to any place (where personal or in rem jurisdiction might be established). The elimination of all such uncertainties by agreeing in advance on a forum acceptable to both parties is an indispensable element in international trade, commerce, and contracting." Id., at 13–14.

An agreement to arbitrate before a specified tribunal is, in effect, a specialized kind of forum-selection clause that posits not only the situs of suit but also the procedure to be used in resolving the dispute. The invalidation of such an agreement in the case before us would not only allow the respondent to repudiate its solemn promise but would, as well, reflect a "parochial concept that all disputes must be resolved under our laws and in our courts.... We cannot have trade and commerce in world markets and international waters exclusively on our terms, governed by our laws, and resolved in our courts." Id., at 9.

For all these reasons we hold that the agreement of the parties in this case to arbitrate any dispute arising out of their international commercial transaction is to be respected and enforced by the federal courts in accord with the explicit provisions of the Arbitration Act.

Accordingly, the judgment of the Court of Appeals is reversed and the case is remanded to that court with directions to remand to the District Court for further proceedings consistent with this opinion.

Mr. Justice Douglas, with whom Mr. Justice Brennan, Mr. Justice White, and Mr. Justice Marshall concur, dissenting:

The basic dispute between the parties concerned allegations that the trademarks which were basic assets in the transaction were encumbered and that their purchase was induced through serious instances of fraudulent representations and omissions by Scherk and his agents within the jurisdiction of the United States. If a question of trademarks were the only one involved, the principle of The Bremen v. Zapata Off-Shore Co., 407 U.S. 1, would be controlling.

We have here, however, questions under the Securities Exchange Act of 1934.... [Section] 29(b) [of that Act provides] that "[e]very contract" made in violation of the Act "shall be void." No exception is made for contracts which have an international character.

The Securities Act of 1933, 48 Stat. 84, 15 U.S.C. § 77n, has a like provision in its § 14:

> Any condition, stipulation, or provision binding any person acquiring any security to waive compliance with any provision of this subchapter or of the rules and regulations of the Commission shall be void.

In Wilko v. Swan, 346 U.S. 427, a customer brought suit against a brokerage house alleging fraud in the sale of stock. A motion was made to stay the trial until arbitration occurred under the United States Arbitration Act, 9 U.S.C. § 3, as provided in the customer's contract. The Court held that an agreement for arbitration was a "stipulation" within the meaning of § 14 which sought to "waive" compliance with the Securities Act. We accordingly held that the courts, not the arbitration tribunals, had jurisdiction over suits under that Act. The arbitration agency, we held, was bound by other standards which were not necessarily consistent with the 1933 Act.... Wilko was held by the Court of Appeals to control this case—and properly so....

It could perhaps be argued that Wilko does not govern because it involved a little customer pitted against a big brokerage house, while we deal here with sophisticated buyers and sellers: Scherk, a powerful German operator, and Alberto-Culver, an American business surrounded and protected by lawyers and experts. But that would miss the point of the problem. The Act does not speak in terms of "sophisticated" as opposed to "unsophisticated" people dealing in securities. The rules when the giants play are the same as when the pygmies enter the market.

If there are victims here, they are not Alberto-Culver the corporation, but the thousands of investors who are the security holders in Alberto-Culver. If there is fraud and the promissory notes are excessive, the impact is on the equity in Alberto-Culver.

Moreover, the securities market these days is not made up of a host of small people scrambling to get in and out of stocks or other securities. The markets are overshadowed by huge institutional traders. The so-called "off-shore funds," of which Scherk is a member, present perplexing problems under both the 1933 and 1934 Acts. The tendency of American investors to invest indirectly as through mutual funds may change the character of the regulation but not its need.

There has been much support for arbitration of disputes; and it may be the superior way of settling some disagreements. If A and B were quarreling over a trade-mark and there was an arbitration clause in the contract, the policy of Congress in implementing the United Nations Convention on the Recognition and Enforcement of Foreign Arbitral Awards, as it did in 9 U.S.C. § 201 et seq., would prevail. But the Act does not substitute an arbiter for the settlement of disputes under the 1933 and 1934 Acts....

But § 29(a) of the 1934 Act makes agreements to arbitrate liabilities under § 10 of the Act "void" and "inoperative." Congress has specified a precise way whereby big and small investors will be protected and the rules under which the Alberto-Culvers of this Nation shall operate. They or their lawyers cannot waive those statutory conditions, for our corporate giants are not principalities of power but guardians of a host of wards unable to care for themselves. It is these wards that the 1934 Act tries to protect. Not a word in the Convention governing awards adopts the standards which Congress has passed to protect the investors under the 1934 Act. It is peculiarly appropriate that we adhere to Wilko—more so even than when Wilko was decided. Huge foreign investments are being made in our companies. It is important that American standards of fairness in security dealings govern the destinies of American investors until Congress changes these standards.

The Court finds it unnecessary to consider Scherk's argument that this case is distinguishable from Wilko in that Wilko involved parties of unequal bargaining strength. Instead, the Court rests its conclusion on the fact that this was an "international" agreement, with an American corporation investing in the stock and property of foreign businesses, and speaks favorably of the certainty which inheres when parties specify an arbitral forum for resolution of differences in "any contract touching two or more countries."

This invocation of the "international contract" talisman might be applied to a situation where, for example, an interest in a foreign company or mutual fund was sold to an utterly unsophisticated American citizen, with material fraudulent misrepresentations made in this country. The arbitration clause could appear in the fine print of a form contract, and still be sufficient to preclude recourse to our courts, forcing the defrauded citizen to arbitration in Paris to vindicate his rights.[7]

It has been recognized that the 1934 Act, including the protections of Rule 10b-5, applies when foreign defendants have defrauded American investors, particularly when, as alleged here, they have profited by virtue of proscribed conduct within our boundaries. This is true even when the defendant is organized under the laws of a foreign country, is conducting much of its activity outside the United States, and is therefore governed largely by foreign law. The language of § 29 of the 1934 Act does not immunize such international transactions, and the United Nations Convention provides that a forum court in which a suit is brought need not enforce an agreement to arbitrate which is "void" and "inoperative" as contrary to its public policy. When a foreign corporation undertakes fraudulent action which subjects it to the jurisdiction of our federal securities laws, nothing justifies the conclusion that only a diluted version of those laws protects American investors.

Section 29(a) of the 1934 Act provides that a stipulation binding one to waive compliance with "any provision" of the Act shall be void, and the Act expressly provides that the federal district courts shall have "exclusive jurisdiction" over suits

---

[7] The Court concedes that there may be situations where foreign contacts were "so insignificant or attenuated" that *Wilko* would apply and an American court would not enforce an arbitration agreement in an international contract. The recognition that 'international' contracts may in fact involve significant direct contacts with this country is realistic and salutary. But the Court by its concession undermines somewhat its reliance on its admonition-itself supported only by speculation-that "[a] contractual provision specifying in advance the forum in which disputes shall be litigated... is... an almost indispensable precondition to achievement of the orderliness and predictability essential to any international business transaction." Uncertainty and a "dicey atmosphere," supposedly destructive of international contracts, may persist for many contracts. The parties to an international contract may not in fact be bound by a "solemn agreement" to arbitrate, for an American court could find, at a much later date, sufficient contacts with this country to require the application of *Wilko*.

brought under the Act. 15 U.S.C. § 78aa. The Court appears to attach some significance to the fact that the specific provisions of the 1933 Act involved in Wilko are not duplicated in the 1934 Act, which is involved in this case. While Alberto-Culver would not have the right to sue in either a state or federal forum as did the plaintiff in Wilko, 346 U.S., at 431, the Court deprives it of its right to have its Rule 10b-5 claim heard in a federal court. We spoke at length in Wilko of this problem, elucidating the undesirable effects of remitting a securities plaintiff to an arbitral, rather than a judicial, forum. Here, as in Wilko, the allegations of fraudulent misrepresentation will involve "subjective findings on the purpose and knowledge" of the defendant, questions ill-determined by arbitrators without judicial instruction on the law. See id., at 435. An arbitral award can be made without explication of reasons and without development of a record, so that the arbitrator's conception of our statutory requirement may be absolutely incorrect yet functionally unreviewable, even when the arbitrator seeks to apply our law. We recognized in Wilko that there is no judicial review corresponding to review of court decisions. Id., at 436–437. The extensive pretrial discovery provided by the Federal Rules of Civil Procedure for actions in district court would not be available. And the wide choice of venue provided by the 1934 Act, 15 U.S.C. § 78aa, would be forfeited. See Wilko v. Swan, supra, at 431. The loss of the proper judicial forum carries with it the loss of substantial rights.

When a defendant, as alleged here, has, through proscribed acts within our territory, brought itself within the ken of federal securities regulation, a fact not disputed here, those laws—including the controlling principles of Wilko—apply whether the defendant is foreign or American, and whether or not there are transnational elements in the dealings. Those laws are rendered a chimera when foreign corporations or funds-unlike domestic defendants-can nullify them by virtue of arbitration clauses which send defrauded American investors to the uncertainty of arbitration on foreign soil, or, if those investors cannot afford to arbitrate their claims in a far-off forum, to no remedy at all.

Moreover, the international aura which the Court gives this case is ominous. We now have many multinational corporations in vast operations around the world-Europe, Latin America, the Middle East, and Asia. The investments of many American investors turn on dealings by these companies. Up to this day, it has been assumed by reason of Wilko that they were all protected by our various federal securities Acts. If these guarantees are to be removed, it should take a legislative enactment. I would enforce our laws as they stand, unless Congress makes an exception.

The virtue of certainty in international agreements may be important, but Congress has dictated that when there are sufficient contacts for our securities laws to apply, the policies expressed in those laws take precedence. Section 29 of the 1934 Act, which renders arbitration clauses void and inoperative, recognizes no exception for fraudulent dealings which incidentally have some international factors. The Convention makes provision for such national public policy in Art. II(3). Federal jurisdiction under the 1934 Act will attach only to some international transactions, but when it does, the protections afforded investors such as Alberto-Culver can only be full-fledged.

Comments and Questions

1. The Court not only applies The Bremen doctrine; it characterizes an arbitration clause as a "super"-forum-selection clause. Are there important differences between enforcing a choice of court clause that effectively sends the matter to State X and enforcing an arbitration clause that effectively sends the matter to Arbitral Forum Y?

2. This Court was divided 5–4. Is the breakdown justifiable (or predictable) based on the ideologies of the justices? Is arbitration "conservative"? Justice Douglas had been head of the Securities Exchange Commission before joining the Court. Whatever the explanation for the split, the decision has stood the test of time and is often cited as evidence of the United States' strong support of arbitration, even where public law issues are involved.

3. The arbitration clause quoted in footnote 1 of the majority opinion in Scherk provides a good example of the content, structure, and function of an international agreement to arbitrate. Consider some of the interpretive issues:

   a. "The parties agree that if any controversy or claim shall arise out of this agreement or the breach thereof...." Is this sufficiently broad to cover related tort claims? If yes, how "related" must they be? And if no, what additional language is missing?

   b. "...the matter shall be settled exclusively by arbitration..." Does the word exclusively preclude the plaintiff from seeking preliminary relief from a court?

   c. "...in accordance with the rules then obtaining of the International Chamber of Commerce, Paris, France ...." And if there are no specific rules governing the gathering or presentation of evidence, the availability of expert witnesses, applicable privileges, contempt sanctions, etc., what rules apply then?

   d. "...each party agrees to comply in all respects with any award made in any such proceeding...." But what if the arbitral proceeding was fraudulent, or if the arbitrator got the law wrong, or if one of the parties was denied a fair opportunity to present their case?

   e. "The laws of the State of Illinois, U.S.A. shall apply to and govern this agreement, its interpretation and performance." Does this include federal laws? Does this include the substantive law of other jurisdictions to the extent that the State of Illinois, pursuant to its principles of conflict of laws, would apply that other law? What result if Illinois law prohibited such an arbitration clause?

4. The arbitrability of statutory rights is not expressly mentioned in Scherk. That issue arose ten years later in *Mitsubishi Motors Corp. v. Soler Chrysler-Plymouth, Inc.*, which follows.

Mitsubishi Motors Corp. v. Soler Chrysler-Plymouth, Inc.

473 U.S. 614 (1985)

MR. JUSTICE BLACKMUN delivered the opinion of the Court:
The principal question presented by these cases is the arbitrability, pursuant to the Federal Arbitration Act, 9 U.S.C. § 1 et seq., and the Convention on the Recognition and Enforcement of Foreign Arbitral Awards (Convention), [1970] 21 U.S.T. 2517, T.I.A.S. No. 6997, of claims arising under the Sherman Act, 15 U.S.C. § 1 et seq., and encompassed within a valid arbitration clause in an agreement embodying an international commercial transaction.

I

Petitioner-cross-respondent Mitsubishi Motors Corporation (Mitsubishi) is a Japanese corporation which manufactures automobiles and has its principal place of business in Tokyo, Japan. Mitsubishi is the product of a joint venture between, on the one hand, Chrysler International, S.A. (CISA), a Swiss corporation registered in Geneva and wholly owned by Chrysler Corporation, and, on the other, Mitsubishi Heavy Industries, Inc., a Japanese corporation. The aim of the joint venture was the distribution through Chrysler dealers outside the continental United States of vehicles manufactured by Mitsubishi and bearing Chrysler and Mitsubishi trademarks. Respondent-cross-petitioner Soler Chrysler-Plymouth, Inc. (Soler), is a Puerto Rico corporation with its principal place of business in Pueblo Viejo, Guaynabo, Puerto Rico.

On October 31, 1979, Soler entered into a Distributor Agreement with CISA which provided for the sale by Soler of Mitsubishi-manufactured vehicles within a designated area, including metropolitan San Juan. On the same date, CISA, Soler, and Mitsubishi entered into a Sales Procedure Agreement (Sales Agreement) which, referring to the Distributor Agreement, provided for the direct sale of Mitsubishi products to Soler and governed the terms and conditions of such sales. Paragraph VI of the Sales Agreement, labeled "Arbitration of Certain Matters," provides:

> All disputes, controversies or differences which may arise between [Mitsubishi] and [Soler] out of or in relation to Articles I-B through V of this Agreement or for the breach thereof, shall be finally settled by arbitration in Japan in accordance with the rules and regulations of the Japan Commercial Arbitration Association.

Initially, Soler did a brisk business in Mitsubishi-manufactured vehicles. As a result of its strong performance, its minimum sales volume, specified by Mitsubishi and CISA, and agreed to by Soler, for the 1981 model year was substantially increased. In early 1981, however, the new-car market slackened. Soler ran into serious difficulties in meeting the expected sales volume, and by the spring of 1981 it felt itself compelled to request that Mitsubishi delay or cancel shipment of several orders. About the same time, Soler attempted to arrange for the transshipment of a quantity of its vehicles for sale in the continental United States and Latin America. Mitsubishi and CISA, however, refused permission for any such diversion, citing a variety of reasons,[1] and no vehicles were transshipped. Attempts to work out these difficulties failed. Mitsubishi eventually withheld shipment of 966 vehicles, apparently representing orders placed for May, June, and July 1981 production, responsibility for which Soler disclaimed in February 1982.

The following month, Mitsubishi brought an action against Soler in the United States District Court for the District of Puerto Rico under the Federal Arbitration Act and the Convention. Mitsubishi sought an order, pursuant to 9 U.S.C. §§ 4 and 201, to compel arbitration in accord with 57 VI of the Sales Agreement. Shortly after filing the complaint, Mitsubishi filed a request for arbitration before the Japan Commercial Arbitration Association.

Soler denied the allegations and counterclaimed against both Mitsubishi and CISA. It alleged numerous breaches by Mitsubishi of the Sales Agreement,[5] raised a pair of defamation claims,[6] and asserted causes of action under the Sherman Act, 15 U.S.C. § 1 et seq.; the federal Automobile Dealers' Day in Court Act, 70 Stat. 1125, 15 U.S.C. § 1221 et seq.; the Puerto Rico competition statute, P.R. Laws Ann., Tit. 10, § 257 et seq. (1976); and the Puerto Rico Dealers' Contracts Act, P.R. Laws Ann., Tit. 10, § 278 et seq. (1978 and Supp.1983). In the counterclaim premised on the Sherman Act, Soler alleged that Mitsubishi and CISA had conspired to divide markets in restraint of trade. To effectuate the plan, according to Soler, Mitsubishi had refused to permit Soler to resell to buyers in North, Central, or South America vehicles it had obligated itself to purchase from Mitsubishi; had refused to ship ordered vehicles or the parts, such as heaters and defoggers, that would be necessary to permit Soler to make its vehicles suitable for resale outside Puerto Rico; and had coercively attempted to replace Soler and its other Puerto Rico distributors with a wholly owned subsidiary which would serve as the exclusive Mitsubishi distributor in Puerto Rico.

After a hearing, the District Court ordered Mitsubishi and Soler to arbitrate each of the issues raised in the complaint and in all the counterclaims save two and a portion of a third. With regard to the federal antitrust issues, it recognized that

---

[1] The reasons advanced included concerns that such diversion would interfere with the Japanese trade policy of voluntarily limiting imports to the United States; that the Soler-ordered vehicles would be unsuitable for use in certain proposed destinations because of their manufacture, with use in Puerto Rico in mind, without heaters and defoggers; that the vehicles would be unsuitable for use in Latin America because of the unavailability there of the unleaded, high-octane fuel they required; that adequate warranty service could not be ensured; and that diversion to the mainland would violate contractual obligations between CISA and Mitsubishi.

[5] The alleged breaches included wrongful refusal to ship ordered vehicles and necessary parts, failure to make payment for warranty work and authorized rebates, and bad faith in establishing minimum-sales volumes.

[6] The fourth counterclaim alleged that Mitsubishi had made statements that defamed Soler's good name and business reputation to a company with which Soler was then negotiating the sale of its plant and distributorship. The sixth counterclaim alleged that Mitsubishi had made a willfully false and malicious statement in an affidavit submitted in support of its application for a temporary restraining order, and that Mitsubishi had wrongfully advised Soler's customers and the public in its market area that they should no longer do business with Soler.

the Courts of Appeals, following American Safety Equipment Corp. v. J.P. Maguire & Co., 391 F.2d 821 (2nd Cir. 1968), uniformly had held that the rights conferred by the antitrust laws were "'of a character inappropriate for enforcement by arbitration.'" App. to Pet. for Cert. in No. 83-1569, p. B9, quoting Wilko v. Swan, 201 F.2d 439, 444 (2nd Cir. 1953), rev'd, 346 U.S. 427 (1953). The District Court held, however, that the international character of the Mitsubishi-Soler undertaking required enforcement of the agreement to arbitrate even as to the antitrust claims. It relied on Scherk v. Alberto-Culver Co., 417 U.S. 506, 515–520 (1974), in which this Court ordered arbitration, pursuant to a provision embodied in an international agreement, of a claim arising under the Securities Exchange Act of 1934 notwithstanding its assumption, arguendo, that Wilko, supra, which held nonarbitrable claims arising under the Securities Act of 1933, also would bar arbitration of a 1934 Act claim arising in a domestic context.

The United States Court of Appeals for the First Circuit affirmed in part and reversed in part. It first rejected Soler's argument that Puerto Rico law precluded enforcement of an agreement obligating a local dealer to arbitrate controversies outside Puerto Rico. It also rejected Soler's suggestion that it could not have intended to arbitrate statutory claims not mentioned in the arbitration agreement. Assessing arbitrability "on an allegation-by-allegation basis," the court then read the arbitration clause to encompass virtually all the claims arising under the various statutes, including all those arising under the Sherman Act.

Finally, after endorsing the doctrine of American Safety, precluding arbitration of antitrust claims, the Court of Appeals concluded that neither this Court's decision in Scherk nor the Convention required abandonment of that doctrine in the face of an international transaction. Accordingly, it reversed the judgment of the District Court insofar as it had ordered submission of "Soler's antitrust claims" to arbitration. Affirming the remainder of the judgment, the court directed the District Court to consider in the first instance how the parallel judicial and arbitral proceedings should go forward.

We granted certiorari primarily to consider whether an American court should enforce an agreement to resolve antitrust claims by arbitration when that agreement arises from an international transaction. 469 U.S. 916 (1984).

II

[W]e find no warrant in the Arbitration Act for implying in every contract within its ken a presumption against arbitration of statutory claims. The Act's centerpiece provision makes a written agreement to arbitrate "in any maritime transaction or a contract evidencing a transaction involving commerce... valid, irrevocable, and enforceable, save upon such grounds as exist at law or in equity for the revocation of any contract." 9 U.S.C. § 2. The "liberal federal policy favoring arbitration agreements," Moses H. Cone Memorial Hospital v. Mercury Construction Corp., 460 U.S. 1, 24 (1983), manifested by this provision and the Act as a whole, is at bottom a policy guaranteeing the enforcement of private contractual arrangements: the

Act simply "creates a body of federal substantive law establishing and regulating the duty to honor an agreement to arbitrate." Id., at 25, n.32. As this Court recently observed, "[t]he preeminent concern of Congress in passing the Act was to enforce private agreements into which parties had entered," a concern which "requires that we rigorously enforce agreements to arbitrate." Dean Witter Reynolds Inc. v. Byrd, 470 U.S. 213, 221 (1985).

Accordingly, the first task of a court asked to compel arbitration of a dispute is to determine whether the parties agreed to arbitrate that dispute.... Thus, as with any other contract, the parties' intentions control, but those intentions are generously construed as to issues of arbitrability.

There is no reason to depart from these guidelines where a party bound by an arbitration agreement raises claims founded on statutory rights. Some time ago this Court expressed "hope for [the Act's] usefulness both in controversies based on statutes or on standards otherwise created," Wilko v. Swan, 346 U.S. 427, 432 (1953) (footnote omitted); see Merrill Lynch, Pierce, Fenner & Smith, Inc. v. Ware, 414 U.S. 117, 135 n.15 (1973), and we are well past the time when judicial suspicion of the desirability of arbitration and of the competence of arbitral tribunals inhibited the development of arbitration as an alternative means of dispute resolution. Just last Term in Southland Corp., supra, where we held that § 2 of the Act declared a national policy applicable equally in state as well as federal courts, we construed an arbitration clause to encompass the disputes at issue without pausing at the source in a state statute of the rights asserted by the parties resisting arbitration. 465 U.S., at 15, and n.7. Of course, courts should remain attuned to well-supported claims that the agreement to arbitrate resulted from the sort of fraud or overwhelming economic power that would provide grounds "for the revocation of any contract." 9 U.S.C. § 2; see Southland Corp., 465 U.S., at 16, n.11; The Bremen v. Zapata Off-Shore Co., 407 U.S. 1, 15 (1972). But, absent such compelling considerations, the Act itself provides no basis for disfavoring agreements to arbitrate statutory claims by skewing the otherwise hospitable inquiry into arbitrability.

That is not to say that all controversies implicating statutory rights are suitable for arbitration. There is no reason to distort the process of contract interpretation, however, in order to ferret out the inappropriate. Just as it is the congressional policy manifested in the Federal Arbitration Act that requires courts liberally to construe the scope of arbitration agreements covered by that Act, it is the congressional intention expressed in some other statute on which the courts must rely to identify any category of claims as to which agreements to arbitrate will be held unenforceable. See Wilko v. Swan, 346 U.S., at 434–435; Southland Corp., 465 U.S., at 16, n. 11; Dean Witter Reynolds Inc., 470 U.S., at 224–225 (concurring opinion). For that reason, Soler's concern for statutorily protected classes provides no reason to color the lens through which the arbitration clause is read. By agreeing to arbitrate a statutory claim, a party does not forgo the substantive rights afforded by the statute; it only submits to their resolution in an arbitral, rather than a judicial, forum. It trades the procedures and opportunity for review of the courtroom for the simplicity, informality, and expedition of arbitration. We must assume that if

Congress intended the substantive protection afforded by a given statute to include protection against waiver of the right to a judicial forum, that intention will be deducible from text or legislative history. See Wilko v. Swan, supra. Having made the bargain to arbitrate, the party should be held to it unless Congress itself has evinced an intention to preclude a waiver of judicial remedies for the statutory rights at issue. Nothing, in the meantime, prevents a party from excluding statutory claims from the scope of an agreement to arbitrate. See Prima Paint Corp., 388 U.S., at 406....

III

We now turn to consider whether Soler's antitrust claims are nonarbitrable even though it has agreed to arbitrate them. In holding that they are not, the Court of Appeals followed the decision of the Second Circuit in American Safety Equipment Corp. v. J.P. Maguire & Co., 391 F.2d 821 (1968). Notwithstanding the absence of any explicit support for such an exception in either the Sherman Act or the Federal Arbitration Act, the Second Circuit there reasoned that "the pervasive public interest in enforcement of the antitrust laws, and the nature of the claims that arise in such cases, combine to make...antitrust claims...inappropriate for arbitration." Id., at 827–828. We find it unnecessary to assess the legitimacy of the American Safety doctrine as applied to agreements to arbitrate arising from domestic transactions. As in Scherk v. Alberto-Culver Co., 417 U.S. 506 (1974), we conclude that concerns of international comity, respect for the capacities of foreign and transnational tribunals, and sensitivity to the need of the international commercial system for predictability in the resolution of disputes require that we enforce the parties' agreement, even assuming that a contrary result would be forthcoming in a domestic context....

The Bremen and Scherk establish a strong presumption in favor of enforcement of freely negotiated contractual choice-of-forum provisions. Here, as in Scherk, that presumption is reinforced by the emphatic federal policy in favor of arbitral dispute resolution. And at least since this Nation's accession in 1970 to the Convention, see [1970] 21 U.S.T. 2517, T.I.A.S. 6997, and the implementation of the Convention in the same year by amendment of the Federal Arbitration Act, that federal policy applies with special force in the field of international commerce. Thus, we must weigh the concerns of American Safety against a strong belief in the efficacy of arbitral procedures for the resolution of international commercial disputes and an equal commitment to the enforcement of freely negotiated choice-of-forum clauses.

At the outset, we confess to some skepticism of certain aspects of the American Safety doctrine. As distilled by the First Circuit, 723 F.2d, at 162, the doctrine comprises four ingredients. First, private parties play a pivotal role in aiding governmental enforcement of the antitrust laws by means of the private action for treble damages. Second, "the strong possibility that contracts which generate antitrust disputes may be contracts of adhesion militates against automatic forum determination by contract." Third, antitrust issues, prone to complication, require sophisticated legal and economic analysis, and thus are "ill-adapted to strengths of the arbitral process, i.e., expedition, minimal requirements of written rationale, simplicity, resort to basic concepts of common sense and simple equity." Finally, just as "issues of war and peace are too important to be vested in the generals,... decisions as to antitrust regulation of business are too important to be lodged in arbitrators chosen from the business community-particularly those from a foreign community that has had no experience with or exposure to our law and values." See American Safety, 391 F.2d, at 826–827.

Initially, we find the second concern unjustified. The mere appearance of an antitrust dispute does not alone warrant invalidation of the selected forum on the undemonstrated assumption that the arbitration clause is tainted. A party resisting arbitration of course may attack directly the validity of the agreement to arbitrate. See Prima Paint Corp. v. Flood & Conklin Mfg. Co., 388 U.S. 395 (1967). Moreover, the party may attempt to make a showing that would warrant setting aside the forum-selection clause-that the agreement was "[a]ffected by fraud, undue influence, or overweening bargaining power"; that "enforcement would be unreasonable and unjust"; or that proceedings "in the contractual forum will be so gravely difficult and inconvenient that [the resisting party] will for all practical purposes be deprived of his day in court." The Bremen, 407 U.S. at 12, 15, 18. But absent such a showing-and none was attempted here-there is no basis for assuming the forum inadequate or its selection unfair.

Next, potential complexity should not suffice to ward off arbitration. We might well have some doubt that even the courts following American Safety subscribe fully to the view that antitrust matters are inherently insusceptible to resolution by arbitration, as these same courts have agreed that an undertaking to arbitrate antitrust claims entered into after the dispute arises is acceptable. See, e.g., Coenen v. R.W. Pressprich & Co., 453 F.2d 1209, 1215 (2nd Cir.), cert. denied, 406 U.S. 949 (1972); Cobb v. Lewis, 488 F. 2d 41, 48 (5th Cir. 1974). See also, in the present cases, 723 F.2d, at 168, n.12 (leaving question open). And the vertical restraints which most frequently give birth to antitrust claims covered by an arbitration agreement will not often occasion the monstrous proceedings that have given antitrust litigation an image of intractability. In any event, adaptability and access to expertise are hallmarks of arbitration. The anticipated subject matter of the dispute may be taken into account when the arbitrators are appointed, and arbitral rules typically provide for the participation of experts either employed by the parties or appointed by the tribunal. Moreover, it is often a judgment that streamlined proceedings and expeditious results will best serve their needs that causes parties to agree to arbitrate their disputes; it is typically a desire to keep the effort and expense required to resolve a dispute within manageable bounds that prompts them mutually to forgo access to judicial remedies. In sum, the factor of potential complexity alone does not persuade us that an arbitral tribunal could not properly handle an antitrust matter.

For similar reasons, we also reject the proposition that an arbitration panel will pose too great a danger of innate hostility to the constraints on business conduct that antitrust law imposes. International arbitrators frequently are drawn from the legal as well as the business community; where the dispute has an important legal component, the parties and the arbitral body with whose assistance they have agreed to settle their dispute can be expected to select arbitrators accordingly.[18] We decline to indulge the presumption that the parties and arbitral body conducting a proceeding will be unable or unwilling to retain competent, conscientious, and impartial arbitrators.

We are left, then, with the core of the American Safety doctrine—the fundamental importance to American democratic capitalism of the regime of the antitrust laws. See, e.g., United States v. Topco Assocs., Inc., 405 U.S. 596, 610 (1972); Northern Pacific R. Co. v. United States, 356 U.S. 1, 4 (1958). Without doubt, the private cause of action plays a central role in enforcing this regime. See, e.g., Hawaii v. Standard Oil Co., 405 U.S. 251, 252 (1972). As the Court of Appeals pointed out:

> A claim under the antitrust laws is not merely a private matter. The Sherman Act is designed to promote the national interest in a competitive economy; thus, the plaintiff asserting his rights under the Act has been likened to a private attorney-general who protects the public's interest. (723 F.2d, at 168, quoting American Safety, 391 F.2d, at 826.)

The treble-damages provision wielded by the private litigant is a chief tool in the antitrust enforcement scheme, posing a crucial deterrent to potential violators. See, e.g., Perma Life Mufflers, Inc. v. International Parts Corp., 392 U.S. 134, 138–139 (1968).

The importance of the private damages remedy, however, does not compel the conclusion that it may not be sought outside an American court. Notwithstanding its important incidental policing function, the treble-damages cause of action conferred on private parties by § 4 of the Clayton Act, 15 U.S.C. § 15, and pursued by Soler here by way of its third counterclaim, seeks primarily to enable an injured competitor to gain compensation for that injury....

There is no reason to assume at the outset of the dispute that international arbitration will not provide an adequate mechanism. To be sure, the international arbitral tribunal owes no prior allegiance to the legal norms of particular states;

---

[18] *See* Craig, Park, & Paulsson, *supra*, § 12.03, p. 28; Sanders, Commentary on UNCITRAL Arbitration Rules § 15.1, in 2 Yearbook Commercial Arbitration, *supra*, at 203.

We are advised by Mitsubishi and amicus International Chamber of Commerce, without contradiction by Soler, that the arbitration panel selected to hear the parties' claims here is composed of three Japanese lawyers, one a former law school dean, another a former judge, and the third a practicing attorney with American legal training who has written on Japanese antitrust law. Brief for Petitioner in No. 83-1569, p. 26; Brief for International Chamber of Commerce as Amicus Curiae 16, n. 28.

The Court of Appeals was concerned that international arbitrators would lack "experience with or exposure to our law and values." 723 F.2d, at 162. The obstacles confronted by the arbitration panel in this case, however, should be no greater than those confronted by any judicial or arbitral tribunal required to determine foreign law. *See, e.g.*, Fed. Rule Civ. Proc. 44.1. Moreover, while our attachment to the antitrust laws may be stronger than most, many other countries, including Japan, have similar bodies of competition law. *See, e.g.*, 1 Law of Transnational Business Transactions, ch. 9 (Banks, Antitrust Aspects of International Business Operations), § 9.03[7] (V. Nanda ed. 1984); H. Iyori & A. Uesugi, The Antimonopoly Laws of Japan (1983).

hence, it has no direct obligation to vindicate their statutory dictates. The tribunal, however, is bound to effectuate the intentions of the parties. Where the parties have agreed that the arbitral body is to decide a defined set of claims which includes, as in these cases, those arising from the application of American antitrust law, the tribunal therefore should be bound to decide that dispute in accord with the national law giving rise to the claim. Cf. Wilko v. Swan, 346 U.S., at 433–434.[19] And so long as the prospective litigant effectively may vindicate its statutory cause of action in the arbitral forum, the statute will continue to serve both its remedial and deterrent function.

Having permitted the arbitration to go forward, the national courts of the United States will have the opportunity at the award-enforcement stage to ensure that the legitimate interest in the enforcement of the antitrust laws has been addressed. The Convention reserves to each signatory country the right to refuse enforcement of an award where the "recognition or enforcement of the award would be contrary to the public policy of that country." Art. V(2)(b), 21 U.S.T., at 2520; see Scherk, 417 U.S., at 519, n. 14. While the efficacy of the arbitral process requires that substantive review at the award-enforcement stage remain minimal, it would not require intrusive inquiry to ascertain that the tribunal took cognizance of the antitrust claims and actually decided them.

As international trade has expanded in recent decades, so too has the use of international arbitration to resolve disputes arising in the course of that trade. The controversies that international arbitral institutions are called upon to resolve have increased in diversity as well as in complexity. Yet the potential of these tribunals for efficient disposition of legal disagreements arising from commercial relations has not yet been tested. If they are to take a central place in the international legal

---

[19] In addition to the clause providing for arbitration before the Japan Commercial Arbitration Association, the Sales Agreement includes a choice-of-law clause which reads: "This Agreement is made in, and will be governed by and construed in all respects according to the laws of the Swiss Confederation as if entirely performed therein." App. 56. The United States raises the possibility that the arbitral panel will read this provision not simply to govern interpretation of the contract terms, but wholly to displace American law even where it otherwise would apply. Brief for United States as Amicus Curiae 20. The International Chamber of Commerce opines that it is "[c]onceivabl[e], although we believe it unlikely, [that] the arbitrators could consider Soler's affirmative claim of anticompetitive conduct by CISA and Mitsubishi to fall within the purview of this choice-of-law provision, with the result that it would be decided under Swiss law rather than the U.S. Sherman Act." Brief for International Chamber of Commerce as Amicus Curiae 25. At oral argument, however, counsel for Mitsubishi conceded that American law applied to the antitrust claims and represented that the claims had been submitted to the arbitration panel in Japan on that basis. Tr. of Oral Arg. 18. The record confirms that before the decision of the Court of Appeals the arbitral panel had taken these claims under submission. *See* District Court Order of May 25, 1984, pp. 2–3.

We therefore have no occasion to speculate on this matter at this stage in the proceedings, when Mitsubishi seeks to enforce the agreement to arbitrate, not to enforce an award. Nor need we consider now the effect of an arbitral tribunal's failure to take cognizance of the statutory cause of action on the claimant's capacity to reinitiate suit in federal court. We merely note that in the event the choice-of-forum and choice-of-law clauses operated in tandem as a prospective waiver of a party's right to pursue statutory remedies for antitrust violations, we would have little hesitation in condemning the agreement as against public policy.

order, national courts will need to "shake off the old judicial hostility to arbitration," Kulukundis Shipping Co. v. Amtorg Trading Corp., 126 F.2d 978, 985 (2nd Cir. 1942), and also their customary and understandable unwillingness to cede jurisdiction of a claim arising under domestic law to a foreign or transnational tribunal. To this extent, at least, it will be necessary for national courts to subordinate domestic notions of arbitrability to the international policy favoring commercial arbitration. See Scherk, supra.

Accordingly, we "require this representative of the American business community to honor its bargain," Alberto-Culver Co. v. Scherk, 484 F.2d 611, 620 (7th Cir. 1973) (Stevens, J., dissenting), by holding this agreement to arbitrate "enforce[able]...in accord with the explicit provisions of the Arbitration Act." Scherk, 417 U.S., at 520.

The judgment of the Court of Appeals is affirmed in part and reversed in part, and the cases are remanded for further proceedings consistent with this opinion.

Justice Powell took no part in the decision of these cases.

Justice Stevens, with whom Justice Brennan joins, and with whom Justice Marshall joins except as to Part II, dissenting:

This Court's holding rests almost exclusively on the federal policy favoring arbitration of commercial disputes and vague notions of international comity arising from the fact that the automobiles involved here were manufactured in Japan. Because I am convinced that the Court of Appeals' construction of the arbitration clause is erroneous, and because I strongly disagree with this Court's interpretation of the relevant federal statutes, I respectfully dissent. In my opinion, (1) a fair construction of the language in the arbitration clause in the parties' contract does not encompass a claim that auto manufacturers entered into a conspiracy in violation of the antitrust laws; (2) an arbitration clause should not normally be construed to cover a statutory remedy that it does not expressly identify; (3) Congress did not intend § 2 of the Federal Arbitration Act to apply to antitrust claims; and (4) Congress did not intend the Convention on the Recognition and Enforcement of Foreign Arbitral Awards to apply to disputes that are not covered by the Federal Arbitration Act.

I

On October 31, 1979, respondent, Soler Chrysler-Plymouth, Inc. (Soler), entered into a "distributor agreement" to govern the sale of Plymouth passenger cars to be manufactured by petitioner, Mitsubishi Motors Corporation of Tokyo, Japan (Mitsubishi). Mitsubishi, however, was not a party to that agreement. Rather the "purchase rights" were granted to Soler by a wholly owned subsidiary of Chrysler Corporation that is referred to as "Chrysler" in the agreement. The distributor agreement does not contain an arbitration clause. Nor does the record contain any other agreement providing for the arbitration of disputes between Soler and Chrysler.

Paragraph 26 of the distributor agreement authorizes Chrysler to have Soler's orders filled by any company affiliated with Chrysler, that company thereby becoming the "supplier" of the products covered by the agreement with Chrysler. Relying on paragraph 26 of their distributor agreement, Soler, Chrysler, and Mitsubishi entered into a separate Sales Procedure Agreement designating Mitsubishi as the supplier of the products covered by the distributor agreement. The arbitration clause the Court construes today is found in that agreement. As a matter of ordinary contract interpretation, there are at least two reasons why that clause does not apply to Soler's antitrust claim against Chrysler and Mitsubishi.

First, the clause only applies to two-party disputes between Soler and Mitsubishi. The antitrust violation alleged in Soler's counterclaim is a three-party dispute. Soler has joined both Chrysler and its associated company, Mitsubishi, as counterdefendants. The pleading expressly alleges that both of those companies are "engaged in an unlawful combination and conspiracy to restrain and divide markets in interstate and foreign commerce, in violation of the Sherman Antitrust Act and the Clayton Act." App. 91. It is further alleged that Chrysler authorized and participated in several overt acts directed at Soler. At this stage of the case we must, of course, assume the truth of those allegations. Only by stretching the language of the arbitration clause far beyond its ordinary meaning could one possibly conclude that it encompasses this three-party dispute.

Second, the clause only applies to disputes "which may arise between MMC and BUYER out of or in relation to Articles I-B through V of this Agreement or for the breach thereof…." Id., at 52. Thus, disputes relating to only 5 out of a total of 15 Articles in the Sales Procedure Agreement are arbitrable. Those five Articles cover: (1) the terms and conditions of direct sales (matters such as the scheduling of orders, deliveries, and payment); (2) technical and engineering changes; (3) compliance by Mitsubishi with customs laws and regulations, and Soler's obligation to inform Mitsubishi of relevant local laws; (4) trademarks and patent rights; and (5) Mitsubishi's right to cease production of any products. It is immediately obviously that Soler's antitrust claim did not arise out of Articles I-B through V and it is not a claim "for the breach thereof." The question is whether it is a dispute "in relation to" those Articles.

Because Mitsubishi relies on those Articles of the contract to explain some of the activities that Soler challenges in its antitrust claim, the Court of Appeals concluded that the relationship between the dispute and those Articles brought the arbitration clause into play. I find that construction of the clause wholly unpersuasive. The words "in relation to" appear between the references to claims that arise under the contract and claims for breach of the contract; I believe all three of the species of arbitrable claims must be predicated on contractual rights defined in Articles I-B through V.

The federal policy favoring arbitration cannot sustain the weight that the Court assigns to it. A clause requiring arbitration of all claims "relating to" a contract surely could not encompass a claim that the arbitration clause was itself part of a contract in restraint of trade. Cf. Paramount Famous Lasky Corp. v. United States, 282 U.S. 30 (1930); see also United States v. Paramount Pictures, Inc., 334 U.S. 131, 176 (1948). Nor in my judgment should it be read to encompass a claim that relies, not on a failure to perform the contract, but on an independent violation of federal law. The matters asserted by way of defense do not control the character, or the source, of the claim that Soler has asserted. Accordingly, simply as a matter of ordinary contract interpretation, I would hold that Soler's antitrust claim is not arbitrable.

II

Section 2 of the Federal Arbitration Act describes three kinds of arbitrable agreements. Two—those including maritime transactions and those covering the submission of an existing dispute to arbitration—are not involved in this case.... The plain language of this statute encompasses Soler's claims that arise out of its contract with Mitsubishi, but does not encompass a claim arising under federal law, or indeed one that arises under its distributor agreement with Chrysler. Nothing in the text of the 1925 Act, nor its legislative history, suggests that Congress intended to authorize the arbitration of any statutory claims.

Until today all of our cases enforcing agreements to arbitrate under the Arbitration Act have involved contract claims. In one, the party claiming a breach of contractual warranties also claimed that the breach amounted to fraud actionable under § 10(b) of the Securities Exchange Act of 1934. Scherk v. Alberto-Culver Co., 417 U.S. 506 (1974). But this is the first time the Court has considered the question whether a standard arbitration clause referring to claims arising out of or relating to a contract should be construed to cover statutory claims that have only an indirect relationship to the contract. In my opinion, neither the Congress that enacted the Arbitration Act in 1925, nor the many parties who have agreed to such standard clauses, could have anticipated the Court's answer to that question.

On several occasions we have drawn a distinction between statutory rights and contractual rights and refused to hold that an arbitration barred the assertion of a statutory right. Thus, in Alexander v. Gardner-Denver Co., 415 U.S. 36 (1974), we held that the arbitration of a claim of employment discrimination would not bar an employee's statutory right to damages under Title VII of the Civil Rights Act of 1964, 42 U.S.C. §§ 2000e-2000e-17, notwithstanding the strong federal policy favoring the arbitration of labor disputes.... In addition, the Court noted that the informal procedures which make arbitration so desirable in the context of contractual disputes are inadequate to develop a record for appellate review of statutory questions.[14] Such review is essential on matters of statutory interpretation in order to assure consistent application of important public rights.

---

[14] "Moreover, the factfinding process in arbitration usually is not equivalent to judicial factfinding. The record of the arbitration proceedings is not as complete; the usual rules of evidence do not apply; and rights and procedures common to civil trials, such as discovery, compulsory process, cross-examination, and testimony under oath, are often severely limited or unavailable. And as this Court has recognized, '[a]rbitrators have no obligation to the court to give their reasons for an award.' *United Steelworkers of America v. Enterprise Wheel & Car Corp.*, 363 U.S. [593], at 598. Indeed, it is the informality of arbitral procedure that enables it to function as an efficient, inexpensive, and expeditious means for dispute resolution. This same characteristic, however, makes arbitration a less appropriate forum for final resolution of Title VII issues than the federal courts." 415 U.S., at 57–58 (footnote omitted).

In Barrentine v. Arkansas-Best Freight System, Inc., 450 U.S. 728 (1981), we reached a similar conclusion with respect to the arbitrability of an employee's claim based on the Fair Labor Standards Act, 29 U.S.C. §§ 201–219. We again noted that an arbitrator, unlike a federal judge, has no institutional obligation to enforce federal legislative policy....

In view of the Court's repeated recognition of the distinction between federal statutory rights and contractual rights, together with the undisputed historical fact that arbitration has functioned almost entirely in either the area of labor disputes or in "ordinary disputes between merchants as to questions of fact," see n. 11, supra, it is reasonable to assume that most lawyers and executives would not expect the language in the standard arbitration clause to cover federal statutory claims. Thus, in my opinion, both a fair respect for the importance of the interests that Congress has identified as worthy of federal statutory protection, and a fair appraisal of the most likely understanding of the parties who sign agreements containing standard arbitration clauses, support a presumption that such clauses do not apply to federal statutory claims.

III

The Court has repeatedly held that a decision by Congress to create a special statutory remedy renders a private agreement to arbitrate a federal statutory claim unenforceable. Thus, as I have already noted, the express statutory remedy provided in the Ku Klux Act of 1871, the express statutory remedy in the Securities Act of 1933, the express statutory remedy in the Fair Labor Standards Act, and the express statutory remedy in Title VII of the Civil Rights Act of 1964, each provided the Court with convincing evidence that Congress did not intend the protections afforded by the statute to be administered by a private arbitrator. The reasons that motivated those decisions apply with special force to the federal policy that is protected by the antitrust laws....

The Sherman and Clayton Acts reflect Congress' appraisal of the value of economic freedom; they guarantee the vitality of the entrepreneurial spirit. Questions arising under these Acts are among the most important in public law.

The unique public interest in the enforcement of the antitrust laws is repeatedly reflected in the special remedial scheme enacted by Congress. Since its enactment in 1890, the Sherman Act has provided for public enforcement through criminal as well as civil sanctions. The preeminent federal interest in effective enforcement once justified a provision for special three-judge district courts to hear antitrust claims on an expedited basis, as well as for direct appeal to this Court bypassing the courts of appeals.

The special interest in encouraging private enforcement of the Sherman Act has been reflected in the statutory scheme ever since 1890. Section 7 of the original Act, used the broadest possible language to describe the class of litigants who may invoke its protection....

The provision for mandatory treble damages-unique in federal law when the statute was enacted-provides a special incentive to the private enforcement of the statute, as well as an especially powerful deterrent to violators. What we have described as "the public interest in vigilant enforcement of the antitrust laws through the instrumentality of the private treble-damage action," Lawlor v. National Screen Service Corp., 349 U.S. 322, 329 (1955), is buttressed by the statutory mandate that the injured party also recover costs, "including a reasonable attorney's fee." 15 U.S.C. § 15(a). The interest in wide and effective enforcement has thus, for almost a century, been vindicated by enlisting the assistance of "private Attorneys General"; we have always attached special importance to their role because "[e]very violation of the antitrust laws is a blow to the free-enterprise system envisaged by Congress." Hawaii v. Standard Oil Co., 405 U.S. 251, 262 (1972).

There are, in addition, several unusual features of the antitrust enforcement scheme that unequivocally require rejection of any thought that Congress would tolerate private arbitration of antitrust claims in lieu of the statutory remedies that it fashioned. As we explained in Blumenstock Brothers Advertising Agency v. Curtis Publishing Co., 252 U.S. 436, 440 (1920), an antitrust treble-damages case "can only be brought in a District Court of the United States." The determination that these cases are "too important to be decided otherwise than by competent tribunals" surely cannot allow private arbitrators to assume a jurisdiction that is denied to courts of the sovereign States....

In view of the history of antitrust enforcement in the United States, it is not surprising that all of the federal courts that have considered the question have uniformly and unhesitatingly concluded that agreements to arbitrate federal antitrust issues are not enforceable....

This Court would be well advised to endorse the collective wisdom of the distinguished judges of the Courts of Appeals who have unanimously concluded that the statutory remedies fashioned by Congress for the enforcement of the antitrust laws render an agreement to arbitrate antitrust disputes unenforceable. Arbitration awards are only reviewable for manifest disregard of the law, 9 U.S.C. §§ 10, 207, and the rudimentary procedures which make arbitration so desirable in the context of a private dispute often mean that the record is so inadequate that the arbitrator's decision is virtually unreviewable.[31] Despotic decisionmaking of this kind is fine for parties who are willing to agree in advance to settle for a best approximation of the correct result in order to resolve quickly and inexpensively any contractual dispute that may arise in an ongoing commercial relationship. Such informality, however, is simply unacceptable when every error may have devastating consequences for important businesses in our national economy and may undermine their ability to compete in world markets. Instead of "muffling a grievance in the cloakroom of arbitration," the public interest in free competitive markets would be better served by having the issues resolved "in the light of impartial

[31] The arbitration procedure in this case does not provide any right to evidentiary discovery or a written decision, and requires that all proceedings be closed to the public. App. 220–221. Moreover, Japanese arbitrators do not have the power of compulsory process to secure witnesses and documents, nor do witnesses who are available testify under oath. *Id.*, at 218–219. *Cf.* 9 U.S.C. § 7 (arbitrators may summon witnesses to attend proceedings and seek enforcement in a district court).

public court adjudication." See Merrill Lynch, Pierce, Fenner & Smith v. Ware, 414 U.S. 117, 136 (1973).

IV

The Court assumes for the purposes of its decision that the antitrust issues would not be arbitrable if this were a purely domestic dispute, but holds that the international character of the controversy makes it arbitrable. The holding rests on vague concerns for the international implications of its decision and a misguided application of Scherk v. Alberto-Culver, Co., 417 U.S. 506 (1974).

International Obligations of the United States

[T]he United States, as amicus curiae, advises the Court that the Convention "clearly contemplates" that signatory nations will enforce domestic laws prohibiting the arbitration of certain subject matters. This interpretation of the Convention was adopted by the Court of Appeals, and the Court declines to reject it. The construction is beyond doubt....

Thus, reading Articles II and V together, the Convention provides that agreements to arbitrate disputes which are nonarbitrable under domestic law need not be honored, nor awards rendered under them enforced.

This construction is also supported by the legislative history of the Senate's advice and consent to the Convention....

International Comity

It is clear then that the international obligations of the United States permit us to honor Congress' commitment to the exclusive resolution of antitrust disputes in the federal courts. The Court today refuses to do so, offering only vague concerns for comity among nations. The courts of other nations, on the other hand, have applied the exception provided in the Convention, and refused to enforce agreements to arbitrate specific subject matters of concern to them.[35]

It may be that the subject-matter exception to the Convention ought to be reserved-as a matter of domestic law-for matters of the greatest public interest which involve concerns that are shared by other nations. The Sherman Act's commitment to free competitive markets is among our most important civil policies. This commitment, shared by other nations which are signatory to the Convention, is hardly the sort of parochial concern that we should decline to enforce in the interest of international comity. Indeed, the branch of Government entrusted with the conduct of political relations with foreign governments has informed us that

---

[35] For example, the Cour de Cassation in Belgium has held that disputes arising under a Belgian statute limiting the unilateral termination of exclusive distributorships are not arbitrable under the Convention in that country, *Audi-NSU Auto Union A.G. v. S.A. Adelin Petit & Cie.* (1979), in 5 Yearbook Commercial Arbitration 257, 259 (1980), and the Corte di Cassazione in Italy has held that labor disputes are not arbitrable under the Convention in that country, *Compagnia Generale Construzioni v. Piersanti,* [1980] Foro Italiano I 190, in 6 Yearbook Commercial Arbitration 229, 230 (1981).

the "United States' determination that federal antitrust claims are nonarbitrable under the Convention...is not likely to result in either surprise or recrimination on the part of other signatories to the Convention." Brief for United States as Amicus Curiae 30....

[I]t is especially distressing to find that the Court is unable to perceive why the reasoning in Scherk is wholly inapplicable to Soler's antitrust claims against Chrysler and Mitsubishi. The merits of those claims are controlled entirely by American law. It is true that the automobiles are manufactured in Japan and that Mitsubishi is a Japanese corporation, but the same antitrust questions would be presented if Mitsubishi were owned by two American companies instead of by one American and one Japanese partner. When Mitsubishi enters the American market and plans to engage in business in that market over a period of years, it must recognize its obligation to comply with American law and to be subject to the remedial provisions of American statutes.

The federal claim that was asserted in Scherk, unlike Soler's antitrust claim, had not been expressly authorized by Congress. Indeed, until this Court's recent decision in Landreth Timber Co. v. Landreth, 471 U.S. 681 (1985), the federal cause of action asserted by Scherk would not have been entertained in a number of Federal Circuits because it did not involve the kind of securities transaction that Congress intended to regulate when it enacted the Securities Exchange Act of 1934. The fraud claimed in Scherk was virtually identical to the breach of warranty claim; arbitration of such claims arising out of an agreement between parties of equal bargaining strength does not conflict with any significant federal policy.

In contrast, Soler's claim not only implicates our fundamental antitrust policies, supra, at 3366–3370, but also should be evaluated in the light of an explicit congressional finding concerning the disparity in bargaining power between automobile manufacturers and their franchised dealers. In 1956, when Congress enacted special legislation to protect dealers from bad-faith franchise terminations, it recited its intent "to balance the power now heavily weighted in favor of automobile manufacturers." 70 Stat. 1125. The special federal interest in protecting automobile dealers from overreaching by car manufacturers, as well as the policies underlying the Sherman Act, underscore the folly of the Court's decision today.

V

The Court's repeated incantation of the high ideals of "international arbitration" creates the impression that this case involves the fate of an institution designed to implement a formula for world peace. But just as it is improper to subordinate the public interest in enforcement of antitrust policy to the private interest in resolving commercial disputes, so is it equally unwise to allow a vision of world unity to distort the importance of the selection of the proper forum for resolving this dispute. Like any other mechanism for resolving controversies, international arbitration will only succeed if it is realistically limited to tasks it is capable of performing well-the prompt and inexpensive resolution of essentially contractual disputes between commercial partners. As for matters involving the political passions and the fundamental interests of nations, even the multilateral convention adopted under the auspices of the United Nations recognizes that private international arbitration is incapable of achieving satisfactory results.

In my opinion, the elected representatives of the American people would not have us dispatch an American citizen to a foreign land in search of an uncertain remedy for the violation of a public right that is protected by the Sherman Act. This is especially so when there has been no genuine bargaining over the terms of the submission, and the arbitration remedy provided has not even the most elementary guarantees of fair process. Consideration of a fully developed record by a jury, instructed in the law by a federal judge, and subject to appellate review, is a surer guide to the competitive character of a commercial practice than the practically unreviewable judgment of a private arbitrator.

Unlike the Congress that enacted the Sherman Act in 1890, the Court today does not seem to appreciate the value of economic freedom. I respectfully dissent.

Comments and Questions

1. Is this really an antitrust case at all? Put another way: what are Soler and Mitsubishi really fighting about? Is Soler genuinely raising an antitrust claim or are they just trying creatively to avoid arbitration and perhaps gain some leverage?

2. Setting aside the doctrine, do you think this arbitral clause is fair? What makes this (or some other) arbitration clause fair? For what kinds of facts and circumstances are you looking to answer these questions?

3. In England, the House of Lords recently ruled that an arbitration clause may be valid and binding on the parties even when the underlying contract is not. Premium Nafta Products Ltd. v. Fili Shipping Company Ltd., UKHL 40 (2007). The decision dismissed an appeal by owners of a company who were attempting to rescind charters that they claimed had been procured through bribery. The question was whether the issue of rescission should be determined by a court or through arbitration. The Law Lords found the arbitration clause binding regardless of the validity of the underlying contract, and thus required the case to be resolved by arbitration. They noted that this decision was consistent with the law of Germany, the United States, and Australia, and expressed their hope that this decision would bring English law into step with that of international commerce.

4. The civil law countries have tended to maintain a somewhat tighter grip on topics that are not arbitrable. Most European states take the position that matters related to public policy are not arbitrable. Yet, in practice, those states—and especially France, a major player in international arbitration—have adopted a very tolerant approach toward arbitration, and (like Mitusbishi) are especially inclined toward arbitration in international matters. Thus, in most European countries, the arbitrability of disputes raising questions of European competition (antitrust) law has been progressively recognized by the courts and legal commentators. Also, arbitrability is not generally limited to private law. Several countries,

including Switzerland and Germany, have recognized that arbitration can also bear on claims derived from public law, namely, on rights conferred by contracts subject to administrative law. There are some important limits, however. Because of the absolute character of the protection conferred by intellectual property regimes, the arbitrability of these disputes is still often subject to restrictions. And several legal provisions restrict or prohibit the arbitrability of certain disputes where the legal relationship involves a party deemed to be economically weak—in labor and employment contracts, for example. See, generally, Jean-Francois Poudret & Sebastien Besson, Comparative Law of International Arbitration (2d ed. 2007).

Concluding Comments and Questions

1. Does the popularity of arbitration among litigants and its support by the courts suggest that the formal court systems are broken and in need of repair? Are courts competing with arbitration? Is arbitration competing with courts?

2. Return to the problem that opened this chapter. When negotiating an agreement with a forum selection clause, what can you include in that agreement (or otherwise do) to make it more likely that the clause would ultimately be enforced?

D. Bibliography of Additional Resources

Andrew S. Bell, FORUM SHOPPING AND VENUE IN TRANSNATIONAL LITIGATION (Oxford 2003)

Barton Legum (ed.), INTERNATIONAL LITIGATION STRATEGIES AND PRACTICE (Am. Bar Ass'n 2005)

4 & 4B Charles Alan Wright & Arthur R. Miller, FEDERAL PRACTICE AND PROCEDURE §§ 1061–1075 (Thomson West 3d ed. 2002)

David Epstein, Jeffrey L. Snyder & Chrales S. Baldwin, INTERNATIONAL LITIGATION: A GUIDE TO JURISDICTION, PRACTICE, AND STRATEGY (Martinus Nijhoff 3d ed. 1998 & Supp. 2007).

Gary B. Born, INTERNATIONAL ARBITRATION AND FORUM SELECTION AGREEMENTS: DRAFTING AND ENFORCING (2d ed. Kluwer 2006)

Hannah L. Buxbaum, Forum Selection in International Contract Litigation: The Role of Judicial Discretion, 12 WILLAMETTE J. INT'L L. & DISP. RESOL. 185 (2004)

James Wm. Moore, MOORE'S FEDERAL PRACTICE (Matthew Bender 3d ed. 1997 & Supp. 2007).

Jason W. Yackee, Choice of Law Considerations in the Validity and Enforcement of International Forum Selection Agreements: Whose Law Applies?, 9 UCLA J. INT'L L. & FOREIGN AFF. 43 (2004)

Pascal De Vareilles-Sommieres, ed., FORUM SHOPPING IN THE EUROPEAN JUDICIAL AREA (Hart 2007)

Philip A. Buhler, Forum Selection and Choice of Law Clauses in International Contracts: A United State Viewpoint with Particular Reference to Maritime Contracts and Bills of Lading, 27 U. MIAMI INTER-AM. L. REV. 1 (1995)

Richard H. Kreindler & Judith L. Holdsworth (eds.), TRANSNATIONAL LITIGATION: A PRACTITIONER'S GUIDE (Oceana 1997 & Supp. 2007)

Richard H. Kreindler, TRANSNATIONAL LITIGATION: A BASIC PRIMER (Oceana 1998)

Russell F. Conn & William P. Corbett, Jr., Defending Your Client's Choice of Forum: Careful Focus and Precise Drafting Pay Off, 66 DEF. COUNS. J. 562 (1999)

Tim Taylor & Nigel Cooper, EUROPEAN LITIGATION HANDBOOK (Sweet & Maxwell 1995)

Ved P. Nanda & David K. Pansius, LITIGATION OF INTERNATIONAL DISPUTES IN U.S. COURTS (Thomson West 2d ed. 2005 & Supp. 2007)

CHAPTER 6

State Immunity

A. Introduction

Countries have long recognized sound policy reasons for granting any state immunity from the jurisdiction of the courts of another. Orginally applied to ambassadors and individual sovereigns themselves, the doctrine of jurisdictional immunity expanded to cover states as well, as they—often through their agencies and vessels—became increasingly active in the private sphere. The doctrine facilitates effective and cordial relations among members of the international community.

> [F]rom the continental point of view, ... the forum rei (if any) [against sovereign persons or bodies] is that of his own country.... [It] is not that a case cannot arise in which, on strict principles of law, parties deemed extraterritorial would be amenable, for even a government may by its agents commit an injury within the jurisdiction; nor that civil process against them would necessarily be without effect, for even a government might have property within the jurisdiction capable of being reached by the sentence; but to avoid the danger of provoking war by wounding the dignity of a foreign state.
>
> John Westlake, A Treatise on Private International Law §§ 133–134 at 83–84 (1859).

The immunity of foreign states from the adjudicatory and enforcement jurisdiction of national courts is rooted in the sovereign equality of states, a basic principle of international law enshrined in Article 2(1) of the United Nations Charter. The United Nations General Assembly has elaborated upon the principle of sovereign equality in a series of resolutions. Resolution 2131 (XX) (1965) declares that "[n]o state has the right to intervene, directly or indirectly, for any reason whatever, in the internal and external affairs of any other state." Resolution 2625 (XXV) (1970) specifically addresses sovereign equality:

> All States enjoy sovereign equality. They have equal rights and duties and are equal members of the international community, notwithstanding differences of an economic, social, political or other nature. In particular, sovereign equality includes the following elements:
>
> (a) States are juridically equal;
> (b) Each State enjoys the rights inherent in full sovereignty;
> (c) Each State has the duty to respect the personality of other States;
> (d) The territorial integrity and political independence of the State are inviolable;
> (e) Each State has the right freely to choose and develop its political, social, economic and cultural systems;
> (f) Each State has the duty to comply fully and in good faith with its international obligations and to live in peace with other States.*

The legal equality of states has a number of important consequences. One of these consequences is that—according to the maxim par in parem non habet imperium—no state can claim jurisdiction over another.†

Notwithstanding its ancient origin and noble purpose, the doctrine of foreign state immunity has evolved considerably in the past century. A doctrine of "restrictive immunity" has largely replaced "absolute immunity," and in doing so, has introduced complexity as to the contours of this defense. Restrictive immunity—so named because sovereign immunity is said to be "restricted" to cases in which the foreign state acts in its public, governmental capacity—recognizes certain exceptions to sovereign immunity that the absolute doctrine did not. A further complication is that the doctrine of immunity is really two separate immunities: immunity from adjudication (or jurisdiction) and immunity from enforcement. In this chapter, we will examine the practice in various national courts and will also consider the United Nations Convention on Jurisdictional Immunities of States and their Property. After two decades of study and negotiations, the United Nations adopted this new multilateral treaty in December 2004. The Convention sets forth a comprehensive approach for determining the immunity of states, their agencies and instrumentalities and properties in litigation in foreign jurisdictions.

---

* This Resolution is titled the Declaration on Principles of International Law Concerning Friendly Relations and Co-operation Among States in Accordance with the Charter of the United Nations. *See* 9 I.L.M. 1292. Although this Resolution is not binding *per se*, it is taken as an authoritative elaboration of the relevant provisions of the U.N. Charter. *See* Stephen C. McCaffrey, Understanding International Law § 5.02[D] at 155–160 (2006).

† This principle should not be given absolute effect, however: "Even the maxim *par in parem imperium non habet* has never been interpreted with such liberality as to give a State unregulated freedom to exercise its sovereignty wherever it pleases and regardless of international law." Sompong Sucharitkul, Fourth Report on Jurisdictional Immunities of States and their Property, 1982 Y.B. Int'l L. Comm'n, vol. 2, pt. 1, 199, at 204. Thus it may be more accurate to formulate the maxim as *par in parem jurisdictionem non habet.*

The Convention will not come into force unless or until thirty states have ratified it. Because the Convention was negotiated on the basis of a draft prepared by the U.N. International Law Commission (ILC),[‡] and was adopted without a vote, the terms of the Convention indicate some emerging consensus about the current rules of customary international law on the subject.

The Problem: Monkey Business[*]

Many years ago, the Bangladesh Ministry of Agriculture granted MOL Inc., an Oregon corporation, a ten-year license to capture and export rhesus monkeys. In exchange for the right to export the monkeys, MOL was required to pay a fee for each exported monkey, and was required to build in Bangladesh a breeding farm for the monkeys. Rhesus monkeys are very valuable research subjects because of their anatomical and behavioral similarity to humans. One condition of the parties' written agreement required that the monkeys be used exclusively for the purposes of humane and expert medical research. To enable Bangladesh to monitor uses of the monkeys, it required MOL to keep available records on each monkey and to arrange for duplicate records in Bangladesh.

Two years into this agreement, India banned the export of its rhesus monkeys. Because India had been the major exporter of these animals, Bangladesh became an increasingly important supplier of these valuable animals. Although world prices for rhesus monkeys rose dramatically while MOL's payments to Bangladesh remained fixed by the agreement, Bangladesh complied with the agreement for another three years.

Bangladesh announced that it was terminating the agreement, and MOL faces an incremental supply cost of $15 million. The government's reason for the termination is one or some combination of the following: (1) Bangladesh can make more money by selling the monkeys at market prices; (2) MOL did not build the breeding farm according to the specifications set forth in the agreement; (3) MOL did not use the monkeys for humanitarian purposes but rather for radiation experiments on behalf of the U.S. military; and/or (4) Bangladesh is limiting trade with the United States in retaliation for American interference in a dispute between the countries of Pakistan and India.

(1) Is Bangladesh immune from the jurisdiction of U.S. courts?
(2) Is immunity more or less justifiable if the plaintiff seeks specific performance instead of damages?
(3) What if the supplier of monkeys were instead a company (i) owned by the government of Bangladesh; (ii) owned in part by the government of Bangladesh; or (iii) that was a wholly owned subsidiary of a company owned by the government of Bangladesh?

---

‡ *See* 1994 Y.B. Int'l L. Comm'n, vol. 2, pt. 2, 13. The ILC was established by the U.N. General Assembly in 1947 to promote the "progressive development of international law and its codification." ILC Stat. Art. 1(1), U.N. Doc. A/CN.4/4/Rev. 2 (1982).

* This hypothetical is based upon *MOL v. Bangladesh,* 736 F.2d 1326 (9th Cir. 1984).

(4) Is it significant that this case deals with natural resources? Put another way, should it make a difference if the transaction involved the supply of widgets rather than monkeys?

B. Doctrinal Justifications

The earliest judicial pronouncement of the doctrine of sovereign immunity by the highest court of a nation was made in 1812 in the case of The Schooner Exchange v. McFaddon. In that case, Chief Justice Marshall said that immunity was rooted in the "perfect equality and absolute independence of sovereigns."

> The jurisdiction of the nation within its own territory is necessarily exclusive and absolute. It is susceptible of no limitation not imposed by itself. Any restriction upon it, deriving validly from an external source, would implay a diminution of its sovereignty to the same extent in that power which could impose such restriction.
>
> All exceptions, therefore, to the full and complete power of a nation within its own territories must be traced up to the consent of the nation itself. They can flow from no other legitimate source. This consent may be either express or implied. In the latter case, it is less determinate, exposed more to the uncertainties of construction; but, if understood, not less obligatory.
>
> The world being composed of distinct sovereignties, possessing equal rights and equal independence, whose mutual benefit is promoted by intercourse with each other, and by an interchange of those good offices which humanity dictates and its wants require, all sovereignties have consented to a relaxation in practice, in cases under certain peculiar circumstances, of that absolute and complete jurisdiction within their respective territories which sovereignty confers.

The Schooner Exchange v. McFaddon, 11 U.S. (7 Cranch) 116, 136 (1812). The defense of immunity obliged domestic courts to avoid resolving disputes that could more effectively be pursued through other methods of conflict resolution—namely, diplomatic channels.

Hazel Fox, The Rationale for Immunity

The Law of State Immunity 56–59 (2d ed. 2008)

[Three main grounds are given for the grant of immunity to foreign States.] The municipal court's inability to enforce its judgments against a foreign State remains the outstanding reason for the retention of immunity, as demonstrated by the fact that a separate immunity from execution is afforded to States and largely remains an absolute bar on enforcement of judgments against State property. This inability is partly legal and partly factual. The application by one State of forcible measures of constraint against the conduct or property of another State is an unfriendly act generally prohibited by international law, except where the State has itself contravened international law....

The basis for a rule of absolute immunity from execution therefore derives, legally, from the rule of non-intervention in the internal conduct of the State's public functions—"à ne rien faire que soit susceptible d'entraver le fonctionnement des services publiques du dit Etat" [transl. to do nothing that might interfere with the functioning of the public services of a particular state], and factually, from the practical impossibility, short of invasion or war, of forcing a State to do what a court may order. It cannot be ignored that lack of means of forcible enforcement remains the underlying political obstacle and hence the justification for a legal plea that avoids forcible confrontation between States. Even where attachment of State assets located in the forum State is legally possible, the political consequences to the friendly relations of the forum State with the foreign State may discourage the forum State's support for such enforcement. The political nature of immunity from execution is well illustrated by the Italian government's enactment of a law referring all decisions on enforcement against foreign States to the Minister of Justice after the Court of Cassation had ruled that attachment of State assets in certain circumstances was legally permissible. In effect, this first ground discloses the policy reasons which underlie the other justifications for a doctrine of State immunity....

The second ground, the independence and equality of States, recognizes this underlying political reality, and gives it expression in legal terms as the lack of competence of one State to exercise jurisdiction over another State. Independence provides a justification for the absolute rule of immunity, and remains a justification for the restrictive rule which restrains the forum State from adjudicating acts in the exercise of sovereign power, jure imperii of another State. It is expressed in the maxim par in parem non habet imperium: one sovereign State is not subject to the jurisdiction of another State....

Lack of competence as a basis of immunity is readily recognized in civil law countries, since their courts, being courts of limited competence over private persons, acknowledge the absence of jurisdiction over other States. A plea of State immunity is therefore a signal to the forum court that jurisdiction belongs to another court or method of adjudication. Thus, the French Cour de Cassation decided in 1849 in an action brought by Lambege and Pujot against the Spanish government for payment in respect of a purchase of army boots, that it had no competence to hear the suit....

In common law countries greater stress is placed on the forum State's own jurisdiction, and independence and equality as attributes of the State are used to justify restricting that jurisdiction. Consequently, stress is placed on the respect for the dignity of the foreign State and for reciprocity of treatment of States as the ground for immunity.... For example, Brett LJ in the case of Le Parlement Belge declared that a State's refusal to exercise territorial jurisdiction over the person of the sovereign, his ambassador, or over public property destined to public use though it be within the territory was a "consequence of the absolute independence of every sovereign authority and of international comity which induces every sovereign State to respect the independence and dignity of every other sovereign."

Inherent in the recognition of the foreign State's independence is an acknowledgement that it alone is responsible for the determination of its policy and conduct of its public administration, and that courts should refrain from hampering the foreign State in the achievement of these purposes....

[Third, the] immunity of the foreign State has been justified by analogy, either by reference to its immune position under its own home law, or by reference to the protected position of the forum State under its national laws. In this context a general argument derived from feudal law, and applied in the United States to afford immunity to the individual States of the union, has been advanced that it is not possible for the State as the source of the law to be subject to the laws which it makes. In the nineteenth century, when the law of State immunity developed, the central government of the forum State enjoyed extensive immunity from proceedings in its own courts and this exemption was a factor in the recognition of similar immunities on the part of the foreign State.

Comments and Questions

1. We shield foreign sovereigns with immunity doctrines yet freely open our courts to suits initiated by them as plaintiffs. Is that asymmetry necessary—or at least justifiable? (Of course, if a foreign state sues, it waives immunity with regard to any counterclaims related to that proceeding.)

2. Are plaintiffs injured by foreign sovereigns less deserving of compensation than plaintiffs injured by anyone else? If the forum state wants to protect the foreign state, should the forum state provide the injured plaintiff with an alternate remedy?

3. Should the immunity vel non of a state instead be addressed under the various substantive laws that assign responsibility? For example, we might imagine that the scope of permissible defendants in a jurisdiction that recognizes a cause of action for breach of contract could be a matter of that jurisdiction's law of contracts; isn't a generalized doctrine of state immunity a rather blunt instrument? Is state immunity a doctrine of substance or of procedure?

C. The Restrictive Theory

Until the twentieth century, sovereign immunity from the jurisdiction of foreign courts seemed to have no exceptions—immunity was "absolute." After World War I, however, governments increasingly engaged in trade and other commercial activities. Moreover, the appearance of socialist and communist states elevated the significance of the public sector in national economies. In short, socialist states became participants in the marketplace. Scholars, governments, litigants, and courts thus queried whether the immunity of states engaged in such activities was required by international law, and whether it was a desirable practice. Some argued that immunity deprived private parties that dealt with a state of their judicial remedies, and gave states an unfair advantage in competition with private commercial enterprise. Immunity for official functions was accepted, but impunity for non-sovereign actions was inequitable.

As early as 1873, the doctrine of immunity was evolving. In *The Charkieh*, a ship owned by the Khedive of Egypt but used as an ordinary merchant vessel caused injury to another after a collision on the Thames River in England. Sir Robert Phillimore held:

> No principle of international law, and no decided case, and no dictum of jurists of which I am aware, has gone so far as to authorize a sovereign prince to assume the character of a trader, when it is for his benefit; and when incurs an obligation to a private subject to throw off, so to speak, his disguise, and appear as a sovereign, claiming for his own benefit, and to the injury of a private person, for the first time, all the attributes of his character.... Assuming the privilege to exist, it has been waived with reference to this ship by the conduct of the person who has claimed it.

The Charkieh [1873] LR 4 A & E 59. This notion of the state as a dual character ultimately became the premise of the modern "restrictive" approach to immunity. Sir Robert, however, was well ahead of his time: his decision in *The Charkieh* was overruled by the Court of Appeal in a later case. Fifty years later, the restrictive doctrine found some traction. A League of Nations report of 1927 and the subsequent case law record the emergence of the restrictive doctrine.

Competence of the Courts in Regard to Foreign States

Publications of the League of Nations, V: Legal. 1927. v. 9 No. 11

The question whether a State may, in any respect, be subject to the jurisdiction of the courts of another State is connected with the right of States to independence. In other words, are the Courts of one State competent to decide disputes to which another State is a party?

That the courts of one State are not competent with regard to another State is unanimously recognized when the foreign State is called to justice on account of acts committed by it, in the exercise of its sovereignty, to ensure the general administration of the country and the working of its public services. To weigh and judge the consequences of such acts would be to interfere in the internal policy of the foreign State and deny its right of independence. As regards acts of its Government and public administration, a State ought to be—as, indeed it is—entirely immune from the jurisdiction of another State. In almost all countries this is the decision which has been reached, and it is followed by most writers on the subject.

There is, however, some difference of opinion when we come to consider acts accomplished by a State, not in fulfillment of one of its sovereign functions or governmental duties, but in the same way as a private individual, and, so to speak, in a private capacity. A State may, for instance, have been engaged in commercial transactions; in many countries the State is responsible for transport by rail. If it fails to execute the contract of transport, may it not be sued abroad by the consignor or consignee who has suffered from the non-fulfillment of the contract?

On this point there are two conflicting views. An imposing body of case law, which has received the general approval of the French, German, British and American courts, renders exemption from jurisdiction an absolute immunity attaching to the very person of the foreign State, independent of the character of particular acts and removable only by express or tacit waiver by the State itself.... States are independent—i.e., the sovereign power of a State cannot extend beyond its own sphere and intrude into the sphere of another State to be exercised over persons and things within the domain of the other State. Nevertheless, a State may to a certain extent forego its sovereign rights in favour of another's sovereignty. This, however, can only take place by means of an agreement between the two States freely consented by both. Failing such agreements, or customary law which has become established de facto apart from any such agreements, there can be no question of admitting the claim of one State to regulate, in accordance with its own views, the affairs or interests of another State....

[Under a contrary perspective,] the State possesses two aspects and practically constitutes two persons. From one point of view it is a person politic: from the other, a private person. What the State does jure imperii is one thing, and what it does jure gestionis is another. As a public person, the foreign State is not subject to the jurisdiction of the judicial authorities; but it may become subject thereto as a private person like foreign private individuals—indeed by analogy thereto—and in accordance with the principles of private international law which apply to private individuals in the matter of jurisdiction.

The rule of the mutual respect of sovereignty cannot claim to go further than the recognition of sovereignty which is its basis. The position of a State alters when, under cover of its civil personality, it enters into relations at private law which, by their nature, normally come within the competence of foreign jurisdictions. Of course, the juridical personality of the State is not really twofold, its mission always being to safeguard the general interests for which it is responsible; but certainly the activities of a State do assume two separate forms, and it is therefore desirable to consider the intrinsic nature of the acts and not merely their political purpose. This seems to be all the more just and equitable in that the sovereignty of a State is only entitled to respect so long as it remains within its proper sphere....

Dralle v. Republic of Czechoslovakia

Supreme Court of Austria. May 10, 1950

ÖJZ, 5 (1950), p. 341, No. 356; 17 I.L.R. 155 (1956)

The appellant was the representative in Austria of the German firm of Georg Dralle (G.D.), manufacturers of cosmetics in Hamburg. The firm of G.D. owned certain trade marks which were registered in the Austria Register of Trade Marks and which were applied to goods manufactured by them and offered for sale by the appellant in Austria. Since 1910 there had been established at Bodenbach, in the province of Bohemia, which subsequently became part of Czechoslovakia, a branch office of the Hamburg firm; this branch office was the registered owner, by consent of the parent firm in Hamburg, of the trade marks registered by the latter in the Austrian Register. In 1945 the branch office was nationalized by virtue of a Czechoslovak nationalization decree, and the nationalized firm thereupon laid claim to the trade marks formerly owned by its predecessor. The nationalized firm having requested the appellant's customers in Austria not to offer for sale under the said trade marks any of the goods supplied by the appellant, the latter applied for an injunction to restrain the Czechoslovak firm (the respondents) from using the said trade marks in the territory of the Austrian Republic. The respondents claimed to be immune from the jurisdiction of the Austrian courts, and claimed to be entitled in any event to use the trade marks concerned....

Before dealing with the merits of the appeal the Supreme Court must decide whether jurisdiction can be exercised in the present case. The respondent is the State of Czechoslovakia, regardless of the fact that it engages in business under a firm name; the firm merely constitutes a name, and by virtue of the use of that name there does not come into existence a new legal entity which is distinguishable from the owner of the firm.

The question whether a foreign State can be sued in the municipal courts has not been answered in a uniform manner by the Austrian courts. The older practice of all countries was to exempt foreign States from municipal jurisdiction, the exceptions being at the most actions in rem and voluntary submission to the jurisdiction. This was also the attitude of Austrian courts until the turn of the century. The first decision to depart from this principle was the judgment of December 17, 1907. (see Röll, Eisenbahnrechtliche Entscheidungen, XXI (1907) No. 122). This judgment states that "the State as entrepreneur is a juridical person within the realm of private law and can, therefore, be sued in the ordinary courts in all matters concerning private law.... This applies undoubtedly to the home State, but there is no reason to depart from this principle in the case of a foreign State. This does not constitute an infringement of territorial sovereignty any more than does the act of suing a foreign national in a municipal court...."

[The Court, having reviewed a number of decisions confirming the principle set out above, continued:]

A further judgment was given on January 5, 1920 (SZ. II/I). In this case the Ottoman State was sued for payment for certain building work carried out at the Embassy in Vienna by order of the Ottoman Ambassador. The Supreme Court decided in favour of municipal jurisdiction on the following ground:

> The view that the concept of sovereignty of a State includes the absolute freedom of that State from the jurisdiction of every court is not correct. It is true that in matters concerning the sovereignty of a foreign State, which sovereignty serves as the basis for the application of the rules of international law, municipal jurisdiction cannot be assumed. Where, on the other hand, the foreign State conducts itself as the holder of ordinary private rights and enters into contracts to be performed within the territory (i.e., Austria), it enters the confines of the legal system of that

> territory and cannot therefore remain entirely independent thereof; in such cases the foreign State too must be subject to the jurisdiction of the State in whose territory the business enterprise is domiciled....

In later judgments the Supreme Court, apparently under the influence of Walker's book on Private International Law, abandoned this practice and returned to earlier case law. Henceforth it again required express submission to municipal jurisdiction. In the case which formed the basis of the judgment of January 20, 1926 (ZBl. 1926, No. 134), the Czechoslovak State Railways had ordered machines from a firm in Vienna. The offer contained a clause that the courts of the supplier's domicile were to exercise jurisdiction. The Supreme Court denied the competence of the municipal court whose jurisdiction had been invoked, on the ground that the agreement between the parties did not clearly provide for the right of the municipal courts to exercise jurisdiction and compulsory powers. Such a clear provision was regarded as all the more necessary in view of the fact that the submission of a foreign State to municipal jurisdiction implies a waiver of exterritoriality, and that, for this reason, such a waiver which runs counter to the essential nature of a sovereign State can only be inferred from such acts of that State as clearly show an intention to waive....

[After reviewing a number of other judgments which upheld claims to immunity, except in cases of express and voluntary submission by the States concerned, the Court continued:]

[I]t cannot be said that there is any uniformity of case law in so far as concerns the extent to which foreign States are subject to Austrian jurisdiction. In view of the fact that we are here concerned with a question of international law we have to examine the practice of the courts of civilised countries and to find out whether from that practice we can deduce a uniform view; this is the only method of ascertaining whether there still exists a principle of international law to the effect that foreign States, even in so far as concerns claims belonging to the realm of private law, cannot be sued in the courts of a foreign State.

The first court to enunciate the principle that in matters belonging purely to the realm of private law foreign States cannot claim immunity was the Court of Cassation of Naples in a judgment of March 27, 1886... [The Court then referred to more recent cases in which this view was affirmed by Italian courts.] In 1903...the Belgian Court of Cassation followed this practice....The recent jurisprudence of the Swiss courts has moved in the same direction....

The judgments of the Mixed Tribunals in Egypt drew the same distinction. In its judgment of November 24, 1920 (Clunet, 1921, 271), concerning a case against the English Crown arising out of a collision at sea, the Mixed Court of Appeal stated that acts done in the exercise of the sovereignty of a foreign State were not subject to the jurisdiction of a foreign court, but that the position was entirely different where an act, as e.g a quasi-delict in the case under review, had been done by the employees of a foreign State in its private interest and without any connection whatever with its political activity. To concede immunity from jurisdiction in such a case would be a denial of justice (negation de la justice) because it would deprive of the protection of the law those individuals whose interests are in conflict with the private interests of the State concerned.... The Court of Appeal added that the lack of jurisdiction of the court of one State over another State is only relative, it being generally acknowledged that a foreign Government could proceed in the courts of another State as plaintiff against those persons who are subject to the jurisdiction of that State, and that it was bound to submit to a suit before a court of that State in matters concerning immovable property there situate. The Court of Appeal argued from this that lack of jurisdiction cannot be pleaded by a foreign State where the latter has acted as an ordinary private individual....

Among States which in principle recognize immunity from jurisdiction even where acta gestionis of private law are concerned are Germany, England, the United States, Czechoslovakia, Poland, Portugal and France [citing cases for each]. The French courts, however, have deviated form this jurisprudence in so far concerns a foreign State regularly engaged in commerce in France.... [The Court then reviewed certain decisions of Greek, Roumanian and Brazilian tribunals which adopted the same view, and continued as follows:] This survey shows that today it can no longer be said that jurisprudence generally recognizes the principle of exemption of foreign States in so far as concerns claims of a private character, because the majority of courts of different civilised countries deny the immunity of a foreign State, and more particularly because exceptions are made even in those countries which today still adhere to the traditional principle that no State is entitled to exercise jurisdiction over another State....

The Resolution passed by the Imperial Economic Conference of the British Empire in 1923 is proof that this movement has also made headway in the Anglo-Saxon countries; the Resolution stated expressly that a Dominion engaged in trade in another Dominion is not, for that reason, entitled to claim freedom from taxation.... A similar recommendation is contained in the Report of the World Economic Conference held at Geneva in 1927.

International treaties too have on several occasions recognised the principle that acta jure gestionis are not exempt from jurisdiction. Thus, Article 233 of the Treaty of St. Germain (and similarly the other Treaties concluded near Paris) provide that the Austrian Government if it engages in international trade shall not, in relation to such trade, be or be regarded as being, entitled to claim rights, privileges and immunities of sovereignty.

The meaning of this clause is controversial. Some regard it as a privilegium odiosum of the Central Powers, others as the manifestation of a new international law. We need not consider which of these two views is correct. As the former Central Powers accepted an obligation, not only in relation to former enemy Powers, but quite generally, to invoke the jurisdiction of foreign courts in commercial matters, we are, in any event, entitled to say that such submission of sovereign States in matters of private law is regarded as being admissible in international law.

Other treaties too contain similar provisions which are not limited in their application to particular States, as e.g. Article 30 of the Paris Air Navigation

Convention of October 13, 1919, and Article 2 of the Warsaw Convention for the Unification of Certain Rules regarding Air Transport, of October 12, 1929. Similarly, the various draft agreements of international associations contain proposals pointing in the same direction.... [A report] prepared by the Harvard Law School in 1932... contains the following provision: "A State may be made a respondent in a proceeding in a court of another State, when in the territory of such other State it engages in an industrial, commercial, financial or other business enterprise in which private persons may there engage, or does an act there in connection with such an enterprise wherever conducted, and the proceeding is based upon the conduct of such enterprise or upon such act."... The various proposals of international associations show that the classic doctrine of unlimited immunity no longer corresponds to the view expressed in legal practice....

[After examining the views of a number of writers of different nationalities, the Court continued:] Accordingly, there clearly is no communis opinio doctorum. The Supreme Court therefore reaches the conclusion that it can no longer be said that by international law so-called acta gestionis are exempt from municipal jurisdiction. This subjection of the act gestionis to the jurisdiction of States has its basis in the development of the commercial activity of States. The classic doctrine of immunity arose at a time when all the commercial activities of States in foreign countries were connected with their political activities, either by the purchase of commodities for their diplomatic representatives abroad, or by the purchase of war material for war purposes, etc. Therefore there was no justification for any distinction between private transactions and acts of sovereignty. Today the position is entirely different; States engage in commercial activities and, as the present case shows, enter into competition with their own nationals and with foreigners. Accordingly the classic doctrine of immunity has lost its meaning and, ratione cessante, can no longer be recognized as a rule of international law....

Baker McCormac (Pvt) Ltd. v. Government of Kenya

Zimbabwe High Court, 16 January 1985

1983 (4) SA 817; 84 I.L.R. 27

Samatta, J

This cases raises some interesting points of law relating to the doctrine of sovereign immunity. Before the Second World War nearly all States treated sovereign immunity as being absolute, regardless of the circumstances of the subject-matter. Since then, however, many States have abandoned the classical or absolute theory of immunity and embraced the restrictive theory under which immunity is granted only with respect to causes of action arising out of a foreign State's public or governmental actions and not with respect to those arising out of its commercial or proprietary actions. Which of these two theories forms part of the law of this country?...

The facts of the case... are as follows. In May 1976 the plaintiff and a company known as "Albermarle (Pvt) Ltd" entered into a lease whereby the former leased from the latter a portion of immovable property situated at 95 Park Lane, Harare, hereinafter referred to as "the property." The duration of the lease was five years, but there was a provision granting the plaintiff an option to renew the lease.... In or about May 1980 the Government of Kenya (the defendant), a foreign sovereign Government, bought the property for the purpose of using it as its High Commission in Zimbabwe. On 2 October 1980, [plaintiff] formally informed Albermarle (Pvt) Ltd, as well as the defendant, that [plaintiff] wished to renew the lease, but the defendant would not allow it to continue occupying the leased premises. In September 1982, after failing to persuade the defendant to change its mind, the plaintiff vacated the premises and leased other premises in the city at a higher rental. About four months later it commenced civil proceedings against the defendant before this Court to recover the sum of $55,691.35, being the difference in the rental....

In Trendtrex Trading Corporation Ltd v. Central Bank of Nigeria [1977] 1 All ER 881 (CA), where one of the issues was whether the rule of international law that the doctrine of sovereign immunity was not applicable to the ordinary commercial transactions, as distinct from the governmental acts of a sovereign State, was part of English law, Lord Denning MR, after he had considered authorities from various jurisdictions which demonstrated that in those respective jurisdictions the doctrine of absolute sovereign immunity had yielded to the doctrine of restrictive immunity, said at 891e:

> Seeing this great cloud of witnesses, I would ask: is there not here sufficient evidence to show that the rule of international law has changed? What more is needed? Are we to wait until every other country save England recognises the change? Ought we to act now? Whenever a change is made, some one some time has to make the first move. One country alone may start the process. Others may follow. At first a trickle, then a stream, last a flood. England should not be left behind on the bank. "... we must take the current when it serves, or lose our ventures." 64 ILR 111 at 130.

Mr De Bourbon [counsel for defendant Kenya] said that if Mr. Mkushi's contention [on behalf of the plaintiff] prevailed, Zimbabwe would "be left behind on the bank."... [Zimbabwe is now] on the other side of the river....

Why have many States abandoned the absolute doctrine and, like Zimbabwe, embraced the restrictive doctrine? I am inclined to think that the answer to that question is to be found in the following passage from the judgment of Lord Wilberforce in I Congreso del Partido [1981] 2 All ER 1064 (HL) at 1070g-h:

> The... exception, or limitation, which has been engrafted on the principle of immunity of States, under the so-called restrictive theory, arises from the willingness of States to enter into commercial, or other private law, transactions with individuals. It appears to have two main foundations: (a) It is necessary in the interest of justice to individuals having such transactions with States to allow them to bring such

> transactions before the courts. (b) To require a State to answer a claim based on such transactions does not involve a challenge to or inquiry into any act of sovereignty or governmental act of that State. It is, in accepted phrases, neither a threat to the dignity of that State nor any interference with its sovereign functions. 64 ILR 307 at 313.

What then are the exact bounds of the immunity?...The principle of restricted immunity only accords immunity to acta jure imperii, i.e. acts of a purely governmental or public nature, and not to acta jure gestionis, i.e. acts of a commercial or proprietary nature. But how do Courts distinguish acta jure imperii from acta jure gestionis?

***

Of course Justice Samatta's questions are not merely rhetorical; they demand answers. And since the emergence of a doctrine of restrictive immunity, courts have undertaken this difficult task. Professor Hill summarizes the various approaches in the following excerpt.

Thomas H. Hill, The Absolute Doctrine and the Restrictive Doctrine

A Policy Analysis of the American Law of Foreign State Immunity

50 Fordham L. Rev. 155, 168 (1981)

Various tests have been formulated to categorize the acts of foreign states according to their public or private character. The two most commonly used tests focus, respectively, on the nature and the purpose of the activity in question. The "nature" test, for example, would deny immunity from legal actions arising out of an ordinary commercial contract, even if the contract had been concluded for the purpose of procuring governmental goods, such as military equipment. The "purpose" test would grant immunity if such a contract had a public purpose, but might deny immunity in the case of a governmental regulation intended to have a commercial effect.

Another line of thought eschews both the "nature" test and the "purpose" test and opts for identifying specific activities that will be immune from judicial inquiry. Actions not falling within the categories identified will not be entitled to immunity. The exempted areas of government activity include such public functions as diplomacy, military operations, and internal administrative acts.

Finally, one scholar argued that a government's acts should be considered public only when a private person would be incapable of performing them. Thus virtually any contract, including debt instruments issued by a government, would be actionable because private persons are able to enter into such transactions. The set of immune activities would be reduced to legislative, military, and similar functions.

The absolute doctrine avoids the difficult distinctions sought to be made by the foregoing tests. It simply extends immunity to activities by a foreign state, irrespective of their public or private nature, unless the state has waived immunity.

Because all acts of a government are by definition "governmental" and serve a public purpose, however indirectly, the proponents of this view argue that the public-private distinction is untenable and that all activities by governments should be immune.

Comments and Questions

1. Apply the nature and purpose tests to the acts taken by Czechoslovakia and Kenya in Dralle and Baker McCormac (Pvt) Ltd., respectively. Is Czechoslovakia's use of the trade marks an act jure gestionis? Was Kenya's breach of the lease agreement with its tenant an act jure imperii? Do these questions fairly or unfairly define the relevant "act"; consider an alternative characterization.

2. As shown by the U.N. Convention, considered below, the restrictive theory based on the "nature" test has emerged as the predominant theory. Was this inevitable? Is it damaging to relations between states? Even if so, is it more important that states and private entities with whom they do business be placed on equal footing?

3. We will return to the exercise of delineating these categories later in this chapter. Before doing so, however, we must appreciate that a state's decision whether to replace a doctrine of absolute immunity with a doctrine of restrictive immunity begs the question whether a state should recognize the immunity of a foreign state at all.

D. Abolition of Immunity

Rejection of the absolute immunity rule could also lead one seriously to consider abolishing immunity in its entirety. Such a proposal has two primary justifications. First, requiring the forum to distinguish, the "public" acts of foreign States (acta jure imperii) from their "private" acts (acta jure gestionis) has no inherent plausibility. Such a categorization requires value judgments about the proper purpose or essential role of state activity, and thus is premised on political assumptions that may not be universally accepted. This point was eloquently expressed by the U.S. Supreme Court in a 1926 opinion rejecting the adoption of a restrictive doctrine of immunity (and retaining absolute immunity): "no international usage which regards the maintenance and advancement of the economic welfare of a people in time of peace has any less a public purpose than the maintenance and training of a naval force." Berizzi Bros. Co. v. The Pesaro, 271 U.S. 562, 574 (1926). Under regimes that undertake to categorize, immunity can be politicized and used by courts as a pretext to favor (or to disfavor, as the case may be) particular States.

A second justification for abolishing immunity simply focuses on the trade-off between state immunity, on the one hand, and justice for individuals, on the other. After all, in each incident in which immunity is successfully invoked, it is possible if not likely that the putative plaintiff is being denied any recourse for the injury caused by the foreign State.

Elihu Lauterpacht, Aspects of the Administration of International Justice

55–57 (Cambridge 1991)*

What would happen if the immunity of foreign States in national courts were totally abolished? In theory, the way would be open to proceedings against States in respect of acts jure imperii. But what would this amount to in practical terms? Would it much matter if those cases that fall just on the jure imperii side of the dividing line were actually litigated if they otherwise lie within the jurisdiction of the Court? And would it not be true that many of the supposedly "dangerous" sources of proceedings, for example, a claim in State A against the government of State B by a person expelled from or denied entry to the latter State, would be found not to give rise to any cause of action justifiable in State A? The probability is that most actions involving acts jure imperii would, on the application of generally accepted rules of international law, be dismissed either because the substantive law applicable to the mater was found to give rise to no cause of action, for example, because the lex loci delicti did not treat that particular kind of conduct as a wrong, or because the forum was non conveniens.

Indeed, it may be suggested that the widespread and remarkable acceptance by States of standards prescribed both in regional and universal conventions on human rights, coupled with the compulsory procedures for their implementation, compellingly evidences the reduction in the importance of the residue of so-called acts jure imperii in respect of which State immunity on the national plane exists....

Still more cogent in demonstrating the extent of the exercise of international jurisdiction in matters hitherto regarded as jurisdictionally sacrosanct because falling within the "reserved domain" of States is the wide range of issues over which the Court of the European Communities may exercise jurisdiction. To reply that this is the court of regional and supra-national system where special considerations prevail is descriptive rather than argumentative; it does not answer the contention that if some States can submit to international jurisdiction in respect of such domestically sensitive matters surely they have by their conduct acknowledged the practical acceptability of a more comprehensive international jurisdiction.

If it is concern over "opening the floodgates" of litigation against States that inhibits a change in the present system, then one needs to probe more deeply the existing causes of, and restraints upon, litigation in the international sphere in those situations where jurisdiction undoubtedly exists. Despite the fact there already exist wide ranges of international activity covered by various kinds of compulsory jurisdiction, there is no evidence that States lightly or wantonly resort to unnecessary litigation against each other—any more than individuals do within national legal systems. The constraints upon resort to unnecessary litigation—apart from those relatively few cases identified as frivolous and vexatious—are of

---

a non-legal character: expense (especially the risk of bearing the costs of the other party if the case is lost); disinclination to take the trouble relative to the gain to be achieved even if optimum expectations are fulfilled; public exposure of the plaintiff's conduct; and the exacerbation of relations between the parties, probably with lasting consequences. There is no reason to doubt the operation of comparable constraints—especially the last—in the international sphere. There really seems to be no functional justification for maintaining the immunity that States retain against actions instituted by other States.

Comments and Questions

1. Does the distinction of "public" and "private" acts for purposes of determining state immunity make certain assumptions about the proper or essential role of a state? Are those assumptions shared? Is the sponsorship of medical care the exercise of a public or a private act? The purchase by a state of drugs to combat HIV-AIDS?

2. Lauterpacht suggests that other doctrines could perform the beneficial work of immunity. Pursuant to the doctrine of forum non conveniens (at least as known in the United States) a judge has broad discretion to decline to hear a case when there exists another more appropriate forum. What are the relative advantages and disadvantages of that method? Understand that the doctrine of forum non conveniens is almost exclusively a phenomenon of common law countries; in civil law countries, a court with jurisdiction is required to hear the case. How would you expect Lauterpacht to respond to this?

3. Lauterpacht also suggests that attention to the extraterritorial reach of the substantive law could replace some of the concerns that are advanced by immunity doctrines. In most jurisdictions, the extraterritorial reach of substantive law can be narrowed or expanded through legislation. Do you trust legislatures to exercise the judgment necessary to maintain positive interstate relations? If not, should that judgment be exercised by the judiciary or the executive?

E. Categorical Exceptions to Immunity

As we have seen, the restrictive immunity doctrine distinguishes between acts jure imperii and those jure gestionis. Because the borderline between these categories is far from obvious, the enumeration of various categories can remove some uncertainty. The United States, the United Kingdom, Australia, Canada, Malaysia, Pakistan, South Africa, Singapore, and many other countries have enacted legislation that delineates the exceptions to immunity. In Kenya, Ireland, New Zealand, Nigeria, Zimbabwe, and elsewhere, there may be no legislation, but the courts have adopted a restrictive doctrine, as Austria did in the Dralle case above. In this section, we will review certain case law and legislation from various jurisdictions. Furthermore, we will study the recently adopted United Nations Convention on Jurisdictional Immunities of States and Their Property. That Convention may be the best depiction of the current international law regarding immunity from adjudication and enforcement. The Convention recognizes proceedings involving the following as ones in which state immunity cannot be invoked: commercial transactions, contracts of employment, personal injuries and damage to property, ownership, possession and use of property, intellectual and industrial property, participation in companies or other collective bodies, ships owned or operated by a state. Consent and waiver are also recognized by the Convention as exceptions to immunity.

A review of the contemporary practice suggests that there are approximately a dozen (overlapping) exceptions under a doctrine of restrictive immunity. Neither any state nor the Convention recognizes all of them. Indeed, some of these exceptions are universally accepted, whereas others are much more controversial. Some of these exceptions are widely accepted in principle but can vary significantly in the scope of their application and in the vigor of their enforcement. And the legislation of some countries, such as the United States, provides for a general exception—"commercial activity," in the U.S. legislation—which embraces many of those contained in the U.N. Convention.

1. Waiver

All jurisdictions recognize express and implied waiver as exceptions to foreign state immunity. Even under regimes of absolute immunity, the courts of the forum state could exercise jurisdiction over a foreign government that had expressly consented to the jurisdiction of the courts of the forum state. A foreign state may renounce its immunity in an international agreement, through contractual negotiation, or by a declaration in a particular proceeding. A foreign state could choose to waive its immunity, for example, because parties might otherwise hesitate to do business with it or because other countries might be reluctant to allow it to operate within its borders.

A foreign state may also be deemed to have waived its sovereign immunity by engaging in certain acts. There is a general consensus, for example, that participation in a court proceeding may constitute an implied waiver. Accordingly, if a state itself institutes or intervenes in a proceeding, that state will ordinarily be deemed to have waived its immunity in respect of that proceeding. Fairness requires that the foreign state not be allowed to avoid the adjudication by forum courts of counterclaims in the same proceeding. Waiver also can be a trap for the unwary, as demonstrated in the next case.

Joseph v. Nigeria

830 F.2d 1018 (9th Cir. 1987), cert. denied, 485 U.S. 905 (1988)

Choy, Senior Circuit Judge

The sovereign defendants in this case are the Federal Republic of Nigeria ("Nigeria") and the Consulate General of Nigeria (the "Consulate"). According to the defendants, the basic function of the Consulate is to protect the interests of Nigerians residing in its consular district, and to encourage cultural exchanges between Nigerian and American organizations.

In 1978, Catherine Joseph ("Joseph") leased a house in San Francisco to the Consulate. O. Effiong, a former consular officer, signed the standard form lease on behalf of the Consulate. The house was used as a residence by employees of the Consulate and their families. One of those consular employees was defendant A.A. Olalandu ("Olalandu"), a finance officer for the Consulate, who began residence at the Joseph property in 1982.

Shortly after the end of the five-year lease period, Joseph allegedly discovered that the tenants had removed property from the house and had left the premises severely damaged. Joseph brought suit in federal district court, seeking, inter alia, compensation for damages to fixtures, landscaping, and appliances.[1] Joseph asserts four causes of action against both Nigeria and the Consulate. The first is for breach of contract; the other three are tort claims for conversion, trespass, and waste. In addition, Joseph asserts three tort claims against Olalandu for conversion, trespass, and waste.

Joseph filed her complaint in district court in August 1984. The defendants did not respond. On September 27, 1985, the court entered a default judgment against the defendants. In January 1986, the defendants filed a motion to set aside the default judgment. The defendants contended that the default judgment was void for lack of jurisdiction on account of the defendants'... immunity.... [We review to determine whether the district court had jurisdiction.]

Discussion

The Foreign Sovereign Immunities Act (FSIA) is the exclusive source of subject matter jurisdiction over suits involving foreign states or their instrumentalities. Nigeria is of course a foreign state. The Consulate, as a separate legal person, also qualifies as a "foreign state" under the FSIA.

Under the FSIA, we presume that actions taken by foreign states or their instrumentalities are sovereign acts and thus are protected from the exercise of our jurisdiction, unless one of the FSIA's exceptions to immunity applies. Once the plaintiff offers evidence that an FSIA exception to immunity applies, the party claiming immunity bears the burden of proving by a preponderance of the evidence that the exception does not apply....

The FSIA's waiver exception denies immunity in any case "in which the foreign state has waived its immunity either explicitly or by implication...." 28 U.S.C. § 1605(a)(1). The waiver exception is narrowly construed. Implicit waivers are ordinarily found only where: "(1) a foreign state has agreed to arbitration in another

---

[1] The defendants' brief states that Joseph alleges "extensive damage to appliances, fixtures, and landscaping; removal of appliances, furniture, light fixtures, solid wood doors, the glass shower door; removal of shutters and drapes from thirty-three windows, removal of fully grown trees; the removal of wood framing from windows and floor boards, the removal of a built-in barbecue."

country; (2) a foreign state has agreed that a contract is governed by the law of a particular country; and (3) a foreign state has filed a responsive pleading in a case without raising the defense of sovereign immunity." Frolova v. Union of Soviet Socialist Republics, 761 F.2d 370, 377 (7th Cir. 1985).

At issue in this case is whether the lease agreement between Joseph and the Consulate implicitly waives sovereign immunity. The relevant lease provision states:

> In the event that any action shall be commenced by either party hereto arising out of, or concerning this lease or any right or obligation derived therefrom, then in addition to all other relief at law or equity, the prevailing party shall be entitled to recover attorney's fees as fixed by the court.

We conclude that this provision constitutes a waiver of sovereign immunity as to all of Joseph's claims against Nigeria and the Consulate.

A foreign state does not waive its sovereign immunity merely by entering into a contract with another party. Nevertheless, at the very least it is clear that a sovereign party has waived immunity where a contract specifically states that the laws of a jurisdiction within the United States are to govern the transaction. Marlowe v. Argentine Naval Commission, 604 F.Supp. 703, 708–09 (D.D.C. 1985) (implicit waiver where contract stated that it "shall be governed by and construed in accordance with the laws of the District of Columbia"); Resource Dynamics International, Ltd. v. General People's Committee for Communications and Maritime Transport in the Socialist People's Libyan Arab Jamahiriya, 593 F. Supp. 572, 575 (N.D. Ga. 1984) (implicit waiver where contract provided that "[t]his Agreement and the performance or breach hereof shall be governed by the... laws in effect in the State of Virginia"). On the other hand, where a contract specifies that the laws of a jurisdiction outside of the United States are to govern, a waiver of sovereign immunity has not been made for the purposes of the FSIA. See Colonial Bank v. Compagnie Generale Maritime et Financiere, 645 F. Supp. 1457, 1461–62 (S.D.N.Y. 1986).

In the instant case, the lease agreement does not specify which jurisdiction's laws will govern disputes under the lease. Joseph argues that it is not necessary for a contract to specify which law will govern a contract in order for the waiver exception to apply. Indeed, there appears to be no justification for requiring a contract to specifically state the governing law in order for there to be a waiver of immunity. Waiver by contract is premised on an agreement by the parties that the United States courts may become involved in disputes arising pursuant to the contract. Cf. Maritime International Nominees Establishment v. Republic of Guinea, 693 F.2d 1094, 1103 (D.C. Cir. 1983) (arbitration agreement case), cert. denied, 464 U.S. 815 (1983). Where an agreement contemplates adjudication of a dispute by the United States courts, the waiver exception should be applied, regardless of whether the governing law is explicitly identified. See id. at 1103–04.

Because the lease at issue provides for adjudication of landlord-tenant disputes in court, we conclude that the lease contemplates participation of the United States courts in disputes between Joseph and her tenants. In light of the wholly local nature of the transaction, it is virtually inconceivable that the Consulate contemplated that adjudication of disputes would occur in a court outside of the United States. Therefore, we believe that the waiver exception is applicable to Joseph's breach of contract and tort claims.

Comments and Questions

1. Do you agree that the attorney's fees clause constituted a waiver of Nigeria's immunity from judicial jurisdiction?

2. Some jurisdictions invoke a doctrine of "implied waiver" to reach foreign states that engage in certain acts that are addressed here as separate exceptions to immunity. For example, the extent to which a state's agreement to arbitrate constitutes an implied waiver is discussed in Section 9, infra.

3. Notice that among the defendants in Joseph was Olalandu in his individual capacity. Olalandu is not a foreign state nor an organ or instrumentality of the state; so the FSIA does not give him immunity. Olalandu thus asserted consular immunity under the Vienna Convention on Consular Relations, April 24, 1963, 21 U.S.T. 77, T.I.A.S. No. 6820, 596 U.N.T.S. 261. Under Article 43 of the Vienna Convention, consular officials are subject to the jurisdiction of the courts of the receiving state except "in respect of acts performed in the exercise of consular functions." The Convention lists twelve specific consular functions, but none of these were availing to Olalandu.

4. Now that we have opened the Pandora's Box of individual immunities, we will also introduce two more types of immunities that can arise in transnational litigation in the United States involving foreign officials: head of state and diplomatic immunity. Depending on the nature of the proceeding, courts may deem a head of state to be an organ or instrumentality of the state, making the FSIA the relevant framework of analysis. Other courts have relied instead on federal common law which recognizes head of state immunity not as a matter of right but, rather, as a matter of grace and comity. Again, however, such immunity generally extends only to official acts.

The rules of international law on diplomatic immunity are outlined in the 1961 Vienna Convention on Diplomatic Relations, 23 U.S.T. 3227, T.I.A.S. No. 7502, 500 U.N.T.S. 95, and codified into U.S. law in 1978 by the Diplomatic Relations Act, 22 U.S.C. §254a-e & 28 U.S.C. § 1364. Under Section 464 of the Restatement (Third) of Foreign Relations Law, which is based on the 1961 Vienna Convention:

> A diplomatic agent of a state, accredited to and accepted by another state, is immune
>
> (1) from the exercise by the receiving state of jurisdiction to prescribe in respect of acts or omissions in the exercise of the agent's official functions, as well as from other regulation that would be incompatible with the agent's diplomatic status; and
>
> (2) from arrest, detention, criminal process, and, in general, civil process in the receiving state.

Diplomatic immunity is substantially similar to consular immunity except that diplomatic immunity is not limited to acts or omissions in the performance of official functions.

2. Immovable property

The ownership, possession, or use of property in the forum state is another long-recognized exception to the immunity doctrine. This exception, often labeled the "immovable property" exception, denies immunity in litigation relating to rights in real estate that is located within the forum state. The reason for an immovable property exception is that the acquisition and continued ownership of property in a foreign country is made possible only by virtue of the application of the internal law or private law of the state of the situs of the property. Because ownership itself is only possible through the operation of local law, the thinking goes, the foreign state must recognize and respect the internal law of the forum state with regard to the foreign state's relationship with the property in the forum state. Because the foreign government's property rights derive from and are protected by that regime, certain burdens of ownership accompany those benefits. When owning property abroad, a foreign state must follow all the same laws that pertain to private owners of such property, except to the extent that it can point to specific exceptions in that country's agreements with the government of the forum state. In the following case, Brazil explores the parameters of its immovable property exception in the context of a larger matter of international relations.

Arab Republic of Syria v. Arab Republic of Egypt

Brazil, Supreme Court (Plenary Session)

Case No 298-Df, 14 April 1982

RTJ, vol. 104, 1983, p. 889 (in Portuguese); 91 I.L.R 289 (1993)

The facts: In 1951 the Government of Syria purchased property in Rio de Janeiro which was subsequently used for its diplomatic service. In 1958 Syria and Egypt merged to form the United Arab Republic ("UAR"), which replaced them at the international level. The UAR was represented by a single ambassador to Brazil. At the time of the dissolution of the UAR in 1961, an Egyptian diplomat was serving as the ambassador of the UAR in Brazil and the property at issue was being used as the embassy premises. The diplomatic mission of the UAR having ceased to exist, Syria reclaimed the property on the basis of its having been the original owner registered in the land registry, no subsequent entry ever having been made. The Egyptian diplomat in question refused to return the premises to Syria and they continued to be used, initially as the seat of the re-established Egyptian embassy and later as Egyptian consular premises.

In 1981 the Syrian Ambassador to Brazil instituted original proceedings before the Brazilian Supreme Court against the Egyptian Ambassador and Consul, claiming repossession of the premises. A writ was issued and service was attempted through the offices of the Brazilian Ministry of Foreign Affairs, which sent a Note Verbale to the Egyptian Ambassador, requesting him to acknowledge the claim and give notice of his intention to defend. The Egyptian Ambassador replied by Note Verbalc stating that his country enjoyed jurisdictional immunity pursuant to international law and that the Brazilian courts were not competent to pronounce in a dispute between two sovereign foreign States....

Judge Moreira Alves

There is no doubt that the predominant doctrine...bearing in mind the increasing commercial activities carried out nowadays by modern States does not any longer support the existence of a customary rule of international law asserting the absolute immunity of sovereign States from the jurisdiction of other foreign States. Recent international practice is favourable to a concept of restrictive immunity...distinguishing between acts performed jure imperii and acts performed jure gestionis.

On the other hand, there is also no doubt that even the most rigorous supporters of the theory of absolute immunity do admit some exceptions, related in particular to real actions and questions of succession concerning immovable property situated on the territory of foreign States.

According to these principles...it could be assumed that the case at issue, concerning a real action whose subject matter is immovable property situated on the territory of a third sovereign State, constitutes one of these exceptions...so that the Brazilian courts should have competence to decide the dispute.

However, the issues are very complex and cannot be solved uniquely on the basis of statements of principle which take account of ordinary cases unrelated to real actions and consider only the legal order of the State where the immovable property is situated. The case at issue raises international issues and involves a procedural problem concerning the jurisdiction of a sovereign State over another sovereign State. In such a case normally the courts of the State where the immovable property is situated must settle the dispute on the basis of the application of municipal law, since no problem of international law arises. For example, in a dispute between an individual and a foreign State, or even between two foreign States, concerning the ownership of immovable property acquired non domino, the question is purely one of municipal law and the international issues are related only to procedure....

The problem changes, however, where in order to decide a dispute concerning immovable property it is necessary to decide not only the real action itself but also questions of public international law arising in a dispute between two foreign States.

In such a case it seems clear that jurisdictional immunity must be granted on the grounds that no sovereign State is entitled to exercise jurisdiction over another sovereign State in order to decide questions of public international law arising between that foreign State and another foreign State.

[The judge referred to the writings of Panebianco and Verdross in support of this assertion and continued:]

There is no doubt that the claim put forward by the plaintiff in this case involves questions of public international law; the establishment of the United Arab Republic by Egypt and Syria in 1958; the circumstance that the UAR used the property at issue as its diplomatic mission; and finally the secession of Syria from the UAR....

The plaintiff maintains...that the law of Brazil applies.... [It is my opinion that] this claim is based on a fundamental defect of principle. It assumes that certain issues have already been proved in order to avoid the problem of the presence of issues of public international law. The plaintiff's contentions are based on the assumption as undisputed fact that Syria allowed the UAR to temporarily take possession of the property in dispute for the use of its diplomatic mission...but this allegation must be proved. In addition, the legal nature of the initial transfer of possession, the title to possession of Egypt so long as the Union lasted and the legal consequences of the secession of Syria in 1961, must all be ascertained. All these points can only be solved by means of the application of public international law....

It therefore seems self-evident that, in order to decide the present dispute...these problems relating to public international law cannot be ignored as if they did not exist. They are closely related to the right of ownership and possession of the immovable property which was used as the seat of the diplomatic mission of the UAR. This complex conflict cannot be solved merely on the basis of the entry in the Brazilian Land Registry which does not show any record of the events at issue and does not appear to mention any transfer of ownership. This fact in itself cannot establish any presumption of truth in relation to the bona fides of third parties....

In the light of the above considerations, and bearing in mind the peculiar facts of this dispute...as between the choices of a denial of justice or the difficulties inherent in enforcing a decision, I have opted for providing a solution to those difficulties since a judge should not avoid his judicial duties even where this may lead to complications in the enforcement of the decision. It is the task of the courts to administer justice and take the appropriate measures to ensure that their decisions are respected and enforced....

[The Supreme Court thus held that it was not competent to exercise jurisdiction and the proceedings were quashed.]

Judge Neri da Silveira, dissenting:
It is my understanding that, in the name of the sovereignty of the State and in compliance with the obligation to guarantee property rights laid down in the Constitution and the laws, the Brazilian State cannot allow the judicial authorities to countenance the infringement of property rights, even where a claim is brought by one foreign State against another foreign State. Indeed, given that the property right in question is in Brazil, a finding that the Brazilian courts lacked competence would meant that the right to property could not be adequately safeguarded because no other foreign court would be competent to rule on the case at issue and to render a decision which would be enforceable on Brazilian

territory.... If the plaintiff were a private person and was denied the right to bring a claim before a Brazilian court similar to the claim brought by the Arab Republic of Syria and based on the same grounds... this would infringe Article 8 of the Universal Declaration on Human Rights, approved by the General Assembly of the United Nations on 10 December 1948, which provides: "Everyone has the right to an effective remedy by the competent national tribunals for acts violating the fundamental rights granted him by the Constitution or by law."...

I would dismiss the preliminary plea of jurisdictional immunity....

Comments and Questions

1. So where does the majority expect Syria to litigate this?

2. Given Judge da Silveira's logic, would it be necessary even to distinguish between acts performed jure imperii and acts performed jure gestionis? Under a regime of absolute immunity, would Judge da Silveira recognize an exception to that principle in order to allow a foreign State to be sued in proceedings concerning a right to property located in the forum state?

3. The U.S. Supreme Court recently addressed the scope of the Foreign Sovereign Immunities Act which excepts from immunity "any case... in which... rights in immovable property situated in the United States are in issue." 28 U.S.C. § 1605(a)(4). See The Permanent Mission of India to the United Nations, et al. v. City of New York, New York, 127 S. Ct. 2352 (2007). In this case, the Government of India owned a 26-story building in New York City that was used in part for diplomatic offices, with the remainder used for residential units for lower-level diplomatic employees of the Permanent Mission of India to the United Nations and those employees' families. The City levied property taxes only on that portion of the building that housed the employees, but the taxes were never paid. The unpaid taxes, totaling $16.4 million, were eventually converted into tax liens held by the City. When the City sought a declaratory judgment to determine the validity of the liens, India argued that it was immune. (The Supreme Court opinion involves a companion suit with substantially similar facts involving property occupied by the Ministry for Foreign Affairs of the People's Republic of Mongolia and owned by the Mongolian Government.)

Writing for a 7–2 majority, Justice Thomas held that a tax lien creates an adverse effect on the property because it is enforceable against any potential purchaser. And because the FSIA does not otherwise limit the meaning of the words in the immovable property exception, a lien involves "a right" that puts the property "in issue." India would thus not be immune. Justice Stevens (with Justice Breyer) dissented, arguing for a more restrained interpretation: "[T]his case is not about the validity of the city's title to immovable property.... Rather, it is a dispute over a foreign soveriegn's tax liability. If Congress had intended the statute to waive sovereign immunity in tax litigation, I think it would have said so." Id. 127 S. Ct. at 2359.

4. Why is there no categorical exception for tax litigation?

3. Participation in associations, companies, and other collective bodies

In some, but not all jurisdictions, there is a specific exception for participation by the State in a company or other collective body which has been established or has its seat or principal place of business in the State of the forum. In the United Kingdom, for example, Section 8 of the State Immunity Act 1978 provides:

> (1) A State is not immune as respects proceedings relating to its membership of a body corporate, an unincorporated body or a partnership which—
> (a) has members other than States; and
> (b) is incorporated or constituted under the laws of the United Kingdom or is controlled from or has its principal place of business in the United Kingdom,
> being proceedings arising between the State and the body or its other members or, as the case may be, between the State and the other partners.
> (2) This section does not apply if provision to the contrary has been made by an agreement in writing between the parties to the dispute or by the constitution or other instrument establishing or regulating the body or partnership in question.

This section tracks the comparable provision of the European Convention on State Immunity of 1972 which the 1978 Act implements in the United Kingdom.

When a state participates in a collective body, such as by acquiring or holding shares in a company or becoming a member of a body corporate which is organized or operated in another State, it voluntarily enters into the legal system of that other State and into a relationship recognized as binding under that legal system. Consequently, the exception is justified on the ground that the State should be bound and obliged to abide by the applicable rules and internal law of the State of incorporation, of registration or of the principal place of business. The State also has rights and obligations under the relevant provisions of the charter of incorporation, articles of association or other similar instruments establishing limited or registered partnerships. The relationship between shareholders inter se or between shareholders and the company or the body of any form in matters relating to the formation, management, direction, operation, dissolution or distribution of assets of the entity in question is governed by the law of the State of incorporation, of registration or of the seat or principal place of business. And the courts of that state are best qualified to apply this specialized branch of their own law. Many jurisdictions, such as the United States, do not recognize this as a separate exception to immunity, but it treat it as being covered by the broader commercial activities exception, which is discussed in Section 5, infra.

4. Intellectual and industrial property

Although this exception applies only to a specialized branch of the law, it is of growing practical importance. The U.S. Foreign Sovereign Immunities Act has no express exception dealing with this matter, although once again the matters addressed in this narrower exception may also be included within the broader commercial activities exception, which is discussed in Section 5, infra. An intellectual and industrial property exception is especially popular in many civil law countries and is recognized in Article 8 of the European Convention on State Immunity. It is also included in Article 14 of the U.N. Convention, which provides as follows:

> Unless otherwise agreed between the States concerned, a State cannot invoke immunity from jurisdiction before a court of another State which is otherwise competent in a proceeding which relates to:
>
> (a) the determination of any right of the State in a patent, industrial design, trade name or business name, trademark, copyright or any other form of intellectual or industrial property which enjoys a measure of legal protection, even if provisional, in the State of the forum; or
>
> (b) an alleged infringement by the State, in the territory of the State of the forum, of a right of the nature mentioned in subparagraph (a) which belongs to a third person and is protected in the State of the forum.

Most states have some system of intellectual property registration in force that is designed to promote inventiveness and creativity yet also to regulate and secure fair competition. The voluntary entrance by a State into the legal system of the State of the forum, for example, by submitting an application for registration of, or registering a copyright, as well as the legal protection offered by the State of the forum, provides the basis for exercise of jurisdiction. This exception may be viewed conceptually as falling somewhere between the exceptions for commercial transactions and for immovable property. The exception allows the courts of the forum state to exercise jurisdiction over a foreign state in matters that regard the determination of any rights of the foreign state in legally protected intellectual or industrial property. The U.N. Convention defines the word "determination" to include not only the ascertainment or verification of the existence of the rights protected, but also to the evaluation or assessment of the substance, including content, scope and extent of such rights.

Importantly, the scope of Article 14(b) is confined to infringements occurring in the State of the forum. Every State is free to pursue its own policy within its own territory. Infringement of such rights in the territory of another State, for instance, the unauthorized reproduction or distribution of copyrighted publications, cannot escape the exercise of jurisdiction by the competent courts of that State in which measures of protection have been adopted. The State of the forum is also equally free to tolerate or permit such infringements or to deny remedies therefor in the absence of an internationally organized system of protection for the rights violated or breached in its own territory.

5. Commercial transactions

A commercial transaction or activity exception is universally recognized by countries that have adopted the restrictive doctrine of State immunity. Indeed, the state's participation in commerce—through acta jure gestionis—fueled if not generated the restrictive immunity theory. We begin this section with two cases interpreting the commercial activities exception that is codified in the United States Foreign Sovereign Immunities Act.

Republic of Argentina v. Weltover, Inc.

504 U.S. 607 (1992)

JUSTICE SCALIA delivered the opinion for a unanimous Court:
This case requires us to decide whether the Republic of Argentina's default on certain bonds issued as part of a plan to stabilize its currency was an act taken "in connection with a commercial activity" that had a "direct effect in the United States" so as to subject Argentina to suit in an American court under the Foreign Sovereign Immunities Act of 1976, 28 U.S.C. § 1602 et seq.

I

Since Argentina's currency is not one of the mediums of exchange accepted on the international market, Argentine businesses engaging in foreign transactions must pay in United States dollars or some other internationally accepted currency. In the recent past, it was difficult for Argentine borrowers to obtain such funds, principally because of the instability of the Argentine currency. To address these problems, petitioners, the Republic of Argentina and its central bank, Banco Central (collectively Argentina), in 1981 instituted a foreign exchange insurance contract program (FEIC), under which Argentina effectively agreed to assume the risk of currency depreciation in cross-border transactions involving Argentine borrowers. This was accomplished by Argentina's agreeing to sell to domestic borrowers, in exchange for a contractually predetermined amount of local currency, the necessary United States dollars to repay their foreign debts when they matured, irrespective of intervening devaluations.

Unfortunately, Argentina did not possess sufficient reserves of United States dollars to cover the FEIC contracts as they became due in 1982. The Argentine Government thereupon adopted certain emergency measures, including refinancing of the FEIC-backed debts by issuing to the creditors government bonds. These bonds, called "Bonods," provide for payment of interest and principal in United States dollars; payment may be made through transfer on the London, Frankfurt, Zurich, or New York market, at the election of the creditor. Under this refinancing program, the foreign creditor had the option of either accepting the Bonods in satisfaction of the initial debt, thereby substituting the Argentine Government for the private debtor, or maintaining the debtor/creditor relationship with the private borrower and accepting the Argentine Government as guarantor.

When the Bonods began to mature in May 1986, Argentina concluded that it lacked sufficient foreign exchange to retire them. Pursuant to a Presidential Decree, Argentina unilaterally extended the time for payment and offered bondholders substitute instruments as a means of rescheduling the debts. Respondents, two

Panamanian corporations and a Swiss bank who hold, collectively, $1.3 million of Bonods, refused to accept the rescheduling and insisted on full payment, specifying New York as the place where payment should be made. Argentina did not pay, and respondents then brought this breach-of-contract action in the United States District Court for the Southern District of New York, relying on the Foreign Sovereign Immunities Act of 1976 as the basis for jurisdiction....

II

The Foreign Sovereign Immunities Act of 1976 (FSIA), establishes a comprehensive framework for determining whether a court in this country, state or federal, may exercise jurisdiction over a foreign state. Under the Act, a "foreign state shall be immune from the jurisdiction of the courts of the United States and of the States" unless one of several statutorily defined exceptions applies. § 1604 (emphasis added). The FSIA thus provides the "sole basis" for obtaining jurisdiction over a foreign sovereign in the United States. See Argentine Republic v. Amerada Hess Shipping Corp., 488 U.S. 428, 434–439 (1989). The most significant of the FSIA's exceptions—and the one at issue in this case—is the "commercial" exception of § 1605(a)(2), which provides that a foreign state is not immune from suit in any case

> in which the action is based upon a commercial activity carried on in the United States by the foreign state; or upon an act performed in the United States in connection with a commercial activity of the foreign state elsewhere; or upon an act outside the territory of the United States in connection with a commercial activity of the foreign state elsewhere and that act causes a direct effect in the United States.
>
> § 1605(a)(2).

In the proceedings below, respondents relied only on the third clause of § 1605(a)(2) to establish jurisdiction, and our analysis is therefore limited to considering whether this lawsuit is (1) "based...upon an act outside the territory of the United States"; (2) that was taken "in connection with a commercial activity" of Argentina outside this country; and (3) that "cause[d] a direct effect in the United States."[1] The complaint in this case alleges only one cause of action on behalf of each of the respondents, viz., a breach-of-contract claim based on Argentina's attempt to refinance the Bonods rather than to pay them according to their terms. The fact that the cause of action is in compliance with the first of the three requirements—that it is "based upon an act outside the territory of the United States" (presumably Argentina's unilateral extension)—is uncontested. The dispute pertains to whether the unilateral refinancing of the Bonods was taken "in

[1] It is undisputed that both the Republic of Argentina and Banco Central are "foreign states" within the meaning of the FSIA. See 28 U.S.C. § 1603(a),(b) ("[F]oreign state" includes certain "agenc[ies] or instrumentalit[ies] of a foreign state").

connection with a commercial activity" of Argentina, and whether it had a "direct effect in the United States." We address these issues in turn.

A

Respondents and their amicus, the United States, contend that Argentina's issuance of, and continued liability under, the Bonods constitute a "commercial activity" and that the extension of the payment schedules was taken "in connection with" that activity. The latter point is obvious enough, and Argentina does not contest it; the key question is whether the activity is "commercial" under the FSIA.

The FSIA defines "commercial activity" to mean:

> [E]ither a regular course of commercial conduct or a particular commercial transaction or act. The commercial character of an activity shall be determined by reference to the nature of the course of conduct or particular transaction or act, rather than by reference to its purpose.
>
> 28 U.S.C. § 1603(d).

This definition, however, leaves the critical term "commercial" largely undefined: The first sentence simply establishes that the commercial nature of an activity does not depend upon whether it is a single act or a regular course of conduct; and the second sentence merely specifies what element of the conduct determines commerciality (i.e., nature rather than purpose), but still without saying what "commercial" means. Fortunately, however, the FSIA was not written on a clean slate. As we have noted, see Verlinden B.V. v. Central Bank of Nigeria, 461 U.S. 480, 486–489 (1983), the Act (and the commercial exception in particular) largely codifies the so-called "restrictive" theory of foreign sovereign immunity first endorsed by the State Department in 1952. The meaning of "commercial" is the meaning generally attached to that term under the restrictive theory at the time the statute was enacted....

This Court did not have occasion to discuss the scope or validity of the restrictive theory of sovereign immunity until our 1976 decision in Alfred Dunhill of London, Inc. v. Republic of Cuba, 425 U.S. 682. Although the Court there was evenly divided on the question whether the "commercial" exception that applied in the foreign-sovereign-immunity context also limited the availability of an act-of-state defense, compare id. at 695–706 (plurality opinion), with id. at 725–730 (Marshall, J., dissenting), there was little disagreement over the general scope of the exception. The plurality noted that, after the State Department endorsed the restrictive theory of foreign sovereign immunity in 1952, the lower courts consistently held that foreign sovereigns were not immune from the jurisdiction of American courts in cases "arising out of purely commercial transactions," id. at 703. [additional citations omitted] The plurality further recognized that the distinction between state sovereign acts, on the one hand, and state commercial and private acts, on the other, was not entirely novel to American law. See 425 U.S. at 695–696 citing Parden v. Terminal Railway of Alabama Docks Dept., 377 U.S. 184, 189–190 (1964) (Eleventh Amendment immunity).... The plurality stated that the restrictive theory of foreign sovereign immunity would not bar a suit based upon a foreign state's participation in the marketplace in the manner of a private citizen or corporation. 425 U.S. at 698–705. A foreign state engaging in "commercial" activities "do[es] not exercise powers peculiar to sovereigns"; rather, it "exercise[s] only those powers that can also be exercised by private citizens." Id. at 704. The dissenters did not disagree with this general description. See id. at 725. Given that the FSIA was enacted less than six months after our decision in Alfred Dunhill was announced, we think the plurality's contemporaneous description of the then-prevailing restrictive theory of sovereign immunity is of significant assistance in construing the scope of the Act.

In accord with that description, we conclude that when a foreign government acts, not as regulator of a market, but in the manner of a private player within it, the foreign sovereign's actions are "commercial" within the meaning of the FSIA. Moreover, because the Act provides that the commercial character of an act is to be determined by reference to its "nature" rather than its "purpose," 28 U.S.C. § 1603(d), the question is not whether the foreign government is acting with a profit motive or instead with the aim of fulfilling uniquely sovereign objectives. Rather, the issue is whether the particular actions that the foreign state performs (whatever the motive behind them) are the type of actions by which a private party engages in "trade and traffic or commerce," Black's Law Dictionary 270 (6th ed. 1990).... Thus, a foreign government's issuance of regulations limiting foreign currency exchange is a sovereign activity, because such authoritative control of commerce cannot be exercised by a private party; whereas a contract to buy army boots or even bullets is a "commercial" activity, because private companies can similarly use sales contracts to acquire goods, see, e.g., Stato di Rumania v. Trutta, [1926] Foro It. I 584, 585–586, 589 (Corte di Cass. del Regno, Italy), translated and reprinted in part in 26 Am. J. Int'l L. 626–629 (Supp.1932).

The commercial character of the Bonods is confirmed by the fact that they are in almost all respects garden-variety debt instruments: They may be held by private parties; they are negotiable and may be traded on the international market (except in Argentina); and they promise a future stream of cash income. We recognize that, prior to the enactment of the FSIA, there was authority suggesting that the issuance of public debt instruments did not constitute a commercial activity. Victory Transport, Inc. v. Comisaria General, 336 F.2d 354, 360 (2nd Cir.) (dicta), cert. denied, 381 U.S. 934 (1956). There is, however, nothing distinctive about the state's assumption of debt (other than perhaps its purpose) that would cause it always to be classified as jure imperii, and in this regard it is significant that Victory Transport expressed confusion as to whether the "nature" or the "purpose" of a transaction was controlling in determining commerciality, id. at 359–360. Because the FSIA has now clearly established that the "nature" governs, we perceive no basis for concluding that the issuance of debt should be treated as categorically different from other activities of foreign states.

Argentina contends that, although the FSIA bars consideration of "purpose," a court must nonetheless fully consider the context of a transaction in order to determine whether it is "commercial." Accordingly, Argentina claims that the Court of Appeals erred by defining the relevant conduct in what Argentina considers an overly generalized, acontextual manner and by essentially adopting a per se rule that all "issuance of debt instruments" is "commercial." See 941 F.2d at 151 ("[I]t is self-evident that issuing public debt is a commercial activity within the meaning of [the FSIA]"), quoting Shapiro v. Republic of Bolivia, 930 F.2d 1013, 1018 (2nd Cir. 1991). We have no occasion to consider such a per se rule, because it seems to us that even in full context, there is nothing about the issuance of these Bonods (except perhaps its purpose) that is not analogous to a private commercial transaction.

Argentina points to the fact that the transactions in which the Bonods were issued did not have the ordinary commercial consequence of raising capital or financing acquisitions. Assuming for the sake of argument that this is not an example of judging the commerciality of a transaction by its purpose, the ready answer is that private parties regularly issue bonds, not just to raise capital or to finance purchases, but also to refinance debt. That is what Argentina did here: By virtue of the earlier FEIC contracts, Argentina was already obligated to supply the United States dollars needed to retire the FEIC-insured debts; the Bonods simply allowed Argentina to restructure its existing obligations. Argentina further asserts (without proof or even elaboration) that it "received consideration [for the Bonods] in no way commensurate with [their] value," Brief for Petitioners 22. Assuming that to be true, it makes no difference. Engaging in a commercial act does not require the receipt of fair value, or even compliance with the common-law requirements of consideration.

Argentina argues that the Bonods differ from ordinary debt instruments in that they "were created by the Argentine Government to fulfill its obligations under a foreign exchange program designed to address a domestic credit crisis, and as a component of a program designed to control that nation's critical shortage of foreign exchange." Id., at 23–24. In this regard, Argentina relies heavily on DeSanchez v. Banco Central de Nicaragua, 770 F.2d 1385 (1985), in which the Fifth Circuit took the view that "[o]ften, the essence of an act is defined by its purpose"; that unless "we can inquire into the purposes of such acts, we cannot determine their nature"; and that, in light of its purpose to control its reserves of foreign currency, Nicaragua's refusal to honor a check it had issued to cover a private bank debt was a sovereign act entitled to immunity. Id. at 1393. Indeed, Argentina asserts that the line between "nature" and "purpose" rests upon a "formalistic distinction [that] simply is neither useful nor warranted." Reply Brief for Petitioners 8. We think this line of argument is squarely foreclosed by the language of the FSIA. However difficult it may be in some cases to separate "purpose" (i.e., the reason why the foreign state engages in the activity) from "nature" (i.e., the outward form of the conduct that the foreign state performs or agrees to perform), see DeSanchez, supra, at 1393, the statute unmistakably commands that to be done, 28 U.S.C. § 1603(d). We agree with the Court of Appeals that it is irrelevant why Argentina participated in the bond market in the manner of a private actor; it matters only that it did so.

We conclude that Argentina's issuance of the Bonods was a "commercial activity" under the FSIA.

B

The remaining question is whether Argentina's unilateral rescheduling of the Bonods had a "direct effect" in the United States, 28 U.S.C. § 1605(a)(2). In addressing this issue, the Court of Appeals rejected the suggestion in the legislative history of the FSIA that an effect is not "direct" unless it is both "substantial" and "foreseeable." 941 F.2d, at 152.... Of course the generally applicable principle de minimis non curat lex ensures that jurisdiction may not be predicated on purely trivial effects in the United States. But we reject the suggestion that § 1605(a)(2) contains any unexpressed requirement of "substantiality" or "foreseeability." As the Court of Appeals recognized, an effect is "direct" if it follows "as an immediate consequence of the defendant's... activity." 941 F.2d, at 152....

[We] have little difficulty concluding that Argentina's unilateral rescheduling of the maturity dates on the Bonods had a "direct effect" in the United States. Respondents had designated their accounts in New York as the place of payment, and Argentina made some interest payments into those accounts before announcing that it was rescheduling the payments. Because New York was thus the place of performance for Argentina's ultimate contractual obligations, the rescheduling of those obligations necessarily had a "direct effect" in the United States: Money that was supposed to have been delivered to a New York bank for deposit was not forthcoming. We reject Argentina's suggestion that the "direct effect" requirement cannot be satisfied where the plaintiffs are all foreign corporations with no other connections to the United States. We expressly stated in Verlinden that the FSIA permits "a foreign plaintiff to sue a foreign sovereign in the courts of the United States, provided the substantive requirements of the Act are satisfied," 461 U.S., at 489.... Accordingly, the judgment of the Court of Appeals is affirmed.

Comments and Questions

1. In footnote 1, the Court mentioned that the Republic of Argentina and Banco Central were "foreign states" within the meaning of the FSIA. Such a determination is not always obvious, however. The FSIA defines a foreign state" to include "a political subdivision of a foreign state or an agency or instrumentality of a foreign state". An "agency or instrumentality of a foreign state means any entity:

(1) which is a separate legal person, corporate or otherwise; and
(2) which is an organ of a foreign state or political subdivision thereof, or a majority of whose shares or other ownership interest is owned by a foreign state or political subdivision thereof; and
(3) which is neither a citizen of a state of the United States as defined in Section 1332(c) and (d) [of Title 28] nor created under the laws of any third country.

28 U.S.C. § 1603(b).

2. In 2003, the U.S. Supreme Court decided a case that involved banana workers from several Latin American countries who sued Dole Food Company for liability arising out of Dole's use of a pesticide known to cause various diseases. Dole Food Co. v. Patrickson, 538 U.S. 468 (2003). When Dole impleaded two Israeli companies (Dead Sea Companies) that manufactured the pesticides, the third party defendants pleaded foreign state immunity. The Court held that a majority of a foreign corporation's shares must be directly owned by a foreign sovereign in order for the corporation to qualify as a foreign government "instrumentality," and hence as a foreign state under the FSIA. Because the State of Israel indirectly owned the defendant companies, the defendants fell outside the scope of the FSIA. Under this interpretation, an entity directly owned 51 percent by a foreign sovereign would qualify under the Act. An entity owned 100 percent by a foreign sovereign but held through another 100 percent–owned holding entity would not qualify even though the foreign sovereign's interests are likely more affected by legal process against the latter.

3. Section 1605(a)(2) requires that an action be "based upon" a commercial activity—or be "based upon" an act "in connection with" a commercial activity. The next case focuses on the meaning of this language.

Saudi Arabia v. Nelson

507 U.S. 349 (1993)

JUSTICE SOUTER delivered the opinion of the Court, in which CHIEF JUSTICE REHNQUIST, and JUSTICES O'CONNOR, SCALIA, and THOMAS joined, and in which JUSTICE KENNEDY joined except for the last paragraph of Part II.

The Foreign Sovereign Immunities Act of 1976 entitles foreign states to immunity from the jurisdiction of courts in the United States, 28 U.S.C. § 1604, subject to certain enumerated exceptions. § 1605. One is that a foreign state shall not be immune in any case "in which the action is based upon a commercial activity carried on in the United States by the foreign state." § 1605(a)(2). We hold that respondents' action alleging personal injury resulting from unlawful detention and torture by the Saudi Government is not "based upon a commercial activity" within the meaning of the Act, which consequently confers no jurisdiction over respondents' suit.

I

Because this case comes to us on a motion to dismiss the complaint, we assume that we have truthful factual allegations before us, though many of those allegations are subject to dispute. Petitioner Kingdom of Saudi Arabia owns and operates petitioner King Faisal Specialist Hospital in Riyadh, as well as petitioner Roysрec Purchasing Services, the hospital's corporate purchasing agent in the United States. The Hospital Corporation of America, Ltd. (HCA), an independent corporation existing under the laws of the Cayman Islands, recruits Americans for employment at the hospital under an agreement signed with Saudi Arabia in 1973.

In its recruitment effort, HCA placed an advertisement in a trade periodical seeking applications for a position as a monitoring systems engineer at the hospital. The advertisement drew the attention of respondent Scott Nelson in September 1983, while Nelson was in the United States. After interviewing for the position in Saudi Arabia, Nelson returned to the United States, where he signed an employment contract with the hospital, satisfied personnel processing requirements, and attended an orientation session that HCA conducted for hospital employees. In the course of that program, HCA identified Royspec as the point of contact in the United States for family members who might wish to reach Nelson in an emergency.

In December 1983, Nelson went to Saudi Arabia and began work at the hospital, monitoring all "facilities, equipment, utilities and maintenance systems to insure the safety of patients, hospital staff, and others." He did his job without significant incident until March 1984, when he discovered safety defects in the hospital's oxygen and nitrous oxide lines that posed fire hazards and otherwise endangered patients' lives. Over a period of several months, Nelson repeatedly advised hospital officials of the safety defects and reported the defects to a Saudi Government commission as well. Hospital officials instructed Nelson to ignore the problems.

The hospital's response to Nelson's reports changed, however, on September 27, 1984, when certain hospital employees summoned him to the hospital's security office where agents of the Saudi Government arrested him.[1] The agents transported Nelson to a jail cell, in which they "shackled, tortured and bea[t]" him, and kept him four days without food. Although Nelson did not understand Arabic, government agents forced him to sign a statement written in that language, the content of which he did not know; a hospital employee who was supposed to act as Nelson's interpreter advised him to sign "anything" the agents gave him to avoid further beatings. Two days later, government agents transferred Nelson to the Al Sijan Prison "to await trial on unknown charges."

At the prison, Nelson was confined in an overcrowded cell area infested with rats, where he had to fight other prisoners for food and from which he was taken only once a week for fresh air and exercise. Although police interrogators repeatedly questioned him in Arabic, Nelson did not learn the nature of the charges, if any, against him. For several days, the Saudi Government failed to advise Nelson's family of his whereabouts, though a Saudi official eventually told Nelson's wife, respondent Vivian Nelson, that he could arrange for her husband's release if she provided sexual favors.

---

[1] Petitioners assert that the Saudi Government arrested Nelson because he had falsely represented to the hospital that he had received a degree from the Massachusetts Institute of Technology and had provided the hospital with a forged diploma to verify his claim. Brief for Petitioners 4–5. The Nelsons concede these misrepresentations, but dispute that they occasioned Scott Nelson's arrest. Brief for Respondents 9.

Although officials from the United States Embassy visited Nelson twice during his detention, they concluded that his allegations of Saudi mistreatment were "not credible" and made no protest to Saudi authorities. It was only at the personal request of a United States Senator that the Saudi Government released Nelson, 39 days after his arrest, on November 5, 1984. Seven days later, after failing to convince him to return to work at the hospital, the Saudi Government allowed Nelson to leave the country.

In 1988, Nelson and his wife filed this action against petitioners in the United States District Court for the Southern District of Florida seeking damages for personal injury. The Nelsons' complaint sets out 16 causes of action, which fall into three categories. Counts II through VII and counts X, XI, XIV, and XV allege that petitioners committed various intentional torts, including battery, unlawful detainment, wrongful arrest and imprisonment, false imprisonment, inhuman torture, disruption of normal family life, and infliction of mental anguish. Counts I, IX, and XIII charge petitioners with negligently failing to warn Nelson of otherwise undisclosed dangers of his employment, namely, that if he attempted to report safety hazards the hospital would likely retaliate against him and the Saudi Government might detain and physically abuse him without legal cause. Finally, counts VIII, XII, and XVI allege that Vivian Nelson sustained derivative injury resulting from petitioners' actions. Presumably because the employment contract provided that Saudi courts would have exclusive jurisdiction over claims for breach of contract, the Nelsons raised no such matters....

The District Court dismissed for lack of subject-matter jurisdiction under the Foreign Sovereign Immunities Act of 1976, 28 U.S.C. §§ 1330, 1602 et seq.... The Court of Appeals reversed.

II

The Foreign Sovereign Immunities Act "provides the sole basis for obtaining jurisdiction over a foreign state in the courts of this country." Argentine Republic v. Amerada Hess Shipping Corp., 488 U.S. 428, 443 (1989). Under the Act, a foreign state is presumptively immune from the jurisdiction of United States courts; unless a specified exception applies, a federal court lacks subject-matter jurisdiction over a claim against a foreign state....

Only one such exception is said to apply here. The first clause of § 1605(a)(2) of the Act provides that a foreign state shall not be immune from the jurisdiction of United States courts in any case "in which the action is based upon a commercial activity carried on in the United States by the foreign state." The Act defines such activity as "commercial activity carried on by such state and having substantial contact with the United States," § 1603(e), and provides that a commercial activity may be "either a regular course of commercial conduct or a particular commercial transaction or act," the "commercial character of [which] shall be determined by reference to" its "nature," rather than its "purpose," § 1603(d).

There is no dispute here that Saudi Arabia, the hospital, and Royspec all qualify as "foreign state[s]" within the meaning of the Act. For there to be jurisdiction in this case, therefore, the Nelsons' action must be "based upon" some "commercial activity" by petitioners that had "substantial contact" with the United States within the meaning of the Act. Because we conclude that the suit is not based upon any commercial activity by petitioners, we need not reach the issue of substantial contact with the United States.

We begin our analysis by identifying the particular conduct on which the Nelsons' action is "based" for purposes of the Act. See Texas Trading & Milling Corp. v. Federal Republic of Nigeria, 647 F.2d 300, 308 (2nd Cir. 1981), cert. denied, 454 U.S. 1148 (1982); Donoghue, Taking the "Sovereign" Out of the Foreign Sovereign Immunities Act: A Functional Approach to the Commercial Activity Exception, 17 Yale J. Int'l L. 489, 500 (1992). Although the Act contains no definition of the phrase "based upon," and the relatively sparse legislative history offers no assistance, guidance is hardly necessary. In denoting conduct that forms the "basis," or "foundation," for a claim... the phrase is read most naturally to mean those elements of a claim that, if proven, would entitle a plaintiff to relief under his theory of the case.

What the natural meaning of the phrase "based upon" suggests, the context confirms.... Section 1605(a)(2) contains two clauses following the one at issue here. The second allows for jurisdiction where a suit "is based... upon an act performed in the United States in connection with a commercial activity of the foreign state elsewhere," and the third speaks in like terms, allowing for jurisdiction where an action "is based... upon an act outside the territory of the United States in connection with a commercial activity of the foreign state elsewhere and that act causes a direct effect in the United States." Distinctions among descriptions juxtaposed against each other are naturally understood to be significant, and Congress manifestly understood there to be a difference between a suit "based upon" commercial activity and one "based upon" acts performed "in connection with" such activity. The only reasonable reading of the former term calls for something more than a mere connection with, or relation to, commercial activity.[4]

In this case, the Nelsons have alleged that petitioners recruited Scott Nelson for work at the hospital, signed an employment contract with him, and subsequently employed him. While these activities led to the conduct that eventually injured the Nelsons, they are not the basis for the Nelsons' suit. Even taking each of the Nelsons' allegations about Scott Nelson's recruitment and employment as true, those facts alone entitle the Nelsons to nothing under their theory of the case. The Nelsons have not, after all, alleged breach of contract, but personal injuries caused by petitioners' intentional wrongs and by petitioners' negligent failure to warn Scott Nelson that they might commit those wrongs. Those torts, and not the

[4] We do not mean to suggest that the first clause of § 1605(a)(2) necessarily requires that each and every element of a claim be commercial activity by a foreign state, and we do not address the case where a claim consists of both commercial and sovereign elements. We do conclude, however, that where a claim rests entirely upon activities sovereign in character, as here, jurisdiction will not exist under that clause regardless of any connection the sovereign acts may have with commercial activity.

arguably commercial activities that preceded their commission, form the basis for the Nelsons' suit.

Petitioners' tortious conduct itself fails to qualify as "commercial activity" within the meaning of the Act, although the Act is too "obtuse" to be of much help in reaching that conclusion. We have seen already that the Act defines "commercial activity" as "either a regular course of commercial conduct or a particular commercial transaction or act," and provides that "[t]he commercial character of an activity shall be determined by reference to the nature of the course of conduct or particular transaction or act, rather than by reference to its purpose." 28 U.S.C. § 1603(d). If this is a definition, it is one distinguished only by its diffidence; as we observed in our most recent case on the subject, it "leaves the critical term 'commercial' largely undefined." Republic of Argentina v. Weltover, Inc., 504 U.S. 607, 612 (1992).... We do not, however, have the option to throw up our hands. The term has to be given some interpretation, and congressional diffidence necessarily results in judicial responsibility to determine what a "commercial activity" is for purposes of the Act....

We explained in Weltover, supra, 504 U.S., at 614 (quoting Alfred Dunhill of London, Inc. v. Republic of Cuba, 425 U.S. 682, 704 (1976)), that a state engages in commercial activity under the restrictive theory where it exercises "only those powers that can also be exercised by private citizens, as distinct from those powers peculiar to sovereigns." Put differently, a foreign state engages in commercial activity for purposes of the restrictive theory only where it acts "in the manner of a private player within" the market. 504 U.S., at 614; see Restatement (Third) of the Foreign Relations Law of the United States § 451 (1987) ("Under international law, a state or state instrumentality is immune from the jurisdiction of the courts of another state, except with respect to claims arising out of activities of the kind that may be carried on by private persons").

We emphasized in Weltover that whether a state acts "in the manner of" a private party is a question of behavior, not motivation:

> [B]ecause the Act provides that the commercial character of an act is to be determined by reference to its 'nature' rather than its 'purpose,' the question is not whether the foreign government is acting with a profit motive or instead with the aim of fulfilling uniquely sovereign objectives. Rather, the issue is whether the particular actions that the foreign state performs (whatever the motive behind them) are the type of actions by which a private party engages in 'trade and traffic or commerce.
>
> Weltover, supra, at 614 (citations omitted) (emphasis in original).

We did not ignore the difficulty of distinguishing "'purpose' (i.e., the reason why the foreign state engages in the activity) from 'nature' (i.e., the outward form of the conduct that the foreign state performs or agrees to perform)," but recognized that the Act "unmistakably commands" us to observe the distinction. 504 U.S., at 617 (emphasis in original). Because Argentina had merely dealt in the bond market in the manner of a private player, we held, its refinancing of the bonds qualified as a commercial activity for purposes of the Act despite the apparent governmental motivation. Ibid.

Unlike Argentina's activities that we considered in Weltover, the intentional conduct alleged here (the Saudi Government's wrongful arrest, imprisonment, and torture of Nelson) could not qualify as commercial under the restrictive theory. The conduct boils down to abuse of the power of its police by the Saudi Government, and however monstrous such abuse undoubtedly may be, a foreign state's exercise of the power of its police has long been understood for purposes of the restrictive theory as peculiarly sovereign in nature. See Arango v. Guzman Travel Advisors Corp., 621 F.2d 1371, 1379 (5th Cir. 1980); Victory Transport Inc. v. Comisaria General de Abastecimientos y Transportes, 336 F.2d 354, 360 (2nd Cir. 1964) (restrictive theory does extend immunity to a foreign state's "internal administrative acts"), cert. denied, 381 U.S. 934 (1965);...K. Randall, Federal Courts and the International Human Rights Paradigm 93 (1990) (the Act's commercial-activity exception is irrelevant to cases alleging that a foreign state has violated human rights).[5] Exercise of the powers of police and penal officers is not the sort of action by which private parties can engage in commerce. "[S]uch acts as legislation, or the expulsion of an alien, or a denial of justice, cannot be performed by an individual acting in his own name. They can be performed only by the state acting as such." Lauterpacht, The Problem of Jurisdictional Immunities of Foreign States, 28 Brit.Y.B.Int'l L. 220, 225 (1952); see also id., at 237.

The Nelsons and their amici urge us to give significance to their assertion that the Saudi Government subjected Nelson to the abuse alleged as retaliation for his persistence in reporting hospital safety violations, and argue that the character of the mistreatment was consequently commercial. One amicus, indeed, goes so far as to suggest that the Saudi Government "often uses detention and torture to resolve commercial disputes." Brief for Human Rights Watch as Amicus Curiae 6. But this argument does not alter the fact that the powers allegedly abused were those of police and penal officers. In any event, the argument is off the point, for it goes to purpose, the very fact the Act renders irrelevant to the question of an activity's commercial character. Whatever may have been the Saudi Government's motivation for its allegedly abusive treatment of Nelson, it remains the case that the Nelsons' action is based upon a sovereign activity immune from the subject-matter jurisdiction of United States courts under the Act....

[T]he judgment of the Court of Appeals is accordingly reversed.

---

[5] The State Department's practice prior to the passage of the Act supports this understanding. Prior to the Act's passage, the State Department would determine in the first instance whether a foreign state was entitled to immunity and make an appropriate recommendation to the courts. *See Verlinden B.V. v. Central Bank of Nigeria*, 461 U.S. 480, 486–488 (1983). A compilation of available materials demonstrates that the Department recognized immunity with respect to claims involving the exercise of the power of the police or military of a foreign state. See Sovereign Immunity Decisions of the Department of State, May 1952 to January 1977 (M. Sandler, D. Vagts, & B. Ristau eds.), in 1977 Digest of United States Practice in International Law 1017, 1045–1046 (claim that Cuban armed guard seized cash from plaintiff at Havana airport); *id.*, at 1053–1054 (claim that Saudi militia fired on plaintiffs and caused personal and property damage)....

Justice White, with whom Justice Blackmun joins, concurring in the judgment:

According to respondents' complaint, Scott Nelson's employer retaliated against him for reporting safety problems by "summon[ing him]...to the hospital's security office from which he was transported to a jail cell." Once there, he allegedly was "shackled, tortured and beaten by persons acting at the direction, instigation, provocation, instruction or request of" petitioners-Saudi Arabia, King Faisal Specialist Hospital, and Royspec. The majority concludes that petitioners enjoy sovereign immunity because respondents' action is not "based upon a commercial activity." I disagree. I nonetheless concur in the judgment because in my view the commercial conduct upon which respondents base their complaint was not "carried on in the United States."

To run and operate a hospital, even a public hospital, is to engage in a commercial enterprise. The majority never concedes this point, but it does not deny it either, and to my mind the matter is self-evident. By the same token, warning an employee when he blows the whistle and taking retaliatory action, such as harassment, involuntary transfer, discharge, or other tortious behavior, although not prototypical commercial acts, are certainly well within the bounds of commercial activity.... Indeed, I am somewhat at a loss as to what exactly the majority believes petitioners have done that a private employer could not....

At the heart of the majority's conclusion...is the fact that the hospital in this case chose to call in government security forces. I find this fixation on the intervention of police officers, and the ensuing characterization of the conduct as "peculiarly sovereign in nature," to be misguided. To begin, it fails to capture respondents' complaint in full. Far from being directed solely at the activities of the Saudi police, it alleges that agents of the hospital summoned Nelson to its security office because he reported safety concerns and that the hospital played a part in the subsequent beating and imprisonment. Without more, that type of behavior hardly qualifies as sovereign. Thus, even assuming for the sake of argument that the role of the official police somehow affected the nature of petitioners' conduct, the claim cannot be said to "res[t] entirely upon activities sovereign in character." At the very least it "consists of both commercial and sovereign elements," thereby presenting the specific question the majority chooses to elude. The majority's single-minded focus on the exercise of police power, while certainly simplifying the case, thus hardly does it justice....

Contrary to the majority's suggestion, this conclusion does not involve inquiring into the purpose of the conduct. Matters would be different, I suppose, if Nelson had been recruited to work in the Saudi police force and, having reported safety violations, suffered retributive punishment, for there the Saudi authorities would be engaged in distinctly sovereign activities.... In this instance, however, the state-owned hospital was engaged in ordinary commercial business and "[i]n their commercial capacities, foreign governments do not exercise powers peculiar to sovereigns. Instead, they exercise only those powers that can also be exercised by private citizens." Alfred Dunhill, supra, 425 U.S., at 704 (plurality opinion). As we recently stated, "when a foreign government acts, not as regulator of a market, but in the manner of a private player within it, the foreign sovereign's actions are 'commercial' within the meaning of the FSIA." Republic of Argentina v. Weltover, Inc., 504 U.S. 607, 614 (1992). That, I believe, is the case here.

Nevertheless, I reach the same conclusion as the majority because petitioners' commercial activity was not "carried on in the United States."...Respondents point to the hospital's recruitment efforts in the United States, including advertising in the American media, and the signing of the employment contract in Miami.... [W]hile these may very well qualify as commercial activity in the United States, they do not constitute the commercial activity upon which respondents' action is based....

JUSTICE KENNEDY, with whom JUSTICE BLACKMUN and JUSTICE STEVENS join as to Parts I-B and II, concurring in part and dissenting in part.

I join all of the Court's opinion except the last paragraph of Part II, where, with almost no explanation, the Court rules that, like the intentional tort claim, the claims based on negligent failure to warn are outside the subject-matter jurisdiction of the federal courts. These claims stand on a much different footing from the intentional tort claims for purposes of the Foreign Sovereign Immunities Act (FSIA). In my view, they ought to be remanded to the District Court for further consideration.

I agree with the Court's holding that the Nelsons' claims of intentional wrongdoing by the hospital and the Kingdom of Saudi Arabia are based on sovereign, not commercial, activity, and so fall outside the commercial activity exception to the grant of foreign sovereign immunity contained in 28 U.S.C. § 1604. The intentional tort counts of the Nelsons' complaint recite the alleged unlawful arrest, imprisonment, and torture of Mr. Nelson by the Saudi police acting in their official capacities. These are not the sort of activities by which a private party conducts its business affairs; if we classified them as commercial, the commercial activity exception would in large measure swallow the rule of foreign sovereign immunity Congress enacted in the FSIA.

By the same token, however, the Nelsons' claims alleging that the hospital, the Kingdom, and Royspec were negligent in failing during their recruitment of Nelson to warn him of foreseeable dangers are based upon commercial activity having substantial contact with the United States. As such, they are within the commercial activity exception and the jurisdiction of the federal courts. Unlike the intentional tort counts of the complaint, the failure to warn counts do not complain of a police beating in Saudi Arabia; rather, they complain of a negligent omission made during the recruiting of a hospital employee in the United States. To obtain relief, the Nelsons would be obliged to prove that the hospital's recruiting agent did not tell Nelson about the foreseeable hazards of his prospective employment in Saudi Arabia. Under the Court's test, this omission is what the negligence counts are "based upon."

Omission of important information during employee recruiting is commercial activity as we have described it. See Republic of Argentina v. Weltover, Inc.,

504 U.S. 607 (1992). It seems plain that recruiting employees is an activity undertaken by private hospitals in the normal course of business. Locating and hiring employees implicates no power unique to the sovereign. In explaining the terms and conditions of employment, including the risks and rewards of a particular job, a governmental entity acts in "the manner of a private player within" the commercial marketplace....

The recruiting activity alleged in the failure to warn counts of the complaint also satisfies the final requirement for invoking the commercial activity exception: that the claims be based upon commercial activity "having substantial contact with the United States." 28 U.S.C. § 1603(e). Nelson's recruitment was performed by Hospital Corporation of America, Ltd. (HCA), a wholly owned subsidiary of a United States corporation, which, for a period of at least 16 years beginning in 1973, acted as the Kingdom of Saudi Arabia's exclusive agent for recruiting employees for the hospital. HCA in the regular course of its business seeks employees for the hospital in the American labor market. HCA advertised in an American magazine, seeking applicants for the position Nelson later filled. Nelson saw the ad in the United States and contacted HCA in Tennessee. After an interview in Saudi Arabia, Nelson returned to Florida, where he signed an employment contract and underwent personnel processing and application procedures. Before leaving to take his job at the hospital, Nelson attended an orientation session conducted by HCA in Tennessee for new employees. These activities have more than substantial contact with the United States; most of them were "carried on in the United States." 28 U.S.C. § 1605(a)(2). In alleging that the petitioners neglected during these activities to tell him what they were bound to under state law, Nelson meets all of the statutory requirements for invoking federal jurisdiction under the commercial activity exception.

Having met the jurisdictional prerequisites of the FSIA, the Nelsons' failure to warn claims should survive petitioners' motion under Federal Rule of Civil Procedure 12(b)(1) to dismiss for want of subject-matter jurisdiction. Yet instead of remanding these claims to the District Court for further proceedings, the majority dismisses them in a single short paragraph....The Court's summary treatment may stem from doubts about the underlying validity of the negligence cause of action....These doubts, however, are not relevant to the analytical task at hand....

Justice Stevens, dissenting.

Under the Foreign Sovereign Immunities Act of 1976 (FSIA), a foreign state is subject to the jurisdiction of American courts if two conditions are met: The action must be "based upon a commercial activity" and that activity must have a "substantial contact with the United States." These two conditions should be separately analyzed because they serve two different purposes. The former excludes commercial activity from the scope of the foreign sovereign's immunity from suit; the second identifies the contacts with the United States that support the assertion of jurisdiction over the defendant.

In this case, as Justice White has demonstrated, petitioner Kingdom of Saudi Arabia's operation of the hospital and its employment practices and disciplinary procedures are "commercial activities" within the meaning of the statute, and respondent Scott Nelson's claim that he was punished for acts performed in the course of his employment was unquestionably "based upon" those activities. Thus, the first statutory condition is satisfied; petitioner is not entitled to immunity from the claims asserted by respondent.

Unlike Justice White, however, I am also convinced that petitioner's commercial activities—whether defined as the regular course of conduct of operating a hospital or, more specifically, as the commercial transaction of engaging respondent "as an employee with specific responsibilities in that enterprise"—have sufficient contact with the United States to justify the exercise of federal jurisdiction. Petitioner Royspec maintains an office in Maryland and purchases hospital supplies and equipment in this country. For nearly two decades the hospital's American agent has maintained an office in the United States and regularly engaged in the recruitment of personnel in this country. Respondent himself was recruited in the United States and entered into his employment contract with the hospital in the United States. Before traveling to Saudi Arabia to assume his position at the hospital, respondent attended an orientation program in Tennessee. The position for which respondent was recruited and ultimately hired was that of a monitoring systems manager, a troubleshooter, and, taking respondent's allegations as true, it was precisely respondent's performance of those responsibilities that led to the hospital's retaliatory actions against him....

Comments and Questions

1. The criteria and methodology of the commercial transactions exception varies across jurisdictions. Article 2 of the U.N. Convention defines a commercial transaction to include:

> (i) any commercial contract or transaction for the sale of goods or supply of services;
> (ii) any contract for a loan or other transaction of a financial nature, including any obligation of guarantee or indemnity in respect of any such loan or transaction;
> (iii) any other contract or transaction of a commercial, industrial, trading or professional nature, but not including a contract of employment of persons.
>
> In determining whether a contract or transaction is a "commercial transaction," ... reference should be made primarily to the nature of the contract or transaction, but its purpose should also be taken into account if the parties to the contract or transaction have so agreed, or if, in the practice of the State of the forum, that purpose is relevant to determining the non-commercial character of the contract or transaction.

Would Scott Nelson's argument to the Court been more persuasive under this definition?

2. Definitions of commercial activity tend to be hopelessly circular. Rather than undertake such a definition, would it be possible to construct within the legislative scheme a positive list which would be presumptively immune sovereign acts? Or conversely would it be possible to elaborate a negative list which would be presumptively private acts? The following case interprets the Australian Foreign Sovereign Immunities Act of 1985.

Victoria Aircraft Leasing Ltd v. United States

Court of Appeal of the Supreme Court of Victoria

[2005] VSCA 76; 218 ALR 640

Cur adv vult

BUCHANAN , JA

5. Wells Fargo Bank Northwest, National Association (Wells Fargo), a Utah company, brought proceedings in the Supreme Court to recover possession of a Boeing 737–400 aircraft from Nauru Aircraft Corporation (NAC).

6. Wells Fargo acted as the security trustee for the mortgagee of the aircraft, the Export Import Bank of the United States (Eximbank), the second-named plaintiff in the action. Eximbank is an agency of the United States of America. The aircraft was purchased by Victoria Aircraft Leasing Limited (VALL) with a loan guaranteed by Eximbank. VALL defaulted in the performance of its obligations as borrower and Eximbank's guarantee was called up. Eximbank paid out the loan and stood in the shoes of the lender.

7. The aircraft was operated by NAC, which carried on the business of an airline under the name "Air Nauru." The Republic of Nauru guaranteed to Eximbank the due performance of the obligations of VALL as borrower of the price of the aircraft.* VALL and NAC are agencies of Nauru. VALL, NAC and the Republic of Nauru were the defendants to the proceeding. In its statement of claim Wells Fargo alleged that VALL failed to make repayments of the loan and committed other breaches which constituted events of default under the mortgage.

8. By their defence and counterclaim the defendants did not deny the debt owing to Eximbank or the mortgage, but pleaded that the obligations alleged by the plaintiffs were not enforceable by reason of an agreement made between Nauru and the United States of America by representatives of both countries. It was alleged that Nauru agreed to assist in the defection of a North Korean scientist to the United States, to co-operate with the United States to investigate the involvement of Nauruan organisations in the transfer of money for the purpose of international terrorism and to reform Nauru's laws to prevent money laundering and the production of false Nauruan passports.

---

* Eds.' Note: Nauru is an island republic of about 9,400 people in the western Pacific Ocean, and is one of the world's smallest states.

9. It was alleged in para 15 of the pleading that if Nauru co-operated with the United States agenda, the United States would:

(a) ensure that Eximbank would give Nauru additional time to pay its debts to Eximbank, sufficient to ensure the operational viability of Air Nauru;
(b) provide funds to Nauru sufficient to eliminate any problems Nauru might have in relation to re-payment of the Eximbank financing; and
(c) not permit Eximbank to exercise any strict contractual rights which it might have to take possession of and sell the aircraft.

10. In the particulars subjoined to this paragraph it was alleged that the agreement and representations were oral. The substance of the conversations constituting the agreement and representations was set out. From the particulars it is apparent that the defendants' case is that the United States promised to provide a broad range of assistance to Nauru as the price of Nauru's co-operation. The United States agreed to arrange to remove Nauru from a list of non-co-operative countries compiled by the Financial Action Task Force, an arm of the Organisation for Economic Cooperation and Development (OECD). Nauru's inclusion on the list made it very difficult for Nauruan companies to do business with United States and OECD banks. The United States agreed to provide substantial assistance, monetary and otherwise, to enable Nauru to establish a modern international banking facility. The United States also agreed to undertake economic projects, such as a satellite research tracking station, to benefit the Nauruan economy. The United States' promise to assist Nauru in dealing with Eximbank was part of a larger promise to deal with Nauru's financial problems, not only with Eximbank, but also with Marriott Properties and GE Finance.

11. It was alleged that in consideration of the promises made by the United States and in reliance upon the United States' representations Nauru appointed representatives of the United States as diplomatic officials, took steps to reform its off-shore banking regime and introduced laws to control the misuse of Nauruan passports.

12. A third party notice was issued against the United States. The allegations in the statement of claim endorsed upon the notice mirrored those in the defence and counterclaim.

13. The third party entered a conditional appearance and applied to set aside the notice on the ground that the Court lacked jurisdiction to entertain the claim as the United States was entitled to immunity pursuant to the provisions of § 9 of the Foreign States Immunities Act 1985 (the Act), which provides: "Except as provided by or under this Act, a foreign State is immune from the jurisdiction of the courts of Australia in a proceeding."

One exception is found in § 11, which provides:

(1) A foreign State is not immune in a proceeding in so far as the proceeding concerns a commercial transaction.
(2) Subsection (1) does not apply:
    (a) if all the parties to the proceeding:

(i) are foreign States or are the Commonwealth and one or more foreign States; or

(ii) have otherwise agreed in writing; or

(b) in so far as the proceeding concerns a payment in respect of a grant, a scholarship, a pension or a payment of a like kind.

(3) In this section, "commercial transaction' means a commercial, trading, business, professional or industrial or like transaction into which the foreign State has entered or a like activity in which the State has engaged and, without limiting the generality of the foregoing, includes:

(a) a contract for the supply of goods or services;

(b) an agreement for a loan or some other transaction for or in respect of the provision of finance; and

(c) a guarantee or indemnity in respect of a financial obligation;

but does not include a contract of employment or a bill of exchange.

"Proceeding" is defined as "a proceeding in a court..." (§ 3(1)).

14. The United States did not concede the truth or accuracy of the case pleaded against it, but for the purposes of the application it was assumed that the allegations contained in the third party statement of claim were true. The application proceeded on the basis that the third party was entitled to immunity unless the arrangement between Nauru and the United States was a commercial transaction within the meaning of § 11. The United States also contended that if the arrangement was a commercial transaction, its immunity was restored by § 11(2)(a)(i). It was submitted that the word "proceeding" in the subsection was a drafting error: the clear intention of the legislature was to preserve immunity where all the parties to a transaction, rather than a proceeding, were foreign states.

15. The judge who heard the application held that the transactions specified in paras (a), (b) and (c) in § 11(3) of the Act were qualified by the opening words of the sub-section. The specified transactions would be commercial transactions only if they had the necessary quality of a "commercial, trading, business, professional or industrial or like transaction". Accordingly, if a transaction was substantially, essentially or predominantly of a political, diplomatic, governmental or intelligence or like character, it was not a "commercial transaction" despite the fact that it incorporated some elements of the transactions specified in § 11(3)(a) to (c). Her Honour said:

> Whether or not the transactions in § 11(3)(a)-(b) are ipso facto commercial, the incorporation of only subsidiary or minor "commercial, trading, business, professional, industrial or like" elements in a transaction which is predominantly one of a political, diplomatic, governmental or intelligence character, or an admixture of those elements, in my view will not render it a "commercial transaction."

16. Her Honour found that the transaction between Nauru and the United States alleged in the third party statement of claim appeared "overwhelmingly non-commercial". Although the promises by the United States included the possible payment of funds which might be the provision of finance within the meaning

of § 11(3)(b), the transaction viewed as a whole was of a diplomatic, governmental, intelligence and national security character.

17. The trial judge also held that § 11(2)(a)(i) should be read as if the word "transaction" replaced the word "proceeding" and thus immunity was conferred on the United States pursuant to the exception, for the only parties to the agreement alleged in the third party notice were Nauru and the United States.

18. Accordingly, her Honour set aside the third party notice on the basis that the Unites States was not amenable to the jurisdiction of Australian courts pursuant to the provisions of the Act.

19. The appellants contend that sovereign immunity was lost once the transaction fell within one of the paras (a), (b) and (c) in § 11(3) and the trial judge erred in also requiring the transaction to be of a type described in the opening words of the sub-section.

20. Relying upon the report of the Australian Law Reform Commission, which drafted the Act, the appellants contended that the legislature intended to wholly replace the common law with a new type of test. In 1975 the absolute doctrine of state immunity at common law was replaced in England by an immunity restricted to claims where the act forming the basis of the claim was a "sovereign or public act" rather than an act of a private law character such as a private citizen might have entered into. The distinction between sovereign and governmental transactions on the one hand and commercial and private transactions on the other hand was difficult to draw. The courts analysed the objective characteristics of transactions and the subjective purposes they were designed to achieve. The outcome generally depended on the particularity with which the evaluation was conducted, and the choice of the degree of particularity was arbitrary.

21. In the United Kingdom the State Immunity Act 1978 (UK) supplanted the common law. Subject to a residual provision preserving the test of restrictive immunity, transactions were classified according to their objective effects, for example, contracts for the supply of services, transactions for the provision of finance. Immunity was conferred or withheld for each type of transaction. If a foreign state entered into a specified transaction, it was a commercial transaction whether or not the foreign state exercised sovereign authority.

22. While I think there is some force in the contention that, despite its different structure, § 11 of the Act was intended to "adopt the substance of the United Kingdom provision," it is not necessary to decide whether paragraphs (a), (b) and (c) are qualified by an additional requirement of commerciality. In my view the transaction entered into by Nauru and the United States did not meet any of the descriptions set out in the paragraphs.

23. In my opinion none of the paragraphs of subsection (3) applied to the promises made by the United States to Nauru. Paragraph (a) had no operation. Paragraph (b) contemplates a loan or like transaction. In my view it does not extend to a promise to influence the creditor to give his debtor extra time to pay or refrain from exercising rights under a security. Nor do I think that the paragraph extends to a promise to pay money which could be used by the recipient to repay

a debt to another. Paragraph (c) is concerned with a guarantee of the performance of another's obligation. I think that the indemnity with which it is coupled connotes the assumption of a primary liability whether or not another makes default. The paragraph does not embrace a promise to prevent a creditor exercising rights under a security.

24. Even if an aspect of the transaction between Nauru and the United States literally fell within one or more of the paragraphs of subsection (3), nevertheless in my view the transaction viewed as a whole was not encompassed by the subsection.

25. Each of the promises alleged to have been made by Nauru and each of the acts which it is alleged to have performed in reliance upon the representations said to have been made by the United States concerned governmental functions of Nauru. None of the promises or acts related to a contract for the supply of goods or services, an agreement for a loan or other transaction for or in respect of the provision of finance or a guarantee or indemnity in respect of a financial transaction. The actions to be undertaken by Nauru comprised activities relating to its diplomatic and foreign relations, national security, intelligence, terrorism and the reform of banking laws and passport abuse. The promises made by the United States did include an offer to assist Nauru to deal with its obligations to repay a loan and may have involved the provision of money to Nauru. The context in which that promise was made was that it was but one component in a number of measures answering the description of economic assistance to the government of Nauru.

26. In my opinion the vagueness of the terms alleged in paragraph 15 tells against the contention that the transaction amounted to an agreement in respect of the provision of finance or a guarantee or indemnity in respect of a financial obligation. The additional time to pay which the United States was alleged to have promised was no more specific than the time sufficient to ensure the operational viability of Air Nauru. Neither the amount of the funds to be provided to Nauru nor the time when that provision was to be made was stated. The promises were somewhat inconsistent. Was the United States to pay the sums owing to Eximbank or was it to arrange time for Nauru to pay those sums? The obligations in commercial agreements are generally expressed in definite, quantifiable terms. The transaction between Nauru and the United States was expressed in terms more akin to political arrangements between states.

27. In my view the promises by the United States to deal with Nauru's difficulties in meeting its obligations to Eximbank were not the most significant or substantial element in the United States' offer of assistance. In the third party statement of claim those promises were alleged as the only consideration for the promises made by Nauru, and counsel for Nauru in his submissions described the promises as those regarded by Nauru as the most important component of the transaction. In my opinion the importance of the promise of assistance to meet Nauru's obligations to Eximbank is to be judged objectively, not from the narrow prism of Nauru's objectives in its negotiations with the United States or in the litigation.

28. I have taken into account the particulars as well as the substantive allegations in the third party statement of claim, for I think the transaction is to be evaluated by considering as a whole the conversations comprising it. The transaction cannot sensibly be segmented by isolating the promises made by the United States which might be said to answer the description of an agreement in respect to the provision of finance. Those promises were part of a package or program of assistance in return for political favours. In my opinion the transaction taken as a whole is not accurately described as one for or in respect of the provision of finance or as a guarantee or indemnity in respect of a financial obligation....

Comments and Questions

1. Isn't the United States' obligation "an agreement for a loan or some other transaction for or in the respect of the provision of finance" or "a guarantee or indemnity in respect of a financial obligation"? If so, then why isn't it a commercial transaction within the meaning of Section 11?

2. What is the authority in the statute for the Court to "evaluate by considering as a whole the conversations comprising the transaction"?

6. Employment contracts

The existence and scope of an exception for employment contracts has become increasingly important as States are more likely to find themselves embroiled in foreign litigation initiated by current and former employees who are located there or in some other country. Naturally, a forum State has a legitimate interest in regulating the conditions under which its local labor force works for foreign governments, whether at embassies, consulates, trade offices, or other official representations within its territory. Yet every state must also be able to manage its activities within foreign countries, to control its own representatives and employees, to mediate the employment relationship in a manner that is consistent with its own laws and regulations, and to avoid outside interference with its internal organization and functions. It would surely be inappropriate, for example, if another State's courts investigated one State's policy with regard to the hiring of heads of diplomatic missions. The challenge, of course, is to strike an appropriate compromise between these competing interests. After reading Professor Garnett's overview of national practice regarding the employment contracts exception, compare the cases from Belgium and Italy.

Richard Garnett, State Immunity in Employment Matters

46 Int'l & Comp. L. Q. 81, 83–86 (1997)

Perhaps the most common approach in the judicial practice of States in relation to employment claims has been to apply the jure imperii / jure gestionis distinction and to consider whether the foreign State, in entering into the contract of employment, is engaging in "private" or "sovereign" activity. However, in resolving this question courts have taken different approaches. First there is the view which states that in determining whether a foreign State should claim immunity, primary regard should be had to the context or location of the employment. Therefore if an employee, at whatever level, is employed in a highly sovereign context such as a military base or an embassy, immunity should be granted on the basis that any enquiry into a foreign State's activities in such places would be excessively intrusive. By contrast, a foreign State-owned school or trading corporation is little different from an equivalent entity in the private sector and allowing an employee's claim to proceed would have little impact on the State's sovereignty. Such an approach has been favoured in the judicial practice of common law countries such as Ireland and New Zealand and civil law countries such as Germany and, until recently, Italy. Other states, such as the United Kingdom, South Africa, Singapore, Pakistan and Australia, have enacted legislation on State immunity but, although not adopting the private/sovereign act distinction, have nonetheless recognised that the context or place of employment should be a significant factor in resolving employment disputes. Under this approach the focus is on the nature of the employer.

In other judicial practice courts have, also in applying the sovereign/commercial act test, chosen to determine the issue of immunity primarily on the basis of the status of the employee. The premise of this approach is that a finding of immunity should be made only in the case of senior employees with great responsibility on the basis that, by their position, they are closer to the sovereign core of the foreign State. By contrast, employees engaged in routine or menial duties are little different from their counterparts in the private sector and so should be entitled to sue. Under this approach, then, the focus is on the employee. Swiss courts, for example, have taken this position.

A third approach evident in State practice, particularly in the national legislation and multilateral conventions on immunity, is to place emphasis on the territorial nexus between the forum and (i) the employee and (ii) the employment contract. This approach has its origins in the doctrine of State jurisdiction, in particular the idea that under international law every municipal forum must have an adequate connection with the subject matter or parties to a claim before it can exercise jurisdiction in either civil or criminal matters. The approach of territoriality is advocated by a number of commentators as a more certain and predictable method of representing the various interests at stake in a dispute over State immunity. This principle typically involves a State making provision for protection of its own nationals and residents by assuming jurisdiction in cases in which such persons are suing as employees of a foreign state and where the employment contract has some connection with the forum. Conversely, the principle recognises that it will be in very few cases that a forum will wish to exercise jurisdiction over a dispute between a foreign State and one of its nationals. Such a situation attracts no interest of the forum in protecting the employee but may certainly offend its interest in comity and good relations with the foreign State. There is similarly little interest in protecting a national of a third State without any residential ties to the forum.... The US Foreign Sovereign Immunity Act 1976... requires a link between the employment, as "commercial activity," and the forum.

A fourth approach apparent in the practice is to resolve the immunity issue in employment cases by reference to the nature of the claim. Under this head may be distinguished actions the nature of which may intrude upon the sovereignty of the foreign State and actions which relate only to the "economic aspects of the employment relationship." As examples of the former category may be included actions by trade unions seeking union protection for certain employees, and actions which may involve investigation into matters of State security. All these situations involve a court having to enquire into hiring practices and policies of a foreign State to an extent incompatible with that State's sovereignty. By contrast, an action for unpaid wages, for example, would involve little questioning of a State's power to organize its offices.

These four approaches are not to be considered mutually exclusive of one another as courts and national parliaments have often relied upon a combination of the above factors, for example a finding of immunity may be made where an employee is a national of the foreign State (and so lacks sufficient territorial nexus with the forum), is in a senior position (and so satisfies the status test) and is working in a highly sovereign area, such as a military installation. Even within the same legislative provision a mixture of the four approaches is apparent. For example, the UK State Immunity Act... relies upon the elements of both context of employment and territorial nexus. The US position... reveals the influence of all four approaches.

Francois v. State of Canada

Belgium, Labor Court of Brussels (First Chamber)

Jurisprudence des jurisdictions du travail de Bruxelles 1989, p. 274

115 ILR 418 (1999)

DEKEYSER, VICE-PRESIDENT

The purpose of these proceedings is to obtain judgment against the defendant for payment of the sum of 191,175 Belgian francs as compensation in lieu of notice with... interest and costs.

The claimant entered into the service of the defendant on 1 October 1978 as a technician at the Cultural and Information Centre of the Embassy of Canada in Brussels, under a letter of engagement of 1 August 1978.

By a letter of 19 June 1986, his contract was terminated with effect from 30 June 1986 subject to the payment of an indemnity in lieu of notice of nine months' salary [that is required by Belgian law]. On 26 June 1986, counsel for the claimant asked for an additional three months' salary.

The defendant raises the lack of jurisdiction of the Court in application of the principle of the jurisdictional immunity of States.

The defendant State is entitled in principle to jurisdictional immunity, but such immunity is not absolute. A distinction must be made between acts performed within the framework of public power, which involve the sovereignty of the defendant State, and those acts performed within the framework of its private administration. It is necessary to determine whether the foreign State acted as a private person or on the basis of its imperium. Only in the latter case will it enjoy jurisdictional immunity (cf. Labour Court of Brussels, 1 February 1980, JTT 1980, p. 274 with references cited there; Rupture du contrat de travail, chronique de jurisprudence, 1982–1984, JTT 1986, p. 103).

In this case the contract between the parties is a contract of employment which relates to the private administration of the defendant State. It is not a governmental act and its sovereignty is not involved. The State acted merely as an ordinary private person without bringing its public power into play.

Furthermore, it is very significant that in terminating the contract of employment, the defendant State allocated an indemnity in lieu of notice, making express reference to Belgian law....

Taking account of the seniority of the claimant (who has been employed for nine years and nine months), his function as a technician, his annual salary of 764,700 Belgian francs and his age (thirty-two years), the period of notice given to him should have been ten months. Since an indemnity of only nine months was paid, an additional indemnity of one month is due. That amounts to 63,725 Belgian francs....

Comments and Questions

1. The opinion does not tell us much about Mr. Francois's job responsibilities as a "technician" at the Cultural and Information Centre of the Canadian Embassy in Brussels. Does it matter—to you or to the court—what his responsibilities, in fact, were? For purposes of class discussion, we might assume that his job included the following responsibilities: (i) arranging and installing art exhibits; (ii) installing and maintaining lights; determining proper placement, intensity, and type of bulb for optimal effect on objects; monitoring light levels in all galleries; (iii) receiving and uncrating incoming pieces of art; packing and crating pieces of art for shipping or return to storage; overseeing staff in transporting objects to and from packing room; and (iv) monitoring exhibitions and permanent collections to detect damage.

2. What is the court using as a touchstone to distinguish governmental and private acts?

3. The Court indicates that it is "very significant" that the State of Canada offered Mr. Francois nine months' salary (referencing Belgian law) when it terminated him. Was it significant enough to change the result in this case? Put another way, did Canada waive its immunity defense?

Perrini v. Académie de France

Italy, Court of Cassation (Plenary Session)

26 May 1994; RDI 1995, p. 229 (in Italian); 114 ILR 536 (1999)

MONTANARI VISCO, PRESIDENT

In an application lodged [with the Rome Magistrate (Pretore)] on 21 July 1992, Anna Felice Perrini stated the following: On 26 April 1986 she had been hired by the Académie de France in Rome in an administrative post with managerial responsibilities, on the standard terms of employment for civil servants. She had in fact been working since December 1982 as archivist and cataloguing assistant to the "art history" department, as well as carrying out general secretarial duties. Between 1982 and 1986 her employment had been artificially interrupted for short periods, in order to preserve its part-time character. On 1 February 1990 the plaintiff had been abruptly dismissed, on the ground that her work as secretary/documentary assistant to Mr. André Castel at the Villa Medici had come to an end. In fact, her work had also involved a whole series of other duties. In the absence of any proper ground for her dismissal, she had requested the Académie to withdraw it, but to no avail. Invoking the provisions of Law No 300 of 1970, she accordingly requested the Pretore, sitting as a labour judge, to declare her dismissal unlawful, to order her immediate reinstatement, and to order the Académie to pay damages.

The defendant, having entered an appearance, disputed the jurisdiction of the Italian courts, on the ground that it was a public administrative body of a foreign State, and lodged an application for a preliminary ruling on the matter....

Grounds of the Decision. The applicant, the Académie de France, contests the jurisdiction of the Italian courts in this dispute under three main heads: the public-law nature of the employment in question; the type of duties carried out by the plaintiff, Ms. Perrini; and the specific content of her claim.

The application is well founded.

With regard to the first head, this Court finds that the Académie de France constitutes an integral part of the administration of the French State, as is clear from the terms of Decree No 71-1140 of 21 December 1971, which defines it as a "national public establishment of an administrative character, possessing legal personality and financial autonomy, and answerable to the Minister for Cultural Affairs"....

Under the Franco-Italian Cultural Agreement, signed in Paris on 4 November 1949 and implemented by Law No 1177 of 30 July 1952, and the Exchange of Notes of 17 May May 1965, implemented by Law No 875 of 4 October 1966, the Académie de France is one of the "establishments of high culture" which the Italian and French Governments have agreed to recognize, "each promising to accord to the other every facility for the creation and operation of such establishments," within the framework of cultural cooperation and "the development of relations in the field of science and the arts"....

The public-law purposes of the Académie are thus clearly established: it directly represents the French Ministry for Cultural Affairs operating in Italy; it pursues the institutional aims of the French State (the diffusion of national culture abroad); and in fact, as the documents before us show, the annual French Budgetary Law makes provision for a sum to cover its operating costs.

Thus in this case there exists an ad hoc agreement between two States, ratified and given effect in domestic law, which reinforces the principle of international law "par in parem non habet jurisdictionem" (a cardinal principle, recognized by Article [ ] of the Constitution and reaffirmed by this Court on numerous occasions in relation to foreign cultural establishments . . .).

As to the second head it is clear, on Ms. Perrini's own admission, that she was recruited to a post carrying managerial responsibilities. Officially archivist and cataloguing assistant to the art history department, in practice she carried out secretarial duties of a particularly skilled and specialized nature (research, loans of works for exhibitions, organization of lectures and conferences, collaboration in the André Castel exhibition at the Villa Medici, etc.). Clearly these were not merely manual or subordinate duties, but involved a position of trust, closely linked with the Académie's public-law activity in pursuance of its institutional functions, and hence characterized by her integration into that entity's organizational structure. Under the case-law of this Court, such a situation excludes the jurisdiction of the Italian courts in relation to employment disputes between Italian citizens and foreign States. The fact that the employment was governed by the terms of a standard collective contract is irrelevant. . . .

Finally, as regards the content of the claim, Ms. Perrini sought a declaration that her dismissal was unlawful, an order for her reinstatement and damages for loss of salary. All three heads of claim fall outside the jurisdiction of the Italian courts, inasmuch as any examination of them directly impugns the public-law powers of the foreign State with regard to the manner in which it organizes its official agencies and services. . . . . We accordingly conclude that the Italian courts do not have jurisdiction in this case.

Comments and Questions

1. Ms. Perrini may have held job duties very similar to those of Mr. Francois. Explain why the courts reached different outcomes. Are the decisions reconcilable?

2. The U.N. Convention offers a different framework for excepting contracts of employment from the scope of sovereign immunity. Article 11 provides as follows:

> 1. Unless otherwise agreed between the States concerned, a State cannot invoke immunity from jurisdiction before a court of another State which is otherwise competent in a proceeding which relates to a contract of employment between the State and an individual for work performed or to be performed, in whole or in part, in the territory of that other State.
> 2. Paragraph 1 does not apply if:
>   (a) the employee has been recruited to perform particular functions in the exercise of governmental authority;

(b) the employee is:
 (i) a diplomatic agent, as defined in the Vienna Convention on Diplomatic Relations of 1961;
 (ii) a consular officer, as defined in the Vienna Convention on Consular Relations of 1963;
 (iii) a member of the diplomatic staff of a permanent mission to an international organization or of a special mission, or is recruited to represent a State at an international conference; or
 (iv) any other person enjoying diplomatic immunity;

(c) the subject-matter of the proceeding is the recruitment, renewal of employment or reinstatement of an individual;

(d) the subject-matter of the proceeding is the dismissal or termination of employment of an individual and, as determined by the head of State, the head of Government or the Minister for Foreign Affairs of the employer State, such a proceeding would interfere with the security interests of that State;

(e) the employee is a national of the employer State at the time when the proceeding is instituted, unless this person has the permanent residence in the State of the forum; or

(f) the employer State and the employee have otherwise agreed in writing, subject to any considerations of public policy conferring on the courts of the State of the forum exclusive jurisdiction by reason of the subject-matter of the proceeding.

Would a court invoking this definition of employment contracts have jurisdiction over Ms. Perrini's claim? What is the "right" result here?

7. Personal injury and damage to property

It is generally recognized that a restrictive immunity doctrine allows a foreign state to be held responsible for deaths or personal injuries or damage to or loss of property that is caused within the forum State. Naturally, there is some variation among countries as to the scope and particulars of this exception. This exception largely grew out of negligent use of motor vehicles by foreign state officials, and we begin with such a case from the Austrian Supreme Court.

Collision With Foreign Government-Owned Motor Car (Austria) Case

Austria Supreme Court. 10 February 1961.

J.B. 84 (1962), p. 43 (in German); 40 ILR 73 (1970)

The plaintiff, an Austrian citizen, alleged that his motor car had been damaged by the negligent driving of a car owned by the Government of the United States of America. He brought an action for damages for negligence against the United States Government. The latter realised a plea to the jurisdiction of the Austrian courts and contended that since at the time of the alleged collision their motor car was carrying mail intended for the United States Embassy, the Austrian courts were not entitled to exercise jurisdiction. The carriage of mail for and on behalf of the United States Embassy constituted the performance of a "sovereign act" by the United States Government....

The Supreme Court, in Rule 28 (new), reported in SZ XXIII, p. 143, has dealt with the question whether, and subject to what conditions, a foreign State may be sued in an Austrian court....

(i) By international law foreign States are exempt from the jurisdiction of the Austrian courts so far as concerns acts undertaken by them in the exercise of their sovereign powers.
(ii) Similarly, by municipal law, foreign States are subject to the jurisdiction of the Austrian courts in relation to all contentious matters arising out of legal relations pertaining to the realm of private law.

The Court, in its earlier judgment, reached the conclusion that in respect of acta jure gestionis a limitation by international law can no longer be recognized. Basing ourselves on this premise, all we have to do in this case is to examine the question whether the plaintiff bases his claim on an act performed by the foreign defendant State in its private or in its sovereign capacity. The lower Courts arrived at different conclusions. Whereas the Court of first instance regarded as decisive the purpose of the journey, viz. the collection of mail for the embassy of the defendant, the Court of Appeal took the view that the defendant State was being sued as the operator of the vehicle and as a person circulating as a road user.

In its appeal the defendant contends that the means whereby a State exercises its sovereign rights are irrelevant because all means at its disposal belong to the sphere of private law, and that the decisive factor is the act performed by the State with the aid of those means. It is contended that in this case the motor car was the means whereby the sovereign act (the collection of mail for the embassy) was carried out, and that the case must be judged in accordance with this act. This Court is unable to accept this contention. The distinction between private and sovereign acts is easily understood if one considers the following: Eminent writers, e.g. Schnitzler (Private International Law, at pp. 833 seq.) point out that an act must be deemed to be a private act where the State acts through its agencies in the same way as a private individual can act. An act must be deemed to be a sovereign act where the State performs an act of legislation or administration (makes a binding decision). Sovereign acts are those in respect of which equality between the parties is lacking, and where the place of equality is taken by subordination of one party to the other. Spruth (Jurisdiction over Foreign States) defined this distinction as follows: 'To act as a sovereign State means to act in the performance of sovereign rights. To enter into private transactions means to put oneself on the basis of equality with private individuals.' Dahm (International Law, p. 229) expresses the same idea when he says that there are cases in which a State descends from its elevated position and makes its appearance in spheres in which private individuals move.

Thus, we must always look at the act itself which is performed by State organs, and not at its motive or purpose. We must always investigate the act of the State from which the claim is derived. Whether an act is of a private or sovereign nature must always be deduced from the nature of the legal transaction, viz. the nature of the action taken or the legal relationship arising....

If we apply the basic principles here outlined to the case before us, we must conclude that the act from which the plaintiff derives his claim for damages against the defendant is not the collection of mail but the operation of a motor car by the defendant and the latter's action as a road user. By operating a motor car and using the public roads the defendant moves in spheres in which private individuals also move. In these spheres the parties face one another on a basis of equality, and there is no indication here of any supremacy and subordination. It follows that, so far as liability for damage is concerned, the foreign State must be treated like a private individual. The damage which the plaintiff alleges was not caused by the collection of mail from the airport but by the operation and management of the motor car and the use of public roads by the defendant. The plaintiff thus derives his claim from a private legal relationship. The development of traffic on public roads and the dangers threatening every road user from such traffic compel us to accept this view. To deny the liability of a foreign State arising from the operation and management of motor vehicles would lead to intolerable results and hardships for private citizens. This is best illustrated by the present case, assuming always that the plaintiff's allegations are true, which will emerge when the case is heard on the merits. Spruth has made certain observations which are apposite in the present case. There is no doubt that the foreign State, in the event of a collision involving a motor vehicle owned by it, would be entitled to bring an action for damages against a private individual in the local courts and in accordance with local law. The foreign State is thus given rights to invoke the jurisdiction of the courts of another State, and it could do so as it pleases for his own benefit. Not so the private individual. The latter would have no rights whatever against the foreign State if the management and operation of motor vehicles and the use of public roads by foreign States were to be regarded as a sovereign act. It could be argued that the claims, however well-founded, of a private individual for damage caused by a collision could not be pursued against the foreign State by a separate action or a counterclaim. The State of the forum would have to deny to its citizens rights which it grants to a foreign State....

For all these reasons the Court is of opinion that the operation of a motor vehicle by a foreign State and the use of public roads by the latter belong to the sphere of the private activities of that State even if, as has been contended, such operation and use have occurred in the performance of official functions, and that accordingly the foreign State can be sued for damages in a local court. A traffic accident creates private legal relations between the foreign State and the private individual, on a basis of equal rights between them. In international jurisprudence, likewise, liability arising out of a private contract is treated on the same basis as liability for a tort which has nothing to do with the political order.

The Court is therefore of opinion that this action has been properly brought in the Austrian courts. The Court did not consider it necessary to consult the Federal Ministry of Justice, as provided in Article IX (3) of the Introductory Law to the Law on Jurisdiction, because no doubt exists as to the exterritoriality as such of the defendant. This question was capable of being determined on the basis of the record before the Court.

Hazel Fox, The Exception for Personal Injuries and Tangible Property

The Law of State Immunity 569–570, 577 (2d ed. 2008)

Whilst initially intended to cover one limited consequence of tortious State conduct in another State, namely the negligent use of motor vehicles by State officials, whether for a public purpose or otherwise, the exception for personal injuries has subsequently been extended in common law jurisdictions without any restriction to private law only. Its justification seems to be based on an assertion of local control or jurisdiction over acts occurring within the territory of the forum State, but the justification is not carried to its logical conclusion; the exception is confined to acts causing personal injury or tangible loss and does not extend to private parties' claims for remoter causation or loss such as economic loss, and damage from published statements, which are recoverable in developed municipal systems of tort.

The first authoritative formulation of such an exception is to be found in the ECSI [European Convention on State Immunity].... Although originally formulated more narrowly to remove immunity in respect of personal injuries resulting from traffic accidents caused by a foreign State within the territory of the forum State, ECSI, Article 11 in its final form was much wider, rendering non-immune "proceedings which relate to redress for injury to the person or damage to tangible property, if the facts which occasioned the injury or damage occurred in the territory of the State of the forum, and if the author of the injury or damage was present in that territory at the time when those facts occurred."....

Types of tortious conduct within the exception.

Neither the U.S. nor the UK acts distinguish between intentional or negligent acts as coming within the exception (the ECSI makes no express reference), although the FSIA excludes most intentional torts by expressly excluding claims arising out of malicious prosecution, abuse of process, libel, slander, misrepresentation, deceit, or interference with contract rights.... [T]he exception was primarily designed to deal with damage caused by the negligent driving of a State official, which if he was a diplomat would not be recoverable personally against him, and hence omission to take care as to the driver and the vehicle on the part of the State is necessarily brought within the exception....

Comments and Questions

1. Article 12 of the U.N. Convention tracks the language of the ECSI and provides the following exception for personal injuries and damage to property:

> Unless otherwise agreed between the States concerned, a State cannot invoke immunity from jurisdiction before a court of another State which is otherwise competent in a proceeding which relates to pecuniary compensation for death or injury to the person, or damage to or loss of tangible property, caused by an act or omission which is alleged to be attributable to the State, if the act or omission occurred in whole or in part in the territory of that other State and if the author of the act or omission was present in that territory at the time of the act or omission.

2. In Article 12 as in other formulations of this exception, there is a physical damage requirement. Certain torts claims, such as damage to reputation or defamation, would not ordinarily include any physical injury. Similarly, tortious interference with contract rights or with any other rights (including economic or social rights) may not involve damage to tangible property. Are plaintiffs suffering these kinds of injuries less deserving of compensation?

3. If a foreign state were responsible for the September 11 attacks, would the personal injury exception authorize suit? We will also consider terrorism as a separate exception in Section 10, infra.

Olsen v. Mexico

729 F.2d 641 (9th Cir.), cert. denied, 469 U.S. 917 (1984)

Nelson, Circuit Judge

Appellants Erin Olsen and Ursula Sanchez, United States citizens domiciled in California, are minor children claiming the wrongful death of their parents. As prisoners of the Mexican government, the parents of appellants were to be transferred to authorities for incarceration in the United States pursuant to the Prisoner Exchange Treaty between the United States and the Government of Mexico ("Mexico").

On the night of October 27, 1979, a twin-propeller plane owned and operated by the Mexican government carrying guards, pilots and appellants' parents departed Monterrey, Mexico for Tijuana, where the transfer was to take place. En route, the pilots, employees of the Mexican Department of Justice, learned of thick fog and diminishing visibility at their destination. They requested an instrument landing which, at Tijuana Airport, requires the airplane to enter United States airspace so it can approach the runway from the west. Following procedures established by a Letter of Agreement between aviation authorities of the United States and Mexico, Tijuana air control sought and received permission for the airplane to cross the border. In addition to providing access to United States airspace during hazardous weather conditions, the Letter also allows for coordinated navigational assistance.

Because its radar and instrument landing navigational system were inoperative, Tijuana air control asked its counterpart in San Diego to radio direction headings, altitude and location data necessary for an instrument landing to the aircraft. Unfortunately, neither the San Diego air controllers nor the pilots were bilingual. Instead, the San Diego air controllers relayed the information via the telephone "hotline" to Tijuana air control who radioed their translation to the pilots.

In this manner, the aircraft penetrated almost 12 miles into United States airspace, made a wide turn and began to descend toward Tijuana Airport. Having strayed one mile off the proper course, the pilot abandoned the approach at the border and re-entered Mexican airspace.

San Diego air control advised the pilot to proceed to other airports where visual landings would be possible. The pilot declined and decided to attempt another instrument landing. With the continued use of navigational data from San Diego air control, the airplane re-entered United States airspace. The pilots aligned the aircraft with the proper compass heading and descended on course, but failed to maintain the proper altitude. After striking a telephone pole, the airplane crashed three-quarters of a mile inside the United States, killing all on board. The crash site was two and one-half miles from the beginning of the runway.

Discussion

The FSIA sets forth criteria which must be satisfied to establish both statutory subject matter jurisdiction and personal jurisdiction. The FSIA confers subject matter jurisdiction upon district courts in nonjury civil actions where the foreign state is not entitled to immunity as defined by its substantive provisions, 28 U.S.C. § 1330(a) (1976)....

As section 1330(a) indicates, sovereign immunity is not merely a defense under the FSIA. Its absence is a jurisdictional requirement. See Verlinden, B.V. v. Central Bank of Nigeria, 103 S.Ct. 1962, 1971 n. 20 (1983) ("Verlinden"). We begin our inquiry, therefore, by considering whether Mexico is entitled to immunity.

The FSIA grants blanket immunity to foreign states, 28 U.S.C. § 1604, and then carves out specific exceptions to immunity in sections 1605 to 1607. Appellants allege that their wrongful death claims come within the so-called "noncommercial torts" exception, section 1605(a)(5), which provides:

> (a) A foreign state shall not be immune from the jurisdiction of courts of the United States or of the States in any case-
>
> (5) not otherwise encompassed in paragraph (2) above, [the commercial activity exception] in which money damages are sought against a foreign state for personal injury or death, or damage to or loss of property, occurring in the United States and caused by the tortious act or omission of that foreign state or of any official or employee of that foreign state while acting within the scope of his office or employment
>
> 28 U.S.C. § 1605(a)(5) (1982).

Mexico argues that section 1605(a)(5) does not apply and it is therefore immune from suit. First, Mexico contends that Congress, in enacting the FSIA, adopted the restrictive theory of sovereign immunity and that Mexico's conduct was of the public nature held to be immune under that theory. Second, Mexico asserts that the 1605(a)(5) exception to immunity requires all the acts or omissions constituting the tort to occur within the United States. Finally, Mexico characterizes its activities which led to the crash as discretionary functions, thus falling within the exception to jurisdiction set forth in section 1605(a)(5)(A). We consider these arguments in turn.

A. The FSIA and the Restrictive Theory of Sovereign Immunity.

It is clear that the FSIA, for the most part, codifies the restrictive principle of sovereign immunity. See Verlinden, 103 S. Ct. at 1968. Under this principle, the immunity of a foreign state is "restricted" to suits involving that state's public acts (jure imperii) and does not extend to suits based on its private or commercial acts (jure qestionis). McKell v. Islamic Republic of Iran, 722 F.2d 582, 587 n. 6 (9th Cir. 1983).

Mexico argues that this public/private distinction applies not only to the FSIA generally, but specifically to section 1605(a)(5), the noncommercial torts exception to immunity. According to Mexico's interpretation, foreign states would be immune from jurisdiction for those torts which otherwise come within the bounds of section 1065(a)(5) but which are public in nature.

Section 1605(a)(5) cannot be read, however, other than in conjunction with section 1605(a)(5)(A), which exempts from the reach of section 1605(a)(5) those torts committed in a foreign state's discretionary capacity. 28 U.S.C. § 1605(a)(5)(A) (1982). Discretionary functions, as discussed below, include those acts or decisions made at the policy-making or planning level of government. Those torts involving acts or omissions of a fundamentally governmental nature are not actionable. Thus, despite section 1605(a)(5) a foreign state remains largely immunized from torts committed in its governmental capacity. Mexico's position, that governmental acts are automatically read out of section 1605(a)(5), would render section 1605(a)(5)(A) superfluous. Its argument is therefore untenable.

B. The Location of the Tortious Conduct.

Section 1605(a)(5) requires the injury complained of to occur in the United States. The provision does not indicate that the conduct causing the tort must also take place in the United States. Ordinarily, this would end our inquiry and there would be no need to consider the location of the tortious conduct. Where, as in the instant case, the injuries occurred in the United States, and all other requirements of section 1605(a)(5) are met, the foreign state would not be immune. However, the legislative history to section 1605(a)(5) indicates that "the tortious act or omission must occur within the jurisdiction of the United States...." House Report at 21, U.S.Code Cong. & Admin.News 1976, p. 6619.

A careful reading of the record in this case suggests that many potentially tortious acts and omissions occurring both in Mexico and the United States caused the crash. Pilot error, the absence of operational radar and navigational aids at Tijuana airport, defective aircraft instruments, the decision to forego a visual landing at another airport, inaccurate data from San Diego air control, and other factors may have contributed causally to the accident.

Mexico, relying on Matter of SEDCO, 543 F.Supp. 561, 567 (S.D. Tex. 1982) (SEDCO), contends that section 1605(a)(5) must be construed to require all of the tortious conduct to occur in the United States before a foreign state will be denied immunity. In SEDCO, an exploratory off-shore well operated by Pemex, the Mexican national oil company, exploded in Mexican waters. The resulting oil slick washed up on the shores of Texas. Citizens there sued Pemex and other parties under section 1605(a)(5). Citing that section's legislative history requiring the tortious act or omission to occur within the United States, the court held that for the noncommercial tort exception to apply, "the tort, in whole, must occur in the United States." SEDCO, 543 F. Supp. at 567. Thus, Mexico argues, because some allegedly tortious acts or omissions took place outside the United States-such as the maintenance of the aircraft and the inoperative radar at Tijuana airport-Mexico should be immune.

The instant case is distinguishable from SEDCO in one crucial respect. In SEDCO, none of the alleged acts or omissions, only the resultant injury, occurred in the United States. By requiring every aspect of the tortious conduct to occur in the United States, a rule such as in SEDCO would encourage foreign states to allege that some tortious conduct occurred outside the United States. The foreign state would thus be able to establish immunity and diminish the rights of injured persons seeking recovery. Such a result contradicts the purpose of the FSIA, which is to "serve the interests of justice and...protect the rights of both foreign states and litigants in United States courts." 28 U.S.C. § 1602. The FSIA requires us to protect the rights of plaintiffs while respecting the sovereignty of foreign states. Consequently, we hold that if plaintiffs allege at least one entire tort occurring in the United States, they may claim under section 1605(a)(5). In this case, appellants allege conduct constituting a single tort-the negligent piloting of the aircraft-which occurred in the United States. We are satisfied that appellants have alleged sufficient conduct occurring in the United States to bring this case within the noncommercial torts exception as expressed in section 1605(a)(5) and its legislative history.

C. The Discretionary Function Exception.

Section 1605(a)(5)(A) provides an exception to noncommercial tort jurisdiction for claims based upon a state's discretionary function.[4] Mexico seeks to bring the

[4] Section 1605(a)(5) does not apply to: "(A) any claim based upon the exercise or performance or the failure to exercise or perform a discretionary function regardless of whether discretion be abused." 28 U.S.C. § 1605(a)(5)(A) (1982).

airplane crash within this exception by contending that the conduct which led to the crash was discretionary.

The FSIA provides considerable guidance as to which acts or decisions constitute discretionary functions. Not only does the language of the FSIA discretionary function exception replicate that of the Federal Tort Claims Act (FTCA), 28 U.S.C. § 2680(a), but the legislative history of the FSIA, in explaining section 1605(a)(5)(A), directs us to the FTCA. House Report at 21. To determine the scope of the discretionary function exception of the FSIA, we therefore turn to the interpretation given the similar FTCA provision.

The seminal case defining the scope of the discretionary function exception within the context of the FTCA, Dalehite v. United States, 346 U.S. 15 (1953), held "discretion" to mean:

> more than the initiation of programs and activities. It also includes determinations made by executives or administrators in establishing plans, specifications or schedules of operations. Where there is room for policy judgment and decision there is discretion.

Id. at 35–36. In so defining discretion, the Court adhered to the legislative purpose behind the exception: to allow government executives to make policy decisions in an atmosphere free of concern over possible litigation. Id. at 32.

Over the years, the definition of discretion has been refined and qualified somewhat. See Driscoll v. United States, 525 F.2d 136, 138 (9th Cir. 1975). This circuit employs a test which distinguishes between the "planning level" of governmental activity and those acts designed to carry out policy, the "operational level." Thompson v. United States, 592 F.2d 1104, 1111 (9th Cir. 1979). Because decisions at the planning level establish governmental policy, they are not actionable. But where decisions occur at the operational level, the discretionary function exemption provides no protection from liability even though such decisions or acts may involve elements of discretion. Lindgren v. United States, 665 F.2d 978, 980 (9th Cir. 1982); see also Thompson, 592 F.2d at 1111; Driscoll, 525 F.2d at 138. In addition to examining the level at which the conduct occurred, we also consider two other factors which are particularly important when determining the immunity of foreign states: The ability of United States courts to evaluate the act or omission of the state, and the potential impairing effect such an evaluation would have on the effective administration of the state's government. Lindgren, 665 F.2d at 980; Driscoll, 525 F.2d at 138.

We conclude that of those alleged acts or omissions on the part of Mexico which contributed to the accident, none was discretionary. First, while Mexico's decision to enter into the Prisoner Exchange Treaty with the United States or to transfer these particular prisoners to United States custody might well be deemed discretionary, those decisions are not implicated in the instant action. Rather, appellants allege that Mexico negligently maintained, directed and piloted the aircraft. Such conduct represents measures taken to implement the broader policy or plan to exchange prisoners. The acts or omissions in question involved the transportation of prisoners, an act remote from the policy decision to transfer them. While the pilot and air controllers had considerable discretion in carrying out their assigned tasks, it is clear they acted on the operational level, far from the centers of policy judgment.

Second, this dispute does not raise questions of policy decisions of Mexico, only issues of historical fact and tort liability. Therefore, the trial court can readily evaluate the allegedly tortious acts as it is well suited to the task of determining facts and applying the relevant law.

Third, we see nothing which suggests that denying immunity will impair the effectiveness of Mexico's penal or aviation authorities. A trial on the merits will call for the testimony of individuals involved in the accident, primarily Mexican air traffic control personnel. There seems little doubt that the air traffic authorities and other relevant governmental entities can function without diminished efficacy while their employees testify in discovery or court proceedings.

In conclusion, the claims asserted by appellants fall within the exception to immunity for noncommercial torts as provided by section 1605(a)(5) of the FSIA. Additionally, the conduct of Mexican personnel which may have led to the crash occurred at the operational level and was not discretionary. Thus, Mexico is not immune under the FSIA and subject matter jurisdiction exists....

Comments and Questions

1. Isn't the implementation of a treaty a quintessentially public act? Does this mean Mexico should have been immune or that the public/private act distinction isn't helpful?

2. The test for the discretionary function exception has continued to evolve. See U.S. v. S.A. Empresa de Viacao Aerea Rio Grandense (Varig Airlines), 467 U.S. 797 (1984). Pursuant to Varig, a new two-pronged test has been developed for determining whether the discretionary function exception applies in FTCA cases. First, the court must examine the nature of the conduct, rather than the status of the actor. And, second, the court must inquire whether the governmental acts at issue were grounded in social, economic, and political policy. In other words, the court should avoid second-guessing policy decisions through the medium of a tort action. The execution of policy decisions by subordinates, even those subordinates at the operational level, comes under the discretionary function exception if the acts involved the exercise of policy judgment.

8. Suits in admiralty

Article 16(1) of the Convention articulates a general rule that a state cannot invoke immunity with regard to proceedings relating to the operation of a ship it owns or operates if, at the time the cause of action arose, the ship was used for "other than government non-commercial purposes." The problem of government-owned or State-operated vessels employed in ordinary commercial activities is not new. Indeed, many of the earliest discussions of sovereign immunity were admiralty cases. See The Schooner Exchange v. McFaddon, 11 U.S. (7 Cranch) 116 (1812). Maritime powers felt it necessary to convene a conference to adopt the International Convention for the Unification of Certain Rules Relating to the Immunity of State-Owned Vessels (Brussels, 1926) and its Additional Protocol (1934) on the subject. The main purpose of the 1926 Brussels Convention was to reclassify seagoing vessels not according to ownership but according to the nature of their operation (exploitation) or their use, whether in "governmental and non-commercial" or in "commercial" service.

The Convention's immunity exception does not apply to warships or naval auxiliaries, or to other vessels owned or operated by a state and used "for the time being, only on government non-commercial service." Nor (unless otherwise agreed) is a state immune from proceedings relating to the carriage of cargo on board a ship owned or operated by the state if, at the time the cause of action arose, the ship was used for "other than government non-commercial purposes" (but not if the cargo was carried on board warships, naval auxiliaries or vessels owned or operated by a state and used "for the time being, only on governmental non-commercial service"). Nor does the exception apply to any cargo owned by a state and used, or intended for use, exclusively for governmental non-commercial purposes.

The Convention acknowledges that in such proceedings, states may plead all measures of defense, prescription, and limitation of liability that are available to private ships and cargoes and their owners. It also provides that, if questions arise relating to "the government and noncommercial character" of a ship or cargo, a certificate signed by a diplomatic representative or other competent authority of the state concerned shall serve as evidence of the character of that ship or cargo.

9. Arbitration agreements

The consent of a State to arbitrate a dispute may be construed as a waiver of immunity in proceedings before a national court relating to the arbitration. However, the uncertainty as to the proper extent of the waiver to be construed from such a consent to arbitration has led some regimes to provide an express exception to immunity in respect of arbitration agreements. Most legal systems are prepared to assume supervisory jurisdiction over arbitrations held within the territory or subject to the law of the forum State.

Article 17 of the U.N. Convention outlines the effect of an arbitration agreement.

> If a State enters into an agreement in writing with a foreign natural or juridical person to submit to arbitration differences relating to a commercial transaction, that State cannot invoke immunity from jurisdiction before a court of another State which is otherwise competent in a proceeding which relates to:
>
> (a) the validity, interpretation or application of the arbitration agreement;
> (b) the arbitration procedure; or
> (c) the confirmation or the setting aside of the award,

unless the arbitration agreement otherwise provides.

This provision reflects the generally-accepted principle that a valid consent to arbitration entails acceptance of a measure of supervisory jurisdiction over the arbitral proceedings by foreign courts that are otherwise competent in the matter.

10. State-sponsored acts of terrorism

In 1996, the U.S. Congress amended its Foreign Sovereign Immunities Act in response to the revelation that the Libyan government assisted in blowing up Pan Am 103 over Lockerbie, Scotland. The following Section 1605(a)(7) was added to the FSIA as part of the Anti-Terrorism and Effective Death Penalty Act 1996. The stated purpose of the Act was to deter terrorist acts against U.S. nationals by foreign sovereigns or their agents and to provide for justice for victims of such terrorism.

> (a) A foreign state shall not be immune from the jurisdiction of the courts of the United States or of the States in any case—
>
> (7) not otherwise covered by paragraph (2) [the commercial activities exception], in which money damages are sought against a foreign state for personal injury or death that was caused by an act of torture, extrajudicial killing, aircraft sabotage, hostage taking, or the provision of material support or resources... for such an act if such act or provision of material support is engaged in by an official, employee, or agent of such foreign state while acting within the scope of his or her office, employment, or agency, except that the court shall decline to hear a claim under this paragraph—
>
> (A) if the foreign state was not designated as a state sponsor of terrorism... at the time the act occurred, unless later so designated as a result of such act....
>
> (B) even if the foreign state is or was so designated, if—
>
> (i) the act occurred in the foreign state against which the claim has been brought and the claimant has not afforded the foreign state a reasonable opportunity to arbitrate the claim in accordance with accepted international rules of arbitration; or
>
> (ii) neither the claimant nor the victim was a national of the United States... when the act upon which the claim is based occurred.

For an application of this statutory language, see Owens v. Republic of Sudan, 412 F.Supp.2d 99 (D.D.C. 2006). This civil action arose out of August 7, 1998, terrorist attacks on the United States embassies in Dar es Salaam, Tanzania, and Nairobi, Kenya.

Comments and Questions

1. Only the United States has recognized an immunity exception for state-sponsored acts of terrorism. The United States' effort to create an exception for state-sponsored acts of terrorism offers a remedy for plaintiffs that may not fit neatly within any of the other categorical exceptions. Why haven't other states or the drafters of the Convention followed this lead?

2. Is the process for determining who is and who isn't a "terrorist" under Section 1605(a)(7) problematic? At various times, the State Department has designated Cuba, Iran, Iraq, Libya, North Korea, Sudan, and Syria as terrorist States and also the Federal Republic of Yugoslavia under President Milosevic's regime. But after the invasion of Iraq the designation of Iraq as a State sponsor of terrorism was lifted and all previously blocked Iraqi assets were vested "in the Department of the Treasury" to be used "to assist the Iraqi people and to assist in the reconstruction of the Treasury." Taken to such extremes, the unilateral discretionary approach to immunity could result in anarchy. A step in that direction is a report that Iran has passed legislation allowing Iranian victims of United States' "interference" to sue the United States. See Hazel Fox, In Defence of State Immunity: Why the UN Convention on State Immunity is Important, 55 Int'l & Comp. L.Q. 399 (2006).

11. Taking of property in violation of international law

The United States Foreign Sovereign Immunities Act is unique in recognizing an exception to immunity for claims involving expropriations of property in violation of international law. This category is especially controversial since expropriation is a quintessentially sovereign act. Nevertheless, Congress grants American courts limited jurisdiction over claims:

> in which rights in property taken in violation of international law are in issue and that property or any property exchanged for such property is present in the United States in connection with a commercial activity carried on in the United States by the foreign state; or that property or any property exchanged for such property is owned or operated by an agency or instrumentality of the foreign state and that agency or instrumentality is engaged in a commercial activity in the United States.
>
> 28 U.S.C. § 1605(a)(3).

The exception has three discrete elements: (1) "rights in property" are at issue; (2) that property was taken in violation of international law; and (3) the jurisdictional nexus with the United States can be satisfied. The first of these elements typically requires that the property be specific and tangible.v

The second element is essential because not all government takings violate international law. For example, a state's expropriation of the property of its own nationals does not violate settled principles of international law. Therefore, to fit an action within this exception the plaintiff must not have been a citizen of the defendant State at the time of the expropriation. Further, according to U.S. courts, the expropriation is a "violation of international law" only if it: (1) fails to serve a public purpose; (2) is discriminatory, i.e., singles out aliens generally, aliens of a specific nationality, or particular individual aliens; or (3) fails to provide just compensation.

The third element demands that plaintiff satisfy a jurisdictional nexus. And this can be met through either of two ways. The first method requires that the subject property or any property exchanged for that property be present in the United

States. Further, plaintiffs must demonstrate that the foreign state, or its political subdivisions, agencies, or instrumentalities use the property in connection with a commercial activity in the United States. A second method is available if the property or the property exchanged therefor is not located in the United States: the plaintiff must show that the property is owned by an agency or instrumentality of the foreign state which is engaged in commercial activity in the United States. As a practical matter, however, the act of state doctrine may bar the adjudication of many claims pursued under this latter method.

Altmann v. Republic of Austria, which follows, explores the scope of the exception in the context of the Nazi's illegal expropriations. Countless works of art and other cultural property were looted by the Nazis; although much of the property has been returned to its original owners, some remains in the hands of public museums and private owners scattered around the world. Ms. Altmann filed this case to retrieve some of her family's art that was hanging in the Austrian Gallery.

In addition to raising issues regarding the applicability of the expropriation exception, the case poses a more general issue about the applicability of the Foreign Sovereign Immunities Act itself—viz., whether the Act can be applied retroactively. The Foreign Sovereign Immunities Act was enacted in 1976, long after the property was looted and the art was hanging in the Austrian Gallery. The court's discussion of these issues will be more meaningful with some additional historical context. Until the middle of the twentieth century, foreign sovereigns enjoyed absolute immunity from the jurisdiction of the U.S. courts. In 1952, the Acting Legal Advisor to the Department of State, Jack B. Tate, wrote to the Acting Attorney General, announcing that it would "thereafter be the Department's policy to follow the restrictive theory of sovereign immunity." The courts typically deferred to the State Department's "suggestions of immunity."

President Ford signed the Foreign Sovereign Immunities Act (FSIA) into law on October 21, 1976. In doing so, the United States codified the restrictive theory of sovereign immunity that had been adopted by the U.S. State Department.

> The central principle of the [FSIA] is to make the question of a foreign state's entitlement to immunity an issue justiciable by the courts, without participation by the Department of State. As the situation now stands, the courts normally defer to the views of the Department of State, which puts the Department in the difficult position of effectively determining whether the plaintiff will have his day in court.... The transfer of this function to the courts will... free the Department from pressures by foreign states to suggest immunity and from any adverse consequences resulting from the unwillingness of the Department to suggest immunity. The Department would be in a position to assert that the question of immunity is entirely one for the courts.*

* Attorney General Richard G. Kleindienst and Secretary of State William Rogers, *Immunities of Foreign States,* hearing before the Sub-committee on Claims and Governmental Relations, House Judiciary Committee, 93rd Cong. (7 June 1973) at 34.)

The FSIA thus shifted the question of sovereign immunity from the political branch to the courts. It also provided an opportunity to delineate certain particulars of the doctrine. Indeed, President Ford's Statement accompanying his signature noted "[i]n this modern world where private citizens increasingly come into contact with foreign government activities, it is important to know when the courts are available to redress legal grievances."**

Altmann v. Republic of Austria

317 F.3d 954 (9th Cir. 2002), aff'd on other grounds, 541 U.S. 677 (2004)

Wardlaw, Circuit Judge

At issue is whether the Foreign Sovereign Immunities Act, 28 U.S.C. §§ 1602–1611, confers jurisdiction in the United States District Court for the Central District of California over the Republic of Austria and the state-owned Austrian Gallery in a suit alleging wrongful appropriation of six Gustav Klimt paintings from their rightful heirs. Maria Altmann, a United States citizen, seeks the recovery of the paintings from the Republic of Austria, which now houses them in the Austrian Gallery. She alleges that (i) the Nazis took the paintings from her Jewish uncle to "Aryanize" them in violation of international law; (ii) the pre-World War II and wartime Austrian government was complicit in their original takings; (iii) the current government, when it learned of the heirs' rights to the paintings, deceived the heirs as to the circumstances of its acquisition of the paintings; and (iv) the Republic and the Gallery now wrongfully assert ownership over the paintings. The Republic of Austria appeals from the district court's denial of its motion to dismiss for want of jurisdiction. Rejecting the Austrian Republic's assertions, the district court found, inter alia, that the FSIA applied retroactively and generally to the events of the late 1930s and 1940s, and that the seizure of the paintings fell within the expropriation exception to the FSIA's grant of immunity.

For the reasons stated below, we determine that the exercise of jurisdiction in this case does not work an impermissible retroactive application of the FSIA. If true, the facts alleged by Altmann establish a taking in violation of international law that confers jurisdiction upon our federal courts, and thus Altmann has presented a substantial and nonfrivolous claim. See Siderman de Blake v. Republic of Argentina, 95 F.2d 699, 711 (9th Cir. 1992) ("At the jurisdictional stage, we need not decide whether the taking actually violated international law; as long as a 'claim is substantial and nonfrivolous, it provides a sufficient basis for the exercise of our jurisdiction.'" (quoting West v. Multibanco Comermex, S.A., 807 F.2d 820, 826 (9th Cir. 1987))), cert. denied, 507 U.S. 1017 (1993). Because Appellants profit from the Klimt paintings in the United States, by authoring, promoting, and distributing books and other publications exploiting these very paintings, these actions are sufficient to constitute "commercial

** Statement by President Gerald Ford on signing HR 11315 into law.

activity" for the purpose of satisfying the FSIA, as well as the predicates for personal jurisdiction....

I. Background

In the early 1900s Ferdinand Bloch, a wealthy Czech sugar magnate, commissioned a portrait of his young wife, Adele Bloch-Bauer, by the Austrian painter Gustav Klimt. Adele and Ferdinand, members of the wealthy Viennese intellectual elite, commissioned Klimt's painting at a time when the artist commanded a fee in excess of a quarter of the price of a furnished country villa. Klimt made hundreds of sketches of Adele, culminating in 1907 with the shimmery golden portrait, Adele Bloch-Bauer I. Before Adele's untimely passing in 1925, she owned six Klimt paintings, including another portrait of herself, a portrait of a close friend, and three landscapes: Adele Bloch-Bauer I & II, Amalie Zuckerkandl, Apple Tree I, Beechwood, and Houses in Unterach am Attersee. Obviously oblivious to the terror to come, which would dramatically affect Austria generally and her husband Ferdinand intimately, Adele left a will "kindly" requesting that Ferdinand donate the paintings to the Austrian Gallery upon his death.

The Nazi invasion of Austria on March 12, 1938, worked a dramatic upheaval on the lives of Ferdinand and all Austrians. Many of the Austrians embraced the Nazis, moving Adolf Hitler to declare the Anschluss-the annexation of Austria to Nazi Germany-the next day. To imbue these actions with a quasi-legal basis, a mock Council of Ministers was convened, which adopted the resolution for the Anschluss. The legitimate Austrian cabinet leaders were arrested and deported to concentration camps. The country was split into single districts under the direct control of Berlin. Even the name "Austria" was abolished. Ferdinand, who was Jewish and had supported anti-Nazi efforts before the annexation of Austria, fled the country to avoid persecution, leaving behind all his holdings, including his paintings, a valuable porcelain collection, and his beautiful home, castle, and sugar factory. He settled in Zurich, Switzerland.

In the meantime, Nazi officials, accompanied by representatives of what later became the Austrian Gallery, convened a meeting to divide up Ferdinand's property. His sugar company was "Aryanized" and his Vienna home was reduced to a German railway headquarters. Reinhardt Heydrich, the author of the infamous Final Solution, moved into Ferdinand's castle. Ferdinand's vast porcelain collection was sold at a public auction, with the best pieces going to Vienna's museums. Hitler and Hermann Göring confiscated some of Ferdinand's Austrian Masters paintings for their private collections. Others were bought for Hitler's planned museum at Linz. Dr. Erich Fuerher, the Nazi lawyer liquidating the estate, chose a few paintings for his personal collection. Dr. Fuerher purported to give two of the paintings at issue, Adele Bloch-Bauer I and Apple Tree I, to the Austrian Gallery in 1941, in exchange for a painting donated by Ferdinand in 1936. He accompanied the transaction with a note claiming to deliver the paintings in fulfillment of the last will and testament of Adele and signed it "Heil Hitler." In March 1943, Dr. Fuerher sold Adele Bloch-Bauer II to the Gallery and Beechwood to the Museum of the City of Vienna. He kept Houses in Unterach am Attersee for his personal collection. It is not clear what immediately happened to Amalie Zuckerkandl, although it ended up in the hands of the art dealer Vita Künstler.

Ferdinand died in Switzerland in November 1945. He left a will, revoking all prior wills, and leaving his entire estate to one nephew and two nieces, including Maria Altmann. Like Ferdinand, Altmann and her husband had been forced to flee Austria. When the Nazis invaded Austria, they imprisoned her husband Fritz in the labor camp at Dachau and moved Altmann to a guarded apartment. Her brother-in-law managed to get Fritz released from Dachau, after which they escaped to Holland. Ultimately, they ended up in Hollywood, California, where Altmann became a United States citizen in 1945.

Also in 1945, the Second Republic of Austria was born and the next year, it declared that all transactions motivated by the Nazis were void. Despite this official policy, Altmann and her family members were unsuccessful in recovering the Klimt paintings. Altmann's brother could retrieve only Houses in Unterach from the private collection of Dr. Fuehrer. In December 1947, the Museum of the City of Vienna offered to return the painting Beechwood, but only in exchange for a refund of the purchase price. This offer was rejected by Ferdinand's heirs. The heirs then unsuccessfully sought return of three of the paintings from the Gallery; the Gallery refused to transfer the paintings, asserting that they had been bequeathed to it by the terms of Adele's will. Under color of the will, the legal effect of which has yet to be determined, the museum even began to prepare suit for return of the Klimt paintings not yet in its possession. Despite the museum's aggressive stance, a private letter from Dr. Karl Garzarolli dated March 8, 1948, of the Gallery to his Nazi-era predecessor revealed that nothing in the files of the Gallery would document the donation of the paintings to the Gallery. This letter was kept hidden from Ferdinand's heirs.

In 1948, an agent of Austria's Federal Monument Agency contacted Dr. Rinesch, the Austrian lawyer hired by the family, to discuss the artworks in question. He informed Dr. Rinesch that the artworks could not be exported without resolution of their ownership. In a practice later declared illegal by the Austrian government, the Agency informed Dr. Rinesch that it would grant export permits on some of the family's other recovered artworks in exchange for a "donation" of the Klimt paintings. With little hope of otherwise exporting the other artworks, Dr. Rinesch agreed that Ferdinand's heirs would acknowledge the will of Adele Bloch-Bauer and allow the Austrian Gallery to keep the six Klimt paintings mentioned in the will. He justified this decision to Robert Bentley, Altmann's brother, by claiming that Adele's will would be sufficient to give the museum a claim to the six paintings. He executed a document, dated April 12, 1948, acknowledging the agreement and gave Houses in Unterach to the Austrian Gallery. As agreed, Dr. Rinesch obtained export permits for almost all of the other recovered artworks.

In early 1998, an international art scandal broke: the City of New York seized two Egon Schiele paintings loaned by Austria to the Museum of Modern Art in New York, claiming that they were stolen by the Nazis. In response to allegations that the

Austrian Gallery still possessed looted art, the Austrian Minister for Education and Culture for the first time opened up the Ministry's archives to permit research into the provenance of the national collection. The Austrian government also created a Committee made up of government officials and art historians to advise the Minister for Education and Culture on which artworks should be returned and to whom. The documents that surfaced in 1998 demonstrated that reliance on Adele's will as the source of legal title to the paintings was questionable at best.

Notwithstanding the discovery of the documents undermining the Austrian Gallery's ownership of the paintings, the Committee recommended against returning the six Klimt paintings at issue. Altmann alleges that the Committee vote was predetermined by the Austrian government before the Committee ever discussed the matter. Altmann points to the resignation of one Committee member who abstained from the vote and later stated that she had been ordered by a superior to vote against return of the six paintings.

In September 1999, Altmann decided to file a lawsuit in Austria to overturn the Committee's recommendation regarding the Klimt paintings. To do so, under Austrian law, Altmann was required to pay a filing fee that is a percentage of the recoverable amount. The standard formula used to calculate the court fees is 1.2% of the amount in controversy plus 13,180 Austrian schillings. Because the amount in controversy here is approximately $135 million, Altmann would have been required to pay about $1.6 million to pursue her claim. Altmann applied for legal aid, seeking reduction of the fees, and was granted a partial waiver. Based on the information detailing her assets, the court determined that Altmann and her co-heirs could afford a fee of 2 million schillings, or approximately $135,000. Although Altmann did not appeal the decision, the Republic of Austria appealed on the grounds that Altmann had not declared the value of various art objects worth almost $700,000 that she had recently recovered from the Austrian government. The petition was rejected as untimely. Regardless of the amount paid, in the event that Altmann prevailed in the Austrian civil action, she would be entitled to recover all of the court fees and her attorney's fees as part of the final judgment.

Because of what they viewed as the prohibitive cost of the lawsuit, Altmann and her family abandoned their Austrian complaint. On August 22, 2000, Altmann filed the present action against the Republic of Austria and the Gallery in the Central District of California. The Republic of Austria and the Gallery moved for dismissal under (i) Fed. R. Civ. P. 12(b)(1) for lack of subject matter jurisdiction; (ii) Fed. R. Civ. P. 12(b)(3) for lack of venue; (iii) Fed. R. Civ. P. 12(b)(7) for failure to join indispensable parties; and (iv) the doctrine of forum non conveniens. The district court denied this motion on May 4, 2001.

II. Subject Matter Jurisdiction—The Foreign Sovereign Immunities Act

A. The Applicability of the FSIA

We must first determine whether the district court properly held that the FSIA may be applied to the alleged wrongful appropriation by the Republic. The FSIA "provides the sole basis for obtaining jurisdiction over a foreign state in the courts of this country." Argentine Republic v. Amerada Hess Shipping Corp., 488 U.S. 428, 443 (1989). The defendants maintain that jurisdiction is lacking because the FSIA may not be retrospectively applied to conduct pre-dating the Department of State's 1952 issuance of the Tate Letter, while the last taking in this case purportedly occurred in 1948. See Letter of Jack B. Tate, Acting Legal Advisor, Department of State, to Acting Attorney General Philip B. Perlman, May 19, 1952 ("1952 Tate Letter"), reprinted in 26 Dep't State Bull. 984 (1952) and in Alfred Dunhill of London, Inc. v. Republic of Cuba, 425 U.S. 682, 711–15 app. 2 (1976). To the extent courts have considered the retroactivity of the FSIA, the consensus appears to be that it would encompass events dating back at least as far as the date of this letter. [citing cases]

We need not reach the broad conclusion of the district court that the FSIA may be generally applied to events predating the 1952 Tate Letter. Instead, we find persuasive the reasoning set forth by Judge Wald, who resigned in 1999 from the Court of Appeals for the District of Columbia Circuit to serve two years as a judge on the International Criminal Tribunal for the Former Yugoslavia. In her dissenting opinion in Princz v. Federal Republic of Germany, Judge Wald agreed with the majority that application of the FSIA to pre-1952 conduct is not impermissibly retroactive, but set forth a narrower rationale for that conclusion. See 26 F.3d 1166, 1178–79 (D.C. Cir. 1994) (Wald, J., dissenting on other grounds), cert. denied, 513 U.S. 1121 (1995)....

We conclude, as did Judge Wald, that the application of the FSIA infringes on no right held at the time the acts at issue occurred, and thus the FSIA is not impermissibly applied to Austria in this case.... [Moreover,] we note that by the 1920s, Austria itself had adopted the restrictive theory, which recognizes sovereign immunity "with regard to sovereign or public acts (jure imperii) of a state, but not with respect to private acts (jure gestionis)."... [And further still,] the cases holding the FSIA inapplicable to pre-1952 events involve economic transactions entered into long before the facts of this case arose and, unlike here, prior to the defendant country's acceptance of the restrictive principle of sovereign immunity and to the widespread acceptance of the restrictive theory....

B. Expropriation Exception to Sovereign Immunity

The FSIA's expropriation exception to immunity provides that:

> A foreign state shall not be immune from the jurisdiction of the courts of the United States or of the States in any case—...
>
> (3) in which rights in property taken in violation of international law are in issue and...that property or any property exchanged for such property is owned or operated by an agency or instrumentality of the foreign state and that agency or instrumentality is engaged in a commercial activity in the United States.
>
> 28 U.S.C. § 1605(a).

This exception to foreign sovereign immunity "is based upon the general presumption that states abide by international law and, hence, violations of international law are not 'sovereign' acts." West, 807 F.2d at 826; H.R. Rep. No. 94-1487, at 14, reprinted in 1976 U.S.C.C.A.N. 6604, 6613 ("[T]he central premise of the bill [is that] decisions on claims by foreign states to sovereign immunity are best made by the judiciary on the basis of a statutory regime which incorporates standards recognized under international law.").... For guidance regarding the norms against takings in violation of international law, we may look to court decisions, United States law, the work of jurists, and the usage of nations. See Siderman de Blake, 965 F.2d at 714–15; West 807 F.2d at 831 n.10. Nevertheless, we recognize that "[a]t the jurisdictional stage, we need not decide whether the taking actually violated international law; as long as a 'claim is substantial and non-frivolous, it provides a sufficient basis for the exercise of our jurisdiction.'" Siderman de Blake, 965 F.2d at 711 (quoting West, 807 F.2d at 826).

The facts alleged by Altmann fall squarely within the expropriation exception to sovereign immunity. There is no question but that "rights in property" are in issue. The Austrian Republic and Gallery insist on Adele's will as the basis for their legal ownership of the Klimt paintings. Altmann, as a true heir and as a representative of other heirs, asserts the will has no such legal effect and the documents unearthed in 1998 revealed that fact to the current Austrian government and to the Austrian Gallery, which nevertheless have retained possession of the paintings without payment therefor.

The next question is whether the property in issue was taken in violation of international law. To constitute a valid taking under international law three predicates must exist. First, "[v]alid expropriations must always serve a public purpose." West, 807 F.2d at 831. Second, "aliens [must] not be discriminated against or singled out for regulation by the state." Id. at 832. Finally, "[a]n otherwise valid taking is illegal without the payment of just compensation." Id. (relying on reports from the Foreign Claims Settlement Commission, international law journals, the Restatement (Second) of Foreign Relations Law of the United States, and federal case law). To fall into this exception, the plaintiff cannot be a citizen of the defendant country at the time of the expropriation, because "'[e]xpropriation by a sovereign state of the property of its own nationals does not implicate settled principles of international law.'" Siderman de Blake, 965 F.2d at 711.

The facts of record, which in this procedural posture we must take as true, show that the Klimt paintings have been wrongfully and discriminatorily appropriated in violation of international law. The Nazis did not even pretend to take the Klimt paintings for a public purpose; instead, Dr. Fuehrer sold them for personal gain or exchanged them to supplement his private collection. In addition, their taking appears discriminatory. Altmann is a Jewish refugee, now a United States citizen, who is a descendant of a Czech family whose property was looted by the Nazis because of their religious heritage. According to Altmann, despite convening a Committee to evaluate expropriation claims and return stolen artwork, the Austrian government intentionally intervened to thwart a fair and impartial vote on the restitution of the Klimt paintings. Further, the Austrian government has not yet returned the paintings to Altmann and her family or justly compensated them for the value of the paintings. Without compensation, this taking cannot be valid.

Finally, the Austrian Gallery is engaged in commercial activity in the United States. Altmann has satisfied the FSIA's statutory nexus requirement by showing that the paintings are owned or operated by an agency or instrumentality of the foreign state, here the Austrian Gallery, which is "engaged in commercial activity in the United States." 28 U.S.C. § 1605(a)(3). The defendants do not contest that the Gallery is an "agency or instrumentality." The FSIA defines "commercial activity" as "either a regular course of commercial conduct or a particular commercial transaction or act," and provides that "[t]he commercial character of an activity shall be determined by reference to the nature of the course of conduct or particular transaction or act, rather than by reference to its purpose." Id. at § 1603(d).

Altmann argues that the Gallery engages in commercial activity in the United States by authoring, editing, and publishing in the United States both a book entitled Klimt's Women, as well as an English-language guidebook, containing photographs of the looted paintings. She also contends that the advertisements in the United States of Gallery exhibitions, particularly those relating to the Klimt paintings, as well as operation of the Gallery itself, constitute commercial activity. The key commercial behavior of the Gallery here is not its operation of the museum exhibition in Austria, however, but its publication and marketing of that exhibition and the books in the United States. Klimt's Women, for example, is published in English in the United States by Yale University Press and capitalizes on the images of three of the paintings at issue. That book was published in conjunction with a large exhibition at the Gallery featuring the expropriated paintings. Furthermore, the Austrian Gallery asserts copyright ownership as "authors"; two employees of the Gallery edited the book; and the director of the Gallery is listed as responsible for its content. The museum guidebook is also published in English and features the painting Adele Bloch-Bauer I on its cover. The publication and sale of these materials and the marketing of the Klimt exhibition in the United States are commercial activities in and of themselves, but are also a means to attract American tourists to the Gallery. Given that the commercial activity is centered around the very paintings at issue in this action and far exceeds that which we found sufficient to justify applying § 1605(a)(3) in Siderman de Blake, 965 F.2d at 709, we must conclude that the Gallery is engaging in commercial activity sufficient to justify jurisdiction under the FSIA....

Comments and Questions

1. The U.S. Supreme Court declined to review the determination that the expropriation exception authorized the suit, but affirmed that the Act could be applied retroactively. 541 U.S. 677 (2004).

2. An exception for expropriation does not fit neatly within the dichotomous framework of acta jure gestionis and acta jure imperii. Private acts undertaken by a sovereign are not immune; public acts are immune. Expropriation is, by definition, a public act (because a private person is incapable of expropriating another's

property). Yet the state is not immune for these public acts, provided they are unlawful. How would you justify this exception? Can it be analogized to the tort exception? Is the public-private distinction outdated? What is the replacement?

12. Jus Cogens

An exception for acts contrary to norms of jus cogens represents the outer edge of state immunity jurisprudence. When acts contrary to international law also trigger the commercial activity or personal injury (or, in the United States, the state-sponsored acts of terrorism or expropriation) exception, the foreign state cannot invoke immunity as a shield for its actions. Often, however, the act cannot be shoehorned into those exceptions. Although there is much discussion about a jus cogens exception, the Convention does not include it, and very few courts have, in fact, recognized it. The Bouzari case and the article by Professor McGregor illustrate the current national practice and also reveal a bearing for future practice.

Bouzari v. Islamic Republic of Iran

Canada, Ontario Superior Court of Justice

1 May 2002; 124 I.L.R. 428 (2003)

Swinton J

1. This action has been brought by the plaintiff Houshang Bouzari, his wife and two children against the Islamic Republic of Iran claiming damages for torture. Mr. Bouzari and his family are landed immigrants in Canada, who are in the process of acquiring Canadian citizenship. The action arises out of events which occurred in Iran in 1993 and 1994.

2. Iran did not file a Statement of Defence and has been noted in default. This matter comes before me as a motion to determine whether the Superior Court of Justice has jurisdiction over this proceeding, both under the common law rules, respecting conflicts of law and under the State Immunity Act, RSC 1985, c. S-18. Section 3 of that Act states,

> (1) Except as provided by this Act, a foreign state is immune from the jurisdiction of any court in Canada.
> (2) In any proceedings before a court, the court shall give effect to the immunity conferred on a foreign state by subsection (1) notwithstanding that the state has failed to take any step in the proceedings.

The plaintiffs argue that they fall within one of three exceptions specified in the Act—the commercial activity exception in § 5, the tort exception in § 6, or the penal proceedings provision in § 18. Alternatively, they argue that a further exception should be read into the Act to permit a civil action for damages for torture against a foreign state. If the State Immunity Act bars this proceeding, they challenge the constitutionality of § 3 under the Canadian Charter of Rights and Freedoms, arguing that it is contrary to § 7 and not justified under § 1.

3. The Attorney General of Canada was granted leave to intervene and present evidence with respect to international law and the constitutional issue, while Amnesty International (Canadian Section) was given leave to intervene and present argument, which it did in support of the plaintiffs' submissions respecting an exception from state immunity for actions for damages caused by torture.

The Facts

4. Since Iran did not defend this proceeding, it is deemed to have admitted the truth of all allegations of fact in the Statement of Claim under the Ontario rules with respect to default judgment (Rule 19.02(1)(a)). Nevertheless, Mr. Bouzari also testified about the events in Iran that led to these proceedings.

5. Mr. Bouzari was born in Iran and worked for the government there for several years in the 1980s. He ended his government employment in late 1987 and began to work as a consultant in the oil and gas industry. In early 1988, he moved his family—his wife, daughter and son—to Rome, and he conducted his business from Rome and Geneva. Essentially, his work consisted of aiding foreign companies to find oil and gas projects in Iran. He was paid commission and consulting fees by these companies.

6. In 1991, he was involved in the South Pars project, a very rich oil and gas field offshore Iran in the Persian Gulf. A consortium retained him to act for them on the project. They sought to provide oil and gas drilling and exploration technology and pipeline and refinery construction to NIOC, the National Iranian Oil Company. This was the main subsidiary of the Ministry of Petroleum for all oil projects and was 100% state-owned.

7. In April, 1992, a consortium of five companies signed a contract with NIOC for $1.8 billion (US). Mr. Bouzari was supposed to be paid 2% of the cost of the entire project for his commission, with the amount payable in installments.

8. From November, 1992 through to May, 1993, Mehdi Hashemi Bahramani, the son of the president of Iran, approached Mr. Bouzari and offered his father's help to bring the project into effect, in return for a commission of around $50 million. Mr. Bouzari refused.

9. On June 1, 1993, three plain clothes police officers broke into Mr. Bouzari's apartment in Tehran and searched it. They took money, jewelry, a computer, and documents. Then he was ordered to drive at gunpoint to Even Prison. He was taken to Section 209, which belongs to the Ministry of Information. He was held in a small cell, blindfolded, for about 40 days. During that time, he was beaten and once had his head pushed into a toilet filled with excrement.

10. Around July 10, 1993, he was transferred by government agents to Towhid Detention Centre. By this time, they demanded a ransom of $1 million for his release, which he refused to pay. While incarcerated, he was subject to fake executions and many beatings with cables, which injured his feet. He was also hung by his shoulders for periods of time, which caused great pain and lasting injury to his shoulders, and beaten around the ears with slippers, which has damaged his hearing.

11. It is Mr. Bouzari's opinion that he was tortured in order to remove him from the South Pars project. In the summer of 1993, NIOC cancelled its contract with the consortium for South Pars. Later, Mehdi established a state-owned company for himself, Offshore Engineering and Construction Company, and signed a contract with the consortium for SouthPars in around 1996.

12. Apparently, Mr. Bouzari's family paid $3 million as ransom in the summer of 1993. According to the Statement of Claim, the funds were transferred to the Foreign Currency Account of the Ministry of Information in a bank in Tehran. Again on January 22, 1994, the family transferred $250,000.00 (US) to the bank account of the Islamic Revolutionary Prosecutor General in Tehran. On January 22, 199, Mr. Bouzari was taken from prison and released by being left, blindfolded in the middle of a traffic circle in Tehran.

13. He ultimately was able to get a passport by promising a further $1.75 million to government agents in the Ministry of Information. He escaped in July, 1994, to Vienna and finally rejoined his family. After his escape, he received telephone threats from Iranian agents, threatening to kill him.

14. Mr. Bouzari and his family emigrated to Canada in July, 1998 as landed immigrants, and he has brought his action here because it is impossible to do so in Iran. He testified that he continues to suffer from his experiences in Iran, including post-traumatic stress disorder, ongoing pain in his shoulders and back, and deafness. He seeks both compensatory and punitive damages personally against Iran, while his wife and children have brought claims for damages under the Family Law Act, RSO 1990, c. F. 3....

18. Historically, in accordance with customary international law, foreign states were granted absolute immunity from proceedings in the courts of other states. This practice was founded on the principles of sovereign equality of states and non-interference of states in the internal affairs of another state. However, over the course of the last century, as certain exceptions developed, the doctrine of restrictive immunity has replaced absolute immunity. Section 3 of the Canadian State Immunity Act makes this clear. Essentially, foreign states are immune from civil suits in Canadian courts, unless one of the exceptions in the Act applies, or the state waives its immunity (§ 4). However, the number of exceptions to immunity is limited in the Act. Most notable in the Canadian legislation are the commercial activity exception found in § 5 and the tort exception in § 6....

The Commercial Activity Exception

22. ...Immunity is not accorded when the act of the foreign state is characterized as private or commercial (acta iure gestionis)....

24. ...The leading Canadian authority on the commercial activity exception...adopt[ed] a contextual approach to determine whether the doctrine of restrictive immunity should apply to a particular claim....This approach requires an examination predominantly of the nature of the activity, but its purpose can also be relevant....

25. Mr. Bouzari has framed his claim in tort for damages for kidnapping, false imprisonment, assault, torture and death threats. He takes the position that he was abducted and held because he refused to pay monies to Mehdi, and the imprisonment and torture were aimed at extracting an advance payment from him on the commission that he had refused to pay Mehdi. As well, Iran sought to obtain ransom monies from him.

26. I cannot characterize the nature of the activity here as commercial. This is far from the usual case where commercial activity is found—for example, where the plaintiff sues on a contract for goods provided to the foreign state, or where the foreign state has entered the marketplace as a trader....

28. In my view, regardless of the state's ultimate purpose, exercises of police, law enforcement and security powers are inherently exercises of governmental authority and sovereignty....

The Tort Exception

30. Section 6 states:

> A foreign state is not immune from the jurisdiction of a court in any proceedings that relate to:
>
> (a) any death or personal or bodily injury; or
> (b) any damage to or loss of property that occurs in Canada.

31. This is a more recent exception to state immunity. However, a number of states have enacted a comparable provision in order to protect their citizens against wrongful acts by a foreign state in the forum state that cause injury to individuals or property. In contrast to the Canadian provision, some of these statutes more clearly say that the act causing injury must occur in the forum. For example, the legislation of the United Kingdom provides that a state is not immune from proceedings in respect of death or personal or injury "caused by an act or omission in the United Kingdom" (State Immunity Act 1978, c. 33, § 5).

32. Section 6 only permits a Canadian court to take jurisdiction if the injury occurs in Canada. The Ontario Court of Appeal has held that this provision can apply to psychological injury or mental distress, but only if that injury arises from or is linked to a physical injury as well, and that injury must occur in Canada.... In this case, the physical injury, as well as the related psychological injury, occurred in Iran because of acts of torture there. While Mr. Bourazzi continues to suffer from those injuries in Canada, both physically and mentally, that does not change the fact that the injury occurred in Iran....

34. Therefore, § 6 does not apply, unless a special exception must be read into the Act for damages caused by acts of torture in a foreign state.

Reading in a Further Exception

35. The plaintiff argued that § 6 of the Act must be read in light of the current state of international law so as to include actions for damages for torture committed in

a foreign state. Alternatively it was submitted that a further exception should be read into § 3 with respect to a civil action for damages for torture by a foreign state. Specifically, it is argued that Canada is a signatory of the Convention against Torture and, therefore, has an obligation to provide a civil remedy for victims of torture, even against foreign states acting within their territorial jurisdiction. Alternatively, the prohibition against torture is jus cogens—that is, a fundamental norm of international law which overrides customary rules of international law, such as state immunity from civil proceedings in the courts of foreign jurisdictions....

The Role of International Law in the Interpretation of Canadian Statutes

39. Customary rules of international law are directly incorporated into Canadian domestic law unless ousted by contrary legislation.... In contrast, an international obligation under a treaty or convention has no direct application in Canada until implemented by legislation by the appropriate level of government. Nevertheless, even when an international obligation has not been implemented, the Supreme Court has observed that "the values reflected in international human rights law may help inform the contextual approach to statutory interpretation and judicial review." (Baker v. Canada, [1999] 2 SCR 817 at 861)....

The Interpretation of the State Immunity Act in Light of International Law

40. There are two bases for the plaintiff's argument that the State Immunity Act must be interpreted so as to permit this action to proceed. The first rests on that fact that Canada is a signatory of the Convention Against Torture (entered into force June 26, 1987, GA/res. 39/46, 39 UN GAOR Supp. (No. 51) UN Doc. A/39/51 (1984)). It was argued that Canada has an obligation to provide victims of torture with a civil remedy by the terms of the Convention. The second argument rested on the principle of jus cogens: as the prohibition on torture is jus cogens, an exception to the doctrine of state immunity for civil actions for damages for torture must be read into the Act in order that Canada not be in violation of international law....

41. The hurdle for the plaintiff here is that the words of the Act seem clear. Section 3 appears to set out a general rule of state immunity and to specify certain exceptions. It appears to codify the law respecting state immunity. If so, any further exception would be for Parliament to specify, not a judge interpreting the legislation. Similarly, § 6 appears to deal with acts causing injury in Canada, and the language does not lend itself to one approach for injury caused by torture outside the country and another approach for other kinds of acts causing injury in Canada.

42. However, even more important than the problem which the plaintiff faces with the language of the Act is the fact that the legislation in its current form, without a further exception, is consistent with both customary international law respecting state immunity and Canada's treaty obligations. Therefore, for the reasons that follow, there is no need to read in a further exception in order to comply with international law.

The Convention Against Torture

46. [Some commentators read the Convention Against Torture to require signatories, such as Canada] to provide a civil remedy for torture, even if the acts are committed outside the jurisdiction.... [However,] no country has enacted legislation to give a civil remedy for torture committed outside its jurisdiction by a foreign state.

47. [Other commentators insist the Convention Against Torture] does not impose an obligation on signatories to provide a civil remedy for all acts of torture, including those committed outside its jurisdiction. [Article 14 of the Convention] is silent with respect to territorial reach....

50. ... [S]tate practice, both at the time the treaty was signed and since, indicates that no state interprets Article 14 to require it to take civil jurisdiction over a foreign state for acts committed outside the forum state.

53. [The court acknowledged that it was quite possible that its interepretation described "where international law had been, but not where it was going."] My task is to determine whether Canada's State Immunity Act should be interpreted to provide a further exception for damages for torture committed by foreign states outside Canada so as to be in compliance with international law, or whether § 3 of the Act is unconstitutional. In making my decision, especially on the interpretation issue, I need to know the current state of international law....

56. Therefore, Canada has no treaty obligation which requires it to provide a civil remedy for acts of torture committed by foreign states.

The Jus Cogens Argument

57. In the alternative, the plaintiff argues that the prohibition against torture is a norm of jus cogens, which obliges Canada to provide a right to sue a foreign state in a Canadian court for damages for torture committed outside Canada....

59. A rule of jus cogens is a higher form of customary international law. It is a peremptory norm from which no derogation is permitted. (Vienna Convention on the Law of Treaties, Article 53). Under international law, a norm of jus cogens overrides other rules of customary international law in conflict with it. As well, Articles 53 and 64 of the Vienna Convention on the Law of Treaties provide that a treaty obligation in conflict with a principle of jus cogens is of no force or effect in international law....

60. With respect to the jus cogens argument, the first question must be whether the prohibition against torture is a norm of jus cogens and, if it is, what is the scope of the norm....

61. Courts of other countries have held the prohibition on torture to be a rule of jus cogens—for example, the House of Lords in R v. Bow Street Metropolitan Stipendiary Magistrate, ex parte Pinochet (No 3), [2000] 1 AC 147. [I accept] that the prohibition on torture is a norm of jus cogens....

62. That still raises the important question of the scope of the norm. [However,] states do not universally embrace the view that there must be a civil remedy for

torture, and [thus] this is not currently accepted as an element of the prohibition of torture....

64. The decisions of the English Courts have consistently respected the principle of state immunity for sovereign acts committed outside of the United Kingdom. This has been the case even where the acts were contrary to rules of jus cogens. For example, in Kuwait Airways Corporation v. Iraqi Airways Co. (No 1), [1995] 1 WLR 1147, the House of Lords held that Iraq and its instrumentalities were entitled to state immunity in the English courts in respect of Iraqi aggression against Kuwait, even though the illegal act was contrary to a rule of jus cogens....

66. Courts in the United States have also refused to take jurisdiction in proceedings in which claims for damages for torture are made arising from acts outside the United States.... In Siderman de Blake v. Republic of Argentina, 965 F.2d 699 (9th Cir. 1992), the Court held that there was no exception to state immunity for acts of torture committed outside the United States, even though those acts were in violation of jus cogens....

67. Mr. Morgan [one of the experts] could point to only one decision of any domestic court in the world in which the court had taken jurisdiction in a civil case involving torture against a foreign state: Prefecture of Voiotia v. Federal Republic of Germany (summarized in (2001), 95 AJIL 198). The Hellenic Supreme Court was dealing with a claim for damages arising from German atrocities in Greece during the Second World War....

73. [After reviewing various decisions of international tribunals that supported and undermined the plaintiffs' position, the Court concluded that there was no "general practice" to support an exception from state immunity.] As a result, there is no conflict between the Canadian State Immunity Act as written, with its limited exceptions, and customary international law. Indeed, the Canadian Act, in its present form, is consistent with current norms of customary international law. While international law may someday evolve to include a further exception for acts of torture, it does not do so now.... Therefore, the action is barred by § 3 of the Act....

Lorna McGregor, State Immunity and Jus Cogens
55 ICLQ 437 (2006)

The [United Nations] General Assembly first proposed that the International Law Commission look into the issue of state immunity in 1977. As State immunity, by its very nature, sits at the interface between traditional and contemporary notions of international law, the span of the negotiations over three decades inevitably exposed the resulting Convention to gaps and inconsistencies with evolving areas of international law. In 1999 the International Law Commission established a Working Group on Jurisdictional immunities of States and their property, "to consider outstanding substantive issues... taking into account the recent developments of State practice and legislation and any other factors related to this issue since the adoption of the draft articles [in 1986]." Beyond the five issues identified by States during informal discussions in 1993,[2] the Working Group highlighted another developing area of international law relating to the "existence or non-existence of jurisdictional immunity in actions arising, inter alia out of violations of jus cogens norms." However, although the Working Group noted the "current interest" in the interaction between immunity and jus cogens norms, it concluded that the issue "did not seem to be ripe enough for the Working Group to engage in a codification exercise over it." The Working Group then referred the issue to the Sixth Committee which did not consider the relationship between the Convention and jus cogens norms any further. The Third Committee also did not look into the interaction, despite the Working Group's suggestion that it might present the more appropriate body in which to address the issue due to its focus on "non-impunity."

As a general matter, the position of the Working Group appropriately excludes the relationship between State immunity and jus cogens norms from the purview of the Convention. The interaction between State immunity and jus cogens norms reflects an area of international law in a state of flux. As the purpose of the Convention is to promote "uniformity and clarity in the law of jurisdictional immunities of States and their property," any definitive treatment of the issue would have been premature. However, the failure of the Convention to expressly exclude jus cogens norms from its coverage could potentially result in regressive development of international law. In this regard, this article first examines the current developments in international law which indicate a progression towards the denial of immunity in cases concerning jus cogens norms. The article then addresses three main ways in which the Convention could restrict the development of international law in this area: namely, the structure of the Convention as providing for a general rule of immunity subject to enumerated exceptions; the understanding in the travaux préparatoires that the Convention should be interpreted to exclude criminal proceedings; and the removal of the clause subjecting the Convention to future developments in international law. Taken together, these aspects of the Convention could potentially freeze rapidly evolving areas of international law. As a result, this article supports the idea of a human rights protocol which would guard against the potentially adverse impact of the Convention on the development and clarification of international law in this area.

I. Developments in the Relationship Between State Immunity and Jus Cogens Norms Under International Law

In drafting the Convention, "all the relevant doctrines as well as treaties, case law and national legislation," were ostensibly taken into account. Yet the majority of

---

[2] Annex to the Report of the International Law Commission on the Work of its Fifty-First Session, A/54/10 (3 May-23 July 1999) para 7 (outlining the five outstanding substantive areas requiring clarification as: '(1) the concept of a State for the purposes of immunity: (2) Criteria for determining the commercial character of a contract or transaction; (3) Concept of a State enterprise or other entity in relation to commercial transactions; (4) Contracts of employment and (5) Measures of constraint against State property.)'

State practice cited in the commentaries to the Convention relates back to the late 1970s and early 1980s. Moreover, in the examination of jus cogens norms, the Working Group only looked at developments up to 1999, at which point only a limited number of cases and scholarly articles had considered the relationship between the two sets of norms. On this basis, the Working Group concluded that "national courts, in some cases, have shown some sympathy for this argument. However, in most cases, the plea of sovereign immunity has succeeded." As this was the last time the interaction was considered before the Convention opened for signature in 2004, the further developments discussed below which have taken place in the intervening years were not addressed. In an area of evolving international law, the lag in the adoption of the Convention renders it outdated. Current jurisprudence..., taken in conjunction with broader developments on the right to reparation, impunity and State responsibility under international law,[11] indicates a move away from the availability of State immunity in cases concerning jus cogens norms.

Since 1999 four national court decisions, in particular, highlight the divide in the approach to the relationship between jus cogens norms and State immunity. On the one hand, the Italian Supreme Court in Ferrini v the Federal Republic of Germany[12] and the Greek Supreme Court in Prefecture of Voiotia v the Federal Republic of Germany[13] have found that State immunity is not available as a bar to jurisdiction in cases concerning jus cogens violations. In contrast, despite underlying allegations of torture, the English Court of Appeal upheld the plea of immunity in Al-Adsani v Kuwait[14] and the Ontario Court of Appeal granted the Islamic Republic of Iran immunity in Bouzari v Iran.[15] Both decisions were based on the lack of an express human rights exception in the respective domestic statutes on immunity. However, as discussed below, the Committee against Torture subsequently made clear in its consideration of Canada's State party report that its failure to provide a civil remedy to all victims of torture did not comport with its obligations under the Convention against Torture. This development, coupled with the decisions of the Greek and Italian Supreme Courts, questions the continuing weight

[11] Basic Principles and Guidelines on the Right to a Remedy and Reparation for Victims of Gross Violations of International Human Rights Law and Serious Violations of International Humanitarian Law UN Doc E/CN.4/RES/2005/35, Annex (20 Apr 2005); Economic and Social Council Promotion and Protection of Human Rights: Impunity: Report of the Independent Expert to Update the Set of Principles to Combat Impunity, Diane Orentlicher: Addendum: Updated Set of Principles for the Protection and Promotion of Human Rights Through Action to Combat Impunity E/CN.4/2005/102/Add 1 (2005); Draft Articles on Responsibility of States for Internationally Wrongful Acts, in Report of the International Law Commission on the Work of Its Fifty-Third Session UN GAOR 56th Sess, Supp No 10, UN Doc A/56/10 (2001).

[12] *Ferrini v Federal Republic of Germany* (Cass Sez Un 5044/04) (reproduced in the original Italian text in (2004) 87 Rivista di diritto internazionale 539).

[13] *Prefecture of Voiotia v FRG* Case No 11/2000, Areios Pagos, (2001) 95 AJIL 198–204, 200 (translating the judgment of the court).

[14] *Al-Adsani v Government of Kuwait* 107 ILR 536 (1996).

[15] *Bouzari v Iran (Islamic Republic)* Ont CA (2004).

to be granted to the European Court of Human Rights decision in Al-Adsani v the United Kingdom,[17] which accorded a wide margin of appreciation to the United Kingdom without a detailed assessment of how the provision of State immunity fulfilled a legitimate aim or met the requirements of proportionality.

In Ferrini v the Federal Republic of Germany, Mr Ferrini brought a civil claim for reparation before the Italian courts, alleging that he was forcibly deported from Italy to Germany by the German military forces during the Second World War, for the purpose of forced labour. He had previously attempted to bring a claim for compensation in Germany but had failed as his case did not fall within the terms of a domestic statute which provided the exclusive basis for reparation claims arising out of the Second World War. The Italian Corte di Cassazione acknowledged that Germany's military actions amounted to acta jure imperii that would normally enjoy the protection of immunity. However, the Court distinguished the case before it from previous cases granting immunity for military activities on the basis of the underlying act involved. By defining the prohibition of forced labour as a peremptory norm under international law, the Court held that jus cogens norms "trump" the plea of state immunity as an "ordinary" customary international law rule.[20] In particular, the Court contrasted the progressive movement away from the principle of absolute immunity which "has become, and continues to become, gradually limited,"[21] to the absolute nature of a jus cogens norm. The court questioned whether "immunity from jurisdiction can exist even in relation to actions which... take on the gravest connotations, and which figure in customary international law as international crimes, since they undermine universal values which transcend the interest of single States." As a result, the Court denied Germany the protection of immunity on the basis that it "would hinder the protection of values whose safeguard is to be considered... essential to the whole international community."

In 2001 the Greek Areios Pagos, in Prefecture of Voiotia v the Federal Republic of Germany,[24] held that Germany did not enjoy immunity in another civil claim for reparation arising out of jus cogens violations committed during the Second World War. Similar to the Italian Corte di Cassazione, the Court found that immunity only applies to acts of a sovereign nature. However, its reasoning differed from the Italian Court in two main respects. First, the Court found that as Germany's actions were, "in breach of rules of peremptory international law... they were not

---

[17] *Al-Adsani v The United Kingdom* (35763/97) [2001] ECHR 752.

[20] For further discussion of the 'trumping' argument or normative hierarchy theory, *see* Lee Caplan *State Immunity, Human Rights and Jus Cogens: A Critique of the Normative Hierarchy Theory* (2003) 97 AJIL 741–81.

[21] *Ferrini v Germany* (n 12) para 5 (translated in Pasquale De Sena and Francesca de Vittor *State Immunity and Human Rights: The Italian Supreme Court Decision on the Ferrini Case* (2005) 16 EJIL 89–112, 94.

[24] *Prefecture of Voiotia v the Federal Republic of Germany* (n 12). See Gavouneli and Bantekas (n 13) 198 (translating the decision of the Areios Pagos).

acts jure imperii," and that "crimes carried out by organs of the occupying power in abuse of their sovereign power do not attract immunity." Secondly, in contrast to the Italian Court, the Areios Pagos did not employ the normative hierarchy theory (or trumping argument). Rather, it based its decision on the theory of implied waiver whereby by violating a peremptory norm under international law, the State is understood to have waived any immunity that might otherwise attach by implication.[27]

In a later case involving war reparations, the First Chamber of the Areios Pagos referred the case to the Special Supreme Court, an ad hoc court composed of a combination of judges and legal scholars convened to decide on whether rules of international law are "generally recognized." By six votes to five, the Greek Special Supreme Court found, "that Germany enjoyed immunity without any restrictions or exceptions and therefore could not be sued before any Greek Civil Court for torts committed." The Court based its decision on "a general norm of customary international law that rendered inadmissible any claim against a foreign state for tortures committed by its armed forces."[30] However, as Supreme Court decisions only carry persuasive and not precedential value, the decision again serves to demonstrate the flux in international law....

Comments and Questions

1. The court's adoption of the waiver argument in Voitia was widely criticized as an acute case of judicial activism. To what extent may or should national courts and legislatures deviate from customary international norms that are long-established yet also slowly shifting?

2. The war reparations cases continue to be litigated. And the law evolves. The Italian Court of Cassation recently ruled that Germany could not rely on an

---

[27] *ibid* 203. For further discussion on the concept of implied waiver, *see* Adam C Belsky, Mark Merva, and Naomi Roht-Arriaza *Implied Waiver under the FSIA: A Proposed Exception to Immunity for Violations of Peremptory Norms of International Law* (1989) 77 Calif. L. Rev. 365–415 and Roger O'Keefe *European Convention on State Immunity and International Crimes* (1999) 2 Cam YB of Euro Legal Studies 507–20, 512–18. However, this theory has recently lost support. In *Ferrini v the Federal Republic of Germany*, the Italian Corte di Cassazione supported the Areios Pagos' findings but noted that "a waiver cannot... be envisaged in the abstract, but only encountered in the concrete" (n 12) para 8.2. (translated in De Sena and De Vittor (n 21) 101–2 (emphasis in translation and original). Notably, in line with the separation under international law, the Areios Pagos upheld the plea of immunity at the enforcement stage, Decision of the Greek Supreme Court No 36/2002 (2003) 51 Nomiko Vima 856. The German Federal Court of Justice also held that the Greek courts did not have jurisdiction to hear the case as the underlying acts constituted *acta jure imperii*, their illegality notwithstanding, and therefore it did not recognize the judgment. Distomo, Bundesgerichtshof (BGH), decision of 26 June 2003, III ZR 245/98, published in (2003) NJW 3488. The European Court of Human Rights subsequently rejected the survivors' claim that the German and Greek courts had violated their right of access to a court under Article 6(1) as inadmissible in *Kalogeropoulou et al v Greece and Germany* (App 59021/00).

[30] *See* Maria Panezi *Sovereign immunity and violation of ius cogens norms* AED 6/2002 56 RHDI 199 (2003).

immunity defense to prevent cases concerning war reparations from being heard in Italian courts. The Italian court held that a state's immunity ends where alleged crimes against humanity are at issue. See 2008 Bulletin of International Legal Developments 145.

3. Is the exception for state-sponsored acts of terrorism under the U.S. Foreign Sovereign Immunites Act, considered above, in effect an exception for one kind of jus cogens violation? If so, does the fact that this one was included while others were not imply rejection of exceptions for other kinds of violations?

4. Should human rights claims be considered a separate category from ordinary civil claims such as those involving automobile accidents and commercial activities? Would this have helped Scott Nelson? (See *Saudi Arabia v. Nelson,* above.)

5. Is immunity or nonimmunity a binary choice or is there some incremental step in between those options?

F. Immunity from Execution

Under contemporary regimes of restrictive immunity, various claims against foreign States may be subject to adjudication. The authority to draw the foreign State into court, however, does not also confer the authority to execute a judgment. Indeed, with regard to the execution of judgments, it is necessary to consider entirely separately the questions of immunity from adjudication and immunity from execution. Because the question of execution of judgments arises only after successful litigation against a state party, this doctrine represents the "last bastion of state immunity."* From the perspective of plaintiffs, however, the defendant's immunity from execution means that plaintiff possesses a right without a remedy. We begin with reprinted excerpts from the U.N. Convention, which reflect a methodology for immunity from enforcement that is typical of many regimes.

Articles 18 and 19 of the Convention establish the operating premise that foreign states are generally immune from coercive judicial measures (or "measures of constraint") against their property both pre- and post-judgment. Any enforcement of a judgment against a foreign state, then, must fit within one of the enumerated exceptions. Article 20 clarifies that consent to enforcement is not to be inferred from a state's express consent to the exercise of jurisdiction. Article 21 carves out specific property that is immune from execution even if a plaintiff finds an exception to immunity from enforcement. And Article 24 enumerates certain privileges that foreign states enjoy in court proceedings. When foreign states appear before them, courts do not have at their disposal the full panoply of sanctions and enforcement mechanisms that they typically employ.

---

* Report of the Draft Articles on the Jurisdictional Immunities of States and Their Property, U.N. Doc. A/46/10, reprinted in [1991] Y.B. Int'l L. Comm., Vol. II (2), at 56.

United Nations Convention on Jurisdictional Immunities of States and Their Property (2004)

Article 18

State immunity from pre-judgment measures of constraint

No pre-judgment measures of constraint, such as attachment or arrest, against a property of a State may be taken in connection with a proceeding before a court of another State unless and except to the extent that:

(a) the State has expressly consented to the taking of such measures as indicated:
   (i) by international agreement;
   (ii) by an arbitration agreement or in a written contract; or
   (iii) by a declaration before the court or by a written communication after a dispute between the parties has arisen; or

(b) the State has allocated or earmarked property for the satisfaction of the claim which is the object of that proceeding.

Article 19

State immunity from post-judgment measures of constraint

No post-judgment measures of constraint, such as attachment, arrest or execution, against property of a State may be taken in connection with a proceeding before a court of another State unless and except to the extent that:

(a) the State has expressly consented to the taking of such measures as indicated:
   (i) by international agreement;
   (ii) by an arbitration agreement or in a written contract; or
   (iii) by a declaration before the court or by a written communication after a dispute between the parties has arisen;

(b) the State has allocated or earmarked property for the satisfaction of the claim which is the object of that proceeding; or

(c) it has been established that the property is specifically in use or intended for use by the State for other than government non-commercial purposes and is in the territory of the State of the forum, provided that post-judgment measures of constraint may only be taken against property that has a connection with the entity against which the proceeding was directed.

Article 20

Effect of consent to jurisdiction to measures of constraint

Where consent to the measures of constraint is required under articles 18 and 19, consent to the exercise of jurisdiction under article 7 shall not imply consent to the taking of measures of constraint.

Article 21

Specific categories of property

1. The following categories, in particular, of property of a State shall not be considered as property specifically in use or intended for use by the State for other than government non-commercial purposes under article 19, subparagraph (c):
   (a) property, including any bank account, which is used or intended for use in the performance of the functions of the diplomatic mission of the State or its consular posts, special missions, missions to international organizations or delegations to organs of international organizations or to international conferences;
   (b) property of a military character or used or intended for use in the performance of military functions;
   (c) property of the central bank or other monetary authority of the State;
   (d) property forming part of the cultural heritage of the State or part of its archives and not placed or intended to be placed on sale;
   (e) property forming part of an exhibition of objects of scientific, cultural or historical interest and not placed or intended to be placed on sale.
6. Paragraph 1 is without prejudice to article 18 and article 19, subparagraphs (a) and (b).

Article 24

Privileges and immunities during court proceedings

1. Any failure or refusal by a State to comply with an order of a court of another State enjoining it to perform or refrain from performing a specific act or to produce any document or disclose any other information for the purposes of a proceeding shall entail no consequences other than those which may result from such conduct in relation to the merits of the case. In particular, no fine or penalty shall be imposed on the State by reason of such failure or refusal.
2. A State shall not be required to provide any security, bond, or deposit, however described, to guarantee the payment of judicial costs or expenses in any proceeding to which it is a respondent party before a court of another State.

1. Enforcement Against the State as a Person

In most countries, immunity remains absolute as to forcible measures of execution against the State as a legal person. In other words, injunctions requiring performance or enjoining certain conduct are typically unenforceable. Such orders against the state as a person are thought to be incapable of enforcement without disrupting relations between States.

Nuclear Power Plan Injunction Case (No 2)

Austria, Superior Provincial Court (Oberlandesgericht) of Linz

(Case No 3 R 273/88) 2 March 1989; 86 I.L.R. 579 (1991)

The plaintiff seeks an order against the defendant State that it should immediately cease the construction of the atomic power stations Temelin 1 to 4 in the neighbourhood of Budweis [Czechoslovakia].

The plaintiff argues as follows: He is the owner of real proerpty within the district of the Provincial Court (LG) of Linz [Austira]. The defendant State is engaged, acting as a subject of private law, in the construction of an atomic power station on land of which it is the sole owner in Temelin in the neighbourhood of Budweis. The installation at issue would affect the plaintiff's own land in such a way as to render its use impossible or at least to seriously impair that use. The Provincial Court (LG) of Linz has territorial competence pursuant to Section 81 of the Jurisdictional Statute (JN). The enforcement of any judgment rendered would in all likelihood be impossible in Czechoslovakia (the CSSR). But a judgment could be executed against the defendant within Austria pursuant to Section 355 of the Enforcement Code (EO) by the imposition of a fine. Violation by the defendant of an order to desist from construction could provide a legal basis for a claim to damages. Furthermore, the complaint has substance.

By the judgment under appeal, the court of first instance rejected the claim for lack of territorial competence.... The appeal is unfounded.... The creation of a judgment which would be no more than a worthless piece of paper is not something within the competence of the municipal courts....

[M]unicipal execution by the imposition of a penalty or imprisonment, in order to enforce an order to desist from certain action abroad, constitutes a deliberate attempt at trans-frontier judicial interference and is therefore an infringement of foreign sovereignty.... An order for execution in this case would be addressed to the CSSR (as a State) so that any penalty would have to be enforced against the constitutionally empowered representative organ of that State.... The interested persons in Austria must in this case take up the matter on the plan of public international law through inter-State representations.

Comments and Questions

1. If there is no immunity from adjudication but there is immunity from enforcement in this case, then why not provide the forum for the adjudication but deny enforcement if and when that time comes? Perhaps the "piece of paper" is a sufficient victory for the plaintiff; why deny him that, too?

2. Some judgments of national courts against foreign states have been paid, or served as the basis of settlements, under diplomatic pressure from the forum state. This was the case, for example, regarding Letelier, which is reprinted below. Importantly, then, a judgment against a foreign foreign state, even when judicially unenforceable, may not be a "worthless piece of paper."

3. The incapacity to enjoin or to demand that a foreign state engage in particular conduct is a generally-accepted principle. Article 24 of the Convention codifies this principle, albeit somewhat less directly than most other regimes. Section 13(2) of the U.K. State Immunity Act, for example, provides that "relief shall not be given against a State by way of injunction or order for specific performance…" The Australian Law Commission has taken an independent line: although accepting that no penalty by way of fine or committal may be ordered against any person by reason of a State's failure to comply with an order of the court, it asserts that a court vested with jurisdiction should also have the authority to make appropriate interim and final orders, whether of a procedural or substantive nature. Australian Law Reform Commission, Report No. 24, Foreign State Immunity (1984), para. 137. Although the former (restrictive) language appears in the text of the Australian Foreign States Immunites Act of 1985, the latter (expansive) language does not.

2. Waivers

In most regimes, separate waivers are required for immunity from adjudication and for immunity from execution. In other words, even an explicit waiver of immunity from jurisdiction will not necessarily allow for execution of any judgment obtained thereby against sovereign property. Articles 18 and 19 of the Convention, supra, detail the rigorous requirements for waivers. Most national courts similarly require an express written waiver as to execution immunity. The following excerpt illustrates a waiver-by-contract, but one that was found to be considerably broader than many courts would allow.

A Company Ltd. v. Republic of X

[1990] 2 Lloyd's Rep 520, QBD (Comm Ct.); Dec. 21, 1989

Mr. Justice Saville

In these proceedings the plaintiffs claim some U.S.$12 m. from the Republic of X under an agreement between these parties dated Oct. 13, 1988. The plaintiffs allege that under this agreement the government of X undertook to pay for rice delivered under an earlier agreement made in July, 1988 by delivering to the plaintiffs quantities of coffee and cocoa, to repay by the same method an advance of U.S.$5 m. to be made by the plaintiffs to the State and to pay on demand in U.S. dollars the total amount remaining outstanding if insufficient cocoa and coffee were shipped to settle the indebtedness by May 31, 1989. The plaintiffs claim that insufficient cocoa and coffee was shipped by this date and that, despite demands, the government of X has failed to pay any part of the amounts remaining outstanding.

On Aug. 3, 1989 Mr. Justice Gatehouse, on an ex parte application, gave the plaintiffs leave to issue and serve a writ containing this claim on X out of the jurisdiction. On Aug. 8, 1989 Judge J., again on an ex parte application, granted Mareva relief against X. [As seen in Chapter 1, a Mareva injunction is a pre-judgment remedy intended to prevent a defendant's removal of specific assets, often those related to the underlying claim, from the forum state.]...

Section 1(1) of the State Immunity Act, 1978 provides as follows:

> A State is immune from the jurisdiction of the courts of the United Kingdom except as provided in the following provisions of this Part of this Act.

One of the exceptions to this general immunity is contained in § 2 of the Act, sub-§§ (1) and (2) of which provide as follows:

> (1) A State is not immune as respects proceedings in respect of which it has submitted to the jurisdiction of the courts of the United Kingdom.
> (2) A State may submit after the dispute giving rise to the proceedings has arisen or by a prior written agreement; but a provision in any agreement that it is to be governed by the law of the United Kingdom is not to be regarded as a submission.

Clauses 6 and 7 of the agreement dated Oct. 13, 1988 provide as follows:

> 6. Sovereign Immunity
> The Ministry of Finance hereby waives whatever defence it may have of sovereign immunity for itself or its property (present or subsequently acquired).
>
> 7. Governing Law & Arbitration
> (a) This agreement shall be governed and construed in accordance with the laws of England without reference to conflict of the laws, and A Co. and the Ministry of Finance hereby submit to the jurisdiction of the English courts.
> (b) Any dispute relating to, referring to or arising from the cocoa and coffee actually delivered to A Co. under section 1 above shall be resolved in London under the auspices of and in accordance with the rules and regulations of the Coffee Trade Federation (in respect of coffee) or the Cocoa Association of London (in respect of cocoa).

Despite the reference to the Ministry of Finance in these clauses, it is common ground between the parties that the agreement was made between the State of X and the plaintiffs.

That State has accepted before me that clauses 6 and 7 of the agreement constitute an effective submission to the jurisdiction of the Court in respect of the claims under the agreement. Accordingly, in this case, since the plaintiffs' claims are indisputably under that agreement, the defendants are not immune in respect of these claims from the jurisdiction of the Court by virtue of § 1 of the Act....

The first question concerns the true construction of § 13, sub-§§ (2)-(4) of the State Immunity Act, 1978 and clause 6 of the agreement. The relevant provisions of § 13 are as follows:

> (2) Subject to subsections (3) and (4) below: (a) relief shall not be given against a State by way of injunction or order for specific performance or for the recovery of land or other property; and (b) the property of a State shall not be subject to any process for the enforcement of a judgment or arbitration award or, in an action in rem, for its arrest, detention or sale.

(3) Subsection (2) above does not prevent the giving of any relief or the issue of any process with the written consent of the State concerned, and any such consent (which may be contained in a prior agreement) may be expressed so as to apply to a limited extent or generally; but a provision merely submitting to the jurisdiction of the courts is not to be regarded as a consent for the purposes of this subsection.

(4) Subsection (2)(b) above does not prevent the issue of any process in respect of property which is for the time being in use or intended for use for commercial purposes; but, in a case not falling within section 10 above, this section applies to property of a State party to the European Convention on State Immunity only if:

(a) the process is for enforcing a judgment which is final within the meaning of section 18(1)(b) below and the State has made a declaration under Article 24 of the Convention, or

(b) the process is for enforcing an arbitration award.

The defendants' first contention is that clause 6 of the agreement does not amount to the written consent of the State concerned within the meaning of sub-§ (3), so that the Court has no power to give relief against the State by way of injunction and should in any event not grant Mareva relief in respect of property that could not, by virtue of § 13(2)(b), be taken to satisfy a judgment unless such property fell within section 13(4).

It was submitted on behalf of the State that clause 6 refers to waiver of defences, not to consent to the granting of the relief referred to in § 13(2)(a) or the processes referred to in § 13(2)(b). It was further submitted that since § 13 deals with privileges rather than immunities, and since clause 6 covers only the latter and not the former, there is no written consent to the relief or processes covered by § 13. Finally it was submitted that even if clause 6 was wide enough to cover the processes of enforcement referred to in § 13(2)(b) it was not wide to cover relief by way of injunction or orders for specific performance.

I am not persuaded by any of these arguments. It seems to me that, read in the context of what was undoubtedly a commercial bargain between the parties, the intent and purpose of the clause is quite clear, namely, to put the State on the same footing as a private individual so that neither in respect of the State nor its property would any question of sovereign immunity arise in connection with the State's obligations to the plaintiffs under the agreement....

It is not, of course, necessary to decide whether clause 6 does amount to consent to other forms of injunction, but to my mind it clearly does amount to the agreement and consent of the State that its property can be made the subject of a Mareva injunction.

3. Scope of Immunity from Execution

Some immunity regimes, such as the Convention, require a "nexus" between a commercial property against which a judgment may be executed and the underlying claim upon which the judgment to be executed is based. See Article 19(c). This burden can be a difficult one for plaintiffs since they must be fortunate enough to find property in the forum state that is related to the subject matter of the claim. The U.S. Foreign Sovereign Immunites Act eases this burden with regard to actions against state agencies and instrumentalities—as distinguished from those against the state itself—any of whose commercial assets in the United States may be executed upon, whether or not used in connection with the activity on which the plaintiff's claim was based. But plaintiffs with contract claims may be able to find tangible property within the forum that is used by the State for other than government noncommercial purposes. Many tort plaintiffs may be less lucky. A nexus requirement (1) assures that an antecedent basis for adjudicative jurisdiction exists; and (2) limits the property at issue to satisfy the judgment to resources that had already been allocated to a commercial transaction. Letelier illustrates an application of the nexus requirement that appears in the U.S. Foreign Sovereign Immunities Act.

Letelier v. Republic of Chile

748 F.2d 790 (2nd Cir. 1984)

CARDAMONE, CIRCUIT JUDGE

The critical question posed on this appeal is whether the assets of a foreign state's wholly owned airline are subject to execution to satisfy a default judgment obtained against the foreign state. The district court, believing that Congress under the Foreign Sovereign Immunities Act of 1976, 28 U.S.C. §§ 1602–11 (1982) (FSIA or the Act), would not have established a right to jurisdiction over the foreign state without also providing a remedy, ordered execution. We reverse although we recognize that our decision may preclude the plaintiffs from collecting on their judgment. How one wishes to decide a case comes lightly to mind, on a wing; but often how one must decide it comes arduously, weighed down by somber thought. To rule otherwise here would only illustrate once again that hard cases make bad law.

Facts

Orlando Letelier, the former Chilean Ambassador to the United States, his aide, Michael Moffitt, and Moffitt's wife, Ronni, were riding to work in Washington, D.C. in September, 1976 when an explosive device planted under the driver's seat in their car was detonated killing both Letelier and Ronni Moffitt and seriously injuring Michael Moffitt. That assassination gives rise to the present appeal.

Investigation by agencies of the United States government into these murders revealed the identity of nine assassins and their alleged connection to the government of Chile. Of the nine only Michael Vernon Townley, an American citizen working for Chilean intelligence, was convicted of a criminal offense. Three of those indicted were members of the Cuban Nationalist Movement who, although found guilty in the trial court, had their convictions reversed on appeal. See United States v. Sampol, 636 F.2d 621, 684 (D.C.Cir. 1980). Of the other five individuals indicted, none was brought to trial: three were Chilean nationals that Chile refused to extradite, and two remain at large.

In August 1978 the personal representatives of Letelier and Moffitt instituted a civil tort action in the United States District Court for the District of Columbia against the indicted individuals and the Republic of Chile. The complaint asserted five causes of action: (1) a conspiracy to deprive Letelier and Moffitt of their civil rights under 42 U.S.C. § 1985; (2) assault and battery; (3) reckless transportation and detonation of explosives; (4) violation of the "law of nations" (international law); and (5) murder of an internationally protected person under 18 U.S.C. § 1116. The complaint alleged that the noncommercial tort exception of § 1605(a)(5) of the FSIA applied and that Chile was not entitled to sovereign immunity in the tort action.

All defendants defaulted, although Chile sent two Diplomatic Notes to the United States Department of State asserting its sovereign immunity and that the allegations against it were false. The State Department forwarded these Notes to the clerk of the district court. In August 1978 the trial court granted default judgments against the individual defendants. During 1979 and 1980 the district court heard plaintiffs' motion for a default judgment against Chile, see Letelier v. Republic of Chile, 488 F. Supp. 665 (D.D.C. 1980), and finally resolved that motion. See Letelier v. Republic of Chile, 502 F. Supp. 259 (D.D.C. 1980). In the former case, the court ruled that it had subject matter jurisdiction pursuant to the exception to immunity found in § 1605(a)(5) of the Act. In the latter case the trial court relying on Townley's testimony at the criminal trial, where he had pled guilty and testified for the prosecution, granted a default judgment against the Republic of Chile and awarded plaintiffs over five million dollars including interest, compensatory and punitive damages, counsel fees and out of pocket expenses. The Republic of Chile did not take an appeal from either of these judgments.

The resulting judgment against the Republic of Chile was entered in the United States District Court for the District of Columbia. Plaintiffs subsequently filed the judgment in the United States District Court for the Southern District of New York, see 28 U.S.C. § 1963 (1982), for the purpose of executing on the property interests that The Republic of Chile has in the Chilean national airline, Linea Aerea Nacional-Chile or LAN, which is located in New York, and for the appointment of Michael Moffitt as a receiver of those interests to satisfy the judgment against Chile pursuant to New York's CPLR 5228 and Fed. R. Civ. P. 69. The application for execution against LAN's assets came before District Court Judge Morris E. Lasker. LAN moved to dismiss claiming that it should not be held to answer for Chilean debts and that its assets were immune from execution. Relying upon a recent decision of the United States Supreme Court, First. National City Bank v. Banco Para El Comercio Exterior de Cuba (Bancec), 462 U.S. 611 (1983), which based a decision to disregard separate corporation identities on "international equitable principles," Judge Lasker first held in an opinion and order dated July 28, 1983 that, were the facts as asserted, LAN's role in the assassination was commercial activity under the Act. He further held that to adhere to LAN's separate corporate identity would, as in Bancec, violate equitable principles. Letelier v. Republic of Chile, 567 F. Supp. 1490, 1496 (S.D.N.Y. 1983).

Having concluded that LAN's assets were subject to execution to satisfy a judgment against Chile, the district court concluded that the language of § 1610(a)(2) did not limit execution only to commercial assets used for commercial purposes, as LAN claimed, but also permitted execution to satisfy tort judgments "so long as the assets on which the judgment creditor seeks to execute were also used commercially in the activity giving rise to the claim." Id. at 1499. The rationale for this reading of the statute was that a statute should not be interpreted to create a right without a remedy. The court reasoned that if jurisdictional immunity is lifted, the presumption is that there will be a right to execute. Id. at 1500 & n.7.

Plaintiffs later sought discovery against The Republic of Chile by serving it with interrogatories and requests to produce documents and admit facts. Chile refused to comply and again filed Diplomatic Notes asserting its refusal to recognize either the validity of the default judgment or the district court's jurisdiction in the supplementary proceedings for enforcement. Judge Lasker in an order dated December 20, 1983 granted plaintiff's motions for Rule 37 sanctions against LAN consisting of adverse findings of fact that provided a basis to disregard LAN's juridical separateness, and appointed Moffitt as a receiver of LAN's assets in the United States. 575 F. Supp. 1217 (S.D.N.Y. 1983). From the rulings of July 28 and December 20, 1983 LAN has appealed and raised a number of issues.

Discussion

The principal issue is whether LAN's assets may be executed upon to satisfy the judgment obtained in the District of Columbia against Chile. This discussion necessarily focuses on the Foreign Sovereign Immunities Act of 1976, which is the exclusive source of subject matter jurisdiction over all suits involving foreign states or their instrumentalities. Rex v. CIA Pervana de Vapores, S.A., 660 F.2d 61, 62 (3d Cir. 1981), cert. denied, 456 U.S. 926 (1982). According to § 1604, foreign states are immune from suit in our courts unless the conduct complained of comes within the exceptions set forth in § § 1605 to 1607 of the Act. Similarly, under § 1609 foreign states are immune from execution upon judgments obtained against them, unless an exception set forth in §§ 1610 or 1611 or of the FSIA applies.

The judgment creditors claim that § 1610(a)(2) allows them to execute upon LAN's assets in this case. Section 1610(a)(2) provides:

> The property in the United States of a foreign state... used for a commercial activity in the United States, shall not be immune from attachment in aid of execution, or from execution...if...the property is or was used for the commercial activity upon which the claim is based....

We consider first whether LAN's separate juridical existence may be ignored, thereby making its assets "[t]he property in the United States of a foreign state."

I. Separate Juridical Existence

In Bancec the Supreme Court determined whether a claim of a foreign agency plaintiff was subject to a set-off for the debts of its parent government. Bancec deserves close scrutiny because it provides a conceptual framework for resolving plaintiff's assertion that LAN's assets should be treated as assets of Chile and because the district court relied on it to reach that conclusion.

In Bancec, the Cuban bank of the same name brought suit against Citibank to collect on a letter of credit issued in its favor in 1960. Citibank counterclaimed arguing that it was entitled to set-off amounts as compensation due it for the Cuban government's expropriation of Citibank's assets in Cuba. We ruled that as Bancec was not the alter ego of the Cuban government, it could not be held to account for Cuban debts. The Supreme Court reversed. Relying on the Act's legislative history, the Court noted that it was not intended to affect the substantive law of liability of a foreign state or the attribution of liability among its entities and proceeded to resolve the appeal on "equitable principles." The Bancec Court recognized that "government instrumentalities established as juridical entities distinct and independent from their sovereign should normally be treated as such." 103 S. Ct. at 2600. FSIA's legislative history provided support for that conclusion:

Section 1610(b) will not permit execution against the property of one agency or instrumentality to satisfy a judgment against another, unrelated agency or instrumentality. There are compelling reasons for this. If U.S. law did not respect the separate juridical identities of different agencies or instrumentalities, it might encourage foreign jurisdictions to disregard the juridical divisions between different U.S. corporations or between a U.S. corporation and its independent subsidiary. However, a court might find that property held by one agency is really the property of another. H.R.Rep. No. 94-1487, pp. 29–30, U.S.Code Cong. & Admin. News 1976, 6604, pp. 6628, 6629 (citation omitted.)

The Supreme Court concluded in Bancec that the presumption of separateness had been overcome. It reasoned that the real beneficiary of any recovery would be the Cuban government, and that Cuba should not be permitted to obtain relief in American courts without answering for its seizure of Citibank's assets. The Court commented that "Cuba cannot escape liability for acts in violation of international law simply by retransferring the assets to separate juridical entities." 103 S. Ct. at 2603.

Thus, Bancec rests primarily on two propositions. First, Courts may use set-off as a unique, equitable remedy to prevent a foreign government from eluding liability for its own acts when it affirmatively seeks recovery in an American judicial proceeding. See National City Bank v. Republic of China, 348 U.S. 356 (1955). The broader message is that foreign states cannot avoid their obligations by engaging in abuses of corporate form. The Bancec Court held that a foreign state instrumentality is answerable just as its sovereign parent would be if the foreign state has abused the corporate form, or where recognizing the instrumentality's separate status works a fraud or an injustice.

The district court analyzed the present case in light of Bancec and ruled that Chile's alleged use of LAN to transport Townley and explosives to the United States were "significant steps in the conspiracy" that if proven "would constitute a gross abuse of the corporate form." 567 F. Supp. at 1496. Accordingly, it held, "If Chile ignored LAN's separate existence in accomplishing the wrong, it may not invoke that separate existence in order to deny the injured a remedy." Id. at 1496.

The district judge "found" the following facts based "on the record" and "established" by evidentiary sanctions imposed pursuant to Rule 37(b)(2)(A): From January 1975 through January 1979 LAN's assets and facilities were under the direct control of Chile, which had the power to use them; Chile could have decreed LAN's dissolution and taken over property interests held in LAN's name; Chile, through its agencies, officers, and employees, intentionally used facilities and personnel of LAN to plan and carry out its conspiracy to assassinate Orlando Letelier by (a) transporting Michael Vernon Townley between Chile and the United States, (b) transporting explosives on several occasions, (c) assisting with currency transactions involved in paying off the co-conspirators in the assassination, (d) providing a meeting place for the co-conspirators, (e) arranging for Townley to exit the United States under an alias after the assassination. By using LAN in these endeavors, the district court found, Chile ignored LAN's separate existence and abused the corporate form.

In our view this is not the sort of "abuse" that overcomes the presumption of separateness established by Bancec. Joint participation in a tort is not the "classic" abuse of corporate form to which the Supreme Court referred. In Bancec the Court relied by analogy on the domestic law of private corporations that ignores separate juridical status "where a corporate entity is so extensively controlled by its owner that a relationship of principal and agent is created," where "the corporate form…is interposed to defeat legislative policies," or where recognition of corporate form "'would work fraud or injustice.'" 103 S. Ct. at 2601. The facts that the district court "found" here do not add up to anything that resembles the abuses in the decisions cited in Bancec. None of these facts shows that Chile ignored LAN's separate status. Instead, they simply demonstrate that Michael Townley was able to enlist the cooperation of certain LAN pilots and officials with whom he had a pre-existing social relationship in pursuing his sinister goal. There was no finding that LAN's separate status was established to shield its owners from liability for their torts or that Chile ignored ordinary corporate formalities.

Plaintiffs had the burden of proving that LAN was not entitled to separate recognition. A creditor seeking execution against an apparently separate entity must prove "the property to be attached is subject to execution." Palmiter v. Action, Inc., 548 F. Supp. 1166, 1172 (N.D. Ind. 1982). The evidence submitted by the judgment creditors does not reveal abuse of corporate form of the nature or degree that Bancec found sufficient to overcome the presumption of separate existence. As both Bancec and the FSIA legislative history caution against too easily overcoming the presumption of separateness, we decline to extend the Bancec holding to do so in this case.

II. Commercial Activity

Even assuming the district court was correct in disregarding LAN's corporate form and finding that LAN's assets were Chile's property in the United States, § 1610(a)(2) also requires that the property be "used for the commercial activity upon which the claim is based." In permitting execution against LAN's assets the court below essentially concluded that LAN's activities aided Townley in the assassination and constituted the "commercial activities" that § 1610(a)(2) requires. We cannot agree because a consistent application of the Act, analysis of the background of its enactment, its language and legislative history, and the case law construing it compel the opposite conclusion.

We first note that the district court for the District of Columbia found that Chile lost its immunity from jurisdiction pursuant to § 1605(a)(5), the "tortious activity" exception to jurisdictional immunity. Section 1605(a)(5) specifically states that it applies to situations "not otherwise encompassed in paragraph (2)." Section 1605(a)(2) is the commercial activity exception. This language suggests that the commercial activity exception to jurisdictional immunity under (2) and the tort exception under (5) are mutually exclusive. If the district court in the District of Columbia lifted jurisdictional immunity based on its finding that the activities complained of were tortious, not commercial, it is inconsistent for this court to lift execution immunity based on a finding that the activities were commercial.

Our disagreement with the finding that LAN's activities were commercial rests on more than the resulting lack of symmetry in application of the FSIA. If LAN, as the trial court found, acted in complicity with the Chilean secret police in the assassination, its activities had nothing to do with its place in commerce. The nature of its course of conduct could not have been as a merchant in the marketplace. Its activities would have been those of the foreign state: governmental, not private or commercial....

FSIA § 1602 contains the findings and declaration of purpose for the Act. That section states:

> Under international law, states are not immune from the jurisdiction of foreign courts insofar as their commercial activities are concerned, and their commercial property may be levied upon for the satisfaction of judgments rendered against them in connection with their commercial activities. (emphasis furnished).

Under § 1603(d) commercial activity is defined as "either a regular course of commercial conduct or a particular commercial transaction or act." S.Rep. No. 94-1310, 94th Cong., 2d Sess. (1976) (Senate Report) recognizes that activities fall along a "spectrum" bounded by "commercial" behavior on one end of the spectrum and "governmental" activity on the other:

> Certainly, if an activity is customarily carried on for profit, its commercial nature could readily be assumed. At the other end of the spectrum, a single contract, if of the same character as a contract which might be made by a private person, could constitute a "particular transaction or act."

Id. at 15. The Senate Report contains examples of commercial activities:

> Activities such as a foreign government's sale of a service or product, its leasing of property, its borrowing of money, its employment or engagement of laborers, clerical staff or public relations or marketing agents or its investment in a security of an American corporation, would be among those included within the definition.

Id. at 16. Congress specifically designed the execution immunity rules to "conform" to the jurisdictional immunity provisions of § 1605. H.R.Rep. No. 94-1487, 94th Cong.2d Sess. (1976), reprinted in 1976 U.S. Code Cong. & Ad.News 6604, 6626 (House Report).

Congress intended the "essential nature" of given behavior to determine its status for purposes of the commercial activities exception, and gave the courts a "great deal of latitude" to decide this issue. Id. at 6615. The legislative history makes clear that courts should not deem activity "commercial" as a whole simply because certain aspects of it are commercial. The example given is that the AID programs remain governmental even though they involve behavior traditionally performed by private persons....

A case that involved facts analogous to those before us is Arango v. Guzman Travel Adivsors Corp., 621 F.2d 1371 (5th Cir. 1980), which was decided under § 1605, not § 1610. In Arango, the plaintiffs sued the wholly owned, national airline of the Dominican Republic after being expelled from a flight because that country's officials would not permit them entry. Although the Court dismissed the appeal because it was taken from a non-appealable order, it discussed (in dicta) whether the "commercial activity" exception of § 1605(a)(2) would allow plaintiffs to bring their tort action against the airline. The Arango court considered the airline's actions in rerouting plaintiffs noncommercial because it concluded that the airline acted merely as the agent of the Dominican government. Id. at 1379.

We agree with the Arango analysis. The Arango court found that alleged "kidnapping" by a foreign state is not "commercial activity" under the FSIA because a private person cannot lawfully engage in that activity. 567 F. Supp. at 1501. A private person cannot lawfully engage in murder any more than he can in kidnapping or criminal assault. Carriage of passengers and packages is an activity in which a private person could engage. But it is not for those activities that LAN's assets are being executed against. Rather, plaintiffs assert that LAN itself participated in the assassination and essentially accuse LAN of being a co-conspirator or joint tortfeasor. In other words, LAN is accused of engaging in state-sponsored terrorism the purpose of which, irrelevant under the FSIA, was to assassinate an opponent of the Chilean government. Politically motivated assassinations are not traditionally the function of private individuals. They can scarcely be considered commercial activity. Viewed in this light, LAN's participation, if any, in the assassination is not commercial activity that falls within the § 1610(a)(2) exception and its assets therefore are not stripped of immunity.

III. Right Without a Remedy

The district court's principal concern with finding LAN immune from execution on its assets was that "[h]aving determined to grant jurisdiction in both commercial and tort claims, it appears out of joint to conclude that Congress intended the surprising result of allowing only commercial creditors to execute on their judgments," 567 F. Supp. at 1499–1500. Hence, it concluded that Congress would not create a right without a remedy. Few would take issue with the district judge's comment as an abstract principle of statutory interpretation. Nevertheless, when drafting the FSIA Congress took into account the international community's view of sovereign immunity. That makes a world of difference in the Act's interpretation. The Act's history and the contemporaneous passage of similar European legislation strongly support the conclusion that under the circumstances at issue in this case Congress did in fact create a right without a remedy. Congress wanted the execution provisions of the FSIA to "remedy, in part, the [pre-FSIA] predicament of a plaintiff who has obtained a judgment against a foreign state." House Report, supra, at 6605–06 (emphasis added). It is to that pre-FSIA plaintiff's predicament that we now turn.

To put the execution immunity provisions of the 1976 Act in proper perspective it is helpful to examine them in light of the European Convention on State Immunity and Additional Protocol adopted in 1972 and the United Kingdom's enactment of The State Immunity Act of 1978. Although these two codifications contain vastly different approaches to execution of judgments, they are relevant to this discussion in that neither Act ensures that a party may execute on a judgment against a foreign state by attaching property, even if it may validly assert jurisdiction over that foreign state. See Note, The International Law Association Draft Convention on Foreign Sovereign Immunity: A Comparative Approach, 23 Va. J. Int'l L. 635, 658 (1983).

The European Convention, because of its members' conflicting views, decided not to provide machinery for the enforcement of judgments by execution. The Convention relied instead on the obligation of an individual State to honor judgments taken against it. A judgment creditor must ordinarily obtain satisfaction through executive or administrative channels, though when both States involved have made certain declarations the European Court of Human Rights provides a judicial remedy. ILA Draft Convention at 662–63. In effect, the European Convention leaves execution by judgment creditors at the mercy of the defendant State's policies. This is scarcely surprising as Article 2, paragraph 7 of the Charter of the United Nations declared the same rule 37 years earlier. Paragraph 7 prohibits the United Nations from intervening "in matters which are essentially within the domestic jurisdiction of any state." S. Goodrich & E. Hambro, Charter of the United Nations, Commentary and Documents 65 (1946).

The State Immunity Act like the FSIA grants general immunity from execution over a foreign state's property except that, unlike the FSIA, which permits execution only on property upon which the claim is based, courts in England may execute on property in use or intended to be used for commercial purposes. ILA Draft Convention at 661. Hence, The State Immunity Act restricts immunity from execution more than the FSIA and subjects any property of the foreign state used for commercial purposes to execution.

The FSIA distinguishes between execution against property of an agency or instrumentality of a foreign state, which may be executed against regardless of whether the property was used for the activity on which the claim is based under § 1610(b)(2), and the property of the foreign state itself, which may be executed against only when the property was used for the commercial activity on which the claim is based under § 1610(a)(2). In so distinguishing, Congress sharply restricted immunity from execution against agencies and instrumentalities, but was more cautious when lifting immunity from execution against property owned by the State itself. Congress passed the FSIA on the background of the views of sovereignty expressed in the 1945 charter of the United Nations and the 1972 enactment of the European Convention, which left the availability of execution totally up to the debtor state, and its own understanding as the legislative history demonstrates, that prior to 1976 property of foreign states was absolutely immune from execution. House Report at 6606. It is plain then that Congress planned to and did lift execution immunity "in part." Yet, since it was not Congress' purpose to lift execution immunity wholly and completely, a right without a remedy does exist in the circumstances here. Our task must be to read the Act as it is expressed, and apply it according to its expressions.

Conclusion

We hold therefore that the Foreign Sovereign Immunities Act does not allow execution against the assets of LAN, the Chilean National Airlines.[4] The court below improperly ignored defendant LAN's separate juridical status from the Republic of Chile. Ordinarily, we would remand for further evidentiary hearings on the separateness issue, but we are further persuaded, even were LAN and Chile found to be alter egos, that Congress did not provide for execution against a foreign state's property under the circumstances of this case. Congress provided for execution against property used in commercial activity upon which the claim is based. An act of political terrorism is not the kind of commercial activity that Congress contemplated. Accordingly, we reverse the orders appealed from and dismiss the supplementary proceedings.

---

[4] Although tenuous, other remedies may still be possible. Chile itself may decide as an act of international good-will to honor the judgment of the United States District Court for the District of Columbia. Alternatively, the United States may be persuaded to bring this claim before some international tribunal as it did in Z&F Assets Realization Corp. v. Hull, 311 U.S. 470, 487 (1941), or there may be a forum in South America or elsewhere equivalent to the European Court of Human Rights that will provide a judicial remedy.

Comments and Questions

1. Are you outraged? Was the Court right? Why or why not? Why did Congress not make it easier to enforce tort judgments against foreign states?

2. Why would the FSIA make it easier to enforce judgments against state agencies or instrumentalities than against the state itself?

3. The Sovereign Immunity Acts of Canada, the United Kingdom, and Australia allow execution without any requirement of a nexus to the underlying claim. Thus any property in the forum used for a commercial purpose is subject to execution.

4. Congress has since made several efforts to provide remedies for plaintiffs with rights against states that sponsor terrorism. The Foreign Sovereign Immunities Act now provides an exception to enforcement immunity if "the judgment relates to a claim for which the foreign is not immune under Section 1605(a)(7), regardless of whether the property is or was involved with the act upon which the claim is based." 28 U.S.C. § 1610(a)(7).

4. Specific Sovereign Assets

Like most national regimes of sovereign immunity, the U.N. Convention provides additional protection for certain classifications of property. See Article 21, supra. These classifications, including diplomatic and embassy property and central bank property receive preferable treatment because (1) they strongly implicate the distinctly sovereign powers of states, and (2) they constitute the form of state property most commonly present in a foreign jurisdiction, but with the understanding that the forum state will not exercise jurisdictional power over it. One might contend that these provisions are unnecessary since the only state property subject to execution is that which is used by the State for other than government noncommercial purposes. See Article 19(c). Yet the additional layer of protection is a common feature of most national regimes.

X v. Republic of Philippines Embassy Bank Account

German Federal Constitutional Court

Bundesverfassungsgericht, vol. 46, p. 342; 13 December 1977

United Nations, Materials on Jurisdictional Immunities of States and Their Property, p. 297 (1982)

In 1975 the judgement creditor in the original proceedings obtained from the Land Court at Bonn a judgment by default against the Republic of the Philippines for the payment of DM 95,231.86 plus interest and costs. The action at trial arose from a rent contract concluded between the creditor and the Republic of the Philippines in 1966 for a house which the Republic of the Philippines had leased for use as offices by its Embassy in the Federal Republic of Germany. On the basis of the enforceable judgement by default, the creditor obtained from the district Court at

Bonn an attachment and assignment order against the Republic of the Philippines under which the reputed claim of the Republic of the Philippines against the "Bonn-Bad Godesberg branch of the D Bank AG...—the garnishee—for payment of the present and all future surpluses (balances) due to the debtor, upon establishment of the balance, from existing transactions on current account, and in particular through accounts Nos...., and all reputed claims and demands...arising from transfers through the aforementioned accounts to and for the crediting of all future receipts, the continued repayment of balances and the execution of transfers to third parties" was attached and assigned to the creditor for collection in the amount attached.

The Republic of the Philippines made a written submission to the District Court at Bonn objecting to the attachment and assignment order on the ground that the Embassy's account was not subject to German jurisdiction. The District Court at Bonn suspended the proceedings in accordance with article 100 (II) of the Basic Law and submitted the question which appears in leading principles 8 and 11 to the Federal Constitutional Court for a ruling.

[After an extensive review of the practice of many States the court concluded that the rules of international law do not impose an outright prohibition on execution by the State of the forum against a foreign State. It then addressed the question whether customary international law imposes material limits on execution.]

1. There is an established general custom among States, backed by a legal consensus, whereby the State of the forum is prohibited by international law from levying execution, under judicial writs against a foreign State, on property of the foreign State which is situated or present in the State of the forum and is used for sovereign purposes of the foreign State, except with the latter's consent. It is true that complete agreement is lacking in State practice concerning the extent of the property which, by its nature, is protected by State immunity; whereas, under the United States Foreign Sovereign Immunities Act of 1976, only property which is or was used for a commercial activity of the foreign State upon which the material claim that is asserted is based is in principle subject to execution (see sect. 1610 (a)(2)), the Italian and Swiss courts lay stress on whether the property on which execution is to be levied is actually used or is intended to be used for non-sovereign or sovereign purposes of the foreign State. For the purposes of the present submission proceedings, there is no need for us to take a conclusive position, as regards German law, on these distinctions and their legal consequences, since there is at least a general agreement and an established custom among States to the effect that, under general international law, property in the State of the forum which is actually used for sovereign purposes of the foreign State is not subject to execution. Occasional doubts—such as those which are mentioned in the statement of position by the Federal Government concerning the levying of execution on embassy accounts, but which the Federal Government itself does not share—cannot alter the fact that a general rule of international law does exist on that point. State practice, as evidenced in treaty practice, in legislation and in the decisions of national courts, and the international law literature are unanimous on this question....

2. As regards trial proceedings, the Federal Constitutional Court has ruled that the determination of whether a State activity is, by its legal nature, a sovereign or a non-sovereign act will in principle have to be effected according to the national law applicable in each case, since international law, at least as a rule, contains no criteria for establishing that distinction (BVerfGE 16, 27 (62 et seq.) = NJW 1963, 1732). The court acknowledged that making the determination of that point a matter for the national law applicable in each in each case rendered the application of general international law more difficult and worked against the desirable uniformity of the law. However, that disadvantage was mitigated by the fact that international law placed limits on the determination, according to national law, of a State activity as an act jure gestionis. Under international law, national law could be applied in that connexion only with the proviso that State acts which, in the view of the overwhelming majority of States, fell within the sphere of State authority in the narrow and true sense could not be taken out of the sphere of sovereignty and thus could not be stripped of immunity. In exceptional cases, international law might require that an activity of a foreign State should be regarded as an act jure imperii because it pertained to the very core of State authority, even though it would have to be regarded under national law as a private-law and not a public-law activity (BVerfGE 16, 27 (63 et seq.) = NJW 1963, 1732).

In the case before us, where only the admissibility of measures of execution in respect of claims arising out of the general current account of the embassy of a foreign State is at issue, there is no need for a ruling on whether the determination that an item of property is used for sovereign purposes must generally be made on the basis of appropriate principles; for in the case of property used for performance of the official functions of the diplomatic mission of a foreign State in the State of the forum, that determination involves special rules of international law which, notwithstanding the fact that they have been partially codified in the Vienna Convention on Diplomatic Relations, constitute general rules of international law within the meaning of article 25 of the Basic Law. They derive both from the principle of the inviolability of diplomatic missions and from the jurisdictional immunity of the foreign State in respect of the official function of its diplomatic mission.

3. According to the established view, which began to emerge even before Grotius (De jure belli ac pacis, L. II, c. XVIII, 9) and Bynkershoek (Foro Legatorum, sec. ed. (1744), Cap. XVI, XXIII), preventive measures or measure of execution against a foreign State may not, under international law, be levied on property which at the relevant time was being used by its diplomatic mission for the performance of its official functions (see, with references in each case, van Praag, Jurisdiction et droit international public (1915), pp. 357 et seq.; C.E. Wilson, Diplomatic Privileges and Immunities 1967), pp. 1 et seq.; Gmür, Gerichtsbarkeit über fremde Staaten (1948), p. 134; Verdross, Völkerrecht, 5th ed. (1964), pp. 338 et seq.; Habscheid, BerDGVR, loc. cit., pp. 264 et seq.). The principle of international law ne impediatur legatio precludes such measures where they might impair the exercise of diplomatic duties, thus, the Federal Constitutional Court has ruled that German jurisdiction in respect of trial proceedings against a foreign State in which consent is sought to rectification of the land register regarding the ownership of premises

used for diplomatic purposes is not precluded by any general rule of international law, because this would not impair the ability of the diplomatic mission to function (BVerfGE 15, 25 (43) = NJW 1963, 435).

Because of the difficulties of delimitation involved in judging whether that ability to function is endangered, and because of the potential for abuse, general international law makes the area of protection enjoyed by the foreign State very wide and refers to the typical abstract danger, but not to the specific threat to the ability of the diplomatic mission to function posed by measures on the part of the receiving State (see Habscheid, BerDGVR, loc. cit., p. 206). For instance, article 22, paragraph 3, of the Vienna Convention on Diplomatic Relations of 18 April 1961, which codifies general international law on the subject, provides that the premises of the missions, their furnishings and other property thereon and the means of transport of the mission shall be immune from search, requisition, attachment or execution. However, this rule of inviolability is not exclusive in the sense that these and other items of property might not also enjoy immunity under international law by reason of the protection afforded to the official functions of the diplomatic mission of the sending State. It is true that, so far as can be seen, this question was not further discussed from the standpoint of inviolability... in the United Nations International Law Commission, whose draft articles constituted the basis for the Vienna Conference.... However, the preamble to the Vienna Convention affirms that the rules of customary international law should continue to govern questions not expressly regulated by the provisions of the Convention.... This and similar treaty provisions confirm the general rule of international law that property used by the sending State for the performance of its diplomatic functions in any event enjoys immunity even if it does not fall within the material or spatial scope of the inviolability provision in article 22 of the Vienna Convention (as agreed by Schaumann, BerDGVR, loc. cit., p. 148, who deduces this from the general immunity of States, although "supported" by diplomatic immunity; see also article 23 of the Harvard draft, loc. cit., AJIL 26 (1932), Suppl., p. 707).

4. (a) The question whether, under general international law, claims arising out of a general current Bank account which the sending State maintains for its diplomatic mission in the receiving State for the purpose of covering and paying the embassy's costs and expenses share the special protection afforded to diplomatic missions is answered by reference to the special purpose of the international-law protection in favour of diplomatic missions. The purpose of both inviolability and immunity in this field is to ensure the unimpeded functioning of the diplomatic mission of the sending State in the receiving State as regards the performance of its diplomatic duties (see C. E. Wilson, Diplomatic Privileges and Immunities, pp. 19 et seq., with many examples from State practice). Under article 3 of the Vienna Convention on Diplomatic Relations, which circumscribes general international law on this point, the functions of a diplomatic mission include:

(a) representing the sending State in the receiving State;
(b) protecting in the receiving State the interest of the sending State and of its nationals, within the limits permitted by international law;

(c) negotiating with the Government of the receiving State;
(d) ascertaining by all lawful means conditions and developments in the receiving State, and reporting thereon to the Government of the sending State;
(e) promoting friendly relations between the sending State and the receiving State, and developing their economic, cultural and scientific relations.

Obviously, the use of funds is essential for the performance of these functions. The maintenance of such funds in connexion with these functions, and the organization and administration of the financial settlement of the diplomatic mission's costs and expenses by the sending State, belong directly to the area of the functions and duties of a diplomatic mission (see also Cahier, Le droit diplomatique contemporain (1962), p. 210, where funds in an embassy's Bank account are expressly stated to be covered by the inviolability rule.)

It is immaterial for our purposes whether the receiving State is obligated under general international law to allow the sending State the possibility of maintaining Bank accounts in the receiving State in order to pay the costs and expenses of its embassy. If, however, the receiving State does afford this possibility and the sending State makes use of it in accordance with the laws of the receiving State, the immunity of the sending State in respect of its claims and other rights arising out of such an account is not extinguished simply because, and to the extent that, the legal relationship between the sending State and the Bank is to be regarded under the laws of the receiving State as non-sovereign. Yet it must be borne in mind that the sending State is not in principle in a position, by virtue of its own sovereign authority, to attribute sovereign status, with binding effect on the laws of the receiving State, to property or rights which directly serve the purposes of the exercise of its diplomatic functions or of the continued operation of its diplomatic mission, for instance by declaring that certain property is public property within the meaning of the laws of the receiving State. In this respect, the sending State is largely bound by the laws of the receiving State. Nevertheless, if those laws enable it, for instance, to act only under private law, that must not be allowed to abridge the immunity afforded by international law with an eye to the ability of its diplomatic mission to function. The financial settlement of the costs and expenses of an embassy through a general current account of the sending State maintained with a Bank in the receiving State pertains directly to the continued discharge of the diplomatic functions of the sending State, notwithstanding the fact that some transactions through such an account may, as regards relations with the Bank or with third parties, be effected in the context of legal relationships or forms of activity which can, by their legal nature, be termed acts jure gestionis. Claims of the sending State on the Bank arising out of such an account therefore enjoy, under general international law, at least the immunity afforded to diplomatic missions in respect of measures of execution.

Taking any other view of the matter would mean that the executing authorities of receiving State might have to ascertain the existence of funds in such an account and the purposes for which the sending State intended such funds or parts of them to be used. In the case of a general current account, it may be doubtful for the purposes of German law, even from the standpoint of the adequate availability of the property to be attached, whether criteria for determining that some of the assets may be liable to attachment can be arrived at in this way (similar doubts were expressed with regard to French law by the Court of Justice of Aix-en-Provence, judgment of 14 February 1966, in Statni Banka et Banque d'Etat tchécoslovaque c. Englander, Clunet 1966, 846, reversed by the Court of Cassation in its judgment of 11 February 1969, Clunet 1969, 923; in Clerget c. Représentation commerciale de la République démocratique du Viet-Nam, judgment of 2 November 1971, Clunet 1972, 267, the Court of Cassation refused to allow the attachment of a Bank account because the origin and intended use of the funds had not been established during the proceedings); but even if this should be possible in isolated cases with respect to claims arising out of such an account, the danger of intrusion into the internal sphere of operation of the diplomatic mission of the sending State is usually evoked and, except with the consent of the sending State, that is prohibited outright under international law relating to embassies. Moreover, for the executing authorities of the receiving State to require the sending State, without its consent, to provide details concerning the existence or the past, present or future purposes of funds in such an account would constitute interference, contrary to international law, in matters within the exclusive competence of the sending State. On the other hand, general international law does not prohibit asking the sending State to substantiate the fact that a given account is one that is used for the continued performance of the functions of its diplomatic mission. As regards the substance and form of such substantiation, the State of the forum must of course, in accordance with international law, be satisfied with due assurances from a competent authority of the sending State.

(b) No radical objections to this finding can be deduced from the practice of State authorities responsible for foreign affairs, from the rulings of national courts or from the international-law literature. As far as can be seen, the levying of execution on claims arising out of a general current account maintained with a Bank by a foreign State on behalf of its embassy for the payment of costs and expenses has never yet been allowed, although there have been isolated decisions—relating for the most part, it is true, to other types of account not opened specially for embassy purposes—which suggest that a distinction according to whether the origin and intended purpose of funds or of an account are sovereign or non-sovereign is not excluded. . . .

Schaumann (BerDGVR, loc. cit., p. 145) considers that a foreign State can obtain immunity even in terms of general State immunity in the case of a general Bank account, and also to a limited extent in respect of other property, simply be declaring some sovereign purpose, since it will seldom be possible to prove the opposite. In his opinion, this conclusion, which is based on diplomatic immunity, is unavoidable if State immunity is viewed as being designed to protect the sovereign functions of the foreign State. For example, if instead of the intended use of certain property for a sovereign purpose, proof of its actual use for that purpose were to be demanded, then protection afforded to the sovereign functions of the State in foreign affairs would be incomplete. According to Habscheid (BerDGVR, loc. cit., pp. 266 et seq.), the important point is the specific purpose for which the funds to be attached are intended. Indications of this might include, for example, which ministry is designated as the account-holder.

(c) This Chamber fully appreciates that the immunity accorded to claims arising out of a general current account of the embassy of a foreign State might in some cases be used as a shield for financial transactions through such an account which were not directly related to the functions of a diplomatic mission. Should such a case occur—and there is no indication of this in the original proceedings—it would be for the competent authorities of the Federal Republic of Germany to counter a "non-functional" use of the immunity of diplomatic missions by diplomatic and other means admissible under international law. There is nothing to prevent a private party wishing to enter into private business relations with a foreign State from protecting his interests as much as possible, for instance through agreements on the manner in which business is to be transacted, the procedure in case of dispute—particularly waiver of immunity, which is in principle irrevocable (see also the relevant provision of the United States Foreign Sovereign Immunities Act of 1976, sect. 1610(a) (1))—or the furnishing of guarantees.

5. Where the question of immunity of the sending State for the benefit of its diplomatic mission is concerned, the financial position of the sending State—for instance, whether it would be in a position, despite the attachment of claims arising out of a general current account of its mission, to continue the operation of the embassy through financial allocations or remittances provided in some other way—is immaterial. The only relevant consideration is the abstract danger posed by measures of execution of this kind. Such a danger exists by reason of the adverse legal consequences which an attachment and assignment order entails under German law for the judgment debtor and the garnishee. Moreover, differentiation according to the financial position of the sending state could lead to differential treatment of foreign States in the field of diplomatic immunity, in contravention of the international-law principle of sovereign equality of States. It is immaterial for our purposes whether that legal principle, as set forth in Article 2, paragraph 1, of the Charter of the United Nations (BGBl 1973 II, 430), applies in the United Nations context only to relations between Member States; the principle of sovereign equality of States is also a fundamental principle of contemporary general international law which, at least in the field of diplomatic intercourse among States, demands formal equality of treatment on a broad scale (see, with regard to the principle of sovereign equality, the United Nations Declaration of 24 October 1970, General Assembly resolution 2625 (XXXV), ILM IX (1970), 1292 et seq., 1296). Any differential treatment of States in the field of diplomatic immunity according to their respective financial capacities would be incompatible with that.

Comments and Questions

1. The "abstract danger" referred to by the court evidently was not of concern to the United States District Court for the District of Columbia in Birch Shipping Corp. v. Embassy of United Republic of Tanzania, 507 F. Supp. 311 (1980). In that

case, the court found that an embassy bank account used for "mixed purposes" was not immune from attachment. Defendant State could protect public purpose funds in the future, according to the court, by segregating them from commercial activity funds.

2. Because bank accounts are perhaps the most common and readily available form of foreign state property, should rules along the lines of that applied in Birch Shipping Corp. be accepted generally?

Concluding Comments and Questions

Return to the problem that opened this chapter and consider anew the questions posed. Which of the categorical exceptions to immunity is MOL likely to invoke? Is MOL likely to succeed? From a purely normative perspective, should Bangladesh be immune from judgment? From execution?

G. Bibliography of Additional Resources

Andrew Dickinson, Rae Lindsay & James P. Loonam, STATE IMMUNITY: SELECTED MATERIALS AND COMMENTARY (Oxford 2004)

Bernard H. Oxman & Ilias Banterkas, International Decision, 95 AM. J. INT'L L. 198 (2001).

14A Charles Alan Wright, Arthur R. Miller & Edward H. Cooper, FEDERAL PRACTICE AND PROCEDURE § 3662 (Thomson West 3d ed. 1998 & Supp. 2007)

Christoph H. Schreuer, STATE IMMUNITY: SOME RECENT DEVELOPMENTS (Grotius 1988)

David Epstein, Jeffrey L. Snyder & Charles S. Baldwin, INTERNATIONAL LITIGATION: A GUIDE TO JURISDICTION, PRACTICE, AND STRATEGY (Marinus Nijhoff 3d ed. 1998 & Supp. 2007)

Dennis Campbell & Dharmendra Popat, Strategies for Effective Management of Crossborder Recognition and Enforcement of American Money Judgments, 56 AM. JUR. TRIALS 529 (1995 & Supp. 2007)

Dhisadee Chamlongrasdr, FOREIGN STATE IMMUNITY AND ARBITRATION (Cameron 2007)

E.H. Schopler, Annotation, Modern Status of the Rules as to Immunity of Foreign Sovereign from Suit in Federal or State Courts, 25 A.L.R. 3rd 322 (1969)

Eleanor W. Allen, THE POSITION OF FOREIGN STATES BEFORE NATIONAL COURTS: CHIEFLY IN CONTINENTAL EUROPE (Gaunt 2001)

Ernest K. Bankas, THE STATE IMMUNITY CONTROVERSY IN INTERNATIONAL LAW: PRIVATE SUITS AGAINST SOVEREIGN STATES IN DOMESTIC COURTS (Springer 2005)

13A FEDERAL PROCEDURE: LAWYERS EDITION §§ 36:395 to 36:509 (Thomson West 2006 & Supp. 2007)

George K. Chamberlin, Annotation, Exceptions to Jurisdicitonal Immunity of Foreign States and Their Property Under the Foreign Sovereign Immunities Act of 1976 (28 U.S.C.A. §§ 1602 et seq.), 59 A.L.R. FED. 99 (1982)

Hazel Fox, THE LAW OF STATE IMMUNITY (Oxford 2d ed. 2008)

15 James Wm. Moore, Moore's Federal Practice § 104.03 (Matthew Bender 3d ed. 1997 & Supp. 2007)

Joseph W. Dellapenna, Suing Foreign Governments and Their Corporations (Transnational Publishers 2d ed. 2003)

Jürgen Brohmer, State Immunity and the Violation of Human Rights (Kluwer 1997)

Richard H. Kreindler & Judith L. Holdsworth (eds.), Transnational Litigation: A Practitioner's Guide (Oceana 1997 & Supp. 2007)

Richard H. Kreindler, Transnational Litigation: A Basic Primer (Oceana 1998)

Susan Breau, Gerhard Hafner & Marcelo G. Kohen (eds.), State Practice Regarding State Immunities (Martinus Nijhoff 2006)

Ved P. Nanda & David K. Pansius, Litigation of International Disputes in U.S. Courts (Thomson West 2d ed. 2005 & Supp. 2007)

CHAPTER 7

The Act of State Doctrine

A. Introduction

This chapter introduces a doctrine developed chiefly by courts in the United States (although less robust versions of it have been applied in other common law countries, as well). The act of state doctrine precludes the courts of one country from examining the validity of acts of the governments of other countries taken in their own territories. The doctrine is consistent with the themes introduced in the previous chapter because it demonstrates a respect for sovereign acts and promotes international comity. However, the act of state doctrine leads neither to abstention nor immunity. Rather, the doctrine provides a binding rule of decision, precluding the parties from challenging the validity of certain acts of a foreign sovereign.

The doctrine is unpopular among certain constituences, including the business community, because it can effectively insulate from the scrutiny of courts the acts of other governments that take the property of, or otherwise injure, foreign nationals (often U.S. corporations or individuals)—even in violation of international law.

The classic statement of the theory behind the doctrine appears in an 1897 decision of the U.S. Supreme Court:

> Every sovereign state is bound to respect the independence of every other sovereign state, and the courts of one country will not sit in judgment on the acts of the government of another, done within its own territory. Redress of grievances by reason of such acts must be obtained through the means open to be availed of by sovereign powers as between themselves.
>
> Underhill v. Hernandez, 168 U.S. 250, 252 (1897).

In other words, the injured party should instead seek to have the claim taken up by the U.S. government and asserted on the international plane, under international law, against the government of the state that allegedly caused the injury. Or, as the Court put it somewhat more specifically in Banco Nacional de Cuba v. Sabbatino, "[b]ecause of [the] peculiar nation-to-nation character [of international law] the usual method for an individual to seek relief is to exhaust local remedies and then repair to the executive authorities of his own state to persuade them to champion his claim in diplomacy or before an international tribunal." 376 U.S. 398, 422–423 (1964).

Among other challenges, the claimant would be required to exhaust remedies in the very state that is alleged to have committed the wrong. When that state has an independent judiciary, recovery may be possible. Otherwise, the claimant must try to persuade their own government to pursue the claim. Even if the government does take up the claim, the vigor with which it pursues it will depend on a variety of factors, ranging from domestic political considerations to those of a diplomatic nature. In fact, because it becomes the state's claim once it is taken up (as explained below), the state can compromise it or even waive it altogether. If the government pursues, prevails, and secures compensation from the foreign state, it is not required by international law to pass the recovery along to the private complainant (although it would usually do so).

Under principles of international law, when a state injures a foreign natural or legal person in violation of international law, that is regarded as an injury to the person's state of nationality. But for the person who actually suffered the harm, litigation against the foreign state is the more direct and familiar avenue for redress, and, as mentioned, is a precondition to espousal of the claim by the person's government.

The Problem: An Olympic Wring

Creative Pennants Ltd. is an English manufacturer of flags, banners, and souvenirs. Creative is an industry leader with a broad reputation for innovative products at low prices for consumers, yet high profits for its shareholders. A few months before the 2010 Winter Olympic Games were to commence in Vancouver, British Columbia, Canadian officials impounded more than £1 million worth of merchandise that Creative had shipped to a Vancouver storage facility. At the time of the seizure, Canadian officials claimed that the merchandise had entered the country illegally and without the usual Customs inspections. Two weeks after the Olympic Games were completed, Canadian officials announced that their investigation had concluded that Creative had engaged in no wrongdoing, and that the confiscated items would be returned immediately.

Creative has suffered damages of approximately £2 million. The returned merchandise was targeted for the Olympic audience, and now has almost no fair market value. Creative recognizes that a seizure of goods under ordinary circumstances would be an exercise of legitimate police authority. But they argue that this case is different, and they have asked you to represent them. Your client has solid evidence that the two major sellers of merchandise at these Olympic Games were both public/private partnerships that earned significant profits for their junior partners, the Canadian Government.

These facts present the opportunity to review several doctrines introduced in previous chapters: (i) If the forum state recognizes some theory of restricted immunity, which of the categorical exceptions might be implicated here? (ii) If the action is filed in England, how likely is a forum non conveniens dismissal? (iii) Where might this defendant be subject to personal jurisdiction? For the remaining questions in this Problem, you should assume that the defendant state is not immune and that the forum has jurisdiction to adjudicate.

(1) Assume that plaintiff files its case against the Canadian government in London. Does an act of state doctrine appear to be applicable on these facts?
(2) What significance should the English court give a letter from the U.K. Foreign Secretary that the court's involvement would impinge on its diplomatic efforts? A letter indicating that a suit would not impinge on the U.K.'s diplomatic efforts?
(3) Assume that plaintiff instead files its case against the Canadian government in the United States. Would a U.S. forum present a stronger or weaker argument for an act of state doctrine defense on these facts?
(4) Which of these facts would present a weaker case for the application of the act of state doctrine: the goods were impounded by authorities in violation of Canadian national laws or the goods were impounded in violation of customary international law?
(5) Is the act of state doctrine something that should be raised by the court sua sponte or only upon motion of the defendant?

B. Doctrinal Justifications

Study of the contemporary act of state doctrine begins with the seminal case *Banco Nacional de Cuba v. Sabbatino.* But some context and a word of caution may be helpful.

First, some history. This case involves an expropriation by Cuba in August, 1960 of the property and enterprises of companies wholly or principally owned by American nationals. Fidel Castro had taken power in Cuba in January 1959. The U.S. military had supported the Cuban military dictator, Fulgencio Batista, ousted by Castro. This support, together with Castro's communist ideology and acts against American interests, soured relations between the two countries and led the U.S. to take acts such as the reduction of the Cuban sugar import quota. That the Supreme Court applied the act of state doctrine and refused to question the validity of Cuba's exproproiation in the face of U.S. enmity toward Cuba demonstrates the force of this doctrine.

Second, the facts of the case can be hard to follow. The relevant parties are (1) Compania Asucarera Vertientes (CAV), a Cuban sugar growing company that was partially owned by Americans; (2) Farr Whitlock, a New York commodities broker who had arranged for the sale of CAV's sugar to a buyer; (3) Sabbatino, who was appointed by the trial court as a receiver to hold the money that the purchaser of the sugar had tendered; and (4) two Cuban banks, Banco Nacional de Cuba and

Banco Exterior. The expropriation occurred on the day that the sugar was being loaded onto a ship for transport. Under the terms of the expropriation, the Cuban banks acquired the Americans' interest in CAV. The sugar was delivered and the buyer paid. In the lawsuit, the Cuban banks are suing the receiver, claiming entitlement to the payments tendered by the buyer.

Third, the opinion is controversial and Congress enacted legislation to overturn this specific holding. See 22 U.S.C. § 2370 (e)(1)-(2) (the "Second Hickenlooper Amendment"). Moreover, later decisions mentioned in the Comments and Questions have eroded Sabbatino's statement of the doctrine. But the opinion remains deeply influential.

Banco Nacional de Cuba v. Sabbatino

376 U.S. 398 (1964)

Mr. Justice Harlan delivered the opinion of the Court:

The question which brought this case here, and is now found to be the dispositive issue, is whether the so-called act of state doctrine serves to sustain petitioner's claims in this litigation. Such claims are ultimately founded on a decree of the Government of Cuba expropriating certain property, the right to the proceeds of which is here in controversy. The act of state doctrine in its traditional formulation precludes the courts of this country from inquiring into the validity of the public acts a recognized foreign sovereign power committed within its own territory.

I

In February and July of 1960, respondent Farr, Whitlock & Co., an American commodity broker, contracted to purchase Cuban sugar, free alongside the steamer, from a wholly owned subsidiary of Compania Azucarera Vertientes-Camaguey de Cuba (C.A.V.), a corporation organized under Cuban law whose capital stock was owned principally by United States residents. Farr, Whitlock agreed to pay for the sugar in New York upon presentation of the shipping documents and a sight draft.

On July 6, 1960, the Congress of the United States amended the Sugar Act of 1948 to permit a presidentially directed reduction of the sugar quota for Cuba. On the same day President Eisenhower exercised the granted power. The day of the congressional enactment, the Cuban Council of Ministers adopted "Law No. 851," which characterized this reduction in the Cuban sugar quota as an act of 'aggression, for political purposes' on the part of the United States, justifying the taking of countermeasures by Cuba. The law gave the Cuban President and Prime Minister discretionary power to nationalize by forced expropriation property or enterprises in which American nationals had an interest. Although a system of compensation was formally provided, the possibility of payment under it may well be deemed illusory.[4] Our State Department has described the Cuban law as "manifestly in violation of those principles of international law which have long been accepted by the free countries of the West. It is in its essence discriminatory, arbitrary and confiscatory."

Between August 6 and August 9, 1960, the sugar covered by the contract between Farr, Whitlock and C.A.V. was loaded, destined for Morocco, onto the S.S. Hornfels, which was standing offshore at the Cuban port of Jucaro (Santa Maria). On the day loading commenced, the Cuban President and Prime Minister, acting pursuant to Law No. 851, issued Executive Power Resolution No. 1. It provided for the compulsory expropriation of all property and enterprises, and of rights and interests arising therefrom, of certain listed companies, including C.A.V., wholly or principally owned by American nationals. The preamble reiterated the alleged injustice of the American reduction of the Cuban sugar quota and emphasized the importance of Cuba's serving as an example for other countries to follow "in their struggle to free themselves from the brutal claws of Imperialism." In consequence of the resolution, the consent of the Cuban Government was necessary before a ship carrying sugar of a named company could leave Cuban waters. In order to obtain this consent, Farr, Whitlock, on August 11, entered into contracts, identical to those it had made with C.A.V., with the Banco Para el Comercio Exterior de Cuba, an instrumentality of the Cuban Government. The S.S. Hornfels sailed for Morocco on August 12.

Banco Exterior assigned the bills of lading to petitioner, also an instrumentality of the Cuban Government, which instructed its agent in New York, Societe Generale, to deliver the bills and a sight draft in the sum of $175,250.69 to Farr, Whitlock in return for payment. Societe Generale's initial tender of the documents was refused by Farr, Whitlock, which on the same day was notified of C.A.V.'s claim that as rightful owner of the sugar it was entitled to the proceeds. In return for a promise not to turn the funds over to petitioner or its agent, C.A.V. agreed to indemnify Farr, Whitlock for any loss.[8] Farr, Whitlock subsequently accepted the shipping documents, negotiated the bills of lading to its customer, and received payment for the sugar. It refused, however, to hand over the proceeds to Societe Generale. Shortly thereafter, Farr, Whitlock was served with an order of the New York Supreme Court, which had appointed Sabbatino as Temporary Receiver of

[4] Payment for expropriated property would consist of bonds with terms of at least thirty years and bearing 2 percent annual interest. The interest was not to be cumulative from year to year and was to be paid only out of 25 percent of the yearly foreign exchange received by sales of Cuban sugar to the United States in excess of 3,000,000 Spanish long tons at a minimum price of 5.75 cents per English pound. (In the preceding ten years, the annual average price had never been that high and in only one of those years had as many as 3,000,000 Spanish long tons been sold.) The bonds were to be amortized only upon the authority of the President of the National Bank. The President and Prime Minister of the Cuban state were empowered to choose the appraisers. It is not clear whether the bonds were to be paid at maturity if funds were insufficient at that time.

[8] C.A.V. also agreed to pay Farr, Whitlock 10 percent of the $175,000 if C.A.V. ever obtained that sum.

C.A.V.'s New York assets, enjoining it from taking any action in regard to the money claimed by C.A.V. that might result in its removal from the State. Following this, Farr, Whitlock, pursuant to court order, transferred the funds to Sabbatino, to abide the event of a judicial determination as to their ownership.

Petitioner then instituted this action in the Federal District Court for the Southern District of New York. Alleging conversion of the bills of lading it sought to recover the proceeds thereof from Farr, Whitlock and to enjoin the receiver from exercising any dominion over such proceeds. Upon motions to dismiss and for summary judgment, the District Court, 193 F.Supp. 375, sustained federal in personam jurisdiction despite state control of the funds. It found that the sugar was located within Cuban territory at the time of expropriation and determined that under merchant law common to civilized countries Farr, Whitlock could not have asserted ownership of the sugar against C.A.V. before making payment. It concluded that C.A.V. had a property interest in the sugar subject to the territorial jurisdiction of Cuba. The court then dealt with the question of Cuba's title to the sugar, on which rested petitioner's claim of conversion. While acknowledging the continuing vitality of the act of state doctrine, the court believed it inapplicable when the questioned foreign act is in violation of international law. Proceeding on the basis that a taking invalid under international law does not convey good title, the District Court found the Cuban expropriation decree to violate such law in three separate respects: it was motivated by a retaliatory and not a public purpose; it discriminated against American nationals; and it failed to provide adequate compensation. Summary judgment against petitioner was accordingly granted.

The Court of Appeals, affirming the decision on similar grounds, relied on two letters (not before the District Court) written by State Department officers which it took as evidence that the Executive Branch had no objection to a judicial testing of the Cuban decree's validity. The court was unwilling to declare that any one of the infirmities found by the District Court rendered the taking invalid under international law, but was satisfied that in combination they had that effect. We granted certiorari because the issues involved bear importantly on the conduct of the country's foreign relations and more particularly on the proper role of the Judicial Branch in this sensitive area. For reasons to follow we decide that the judgment below must be reversed.

Subsequent to the decision of the Court of Appeals, the C.A.V. receivership was terminated by the State Supreme Court; the funds in question were placed in escrow, pending the outcome of this suit. C.A.V. has moved in this Court to be substituted as a party in the place of Sabbatino. Although it is true that Sabbatino's defensive interest in this litigation has largely, if not entirely, reflected that of C.A.V., this is true also of Farr, Whitlock's position. There is no indication that Farr, Whitlock has not adequately represented C.A.V.'s interest or that it will not continue to do so. Moreover, insofar as disposition of the case here is concerned, C.A.V. has been permitted as amicus to brief and argue its position before this Court. In these circumstances we are not persuaded that the admission of C.A.V. as a party is necessary at this stage to safeguard any claim either that it has already presented or that it may present in the future course of this litigation. Accordingly, we are constrained to deny C.A.V.'s motion to be admitted as a party, without prejudice however to the renewal of such a motion in the lower courts if it appears that C.A.V.'s interests are not adequately represented by Farr, Whitlock and that the granting of such a motion will not disturb federal jurisdiction....

II

The classic American statement of the act of state doctrine, which appears to have taken root in England as early as 1674, Blad v. Bamfield, 3 Swans. 604, 36 Eng.Rep. 992, and began to emerge in the jurisprudence of this country in the late eighteenth and early nineteenth centuries,...is found in Underhill v. Hernandez, 168 U.S. 250, p. 252, where Chief Justice Fuller said for a unanimous Court:

> Every sovereign state is bound to respect the independence of every other sovereign state, and the courts of one country will not sit in judgment on the acts of the government of another, done within its own territory. Redress of grievances by reason of such acts must be obtained through the means open to be availed of by sovereign powers as between themselves.

Following this precept the Court in that case refused to inquire into acts of Hernandez, a revolutionary Venezuelan military commander whose government had been later recognized by the United States, which were made the basis of a damage action in this country by Underhill, an American citizen, who claimed that he had had unlawfully assaulted, coerced, and detained in Venezuela by Hernandez.

None of this Court's subsequent cases in which the act of state doctrine was directly or peripherally involved manifest any retreat from Underhill. See American Banana Co. v. United Fruit Co., 213 U.S. 347; Oetjen v. Central Leather Co., 246 U.S. 297; Ricaud v. American Metal Co., 246 U.S. 304; Shapleigh v. Mier, 299 U.S. 468; United States v. Belmont, 301 U.S. 324; United States v. Pink, 315 U.S. 203. On the contrary in two of these cases, Oetjen and Ricaud, the doctrine as announced in Underhill was reaffirmed in unequivocal terms.

Oetjen involved a seizure of hides from a Mexican citizen as a military levy by General Villa, acting for the forces of General Carranza, whose government was recognized by this country subsequent to the trial but prior to decision by this Court. The hides were sold to a Texas corporation which shipped them to the United States and assigned them to defendant. As assignee of the original owner, plaintiff replevied the hides, claiming that they had been seized in violation of the Hague Conventions. In affirming a judgment for defendant, the Court suggested that the rules of the Conventions did not apply to civil war and that, even if they did, the relevant seizure was not in violation of them. Nevertheless, it chose to rest its decision on other grounds. It described the designation of the sovereign as a political question to be determined by the legislative and executive departments rather than the judicial department, invoked the established rule that such recognition operates retroactively to validate past acts, and found the basic tenet of Underhill to be applicable to the case before it.

> The principle that the conduct of one independent government cannot be successfully questioned in the courts of another is as applicable to a case involving the title to property brought within the custody of a court, such as we have here, as it was held to be to the cases cited, in which claims for damages were based upon acts done in a foreign country, for its rests at last upon the highest considerations of international comity and expediency. To permit the validity of the acts of one sovereign state to be ree xamined and perhaps condemned by the courts of another would very certainly 'imperil the amicable relations between governments and vex the peace of nations.
>
> 246 U.S. at 303–304.

In Ricaud the facts were similar—another general of the Carranza forces seized lead bullion as a military levy—except that the property taken belonged to an American citizen. The Court found Underhill, American Banana, and Oetjen controlling. Commenting on the nature of the principle established by those cases, the opinion stated that the rule

> does not deprive the courts of jurisdiction once acquired over a case. It requires only that when it is made to appear that the foreign government has acted in a given way on the subject-matter of the litigation, the details of such action or the merit of the result cannot be questioned but must be accepted by our courts as a rule for their decision. To accept a ruling authority and to decide accordingly is not a surrender or abandonment of jurisdiction but is an exercise of it. It results that the title to the property in this case must be determined by the result of the action taken by the military authorities of Mexico....
>
> 246 U.S. at 309.

To the same effect is the language of Mr. Justice Cardozo in the Shapleigh case, supra, where, in commenting on the validity of a Mexican land expropriation, he said (299 U.S. at 471): "The question is not here whether the proceeding was so conducted as to be a wrong to our nationals under the doctrines of international law, though valid under the law of the situs of the land. For wrongs of that order the remedy to be followed is along the channels of diplomacy."

In deciding the present case the Court of Appeals relied in part upon an exception to the unqualified teachings of Underhill, Oetjen, and Ricaud which that court had earlier indicated. In Bernstein v. Van Heyghen Freres Societe Anonyme, 2 Cir., 163 F.2d 246, suit was brought to recover from an assignee property allegedly taken, in effect, by the Nazi Government because plaintiff was Jewish. Recognizing the odious nature of this act of state, the court, through Judge Learned Hand, nonetheless refused to consider it invalid on that ground. Rather, it looked to see if the Executive had acted in any manner that would indicate that United States Courts should refuse to give effect to such a foreign decree. Finding no such evidence, the court sustained dismissal of the complaint. In a later case involving similar facts the same court again assumed examination of the German acts improper, Bernstein v. N.V. Nederlandsche-Amerikaansche Stoomvaart-Maatschappij, 2 Cir., 173 F.2d 71, but, quite evidently following the implications of Judge Hand's opinion in the earlier case, amended its mandate to permit evidence of alleged invalidity, 2 Cir., 210 F.2d 375, subsequent to receipt by plaintiff's attorney of a letter from the Acting Legal Adviser to the State Department written for the purpose of relieving the court from any constraint upon the exercise of its jurisdiction to pass on that question.[18]

This Court has never had occasion to pass upon the so-called Bernstein exception, nor need it do so now. For whatever ambiguity may be thought to exist in the two letters from State Department officials on which the Court of Appeals relied, 307 F.2d at 858, is now removed by the position which the Executive has taken in this Court on the act of state claim; respondents do not indeed contest the view that these letters were intended to reflect no more than the Department's then wish not to make any statement bearing on this litigation.

The outcome of this case, therefore, turns upon whether any of the contentions urged by respondents against the application of the act of state doctrine in the premises is acceptable: (1) that the doctrine does not apply to acts of state which violate international law, as is claimed to be the case here; (2) that the doctrine is inapplicable unless the Executive specifically interposes it in a particular case; and (3) that, in any event, the doctrine may not be invoked by a foreign government plaintiff in our courts.

III

Preliminarily, we discuss the foundations on which we deem the act of state doctrine to rest, and more particularly the question of whether state or federal law governs its application in a federal diversity case.

We do not believe that this doctrine is compelled either by the inherent nature of sovereign authority, as some of the earlier decision seem to imply, see Underhill, supra; American Banana, supra; Oetjen, supra, 246 U.S. at 303, or by some principle of international law. If a transaction takes place in one jurisdiction and the forum is in another, the forum does not by dismissing an action or by applying its own law purport to divest the first jurisdiction of its territorial sovereignty; it

---

[18] The letter stated:

1. This government has consistently opposed the forcible acts of dispossession of a discriminatory and confiscatory nature practiced by the Germans on the countries or peoples subject to their controls.

3. The policy of the Executive, with respect to claims asserted in the United States for the restitution of identifiable property (or compensation in lieu thereof) lost through force, coercion, or duress as a result of Nazi persecution in Germany, is to relieve American courts from any restraint upon the exercise of their jurisdiction to pass upon the validity of the acts of Nazi officials."

State Department Press Release, April 27, 1949, 20 Dept. State Bull. 592.

merely declines to adjudicate or makes applicable its own law to parties or property before it. The refusal of one country to enforce the penal laws of another (supra, pp. 932–933) is a typical example of an instance when a court will not entertain a cause of action arising in another jurisdiction. While historic notions of sovereign authority do bear upon the wisdom or employing the act of state doctrine, they do not dictate its existence.

That international law does not require application of the doctrine is evidenced by the practice of nations. Most of the countries rendering decisions on the subject [d]o followthe rule rigidly.[21] No international arbitral or judicial decision discovered suggests that international law prescribes recognition of sovereign acts of foreign governments, see 1 Oppenheim's International Law, § 115aa (Lauterpacht, 8th ed. 1955), and apparently no claim has ever been raised before an international tribunal that failure to apply the act of state doctrine constitutes a breach of international obligation. If international law does not prescribe use of the doctrine, neither does it forbid application of the rule even if it is claimed that the act of state in question violated international law. The traditional view of international law is that it establishes substantive principles for determining whether one country has wronged another. Because of its peculiar nation-to-nation character the usual method for an individual to seek relief is to exhaust local remedies and then repair to the executive authorities of his own state to persuade them to champion his claim in diplomacy or before an international tribunal. Although it is, of course, true that United States courts apply international law as a part of our own in appropriate circumstances, Ware v. Hylton, 3 Dall. 199, 281; The Nereide, 9 Cranch 388, 423; The Paquete Habana, 175 U.S. 677, 700, the public law of nations can hardly dictate to a country which is in theory wronged how to treat that wrong within its domestic borders.

Despite the broad statement in Oetjen that "The conduct of the foreign relations of our government is committed by the Constitution to the executive and

---

[21] In English jurisprudence, in the classic case of *Luther v. James Sagor & Co.*, (1921) 3 K.B. 532, the act of state doctrine is articulated in terms not unlike those of the United States cases. *See Princess Paley Olga v. Weisz*, (1929) 1 K.B. 718. *But see Anglo-Iranian Oil Co. v. Jaffrate*, (1953) 1 Weekly L.R. 246, (1953) Int'l L.Rep. 316 (Aden Sup.Ct.) (exception to doctrine if foreign act violates international law). Civil law countries, however, which apply the rule make exceptions for acts contrary to their sense of public order. *See, e.g., Ropit* case, Cour de Cassation (France), (1929) Recueil General Des Lois et Des Arrets (Sirey) Part I, 217; 55 Journal Du Droit International (Clunet) 674 (1928), (1927–1928) Ann. Dig., No. 43; Graue, *Germany: Recognition of Foreign Expropriations*, 3 Am. J. Comp. L. 93 (1954); Domke, *Indonesian Nationalization Measures Before Foreign Court*, 54 Am. J. Int'l L. 305 (1960) (discussion of and excerpts from opinions of the District Court in Bremen and the Hanseatic Court of Appeals in N.V. Verenigde Deli-Maatschapijen v. Deutsch-Indonesische Tabak-Handelsgesellschaft m.b.H., and of the Amsterdam District Court and Appellate Court in Senembah Maatschappij N.V. v. Republiek Indonesie Bank Indonesia); Massouridis, *The Effects of Confiscation, Expropriation, and Requisition by a Foreign Authority*, 3 Revue Helle nique De Droit International 62, 68 (1950) (recounting a decision of the court of the first instance of Piraeus); *Anglo-Iranian Oil Co. v. S.U.P.O.R. Co.*, (1955) Int'l L. Rep. 19, (Ct. of Venice), 78 Il Foro Italiano Part I, 719; 40 Blatter fur Zurcherische Rechtsprechung No. 65, 172–173 (Switzerland). *See also Anglo-Iranian Oil Co. v. Idemitsu Kosan Kabushiki Kaisha*, (1953) Int'l L.Rep. 312 (High Ct. of Tokyo).

legislative...departments," 246 U.S. at 302, it cannot of course be thought that "every case or controversy which touches foreign relations lies beyond judicial cognizance." Baker v. Carr, 369 U.S. 186, 211. The text of the Constitution does not require the act of state doctrine; it does not irrevocably remove from the judiciary the capacity to review the validity of foreign acts of state.

The act of state doctrine does, however, have "constitutional" underpinnings. It arises out of the basic relationships between branches of government in a system of separation of powers. It concerns the competency of dissimilar institutions to make and implement particular kinds of decisions in the area of international relations. The doctrine as formulated in past decisions expresses the strong sense of the Judicial Branch that its engagement in the task of passing on the validity of foreign acts of state may hinder rather than further this country's pursuit of goals both for itself and for the community of nations as a whole in the international sphere. Many commentators disagree with this view; they have striven by means of distinguishing and limiting past decisions and by advancing various considerations of policy to stimulate a narrowing of the apparent scope of the rule. Whatever considerations are thought to predominate, it is plain that the problems involved are uniquely federal in nature. If federal authority, in this instance this Court, orders the field of judicial competence in this area for the federal courts, and the state courts are left free to formulate their own rules, the purposes behind the doctrine could be as effectively undermined as if there had been no federal pronouncement on the subject....

We could perhaps in this diversity action avoid the question of deciding whether federal or state law is applicable to this aspect of the litigation.... However, we are constrained to make it clear that an issue concerned with a basic choice regarding the competence and function of the Judiciary and the National Executive in ordering our relationships with other members of the international community must be treated exclusively as an aspect of federal law....

IV

If the act of state doctrine is a principle of decision binding on federal and state courts alike but compelled by neither international law nor the Constitution, its continuing vitality depends on its capacity to reflect the proper distribution of functions between the judicial and political branches of the Government on matters bearing upon foreign affairs. It should be apparent that the greater the degree of codification or consensus concerning a particular area of international law, the more appropriate it is for the judiciary to render decisions regarding it, since the courts can then focus on the application of an agreed principle to circumstances of fact rather than on the sensitive task of establishing a principle not inconsistent with the national interest or with internationl justice. It is also evident that some aspects of international law touch much more sharply on national nerves than do others; the less important the implications of an issue are for our foreign relations, the weaker the justification for exclusivity in the political branches. The balance of relevant considerations may also be shifted if the government which perpetrated the challenged act of state is no longer in existence, as in the Bernstein case, for the political interest of this country may, as a result, be measurably altered. Therefore, rather than laying down or reaffirming an inflexible and all-encompassing rule in this case, we decide only that the (Judicial Branch) will not examine the validity of a taking of property within its own territory by a foreign sovereign government, extant and recognized by this country at the time of suit, in the absence of a treaty or other unambiguous agreement regarding controlling legal principles, even if the complaint alleges that the taking violates customary international law.

There are few if any issues in international law today on which opinion seems to be so divided as the limitations on a state's power to expropriate the property of aliens. There is, of course, authority, in international judicial and arbitral decisions, in the expressions of national governments, and among commentators for the view that a taking is improper under international law if it is not for a public purpose, is discriminatory, or is without provision for prompt, adequate, and effective compensation. However, Communist countries, although they have in fact provided a degree of compensation after diplomatic efforts, commonly recognize no obligation on the part of the taking country. Certain representatives of the newly independent and underdeveloped countries have questioned whether rules of state responsibility toward aliens can bind nations that have not consented to them and it is argued that the traditionally articulated standards governing expropriation of property reflect "imperialist" interests and are inappropriate to the circumstances of emergent states.

The disagreement as to relevant international law standards reflects an even more basic divergence between the national interests of capital importing and capital exporting nations and between the social ideologies of those countries that favor state control of a considerable portion of the means of production and those that adhere to a free enterprise system. It is difficult to imagine the courts of this country embarking on adjudication in an area which touches more sensitively the practical and ideological goals of the various members of the community of nations.

When we consider the prospect of the courts characterizing foreign expropriations, however justifiably, as invalid under international law and ineffective to pass title, the wisdom of the precedents is confirmed. While each of the leading cases in this Court may be argued to be distinguishable in its facts from this one—Underhill because sovereign immunity provided an independent ground and Oetjen, Ricaud, and Shapleigh because there was actually no violation of international law—the plain implication of all these opinions, and the import of express statements in Oetjen, 246 U.S. at 304, and Shapleigh, 299 U.S. at 471, is that the act of state doctrine is applicable even if international law has been violated.

The possible adverse consequences of a conclusion to the contrary of that implicit in these cases in highlighted by contrasting the practices of the political branch with the limitations of the judicial process in matters of this kind. Following an expropriation of any significance, the Executive engages in diplomacy aimed to assure that United States citizens who are harmed are compensated fairly.

Representing all claimants of this country, it will often be able, either by bilateral or multilateral talks, by submission to the United Nations, or by the employment of economic and political sanctions, to achieve some degree of general redress. Judicial determinations of invalidity of title can, on the other hand, have only an occasional impact, since they depend on the fortuitous circumstance of the property in question being brought into this country. Such decisions would, if the acts involved were declared invalid, often be likely to give offense to the expropriating country; since the concept of territorial sovereignty is so deep seated, any state may resent the refusal of the courts of another sovereign to accord validity to acts within its territorial borders. Piecemeal dispositions of this sort involving the probability of affront to another state could seriously interfere with negotiations being carried on by the Executive Branch and might prevent or render less favorable the terms of an agreement that could otherwise be reached. Relations with third countries which have engaged in similar expropriations would not be immune from effect.

The dangers of such adjudication are present regardless of whether the State Department has, as it did in this case, asserted that the relevant act violated international law. If the Executive Branch has undertaken negotiations with an expropriating country, but has refrained from claims of violation of the law of nations, a determination to that effect by a court might be regarded as a serious insult, while a finding of compliance with international law would greatly strengthen the bargaining hand of the other state with consequent detriment to American interests.

Even if the State Department has proclaimed the impropriety of the expropriation, the stamp of approval of its view by a judicial tribunal, however, impartial, might increase any affront and the judicial decision might occur at a time, almost always well after the taking, when such an impact would be contrary to our national interest. Considerably more serious and far-reaching consequences would flow from a judicial finding that international law standards had been met if that determination flew in the face of a State Department proclamation to the contrary. When articulating principles of international law in its relations with other states, the Executive Branch speaks not only as an interpreter of generally accepted and traditional rules, as would the courts, but also as an advocate of standards it believes desirable for the community of nations and protective of national concerns. In short, whatever way the matter is cut, the possibility of conflict between the Judicial and Executive Branches could hardly be avoided.

Respondents contend that, even if there is not agreement regarding general standards for determining the validity of expropriations, the alleged combination of retaliation, discrimination, and inadequate compensation makes it patently clear that this particular expropriation was in violation of international law. If this view is accurate, it would still be unwise for the courts so to determine. Such a decision now would require the drawing of more difficult lines in subsequent cases and these would involve the possibility of conflict with the Executive view. Even if the courts avoided this course, either by presuming the validity of an act of state whenever the international law standard was thought unclear or by following the State Department declaration in such a situation, the very expression of judicial uncertainty might provide embarrassment to the Executive Branch.

Another serious consequence of the exception pressed by respondents would be to render uncertain titles in foreign commerce, with the possible consequence of altering the flow of international trade. If the attitude of the United States courts were unclear, one buying expropriated goods would not know if he could safely import them into this country. Even were takings known to be invalid, one would have difficulty determining after goods had changed hands several times whether the particular articles in question were the product of an ineffective state act.

Against the force of such considerations, we find respondents' countervailing arguments quite unpersuasive. Their basic contention is that United States courts could make a significant contribution to the growth of international law, a contribution whose importance, it is said, would be magnified by the relative paucity of decisional law by international bodies. But given the fluidity of present world conditions, the effectiveness of such a patchwork approach toward the formulation of an acceptable body of law concerning state responsibility for expropriations is, to say the least, highly conjectural. Moreover, it rests upon the sanguine presupposition that the decisions of the courts of the world's major capital exporting country and principal exponent of the free enterprise system would be accepted as disinterested expressions of sound legal principle by those adhering to widely different ideologies.

It is contended that regardless of the fortuitous circumstances necessary for United States jurisdiction over a case involving a foreign act of state and the resultant isolated application to any expropriation program taken as a whole, it is the function of the courts to justly decide individual disputes before them. Perhaps the most typical act of state case involves the original owner or his assignee suing one not in association with the expropriating state who has had "title" transferred to him. But it is difficult to regard the claim of the original owner, who otherwise may be recompensed through diplomatic channels, as more demanding of judicial cognizance than the claim of title by the innocent third party purchaser, who, if the property is taken from him, is without any remedy.

Respondents claim that the economic pressure resulting from the proposed exception to the act of state doctrine will materially add to the protection of United States investors. We are not convinced, even assuming the relevance of this contention. Expropriations take place for a variety of reasons, political and ideological as well as economic. When one considers the variety of means possessed by this country to make secure foreign investment, the persuasive or coercive effect of judicial invalidation of acts of expropriation dwindles in comparison. The newly independent states are in need of continuing foreign investment; the creation of a climate unfavorable to such investment by wholesale confiscations may well work to their long-run economic disadvantage. Foreign aid given to many of these countries provides a powerful lever in the hands of the political branches to ensure fair treatment of United States nationals. Ultimately the sanctions of economic embargo and the freezing of assets in this country may be employed. Any country willing to brave any or all of these consequences is unlikely to be deterred by sporadic judicial decisions directly affecting only property brought to our shores. If the political branches are unwilling to exercise their ample powers to effect compensation, this reflects a judgment of the national interest which the judiciary would be ill-advised to undermine indirectly.

It is suggested that if the act of state doctrine is applicable to violations of international law, it should only be so when the Executive Branch expressly stipulates that it does not wish the courts to pass on the question of validity. See Association of the Bar of the City of New York, Committee on International Law, A Reconsideration of the Act of State Doctrine in United States Courts (1959). We should be slow to reject the representations of the Government that such a reversal of the Bernstein principle would work serious inroads on the maximum effectiveness of United States diplomacy. Often the State Department will wish to refrain from taking an official position, particularly at a moment that would be dictated by the development of private litigation but might be inopportune diplomatically. Adverse domestic consequences might flow from an official stand which could be assuaged, if at all, only by revealing matters best kept secret. Of course, a relevant consideration for the State Department would be the position contemplated in the court to hear the case. It is highly questionable whether the examination of validity by the judiciary should depend on an educated guess by the Executive as to probable result and, at any rate, should a prediction be wrong, the Executive might be embarrassed in its dealings with other countries. We do not now pass on the Bernstein exception, but even if it were deemed valid, its suggested extension is unwarranted.

However offensive to the public policy of this country and its constituent States an expropriation of this kind may be, we conclude that both the national interest and progress toward the goal of establishing the rule of law among nations are best served by maintaining intact the act of state doctrine in this realm of its application....

Since the act of state doctrine proscribes a challenge to the validity of the Cuban expropriation decree in this case, any counterclaim based on asserted invalidity must fail. Whether a theory of conversion or breach of contract is the proper cause of action under New York law, the presumed validity of the expropriation is unaffected....

[The dissenting opinion of Justice White is omitted.]

Comments and Questions

1. For the doctrine to be invoked in U.S. courts, a threshold inquiry demands that three conditions be satisfied: First, the act must be an official act of a sovereign. Second, the act must have been performed within the sovereign's territory. And, third, the relief sought in the lawsuit must require the court to declare the sovereign's act invalid.

2. Because of the sheer force of this doctrine, it is critical to understand the primary exceptions to its applicability.

First, "a treaty or other unambiguous agreement [between countries] regarding controlling legal principles," such as a bilateral investment treaty, may supersede the doctrine. Sabbatino, 376 U.S. at 428. The large and growing number of bilateral investment treaties ("BITs") between the United States and other nations increases the likelihood that such a treaty will be present.

Second, a "Bernstein letter" from the Executive Branch (e.g., the State Department Legal Adviser) indicating that litigation of the issue would not disturb the president's conduct of foreign relations could provide the basis for an exception.[†] Although the court is not bound by the proclamation, the letter alleviates the separation of powers concern that underlies the act of state doctrine in the United States.

Third, particular applications of the doctrine may be displaced by congressional legislation. In response to the Sabbatino decision, for example, the Second Hickenlooper Amendment provided that the act of state doctrine is not to be applied by courts in the United States in cases involving certain types of claims that a foreign state confiscated property in violation of international law. See Foreign Assistance Act of 1961, § 620(e)(2), as amended, 22 U.S.C. § 2370(e)(2). However, the courts have generally interpreted the amendment to apply only where the claim is made to specific property that is before the court.

Fourth, in Alfred Dunhill of London, Inc. v. Cuba, 425 U.S. 682, 704 (1976), a plurality of Justices invoked commercial acts as an exception to the act of state doctrine by analogizing the doctrine to sovereign immunity. Four dissenters disputed the analogy and warned against its use. Some, though not all, lower courts recognize the exception. (Could matters that are commercial in nature also raise sensitive issues of foreign policy?)

Fifth, the enforcement of agreements to arbitrate and the execution of arbitration awards "shall not be refused on the basis of the act of state doctrine." 9 U.S.C. § 15.

Finally, there are additional considerations that may be characterized either as "exceptions" to the act of state doctrine or as a narrowing of the meaning of validity—the third prerequisite that the party seeking application of the act of state doctrine must establish. For example, acts that can be characterized as torture, genocide, terrorism, crimes against humanity, acts of "illegitimate warfare," or other human rights abuses will not enjoy any presumption of validity.[**] The Supreme Court has indicated that it intends to confine the doctrine's application rather strictly.

[†] *See Bernstein v. N.V. Nederlandsche-Amerikaansche Stoomvaart-Maatschappij*, 173 F.2d 71 (2nd Cir. 1949), 210 F.2d 375 (2nd Cir. 1954).

[**] *See, e.g., Kadic v. Karadzic*, 70 F.3d 232 (2nd Cir. 1995), *cert. denied*, 518 U.S. 1005 (1996). Of course many of these acts may also be violations of treaties and thus would (also) fall within the exception for treaties and other unambiguous agreements.

W.S. Kirkpatrick & Co., Inc. v. Envtl. Tectonics Corp., Int'l

493 U.S. 400 (1990)

JUSTICE SCALIA delivered the opinion of the Court:
In this case we must decide whether the act of state doctrine bars a court in the United States from entertaining a cause of action that does not rest upon the asserted invalidity of an official act of a foreign sovereign, but that does require imputing to foreign officials an unlawful motivation (the obtaining of bribes) in the performance of such an official act.

I

The facts as alleged in respondent's complaint are as follows: In 1981, Harry Carpenter, who was then chairman of the board and chief executive officer of petitioner W.S. Kirkpatrick & Co., Inc. (Kirkpatrick), learned that the Republic of Nigeria was interested in contracting for the construction and equipment of an aeromedical center at Kaduna Air Force Base in Nigeria. He made arrangements with Benson "Tunde" Akindele, a Nigerian citizen, whereby Akindele would endeavor to secure the contract for Kirkpatrick. It was agreed that, in the event the contract was awarded to Kirkpatrick, Kirkpatrick would pay to two Panamanian entities controlled by Akindele a "commission" equal to 20% of the contract price, which would in turn be given as a bribe to officials of the Nigerian Government. In accordance with this plan, the contract was awarded to petitioner W.S. Kirkpatrick & Co., International (Kirkpatrick International), a wholly owned subsidiary of Kirkpatrick; Kirkpatrick paid the promised "commission" to the appointed Panamanian entities; and those funds were disbursed as bribes. All parties agree that Nigerian law prohibits both the payment and the receipt of bribes in connection with the award of a government contract.

Respondent Environmental Tectonics Corporation, International, an unsuccessful bidder for the Kaduna contract, learned of the 20% "commission" and brought the matter to the attention of the Nigerian Air Force and the United States Embassy in Lagos. Following an investigation by the Federal Bureau of Investigation, the United States Attorney for the District of New Jersey brought charges against both Kirkpatrick and Carpenter for violations of the Foreign Corrupt Practices Act of 1977, 91 Stat. 1495, as amended, 15 U.S.C. § 78dd-1 et seq., and both pleaded guilty.

Respondent then brought this civil action in the United States District Court for the District of New Jersey against Carpenter, Akindele, petitioners, and others, seeking damages under the Racketeer Influenced and Corrupt Organizations Act, 18 U.S.C. § 1961 et seq., the Robinson-Patman Act, 49 Stat. 1526, 15 U.S.C. § 13 et seq., and the New Jersey Anti-Racketeering Act, N.J.Stat.Ann. § 2C:41–2 et seq. (West 1982). The defendants moved to dismiss the complaint under Rule 12(b)(6) of the Federal Rules of Civil Procedure on the ground that the action was barred by the act of state doctrine.

The District Court, having requested and received a letter expressing the views of the legal adviser to the United States Department of State as to the applicability of the act of state doctrine, treated the motion as one for summary judgment under Rule 56 of the Federal Rules of Civil Procedure and granted the motion. 659 F. Supp. 1381 (1987). The District Court concluded that the act of state doctrine applies "if the inquiry presented for judicial determination includes the motivation of a sovereign act which would result in embarrassment to the sovereign or constitute interference in the conduct of foreign policy of the United States." Id., at 1392–1393. Applying that principle to the facts at hand, the court held that respondent's suit had to be dismissed because in order to prevail respondent would have to show that "the defendants or certain of them intended to wrongfully influence the decision to award the Nigerian Contract by payment of a bribe, that the Government of Nigeria, its officials or other representatives knew of the offered consideration for awarding the Nigerian Contract to Kirkpatrick, that the bribe was actually received or anticipated and that 'but for' the payment or anticipation of the payment of the bribe, ETC would have been awarded the Nigerian Contract." 659 F.Supp., at 1393 (footnote omitted).

The Court of Appeals for the Third Circuit reversed. 847 F.2d 1052 (1988). Although agreeing with the District Court that "the award of a military procurement contract can be, in certain circumstances, a sufficiently formal expression of a government's public interests to trigger application" of the act of state doctrine, id., at 1058, it found application of the doctrine unwarranted on the facts of this case. The Court of Appeals found particularly persuasive the letter to the District Court from the legal adviser to the Department of State, which had stated that in the opinion of the Department judicial inquiry into the purpose behind the act of a foreign sovereign would not produce the "unique embarrassment, and the particular interference with the conduct of foreign affairs, that may result from the judicial determination that a foreign sovereign's acts are invalid." Id., at 1061. The Court of Appeals acknowledged that "the Department's legal conclusions as to the reach of the act of state doctrine are not controlling on the courts," but concluded that "the Department's factual assessment of whether fulfillment of its responsibilities will be prejudiced by the course of civil litigation is entitled to substantial respect." Id., at 1062. In light of the Department's view that the interests of the Executive Branch would not be harmed by prosecution of the action, the Court of Appeals held that Kirkpatrick had not met its burden of showing that the case should not go forward; accordingly, it reversed the judgment of the District Court and remanded the case for trial. Id., at 1067.

II

This Court's description of the jurisprudential foundation for the act of state doctrine has undergone some evolution over the years. We once viewed the doctrine as an expression of international law, resting upon "the highest considerations of international comity and expediency," Oetjen v. Central Leather Co., 246 U.S. 297,

303–304 (1918). We have more recently described it, however, as a consequence of domestic separation of powers, reflecting "the strong sense of the Judicial Branch that its engagement in the task of passing on the validity of foreign acts of state may hinder" the conduct of foreign affairs, Banco Nacional de Cuba v. Sabbatino, 376 U.S. 398, 423 (1964). Some Justices have suggested possible exceptions to application of the doctrine, where one or both of the foregoing policies would seemingly not be served: an exception, for example, for acts of state that consist of commercial transactions, since neither modern international comity nor the current position of our Executive Branch accorded sovereign immunity to such acts, see Alfred Dunhill of London, Inc. v. Republic of Cuba, 425 U.S. 682, 695–706 (1976) (opinion of White, J.); or an exception for cases in which the Executive Branch has represented that it has no objection to denying validity to the foreign sovereign act, since then the courts would be impeding no foreign policy goals, see First National City Bank v. Banco Nacional de Cuba, 406 U.S. 759, 768–770 (1972) (opinion of Rehnquist, J.).

The parties have argued at length about the applicability of these possible exceptions, and, more generally, about whether the purpose of the act of state doctrine would be furthered by its application in this case. We find it unnecessary, however, to pursue those inquiries, since the factual predicate for application of the act of state doctrine does not exist. Nothing in the present suit requires the Court to declare invalid, and thus ineffective as "a rule of decision for the courts of this country," Ricaud v. American Metal Co., 246 U.S. 304, 310 (1918), the official act of a foreign sovereign.

In every case in which we have held the act of state doctrine applicable, the relief sought or the defense interposed would have required a court in the United States to declare invalid the official act of a foreign sovereign performed within its own territory. In Underhill v. Hernandez, 168 U.S. 250, 254 (1897), holding the defendant's detention of the plaintiff to be tortious would have required denying legal effect to "acts of a military commander representing the authority of the revolutionary party as government, which afterwards succeeded and was recognized by the United States." In Oetjen v. Central Leather Co., supra, and in Ricaud v. American Metal Co., supra, denying title to the party who claimed through purchase from Mexico would have required declaring that government's prior seizure of the property, within its own territory, legally ineffective. See Oetjen, supra, 246 U.S., at 304; Ricaud, supra, 246 U.S., at 310. In Sabbatino, upholding the defendant's claim to the funds would have required a holding that Cuba's expropriation of goods located in Havana was null and void. In the present case, by contrast, neither the claim nor any asserted defense requires a determination that Nigeria's contract with Kirkpatrick International was, or was not, effective.

Petitioners point out, however, that the facts necessary to establish respondent's claim will also establish that the contract was unlawful. Specifically, they note that in order to prevail respondent must prove that petitioner Kirkpatrick made, and Nigerian officials received, payments that violate Nigerian law, which would, they assert, support a finding that the contract is invalid under Nigerian law. Assuming that to be true, it still does not suffice. The act of state doctrine is not some vague doctrine of abstention but a "principle of decision binding on federal and state courts alike." Sabbatino, supra, 376 U.S., at 427 (emphasis added). As we said in Ricaud, "the act within its own boundaries of one sovereign State... becomes... a rule of decision for the courts of this country." 246 U.S., at 310. Act of state issues only arise when a court must decide-that is, when the outcome of the case turns upon-the effect of official action by a foreign sovereign. When that question is not in the case, neither is the act of state doctrine. That is the situation here. Regardless of what the court's factual findings may suggest as to the legality of the Nigerian contract, its legality is simply not a question to be decided in the present suit, and there is thus no occasion to apply the rule of decision that the act of state doctrine requires.

In support of their position that the act of state doctrine bars any factual findings that may cast doubt upon the validity of foreign sovereign acts, petitioners cite Justice Holmes' opinion for the Court in American Banana Co. v. United Fruit Co., 213 U.S. 347 (1909). That was a suit under the United States antitrust laws, alleging that Costa Rica's seizure of the plaintiff's property had been induced by an unlawful conspiracy. In the course of a lengthy opinion Justice Holmes observed, citing Underhill, that "a seizure by a state is not a thing that can be complained of elsewhere in the courts." 213 U.S., at 357–358. The statement is concededly puzzling. Underhill does indeed stand for the proposition that a seizure by a state cannot be complained of elsewhere—in the sense of being sought to be declared ineffective elsewhere. The plaintiff in American Banana, however, like the plaintiff here, was not trying to undo or disregard the governmental action, but only to obtain damages from private parties who had procured it. Arguably, then, the statement did imply that suit would not lie if a foreign state's actions would be, though not invalidated, impugned.

Whatever Justice Holmes may have had in mind, his statement lends inadequate support to petitioners' position here, for two reasons. First, it was a brief aside, entirely unnecessary to the decision. American Banana was squarely decided on the ground (later substantially overruled, see Continental Ore Co. v. Union Carbide & Carbon Corp., 370 U.S. 690, 704–705 (1962)) that the antitrust laws had no extraterritorial application, so that "what the defendant did in Panama or Costa Rica is not within the scope of the statute." 213 U.S., at 357. Second, whatever support the dictum might provide for petitioners' position is more than overcome by our later holding in United States v. Sisal Sales Corp., 274 U.S. 268 (1927). There we held that, American Banana notwithstanding, the defendant's actions in obtaining Mexico's enactment of "discriminating legislation" could form part of the basis for suit under the United States antitrust laws. 274 U.S., at 276. Simply put, American Banana was not an act of state case; and whatever it said by way of dictum that might be relevant to the present case has not survived Sisal Sales.

Petitioners insist, however, that the policies underlying our act of state cases—international comity, respect for the sovereignty of foreign nations on their own territory, and the avoidance of embarrassment to the Executive Branch in its conduct of foreign relations—are implicated in the present case because, as the District Court found, a determination that Nigerian officials demanded and accepted a bribe "would impugn or question the nobility of a foreign nation's motivations," and would "result in embarrassment to the sovereign or constitute interference in the conduct of foreign policy of the United States." 659 F. Supp., at 1392–1393. The United States, as amicus curiae, favors the same approach to the act of state doctrine, though disagreeing with petitioners as to the outcome it produces in the present case. We should not, the United States urges, "attach dispositive significance to the fact that this suit involves only the 'motivation' for, rather than the 'validity' of, a foreign sovereign act," Brief for United States as Amicus Curiae 37, and should eschew "any rigid formula for the resolution of act of state cases generally,"id., at 9. In some future case, perhaps, "litigation... based on alleged corruption in the award of contracts or other commercially oriented activities of foreign governments could sufficiently touch on 'national nerves' that the act of state doctrine or related principles of abstention would appropriately be found to bar the suit," id., at 40 (quoting Sabbatino, 376 U.S., at 428), and we should therefore resolve this case on the narrowest possible ground, viz., that the letter from the legal adviser to the District Court gives sufficient indication that, "in the setting of this case," the act of state doctrine poses no bar to adjudication, ibid.*

These urgings are deceptively similar to what we said in Sabbatino, where we observed that sometimes, even though the validity of the act of a foreign sovereign within its own territory is called into question, the policies underlying the act of state doctrine may not justify its application. We suggested that a sort of balancing approach could be applied-the balance shifting against application of the doctrine, for example, if the government that committed the "challenged act of state" is no longer in existence. 376 U.S., at 428. But what is appropriate in order to avoid unquestioning judicial acceptance of the acts of foreign sovereigns is not similarly appropriate for the quite opposite purpose of expanding judicial incapacities where such acts are not directly (or even indirectly) involved. It is one thing to suggest, as we have, that the policies underlying the act of state doctrine should be considered in deciding whether, despite the doctrine's technical availability, it should nonetheless not be invoked; it is something quite different to suggest that those underlying policies are a doctrine unto themselves, justifying expansion of the act of state doctrine (or, as the United States puts it, unspecified "related principles of abstention") into new and uncharted fields.

The short of the matter is this: Courts in the United States have the power, and ordinarily the obligation, to decide cases and controversies properly presented

---

* Even if we agreed with the Government's fundamental approach, we would question its characterization of the legal adviser's letter as reflecting the absence of any policy objection to the adjudication. The letter, which is reprinted as an appendix to the opinion of the Court of Appeals, *see* 847 F.2d 1052, 1067–1069 (CA3 1988), did not purport to say whether the State Department would like the suit to proceed, but rather responded (correctly, as we hold today) to the question whether the act of state doctrine was applicable.

to them. The act of state doctrine does not establish an exception for cases and controversies that may embarrass foreign governments, but merely requires that, in the process of deciding, the acts of foreign sovereigns taken within their own jurisdictions shall be deemed valid. That doctrine has no application to the present case because the validity of no foreign sovereign act is at issue.

The judgment of the Court of Appeals for the Third Circuit is affirmed.

Comments and Questions

1. The State Department's Legal Adviser, Abraham Sofaer, made three principal points in his letter to the trial judge.

> [First,] If the adjudication of this suit were to involve a judicial inquiry into the motivations of the Governmet of Nigeria's decision to award the contract, the Department does not believe the act of state doctrine would bar the Court from adjudicating this dispute.
>
> [Second,] Moreover, the Department is of the view that the act of state doctrine may not appy to the award of the contract in question, to the extent that such award does not constitute a sufficiently formal expression of Nigeria's public policy or interests.
>
> [And third,] Apart from the act of state question, however, inquiries into the motivation and validity of foreign states' actions and discovery against foreign government officials may seriously affect United States foreign relations. These concerns, in the context of this litigation, counsel that caution and due regard for foreign sovereign sensibilities be exercised at each relevant stage in the proceedings. Moreover, the court should endeavor to assure that no unnecessary inquiries are made, or allegations tested, during the course of discovery or trial.

The district judge was not sure what to make of the Legal Advisor's letter. What do you think it means? Is it a Bernstein letter? Is this letter mentioned or reflected in the Supreme Court's opinion?

2. Isn't the rationale for an act of state doctrine equally compelling in a situation where the court would be imputing unlawful conduct to a foreign sovereign (even if not declaring it invalid)? Would the Court have reached the same result if the Nigerian government had been a party in this suit?

3. Consider the act of state doctrine in the context of the Ferdinand Marcos litigation. Efforts by 9,539 victims of human rights violations in the Philippines to enforce a judgment for $1,964,005,859.90 against the Estate of Ferdinand Marcos were barred by the act of state doctrine. See Credit Suisse v. U.S. District Court for the Central District of California, 130 F.3d 1342 (9th Cir. 1997).

Plaintiffs had registered their judgment in the Central District of California and served writs of execution and notices of levy on the California offices of Credit Suisse and Swiss Bank Corp. ("the Banks"). However, because none of the Marcos' accounts were maintained at the California offices of either of the Banks, the service of notice of levy was ineffective under California law. That law requires that personal service of notice of levy be made at the office of the financial institution at which the account is actually carried—here, the Banks' offices in Switzerland.

Plaintiffs then brought an action directly against the Banks, seeking to enjoin any transfer of funds on behalf of the Marcos Estate. The Banks moved to dismiss, inter alia, on the ground that the injunctive relief sought would violate the act of state doctrine. The district court denied the Banks' motion, whereupon the Banks petitioned for a writ of mandamus to compel dismissal of the action.

The court granted the Banks' petition. It reasoned that because Switzerland had previously frozen all Estate assets at the request of the Philippine government, "Subjecting Estate assets held by the Banks to the district court's further orders would . . . allow a United States court to question and, in fact, 'declare invalid the official act of a foreign sovereign.' [citing Kirkpatrick]" Furthermore, according to the court, the relief requested by plaintiffs would also "render nugatory Switzerland's attempts to render legal assistance to The Republic of the Philippines by protecting the Estate assets." The court concluded that "If the . . . plaintiffs want to contest the legality of the Swiss freeze orders, . . . or seek an injunction compelling the Banks to turn over the assets, they should do so via the Swiss judicial system."

Do you agree with the court's analysis? Would the requested relief in fact require the court to "declare invalid" a foreign sovereign's official act? Or would it simply place the Banks under another, and possibly conflicting, set of orders? Is the latter prohibited by the act of state doctrine?

Concluding Comments and Questions

1. The act of state doctrine has no equivalent in any civil law law country. Even in some common law countries—namely, Canada—courts can be reluctant to invoke the doctrine. See Crown Resources Corp. S.A. v. National Iranian Drilling Co. (Unreported, Ontario Superior Court of Justice, Greer, J, 14 September 2005). See also Buttes Gas & Oil Co. v. Hammer, 1982 A.C. 888 (H.L.) (recognizing an act of state doctrine for Great Britain). Why should a country like the United States invoke the act of state doctrine in favor of countries who would not do the same for the U.S. if the positions were reversed?

2. The doctrine's lack of definition is capable of conflicting results on the same set of facts. Is that problematic? Avoidable?

C. Bibliography of Additional Resources

American Bar Association, ACT OF STATE AND EXTRATERRITORIAL REACH: PROBLEMS OF LAW AND POLICY (Am. Bar Assoc. 1983)

David Epstein, Jeffrey L. Snyder & Charles S. Baldwin, INTERNATIONAL LITIGATION: A GUIDE TO JURISDICTION, PRACTICE, AND STRATEGY (Marinus Nijhoff 3d ed. 1998 & Supp. 2007)

Dennis Campbell & Dharmendra Popat, Strategies for Effective Management of Crossborder Recognition and Enforcement of American Money Judgments, 56 AM. JUR. TRIALS 529 (1995 & Supp. 2007)

13A Federal Procedure: Lawyers Edition §§ 36:395 to 36:509 (Thomson West 2006 & Supp. 2007)

James B. Whisker, The Supremacy of the State in International Law: The Act of State Doctrine (Edwin Mellen 2003)

15 James Wm. Moore, Moore's Federal Practice § 104.03 (Matthew Bender 3d ed. 1997 & Supp. 2007)

Joseph W. Dellapenna, Suing Foreign Governments and Their Corporations (Transnational Publishers 2d ed. 2003)

Paul Vishny, Litigating with Foreign Governments: Sovereign Immunity and the Act of State Doctrine, A.L.I.-A.B.A. Continuing Legal Education (May 8, 2008)

Richard H. Kreindler & Judith L. Holdsworth (eds.),Transnational Litigation: A Practitioner's Guide (Oceana 1997 & Supp. 2007)

Richard H. Kreindler, Transnational Litigation: A Basic Primer (Oceana 1998)

Ved P. Nanda & David K. Pansius, Litigation of International Disputes in U.S. Courts (Thomson West 2d ed. 2005 & Supp. 2007)

CHAPTER 8

Service of Process

A. Introduction

Service of process is among the most fundamental litigation procedures. In one form or another, every legal system in the world has some method of notifying the defendant of the filing of the suit:

> For at least four thousand years, claimants have been required to take concrete steps to bring a putative defendant before the governing tribunal. In the Code of Eshnunna, one of the earliest known legal codes, some of the terms for a plaintiff's commencing an action literally meant to "speak" or "shout." The Eshnunna plaintiff could not have the action heard, however, unless the defendant joined in submitting it to the power of the court.[11]
>
> In medieval times, the most common procedure for summoning a defendant in actions at law was for the sheriff to locate the defendant and summon his presence for a hearing.[12] Some jurisdictions charged direct monetary costs to a plaintiff in return for this service. The regularity of the mechanism of delivery by a sheriff

[11] R. Yaron, The Laws of Eshnunna 81 (1969). A similar requirement for submission to the jurisdiction of the court is found in the earliest Russian codified civil rules. *See* A. Evans, Medieval Russian Laws 7, 89 (1947) (Charter of Novgorod arts. 30–31 (ca. 1471) (required both disputants to express submission to the jurisdiction of the court to commence a proceeding).... The Charter of Dvina Land (1397) called upon plaintiff to kiss the cross before the authorities undertook steps calculated to summon defendant. *See* A. Evans, *supra,* at 7, 59.

[12] The oath of office for early sheriffs in both England and the American colonies bound them to serve writs to the fullest extent of their abilities. *See* C. Karraker, The Seventeenth Century Sheriff 166–168 (1930) (illustrative oath of office administered in England to Sheriff William Ffraington in 1636, including the undertaking that "yee shall trulye return and trulye serve all the Kings Writs as far forth as it shallbee in your cunnige"); id. at 167–168 (Sheriff's Oath of Office, Virginia, 1641: "You shall truly retorne and truely serve all the Kings writs as farr forth as shall be to you Cunning.")....

gave legal systems the confidence to hold a defendant at risk for nonappearance after such service.

By contrast, today's service of process is characterized by photocopied forms and impersonal methods of delivery, perhaps reaching its nadir with modern mail service. With little of the element of confrontation that characterized some early procedures, and an absence of the personal interaction with the lawgivers that still attends commencement of an action in some primitive cultures,[18] service of process today is several steps removed from the personal participation of a plaintiff. The awesome impact of the sheriff arriving in armor and on horseback to deliver a writ in medieval England and the authority of the sovereign sealed in hot, red wax of earlier times has been replaced....

Kent Sinclair, Service of Process: Rethinking the Theory and Procedure of Service Process Under Federal Rule 4(c), 73 Va. L. Rev. 1183, 1187–89 (1987).

In most jurisdictions today, service of process is governed by detailed but generally straightforward rules. Procedural codes or rules typically prescribe methods that may vary depending on whether the defendant is an individual, a corporation, a government, or some other entity. For example, a corporate defendant may be properly notified by personal delivery to an officer of that company or by certain forms of mail requiring a signed receipt. Service on individuals may require personal notification or delivery to the individual's residence. Each country, of course, has its own law and practice.

In many common law jurisdictions, and in countries such as those in Scandinavia with a similar approach, the responsibility for service is often assigned to plaintiffs or to individuals retained by them (e.g., agents, solicitors, process-servers). By contrast, in many civil law countries, service is usually an action that must be undertaken either by the court itself or by some other public authority. In these circumstances, the court is exercising a power of the state, and its actions have sovereign character. The initiating documents may be served by an officer of the court, who may be the clerk to the court (as in Switzerland), or an officer with specific functions including the service of process (such as the ufficiale giudiziario in Italy), or in some countries such as France a huissier de justice, a process-server

[18] Those who believe that service of process is a dry subject would do well to study the litigation procedures of the Zinacantan, a Mayan tribe in Mexico adhering to ancient traditions. A would-be plaintiff among the Zinacantan must personally help to move the judicial apparatus to cause service of process upon the defendant. Normal litigation protocol calls for the plaintiff to visit the local liquor store, purchase a bottle of rum, and then appear before El Presidente, a ranking administrative and judicial authority. The plaintiff may place the bottle of rum and the fee of El President at the outset of the audience or may elect to keep it in his pocket while describing the background of the action, producing and offering it only when making a formal prayer for relief. If El Presidente is satisfied with the composite liability and libation application, he directs the Mayores, minor officials, to summon the defendant for further proceedings in the matter. *See* J. Collier, Law and Social Change in Zinacantan 36–38 (1973).

appointed by the state authorities but engaged in a professional capacity by the plaintiff. These "formal" methods of service are often closely regulated by legislation. Many civil law countries also recognize certain "informal" and "voluntary" forms of service that are effective in particular contexts.

In some jurisdictions the act of service may, in addition to effecting notice, also constitute a basis for the exercise of personal jurisdiction. In the United States, the United Kingdom, Ireland, Finland, and elsewhere, the in-hand service of process upon a defendant who is then within the forum state is an exercise of the court's territorial authority that may establish jurisdiction to adjudicate. See Chapter 3.

Complications may arise when the plaintiff and defendant are located in different countries. The participants (and their respective court systems) may have very different assumptions about service, with each projecting on to the international plane the familiar features of their own national systems. For example, systems that view service of process as a judicial act may have unrealistic expectations that another system's government will offer formal assistance. More problematically, litigants from systems that view service as a largely private act may interfere with the sovereignty of another country by performing what is there perceived to be an official act. Indeed, some systems make it an offense to perform, without express permission from the local government, judicial functions within their territories. "Ignorance or disregard of [such prohibitions] has led to a damage suit abroad for malicious trespass against an Assistant U.S. Attorney who served a subpoena at a private residence in the Bahamas, and to a criminal indictment of an SEC staff attorney who served an administrative subpoena in France." U.S. Dept. Justice Mem. No. 386, at 20 (1977), reprinted in 16 Int'l Legal Materials 1331, 1338 (1977). Similarly, Article 271 of the Swiss Penal Code provides:

> Whoever, without authorization, executes acts on Swiss territory which are attributed to an administrative or government authority, on behalf of a foreign state, and whoever executes such acts on behalf of a foreign person or another foreign organization, and whoever encourages or otherwise participates in such acts, will be punished with prison, and in severe cases with penitentiary.

See Yvonne A. Tamayo, Catch Me If You Can: Serving United States Process on an Elusive Defendant broad, 17 Harv. J.L. & Tech. 211, 239 n.192 (2003).

The Problem: Navigating Service*

Approximately six months ago, the cargo vessel *Sky One* was loaded with marble at Marina di Carrara in Italy for carriage to Jeddah in Saudi Arabia. Several days after the vessel set sail, it sank a few miles off the coast of Crete. At the time that

---

* This hypothetical is derived from *Ferrarini SpA v. Magnol Shipping Co., Inc., The Sky One* [1988] 1 Lloyd's Rep 238 (aff'd CA, ibid).

the ship sank, the cargo was owned by Contintental Ltd., an English corporation. Continental argues that the accident occurred because of the age and unseaworthiness of the vessel, and claims £280,000 in damages. The owner of the *Sky One*, a Panamanian corporation, disclaims responsibility and ascribes the accident to a collision with an as-yet unidentified underwater object.

Continental would prefer to file suit against the owners of the *Sky One* in an English court, assuming that court has personal jurisdiction. But the Panamanian defendants cannot be served in England. The defendant must be given proper notice of the fact that litigation is pending against it, of the nature of the case, and of the date by which action on its part is required. Moreover, the notice must be given promptly and in time for the defendant to adequately prepare a defense. But which court system defines whether the notice that defendant receives is "proper," "timely," "adequate" and so forth? Does it matter—and should it matter—whether defendant is served in England, Panama, or elsewhere?

(1) If the suit is filed in England, is this purely a matter of English law even if the defendants are served in Panama? Regardless of what substantive law applies to this dispute by virtue of rules of private international law (or conflict of laws), procedural matters are typically governed by the lex fori. The English courts thus might look only to their own law to determine whether there has been sufficient notice ("service of process"). This law would also identify the steps required to set running the time which must elapse before a default judgment can be entered; and the same law would, in some countries, be applied to determine whether service was so defective that a default judgment must be set aside.

(2) If the defendants are served in Panama, should Panama be able to properly exercise some measure of control over acts done within their borders? If a country understands service of process to be an official government act, that country may be especially reluctant to welcome or permit an expression of sovereignty by some other state within its borders. Indeed, service on behalf of the plaintiff of foreign process could even be an offense punishable by imprisonment. Would such punishment under Panamanian law interfere with the sovereignty of the forum state?

(3) Assume that you represent the plaintiff and are able to serve the defendant in a manner that complies with English law at a cost of £1,000. Compliance also with the much more elaborate Panamanian law will cost an additional £9,000. Failure to comply with the Panamanian law will not subject you or anyone else to imprisonment or any other punishment, but the Panamanian courts are likely to view any English judgment as void. Under what circumstances would you undertake the additional expense?

(4) Perhaps the English and Panamanian (and other) governments should anticipate such litigation and coordinate transnational service of process by treaty. Is this likely or even feasible?

B. The Functions of Service of Process

Haimo Schack, Transnational Service of Process
6 Unif. L. Rev. n.s. 827, 830–832 (2001)

Service—the formalized, documented handing over of specific documents (pleadings, judicial decisions)—is provided for by all legal systems. Formal proof in the shape of a certificate of service is needed for the introduction and pursuit of legal proceedings and is therefore primarily of service to the plaintiff. The documentary procedure, i.e., remittance of the document, is intended to inform the addressee of the legal action being taken against it and to enable it to make use of its opportunity and right to be heard. Timely service of the statement of claim and other documents instituting proceedings is of elementary importance to the defendant.

Conflicts of interest arise when it is impossible or difficult physically to hand over the documents to the addressee. This may be because the addressee lives abroad, or because its place of abode is unknown, or because it purposely seeks to evade service. In such cases, the legislator must weigh the plaintiff's interest in a speedy trial against the defendant's interest in obtaining actual knowledge of the content of the documents in question. For both parties, the problem is one of guaranteeing the effectiveness of judicial relief.

That being so, extreme solutions are out of the question. The plaintiff is no more entitled to disregard the normal complexities of service and go ahead with the proceedings than the defendant is allowed to torpedo the proceedings simply by refusing to accept delivery of the document. But as long as the defendant is not aware of the action brought against it, it is entitled to maximum legal protection as the only guarantee of fair process.

In other words, the method of service must be such as to ensure that the defendant is informed of the action against it in a reliable and timely manner, so that it can defend itself. How this information is transmitted is of secondary importance; even roundabout ways are harmless provided the period for filing a defence is sufficiently long. The notice will, however, only be useful if the document is written in a language the addressee understands....

[Another] element concerns the warning function of service. Service must be in a form distinct from ordinary letters or e-mails, since these latter are too easily overlooked. This need for special attention is one reason to adhere to the principle (valid in Germany and Austria) that service of process be ex officio. Service by the parties themselves is liable to denegrate; moreover, the court would have no opportunity to inspect the document prior to service. If the purpose is to facilitate the form of service, then the sender's seriousness must be beyond all doubt. The court also has a duty to protect the defendant.

The widespread continental view of service as an act of sovereignty would seem to suggest that the sovereignty of the State of residence can protect the defendant from encroachments of service from abroad. This is a misconception, however, since, even if the State of residence declines to participate in the transnational service of process, the proceedings in the State where judgment is to be rendered will nevertheless continue, if necessary after service by publication. If we take Germany as an example, it is simply not true that a party that is resident abroad can only be drawn into German proceedings in accordance with the laws of its home country. In point of fact, the home country can only refuse to recognise a foreign judgment once rendered, and only insofar as it pertains to such of defendant's property as is located in the State of recognition....

In order to fulfil its legitimate functions, service must be simple, quick, reliable and fair. Certainly, these conditions leave much to be desired, both in Germany and abroad, when, e.g., service to "Bronx N.Y." is held ineffective because the country designation "USA" is missing; when service of process in Spain, for example (even though it is part of the EU!) involves up to two years of judicial assistance; when substituted service all too easily becomes fictitious service; or when the period for filing a defence—such as might occur following a remise au parquet or constructive service by mail, is so short that time runs out before the document actually reaches the defendant. Even though the defendant is sometimes helped by reinstatement, such service of process remains unfair.

Comments and Questions

1. Consider whether service of process is necessarily a solemn act. Is casual service by e-mail, voice mail, or ordinary mail in some way inferior—i.e., less "notice"? Is formality a process norm or a cultural expectation?

2. What is the resident state's "interest" when one of its citizens is named as a defendant in foreign litigation? Does a state have a similar interest whenever one of its citizens enters into a significant contract with a foreigner? ((How) Is that state "interest" protected?)

C. National Practice

In this section, we review several national approaches to transnational service of process. In most systems, a court cannot exercise jurisdiction without proper service of process. Indeed, in many jurisdictions service is the very basis on which jurisdiction rests. Service provides the defendant with notice of the claims against it and announces the opportunity to be heard. The date of service may also constitute the formal commencement of the action for various timing purposes.

David McClean, Differing Approaches to Transnational Service

International Co-operation in Civil and Criminal Matters 14–18 (Oxford 2002)

The form which is taken by international assistance in the service of process depends upon a number of necessarily interrelated factors. International discussion is eased if they are distinguished as far as possible. The first issue concerns the initiation of international action within the state of origin. The law of that state, as lex fori, will prescribe any special procedures to be followed where service is to be effected abroad. Where the common law approach of treating service as a matter for the plaintiff prevails, there are usually few special requirements. The leave of the court or of some other official agency may be required and official assistance may be available to those who choose to avail themselves of it; but no special steps to initiate the actual business of service abroad will be mandatory. The lex fori will be satisfied by proof that the plaintiff has secured the service of the documents on the defendant abroad, either by taking them personally or (much more usually) by employing an agent.

The more formal civil law tradition requires international service to be initiated by specified officials. Action may be required by the court itself, the court issuing a Letter of Request asking either a foreign court or another competent authority in the state of destination to assist in having the documents served; this practice is particularly entrenched in Latin America. In many other countries the initiating steps will be taken by an officer attached to the court. Taking the French system as an example, the huissier de justice engaged by the plaintiff will deliver the documents to the ministère public; this is a body of officers attached to the court and primarily responsible for the public prosecution function in the criminal jurisdiction, and customarily and conveniently referred to as the parquet (which literally means "the well of the court" where these officers used to be placed). The parquet is responsible for the onward transmission of the documents via central government agencies. The law may allow the huissier himself, given his semi-official position, to initiate contact with the competent authorities (or a brother huissier) in the state of destination, or may (as has French law since 1966) require the huissier to take informal steps such as the use of the post to supplement the official service initiated by the parquet.

The second issue is in a sense the counterpart of the first, for it concerns the proper addressee in the state of destination. The law of that state as to the service of documents originating abroad may permit documents to be sent directly to the defendant without the use of any local official acting as intermediary, or it may insist on the documents passing through, for example, the court having jurisdiction at the defendant's place of residence, the parquet attached to that court, or a huissier practicing in the relevant area....

The interaction of these issues affects the final point, the actual mode of transmission of documents from country to country. Official modes, such as the diplomatic channel, are more likely to be associated with communications which must pass between officials in the two countries, whilst the post may be more appropriate for communications between huissiers or directly to the defendant....

Taking these factors into account, it is possible to list a range of forms of procedure which are, or have in the past been, found in national legislation and in practice under international conventions.

(a) The Diplomatic Channel

The most venerable and most formal mode of communications is the diplomatic channel. It may lend a certain dignity to the whole transaction but is notoriously slow. This is due to the number of distinct administrative hierarchies whose active co-operation is required, and whose officers frankly have other tasks of much greater priority and interest. Under this procedure, documents emanating from, say, a court or parquet in the state of origin are transmitted (perhaps via the Ministry of Justice of that state) to its Ministry for External Affairs. They are then sent to the embassy maintained in the state of destination which conveys them to the External Affairs Ministry of that state, which will pass them over to its Ministry of Justice to be sent down to the appropriate local agency for delivery to the addressee. If some acknowledgement of due service is required, it may have to retrace the path of the original documents.

(b) The (Direct) Consular Channel

The service of judicial documents is a well-recognized consular function. Its exercise depends very much on the conventions governing consular relations between the states concerned. It may be that the consul for the state of origin can serve documents only on nationals of his state, or he may be allowed to effect service on anyone in the area of his responsibility. In some cases, notably where consuls are not in post, these consular functions may actually be performed by diplomatic officers.

(c) The Indirect Consular Channel

Many writers treat the diplomatic and (direct) consular channels as part of the customary practice of states. Arguably the indirect consular channel, like the modes of transmission still to be noted, is solely a creature of conventions. The "indirectness" lies in the fact that the consul does not approach the defendant directly, but the appropriate authority in the state of destination; this will usually be some central government agency, within the Ministry of Justice for example, but local officers can be specified.

(d) Ministry of Justice (or Central Authority) to Ministry of Justice (or Central Authority)

It is considerably simpler to exclude the relevant Ministries for External Affairs and their diplomatic or consular staffs from the process. The administration of justice is a central concern of a Ministry of Justice, and direct communication between the two Justice Ministries is likely to produce greater understanding and a speedier response. What is essential to this mode is that each country should communicate via some agency of central government located in that part of the state's apparatus which is concerned with the administration of justice. This agency can have a title other than that of Ministry of Justice (for example, Attorney-General's Department) or may be located in the courts service or form a specialist bureau. In every case, the agency will communicate with its counterpart in the other country.

(e) Competent Official to Ministry of Justice (or Central Authority)

Most of the modes considered so far require the involvement in each state of an agency of central government as well as the competent official (parquet, etc.) at the local level. There is a readily identified "central government interest" within the state of destination where considerations of sovereignty may be seen to be involved and where some knowledge of the nature of the documents is necessary if the state of destination is to be sure that its public policy (for example as to bank secrecy) is not offended. The interest of central government in the outward transmission of documents intended for service abroad is less pressing. There may be real practical advantages in having a central source of expertise; such a source is more likely to send documents in a form, and with accompanying material, required by the state of destination or specified in the applicable bilateral or multilateral convention. If however the local officials in the state of origin have access to appropriate procedural guidance, there is no strong reason of principle not to allow them to communicate directly with the Justice Ministry or other central authority of the state of destination. This mode comprises just that procedure.

One theoretical possibility which is thought not to be found in actual practice would be for the plaintiff, in a state of origin which regarded service as a matter for the parties to handle, to be allowed to make a direct approach to the Justice Ministry or other central authority of the state of destination. Ministries of Justice are, however, quite properly unwilling to enter into dialogue with private citizens of other states in this context, or to operate an advisory service for foreign lawyers.

(f) Competent Official to Competent Official

The argument supporting mode (e) can be taken a stage further. Provided the competent local officials in the state of destination have adequate administrative guidance, their Justice Ministry may be content, or even happy, to withdraw from active involvement. This opens the way for direct communication between the appropriate officer (parquet, etc.) in the state of origin and his counterpart in the state of destination.

(g) Huissier de Justice to Huissier de Justice

Where both concerned states have the institution of huissier de justice, a variant of the last mode is possible. The facts that huissiers are appointed or licensed by the state and have a defined role in codes of civil procedure in respect of service enable them to be treated as in a similar position to the competent state officials, and direct communication from huissier to huissier (who will then act in the state of destination to involve the local parquet) can be authorized.

(h) Plaintiff to Competent Official

This mode represents the ultimate "deregulation," always supposing that service by some official of the state of destination is required. It allows a direct approach by the plaintiff or his agent to the competent local official in that state. No official of the state of origin is involved.

(i) Service by Post

The final mode eliminates all official involvement and permits the plaintiff or his agent to send the documents, with some appropriate means of obtaining confirmation of their delivery, by post. It may be that "post" will need progressive reinterpretation to include telex, facsimile transmission and other forms of electronic mail but only the most recent international instruments reflect these newer possibilities. This means that the older conventions requiring the use of the post impose delays which any commercial firm with access to modern technology would not tolerate in its normal practice.

Comments and Questions

1. A formal request from the courts of one country to those of another is often called a "letter rogatory" of "letter or request." Specific treaties may authorize the transmission of letters through diplomatic or other channels. Even where there is no convention in force, the request for judicial assistance could be executed upon principles of comity and reciprocity.

2. Is the issuance of letters rogatory an inherent judicial function? An executive function? Should its exercise require legislative authority?

3. The form of a sample letter rogatory (or letter of request) to the Republic of Iceland follows:

UNITED STATES DISTRICT COURT
FOR THE DISTRICT OF MASSACHUSETTS

CaiCay Indus., Inc.,
Plaintiff

v. Civil Action No. 4843-NRVD

Keisha Naig,
Defendant

REQUEST FOR INTERNATIONAL JUDICIAL ASSISTANCE
(LETTER ROGATORY)

The United States District Court for the District of Massachusetts presents its compliments to the appropriate judicial authority of the Republic of Iceland, and requests international judicial assistance to effect service of process to be used in a civil proceeding before this court in the above captioned matter.

This action was filed in the United States District Court for the District of Massachusetts on July 12, 20xx, and a hearing on this matter is scheduled at present for December 15, 20xx in Boston, Massachusetts, U.S.A.

The defendant in the above captioned matter is a resident of the City of Grindavík in the Republic of Iceland. The last known address of Ms. Naig is Bluelagoon Road, Grindavik 240, Iceland.

The court requests the assistance described herein as necessary in the interests of justice. The assistance requested is that the appropriate judicial authority of the Republic of Iceland cause the attached copies of the summons and complaint to be served upon defendant Ms. Keisha Naig, in such a manner as is reasonably calculated to give the defendant actual notice of this action.

We further request that you cause the sworn statement of the person actually serving the summons and complaint on defendant to be taken, according to the proper and usual process of your court, stating the date and manner in which service was made, and to cause this statement to be reduced to writing and returned to us under cover, duly closed and sealed, endorsed with the title of this action, together with these presents, addressed to the Clerk of the United States District Court for the District of Massachusetts, at 1 Courthouse Way, Boston, Massachusetts 02210 U.S.A.

The United States District Court for the District of Massachusetts will reimburse the judicial authorities of the Republic of Iceland for costs incurred in executing this Request.

Further, the United States District Court for the District of Massachusetts hereby expresses its willingness to provide similar assistance to judicial authorities of the Republic of Iceland when required.

Witness the Honorable Eloise Francis, District Judge of the United States District Court for the District of Massachusetts, the United States of America.

Dated: /d/ [Signature] [Court seal]

1. United States

Rule 4 of the Federal Rules of Civil Procedure specifies the methods for service of process in cases brought in United States federal courts. In particular, Rule 4(f) and 4(h) describe methods for service of process outside the United States:

> (f) Service Upon Individuals in a Foreign Country
>
> Unless otherwise provided by federal law, service upon an individual from whom a waiver has not been obtained and filed, other than an infant or an incompetent person, may be effected in a place not within any judicial district of the United States:
>
> (1) by any internationally agreed means reasonably calculated to give notice, such as those means authorized by the Hague Convention on the Service Abroad of Judicial and Extrajudicial Documents;
>
> (2) if there is no internationally agreed means of service or the applicable international agreement allows other means of service, provided that service is reasonably calculated to give notice:
>
> (A) in the manner prescribed by the law of the foreign country for service in that country in an action in any of its courts of general jurisdiction; or
>
> (B) as directed by the foreign authority in response to a letter rogatory or letter of request; or

(C) unless prohibited by the law of the foreign country, by
  (i) delivery to the individual personally of a copy of the summons and the complaint; or
  (ii) any form of mail requiring a signed receipt, to be addressed and dispatched by the clerk of the court to the party to be served; or

(3) by other means not prohibited by international agreement as may be directed by the court....

(h) Service Upon Corporations and Associations

Unless otherwise provided by federal law, service upon a domestic or foreign corporation or upon a partnership or other unincorporated association that is subject to suit under a common name, and from which a waiver of service has not been obtained and filed, shall be effected:...

(1) in a judicial district of the United States..., or

(2) in a place not within any judicial district of the United States in any manner prescribed for individuals by subdivision (f) except personal delivery as provided in paragraph (2)(C)(i) thereof.

"Internationally agreed means of service" are discussed later in this chapter. The following case focuses on methods of service available under Fed. R. Civ. P. 4(f)(2) and (3).

Prewitt Enterprises, Inc. v. Organization of Petroleum Exporting Countries

353 F.3d 916 (11th Cir. 2003), cert. denied, 543 U.S. 814 (2004)

Barkett, Circuit Judge

Prewitt Enterprises, Inc. ("Prewitt") appeals from the dismissal of its complaint against the Organization of the Petroleum Exporting Countries ("OPEC") for insufficient service of process and from the denial of its motion for alternative service of process. Prewitt's complaint against OPEC alleged a violation of the Sherman Act, 15 U.S.C. § 1 for illegal price-fixing agreements on production and export of crude oil and claimed equitable relief pursuant to the Clayton Act, 15 U.S.C. § 26. Because OPEC initially did not respond to the complaint, the district court entered a default final judgment against OPEC enjoining it from entering into, implementing or enforcing any agreements to fix and control the production and export of crude oil for one year. OPEC then appeared and moved to vacate the default judgment and injunction on the grounds that OPEC had never been properly served with process, and thus, the court lacked jurisdiction over it. The district court concluded that, because OPEC resides in Austria and the applicable Austrian law prohibits service without OPEC's consent, Prewitt's complaint must be dismissed for lack of jurisdiction. We agree and affirm the dismissal of Prewitt's complaint for lack of jurisdiction because service of process on OPEC has not been effectuated. We also affirm the district court's denial of alternative service of process because, in this case, there are no means available for service upon OPEC under the Federal Rules of Civil Procedure.

I Background

Prewitt is a corporation organized and existing under the laws of Alabama with its principal place of business in Birmingham, Alabama. Prewitt purchases substantial quantities of gasoline and other refined petroleum products for resale at its Eastwood Texaco Service Center gasoline station.

OPEC is an intergovernmental organization originally established in 1960 via resolutions promulgated at the Conference of the Representatives of the Governments of Iran, Iraq, Kuwait, Saudi Arabia and Venezuela in Baghdad, Iraq. The principal aim of OPEC is "the co-ordination and unification of the petroleum policies of Member Countries and the determination of the best means for safeguarding their interests, individually and collectively." OPEC Stat. art. 2(A) (2000). Presently, OPEC's membership consists of: Algeria, Indonesia, Iran, Iraq, Kuwait, Libya, Nigeria, Qatar, Saudi Arabia, the United Arab Emirates and Venezuela. Since September 1, 1965, OPEC has been headquartered in Vienna, Austria. Its relationship with the Austrian government is governed by the Agreement Between the Republic of Austria and the Organization of the Petroleum Exporting Countries Regarding the Headquarters of the Organization of the Petroleum Exporting Countries, February 18, 1974, BGBL 1974/382 ("Austrian/OPEC Headquarters Agreement" or "Headquarters Agreement").

Prewitt filed a complaint with the district court against OPEC on behalf of itself and as the representative of all persons or entities who have indirectly purchased petroleum or petroleum products in the United States since March 1999. Prewitt claimed that OPEC has been coordinating an international conspiracy through agreements among its Member States and non-OPEC members to limit the production and export of oil in order to fix world oil prices above competitive levels. Prewitt argued that these agreements constitute violations of United States antitrust laws, specifically the Sherman and Clayton Acts, and have resulted in a substantial and adverse impact on United States trade and commerce. Prewitt claimed that as a result of OPEC's illegal conduct, its own acquisition and inventory costs for gasoline have increased significantly. Consequently, Prewitt requested that the court declare the OPEC-coordinated agreements illegal under United States law, enjoin implementation of the agreements, grant any other appropriate equitable relief, and award costs of the suit against OPEC for injuries sustained by Prewitt.

Prewitt attempted service on OPEC by requesting that the trial court send a copy of the complaint to OPEC by international registered mail, return receipt requested. The court clerk did so, mailing Prewitt's summons and complaint to OPEC at its headquarters in Vienna. The pleadings were signed for, stamped "received" by OPEC's Administration and Human Resources Department, and forwarded to the Director of OPEC's Research Division as well as other departments including the Secretary General's office. Ultimately, the Secretary General decided that the OPEC Secretariat would not take any action with regard to the summons and complaint.

Without the participation of OPEC, the district court certified a class defined as all persons or entities who purchased refined petroleum products in the United States from March 1999 to the present and entered a default final judgment and order of injunction against OPEC. The court found that there was a conspiracy between OPEC, its Member States, and non-OPEC members, namely Norway, Mexico, the Russian Federation and Oman, to fix and control crude oil prices; that the agreements coordinated and implemented by OPEC were illegal under United States antitrust laws; that OPEC's illegal conduct has resulted in substantial and adverse impact on United States trade and commerce of approximately $80–120 million per day; and that OPEC and those acting in concert with OPEC should be enjoined from entering into, implementing, and enforcing any further oil price-fixing agreements for a period of twelve months. Copies of the court's orders were delivered to each of the United States embassies for the Member States of OPEC.

In response, OPEC made a special appearance and filed a motion to set aside the default judgment and stay its enforcement pursuant to Rule 60(b)(1), (4), (5) and (6) of the Federal Rules of Civil Procedure, which the district court granted, vacating the default judgment and injunction. OPEC then filed a motion to dismiss Prewitt's complaint on various grounds including insufficient service of process pursuant to Fed. R. Civ. P. 12(b)(5). The district court dismissed the case without prejudice, finding that Prewitt had failed to serve OPEC its summons and complaint properly under the Federal Rules. Prewitt then filed a motion to pursue alternative means of effecting service or to amend the judgment. The district court denied the motion finding that, in this case, OPEC cannot be effectively served with process.

II Discussion

We review the district court's grant of a motion to dismiss for insufficient service of process under Fed. R. Civ. P. 12(b)(5) by applying a de novo standard to the law and a clear error standard to any findings of fact. We generally review the district court's interpretation of Fed. R. Civ. P. 4 on service of process as a matter of law de novo. Likewise, the district court's interpretation of foreign law in determining sufficiency of service of process is subject to de novo review. However, we join our sister circuit in holding that the district court's denial of a motion for alternative service of process under Fed. R. Civ. P. 4(f)(3) is subject to an abuse of discretion standard because the plain language of the rule stipulates that the district court "may" direct alternative means of service. Rio Properties, Inc. v. Rio Int'l Interlink, 284 F.3d 1007, 1014 (9th Cir. 2002).

The threshold issue in this case is whether OPEC has been effectively served under the Federal Rules of Civil Procedure. If it has not, we must then determine whether extraterritorial service of process on OPEC may be effectuated at all under the circumstances here.... There are two rules of federal civil procedure that apply to service of process upon an international entity located outside of United States jurisdiction: Fed. R. Civ. P. 4(f) (Service Upon Individuals in a Foreign Country) and Fed. R. Civ. P. 4(h) (Service of Process Upon Corporations and Associations). The latter governs service on unincorporated associations located outside of the United States and provides that:

> Unless otherwise provided by federal law, service upon a[n]...unincorporated association that is subject to suit under a common name, and from which a waiver of service has not been obtained and filed, shall be effected:...
>
> (2) in a place not within any judicial district of the United States in any manner prescribed for individuals by subdivision (f) except personal delivery....

Fed. R. Civ. P. 4(h)(2) (emphasis added). Thus, an "unincorporated association"[6] headquartered outside of the United States that is (1) subject to suit under a common name and (2) has not waived service may be served in any manner authorized under Fed. R. Civ. P. 4(f) for individuals in a foreign country except for personal delivery.

Turning to Fed. R. Civ. P. 4(f),... [i]n this case, no other means of service has been "otherwise provided by federal law" nor is there an "internationally agreed means reasonably calculated to give notice such as those means authorized by the Hague Convention on the Service Abroad of Judicial and Extrajudicial Documents...."[10]

Thus, we must look to the remainder of Fed. R. Civ. P. 4(f), which provides for other methods by which an unincorporated association may be served in the absence of relevant federal law or international agreements. ....Prewitt originally chose to attempt service of process on OPEC under Fed. R. Civ. P. 4(f)(C)(ii). However, the method set forth under that provision applies only if it is not

---

[6] The district court treated OPEC as an unincorporated association pursuant to Fed. R. Civ. P. 17(b)(1). Under this Circuit's jurisprudence, an unincorporated association is defined as "a body of persons acting together, without a charter, but upon the methods and forms used by corporations, for the prosecution of some common enterprise." *Penrod Drilling Co. v. Johnson,* 414 F.2d 1217, 1222 (5th Cir. 1969) (holding that labor unions, agricultural societies, co-ops, banking associations, charitable associations, news associations, and religious societies may all be considered unincorporated associations)....In this case, OPEC is an administrative body joined together for the common purpose of acting on behalf of the business and political interests of its members with regard to their petroleum resources. While its members are sovereign nation states rather than private individuals, OPEC is not a governmental unit or subdivision and is not incorporated under the laws of any one Member State. Thus, under the facts of this case, we agree that it is amenable to the designation of "unincorporated association."...

[10] The Hague Convention on the Service Abroad of Judicial and Extrajudicial Documents in Civil or Commercial Matters Done at The Hague, the Netherlands, November 15, 1965, 658 U.N.T.S. 163 ("Hague Service Convention"), provides rules governing service of process between signatory states. However, while the United States is party to the Hague Service Convention, Austria is not. Austria *is* party to the Hague Convention on Civil Procedure, entered into force March 1, 1954, 286 U.N.T.S. 265, 1 Am. J. Comp. L. 282 (1952) (translation), but the United States is not.

prohibited by the law of the foreign country. Based on the evidence presented,[11] the district court correctly found that service on OPEC was prohibited by the law of Austria. Article 5(2) of the Austrian/OPEC Headquarters Agreement provides that: "the service of legal process... shall not take place within the [OPEC] headquarters seat except with the express consent of, and under conditions approved by, the Secretary General."[12] Since the Headquarters Agreement was enacted into law by resolution of the Austrian Parliament and published in the Austrian Official Gazette pursuant to the Austrian Constitution, the district court found it to be an integral part of Austrian law. Thus, because service was prohibited by Austrian law, Prewitt could not have effectively served OPEC under Fed. R. Civ. P. 4(f)(2)(C)(ii).

Prewitt nonetheless suggests that we should liberally construe the formal requirements for service under the Federal Rules because OPEC received actual notice but simply chose to "ignore the whole thing." Br. of Appellant at 23. However, we find no support for such an argument. Due process under the United States Constitution requires that "before a court may exercise personal jurisdiction over a defendant, there must be more than notice to the defendant... [t]here also must be a basis for the defendant's amenability to service of summons. Absent consent, this means there must be authorization for service of summons on the defendant." Omni Capital Int'l v. Rudolf Wolff & Co., 484 U.S. 97, 104 (1987) (emphasis added). In other words, an individual or entity "is not obliged to engage in litigation unless [officially] notified of the action... under a court's authority, by formal process." Murphy Bros., Inc. v. Michetti Pipe Stringing, Inc., 526 U.S. 344, 347 (1999). In this case, Fed. R. Civ. P. 4(f)(2)(C)(ii) clearly states that service of process

---

[11] Evidence on service of process in Austria under Austrian and international law was considered by the district court pursuant to Fed. R. Civ. P. 44.1 (Determination of Foreign Law), which provides that:

> A party who intends to raise an issue concerning the law of a foreign country shall give notice by pleadings or other reasonable written notice. The court, in determining foreign law, may consider any relevant material or source, including testimony, whether or not submitted by a party or admissible under the Federal Rules of Evidence. The court's determination shall be treated as a ruling on a question of law.

The evidence before the district court included: sections of Austrian law from the Austrian Constitution, the Austrian Service Act, and the Austrian Code of Civil Procedure; articles of international treaties such as the Vienna Convention on the Law of Treaties, entered into force January 27, 1980, 1155 U.N.T.S. 331, and the Austrian/OPEC Headquarters Agreement; expert affidavits and testimony from Austrian lawyers and professors on Austrian law; correspondence between Austrian law experts; "Notes Verbales" between the Austrian Ministry of Foreign Affairs and OPEC; correspondence from the Austrian Embassy to the District Court for the Northern District of Alabama on service of process in Austria; the United States State Department circular on service of process abroad; the Austrian Foreign Ministry website on Austrian law; and academic treatises on transnational litigation.

[12] As noted in some of the amicus curiae briefs submitted to this Court, this provision is commonly found in numerous other Headquarters Agreements between sovereign states and international organizations around the world....

by registered mail is only authorized where it is not prohibited by foreign law. Here, the Headquarters Agreement constitutes Austrian law and, under Article 5(2), expressly prohibits all service of process upon OPEC within the headquarters seat that has not been consented to by its Secretary General. Thus, we agree with the district court that even though OPEC had actual notice of the filing of the suit, service of process was ineffective because it was clearly not in substantial compliance with the requirements of Fed. R. Civ. P. 4(f)(2)(C)(ii).

Alternatively, Prewitt argues that even if service failed under Fed. R. Civ. P. 4(f)(2)(C)(ii), service by registered mail upon OPEC nonetheless complied with Fed. R. Civ. P. 4(f)(2)(A), which permits service if it is effectuated "in the manner prescribed by the law of the foreign country for service in that country in an action in any of its courts of general jurisdiction." The provisions of Austrian law that Prewitt references from Austria's Civil Procedure Code and regulations for service of process by mail relate to service by Austrian courts on persons resident in Austria and abroad. None of these Austrian law provisions directly pertain to service mailed from abroad upon international organizations resident in Austria. Prewitt argues that we should look only to the approved "method" of service within the foreign jurisdiction and not to the substance of Austrian law. However, the substance of the law specifically relating to service of process cannot be divorced from the "method" of service. Indeed, §§ 12(1) and 11(2) of the Austrian Service Act specifically address service from authorities abroad upon residents in Austria and trump the more general provisions cited by Prewitt from the Austrian Code of Civil Procedure and regulations for service of process by Austrian courts on residents in Austria or abroad. Moreover, the Regulation Regarding the Service of Process by Mail upon Persons Abroad in Civil Proceedings that Prewitt argues applies in this case specifically states that it does not apply to service on entities specified under § 11(2) of the Austrian Service Act. Dist. Ct. Doc. 87, Exh. 4B. Section 12(1) (as amended 1990) of the Austrian Service Act requires that:

> The service of documents generated by authorities abroad to recipients in Austria shall be carried out in accordance with the existing international conventions, in the absence of which it has to be done in accordance with this law.... (emphasis added).

Section 11(2) (as amended 1998) of the Austrian Service Act directly addresses service from abroad upon international organizations such as OPEC requiring that:

> the mediation of the Federal Ministry for Foreign Affairs shall be enlisted in undertaking service of process on foreigners or international organizations that enjoy privileges and immunities under international law, regardless of their place of residence or headquarters.

There would be no way for Prewitt to serve OPEC under § 11(2) of the Austrian Service Act because we must assume that if it had gone to the Austrian Federal Ministry of Foreign Affairs, the Ministry would have applied the laws of its own country and obeyed the dictates of the Austrian/OPEC Headquarters Agreement prohibiting service without OPEC's consent.

In response, Prewitt again argues that actual notice can cure defective service of process pursuant to Section 7 of the Austrian Service Act, which provides:

> Should defects in service of process occur, service shall be deemed effectuated at the time when the document has actually reached the recipient designated by the authority.

Section 7 (as amended January 1, 1991) of the Austrian Service Act. However, this section has specifically been interpreted in Austria not to apply to defects in service of process that are in breach of the requirements for service under an international agreement such as the Austrian/OPEC Headquarters Agreement.[17] Moreover, Section 7 may not cure a failure to obtain OPEC's express consent because under the Austrian law of lex specialis, the more specific provision in the Headquarters Agreement for service of process upon OPEC takes precedence over the more general language of the Austrian Service Act. Expert Decl. of Dr. Wolfgang Hahnkamper, Dist. Ct. Doc. 80, Exh. 5 at 416–17, 420–21.[18] Finally, Prewitt contends that even if its service by registered mail on OPEC could not be effectuated pursuant to any of the provisions of Fed. R. Civ. P. 4(f)(2), the district court still had the discretion to order service of process pursuant to Fed. R. Civ. P. 4(f)(3), which provides that service may be effected "by other means not prohibited by international agreement as may be directed by the court." (emphasis added). We agree with Prewitt that a district court's denial of relief under 4(f)(3) is reviewed under an abuse of discretion standard. However, there is no abuse of discretion here; on the contrary, any circumvention of 4(f)(2)(C)(ii) by the district court in directing service again by registered mail would constitute such an abuse. On these facts, we cannot read 4(f)(3) as permitting that which has already been specifically prohibited under 4(f)(2).

Prewitt then argues that, even if service by registered mail is prohibited by 4(f)(2), other means of giving actual notice, such as fax or e-mail, that are not

[17] The Austrian Administrative Court ("Verwaltungsgerichtshof") has held that a breach of a rule in an international agreement on service of process was not a "simple defect of service" that could be cured by Section 7 of the Austrian Service Act. The court stated the rule that: "[S]imple consideration of the generally acknowledged rules of public law, which apply according to Art. 9(1) B-VG [Federal Constitutional Act] as constituents of Federal law, and which include the principle that contracts are to be performed in good faith... prohibits § 7 of the Service Act from being afforded the content that it should also reform breaches of explicit prohibitions on service contained in international agreements...." Verwaltungsgerichtshof [VwGH] Beschluß, December 18, 1997, No. 97/11/0274 (Aus.).

[18] Prewitt similarly argues that because OPEC failed to immediately reject the pleadings sent to it by international registered mail, return them, or lodge diplomatic protests with the United States, its actual receipt of the pleadings constituted constructive consent or waiver of the protection under Article 5(2) of the Headquarters Agreement that OPEC may only be served where it has expressly consented to service of process. Br. of Appellant at 31 n.9. We reject this argument because Article 5(2) must be read together with Article 9 of the Headquarters Agreement, which provides that "OPEC ... shall enjoy immunity from *every form of legal process* except in so far as in any particular case OPEC shall have *expressly waived* its immunity ... (emphasis added)."

mentioned in the rule or prohibited by international agreement could be employed to serve OPEC under Fed. R. Civ. P. 4(f)(3), even if the service is contrary to the laws of Austria. However, the 1993 Advisory Committee Notes to Fed. R. Civ. P. 4(f)(3) instruct that:

> Paragraph (3) authorizes the court to approve other methods of service not prohibited by international agreements.... Inasmuch as our Constitution requires that reasonable notice be given, an earnest effort should be made to devise a method of communication that is consistent with due process and minimizes offense to foreign law.

Rather than minimizing offense to Austrian law, the failure to obtain OPEC's consent would constitute a substantial affront to Austrian law. We can find no support permitting such a consequence in the face of Austria's direct prohibition of service on OPEC without its consent. The case relied upon as persuasive by Prewitt, Rio Properties, Inc. v. Rio Int'l Interlink, 284 F.3d 1007, 1014 (9th Cir. 2002), is not at all applicable to the circumstances here. In Rio, the court held that the district court did not abuse its discretion by ordering service by email upon an international corporation based in Costa Rica. However, the primary issue in that case was whether Fed. R. Civ. P. 4(f) should be read to create a hierarchy of preferred methods of service of process, requiring a party to attempt service by the methods enumerated in Fed. R. Civ. P. 4(f)(2) before petitioning the court for alternative relief under Fed. R. Civ. P. 4(f)(3). More importantly, the facts supporting the district court's direction of alternative service in Rio are completely different from the facts here. In Rio, the court determined that the defendant, an international internet company doing business in the United States, had a viable presence in the United States; that physical personal service had been legally attempted by actually serving a legitimate agent of the defendant in the United States; and that the defendant had evaded the attempted service. The most important distinction, however, is that in Rio, there was no discussion of Costa Rican law at all, much less of any prohibitions relating to service of process and thus, no need to take into account the advisory note to Fed. R. Civ. P. 4(f)(3) directing that alternative service of process should minimize offense to foreign law.[21]

Austrian law clearly provides protection to OPEC as an international organization from all methods of service of process without its consent and also requires that any service of process from abroad be effected through Austrian authorities. In this case, OPEC has made clear that it refuses to consent expressly to service of process by Prewitt; thus, the district court did not abuse its discretion in denying Prewitt's motion to authorize alternative means of service.

---

[21] We do not say that a district court *never* has discretion to direct service of process under Fed. R. Civ. P. 4(f)(3) that is in contravention of a foreign law. Rather, we are satisfied that under the facts and circumstances of this case, directing service of process would constitute a clear abuse of discretion.

III Conclusion

Based on the foregoing, we affirm the district court's [order granting defendant's] motion to dismiss this case for insufficient service of process and its denial of [the request for] alternative service of process on OPEC.

Comments and Questions

1. There is no question here that OPEC had actual notice that the lawsuit was filed. Other than ensuring that the defendant has actual notice, what purpose(s) do formal requirements advance?

2. Pursuant to Fed. R. Civ. P. 4(f)(3) and its predecessor, courts have authorized a wide variety of alternative methods of service including publication, ordinary mail, mail to the defendant's last known address, delivery to the defendant's attorney, telex, and most recently, e-mail. "[W]hen faced with an international e-business scofflaw, playing hide-and-seek with the federal court, email may be the only means of effective service of process." Rio Props., Inc. v. Rio Int'l Interlink, 284 F.3d 1007, 1016 (9th Cir. 2002). See also Smith v. Islamic Emirate, Nos. 01 Civ. 10132, 01. Civ. 10144, 2001 WL 1658211 (S.D.N.Y. Dec. 26, 2001) (authorizing service of process on Osama bin Laden and Al Qaeda by publication); SEC v. Tome, 833 F.2d 1086, 1094 (2nd Cir. 1987) (condoning service of process by publication in the International Herald Tribune); New Eng. Merchs. Nat'l Bank v. Iran Power Generation & Transmission Co., 495 F. Supp. 73, 80 (S.D.N.Y. 1980) (allowing service by telex for Iranian defendants). The Constitution guarantees that notice must be reasonably calculated to apprise the defendant of the pendency of the action. Mullane v. Central Hanover Bank & Trust Co., 339 U.S. 306 (1950).

Illustrative of the flexibility allowed by rule is the fantastic case of International Controls Corp. v. Vesco, 593 F.2d 155 (2nd Cir.), cert. denied, 442 U.S. 941 (1979). The case was one of many involving Robert L. Vesco, a financier whom the U.S. Securities and Exchange Commission accused of masterminding a "scheme of extraordinary magnitude, deviousness and ingenuity in violation of the anti-fraud provisions of the Securities and Exchange Act of 1934...." Vesco's deviousness and ingenuity also led to his absenting himself from the territorial limits of the United States. He refused to return to face charges or the many lawsuits filed against him and, for a time, remained ensconced in Nassau, the Bahamaian capital.

> Miss Yohonn [Plaintiff's process server] proceeded to Nassau on Saturday, July 28, 1973.... [S]he spent the afternoon and evening of Sunday, July 29, and most of Monday, July 30, searching for Vesco at various locations in Nassau and Paradise Island. Unsuccessful in these efforts, Miss Yohonn drove herself to [Vesco's] Brace Ridge Road residence. There she found a bolted gate and two men who appeared to be bodyguards. One of them inquired as to her business. She asked if this was Vesco's residence. After some evasion one of the two men said it was [Vesco's] residence. Miss Yohonn represented that she was a friend of Vesco's and wished to speak with him. One of the guards left to go into the house and said he would make inquiry.

While the one guard was in the house . . . a car drove up to the gate and was admitted. Inside, according to Miss Yohonn . . . were Mrs. Vesco and two children. Later a boy of approximately 16 years came out of the house and, approaching the gate, stated to Miss Yohonn, "My father said to ask what you want." Miss Yohonn responded that she wished to serve a summons and complaint and threw the papers at the boy. The boy threw them back and returned into the house.

In the meantime, the first guard had returned. When Miss Yohonn attempted to serve one of the guards, the response was: "You get out of here. We don't want no papers on this property. Don't you put anything on this property." They then threw the papers onto the road. Miss Yohonn ran back to her car, afraid of the guards, and drove to her hotel. . . .

Miss Yohonn hired a taxi for the second trip to Vesco's residence. There she threw a copy of the summons and complaint folded and tied with a blue ribbon over the fence and photographed the papers as they remained on the law in front of the house. The two guards immediately ran out to the gate, one armed with a stick and the other with a piece of pipe. One pulled open the door of the car and demanded that Miss Yohonn come out. The cab driver remonstrated with the guards and told them they could do nothing to Miss Yohonn while she was in his cab. When she told the guard that he had no right to touch the cab, he replied that she had no right to put anything on the property.

After they had driven a short distance the driver informed Miss Yohonn that the guards were following them in a car. Fearing for her safety, Miss Yohonn directed the driver to proceed to a different hotel that was connected with her hotel by a series of corridors. She asked that the driver keep secret her whereabouts and returned to her hotel by a circuitous route, where she put the film in a safe deposit box. She arrived at her room at approximately 7:00 pm and remained there for some time during which the phone rang on several occasions, each time with no one on the other end. Miss Yohonn returned to New York on the following day, July 31, 1973.

On August 1, 1973 Miss Yohonn mailed a copy of the summons and complaint to Vesco at his Brace Ridge Road residence by ordinary first class mail.

593 F.2d at 177–178.

3. Does Fed. R. Civ. P. 4(f)(3) authorize a court to devise alternative methods of service that violate the national law of the target country? What should Prewitt Enterprises' lawyers have done differently?

4. When applying Fed. R. Civ. P. 4(f)(2), a court must determine which methods of service are prescribed and which are prohibited by the law of the foreign country. Revisit footnote 11 of Judge Barkett's opinion. Again, is there anything that Prewitt Enterprises' lawyers should have done differently?

5. Even if OPEC could be properly served, would OPEC enjoy state immunity in any event? See Chapter 6. Is there any reason to sue them and serve them (properly) if they are immune?

6. The Restatement (Third) of Foreign Relations Law supports the view that international law forbids one state from effecting service within another state's territory without consent, even absent local legislation restricting foreign service. An Introductory Note to Chapter 7 of that Restatement emphasizes that an "underlying principle of international law [is] that a state may not conduct official activities in the territory of another state without that state's consent, express or implied. That principle is generally applied as well to the service of judicial documents...." Section 471(1) then provides:

> Under international law, a state may determine the conditions for service of process in its territory in aid of litigation in another state, but the state where the litigation is pending may determine the effect of such service.

But not all commentators agree that international law forbids the service of process abroad without the consent of the state where service is carried out. According to Professor Smit, "[t]here appears to be no authoritative source of international law specifically supporting the claim that the making of service by...a private person may be forbidden in the absence of prohibitions validly created by domestic law. Nor can the conduct of the private person who makes service ....possibly qualify as official conduct that may validly be forbidden....The making of service by...private persons does not in any way involve the exercise of judicial or other official powers." Hans Smit, International Cooperation in Civil Litigation: Some Observations on the Roles of International Law and Reciprocity, 9 Netherlands Int'l L. Rev. 137 (1962). Is this position more or less defensible than the Restatement's?

7. Whether or not service by a private person in another state would be lawful in that state, it may not be considered objectionable in the forum state. Thus, P might be regarded as having effectively served D under the law of forum state F even though the service would be considered ineffective, and possibly a violation of sovereignty, in State X, the state of D's domicile where service was effected. Under what circumstances would you advise P that service should be made on D in State X? Does your answer depend on where D's assets are located?

8. Special requirements for serving foreign, state or local governments proper are found in Fed. R. Civ. P. 4(j) and in 28 U.S.C. §§ 1602 et seq.

2. Portugal

As a civil law country, Portugal generally follows that tradition in its law of service of process. Portuguese law identifies three familiar objectives for service of process: (1) the defendant is notified of the existence and location of the suit; (2) the defendant is informed of her right to present a defense; and (3) the date of service of process determines the interruption of the statute of limitations. As in most jurisdictions, service of process is governed almost exclusively by statutes and international accords.

Joao Paulo Teixeira de Matos, Service of Process Abroad

Serving Process and Obtaining Evidence Abroad 294–298 (Campbell, ed. 1999)

Service of Process in the National State

In Portugal, service of process must be carried out personally on the defendant. The most common way is service by post. In this case, the clerk of the court will send to the defendant, by registered mail, a copy of the writ and all of the information mentioned above. The law considers that service of process is effective when the defendant receives and signs the receipt presented to him by the mail officer. When service of process by post is not possible, for example, because the defendant refuses to receive the letters sent by the court, the clerk of the court will try to deliver the writ personally to the defendant. As an alternative, service of process can be made via the plaintiff's attorney. In this case, the plaintiff's attorney will receive from the court a copy of the writ and will be obliged to deliver it to the defendant. If it is not possible to effect service of process personally on the defendant, for example, because he is at an unknown place, it will be effected by publication in a newspaper of the place of his last domicile. A notice will also be fixed at the court where the lawsuit is pending.

Service of Process in Foreign States

If a lawsuit was filed before a Portuguese court of law, but the defendant is domiciled in a different country, service of process must be in accordance with any existent and applicable international treaty or convention. Thus, the first step is to determine whether Portugal has entered into any bilateral or multilateral international treaty or convention applicable to the country where the defendant has his domicile. If this is the case, the Portuguese court has to comply with the rules of such treaty or convention. Service of process will be effected in accordance with the rules established therein. If there is no international treaty or convention applicable to the case, service will be governed by the rules of the Código de Processo Civil ("CPC"). According to its Article 247, service of process must be by post. The clerk of the court will send a letter with a copy of the writ, by registered mail, to the domicile of the defendant.

In cases where service of process by post is not possible, service will be carried out by the Portuguese consulate nearest to the domicile of the defendant. However, it should be noted that Portuguese consulates are not allowed to effect service of process on defendants of foreign nationality. Only Portuguese citizens living abroad may receive service of process through Portuguese consulates. In the majority of cases, defendants domiciled in foreign countries will not be Portuguese nationals. In this case, and in the absence of any applicable international treaty or convention, the Portuguese court must send a letter rogatory to a court of the state where the defendant is domiciled asking that court to effect service of process. In cases where it is not possible to determine the domicile of the defendant, process will be served by publication in a newspaper of the place of his last domicile in Portugal. A notice will also be fixed at the court of law where the lawsuit was filed.

How to Avoid Serving Process Abroad

As Portuguese law imposes the rule that service of process be effected personally on the defendant, and the CPC contains precise rules applicable to defendants domiciled in foreign countries, it is almost impossible to avoid the need to serve process abroad. However, it will be possible to avoid service of process in a foreign country when the defendant has appointed a proxy in Portugal specific powers to accept service. The plaintiff must know the existence of such a proxy in order to inform the court that service of process can be effected in Portugal. Most of the time, however, the proxy does not exist and, when he exists, the plaintiff has no knowledge of that fact.

Although not very common, the appointment of a proxy can be a useful and effective way of avoiding the need to serve process abroad. For example, in contracts entered into between parties domiciled in different countries, it can be convenient to establish that parties will appoint proxies in Portugal (if litigation is supposed to take place in Portugal) in order to facilitate service of process. It should be noted that the proxy must be executed before a notary public and must contain specific powers to accept service of process in any jurisdiction....

Service in Violation of Foreign and Domestic Law

Portuguese law has a very practical way of dealing with this matter. The consequences of service of process in violation of foreign law is irrelevant for national courts. In fact, if service of process in a lawsuit pending before a Portuguese court is effected abroad, or even in Portugal, in violation of foreign law, but with full respect to the relevant provisions of Portuguese law, the service will be valid for Portuguese courts. If the lawsuit is pending before a foreign court and Portuguese courts are requested by that jurisdiction to effect service of process, the national courts will make their best efforts to comply with all of the relevant provisions of such law. However, if Portuguese courts fail to comply with the foreign law, the consequences must be evaluated by the foreign court in accordance with that law.

Obviously, the situation is completely different in lawsuits pending before a Portuguese court. Service of process in Portugal or abroad must follow the relevant provisions of Portuguese law. If there is a lack of service of process or if the service procedures established by the law are not followed, service of process will be null and void. In addition, when service of process is null and void, all of the proceedings will also be null and void. The nullity of service of process is to be invoked by the defendant but, even when it is not invoked, the judge is empowered to verify the validity of service and to declare it null and void.

Comments and Questions

1. The Código de Processo Civil went into effect in April 1962, but was amended substantially in the 1990s. The amendments were a result of efforts to modernize the court system and to minimize delay. Among other reforms, the service rules were amended to streamline the proceedings. Service by mail is surely the most efficient form of service. Does the pursuit of efficiency, however, compromise some other procedural value?

2. Actual notice is no excuse for failure to comply with the service procedures established by Portuguese law. Thus if the procedures are not followed, the service and the proceedings are null and void. Is that efficient? (Is it necessary?)

3. Foreign service of process can be valid in Portugal even when that service is in violation of foreign law. Why are the Portuguese (and American and other) courts unwilling or unable to defer?

3. China

The civil dispute resolution system of the People's Republic of China has been transformed by and with the remarkable growth of an economy that is socialist yet also market-driven. "As a country that has traditionally eschewed legal formality, China's experience in its construction of a formal, legal system is informative of the assumed effectiveness of legal transformation, and of the widespread predictions of globalization and harmonization of legal systems." Margaret Woo & Yaxin Wang, Civil Justice in China, 53 Am. J. Comp. L. 911, 911–912 (2005). The following excerpt describing the statutory law on domestic and transnational service of process echoes the challenges and solutions detailed throughout this chapter.

Shizhou Wang & Hong Yao, Notice Service

International Encyclopaedia of Laws

I Civil Procedure 80–81 (Kluwer 2001)

It is an important measure to timely inform the parties of their relevant litigation rights and obligations in this "pre-trial proceedings," so that the parties may avoid their rights to be damaged from the very beginning of the proceedings.

In accordance with the Civil Procedure Law of the People's Republic of China (CCPL), a receipt shall be required for every litigation document that is served and it shall bear the date of receipt noted by the signature or seal of the person on whom the document was served. The date noted on the receipt by the person on whom the document was served shall be regarded as the date of service of the document (Article 77).

Litigation documents shall be sent or delivered directly to the person on whom they are to be served. If that person is a citizen, the documents shall, in case of his absence, be received by an adult member of his family living with him. If the person on whom they are to be served is a legal person or any other organisation, the documents shall be received by the legal representatives of the legal person or the principal heads of the other organisation or anyone of the legal person or the other organisation responsible for receiving such documents.... The date put down in the receipt and signed by [the recipient] shall be deemed the date of service of the documents (Article 78).

If the person on whom the litigation documents are to be served or the adult family member living with him refuses to receive the documents, the person serving the documents shall ask representatives from the relevant grass-roots organisation of the unit to which the person on whom the documents are to be served belongs to appear on the scene, explain the situation to them, and record on the receipt the reasons of the refusal and the date of it. After the person serving the documents and the witnesses have affixed their signatures or seals to the receipt, the documents shall be left at the place where the person on whom they are to be served lives and the service shall be deemed completed (Article 79).

If direct service [proves] to be difficult, service of litigation documents may be entrusted to another people's court, or done by mail. If the documents are served by mail, the date stated on the receipt for postal delivery shall be deemed the date of service of the documents (Article 80).

If the whereabouts of the person on whom the litigation documents are to be served is unknown, or if the documents cannot be served by the other methods specified in this section, the documents shall be served by public announcement. Sixty days after the public announcement is made, the documents shall be deemed to have been served. The reasons for service by public announcement and the process gone through shall be recorded in the case files (Article 84)....

A people's court may serve litigation documents on a party who has no domicile within the territory of the People's Republic of China (PRC) in the following ways:

(1) in the way specified in the international treaties concluded or acceded to by both the PRC and the country where the person on whom service is to be made resides;
(2) by making the service through diplomatic channels;
(3) with respect to the person on whom the service is to be made and who is of the nationality of the PRC, service may be entrusted to the embassy or consulate of the PRC accredited to the country where the person resides;
(4) by making the service on the agent ad litem who is authorised to receive the documents served;
(5) by serving the documents on the representative office established in the PRC by the person on whom the service is to be made or on his branch office or business agents there who have the right to receive the documents;
(6) by making service by mail if the law of the country where the person on whom the service is to be made resides so permits. In the event that the receipt of delivery is not returned six months after the date on which the documents were mailed, and that circumstances justify the assumption that service has been made, the service shall be deemed completed upon the expiration of the said time limit; and

(7) by making service by public notice, if none of the above-mentioned methods can be employed. The service shall be deemed completed six months after the date on which the public notice was issued.

Comments and Questions

1. One might expect the unique history, tradition, and culture of the People's Republic of China to yield a unique approach to service of process. Yet the service of process rules for China and all national systems tend to be substantially similar. Is service of process immune from the social, political, and cultural influences that can shape—and differentiate—other aspects of procedure?

2. Rules pertaining to service of process tend to be trans-substantive—meaning that the same rules apply to all substantive categories of cases. Is that necessary? Or would it be useful to tailor service rules for contract, antitrust, tort, and civil rights cases?

4. Mexico

This chapter has already highlighted the overlap between issues of personal jurisdiction and sovereign immunity. The following excerpt draws a connection to the enforcement of judgments, which is the topic of Chapter 11.

Alejandro Suarez-Mendez, The Agent for Service of Process in Mexico

Amer. Bar Assoc., 35 Int'l Law News 14 (Winter 2006)

A Mexican party may enter into an agreement with one or more foreign parties, governed by foreign law that accepts the appointment of an agent for service of process in that foreign country. For the purpose of service of process, a "Mexican party" is an individual or entity whose domicile and/or main business and/or main assets are located in Mexico. In the same context, a "foreign party" is any non-Mexican party. Though such an agreement is fully valid, a final judgment, issued by a foreign judge as a result of the process served to the agent of the Mexican party, may still not be enforceable in Mexico. This could be an issue of major concern because the awarded foreign party may be impeded to execute its final judgment against the main business and assets of the Mexican party located in the Mexican territory.

Article 571, paragraph IV, of the Mexican Federal Code of Civil Procedure and Article 1347A, paragraph IV, of the Mexican Commercial Code provide that any final judgment issued by a foreign court may be recognized and enforced by the courts of Mexico without reexamination of the issues, but only if the service of process was made personally on the defendant.

A service of process conducted through an agent appointed in a private agreement would not constitute a personal service of process under Mexican law.

Personal service of process is considered a basic procedural requirement under Mexican law and therefore protected by the Mexican constitution. Thus, a final foreign judgment based on process served on an agent may not be recognized and enforced by the courts of Mexico.

D. International Cooperation

States have found it worthwhile to try to ease the difficulties experienced by their citizens in pursuing claims involving persons or entities in other countries. Accordingly, there are various bilateral, regional, and multilateral agreements facilitating cooperation among member states. Indeed, in most cases service in a foreign country can be effected through the Hague Convention or some other agreement that provides a uniform framework for serving process in civil or commercial cases.

1. Hague Service Convention

The Hague Conference on Private International Law is a global inter-governmental organization with member states representing all continents and legal traditions. The Conference undertakes to develop and service multilateral legal instruments that respond to global needs. The Conference held its first meeting in 1893 under the leadership of T.M.C. Asser, a notable Dutch scholar who won the Nobel Peace Prize in 1911. Its present Statute entered into force on 15 July 1955, declaring the Hague Conference's objective to be: "the progressive unification of the rules of private international law." Notwithstanding its international character, the Conference functions under the supervision of a Commission of the State of the Netherlands established by Royal Decree in 1897, and the Netherlands Government bears the costs of the quadrennial sessions.

Although the Conference was initially a civil law and European institution, its membership has expanded and is now much more representative of the various legal traditions. Member states presently include not only common law countries such as Australia, Canada, Ireland, the United Kingdom, and the United States, but also countries such as China representing the socialist tradition. There are also some Latin American members, although their participation was delayed because Spanish translations were not introduced until the early 1990s. (As discussed in section 3 below, cooperation in the field of private international law in the Americas has taken place chiefly through the Inter-American Specialized Conferences on Private International Law, known by their acronym in Spanish, CIDIP. These meetings, which have produced over twenty-five agreements, are held under the auspices of the Organization of American States (OAS).) Even the first English text was not adopted until 1961 (French was formerly the official language of the Conference). Most of the conventions prepared under the auspices of the Conference are open to non-Member States and as a result, its work encompasses more than 120 countries around the world.

Civil procedure is a frequent item on the Conference's agenda. In particular, a draft convention with regard to transnational service of process was prepared by a Special Commission of the Hague Conference in February 1964 and agreed by the 10th Session of the Conference the following October. The starting points for the project were dissatisfaction with the indirect consular channel and concern that the non-obligatory nature of the channels provided for in the then-existing practice enabled some countries to make use of the system of notification au parquet to which increasing exception was being taken. This latter system, which was then available in at least some cases in Belgium, France, Greece, Italy and the Netherlands, allows legally effective service on a defendant resident abroad to be made by leaving the relevant document at the office of the parquet in the forum state. (The parquet was introduced in Part C of this chapter) Although the parquet was then expected to take steps to bring the document to the attention of the defendant, service was already complete and time began to run for various purposes regardless of the date upon which the defendant received actual notice of the proceedings. One of the goals of a new convention was to safeguard the position of defendants who remained in ignorance of the proceedings being taken against them.*

The result of this effort was the Hague Convention of 15 November 1965 that is excerpted below. The framework for the Hague Service Convention, as it is commonly referred to, is relatively straightforward and is generally considered to have been a success. Among the dozens of member states of this convention are Argentina, Belarus, Canada, China, Denmark, Egypt, Israel, Japan, Korea, Mexico, Poland, Russia, Sri Lanka, Turkey, the United Kingdom, the United States, and Venezuela. Non-member states (of the Conference) who are members of the Hague Service Convention include Botswana, Malawi, and Pakistan.*

Hague Convention on the Service Abroad of Judicial and Extrajudicial Documents in Civil and Commercial Matters

20 U.S.T. 361 (Concluded 15 Nov 1965; Entered into force 10 Feb 1969)

Article 1

The present Convention shall apply in all cases, in civil or commercial matters, where there is occasion to transmit a judicial or extrajudicial document for service abroad.

This Convention shall not apply where the address of the person to be served with the document is not known.

---

* *See* David McClean, International Co-operation in Civil and Criminal Matters 5–6 (Oxford 2002).

* The Hague Conference on Private International Law maintains an excellent website, including a list of the contracting states to conventions such as the Convention on Service Abroad of Judicial and Extrajudicial Documents. *See* http://hcch.e-vision.nl/index_en.php?act=conventions.text&cid=17 (last visited November 19, 2008).

Article 2

Each Contracting State shall designate a Central Authority which will undertake to receive requests for service coming from other Contracting States and to proceed in conformity with the provisions of Articles 3 to 6.

Each State shall organise the Central Authority in conformity with its own law.

Article 3

The authority or judicial officer competent under the law of the State in which the documents originate shall forward to the Central Authority of the State addressed a request conforming to the model annexed to the present Convention, without any requirement of legalisation or other equivalent formality.

The document to be served or a copy thereof shall be annexed to the request. The request and the document shall both be furnished in duplicate.

Article 4

If the Central Authority considers that the request does not comply with the provisions of the present Convention it shall promptly inform the applicant and specify its objections to the request.

Article 5

The Central Authority of the State addressed shall itself serve the document or shall arrange to have it served by an appropriate agency, either—

a) by a method prescribed by its internal law for the service of documents in domestic actions upon persons who are within its territory, or
b) by a particular method requested by the applicant, unless such a method is incompatible with the law of the State addressed.

Subject to sub-paragraph (b) of the first paragraph of this Article, the document may always be served by delivery to an addressee who accepts it voluntarily.

If the document is to be served under the first paragraph above, the Central Authority may require the document to be written in, or translated into, the official language or one of the official languages of the State addressed....

Article 6

The Central Authority of the State addressed or any authority which it may have designated for that purpose, shall complete a certificate in the form of the model annexed to the present Convention.

The certificate shall state that the document has been served and shall include the method, the place and the date of service and the person to whom the document was delivered. If the document has not been served, the certificate shall set out the reasons which have prevented service....

The certificate shall be forwarded directly to the applicant.

Article 7

The standard terms in the model annexed to the present Convention shall in all cases be written either in French or in English. They may also be written in the official language, or in one of the official languages, of the State in which the documents originate....

Article 8

Each Contracting State shall be free to effect service of judicial documents upon persons abroad, without application of any compulsion, directly through its diplomatic or consular agents.

Any State may declare that it is opposed to such service within its territory, unless the document is to be served upon a national of the State in which the documents originate.

Article 9

Each Contracting State shall be free, in addition, to use consular channels to forward documents, for the purpose of service, to those authorities of another Contracting State which are designated by the latter for this purpose.

Each Contracting State may, if exceptional circumstances so require, use diplomatic channels for the same purpose.

Article 10

Provided the State of destination does not object, the present Convention shall not interfere with—

(a) the freedom to send judicial documents, by postal channels, directly to persons abroad,
(b) the freedom of judicial officers, officials or other competent persons of the State of origin to effect service of judicial documents directly through the judicial officers, officials or other competent persons of the State of destination,
(c) the freedom of any person interested in a judicial proceeding to effect service of judicial documents directly through the judicial officers, officials or other competent persons of the State of destination.

Article 11

The present Convention shall not prevent two or more Contracting States from agreeing to permit, for the purpose of service of judicial documents, channels of transmission other than those provided for in the preceding Articles and, in particular, direct communication between their respective authorities....

Article 13

Where a request for service complies with the terms of the present Convention, the State addressed may refuse to comply therewith only if it deems that compliance would infringe its sovereignty or security.

It may not refuse to comply solely on the ground that, under its internal law, it claims exclusive jurisdiction over the subject-matter of the action or that its internal law would not permit the action upon which the application is based.

The Central Authority shall, in case of refusal, promptly inform the applicant and state the reasons for the refusal. . . .

Article 15

When a writ of summons or an equivalent document had to be transmitted abroad for the purpose of service, under the provisions of the present Convention, and the defendant has not appeared, judgment shall not be given until it is established that—

(a) the document was served by a method prescribed by the internal law of the State addressed for the service of documents in domestic actions upon persons who are within its territory, or

(b) the document was actually delivered to the defendant or to his residence by another method provided for by this Convention,

and that in either of these cases the service or the delivery was effected in sufficient time to enable the defendant to defend.

Each Contracting State shall be free to declare that the judge, notwithstanding the provisions of the first paragraph of this Article, may give judgment even if no certificate of service or deliver has been received, if all the following conditions are fulfilled—

(a) the document was transmitted by one of the methods provided for in this Convention,

(b) a period of time not less than six months, considered adequate by the judge in the particular case, has elapsed since the date of the transmission of the document,

(c) no certificate of any kind has been received, even though every reasonable effort has been made to obtain it through the competent authorities of the State addressed.

Notwithstanding the provisions of the preceding paragraphs the judge may order, in case of urgency, any provisional or protective measures.

Article 16

When a writ of summons or an equivalent document had to be transmitted abroad for the purpose of service, under the provisions of the present Convention, and a judgment has been entered against a defendant who has not appeared, the judge shall have the power to relieve the defendant from the effects of the expiration of the time for appeal from the judgment if the following conditions are fulfilled—

(a) the defendant, without any fault on his part, did not have knowledge of the document in sufficient time to defend, or knowledge of the judgment in sufficient time to appeal, and

(b) the defendant has disclosed a prima facie defence to the action on the merits.

An application for relief may be filed only within a reasonable time after the defendant has knowledge of the judgment.

Each Contracting State may declare that the application will not be entertained if it is filed after the expiration of a time to be stated in the declaration, but which shall in no case be less than one year following the date of the judgment.

This Article shall not apply to judgments concerning status or capacity of persons.

Article 19

To the extent that the internal law of a Contracting State permits methods of transmission, other than those provided for in the preceding Articles, of documents coming from abroad, for service within its territory, the present Convention shall not affect such provisions....

Comments and Questions

1. According to Article 1, the Convention applies to "civil and commercial matters." Although this is a common phrase used in civil procedure conventions throughout the past century, it is subject to different interpretations. Common law countries tend to interpret this phrase as including almost anything which is not a criminal matter. Civil law systems recognize a larger number of categories than simply civil and criminal, and thus, for example, might assign certain administrative or public law matters to a separate category.

2. The Convention does not apply in cases in which the address of the person on whom documents were to be served is unknown. See Art. 1. The notion of an "unknown address" is often interpreted strictly. If the person seeking service gives an address for service, having reason to believe that it is accurate, the case is not made one of an "unknown address" merely by the fact that the person to be served has disappeared from that address and cannot be found. Does this mean that service can be deemed effective under the Convention even if it is sent to what turns out to be the wrong address?

3. The main innovation in the 1965 Convention was the creation of the system of Central Authorities. Each Contracting State must designate such a Central Authority to receive requests for service from other Contracting States. Most Contracting States have designated their departments (or ministries) of justice; others use their state departments or foreign ministries; others designate political subdivisions; and still others place the Central Authority within their court system.

4. The Convention provides that the request is initiated by an "authority or judicial officer competent under the law of the State in which the documents originate." Some countries, including the United Kingdom, have chosen to provide that outgoing requests must be forwarded through the Central Authority of the originating state; others allow local court officials or huissiers to act. Private parties may not themselves originate requests, but a party's lawyer may do so if the law of the state of origin so allows, as is often the case in the United States.

5. The Convention prescribes in some detail the documentation to be used, the extent to which translations may be required, and the actual mode of service to be employed in the state of destination; these various issues are interconnected. An Annex to the Convention prescribes a form of "Request for Service" which is to be used.

6. Each Central Authority has a preferred method of dealing with requests for service. For example, in the United States where the Central Authority is an agency of the Federal Government, service is effected by the use of U.S. Marshals attached to the (Federal) District Courts. In France and Germany, by contrast, the informal method of "simple delivery" is preferred. If a Central Authority considers that a request for service does not fall within the Convention it may reject it. Otherwise, a request may only be rejected on the ground of infringement of "sovereignty or security;" neither a claim to exclusive jurisdiction by the state of destination over the subject matter with which the documents deals, nor the fact that no cause of action would exist under the law of that state, is a proper ground for rejection.

7. Service of process under the Convention is generally cost-free. Thus, no fee is to be charged by the State addressed. However, the person requesting service must pay or reimburse any costs due to the need to employ a judicial officer or other competent person, or due to the use of a particular method of service.

8. In addition to establishing a network of Central Authorities, the Convention also provides, in Article 10(a), that it "shall not interfere with . . . the freedom to send judicial documents, by postal channels, directly to persons abroad. . . ." (emphasis added). Looking at The Hague Convention's purpose of facilitating service abroad, some courts have decided that this article permits service by mail on foreign parties because article 10(a) would be superfluous unless it was related to the sending of such documents for the purpose of service. See, e.g., Brockmeyer v. May, 383 F.3d 798 (9th Cir. 2004); Ackermann v. Levine, 788 F.2d 830, 839 (2d Cir. 1986); Case C-412/97, E.D. Srl. v. Italo Fenocchio, 1999 E.C.R. I-3845, [2000] C.M.L.R. 855 (Court of Justice of the European Communities) ("Article 10(a) of [the Hague Convention] allows service by post."); Integral Energy & Envtl. Eng'g Ltd. v. Schenker of Canada Ltd., (2001) 295 A.R. 233, 2001 WL 454163 (Alberta Queens Bench) ("Article 10(a) of the Hague Convention provides that if the state of destination does not object, judicial documents may be served by postal channels"), rev'd on other grounds, (2001) 293 A.R. 327; R. v. Re Recognition of an Italian Judgment, [2002] I.L.Pr. 15, 2000 WL 33541696 (Thessaloniki Court of Appeal, Greece) ("It should be noted that the possibility of serving judicial documents in civil and

commercial cases through postal channels...is envisaged in Article 10(a) of the Hague Convention."). A minority of courts, however, have held that the meaning of the word "send" does not include "serve"; these courts interpret this language of the Convention to authorize the sending of judicial documents by mail, but only after service of process is accomplished by some other means. See, e.g., Bankston v. Toyota Motor Corp., 889 F.2d 172, 173–74 (8th Cir. 1989); Nuovo Pignone v. Storman Asia M/V, 310 F.3d 374, 384 (5th Cir. 2002).

9. Articles 15 and 16 of the Convention provide some safeguards for defendants. Do these provisions achieve a meaningful balance given what the Convention offers plaintiffs?

10. Article 1 provides that the Convention applies "in all cases...where there is occasion to transmit a...document for service abroad." Yet exactly what the Convention obliges member states to do remains a subject of dispute. There is consensus that transnational service is invalid if it meets the requirement of forum law but fails to meet the terms of the Convention. However, the Convention does not specify under what circumstances transnational service is required. And by failing to do so, the Convention leaves untouched those cases in which the procedural law of the forum recognizes some action within the jurisdiction as legally sufficient to constitute service on a defendant who is actually resident abroad. In the following case, the U.S. Supreme Court confronts this dilemma.

Volkswagenwerk AG v. Schlunk
486 U.S. 694 (1988)

Justice O'Connor delivered the opinion of the Court

This case involves an attempt to serve process on a foreign corporation by serving its domestic subsidiary which, under state law, is the foreign corporation's involuntary agent for service of process. We must decide whether such service is compatible with the Convention on Service Abroad of Judicial and Extrajudicial Documents in Civil and Commercial Matters, Nov. 15, 1965 (Hague Service Convention), [1969] 20 U.S.T. 361, T.I.A.S. No. 6638.

I

The parents of respondent Herwig Schlunk were killed in an automobile accident in 1983. Schlunk filed a wrongful death action on their behalf in the Circuit Court of Cook County, Illinois. Schlunk alleged that Volkswagen of America, Inc. (VWoA), had designed and sold the automobile that his parents were driving, and that defects in the automobile caused or contributed to their deaths. Schlunk also alleged that the driver of the other automobile involved in the collision was negligent; Schlunk has since obtained a default judgment against that person, who is no longer a party to this lawsuit. Schlunk successfully served his complaint on VWoA, and VWoA filed an answer denying that it had designed or assembled the automobile in question. Schlunk then amended the complaint to add as a defendant Volkswagen Aktiengesellschaft (VWAG), which is the petitioner here. VWAG, a corporation established under the laws of the Federal Republic of Germany, has its place of business in that country. VWoA is a wholly owned subsidiary of VWAG. Schlunk attempted to serve his amended complaint on VWAG by serving VWoA as VWAG's agent.

VWAG filed a special and limited appearance for the purpose of quashing service. VWAG asserted that it could be served only in accordance with the Hague Service Convention, and that Schlunk had not complied with the Convention's requirements. The Circuit Court denied VWAG's motion. It first observed that VWoA is registered to do business in Illinois and has a registered agent for receipt of process in Illinois. The court then reasoned that VWoA and VWAG are so closely related that VWoA is VWAG's agent for service of process as a matter of law, notwithstanding VWAG's failure or refusal to appoint VWoA formally as an agent. The court relied on the facts that VWoA is a wholly owned subsidiary of VWAG, that a majority of the members of the board of directors of VWoA are members of the board of VWAG, and that VWoA is by contract the exclusive importer and distributor of VWAG products sold in the United States. The court concluded that, because service was accomplished within the United States, the Hague Service Convention did not apply.

The Circuit Court certified two questions to the Appellate Court of Illinois. For reasons similar to those given by the Circuit Court, the Appellate Court determined that VWoA is VWAG's agent for service of process under Illinois law, and that the service of process in this case did not violate the Hague Service Convention. After the Supreme Court of Illinois denied VWAG leave to appeal, 112 Ill.2d 595 (1986), VWAG petitioned this Court for a writ of certiorari to review the Appellate Court's interpretation of the Hague Service Convention. We granted certiorari to address this issue, which has given rise to disagreement among the lower courts....

II

The Hague Service Convention is a multilateral treaty that was formulated in 1964 by the Tenth Session of the Hague Conference of Private International Law. The Convention revised parts of the Hague Conventions on Civil Procedure of 1905 and 1954. The revision was intended to provide a simpler way to serve process abroad, to assure that defendants sued in foreign jurisdictions would receive actual and timely notice of suit, and to facilitate proof of service abroad. 3 1964 Conférence de la Haye de Droit International Privé, Actes et Documents de la Dixième Session (Notification) 75–77, 363 (1965) (3 Actes et Documents); 1 B. Ristau, International Judicial Assistance (Civil and Commercial) § 4-1 (1984 and 1 Supp.1986) (1 Ristau)....

The primary innovation of the Convention is that it requires each state to establish a central authority to receive requests for service of documents from other countries. 20 U.S.T. 362, T.I.A.S. 6638, Art. 2. Once a central authority receives a request in the proper form, it must serve the documents by a method prescribed by the internal law of the receiving state or by a method designated by the requester and compatible with that law. Art. 5. The central authority must then provide a certificate of service that conforms to a specified model. Art. 6. A state also may consent to methods of service within its boundaries other than a request to its central authority. Arts. 8–11, 19. The remaining provisions of the Convention that are relevant here limit the circumstances in which a default judgment may be entered against a defendant who had to be served abroad and did not appear, and provide some means for relief from such a judgment. Arts. 15, 16.

Article 1 defines the scope of the Convention, which is the subject of controversy in this case. It says: "The present Convention shall apply in all cases, in civil or commercial matters, where there is occasion to transmit a judicial or extrajudicial document for service abroad." 20 U.S.T., at 362. The equally authentic French version says, "La présente Convention est applicable, en matière civile ou commerciale, dans tous les cas où un acte judiciaire ou extrajudiciaire doit être transmis à l'étranger pour y être signifié ou notifié." IbId. This language is mandatory, as we acknowledged last Term in Société Nationale Industrielle Aérospatiale v. U.S. District Court, 482 U.S. 522, 534, n.15 (1987). By virtue of the Supremacy Clause, U.S. Const., Art. VI, the Convention pre-empts inconsistent methods of service prescribed by state law in all cases to which it applies. Schlunk does not purport to have served his complaint on VWAG in accordance with the Convention. Therefore, if service of process in this case falls within Article 1 of the Convention, the trial court should have granted VWAG's motion to quash.

When interpreting a treaty, we "begin 'with the text of the treaty and the context in which the written words are used.'" Société Nationale, supra, at 534. (quoting Air France v. Saks, supra, 470 U.S. 392, 397 (1985)). Other general rules of construction may be brought to bear on difficult or ambiguous passages. "'Treaties are construed more liberally than private agreements, and to ascertain their meaning we may look beyond the written words to the history of the treaty, the negotiations, and the practical construction adopted by the parties.'" Air France v. Saks, supra, at 396...

The Convention does not specify the circumstances in which there is "occasion to transmit" a complaint "for service abroad." But at least the term "service of process" has a well-established technical meaning. Service of process refers to a formal delivery of documents that is legally sufficient to charge the defendant with notice of a pending action. The legal sufficiency of a formal delivery of documents must be measured against some standard. The Convention does not prescribe a standard, so we almost necessarily must refer to the internal law of the forum state. If the internal law of the forum state defines the applicable method of serving process as requiring the transmittal of documents abroad, then the Hague Service Convention applies.

The negotiating history supports our view that Article 1 refers to service of process in the technical sense. The committee that prepared the preliminary draft deliberately used a form of the term "notification" (formal notice), instead of the more neutral term "remise" (delivery), when it drafted Article 1. 3 Actes et Documents, at 78–79. Then, in the course of the debates, the negotiators made the language even more exact. The preliminary draft of Article 1 said that the present Convention shall apply in all cases in which there are grounds to transmit or to give formal notice of a judicial or extrajudicial document in a civil or commercial matter to a person staying abroad. Id., at 65 ("La présente Convention est applicable dans tous les cas où il y a lieu de transmettre ou de notifier un acte judiciaire ou extrajudiciaire en matière civile ou commerciale à une personne se trouvant à l'étranger") (emphasis added). To be more precise, the delegates decided to add a form of the juridical term "signification" (service), which has a narrower meaning than "notification" in some countries, such as France, and the identical meaning in others, such as the United States. Id., at 152–153, 155, 159, 366. The delegates also criticized the language of the preliminary draft because it suggested that the Convention could apply to transmissions abroad that do not culminate in service. Id., at 165–167. The final text of Article 1, supra, eliminates this possibility and applies only to documents transmitted for service abroad. The final report (Rapport Explicatif) confirms that the Convention does not use more general terms, such as delivery or transmission, to define its scope because it applies only when there is both transmission of a document from the requesting state to the receiving state, and service upon the person for whom it is intended. Id., at 366.

The negotiating history of the Convention also indicates that whether there is service abroad must be determined by reference to the law of the forum state. The preliminary draft said that the Convention would apply "where there are grounds" to transmit a judicial document to a person staying abroad. The committee that prepared the preliminary draft realized that this implied that the forum's internal law would govern whether service implicated the Convention. Id., at 80–81. The reporter expressed regret about this solution because it would decrease the obligatory force of the Convention. Id., at 81. Nevertheless, the delegates did not change the meaning of Article 1 in this respect.

The Yugoslavian delegate offered a proposal to amend Article 1 to make explicit that service abroad is defined according to the law of the state that is requesting service of process. Id., at 167. The delegate from the Netherlands supported him. Ibid. The German delegate approved of the proposal in principle, although he thought it would require a corresponding reference to the significance of the law of the state receiving the service of process, and that this full explanation would be too complicated. Id., at 168. The President opined that there was a choice to be made between the phrase used by the preliminary draft, "where grounds exist," and the Yugoslavian proposal to modify it with the phrase, "according to the law of the requesting state." Ibid. This prompted the Yugoslavian delegate to declare that the difference was immaterial, because the phrase "where grounds exist" necessarily refers to the law of the forum. Ibid. The French delegate added that, in his view, the law of the forum in turn is equivalent to the law of the requesting state.

Id., at 169. At that point, the President recommended entrusting the problem to the drafting committee.

The drafting committee then composed the version of Article 1 that ultimately was adopted, which says that the Convention applies "where there is occasion" to transmit a judicial document for service abroad. Id., at 211. After this revision, the reporter again explained that one must leave to the requesting state the task of defining when a document must be served abroad; that this solution was a consequence of the unavailability of an objective test; and that while it decreases the obligatory force of the Convention, it does provide clarity. Id., at 254. The inference we draw from this history is that the Yugoslavian proposal was rejected because it was superfluous, not because it was inaccurate, and that "service abroad" has the same meaning in the final version of the Convention as it had in the preliminary draft.

VWAG protests that it is inconsistent with the purpose of the Convention to interpret it as applying only when the internal law of the forum requires service abroad. One of the two stated objectives of the Convention is "to create appropriate means to ensure that judicial and extrajudicial documents to be served abroad shall be brought to the notice of the addressee in sufficient time." 20 U.S.T., at 362. The Convention cannot assure adequate notice, VWAG argues, if the forum's internal law determines whether it applies. VWAG warns that countries could circumvent the Convention by defining methods of service of process that do not require transmission of documents abroad. Indeed, VWAG contends that one such method of service already exists and that it troubled the Conference: notification au parquet.

Notification au parquet permits service of process on a foreign defendant by the deposit of documents with a designated local official. Although the official generally is supposed to transmit the documents abroad to the defendant, the statute of limitations begins to run from the time that the official receives the documents, and there allegedly is no sanction for failure to transmit them. 3 Actes et Documents, at 167–169; S.Exec.Rep. No. 6, 90th Cong., 1st Sess., 12 (1967) (statement of Philip Amram, member of the United States delegation); 1 Ristau § 4–33, p. 172. At the time of the 10th Conference, France, the Netherlands, Greece, Belgium, and Italy utilized some type of notification au parquet. 3 Actes et Documents, at 75.

There is no question but that the Conference wanted to eliminate notification au parquet. Id., at 75–77. It included in the Convention two provisions that address the problem. Article 15 says that a judgment may not be entered unless a foreign defendant received adequate and timely notice of the lawsuit. Article 16 provides means whereby a defendant who did not receive such notice may seek relief from a judgment that has become final. 20 U.S.T., at 364–365. Like Article 1, however, Articles 15 and 16 apply only when documents must be transmitted abroad for the purpose of service. 3 Actes et Documents, at 168–169. VWAG argues that, if this determination is made according to the internal law of the forum state, the Convention will fail to eliminate variants of notification au parquet that do not expressly require transmittal of documents to foreign defendants. Yet such methods of service of process are the least likely to provide a defendant with actual notice.

The parties make conflicting representations about whether foreign laws authorizing notification au parquet command the transmittal of documents for service abroad within the meaning of the Convention. The final report is itself somewhat equivocal. It says that, although the strict language of Article 1 might raise a question as to whether the Convention regulates notification au parquet, the understanding of the drafting Commission, based on the debates, is that the Convention would apply. Id., at 367. Although this statement might affect our decision as to whether the Convention applies to notification au parquet, an issue we do not resolve today, there is no comparable evidence in the negotiating history that the Convention was meant to apply to substituted service on a subsidiary like VWoA, which clearly does not require service abroad under the forum's internal law. Hence neither the language of the Convention nor the negotiating history contradicts our interpretation of the Convention, according to which the internal law of the forum is presumed to determine whether there is occasion for service abroad.

Nor are we persuaded that the general purposes of the Convention require a different conclusion. One important objective of the Convention is to provide means to facilitate service of process abroad. Thus the first stated purpose of the Convention is "to create" appropriate means for service abroad, and the second stated purpose is "to improve the organization of mutual judicial assistance for that purpose by simplifying and expediting the procedure." 20 U.S.T., at 362. By requiring each state to establish a central authority to assist in the service of process, the Convention implements this enabling function. Nothing in our decision today interferes with this requirement.

VWAG correctly maintains that the Convention also aims to ensure that there will be adequate notice in cases in which there is occasion to serve process abroad. Thus compliance with the Convention is mandatory in all cases to which it applies, see supra, at 2109, and Articles 15 and 16 provide an indirect sanction against those who ignore it, see 3 Actes et Documents, at 92, 363. Our interpretation of the Convention does not necessarily advance this particular objective, inasmuch as it makes recourse to the Convention's means of service dependent on the forum's internal law. But we do not think that this country, or any other country, will draft its internal laws deliberately so as to circumvent the Convention in cases in which it would be appropriate to transmit judicial documents for service abroad. For example, there has been no question in this country of excepting foreign nationals from the protection of our Due Process Clause. Under that Clause, foreign nationals are assured of either personal service, which typically will require service abroad and trigger the Convention, or substituted service that provides "notice reasonably calculated, under all the circumstances, to apprise interested parties of the pendency of the action and afford them an opportunity to present their objections." Mullane v. Central Hanover Bank & Trust Co., 339 U.S. 306, 314 (1950).*

Furthermore, nothing that we say today prevents compliance with the Convention even when the internal law of the forum does not so require. The Convention provides simple and certain means by which to serve process on a foreign national. Those who eschew its procedures risk discovering that the forum's internal law required transmittal of documents for service abroad, and that the Convention therefore provided the exclusive means of valid service. In addition, parties that comply with the Convention ultimately may find it easier to enforce their judgments abroad. See Westin, Enforcing Foreign Commercial Judgments and Arbitral Awards in the United States, West Germany, and England, Law & Policy Int'l Bus. 325, 340–341 (1987). For these reasons, we anticipate that parties may resort to the Convention voluntarily, even in cases that fall outside the scope of its mandatory application.

III

In this case, the Illinois long-arm statute authorized Schlunk to serve VWAG by substituted service on VWoA, without sending documents to Germany. See Ill. Rev.Stat., ch. 110, ¶ 2-209(a)(1) (1985). VWAG has not petitioned for review of the Illinois Appellate Court's holding that service was proper as a matter of Illinois law. VWAG contends, however, that service on VWAG was not complete until VWoA transmitted the complaint to VWAG in Germany. According to VWAG, this transmission constituted service abroad under the Hague Service Convention.

VWAG explains that, as a practical matter, VWoA was certain to transmit the complaint to Germany to notify VWAG of the litigation. Indeed, as a legal matter, the Due Process Clause requires every method of service to provide "notice reasonably calculated, under all the circumstances, to apprise interested parties of the pendency of the action and afford them an opportunity to present their objections." Mullane v. Central Hanover Bank & Trust Co., supra, at 314. VWAG

* The concurrence believes that our interpretation does not adequately guarantee timely notice, which it denominates the "primary" purpose of the Convention, albeit without authority. The concurrence instead proposes to impute a substantive standard to the words, "service abroad." Evidently, a method of service would not be deemed to be "service abroad" within the meaning of Article 1 unless it provides notice to the recipient "in due time." This due process notion cannot be squared with the plain meaning of the words, "service abroad." The contours of the concurrence's substantive standard are not defined, and we note that it would create some uncertainty even on the facts of this case. If the substantive standard tracks the Due Process Clause of the Fourteenth Amendment, it is not self-evident that substituted service on a subsidiary is sufficient with respect to the parent. In the only cases in which it has considered the question, this Court held that the activities of a subsidiary are not necessarily enough to render a parent subject to a court's jurisdiction, for service of process or otherwise. *Cannon Mfg. Co. v. Cudahy Packing Co.*, 267 U.S. 333, 336–337 (1925); *Consol. Textile Corp. v. Gregory*, 289 U.S. 85, 88 (1933); *see* 18A W. Fletcher, *Cyclopedia of Law of Private Corporations* § 8773 pp. 250–254 (rev.ed. 1988). Although the particular relationship between VWAG and VWoA might have made substituted service valid in this case, a question that we do not decide, the factbound character of the necessary inquiry makes us doubt whether the standard suggested by the concurrence would in fact be "remarkably easy" to apply.

argues that, because of this notice requirement, every case involving service on a foreign national will present an "occasion to transmit a judicial... document for service abroad" within the meaning of Article 1. Tr. of Oral Arg. 8. VWAG emphasizes that in this case, the Appellate Court upheld service only after determining that "the relationship between VWAG and VWoA is so close that it is certain that VWAG 'was fully apprised of the pendency of the action' by delivery of the summons to VWoA." 145 Ill.App.3d, at 606 (quoting Maunder v. DeHavilland Aircraft of Canada, Ltd., 102 Ill.2d 342, 353, cert. denied, 469 U.S. 1036 (1984)).

We reject this argument. Where service on a domestic agent is valid and complete under both state law and the Due Process Clause, our inquiry ends and the Convention has no further implications. Whatever internal, private communications take place between the agent and a foreign principal are beyond the concerns of this case. The only transmittal to which the Convention applies is a transmittal abroad that is required as a necessary part of service. And, contrary to VWAG's assertion, the Due Process Clause does not require an official transmittal of documents abroad every time there is service on a foreign national. Applying this analysis, we conclude that this case does not present an occasion to transmit a judicial document for service abroad within the meaning of Article 1. Therefore the Hague Service Convention does not apply, and service was proper. The judgment of the Appellate Court is Affirmed.

Justice Brennan, with whom Justice Marshall and Justice Blackmun join, concurring in the judgment.

We acknowledged last Term, and the Court reiterates today that the terms of the Convention on Service Abroad of Judicial and Extrajudicial Documents in Civil or Commercial Matters, Nov. 15, 1965, [1969] 20 U.S.T. 361, T.I.A.S. No. 6638, are "mandatory," not "optional" with respect to any transmission that Article 1 covers. Société Nationale Industrielle Aérospatiale v. U.S. District Court, 482 U.S. 522, 534, and n. 15 (1987). Even so, the Court holds, and I agree, that a litigant may, consistent with the Convention, serve process on a foreign corporation by serving its wholly owned domestic subsidiary, because such process is not "service abroad" within the meaning of Article 1. The Court reaches that conclusion, however, by depriving the Convention of any mandatory effect, for in the Court's view the "forum's internal law" defines conclusively whether a particular process is "service abroad," which is covered by the Convention, or domestic service, which is not. I do not join the Court's opinion because I find it implausible that the Convention's framers intended to leave each contracting nation, and each of the 50 States within our Nation, free to decide for itself under what circumstances, if any, the Convention would control. Rather, in my view, the words "service abroad," read in light of the negotiating history, embody a substantive standard that limits a forum's latitude to deem service complete domestically.

The first of two objectives enumerated in the Convention's preamble is "to create appropriate means to ensure that judicial... documents to be served abroad shall be brought to the notice of the addressee in sufficient time...." 20 U.S.T., at 362. Until the Convention was implemented, the contracting nations followed widely divergent practices for serving judicial documents across international borders, some of which did not ensure any notice, much less timely notice, and therefore often produced unfair default judgments. See generally International Co-Operation in Litigation: Europe (H. Smit ed. 1965); 3 1965 Conférence de la Haye de Droit International Privé, Actes et Documents de la Dixième Session (Notification) 11–12 (1965) (hereinafter 3 Actes et Documents). Particularly controversial was a procedure, common among civil-law countries, called notification au parquet, which permitted delivery of process to a local official who was then ordinarily supposed to transmit the document abroad through diplomatic or other channels. See S.Exec.Rep. No. 6, 90th Cong., 1st Sess., 11–12, 14–16 (1967) (S.Exec.Rep. No. 6); S.Doc. C, 90th Cong., 1st Sess., 5–6, 21 (1967) (S.Exec.Doc. C). Typically, service was deemed complete upon delivery of the document to the official whether or not the official succeeded in transmitting it to the defendant and whether or not the defendant otherwise received notice of the pending lawsuit.[1]

The United States delegation to the Convention objected to notification au parquet as inconsistent with "the requirements of 'due process of law' under the Federal Constitution." 3 Actes et Documents 128 (citations omitted). The head of the delegation has derided its "'[i]njustice, extravagance, [and] absurdity....'" Amram 651 (citation omitted). In its classic formulation, he observed, notification au parquet "'totally sacrificed all rights of the defense in favor of the plaintiff.'" Id., at 652, n. 9 (citation omitted). The Convention's official reporter noted similar "'spirited criticisms of the system'... which we wish to see eliminated." 3 Actes et Documents 76 (translated).

In response to this and other concerns, the Convention prescribes the exclusive means for service of process emanating from one contracting nation and culminating in another. As the Court observes, the Convention applies only when the document is to be "transmit[ted]... for service abroad"; it covers not every transmission of judicial documents abroad, but only those transmissions abroad that constitute formal "service." It is common ground that the Convention governs when the procedure prescribed by the internal law of the forum nation or state provides that service is not complete until the document is transmitted abroad.

[1] The head of the U.S. delegation to the Convention described *notification au parquet* as follows:

"This is a system which permits the entry of judgments in personam by default against a nonresident defendant without requiring adequate notice. There is also no real right to move to open the default judgment or to appeal, because the time to move to open judgment or to appeal will generally have expired before the defendant finds out about the judgment.

"Under this system of service, the process-server simply delivers a copy of the writ to a public official's office. The time for answer begins to run immediately. Some effort is supposed to be made through the Foreign Office and through diplomatic channels to give the defendant notice, but failure to do this has no effect on the validity of the service....

"There are no ... limitations and protections [comparable to due process or personal jurisdiction] under the *notification au parquet* system. Here jurisdiction lies merely if the plaintiff is a local national; nothing more is needed." S.Exec.Rep. No. 6, at 11–12 (statement by Philip W. Amram).

See also S.Exec.Doc. C, at 5 (letter of submittal from Secretary of State Rusk); Amram, The Revolutionary Change in Service of Process Abroad in French Civil Procedure, 2 Int'l Law 650, 650–651 (1968) (Amram).

That is not to say, however, as does the Court, that the forum nation may designate any type of service "domestic" and thereby avoid application of the Convention.

Admittedly, as the Court points out, the Convention's language does not prescribe a precise standard to distinguish between "domestic" service and "service abroad." But the Court's solution leaves contracting nations free to ignore its terms entirely, converting its command into exhortation. Under the Court's analysis, for example, a forum nation could prescribe direct mail service to any foreigner and deem service effective upon deposit in the mailbox, or could arbitrarily designate a domestic agent for any foreign defendant and deem service complete upon receipt domestically by the agent even though there is little likelihood that service would ever reach the defendant. In fact, so far as I can tell, the Court's interpretation permits any contracting nation to revive notification au parquet so long as the nation's internal law deems service complete domestically, even though, as the Court concedes, "such methods of service are the least likely to provide a defendant with actual notice," and even though "[t]here is no question but that the Conference wanted to eliminate notification au parquet" (citation omitted)....

The negotiating history and the uniform interpretation announced by our own negotiators confirm that the Convention limits a forum's ability to deem service "domestic," thereby avoiding the Convention's terms. Admittedly, the Convention does not precisely define the contours. But that imprecision does not absolve us of our responsibility to apply the Convention mandatorily, any more than imprecision permits us to discard the words "due process of law," U.S. Const., Amdt. 14, § 1. And however difficult it might be in some circumstances to discern the Convention's precise limits, it is remarkably easy to conclude that the Convention does not prohibit the type of service at issue here. Service on a wholly owned, closely controlled subsidiary is reasonably calculated to reach the parent "in due time" as the Convention requires. See, e.g., 9 W. Fletcher, Cyclopedia of Law of Private Corporations § 4412, p. 400 (rev.ed. 1985). That is, in fact, what our own Due Process Clause requires, see Mullane v. Central Hanover Bank & Trust Co., 339 U.S. 306, 314–315 (1950), and since long before the Convention's implementation our law has permitted such service, see, e.g., Perkins v. Benguet Consol. Mining Co., 342 U.S. 437, 444–445 (1952); Latimer v. S/A Industrias Reunidas F. Matarazzo, 175 F.2d 184, 185 (2nd Cir. 1949) (L. Hand, J.). This is significant because our own negotiators made clear to the Senate their understanding that the Convention would require no major changes in federal or state service-of-process rules.[6] Thus, it is unsurprising that nothing in the negotiating history suggests that

[6] In words reiterated by Secretary of State Rusk, the delegation observed that "[i]n its broadest aspects the convention makes no basic changes in U.S. practices." S.Exec.Doc. C, at 20. See also id., at 8 ("The most significant aspect of the convention is the fact that it requires so little change in the present procedures in the United States") (letter of submittal of Secretary of State Rusk). The delegation's head likewise repeatedly observed that the Convention "leaves our common-law due-process principles unaffected and unchanged." S.Exec.Rep. No. 6, at 11. See also id., at 9 ("By our internal law... we already give to foreign litigants all that this convention would require us to provide"); id., at 16 (Convention "requires no changes in our law of judicial assistance").

the contracting nations were dissatisfied with the practice at issue here, which they were surely aware, much less that they intended to abolish it like they intended to abolish notification au parquet. And since notice served on a wholly owned domestic subsidiary is infinitely more likely to reach the foreign parent's attention than was notice served au parquet (or by any other procedure that the negotiators singled out for criticism) there is no reason to interpret the Convention to bar it.

My difference with the Court does not affect the outcome of this case, and, given that any process emanating from our courts must comply with due process, it may have little practical consequence in future cases that come before us. But cf. S.Exec.Rep. No. 6, at 15 (statement by Philip W. Amram suggesting that Convention may require "a minor change in the practice of some of our States in long-arm and automobile accident cases" where "service on the appropriate official need be accompanied only by a minimum effort to notify the defendant"). Our Constitution does not, however, bind other nations haling our citizens into their courts. Our citizens rely instead primarily on the forum nation's compliance with the Convention, which the Senate believed would "provide increased protection (due process) for American Citizens who are involved in litigation abroad." Id., at 3. And while other nations are not bound by the Court's pronouncement that the Convention lacks obligatory force, after today's decision their courts will surely sympathize little with any United States national pleading that a judgment violates the Convention because (notwithstanding any local characterization) service was "abroad."

It is perhaps heartening to "think that [no] countr[y] will draft its internal laws deliberately so as to circumvent the Convention in cases in which it would be appropriate to transmit judicial documents for service abroad," although from the defendant's perspective "circumvention" (which, according to the Court, entails no more than exercising a prerogative not to be bound) is equally painful whether deliberate or not. The fact remains, however, that had we been content to rely on foreign notions of fair play and substantial justice, we would have found it unnecessary, in the first place, to participate in a Convention "to ensure that judicial...documents to be served abroad [would] be brought to the notice of the addressee in sufficient time," 20 U.S.T., at 362.

Comments and Questions

1. Does the Convention eliminate notification au parquet and other forms of service that may not provide adequate notice?

2. Assume that the forum state authorizes notice against a foreign defendant by publication. Is this service "abroad"?

3. Does compliance with the Convention inflict some hardship that the Court is reluctant to impose?

4. Assume that Schlunk is inconsistent with the intention of the drafters of the Convention. Propose an amendment to the "where there is occasion to transmit" language that would cure any ambiguity.

2. European Regulation

Since May 2001, transnational service within the European Union has been governed by a Council Regulation. This Regulation replaces the Hague Convention for most disputes between citizens of Member States, but it also builds on the decades of experience with the Convention and, in large part, replicates it. Perhaps the most significant reform is that the Regulation establishes an option for more direct and rapid means of communication than the Convention's framework of Central Authorities. In the following case, Plumex, a Portuguese company, received notice of the Belgian court's judgment through both traditional means and through the more accelerated process, to-wit: certified mail. Under Belgian law, Plumex had a certain period of time from the date that notice was served to file an appeal.

Plumex v. Young Sports NV

[2006] ECR I-1417

European Court of Justice

The Court (Third Chamber)

1. This reference for a preliminary ruling [from the Hof van Cassatie (Belgium)] concerns the interpretation of Articles 4 to 11 and 14 of Council Regulation (EC) No 1348/2000 of 29 May 2000 on the service in the Member States of judicial and extrajudicial documents in civil or commercial matters (OJ 2000 L 160, p. 37, "the Regulation").

2. The reference was made in the course of an appeal brought by Plumex against the Hof van Beroep te Gent's dismissal for being out of time of an appeal against a judgment at first instance ruling on a dispute between Plumex and Young Sports NV.

Relevant provisions

Community legislation

3. In the words of the second recital in the preamble to the Regulation, the proper functioning of the internal market entails the need to improve and expedite the transmission of judicial and extrajudicial documents in civil or commercial matters for service between the Member States.

4. The Regulation thus has the objective of improving efficiency and speed in judicial procedures by establishing the principle of direct transmission of judicial and extrajudicial documents.

5. Article 1(1) provides that the Regulation is to apply in civil and commercial matters where a judicial or extrajudicial document has to be transmitted from one Member State to another for service there.

6. Chapter II of the Regulation contains provisions which provide for various means of transmission and service of judicial documents. It is divided into two sections.

7. Section 1 of that chapter, comprised of Articles 4 to 11, relates to the first method of transmission and service ("service through agencies"), under which a judicial document to be served is first to be transmitted directly and as soon as possible between the agencies designated by the Member States, referred to as "transmitting agencies" and "receiving agencies." Next, the receiving agency is itself to serve that document or have it served, either in accordance with the law of the Member State addressed or in the particular manner requested by the transmitting agency, unless such a method is incompatible with the law of that Member State.

8. Article 7 of the Regulation provides that all steps required for service of the document are to be effected as soon as possible.

9. Section 2 of Chapter II of the Regulation provides for "[o]ther means of transmission and service of judicial documents," namely transmission by consular or diplomatic channels (Article 12), service by diplomatic or consular agents (Article 13), service by post (Article 14) and direct service (Article 15).

10. As regards service by post in particular, Article 14 of the Regulation provides:

1. Each Member State shall be free to effect service of judicial documents directly by post to persons residing in another Member State.
2. Any Member State may specify... the conditions under which it will accept service of judicial documents by post.

11. According to the information communicated by the Member States..., the Portuguese Republic has accepted service by post, provided it is made by registered letter with advice of delivery and is accompanied by a translation.

National legislation

12. Under Article 1051 of the Belgian Judicial Code the time-limit for lodging an appeal is one month from service of the judgment.

13. Under the same provision, read in conjunction with Article 55 of the Judicial Code, the time-limit for an appeal is extended by 30 days if one of the parties on which the judgment is served does not reside or have a registered address or an address for service in Belgium, where that party resides in a European country other than the United Kingdom or the countries bordering on Belgium.

14. Article 40(1) of the Judicial Code provides that, as regards persons who do not have a known residence or registered address or address for service in Belgium, the copy of the document is to be sent by the process server by letter registered with the postal service to their residence or their registered address abroad and service is deemed to have been effected when the document is handed to the postal service in return for a certificate of posting, in accordance with the formal requirements under that article.

The main proceedings and the questions referred for a preliminary ruling

15. Plumex, a company incorporated under Portuguese law with a registered office in Portugal, was served at its address in Portugal with a judgment from a Belgian

court of first instance delivered in a case between Plumex and Young Sports NV. Service was effected both through agencies and by post.

16. On 17 December 2001, Plumex lodged an appeal against that judgment before the Hof van Beroep. That court dismissed the appeal for being out of time, holding that the time-limit for an appeal provided for in Article 1051 of the Belgian Judicial Code had expired on 11 December 2001 since the period had begun to run on the day on which the first service was validly effected, in this case the service by post.

17. Plumex brought an appeal against that decision before the Hof van Cassatie, claiming that the Regulation had to be interpreted as meaning that service through agencies constituted the primary method of service taking precedence over service by post. Accordingly, the time-limit for an appeal must be calculated from the date of the "primary" service—which took place after the service by post—since the latter was only "secondary" service.

18. In those circumstances, the Hof van Cassatie decided to stay the proceedings and to refer the following questions to the Court for a preliminary ruling:

(1) Is the service contemplated by Articles 4 to 11 the primary method of service and service directly by post contemplated by Article 14 a secondary method of service, whereby the former method takes precedence over the latter when both are effected in accordance with the legal requirements?

(2) In the case of service being effected twice, once in accordance with Articles 4 to 11, and once directly by post in accordance with Article 14, does the time-limit for an appeal begin to run against the person on whom service was effected on the date of the service effected in accordance with Articles 4 to 11 and not on the date of service in accordance with Article 14?'

On the questions referred for a preliminary ruling

The first question

19. By its first question, the national court asks, essentially, whether any hierarchy exists between service through agencies and service by post, whereby the first method takes precedence over the second where both have been validly effected.

20. It must be observed at the outset that there is nothing in the wording of the Regulation to indicate that it introduced a hierarchy between those methods of service. Neither the recitals in its preamble nor its provisions state that a method of transmission and service, used in accordance with the rules of the Regulation, would rank below the method of service through agencies.

21. Moreover, it follows from the spirit and purpose of the Regulation that it is intended to ensure that judicial documents are served effectively, while respecting the legitimate interests of the persons on whom they are served. Although all the methods of service provided for by the Regulation can ensure, as a rule, that those interests are respected, it must be conceivable, in view of that purpose, to use one or other, or indeed two or more at once of those methods of service which appear the most suitable or appropriate in light of the circumstances of the case.

22. In view of the foregoing, the answer to the first question must be that the Regulation does not establish any hierarchy between service through agencies and service by post and, consequently, it is possible to serve a judicial document by one or other or both of those methods.

The second question

23. By its second question, the national court asks, essentially, to the date of which service must reference be made to determine vis-à-vis the person on whom service is effected the point from which time starts to run for the purposes of a procedural time-limit linked to effecting service where service is being effected both through agencies and by post.

24. In the observations which they submitted to the Court, the Austrian Government and the Commission of the European Communities state that they are uncertain as to whether the Court has jurisdiction to answer that question, since it concerns only the interpretation of national law. Where a Member State makes it possible to serve a judgment in various ways, the time-limit for an appeal starts to run under Belgian law, as a rule, from the first service which was valid. That date is determined in accordance with the law of the Member State addressed and, in any event, in accordance with national law.

25. In that respect, it should be recalled that, according to settled case-law, it is solely for the national courts before which actions are brought, and which must bear the responsibility for the subsequent judicial decision, to determine in the light of the special features of each case both the need for a preliminary ruling in order to enable them to deliver judgment and the relevance of the questions which they submit to the Court. Consequently, where the questions referred involve the interpretation of Community law, the Court is, in principle, obliged to give a ruling.

26. The second question relates to the relationship between the various methods of service provided for by the Regulation and it therefore involves the interpretation of Community law.

27. Accordingly, the Court is obliged to give a ruling.

28. As to the substance, first of all it follows from the answer to the first question that no hierarchy exists between service through agencies and service by post.

29. Secondly, in order not to render meaningless the provisions of the Regulation governing those methods of service, all the legal effects which follow when one of those methods is validly effected must be taken into account irrespective of subsequent successful service by another method.

30. Finally, it must be observed that, in accordance with the second recital in the preamble thereof, the Regulation is intended to expedite the transmission of judicial documents for service and, therefore, the conduct of judicial proceedings. If, for the purposes of computing a procedural time-limit, the first service of the document in question is taken into consideration, the person on whom that document is served—to whom such a time-limit applies—is required to defend judicial proceedings earlier, which can enable the competent court to give a ruling within shorter time-limits.

31. It follows from all those considerations that, where service is effected more than once in accordance with the Regulation, account must be taken of the service effected first. There is nothing in the Regulation to preclude the application of such an approach to the relationship between service through agencies and service by post. Accordingly, where service is effected by both those methods, in order to determine vis-à-vis the person on whom service is effected the point from which time starts to run for the purposes of a procedural time-limit linked to effecting service, reference must be made to the date of service by post, where that occurred first.

32. That conclusion does not adversely affect in any way the interests of the person on whom a judicial document is served since the first service validly effected enables him in fact to become acquainted with the document and to have a sufficient period of time in which to defend the proceedings. The fact that he is subsequently served with the same judicial document by a different method does not alter the fact that the first service has already complied with those requirements.

33. The answer to the second question must therefore be that, where service is being effected both through agencies and by post, in order to determine vis-a-vis the person on whom service is effected the point from which time starts to run for the purposes of a procedural time-limit linked to effecting service, reference must be made to the date of the first service validly effected....

Comments and Questions

1. Why was Plumex served twice?

2. Does the Court disagree with the observation of the Commission (and the Austrian Government) in paragraph 24 that the date of notice involves only the interpretation of national law?

3. Article 1 defines the scope of the Regulation:

> 1. This Regulation shall apply in civil and commercial matters where a judicial or extrajudicial document has to be transmitted from one Member State to another for service there.
> 2. This Regulation shall not apply where the address of the person to be served with the document is not known.

Is the applicability of this Regulation more definite than the scope of the Hague Convention? Could the Regulation be Schlunked by national laws permitting notification au parquet?

3. Inter-American Arrangements

As first mentioned in Section 1 of this part of the chapter, Latin American countries do not have deep roots in the Hague Conference. Accordingly, Brazil, Chile, Ecuador, Guatemala, Panama, Peru, Uruguay, and many others are not parties to the Hague Service Convention. Moreover, some Latin American countries that are parties to the Hague Convention (e.g., Argentina, Mexico, Venezuela) may require compliance also with additional protocols that supplement the Convention.

David McClean, Inter-American Arrangements

International Co-operation in Civil and Criminal Matters 60–70 (Oxford 2002)

Latin American lawyers are conscious of a strong regional tradition in private international law. An early expression of this was the great Congreso Sudamericano de Derecho Internacional Privado held in Montevideo in 1888 to 1889. One result of that Congress was the Convention on Civil Procedure of 11 January 1889, article 9 of which read as follows:

> Letters rogatory which have as their object the service of legal notices, the taking of testimony of witnesses, or the performance of any other judicial act, shall be complied with in any Contracting State provided such Letters meet the requirements of this Convention.

Just over fifty years later a second Montevideo Congress produced a revised Convention, that on International Procedural Law of 19 March 1940. To the existing text of what became article 11 were added two further sentences, one requiring that letters rogatory be translated into the language of the state of destination and the other dispensing with the requirement of legalization provided transmission was through the diplomatic (or, in their absence, consular) agents of the state of origin. Meanwhile the Bustamente Code of 1928 contained similar provisions, dealing additionally with the power of the judges issuing and receiving letters rogatory to determine questions as to the jurisdiction they were asked to exercise.

It has been commented, not unfairly, that a reader from the common law tradition finds the sparse language of these texts almost unintelligible. They take for granted that the service of process requires involvement of state officials, the usual civil law approach; that international co-operation between officials of different states in matters of civil procedure is initiated by letters rogatory transmitted by the diplomatic channel; and that in these respects the service of documents is in exactly the same category as the taking of evidence abroad. For many years, courts in the United States failed to understand the Latin American approach; the failure was so fundamental that a plaintiff in a Latin American republic had no means of service process on a defendant in the United States.

In 1919, a United States District Court held that foreign letters rogatory seeking the service of process could not be executed. The judgment in the case, Re Letters Rogatory out of the First Civil Court of City of Mexico, 261 F. 652 (S.D.N.Y. 1919), is badly flawed but was followed almost without exception for half a century. Judge Hand's refusal to comply with the request addressed to him in the Mexico City case rested on two grounds. The first was the narrow perception of letters rogatory as "exclusively limited by understanding and in practice" to requests for the taking of evidence; their use in the context of service of process he described as "novel," one requiring express statutory authority. The second was that, on theories of jurisdiction then prevailing in the United States, Mexico's claim to assert personal jurisdiction against a non-resident defendant was regarded as exorbitant; Judge Hand thought that he should not "aid a foreign tribunal to acquire jurisdiction" in these circumstances, a phrase really quite inappropriate, since a civil law system would not regard the service of process as a basis for jurisdiction.

Practitioners gradually became aware of the extent of the problems created not only by this approach but also by the inability of any Latin American country to recognize a United States judgment given after service had been effected by post on a defendant resident in such a country. The pressure grew for some international action....

Eventually, the Inter-American Council of Jurists, meeting at Rio de Janeiro in 1950, asked the Inter-American Juridical Committee to examine the matter. Its report suggested some principles which might provide a basis for action. These principles would accept both the formal approach of letters rogatory and the informal approach of direct (and usually postal) service, but would also note that no such service would be sufficient of itself to extend the jurisdiction of the state of origin. The Hague Convention of 1965 reflects this general approach and in later inter-American discussions the United States pressed for the acceptance of that Convention as the basis for regional co-operation, but unavailingly. The absence of any authentic Spanish or Portuguese text of any of the Hague Conventions militates against their acceptance in Latin America (and is responsible in part for the limited number of South American states which are members of the Hague Conference), and the Latin American attachment to the letters rogatory procedure proved too strong to allow a more broadly based solution in that region. What was there seen as more desirable was clear international agreement on the operation of the letters rogatory procedure.

After a good deal of further debate in the various inter-American bodies, the General Assembly of the Organization of American States resolved in 1971 to convene an Inter-American Specialized Conference on Private International Law (CIDIP from its Spanish title, Conferencia Especializada Inter-Americana sobre Derecho Internacional Privado). This produced six conventions, including the Inter-American Convention on Letters Rogatory signed in Panama on 30 January 1975. This convention retained something of the laconic style of drafting of its Latin American predecessors, and like them applied in principle to both the service of documents and the taking of evidence. It found little favour in the United States, where there was however considerable interest in securing some workable arrangement. As a result, the United States delegation at the Second Inter-American Specialized Conference on Private International Law (CIDIP 2), held in Montevideo in 1979, secured the adoption of an Additional Protocol, limited to service of documents but containing a fuller treatment of that topic drawing inspiration from some aspects of the Hague Convention. Of the total of fourteen states now party to the Convention, half have ratified the Protocol.[278]

---

[278] Parties to the Protocol are Argentina, Ecuador, Mexico, Paraguay, Peru, the United States, and Uruguay; parties only to the Convention are Chile, Costa Rica, El Salvador, Guatemala, Honduras, Panama, and Venezuela.

The Inter-American Protocol of 1979

The Protocol was prepared by Committee I of the Second Inter-American Specialized Conference on Private International Law, almost entirely on the basis of successive proposals from the United States delegation. Although in form supplementary to the 1975 Convention, it is in truth a substantial revision of it, creating an alternative treaty regime.

Scope and Modes of Transmission. This is best illustrated by reference to article 1 of the Protocol. This declares that the Protocol applies only to those procedural acts set forth in article 2(a) of the Convention. This immediately excludes from the scope of the Protocol the whole area of taking evidence and obtaining information abroad; this area could be excluded by reservation from the scope of the Convention, and is also the object of a distinct Inter-American Convention. Remaining within the scope of the present instrument were only "the performance of procedural acts of a merely formal nature, such as service of process, summonses or subpoenas abroad." These are redefined for the purposes of the Protocol as

> procedural acts (pleadings, motions, orders and subpoenas) that are served and requests for information that are made by a judicial or administrative authority of a State Party to a judicial or administrative authority of another State Party and are transmitted by a letter rogatory from the Central Authority of the State of origin to the Central Authority of the State of destination.

Not only does this clarify the nature of the authorities competent to issue and execute letters rogatory but it makes mandatory as between parties to the Protocol the use of Central Authorities both for the outward transmission and inward receipt of letters rogatory; that there is an obligation to designate a Central Authority, a matter not wholly clear in the text of the Convention, is specifically provided in article 2 of the Protocol. The duties of the receiving Central Authority are set out in detail in article 4. The understanding of the United States in drafting the Protocol was that while the United States would ratify the Convention as well as the Protocol, ratification of the latter alone not being permitted, this would create treaty obligations binding upon the United States only with other states which had ratified the Protocol and in accordance with its terms. It is submitted that this leaves in place the binding character of article 13 of the original Convention as to service of documents by accredited consular or diplomatic agents.

Documentation. There are elaborate provisions in articles 3 and 4 of the Protocol as to the appropriate documentation, and these provisions are very obviously inspired by provisions of the Hague Convention. In particular three forms are prescribed, which to minimize translation problems are required to be printed either in all four official languages of the Organization of American States (English, French, Portuguese and Spanish) or at least in the languages of the states of origin and destination. The forms are of the Letter Rogatory itself, which follows the functional layout of the Hague "Request" rather than the formal, almost supplicatory, style of a traditional letter rogatory; a statement of Essential Information for the Addressee, corresponding to the Hague "Summary of the Document to be Served"; and a Certificate of Execution or Non-execution again on the model of the corresponding Hague document. Two copies, in addition to the originals, are to be supplied; one is for service, one for retention by the state of destination; one for return with the relevant Certificate to the Central Authority of the state of origin.

The translation requirements are considerably lightened. As the Report of Committee I observed, "One of the greatest obstacles to international judicial co-operation is the necessity of translating innumerable documents into the official language of the country of destination for each international procedural act, given the high cost of translation services." Under the Protocol the only document which need be translated is the complaint or pleading that initiated the action in which the letter rogatory was issued. Attached documents and the actual rulings ordering that a letter rogatory be issued are to be supplied, but need not be translated. The precise scope of the translation requirements is not completely clear, especially in cases in which the letter rogatory is issued at some interlocutory stage; the specific motion there relevant surely should be translated, but the Protocol speaks only of the document which "initiated the action." The interpretation of this would appear to be within the competence of the state of origin, and it is to be hoped that an interpretation reflecting the realities of the position would always be adopted; what is important to the defendant [is] prompt access to the information necessary to judge how to respond to the current move by the other party.

Legalization is not required, as the Convention already provided for the exclusion of this requirement when transmission was through a Central Authority....

4. Asian-African Model Arrangements

David McClean, Asian-African Model Arrangements

International Co-operation in Civil and Criminal Matters 71–71 (Oxford 2002)

The Asian-African Legal Consultative Committee adopted at its Seventh Session in 1965 a set of Model Rules for the Service of Judicial Process and the Recording of Evidence in Civil and Commercial Cases. This is a remarkably brief document, providing so far as service of documents is concerned for letters or request to be addressed by a diplomatic or consular officer of the requesting state to the competent authority of the requested state, and for the execution of any request the authenticity of which was not in doubt unless the requested state considered that this would be contrary to its public policy. The Model Rules did not prove influential in practice, but they did serve to establish a commitment on the part of the Committee to a comprehensive approach covering criminal as well as civil matters.

The question of a regional convention in this whole field was put on the agenda of the Committee in 1975 and detailed reports were considered at its Twentieth Session in 1979 and its Twenty-Second Session is 1981. The Committee's Secretariat reviewed the existing models, particularly the Hague and Inter-American instruments and an Agreement Relating to Writs and Letters of Request adopted in 1952 by the Council of the League of Arab States, but recommended a "common integrated and comprehensive approach" which would cover civil and criminal matters, and both service and the taking of evidence. This proved too ambitious; the Twenty-Second Session favoured separate texts for civil and for criminal matters, and a subsequent Expert Group, meeting in New Delhi in 1982, decided that a model bilateral agreement in each of these areas was more appropriate than a draft convention.

After a further Expert Group had met, unusually for an Asian-African body, in The Hague with participation from the Permanent Bureau of the Hague Conference, the Arab League and the Commonwealth Secretariat, a Model for Bilateral Agreement for the Service of Process and Taking of Evidence Abroad in Civil or Commercial Matters was adopted at the Twenty-Fifth Session of the Committee in 1986. Its text is clearly influenced by both the Hague Convention and the Inter-American instruments.

Chapter I of the Model contains general provisions applying to both service of documents and the taking of evidence and adopting the system of transmission through central authorities (called "Central Agencies" in this text) in both the state of origin and that of destination. The provisions as to service of process in Chapter II are in other respects very close to the Hague Convention's provisions, especially in relation to the prescribed forms of Request, Summary and Certificate, and in the range of other modes of transmission, such as service by post or by direct communication between judicial or other personnel in the two states, which may be allowed in addition to the Central Agency channel. There are no provisions corresponding to the "guarantees" of articles 15 and 16 of the Hague Convention, but there is a provision as to non-commitment to recognition of a judgment based on the Inter-American Convention.

No information is available as to the extent to which this Model has been relied upon in international negotiations.

E. A Call for Uniform and Mandatory Rules

Haimo Schack, Need for and Extent of Unified Rules on Service

Transnational Service of Process, 6 Unif. L. Rev. 827, 836–838 (2001)

(1) The orderly international administration of justice demands a fine balance in protecting plaintiff's and defendant's interests. Since the plaintiff has the choice of the forum, the disadvantages accruing to the party that has to defend itself in a foreign country must be kept to a minimum. It is for that reason that rules such as the remise au parquet that favour only the plaintiff's enforcement interests are absolutely inadmissible. Neither the HSC [Hague Service Convention] nor the EuSR [European Service Regulation] are capable of preventing the proliferation of such national methods of fictitious service according to a "catch as catch can" philosophy, since these legal instruments apply only to service abroad, and even Articles 15 HSC and 19 EuSR provide for postponement of judgment only "where a writ of

summons or an equivalent document had to be transmitted abroad for the purpose of service" according to the law of the State where judgment is to be rendered. Even in the extreme cases of service by publication when the foreign addressee's address is known, or service upon fictitiously authorised agents, both the HSC and EuSR are quite helpless. It is not enough, therefore, to regulate only the modalities of service abroad if its prerequisites are left to national law. This imbalance of fictitious service in the forum State to the benefit of resident plaintiffs must be adjusted, preferably through a multilateral convention creating uniform service rules rather than by unilaterally denying recognition of a foreign judgment.

Insofar as national rules on service of process deny the defendant's right to be heard, they infringe the fair proceeding requirement of Article 6(1) ECHR [European Convention on Human Rights]. In order better to protect the defendant while at the same time improving the chances of recognition of a judgment rendered against the defendant, the prerequisites of a fair proceeding must be more clearly defined. An important point is the length of the period for filing a defence, the need for translation and cure of defective service. Additionally, within the EU, Article 12(1) of the EC Treaty [Treaty Establishing the European Community] forbids even disguised discrimination on the ground of the defendant's nationality.

(2) While the need for standardisation of the substantive rules on service of process is evident, the scope of the prospective uniform law is not. Certainly, the prerequisites of mandatory service abroad must be uniformly defined. Treaties such as the Hague Service and Evidence Conventions or the European Service Regulation are worthless if they fail to define the conditions of their applicability and rather leave these to the (different) national laws of the Contracting States. Once national peculiarities have been shed, the following prerequisites of service abroad are obvious: in all cases where the foreign defendant's address is known but the document cannot be delivered personally to the addressee or its authorised agent, the treaty rules on service abroad must be obeyed.

The question of whether the forms of service should also be standardized is another matter. This would require at least some intrusion into national laws on service of process. Much more important than a uniform method of service is agreement on minimum substantive guarantees to safeguard the defendant's right to be heard without violating the plaintiff's right to effective legal protection. The result would be an additional form of service created by the treaty which would in practice assert itself through its very quality.

In regard of substance, care should be taken that the period for filing a defence does not start to run before the date on which the defendant actually received the document. The reference made in Article 9(1) EuSR to the law of the receiving State does not guarantee this. Instead, periods of different length within the EU and outside it must be provided for; it should be possible to provide a flexible extension of the legally prescribed period....

A regular point of controversy is the need to translate the document to be served. While Article 5(3) HSC allows the requested State to insist on translation into one of its official languages, under Article 8(1)(b) EuSR the addressee is not entitled to refuse acceptance of a document in a language of the member State of transmission "which the addressee understands." However, the addressee's sufficient (!) command of the foreign language is difficult to prove in practice. A rule in the following terms would be preferable: "Notice of the suit shall be in the language of the forum and in the language of the State of which the defendant is a habitual resident." Habitual residence is a common concept in international civil procedure and quite easy to ascertain.

Similar considerations apply to the provisions on cure of defective service abroad. Treaties which leave it to the judgment State whether and how to cure a violation of the unified service rules again place themselves at the mercy of Contracting States. It is not to be supposed that this was the intention of the Hague Service Convention which itself does not contain any rules on cure of defective service. As a consequence, insofar as the Convention is applicable, there is no room for a cure in accordance with national rules.... In essence, there is nothing to be said against curing the quite common defects of service abroad once it has achieved its function of informing the defendant in a reliable and timely manner, but in that case the prerequisites for achieving such must likewise be defined in a uniform manner so as to prevent the judgment State from hollowing out its contractual obligations at will.

Comments and Questions

1. The American Law Institute ("ALI") and the International Institute for the Unification of Private Law ("UNIDROIT") recently undertook a next step in the international harmonization of private law. Rule 11 of their non-binding Transnational Rules of Civil Procedure addresses "Commencement of the Proceeding and Notice":

> 11.1 The plaintiff shall submit to the court a statement of claim, as provided in Rule 12. The court shall thereupon give notice of the proceeding, as provided in Rule 7.
>
> 11.2 The time of lodging of the complaint with the court determines compliance with statutes of limitations, lis pendens, and other requirements of timeliness, subject to compliance with requirements of timely notice to the party affected thereby.
>
> Comment:
>
> R-11A. Rule 11 specifies the rule for commencement of suit for purposes of determining the competence of the court, lis pendens, interruption of statutes of limitations, and other purposes as provided by the forum law.
>
> R-11B. Rule 11 also provides for giving notice of the proceeding to the defendant, or "service of process" as it is called in common-law procedure. The Hague Service Convention specifies rules of notice that govern proceedings in countries signatory to that Convention. When judicial assistance from the courts of another country is required in order to effect notice, the procedure

> for obtaining such assistance should be followed. In any event, the notice must include a copy of the statement of claim, a statement that the proceeding is conducted under these Rules, and a warning that default judgment may be taken against a defendant that does not respond.... Beyond these requirements, the rules of the forum govern the mechanisms and formalities for giving notice of the proceeding. In some states it is sufficient to mail the notice; some states require that notice, such as a summons, be delivered by an officer of the court.

Did the drafters of this proposed Rule meet Professor Schack's concerns?

Concluding Comments and Questions

1. Revisit the problem that opened this chapter. Should it matter whether defendant is served in England, Panama, or elsewhere?

2. Almost all of the questions presented in the problem reveal complications that disappear if the parties involved agreed to arbitration. If arbitrating parties can dispense with service of process and all of its attendant baggage, why can't courts?

F. Bibliography of Additional Resources

Barton Legum (ed.), INTERNATIONAL LITIGATION STRATEGIES AND PRACTICE (Am. Bar Ass'n 2005)

Beverly L. Jacklin, Annotation, Service of process by mail in international civil action as permissible under Hague Convention, 18 A.L.R. FED.2D 241 (1993)

4B Charles Alan Wright & Arthur R. Miller, FEDERAL PRACTICE AND PROCEDURE §§ 1061–1075 (Thomson West 3d ed. 2002)

Chritophe Bernasconi & Laurence Thébault, PRACTICAL HANDBOOK ON THE OPERATION OF THE HAGUE CONVENTION OF 15 NOVEMBER 1965 ON THE SERVICE ABROAD of JUDICIAL AND EXTRAJUDICIAL DOCUMENTS IN CIVIL or COMMERCIAL MATTERS (3d ed. Wilson & Lafleur 2006)

Daniel J. Smith, Invalidity of Judgment of Court of Foreign Country, 9 AM. JUR. PROOF OF FACTS 3d (1990 & Supp. 2007)

David Epstein, Jeffrey L. Snyder & Chrales S. Baldwin, INTERNATIONAL LITIGATION: A GUIDE TO JURISDICTION, PRACTICE, AND STRATEGY (Martinus Nijhoff 3d ed. 1998 & Supp. 2007).

1 James Wm. Moore, MOORE'S FEDERAL PRACTICE § 4.52 (Matthew Bender 3d ed. 1997 & Supp. 2007).

Marjorie A. Shields, Annotation, When is Compliance with Hague Convention on Service Abroad of Judicial and Extrajudicial Documents in Civil and Commerical Matters, Art. 1 et seq., Required, 1 A.L.R. FED.2D 185 (2007)

Richard H. Kreindler & Judith L. Holdsworth (eds.),TRANSNATIONAL LITIGATION: A PRACTITIONER'S GUIDE Oceana 1997 & Supp. 2007)

Richard H. Kreindler, TRANSNATIONAL LITIGATION: A BASIC PRIMER (Oceana 1998)

Stephen J. Newman, Proof of Personal Jurisdiction in the Internet Age, 59 Am. Jur. Proof of Facts 3d 1 (2000 & Supp. 2007)

Tim Taylor & Nigel Cooper, European Litigation Handbook (Sweet & Maxwell 1995)

Ved P. Nanda & David K. Pansius, Litigation of International Disputes in U.S. Courts (Thomson West 2d ed. 2005 & Supp. 2007)

Yvonne A. Tamayo, Sometimes the Postman Doesn't Ring at All: Service Process by Mail to a Post Office Box Abroad, 13 Willamett J. Int'l L.& Disp. Resol. 269 (2005)

CHAPTER 9

Gathering Evidence Abroad

A. Introduction

American discovery practice is notorious around the world. The standard perception is that U.S. lawyers file lawsuits on minimal bases, and then rely on discovery to develop or even find a case. To be sure, the scope of American discovery is broad—and it is thus by design. "No longer can the time-honored cry of 'fishing expedition' serve to preclude a party from inquiring into the facts underlying his opponent's case," the U.S. Supreme Court announced in 1947.* But since, discovery has been the scapegoat for the high costs of litigation (and of doing business).

> [L]awyers, I submit, are so widely disliked in this country because they are so very widely, and correctly, feared for the power without responsibility they wield.... Nowhere else can a lawyer show up, dump a pile of papers on your front lawn, tie you up for years responding to untold damage to your business and reputation, and then walk away with so few consequences if he is proven wrong.... Lawyers have plummeted in the occupational-esteem standing... because people think [lawyers] have nosed into too many areas of American life.**

Discovery practice is often labeled "the single most troubling element of contemporary procedure."***

This chapter offers comparative perspective on the discovery (or evidence-gathering) practices of different countries and introduces the mechanics of gathering evidence that is located in another country. With an increasing number of individuals, companies, transactions, and occurrences having multinational

---

* Hickman v. Taylor, 329 U.S. 495, 507 (1947).

** Walter Olson, Dentists, Bartenders, and Lawyer Unpopularity, Manhattan Institute, Civil Justice Memo No. 37 (April 1999).

*** Edward H. Cooper, *Discovery Cost Allocation: Comment on Cooter and Rubinfeld*, 23 J. Legal Stud. 465, 475 (1994).

components, it is important to appreciate the special challenges that are presented when evidence needed or desired within the forum is located elsewhere.

Some countries have bank or business secrets laws prohibiting the production of evidence for use in foreign proceedings. Many other countries require compliance with internal laws and procedures. These policies can be motivated by a desire to safeguard privacy, to minimize government intrusion, to promote sovereignty, to protect the rights of parties from whom discovery is sought, and/or to alleviate the burdens on non-parties from whom discovery is sought. Whatever their motive(s), most countries are not inclined to cooperate with the broad, burdensome, invasive, and expensive discovery techniques that epitomize American litigation.

Problem: Mitigating the Shotgun Approach

Following a path paved by the tobacco litigation, many plaintiffs in the United States filed suits against gun manufacturers. Among the theories of liability are misrepresentation in advertising, unfair business practices, and negligent design. In particular, plaintiffs allege that the manufacturers did not include safety features that they could and should have; and that they marketed the guns as safe when, in fact, they were not. According to plaintiffs, the entire gun industry may well have conspired to conceal information—greedily pursuing profits and needlessly endangering the public. These allegations will require extensive discovery. To prove these cases, plaintiffs will need to know and, ultimately, prove inter alia what the manufacturers knew about safety hazards and alternatives, and when they knew it.

Among the defendant gun manufacturers are many international companies including Heckler & Koch GmbH and Carl Walther GmbH Sportwaffen, which are both German companies; Forjas Taurus, S.A. is a Brazilian corporation; Glock GmbH. is an Austrian manufacturer located in Deutsch-Wagram, near Vienna; Fabbrica d'Armi Pietro Beretta S.p.A., one of the world's oldest corporations, has been owned by the same Italian family for nearly 500 years; Smith & Wesson was, until recently, owned by Tomkins PLC, a U.K. conglomerate.

To prove their case these American plaintiffs seek discovery of evidence that is located in these various foreign countries—and not only from the defendant-manufacturers and their employees but also each company's customers, vendors, suppliers, partners, affiliates, trade groups and so forth.

(1) If the case is filed in a U.S. court, should the scope of inquiry and the available discovery mechanisms be determined by the law of the forum or by the (more restrictive foreign) law where the putatively discoverable evidence is located? Or by some hybrid of the two extremes?

(2) What if that foreign law criminalized the disclosure of information for use in a foreign judicial proceeding. Should an American court be able to require the foreign defendant appearing before it to do something that would violate the laws of the defendant's own country? Is this something that can be left to the discretion of a trial judge or is there a need for greater predictability and certainty?

(3) Assume that the above case is filed in a court in California and that the parties agree that the substantive law of California applies to the case. Wouldn't the elements of the substantive law of California presume the availability of broad discovery? Put another way, wouldn't the substantive law be worded differently if discovery were not available?
(4) Assume that the plaintiffs are governmental regulatory agencies (instead of private individuals). In the tobacco litigation, for example, state governments were plaintiffs seeking reimbursement for medical expenses. Would such plaintiffs have a stronger or weaker argument for the application of the discovery rules of the forum state?
(5) Now imagine that the jurisdictions are reversed so that the litigation is pending in a jurisdiction with narrow discovery rules; and the evidence is located in a jurisdiction with broader discovery rules. Do you reach the same result as in (1) above?

B. Discovery in Context

Discovery practice is best understood when one can appreciate the role that discovery plays within the larger context of a litigation system. The following excerpt provides useful background about the civil and common law traditions.

Rolf Stürner, Discovery and Sanctions Against Non-Compliance

6 Unif. L. Rev. 871 (2001)

One of the most difficult problems besetting [transnational litigation] is how to strike a reasonable compromise between the broad American discovery with its rigid and direct compulsory sanctions and the more limited taking of evidence of Continental procedure which prefers indirect means of compulsion in the form of procedural disadvantages if a party refuses to cooperate. A careful discussion of this problem demands a thoroughly prepared broad basis and sufficient understanding of the different procedural conceptions. [T]his article analyses the present situation of American, Continental and English civil procedure, the basic procedural structures, and the purpose of the pre-trial phase, the scope of discovery and privileges, and existing sanctions for non-compliance; a short description of the historical genesis of the different procedural conceptions may help to further mutual understanding....

I Basic Procedural Structures

1. U.S. Procedure

(a) *Pleading phase.* In the pleading phase, the parties present "a short and plain statement" of the claims and defenses. The pleadings intend only to give the parties general notice of their opponent's case ("notice pleading"). The pleading stage does not identify the exact legal and factual contentions of the parties; a party is not completely prepared to meet the opponent's case at this point. The parties may use later stages to find the real legal and factual issues of the case. Fact pleading and relevancy requirement, systematically repudiated since the mid-20th century, are of scant importance.

(b) *Discovery phase.* In the pre-trial phase, the parties are concerned with gathering facts and evidence and finding the most effective and concentrated way of presenting their case and evidence at trial. Fact development occurs at this stage more or less apart from a later adjudication of the law. The importance of fact development increases in jury proceedings because the layperson jury assesses a dispute predominantly on its perception of the real and true facts of the case rather than on strict legal relevance. The purpose of American discovery is information of the parties and their lawyers as well as preparation of the trial and not the information of the court.

(c) *Trial phase.* In the final hearing or trial phase, it is up to the parties to present their final legal arguments and the evidence for the facts justifying their claims and affirmative defenses. If the judge is convinced that a party's allegations, accepted as true, do not justify the claim or affirmative defense (relevancy test) although the party had good opportunity to use helpful discovery measures to obtain further and better information, the court may render a summary judgment without trial. If asserted relevant facts are in dispute, the case must be set for trial or jury trial. All evidence, even documents, pictures, or other tangible items must be introduced by the oral testimony of witnesses, unless their admissibility has been stipulated in advance.

2. Continental Europe

(a) *Pleading phase.* In the pleading phase, the parties in Continental civil procedure furnish the detailed factual basis of the legal contentions which justify their claims or affirmative defenses. The European pleading phase permits the court strict control of the relevance of the alleged facts. It depends on the courts' discretion whether to allow the assertion of more general facts or to ask for more and better particulars. If the events in dispute occurred in the sphere of the opponent or of a third person without actual knowledge of the party that alleges them, the court may be satisfied with very broad and general factual assertions, so that the "burden of allegation" does not prevent a party from presenting its case and evidence. Continental pleadings are intended to establish in advance not only the facts to be proved, but also the means of evidence a party wants to present in the following hearings or trial. If the asserted facts do not justify the claims or affirmative defenses, the court may render judgment without further discovery or taking of evidence; the same is true when a party fails to offer evidence for alleged but disputed facts. In most Continental jurisdictions, the court has the power, indeed obligation, to give hints and feedback to the failing party before judgment is rendered, giving it a fair chance to improve its pleadings.

(b) *Preparatory phase.* The characteristic features of the second stage of the Continental proceeding are different in some aspects. Since the common purpose of this second phase is to prepare the final hearing, its organization depends on the purpose and contents of that final hearing, and these vary from country to country.

In France and Italy, the taking of evidence in the final hearing is a very rare exception (Romanic tradition); in the final hearing the parties present only their legal arguments and their arguments for the deliberation of proof. Normally, all evidence is taken before the final hearing by the "instructing judge," who often needs a sequence of different hearings to gather all facts and to take all evidence. In these countries, the main purpose of this second stage ("instructing phase") is the taking of evidence and the information of the court, not the information of the parties.

According to the procedural conception of the Code of Germany and most recently of Spain, the taking of evidence takes place[ ] during the main hearing. The second stage of German civil procedure, between pleadings and main hearing or trial, has a preparatory character: exchange of documents; preparation of expertise by court appointed experts; written hints by the court to supply more and better particulars, to admit facts, to offer better or more evidence, to improve legal arguments; also sometimes written testimony to prepare a possible oral examination; an early hearing to discuss the management of the case. The idea is to prepare a concentrated, final main hearing, very similar to the Anglo-American trial. In practice, some courts hold more than one preparatory hearing and they sometimes take evidence in the hearings of the preparatory phase, so that only part of the taking of evidence occurs in the course of the main hearing. There is very little difference with the Franco-Italian model when the court chooses this alternative case management.

Some common law observers argue that the Continental model has no real discovery stage. While it is true that the purpose of the taking of evidence in a sequence of hearings in some civil law countries is primarily information of the court and not—as in the American discovery phase—that of the parties to litigation, there is no denying that this sequence of hearings also provides additional pieces of information for the parties—information which often motivates them to change or modify their claims or other applications or to present additional facts, evidence, or legal arguments. The purpose of the preparatory stage in the German procedure is clearly to inform the court and the parties. The strict separation between party information ("discovery phase") and court information ("trial phase") in the American procedure is dictated by the need for an oral presentation of the results of the discovery stage in the American jury trial. In non-jury cases, American parties often stipulate the admissibility of discovery results as evidence, especially when the same judge leads the pre-trial and the trial. Hence, in non-jury cases the sharp distinction between discovery and the taking of evidence may not be so important, and there the convergence between the different systems and especially between the American and German models is remarkable.

(c) *Final or main hearing.* As mentioned supra, it is the purpose of the final hearing in France and Italy to hear the final arguments and statements of the parties to litigation. In Germany, the main hearing begins with the judge's report of the results of the pleading stage and the preparatory phase, following which the parties make their opening statements. The court and the parties then take all evidence needed to decide the case which was not taken in the preparatory phase. At the close of the main hearing, the parties make their final arguments to the court. The court renders judgment four weeks later.

3. England

(a) *Pleading phase.* The new rules emphasize the need for fact pleading. The claim form must contain not only a concise, brief statement of the claim and a specification of the remedy sought—in so far the rules describe the requirements of "notice pleading"—but also the particulars of the claim and the details of any interest claimed; furthermore, a claim may include a reference to any point of law on which the claim is based, the name of any witness or expert witness whom the claimant wishes to call and, by way of service or attachment, a copy of any document which the claimant considers necessary to its claim (including pre-action expert reports). In a similar manner, it is incumbent upon the defendant to state full particulars of its case.

The English reform attempts somewhat to keep the parties under greater judicial control, to limit the scope of discovery at the subsequent pre-trial stage and to determine exactly the issues that require evidence in a later trial. Traditionally, scrutiny of the relevancy of facts at the pleading or pre-trial stage has tended to be rather generous: a reasonable connection of alleged facts with the case at hand has been sufficient basis for discovery ("relating to any matter in question between the parties"). It has been up to the parties to aver the applicable law and legal arguments at the latest at trial, so that the pre-trial judge has been less in a position than his or her Continental counterpart to manage the proceeding on the basis of a self-determined legal framework. In [the] future, courts will probably be increasingly required to acquaint themselves with and scrutinize the legal arguments as early as the pleading stage and the start of the pre-trial stage. More judicial control of relevance may accordingly be expected, but there will be no really strict pertinence test. The difference with Continental practice will not vanish entirely, but it will probably diminish.

It should be mentioned that in many cases, the "burden of allegation" in the pleading phase of the new English procedure [means] no unprepared and uninformed parties. The new rules provide obligations on the parties to exchange information before the proceedings commence; non-compliance with the requirements of the pre-action protocols, which contain special rules for certain types of claims, may lead to a cost[ly] decision that takes account of the party's misconduct.

(b) *Disclosure and discovery phase.* The traditional purpose of the English pre-trial discovery was to inform the parties and prepare the trial. The trial judge was not informed of the results of the pre-trial discovery proceeding before the master or district judge. The reformed English procedure, which is the outcome of developments in the last decades, reflects a different understanding of the discovery stage. An important part of the results of the discovery phase replaces the taking of evidence at trial and forms, together with the results of the pre-trial stage, the evidentiary basis of the judgment (witness statements as evidence in chief, written expertise and the result of expert meetings and discussions, etc.). In other words, the modern English discovery phase has—in much the same way as the German preparatory stage—a double purpose: information of the party and of the court. Discovery and the taking of evidence converge and coincide. Typically, the jury no longer plays a significant role in English civil procedure.

(c) *Trial phase and final hearing.* The trial is the place where final legal arguments are presented and all evidence is produced that is necessary for the success of the case and which cannot be replaced by the results of discovery. The requirements for summary judgment without trial are virtually the same as in the American procedure.

II The Scope of Discovery and Taking of Evidence

1. Continental Procedure

In modern Continental procedure, parties are obliged to make truthful written or oral statements, testify in person and under oath, disclose documents and real evidence and—under exceptional circumstances—submit to medical examination. Non-parties are required to give written or oral testimony, present documents and permit inspection of things and entry upon land, while some European countries also provide for medical examination of third persons in paternity suits. The requirements of the opponent's obligation to cooperate are usually strict and quite restrictive. The party applying for a court order must give sufficient particulars and specify exactly the means of evidence to be produced or inspected. In principle, fishing expeditions are not permitted. Only in more exceptional cases, when a party has no exact knowledge of facts and means of evidence in the sphere of its opponent and shows a good cause for the alleged fact, a more general description of a class of documents or means of evidence may suffice and the court may order the production and inspection of a category of documents or tangible things. But each case depends on its own circumstances, no hard and fast rule can be given and the practice of the Continental judge differs from country to country and from court to court. The requirements of fair trial of a case (Article 6 of the European Convention of Human Rights) may today recommend a more generous standard of specification.

2. U.S. Procedure

U.S. procedure undoubtedly offers the broadest range of discovery measures and prescribes an impressive number of duties to cooperate in the taking of evidence. The requirements for parties include deposition upon oral examination or written questions, production of documents or things or permission to enter upon land or other property for inspection and other purposes, physical and mental examinations and requests for admission. Third parties are required to submit to depositions and produce movable things. Permission to enter upon land, in particular, gives comprehensive, detective-like investigatory opportunities in office areas, files, computer programs, registries and documents. Private searches for evidence and fishing expeditions are basic strategies in the U.S.

3. England

The reformed English pre-trial seeks a compromise between a system with little information and a system with nearly unlimited obligations of disclosure. It imposes on the parties obligations to exchange information and means of evidence (disclosure of documents, service and exchange of witness statements and reports, exchange of pre-action expertise, exchange of statements of truth, etc.). Specific disclosure, where a party applies for further discovery, or third party disclosure of documents must be granted by special court order and the application must be supported by evidence. Third persons and parties to litigation are obliged to give oral testimony at trial. Search orders may permit an experienced and independent person to enter premises and carry out a search for means of evidence described in the order. Applications for search orders must disclose very fully a good cause why the order is sought, including the probability that relevant material might disappear. While American orders for entry upon land intend to further private investigations for more and better evidentiary material, the main purpose of the English search orders as described above is to preserve relevant evidence; fishing expeditions are, in principle, not permitted.

III Sanctions

1. The Continental System

The majority of Continental rules of civil procedure and those influenced by them impose no direct compulsory sanctions (contempt sanctions) on the parties to litigation, but rely on indirect means of compulsion in the form of procedural disadvantages in the event discovery does not take place or cooperation in the taking of evidence is refused. By contrast, direct contempt sanctions can be imposed on non-parties not likely to be affected by a procedural disadvantage. French law has adopted two policies that contrast with the other Continental rules of procedure: on the one hand, if a party refuses to cooperate, a court may consider this to the disadvantage of the party; on the other hand, there is the possibility of astreinte, a form of procedural fine. However, in practice, negative evaluation tends to be the rule, with the astreinte a very rare exception.

2. The Anglo-American Tradition

As in Continental procedure, the rules of procedure in the Anglo-American tradition provide for contempt sanctions against non-parties when they refuse to testify or do not produce evidence. When parties refuse to submit to discovery, English and American rules of procedure provide for procedural disadvantages or, alternatively, imprisonment or fines for contempt of court. Procedural disadvantages include not only—as in Continental procedure—negative evaluation ("designated facts shall be taken to be established"), but even more than on the Continent also "judgment by default" or the "striking out" of an entire complex of allegations or defenses already in the pre-trial phase. While an English judge seldom resorts to imprisonment or fines for contempt as the ultima ratio, the contempt sanction even against parties to litigation is very common in U.S. proceedings. However, it must always be made clear that a party can avoid sanctions by admissions or stipulations and, therefore, limit the compulsion to the effect of the disadvantages under European procedure. Despite the leveling of differences, the fact cannot be overlooked that American procedure allows for extremely forceful means of compulsion to establish substantive truth.

IV Privileges

1. Non-parties

Privileges of non-parties are similar in Continental and Anglo-American procedure to the extent that both systems seek to protect from self-incrimination. It is striking that, under German law for example, this protection is extended to protection from disclosure of acts of dishonesty and from consequential civil damages, while U.S. law restricts this protection in the case of business documents of corporations and by the granting of immunity in parallel with or following criminal proceedings.

Most Continental procedures provide well-nigh absolute privileges for spouses and relatives; by contrast, this privilege no longer exists in England, and American law recognizes it at best reluctantly and inconsistently. Continental procedure protects professional confidentiality very broadly, for the most part by means of privileges; U.S. procedure by contrast grants only a few guaranteed privileges and not always uniformly so. American and English procedure is restricted to a clear "legal professional privilege"; it grants similar privileges to other professions such as physicians, priests, social workers and journalists, but sometimes only as a more limited exception from their general duty to give testimony or on a case-by-case basis. While business secrets, including a banker's duty of secrecy toward third persons, enjoy nearly absolute protection and are very broadly defined in some Continental countries, American law defines secrecy much more narrowly, protects secrets in the pre-trial phase by protective orders, and ultimately at trial does not protect them from disclosure.

The significance of non-party privileges for the protection of the sphere of parties to litigation should not be overestimated. If a privilege is asserted by a non-party but only for the protection of the party, the party's failure to "unlock" the privilege without good grounds may be the basis of an inference against it, especially when it is clear that the decision lies solely in its own hands, for example, when a party blocks the discovery of bank accounts with relevant data by refusing permission to the banker who is under the control of the party. Only if the privilege is solely that of the non-party, and the party has no means of compelling it to waive the privilege or otherwise permit access, no inference could and should ordinarily be drawn against the party by reason of the claim of privilege.

2. Parties

In Continental procedure, party privileges are for the most part not expressly regulated; rather, they are subject to judicial discretion, the result being that a privilege asserted by a party often ends up by creating a disadvantage for that party if the court draws negative inferences from its refusal to give information and to cooperate. Equal treatment of privileges of the parties and witnesses is under discussion in theory but it is not a reality in Continental procedure. The protection of a party from unfavorable consequences, in particular, is not a recognized privilege and is not accepted ground for refusing discovery and cooperation. In some countries, it may be an argument against fishing expeditions that one party need not deliver the procedural weapons for the other party's case, but there exists no general privilege protections from disclosure of unfavorable facts and means of evidence.

The optional contempt sanctions of the American procedure apply to parties and witnesses or non-parties alike. This is why parties may claim "privileges" just as non-parties may. From this it may be seen that "privileges" in Anglo-American procedure necessarily have to be defined more narrowly, or the substance of the case would be much too limited and the proper preparation of the trial before layperson juries by means of discovery measures would be burdensome and more difficult, though it may be permissible for juries to drawn an adverse inference from a party's claim of a privilege.

All in all, despite many similarities, the fact is that Anglo-American litigation curtails privileges to a much greater extent than is done in proceedings according to the Continental tradition. For European or Far Eastern parties, and defendants in particular, this is a very intractable problem since there is always the risk that an American lawsuit is brought only to obtain disclosure of industrial secrets or trade secrets.

Comments and Questions

1. Broad discovery is an integral part of American litigation. Is broad discovery a sine qua non of an adversarial system? Can a system tolerate "broad discovery" but not also "fishing expeditions"?

2. Why would the Continental system not embrace contempt sanctions to bolster discovery rules and obligations?

3. Why would a party accept the penalty of allowing a negative inference to be drawn rather than endure the pain of disclosing a document?

C. National Practice

National approaches to discovery (or evidence-gathering) can vary widely—even among neighboring countries whose systems are derivative of the same legal tradition. Explanations for these variations would include politics and culture, perceptions about the purposes of litigation and, given the interrelatedness of procedure, other rules and doctrines. Systems can be differentiated by examining their approach as to each of the following protocols: (i) the available mechanisms; (ii) the scope of inquiry; (iii) timing; (iv) the extent of judicial involvement; and (v) the participation of experts.

Discovery Mechanisms. American litigators have at their disposal a number of formal discovery techniques, including document requests, interrogatories, depositions, requests for admissions, and physical examinations. This set is unusually broad. Other common law systems, including Australia, England, Hong Kong, India, the Philippines, and Singapore, offer only a subset of this list. In particular, no common law countries other than the United States and (parts of) Canada liberally allow pretrial depositions for the purpose of gathering evidence.

The civil law countries tend to maintain a still narrower set of pretrial discovery mechanisms. In many countries, only documents are exchanged in advance of trial. Pretrial discovery in Japan is limited primarily to document requests and interrogatories. In Belgium, other than receiving documents, the most that a party can do to elicit detail from their opponent is to use their written submissions to the court to ask questions challenging the other party openly to respond. Many civil and common law countries have other discovery mechanisms (including depositions) available, but these techniques are for the limited use of preserving testimony that might be impossible to obtain at trial.

Among the discovery tools of almost all systems are automatic disclosure requirements. Either with the pleadings or at some later point, parties typically are obliged to disclose documents. Some require the disclosure only of documents that support the disclosing party's position; many others require the disclosure of all relevant documents.

Scope of Inquiry. A system's philosophy toward the gathering of evidence is also reflected in the permissible scope of discovery. At one end of that spectrum, the United States' Federal Rules of Civil Procedure permit the discovery of any unprivileged matter that is relevant to the claim or defense of any party (provided the request is not unreasonably cumulative or burdensome). Under this regime, litigants tend to make broad requests, seeking unspecified information for the purpose of turning up anything that might be (or become) relevant to the case. These are the sort of "fishing expeditions" that are frequently derided by other systems. In other systems—whether of the common law or the civil law tradition—discovery requests must be more narrowly tailored and must correspond to the allegations and theories in the pleadings. These constraints are especially significant because, in other systems, the pleadings are both fixed and more precise. Whether a particular request is sufficiently specific depends on the circumstances leading to the request and the system's tolerance for discovery.

Timing. The timing and sequence of gathering evidence are fundamentally different in the common law and civil law traditions. In the common law tradition, the discovery stage occurs in preparation for trial where the evidence is then presented in full. In the civil law tradition, certain documents and evidence may be disclosed early in the action, but otherwise the evidence is simultaneously gathered and evaluated by the judge in a series of hearings. In Italy, for example, the discovery of evidence occurs over the course of a number of separate hearings spanning months or years. The purpose of the earlier hearings is to determine which mechanisms of evidence will be used; the latter hearings involve the "taking" of evidence.

Judicial Involvement. In most common law systems, certain initial disclosures may be required by procedural rule, but discovery otherwise is largely party-controlled. Under the U.S. Federal Rules, discovery requests and responses ordinarily are not filed with the court, and only if there is some dispute between the parties is the judge likely even to know whether or what discovery is underway.

In most civil law systems, however, the parties may not compel one another to produce evidence without the participation of the court. Because of the interrelatedness of discovery and trial, civil law systems view discovery (or, more precisely, evidence-gathering) as a judicial function. Although the parties may offer the names of witnesses, and will suggest questions to be put to the witnesses, the civil law judge typically decides which witnesses to summon, conducts the questioning and records the evidence. The gathering and evaluation of the evidence are intertwined, and both tasks are undertaken as an exercise of the judicial function.

Expert Evidence. Under the U.S. Federal Rules, the use and selection of experts are largely within the control of the parties. It is not uncommon, then, that so-called hired guns engage in a "battle of the experts." Not all common law systems, however, follow this model. In England, the new Civil Practice Rules restrict the use of expert witnesses "to that which is reasonably required to resolve the proceedings."* In particular, no expert witness can be used in any civil proceeding without the court's permission.

The civil law countries tend to be even more restrictive. Parties ordinarily cannot bring their own expert witnesses or present reports from their own experts. Instead, the court, on acknowledging the need for expert testimony, appoints a neutral expert who submits a report answering the parties' questions and appears for questioning at trial. In Belgium, for example, the judge determines both the need for and the tasks of any expert. At a meeting with the expert, the parties give an overview of their respective positions and the evidence necessary for the expert to offer her opinion. The expert prepares a preliminary report on which the parties are permitted comment. The expert then prepares a final report that incorporates and responds to the parties' comments. The court is not bound by the conclusions of the expert although, in practice, most courts follow the findings.

The following excerpt offers some context for the broad discovery that dominates U.S. practice. As you read it, consider whether Professor Subrin is defending or merely explaining the American approach.

---

* Civil Procedure Rule 35.1.

Stephen N. Subrin, Discovery in Global Perspective: Are We Nuts?
52 DePaul L. Rev. 299, 309–312 (2002)

Our discovery mechanisms are not so irrational when seen in context. Let me sketch out some examples. Consider our historic distrust of concentrated power. Our doctrines of federalism and separation of powers, the right to a jury trial, and the adversary system, including party control, reflect our historic distrust of residing power in one person or limited groups. We do not think that judges would ferret out negative aspects of our opponent's case and positive information to prove our own claims or defenses with the same motivation and intensity that self-interest propels. Perhaps if we had more experience with career judges, elevated as the result of performance based on objective criteria, as opposed to politically-appointed or elected judges, we would have more confidence in turning over discovery to the judiciary....

In the United States, civil litigation plays a more substantial role in the governmental and societal structure than in most other countries. Alexis de Tocqueville noted in the 1830s how many hotly contested political issues end up in the United States courts. These issues are frequently, if not usually, raised by private litigants in civil litigation, as opposed to law enforcement by the state itself. A recent article about the Japanese legal system emphasizes how unusual the United States is in utilizing civil litigation, often through the tort system, to enforce social norms.[53] In this article, the author notes that in Japan, after private individuals sought to enforce environmental and anti-discrimination laws through civil litigation, the government, particularly "the entrenched bureaucracy," sought to curtail private enforcement so that the state could retain its power "as the appropriate enforcer of legal norms." Perhaps a truer comparison of the utilization of discovery in the United States would be between our civil discovery and the methods used in other countries to gain information, through force or otherwise, by the police, prosecutors, and administrative agencies in their attempt to enforce laws. It may well be that other countries permit so little discovery because the bulk of their civil cases are like the routine cases in the United States that engender modest discovery.

Broad discovery seems critical in many situations in which private individuals in the United States use civil litigation to enforce rights. This is particularly true in such cases as civil rights, products liability, securities, and antitrust, in which evidence to make a prima facie case frequently resides in the files and minds of the defendants. In these lawsuits, it would often be very difficult, if not impossible, for the plaintiff to plead her facts or evidence with particularity in the complaint, as is required in the pleading rules of other countries. The lack of precise pleading means that the defendant also frequently needs extensive discovery. The United States Supreme Court has repeatedly drawn the connection between notice

[53] Carl F. Goodman, *The Somewhat Less Reluctant Litigant: Japan's Changing View Towards Civil Litigation*, 32 Law & Pol'y Int'l Bus. 769 (2001).

pleading and liberal discovery.... In short, it would be difficult to eliminate extensive discovery in United States civil litigation without also changing the relative places of civil litigation, lawyers, judges, and juries in our culture and the relative roles of pleading, discovery, summary judgment, and other elements of procedure. The rules and the culture are interrelated in complex ways that would be very difficult to disentangle, even if such rearrangements were deemed desirable.

D. Transnational Conflict

National differences in discovery practice present circumstances ripe not only for comparative study, but also for transnational conflict. Indeed "no aspect of international litigation has caused as much friction as the issue of discovery."* Most of these conflicts tend to develop when documents or other evidence is located in another country that has a more restrictive approach to discovery.

Bernard H. Oxman, Direct Discovery and Other Means of Obtaining Evidence Abroad

37 U. Mia. L. Rev. 733, 749–752 (1983)

Territoriality

It is a basic principle of international law that each state has sovereignty over all activities taking place within its territory.[41] No state may perform an act in the territory of a foreign state without the latter state's consent.[42] This principle holds true whether a government purports to act through its political or judicial branches, or through its central government or political subdivisions.[43]

Consent may be express or implied. It may also flow from the right of another state under international law, such as the right of each state to regulate the activities of its own nationals wherever they are. The attempt to balance the two competing

---

* Andreas Lowenfeld, International Litigation and the Quest for Reasonableness 137 (1996).

41 Chief Justice Marshall authored the classic American formulation of the principle of territorial sovereignty in *The Schooner Exchange v. M'Faddon*, 11 U.S. (7 Cranch) 116 (1812): "The jurisdiction of the nation within its own territory is necessarily exclusive and absolute. It is susceptible of no limitation not imposed by itself. Any restriction upon it, deriving validity from an external source, would imply a diminution of its sovereignty to the extent of the restriction. ..." *Id.* at 136; accord *Wilson v. Girard*, 354 U.S. 524, 529 (1957).

42 "All exceptions, therefore, to the full and complete power of a nation within its own territories, must be traced up to the consent of the nation itself. They can flow from no other legitimate source." *The Schooner Exchange*, *supra*, at 136.

43 "The jurisdiction of courts is a branch of that which is possessed by the nation as an independent sovereign power." *Id.*; *see* Restatement (Second) of Foreign Relations Law of the United States §§ 169–170 (1965).

jurisdictional principles of territoriality and nationality may on occasion lead to serious international conflict.

The dilemma exists on two levels: first, fairness to the individual litigants, and second, rational ordering of relations between states. On the level of fairness, the individuals involved may face sanctions under the law of one country if they obey the law of the other.[46] On the level of rational ordering of relations between states, conflict must inevitably yield to some principles of self-restraint, perhaps voluntary at the start, but sooner or later ripening into law.[47]

The typical foreign discovery problem does not usually present a clash between territoriality and nationality as such. Evidence is sought from a national of a foreign state in the territory either of that state or of a third state. In theory, the sovereignty exercised by the forum state might be based on either territoriality or nationality, the former on the ground that the conduct of trials is an exercise of territorial sovereignty, the latter on the ground that persons subject to the jurisdiction of the court owe it "temporary allegiance" with respect to the litigation in question. In either case, the interest of the forum state as such is in the proper conduct of the litigation. That interest is distinguishable from the "substantive" interests of a state in controlling all events within its territory or in controlling the global conduct of its nationals. The subject matter of the litigation may indeed involve the latter "substantive" interests of the forum, and those interests are relevant to the existence of jurisdiction, but they are not strictly relevant to the collection of evidence, i.e., the search for truth, in a civil case.[48]

---

[46] This dilemma is particularly acute for corporations that may have subsidiaries, affiliates, or licensees in a large number of countries. An attempt by one country to use its power over a corporation or the corporation's employees and property located in its territory to compel acts to be done in the territory of a foreign state that are illegal under the latter's laws places the corporation or its officers or employees in a situation in which they cannot avoid committing a crime in one of those countries. Assertions that each country has jurisdiction to apply its laws in that situation are beside the point. In Western tradition and, increasingly, under general international law an individual is entitled to elementary fairness—in our terms, "due process"—in a government's exercise of jurisdiction over him. That demands mutual restraint and accommodation by the governments asserting concurrent jurisdiction. The fairness question thus implicates the sovereignty question.

[47] "A person may not ordinarily be required by authority of the United States...to do an act prohibited by the law of the state where the act is to be done or, if he is an alien, by the law of the state of which he is a national." Restatement of Foreign Relations Law of the United States (Revised) § 419(1)(a) (Tent. Draft No. 3, 1982). This rule is qualified in the case of orders to do acts in the United States prohibited by the state of nationality. The "territorial preference" is clear: "[P]rohibitions by the state in whose territory the act is to be carried out ordinarily prevail over orders of other states." Id. § 419 comment b.

[48] It may be argued that this analysis is too neat, since the choice of forum may affect the outcome in several ways, including cost, differences in the substantive rules establishing the rights of the parties, differences in the applicable choice of law rules, and differences in the procedural rules regarding burdens of proof. Inability to obtain evidence for use in a particular forum may therefore result in a party's having no remedy at all. Nontheless, the presence of these factors does not contradict the analysis. Rather it underscores the fact that the "substantive" territorial or nationality interests of a forum state may be substantial in a given case.

It is established that a state may not directly invoke its compulsory process against foreign nationals in the territory of a foreign state without the latter state's consent.[49] There is thus no question of a United States court dispatching a marshal to seize a person or property in a foreign country. It is not merely that a policeman of one state has no privilege to use force in a foreign state; he may not purport to act there as a policeman, particularly with respect to a foreign national on foreign soil. Even if a court may coerce a foreign national to "consent" in advance to the discovery of evidence controlled by him in his home country, the court may not dispatch a policeman to collect the evidence in the territory of the foreign state without the consent of that state.[50] Thus, one issue posed is whether counsel for a private litigant seeking evidence is a private citizen or an agent of a foreign governmental entity—in effect, a policeman. Does the arrival in a country of counsel for a private litigant armed with a foreign state's authorization to take a deposition or examine records or other property (which necessarily involves the possibility of sanctions for failure to comply) amount to an unlawful attempt at direct execution of foreign process in that country? Another issue posed is whether "indirect" execution, namely, ordering a party or witness already before a United States court to transport employees or documents from a foreign country to the United States or a third state for examination, entirely avoids the difficulty.

---

[49] *See The S.S. "Lotus" (Fr. v. Turk.),* 1927 P.C.I.J., ser. A, No. 10 (Judgment of Sept. 7); Restatement (Second) of Foreign Relations Law of the United States § 8 comments e & f, § 20 comment b, § 44 (1962); Restatement (Second) of Conflict of Laws § 53 comment d (1969); G. Stumberg, Principles of Conflict of Laws 100 (3d ed. 1963); Mann, *The Doctrine of Jurisdiction in International Law,* 111 Recueil des Cours 1, 128, 138 (1964).

In *The S.S. "Lotus,"* the Permanent Court of International Justice drew a clear distinction between the power to legislate and adjudicate and the power to take evidence in foreign territory. In upholding the power of Turkey to arrest in Turkish territory, and to try an officer of a French ship that collided with a Turkish ship on the high seas, the court analogized ships on the high seas to national territory, finding that the alleged involuntary homicide on board the Turkish ship occurred within Turkish territory for jurisdictional purposes. The court based its conclusion on Turkey's power to exercise its jurisdiction in its own territory, stating, "[T]he first and foremost restriction imposed by international law upon a State is that—failing the existence of a permissive rule to the contrary—it may not exercise its power in any form in the territory of another State." 1927 P.C.I.J., ser. A, No. 10, at 18. Elaborating on this point, the court stated, "Thus, if a war vessel, happening to be at the spot where a collision occurs between a vessel flying its flag and a foreign vessel, were to send on board the latter an officer to make investigations or to take evidence, such an act would undoubtedly be contrary to international law." Id. at 25. In this connection, the court noted that "by virtue of the principle of the freedom of the high seas, a ship is placed in the same position as national territory." Id. Despite its restrictive view of jurisdiction to take evidence, the court's expansive view of Turkey's jurisdiction to try the case was narrowed if not completely rejected with respect to collision cases by subsequent treaty. See Convention on the High Seas, Apr. 29, 1958, art. 11, 13 U.S.T. 2312, 2316, T.I.A.S. No. 5200, at 3, 450 U.N.T.S. 82, 88; accord Convention on the Law of the Sea, art. 97, U.N. Doc. A/CONF.62/122 (1982).

[50] The United States government sought the express consent of the government of the Federal Republic of Germany and the government of Iraq for its own consular officials to take depositions in the territories of those states, without compulsion, even on the premises of United States embassies and consulates in those countries. 6 M. Whiteman, Digest of International Law 221–25 (1968).

Implied Consent

Governments routinely permit foreign nationals in their territories to engage in activities that may further a foreign government's policies. Express consent to the presence of diplomatic officers, consular agents, and visitors of high rank implies consent for them to engage in their official activities. In other situations, patterns of tolerance may give rise to implied consent to do certain acts.

In principle, friendly countries may have no interest in frustrating the processes by which their respective courts endeavor to ascertain truth in civil cases, at least where jurisdiction over the parties is uncontested. Surely, strict territorialization of evidence gathering could complicate or frustrate the administration of justice in many cases. Absent indications to the contrary, a court may be justified in reaching the conclusion that there is implied consent for obtaining documents or testimony abroad from a "willing" witness. The parties may then proceed to take [discovery].... In the United States and to some degree in other common law countries, patterns of tolerance have arisen with respect to the taking of evidence from willing witnesses in foreign civil litigation.... That tolerance does not, however, exist to the same degree, if at all, in many countries, particularly civil law countries. The tendency of some American lawyers to proceed as though the liberal American policy were universal is not founded on fact.

Express Consent

By domestic legislation, bilateral treaty, or multilateral treaty, a state may consent to the taking of evidence within its territory for use in foreign litigation. [One example of express consent is 28 U.S.C. § 1782. This Section provides that a federal district court "may order" a person "resid[ing]" or "found" in the district to produce documents or provide testimony "for use in a proceeding in a foreign or international tribunal... upon application of any interested person." We will revisit Section 1782 later in this Chapter.]

Comments and Questions

1. Many countries are uncomfortable with—even incensed by—the unilateral export of American-style discovery. From their perspective, American courts act outside their territorial boundaries and flout the rights and protections granted by the foreign law. Moreover, American discovery essentially privatizes the gathering of evidence, which in the civil law tradition is a sovereign act performed by the judiciary.

A number of countries have adopted statutes to address the extraterritorial application of United States laws generally, and in particular discovery procedures, against foreign persons. To protect their citizens and information within their territories, if not also to defend the integrity of their court system, many countries prohibited the disclosure of such information. For example, in 1980 France added to its Penal Code the following offense:

> [I]t is prohibited for any party to request, seek or disclose, in writing, orally or otherwise, economic, commercial, industrial, financial or technical documents or

> information leading to the constitution of evidence with a view to foreign judicial or administrative proceedings or in connection therewith.

These "blocking statutes" took various forms, including the constructive "seizure" by the (foreign) government of documents otherwise subject to discovery. By invoking these statutes, foreign litigants in American courts could thus argue that they could not perform their discovery obligations without violating the law of their own countries. Through the wonder of globalization, then, a discovery dispute becomes a question of international relations and diplomacy: which country's laws and values should prevail?

> Blocking statutes generally take one of three basic forms. First...there are older laws like the Swiss banking secrecy statutes....Second, the most comprehensive foreign laws create blanket protection for large categories of documents and/or vest relatively broad discretion over disclosure issues in some government official. Especially around 1980 some of our most important trading partners attempted to cut back on the extraterritorial application of American laws by enacting broad nondisclosure statutes. For instance, the British Protection of Trading Interests Act of 1980 (PTIA) gives the British government the power to block most types of discovery....Finally, a third type of law, such as Canada's Uranium Information Security Regulations has been aimed directly at frustrating specific American claims. The Canadian law arose out of the attempt by the Canadian government, along with several other foreign sovereigns, to quash American antitrust litigation concerning a worldwide uranium cartel. This was done by forbidding the production of any information relating to "conversations, discussions or meetings that took place between January 1, 1972 and December 31, 1975...in respect of the production, import, export...use or sale of uranium."
>
> David E. Teitelbaum, Strict Enforcement of Extraterritorial Discovery, 38 Stan. L. Rev. 841, 847–849 (1986).

Courts balanced the interests of the countries involved and, generally speaking, during the 1950s and 1960s the blocking statutes worked. Judges recognized that litigants were faced with the choice of violating either forum or foreign law. The blocking statutes created enough friction to moderate the application abroad of discovery techniques, "consistent with the overall principle of reasonableness in the exercise of jurisdiction." Restatement of Foreign Relations Law of the United States § 437, Reporter's Note 5, p. 42.

E. International Solutions

1. Hague Evidence Convention

Foreign resistance to U.S.-style discovery prompted the United States to propose the adoption of a convention on transnational discovery. The 1970 Hague Convention on the Taking of Evidence Abroad in Civil or Commercial Matters was intended to establish a system that would be tolerable to the state executing the request yet useful to the requesting state. The United States ratified the Convention after a unanimous vote of the Senate in 1972. Dozens of other countries have since joined.*

There are three alternative methods for obtaining evidence abroad under the Convention.

(1) A litigant may request the court where the action is pending to transmit a "Letter of Request" to the "Central Authority"† in the country where the evidence is to be obtained. The Central Authority transmits the request to the appropriate foreign court, which conducts an evidentiary proceeding under procedures of the foreign country.
(2) A litigant may request that the evidence be taken before a diplomatic or consular officer in the country where the action is pending. The Convention provides that a contracting state may reserve the right not to allow the taking of evidence before a diplomatic or consular officer.
(3) A litigant may request that a specially appointed commissioner take evidence in the foreign country.

Of the three procedures, the Letter of Request is the most useful. It is the only method which applies to compulsory evidentiary proceedings. The other two methods are subject to limitations in the Convention and many countries have limited the use of these procedures in a variety of ways. Some of the key provisions of the Convention regarding the procedure for Letters of Request are printed below.

Hague Convention on the Taking of Evidence Abroad in Civil and Commercial Matters

23 U.S.T. 2555 (Concluded 18 March 1970; Entered into force 7 October 1972)

The States signatory to the present Convention,

Desiring to facilitate the transmission and execution of Letters of Request and to further the accommodation of the different methods which they use for this purpose,

Desiring to improve mutual judicial co-operation in civil or commercial matters,

Have resolved to conclude a Convention to this effect and have agreed upon the following provisions:

---

* The Hague Conference on Private International Law maintains an excellent website, including a list of the contracting states to conventions such as the Convention on the Taking of Evidence Abroad. *See* http://hcch.net (last visited November 15, 2008).

† Article 2 of the Convention requires each Contracting State to designate a Central Authority to receive Letters of Request emanating from other countries and to transmit them to the authority competent to execute them. In the United States, the Department of Justice serves as the Central Authority for incoming requests. For a list of Central Authorities, *see* the Hague Conference Web site, cited in the previous note.

Article 1

In civil or commercial matters a judicial authority of a Contracting State may, in accordance with the provisions of the law of that State, request the competent authority of another Contracting State, by means of a Letter of Request, to obtain evidence, or to perform some other judicial act.

A Letter shall not be used to obtain evidence which is not intended for use in judicial proceedings, commenced or contemplated....

Article 2

A Contracting State shall designate a Central Authority which will undertake to receive Letters of Request coming from a judicial authority of another Contracting State and to transmit them to the authority competent to execute them. Each State shall organize the Central Authority in accordance with its own law.

Letters shall be sent to the Central Authority of the State of execution without being transmitted through any other authority of that State.

Article 3

A Letter of Request shall specify—

a) the authority requesting its execution and the authority requested to execute it, if known to the requesting authority;
b) the names and addresses of the parties to the proceedings and their representatives, if any;
c) the nature of the proceedings for which the evidence is required, giving all necessary information in regard thereto;
d) the evidence to be obtained or other judicial act to be performed.

Where appropriate, the Letter shall specify, inter alia—

e) the names and addresses of the persons to be examined;
f) the questions to be put to the persons to be examined or a statement of the subject-matter about which they are to be examined;
g) the documents or other property, real or personal, to be inspected;
h) any requirement that the evidence is to be given on oath or affirmation, and any special form to be used;
i) any special method or procedure to be followed under Article 9.

A Letter may also mention any information necessary for the application of Article 11. No legalization or other like formality may be required.

Article 4

A Letter of Request shall be in the language of the authority requested to execute it or be accompanied by a translation into that language.

Nevertheless, a Contracting State shall accept a Letter in either English or French, or a translation into one of these languages, unless it has made the reservation authorized by Article 33.

A Contracting State which has more than one official language and cannot, for reasons of internal law, accept Letters in one of these languages for the whole of its territory, shall, by declaration, specify the language in which the Letter or translation thereof shall be expressed for execution in the specified parts of its territory. In case of failure to comply with this declaration, without justifiable excuse, the costs of translation into the required language shall be borne by the State of origin.

A Contracting State may, by declaration, specify the language or languages other than those referred to in the preceding paragraphs, in which a Letter may be sent to its Central Authority.

Any translation accompanying a Letter shall be certified as correct, either by a diplomatic officer or consular agent or by a sworn translator or by any other person so authorized in either State. . . .

Article 9

The judicial authority which executes a Letter of Request shall apply its own law as to the methods and procedures to be followed.

However, it will follow a request of the requesting authority that a special method or procedure be followed, unless this is incompatible with the internal law of the State of execution or is impossible of performance by reason of its internal practice and procedure or by reason of practical difficulties.

A Letter of Request shall be executed expeditiously. . . .

Article 11

In the execution of a Letter of Request the person concerned may refuse to give evidence in so far as he has a privilege or duty to refuse to give the evidence—

a) under the law of the State of execution; or
b) under the law of the State of origin, and the privilege or duty has been specified in the Letter, or, at the instance of the requested authority, has been otherwise confirmed to that authority by the requesting authority.

A Contracting State may declare that, in addition, it will respect privileges and duties existing under the law of States other than the State of origin and the State of execution, to the extent specified in that declaration.

Article 12

The execution of a Letter of Request may be refused only to the extent that–

a) in the State of execution the execution of the Letter does not fall within the functions of the judiciary; or
b) the State addressed considers that its sovereignty or security would be prejudiced thereby.

Execution may not be refused solely on the ground that under its internal law the State of execution claims exclusive jurisdiction over the subject-matter of the action or that its internal law would not admit a right of action on it. . . .

Article 14

The execution of the Letter of Request shall not give rise to any reimbursement of taxes or costs of any nature.

Nevertheless, the State of execution has the right to require the State of origin to reimburse the fees paid to experts and interpreters and the costs occasioned by the use of a special procedure requested by the State of origin under Article 9, paragraph 2. . . .

Article 23

A Contracting State may at the time of signature, ratification or accession, declare that it will not execute Letters of Request issued for the purpose of obtaining pre-trial discovery of documents as known in Common Law countries.

Article 27

The provisions of the present Convention shall not prevent a Contracting State from—

a) declaring that Letters of Request may be transmitted to its judicial authorities through channels other than those provided for in Article 2;
b) permitting, by internal law or practice, any act provided for in this Convention to be performed upon less restrictive conditions;
c) permitting, by internal law or practice, methods of taking evidence other than those provided for in this Convention. . . .

With regard to the Articles omitted here, Articles 5–8, 10 and 13 concern technical requirements about Letters of Request; Articles 15–22 outline a process for taking of evidence by diplomatic officers, consular agents, and commissioners; and Articles 24–26 and 28–42 detail certain "general clauses" regarding participation by contracting states.]

Comments and Questions

1. Article 1 appears to delineate a scope that includes evidence for use at trial, rather than for pretrial discovery. Is there a difference? If so, why should that matter?

2. Professor Stürner emphasized evidentiary privileges as a distinguishing characteristic. How does the Hague Evidence Convention mediate a conflict between systems with different privileges? (Are the relevant privileges those of the country where the evidence is given or those where the evidence is requested and used?)

3. A majority of contracting states have made the declaration permitted by Article 23 of the Convention. If there were a hierarchy of forms of evidence that are crucial to determining the truth, where would documents appear on that list? Are the civil law countries that made the Article 23 declaration more comfortable with depositions (than with document discovery)? Justify their approach.

4. The Evidence Convention outlined a scope and procedure for foreign evidence gathering that, although narrow and administratively cumbersome in comparison with the Federal Rules, identified important common ground. But this common ground confined American litigators familiar with American discovery, who "needed" broader discovery in order to meet their burdens of proof—or at least wished to use the discovery methods with which they were familiar. Those litigators tested the limits and durability of the Convention.

The Court's decision in the Aérospatiale case, which follows, addressed the extent to which litigants and courts were obliged to follow the Convention when engaged in transnational discovery. The petitioners to the Court (SNIA) were corporations owned by the Republic of France engaged in the business of designing, manufacturing and marketing aircraft. One of their planes, the "Rallye," was allegedly advertised in American aviation publications as "the World's safest and most economical STOL plane." STOL is an acronym for "short takeoff and landing," and it refers to a fixed-wing aircraft that either takes off or lands with only a short taxi. On August 19, 1980, a Rallye crashed in Iowa, injuring the pilot and a passenger.

The plaintiffs (later the respondents in the Supreme Court action) brought separate suits based upon this accident in the United States District Court for the Southern District of Iowa, alleging that petitioners had manufactured and sold a defective plane and were thus liable under theories of negligence and breach of warranty. Plaintiffs sought discovery under the Federal Rules, and SNIA filed a motion for a protective order. SNIA argued that, because it was a French corporation, the Hague Evidence Convention was the only means through which the plaintiffs could conduct discovery. After all, defendants argued, the Hague Evidence Convention had been accepted by the Senate, ratified by the President, and thus, was the law of the land. The plaintiffs argued, however, that compliance with the Convention was not mandatory. The district court agreed with the plaintiffs, and denied the motion for a protective order. The case ultimately found its way to the Supreme Court.

Société Nationale Industrielle Aérospatiale v. United States District Court

482 U.S. 522 (1987)

Justice Stevens delivered the opinion of the Court:

[I]

In arguing their entitlement to a protective order, petitioners correctly assert that both the discovery rules set forth in the Federal Rules of Civil Procedure and the Hague Convention are the law of the United States. This observation, however, does not dispose of the question before us; we must analyze the interaction between these two bodies of federal law. Initially, we note that at least four different interpretations of the relationship between the federal discovery rules and the Hague Convention are possible. Two of these interpretations assume that the Hague Convention by its terms dictates the extent to which it supplants normal discovery rules. First, the Hague Convention might be read as requiring its use to the exclusion of any other discovery procedures whenever evidence located abroad is sought for use in an American court. Second, the Hague Convention might be interpreted to require first, but not exclusive, use of its procedures. Two other interpretations assume that international comity, rather than the obligations created by the treaty, should guide judicial resort to the Hague Convention. Third, then, the Convention might be viewed as establishing a supplemental set of discovery procedures, strictly optional under treaty law, to which concerns of comity nevertheless require first resort by American courts in all cases. Fourth, the treaty may be viewed as an undertaking among sovereigns to facilitate discovery to which an American court should resort when it deems that course of action appropriate, after considering the situations of the parties before it as well as the interests of the concerned foreign state....

We reject the first two of the possible interpretations as inconsistent with the language and negotiating history of the Hague Convention. The preamble of the Convention specifies its purpose "to facilitate the transmission and execution of Letters of Request" and to "improve mutual judicial co-operation in civil or commercial matters." 23 U.S.T., at 2557, T.I.A.S. No. 7444. The preamble does not speak in mandatory terms which would purport to describe the procedures for all permissible transnational discovery and exclude all other existing practices.[15] The text of the Evidence Convention itself does not modify the law of any contracting state, require any contracting state to use the Convention procedures, either in requesting evidence or in responding to such requests, or compel any contracting state to change its own evidence-gathering procedures.

The Convention contains three chapters. Chapter I, entitled "Letters of Requests," and chapter II, entitled "Taking of Evidence by Diplomatic Officers, Consular Agents and Commissioners," both use permissive rather than mandatory language. Thus, Article 1 provides that a judicial authority in one contracting state "may" forward a letter of request to the competent authority in another contracting state for the purpose of obtaining evidence. Similarly, Articles 15, 16, and 17 provide that diplomatic officers, consular agents, and commissioners "may...without compulsion," take evidence under certain conditions. The absence

---

[15] The Hague Conference on Private International Law's omission of mandatory language in the preamble is particularly significant in light of the same body's use of mandatory language in the preamble to the Hague Service Convention, 20 U.S.T. 361, T.I.A.S. No. 6638. Article 1 of the Service Convention provides: "The present Convention shall apply in all cases, in civil or commercial matters, where there is occasion to transmit a judicial or extrajudicial document for service abroad."...[T]he Service Convention was drafted before the Evidence Convention, and its language provided a model exclusivity provision that the drafters of the Evidence Convention could easily have followed had they been so inclined. Given this background, the drafters' election to use permissive language instead is strong evidence of their intent.

of any command that a contracting state must use Convention procedures when they are not needed is conspicuous.

Two of the Articles in chapter III, entitled "General Clauses," buttress our conclusion that the Convention was intended as a permissive supplement, not a pre-emptive replacement, for other means of obtaining evidence located abroad. Article 23 expressly authorizes a contracting state to declare that it will not execute any letter of request in aid of pretrial discovery of documents in a common-law country. Surely, if the Convention had been intended to replace completely the broad discovery powers that the common-law courts in the United States previously exercised over foreign litigants subject to their jurisdiction, it would have been most anomalous for the common-law contracting parties to agree to Article 23, which enables a contracting party to revoke its consent to the treaty's procedures for pretrial discovery.[22] In the absence of explicit textual support, we are unable to accept the hypothesis that the common-law contracting states abjured recourse to all preexisting discovery procedures at the same time that they accepted the possibility that a contracting party could unilaterally abrogate even the Convention's procedures. Moreover, Article 27 plainly states that the Convention does not prevent a contracting state from using more liberal methods of rendering evidence than those authorized by the Convention. Thus, the text of the Evidence Convention, as well as the history of its proposal and ratification by the United States, unambiguously supports the conclusion that it was intended to establish optional procedures that would facilitate the taking of evidence abroad.

An interpretation of the Hague Convention as the exclusive means for obtaining evidence located abroad would effectively subject every American court hearing a case involving a national of a contracting state to the internal laws of that state. Interrogatories and document requests are staples of international commercial litigation, no less than of other suits, yet a rule of exclusivity would subordinate the court's supervision of even the most routine of these pretrial proceedings to the actions or, equally, to the inactions of foreign judicial authorities....

We conclude accordingly that the Hague Convention did not deprive the District Court of the jurisdiction it otherwise possessed to order a foreign national party before it to produce evidence physically located within a signatory nation.[25]...

[II]

Petitioners contend that even if the Hague Convention's procedures are not mandatory, this Court should adopt a rule requiring that American litigants first resort

[22] Thirteen of the seventeen signatory states have made declarations under Article 23 of the Convention that restrict pretrial discovery of documents.

[25] The opposite conclusion of exclusivity would create three unacceptable asymmetries. First, within any lawsuit between a national of the United States and a national of another contracting party, the foreign party could obtain discovery under the Federal Rules of Civil Procedure, while the domestic party would be required to resort first to the procedures of the Hague Convention. This imbalance would run counter to the fundamental maxim of discovery that "[m]utual knowledge of all the

to those procedures before initiating any discovery pursuant to the normal methods of the Federal Rules of Civil Procedure. The Court of Appeals rejected this argument because it was convinced that an American court's order ultimately requiring discovery that a foreign court had refused under Convention procedures would constitute "the greatest insult" to the sovereignty of that tribunal. We disagree with the Court of Appeals' view. It is well known that the scope of American discovery is often significantly broader than is permitted in other jurisdictions, and we are satisfied that foreign tribunals will recognize that the final decision on the evidence to be used in litigation conducted in American courts must be made by those courts. We therefore do not believe that an American court should refuse to make use of Convention procedures because of a concern that it may ultimately find it necessary to order the production of evidence that a foreign tribunal permitted a party to withhold.

Nevertheless, we cannot accept petitioners' invitation to announce a new rule of law that would require first resort to Convention procedures whenever discovery is sought from a foreign litigant. Assuming, without deciding, that we have the lawmaking power to do so, we are convinced that such a general rule would be unwise. In many situations the Letter of Request procedure authorized by the Convention would be unduly time consuming and expensive, as well as less certain to produce needed evidence than direct use of the Federal Rules. A rule of first resort in all cases would therefore be inconsistent with the overriding interest in the "just, speedy, and inexpensive determination" of litigation in our courts. See Fed. R. Civ. P. 1.

Petitioners argue that a rule of first resort is necessary to accord respect to the sovereignty of states in which evidence is located. It is true that the process of obtaining evidence in a civil-law jurisdiction is normally conducted by a judicial officer rather than by private attorneys. Petitioners contend that if performed on French soil, for example, by an unauthorized person, such evidence-gathering might violate the "judicial sovereignty" of the host nation. Because it is only through the Convention that civil-law nations have given their consent to evidence-gathering activities within their borders, petitioners argue, we have a

---

relevant facts gathered by both parties is essential to proper litigation." *Hickman v. Taylor*, 329 U.S. 495, 507 (1947). Second, a rule of exclusivity would enable a company which is a citizen of another contracting state to compete with a domestic company on uneven terms, since the foreign company would be subject to less extensive discovery procedures in the event that both companies were sued in an American court. Petitioners made a voluntary decision to market their products in the United States. They are entitled to compete on equal terms with other companies operating in this market. But since the District Court unquestionably has personal jurisdiction over petitioners, they are subject to the same legal constraints, including the burdens associated with American judicial procedures, as their American competitors. A general rule according foreign nationals a preferred position in pretrial proceedings in our courts would conflict with the principle of equal opportunity that governs the market they elected to enter. Third, since a rule of first use of the Hague Convention would apply to cases in which a foreign party is a national of a contracting state, but not to cases in which a foreign party is a national of any other foreign state, the rule would confer an unwarranted advantage on some domestic litigants over others similarly situated.

duty to employ those procedures whenever they are available. We find that argument unpersuasive. If such a duty were to be inferred from the adoption of the Convention itself, we believe it would have been described in the text of that document. Moreover, the concept of international comity[27] requires in this context a more particularized analysis of the respective interests of the foreign nation and the requesting nation than petitioners' proposed general rule would generate. We therefore decline to hold as a blanket matter that comity requires resort to Hague Evidence Convention procedures without prior scrutiny in each case of the particular facts, sovereign interests, and likelihood that resort to those procedures will prove effective.[29]

Some discovery procedures are much more "intrusive" than others. In this case, for example, an interrogatory asking petitioners to identify the pilots who flew flight tests in the Rallye before it was certified for flight by the Federal Aviation Administration, or a request to admit that petitioners authorized certain advertising in a particular magazine, is certainly less intrusive than a request to produce all of the "design specifications, line drawings and engineering plans and all engineering change orders and plans and all drawings concerning the leading edge slats for the Rallye type aircraft manufactured by the Defendants." Even if a court might be persuaded that a particular document request was too burdensome or too "intrusive" to be granted in full, with or without an appropriate protective order, it might well refuse to insist upon the use of Convention procedures before requiring responses to simple interrogatories or requests for admissions. The exact line between reasonableness and unreasonableness in each case must be drawn by the trial court, based on its knowledge of the case and of the claims and interests of the parties and the governments whose statutes and policies they invoke.

---

[27] Comity refers to the spirit of cooperation in which a domestic tribunal approaches the resolution of cases touching the laws and interests of sovereign states....

[29] The French "blocking statute"... does not alter our conclusion. It is well settled that such statutes do not deprive an American court of the power to order a party subject to its jurisdiction to produce evidence even though the act of production may violate that statute. *See Societe Internationale Pour Participations Industrielles et Commerciales, S.A. v. Rogers*, 357 U.S. 197, 204–06 (1958). Nor can the enactment of such a statute by a foreign nation require American courts to engraft a rule of first resort onto the Hague Convention, or otherwise to provide the nationals of such a country with a preferred status in our courts. It is clear that American courts are not required to adhere blindly to the directives of such a statute. Indeed, the language of the statute, if taken literally, would appear to represent an extraordinary exercise of legislative jurisdiction by the Republic of France over a United States district judge, forbidding him or her to order any discovery from a party of French nationality, even simple requests for admissions or interrogatories that the party could respond to on the basis of personal knowledge. It would be particularly incongruous to recognize such a preference for corporations that are wholly owned by the enacting nation. Extraterritorial assertions of jurisdiction are not one-sided. While the District Court's discovery orders arguably have some impact in France, the French blocking statute asserts similar authority over acts to take place in this country. The lesson of comity is that neither the discovery order nor the blocking statute can have the same omnipresent effect that it would have in a world of only one sovereign. The blocking statute thus is relevant to the court's particularized comity analysis only to the extent that its terms and its enforcement identify the nature of the sovereign interests in nondisclosure of specific kinds of material....

American courts, in supervising pretrial proceedings, should exercise special vigilance to protect foreign litigants from the danger that unnecessary, or unduly burdensome, discovery may place them in a disadvantageous position. Judicial supervision of discovery should always seek to minimize its costs and inconvenience and to prevent improper uses of discovery requests. When it is necessary to seek evidence abroad, however, the district court must supervise pretrial proceedings particularly closely to prevent discovery abuses. For example, the additional cost of transportation of documents or witnesses to or from foreign locations may increase the danger that discovery may be sought for the improper purpose of motivating settlement, rather than finding relevant and probative evidence. Objections to "abusive" discovery that foreign litigants advance should therefore receive the most careful consideration. In addition, we have long recognized the demands of comity in suits involving foreign states, either as parties or as sovereigns with a coordinate interest in the litigation. American courts should therefore take care to demonstrate due respect for any special problem confronted by the foreign litigant on account of its nationality or the location of its operations, and for any sovereign interest expressed by a foreign state. We do not articulate specific rules to guide this delicate task of adjudication.

Comments and Questions

1. The French government submitted an amicus brief, seeking to assure the Court that, notwithstanding the Republic's declaration pursuant to Article 23, the Convention procedures provided American litigants with a "fair and reasonable opportunity" to gather evidence in France. France had submitted its declaration under Article 23 in order to prohibit "legal tourism," that is, "unfocused demands for documents by foreign lawyers acting without court supervision," but not to prohibit production of enumerated documents that have "a direct and clear nexus with the subject matter of the litigation." On January 19, 1987, five days after Aérospatiale was argued and five months before the decision came down, France formally filed an amended declaration confirming that its Article 23 declaration "does not apply when the requested documents are enumerated limitatively in the Letter of Request and have a direct and precise link with the object of the procedure." Germany and Switzerland also filed amicus briefs. All three countries supported the mandatory applicability of the Hague Convention.

2. After Aérospatiale, district courts must balance the need for discovery against the policies reflected in a treaty. There have been some cases where the plaintiff was forced to use Hague Convention procedures. See, e.g., Hudson v. Hermann Pfauter GmbH, 117 F.R.D. 33 (N.D.N.Y. 1987). But in the vast majority of cases recourse to the Hague Convention is held not to be mandatory. See, e.g., Haynes v. Kleinewefers GmbH, 119 F.R.D. 335 (E.D.N.Y. 1988). Justice Blackmun's dissent noted that "it is the Executive that normally decides when a course of action is important enough to risk affronting a foreign nation or placing a strain on foreign commerce. It is the Executive, as well, that is best equipped to determine how to accommodate foreign

interests along with our own." Is the question of foreign discovery more appropriately considered by the Executive and by Congress? But isn't the reasonableness of a particular discovery request more appropriately considered by a judge? How should these competing concerns be reconciled?

4. Does the enactment of a "blocking statute" disrespect the laws and institutions of other nations? Is it too blunt an instrument?

5. On remand in Aérospatiale, the French manufacturer agreed to provide the requested information so the "delicate task" requiring "special vigilance" was not undertaken in this case. But since then, U.S. courts have adopted a balancing test to implement Justice Stevens's test. That test is reflected in the Restatement, which follows.

Restatement (Third) of Foreign Relations Law of the United States (1987)

§ 442. Requests For Disclosure; Law Of The United States

(1) (a) A court or agency in the United States, when authorized by statute or rule of court, may order a person subject to its jurisdiction to produce documents, objects, or other information relevant to an action or investigation, even if the information or the person in possession of the information is outside the United States.

(b) Failure to comply with an order to produce information may subject the person to whom the order is directed to sanctions, including finding of contempt, dismissal of a claim or defense, or default judgment, or may lead to a determination that the facts to which the order was addressed are as asserted by the opposing party.

(c) In deciding whether to issue an order directing production of information located abroad, and in framing such an order, a court or agency in the United States should take into account the importance to the investigation or litigation of the documents or other information requested; the degree of specificity of the request; whether the information originated in the United States; the availability of alternative means of securing the information; and the extent to which noncompliance with the request would undermine important interests of the United States, or compliance with the request would undermine important interests of the state where the information is located.

(2) If disclosure of information located outside the United States is prohibited by a law, regulation, or order of a court or other authority of the state in which the information or prospective witness is located, or of the state of which a prospective witness is a national,

(a) a court or agency in the United States may require the person to whom the order is directed to make a good faith effort to secure permission from the foreign authorities to make the information available;

(b) a court or agency should not ordinarily impose sanctions of contempt, dismissal, or default on a party that has failed to comply with the order for production, except in cases of deliberate concealment or removal of information or of failure to make a good faith effort in accordance with paragraph (a);

(c) a court or agency may, in appropriate cases, make findings of fact adverse to a party that has failed to comply with the order for production, even if that party has made a good faith effort to secure permission from the foreign authorities to make the information available and that effort has been unsuccessful.

Comments and Questions

1. The Restatement in this and other areas reflect experts' judgments about the trends in case law. Restatements are published by the American Law Institute (ALI), which has an elected membership that includes judges, practitioners, and academics. Although some Restatements have been very influential in the United States (by recognizing trends in case law and by reshaping them), the publications are not binding on any jurisdiction. Although the ALI has made efforts to broaden its membership to include more international perspectives (and to undertake more international projects), it remains the American Law Institute.

2. When engaged in the evaluation of factors contemplated in paragraph 1(c), which factor deserves the most weight, and which the least weight?

3. Which party has the burden of proving "good faith" in paragraph (2)?

4. The following case does not involve the Hague Convention; indeed, the People's Republic of China was not then a party. However, the case illustrates well the difficult task of determining whether to require disclosure notwithstanding contrary foreign compulsion. As you read this case, consider whether the standard is (or should be) predictable and certain or discretionary and flexible.

Richmark Corp. v. Timber Falling Consultants

959 F.2d 1468 (9th Cir. 1992)

D.W. Nelson, Circuit Judge

This case presents a number of difficult questions regarding a sensitive area of law and foreign relations. Timber Falling Consultants, Inc. (TFC) won a default judgment for fraud and breach of contract against Beijing Ever Bright Industrial Co. (Beijing), a corporation organized under the laws of the People's Republic of China (PRC) and an arm of the PRC government. As part of an effort to execute that judgment, TFC sought discovery of Beijing's assets worldwide. Beijing resisted those discovery efforts, and refused to comply when ordered to do so by the district court. The district court imposed discovery sanctions, held Beijing in contempt, and ordered contempt fines of $10,000 a day. Beijing contends that PRC secrecy laws prevent it from complying with the discovery order and that it would be subject to prosecution in the PRC were it to comply....

Factual and Procedural Background

Beijing contracted to purchase lumber from Richmark Corp. Richmark in turn retained TFC to procure the timber. After the contract fell through, Richmark sued TFC. TFC counterclaimed against Richmark and cross-claimed against all other parties involved, including Beijing, alleging fraud and breach of contract. Beijing failed to appear, apparently because of the interruption in United States-PRC relations which followed the Tienanmen Square incident. All other claims on both sides were dismissed by the district court, but TFC was awarded a $2.2 million default judgment against Beijing. This judgment was entered on June 5, 1990.

Beijing appealed this judgment to the Ninth Circuit. Beijing did not post a supersedeas bond or letter of credit, however, so TFC was free to begin efforts to collect the judgment while the appeal was pending. In an attempt to do so, TFC served Beijing with a number of discovery requests and interrogatories which sought to identify Beijing's assets worldwide. Beijing did not respond to those requests, and instead moved for a stay of discovery pending resolution of its Rule 60(b) motion for relief from the judgment. TFC in turn filed a motion to compel discovery.

On October 15, 1990, the district court denied Beijing's Rule 60(b) motion, mooting Beijing's request for a stay, and granted TFC's motion to compel discovery. Richmark Corp. v. Timber Falling Consultants, 747 F. Supp. 1409 (D. Or. 1990). Beijing then appealed the denial of its Rule 60(b) motion, and on November 27, 1990, petitioned the district court for a stay of discovery pending appeal. The district court denied this motion on January 11, 1991. Beijing promptly petitioned the Ninth Circuit for a stay of discovery. Its petition was denied on February 19, 1991.

On January 28, 1991, Beijing for the first time requested advice from its government on how to respond to TFC's discovery requests. Specifically, Beijing sought guidance as to whether PRC "State Secrecy Laws" prohibited it from disclosing the requested information concerning its assets. This request was passed by the State Secrecy Bureau to another arm of the State Council, the Ever Bright Group, which was in charge of overseeing Beijing's operations. On April 16, 1991, the Ever Bright Group sent written notification to Beijing that almost all of its financial information was classified a state secret and could not be disclosed.

Meanwhile, following the denial of the stay petition by the Ninth Circuit, TFC moved for contempt and discovery sanctions against Beijing. In its answer, Beijing for the first time raised the issue of the State Secrecy Laws. The district court denied the request for sanctions on March 4, but it rejected Beijing's contention that PRC law prevented it from complying as "untimely and without merit," and again ordered Beijing to respond to TFC's discovery requests. On March 5, Beijing moved the district court for a protective order against discovery, on the same grounds. The district court denied this motion on March 14.

Beijing still refused to comply with the discovery orders. On April 4, 1991, the district court held Beijing in contempt of its October 15 and March 4 orders. It awarded TFC its attorney's fees and costs incurred in seeking discovery as a discovery sanction, and imposed contempt fines of $10,000 a day, payable to TFC, until Beijing complied with the discovery orders. However, the district court indicated that it would vacate the contempt order if Beijing complied with the discovery orders within 60 days.

On May 15, 1991, Beijing provided the limited amount of information the Ever Bright Group allowed it to disclose,[4] and moved the district court to vacate the contempt sanctions. On July 24, 1991, the district court denied the motion to vacate. Beijing appeals on a variety of grounds from the March 4 discovery order, the April 4 contempt order, and the July 24 denial of its motion to vacate.

I. Propriety of Discovery Orders and Sanctions

A. Timeliness of Objection

TFC served its discovery requests and interrogatories on Beijing in July 1990. Beijing did not object to those requests on the grounds that PRC law did or might interfere with its ability to comply. When TFC filed a motion to compel a response, Beijing's answer did not raise the potential problem of PRC secrecy law. Nor did Beijing raise the issue in its motion for stay of discovery before the district court, or before the Ninth Circuit. Beijing first raised this issue in February 1991 in its reply to TFC's motion for contempt sanctions.

Because of this delay, TFC contends that Beijing has waived any objection based on the secrecy laws. Fed. R. Civ. P. 33 and 34 provide that discovery requests must be responded to within 30 (or in some cases 45) days. It is well established that a failure to object to discovery requests within the time required constitutes a waiver of any objection. Beijing clearly did not object within the time required by the Federal Rules.

Beijing contends that it raised the issue as soon as possible, and cites a declaration from its counsel in the PRC that the State Secrecy Bureau normally will not advise companies about the impact of the secrecy laws until every legal effort has been made to avoid discovery of the information. This argument might justify Beijing's delay in requesting guidance from the Ministry of Justice, although the

[4] Specifically, Beijing disclosed the nature of its business, the names and addresses of its offices, and the value and location of its furniture, equipment, and machinery. It refused to disclose the value and location of its cash, real property, bank accounts, stock and bond holdings, other financial portfolios, notes, inventories, accounts receivable, or any other information concerning its assets.

validity of this argument is open to question, given that Beijing actually requested such guidance before the resolution of its stay petition in the Ninth Circuit. But in any event, the argument cannot justify Beijing's failure to raise the issue before the district court as an objection to TFC's discovery request, or at the very least in response to the motion to compel. Its objections to the discovery orders and the contempt adjudication based on the PRC secrecy laws were therefore waived.

Although Beijing did not invoke the State Secrecy laws in a timely fashion in opposition to the discovery and contempt orders, we cannot resolve this case without reaching the merits. In its April 4 order, the district court indicated that it would be willing to vacate the contempt order if Beijing complied with the discovery order within 60 days. On May 15, Beijing produced some information and produced a document from the Ever Bright Group, an arm of the PRC, indicating that PRC law barred it from disclosing the remainder of the requested information. While the issue of the validity of the discovery orders was waived by Beijing, the issue of whether it complied with those orders arose only on May 15, 1991. In order to decide whether Beijing's compliance was adequate, we must consider the effect of the PRC secrecy statutes.

B. Deference to PRC Law

Beijing contends that the state secrecy laws prohibit it from disclosing the information the district court ordered it to provide, that it would be subject to criminal prosecution if it did disclose such information, and that this prohibition necessitates the reversal of the discovery order and the contempt sanctions against it. The district court explicitly accepted Beijing's contention that the PRC's State Secrets Act barred disclosure of the information in question. We do so as well.

That does not end the inquiry, however. The PRC's admitted interest in secrecy must be balanced against the interests of the United States and the plaintiffs in obtaining the information. In Societe Internationale Pour Participations Industrielles et Commerciales v. Rogers, 357 U.S. 197 (1958) (Societe Internationale), the Supreme Court confronted a similar issue. In that case, the petitioner, a Swiss company, objected to discovery requests on the grounds that producing Swiss bank records would violate Swiss law. The Swiss Federal Attorney had issued an order prohibiting their disclosure. The district court expressly concluded that the Swiss company acted in good faith in seeking to comply, and the company did disclose over 190,000 documents during discovery. The Supreme Court held that the company had failed to comply with the order, id. at 208, but concluded that the sanction of dismissal of its complaint was inappropriate. It reached this conclusion because "petitioner's failure to satisfy fully the requirements of this production order was due to inability fostered neither by its own conduct nor by circumstances within its control. It is hardly debatable that fear of criminal prosecution constitutes a weighty excuse for nonproduction.... " Id. at 211.

Cases since Societe Internationale, however, have emphasized that a foreign-law prohibition will not always excuse compliance with a discovery order. In Societe Nationale Industrielle Aerospatiale v. United States District Court, 482 U.S. 522,

544 n. 29 (1987) (Aerospatiale), the Supreme Court stated that "[i]t is well settled that such [foreign "blocking"] statutes do not deprive an American court of the power to order a party subject to its jurisdiction to produce evidence even though the act of production may violate that statute."...Instead, Aerospatiale endorsed the balancing test contained in the Restatement (Third) of Foreign Relations Law § 442(1)(c). Under that test, factors that are relevant in deciding whether or not foreign statutes excuse noncompliance with discovery orders include:

> the importance to the investigation or litigation of the documents or other information requested; the degree of specificity of the request; whether the information originated in the United States; the availability of alternative means of securing the information; and the extent to which noncompliance with the request would undermine important interests of the United States, or compliance with the request would undermine important interests of the state where the information is located.
>
> Id.; Aerospatiale, 482 U.S. at 544 n. 28.

As the Court noted, this list of factors is not exhaustive. Other factors that we have considered relevant are "'the extent and the nature of the hardship that inconsistent enforcement would impose upon the person,... [and] the extent to which enforcement by action of either state can reasonably be expected to achieve compliance with the rule prescribed by that state.'" United States v. Vetco, Inc., 691 F.2d 1281, 1288 (9th Cir.) (quoting the Restatement (Second) of Foreign Relations Law § 40), cert. denied, 454 U.S. 1098. We consider each factor in turn.

Importance of the Documents. Where the outcome of litigation "does not stand or fall on the present discovery order," or where the evidence sought is cumulative of existing evidence, courts have generally been unwilling to override foreign secrecy laws. See In re Westinghouse Elec. Corp. Uranium Contracts Litigation, 563 F.2d 992, 999 (10th Cir. 1977). Where the evidence is directly relevant, however, we have found this factor to weigh in favor of disclosure. Vetco, 691 F.2d at 1290. In this case, the information sought is not only relevant to the execution of the judgment, it is crucial. Without information as to Beijing's assets, TFC cannot hope to enforce the judgment. The execution proceedings, and in some sense the underlying judgment itself, will be rendered meaningless. The importance of the documents to the litigation weighs in favor of compelling disclosure.

Specificity of the Request. A second consideration in evaluating a discovery request is how burdensome it will be to respond to that request. Generalized searches for information, the disclosure of which is prohibited under foreign law, are discouraged. In this case, Beijing has not objected to the burdensome nature of the discovery request, apart from the fact of its illegality. While TFC sought a great deal of information, all of it was directed at identifying Beijing's current assets in order to execute the judgment. Further, TFC's request was reasonably limited in time: it sought only recent financial documents. Beijing has not made this factor an issue, and it does not favor nondisclosure here.

Location of Information and Parties. The fact that all the information to be disclosed (and the people who will be deposed or who will produce the documents) are located in a foreign country weighs against disclosure, since those people and documents are subject to the law of that country in the ordinary course of business. Reinsurance Co. of America v. Administratia Asigurarilor de Stat, 902 F.2d 1275, 1281 (7th Cir. 1990); Westinghouse, 563 F.2d at 998. In this case, Beijing has no United States office. All of its employees, and all of the documents TFC has requested, are located in the PRC. This factor weighs against requiring disclosure.

Alternate Means of Obtaining Information. If the information sought can easily be obtained elsewhere, there is little or no reason to require a party to violate foreign law. Cf. In re Sealed Case, 825 F.2d 494, 499 (D.C.Cir.) (reversing contempt sanction, noting that it is "relevant to our conclusion that the grand jury is not left empty-handed by today's decision"), cert. denied, 484 U.S. 963 (1987). In this circuit, the alternative means must be "substantially equivalent" to the requested discovery. Vetco, 691 F.2d at 1290; see SEC v. Minas de Artemisa, 150 F.2d 215, 219 (9th Cir. 1945). Beijing has not suggested any such alternatives, as did the appellants in Vetco.

One possible alternative would be to seek information from Beijing's nominal parent corporation, China Ever Bright Holdings Co., which is incorporated in Hong Kong. However, as Beijing itself takes pains to note, China Ever Bright is a separate entity from Beijing, and financial information about China Ever Bright is not relevant to Beijing's financial position. A second alternative would be to subpoena information from sources in the United States who have dealt with Beijing and might have financial information. TFC in fact has attempted to do this, issuing subpoenas to the Bank of China, Mesta Engineering Corp., Shougang Mechanical Equipment of Pennsylvania, and Solid Beam Industrial Co. TFC was not successful in obtaining information from these sources. Indeed, it failed in part because Beijing and its affiliates actively opposed those subpoenas. Further, Beijing concedes that any information received from these sources would not include the core financial information requested by TFC. Finally, TFC has requested depositions of various Beijing officials, which obviously cannot be provided by anyone other than Beijing.

TFC appears to have done everything in its power to collect information which will enable it to enforce the judgment. To date, it has been unsuccessful. The absence of other sources for the information TFC seeks is a factor which weighs strongly in favor of compelling disclosure.

Balance of National Interests. This is the most important factor. We must assess the interests of each nation in requiring or prohibiting disclosure, and determine whether disclosure would "affect important substantive policies or interests" of either the United States or the PRC. Restatement (Third) of Foreign Relations Law § 442 comment c.10 In assessing the strength of the PRC's interests, we will consider "expressions of interest by the foreign state," "the significance of disclosure in the regulation... of the activity in question," and "indications of the foreign state's concern for confidentiality prior to the controversy." Id. (emphasis added).

In this case, the PRC's State Secrecy Bureau has directly expressed an interest in the outcome of this case. In its response to Beijing's request for guidance, the

Bureau wrote: "[T]his Bureau hereby orders your Company not to disclose or provide the information and documents requested by the United States District Court for the District of Oregon except Items 1, 2, 3(f), 9 and 10. Your Company shall bear any or all legal consequences should you not comply with this order."

However, the State Secrecy Bureau did not express interest in the confidentiality of this information prior to the litigation in question.[10] Indeed, Beijing routinely disclosed information regarding its assets, inventory, bank accounts, and corporate structure to the general public, for example through a trade brochure, and to companies with whom it did business, see Richmark, 937 F.2d at 1447; Timber Falling, No. 90 Civ. 6838 (KTD) (S.D.N.Y. July 19, 1991). The State Secrecy Bureau did not object to the voluntary disclosure of any of this information. It is only now, when disclosure will have adverse consequences for Beijing, that the PRC has asserted its interest in confidentiality.

Further, neither Beijing nor the PRC has identified any way in which disclosure of the information requested here will significantly affect the PRC's interests in confidentiality. Those interests, as set forth by the State Secrecy Laws themselves, are in "matters involving national security and interest." Collection of the Laws of the People's Republic of China 1363 Art. 2 (1989). This is defined to include information which "concern[s] the national economy and social development" or disclosure of which may "diminish the country's economic, technological and scientific strength." Id. at Art. 8, Art. 4(7). There is no indication that Beijing, much less the economy of the PRC as a whole, will be adversely affected at all by disclosure of this information. The only likely "adverse" effect on the PRC economy will be that TFC may be able to collect its judgment, something the PRC has no legitimate state interest in preventing.

The PRC, then, has asserted an interest (albeit one whose strength is unknown) in the confidentiality of the information in question. This interest must be weighed against the United States' interests in vindicating the rights of American plaintiffs and in enforcing the judgments of its courts. The former interest has been described as "substantial," see In re Insurance Antitrust Litigation, 938 F.2d 919, 933 (9th Cir. 1991), petitions for cert. filed Jan. 9 and 13, 1992, and the latter as "vital," Reinsurance, 902 F.2d at 1280. To be sure, these interests are not so strong that they would compel disclosure in all cases. See id. at 1281 (Romanian interest in secrecy outweighs United States' interest in enforcing private judgments). In this case, however, because Beijing and the PRC have been unable to identify any way in which the PRC's interests will be hurt by disclosure, the interests of the United States must prevail. The balancing of national interests is therefore a factor which weighs in favor of disclosure.

---

[10] Initially, Beijing contends that the court is not empowered to look beyond the Chinese government's assertion of its interest in preventing disclosure to determine the strength of that interest. Beijing is in error. As we have recognized, in balancing sovereign interests the court is "necessarily interested in the depth and nature of [the foreign sovereign's] interest." *Timberlane Lumber Co. v. Bank of America*, 549 F.2d 597, 607 (9th Cir. 1976). Indeed, Beijing itself appears to concede in its brief that the court must balance the competing national interests at stake.

Hardship to Beijing. The effect that a discovery order is likely to have on the foreign company is another factor to be considered. If Beijing is likely to face criminal prosecution in the PRC for complying with the United States court order, that fact constitutes a "weighty excuse" for nonproduction. Societe Internationale, 357 U.S. at 211. In this case, Beijing has in fact been ordered by the Chinese government to withhold the information, and has been told that it will bear the "legal consequences" of disclosing the information.[11] Beijing therefore seems to be placed in a difficult position, between the Scylla of contempt sanctions and the Charybdis of possible criminal prosecution.

However, if the hardship is self-imposed, or if Beijing could have avoided it, the fact that it finds itself in an undesirable position will not work against disclosure of the requested information. See Vetco, 691 F.2d at 1289–90 (hardship not a factor because it was "avoidable"). In this case, the discovery dispute arose only because Beijing refused to post a supersedeas bond or letter of credit to stay execution of the judgment pending appeal, as required by Fed. R. Civ. P. 62(d). See United States v. $2,490.00 in United States Currency, 825 F.2d 1419, 1421 (9th Cir. 1987). Beijing even now could post a supersedeas bond pending the outcome of its petition for certiorari, or it could pay the judgment. Either of these courses of action would keep it from having to violate either the district court's orders or the PRC's laws.

Beijing objects that requiring either course of action would violate its "immunity" from execution under the Foreign Sovereign Immunities Act, 28 U.S.C. § 1610(b). Beijing misreads that provision. Section 1610 provides for the execution of judgments against foreign sovereigns. It is true that section 1610 does not empower United States courts to levy on assets located outside the United States. That provision merely limits the power of United States courts, however; it does not vest in Beijing a "right" not to pay a valid judgment against it. See Frolova v. Union of Soviet Socialist Republics, 558 F. Supp. 358, 361 (N.D. Ill. 1983) (purpose of section 1610 is to provide a remedy against foreign states who fail to pay judgments against them), aff'd, 761 F.2d 370 (7th Cir. 1985). TFC can seek to execute the judgment in whatever foreign courts have jurisdiction over Beijing's assets, see Nippon Emo-Trans Co. v. Emo-Trans, Inc., 744 F. Supp. 1215, 1218 (E.D.N.Y. 1990), but TFC needs discovery in order to determine which courts those are. Beijing may be able as a practical matter to conceal its assets from the district court and therefore avoid execution of TFC's judgment, but it has no right to do so, and it certainly has no right to avail itself of the United States judicial system for purposes of appeal while at the same time seeking to evade the judgments of that judicial system.

Because Beijing could—and still can—avoid the hardship disclosure would place on it, that hardship is not a factor weighing against disclosure.

Likelihood of Compliance. If a discovery order is likely to be unenforceable, and therefore to have no practical effect, that factor counsels against requiring compliance with the order. In this case, it may be impossible to force Beijing to comply. The imposition of sanctions in the amount of $10,000 a day, sanctions

---

[11] Beijing has not, however, provided any indication of what those consequences are likely to be.

which have already grown larger than the underlying judgment, has failed to move Beijing. It is perhaps unrealistic to expect that a PRC court will enforce an order requiring Beijing to violate PRC law. Compliance therefore seems unlikely, a factor counseling against compelling discovery.

Nonetheless, the discovery and contempt orders may be of some significance. While Beijing apparently has no assets in the United States, it has in the past done substantial business in this country. Should it wish to do business here in the future, it would have to pay the judgment or risk having its assets seized and its business interrupted. In addition, a clear statement that foreign corporations which avail themselves of business opportunities in the United States must abide by United States laws might have a substantial effect on the way Beijing and other corporations do business in the United States in the future. Our recent decision in Insurance Antitrust is instructive. In that case, the court concluded that an injunction against Lloyd's of London would not be enforced by the British courts. It nonetheless upheld the injunction because it could be enforced within the United States, and because it would send a message to companies who wished to do business in the United States in the future. 938 F.2d at 933.

In short, full compliance by Beijing with the order of the district court is unlikely. The order may nonetheless produce partial compliance, and might be effective in other ways as well. While the likelihood of noncompliance does weigh against compelling disclosure, we think the weight of this factor is lessened by these mitigating circumstances.

Conclusion. Taking all of the aforementioned factors into consideration, the balance tips significantly (although not overwhelmingly) in TFC's favor. The United States has a strong interest in enforcing its judgments which outweighs the PRC's interest in confidentiality in this case. The information sought is vital to the litigation and cannot be obtained elsewhere. Finally, Beijing can avoid any hardship it may face by following normal litigation procedure and posting a supersedeas bond. If it does so, both the district court and TFC have indicated a willingness to forego contempt sanctions. The only factors weighing against compelling disclosure are that Beijing has the information in the PRC and may choose not to disclose it in spite of the court's order. Were these factors alone sufficient, a foreign corporation could avoid its discovery obligations in almost every instance. We therefore conclude that the order compelling discovery should be upheld in spite of the PRC secrecy statute.

In reaching this conclusion, we are not unmindful of the difficulties foreign corporations face in doing business in the United States, nor of the rather delicate nature of relations between sovereign states. We sincerely hope that today's decision will not adversely affect the cordial business relationship between the United States and the PRC. However, international business requires the accommodation of different legal climates. Just as United States companies doing business in the PRC must expect to abide by PRC law, when Beijing availed itself of business opportunities in this country, it undertook an obligation to comply with the lawful orders of United States courts. We do not minimize the difficult situation in which Beijing has been placed. Here, however, where the PRC has not demonstrated a strong interest in keeping the requested information confidential, and where Beijing has options open to it which violate neither United States nor PRC law, Beijing cannot escape compliance with the district court's discovery orders.

C. Good Faith Compliance

Beijing next contends that, even if the discovery order was valid, the contempt sanction should be vacated because Beijing has attempted in good faith to comply with the court's orders. It is true that contempt is inappropriate where a party has taken "all the reasonable steps" it can take to comply. Balla v. Idaho State Bd. of Corrections, 869 F.2d 461, 466 (9th Cir. 1989). The Restatement (Third) of Foreign Relations Law § 442(2)(b) provides that "a court or agency should not ordinarily impose sanctions of contempt... on a party that has failed to comply with the order for production, except in cases of deliberate concealment or removal of information or of failure to make a good faith effort" to secure permission from the foreign government to disclose the information.

In Vetco, we required a foreign corporation asserting a blocking statute as a defense to make an affirmative showing of its good faith in seeking permission to disclose the information. 691 F.2d at 1287 ("This case is not controlled by Societe Internationale. We have no finding that appellants have made good faith efforts to comply with the summonses. Compare Societe Internationale, 357 U.S. at 201 (explicit finding by Special Master of good faith confirmed by district court)."); see also Restatement (Third) of Foreign Relations Law § 442 comment h ("Parties to litigation... may be required to show that they have made serious efforts before appropriate authorities of states with blocking statutes to secure release or waiver from a prohibition against disclosure.") (emphasis added).

Beijing has made no such affirmative showing here. The district court did not find that Beijing acted in good faith in attempting to obtain a waiver. Nor is good faith evident from the record. Beijing fought disclosure for several months before raising the foreign law problem, even after the district court issued an order on October 15, 1990 compelling disclosure. Beijing's effort to seek a waiver consisted of a letter to the Ministry of Justice on January 28, 1991, in which it noted the "broad scope" of the discovery order, pointed out to the Ministry the legal provision it felt barred disclosure, and asked whether it was permitted to disclose the information under the State Secrets Act. While Beijing did ask whether there was "a procedure through which Beijing Ever Bright may seek the permission of the government to disclose the information it is not presently permitted to disclose," it did not in fact seek such permission, but rather requested only "guidance" on the legal question. In spite of this, Beijing asserted that the State Secrets Act prevented it from complying in February 1991, two months before the Ministry even responded to this request. Beijing does not appear to have made a good faith effort to clarify PRC law or to seek a waiver of the secrecy statutes before refusing to comply with the district court order. For these reasons, the district court acted within its discretion in sanctioning Beijing for its noncompliance....

Comments and Questions

1. Would it also have been within the district court's discretion to decline to enforce TFC's discovery efforts? Would it have been within the district court's discretion to require the disclosure but to reject any sanction for noncompliance?

2. What specific evidence should Beijing have introduced to demonstrate its good faith in attempting to obtain a waiver?

3. Why is the balance of national interests "the most important factor"? Is a federal judge well suited for this task?

4. The People's Republic of China has since become a member of the Hague Evidence Convention. How would this affect the decision if this same conflict were to arise today?

5. The taking of evidence in transnational litigation within Europe has been the subject of recent legislation. In 2004, Council Regulation 1206/2001 of 28 May 2001 on Cooperation between the Courts of the Member States in the Taking of Evidence in Civil and Commercial Matters took effect. The Regulation relies heavily on the basic structure and mechanics of the Hague Evidence Convention but also expands on that Convention in two important respects. First, the Regulation reaches that handful of EC countries that are not (also) members of the Hague Convention. Second, the Regulation tries to improve upon some of the perceived deficiencies of the Hague Convention with decentralized mechanisms of transmission (rather than relying on courts) and more rigid time limits. The Regulation places less emphasis on the sovereignty concerns that animate the Hague Convention and more emphasis on the facilitation of effective and fair transnational litigation.

2. Harmonization

With the decision in Aérospatiale diluting the significance of the Hague Convention on the Taking of Evidence Abroad in the United States, the search for international common ground resumed. The ALI/UNIDROIT Transnational Rules are a proposed set of model discovery rules that reflect a compromise: they are based on a generalized version of a common law system outside the United States. If adopted, they would apply to transnational commercial disputes.

ALI/UNIDROIT, Principles of Transnational Civil Procedure

Cambridge University Press (2006)

21. Disclosure

21.1 In accordance with the court's scheduling order, a party must identify to the court and other parties the evidence on which the party intends to rely, in addition to that provided in the pleading, including:

- 21.1.1. Copies of documents or other records, such as contracts and correspondence; and
- 21.1.2 Summaries of expected testimony of witnesses, including parties, witnesses, and experts, then known to the party. Witnesses must be identified, so far as practicable, by name, address, and telephone number.
- 21.1.3 In lieu of a summary of expected testimony, a party may present a written statement of testimony.

21.2 A party must amend the specification required in Rule 21.1 to include documents or witnesses not known when the list was originally prepared....

21.3 To facilitate compliance with this Rule, a lawyer for a party may have a voluntary interview with a potential nonparty witness. The interview may be on reasonable notice to other parties, who may be permitted to attend the interview.

Comment [to Rule 21]

R-21B. Under the concept of professional ethics in some civil-law systems, a lawyer should not discuss the matters in dispute with prospective witnesses (other than the lawyer's own client). That norm is designed to protect testimony from improper manipulation, but it also has the effect of limiting the effectiveness of a lawyer in investigating and organizing evidence for consideration by the court. In discussion with a prospective witness, the lawyer should not suggest what the testimony should be nor offer improper inducement. Although there is some risk of abuse in allowing lawyers to confer with prospective witnesses, that risk is less injurious to fair adjudication than is the risk that relevant and important evidence may remain undisclosed.

22. Exchange of Evidence

22.1 A party who has complied with disclosure duties prescribed in Rule 21, on notice to the other parties, may request the court to order production by any person of any evidentiary matter, not protected by confidentiality or privilege, that is relevant to the case and that may be admissible, including:

- 22.1.1 Documents and other records of information that are specifically identified or identified within specifically defined categories;
- 22.1.2 Identifying information, such as name and address, about specified persons having knowledge of a matter in issue; and
- 22.1.3 A copy of the report of any expert that another party intends to present.

22.2 The court must determine the request and order production accordingly. The court may order production of other evidence as necessary in the interest of justice. Such evidence must be produced within a reasonable time prior to the final hearing....

22.4. The requesting party may present the request directly to the opposing party. That party may acquiesce in the request, in whole or in part, and provide the evidence accordingly. If the party refuses in whole or in part, the requesting party, on notice to the opposing party, may request the court to order production of specified evidence....

22.6 The fact that the demanded information is adverse to the interest of the party to which the demand is directed is not a valid objection to its production....

Comments [to Rule 22]

R-22A. These Rules adopt, as a model of litigation, a system consisting of preliminary hearings followed by a concentrated form of final hearing. The essential core of the first stage is preliminary disclosure and clarification of the evidence. The principal consideration in favor of a unitary final hearing is that of expeditious justice. To achieve this objective, a concentrated final hearing should be used, so that arguments and the taking of evidence are completed in a single hearing or in a few hearings on consecutive judicial days. A concentrated final hearing requires a preliminary phase (called pretrial in common-law systems) in which evidence is exchanged and the case is prepared for concentrated presentation.

R-22B. Rules 21 and 22 define the roles and the rights of the parties, the duty of voluntary disclosure, the procedure for exchange of evidence, the role of the court, and the devices to ensure that the parties comply with demands for evidence. Proper compliance with these obligations is not only a matter of law for the parties, but also a matter of professional honor and obligation on the part of the lawyers involved in the litigation.

R-22C. The philosophy expressed in Rules 21 and 22 is essentially that of the common-law countries other than the United States. In those countries, the scope of discovery or disclosure is specified and limited, as in Rules 21 and 22. However, within those specifications disclosure is generally a matter of right....

R-22G. Rule 22.1 provides that every party is entitled to obtain from any person the disclosure of any unprivileged relevant evidence in possession of that person. Formal requests for evidence should be made to the court, and the court should direct the opposing party to comply with an order to produce evidence or information. This procedure can be unnecessarily burdensome on the parties and on the courts, especially in straightforward requests. Ideally, full disclosure of relevant evidence should result through dialogue among the parties, whereby the parties voluntarily satisfy each other's demands without intervention of the court. A party therefore may present the request directly to the opposing party, which must comply with an adequate request within a reasonable time....

R-22H. According to Rule 22.1, compulsory exchange of evidence is limited to matters directly relevant to the issues in the case as they have been stated in the pleadings. See rule 25.2. A party is not entitled to disclosure of information merely that "appears reasonably calculated to lead to the discovery of admissible evidence," which is permitted under Rule 26 of the Fed. R. Civ. P. in the United

States. "Relevant" evidence is that which supports or contravenes the allegations of one of the parties. This Rule is aimed at preventing overdiscovery or unjustified "fishing expeditions."...

R-22M. If a party fails to comply with a demand for exchange of evidence, the court may impose sanctions to make disclosure effective. The determination of sanctions is within the discretion of the court, taking into account relevant features of the parties' behavior.... The sanctions are: (1) Adverse inferences against the noncomplying party including conclusive determination of the facts; (2) A monetary penalty, fixed by the court in its discretion, or other means of legal compulsion permitted by forum law, including contempt of court....; (3) The most severe sanction against noncompliance with disclosure demands or orders is entry of adverse judgment with respect to one or more of the claims. The court may enter a judgment of dismissal with prejudice against the plaintiff or a judgment by default against the defendant, or dismiss claims, defenses, or allegations to which the evidence is relevant....

23. Deposition and Testimony by Affidavit

23.1 A deposition of a party or other person may be taken by order of the court. Unless the court orders otherwise, a deposition may be presented as evidence in the record....

23.4 With written permission of the court, a party may present a written statement of sworn testimony of any person, containing statements in their own words about relevant facts....

Comment [to Rule 23]

R-23D. The general principle governing presentation of evidence is that evidence will be presented orally at the final hearing. However, oral examination of a witness at the final hearing may be impossible, burdensome, or impractical. Rule 23.1 permits the transcript of a deposition taken in accordance with this Rule to be presented to the court as a substitute for reception of testimony of a witness....

Comments and Questions

1. These Rules purport to strike a compromise between the regimes of broad and narrow discovery. Which of the two extremes is being asked to make the greater sacrifice?

2. Can you foresee any country adopting these rules? If yes, do you expect it to be a civil law or common law country? If no, are you also suggesting that the promulgation of model rules was a wasted effort—or might the rules serve some other purpose?

3. Is it realistic to suggest that transnational and domestic cases could be litigated under different discovery regimes? Could discovery in domestic litigation in the United States be conducted successfully pursuant to rules similar to the Transnational Rules?

F. U.S. Discovery for Use Abroad

In addition to or in lieu of offering judicial assistance to foreign proceedings pursuant to the Hague Evidence Convention, a country might adopt some unilateral measure. Indeed, coincident with the reform initiative that led to the Hague Evidence Convention, in 1964 the U.S. Congress enacted what became 28 U.S.C. §§ 1696 and 1781–1784 to make it easy for information located abroad to be used in litigation in the United States, and for information located in the United States to be used in litigation abroad.*

In particular, Section 1782 provides that the process of the U.S. district courts, including subpoenas, is available for the taking of testimony or production of documents and other things for use in a foreign or international tribunal.

Section 1782. Assistance to foreign and international tribunals and to litigants before such tribunals

> (a) The district court of the district in which a person resides or is found may order him to give his testimony or statement or to produce a document or other thing for use in a proceeding in a foreign or international tribunal, including criminal investigations conducted before formal accusation. The order may be made pursuant to a letter rogatory issued, or request made, by a foreign or international tribunal or upon the application of any interested person and may direct that the testimony or statement be given, or the document or other thing be produced, before a person appointed by the court. By virtue of his appointment, the person appointed has power to administer any necessary oath and take the testimony or statement. The order may prescribe the practice and procedure, which may be in whole or part the practice and procedure of the foreign country or the international tribunal, for taking the testimony or statement or producing the document or other thing. To the extent that the order does not prescribe otherwise, the testimony or statement shall be taken, and the document or other thing produced, in accordance with the Federal Rules of Civil Procedure.
>
> A person may not be compelled to give his testimony or statement or to produce a document or other thing in violation of any legally applicable privilege.
>
> (b) This chapter does not preclude a person within the United States from voluntarily giving his testimony or statement, or producing a document or other thing, for use in a proceeding in a foreign or international tribunal before any person and in any manner acceptable to him.

Notice that Section 1782 does not require any showing of reciprocity, and indeed does not require a request from the foreign court. The order may be made pursuant to a letter rogatory or request of the court or tribunal where the action is pending, "or upon the application of any interested person." Most of the cases under Section 1782, including those that you will review here, involve applications to U.S.

* A statute allowing federal courts to assist foreign courts had been on the books for 140 years, but was much narrower in scope before the 1964 legislation. For the earliest version of such a statute, *see* 10 Stat. 630, ch 140 § 2 (Mar. 2, 1855).

courts by litigants in foreign proceedings, in situations where the foreign court would never itself have sought such "assistance."

The Supreme Court recently addressed the parameters of Section 1782 in a case involving an intellectual property dispute between microprocessor competitors Advanced Micro Devices, Inc. ("AMD") and Intel Corporation. AMD had filed a complaint with the Directorate-General for Competition of the Commission of the European Communities alleging that Intel was abusing its dominant market position in violation of EU law. The European Commission opened an "investigation" in accordance with its normal procedures, and AMD suggested that the Commission seek discovery from Intel of materials previously produced in a private U.S. antitrust action brought against Intel by Intergraph Corporation. The Commission declined that suggestion, so AMD undertook the effort itself. Pursuant to Section 1782, AMD filed an action in the U.S. District Court for the Northern District of California demanding that Intel produce (sealed) materials from the Intergraph action for the benefit of the ongoing European Commission investigation.

The district judge declined to issue the order because the European Commission was not a court, and therefore the Commission's investigation was not a proceeding within the meaning of Section 1782. When AMD appealed, the Court of Appeals for the Ninth Circuit reversed because the investigation was an adversary "quasi-judicial" proceeding. Addressing another of Intel's arguments, the Ninth Circuit also held that Section 1782 did not require a showing that the information sought could be obtained in the foreign proceeding if it were located in the foreign jurisdiction. In addressing this latter issue the Ninth Circuit contributed to a circuit split—siding with the Second and Third Circuits, and against the First and Eleventh Circuits. Finally, the Court of Appeals wrote that "allowance of liberal discovery seems entirely consistent with the aims of Section 1782: providing efficient assistance to participants in international litigation and encouraging foreign countries by example to provide similar assistance to our courts." The Supreme Court granted certiorari.

The European Commission, as amicus curiae, opposed granting discovery; the U.S. government, also as amicus curiae, urged affirmance of the decision of the Ninth Circuit, that is, that Section 1782 authorized discovery, subject to the discretion of the district court in individual cases.

Intel Corporation v. Advanced Micro Devices, Inc.

542 U.S. 2241 (2004)

Justice Ginsburg delivered the opinion of the Court, in which Chief Justice Rehnquist and Justices Stevens, Kennedy, Souter, and Thomas, joined.

II

To place this case in context, we sketch briefly how the European Commission, acting through the [Directorate-General for Competition ("DG-Competition")], enforces European competition laws and regulations. The DG-Competition's "overriding responsibility" is to conduct investigations into alleged violations of the European Union's competition prescriptions. On receipt of a complaint or sua sponte, the DG-Competition conducts a preliminary investigation. In that investigation, the DG-Competition "may take into account information provided by a complainant, and it may seek information directly from the target of the complaint." "Ultimately, DG Competition's preliminary investigation results in a formal written decision whether to pursue the complaint. If [the DG-Competition] declines to proceed, that decision is subject to judicial review" by the Court of First Instance and, ultimately, by the court of last resort for European Union matters, the Court of Justice for the European Communities (European Court of Justice)....

If the DG-Competition decides to pursue the complaint, it typically serves the target of the investigation with a formal "statement of objections" and advises the target of its intention to recommend a decision finding that the target has violated European competition law. The target is entitled to a hearing before an independent officer, who provides a report to the DG-Competition. Once the DG-Competition has made its recommendation, the European Commission may "dismis[s] the complaint, or issu[e] a decision finding infringement and imposing penalties." The Commission's final action dismissing the complaint or holding the target liable is subject to review in the Court of First Instance and the European Court of Justice.

Although lacking formal "party" or "litigant" status in Commission proceedings, the complainant has significant procedural rights. Most prominently, the complainant may submit to the DG-Competition information in support of its allegations, and may seek judicial review of the Commission's disposition of a complaint.

III

A

We turn first to Intel's contention that the catalog of "interested person[s]" authorized to apply for judicial assistance under § 1782(a) includes only "litigants, foreign sovereigns, and the designated agents of those sovereigns," and excludes AMD, a mere complainant before the Commission, accorded only "limited rights." Highlighting § 1782's caption, "[a]ssistance to foreign and international tribunals and to litigants before such tribunals," Intel urges that the statutory phrase "any interested person" should be read, correspondingly, to reach only "litigants."

The caption of a statute, this Court has cautioned, "cannot undo or limit that which the [statute's] text makes plain." The text of § 1782(a), "upon the application of any interested person," plainly reaches beyond the universe of persons designated "litigant." No doubt litigants are included among, and may be the most common example of, the "interested person[s]" who may invoke § 1782; we read § 1782's caption to convey no more.

The complainant who triggers a European Commission investigation has a significant role in the process. As earlier observed, in addition to prompting an investigation, the complainant has the right to submit information for the DG-Competition's consideration, and may proceed to court if the Commission discontinues the investigation or dismisses the complaint. Given these participation rights, a complainant "possess[es] a reasonable interest in obtaining [judicial] assistance," and therefore qualifies as an "interested person" within any fair construction of that term. See Smit, International Litigation 1027 ("any interested person" is "intended to include not only litigants before foreign or international tribunals, but also foreign and international officials as well as any other person whether he be designated by foreign law or international convention or merely possess a reasonable interest in obtaining the assistance").

B

We next consider whether the assistance in obtaining documents here sought by an "interested person" meets the specification "for use in a foreign or international tribunal." Beyond question the reviewing authorities, both the Court of First Instance and the European Court of Justice, qualify as tribunals. But those courts are not proof-taking instances. Their review is limited to the record before the Commission. Hence, AMD could "use" evidence in the reviewing courts only by submitting it to the Commission in the current, investigative stage.... We have no warrant to exclude the European Commission, to the extent that it acts as a first-instance decisionmaker, from § 1782(a)'s ambit.

C

Intel also urges that AMD's complaint has not progressed beyond the investigative stage; therefore, no adjudicative action is currently or even imminently on the Commission's agenda. Section 1782(a) does not limit the provision of judicial assistance to "pending" adjudicative proceedings. In 1964, when Congress eliminated the requirement that a proceeding be "judicial," Congress also deleted the requirement that a proceeding be "pending."...The legislative history of the 1964 revision is in sync; it reflects Congress' recognition that judicial assistance would be available "whether the foreign or international proceeding or investigation is of a criminal, civil, administrative, or other nature." S.Rep. No. 1580, at 9, U.S.Code Cong. & Admin.News 1964, pp. 3782, 3789 (emphasis added).

In 1996, Congress amended § 1782(a) to clarify that the statute covers "criminal investigations conducted before formal accusation." Nothing suggests that this amendment was an endeavor to rein in, rather than to confirm, by way of example, the broad range of discovery authorized in 1964.

In short, we reject the view...that § 1782 comes into play only when adjudicative proceedings are "pending" or "imminent."...Instead, we hold that § 1782(a) requires only that a dispositive ruling by the Commission, reviewable by the European courts, be within reasonable contemplation.

D

We take up next the foreign-discoverability rule on which lower courts have divided: Does § 1782(a) categorically bar a district court from ordering production of documents when the foreign tribunal or the "interested person" would not be able to obtain the documents if they were located in the foreign jurisdiction?

We note at the outset, and count it significant, that § 1782(a) expressly shields privileged material: "A person may not be compelled to give his testimony or statement or to produce a document or other thing in violation of any legally applicable privilege." Beyond shielding material safeguarded by an applicable privilege, however, nothing in the text of § 1782 limits a district court's production-order authority to materials that could be discovered in the foreign jurisdiction if the materials were located there....

Nor does § 1782(a)'s legislative history suggest that Congress intended to impose a blanket foreign-discoverability rule on the provision of assistance under § 1782(a). The Senate Report observes in this regard that § 1782(a) "leaves the issuance of an appropriate order to the discretion of the court which, in proper cases, may refuse to issue an order or may impose conditions it deems desirable."

Intel raises two policy concerns in support of a foreign-discoverability limitation on § 1782(a) aid—avoiding offense to foreign governments, and maintaining parity between litigants. See In re Application of Asta Medica, S.A., 981 F.2d 1, 6 (1st Cir. 1992) ("Congress did not seek to place itself on a collision course with foreign tribunals and legislatures, which have carefully chosen the procedures and laws best suited to their concepts of litigation."). While comity and parity concerns may be important as touchstones for a district court's exercise of discretion in particular cases, they do not permit our insertion of a generally applicable foreign-discoverability rule into the text of § 1782(a).

We question whether foreign governments would in fact be offended by a domestic prescription permitting, but not requiring, judicial assistance. A foreign nation may limit discovery within its domain for reasons peculiar to its own legal practices, culture, or traditions—reasons that do not necessarily signal objection to aid from United States federal courts.... A foreign tribunal's reluctance to order production of materials present in the United States similarly may signal no resistance to the receipt of evidence gathered pursuant to § 1782(a). See South Carolina Ins. Co. v. Assurantie Maatschappij "De Zeven Provincien" N.V., [1987] 1 App. Cas. 24 (House of Lords ruled that nondiscoverability under English law did not stand in the way of a litigant in English proceedings seeking assistance in the United States under § 1782). When the foreign tribunal would readily accept relevant information discovered in the United States, application of a foreign-discoverability rule would be senseless. The rule in that situation would serve only to thwart § 1782(a)'s objective to assist foreign tribunals in obtaining relevant information that the tribunals may find useful but, for reasons having no bearing on international comity, they cannot obtain under their own laws.

Concerns about maintaining parity among adversaries in litigation likewise do not provide a sound basis for a cross-the-board foreign-discoverability rule. When information is sought by an "interested person," a district court could condition relief upon that person's reciprocal exchange of information. See Euromepa, S.A. v. R. Esmerian, Inc., 51 F.3d 1095, 1102 (2nd Cir. 1995). Moreover, the foreign tribunal can place conditions on its acceptance of the information to maintain whatever measure of parity it concludes is appropriate.

We also reject Intel's suggestion that a § 1782(a) applicant must show that United States law would allow discovery in domestic litigation analogous to the foreign proceeding. Section 1782 is a provision for assistance to tribunals abroad. It does not direct United States courts to engage in comparative analysis to determine whether analogous proceedings exist here. Comparisons of that order can be fraught with danger. For example, we have in the United States no close analogue to the European Commission regime under which AMD is not free to mount its own case in the Court of First Instance or the European Court of Justice, but can participate only as complainant, an "interested person," in Commission-steered proceedings.[16]

IV

As earlier emphasized, a district court is not required to grant a § 1782(a) discovery application simply because it has the authority to do so. We note below factors that bear consideration in ruling on a § 1782(a) request.

First, when the person from whom discovery is sought is a participant in the foreign proceeding (as Intel is here), the need for § 1782(a) aid generally is not as apparent as it ordinarily is when evidence is sought from a nonparticipant in the matter arising abroad. A foreign tribunal has jurisdiction over those appearing before it, and can itself order them to produce evidence.... In contrast, nonparticipants in the foreign proceeding may be outside the foreign tribunal's jurisdictional reach; hence, their evidence, available in the United States, may be unobtainable absent § 1782(a) aid.

Second, as the 1964 Senate Report suggests, a court presented with a § 1782(a) request may take into account the nature of the foreign tribunal, the character of the proceedings underway abroad, and the receptivity of the foreign government or the court or agency abroad to U.S. federal-court judicial assistance.... Further, the grounds Intel urged for categorical limitations on § 1782(a)'s scope may be relevant in determining whether a discovery order should be granted in a particular case.... Specifically, a district court could consider whether the § 1782(a) request conceals an attempt to circumvent foreign proof-gathering restrictions or other policies of a foreign country or the United States.... Also, unduly intrusive or burdensome requests may be rejected or trimmed....

Intel maintains that, if we do not accept the categorical limitations it proposes, then, at least, we should exercise our supervisory authority to adopt rules barring § 1782(a) discovery here.... We decline, at this juncture, to adopt supervisory rules. Any such endeavor at least should await further experience with § 1782(a)

---

[16] At oral argument, counsel for AMD observed: "In the United States, we could have brought a private action in the district court for these very same violations. In Europe, our only Europe-wide remedy was to go to the [European Commission]."

applications in the lower courts. The European Commission has stated in amicus curiae briefs to this Court that it does not need or want the District Court's assistance. It is not altogether clear, however, whether the Commission, which may itself invoke § 1782(a) aid, means to say "never" or "hardly ever" to judicial assistance from United States courts. Nor do we know whether the European Commission's views on § 1782(a)'s utility are widely shared in the international community by entities with similarly blended adjudicative and prosecutorial functions.

Several facets of this case remain largely unexplored. Intel and its amici have expressed concerns that AMD's application, if granted in any part, may yield disclosure of confidential information, encourage "fishing expeditions," and undermine the European Commission's Leniency Program.[18] Yet no one has suggested that AMD's complaint to the Commission is pretextual. Nor has it been shown that § 1782(a)'s preservation of legally applicable privileges, and the controls on discovery available to the District Court, see, e.g., Fed. Rule Civ. Proc. 26(b)(2) and (c), would be ineffective to prevent discovery of Intel's business secrets and other confidential information.

On the merits, this case bears closer scrutiny than it has received to date. Having held that § 1782(a) authorizes, but does not require, discovery assistance, we leave it to the courts below to ensure an airing adequate to determine what, if any, assistance is appropriate....

For the reasons stated, the judgment of the Court of Appeals for the Ninth Circuit is affirmed.

Justice O'Connor took no part in the consideration or decision of this case.

Justice Scalia, concurring in the judgment: As today's opinion shows, the Court's disposition is required by the text of the statute. None of the limitations urged by petitioner finds support in the categorical language of 28 U.S.C. § 1782(a). That being so, it is not only (as I think) improper but also quite unnecessary to seek repeated support in the words of a Senate Committee Report—which, as far as we know, not even the full committee, much less the full Senate, much much less the House, and much much much less the President who signed the bill, agreed with. Since, moreover, I have not read the entire so-called legislative history, and have no need or desire to do so, so far as I know the statements of the Senate Report may be contradicted elsewhere. Accordingly, because the statute—the only sure expression of the will of Congress—says what the Court says it says, I join in the judgment.

Justice Breyer, dissenting.

The Court reads the scope of 28 U.S.C. § 1782 to extend beyond what I believe Congress might reasonably have intended....

One might ask why it is wrong to read the statute as permitting the use of America's court processes to obtain information in such circumstances. One might

[18] The European Commission's "Leniency Program" allows "cartel participants [to] confess to their own wrongdoing" in return for prosecutorial leniency.

also ask why American courts should not deal case by case with any problems of the sort mentioned. The answer to both of these questions is that discovery and discovery-related judicial proceedings take time, they are expensive, and cost and delay, or threats of cost and delay, can themselves force parties to settle underlying disputes.... To the extent that expensive, time-consuming battles about discovery proliferate, they deflect the attention of foreign authorities from other matters those authorities consider more important; they can lead to results contrary to those that foreign authorities desire; and they can promote disharmony among national and international authorities, rather than the harmony that § 1782 seeks to achieve. They also use up domestic judicial resources and crowd our dockets.

That is why I believe the statute, while granting district courts broad authority to order discovery, nonetheless must be read as subject to some categorical limits, at least at the outer bounds—a matter that today's decision makes even more important. Those limits should rule out instances in which it is virtually certain that discovery (if considered case by case) would prove unjustified.

This case does not require us to find a comprehensive set of limits. But it does suggest two categorical limitations, which I would adopt. First, when a foreign entity possesses few tribunal-like characteristics, so that the applicability of the statute's word "tribunal" is in serious doubt, then a court should pay close attention to the foreign entity's own view of its "tribunal" -like or non-" tribunal" -like status....

Second, a court should not permit discovery where both of the following are true: (1) A private person seeking discovery would not be entitled to that discovery under foreign law, and (2) the discovery would not be available under domestic law in analogous circumstances. The Federal Rules of Civil Procedure, for example, make only limited provisions for nonlitigants to obtain certain discovery. See Fed. Rule Civ. Proc. 27. The limitations contained in the Rules help to avoid discovery battles launched by firms simply seeking information from competitors. Where there is benefit in permitting such discovery, and the benefit outweighs the cost of allowing it, one would expect either domestic law or foreign law to authorize it. If, notwithstanding the fact that it would not be allowed under either domestic or foreign law, there is some special need for the discovery in a particular instance, one would expect to find foreign governmental or intergovernmental authorities making the case for that need. Where none of these circumstances is present, what benefit could offset the obvious costs to the competitor and to our courts? I cannot think of any.

Application of either of these limiting principles would require dismissal of this discovery proceeding....

Comments and Questions

1. On remand, the district court went through the four factors and found "in its discretion" that at least the first three, and probably all four, weighed against granting AMD's application. Accordingly, the request for discovery was denied. Is that the right result?

2. This case is typical in that the applicant for discovery comes to the U.S. court without an order or the imprimatur of the (foreign) forum where the proceeding is pending. Is this form of assistance offensive to foreign systems? If so, what is the offense—that the foreign forum is unable to find the truth? Should Congress redraft the statute so that it offers assistance to foreign governmental officials or foreign courts rather than to an "interested person"?

3. Is substantive law drafted with certain assumptions about the availability (or not) of discovery? Is Section 1782, then, useful or destructive?

4. Legislation providing federal court assistance in gathering evidence in the United States for use in foreign tribunals dates back more than 150 years. Amended episodically, each iteration of the statutory authorization allowed more discovery, and for use in more types of foreign proceedings. Does a broad Section 1782 encourage foreign countries to emulate the United States' example by providing similar assistance?

5. Why should the United States facilitate discovery against Americans for use in foreign litigation?

6. Consider this hypothetical: In May 1999, Time, Inc. published an article in the Asian edition of its *Time* magazine that was highly critical of former Indonesian president General Suharto. The article asserted that "during his thirty-two year reign, General Suharto, his children, and his close friends amassed a vast fortune through rampant corruption, hidden ownership, nepotism, and abuse of power." General Suharto responded to the article by filing in Indonesia a civil suit for defamation against Time Asia and six of its editors and reporters in the Central Jakarta District Court of Indonesia. General Suharto alleged in the complaint that the article defamed him by falsely reporting that (1) he amassed a fortune for himself, family members, and close friends through an entity known as "Suharto Inc." which he says does not exist; (2) he shifted billions of dollars from a Swiss bank account to an Austrian bank account, when General Suharto says that he never possessed money in either country; (3) the "Suharto companies" very likely never paid more than 10 percent of their real tax obligations, which General Suarto denies and alleges that no such company exists; (4) and by publishing a picture of General Suharto hugging a picture of a house that General Suharto says he does no own, which painted a false portrait of him as a greedy man. The complaint demands a retraction, an apology, and $27 billion in damages.

(a) Imagine that Time Inc. has moved, pursuant to 28 U.S.C. § 1782 for the issuance of subpoenas to Freeport Gold Mines and its chief executive officer to obtain deposition testimony and documents for use in the Indonesian proceedings. Time seeks deposition testimony and documents concerning a broad expanse of topics, primarily concerned with the financial dealings of General Suharto, his family members, and close friends in connection with the Indonesian mine. May the U.S. court offer judicial assistance by facilitating this discovery? Does it matter that Freeport and the CEO are not parties?

(b) Imagine that the Suharto plaintiffs have similarly moved, pursuant to the same statute, for the issuance of subpoenas to certain employees of Time. In particular, the plaintiffs want to ascertain whether and in what amounts Time has insurance that could satisfy any judgment against it. It is undisputed that such information is not discoverable in the Indonesian courts because it is highly prejudicial. May the U.S. court offer this judicial assistance?

(c) Does the court have the discretion to assist with one or the other of the party's requests but not both?

(d) Must the court know something—or anything—about the Indonesian proceeding? The Indonesian court system?

G. Arbitration

The subject of discovery is closely tied with the subject of arbitration. Indeed, the popularity of arbitration in the United States has been fueled, in large part, by the search for alternatives to a litigation process that has become overwhelmed by discovery. Because the arbitral panel is not bound to follow the formal discovery rules, discovery can be not only limited in some general sense, but also tailored to fit the transaction or dispute. Occasionally, the parties' agreement to arbitrate will include certain parameters about the scope of discovery in the event of a dispute and arbitration. Or, at the commencement of the arbitration (in the "Terms of Reference"), the parties might find some common ground on the scope and limits of discovery.

In the absence of any agreement between the parties, the arbitrator(s) has considerable authority to determine the operating principles governing the gathering and presentation of evidence. In most cases, the parties will freely exchange the relevant documents rather than risk involving (or aggravating) the arbitrator. Parties may exchange affidavits and witness statements, or (although less common) take depositions. Arbitrators can police discovery abuse with the threat or imposition of an inference. For example, if a party fails to produce a requested document, the arbitrators may assume that document contains information adverse to the non-producing party. In some countries, such as the United States, arbitrators may also subpoena witnesses and direct witnesses to bring material documentary evidence to a hearing; if witnesses fail to comply, the district court for the district in which the arbitrators are sitting may compel compliance with the subpoenas.

Although arbitral proceedings have adopted many of the characteristics of litigation (positive and negative), arbitration offers many opportunities for more flexibility. The "trial" may be divided into parts to accommodate the schedules of the parties involved; and such a sequence of hearings may even occur in different cities to accommodate witnesses or the arbitrators.

Comments and Questions

1. Some arbitration agreements drafted by American counsel will contain specific reference to the Federal Rules of Civil Procedure. What are the advantages and disadvantages of such an approach?

2. Could parties to a private arbitration proceeding in the United States invoke the procedures of the Hague Evidence Convention to obtain discovery from parties and/or non-parties located in Germany? Find the language in the Convention to justify your position.

3. Could parties to a private arbitration proceeding in Paris invoke Section 1782 to obtain discovery from parties and/or non-parties located in the United States? Find the language in the statute to justify your position.

Concluding Comments and Questions

Return to the problem that opened this chapter and revisit the questions posed anew. Do the readings in this chapter make those questions (and your answers to them) more or less complicated? Is broad discovery an essential component of a fair system? Is discovery an essential component of a fair system?

H. Bibliography of Additional Resources

Andr R. Fiebig (ed.), OBTAINING DISCOVERY ABROAD (Am. Bar Ass'n, 2d ed. 2005)

Barton Legum (ed.), INTERNATIONAL LITIGATION STRATEGIES AND PRACTICE (Am. Bar Ass'n 2005)

8 Charles Alan Wright, Arthur R. Miller & Richard L. Marcus, FEDERAL PRACTICE AND PROCEDURE §§ 1083, 2005.1 (Thomson West 2nd ed. 1994 & Supp. 2007)

David Epstein, Jeffrey L. Snyder & Charles S. Baldwin, INTERNATIONAL LITIGATION: A GUIDE TO JURISDICTION, PRACTICE, AND STRATEGY (Martinus Nijhoff 3d ed. 1998 & Supp. 2007)

FEDERAL PROCEDURE: LAWYERS EDITION §§ 26:895, 26.935 (Thomson West 2007)

6 James Wm. Moore, MOORE'S FEDERAL PRACTICE §§ 28.10 to 28.17 (Matthew Bender 3d ed. 1997 & Supp. 2007)

Kenneth R. Adamo, Robert L. Canala & Susan M. Gerber, Section 1782: A Powerful Tool for Obtaining Discovery to Assist Foreign Litigation, 33 AIPLA Q.J. 337 (2005)

Kuo-Chang Huang, INTRODUCING DISCOVERY INTO CIVIL LAW (Carolina Acad. Press 2003)

Laura W. Smalley, How to Conduct International Discovery, 71 AM. JUR. TRIALS 1 (Thomson West 1999 & Supp. 2007)

D.H. Martens, German Civil Procedure and the Implementation of the Hague Evidence Convention, 1 INT'L LITIG. Q. 115 (1985)

Richard H. Kreindler & Judith L. Holdsworth (eds.), TRANSNATIONAL LITIGATION: A PRACTITIONER'S GUIDE (Oceana 1997 & Supp. 2007)

Richard H. Kreindler, TRANSNATIONAL LITIGATION: A BASIC PRIMER (Oceana 1998)

Richard L. Marcus, Retooling American Discovery for the Twenty-First Century: Toward a New World Order? 7 TUL. J. OF INT'L & COMP. L. 153 (1999)

Tim Taylor & Nigel Cooper, EUROPEAN LITIGATION HANDBOOK (Sweet & Maxwell 1995)

Ved P. Nanda & David K. Pansius, LITIGATION OF INTERNATIONAL DISPUTES IN U.S. COURTS (Thomson West 2d ed. 2005 & Supp. 2007)

CHAPTER 10

Choice of Law

A. Introduction

Choice of law is a discipline that seeks to determine the application of law when the administration of justice requires a choice between two or more systems of law. European lawyers tend to use the term "Private International Law" to refer to this field, whereas American lawyers are more familiar with the term "Conflict of Laws." Ironically, the common American term was coined by seventeenth-century Dutch scholars and Joseph Story, an American, is often credited for the European term.

Conflict cases arise because law-making bodies of various jurisdictions see the world differently; if the law were uniform in all jurisdictions there would be no conflict. Conflict doctrines must mediate a tension between concepts of sovereignty and fairness. On the one hand, we may be inclined to respect policy determinations of different jurisdictions. Yet we also want to decide cases in ways that make good sense and do not violate the parties' ability to prosecute and defend the action effectively.

What has long been sought is a lingua franca of the law that permits the courts of different states to respect each other's persons and policies, while fairly and effectively resolving private disputes. As Professor Juenger and his colleagues have demonstrated, a perfect formula for transmuting legal diversity into equivalence continues to elude both savants and practitioners. See Friedrich Juenger, Choice of Law and Multistate Justice (1993).

Conflict of Laws is a separate course in the curriculum, and deservedly so. In this chapter we can provide only an introduction to some of the topics that are at the core of transnational litigation.

The Problem: 007 Wonders*

Warner Brothers Inc. ("WB") is the owner of the copyright of the James Bond movie *Never Say Never Again,* which was produced in the United Kingdom. WB sold videos of the movie there, and Mr. Erik Viuff Christiansen, who manages a video shop in Copenhagen, purchased a copy in London with a view to renting it out in Denmark. Mr. Christiansen advertised that the film was in its original version (that is, without Danish subtitles). The local James Bond fans were delighted because until then the film had not been obtainable on the Danish market.

Under Danish copyright legislation, the owner of the copyright has a right to authorize or refuse rental and a right to a royalty whenever the video is rented out. In contrast, at all time relevant to this incident,** English copyright law allowed WB to control the initial sale, but gave no right to prohibit or condition rentals of the work.

Which jurisdiction's law should be invoked to determine the respective rights and responsibilities of WB and Mr. Christiansen? Does and should your answer change depending on whether the action is filed in London, Copenhagen, or Lisbon?

For additional context, you may assume that at all times relevant to this incident, the laws of Ireland, the Netherlands, and Germany were similar to the English. French law was substantially similar to the Danish legislation. In Greece, Italy, Luxembourg, and Spain, among others, the matter had not been resolved by specific provisions. (Is this additional context relevant to the choice of law question?)

B. Theoretical Approaches

In this section we consider several theoretical approaches for determining the applicable law. Before engaging this reading, however, consider the answer(s) that you gave to the problem that opened this chapter and analyze the theoretical underpinnings of your intuition—how and why did you reach the conclusion that you did? If you wanted more information before answering, what exactly did you want or need to know?

1. Lex Fori

One approach to the question what country's law applies is simply not to pose the question at all. The court in which the transaction is litigated may simply apply its own law. In support of this solution, it can be argued that judges are, after all, most familiar with the law of the forum, or lex fori. Its application is therefore easier, less time-consuming, and (there being no need for a foreign law expert) more efficient than resort to the rules of decision of some alien legal system. Moreover, an erroneous application of the pertinent law will be less likely. That was indeed the way

* This hypothetical is based largely on *Warner Bros., Inc. v. Christiansen,* Case 158/86 [1988] ECR 2605.

** The actual case invoked the Copyright Act of 1956, which has since been amended.

English common-law courts, after initially refusing even to hear cases involving foreign facts because the juries had to be drawn from the vicinage, used to deal with the problem some centuries ago. Rather than simply dismissing such cases, the common law courts resorted to the fiction that the foreign facts transpired in England, so that they could be tried before a jury and adjudicated by applying English law. Is there any contemporary justification or use for this seemingly archaic approach?

Albert A. Ehrenzweig, The Lex Fori—Basic Rule in the Conflict of Laws

58 Mich. L. Rev. 637, 637–641 (1960)*

Once a court has taken jurisdiction it will usually apply its own law, unless the parties' own choice or an important foreign fact, such as a foreign domicile, a foreign situs, or a foreign conduct, appears to require application of another law. Most judges and lawyers will agree with this simple proposition—and yet text books, class notes, the Restatement, and even much language of the courts, would have it otherwise: foreign domicile, foreign situs, foreign conduct and other foreign "contacts" are said a priori to require application of a foreign law, unless the court can be persuaded for special reasons to turn to its own law or to the law chosen by the parties. This blatant discrepancy between the actual doing of the courts and "official" theory in the law of conflict of laws has made an awesome mystery or an object of ridicule of this subject in the eyes of many....

For several centuries courts have, in varying ways and degrees, recognized foreign contracts or testaments which were valid under the law of their execution, permitted an alleged wrongdoer to show that he acted lawfully under the law of his conduct, or treated the transfer of foreign land in accordance with the law of its situs. Refinements have resulted in longer lists of such exceptions from the basic rule of the law of the forum. But it should not have been forgotten that foreign laws originally assumed these functions only to fill vacua created by the superior legal orders or the forum's self-limitation. The Pope could and did prohibit the bishop from enforcing the law of his diocese against foreigners.... Sister state customs were admitted in medieval Italy, where city ordinances would in terms limit themselves to citizens....

These situations in which foreign laws have thus been called upon to fill a vacuum could well have been collected and classified in a catalogue of exceptions from the basic rule of the law of the forum.... Instead, in a gradual process of academic petrification,... doctrine has traded the fertile inconsistencies and intricacies which would have characterized this scheme, for the sterile consistencies and simplicities of dogmatic formulas, which distinguish our current "official" law of conflict of laws....

A California citizen was killed in an automobile accident in Arizona. In a California law suit the California defendant claimed that the plaintiff's cause of

* Reprinted from Michigan Law Review, March 1960, Vol. 58, No. 5. Copyright 1960 by The Michigan Law Review Association.

action had died under "applicable" Arizona law, although California had long abolished what even a hundred years ago was felt to be a rule contrary to "justice," and permitted the survival of tort actions. Nevertheless it took the imaginativeness and scholarship of a progressive court to defeat the defendant's seemingly conclusive insistence on the law of the "place of the wrong" in order to do justice between two California citizens according to California law. And in order to be able to do so, the court had to resort to dogmatic language devised 700 years ago for totally different purposes. [See Grant v. McAuliffe, 41 Cal. 2d 859, 264 P.2d 944 (1953).] . . . Decisions of this kind could be multiplied at will. . . .

Less frequent, though more disturbing, are those cases in which less courageous judges, or judges less familiar with the tools at their disposal, have more or less grudgingly acquiesced in what they thought to be compelling precedent, and have done injustice by refusing to apply their own laws. . . .

Sutherland v. Kennington Truck Service, Ltd.

562 N.W.2d 466 (Mich. 1997)

[Ohio plaintiffs brought suit against Ontario, Canada, defendants to recover for injuries sustained in vehicle accident in Michigan. A Michigan trial judge, applying Ontario's statute of limitations, granted a defense motion for summary judgment. Plaintiffs appealed and a majority of the Michigan Supreme Court held that neither Ohio nor Ontario had interest in having its law applied, and therefore, Michigan law applied.]

Brickley, Justice (concurring in part and dissenting in part).

I concur in the result reached by the majority. However, I write separately to express my view that the time has come for this state to . . . adopt a lex fori approach to choice of law questions. . . .

[T]he problems in the majority's opinion stem from this underlying methodology. The most fundamental flaw in this approach to choice of law is that it requires the courts of this state to choose between the laws of Michigan and those of foreign jurisdictions. As a matter of policy, the courts of this state should apply Michigan law. The application of foreign law requires a Michigan court to interpret and apply that law as if the court was sitting in that foreign jurisdiction. State courts should not presume to speak for other jurisdictions in this manner. Further, the majority's analysis requires Michigan courts to apply the law of another jurisdiction in certain cases. However, before a court can do this, it must first expressly refuse to apply the laws of this state. This refusal ignores and defeats the express will of the Legislature. Clearly, the courts of this state should avoid this outcome.[4]

---

[4] It should be noted that choosing another jurisdiction's law is fundamentally different from adopting another state's approach to a given issue. In the choice of law context, a Michigan court acts as if it is a court in a foreign jurisdiction and purports to speak on that jurisdiction's laws. However, when a Michigan court finds another state's approach on an issue persuasive and adopts it, the court merely refines Michigan law. Thus, its holding only addresses the laws of this state.

Moreover, there is an increased likelihood of error when Michigan courts attempt to rule on foreign laws....

A second flaw with this state's choice of law methodology is that it is unpredictable. [The doctrine has] sought to create a system that would allow parties to accurately forecast the law that governs any given litigation. However, this case shows that this has not been the result. Rather, these parties have been delayed for over five years as the courts of this state have struggled to determine the governing law. Further, the majority does not make this system any more predictable. Instead, it fails to define a systematic approach for determining the interests of other jurisdictions. It examines two factors in determining that neither Ontario nor Ohio can be interested in this case. Yet, it is far from clear that these are the only factors to be considered....

The third flaw in this choice of law approach is that it allows hidden, pro-forum manipulation. The majority recognizes that courts manipulate apparently neutral choice of law rules in order to justify the application of forum law. This defeats the parties' expectation that choice of law rules will be neutrally applied. I agree with the majority's comment that this preference is not surprising. However, the majority fails to take steps to eliminate this problem. Indeed, the analysis that the majority uses to determine that Ohio and Ontario have no interest in this litigation is an example of that approach....

I feel that lex fori should be adopted. This approach will avoid the three evils of the majority's methodology. First, under lex fori, Michigan courts will only apply Michigan law in most cases. This eliminates the problems that result when a Michigan court applies the laws of another jurisdiction. Second, a lex fori approach will bring clarity and predictability to this area of the law. All parties entering a Michigan court would know that they are to be governed by Michigan law. Finally, courts would not be tempted to manipulate the choice of law rules....

I am aware that the lex fori approach has been criticized for encouraging forum shopping. This supposed evil is greatly exaggerated and should not deter this state's adoption of the lex fori approach. Forum shopping is thought to be an evil because it allows a plaintiff to expose a defendant to the laws of a forum that has little involvement in the litigation, assuming that the forum has jurisdiction over the defendant. Under the approach I propose, an entity may be subjected to Michigan law concerning a cause of action that may have arisen elsewhere, if all constitutional requirements are satisfied. However, this should not prevent the adoption of the lex fori approach in this state.

Initially, it is important to recognize that a forum shopping party who chooses Michigan is asking the courts of this state to effectuate the laws and policies of Michigan. There is no reason why Michigan courts should summarily refuse this request. Rather, it is the duty of Michigan courts to effectuate these laws and policies. Assume that a plaintiff chooses to file suit in Michigan because Michigan law recognizes his claim. The application of Michigan law to this plaintiff's claim will fulfill the policy expressed by the Michigan Legislature, which recognizes the claim. Thus, forum shopping is not necessarily problematic....

Forum shopping is also commonly assumed to be unfair to defendants. This view is based on the premise that the plaintiff has selected an unfair forum. However, the law that the defendant would have the court apply is likely to be just as unfair. Indeed, the defendant will likely urge the court to apply the law of the jurisdiction that is most certain to lead to a dismissal. Thus, while the plaintiff may "shop" for a forum whose law is beneficial to its case, the defendant is just as likely to "shop" for law favorable to it. Thus, there is really no innocent party in these situations. The fairest way to resolve this is to rely on the traditional notion that the plaintiff is the master of his lawsuit, and, as such, is entitled to choose the forum. Also, in the vast majority of cases, an entity that has sufficiently connected itself to Michigan so that a Michigan court has jurisdiction over it will not be unfairly burdened by the application of Michigan's laws....

Thus, I concur with the majority that Michigan's statute of limitations should apply in this case. However, I cannot agree with the choice of law methodology employed by the majority. I would adopt a lex fori approach.

Leary v. Gledhill
8 N.J. 260 (1951)

VANDERBILT, CJ

The plaintiff and the defendant were friends who had become acquainted while in the military service. They first met in 1943 and occasionally thereafter through 1945. They corresponded but did not meet again until Christmas, 1948, when the defendant visited the plaintiff in Germany where he was stationed. At that time the defendant was no longer in the military service but was in Europe attempting to sell tractors for the Franam Corporation. Prior to the defendant's trip to Europe he had corresponded with the plaintiff with reference to an investment in the Franam Corporation as one which would be very profitable. Their correspondence resulted in the plaintiff purchasing $1,000 worth of stock when the defendant went to see him in Germany, the defendant delivering to the plaintiff certificates of stock which he had brought with him to Europe in exchange for the plaintiff's check for $1,000.

In April, 1949, the plaintiff at the defendant's invitation visited him in Paris. The defendant had left the United States with $500 in his possession and after arriving in Europe had been in constant need of money to meet his expenses. In a conversation in a hotel in Paris the defendant told the plaintiff that he needed about $4,000 and that he could raise about $2,000 by selling his Cadillac car. In the plaintiff's presence the defendant made a telephone call to his wife in the United States and instructed her to sell the automobile. The defendant asked the plaintiff to help him, but did not mention anything about selling the plaintiff any shares of stock. The plaintiff said he would think it over for a few days and see what he could do. After returning to his base in Germany the plaintiff mailed the defendant a check payable to the defendant's order for $1,500 without indicating on the check or in the accompanying letter what the money was for. The defendant endorsed the check and converted it into traveler's checks. The parties did not see each other again until the day of the trial, although the plaintiff had made many attempts to see the defendant after they both had returned to the United States, seeking him at his home and calling him on the telephone at various times, but always without success.

The plaintiff instituted this suit against the defendant on two counts, the first for $1,000 and the second for $1,500, but at the outset of the trial the plaintiff moved for a voluntary dismissal of the first count and the pretrial order was amended accordingly. The issue as stated in the amended pretrial order was limited to whether the money given by the plaintiff to the defendant was a loan or an investment in a business venture. At the trial the plaintiff testified that the check for $1,500 was a personal loan to the defendant but this the defendant denied, contending that he had never borrowed any money from the plaintiff. At the end of the plaintiff's case and again at the end of the entire case the defendant moved for an involuntary dismissal on the ground that the plaintiff's proofs were insufficient, there being no promise to repay, no demand for repayment, and no pleading or proof of the law of France where the transaction occurred. These motions were denied, the trial court holding that while it would not take judicial notice of the law of France it would proceed, first, on the presumption that the law involving loans is the same there as in other civilized countries, and, secondly, on the ground that the issue with respect to the law of France had not been set forth in the pretrial order. When the case was submitted to the jury, the defendant objected to the charge on the ground that it did not instruct the jury to find as a fact what the law of France was. The jury returned a verdict in favor of the plaintiff in the sum of $1,500, and from the judgment entered thereon the defendant took this appeal. It is significant that the defendant never proved or even attempted to prove either the delivery of any stock to the plaintiff or a tender thereof. Neither did the defendant attempt to prove or even suggest that the law of France was such as to preclude recovery in the circumstances.

The defendant argues five points on this appeal, none of which has merit:

...3. "The rules of law for a foreign country must be pleaded and proved as facts along with the other elements of a cause of action to enable a plaintiff to recover against the defendant." A court will in general take judicial notice of and apply the law of its own jurisdiction without pleading or proof thereof, the judges being deemed to know the law or at least where it is to be found, 9 Wigmore on Evidence (3rd ed., 1940), 551. Under the common law of England as adopted in this country, however, the law of other countries, including sister states, would not be so noticed and applied by a court, but it was deemed an issue of fact to be pleaded and proved as other material facts had to be.... This common law rule had two great disadvantages; it made every jury pass on questions of law quite beyond its competence and the decision of the jury as to the foreign law was unappealable at common law as were its findings on all questions of fact.

The courts, however, were reluctant to dismiss an action for a failure to plead and prove the applicable foreign law as they would have dismissed it for a failure to prove other material facts necessary to establish a cause of action or a defense. Accordingly the courts frequently indulged in one or another of several presumptions: that the common law prevails in the foreign jurisdiction; that the law of the foreign jurisdiction is the same as the law of the forum, be it common law or statute; or that certain fundamental principles of the law exist in all civilized countries. As a fourth alternative, instead of indulging in any presumption as to the law of the foreign jurisdiction, the courts would merely apply the law of the forum as the only law before the court, on the assumption that by failing to prove the foreign law the parties acquiesce in having their controversy determined by reference to the law of the forum, be it statutory or common law. By the application of these various presumptions the courts have in effect treated the common law rule that foreign law could not be noticed but must be pleaded and proved as if it were a matter of fact merely as a permissive rule whereby either party could, if it were to his advantage, plead and prove the foreign law. Thus the failure to plead and prove the foreign law has not generally been considered as fatal....

In New Jersey, in the absence of proof as to the applicable foreign law, the courts have frequently applied the presumption that the common law exists in the foreign jurisdiction....

While our attention has not been directed to any New Jersey cases on the point, this presumption as to the existence of the common law in a foreign jurisdiction is equally applicable in cases involving other common law countries such as England in the absence of proof to the contrary....

In the instant case the transaction occurred in France. Our courts may properly take judicial knowledge that France is not a common law, but rather a civil jurisdiction. It would, therefore, be inappropriate and indeed contrary to elementary knowledge to presume that the principles of the common law prevail there. This does not mean, however, that the plaintiff must fail in his cause of action because of the absence of any proof at the trial as to the applicable law of France. In these circumstances any one of the other three presumptions may be indulged in, i.e., that the law of France is the same as the law of the forum; that the law of France, like all civilized countries, recognizes certain fundamental principles, as, e.g., that the taking of a loan creates an obligation upon the borrower to make repayment; that the parties by failing to prove the law of France have acquiesced in having their dispute determined by the law of the forum.

The court below based its decision upon the presumption that the law of France in common with that of other civilized countries recognizes a liability to make repayment under the facts here present, and its decision is not without substantial merit in reason and support in the authorities.... The utilization of this presumption has decided limitations, however, for in many cases it would be difficult to determine whether or not the question presented was of such a fundamental nature as reasonably to warrant the assumption that it would be similarly treated by the laws of all civilized countries. The presumption that in the absence of proof the parties acquiesce in the application of the law of the forum, be it statutory law or common law, does not present any such difficulties for it may be universally applied regardless of the nature of the controversy. This view, moreover, is favored by the authorities.... We are of the opinion, therefore, that in the instant case the rights of the parties are to be determined by the law of New Jersey which unquestionably permits recovery on the facts proven.

We recognize, of course, that in certain cases there might be present factors which would make it unreasonable for the court to indulge in any presumption and where the court in the exercise of its sound discretion might require proof of applicable foreign law to be laid before the court, but such is certainly not the situation here. The defendant is in no way prejudiced by the application of the law of this State. If he had desired to raise an issue as to the foreign law, he might have done so in his answer or at the pretrial conference or, with permission of the court, at the trial itself, and himself have introduced proof as to the law of France. It is against the letter and the spirit of our practice to permit him to make the failure of the plaintiff to plead and prove foreign law the basis of a surprise motion addressed to the court either in the course of or at the conclusion of the case....

The judgment below is affirmed.

2. Multilateralism

A different way for judicial systems to deal with conflicts of law is the so-called multilateral approach. Multilateral approaches articulate rules to conceptually locate an incident or transaction within a particular jurisdiction. These rules typically identify a determinative contact for the controversy—whether an individual's domicile or the place where an event occurred or where certain property is located—to identify the state whose law should govern all conflicts within a particular substantive field. One purpose of such a system is to ensure predictable and uniform results irrespective of where the litigation takes place. Forum shopping thus would be discouraged, provided the alternative fora have adopted the same jurisdiction-selection rules.

As you read the materials that follow to develop a deeper understanding of multilateral approaches, focus on two questions in particular: (1) What is the theoretical justification for a court to ignore forum law? (2) Are fixed rules of choice appropriate for conflicts questions?

Ernst Rabel, The Purposes of Conflicts Law

I The Conflict of Laws: A Comparative Study 94–95 (2d ed. 1958)

[I]t has been customary to regard the attainment of uniform solutions as the chief purpose of private international law. Cases should be decided under the same substantive rules, irrespective of the court where they are pleaded. We may gratefully note that this postulate has continued in favor, if only as an ideal remote from reality, at a time when separate conflicts laws have grown up in the various countries and their diversities have been prized. The real value of this postulate under present conditions is that it forms a test for the relative convenience of conflicts rules. The time has come to approach the goal with more energy.

One of the considerations leading to a universally useful rule is the legitimate expectation of the parties. Not to disappoint fair assumptions by persons disposing of property or entering into engagements, was the justified motive of the twisted doctrines protecting vested rights. For example, formalities are subject to the law of the place where a transaction has been concluded; the acquisition of property is governed by the law of the situs as of the time of the acquisition; capacity to contract a business obligation partly is, or should be, determined by the law governing the validity of the contract, et cetera. "When a matter has been settled, in conformity with the law then and there controlling the actions of the parties, the settlement should not be disturbed because the point arises for litigation somewhere else."[75] This fundamental premise suggests that courts should search, in the absence of express intentions with respect to the applicable law, for the "tacit" and eventually the "presumed" intentions of the parties.

Moreover, as a European writer has recently postulated, when a fact or an act is governed by a certain law according to all the conflicts laws practically involved, this law should be applied by any court before which the case may come as a result of subsequent circumstances.[76]

In a more general way, Savigny regarded it a guarantee of uniform treatment of legal relations that the law of that place where the relation has its legal "seat" should be applied everywhere—a conception that through Wharton has been admitted in the Supreme Court of the United States.[77] Gierke substituted for "seat" "center of gravity"; Bar sought localization "according to the nature of things"; and Westlake recommended the law of the state with which the relation has closest connection. All these formulas tend toward the same goal, the importance of which still is in no wise impaired. But the obstacles barring the way to the goal have increased since the world order envisaged by Savigny has been dissolved into more than a hundred national legal systems.

Comments and Questions

1. Is the multilateralist approach appropriate only if a country's peer jurisdictions have also adopted it? (Put another way, is a multilateralist approach appropriate only in the context of multilateral agreement?) Or is it appropriate for a jurisdiction to adopt such an approach even if no other jurisdiction reciprocates?

Raleigh C. Minor, The Basis of Private International Law

Conflict of Laws § 4 at 5–10 (1901)

Effect is given to a foreign law, not through any convention or agreement of nations, but merely because justice and policy often demand that, in the enforcement and

---

[75] Goodrich, *Public Policy in the Law of Conflicts*, 36 W. Va. L.Q. 156, 164 (1930).

[76] Meijers, *La question du renvoi*, 38 Bull. Inst. Int. 225 (1938).

[77] *Pritchard v. Norton*, 106 U.S. 124, 130 (1882).

interpretation of contracts and other transactions possessing a foreign element, the court should be governed by some other than the domestic law.

When one voluntarily does an act in a particular country, it is, as a general rule, just and proper that the effect of the act should be measured by the law under which it is done. The party need not do the act there unless he chooses, and if he elects to do it there, the just measure of its operation is the law to which he has thus voluntarily submitted himself. In other words, the situs or locality of the act in question furnishes the law which will govern it. And the same general principle, as we shall hereafter see, applies to transactions and circumstances which are not the result of voluntary action. The law of the situs of the particular matter will control.

It is often said that a court, in enforcing a foreign law, acts ex comitate, and if care is observed to note the meaning of the term "comity," the expression is not erroneous. The basis of private international law may be said to be comity, but it is as much a comity shown to the litigants in referring to the law of the situs, as above explained, as a comity to the State whose law is thus enforced. In truth, it is something more even than comity to the litigants. It is in answer to the demands of justice and an enlightened policy.

It is to be observed that the rules of private international law do not derive force from a power superior to the sovereign States which recognize and enforce them. On the contrary, the very essence of a sovereign State is that is has no superior. It is one of the fundamental principles of this branch of the law that each sovereign State is supreme within its own limits. It is therefore within the power of such a State at any time to exclude any or all foreign laws from operation within its borders. To the extent that it cannot do this, it is not sovereign. Hence, when effect is given to a foreign law in any territory, it is only because the municipal law of that State temporarily abdicates its supreme authority in favor of the foreign law, which, for the time being, with reference to that particular matter, becomes itself, by the will of that State, its municipal law....

It is of the utmost importance to observe at the outset that every point that may come up before a court for its decision must have a situs somewhere, and each point that arises will in general be governed by the law of the State where that situs is ascertained to be. Whether the interest before the court be one arising from the voluntary action of the individual, or whether it be created, without voluntary action, merely by the law itself, is immaterial. It must have its situs, assigned by the individual or by the law.... A Tort, a contract, a conveyance of property, the devise or descent of land or personalty, marriage, all have their situs, whose law will generally govern with respect to them....

[E]very sovereign State has absolute control over the persons and property within its borders, and may regulate them as its own notions of propriety and policy dictate. The question in all such cases is, shall it exercise the right to control these matters by its own law, or shall it yield to the law of another State? If it chooses the latter course, it does so not because the foreign legislation or institutions have an extraterritorial force within its limits, but simply because policy and justice demand it.

It may be said that the legislature of the State in which the question arises has foreseen and provided for the contingency, and has expressly laid down the rule that shall govern its courts should a foreign element creep into a particular case. In such event the legislature may enact that the foreign law is to control, or that, notwithstanding the foreign element, the domestic law shall still govern. This is a matter of policy wholly in the discretion of the legislature, into which the courts cannot inquire. In the latter case, there would be no room for the operation of the rules of private international law. It is merely a question of the court's obedience to the mandates of the State's municipal law.

But it rarely happens that the legislature, in enacting a statute, expressly deals with cases involving a foreign element. Primarily the legislature enacts laws for its own citizens, touching property and transactions within the State, and does not usually notice expressly those cases in which the person, the property, or the transaction affected may be without the State, in whole or in part. Under these circumstances therefore the duty devolves upon the courts to determine whether the municipal law, by its silence, means to include or to exclude these cases. Here it is that the rules of private international law come into play, and guide the courts in the solution of problems that often intricate.

There may be said to be five instances wherein it is generally considered that the municipal law of the State where the question is raised (lex fori) forbids the enforcement of a foreign law. (1) Where the enforcement of the foreign law would contravene some established and important policy of the State of the forum; (2) where the enforcement of such foreign law would involve injustice and injury to the people of the forum; (3) where such enforcement would contravene the canons of morality established by civilized society; (4) where the foreign law is penal in its nature; and (5) where the question relates to real property.

These exceptions are of supreme importance in the study of this subject, and must be constantly borne in mind, for they constitute standing exceptions to almost every proposition that can be laid down. Yet they are often lost sight of by the courts, or are confounded with the principles themselves. The unnoticed existence and enforcement of them in many of the cases is one main cause of the confusion that envelops the subject....

Joseph Story, Commentaries on the Conflict of Laws
(1834)

§ 4. [I]n the present times, without some general rules of right and obligation, recognised by civilized nations to govern their intercourse with each other, the most serious mischief and most injurious conflicts would arise. Commerce is now so absolutely universal among all countries; the inhabitants of all have such a free intercourse with each other; contracts, marriages, nuptial settlements, wills and successions, are so common among persons, whose domicils are in different countries, having different and even opposite laws on the same subjects; that without some common principles adopted by all nations in this regard there would be an utter confusion of all rights and remedies; and intolerable grievances would grow up to weaken all the domestic relations, as well as to destroy the sanctity of contracts and the security of property.

§ 5. A few simple cases will sufficiently illustrate the importance of some international principles in matters of mere private right and duty. Suppose a contract, valid by the laws of the country, where it is made, is sought to be enforced in another country, where such a contract is positively prohibited by its laws; or vice versa, suppose a contract, invalid by the laws of the country, where it is made, but valid by that of the country, where it is sought to be enforced; it is plain, that unless some uniform rules are adopted to govern such cases, (which are not uncommon), the grossest inequalities will arise in the administration of justice between the subjects of the different countries in regard to such contracts....

§ 6. Questions of this sort must be of frequent occurrence, not only in different countries wholly independent of each other; but also in provinces of the same empire, governed by different laws, as was the case in France before the Revolution; and also in countries acknowledging a common sovereign, but yet organized as distinct communities.... Innumerable suits must be litigated in the judicial forums of these countries and provinces, in which the decision must depend upon the point, whether the nature of a contract should be determined by the law of the place, where it is litigated; or by the law of the domicil of one or both of the parties; or by the law of the place, where the contract was made; whether the capacity to make a testament should be regulated by the law of the testator's domicil, or that of the location of his property; whether the form of his testament should be prescribed the law of his domicil, or of that of the location of his property, or of that of the place, where the testament is made; and in like manner, whether the law of the domicil, or what other law should govern in cases of succession of intestate estates.

§ 7. It is plain, that the laws of one country can have no intrinsic force, proprio vigore, except within the territorial limits and jurisdiction of that country. They can bind only its own subjects, and others, who are within its jurisdictional limits; and the latter only while they remain there. No other nation, or its subjects, are bound to yield the slightest obedience to those laws. Whatever extra-territorial force they are to have, is the result, not of any original power to extend them abroad, but of that respect, which from motives of public policy other nations are disposed to yield to them, giving them effect, as the phrase is, sub mutuae vicissitudinis obtentu, with a wise and liberal regard to common convenience and mutual necessities....

Joseph H. Beale, Vested Rights Doctrine

A Treatise on the Conflict of Laws, 1967–1969 app. (1935)

Instead of the... theory of comity, the common law has worked out indigenously a theory of vested rights, which serves the same purpose, that is, the desire to reach a just result, and is not subject to the objections which can be urged against the doctrine of comity.

As early as the time of Story the courts were already saying that an act or obligation valid by the laws of the place where made was valid everywhere; and that a foreign judgment by a court of competent jurisdiction was conclusive of the right it decided. The fullest statement of this new doctrine was by Sir William Scott in Dalrymple v. Dalrymple: "The cause being entertained in an English court it must be adjudicated according to the principles of English law applicable to such a case. But the only principle applicable to such a case by the law of England is that the validity of Miss Gordon's marriage rights must be tried by reference to the law of the country where, if they exist at all, they had their origin." Story accepted and developed this theory, which from his time has been the accepted theory in the English and American courts.

This doctrine may be stated and explained as follows. Although the law to be applied to the solution of the Conflict of Laws is the territorial law, this does not mean the law by which such right as those brought in question would be created within the territory.... The will which imposes a national law within territorial limits does not necessarily decree the application of that law to all the cases there arising, when great inconvenience would result from so doing. The national law which is applied to the solution of conflicts is that portion of the national law which deals with the solution of conflicts. If by the national law the validity of a contract depends upon the law of the place where the contract was made, then that law is applied for determining the validity of a contract made abroad, not because the foreign law has any force in the nation, nor because of any constraint exercised by an international principle, but because the national law determines the question of the validity of a contract by the lex loci contractus. If it were really a case of conflicting laws, and the foreign law prevailed in the case in question, the decision would be handed over bodily to the foreign law. By the national doctrine, the national law provides for a decision according to certain provisions of the foreign law; in the case considered, according to the foreign contract law. The provisions of this law having been proved as a fact, the question is solved by the national law, the foreign factor in the solution—i.e., the foreign contract law—being present as mere fact, one of the facts upon which the decision is to be based.

To explain the territorial theory in other terms, all that has happened outside the territory, including the foreign laws which have in some way or other become involved in the problem, is regarded merely as fact to be considered by the national law in arriving at its decision, and to be given such weight in determining the decision as the national law may choose to give it. The author summarized this theory in 1902 as follows:

> The topic called "Conflict of Laws" deals with the recognition and enforcement of foreign created rights. In the legal sense, all rights must be created by some law. A right is artificial, not a mere natural fact; no legal right exists by nature. A Right is a political, not a social thing; no legal right can be created by the mere will of parties. Law being a general rule to govern future transaction, its method of creating rights is to provide that upon the happening of a certain event a right shall accrue.

> The law annexes to the event a certain consequence, namely, the creation of a legal right. The creation of a right is therefore conditioned upon the happening of an event. Events which the law acts upon may be of two sorts; acts of human beings and so-called "acts of God," that is, events in which no human being has a share. Rights generally follow acts of men; though sometimes a right is created as a result solely of an act of God (as lapse of time: accretion). When a right has been created by law, this right itself becomes a fact; and its existence may be a factor in an event which the same or some other law makes the condition of a new right. In other words, a right may be changed by the law that created it, or by any other law having power over it. If no law having power to do so has changed a right, the existing right should everywhere be recognized; since to do so is merely to recognize the existence of a fact.

Comments and Questions

1. According to the vested rights theory, the state in which the events assertedly giving rise to a tort or contract obligation occurred, and only that state, had the power to create such an obligation and define its scope and content. If that state did so, the obligation became a "vested right" which every other state was bound to enforce. Because the elements of the underlying transaction might be dispersed among two or more states, a single crucial act or event had to be designated whose location would identify the source of the governing law. In contract cases, this is typically the "place of contracting" and in tort cases, the place of injury or the place of the conduct that caused the injury.

2. One frequent criticism is that absolute rules decide concrete cases on generalities that cannot account for the unique considerations that might be presented in a particular application. Might certain applications of an absolute rule be unjust or unwise? Or are those the circumstances that especially require the certainty and predictability of a mechanical and dispassionate formula that ensures decisional harmony?

3. One method of avoiding mischief would be to draft a truly comprehensive set of rules. However, it would be surprising if any corpus of rules could anticipate all of the possible scenarios, and for this reason choice of law is often thought to be among those fields that does not lend itself to codification. Do you agree?

4. Another method of avoiding mischief would be to incorporate an "escape hatch" or "safety valve" into the schemata of rules. For example, what if the rules permitted a judge to decline to apply a designated law that was against the public policy of the forum state?

3. Unilateralism

Although multilateralists attempt to allocate transactions to a particular legal system, unilateralists approach choice-of-law problems in a rather different manner. Instead of focusing on a rigid framework of rules, unilateral approaches favor a process of more discretionary decision making that can be tailored to the needs of each particular case. Unilateral approaches encourage judges to look beyond the locus or forum or domicile, and allow a broader range of contacts to inform the choice-of-law inquiry and to improve the quality of that determination. Thus, rather than locate a given legal transactions in one legal system or another, unilateralists inquire into the spatial purport of the potentially applicable domestic and foreign rules of decision, such as statutory provisions or case law rules on consideration. The foundation of this approach is that: "[j]ustice, fairness and, the best practical result, may best be achieved by giving controlling effect to the law of the jurisdiction which, because of its relationship or contact with the occurrence or the parties has the greatest concern with the specific issue raised in the litigation." Babcock v. Jackson, 12 N.Y.2d at 481, 191 N.E.2d 279.

This section allows you to explore again one of the fundamental themes of this course: the proper balance between the certainty and predictability and simplicity of rules, on one hand, and the flexible and discretionary standards of fairness and justice, on the other.

Ernst Rabel, The Purposes of Conflicts Law

I The Conflict of Laws: A Comparative Study 95–98 (2d ed. 1958)

In view of the difficulties of reaching uniformity, a more modest aspiration has been... to attain "as much certainty as may be reasonably hoped for in a changing world" and is compatible with "needed flexibility."[78] A just result or the realization of prescribed policies is now often viewed as the main purpose of conflicts law. This is right without doubt, if certain fundamental distinctions be borne in mind.

(a) The usual confusion of private and conflicts laws has engendered the conception that both have to follow the same pattern of values and purposes. If this were true, all the differences that permeate the national laws with respect to the organization of the family, the categories of property rights, freedom of contract, privileges and duties, public interests, and so on, would be reflected, nay reproduced, in the conflicts rules of the divers countries. The writers have formulated their axioms according to their particular views. Kahn,[81] for instance, who considered relationships created by internal law to be the subject matter of conflicts rules, required conformity with the fundamental idea of the internal institution. If, in the doctrine of the internal law, parental power is regarded as a mere right, the father's personal law should govern; if the father's duty is accentuated, the law of the child. Under Pillet's leadership, French writers transformed their doctrine of sovereignty so as to require the determination of what law ought to govern capacity to contract, succession on death, etc., in conformity with the "social purpose" of the state regulations pertaining to personality, family, security of commerce,

[78] Walter Wheeler Cook, the Logical and Legal Bases of the Conflict of Laws 432 (1942).

[81] Franz Kahn, 1–2 Abhandlungen zum internationalen Privatrecht (1928).

etc.; the applicable law is that which most efficiently protects the purpose fostered by the forum's own domestic legislation.

This identification of motives, sometimes extremely consequential, aggravates the difficult task of the conflicts law beyond all limits. To care for social prosperity is the responsibility of the municipal private laws, which have to resolve the merits of each particular problem. The principle, jus suum cuique tribuere, instructs legislators and judges to ponder carefully private and public interests. But this is what each private law does for itself; the function of private international rules is to choose the applicable law with all its evaluations whatever they may be. Existing conflicts law presumes that all laws of civilized countries are of equal rank, not to speak of sister states in a federation. Assuredly, the origin of this idea was political, and its modern theoretical foundation came from its connection with the law of nations. But, as things are, to inject national policies directly into conflicts law, will destroy it. In such event, "international public order" would embrace all internal laws.

(b) When preconceptions are eliminated, policy in the field of conflicts law is of course the main object of concern. Conflicts rules have never been entirely uninfluenced by the underlying social situation. This is pioneer ground. How the interest of the state, of other states, of the parties, of third persons in good faith, of commerce or trade in general, are to be valued against each other in various situations and best reconciled with the postulate of certainty, needs renewed and detailed deliberation. For the time being, it would be entirely premature to try to enumerate or to analyze such considerations in a general way.

(c) The postulate that conflicts rules should have juts results may be understood—or perhaps misunderstood—as signifying that the outcome of lawsuits in every case should conform, not to the lex fori, but to the judge's sense of justice.

We well know that courts will try many direct or devious ways to satisfy this sense of justice. They will use the faculty to reject a foreign rule on the ground of a public policy of the forum. They will classify an unwelcome foreign rule as inapplicable foreign procedure. They will, with a desired end in view, affirm or deny a person's domicil. And we may trust the courts always to select, of two accessible ways, that which leads to the result to them appearing preferable. These expedients of judicial wisdom cannot be closed entirely, and should not be, while conflicts rules remain crude and vague. It is good to know that inscrutable judgments occasionally alleviate the conflicts chaos.

Yet, subservience to subjective and local values would be dangerous and unsound as a general policy. Cavers seems to envisage disintegration of conflicts rules as the consequence of his postulate of just results and, by way of palliation, recommends re-enforcement of the doctrine of stare decisis and recourse to standards.[85] Such programs, not sufficiently detailed, are disturbing.

---

[85] Cavers, *A Critique of the Choice-of-Law Problem,* 47 Harv. L. Rev. 173, 196 (1933). Recently Cavers himself has confessed troublesome doubts concerning his reference to social and economic considerations. Book Review, 56 Harv. L. Rev. 1170, 1173 (1943).

Brainerd Currie, Methods and Objectives in the Conflict of Laws
1959 Duke L.J. 171

The central problem of conflict of laws may be defined... as that of determining the appropriate rule of decision when the interests of two or more states are in conflict—in other words, of determining which interest shall yield. The problem would not exist if this were one world, with an all-powerful central government. It would not exist (though other problems of "conflict of laws" would) if the independent sovereignties in the real world had identical laws. So long, however, as we have a diversity of laws, we shall have conflicts of interest among states. Hence, unless something is done, the administration of private law where more than one state is concerned will be affected with disuniformity and uncertainty. To avoid this result by all reasonable means is certainly a laudable objective; but how? Not by establishing a single government; even if such a thing were remotely thinkable as a practical possibility, we attribute positive values to the principle of self-determination for localities and groups. The attainment of uniformity of laws among diverse states is, to put it mildly, a long-range undertaking. Federations could be established wherein the central government, while not disturbing the autonomy of the states in their internal policies, would determine which of several interests must yield in case of conflict. Treaties might be useful in the accomplishment of the same purpose, but this approach to solution has certain inherent difficulties. For various reasons, the political measures which would seem to be the only possible means of avoiding or adequately solving such problems have not done the job.

We do not, however, despair. We turn, instead, to the resources of jurisprudence, placing our faith primarily in the judges rather than the lawmakers. The judicial function is not narrowly confined; we indulge the hope that it may even be equal to the ambitious task of bringing uniformity and certainty into a world whose conflicts political action has failed to resolve. At first, of course, the judges will not be so bold (or so frank) as to avow that they are assuming the high political function of passing upon the relative merits of the conflicting policies, or interests, of sovereign states. They will address themselves to metaphysical question concerning the nature of law and its abstract operation in space—matters remote from mundane policies and conflicts of interest—and will evolve a set of rules for determining which state's law must, in the nature of things, control. If all states can be persuaded to adhere to these rules, the seemingly impossible will have been accomplished: there will be uniformity and certainty in the administration of private law from state to state. The fact that this goal will be achieved at the price of sacrificing state interests is not emphasized; rather, it is obscured by the metaphysical apparatus of the method.

The rules so evolved have not worked and cannot be made to work. In our times, we have suffered particularly from the jurisprudential theory which has been compounded in order to explain and justify the assumption by the courts of so extraordinary a function. The territorialist conception has been directly responsible for indefensible results and, what is perhaps worse, has therefore driven some of our ablest scholars to consume their energies in purely defensive action against it. But the root of the trouble goes deeper. In attempting to use the rules we encounter difficulties which do not stem from the fact that the particular rules are bad, nor from the fact that a particular theoretical explanation is unsound, but rather from the fact that we have such rules at all.

First, such rules create problems which did not exist before. . . .

Second, the false problems created by the rules may be solved in a quite irrational way—e.g., by defeating the interest of one state without advancing the interest of another. In at least some instances, this result could be avoided by contriving a different rule; but the substitute rule may be objectionable on other grounds. . . .

Third, despite the camouflage of discourse, the rules do operate to nullify state interests. The fact that this is often done capriciously, without reference to the merits of the respective policies and even without recognition of their existence, is only incidental. Trouble enough comes from the mere fact that interests are defeated. The courts simply will not remain always oblivious to the true operation of a system which, though speaking the language of metaphysics, strikes down the legitimate application of the policy of a state, especially when that state is the forum. Consequently, the system becomes complicated. It is loaded with escape devices: the concept of "local public policy" as a basis for not applying the "applicable" law; the concept of "fraud on the law"; the device of novel or disingenuous characterization; the device of manipulating the connecting fact; and, not least, the provision of sets of rules which are interchangeable at will. The tensions which are induced by imposing such a system on a setting of conflict introduce a very serious element of uncertainty and unpredictability even if there is fairly general agreement on the rules themselves. A sensitive and ingenious court can detect an absurd result and avoid it; I am inclined to think that this has been done more often than not and that therein lies a major reason why the system has managed to survive. At the same time, we constantly run the risk that the court may lack sensitivity and ingenuity; we are handicapped in even presenting the issue in its true light; and instances of mechanical application of the rules to produce indefensible results are by no means rare. Whichever of these phenomena is the more common, it is a poor defense of the system to say that the unacceptable results which will inevitably produce can be averted by disingenuousness if the courts are sufficiently alert.

Fourth, where several states have different policies, and also legitimate interests in the application of their policies, a court is in no position to "weigh" the competing interests, or value their relative merits, and choose between them accordingly. This is especially evident when we consider two coordinate states, with such decisions being made by the courts of one or the other. A court need never hold the interest of the foreign state inferior; it can simply apply it own law as such. But when the court, in a true conflict situation, holds the foreign law applicable, it is assuming a great deal: it is holding the policy, or interest, of its own state inferior and preferring the policy or interest of the foreign state. Nor are we much better off if we vest this extraordinary power in a superior judicial establishment, such as our federal courts in the exercise of their diversity jurisdiction, or the Supreme Court tin the exercise of its power to review state court decisions. True, such a superimposed tribunal escapes the embarrassment of having to nullify the interests of its own sovereign; but the difficulty remains that the task is not one be performed by a court. I know that courts make law, and that in the process they "weigh conflicting interests" and draw upon all sorts of "norms" to inform and justify their action. I do not know where to draw the line between the judicial legislation which is "molecular," or permissible, and that which is "molar," or impermissible. But assessment of the respective values of the competing legitimate interests of two sovereign states, in order to determine which is to prevail, is a political function of a very high order. This is a function which should not be committed to courts in a democracy. It is a function which the courts cannot perform effectively, for they lack the necessary resources. Not even a very ponderous Brandeis brief could marshall the relevant considerations in choosing, for example, between the interest of the state of employment and that of the state of injury in matters concerning workmen's compensation. This is a job for a legislative committee, and determining the policy to be formulated on the basis of the information assembled is a job for a competent legislative body. We, of course, have such a competent legislative body in Congress; but it has not seen fit to exercise its powers under the full-faith-and-credit clause in such a way as to contribute to the resolution of true conflicts of interest. . . .

We would be better off without choice-of-law rules. We would be better off if Congress were to give some attention to problems of private law, and were to legislate concerning the choice between conflicting state interests in some of the specific area in which the need for solutions is serious. In the meantime, we would be better off if we would admit the teachings of sociological jurisprudence into the conceptualistic precincts of conflict of laws. This would imply a basic method along the following lines:

1. Normally, even in cases involving foreign elements, the court should be expected, as a matter of course, to apply the rule of decision found in the law of the forum.
2. When it is suggested that the law of a foreign state should furnish the rule of decision, the court should, first of all, determine the governmental policy expressed in the law of the forum. It should then inquire whether the relation of the forum to the case is such as to provide a legitimate basis for the assertion of an interest in the application of that policy. This process is essentially the familiar one of construction or interpretation. Just as we determine by that process how a statute applies in time, and how it applies to marginal domestic situations, so we may determine how it should be applied to cases involving foreign elements in order to effectuate the legislative purpose.
3. If necessary, the court should similarly determine the policy expressed by the foreign law, and whether the foreign state has an interest in the application of its policy.

4. If the court finds that the forum state has no interest in the application of its policy, but that the foreign state has, it should apply the foreign law.
5. If the court finds that the forum state has an interest in the application of its policy, it should apply the law of the forum, even though the foreign also has an interest in the application of its contrary policy, and, a fortiori, it should apply the law of the forum if the foreign state has no such interest....

The suggested analysis does not imply the ruthless pursuit of self-interest by the states.... [T]here is no need to exclude the possibility of rational altruism: for example, when a state has determined upon the policy of placing upon local industry all the social costs of the enterprise, it may well decide to adhere to this policy regardless of where the harm occurs and who the victim is. [Moreover,] there is room for restraint and enlightenment in the determination of what state policy is and where state interests lie....

I have been told that I give insufficient recognition to governmental policies other than those which are expressed in specific statutes and rules: the policy of promoting a general legal order, that of fostering amicable relations with other states, that of vindicating reasonable expectations, and so on. If this is so, it is not, I hope, because of a provincial lack of appreciation of the worth of those ideals, but because of a felt necessity to emphasize the obstacles which the present system interposes to any intelligent approach to the problem. Let us first clear away the apparatus which creates false problems and obscures the nature of the real ones. Only then can we effectively set about ameliorating the ills which arise from a diversity of laws by bringing to bear all the resources of jurisprudence, politics, and humanism—each in its appropriate way.

Comments and Questions

1. Professor Currie's approach has been very influential. But do you agree with him that the basic problem in conflicts of law is reconciling or resolving the conflicting interests of different jurisdictions?

2. Is Currie's approach unduly biased toward forum law?

3. (How) Does Currie's approach incorporate multistate values into his model? What are some multistate values?

4. Harmonization of Substantive Law

A fourth way of dealing with the problem focuses on commonalities rather than on differences. The substantive law approach asks whether there is an interstate or international rule on point. This was the way in which Justice Joseph Story, the great conflicts scholar, dealt with an interstate negotiable instruments problem in *Swift v. Tyson*. Justice Story's opinion in Swift eliminated the possible conflict between the asserted New York requirement of consideration and whatever rule may have prevailed in Maine, where the bill of exchange at bar was dated, by invoking a federal common-law rule derived from a supranational law merchant.

As far as sales contracts are concerned, Justice Story's approach has, in a way, become positive law: Article 2 of the Uniform Commercial Code largely eliminates conflicts within the United States. And internationally, the 1980 Vienna Convention on Contracts for the International Sale of Goods, which the United States and most developed countries have ratified, lays down substantive rules governing the sale of merchandise across national boundaries. Thus, both within the United States and worldwide there now exists, once again, a uniform commercial law of sales.

Of course, American sales law is not entirely uniform because the versions of Article 2 enacted by different states vary and the courts of each state may construe even identical provisions differently. As far as international sales are concerned, the modern lex mercatoria had to take the form of an international compact to become the supreme law of the land. This is not what Justice Story had in mind when, in Swift v. Tyson, he talked about "the law...of the commercial world," which is to say a set of rules that is not the law of any particular state and does not owe its existence to treaties among nations. Rules of international commercial law do not necessarily require the exercise of sovereign prerogatives. The law merchant to which the great judge and conflicts scholar referred, the roots of which reach back to the Roman ius gentium, emerged from commercial custom during the Middle Ages, when it helped Europe to escape from the Dark Ages that followed the fall of the Roman Empire.

This revival of Western culture preceded the existence of territorial states and their claim to a monopoly in law making. Once the world was divided into nation states, legal positivists, such as Justice Holmes, denied that such a set of rules on the practice of private parties could still exist. But, while the U.S. Supreme Court has adopted Holmes' view, see Erie R.R. v. Tompkins, 304 U.S. 64 (1938), a respectable array of current scholarly opinion maintains that modern realities, in particular the prevalence of arbitration as the means of resolving commercial disputes, have spawned a new law merchant. Accordingly, the substantive law approach to multistate and multinational problems presents, even now, a possible alternative to the traditional multilateral and unilateral methodologies.

C. National Practice

1. United States

Stephen C. McCaffrey, Conflict of Laws in the United States

The U.S. Legal System: A Practice Handbook 119 (1983)

This brief treatment of choice-of-law in the United States will be divided into three parts: The first will describe the traditional approaches to choice-of-law as well as the endemic problems that have led to their substantial abandonment; the second will survey some of the leading modern choice-of-law approaches; and the third will discuss statutory choice-of-law rules.

Traditional Choice of Law Doctrine

Historical Background

... Professor Joseph H. Beale... was the Reporter for the American Law Institute's first Restatement of the Law of Conflict of Laws, which appeared in 1934, and published his own three-volume treatise on the subject a year later. While Beale's theories did not go unquestioned among conflicts scholars, together they formed a body of rules which were generally accepted by American courts.

The "Vested Rights" Doctrine of Joseph Beale and the First Restatement of Conflicts

This theory reconciled giving extraterritorial effect to foreign causes of action with the then-popular notion that all laws are territorial by reasoning that the court, rather than applying the foreign law, merely enforced a "foreign-created right."...

The hallmark of the Bealean vested rights approach to choice of law was its mechanistic simplicity. The first Restatement of Conflicts laid down hard-and-fast rules; it did not offer loose guidelines or flexible principles. Ambiguity was an anathema, and therein lay the doctrine's greatest theoretical advantages: its proponents maintained that it produced uniformity of results, and thus discouraged "forum shopping"; and that it produced results that were certain and predictable, ensuring what has been referred to as "conflicts justice". But, as Professor Currie has observed, uniformity of result will occur only if all courts use the system in precisely the same way. Thus, courts in two different states would decide a case in the same way under the traditional method only

> if both states (a) characterize the problem in the same way, as [e.g.,] one involving the validity of a contract, and (b) apply the rule that the law of the place of making governs (rather than some alternative rule), and (c) locate the connecting factor (the place of making) in the same way, and (d) not invoke any second-line defenses, such as local public policy. This is a long list of 'ifs'.... The ideal of uniformity of result is, therefore, to some extent illusory.

The very rigidity of the first Restatement's vested rights doctrine proved to be its ultimate undoing. Courts concerned with reaching a just result in the individual case on a principled basis began to resort to various techniques which would allow them to avoid undesirable outcomes that would have been produced by straightforward applications of the Restatement's rules. These "escape devices" included the use of characterization of the issue at hand—both in terms of whether it was substantive or procedural in nature, and as to the nature of the cause of action (such as, tort or contract); the use of renvoi to reach a pre-ordained result; and the invocation of forum public policy as a bar to the application of an "offensive" foreign law. This section will consider the operation of these escape devices in greater detail after surveying the first Restatement's choice-of-law rules in tort and contract cases as representative examples of its general approach.

(a) Torts

Section 378 of the first Restatement sets forth the generally applicable law in tort cases, the lex loci delicti: "The law of the place of wrong determines whether a person has sustained a legal injury." Section 377 defines the "place of wrong" to be "the state where the last event necessary to make an actor liable for an alleged tort takes place." Thus, the place of wrong, and therefore the jurisdiction whose law would be applied, would be, e.g. the place where the bullet enters the victim's body, not the place from which it is shot; the place where poison "takes effect within the body", i.e., produces illness, not the place from which it is sent to the victim, where it is ingested, or where the victim dies; the place where noxious fumes cause property damage, not the place from which the emanate; the place where loss is sustained as the result of fraudulent misrepresentations, not the place where those representations are made; and the place where a defamatory statement is communicated, not the place from which it is broadcast.

(b) Contracts

The Law made applicable in contract cases by the first Restatement depends upon the issue involved: matters concerning the validity of a promise (including the capacity of the parties to enter into a contract) and its effect are governed by the law of the place of contracting;[39] matters concerning performance of the contract are governed by the law of the place of performance.[40] In general, the "place of contracting" was the place where the last act occurred that was necessary under the "general law of contracts" to make the contract binding, assuming hypothetically that the local law of the place where such act occurred rendered the contract binding.... The Restatement also specifies in great detail where the place of contracting would be when the acceptance of an offer is authorized to be communicated in various different ways, such as by mail (where the acceptance is mailed); by telegraph (where the acceptance is received by the telegraph company for transmission); and by telephone (where the acceptance is spoken). It even provides for the unlikely situation where "a contract is made by word of mouth between two persons standing on opposite sides of a state boundary line," in which case "the place of contracting is where the acceptor speaks at the time he makes his acceptance".

The "place of performance" is defined by Section 355 as "the State where, either by specific provision or by interpretation of the language of the promise, the promise is to be performed". The law of the place governs the details of performance, including the manner, time and locality, and sufficiency of performance, as well as the persons by whom or to whom performance is to be made and excuses for non-performance.

It is obvious that the first Restatement's entire system of rules concerning the law applicable in contract cases assumes that contract issues are neatly divisible into two groups: those concerning the underlying obligation and those concerning

[39] Ibid., Section 332.

[40] Ibid., Section 358.

performance. Yet the Restatement itself admits, in an uncharacteristic display of candid realism, that "there is no logical line which separates questions of the obligation of the contract, which is determined by the law of the place of contracting, from questions of performance, determined by the law of the place of performance". But while logic is useless, the Restatement asserts that "a practical line is drawn in every case by the particular circumstances thereof". Such a "practical line" is reached, according to the Restatement, when, e.g., application of the law of the place of contracting would determine issues concerning the details of performance. Yet, it is recognized that even this line is not one "which can be fixed by any rule of law of universal application to all cases. Like all questions of degree," the Restatement concluded, "the solution must depend upon the circumstances of each case and must be governed by the exercise of judgment".

Thus, while the Restatement's rules themselves are typified by dogmatic rigidity, a court applying those rules may still have some latitude. This would be true in situations like the present one, where the issue involved does not fit clearly within one of the Restatement's categories. The need for the "exercise of judgment" in such cases obviously leaves the door open to result-conscious application of the Restatement's rules, which in turn frustrates its primary objectives of certainty, predictability, and uniformity of result. Characterization of an issue as relating either to the contractual obligation or to performance of the contract is one form of "escape device" courts could use to avoid results they perceive as undesirable. This and other escape devices are the subject of the next section.

Circumvention of Rigid Rules through "Escape Devices"

As stated above, the devices used by courts to escape the confining choice-of-law rules of the traditional approach are of three types: characterization; renvoi; and public policy. This section will briefly illustrate the use of these techniques in order to indicate the need perceived by many courts for more flexible approaches to selecting the applicable law.

(a) Characterization

This type of escape device may be subdivided into two categories: characterization of the issue as substantive or procedural; and characterization of the nature of the cause of action.

(1) Substance versus procedure—The first Restatement provides in Section 585 that "[a]ll matters of procedure are governed by the law of the forum."[54] And the determination of whether a given question is one of substance or procedure is made by the forum court according to its own conflicts rules (Section 584). The Restatement does, however, contain a number of specific directives concerning

---

[54] The rationale for this rule is given in the Introductory Note to Chapter 12 of the *Restatement*. The purpose of the rule is to allow courts to conduct proceedings in accordance with procedures with which they are familiar. The *Restatement* counsels, however, that the "procedural" label is to be used restrictively in order to allow application of the appropriate foreign law to the greatest extent possible, toward the end of the uniformity of result.

issues to which the law of the forum is to apply (Sections, 585 et. seq.). But it is impossible to provide for every situation, and, to the extent that the Restatement's provisions have not been specifically adopted by statutory or case law, the courts are not bound to follow them in any event. As a result, procedural labels were sometimes attached to issues that seemed clearly substantive. In Kilberg v. Northeast Airlines, Inc.,[55] for example, the New York Court of Appeals (the highest court in the state of New York) refused to apply a Massachusetts limitation on wrongful death recoveries on the ground, inter alia, that the measure of damages was a remedial, or "procedural" issue, and was thus governed by the law of the forum. Thus, while there are good reasons for applying the lex fori to matters of procedure, the need to decide which issues are "procedural" and which are "substantive" gave courts an opportunity to manipulate the first Restatement's rules with a view toward reaching a pre-ordained result.

(2) Nature of the action—Use of the vested rights approach necessitates identification of the type of action before the court—such as, tort or contract. While in many cases the cause of action will admit only one characterization, it will often be possible for plaintiff and defendant to take different views as to the nature of the action. This can be used to the litigant's advantage by selecting that category which will lead to the law most favorable to their respective positions. Thus, in Haumschild v. Continental Cas. Co.,[58] a woman sued her husband in Wisconsin, the state of their domicile, to recover for injuries she had sustained in a California automobile accident. Under California law, a woman could not sue her husband in tort; under Wisconsin law, she could. The trial court treated the suit as a tort action and applied California law as the lex loci delicti. The Supreme Court of Wisconsin reversed, finding that "incapacity to sue because of marital status presents a question of family law rather than tort law," and that therefore the law of the spouses' domicile should apply.

(b) Renvoi

The term "renvoi" applies to the situation encountered when the choice-of-law rule of the State of the applicable law refers back to the law of the forum State (remission) or on to the law of a third State (transmission). Thus, for example, in a case involving the validity of a testamentary disposition of movables, the forum's choice-of-law rule might refer to the law of the decedent's domicile at death; but the choice-of-law rule of the state of the decedent's domicile might refer back to the lex fori as the law of the state of the decedent's nationality. If the latter reference is taken as being to the "whole law" of the forum (including its choice-of-law rules), the court is presented with the problem of how to escape the potentially endless oscillation between the conflicts rules of the forum and the state of the decedent's domicile. Three solutions are possible:

(1) Rejection of the renvoi: Here, the court takes the initial reference of the forum's choice-of-law rule as being to the internal law of the foreign state, not to

---

[55] 9 N.Y.2d 34, 172 N.E.2d 526 (1961). *Kilberg* was an action to recover for the wrongful death of a New York resident who had been killed when the plane in which he was traveling crashed at Nantucket, Massachusetts, in the course of a flight from New York to Nantucket.

[58] 7 Wis.2d 130, 95 N.W.2d 814 (1959).

its whole law. In the above hypothetical case, this would result in forum's applying the domiciliary state's local substantive law rules concerning validity of wills, and never looking to its choice-of-law rule.

(2) Partial acceptance of the renvoi: Here, the court takes the reference of the forum's conflicts rule as being to the whole law of the foreign State, but treats the foreign choice-of-law rules as referring back to the internal law of the forum State.

(3) Total acceptance of the renvoi: Here, the court endeavors to place itself in the position of the foreign court and decide the case as it would. Thus, in the above hypothetical case, if a court in the domiciliary State would refer to the whole law of the nationality State, the forum would do likewise, but would then treat the forum/nationality State's conflicts rule as referring to the local law of the domiciliary State. It will be noted that this result is the same as would have been reached had the renvoi been rejected altogether.

Renvoi affords courts manifest opportunities to circumvent hard-and-fast choice-of-law rules: In the absence of controlling statutory or decisional law, a court may simply decide which state's law it wishes to apply, and get off the renvoi merry-go-round in that jurisdiction. The first Restatement, however, rejected the renvoi, providing that where the forum's choice-of-law refers to the law of a foreign state, that reference should be taken as being to the internal law of such State (Section 7). But the Restatement did create exceptions for cases involving title to land and validity of a divorce, as to which it provided that the applicable law would be that of the situs, and of the domicile of the parties, respectively, including the conflict rules of those states. The reason usually given for this exception is that uniformity of result, irrespective of where the suit is brought, is particularly important in these kinds of cases. Yet, the exception does leave the door open to judicial result selection.

(c) Public Policy

The first conflicts Restatement provides in Section 612 that "[n]o action can be maintained upon a cause of action created in another state the enforcement of which is contrary to the strong public policy of the forum". In the comments to that section, the Restatement emphasizes that its "application . . . is extremely limited".[64] Still, the claim that otherwise applicable foreign law violates forum public policy is just one more weapon in the arsenal of courts wishing to avoid applying the law mandated by the traditional rules. Thus, in the Kilberg case adverted to above, one of the grounds used by the New York court for refusing to give effect to the wrongful death damages limitation of the place of the injury (Massachusetts) was that such limitations on recovery are offensive to New York's public policy of providing full compensation to the estates of its residents.[66] . . .

---

64 *Restatement*, *supra* n. 9, Section 612, Comment *c*.

66 See also *Rosenthal v. Warren* 475 F.2d 438 (2d. Cir. 1973) (applying New York law); and *Mertz v. Mertz*, 271 N.Y. 466 (1936) (New York public policy of interspousal immunity prevents suit by wife against husband for a tort occurring where such suits were allowed). Cf. *Miller v. Miller*, 42 N.Y. 2d 12 (1968)

"Modern" Choice-of-Law Approaches

The vested rights doctrine had come under heavy attack even before publication of the first conflicts Restatement in 1934. Disquieted by the rigidity of the traditional approach, a number of scholars began in the 1920's to advocate the use of choice-of-law methodologies which took social and economic policies into account and which would permit a court to consider the justness of the result that a particular choice-of-law would produce....

In 1953, the American Law Institute began work on the Restatement of the Law Second, Conflict of Laws (hereinafter referred to as the Second Restatement), which was not to be published in final form until 1971. The Reporter for the Second Restatement was Professor Willis L.M. Reese of Columbia University. The project, which "started as a modest update and expansion of Professor Beale's Restatement—one which would provide...somewhat more flexible jurisdiction-selecting rules—was gradually compromised by a grudging and finally more whole-hearted acceptance of Policy analysis."...

Courts and commentators differ sharply on the question of whether the "cure" (the modern approaches) is worse than the "malady" (the traditional approach). Not only do most of the modern approaches sacrifice certainty and predictability on the alter of policy analysis; their complexity and sheer number is enough to bewilder even the most dedicated judge. This latter phenomenon alone has prompted one scholar to caution that judges cannot be expected to invest in a choice-of-law question the time it would take to stay current on, and properly apply, the modern theories.[74]

This section on "modern" choice-of-law theories will focus principally on the approach of the Second Restatement but will also offer a brief description of the approaches of four prominent writers to illustrate current American thought in the choice-of-law field.

The "Most Significant Relationship" Doctrine of the Second Restatement

As mentioned above, the Second Restatement of Conflicts, which entirely superseded the first, took a wholly different approach to choice-of-law from that of its predecessor. The nub of the difference between the two approaches is illustrated as follows in the "Introduction" to the Second Restatement:

The earlier Restatement treated choice-of-law in torts and contracts by articulating a closed set of rules derived from vested rights analysis. The governing law in torts was determined by the place in which the injury occurred; that in contracts by the place in which the contract became binding or, when performance was in issue, where the contract was to be performed. Restatement Second supplants these rules by the broad principle that rights and liabilities with respect to a particular issue are determined by the local law of the State, which, as to that issue, has the most significant relationship to the occurrence and the parties. The factors

---

[74] Leflar, "Choice of Law; A Well-Watered Plateau," *Law Contemporary Problems* (1977), Volume 41, pp. 10, 11, 12.

relevant to that appraisal, absent a binding statutory mandate, are enumerated generally (Section 6) to include:

(a) the needs of the interstate and international systems,
(b) the relevant policies of the forum,
(c) the relevant policies of the other interested states and the relative interests of those states in the determination of the particular issue,
(d) the protection of justified expectations,
(e) the basic policies underlying the particular field of law,
(f) certainty, predictability and uniformity of result, and
(g) ease in the determination and application of the law to be applied

The Institute recognized that "the jettisoning of...rigid rules in favor of standards of greater flexibility...reduces certitude", and "leaves the answer to specific problems very much at large." Therefore, after laying down "general principles" for each field of law, the Second Restatement provides a "secondary statement...setting forth the choice-of-law the courts will usually make in given situations."[78]...

The balance of this section will be devoted to surveying the Second Restatement's approach to identifying the applicable law in tort and contract cases, as was done with the first Restatement, and to taking a brief look at the manner in which the Second Restatement deals with the three kinds of "escape devices" used in conjunction with the traditional approach.

(a) Torts

...Section 145 sets forth the "general principle" applicable "to all torts and to all issues in tort. ..."

(1) The rights and liabilities of the parties with respect to an issue in tort are determined by the local law of the state which, with respect to that issue, has the most significant relationship to the occurrence and the parties under the principles stated in Section 6.
(2) Contacts to be taken into account in applying the principles of Section 6 to determine the law applicable to an issue include:
    (a) the place where the injury occurred,
    (b) the place where the conduct causing the injury occurred,
    (c) the domicile, residence, nationality, place of incorporation and place of business of the parties, and
    (d) the place where the relationship, if any, between the parties is centered."

These contacts are to be evaluated according to their relative importance with respect to the particular issue....

The comments to Section 146 provide some guidance for the evaluation process, suggesting that the extent to which another State has a more significant relationship to the occurrence and the parties than the injury State will depend largely upon

[78] Ibid., p. VIII.

whether the "other State has a greater interest in the determination of the particular issue than the state where the injury occurred... The likelihood that some State other than that where the injury occurred is the State of most significant relationship is greater in those relatively rare situations where, with respect to the particular issue, the state of injury bears little relation to the occurrence and the parties."[83]...

(b) Contracts

...It will be recalled that the original Restatement divided contract issues into those concerning validity and those concerning performance, for choice-of-law purposes. It provided that issues of validity are governed by the law of the place where the last act occurred that was necessary to give the contract binding effect (Section 332), and that issues of performance are governed by the law of the place where the last act occurred that was necessary to give the contract binding effect (Section 332), and that issues of performance are governed by the law of the place of performance (Section 358). The Second Restatement's approach differs from that of its predecessor in four principal respects:[93] First, while the original Restatement did not acknowledge that the parties had the power to choose the law governing their contract, the Second Restatement does (Section 187); second, issues of validity are no longer governed by the law of the place of contracting, but, following the Second Restatement's general formula, by the law of the State which, with respect to the particular issue, has the most significant relationship to the transaction and the parties (Section 188); third, the Second Restatement does not draw the sharp distinction between issues of validity and performance that characterized the first Restatement's approach; and finally, while the original Restatement distinguished between different kinds of contracts only with respect to locating the place of contracting, the Second Restatement provides special choice-of-law for nine different kinds of contracts.

Section 186 of the Second Restatement states the basic principal that "[i]ssues in contract are determined by the law chosen by the parties in accordance with the rule of Section 187 and otherwise by the law selected in accordance with the rule of Section 188". Section 187 sets forth in some detail the circumstances under which party choice of law will be respected. The first paragraph directs the court to apply the law chosen by the parties "if the particular issue is one which the parties could have resolved by an explicit provision in their agreement directed to that issue". As examples of issues the parties could not have resolved by such a provision the Restatement gives questions involving capacity, formalities and substantial validity.[94] Paragraph 2 of Section 187 provides that the law chosen by the parties will be applied even if the issue involved is not one that the parties could have resolved by a provision in their agreement, unless:

---

83 *Restatement* 2d, Section 146, Comment C, referring implicitly to factors (b) and (c) of Section 6.

93 *Restatement* 2d, Introductory Note to Chapter 8, Contracts, p. 558.

94 Ibid., Section 187, Comment d. "A person cannot vest himself with contractual capacity by stating in the contract that he has such capacity. He cannot dispense with formal requirements such as that of a writing, by agreeing with the other party that the contract shall be binding without them. Not can he by a similar device, avoid issues of substantial validity, such as whether the contract is illegal."

(a) the chosen State has no substantial relationship to the parties or the transaction and there is no other reasonable basis for the parties' choice, or
(b) application of the law of the chosen State would be contrary to a fundamental policy of a state which has a materially greater interest than the chosen State in the determination of the particular issue and which, under the rule of Section 188, would be the State of the applicable law in the absence of an effective choice-of-law by the parties."

The rule of Section 187 applies even where there is no express provision in the contract concerning the applicable law, so long as the court can determine from the contract's provisions that the parties had the law of a particular State in mind. "So the fact that the contract contains legal expressions, or makes reference to legal doctrines, that are peculiar to the local law of a particular State may provide persuasive evidence that the parties wished to have this law applied."

The rationale given by the Second Restatement for allowing the chosen law to govern even issues that the parties could not have determined by an explicit agreement is essentially that this furthers the prime objective of contract law, protecting the parties' justified expectations and enabling them to predict accurately what their rights and liabilities will be under the contract. The qualifications to party autonomy given in subparagraph (a) of Section 187 simply require that the State whose law is selected have some substantial relationship to the parties or the contract. If so, the parties will be considered to have had a reasonable basis for their choice. Such a relationship could be supplied, for example by the fact that the chosen State was the place of performance or the domicile of one of the parties. But the Second Restatement recognizes that the parties may have a reasonable basis for choosing a given State's law even where neither they nor the contract may have any contacts with the State whose law is chosen. This would be the case, for example, where the parties were unfamiliar with each other's legal systems but were familiar with that of a third State, and where the latter was particularly well developed in the field of the contract's subject matter.

The qualification to party autonomy given in subparagraph (b) of Section 187 allows the court to refuse to respect the parties' choice on the ground that the law chosen would contravene "a fundamental policy", not necessarily of the forum, but of a State which has a greater interest than the chosen State and whose law would be applicable in the absence of an effective party choice. The Restatement points out that mere difference in the two laws will not justify a court in refusing to apply the chosen law; rather, the court is to decline to honor the parties' choice only:

(1) to protect a fundamental policy of the State which, under rule of Section 188, would be the State of the otherwise applicable law, provided
(2) that this State has a materially greater interest than the State of the chosen law in the determination of the particular issue.

The forum is to apply its own law in determining whether the policy is a "fundamental" one. As illustrations of policies which are likely to be considered "fundamental" the Restatement cites those embodied in statutes making certain contracts illegal, or those designed to protect parties with relatively weak bargaining positions. Those not likely to be found fundamental, on the other hand, are policies relating to formalities (such as the statute of frauds) or those represented by rules "tending to become obsolete", such as those relating to the capacity of married women. The "fundamental policy" as used in Section 187 and "public policy": "To be fundamental within the meaning of the present rule, a policy need not be as strong as would be required to justify the forum in refusing to entertain suit upon a foreign cause of action...."

The Second Restatement's final "general principle" concerning contracts covers cases in which there is no effective choice-of-law by the parties. Section 188 provides that, in the absence of effective party choice, the applicable law will be that of the State with the most significant relationship to the transaction and the parties. The State of the most significant relationship is to be determined by evaluating the following factual contracts in light of the choice-of-law principles stated in Section 6: the place of contracting; the place of negotiation; the place of performance; the location of the subject matter of the contract; and the domicile, residence, nationality, place of incorporation and place of business of the parties. The third paragraph of Section 188 provides that where "the place of negotiating the contract and the place of performance are in the same State, the local law of this State will usually be applied, except as otherwise provided in Sections 189–199 [concerning particular kinds of contracts and the issues of capacity and formalities] and 203 [concerning usury]".

The Second Restatement's rules concerning "Particular Contracts" create what amounts to a presumptively applicable law, but then allow that law to be displaced if there is another State with a more significant relationship to the transaction and the parties. The types of contracts covered and the law made presumptively applicable are as follows: transfer of interest in land (situs); contractual duties arising from the transfer of interests in land (situs); sale of interests in chattels (State where seller is to deliver chattel); life insurance contracts (domicil of insured at time policy was applied for); fire, surety or casualty insurance contracts (principal location of insured risk); suretyship (law governing principal obligation); repayment of loans (place of repayment); rendition of services (place where services, or major portion thereof, to be rendered); and transportation (place of departure or dispatch)....

(c) The Second Restatement's Treatment of "Escape Devices"

Inasmuch as many of the Restatement's rules eventually came to be circumvented through the use of the "escape devices" of characterization, renvoi and forum policy, the question of whether the Second Restatement has made any efforts to seal off these escape routes merits brief attention. It will be recalled that the first Restatement provided that "all matters of procedure are governed by the law of the forum" (Section 585), thus giving courts an open invitation to characterize those issues as procedural to which they wished forum law to apply. The Second Restatement devotes an entire chapter to "Procedure" (Chapter 6), dividing the subject into three topic: "The General Principle" (Topic 1, (Section 122); "Specific Applications of General Principle" (Topic 2, Sections 123–143) and "Conversion of

Foreign Currency" (Topic 3, Section 144). It eschews the broad "substance-procedure dichotomy" in favor of a narrower and more specific definition of the types of issues to which the law of the forum should apply. As to those issues, the forum is that State of the most significant relationship "merely because it is the State where the litigation is conducted...."[104] Uncharacteristically, the Second Restatement finds that as to most of the issues treated in the Chapter on Procedure, "it is possible to state categorically that the local law of the forum will be applied."[105]

The "General Principle" concerning procedure is stated in Section 122, which provides as follows:

Section 122. Issues Relating to Judicial Administration

> A court usually applies its own local law rules prescribing how litigation shall be conducted even when it applies the local rules of another State to resolve other issues in the case.

As examples of issues relating to judicial administration the Second Restatement gives "the proper form of action, service of process, pleading, rules of discovery, mode of trial and execution and costs".[106] The Second Restatement recognizes that some issues clearly relate to judicial administration, others clearly relate to the rights and liabilities of the parties, and still others "fall into a gray area [in] between...."[107] As mentioned, it undertakes to provide "categorical rules" calling for those issues falling clearly into the former area to be governed by the law of the forum.[108] Other issues susceptible of being categorized as "procedural" are generally subjected to the law of the forum, unless they would affect the outcome of the case (Sections 128, 133, 134) or unless another State has dominant interest in the issue (Section 132).

The other type of characterization, that concerning the nature of the action, is dealt with in Section 7 of the Second Restatement, which provides in paragraph three that "classification and interpretation of local law concepts and terms are determined in accordance with the law that governs the issue involved". Thus, forum case law would not be determinative of the nature of the action in a given case unless the forum were the State of the applicable law under its conflicts rules. The problem with this approach, of course, is that characterization of the issue may well be a precondition to determining what law applies.

Section 8 of the Second Restatement deals with renvoi. It provides that, with two exceptions, the forum applies the local law (excluding choice-of-law rules) of

---

[104] *Restatement* 2d, introductory note to Chapter 6.

[105] Ibid.

[106] Ibid., Section 122, Comment A.

[107] Ibid.

[108] See Section 123 (Proper Court), 124 (Form of Action), 126 (Service of Process) 127 (Pleading and Conduct of Proceedings), 129 (Trial by Court or Jury), 130 (Methods of Securing Obedience to Orders of the Court), 131 (Manner of Enforcing Judgement), 136 (Notice and Proof of Foreign Law), 137 (Competency of Witnesses), 138 (Admissibility of Evidence), and 142 (Statute of Limitations, exclusive of "borrowing statutes").

the State whose law it is directed to apply by its own choice-of-law rule. Thus, the Restatement basically rejects the renvoi. The two exceptions to this general rule are contained in subsections 2 and 3 of Section 8 which provide as follows:

> (2) When the objective of the particular choice-of-law rule is that the forum reach the same result on the very facts involved as would the courts of another State, the forum will apply the choice-of-law rules of the other State, subject to considerations of practicability and feasibility.
> (3) When the State of forum has no substantial relationship to the particular issue or the pa rties and the courts of all interested States would concur in selecting the local law rule applicable to this issue, the forum will usually apply this rule.

As examples of cases in which the first exception would apply the Second Restatement gives questions relating to the validity and effect of transfers of interests in land (because the situs State clearly has the dominant interest) and those relating to succession to interests in movables (because "there is an urgent need that all States should apply a single law [here, that of the decedent's domicile at death] in resolving [this] question".). But where these reasons for applying the foreign State's conflicts rules would not be served because the rules are difficult of ascertainment or imprecise, the forum is to apply its own choice-of-law rules. Contract and tort choice-of-law rules are cited as being imprecise; those directing application of the law of the situs of land, of a chattel, or of a person's domicile as being sufficiently precise.

The second exception is subject to the qualification that it only applies when "it is clear that the courts of all interested States would have applied the same local law..." When this is not clear, the exception does not apply and the forum applies its own conflicts rules.

The final type of escape device, public policy, is dealt with in the chapter of the Second Restatement on "Judicial Jurisdiction". Section 90 provides that "[n]o action will be entertained on a foreign cause of action the enforcement of which is contrary to the strong public policy of the forum". The comments to Section 90 emphasize that it "has a narrow scope of application", since it does not apply to situations where the court refuses to give effect to a foreign law on public policy grounds but proceeds to decide the controversy, applying its own local law. Thus, one of the most common uses of public policy as an escape device is not covered. Where Section 90 does apply, the comments caution that "[a]ctions should rarely be dismissed because of the rule of this Section". For example, the mere fact that the foreign rule is different from that of the forum will not justify dismissal on public policy grounds. Rather, the test is whether applying the foreign rule " 'would violate some fundamental principle of justice, some prevalent conception of morals, some deep-seated tradition of the commonwealth'."

Professor Brainerd Currie's "Governmental Interest Analysis"

Professor Currie rejected choice-of-law "rules" in favor of evaluation of the interests of the States involved in the case at hand. He essentially called upon the court to identify the policies underlying the conflicting laws, and to determine whether each of the States involved has an interest in giving effect to its respective policy. If only one State has such an interest, that State's law should be applied, but if the forum and another State both have interests (and the conflict cannot be avoided through reconsideration as explained below) the forum should apply its own law. It is important to note that whereas the Second Restatement calls for the court to weigh the relative interests of the States involved in the determination of the particular issue, Professor Currie views this as not being a proper judicial function. It is for this reason that his approach calls for the forum to apply its law automatically in the event that both it and another State are interested, rather than to attempt to determine which State has a greater interest.

Professor Currie prepared the following summary of his approach for inclusion in one of the leading American conflicts casebooks:

1. When a court is asked to apply the law of a foreign State different from the law of the forum, it should inquire into the policies expressed in the respective laws, and into the circumstances in which it is reasonable for the respective States to assert an interest in the application of those policies. In making these determinations the court should employ the ordinary processes of construction and interpretation.
2. If the court finds that one State has an interest in the application of its policy in the circumstances of the case and the other has none, it should apply the law of the only interested State.
3. If the court finds an apparent conflict between the interests of the two States it should reconsider. A more moderate and restrained interpretation of the policy or interest of one State or the other may avoid conflict.
4. If, upon reconsideration, the court finds that a conflict between the legitimate interests of the two States is unavoidable, it should apply the law of the forum.
5. If the forum is disinterested, but an unavoidable conflict exists between the interests of two other States, and the court cannot with justice decline to adjudicate the case, it should apply the law of the forum, at least if that law corresponds with the law of one of the other States. Alternatively, the court might decide the case by a candid exercise of legislative discretion, resolving the conflict as it believes it would be resolved by a supreme legislative body having power to determine which interest should be required to yield.
6. The conflict of interest between States will result in different dispositions of the same problem, depending on where the action is brought. If with respect to a particular problem this appears seriously to infringe a strong national interest in uniformity of decision, the court should not attempt to improvise a solution sacrificing the legitimate interest of its own State, but should leave to Congress, exercising its powers under the full faith and credit clause, the determination of which interests shall be required to yield.

Thus, under the Currie approach, there are potentially three different types of "conflicts" between the laws in question: The second step of his methodology involves the situation where there is a "false conflict" because one of the rules, when given its intended scope of application, would simply not apply since the policy it embodies would not be furthered by such application. The third step deals with the situation where there is an "apparent conflict", in which case the forum is to attempt to avoid the conflict by endeavoring to interpret the policies or interests of the States involved in a "more moderate and restrained" manner in an effort to avoid the conflict. If this proves impossible, there is a "true conflict" (the fourth step) which can only be resolved by applying the law of the forum (assuming the forum is one of the interested States). It perhaps bears reemphasis that the court is to apply its own law in the event of a true conflict even where it views another State as having a greater interest in the resolution of the issue.

Choice-of-Law Statutes

There are no comprehensive choice-of-law codifications in the United States, either at the State or the Federal level. This is in marked contrast to the situation in Europe. There are, however, several "uniform acts" containing choice-of-law provisions, which have been adopted widely by the States. Of course, any Intra-United States conflicts would be eliminated (and these choice-of-law provisions would be unnecessary) to the extent that the adoption of these acts was indeed "uniform" among all American jurisdictions—a goal which has, as yet, proved elusive.

The Uniform Commercial Code (UCC) has enjoyed the most widespread acceptance of all the uniform laws, having been adopted in all but one of the States. Section 1-105(1) of the UCC allows party choice when the transaction involved "bears a reasonable relation" to the State whose law is chosen. Section 1-105(2) provides, however, that in situations governed by five other Sections of the UCC, the law made applicable by those Sections applies, "and a contrary agreement (party choice) is effective only to the extent permitted by the law (including the conflict of law rules) so specified...."

The Uniform Probate Code contains a provision which validates wills that comply with the requirements of the place of execution or of "the place where at the time of execution or at the time of death the testator is domiciled, has a place of abode or is a national". And the Uniform Securities Act contains a detailed set of mechanical rules that specify the jurisdiction whose law governs a number of different issues.

Choice-of-law directives also may be found in the legislation of individual States governing such fields as worker's compensation and insurance. Another common variety of State conflicts legislation is the so-called "borrowing statute". These statutes are so named because they "borrow" the statute of limitations of the foreign State where the cause of action arose. Thus, for example, if P sued D in State X (where the statute of limitations had not run) for injuries negligently inflicted by D in State Y (where the statute of limitations had run), a State X borrowing statute would require the X court to apply the Y statute of limitations to bar the action.

The principal Federal choice-of-law statute of note is that contained in the Federal Tort Claims Act. This Act prescribes what has been described as "a completely inept and inappropriate choice-of-law rule...," that "the law of the place where the act or omission occurred" determines whether the Federal government is liable in tort. In order to bring this provision into line with the then-prevailing rule that the law of the place of the injury governed tort cases, the United States Supreme Court interpreted the Act as referring to the whole law of the place of the act, including its conflicts rules.

Comments and Questions

1. A contemporary snapshot of the choice-of-law methodologies for each of the states is provided in the following table. Note that some states use different methodologies for torts (T) and contracts (C) cases, respectively.

States	Traditional	Signif. Contacts	Rest. 2d	Interest Analysis	Lex Fori	Better Law	Combined Modern
Alabama	T+C						
Alaska			T+C				
Arizona			T+C				
Arkansas		C				T	
California				T			C
Colorado			T+C				
Connecticut			T+C				
Delaware			T+C				
D.C.				T			C
Florida	C		T				
Georgia	T+C						
Hawaii							T+C
Idaho			T+C				
Illinois			T+C				
Indiana		T+C					
Iowa			T+C				
Kansas	T+C						
Kentucky			C		T		
Louisiana							T+C
Maine			T+C				
Maryland	T+C						
Mass.							T+C
Michigan			C		T		
Minnesota						T+C	
Mississippi			T+C				
Missouri			T+C				
Montana			T+C				

(continued)

States	Traditional	Signif. Contacts	Rest. 2d	Interest Analysis	Lex Fori	Better Law	Combined Modern
Nebraska			T+C				
Nevada		C	T				
New Hamp.			C			T	
New Jersey				T			C
New Mex.	T+C						
New York							T+C
N. Carolina	T	C					
N. Dakota		T					C
Ohio			T+C				
Oklahoma	C		T				
Oregon							T+C
Penna.							T+C
Puerto Rico		T+C					
Rhode Isl.	C					T	
S. Carolina	T+C						
So. Dakota			T+C				
Tennessee	C		T				
Texas			T+C				
Utah			T+C				
Vermont			T+C				
Virginia	T+C						
Washington			T+C				
W. Virginia	T		C				
Wisconsin						T+C	
Wyoming	T+C						
Total (52)	T: 10 C: 12	T: 3 C: 5	T: 23 C: 23	T: 3 C: 0	T: 2 C: 0	T: 5 C: 2	T: 6 C: 10

For more than two decades, Dean and Professor Symeon Symeonides of the Willamette University College of Law has published an annual survey of choice of law doctrine. See, e.g., Symeon Symeonides, Choice of Law in the American Courts in 2007: Twenty-First Annual Survey, 56 Am. J. Comp. L. 243 (2008). His survey includes the methodological table reprinted above.

2. Generally speaking, states use the same system of conflicts rules for both domestic and international conflicts. But because there is considerable flexibility in those conflicts rules, you might anticipate that judges might reach different conclusions as to the applicable law even on similar facts when the conflict is between the laws of California and Texas, in one case, and between California and Brazil, in another. Consider why an American judge might be more inclined to apply the

law of another state rather than that of another country. And consider why an American judge might be less inclined to apply the law of another state rather than that of another country.

3. Of course, contracting parties may be able to negotiate what body of law should govern the interpretation and enforcement of their agreement. Perhaps in exchange for a price concession or perhaps merely to confirm what then is manifest common sense, a provision in an agreement may provide: "This agreement shall be interpreted in accordance with, and governed by, the laws of California." (Would this include California's choice-of-law rules?) Recognizing party autonomy has many obvious benefits, including certainty and predictability for the parties at the time of contracting, and in the event of litigation, the conservation of judicial (and party) resources.

Reread § 187 of the Restatement (Second) of Conflict of Laws quoted above in the excerpt by Professor McCaffrey, and focus on the prerequisites for enforcing a choice-of-law clause. Until very recently, Section 1-105(1) of the Uniform Commercial Code similarly required that a choice of law clause have some "reasonable relationship" to the parties or their transaction. Why impose any prerequisites if the clause was the product of a full and fair bargain? Should a decision by contracting parties to choose some "neutral" state's law be enforced?

As we saw in the context of enforcing forum selection clauses, see Chapter 5, a dispute even among private parties may implicate others' interests. A choice of law clause may oblige the court to apply the substantive law of some foreign jurisdiction with which it is not familiar. More significantly, the substantive law that would apply but for the choice of law clause is displaced—ousting whatever values and public policy that law embodied. Yet choice of law clauses are presumptively valid. Why?

The doctrinal framework for enforcing choice of law clauses is analogous to the doctrinal framework for enforcing forum selection clauses. Is there any reason for courts to be more cautious or suspicious of one or the other?

Lauritzen v. Larsen

345 U.S. 571 (1953)

Mr. Justice Jackson delivered the opinion of the Court.

The key issue in this case is whether statutes of the United States should be applied to this claim of maritime tort. Larsen, a Danish seaman, while temporarily in New York joined the crew of the Randa, a ship of Danish flag and registry, owned by petitioner, a Danish citizen. Larsen signed ship's articles, written in Danish, providing that the rights of crew members would be governed by Danish law and by the employer's contract with the Danish Seamen's Union, of which Larsen was a member. He was negligently injured aboard the Randa in the course of employment, while in Havana harbor.

Respondent brought suit under the Jones Act[1] on the law side of the District Court for the Southern District of New York and demanded a jury. Petitioner contended that Danish law was applicable and that, under it, respondent had received all of the compensation to which he was entitled. He also contested the court's jurisdiction. Entertaining the cause, the court ruled that American rather than Danish law applied, and the jury rendered a verdict of $4,267.50. The Court of Appeals, Second Circuit, affirmed. Its decision, at least superficially, is at variance with its own earlier ones and conflicts with one by the New York Court of Appeals. We granted certiorari.

The shipowner, supported here by the Danish Government, asserts that the Danish law supplies the full measure of his obligation and that maritime usage and international law as accepted by the United States exclude the application of our incompatible statute.

That allowance of an additional remedy under our Jones Act would sharply conflict with the policy and letter of Danish law is plain from a general comparison of the two systems of dealing with shipboard accidents. Both assure the ill or injured seafaring worker the conventional maintenance and cure at the shipowner's cost, regardless of fault or negligence on the part of anyone. But, while we limit this to the period within which maximum possible cure can be effected, the Danish law limits it to a fixed period of twelve weeks, and the monetary measurement is different. The two systems are in sharpest conflict as to treatment of claims for disability, partial or complete, which are permanent, or which outlast the liability for maintenance and cure, to which class this claim belongs. Such injuries Danish law relieves under a state-operated plan similar to our workmen's compensation systems. Claims for such disability are not made against the owner but against the state's Directorate of Insurance Against the Consequences of Accidents. They may be presented directly or through any Danish Consulate. They are allowed by administrative action, not by litigation, and depend not upon fault or negligence but only on the fact of injury and the extent of disability. Our own law, apart from indemnity for injury caused by the ship's unseaworthiness, makes no such compensation for such disability in the absence of fault or negligence. But, when such fault or negligence is established by litigation, it allows recovery for elements such as pain and suffering not compensated under Danish law and lets the damages be fixed by jury. In this case, since negligence was found, United States law permits a larger recovery than Danish law. If the same injury were sustained but negligence was absent or not provable, the Danish law would appear to provide compensation where ours would not.

Respondent does not deny that Danish law is applicable to his case. The contention as stated in his brief is rather that "A claimant may select whatever forum

---

1 "Any seaman who shall suffer personal injury in the course of his employment may, at his election, maintain an action for damages at law, with the right of trial by jury, and in such action all statutes of the United States modifying or extending the common-law right or remedy in cases of personal injury to railway employees shall apply...." 46 U.S.C. § 688.

he desires and receive the benefits resulting from such choice" and "A ship owner is liable under the laws of the forum where he does business as well as in his own country." This contention that the Jones Act provides an optional cumulative remedy is not based on any explicit terms of the Act, which makes no provision for cases in which remedies have been obtained or are obtainable under foreign law. Rather he relies upon the literal catholicity of its terminology. If read literally, Congress has conferred an American right of action which requires nothing more than that plaintiff be "any seaman who shall suffer personal injury in the course of his employment." It makes no explicit requirement that either the seaman, the employment or the injury have the slightest connection with the United States. Unless some relationship of one or more of these to our national interest is implied, Congress has extended our law and opened our courts to all alien seafaring men injured anywhere in the world in service of watercraft of every foreign nation—a hand on a Chinese junk, never outside Chinese waters, would not be beyond its literal wording.

But Congress in 1920 wrote these all-comprehending words, not on a clean slate, but as a postscript to a long series of enactments governing shipping. All were enacted with regard to a seasoned body of maritime law developed by the experience of American courts long accustomed to dealing with admiralty problems in reconciling our own with foreign interests and in accommodating the reach of our own laws to those of other maritime nations.

The shipping laws of the United States, set forth in Title 46 of the United States Code, 46 U.S.C.A., comprise a patchwork of separate enactments, some tracing far back in our history and many designed for particular emergencies. While some have been specific in application to foreign shipping and others in being confined to American shipping, many give no evidence that Congress addressed itself to their foreign application and are in general terms which leave their application to be judicially determined from context and circumstance. By usage as old as the Nation, such statutes have been construed to apply only to areas and transactions in which American law would be considered operative under prevalent doctrines of international law. Thus, in United States v. Palmer, 3 Wheat. 610, this Court was called upon to interpret a statute of 1790, 1 Stat. 115, punishing certain acts when committed on the high seas by "any person or persons," terms which, as Mr. Chief Justice Marshall observed, are "broad enough to comprehend every human being." But the Court determined that the literal universality of the prohibition "must not only be limited to cases within the jurisdiction of the state, but also to those objects to which the legislature intended to apply them," and therefore would not reach a person performing the proscribed acts aboard the ship of a foreign state on the high seas.

This doctrine of construction is in accord with the long-heeded admonition of Mr. Chief Justice Marshall that "an Act of Congress ought never to be construed to violate the law of nations if any other possible construction remains. . . ." And it has long been accepted in maritime jurisprudence that ". . . if any construction otherwise be possible, an Act will not be construed as applying to foreigners in respect to acts done by them outside the dominions of the sovereign power enacting. That is a rule based on international law, by which one sovereign power is bound to respect the subjects and the rights of all other sovereign powers outside its own territory." Lord Russell of Killowen in The Queen v. Jameson (1896), 2 Q.B. 425, 430. This is not, as sometimes is implied, any impairment of our own sovereignty, or limitation of the power of Congress. "The law of the sea," we have had occasion to observe, "is in a peculiar sense an international law, but application of its specific rules depends upon acceptance by the United States." Farrell v. United States, 336 U.S. 511, 517. On the contrary, we are simply dealing with a problem of statutory construction rather commonplace in a federal system by which courts often have to decide whether "any" or "every" reaches to the limits of the enacting authority's usual scope or is to be applied to foreign events or transactions....

Congress could not have been unaware of the necessity of construction imposed upon courts by such generality of language and was well warned that in the absence of more definite directions than are contained in the Jones Act it would be applied by the courts to foreign events, foreign ships and foreign seamen only in accordance with the usual doctrine and practices of maritime law.

Respondent places great stress upon the assertion that petitioner's commerce and contacts with the ports of the United States are frequent and regular, as the basis for applying our statutes to incidents aboard his ships. But the virtue and utility of sea-borne commerce lies in its frequent and important contacts with more than one country. If, to serve some immediate interest, the courts of each were to exploit every such contact to the limit of its power, it is not difficult to see that a multiplicity of conflicting and overlapping burdens would blight international carriage by sea....

Maritime law, like our municipal law, has attempted to avoid or resolve conflicts between competing laws by ascertaining and valuing points of contact between the transaction and the states or governments whose competing laws are involved. The criteria, in general, appear to be arrived at from weighing of the significance of one or more connecting factors between the shipping transaction regulated and the national interest served by the assertion of authority. It would not be candid to claim that our courts have arrived at satisfactory standards or apply those that they profess with perfect consistency. But in dealing with international commerce we cannot be unmindful of the necessity for mutual forbearance if retaliations are to be avoided; nor should we forget that any contact which we hold sufficient to warrant application of our law to a foreign transaction will logically be as strong a warrant for a foreign country to apply its law to an American transaction.

In the case before us, two foreign nations can claim some connecting factor with this tort—Denmark, because, among other reasons, the ship and the seaman were Danish nationals; Cuba, because the tortious conduct occurred and caused injury in Cuban waters. The United States may also claim contacts because the seaman had been hired in and was returned to the United States, which also is the state of the forum. We therefore review the several factors which, alone or in combination, are generally conceded to influence choice of law to govern a tort claim, particularly a maritime tort claim, and the weight and significance accorded them.

1. Place of the Wrongful Act.—The solution most commonly accepted as to torts in our municipal and in international law is to apply the law of the place where the acts giving rise to the liability occurred, the lex loci delicti commissi. This rule of locality, often applied to maritime torts, would indicate application of the law of Cuba, in whose domain the actionable wrong took place. The test of location of the wrongful act or omission, however sufficient for torts ashore, is of limited application to shipboard torts, because of the varieties of legal authority over waters she may navigate. These range from ports, harbors, roadsteads, straits, rivers and canals which form part of the domain of various states, through bays and gulfs, and that band of the littoral sea known as territorial waters, over which control in a large, but not unlimited, degree is conceded to the adjacent state. It includes, of course, the high seas as to which the law was probably settled and old when Grotius wrote that it cannot be anyone's property and cannot be monopolized by virtue of discovery, occupation, papal grant, prescription or custom.

We have sometimes uncompromisingly asserted territorial rights, as when we held that foreign ships voluntarily entering our waters become subject to our prohibition laws and other laws as well, except as we may in pursuance of our own policy forego or limit exertion of our power. This doctrine would seem to indicate Cuban law for this case. But the territorial standard is so unfitted to an enterprise conducted under many territorial rules and under none that it usually is modified by the more constant law of the flag. This would appear to be consistent with the practice of Cuba, which applies a workmen's compensation system in principle not unlike that of Denmark to all accidents occurring aboard ships of Cuban registry. The locality test, for what it is worth, affords no support for the application of American law in this case and probably refers us to Danish in preference to Cuban law, though this point we need not decide, for neither party urges Cuban law as controlling.

2. Law of the Flag.—Perhaps the most venerable and universal rule of maritime law relevant to our problem is that which gives cardinal importance to the law of the flag. Each state under international law may determine for itself the conditions on which it will grant its nationality to a merchant ship, thereby accepting responsibility for it and acquiring authority over it. Nationality is evidenced to the world by the ship's papers and its flag. The United States has firmly and successfully maintained that the regularity and validity of a registration can be questioned only by the registering state.

This Court has said that the law of the flag supersedes the territorial principle, even for purposes of criminal jurisdiction of personnel of a merchant ship, because it "is deemed to be a part of the territory of that sovereignty (whose flag it flies), and not to lose that character when in navigable waters within the territorial limits of another sovereignty."... Some authorities reject, as a rather mischievous fiction, the doctrine that a ship is constructively a floating part of the flagstate, but apply the law of the flag on the pragmatic basis that there must be some law on shipboard, that it cannot change at every change of waters, and no experience shows a better rule than that of the state that owns her.

It is significant to us here that the weight given to the ensign overbears most other connecting events in determining applicable law.... These considerations are of such weight in favor of Danish and against American law in this case that it must prevail unless some heavy counterweight appears.

3. Allegiance or Domicile of the Injured.—Until recent times there was little occasion for conflict between the law of the flag and the law of the state of which the seafarer was a subject, for the long-standing rule, as pronounced by this Court after exhaustive review of authority, was that the nationality of the vessel for jurisdictional purposes was attributed to all her crew. Surely during service under a foreign flag some duty of allegiance is due. But, also, each nation has a legitimate interest that its nationals and permanent inhabitants be not maimed or disabled from self-support. In some later American cases, courts have been prompted to apply the Jones Act by the fact that the wrongful act or omission alleged caused injury to an American citizen or domiciliary. We need not, however, weigh the seaman's nationality against that of the ship, for here the two coincide without resort to fiction. Admittedly, respondent is neither citizen nor resident of the United States. While on direct examination he answered leading questions that he was living in New York when he joined the Randa, the articles which he signed recited, and on cross-examination he admitted, that his home was Silkeburg, Denmark. His presence in New York was transitory and created no such national interest in, or duty toward, him as to justify intervention of the law of one state on the shipboard of another.

4. Allegiance of the Defendant Shipowner.—... [I]n recent years a practice has grown, particularly among American shipowners, to avoid stringent shipping laws by seeking foreign registration eagerly offered by some countries. Confronted with such operations, our courts on occasion have pressed beyond the formalities of more or less nominal foreign registration to enforce against American shipowners the obligations which our law places upon them. But here again the utmost liberality in disregard of formality does not support the application of American law in this case, for it appears beyond doubt that this owner is a Dane by nationality and domicile.

5. Place of Contract.—Place of contract, which was New York, is the factor on which respondent chiefly relies to invoke American law. It is one which often has significance in choice of law in a contract action. But a Jones Act suit is for tort, in which respect it differs from one to enforce liability for maintenance and cure. As we have said of the latter, "In the United States this obligation has been recognized consistently as an implied provision in contracts of marine employment. Created thus with the contract of employment, the liability, unlike that for indemnity or that later created by the Jones Act, in no sense is predicated on the fault or negligence of the shipowner." But this action does not seek to recover anything due under the contract or damages for its breach.

The place of contracting in this instance, as is usual to such contracts, was fortuitous. A seaman takes his employment, like his fun, where he finds it; a ship takes on crew in any port where it needs them. The practical effect of making the lex loci contractus govern all tort claims during the service would be to subject a ship to a multitude of systems of law, to put some of the crew in a more advantageous position than others, and not unlikely in the long run to diminish hirings in ports of countries that take best care of their seamen.

But if contract law is nonetheless to be considered, we face the fact that this contract was explicit that the Danish law and the contract with the Danish union were to control....

We do not think the place of contract is a substantial influence in the choice between competing laws to govern a maritime tort.

6. Inaccessibility of Foreign Forum.—It is argued, and particularly stressed by an amicus brief, that justice requires adjudication under American law to save seamen expense and loss of time in returning to a foreign forum. This might be a persuasive argument for exercising a discretionary jurisdiction to adjudge a controversy; but it is not persuasive as to the law by which it shall be judged. It is pointed out, however, that the statutes of at least one maritime country (Panama) allow suit under its law by injured seamen only in its own courts. The effect of such a provision is doubtful in view of our holding that such venue restrictions by one of the states of the Union will not preclude action in a sister state.

Confining ourselves to the case in hand, we do not find this seaman disadvantaged in obtaining his remedy under Danish law from being in New York instead of Denmark. The Danish compensation system does not necessitate delayed, prolonged, expensive and uncertain litigation. It is stipulated in this case that claims may be made through the Danish Consulate. There is not the slightest showing that to obtain any relief to which he is entitled under Danish law would require his presence in Denmark or necessitate his leaving New York. And, even if it were so, the record indicates that he was offered and declined free transportation to Denmark by petitioner.

7. The Law of the Forum.—It is urged that, since an American forum has perfected its jurisdiction over the parties and defendant does more or less frequent and regular business within the forum state, it should apply its own law to the controversy between them. The "doing business" which is enough to warrant service of process may fall quite short of the considerations necessary to bring extraterritorial torts to judgment under our law. Under respondent's contention, all that is necessary to bring a foreign transaction between foreigners in foreign ports under American law is to be able to serve American process on the defendant. We have held it a denial of due process of law when a state of the Union attempts to draw into control of its law otherwise foreign controversies, on slight connections, because it is a forum state. Hartford Acc. & Indem. Co. v. Delta & Pine Land Co., 292 U.S. 143; Home Ins. co. v. Dick, 281 U.S. 397. The purpose of a conflict-of-laws doctrine is to assure that a case will be treated n the same way under the appropriate

law regardless of the fortuitous circumstances which often determine the forum. Jurisdiction of maritime cases in all countries is so wide and the nature of its subject matter so far-flung that there would be no justification for altering the law of a controversy just because local jurisdiction of the parties is obtainable.

It is pointed out that our statute on limitation of shipowner's liability which formerly applied in terms to "any vessel" was applied by our courts to foreign causes. Hence, it is argued by analogy that "any seaman" should be construed so to apply. But the situation is inverted. The limitation-of-liability statute was construed to thus apply only against those who had chosen to sue in our courts on foreign transactions. Because a law of the forum is applied to plaintiffs who voluntarily submit themselves to it is no argument for imposing the law of the forum upon those who do not. Furthermore, this application of the limitation on liability brought our practice into harmony with that of all other maritime nations, while the application of the Jones Act here advocated would bring us into conflict with the maritime world.

This review of the connecting factors which either maritime law or our municipal law of conflicts regards as significant in determining the law applicable to a claim of actionable wrong shows an overwhelming preponderance in favor of Danish law. The parties are both Danish subjects, the events took place on a Danish ship, not within our territorial waters. Against these considerations is only the fact that the defendant was served here with process and that the plaintiff signed on in New York, where the defendant was engaged in our foreign commerce. The latter event is offset by provision of his contract that the law of Denmark should govern. We do not question the power of Congress to condition access to our ports by foreign-owned vessels upon submission to any liabilities it may consider good American policy to exact. But we can find no justification for interpreting the Jones Act to intervene between foreigners and their own law because of acts on a foreign ship not in our waters.

In apparent recognition of the weakness of the legal argument, a candid and brash appeal is made by respondent and by amicus briefs to extend the law to this situation as a means of benefiting seamen and enhancing the costs of foreign ship operation for the competitive advantage of our own. We are not sure that the interest of this foreign seaman, who is able to prove negligence, is the interest of all seamen or that his interest is that of the United States. Nor do we stop to inquire which law does whom the greater or the lesser good. The argument is misaddressed. It would be within the proprieties if addressed to Congress. Counsel familiar with the traditional attitude of this Court in maritime matters could not have intended it for us.

The judgment below is reversed and the cause remanded to District Court for proceedings consistent herewith.

Comments and Questions

1. What are the origins of the law of the flag rule? What is its relevance or virtue today?

2. Is the court applying interest analysis here?

3. Will foreign ships be less inclined to visit American shipping ports if the Jones Act applies in cases like this? What retaliatory acts does the Court contemplate?

4. In the next case that you read, the Court makes no mention of Lauritzen. Consider why not. (Is it overruling Lauritzen? Is Lauritzen irrelevant?)

E.E.O.C. v Arabian-American Oil Co
499 U.S. 244 (1991)

Chief Justice Rehnquist delivered the opinion of the Court:
These cases present the issue whether Title VII applies extraterritorially to regulate the employment practices of United States employers who employ United States citizens abroad. The United States Court of Appeals for the Fifth Circuit held that it does not, and we agree with that conclusion.

Petitioner Boureslan is a naturalized United States citizen who was born in Lebanon. The respondents are two Delaware corporations, Arabian American Oil Company (Aramco), and its subsidiary, Aramco Service Company (ASC). Aramco's principal place of business is Dhahran, Saudi Arabia, and it is licensed to do business in Texas. ASC's principal place of business is Houston, Texas.

In 1979, Boureslan was hired by ASC as a cost engineer in Houston. A year later he was transferred, at his request, to work for Aramco in Saudi Arabia. Boureslan remained with Aramco in Saudi Arabia until he was discharged in 1984. After filing a charge of discrimination with the Equal Employment Opportunity Commission (EEOC or Commission), he instituted this suit in the United States District Court for the Southern District of Texas against Aramco and ASC. He sought relief under both state law and Title VII of the Civil Rights Act of 1964, 78 Stat. 253, as amended, 42 U.S.C. §§ 2000e-2000e-17, on the ground that he was harassed and ultimately discharged by respondents on account of his race, religion, and national origin.

Respondents filed a motion for summary judgment on the ground that the District Court lacked subject-matter jurisdiction over Boureslan's claim because the protections of Title VII do not extend to United States citizens employed abroad by American employers. The District Court agreed and dismissed Boureslan's Title VII claim; it also dismissed his state-law claims for lack of pendent jurisdiction and entered final judgment in favor of respondents. A panel for the Fifth Circuit affirmed. After vacating the panel's decision and rehearing the case en banc, the court affirmed the District Court's dismissal of Boureslan's complaint. Both Boureslan and the EEOC petitioned for certiorari. We granted both petitions for certiorari to resolve this important issue of statutory interpretation.

Both parties concede, as they must, that Congress has the authority to enforce its laws beyond the territorial boundaries of the United States. Cf. Foley Bros., Inc. v. Filardo, 336 U.S. 281, 284–85 (1949). Whether Congress has in fact exercised that authority in these cases is a matter of statutory construction. It is our task to determine whether Congress intended the protections of Title VII to apply to United States citizens employed by American employers outside of the United States.

It is a longstanding principle of American law "that legislation of Congress, unless a contrary intent appears, is meant to apply only within the territorial jurisdiction of the United States." Foley Bros., 336 U.S. at 285. This "canon of construction ... is a valid approach whereby unexpressed congressional intent may be ascertained." Ibid. It serves to protect against unintended clashes between our laws and those of other nations which could result in international discord. See McCulloch v. Sociedad Nacional de Marineros de Honduras, 372 U.S 10, 20–22 (1963).

In applying this rule of construction, we look to see whether "language in the [relevant Act] gives any indication of a congressional purpose to extend its coverage beyond places over which the United States has sovereignty or has some measure of legislative control." Foley Bros, 336 U.S. at 285. We assume that Congress legislates against the backdrop of the presumption against extraterritoriality. Therefore, unless there is "the affirmative intention of the Congress clearly expressed," we must presume it "is primarily concerned with domestic conditions." Foley Bros, 336 U.S. at 285.

Boureslan and the EEOC contend that the language of Title VII evinces a clearly expressed intent on behalf of Congress to legislate extraterritorially. They rely principally on two provisions of the statute. First, petitioners argue that the statute's definitions of the jurisdictional terms "employer" and "commerce" are sufficiently broad to include United States firms that employ American citizens overseas. Second, they maintain that the statute's "alien exemption" clause, 42 U.S.C. § 2000e-1, necessarily implies that Congress intended to protect American citizens from employment discrimination abroad. Petitioners also contend that we should defer to the EEOC's consistently held position that Title VII applies abroad. We conclude that petitioners' evidence, while not totally lacking in probative value, falls short of demonstrating the affirmative congressional intent required to extend the protections of Title VII beyond our territorial borders.

Title VII prohibits various discriminatory employment practices based on an individual's race, color, religion, sex, or national origin. See §§ 2000e-2, 2000e-3. An employer is subject to Title VII if it has employed 15 or more employees for a specified period and is "engaged in an industry affecting commerce." An industry affecting commerce is "any activity, business, or industry in commerce or in which a labor dispute would hinder or obstruct commerce or the free flow of commerce and includes any activity or industry 'affecting commerce' within the meaning of the Labor-Management Reporting and Disclosure Act of 1959 [(LMRDA)] [29 U.S.C. §§ 401 et seq.]." § 2000e(h). "Commerce," in turn, is defined as "trade, traffic, commerce, transportation, transmission, or communication among the several States; or between a State and any place outside thereof; or within the District of Columbia, or a possession of the United States; or between points in the same State but through a point outside thereof." § 2000e(g).

Petitioners argue that by its plain language, Title VII's "broad jurisdictional language" reveals Congress' intent to extend the statute's protections to employment discrimination anywhere in the world by a United States employer who affects trade "between a State and any place outside thereof." More precisely, they assert that since Title VII defines "States" to include States, the District of Columbia, and specified territories, the clause "between a State and any place outside thereof" must be referring to areas beyond the territorial limit of the United States.

Respondents offer several alternative explanations for the statute's expansive language. They contend that the "or between a State and any place outside thereof" clause "provide[s] the jurisdictional nexus required to regulate commerce that is not wholly within a single state, presumably as it affects both interstate and foreign commerce" but not to "regulate conduct exclusively within a foreign country." They also argue that since the definitions of the terms "employer," "commerce," and "industry affecting commerce" make no mention of "commerce with foreign nations," Congress cannot be said to have intended that the statute apply overseas. In support of this argument, respondents point to Title II of the Civil Rights Act of 1964, governing public accommodation, which specifically defines commerce as it applies to foreign nations. Finally, respondents argue that while language present in the first bill considered by the House of Representatives contained the terms "foreign commerce" and "foreign nations," those terms were deleted by the Senate before the Civil Rights Act of 1964 was passed. They conclude that these deletions "[are] inconsistent with the notion of a clearly expressed congressional intent to apply Title VII extraterritorially." Id., at 7.

We need not choose between these competing interpretations as we would be required to do in the absence of the presumption against extraterritorial application discussed above. Each is plausible, but no more persuasive than that. The language relied upon by petitioners—and it is they who must make the affirmative showing—is ambiguous, and does not speak directly to the question presented here. The intent of Congress as to the extraterritorial application of this statute must be deduced by inference from boilerplate language which can be found in any number of congressional Acts, none of which have ever been held to apply overseas. See, e.g., Consumer Product Safety Act, 15 U.S.C. § 2052(a)(12)....

Petitioners' reliance on Title VII's jurisdictional provisions also finds no support in our case law; we have repeatedly held that even statutes that contain broad language in their definitions of "commerce" that expressly refer to "foreign commerce" do not apply abroad....

The EEOC places great weight on an assertedly similar "broad jurisdictional grant in the Lanham Act" that this Court held applied extraterritorially in Steele v. Bulova Watch Co., 344 U.S. 280, 286 (1952). In Steele, we addressed whether the Lanham Act, designed to prevent deceptive and misleading use of trademarks, applied to acts of a United States citizen consummated in Mexico. The Act defined commerce as "all commerce which may lawfully be regulated by Congress." 15 U.S.C. § 1127. The stated intent of the statute was "to regulate commerce within the control of Congress by making actionable the deceptive and misleading use of marks in such commerce." Ibid. While recognizing that "the legislation of Congress will not extend beyond the boundaries of the United States unless a contrary legislative intent appears," the Court concluded that in light of the fact that the allegedly unlawful conduct had some effects within the United States, coupled with the Act's "broad jurisdictional grant" and its "sweeping reach into 'all commerce which may lawfully be regulated by Congress,' " the statute was properly interpreted as applying abroad. Steele, 344 U.S. at 285, 287.

The EEOC's attempt to analogize these cases to Steele is unpersuasive. The Lanham Act by its terms applies to "all commerce which may lawfully be regulated by Congress." The Constitution gives Congress the power "[t]o regulate Commerce with foreign Nations, and among the several States, and with the Indian Tribes." U.S. Const. Art. I, § 8, cl. 3. Since the Act expressly stated that it applied to the extent of Congress' power over commerce, the Court in Steele concluded that Congress intended that the statute apply abroad. By contrast, Title VII's more limited, boilerplate "commerce" language does not support such an expansive construction of congressional intent. Moreover, unlike the language in the Lanham Act, Title VII's definition of "commerce" was derived expressly from the LMRDA, a statute that this Court had held, prior to the enactment of Title VII, did not apply abroad. McCulloch, 372 U.S. at 15.

Thus petitioners' argument based on the jurisdictional language of Title VII fails both as a matter of statutory language and of our previous case law. Many Acts of Congress are based on the authority of that body to regulate commerce among the several States, and the parts of these Acts setting forth the basis for legislative jurisdiction will obviously refer to such commerce in one way or another. If we were to permit possible, or even plausible, interpretations of language such as that involved here to override the presumption against extraterritorial application, there would be little left of the presumption.

Petitioners argue that Title VII's "alien-exemption provision," 42 U.S.C. § 2000e-1, "clearly manifests an intention" by Congress to protect United States citizens with respect to their employment outside of the United States. The alien exemption provision says that the statute "shall not apply to an employer with respect to the employment of aliens outside any State." Petitioners contend that from this language a negative inference should be drawn that Congress intended Title VII to cover United States citizens working abroad for United States employers. There is "[n]o other plausible explanation [that] the alien exemption exists," they argue, because "[i]f Congress believed that the statute did not apply extraterritorially, it would have had no reason to include an exemption for a certain category of individuals employed outside the United States." Since "[t]he statute's jurisdictional provisions cannot possibly be read to confer coverage only upon aliens employed outside the United States," petitioners conclude that "Congress could not rationally have enacted an exemption for the employment of aliens abroad if it intended to foreclose all potential extraterritorial applications of the statute."

Respondents resist petitioners' interpretation of the alien-exemption provision and assert two alternative raisons d'être for that language. First, they contend that since aliens are included in the statute's definition of employee,* and the definition of commerce includes possessions as well as "States," the purpose of the exemption is to provide that employers of aliens in the possessions of the United States are not covered by the statute. Thus, the "outside any State" clause means outside any State, but within the control of the United States. Respondents argue that "[t]his reading of the alien exemption provision is consistent with and supported by the historical development of the provision".... Second, respondents assert that by negative implication, the exemption "confirm[s] the coverage of aliens in the United States."

If petitioners are correct that the alien-exemption clause means that the statute applies to employers overseas, we see no way of distinguishing in its application between United States employers and foreign employers. Thus, a French employer of a United States citizen in France would be subject to Title VII—a result at which even petitioners balk. The EEOC assures us that in its view the term "employer" means only "American employer," but there is no such distinction in this statute and no indication that the EEOC in the normal course of its administration had produced a reasoned basis for such a distinction. Without clearer evidence of congressional intent to do so than is contained in the alien-exemption clause, we are unwilling to ascribe to that body a policy which would raise difficult issues of international law by imposing this country's employment-discrimination regime upon foreign corporations operating in foreign commerce.

This conclusion is fortified by the other elements in the statute suggesting a purely domestic focus. The statute as a whole indicates a concern that it not unduly interfere with the sovereignty and laws of the States. See, e.g., 42 U.S.C. § 2000h-4 (stating that the Act should not be construed to exclude the operation of state law or invalidate any state law unless inconsistent with the purposes of the Act); § 2000e-5 (requiring the EEOC to accord substantial weight to findings of state or local authorities in proceedings under state or local law); § 2000e-7 (providing that nothing in Title VII shall affect the application of state or local law unless such law requires or permits practices that would be unlawful under Title VII); § § 2000e-5(c), (d), and (e) (provisions addressing deferral to state discrimination proceedings). While Title VII consistently speaks in terms of "States" and state proceedings, it fails even to mention foreign nations or foreign proceedings.

Similarly, Congress failed to provide any mechanisms for overseas enforcement of Title VII. For instance, the statute's venue provisions, § 2000e-5(f)(3), are ill-

---

* Title VII defines "employee" as: "an individual employed by an employer, except that the term 'employee' shall not include any person elected to public office in any State or political subdivision of any State by the qualified voters thereof, or any person chosen by such officer to be on such officer's personal staff, or an appointee on the policy making level or an immediate adviser with respect to the exercise of the constitutional or legal powers of the office. The exemption set forth in the preceding sentence shall not include employees subject to the civil service laws of a State government, governmental agency or political subdivision." 42 U.S.C. § 2000e(f).

suited for extraterritorial application as they provide for venue only in a judicial district in the State where certain matters related to the employer occurred or were located. And the limited investigative authority provided for the EEOC, permitting the Commission only to issue subpoenas for witnesses and documents from "any place in the United States or any Territory or possession thereof," 29 U.S.C. § 161 incorporated by reference into 42 U.S.C. § 2000e-9, suggests that Congress did not intend for the statute to apply abroad.

It is also reasonable to conclude that had Congress intended Title VII to apply overseas, it would have addressed the subject of conflicts with foreign laws and procedures. In amending the Age Discrimination in Employment Act of 1967 (ADEA), 81 Stat. 602, as amended, 29 U.S.C. § 621 et seq. to apply abroad, Congress specifically addressed potential conflicts with foreign law by providing that it is not unlawful for an employer to take any action prohibited by the ADEA "where such practices involve an employee in a workplace in a foreign country, and compliance with [the ADEA] would cause such employer ... to violate the laws of the country in which such workplace is located." § 623(f)(1). Title VII, by contrast, fails to address conflicts with the laws of other nations....

Our conclusion today is buttressed by the fact that "[w]hen it desires to do so, Congress knows how to place the high seas within the jurisdictional reach of a statute." Argentine Republic v. Amerada Hess Shipping Corp., 488 U.S. 428, 440 (1989). Congress' awareness of the need to make a clear statement that a statute applies overseas is amply demonstrated by the numerous occasions on which it has expressly legislated the extraterritorial application of a statute.... Indeed, after several courts had held that the ADEA did not apply overseas, Congress amended § 11(f) to provide: "The term 'employee' includes any individual who is a citizen of the United States employed by an employer in a workplace in a foreign country." 29 U.S.C. § 630(f). Congress also amended § 4(g)(1), which states: "If an employer controls a corporation whose place of incorporation is in a foreign country, any practice by such corporation prohibited under this section shall be presumed to be such practice by such employer." § 623(h)(1). The expressed purpose of these changes was to "mak[e] provisions of the Act apply to citizens of the United States employed in foreign countries by U.S. corporations or their subsidiaries." S. Rep. No. 98-467, p. 2 (1984), U.S.Code Cong. & Admin.News 1984, pp. 2974, 2975. Congress, should it wish to do so, may similarly amend Title VII and in doing so will be able to calibrate its provisions in a way that we cannot.

Petitioners have failed to present sufficient affirmative evidence that Congress intended Title VII to apply abroad. Accordingly, the judgment of the Court of Appeals is Affirmed.

Justice Marshall, with whom Justice Blackmun and Justice Stevens join, dissenting.

Like any issue of statutory construction, the question whether Title VII protects United States citizens from discrimination by United States employers abroad turns solely on congressional intent. As the majority recognizes, our inquiry into congressional intent in this setting is informed by the traditional "canon of construction which teaches that legislation of Congress, unless a contrary intent appears, is meant to apply only within the territorial jurisdiction of the United States." Foley Bros., Inc. v. Filardo, 336 U.S. 281, 285 (1949). But contrary to what one would conclude from the majority's analysis, this canon is not a "clear statement" rule, the application of which relieves a court of the duty to give effect to all available indicia of the legislative will. Rather, as our case law applying the presumption against extraterritoriality well illustrates, a court may properly rely on this presumption only after exhausting all of the traditional tools "whereby unexpressed congressional intent may be ascertained." Ibid. When these tools are brought to bear on the issue in this case, the conclusion is inescapable that Congress did intend Title VII to protect United States citizens from discrimination by United States employers operating overseas. Consequently, I dissent.

I

Because it supplies the driving force of the majority's analysis, I start with "[t]he canon ... that legislation of Congress, unless a contrary intent appears, is meant to apply only within the territorial jurisdiction of the United States." Ibid. The majority recasts this principle as "the need to make a clear statement that a statute applies overseas." (emphasis added). So conceived, the presumption against extraterritoriality allows the majority to derive meaning from various instances of statutory silence—from Congress' failure, for instance, "to mention foreign nations or foreign proceedings," "to provide any mechanisms for overseas enforcement," or to "addres[s] the subject of conflicts with foreign laws and procedures.". At other points, the majority relies on its reformulation of the presumption to avoid the "need [to] choose between ... competing interpretations" of affirmative statutory language that the majority concludes "does not speak directly to the question" of extraterritoriality. (emphasis added). In my view, the majority grossly distorts the effect of this rule of construction upon conventional techniques of statutory interpretation....

[T]he presumption against extraterritoriality is not a "clear statement" rule. Clear-statement rules operate less to reveal actual congressional intent than to shield important values from an insufficiently strong legislative intent to displace them. When they apply, such rules foreclose inquiry into extrinsic guides to interpretation, and even compel courts to select less plausible candidates from within the range of permissible constructions. The Court's analysis in Foley Brothers was by no means so narrowly constrained. Indeed, the Court considered the entire range of conventional sources "whereby unexpressed congressional intent may be ascertained," including legislative history, statutory structure, and administrative interpretations. Subsequent applications of the presumption against extraterritoriality confirm that we have not imposed the drastic clear-statement burden upon Congress before giving effect to its intention that a particular enactment apply beyond the national boundaries....

II

...Confirmation that Congress did in fact expect Title VII's central prohibition to have an extraterritorial reach is supplied by the so-called "alien exemption" provision. The alien-exemption provision states that Title VII "shall not apply to an employer with respect to the employment of aliens outside any State." 42 U.S.C. § 2000e-1 (emphasis added). Absent an intention that Title VII apply "outside any State," Congress would have had no reason to craft this extraterritorial exemption. And because only discrimination against aliens is exempted, employers remain accountable for discrimination against United States citizens abroad.

The inference arising from the alien-exemption provision is more than sufficient to rebut the presumption against extraterritoriality....

Notwithstanding the basic rule of construction requiring courts to give effect to all of the statutory language, the majority never advances an alternative explanation of the alien-exemption provision that is consistent with the majority's own conclusion that Congress intended Title VII to have a purely domestic focus. The closest that the majority comes to attempting to give meaning to the alien-exemption provision is to identify without endorsement "two alternative raisons d'être for that language" offered by respondents. Neither of these explanations is even minimally persuasive....

IV

In the hands of the majority, the presumption against extraterritoriality is transformed from a "valid approach whereby unexpressed congressional intent may be ascertained," Foley Bros., 336 U.S. at 285, into a barrier to any genuine inquiry into the sources that reveal Congress' actual intentions. Because the language, history, and administrative interpretations of the statute all support application of Title VII to United States companies employing United States citizens abroad, I dissent.

Comments and Questions

1. Do you find the majority or the dissent more persuasive?

2. What does the Court know about the substantive content of Saudi law? What does the Court need to know about Saudi law?

3. In order to overcome the presumption against extraterritoriality, what exactly must the plain statement include?

Hartford Fire Ins. Co. v. California et al.

509 U.S. 764 (1993)

Justice Souter announced the judgment of the Court and delivered the opinion of the Court with respect to Parts I, II-A, III, and IV, and an opinion with respect to Part II(B) in which Justice White, Justice Blackmun and Justice Stevens joined.

The Sherman Act makes every contract, combination, or conspiracy in unreasonable restraint of interstate or foreign commerce illegal. 26 Stat. 209, as amended, 15 U.S.C. § 1. These consolidated cases present questions about the application of that Act to the insurance industry, both here and abroad. The plaintiffs (respondents here) allege that both domestic and foreign defendants (petitioners here) violated the Sherman Act by engaging in various conspiracies to affect the American insurance market. A group of domestic defendants argues that the McCarran-Ferguson Act, 59 Stat. 33, as amended, 15 U.S.C. § 1011 et seq., precludes application of the Sherman Act to the conduct alleged; a group of foreign defendants argues that the principle of international comity requires the District Court to refrain from exercising jurisdiction over certain claims against it. We hold that most of the domestic defendants' alleged conduct is not immunized from antitrust liability by the McCarran-Ferguson Act, and that, even assuming it applies, the principle of international comity does not preclude District Court jurisdiction over the foreign conduct alleged.

I

The two petitions before us stem from consolidated litigation comprising the complaints of 19 States and many private plaintiffs alleging that the defendants, members of the insurance industry, conspired in violation of § 1 of the Sherman Act to restrict the terms of coverage of commercial general liability (CGL) insurance available in the United States. Because the cases come to us on motions to dismiss, we take the allegations of the complaints as true.

A

According to the complaints, the object of the conspiracies was to force certain primary insurers (insurers who sell insurance directly to consumers) to change the terms of their standard CGL insurance policies to conform with the policies the defendant insurers wanted to sell. The defendants wanted four changes.

First, CGL insurance has traditionally been sold in the United States on an "occurrence" basis, through a policy obligating the insurer "to pay or defend claims, whenever made, resulting from an accident or 'injurious exposure to conditions' that occurred during the [specific time] period the policy was in effect." In place of this traditional "occurrence" trigger of coverage, the defendants wanted a "claims-made" trigger, obligating the insurer to pay or defend only those claims made during the policy period. Such a policy has the distinct advantage for the insurer that when the policy period ends without a claim having been made, the insurer can be certain that the policy will not expose it to any further liability. Second, the defendants wanted the "claims-made" policy to have a "retroactive date" provision, which would further restrict coverage to claims based on incidents that occurred after a certain date. Such a provision eliminates the risk that an insurer, by issuing a claims-made policy, would assume liability arising from incidents that occurred before the policy's effective date, but remained undiscovered or caused no immediate harm. Third, CGL insurance has traditionally covered "sudden and accidental" pollution; the defendants wanted to eliminate that coverage. Finally, CGL insurance has traditionally provided that the insurer would bear the legal costs of defending covered claims against the insured without regard to the policy's stated limits of coverage; the defendants wanted legal defense costs to be counted against the stated limits (providing a "legal defense cost cap").

[The Court then discussed the various allegations in the complaint.]

C

Nineteen States and a number of private plaintiffs filed 36 complaints against the insurers involved in this course of events, charging that the conspiracies described above violated § 1 of the Sherman Act, 15 U.S.C. § 1. After the actions had been consolidated for litigation in the Northern District of California, the defendants moved to dismiss for failure to state a cause of action, or, in the alternative, for summary judgment. The District Court granted the motions to dismiss. The Court of Appeals reversed. We granted certiorari in No. 91-1111 to address two narrow questions about the scope of McCarran-Ferguson Act antitrust immunity,[8] and in No. 91-1128 to address the application of the Sherman Act to the foreign conduct at issue.[9] We now affirm in part, reverse in part, and remand.

[The Court first discussed the liability of the domestic insurance companies.]

III

Finally, we take up the question presented by No. 91-1128, whether certain claims against the London reinsurers should have been dismissed as improper applications of the Sherman Act to foreign conduct. The Fifth Claim for Relief in the California Complaint alleges a violation of §1 of the Sherman Act by certain London reinsurers who conspired to coerce primary insurers in the United States to offer CGL coverage on a claims-made basis, thereby making "occurrence CGL coverage ... unavailable in the State of California for many risks." The Sixth Claim for Relief in the California Complaint alleges that the London reinsurers violated § 1 by a conspiracy to limit coverage of pollution risks in North America, thereby rendering "pollution liability coverage ... almost entirely unavailable for the vast majority of casualty insurance purchasers in the State of California." The Eighth Claim for Relief in the California Complaint alleges a further § 1 violation by the London reinsurers who, along with domestic retrocessional reinsurers, conspired

---

[8] We limited our grant of certiorari in No. 91-1111 to these questions: "1. Whether domestic insurance companies whose conduct otherwise would be exempt from the federal antitrust laws under the McCarran-Ferguson Act lose that exemption because they participate with foreign reinsurers in the business of insurance," and "2. Whether agreements among primary insurers and reinsurers on such matters as standardized advisory insurance policy forms and terms of insurance coverage constitute a 'boycott' outside the exemption of the McCarran-Ferguson Act."

[9] The question presented in No. 91-1128 is: "Did the court of appeals properly assess the extraterritorial reach of the U.S. antitrust laws in light of this Court's teachings and contemporary understanding of international law when it held that a U.S. district court may apply U.S. law to the conduct of a foreign insurance market regulated abroad?"

to limit coverage of seepage, pollution, and property contamination risks in North America, thereby eliminating such coverage in the State of California.

At the outset, we note that the District Court undoubtedly had jurisdiction of these Sherman Act claims, as the London reinsurers apparently concede. See Tr. of Oral Arg. 37 ("Our position is not that the Sherman Act does not apply in the sense that a minimal basis for the exercise of jurisdiction doesn't exist here. Our position is that there are certain circumstances,and that this is one of them, in which the interests of another State are sufficient that the exercise of that jurisdiction should be restrained"). Although the proposition was perhaps not always free from doubt, see American Banana Co. v. United Fruit Co., 213 U.S.347 (1909), it is well established by now that the Sherman Act applies to foreign conduct that was meant to produce and did in fact produce some substantial effect in the United States. Restatement (Third) of Foreign Relations Law of the United States § 415 and Reporters' Note 3 (1987). Such is the conduct alleged here: that the London reinsurers engaged in unlawful conspiracies to affect the market for insurance in the United States and that their conduct in fact produced substantial effect.[23] See 938 F.2d at 933.

According to the London reinsurers, the District Court should have declined to exercise such jurisdiction under the principle of international comity.[24] The Court of Appeals agreed that courts should look to that principle in deciding whether to exercise jurisdiction under the Sherman Act. This availed the London reinsurers nothing, however. To be sure, the Court of Appeals believed that "application of [American] antitrust laws to the London reinsurance market 'would lead to significant conflict with English law and policy,'" and that "[s]uch a conflict, unless outweighed by other factors, would by itself be reason to decline exercise of jurisdiction." But other factors, in the court's view, including the London reinsurers' express purpose to affect United States commerce and the substantial nature of the effect produced, outweighed the supposed conflict and required the exercise of jurisdiction in this litigation.

[23] Under § 402 of the Foreign Trade Antitrust Improvements Act of 1982 (FTAIA), 96 Stat. 1246, 15 U.S.C. § 6a, the Sherman Act does not apply to conduct involving foreign trade or commerce, other than import trade or import commerce, unless "such conduct has a direct, substantial, and reasonably foreseeable effect" on domestic or import commerce. § 6a(1)(A). The FTAIA was intended to exempt from the Sherman Act export transactions that did not injure the United States economy, see H.R. Rep. No. 97-686, pp. 2–3, 9–10 (1982); P. Areeda & H. Hovenkamp, Antitrust Law ¶ 236'a, pp. 296–297 (Supp.1992), and it is unclear how it might apply to the conduct alleged here. Also unclear is whether the Act's "direct, substantial, and reasonably foreseeable effect" standard amends existing law or merely codifies it. See id., ¶ 236'a, p. 297. We need not address these questions here. Assuming that the FTAIA's standard affects this litigation, and assuming further that that standard differs from the prior law, the conduct alleged plainly meets its requirements.

[24] Justice Scalia contends that comity concerns figure into the prior analysis whether jurisdiction exists under the Sherman Act. This contention is inconsistent with the general understanding that the Sherman Act covers foreign conduct producing a substantial intended effect in the United States, and that concerns of comity come into play, if at all, only after a court has determined that the acts complained of are subject to Sherman Act jurisdiction.

When it enacted the FTAIA, 96 Stat. 1246, 15 U.S.C. § 6a, Congress expressed no view on the question whether a court with Sherman Act jurisdiction should ever decline to exercise such jurisdiction on grounds of international comity. See H.R. Rep. No. 97-686, p. 13 (1982) ("If a court determines that the requirements for subject matter jurisdiction are met, [the FTAIA] would have no effect on the court['s] ability to employ notions of comity … or otherwise to take account of the international character of the transaction"). We need not decide that question here, however, for even assuming that in a proper case a court may decline to exercise Sherman Act jurisdiction over foreign conduct (or, as Justice SCALIA would put it, may conclude by the employment of comity analysis in the first instance that there is no jurisdiction), international comity would not counsel against exercising jurisdiction in the circumstances alleged here.

The only substantial question in this litigation is whether "there is in fact a true conflict between domestic and foreign law." Société Nationale Industrielle Aérospatiale v. U.S. Dist. Ct. for Southern Dist. Of Ia., 482 U.S. 522, 555 (1987) (Blackmun, J., concurring in part and dissenting in part). The London reinsurers contend that applying the Act to their conduct would conflict significantly with British law, and the British Government, appearing before us as amicus curiae, concurs. They assert that Parliament has established a comprehensive regulatory regime over the London reinsurance market and that the conduct alleged here was perfectly consistent with British law and policy. But this is not to state a conflict. "[T]he fact that conduct is lawful in the state in which it took place will not, of itself, bar application of the United States antitrust laws," even where the foreign state has a strong policy to permit or encourage such conduct. Restatement (Third) Foreign Relations Law § 415, Comment j. No conflict exists, for these purposes, "where a person subject to regulation by two states can comply with the laws of both." Restatement (Third) Foreign Relations Law § 403, Comment e.[25] Since the London reinsurers do not argue that British law requires them to act in some fashion prohibited by the law of the United States, or claim that their compliance with the laws of both countries is otherwise impossible, we see no conflict with British law. See Restatement (Third) Foreign Relations Law § 403, Comment e, § 415, Comment j. We have no need in this litigation to address other considerations that might inform a decision to refrain from the exercise of jurisdiction on grounds of international comity.

IV

The judgment of the Court of Appeals is affirmed in part and reversed in part, and the cases are remanded for further proceedings consistent with this opinion.

Justice Scalia delivered the opinion of the Court with respect to Part I, and delivered a dissenting opinion with respect to Part II, in which Justice O'Connor, Justice Kennedy, and Justice Thomas have joined.

[25] Justice Scalia says that we put the cart before the horse in citing this authority, for he argues it may be apposite only after a determination that jurisdiction over the foreign acts is reasonable. But whatever the order of cart and horse, conflict in this sense is the only substantial issue before the Court.

... Petitioners in No. 91-1128, various British corporations and other British subjects, argue that certain of the claims against them constitute an inappropriate extraterritorial application of the Sherman Act. It is important to distinguish two distinct questions raised by this petition: whether the District Court had jurisdiction, and whether the Sherman Act reaches the extraterritorial conduct alleged here. On the first question, I believe that the District Court had subject-matter jurisdiction over the Sherman Act claims against all the defendants (personal jurisdiction is not contested). Respondents asserted nonfrivolous claims under the Sherman Act, and 28 U.S.C. § 1331 vests district courts with subject-matter jurisdiction over cases "arising under" federal statutes. As precedents such as Lauritzen v. Larsen, 345 U.S. 571 (1953), make clear, that is sufficient to establish the District Court's jurisdiction over these claims....

The second question—the extraterritorial reach of the Sherman Act—has nothing to do with the jurisdiction of the courts. It is a question of substantive law turning on whether, in enacting the Sherman Act, Congress asserted regulatory power over the challenged conduct. See EEOC v. Arabian American Oil Co., 499 U.S. 244, 248 (1991) ("It is our task to determine whether Congress intended the protections of Title VII to apply to United States citizens employed by American employers outside of the United States"). If a plaintiff fails to prevail on this issue, the court does not dismiss the claim for want of subject-matter jurisdiction—want of power to adjudicate; rather, it decides the claim, ruling on the merits that the plaintiff has failed to state a cause of action under the relevant statute.

There is, however, a type of "jurisdiction" relevant to determining the extraterritorial reach of a statute; it is known as "legislative jurisdiction," This refers to "the authority of a state to make its law applicable to persons or activities," and is quite a separate matter from "jurisdiction to adjudicate," see id., at 231. There is no doubt, of course, that Congress possesses legislative jurisdiction over the acts alleged in this complaint: Congress has broad power under Article I, § 8, cl. 3, "[t]o regulate Commerce with foreign Nations," and this Court has repeatedly upheld its power to make laws applicable to persons or activities beyond our territorial boundaries where United States interests are affected. But the question in this litigation is whether, and to what extent, Congress has exercised that undoubted legislative jurisdiction in enacting the Sherman Act.

Two canons of statutory construction are relevant in this inquiry. The first is the "longstanding principle of American law 'that legislation of Congress, unless a contrary intent appears, is meant to apply only within the territorial jurisdiction of the United States.' "Applying that canon in Aramco, we held that the version of Title VII of the Civil Rights Act of 1964 then in force, 42 U.S.C. §§ 2000e to 2000e-17 (1988 ed.), did not extend outside the territory of the United States even though the statute contained broad provisions extending its prohibitions to, for example, "'any activity, business, or industry in commerce.' " We held such "boilerplate language" to be an insufficient indication to override the presumption against extraterritoriality. The Sherman Act contains similar "boilerplate language," and if the question were not governed by precedent, it would be worth considering whether that presumption controls the outcome here. We have, however, found the presumption to be overcome with respect to our antitrust laws; it is now well established that the Sherman Act applies extraterritorially.

But if the presumption against extraterritoriality has been overcome or is otherwise inapplicable, a second canon of statutory construction becomes relevant: "[A]n act of congress ought never to be construed to violate the law of nations if any other possible construction remains." Murray v. Schooner Charming Betsy, 2 Cranch. 64, 118 (Marshall, C.J.). This canon is "wholly independent" of the presumption against extraterritoriality. Aramco, 499 U.S. at 264. It is relevant to determining the substantive reach of a statute because "the law of nations," or customary international law, includes limitations on a nation's exercise of its jurisdiction to prescribe. See Restatement (Third) §§ 401–416. Though it clearly has constitutional authority to do so, Congress is generally presumed not to have exceeded those customary international-law limits on jurisdiction to prescribe.

Consistent with that presumption, this and other courts have frequently recognized that, even where the presumption against extraterritoriality does not apply, statutes should not be interpreted to regulate foreign persons or conduct if that regulation would conflict with principles of international law. For example, in Romero v. Intl. Terminal Operating Co., 358 U.S. 354 (1959), the plaintiff, a Spanish sailor who had been injured while working aboard a Spanish-flag and Spanish-owned vessel, filed a Jones Act claim against his Spanish employer. The presumption against extraterritorial application of federal statutes was inapplicable to the case, as the actionable tort had occurred in American waters. See id. at 383. The Court nonetheless stated that, "in the absence of a contrary congressional direction," it would apply "principles of choice of law that are consonant with the needs of a general federal maritime law and with due recognition of our self-regarding respect for the relevant interests of foreign nations in the regulation of maritime commerce as part of the legitimate concern of the international community." Id. at 382–83. "The controlling considerations" in this choice-of-law analysis were "the interacting interests of the United States and of foreign countries." Id. at 383.

Romero referred to, and followed, the choice-of-law analysis set forth in Lauritzen v. Larsen, 345 U.S. 571 (1953). As previously mentioned, Lauritzen also involved a Jones Act claim brought by a foreign sailor against a foreign employer. The Lauritzen Court recognized the basic problem: "If [the Jones Act were] read literally, Congress has conferred an American right of action which requires nothing more than that plaintiff be 'any seaman who shall suffer personal injury in the course of his employment.'" The solution it adopted was to construe the statute "to apply only to areas and transactions in which American law would be considered operative under prevalent doctrines of international law." (emphasis added). To support application of international law to limit the facial breadth of the statute, the Court relied upon—of course—Chief Justice Marshall's statement in Schooner Charming Betsy quoted supra. It then set forth "several factors which, alone or in combination, are generally conceded to influence choice of law to govern a tort claim."

Lauritzen, Romero and McCulloch were maritime cases, but we have recognized the principle that the scope of generally worded statutes must be construed in light of international law in other areas as well. More specifically, the principle was expressed in U.S. v. Aluminum Co. of America, 148 F.2d 416 (2nd Cir. 1945), the decision that established the extraterritorial reach of the Sherman Act. In his opinion for the court, Judge Learned Hand cautioned "we are not to read general words, such as those in [the Sherman] Act, without regard to the limitations customarily observed by nations upon the exercise of their powers; limitations which generally correspond to those fixed by the 'Conflict of Laws.'"Id. at 443.

More recent lower court precedent has also tempered the extraterritorial application of the Sherman Act with considerations of "international comity." The "comity" they refer to is not the comity of courts, whereby judges decline to exercise jurisdiction over matters more appropriately adjudged elsewhere, but rather what might be termed "prescriptive comity": the respect sovereign nations afford each other by limiting the reach of their laws. That comity is exercised by legislatures when they enact laws, and courts assume it has been exercised when they come to interpreting the scope of laws their legislatures have enacted. It is a traditional component of choice-of-law theory. See J. Story, Commentaries on the Conflict of Laws § 38 (1834) (distinguishing between the "comity of the courts" and the "comity of nations," and defining the latter as "the true foundation and extent of the obligation of the laws of one nation within the territories of another"). Comity in this sense includes the choice-of-law principles that, "in the absence of contrary congressional direction," are assumed to be incorporated into our substantive laws having extraterritorial reach. Considering comity in this way is just part of determining whether the Sherman Act prohibits the conduct at issue.[9]

In sum, the practice of using international law to limit the extraterritorial reach of statutes is firmly established in our jurisprudence. In proceeding to apply that practice to the present cases, I shall rely on the Restatement (Third) for the relevant principles of international law. Its standards appear fairly supported in the decisions of this Court construing international choice-of-law principles (Lauritzen, Romero, and McCulloch) and in the decisions of other federal courts, especially Timberlane. Whether the Restatement precisely reflects international law in every detail matters little here, as I believe this litigation would be resolved the same way under virtually any conceivable test that takes account of foreign regulatory interests.

---

[9] Some antitrust courts, including the Court of Appeals in the present cases, have mistaken the comity at issue for the "comity of courts," which has led them to characterize the question presented as one of "abstention," that is, whether they should "exercise or decline jurisdiction." *Mannington Mills, Inc. v. Congoleum Corp.*, 595 F.2d 1287, 1294 (3rd Cir. 1979); see also *In re Insur. Antitrust Litig.*, 938 F.2d 919, 932 (9th Cir. 1991). As I shall discuss, that seems to be the error the Court has fallen into today. Because courts are generally reluctant to refuse the exercise of conferred jurisdiction, confusion on this seemingly theoretical point can have the very practical consequence of greatly expanding the extraterritorial reach of the Sherman Act.

Under the Restatement, a nation having some "basis" for jurisdiction to prescribe law should nonetheless refrain from exercising that jurisdiction "with respect to a person or activity having connections with another state when the exercise of such jurisdiction is unreasonable." Restatement (Third) § 403(1). The "reasonableness" inquiry turns on a number of factors including, but not limited to: "the extent to which the activity takes place within the territory [of the regulating state]," id., § 403(2)(a); "the connections, such as nationality, residence, or economic activity, between the regulating state and the person principally responsible for the activity to be regulated," id., § 403(2)(b); "the character of the activity to be regulated, the importance of regulation to the regulating state, the extent to which other states regulate such activities, and the degree to which the desirability of such regulation is generally accepted," id., § 403(2)(c); "the extent to which another state may have an interest in regulating the activity," id., § 403(2)(g); and "the likelihood of conflict with regulation by another state," id., § 403(2)(h). Rarely would these factors point more clearly against application of United States law.

The activity relevant to the counts at issue here took place primarily in the United Kingdom, and the defendants in these counts are British corporations and British subjects having their principal place of business or residence outside the United States.[10] Great Britain has established a comprehensive regulatory scheme governing the London reinsurance markets, and clearly has a heavy "interest in regulating the activity," id., § 403(2)(g). Finally, § 2(b) of the McCarran-Ferguson Act allows state regulatory statutes to override the Sherman Act in the insurance field, subject only to the narrow "boycott" exception set forth in § 3(b)—suggesting that "the importance of regulation to the [United States]," Restatement (Third) § 403(2)(c), is slight. Considering these factors, I think it unimaginable that an assertion of legislative jurisdiction by the United States would be considered reasonable, and therefore it is inappropriate to assume, in the absence of statutory indication to the contrary, that Congress has made such an assertion.

It is evident from what I have said that the Court's comity analysis, which proceeds as though the issue is whether the courts should "decline to exercise ... jurisdiction," rather than whether the Sherman Act covers this conduct, is simply misdirected. I do not at all agree, moreover, with the Court's conclusion that the issue of the substantive scope of the Sherman Act is not in the cases. To be sure, the parties did not make a clear distinction between adjudicative jurisdiction and the scope of the statute. Parties often do not, as we have observed .... It is not realistic, and also not helpful, to pretend that the only really relevant issue in this litigation is not before us. In any event, if one erroneously chooses, as the Court does, to make adjudicative jurisdiction (or, more precisely, abstention) the vehicle for taking account of the needs of prescriptive comity, the Court still gets it wrong.

[10] Some of the British corporations are subsidiaries of American corporations, and the Court of Appeals held that "[t]he interests of Britain are at least diminished where the parties are subsidiaries of American corporations." 938 F.2d at 933. In effect, the Court of Appeals pierced the corporate veil in weighing the interests at stake. I do not think that was proper.

It concludes that no "true conflict" counseling nonapplication of United States law (or rather, as it thinks, United States judicial jurisdiction) exists unless compliance with United States law would constitute a violation of another country's law. That breathtakingly broad proposition, which contradicts the many cases discussed earlier, will bring the Sherman Act and other laws into sharp and unnecessary conflict with the legitimate interests of other countries—particularly our closest trading partners.

In the sense in which the term "conflic[t]" was used in Lauritzen, 345 U.S. at 582, 592, and is generally understood in the field of conflicts of laws, there is clearly a conflict in this litigation. The petitioners here, like the defendant in Lauritzen, were not compelled by any foreign law to take their allegedly wrongful actions, but that no more precludes a conflict-of-laws analysis here than it did there. Where applicable foreign and domestic law provide different substantive rules of decision to govern the parties' dispute, a conflict-of-laws analysis is necessary. See generally R. Weintraub, Commentary on Conflict of Laws 2–3 (1980); Restatement (First) of Conflict of Laws § 1, Comment c and Illustrations (1934).

Literally the only support that the Court adduces for its position is § 403 of the Restatement (Third)—or more precisely Comment e to that provision, which states:

> Subsection (3) [which says that a State should defer to another state if that State's interest is clearly greater] applies only when one state requires what another prohibits, or where compliance with the regulations of two states exercising jurisdiction consistently with this section is otherwise impossible. It does not apply where a person subject to regulation by two states can comply with the laws of both....

The Court has completely misinterpreted this provision. Subsection (3) of § 403 (requiring one State to defer to another in the limited circumstances just described) comes into play only after subsection (1) of § 403 has been complied with—i.e., after it has been determined that the exercise of jurisdiction by both of the two States is not "unreasonable." That prior question is answered by applying the factors (inter alia) set forth in subsection (2) of § 403, that is, precisely the factors that I have discussed in text and that the Court rejects.

I would reverse the judgment of the Court of Appeals on this issue, and remand to the District Court with instructions to dismiss for failure to state a claim on the three counts at issue in No. 91-1128.

Comments and Questions

1. Can you reconcile the Court's opinion with *EEOC v. Arabian American Oil Co.*? Put another way, under what circumstances should courts apply the strong presumption against extraterritoriality?

2. Which of the following seems to have greater influence on the Court's reasoning: the particular facts of this case or the concern for comity in this type of case?

2. England

Roerig v. Valiant Trawlers Ltd.

[2002] 1 Lloyd's Rep. 681 (Court of Appeal)

LORD JUSTICE WALLER

Introduction

[1] This is an appeal from the judgment of His Honour Judge Reddihough dated Mar. 15, 2001. He decided certain preliminary issues in relation to the assessment of damages in favour of the claimant. Although the Judge was asked to answer four issues summarized at par. 5 of his judgment, the issues were drafted in order to enable the Court to answer one question, namely in assessing damages for loss of dependency should benefits resulting from the loss be deducted from the damages?

[2] The claimant is a Dutch lady and brings the action as a dependant of a Dutchman. She does so on her own behalf and on behalf of their Dutch children in the English Courts under the Fatal Accidents Act, 1976, the Dutchman having been tragically killed on a trawler registered in England and owned by the defendants, an English registered company. There is no dispute about liability or about the claimant's entitlement to bring the action under the above Act. It is furthermore not in issue that under § 4 of the Fatal Accidents Act it is provided that in relation to actions brought under that Act:

> Assessment of damages: disregard of benefits. In assessing damages in respect of a person's death in an action under this Act, benefits which have accrued or will or may accrue to any person from his estate or otherwise as a result of his death shall be disregarded.

[3] The defendants (appellants in this Court) however contend, and for the present it must be assumed, accurately, that under Dutch law the position is different. In the witness statement of Mr. Van der Zwan, par. 23 which is the limit of the evidence that has been obtained on Dutch law, the position is put in this way:

> Compensation is also paid to accident victims and their dependants through civil court proceedings. However, under Dutch law the level of compensation is determined by the financial requirements of the claimant. All benefits received by the claimant-whether emanating from social security or from a collective labour agreement's provision-will be taken into account and deducted from compensation. The reasoning behind this is that society provides for its victims and their dependants to an acceptable and reasonably high minimum, which is usually elevated by provisions arranged by the industry they are/were working in. In Ms. Roerig's and her children's case this social security system works out as follows: . . .

[4] There then follows a full explanation of the various benefits which have been paid, or will be payable to the claimant and her children following the death of Mr. Van der Plas. From preceding paragraphs of Mr. Van der Zwan's statement

it seems that the benefits are accrued as a result of substantial contributions deducted from the deceased's earnings, as well as substantial contributions by the deceased's employers in Holland. The benefits include (i) a payment under Dutch labour law; (ii) a payment made without legal obligation covered by a personal accident insurance; (iii) a state surviving relatives' pension including amounts for the children; (iv) a widow and orphans' pension from the Workers' pension fund for the Off-shore Fishing Industry. It is further said that in relation to this last pension, the deceased's employers after his death negotiated with the relevant authorities to ensure the benefits were available to the claimant and her children despite the fact that he and the claimant were not married. The preliminary issues are thus designed to find the answer to the one question—does s. 4 of the Fatal Accidents Act apply to the claimant's claim, or must she give credit for the benefits which she and her children would have to give if the damages were being assessed under Dutch law?

[5] To succeed on this issue in the Court of Appeal the appellants must establish that the Judge was wrong in relation to all, or practically all, the issues he decided.

[6] The first issue he decided related to the proper law of the tort. Section 11 of the Private International Law (Miscellaneous Provisions) Act, 1995 provides as follows:

> Choice of applicable law: the general rule
>
> (1) The general rule is that the applicable law is the law of the country in which the events constituting the tort or delict in question occur.
>
> (2) Where elements of those events occur in different countries, the applicable law under the general rule is to be taken as being-(a) for a cause of action in respect of personal injury caused to an individual or death resulting from personal injury, the law of the country where the individual was when he sustained the injury; (b) for a cause of action in respect of damage to property, the law of the country where the property was when it was damaged; and (c) in any other case, the law of the country in which the most significant element or elements of those events occurred.
>
> (3) In this section "personal injury" includes disease or any impairment of physical or mental condition.

[7] It is not in dispute that under the general rule there laid down the applicable law is English law because the accident to the deceased occurred on an English registered trawler, and thus that is the law "in which the events constituting the tort or delict in question" occurred, or at the very least, the law of the country "where the individual was when he sustained the injury". But the appellants rely on § 12 of the same Act which provides as follows:

> Choice of applicable law: displacement of general rule
>
> (1) If it appears, in all the circumstances, from a comparison of-(a) the significance of the factors which connect a tort or delict with the country whose law would be the applicable law under the general rule; and (b) the significance of any factors connecting the tort or delict with another country, that it is substantially

more appropriate for the applicable law for determining the issues arising in the case, or any of those issues, to be the law of the other country, the general rule is displaced and the applicable law for determining those issues or that issue (as the case may be) is the law of that other country.

(2) The factors that may be taken into account as connecting a tort or delict with a country for the purposes of this section include, in particular, factors relating to the parties, to any of the events which constitute the tort or delict in question or to any of the circumstances or consequences of those events.

[8] They contended accordingly that when a comparison is made of the significant factors connecting the tort with England, and the significant factors connecting the tort with Holland, it is substantially more appropriate for the applicable law relating to the issue of damages to be the law of Holland. The Judge found against the appellants on that issue.

[9] As regards the second issue it seems that after liability was admitted, and one presumes in case the Judge were to be against the claimant on the first issue, the claimant amended her claim to allege a claim in contract as between the deceased and the defendants. The claim as pleaded alleged a contract of employment. It also alleged that the proper law of the contract was English. There thus were two aspects of this issue. The contract relied on was a contract in writing which on its face purported to be such. It was (indeed is) in English and purports to be made between the defendant and the deceased (see p. 208A of the bundle). On the trial of the preliminary issue the Judge found (contrary to the claimant's argument), that the deceased had a contract of employment with a Dutch company (Diepzee) not with the defendants, and that the arrangement was that Diepzee provided its employees to the defendants. Those findings are not challenged. But the Judge, by virtue of the document at p. 208A, spelt out another form of contract, and he further found that that contract was governed by English law. He thus decided both aspects of this issue in favour of the claimant.

[10] The final issue, which the Judge resolved on the basis that he might be wrong about both the previous issues, was whether s. 4 of the Fatal Accidents Act was substantive or procedural. If it was procedural, then (as was common ground) even if the proper law of the tort was Dutch and/or even if the proper law of any relevant contract was Dutch, the English Court would apply § 4. The Judge found that § 4 was procedural, and thus ruled against the appellant on this aspect also.

[11] We have been very much assisted by a full and comprehensive judgment, and by full and comprehensive skeleton arguments, all of a high standard. At the oral hearing we heard full submissions from Mr. Leonard for the appellants on all issues. At the invitation of the Court Mr. Weir concentrated his submissions entirely on issues 1 (proper law of the tort) and 3 (procedural or substantive), success on either of which would be enough for his client to succeed. The Court further suggested to Mr. Weir that if he did not succeed on one or other of those issues he was in fact unlikely to be able to uphold the Judge on issue 2 (the contract issue). It would not have been possible to complete the oral hearing on the day allotted for the appeal if issue 2 had been further developed. Mr. Weir was offered the

opportunity of considering whether he wanted to address further oral argument to the Court on some other day on issue 2 with (as was made clear) possible costs consequences if that issue were to be determined against his client. Since there also remained at the conclusion of the oral hearing a further point on the procedure adopted by the appellants in seeking permission to appeal and the costs consequences of adopting that procedure on which both sides were content to put in written submissions, we invited Mr. Weir to make clear by those written submissions what his position was in relation to issue 2. In the result Mr. Weir has confirmed that his client does not seek to be allowed further oral argument on issue 2 and relies simply on the full skeleton argument previously lodged. Mr. Weir has also put in written submissions on the appeal procedure point.

Issue 1: Proper law of the tort

[12] (i) At first sight § 12 seems less than clear when the question is whether some other law should be applied in relation to an issue such as damages or a head of damage. It requires comparison of the significance of the factors which connect a tort (not the issue) with the country whose law would be the applicable law under the general law, and the significance of any factors connecting the tort (not the issue) with another country, and from that comparison to decide in all the circumstances whether it is substantially more appropriate for the law of that other country to be the law to determine the issue. It may be that the words "or any of those issues" were inserted in the section as an amendment without further amendment of (a) or (b) of the sub-section [that seems possible since those words were apparently not in the Bill originally put forward by the Law Commission and not in the Bill originally placed before Parliament (see par. 35-095 of Dicey and Morris)]. It may also be that it was a deliberate decision to draft the section in a way which forced concentration primarily on factors which connected the tort generally to a particular country, even in considering whether there should be an exception for a particular issue. For our purposes it matters not how it happened, the section requires an approach by reference to factors that connect the tort generally to a particular country, and an assessment by reference to those factors as to whether it is substantially more appropriate that an issue be tried by some law other than the law which governs the tort generally.

(ii) The first exercise is to identify the issue in relation to which it might be suggested that the general rule should not be applicable. It is not I think seriously argued that in relation to issues giving rise to liability the general rule should not have applied. The argument relates to the assessment of damages, and in particular to the assessment of a particular head of damage accepted as recoverable under both Dutch and English law "dependency", and ultimately to the question whether benefits accruing from the death of the deceased should be deducted when making that assessment. The characterization for the purposes of private international law of issues arising in a claim as issues relating to tort or delict is a matter for the Courts of the forum (see § 9(2)). This will be relevant again when considering issue 3 (procedural or substantive). The question is whether the issue in the instant case should be defined as damages generally, or that head of damage "dependency" or even more refined to the issue whether benefits should be deducted. In Chaplin v. Boys [1969 2 Lloyd's Rep. 487; [1971] A.C. 356 the House of Lords wrestled with the question whether damages for pain and suffering which were irrecoverable under Maltese law, Malta being the country where the motor accident took place, but recoverable under English law, the law of the country of both parties, and of the forum, should be decided under English law or Maltese law. That points the way as it seems to me to defining and refining the issue in this case at least to that relating to recoverability of damages for loss of dependency. I would however limit the refinement of the issue to "loss of dependency" as opposed to further refining the issue as to whether "benefits should be deducted in assessing loss of dependency". This may not be so important when considering this issue, but it is at this stage that there seems to me to be an overlap between issue 3 and issue 1. The question whether a head of damage is recoverable is clearly a matter of substantive law which could be decided by reference to a law other than the law of the forum. An issue of what should be deducted in calculating the damages under a specific head should be for the law of the forum. For reasons which I shall develop when considering issue 3, the deduction of benefits seems to me a matter of calculation and thus for the forum. Under § 12 the law of the forum is not an option unless that law is also a law of a country with which the tort has significant connecting factors. Thus an issue which is for the law of the forum cannot be a relevant issue under § 12. I accept that at this stage in the context of this case in any event that distinction may be unimportant.

(iii) The next task is to identify the factors that connect the tort with England and those that connect the tort with Holland. The factors that connect with England seem to me to be that the events occurred on a boat registered in England, and that the defendant is an English company. What then are the factors that connect with Holland? The deceased was a Dutchman, and his death would lead to damage being suffered by his dependants, who are Dutch, in Holland where they live. The incident occurred when the deceased was under the supervision of the Dutch fishing master albeit the skipper of the boat was English. In real terms the vessel was on a Dutch fishing expedition in that the boat set off from a Dutch port and would return with its catch to a Dutch port. The defendant was a subsidiary of a Dutch company, and the deceased was on board the trawler as an employee of a Dutch company also a member of the same group.

(iv) What then is the significance of the Dutch factors when compared to the significance of the English factors which might make it substantially more appropriate for Dutch law to determine the loss of dependency issue? Mr. Leonard submits that it is the fact that the deceased was Dutch, employed by a Dutch company paying Dutch taxes and making contributions to obtain Dutch security benefits, and the fact that the dependants will suffer their loss of dependency in Holland as Dutch citizens, which are the most significant factors. That, he submits, makes it logical to assess this aspect of the damages by Dutch law. But it seems to me that the logic of that argument leads almost inevitably to the consequence that where a claimant, injured in England, is a foreigner living and employed in that foreign country, any head of damage should be assessed in accordance with the law of his or her country. Indeed in one sense I suppose it could be said to be "appropriate" that that should be so since the injured party or the dependants thereof are likely to feel their loss only in that foreign country. But it seems to me that it was not intended that the general rule should be dislodged so easily. Where the defendant is English, and the tort took place in England, it cannot surely be said that it is substantially more appropriate for damages to be assessed by Dutch law simply because the claimant or the deceased is Dutch. One can entirely understand that if fortuitously two English persons are in a foreign country on holiday and one tortiously injures the other, the significant factors in favour of England being the place by reference to which the damages should be assessed may make it substantially more appropriate that damages should be assessed by English law. But say the position were that an English defendant under English principles relevant to assessment of damage would have to pay aggravated damages to a claimant, and would thus have to pay English plaintiffs such damages, why should a foreigner not be entitled to have such damages awarded in his or her favour simply because by the law of where they reside those damages would be unavailable?

(v) In my view the word "substantially" is the key word. The general rule is not to be dislodged easily. I thus think the Judge was right in the view he formed that the defendants had failed in their attempt to do so....

Comments and Questions

1. So under what circumstances might a foreign residence make it substantially more appropriate to apply that law?

2. Even if the Court had applied Dutch law with regard to matters involving whether the claimant could recover for loss of dependency, it might have applied English law to determine the amount of damages. Why? The following excerpt provides an answer.

Russell J. Weintraub, Choice of Law for Quantification of Damages

42 Tex. Int'l L.J. 311 (2007)*

I. Choice of Law for Quantification of Tort Damages

In discussing choice of law for determining damages for torts, it is necessary to distinguish between "heads" of damages and "quantification" of damages under those heads. Heads of damages list the items for which a court or jury may award damages—medical expenses, lost wages, pain and suffering, punitive damages,

* Published with the permission of the copyright holder, Russell J. Weintraub, and the Texas International Law Journal.

and perhaps others. Quantification of damages measures the proper amount under each allowable head—how much for pain and suffering?

It is also necessary to focus on the meaning of "substantive" and "procedural" as those terms are used for choice of law. For "substantive" issues a court applies the forum's choice-of-law rule to select the applicable law. "Procedural" in conflicts jargon is simply shorthand for saying that the forum's rule applies.

"Procedural" is a term used in many contexts. It may refer to the rules that govern the workings of the forum's courts—pleading, preserving objections for appeal, discovery. In the United States it may refer to a federal court's freedom to apply a federal rule when the court has subject-matter jurisdiction because of the parties' diversity of citizenship and is applying state, not federal, law to "substantive" issues. Or, as indicated above, a "procedural" issue might be one for which the forum court will not engage in its usual choice-of-law analysis, but will simply apply its own rule.

Justice Frankfurter said it as well as anyone:

> Matters of "substance" and matters of "procedure" are much talked about in the books as though they defined a great divide cutting across the whole domain of law. But, of course, "substance" and "procedure" are the same key-words to very different problems. Neither "substance" nor "procedure" represents the same invariants. Each implies different variables depending upon the particular problem for which it is used.[7]

Therefore, in deciding when to apply the "procedural" label in the context of choice of law, the question is: what justifies a forum in insisting on applying its local rule when under the forum's choice-of-law rule the law of another jurisdiction applies to all "substantive" issues? The proper standard is one that balances the difficulty of finding and applying the foreign rule against the likelihood that applying the forum's rule will affect the result in a manner that will induce forum shopping. Pleading, serving process, preserving objections for appeal, and similar issues relating to the day-to-day operation of courts are properly labeled "procedural" for choice-of-law purposes. Flouting those rules will affect the outcome, but an attorney is not likely to choose one forum over another to take advantage of such housekeeping provisions. Discovery rules require more balancing. A forum that permits massive pre-trial discovery is likely to attract plaintiffs. U.S.-style discovery is one of the reasons that American forums are magnets for the aggrieved and injured of the world.[9] Nevertheless, it would be unthinkable to require U.S. judges and lawyers to learn and apply foreign discovery rules. Discovery is properly labeled "procedural" for choice-of-law purposes.

---

[7] Guaranty Trust Co. v. York, 326 U.S. 99, 108 (1945).

[9] *See* Piper Aircraft Co. v. Reyno, 454 U.S. 235, 252 n.19 (1981) (listing the fact that "discovery is more extensive in American than in foreign courts" as one of the reasons that American courts are attractive to foreign plaintiffs). *But cf.* 28 U.S.C. § 1782(a) (2005) (giving a federal district court discretion to order "a person [who] resides or is found" within the district "to give his testimony or statement or to produce a document or other thing for use in a proceeding in a foreign or international tribunal").

What about damages? Heads of damages, the items that a court or jury may include in computing the amount awarded to the plaintiff, are universally regarded as substantive. If the forum's choice-of-law rule for torts points to a Mexican state, that Mexican state's law determines the heads of damages. Quantification of damages under these heads, however, is regarded as "procedural" and forum standards apply.

The standard rule treating quantification of damages as procedural makes no sense. Quantification is the bottom line—what all the huffing and puffing at trial is about. The American devotion to jury trials in civil cases and the tendency of American juries to award "fabulous damages"are the primary reasons that foreign plaintiffs attempt to litigate their cases in U.S. courts. I have opposed this silliness, but the windmills show little sign of weakening....

One bit of sanity that survives in this choice-of-law madness is that courts regard statutory limits on recovery as "substantive." They apply these limits when their choice-of-law rules select the tort law of the jurisdiction where the statute is in force. In Harding v. Wealands, however, the House of Lords, construing the Private International Law (Miscellaneous Provisions) Act 1995, has rejected even this limit on the "procedural" label when quantifying damages.[19] Now to turn to that opinion.

II. Harding v. Wealands

Mr. Harding, an Englishman, and Ms. Wealands, an Australian, began a relationship in Australia. She moved to England to live with him. Ms. Wealands returned to Australia to attend a family wedding. He later joined her for a holiday and to visit her parents. While she was driving in New South Wales (NSW) with Mr. Harding as a passenger, she lost control and the vehicle turned over. He was badly injured and became tetraplegic as a result of the injury. Ms. Wealands owned the vehicle and carried liability insurance issued by an Australian company. Both Mr. Harding and Ms. Wealands returned to England.

A NSW statute places limits on compensation for various damages including lost earnings and non-economic damages, and in other ways restricts recovery. Under NSW law the plaintiff would recover about thirty percent less than under English law. The United Kingdom Private International Law Act 1995 abolished the double actionability choice-of-law rule for torts[30] and created a presumption that that the law of the place of injury governs unless it is "substantially more appropriate" to apply some other law. Section 14(3)(b) states that the statute does not authorize "questions of procedure in any proceedings to be determined otherwise than in accordance with the law of the forum."

---

[19] Harding v. Wealands [2006] UKHL 32, [2006] 3 W.L.R. 83 (appeal taken from Eng.).

[30] Private International Law (Miscellaneous Provisions) Act 1995, § 10. The double actionability rule required that the tort be actionable under the laws of both the forum and of the jurisdiction where the tort was committed. *See* Chaplin v. Boys, [1971] A.C. 356 (H.L. 1969) (appeal taken from Eng.).

Mr. Harding sued Ms. Wealands in the High Court of Justice in London. That court ruled that English law determined the damages. Justice Elias gave two reasons: (1) the NSW caps on damages were "procedural"; (2) even if damages were substantive it was "substantially more appropriate" to apply English law because the parties "were living together in a settled relationship and resident in England," and "the costs of alleviating the consequences of the accident will be borne in" England. The Court of Appeal allowed the appeal and applied Australian law. The judges of the Court of Appeal agreed that it was not more appropriate to apply English law if the NSW statutory caps on damages were substantive, but they split 2-1 on the issue of whether the caps were substantive, the majority voting for the substantive classification. With five Law Lords participating, the House of Lords unanimously allowed the appeal and restored the judgment of the trial court on the ground that quantification of damages is procedural.

Lord Hoffman stated that he found no ambiguity in the meaning of "procedure" as used in section 14(3)(b) of the Private International Law Act 1995. Procedure in English private international law had always included all issues relating to quantification of damages. The only authority that statutory limits on recovery are substantive is found in one of the leading English treatises on conflict of laws:

> But Mr. Palmer, who appeared for the defendant, submitted that in English private international law a limit or "cap" on the damages recoverable is regarded as substantive. There is, it is true, some authority for this proposition. The 7th edition (1958) of Dicey's Conflict of Laws edited by Dr. JHC Morris, contained the statement, at p 1092, "statutory provisions limiting a defendant's liability are prima facie substantive; but the true construction of the statute may negative this view."

Lord Hoffman rejected this statement in Dicey's treatise as "too widely stated" because the case cited by Dicey is only "authority for the proposition that a contractual term which limits the obligation to pay damages for a breach of contract or a tort, or a statutory provision which is deemed to operate as such a term, qualifies the substantive obligation."

On the question of whether the NSW statutory limits on recovery are procedural, Lord Hoffman states "we could not have better authority than that of the High Court of Australia in Stevens v Head." Stevens v. Head held that the damage limits in an earlier version of the NSW statute were procedural and did not apply to a suit in Queensland by a New Zealand citizen against a Queensland resident.[48] The defendant struck the plaintiff in NSW near the Queensland border with a motor vehicle that was insured and registered in Queensland. Lord Hoffman noted that the High Court of Australia had overruled Stevens v. Head in John Pfeiffer Pty. Ltd. v. Rogerson.[51] Pfeiffer held that limits on non-economic damages in the NSW Workers' Compensation Act were substantive, and applied to a suit in the Australian Capital Territory. A Capital Territory employee of a Capital Territory

[48] Stevens v. Head (1993) 176 C.L.R. 433 (Austl.).

[51] *See* John Pfeiffer Pty. Ltd. v. Rogerson (2000) 203 C.L.R. 503, paras. 182–83, 199–200 (Austl.).

employer had been injured on the job in NSW. Lord Hoffman dismissed this overruling as "required by constitutional imperatives of Australian federalism."

Pfeiffer states:

> Within a federal nation such as Australia, the capacity of a party to legal proceedings to choose the forum within which to bring such proceedings can be one of the advantages of the interconnected polity. However, such a facility ought not to involve the capacity of one party seriously to prejudice the legal rights of an opponent.
>
> It may be reasonable to recognize the right of a litigant to choose different courts in the one nation by reason of their advantageous procedures, better facilities, or greater expedition. However, it is not reasonable that such a choice, made unilaterally by the initiating party, should materially alter that party's substantive legal entitlements to the disadvantage of its opponents. If this could be done, the law would no longer provide a certain and predictable norm, neutrally applied as between the parties. Instead, it would afford a variable rule which particular parties could manipulate to their own advantage. Such a possibility would be obstructive to the integrity of a federal nation, the reasonable expectations of those living within it, and the free mobility of people, goods, and services within its borders—upon the assumption that such movement would not give rise to a significant alteration of accrued legal rights.

This statement expresses, not some peculiar aspect of "Australian federalism," but sound general choice-of-law principles that would mandate the opposite result in Harding.

Lord Hoffman writes that if the word "procedure" were ambiguous in section 14(3)(b) of the Private International Law Act, "this is as clear a case... as anyone could hope to find" where resort to legislative history would demonstrate that Parliament intended that term to include quantification of damages:

> At the Report stage in the House of Lords, Lord Howie of Troon put down an amendment to add a further paragraph to what is now section 14(3), so that it would read: "[nothing in this Part] (d) authorises any court of the forum to award damages other than in accordance with the law of the forum." Lord Howie declared an interest on behalf of Cape Industries plc, which had a few years earlier been sued in Texas for asbestos-related injuries and was anxious that Part III should not import American scales of compensation into English courts. In the debate on 27 March 1995 Lord Mackay of Clashfern LC [Lord Chancellor] made what was obviously a carefully prepared statement: "With regard to damages, issues relating to the quantum or measure of damages are at present and will continue under Part III to be governed by the law of the forum; in other words, by the law of one of the three jurisdictions in the United Kingdom. Issues of this kind are regarded as procedural and, as such, are covered by clause 14(3)(b). It follows from this that the kind of awards to which the noble Lord referred of damages made in certain states, in particular in parts of the United States, will not become a feature of our legal system by virtue of Part III. Our courts will continue to apply our own rules

> on quantum of damages even in the context of a tort case where the court decides that the "applicable law" should be some foreign system of law so far as concerns the merits of the claim. Some aspects of the law of damages are not regarded as procedural and, in accordance with the views of the Law Commissions in their report on the subject, Part III does not alter this. These aspects concern so-called "heads of damages"—the basic matter which is being compensated for—such as special damage relating to direct financial loss. Whether a particular legal system permits such a head of damage is not regarded as procedural but substantive and therefore not automatically subject to the law of the forum. This seems right given the intimate connection between such a concept and the particular nature of the case in issue. But again, I foresee no significant increase in awards of damages because a particular head of damage permitted by some foreign system of law would continue, so far as the quantum allocated to it in any finding is concerned, to be regulated by our own domestic law of damages. I hope the noble Lord will feel reassured."

This excerpt from the Parliamentary proceedings focuses on avoiding introducing "American scales of compensation into English Courts." That policy would not apply to rejecting statutory limits on damages that would reduce recovery below the English standard. Lord Roger of Earlferry recognizes this distinction:

> The particular problem raised by Lord Howie related to the high level of damages in the United States which he was anxious should not be replicated here. But it would be equally unacceptable if, say, United Kingdom courts had to award damages according to a statutory scale which, while adequate in another country because of the relatively low cost of services etc there, would be wholly inadequate in this country, having regard to the cost of the corresponding items here.

This is an argument, not for treating the NSW statutory limits on recovery as procedural, but for applying English substantive law on one of the grounds stated by Justice Elias in his High Court of Justice decision—that it was "substantially more appropriate" to apply English law because the parties "were living together in a settled relationship and resident in England."

The fact that Ms. Wealands carried liability insurance issued by an Australian company does not make it less appropriate to apply English law. Justice Elias also addressed the effect of Australian insurance. He referred to Justice Garland's opinion in Edmunds v. Simmonds,[63] which applied English law in a suit between English residents to recover compensation for injuries incurred in a motor vehicle accident in Spain:

> The judge accepted that the fact that the insurers were Spanish was a relevant factor, but he did not consider that it was sufficiently strong in that case to prevent section 12 dis-applying Spanish law. He accepted a submission that the insurers would contemplate that many of their clients hiring cars would be foreign and there was

[63] Edmunds v. Simmonds [2001] 1 W.L.R. 1003 (Q.B. 2000).

> always a possibility that damages would be assessed in accordance with another system of law.

Another way of saying this is that the payment in Edmunds v. Simmonds was just grist for the actuarial mill. The payment is added to costs that are used to calculate future premiums.

In this context, the only viable unfair surprise argument concerning insurance focuses on unfair surprise to the insured. This may occur if the liability regimes of the place of injury and a distant forum are so different that liability insurance adequate at the place of injury is inadequate to meet forum standards for quantifying damages. If the tortfeasor cannot reasonably foresee the need for insuring at the higher level, it is unfair to impose forum law to compensate a forum resident. For example, suppose a Texas resident vacationing in Mazatlán on the Pacific coast of Mexico is run over by a Mexican driver. The law of Sinaloa, the Mexican state where Mazatlán is located, does not permit recovery for pain and suffering, and has low statutory limits on the recovery of economic damages. Under Sinaloa law, the Texan would recover a small fraction of what he would recover under Texas law. Then further suppose that a Texas court acquires personal jurisdiction over the Mexican driver in Texas by personal service while the Mexican is visiting Texas. The Mexican defendant has liability insurance that is adequate under Sinaloa compensation standards, but is wholly inadequate under Texas measurements of recovery. It would be outrageous to apply Texas law to determine either heads of damages or compensation under those heads. On the other hand, if two Texas friends vacation together in Mazatlán and one injures the other while driving in that city, the driver had better have liability insurance keyed to Texas compensation standards. A Texas court will apply Texas law as the jurisdiction that has the "most significant relationship" to the parties and the occurrence. If the defendant is surprised, it is because he did not heed the warning that the Supreme Court of Texas issued in 1979.[68]

Lord Hoffman gives mixed signals on whether he would invoke the "substantially more appropriate" avoidance of the law of the place of wrong if he were not compelled by legislative history to consider foreign statutory limits on recovery as procedural. One passage seems to say, "yes": "Even if there appeared to be more logic in the principle in Pfeiffer's case [in which the High Court of Australian treated statutory limits on recovery as substantive]...the question is not what the law should be but what Parliament thought it was in 1995." At the end of his opinion he states, however, that because the NSW statutory limits on recovery are procedural:

> it is unnecessary to decide whether, if they had been properly characterised as substantive, it was open to the Court of Appeal to reverse [the trial judge's] judgment that it was substantially more appropriate to apply English law. The hypothesis necessary to raise this question is in my view somewhat artificial, because most of the

[68] *See* Gutierrez v. Collins, 583 S.W.2d 312, 318–19 (Tex. 1979).

> reasons why it may be more appropriate to apply English law are the reasons why the assessment of damages is traditionally characterised as a matter for the lex fori. I would therefore prefer not to express a view on this question.

On the contrary, as demonstrated above by the two hypothetical cases concerning automobile accidents in Mexico, it will sometimes be appropriate to ignore foreign limits on damages and sometimes outrageous, depending on the forum's contacts with the parties and the occurrence.

Lord Woolf offers another reason for regarding the NSW statutory limits on recovery as procedural:

> The limits on the amount of damages on which the defendant seeks to rely are contained in the Motor Accidents Compensation Act 1999 of New South Wales. That Act contains in Chapters 3, 4, 5 and 6 a detailed statutory procedural code containing the machinery for recovering compensation for motor accident injuries, including the way damages are to be assessed. The code is clearly one that has provisions which it would be very difficult, if not impossible, to apply in proceedings brought in this country, even though they may be capable of being applied in other parts of Australia. To have different parts of that code dealt with by different systems of law would not be an attractive result and in some cases this would produce an impractical result. (See for example section 132 which requires, in the case of a dispute over non economic loss, for the degree of impairment to be assessed by a medical assessor in New South Wales.) The greater part of the code is clearly procedural and those parts which could be arguably regarded as substantive should be treated as being procedural as well.[73]

That some provisions of the NSW statutory scheme cannot be applied in England is not a reason for ignoring limits on compensation included in that scheme. If, for example, Mr. Harding had been injured by a stranger in NSW and the stranger, a resident of NSW, was served with process while visiting England to obtain personal jurisdiction over him,[74] an English court should not deprive the defendant of the protection of the NSW statutory limits on recovery.

III. Public Policy

There is no reasonable objection to the U.K., through its Parliament or courts, declaring that it is against public policy to award compensation that is excessive by U.K. standards. This declaration would not justify a court's awarding higher

[73] *Harding*, [2006] UKHL, para. 11.

[74] Although the Brussels Regulation setting out permissible bases for personal jurisdiction in European Union courts excludes personal service on someone temporarily present in the forum, this exclusion does not apply if the defendant is not domiciled in the EU. See Council Regulation 44/2001, On Jurisdiction and the Recognition and Enforcement of Judgments in Civil and Commercial Matters, art. 4, Annex I, 2001 O.J. (L 12) 1, 4, 18. England retains personal service in England as a basis for personal jurisdiction over defendants not domiciled in the EU. See Chellaram v. Chellaram, [2002] EWHC (Ch) 632, [2002] 3 All E.R. 17....

damages than available under the law of the place of wrong, as the House of Lords did in Harding. The only justification for awarding higher damages would be that substantive choice-of-law analysis pointed to English law as applicable; to use the wording of the Private International Law Act, it was "substantially more appropriate" to apply English law.

Suppose the opposite situation when English quantification of damages is lower than that of the place of wrong. A New Yorker negligently injures a fellow New Yorker in New York. The tortfeasor moves to England with all his assets. The injured party can obtain personal jurisdiction over the tortfeasor in New York under the New York long-arm statute, but wisely declines to do so. Because all the tortfeasor's assets are in England, any New York judgment could not be satisfied in the United States. The injured party would have to get the New York judgment recognized and enforced by an English court. An English court will not recognize the New York judgment. Although a tort committed in England is a basis for personal jurisdiction over the tortfeasor in an English court, an English court will not recognize that basis for jurisdiction in countries with which it does not have a judgment-recognition treaty. An English court is compelled by the Private International Law Act to quantify damages by English standards rather than New York Standards. This is especially relevant for non-economic damages such as pain and suffering, for which New York standards are likely to produce a much higher award.

Is this a just result? The Act compels an English court to apply English law when proper choice-of-law analysis would not. The forum's public policy is a legitimate basis for refusing to apply a foreign rule that, to use Cardozo's classic statement, "would violate some fundamental principle of justice, some prevalent conception of good morals, some deep-rooted tradition of the common weal."[79] Cardozo assumed that a forum thus rejecting a foreign rule selected by the forum's choice-of-law rule should dismiss the case. Rejecting the foreign rule does not justify the forum in applying its own substantive law. True, a number of United States courts, not prepared to replace the place-of-wrong tort choice-of-law rule, but dissatisfied with the result of applying that rule, have used public policy to substitute forum law. Lord Hope of Craighead stated a better approach to using public policy to reject a foreign rule and, instead of dismissing the case, rendering a judgment on the merits under a different law. In Kuwait Airways Corp. v. Iraqi Airways Co., the House of Lords rejected Iraqi law that would justify the conversion of aircraft belonging to the Kuwati State.[82] In his opinion, Lord Hope noted that the public policy under which the Lords refused to apply Iraqi law was "based on the Charter of the United Nations and the resolutions which were made under it." He stated that "a principle of English public policy which was purely domestic or parochial in character would not provide clear and satisfying grounds for disapplying the primary rule which favours the lex loci delicti."

---

[79] Loucks v. Standard Oil Co., 120 N.E. 198, 202 (N.Y. 1918).

[82] Kuwait Airways Corp. v. Iraqi Airways Co., [2002] UKHL 19, [2002] 2 A.C. 883 (appeal taken from Eng.).

In the case suggested above, of a New York torfeasor fleeing to England with all his assets, it should not offend English public policy to apply New York law for quantification of damages. If the tortfeasor was an Englishman visiting in New York, an English court would be more justified, as Lord Howie suggested in Parliament, in refusing to "import American scales of compensation into English courts." Reasonable people may differ as to whether the Englishman should be able to injure an American in the U.S. and then draw around him the protective cloak of English law. The standard choice-of-law would point to English law. It would make more sense to someone who has not had their mind numbed by a legal education to reach this result on the basis of public policy rather than pretending that the matter is procedural. If adequately counseled, the injured American will know that if he sues in England, he will get a smaller judgment than if he sued in the U.S. He would sue in England only if his choice was a partial loaf or none at all.

IV. Conclusion

Contrary to the House of Lords' holding in Harding, the Private International Law Act 1995 did not compel depriving the defendant of statutory limits on damages under the law of the place of wrong. If the result in Harding is correct it is because, in the wording of the Act, it was "substantially more appropriate" to apply English law because of the relationship between the parties and their residence in England. The real harm of the House of Lords decision is that it makes it less likely that courts will change the standard rule that characterizes quantification of damages as procedural, and therefore determined by forum criteria. This standard rule should change to accord with a functional view of "procedural" in the context of choice of law. This functional view would preclude the procedural label for any rule that is likely to affect the result in a manner that would invite forum shopping unless it would be unreasonably difficult for local lawyers and judges to apply foreign law to the issue. More undesirable still is that Harding v. Wealands extends the procedural characterization of quantification of damages to the one area where U.S. and Australian courts have had the good sense not to apply it—statutory limits on recovery.

Fortunately, Harding may have a short life in the United Kingdom. A draft Regulation of the European Parliament and the Council on the Law Applicable to Non-Contractual Obligations, referred to as "Rome II," which seems ready for enactment in 2007, includes among the issues governed by the Regulation's choice-of-law rules "the existence, the nature and the assessment of damage or the remedy claimed." This language appears broad enough to include quantification of damages. If so, this would constitute a desirable reversal of the standard rule treating quantification of damages as a procedural matter to be resolved under forum standards. The United Kingdom has agreed to be bound by Rome II.

Comments and Questions

1. Later in this chapter, we will read the recently-promulgated "Rome II" regulation and will consider whether it addresses Professor Weintraub's concerns.

2. In the next several sections, we explore civilian approaches to choice of law analysis. A survey of various code provisions invites comparison and contrast to the common law approach.

3. Japan

The following excerpt offers a translation of Japan's conflict of laws rules. The approach—a discrete code—is typical of a civil law system.

Act on the General Rules of Application of Laws, Law No. 10 of 1898 (Newly Titled and Amended 21 June 2006)

Reprinted from Kent Anderson & Yasuhiro Okuda, Translation of Japan's Private International Law: Act on the General Rules of Application of Laws [Ho no Tekiyo ni Kansuru Tsusokuho], 8 Asian-Pac. L. & Pol'y J. 138 (2006)

Section 2 Juristic Acts

Article 7. Choice of Applicable Law by the Parties.

The formation and effect of a juristic act shall be governed by the law of the place chosen by the parties at the time of the act.

Article 8. In the Absence of a Choice of Applicable Law by the Parties.

(1) Where there is no choice under the preceding Article, the formation and effect of a juristic act shall be governed by the law of the place with which the act is most closely connected at the time of the act.

(2) For the purpose of the preceding paragraph, where only one party is to effect the characteristic performance of the juristic act, it shall be presumed that the juristic act is most closely connected with the law of his or her habitual residence (i.e., the law of his or her place of business where that place of business is related to the act, or the law of his or her principal place of business where he or she has two or more places of business related to the act and where those laws differ).

(3) For the purpose of the first paragraph of this Article, where the subject matter of the juristic act is immovables, notwithstanding the preceding paragraph, it shall be presumed that the act is most closely connected with the law of the place where the immovables are situated.

Article 9. Variation of Applicable Law by the Parties.

The parties may vary the law otherwise applicable to the formation and effect of a juristic act. However, such variation shall not be asserted against third parties where it would be prejudicial to their rights.

Article 10. Formalities of a Juristic Act.

(1) The formalities of a juristic act shall be governed by the law applicable to the formation of the act (where under the preceding Article the law was varied after the juristic act, the law applicable before the variation shall govern).

(2) Notwithstanding the preceding paragraph, formalities that satisfy the requirements of the law of the place where the act was done (lex loci actus) shall be effective.

(3) For the purpose of the preceding paragraph, where a declaration of intent is addressed to a person situated in a place under a different law, the place from where the notice was sent shall be deemed as the place of the act (locus actus).

(4) The second and third paragraphs of this Article shall not apply to the formalities of a contract concluded between parties situated in places having different laws. In this case, notwithstanding the first paragraph of this Article, contract formalities that satisfy the requirements of either the law of the place from where the notice of offer was sent or the law of the place from where the notice of acceptance was sent shall be effective.

(5) The second, third, and fourth paragraphs of this Article shall not apply to the formalities of a juristic act that establishes or disposes of a right in rem to movables or immovables, or of a right requiring registration.

Article 11. Special Rules for Consumer Contracts.

(1) Regarding the formation and effect of a contract (excluding labor contracts; hereinafter referred to in this Article as "consumer contract") between a consumer (i.e., an individual, excluding those cases where the party acts as a business or for a business) and a business operator (i.e., a juridical person or other corporate association, or an individual in those cases where the party is acting as a business or for a business), even where by choice under Article 7 or variation under Article 9, the applicable law would be a law other than that of the consumer's habitual residence, when the consumer indicates to the business operator his or her intention that a particular mandatory rule from within the law of the consumer's habitual residence should apply, this mandatory rule shall also apply to the matters covered by the rule concerning the consumer contract's formation and effect.

(2) Notwithstanding Article 8, where no choice under Article 7 has been made, the formation and effect of a consumer contract shall be governed by the law of the consumer's habitual residence.

(3) In regards to the formation of a consumer contract, even where a law other than the law of a consumer's habitual residence is chosen under Article 7, when the consumer indicates to the business operator his or her intention that a particular mandatory rule from within the law of the consumer's habitual residence should apply to the formalities of the consumer contract, only the mandatory rule shall apply to the matters covered by the rule concerning the consumer contract's formalities, irrespective of Article 10, paragraphs 1, 2, and 4.

(4) Where the law of a consumer's habitual residence is chosen under Article 7 with regards to the formation of a consumer contract, and when the consumer indicates to the business operator his or her intention that the law of the consumer's habitual residence should only apply to the formalities of a consumer contract, the formalities of the consumer contract shall be governed only by the law of the consumer's habitual residence, irrespective of Article 10, paragraphs 2 and 4.

(5) Notwithstanding Article 10, paragraphs 1, 2, and 4, where there is no choice under Article 7 with regards to the formation of the contract, the formalities of a consumer contract shall be governed by the law of the consumer's habitual residence.

(6) The preceding paragraphs shall not apply in any of the following cases:

(i) Where the business operator's place of business that is associated with a consumer contract is in a place under a law that is different from the law of the consumer's habitual residence, and where the consumer comes to a place that has the same law as that place of business to conclude the contract. However, excluding cases where the consumer, who is in the place of his or her habitual residence, is invited by the business operator to conclude the consumer contract in the place that has the same law as the place of business;

(ii) Where the business operator's place of business that is associated with a consumer contract is in a place under a law that is different from the law of the consumer's habitual residence, and where the consumer has received or should receive the performance of all obligations under the consumer contract in a place that has the same law as that place of business. However, excluding cases where the consumer, who is in the place of his or her habitual residence, is invited by the business operator to have all obligations performed under the consumer contract in a place that has the same law as that place of business;

(iii) Where at the time of contracting the business operator did not know the consumer's habitual residence and there were reasonable grounds for not knowing this; or

(iv) Where at the time of contracting the business operator mistook the other party of the contract for not being a consumer and there were reasonable grounds for this mistake.

Article 12. Special Rules for Labor Contracts.

(1) Even where by choice under Article 7 or variation under Article 9, the applicable law to the formation and effect of a labor contract is a law other than the law with which the contract is most closely connected, when the employee indicates to the employer his or her intention that a particular mandatory rule from within the law of the place with which the employee is most closely connected should apply, this mandatory rule shall apply to the matters covered by the rule concerning the labor contract's formation and effect.

(2) For the purpose of the preceding paragraph, it shall be presumed that a labor contract is most closely connected with the law of the place where the work should be carried out under the contract (i.e., the law of the place of business through which the employee was engaged, where the work is not to be carried out in a particular place. The same applies for the next paragraph).

(3) Notwithstanding Article 8, paragraph 2, where no choice under the provision of Article 7 has been made with regards to the formation and effect of a labor

contract, it shall be presumed that regarding its formation and effect the contract is most closely connected with the law of the place where the work should be carried out under the contract.

Section 3 Rights in Rem and so forth

Article 13. Rights in Rem and Rights Requiring Registration.

(1) Rights in rem to movables and immovables and any other rights requiring registration shall be governed by the law of the place where the property is situated (lex rei sitae).

(2) Notwithstanding the preceding paragraph, the acquisition and loss of the rights mentioned in the preceding paragraph shall be governed by the place where the property is situated (lex rei sitae) at the time when the events causing the acquisition or loss were completed.

Section 4 Claims

Article 17. Tort.

The formation and effect of claims arising from tort shall be governed by the law of the place where the results of the acts causing the damage arose. However, where the occurrence of the results in such place would usually be unforeseeable, the law of the place where the acts causing the damage occurred shall govern.

Article 18. Special Rules for Product Liability.

Notwithstanding the preceding Article, where a claim against a producer (i.e., a person who produces, processes, imports, exports, distributes, or sells a product in the course of trade) or a person who makes a representation that leads others to believe he or she is a producer of a product (hereinafter referred to jointly in this Article as "producer or similar person") arises from a tort injuring the life, body, or property of others caused by the defect of a delivered product (i.e., a produced or processed thing), the formation and effect of those claims shall be governed by the law of the place where the injured person has been delivered the product. However, where the delivery of the product to that place could not usually be foreseen, the law of the principal place of business of the producer or similar person (or the law of his or her habitual residence where he or she has no place of business) shall govern.

Article 19. Special Rules for Defamation.

Notwithstanding Article 17, the formation and effect of claims arising from the tort of defamation of another shall be governed by the law of the injured person's habitual residence (i.e., the law of its principal place of business where the injured person is a juridical person or other corporate association).

Article 20. Exception for Cases with a Clearly Closer Connection to Another Place.

Notwithstanding Articles 17, 18, and 19, the formation and effect of claims arising from tort shall be governed by the law of the place with which they are clearly more closely connected in light of the circumstances such as where at the time of the tort both of the parties had their habitual residence in a place under the same law, or where the tort occurred by breaching obligations in a contract between the parties.

Article 21. Variation of Applicable Law by the Parties.

After a tort occurs, the parties to the tort may vary the law that would otherwise be applicable to the formation and effect of claims. However, such variation shall not be asserted against third parties where it would be prejudicial to their rights.

Article 22. Public Policy Limits in Tort.

(1) Where events that should otherwise be governed by the foreign law applicable in tort do not constitute a tort under Japanese law, recovery of damages or any other remedy under the foreign law may not be demanded.

(2) Even where the events that should otherwise be governed by the foreign law applicable in tort constitute a tort both under the foreign law and under Japanese law, the injured person may not demand recovery of damages or any other remedy not recognized under Japanese law.

Section 7 Supplementary Rules

Article 41. Renvoi.

Where a case should be governed by a person's national law and pursuant to the rules of that law the case should be governed by Japanese law, the case shall be governed by Japanese law. . . .

Article 42. Public Policy (Ordre Public)

Where a case should be governed by a foreign law but application of those provisions would contravene public policy (ordre public), those provisions shall not apply.

Comments and Questions

1. Do (Can) codes achieve greater certainty and predictability for determining the applicable law? How much certainty and predictability does this code accomplish?

2. What is the "special" treatment accorded consumer and labor contracts (Articles 11 and 12)? Are consumer and labor contracts the only categories of contract cases that deserve special treatment?

3. Consider the meaning(s) of "habitual residence." Where is your habitual residence? Can you draft two plausible definitions of habitual residence that would lead to different locations (whether streets, cities, states, or countries) for you?

4. Germany

Germany codified certain components of its conflicts law in 1999. Translated excerpts from the tort rules follow:

Act on the Revision of the Private International Law (1999)

Article 40: Tort

(1) Claims arising from tort are governed by the law of the sate in which the person liable to provide compensation acted. The injured person may demand, however, that the law of the state where the result took effect be applied instead. The right to make this election may be exercised only in the court of first instance and then only until the end of the first oral proceeding or the end of written trial proceeding.

(2) If the person liable to provide compensation and the injured person had their habitual residence in the same state at the time the act took place, the law of that state shall be applied. In the case of enterprises, associations, or legal persons the place of their principal administration, or, in the case of a branch, its location, shall be the equivalent of a habitual residence.

(3) Claims that are governed by the law of another state may not be entertained to the extent that they

1. go substantially beyond that which is required for appropriate compensation for the injured person,
2. obviously serve purposes other than provision of appropriate compensation for the injured person, or
3. conflict with provisions concerning liability contained in a treaty that is in force with respect to the Federal Republic of Germany.

(4) The injured person may bring his or her claim directly against the insurer of the person liable to provide compensation if the law applicable to the tort or the law applicable to the insurance contract so provides.

Article 41: Substantially Closer Connection

(1) If there is a substantially closer connection to the law of a state other than the law that would be applicable under [Article 40 paragraphs 1 and 2] the law of that state shall be applied.

(2) In particular, a substantially closer connection may be the result of a special legal or factual relationship between the parties in connection with an obligation...

Article 42: Party Autonomy

After the event giving rise to a non-contractual obligation has occurred, the parties may choose the law that shall apply to the obligation; rights of third parties remain unaffected.

5. Austria

Federal Statute of 15 June 1978 on Private International Law

§1(1). Factual situations with foreign contracts shall be judged, in regard to private law, according to the legal order to which the strongest connections exists.

§48(1). Noncontractual damage claims shall be judged according to the law of the state in which the damage-causing conduct occurred. However, if the persons involved have a stronger connection to the law of one and the same other state, that law shall be determinative.

6. Switzerland

Statute on Private International law

Entered into force January 1, 1989

29 I.L.M. 1254, Article 133

1. When the tortfeasor and the injured party have their habitual residence in the same State, claims based on tort are governed by the law of that State.

2. When the tortfeasor and the injured party have no habitual residence in the same state, these claims are governed by the law of the State where the tort was committed. However, if the result occurred in another State, the law of this State shall be applied if the tortfeasor could have foreseen that the damage would be suffered in that state.

3. Notwithstanding the preceding paragraphs, if and when a tort violates a judicial relationship between the tortfeasor and the injured party, claims based on this act are governed by the law applying to this judicial relationship.

7. The Rome Regulations

Drawing on the rich tradition and experience of codification, the EU Member States have agreed on the text of two Regulations to create harmonized conflicts principles for contractual claims and extracontractual claims, respectively. The nicknames "Rome I" and "Rome II" deserve some attention because they are likely to endure for quite some time. Opened for signature in Rome in 1980, the EC Convention on the Law Applicable to Contractual Obligations represented a dramatic step toward economic integration. That Convention, the so-called Rome Convention, provided a framework for resolving conflicts between the laws of different states of the EU in contract disputes. A subsequent effort that undertook to harmonize the conflicts principles for extracontractual claims was dubbed "Rome II" because it built on "Rome I" (nee: the Rome Convention). Excerpts from the new Rome I and Rome II regulations follow.

Council Regulation (EC) No 593/2008 of 31 March 2008 on The Law Applicable to Contractual Obligations

("Rome I")

Chapter I: Scope

Article 1: Material Scope

1. This Regulation shall apply, in situations involving a conflict of laws, to contractual obligations in civil and commercial matters. It shall not apply, in particular, to revenue, customs or administrative matters.

2. The following shall be excluded from the scope of this Regulation:
   (a) questions involving the status or legal capacity of natural persons, without prejudice to Article 13;
   (b) obligations arising out of family relationships...;...
   (c) obligations arising out of matrimonial property regimes...;...
   (d) obligations arising...under...negotiable instruments...;...
   (e) arbitration agreements and agreements on the choice of court;
   (f) questions governed by the law of companies...;...
   (g) the question whether an agent is able to bind a principal...;...
   (h) the constitution of trusts...;...
   (i) obligations arising out of dealings prior to the conclusion of a contract;
   (j) [certain] insurance contracts....
3. This Regulation shall not apply to evidence and procedure....
4. In this Regulation, the term "Member State" shall mean Member States to which this regulation applies. However, in Article 3(4) and Article 7 the term shall mean all the Member States.

Article 2: Universal application

Any law specified by this Regulation shall be applied whether or not it is the law of a Member State.

Chapter II: Uniform Rules

Article 3: Freedom of choice

1. A contract shall be governed by the law chosen by the parties. The choice shall be made expressly or clearly demonstrated by the terms of the contract or the circumstances of the case. By their choice the parties can select the law applicable to the whole or a part only of the contract.

2. The parties may at any time agree to subject the contract to a law other than that which previously governed it, whether as a result of an earlier choice under this Article or of other provisions of this Regulation. Any change in the law to be applied that is made after the conclusion of the contract shall not prejudice its formal validity under Article 11 or adversely affect the rights of third parties.

3. Where all other elements relevant to the situation at the time of the choice are located in a country other than the country whose law has been chosen, the choice of the parties shall not prejudice the application of provisions of the law of that other country which cannot be derogated from by agreement.

4. Where all other elements relevant to the situation at the time of the choice are located in one or more Member States, the parties' choice of applicable law other than that of a Member State shall not prejudice the application of provisions of Community law, where appropriate as implemented in the Member State of the forum, which cannot be derogated from by agreement.

5. The existence and validity of the consent of the parties as to the choice of the applicable law shall be determined in accordance with the provisions of Articles 10, 11 and 13.

Article 4: Applicable law in the absence of choice

1. To the extent that the law applicable to the contract has not been chosen in accordance with Article 3 and without prejudice to Articles 5 to 8, the law governing the contract shall be determined as follows:

(a) a contract for the sale of goods shall be governed by the law of the country where the seller has his habitual residence;
(b) a contract for the provision of services shall be governed by the law of the country where the service provider has his habitual residence;
(c) a contract relating to a right in rem in immovable property or to a tenancy of immovable property shall be governed by the law of the country where the property is situated;
(d) notwithstanding point (c), a tenancy of immovable property concluded for temporary private use for a period of no more than six consecutive months shall be governed by the law of the country where the landlord has his habitual residence, provided that the tenant is a natural person and has his habitual residence in the same country;
(e) a franchise contract shall be governed by the law of the country where the franchisee has his habitual residence;
(f) a distribution contract shall be governed by the law of the country where the distributor has his habitual residence;
(g) a contract for the sale of goods by auction shall be governed by the law of the country where the action takes place, if such a place can be determined;
(h) a contract concluded within a multilateral system which brings together... multiple third-party buying and selling interests in [certain] financial instruments....

2. Where the contract is not covered by paragraph 1 or where the elements of the contract would be covered by more than one of points (a) to (h) of paragraph 1, the contract shall be governed by the law of the country where the party required to effect the characteristic performance of the contract has his habitual residence.

3. Where it is clear from all the circumstances of the case that the contract is manifestly more closely connected with a country other than that indicated in paragraphs 1 or 2, the law of that other country shall apply.

4. Where the law applicable cannot be determined pursuant to paragraphs 1 or 2, the contract shall be governed by the law of the country with which it is most closely connected.

Article 5: Contracts of carriage

1. To the extent that the law applicable to a contract for the carriage of good has not been chosen in accordance with Article 3, the law applicable shall be the law of the country of habitual residence of the carrier, provided that the place of receipt or the place of delivery or the habitual residence of the consignor is also situated in that country. If those requirements are not met, the law of the country where the place of delivery as agreed by the parties is situated shall apply.

2. To the extent that the law applicable to a contract for the carriage of passengers has not been chosen by the parties in accordance with the second subparagraph, the law applicable shall be the law of the country where the passenger has his habitual residence, provided that either the place of departure or the place of destination is situated in that country. If these requirements are not met, the law of the country where the carrier has his habitual residence shall apply.

The parties may choose as the law applicable to a contract for the carriage of passengers in accordance with Article 3 only the law of the country where:

(a) the passenger has his habitual residence; or
(b) the carrier has his habitual residence; or
(c) the carrier has his place of central administration; or
(d) the place of departure is situated; or
(e) the place of destination is situated.

3. Where it is clear from all the circumstances of the case that the contract, in the absence of a choice of law, is manifestly more closely connected with a country other that indicated in paragraphs 1 or 2, the law of that other country shall apply.

Article 6: Consumer contracts

1. Without prejudice to Articles 5 and 7, a contract concluded by a natural person for a purpose which can be regarded as being outside his trade or profession ("the consumer") with another person acting in the exercise of his trade or profession ("the professional") shall be governed by the law of the country where the consumer has his habitual residence, provided that the professional:

(a) pursues his commercial or professional activities in the country where the consumer has his habitual residence, or
(b) by any means, directs such activities to that country or to several countries including that country.

and the contract falls within the scope of such activities.

2. Notwithstanding paragraph 1, the parties may choose the law applicable to a contract which fulfills the requirements of paragraph 1, in accordance with Article 3. Such a choice may not, however, have the result of depriving the consumer of the protection afforded to him by provisions that cannot be derogated from by agreement or by virtue of the law which, in the absence of choice, would have been applicable on the basis of paragraph 1.

3. If the requirements in points (a) or (b) of paragraph1 are not fulfilled, the law applicable to a contract between a consumer and a professional shall be determined pursuant to Articles 3 and 4

4. Paragraphs 1 and 2 shall not apply to:

(a) a contract for the supply of services where the services are to be supplied to the consumer exclusively in a country other than that in which he has his habitual residence;
(b) [certain contracts of carriage];
(c) a contract relating to a right in rem in immovable property...;
(d) rights and obligations which constitute a financial instruments and obligations constituting the terms and conditions [of investment securities];

(e) a contract concluded within the type of system falling within the scope of Article 4(1), point (h).

Article 7: Insurance contracts

[Includes provisions analogous to Article 6.]

Article 8: Individual employment contracts

1. An individual employment contract shall be governed by the law chosen by the parties in accordance with Article 3. Such a choice of law may not, however, have the result of depriving the employee of the protection afforded to him by provisions that cannot be derogated from by agreement under the law that, in the absence of choice, would have been applicable pursuant to paragraphs 2, 3 and 4 of this Article.

2. To the extent that the applicable to the individual employment contract has not been chosen by the parties, the contract shall be governed by the law of the country in which or, failing that, from which the employee habitually carries out his work in performance of the contract. The country where the work is habitually carried out shall not be deemed to have changed if he is temporarily employed in another country.

3. Where the law applicable cannot be determined pursuant to paragraph 2, the contract shall be governed by the law of the country where the place of business through which the employee was engaged is situated.

4. Where it appears from the circumstances as a whole that the contract is more closely connected with a country other than that indicated in paragraphs 2 or 3, the law of that other country shall apply.

Article 9: Overriding mandatory provisions

1. Overriding mandatory provisions are provisions the respect for which is regarded as crucial by a country for safeguarding its public interests, such as its political, social or economic organisation, to such an extent that they are applicable to any situation falling within their scope, irrespective of the law otherwise applicable to the contract under this Regulation.

2. Nothing in this Regulation shall restrict the application of the overriding mandatory provisions of the law of the forum.

3. Effect may be given to the overriding mandatory provisions of the law of the country where the obligations arising out of the contract have to be or have been performed, in so far as those overriding mandatory provisions render the performance of the contract unlawful. In considering whether to give effect to those provisions, regard shall be had to their nature and purpose and to the consequences of their application or non-application....

Chapter III: Other Provisions

...

Article 20: Exclusion of renvoi

The application of the law of any country specified by this Regulation means the application of the rules of law in force in that country other than its rules of private international law, unless provided otherwise in this Regulation.

Article 21: Public policy of the forum

The application of a provision of the law of any country specified by this Regulation may be refused only if such application is manifestly incompatible with the public policy ("ordre public") of the forum.

Council Regulation (EC) No 864/2007 of 11 July 2007 on The Law Applicable to Non-Contractual Obligations ("Rome II")

Chapter I: Scope

Article 1: Scope

1. This Regulation shall, in situations involving a conflict of laws, to non-contractual obligations in civil and commercial matters. It shall not apply, in particular, to revenue, customs or administrative matters or to the liability of the State for acts and omissions in the exercise of State authority (acta iure imperii).

2. The following shall be excluded from the scope of this Regulation:
   - (a) non-contractual obligations arising out of family relationships...;...
   - (b) non-contractual obligations arising out of matrimonial property regimes...;...
   - (c) non-contractual obligations arising under bills of exchanges, cheques and promissory notes or other negotiable instruments...;...
   - (d) non-contractual obligations arising out of the law of companies...;...
   - (e) non-contractual obligations arising out of the relations between the settlors, trustees and beneficiaries of a trust created voluntarily;...
   - (f) non-contractual obligations arising out of nuclear damage;...
   - (g) non-contractual obligations arising out of violations of privacy and rights relating to personality, including defamation....

Article 2: Non-contractual obligations

1. For the purposes of this Regulation, damage shall cover any consequence arising out of tort/delict, unjust enrichment, negotiorum gestio or culpa in contrahendo.

2. This Regulation shall apply also to non-contractual obligations that are likely to arise....

Article 3: Universal application

Any law specified by this Regulation shall be applied whether or not it is the law of a Member State.

Chapter II: Torts/Delicts

Article 4: General rule

1. Unless otherwise provided for in this Regulation, the law applicable to a non-contractual obligation arising out of a tort/delict shall be the law of the country in

which the damage occurs irrespective of the country in which the event giving rise to the damage occurred and irrespective of the country or countries in which the indirect consequences of that event occur.

2. However, where the person claimed to be liable and the person sustaining damage both have their habitual residence in the same country at the time when the damage occurs, the law of that country shall apply.

3. Where it is clear from all the circumstances of the case that the tort/delict is manifestly more closely connected with a country other than that indicated in paragraphs 1 or 2, the law of that other country shall apply. A manifestly closer connection with another country might be based in particular on a pre-existing relationship between the parties, such as a contract, that is closely connected with the tort/delict in question.

Article 5: Product liability

1. Without prejudice to Article 4(2), the applicable to a non-contractual obligation arising out of damage caused by a product shall be:

(a) the law of the country in which the person sustaining the damage had his or her habitual residence when the damage occurred, if the product was marketed in that country; or, failing that,

(b) the law of the country in which the product was acquired, if the product was marketed in that country; or, failing that,

(c) the law of the country in which the damage occurred, if the product was marketed in that country.

However, the law applicable shall be the law of the country in which the person claimed to be liable is habitually resident if he or she could not reasonably foresee the marketing of the product, or a product of the same type, in the country the law of which is applicable under (a), (b) or (c).

2. Where it is clear from all the circumstances of the case that the tort/delict is manifestly more closely connected with a country other than that indicated in paragraph 1, the law of that other country shall apply. A manifestly closer connection with another country might be based in particular on a pre-existing relationship between the parties, such as a contract, that is closely connected with the tort/delict in question.

Article 6: Unfair competition and acts restricting free competition

1. The law applicable to a non-contractual obligation arising out of an act of unfair competition shall be the law of the country where competitive relations or the collective interests of consumers are, or are likely to be, affected.

2. Where an act of unfair competition affects exclusively the interests of a specific competitor, Article 4 shall apply.

3. (a) The law applicable to a non-contractual obligation arising out of a restriction of competition shall be the law of the country where the market is, or is likely to be, affected.

(b) When the market is, or is likely to be, affected in more than one country, the person seeking compensation for damage who sues in the court of the domicile of the defendant, may instead choose to base his or her claim on the law of the court seised, provided that the market in that Member State is amongst those directly and substantially affected by the restriction of competition out of which the non-contractual obligation on which the claim is based arises; where the claimant sues, in accordance with the applicable rules on jurisdiction, more than one defendant in that court, he or she can only choose to base his or her claim on the law of that court if the restriction of competition on which the claim against each of these defendants relies directly and substantially affects also the markets in the Member State of that court.

Article 7: Environmental damage

The law applicable to a non-contractual obligation arising out of environmental damage or damage sustained by persons or property as a result of such damage shall be the law determined pursuant to Article 4(1), unless the person seeking compensation for damage chooses to base his or her claim on the law of the country in which the event giving rise to the damage occurred.

Article 8: Infringement of intellectual property rights

1. The law applicable to a non-contractual obligation arising from an infringement of an intellectual property right shall be the law of the country for which protection is claimed.

2. In the case of a non-contractual obligation arising from an infringement of a unitary Community intellectual property right, the law applicable shall, for any question that is not governed by the relevant Community instrument, be the law of the country in which the act of infringement was committed.

3. The law applicable under this Article may not be derogated from by an agreement pursuant to Article 14.

Article 9: Industrial action

Without prejudice to Article 4(2), the law applicable to a non-contractual obligation in respect of the liability of a person in the capacity of a worker or an employer or the organisations representing their professional interests for damages caused by an industrial action, pending or carried out, shall be the law of the country where the action is to be, or has been taken.

Chapter III: Unjust Enrichment, Negotiorum Gestio and Culpa in Contrahendo

Article 10: Unjust Enrichment

1. If a non-contractual obligation arising out of unjust enrichment, including payment of amounts wrongly received, concerns a relationship existing between the parties, such as one arising out of a contract or a tort/delict, that is closely connected with that unjust enrichment, it shall be governed by the law that governs that relationship.

2. Where the law applicable cannot be determined on the basis of paragraph 1 and the parties have their habitual residence in the same country when the event giving rise to unjust enrichment occurs, the law of that country shall apply.

3. Where the law applicable cannot be determined on the basis of paragraphs 1 or 2, it shall be the law of the country in which the unjust enrichment took place.

4. Where it is clear from all the circumstances of the case that the non-contractual obligation arising out of unjust enrichment is manifestly more closely connected with a country other than that indicated in paragraphs 1, 2 and 3, the law of that other country shall apply.

Article 11: Negotiorum gestio

[Includes provisions analogous to Article 10.]

Article 12: Culpa in contrahendo

[Includes provisions analogous to Article 10.]

. . .

Chapter IV: Freedom of Choice

Article 14: Freedom of choice

1. The parties may agree to submit non-contractual obligations to the law of their choice:

(a) by an agreement entered into after the event giving rise to the damage occurred; or

(b) where all the parties are pursuing a commercial activity, also by an agreement freely negotiated before the event giving rise to the damage occurred.

The choice shall be expressed or demonstrated with reasonable certainty by the circumstances of the case and shall not prejudice the rights of third parties.

2. Where all the elements relevant to the situation at the time when the event giving rise to the damage occurs are located in a country other than the country whose law has been chosen, the choice of the parties shall not prejudice the application of provisions of the law of that other country which cannot be derogated from by agreement.

3. Where all the elements relevant to the situation at the time when the event giving rise to the damage occurs are located in one or more of the Member States, the parties' choice of the law applicable other than that of a Member State shall not prejudice the application of provisions of Community law, where appropriate as implemented in the Member State of the forum, which cannot be derogated from by agreement.

Chapter V: Common Rules

Article 15: Scope of the law applicable

The law applicable to non-contractual obligations under this Regulation shall govern in particular:

(a) the basis and extent of liability, including the determination of persons who may be held liable for acts performed by them;
(b) the grounds for exemption from liability, any limitation of liability and any division of liability;
(c) the existence, the nature and the assessment of damage or the remedy claimed;
(d) within the limits of powers conferred on the court by its procedural law, the measures which a court may take to prevent or terminate injury or damage or to ensure the provision of compensation;
(e) the question whether a right to claim damages or a remedy may be transferred, including by inheritance;
(f) persons entitled to compensation for damage sustained personally;
(g) liability for the acts of another person;
(h) the manner in which an obligation may be extinguished and rules of prescription and limitation, including rules relating to the commencement, interruption and suspension of a period of prescription or limitation.

Article 16: Overriding mandatory provisions

Nothing in this Regulation shall restrict the application of the provisions of the law of the forum in a situation where they are mandatory irrespective of the law otherwise applicable to the non-contractual obligation.

Article 17: Rules of safety and conduct

In assessing the conduct of the person claimed to be liable, account shall be taken, as a matter of fact and in so far as is appropriate, of the rules of safety and conduct which were in force at the place and time of the event giving rise to the liability....

Chapter VI: Other Provisions

...

Article 24: Exclusion of renvoi

The application of the law of any country specified by this Regulation means the application of the rules of law in force in that country other than its rules of private international law....

Article 26: Public policy of the forum

The application of a provision of the law of any country specified by this Regulation may be refused only if such application is manifestly incompatible with the public policy ("ordre public") of the forum.

Comments and Questions

1. How respectful are the Rome Regulations of party autonomy (freedom of choice)?

2. Does Rome II address the concerns expressed by Professor Weintraub above about the characterization of the quantification of damages as procedural?

3. Compare the provisions of Rome II to the quoted excerpts above from the German, Austrian, and Swiss national codes. If you were a practitioner in one of those countries, would the Rome II regulation represent a significant reform in conflicts doctrine?

4. If you were a practitioner in the U.S. would local adoption of principles reflected in Rome II represent a significant reform?

D. Hague Conventions

As we have seen, the determination of the applicable law can raise intriguing and difficult questions. Only a few international conventions are in force to regulate the question, and countries have only to a very limited degree adopted uniform principles as to the determination of the applicable law. Three examples follow.

Hague Conference on Private International Law, Convention on Celebration and Recognition of Validity of Marriages

Concluded March 14, 1978

The States signatory to the present Convention,*

Desiring to facilitate the celebration of marriages and the recognition of the validity of marriages,

Have resolved to conclude a Convention to this effect, and have agreed on the following provisions—

Chapter I—Celebration of Marriages

Article 1

This Chapter shall apply to the requirements in a Contracting State for celebration of marriages.

Article 2

The formal requirements for marriages shall be governed by the law of the State of celebration.

Article 3

A marriage shall be celebrated—

(1) where the future spouses meet the substantive requirements of the internal law of the State of celebration and one of them has the nationality of that State or habitually resides there; or

(2) where each of the future spouses meets the substantive requirements of the internal law designated by the choice of law rules of the State of celebration.

* The three Member States of the Hague Conference that are Contracting States to this Convention are Australia, Luxembourg, and the Netherlands.

Article 4

The State of celebration may require the future spouses to furnish any necessary evidence as to the content of any foreign law which is applicable under the preceding Articles.

Article 5

The application of a foreign law declared applicable by this Chapter may be refused only if such application is manifestly incompatible with the public policy ("ordre public") of the State of celebration.

Article 6

A Contracting State may reserve the right, by way of derogation from Article 3, sub-paragraph 1, not to apply its internal law to the substantive requirements for marriage in respect of a future spouse who neither is a national of that State nor habitually resides there.

Chapter II—Recognition of the Validity of Marriages

Article 7

This Chapter shall apply to the recognition in a Contracting State of the validity of marriages entered into in other States.

Article 8

This Chapter shall not apply to—

(1) marriages celebrated by military authorities;
(2) marriages celebrated aboard ships or aircraft;
(3) proxy marriages;
(4) posthumous marriages;
(5) informal marriages.

Article 9

A marriage validly entered into under the law of the State of celebration or which subsequently becomes valid under that law shall be considered as such in all Contracting States, subject to the provisions of this Chapter.

A marriage celebrated by a diplomatic agent or consular official in accordance with his law shall similarly be considered valid in all Contracting States, provided that the celebration is not prohibited by the State of celebration.

Article 10

Where a marriage certificate has been issued by a competent authority, the marriage shall be presumed to be valid until the contrary is established.

Article 11

A Contracting State may refuse to recognize the validity of a marriage only where, at the time of the marriage, under the law of that State—

(1) one of the spouses was already married; or

(2) the spouses were related to one another, by blood or by adoption, in the direct line or as brother and sister; or
(3) one of the spouses had not attained the minimum age required for marriage, nor had obtained the necessary dispensation; or
(4) one of the spouses did not have the mental capacity to consent; or
(5) one of the spouses did not freely consent to the marriage.

However, recognition may not be refused where, in the case mentioned in subparagraph 1 of the preceding paragraph, the marriage has subsequently become valid by reason of the dissolution or annulment of the prior marriage.

Article 12

The rules of this Chapter shall apply even where the recognition of the validity of a marriage is to be dealt with as an incidental question in the context of another question.

However, these rules need not be applied where that other question, under the choice of law rules of the forum, is governed by the law of a non-Contracting State.

Article 13

This Convention shall not prevent the application in a Contracting State of rules of law more favourable to the recognition of foreign marriages.

Article 14

A Contracting State may refuse to recognize the validity of a marriage where such recognition is manifestly incompatible with its public policy ("ordre public").

Article 15

This Chapter shall apply regardless of the date on which the marriage was celebrated.

However, a Contracting State may reserve the right not to apply this Chapter to a marriage celebrated before the date on which, in relation to that State, the Convention enters into force.

Chapter III—General Clauses

Article 16

A Contracting State may reserve the right to exclude the application of Chapter I.

Article 17

Where a State has two or more territorial units in which different systems of law apply in relation to marriage, any reference to the law of the State of celebration shall be construed as referring to the law of the territorial unit in which the marriage is or was celebrated.

Article 18

Where a State has two or more territorial units in which different systems of law apply in relation to marriage, any reference to the law of that State in connection with the recognition of the validity of a marriage shall be construed as referring to the law of the territorial unit in which recognition is sought.

Article 19

Where a State has two or more territorial units in which different systems of law apply in relation to marriage, this Convention need not be applied to the recognition in one territorial unit of the validity of a marriage entered into in another territorial unit.

Article 20

Where a State has, in relation to marriage, two or more systems of law applicable to different categories of persons, any reference to the law of that State shall be construed as referring to the system of law designated by the rules in force in that State.

Article 21

The Convention shall not affect the application of any convention containing provisions on the celebration or recognition of the validity of marriages to which a Contracting State is a Party at the time this Convention enters into force for that State.

This Convention shall not affect the right of a Contracting State to become a Party to a convention, based on special ties of a regional or other nature, containing provisions on the celebration or recognition of validity of marriages.

Article 22

This Convention shall replace, in the relations between the States who are Parties to it, the Convention Governing Conflicts of Laws Concerning Marriage, concluded at The Hague, the 12th of June 1902.

Article 23

Each Contracting State shall, at the time of signature, ratification, acceptance, approval or accession, inform the Ministry of Foreign Affairs of the Netherlands of the authorities which under its law are competent to issue a marriage certificate as mentioned in Article 10 and, subsequently, of any changes relating to such authorities.

Chapter IV—Final Clauses

Article 24

The Convention shall be open for signature by the States which were Members of the Hague Conference on Private International Law at the time of its Thirteenth Session.

It shall be ratified, accepted or approved and the instruments of ratification, acceptance or approval shall be deposited with the Ministry of Foreign Affairs of the Netherlands.

Article 25

Any other State may accede to the Convention.

The instrument of accession shall be deposited with the Ministry of Foreign Affairs of the Netherlands.

Article 26

Any State may, at the time of signature, ratification, acceptance, approval or accession, declare that the Convention shall extend to all the territories for the international relations of which it is responsible, or to one or more of them. Such a declaration shall take effect at the time the Convention enters into force for that State.

Such declaration, as well as any subsequent extension, shall be notified to the Ministry of Foreign Affairs of the Netherlands.

Article 27

A Contracting State which has two or more territorial units in which different systems of law apply in relation to marriage may, at the time of signature, ratification, acceptance, approval or accession, declare that the Convention shall apply to all its territorial units or only to one or more of them, and may extend its declaration at any time thereafter.

These declarations shall be notified to the Ministry of Foreign Affairs of the Netherlands, and shall state expressly the territorial unit to which the Convention applies.

Article 28

Any State may, not later than the time of ratification, acceptance, approval or accession, make one or more of the reservations provided for in Articles 6, 15 and 16. No other reservation shall be permitted.

Any State may at any time withdraw a reservation it has made.

The withdrawal shall be notified to the Ministry of Foreign Affairs of the Netherlands.

The reservation shall cease to have effect on the first day of the third calendar month after the notification referred to in the preceding paragraph.

Article 29

The Convention shall enter into force on the first day of the third calendar month after the deposit of the third instrument of ratification, acceptance, approval or accession referred to in Articles 24 and 25.

Thereafter the Convention shall enter into force—

(1) for each State ratifying, accepting, approving or acceding to it subsequently, on the first day of the third calendar month after the deposit of its instrument of ratification, acceptance, approval or accession;

(2) for a territory to which the Convention has been extended in conformity with Article 26, on the first day of the third calendar month after the notification referred to in that Article.

Article 30

The Convention shall remain in force for five years from the date of its entry into force in accordance with the first paragraph of Article 29 even for States which subsequently have ratified, accepted, approved it or acceded to it.

If there has been no denunciation, it shall be renewed tacitly every five years.

Any denunciation shall be notified to the Ministry of Foreign Affairs of the Netherlands, at least six months before the expiry of the five year period. It may be limited to certain of the territories or territorial units to which the Convention applies.

The denunciation shall have effect only as regards the State which has notified it. The Convention shall remain in force for the other Contracting States.

Article 31

The Ministry of Foreign Affairs of the Netherlands shall notify the States Members of the Conference, and the States which have acceded in accordance with Article 25, of the following—

(1) the signatures and ratifications, acceptances and approvals referred to in Article 24;
(2) the accessions referred to in Article 25;
(3) the date on which the Convention enters into force in accordance with Article 29;
(4) the extensions referred to in Article 26;
(5) the declarations referred to in Article 27;
(6) the reservations referred to in Articles 6, 15 and 16, and the withdrawals referred to in Article 28;
(7) the information communicated under Article 23;
(8) the denunciations referred to in Article 30.

In witness whereof the undersigned, being duly authorised thereto, have signed this Convention.

Done at The Hague, on the 14th day of March, 1978, in the English and French languages, both texts being equally authentic, in a single copy which shall be deposited in the archives of the Government of the Netherlands, and of which a certified copy shall be sent, through the diplomatic channel, to each of the States Members of the Hague Conference on Private International Law at the date of its Thirteenth Session.

Hague Conference on Private International Law, Convention on the Law Applicable to Traffic Accidents

Concluded May 4, 1971

The States signatory to the present Convention,*

Desiring to establish common provisions on the law applicable to civil non-contractual liability arising from traffic accidents,

* The nineteen Member States of the Hague Conference that are Contracting States to this Convention are Austria, Belarus, Belgium, Bosnia and Herzegovina, Croatia, Czech Republic, the Former Yugoslav Republic of Macedonia, France, Latvia, Lithuania, Luxembourg, Montenegro, Netherlands, Poland, Serbia, Slovakia, Slovenia, Spain, and Switzerland.

Have resolved to conclude a Convention to this effect and have agreed upon the following provisions:

Article 1

The present Convention shall determine the law applicable to civil non-contractual liability arising from traffic accidents, in whatever kind of proceeding it is sought to enforce this liability.

For the purpose of this Convention, a traffic accident shall mean an accident which involves one or more vehicles, whether motorized or not, and is connected with traffic on the public highway, in grounds open to the public or in private grounds to which certain persons have a right of access.

Article 2

The present Convention shall not apply—

(1) to the liability of manufacturers, sellers or repairers of vehicles;
(2) to the responsibility of the owner, or of any other person, for the maintenance of a way open to traffic or for the safety of its users;
(3) to vicarious liability, with the exception of the liability of an owner of a vehicle, or of a principal, or of a master;
(4) to recourse actions among persons liable;
(5) to recourse actions and to subrogation in so far as insurance companies are concerned;
(6) to actions and recourse actions by or against social insurance institutions, other similar institutions and public automobile guarantee funds, and to any exemption from liability laid down by the law which governs these institutions.

Article 3

The applicable law is the internal law of the State where the accident occurred.

Article 4

Subject to Article 5, the following exceptions are made to the provision of Article 3—

a) Where only one vehicle is involved in the accident and it is registered in a State other than that where the accident occurred, the internal law of the State of registration is applicable to determine liability
— towards the driver, owner or any other person having control of or an interest in the vehicle, irrespective of their habitual residence,
— towards a victim who is a passenger and whose habitual residence is in a State other than that where the accident occurred,
— towards a victim who is outside the vehicle at the place of the accident and whose habitual residence is in the State of registration.
Where there are two or more victims the applicable law is determined separately for each of them.
b) Where two or more vehicles are involved in the accident, the provisions of a) are applicable only if all the vehicles are registered in the same State.

c) Where one or more persons outside the vehicle or vehicles at the place of the accident are involved in the accident and may be liable, the provisions of a) and b) are applicable only if all these persons have their habitual residence in the State of registration.

The same is true even though these persons are also victims of the accident.

Article 5

The law applicable under Articles 3 and 4 to liability towards a passenger who is a victim governs liability for damage to goods carried in the vehicle and which either belong to the passenger or have been entrusted to his care.

The law applicable under Articles 3 and 4 to liability towards the owner of the vehicle governs liability for damage to goods carried in the vehicle other than goods covered in the preceding paragraph.

Liability for damage to goods outside the vehicle or vehicles is governed by the internal law of the State where the accident occurred.

However the liability for damage to the personal belongings of the victim outside the vehicle or vehicles is governed by the internal law of the State of registration when that law would be applicable to the liability towards the victim according to Article 4.

Article 6

In the case of vehicles which have no registration or which are registered in several States the internal law of the State in which they are habitually stationed shall replace the law of the State of registration. The same shall be true if neither the owner nor the person in possession or control nor the driver of the vehicle has his habitual residence in the State of registration at the time of the accident.

Article 7

Whatever may be the applicable law, in determining liability account shall be taken of rules relating to the control and safety of traffic which were in force at the place and time of the accident.

Article 8

The applicable law shall determine, in particular—

(1) the basis and extent of liability;
(2) the grounds for exemption from liability, any limitation of liability, and any division of liability;
(3) the existence and kinds of injury or damage which may have to be compensated;
(4) the kinds and extent of damages;
(5) the question whether a right to damages may be assigned or inherited;
(6) the persons who have suffered damage and who may claim damages in their own right;
(7) the liability of a principal for the acts of his agent or of a master for the acts of his servant;

(8) rules of prescription and limitation, including rules relating to the commencement of a period of prescription or limitation, and the interruption and suspension of this period.

Article 9

Persons who have suffered injury or damage shall have a right of direct action against the insurer of the person liable if they have such a right, under the law applicable according to Articles 3, 4 or 5.

If the law of the State of registration is applicable under Articles 4 or 5 and that law provides no right of direct action, such a right shall nevertheless exist if it is provided by the internal law of the State where the accident occurred.

If neither of these laws provides any such right it shall exist if it is provided by the law governing the contract of insurance.

Article 10

The application of any of the laws declared applicable by the present Convention may be refused only when it is manifestly contrary to public policy ("ordre public").

Article 11

The application of Articles 1 to 10 of this Convention shall be independent of any requirement of reciprocity. The Convention shall be applied even if the applicable law is not that of a Contracting State....

Hague Conference on Private International Law, Convention on the Law Applicable to Products Liability

Concluded October 2, 1973

The States signatory to the present Convention,*

Desiring to establish common provisions on the law applicable, in international cases, to products liability,

Have resolved to conclude a Convention to this effect and have agreed upon the following provisions:

Article 1

This Convention shall determine the law applicable to the liability of the manufacturers and other persons specified in Article 3 for damage caused by a product, including damage in consequence of a misdescription of the product or of a failure to give adequate notice of its qualities, its characteristics or its method of use.

* The eleven Member States of the Hague Conference that are Contracting States to this Convention are Croatia, Finland, the Former Yugoslav Republic of Macedonia, France, Luxembourg, Montenegro, Netherlands, Norway, Serbia, Slovenia, and Spain.

Where the property in, or the right to use, the product was transferred to the person suffering damage by the person claimed to be liable, the Convention shall not apply to their liability inter se.

This Convention shall apply irrespective of the nature of the proceedings.

Article 2

For the purposes of this Convention—

a) the word "product" shall include natural and industrial products, whether raw or manufactured and whether movable or immovable;
b) the word "damage" shall mean injury to the person or damage to property as well as economic loss; however, damage to the product itself and the consequential economic loss shall be excluded unless associated with other damage;
c) the word "person" shall refer to a legal person as well as to a natural person.

Article 3

This Convention shall apply to the liability of the following persons—

(1) manufacturers of a finished product or of a component part;
(2) producers of a natural product;
(3) suppliers of a product;
(4) other persons, including repairers and warehousemen, in the commercial chain of preparation or distribution of a product.

It shall also apply to the liability of the agents or employees of the persons specified above.

Article 4

The applicable law shall be the internal law of the State of the place of injury, if that State is also—

a) the place of the habitual residence of the person directly suffering damage, or
b) the principal place of business of the person claimed to be liable, or
c) the place where the product was acquired by the person directly suffering damage.

Article 5

Notwithstanding the provisions of Article 4, the applicable law shall be the internal law of the State of the habitual residence of the person directly suffering damage, if that State is also—

a) the principal place of business of the person claimed to be liable, or
b) the place where the product was acquired by the person directly suffering damage.

Article 6

Where neither of the laws designated in Articles 4 and 5 applies, the applicable law shall be the internal law of the State of the principal place of business of the person claimed to be liable, unless the claimant bases his claim upon the internal law of the State of the place of injury.

Article 7

Neither the law of the State of the place of injury nor the law of the State of the habitual residence of the person directly suffering damage shall be applicable by virtue of Articles 4, 5 and 6 if the person claimed to be liable establishes that he could not reasonably have foreseen that the product or his own products of the same type would be made available in that State through commercial channels.

Article 8

The law applicable under this Convention shall determine, in particular—

(1) the basis and extent of liability;
(2) the grounds for exemption from liability, any limitation of liability and any division of liability;
(3) the kinds of damage for which compensation may be due;
(4) the form of compensation and its extent;
(5) the question whether a right to damages may be assigned or inherited;
(6) the persons who may claim damages in their own right;
(7) the liability of a principal for the acts of his agent or of an employer for the acts of his employee;
(8) the burden of proof insofar as the rules of the applicable law in respect thereof pertain to the law of liability;
(9) rules of prescription and limitation, including rules relating to the commencement of a period of prescription or limitation, and the interruption and suspension of this period.

Article 9

The application of Articles 4, 5 and 6 shall not preclude consideration being given to the rules of conduct and safety prevailing in the State where the product was introduced into the market.

Article 10

The application of a law declared applicable under this Convention may be refused only where such application would be manifestly incompatible with public policy ("ordre public").

Article 11

The application of the preceding Articles shall be independent of any requirement of reciprocity. The Convention shall be applied even if the applicable law is not that of a Contracting State....

Concluding Comments and Questions

1. Return to the problem that opened this chapter. Does the additional perspective offered by the theory and practice change your answer as to what law should apply?

2. Is the question what law applies something that the law should resolve with certain and predictable rules or with flexible and discretionary standards?

E. Bibliography of Additional Resources

Dicey & Morris, The Conflict of Laws (David McClean ed., Sweet & Maxwell 5th ed. 2000)

Eckart Gottschalk, Ralf Michaels, Giesela Ruhl & Jan Von Hein, Conflict of Laws in a Globalized World (Cambridge 2007)

Giesela Ruhl, Methods and Approaches in Choice of Law: An Economic Perspective, 24 Berkeley J. Int'l L. 801 (2006)

Janeen M. Carruthers, Substance and Procedure in the Conflict of Laws: A Continuing Debate in Relation to Damages, 53 Int'l & Comp. L.Q. 691 (2004)

Peter Stone, EU Private International Law: Harmonization of Laws (Edward Elgar 2008)

Richard H. Kreindler & Judith L. Holdsworth (eds.), Transnational Litigation: A Practitioner's Guide (Oceana 1997 & Supp. 2007)

Richard H. Kreindler, Transnational Litigation: A Basic Primer (Oceana 1998)

Symeon Symeonides, The American Choice of Law Revolution: Past, Present and Future (Martinus Nijhoff 2006)

Winston Anderson, Elements of Private International Law (Ian Randle 2003)

CHAPTER 11

Recognition and Enforcement of Foreign Judgments

A. Introduction

In this chapter, we consider the significance of the fact that a controversy or an issue has already been litigated in some foreign court. A civil judgment has no formal effect beyond the national boundary of the court that rendered the judgment. A foreign judgment thus will have local effect only if the state acquiesces or is bound by treaty to give the foreign judgment effect. We will examine the role of such treaties and also the elastic rationale for according preclusive effect to foreign judgments.

The basic tension that underlies the study of interjurisdictional preclusion is rather straightforward. On the one hand, a state may be inclined to recognize and enforce foreign judgments because it may be inefficient or unfair to allow parties to relitigate what has already been adjudicated elsewhere. Recognition and enforcement of foreign judgments also fosters stability and collaboration among participants in a global community where an increasing number of social and economic activities have multinational contacts. Yet, on the other hand, because any civil judgment is a product of the rendering jurisdiction's procedural and substantive laws, judgments carry the baggage of political, social, and cultural norms that may conflict with the norms of another country. Respecting or ratifying a foreign judgment that flouts domestic values thus can create serious political problems or run afoul of local values. Most countries have adopted an intermediate position somewhere between the extremes of minimal and universal enforcement of foreign judgments. Articulating an intermediate position has proved difficult, however, as contemporary practices vary widely and may seem inconsistent and unfair.

We begin with a hypothetical that brings the complexity of issues into relief.

The Problem: Yahoo! and a Seamless Web*

Yahoo! is an Internet service provider that operates various Internet Web sites and services that any computer user can access at the Uniform Resource Locator ("URL") http://www.yahoo.com. Yahoo! services ending in the suffix, ".com," without an associated country code as a prefix or extension use the English language and target users who are residents of, utilize servers based in and operate under the laws of the United States. Yahoo! subsidiary corporations operate regional Yahoo! sites and services in twenty other nations, including, for example, Yahoo! France, Yahoo! India, and Yahoo! Spain. Each of these regional Web sites contains the host nation's unique two-letter code as either a prefix or a suffix in its URL (e.g., Yahoo! France is found at http://www.yahoo.fr and Yahoo! Korea at http://www.yahoo.kr). Yahoo!'s regional sites use the local region's primary language, target the local citizenry, and operate under local laws.

Yahoo! provides a variety of means by which people from all over the world can communicate and interact with one another over the Internet. Examples include an Internet search engine, e-mail, an automated auction site, personal Web page hostings, shopping services, chat rooms, and a listing of clubs that individuals can create or join. Any computer user with Internet access is able to post materials on many of these Yahoo! sites, which in turn are instantly accessible by anyone who logs on to Yahoo!'s Internet sites. Yahoo!'s auction site allows anyone to post an item for sale and solicit bids from any computer user from around the globe. Yahoo! records when a posting is made and after the requisite time period lapses sends an e-mail notification to the highest bidder and seller with their respective contact information. Yahoo! is never a party to a transaction, and the buyer and seller are responsible for arranging privately for payment and shipment of goods. Yahoo! monitors the transaction through limited regulation by prohibiting particular items from being sold (such as stolen goods, body parts, prescription and illegal drugs, weapons, and goods violating U.S. copyright laws) and by providing a rating system through which buyers and sellers have their transactional behavior evaluated for the benefit of future consumers. Yahoo! informs auction sellers that they must comply with Yahoo!'s policies and may not offer items to buyers in jurisdictions in which the sale of such item violates the jurisdiction's applicable laws. Yahoo! does not actively regulate the content of each posting, and individuals are able to post, and have in fact posted, highly offensive matter, including Nazi-related propaganda and Third Reich memorabilia, on Yahoo!'s auction sites.

French law prohibits exhibition of Nazi propaganda and artifacts for sale and a lawsuit against Yahoo! was filed in the Tribunal de Grande Instance de Paris (the "French Court") by La Ligue Contre Le Racisme Et l'Antisemitisme ("LICRA"), a French nonprofit organization dedicated to eliminating racism and anti-Semitism. Yahoo! defended the lawsuit and, after a full and contested hearing on the merits, the French Court found that approximately 1,000 Nazi- and Third Reich–related

---

* This hypothetical is based largely on *Yahoo!, Inc. v. La Ligue Contre Le Racisme Et l'Antisemitisme and L'Union Des Etudiants Juifs De France*, 379 F.3d 1120 (9th Cir. 2004).

objects, including Adolf Hitler's *Mein Kampf,* The Protocol of the Elders of Zion (an infamous anti-Semitic report produced by the tsarist secret police in the early 1900s), and purported "evidence" that the gas chambers of the Holocaust did not exist were being offered for sale on Yahoo.com's auction site. Because any French citizen is able to access these materials on Yahoo.com directly or through a link on Yahoo.fr, the French Court concluded that the Yahoo.com auction site violated French law and ordered Yahoo! to (1) pay LICRA 250,000 Euros in civil damages (an amount presumed under the applicable French law based on the number of items advertised for sale); (2) pay LICRA's attorneys' fees in the amount of 75,000 Euros; (3) eliminate French citizens' access to any material on the Yahoo.com auction site that offers for sale any Nazi objects, relics, insignia, emblems, and flags; (4) eliminate French citizens' access to web pages on Yahoo.com displaying text, extracts, or quotations from Mein Kampf and The Protocols of the Elders of Zion; (5) remove from all browser directories accessible in the French Republic index headings entitled "negationists" and from all hypertext links the equation of "negationists" under the heading "Holocaust"; and (6) take all necessary measures to dissuade and render impossible any access via Yahoo.com to the Nazi artifact auction service and to any other site or service that may be construed as constituting an apology for Nazism or a contesting of Nazi crimes. The order subjects Yahoo! to a penalty of 100,000 Euros for each day that it fails to comply with the order. French appellate courts have affirmed the order.

Yahoo! has added "warnings" to its auction sites but lacks the technology to block (only) French citizens from accessing the Yahoo.com auction site to view materials which violate the French Order or from accessing other Nazi-based content of Web sites on Yahoo.com. Indeed, it cannot comply with the French order without banning Nazi-related material from Yahoo.com altogether. Yahoo! has no assets nor corporate presence in France. LICRA has filed an action in a district court in the United States to enforce the foreign decree, but Yahoo! contends that such enforcement would infringe on its rights under the First Amendment to the United States Constitution. Assume that the French order (though consistent with French law) would have violated the United States Constitution were it issued by an American court.

1. Examine each of the six components of the French judgment and determine whether the American court should enforce all, part, or none of the foreign judgment? Why might the arguments for enforcing legal remedies differ from the arguments for enforcing equitable remedies?
2. Would you reach the same result if the French foreign judgment were raised as part of a res judicata defense to a declaratory judgment action initiated by Yahoo! (seeking a determination of the legality of its website)?

B. Theoretical Bases

The U.N. Charter explicitly protects "the principle of the sovereign equality of all its Members." The sovereignty of a state suggests an exclusive right to govern. Why, then, would a sovereign state recognize or enforce the judgment of some other sovereign?

The most common answer is that one court might enforce the judgment rendered by another because that judgment would not be enforceable in the rendering court—maybe the defendant's only assets are in the jurisdiction of the enforcing court, for example. To be sure, it would be inefficient to retry the case in the enforcing court. But why was the case tried in the rendering court in the first instance if those courts did not have the authority to enforce a final judgment? Perhaps this is some indication that the case should not have been litigated there. Aren't we encouraging promiscuous forum-shopping if we allow a plaintiff to obtain a judgment from a court that cannot enforce its own judgment, and then expect some other court to enforce it?

Moreover, although it surely would be inefficient to retry the case in the enforcing court, how much efficiency should we expect? An enforcing court may be willing to invoke its authority and lend its legitimacy to enforce the judgments of other systems under certain circumstances—perhaps, for example, where the defendant was given a full and fair opportunity to present its defenses, and the substantive law was reasonable and was accurately applied. But doesn't confirmation of these prerequisites require some investigation into the underlying facts and law, and some review into the procedures of the court that rendered the judgment? And what significance will be given the tremendous variation among court systems regarding discovery, jury trials, representative actions, the right to counsel, and so forth?

As you read about the conceptual bases for recognizing and enforcing foreign judgments, appreciate both of the extreme positions—that is, enforcing no and enforcing all foreign judgments—and also the intermediate positions that would enforce some foreign judgments. Envision that continuum of approaches and use the theoretical bases to plumb your intuition.

1. Efficiency and Commerce

You have seen in previous chapters the consequences of the economic interdependence of participants in a global economy. This growth of international finance, trade, and travel inevitably spawns increased international conflict. Because when things go wrong—for example, when the transnational corporation becomes insolvent; the manufacturer's product is defective; intellectual property rights are violated; environmental degradation has occurred—the dispute is likely to transcend national boundaries. And if some controversy or issue is litigated once in Country X, to what extent should the controversy or issue be relitigated in Country Y?

Friedrich K. Juenger, The Recognition Problem

36 Am. J. Comp. L. 1, 3–5 (1988)

Judge Learned Hand once said, "I must say that, as a litigant, I should dread a lawsuit beyond almost anything else short of sickness and death." If one lawsuit is bad, two are worse. Within each legal system, the salutary principle of res judicata avoids the expense and inconvenience of having to try the same dispute more than once.

But while that principle is universal, state and national borders diminish its efficacy. A case conclusively determined in one state may have to be relitigated in another because foreign adjudications are not entitled to automatic respect. The credit they receive depends on the vagaries of each recognition state's rules and practices....

The consequences of a narrow-minded attitude toward recognition are deplorable. To retry cases that have been authoritatively decided violates fundamental tenets of judicial economy. Moreover, it is presumptuous for the courts of one country to review the judgments of another, especially if the underlying transaction has but a slight connection with the jurisdiction in which [a party] seeks enforcement. And yet, there are reported decisions of cases fully tried—and even appealed—in the courts of one country, which then had to wind their way through the entire judicial hierarchy of another, remote from the situs of the facts that gave rise to the dispute, for the disappointing determination that the foreign adjudication was not binding after all. Such duplication is not only wasteful; it punishes private litigants and exacts a toll from international commerce. ....

Comments and Questions

1. Does relitigation of an issue "punish" both litigants or only the litigant who prevailed in the prior suit? Should the litigant who did not prevail in the prior suit have the opportunity to relitigate if there are different procedures or remedies—for example, discovery, jury trial, punitive damages—in the jurisdiction that is being asked to recognize the prior judgment? Can a court accommodate one party without also punishing the other?

2. The threat to international commerce of nonrecognition troubled many—and for centuries prior to Professor Juenger. In an action for trover before the English Court of King's Bench, the proffered defense was a judgment in defendant's favor that had been rendered by a French admiralty court. The court ruled:

> Per curiam agreed and adjudged, that as we are to take notice of a sentence in the Admiralty here, so ought we of those abroad in other nations, and we must not set them at large again, for otherwise the merchants would be in a pleasant condition; for suppose a decree here in the Exchequer, and the goods happened to be carried into another nation, should the courts abroad unravel this? It is but agreeable with the law of nations that we should take notice and approve of the laws of their countries in such particulars.
>
> Hughes v. Cornelius, 2 Show. 232 (1680) as quoted in Horace Emerson Read, Recognition and Enforcement of Foreign Judgments 57–58 (Harvard University Press 1938).

See also Re Davidson's Settlement Trusts, L.R., 15 Eq. 383, 386 (1873) ("It would be impossible to carry on the business of the world if Courts refused to act upon what had been done by other Courts of competent jurisdiction."); Maguire v. Maguire, 50 Ont. L. Rev. 100, 111 (1921) ("[I]t is the needs of mercantile and other intercourses the world over that must govern.").

3. We might expect sophisticated parties engaged in multinational transactions to avoid the problems associated with the uncertainty of nonenforcement. How might parties resolve this uncertainty by contract as part of the underlying transaction? If contracting parties can resolve these problems through ex ante negotiation, how compelling are the demands of efficiency and commerce in other contexts?

4. Most commentators, practitioners, and judges would likely agree that, generally speaking, civil procedure aspires to the certain, prompt, inexpensive and effective enforcement of substantive rights. Should these also be the measuring criteria for the enforcement of rights embodied in foreign judgments? If not these, then what are the relevant criteria?

2. Comity and Reciprocity

For centuries, notions of territorial sovereignty focused on the exclusive jurisdiction of a nation over incidents and persons within the bounds of its territory. In the seventeenth century, Ulrich Huber, a Dutch professor of international law, enunciated three maxims of international law:

1. Every state's laws apply within the state but not beyond;
2. All persons within a state are subjects of the state; and
3. Comity calls on states to recognize and enforce rights created by other states, provided that such recognition does not prejudice the state or its subjects.

Huber's concept of comity laid an important foundation in principle for the enforcement of foreign judgments. In this part, we explore the concept of comity and its adjunct, reciprocity.

Hilton v. Guyot
159 U.S. 113

[A.T. Stewart & Co. ("Stewart") was a large retail store in New York City. The retailer had entered into a business partnership with Charles Fortin & Co. ("Fortin"), a French company, to manufacture kid gloves for import into the United States. The partners later disagreed about the allocation of profits and losses, and Fortin filed suit in Paris against Stewart. Stewart defended the suit and, in fact, asserted claims of its own against Fortin. In January 1883, the French tribunal found for Fortin in the amount of (US$) 195,122.47, and that judgment was upheld on appeal. Prior to the entry of a final judgment, Stewart removed all of its property from its Paris warehouse. Thus Fortin would have to come to the United States to enforce its judgment.

During this litigation, Charles Fortin died, and Gustave Bertin Guyot was appointed to liquidate his firm. Alexander T. Stewart had also died, and his interest was held by Henry Hilton and William Libbey. Guyot thus initiated a collection action against Hilton and Libbey in a New York federal court. The trial court was prepared to enforce the French judgment, but the Supreme Court reversed.]

Mr. Justice Gray, after stating the case, delivered the opinion of the court.
...International law, in its widest and most comprehensive sense,-including not only questions of right between nations, governed by what has been appropriately called the "law of nations," but also questions arising under what is usually called "private international law," or the "conflict of laws," and concerning the rights of persons within the territory and dominion of one nation, by reason of acts, private or public, done within the dominions of another nation,-is part of our law, and must be ascertained and administered by the courts of justice as often as such questions are presented in litigation between man and man, duly submitted to their determination.

The most certain guide, no doubt, for the decision of such questions is a treaty or a statute of this country. But when, as is the case here, there is no written law upon the subject, the duty still rests upon the judicial tribunals of ascertaining and declaring what the law is, whenever it becomes necessary to do so, in order to determine the rights of parties to suits regularly brought before them. In doing this, the courts must obtain such aid as they can from judicial decisions, from the works of jurists and commentators, and from the acts and usages of civilized nations....

No law has any effect, of its own force, beyond the limits of the sovereignty from which its authority is derived. The extent to which the law of one nation, as put in force within its territory, whether by executive order, by legislative act, or by judicial decree, shall be allowed to operate within the dominion of another nation, depends upon what our greatest jurists have been content to call "the comity of nations." Although the phrase has been often criticised, no satisfactory substitute has been suggested.

"Comity," in the legal sense, is neither a matter of absolute obligation, on the one hand, nor of mere courtesy and good will, upon the other. But it is the recognition which one nation allows within its territory to the legislative, executive or judicial acts of another nation, having due regard both to international duty and convenience, and to the rights of its own citizens, or of other persons who are under the protection of its laws.

Mr. Justice Story, in his Commentaries on the Conflict of Laws, treating of the question in what department of the government of any state, in the absence of any clear declaration of the sovereign will, resides the authority to determine how far the laws of a foreign state shall have effect, and observing that this differs in different states, according to the organization of the departments of the government of each, says: "In England and America the courts of justice have hitherto exercised the same authority in the most ample manner, and the legislatures have in no instance (it is believed) in either country interfered to provide any positive regulations. The common law of both countries has been expanded to meet the exigencies of the times as they have arisen, and, so far as the practice, of nations, or the "jus gentium privatum," has been supposed to furnish any general principle, it has been followed out." Story, Confl. Laws, §§ 23, 24.

Afterwards, speaking of the difficulty of applying the positive rules laid down by the Continental jurists, he says that "there is, indeed, great truth" in these remarks of Mr. Justice Porter, speaking for the supreme court of Louisiana: "They have attempted to go too far, to define and fix that which cannot, in the nature of things, be defined and fixed. They seem to have forgotten that they wrote on a question which touched the comity of nations, and that that comity is, and ever must be, uncertain; that it must necessarily depend on a variety of circumstances which cannot be reduced to any certain rule; that no nation will suffer the laws of another to interfere with her own to the injury of her citizens; that whether they do or not must depend on the condition of the country in which the foreign law is sought to be enforced, the particular nature of her legislation, her policy, and the character of her institutions; that in the conflict of laws it must often be a matter of doubt which should prevail; and that, whenever a doubt does exist, the court which decides will prefer the laws of its own country to that of the stranger." Story, Confl. Laws, § 28; Saul v. His Creditors (1827) 5 Mart. (N. S.) 569, 596.

Again, Mr. Justice Story says: "It has been thought by some jurists that the term "comity" is not sufficiently expressive of the obligation of nations to give effect to foreign laws when they are not prejudicial to their own rights and interests. And it has been suggested that the doctrine rests on a deeper foundation; that it is not so much a matter of comity or courtesy, as a matter of paramount moral duty. Now, assuming that such a moral duty does exist, it is clearly one of imperfect obligation, like that of beneficence, humanity, and charity. Every nation must be the final judge for itself, not only of the nature and extent of the duty, but of the occasions on which its exercise may be justly demanded." And, after further discussion of the matter, be concludes: "There is, then, not only no impropriety in the use of the phrase "comity of nations," but it is the most appropriate phrase to express the true foundation and extent of the obligation of the laws of one nation within the territories of another." Story, Confl. Laws, §§ 33–38.

Chief Justice Taney, likewise, speaking for this court, while Mr. Justice Story was a member of it, and largely adopting his words, said: "It is needless to enumerate here the instances in which, by the general practice of civilized countries, the laws of the one will, by the comity of nations, be recognized and executed in another, where the rights of individuals are concerned." "The comity thus extended to other nations is no impeachment of sovereignty. It is the voluntary act of the nation by which it is offered, and is inadmissible when contrary to its policy, or prejudicial to its interests. But it contributes so largely to promote justice between individuals, and to produce a friendly intercourse between the sovereignties to which they belong, that courts of justice have continually acted upon it as a part of the voluntary law of nations." "It is not the comity of the courts, but the comity of the nation, which is administered and ascertained in the same way, and guided by the same reasoning, by which all other principles of municipal law are ascertained and guided." Bank v. Earle (1839) 13 Pet. 519, 589; Story, Confl. Laws, § 38.

Mr. Wheaton says:... "No sovereign is bound, unless by special compact, to execute within his dominions a judgment rendered by the tribunals of another state; and, if execution be sought by suit upon the judgment or otherwise, the tribunal in which the suit is brought, or from which execution is sought, is, on principle, at liberty to examine into the merits of such judgment, and to give effect to it or not, as may be found just and equitable. The general comity, utility, and convenience of nations have, however, established a usage among most civilized states, by which the final judgments of foreign courts of competent jurisdiction are reciprocally carried into execution, under certain regulations and restrictions, which differ in different countries." [H. Wheaton, Elements of International Law § 147 (8th ed. 1866).]...

In order to appreciate the weight of the various authorities cited at the bar, it is important to distinguish different kinds of judgments. Every foreign judgment, of whatever nature, in order to be entitled to any effect, must have been rendered by a court having jurisdiction of the cause, and upon regular proceedings, and due notice. In alluding to different kinds of judgments, therefore, such jurisdiction, proceedings, and notice will be assumed. It will also be assumed that they are untainted by fraud, the effect of which will be considered later.

A judgment in rem, adjudicating the title to a ship or other movable property within the custody of the court, is treated as valid everywhere.... A judgment affecting the status of persons, such as a decree confirming or dissolving a marriage, is recognized as valid in every country, unless contrary to the policy of its own law....

Other judgments, not strictly in rem, under which a person has been compelled to pay money, are so far conclusive that the justice of the payment cannot be impeached in another country, so as to compel him to pay it again. For instance, a judgment in foreign attachment is conclusive, as between the parties, of the right to the property or money attached.... Other foreign judgments which have been held conclusive of the matter adjudged were judgments discharging obligations contracted in the foreign country between citizens or residents thereof....

The extraterritorial effect of judgments in personam, at law, or in equity may differ, according to the parties to the cause. A judgment of that kind between two citizens or residents of the country, and thereby subject to the jurisdiction in which it is rendered, may be held conclusive as between them everywhere. So, if a foreigner invokes the jurisdiction by bringing an action against a citizen, both may be held bound by a judgment in favor of either; and if a citizen sues a foreigner, and judgment is rendered in favor of the latter, both may be held equally bound....

The effect to which a judgment, purely executory, rendered in favor of a citizen or resident of the country, in a suit there brought by him against a foreigner, may be entitled in an action thereon against the latter in his own country, as is the case now before us, presents a more difficult question, upon which there has been some diversity of opinion....

[W]hat was the English law, being then our own law, before the Declaration of Independence? They demonstrate that by that law ... a judgment recovered in a foreign country for a sum of money, when sued upon in England, was only prima facie evidence of the demand, and subject to be examined and impeached....

The law upon this subject as understood in the United States at the time of their separation from the mother country was clearly set forth by Chief Justice Parsons, speaking for the supreme judicial court of Massachusetts, in 1813, and by Mr. Justice Story in his Commentaries on the Constitution of the United States, published in 1833. Both those eminent jurists declared that by the law of England the general rule was that foreign judgments were only prima facie evidence of the matter which they purported to decide; and that by the common law, before the American Revolution, all the courts of the several colonies and states were deemed foreign to each other, and consequently judgments rendered by any one of them were considered as foreign judgments, and their merits re-examinable in another colony, not only as to the jurisdiction of the court which pronounced them, but also as to the merits of the controversy, to the extent to which they were understood to be re-examinable in England....

It was because of that condition of the law, as between the American colonies and states, that the United States, at the very beginning of their existence as a nation, ordained that full faith and credit should be given to the judgments of one of the states of the Union in the courts of another of those states....

From this review of the authorities, it clearly appears that, at the time of the separation of this country from England, the general rule was fully established that foreign judgments in personam were prima facie evidence only, and not conclusive of the merits of the controversy between the parties. But the extent and limits of the application of that rule do not appear to have been much discussed, or defined with any approach to exactness, in England or America, until the matter was taken up by Chancellor Kent and by Mr. Justice Story....

Mr. Justice Story, in his Commentaries on the Conflict of Laws, first published in 1834, after reviewing many English authorities, said: "The present inclination of the English courts seems to be to sustain the conclusiveness of foreign judgments,"—to which, in the second edition, in 1841, he added: "Although, certainly, there yet remains no inconsiderable diversity of opinion among the learned judges of the different tribunals."...

He then proceeded to state his own view of the subject, on principle, saying: "It is, indeed, very difficult to perceive what could be done if a different doctrine were maintainable to the full extent of opening all the evidence and merits of the cause anew on a suit upon the foreign judgment. Some of the witnesses may be since dead; some of the vouchers may be lost or destroyed. The merits of the cause, as formerly before the court upon the whole evidence, may have been decidedly in favor of the judgment; upon a partial possession of the original evidence, they may now appear otherwise. Suppose a case purely sounding in damages, such as an action for an assault, for slander, for conversion of property, for a malicious prosecution, or for a criminal conversation; is the defendant to be at liberty to retry the whole merits, and to make out, if he can, a new case upon new evidence? Or is the court to review the former decision, like a court of appeal, upon the old evidence? In a case of covenant, or of debt, or of a breach of contract, are all the circumstances to be re-examined anew? If they are, by what laws and rules of evidence and principles of justice is the validity of the original judgment to be tried? Is the court to open the judgment, and to proceed ex aequo et bono? Or is it to administer strict law, and stand to the doctrines of the local administration of justice? Is it to act upon the rules of evidence acknowledged in its own jurisprudence, or upon those of the foreign jurisprudence? These and many more questions might be put to show the intrinsic difficulties of the subject. Indeed, the rule that the judgment is to be prima facie evidence for the plaintiff would be a mere delusion if the defendant might still question it by opening all or any of the original merits on his side; for, under such circumstances, it would be equivalent to granting a new trial. It is easy to understand that the defendant may be at liberty to impeach the original justice of the judgment by showing that the court had no jurisdiction, or that he never had any notice of the suit, or that it was procured by fraud, or that upon its face it is founded in mistake, or that it is irregular and bad by the local law, fori rei judicatae. To such an extent the doctrine is intelligible and practicable. Beyond this, the right to impugn the judgment is in legal effect the right to retry the merits of the original cause at large, and to put the defendant upon proving those merits." . . .

In view of all the authorities upon the subject, and of the trend of judicial opinion in this country and in England, following the lead of Kent and Story, we are satisfied that where there has been opportunity for a full and fair trial abroad before a court of competent jurisdiction, conducting the trial upon regular proceedings, after due citation or voluntary appearance of the defendant, and under a system of jurisprudence likely to secure an impartial administration of justice between the citizens of its own country and those of other countries, and there is nothing to show either prejudice in the court, or in the system of laws under which it was sitting, or fraud in procuring the judgment, or any other special reason why the comity of this nation should not allow it full effect, the merits of the case should not, in an action brought in this country upon the judgment, be tried afresh, as on a new trial or an appeal, upon the mere assertion of the party that the judgment was erroneous in law or in fact. The defendants, therefore, cannot be permitted, upon that general ground, to contest the validity or the effect of the judgment sued on.

But they have sought to impeach that judgment upon several other grounds, which require separate consideration.

It is objected that the appearance and litigation of the defendants in the French tribunals were not voluntary, but by legal compulsion, and, therefore, that the French courts never acquired such jurisdiction over the defendants that they should be held bound by the judgment. . . .

The present case is not one of a person traveling through or casually found in a foreign country. The defendants, although they were not citizens or residents of

France, but were citizens and residents of the state of New York, and their principal place of business was in the city of New York, yet had a storehouse and an agent in Paris, and were accustomed to purchase large quantities of goods there, although they did not make sales in France. Under such circumstances, evidence that their sole object in appearing and carrying on the litigation in the French courts was to prevent property in their storehouse at Paris, belonging to them, and within the jurisdiction, but not in the custody, of those courts, from being taken in satisfaction of any judgment that might be recovered against them, would not, according to our law, show that those courts did not acquire jurisdiction of the persons of the defendants.

It is next objected that in those courts one of the plaintiffs was permitted to testify not under oath, and was not subjected to cross-examination by the opposite party, and that the defendants were therefore deprived of safeguards which are by our law considered essential to secure honesty and to detect fraud in a witness; and also that documents and papers were admitted in evidence, with which the defendants had no connection, and which would not be admissible under our own system of jurisprudence. But it having been shown by the plaintiffs, and hardly denied by the defendants, that the practice followed and the method of examining witnesses were according to the laws of France, we are not prepared to hold that the fact that the procedure in these respects differed from that of our own courts is, of itself, a sufficient ground for impeaching the foreign judgment....

There is no doubt that both in this country, as appears by the authorities already cited, and in England, a foreign judgment may be impeached for fraud....

It has often, indeed, been declared by this court that the fraud which entitles a party to impeach the judgment of one of our own tribunals must be fraud extrinsic to the matter tried in the cause, and not merely consist in false and fraudulent documents or testimony submitted to that tribunal, and the truth of which was contested before it and passed upon by it....

But it is now established in England, by well-considered and strongly-reasoned decisions of the court of appeal, that foreign judgments may be impeached, if procured by false and fraudulent representations and testimony of the plaintiff, even if the same question of fraud was presented to and decided by the foreign court....

[W]hether those decisions can be followed in regard to foreign judgments, consistently with our own decisions as to impeaching domestic judgments for fraud, it is unnecessary in this case to determine, because there is a distinct and independent ground upon which we are satisfied that the comity of our nation does not require us to give conclusive effect to the judgments of the courts of France; and that ground is the want of reciprocity, on the part of France, as to the effect to be given to the judgments of this and other foreign countries.

In France, the royal ordinance of June 15, 1629 (article 121), provided as follows: "Judgments rendered, contracts or obligations recognized, in foreign kingdoms and sovereignties, for any cause whatever, shall have no lien or execution in our kingdom. Thus the contracts shall stand for simple promises; and, notwithstanding the judgments, our subjects against whom they have been rendered may contest their rights anew before our judges." Touillier, Droit Civil, lib. 3, tit. 3, c. 6, § 3, No. 77.

By the French Code of Civil Procedure (article 546), "judgments rendered by foreign tribunals, and acts acknowledged before foreign officers, shall not be capable of execution in France, except in the manner and in the cases provided by articles 2123 and 2128 of the Civil Code," which are as follows: By article 2123, "a lien cannot arise from judgments rendered in a foreign country, except so far as they have been declared executory by a French tribunal; without prejudice to provisions to the contrary which may exist in public laws and treaties." By article 2128, "contracts entered into in a foreign country cannot give a lien upon property in France, if there are no provisions contrary to this principle in public laws or in treaties." Touillier, ubi supra, No. 84.

The defendants, in their answer, cited the above provisions of the statutes of France, and alleged, and at the trial offered to prove, that by the construction given to these statutes by the judicial tribunals of France, when the judgments of tribunals of foreign countries against the citizens of France are sued upon in the courts of France, the merits of the controversies upon which those judgments are based are examined anew, unless a treaty to the contrary effect exists between the republic of France and the country in which such judgment is obtained (which is not the case between the republic of France and the United States), and that the tribunals of the republic of France give no force and effect, within the jurisdiction of that country, to the judgments duly rendered by courts of competent jurisdiction of the United States against citizens of France after proper personal service of the process of those courts has been made thereon in this country. We are of opinion that this evidence should have been admitted....

By the law of France, settled by a series of uniform decisions of the court of cassation, the highest judicial tribunal, for more than half a century, no foreign judgment can be rendered executory in France without a review of the judgment au fond (to the bottom), including the whole merits of the cause of action on which the judgment rests....

[The Court then summarized the systems of reciprocity under the laws of Belgium, Holland, Denmark, Germany, Switzerland, Russia, Poland, Roumania, Bulgaria, Austria, Italy, Monaco, Spain, Portugal, Greece, Egypt, Cuba, Porto Rico, Hayti, Peru, Chili, Brazil, and Argentina.]

It appears, therefore, that there is hardly a civilized nation on either continent which, by its general law, allows conclusive effect to an executory foreign judgment for the recovery of money. In France and in a few smaller states—Norway, Portugal, Greece, Monaco, and Hayti—the merits of the controversy are reviewed, as of course, allowing to the foreign judgment, at the most, no more effect than of being prima facie evidence of the justice of the claim. In the great majority of the countries on the continent of Europe,—in Belgium, Holland, Denmark, Sweden, Germany, in many cantons of Switzerland, in Russia and Poland, in Roumania, in Austria and Hungary (perhaps in Italy), and in Spain,—as well as in Egypt, in Mexico, and in a great part of South America, the judgment rendered in a foreign country is allowed the same effect only as the courts of that country allow to the judgments of the country in which the judgment in question is sought to be executed.

The prediction of Mr. Justice Story in section 618 of his Commentaries on the Conflict of Laws, already cited, has thus been fulfilled, and the rule of reciprocity has worked itself firmly into the structure of international jurisprudence.

The reasonable, if not the necessary, conclusion appears to us to be that judgments rendered in France, or in any other foreign country, by the laws of which our own judgments are reviewable upon the merits, are not entitled to full credit and conclusive effect when sued upon in this country, but are prima facie evidence only of the justice of the plaintiffs' claim.

In holding such a judgment, for want of reciprocity, not to be conclusive evidence of the merits of the claim, we do not proceed upon any theory of retaliation upon one person by reason of injustice done to another, but upon the broad ground that international law is founded upon mutuality and reciprocity, and that by the principles of international law recognized in most civilized nations, and by the comity of our own country, which it is our judicial duty to known and to declare, the judgment is not entitled to be considered conclusive.

By our law, at the time of the adoption of the constitution, a foreign judgment was considered as prima facie evidence, and not conclusive. There is no statute of the United States, and no treaty of the United States with France, or with any other nation, which has changed that law, or has made any provision upon the subject. It is not to be supposed that, if any statute or treaty had been or should be made, it would recognize as conclusive the judgments of any country, which did not give like effect to our own judgments. In the absence of statute or treaty, it appears to us equally unwarrantable to assume that the comity of the United States requires anything more.

If we should hold this judgment to be conclusive, we should allow it an effect to which, supposing the defendants' offers to be sustained by actual proof, it would, in the absence of a special treaty, be entitled in hardly any other country in Christendom, except the country in which it was rendered. If the judgment had been rendered in this country, or in any other outside of the jurisdiction of France, the French courts would not have executed or enforced it, except after examining into its merits. The very judgment now sued on would be held inconclusive in almost any other country than France. In England, and in the colonies subject to the law of England, the fraud alleged in its procurement would be a sufficient ground for disregarding it. In the courts of nearly every other nation, it would be subject to re-examination, either merely because it was a foreign judgment, or because judgments of that nation would be reexaminable in the courts of France.

Mr. Chief Justice Fuller, dissenting.
...I regard [this case] as one to be determined by the ordinary and settled rule in respect of allowing a party who has had an opportunity to prove his case in a competent court to retry it on the merits; and it seems to me that the doctrine of res

judicata applicable to domestic judgments should be applied to foreign judgments as well, and rests on the same general ground of public policy, that there should be an end of litigation.

This application of the doctrine is in accordance with our own jurisprudence, and it is not necessary that we should hold it to be required by some rule of international law....

[I]t is difficult to see why rights acquired under foreign judgments do not belong to the category of private rights acquired under foreign laws. Now, the rule is universal in this country that private rights acquired under the laws of foreign states will be respected and enforced in our courts unless contrary to the policy or prejudicial to the interests of the state where this is sought to be done; and, although the source of this rule may have been the comity characterizing the intercourse between nations, it prevails to-day by its own strength, and the right to the application of the law to which the particular transaction is subject is a juridical right....

I cannot yield my assent to the proposition that, because by legislation and judicial decision in France that effect is not there given to judgments recovered in this country which, according to our jurisprudence, we think should be given to judgments wherever recovered (subject, of course, to the recognized exceptions), therefore we should pursue the same line of conduct as respects the judgments of French tribunals. The application of the doctrine of res judicata does not rest in discretion; and it is for the government, and not for its courts, to adopt the principle of retorsion, if deemed under any circumstances desirable or necessary....

Comments and Questions

1. The notion of a reciprocity requirement has largely faded, especially in the United States. Both the Restatement (Second) of Conflict of Laws and the Restatement (Third) of Foreign Relations Law of the United States indicate that the majority of jurisdictions do not require reciprocity.

2. Does comity presume that mutuality between countries is a precondition to the recognition of a foreign judgment? This issue of reciprocity requires courts to consider whether enforcement should be withheld if the judgment emanates from a country that refuses to grant a similar measure of credit to the judgments of its courts. And conversely, the issue of reciprocity requires courts to consider whether enforcement should be compelled by comity if the judgment emanates from a country that would recognize the foreign judgment.

3. The practical effect of a reciprocity requirement is to retaliate against countries that do not recognize foreign judgments. Does a foreign state's theory as to recognition of our foreign judgments tell us anything about the quality of justice or process afforded litigants in that system? Does a policy that punishes non-cooperation ultimately encourage cooperation? Or does the policy create a Catch-22? If both the judgment-rendering state and the judgment-enforcing state adopted the reciprocity requirement, then State X would not give automatic effect to the

judgments of State Y and, as a result, vice versa. For a game theoretic explanation of this phenomenon, see Antonio F. Perez, The International Recognition of Judgments: The Debate Between Private and Public Law Solutions, 19 Berkeley J. Int'l L. 44, 59–60 (2001).

4. Does a reciprocity rule encourage nationalistic and parochial views? Does reciprocity expose comity as a political theory? If so, is the invocation of reciprocity by courts an unwarranted intrusion into international relations and political questions? See generally Adolf Homburger, Recognition and Enforcement of Foreign Judgments: A New Yorker Reflects on Uniform Acts, 18 Am. J. Comp. L. 367, 390 (1970); Courtland H. Peterson, Foreign Country Judgments and the Second Restatement of Conflict of Laws, 72 Colum. L. Rev. 220, 235 (1972).

5. Comity denies the intrinsic force of foreign judgments from the point of view of international law yet endeavors to provide an international basis for their recognition and enforcement. Can you reconcile this apparent inconsistency?

6. How does the (pure) doctrine of comity recognize any exceptions to enforcement? Are the bases of these exceptions tenuous and arbitrary? Consider the theory in application: who must persuade whom of what? Must the party seeking recognition, as an affirmative matter, prove the fairness and impartiality of the foreign court, the foreign laws, and the foreign legal system?

7. For a terrific article about the background and significance of Hilton v. Guyot, see Louise E. Teitz, The Story of Hilton: From Globes to Globalization in Kevin M. Clermont, ed., Civil Procedure Stories 445 (2d ed. 2008).

3. Vested Rights and Legal Obligation

Commentators who found the theory of comity ambiguous and imprecise proposed alternative theories to justify the recognition and enforcement of foreign judgments. For example, "vested rights" theorists suggested that respect for universal notions of due process required courts to accept the findings and conclusions of a foreign court. Under this theory, the rights and responsibilities of the parties had vested conclusively on determination by the foreign system. The "legal obligation" theory is a slight variation of the vested rights theory.

G.C. Cheshire & P.M. North, Principles of Recognition

Cheshire's Private International Law 613 (8th ed. 1970)

It is unnecessary...to consider the theory of comity further, for it has been supplanted by a far more defensible principle that has been called "the doctrine of obligation." This doctrine...is that where a foreign court of competent jurisdiction has adjudicated a certain sum to be due from one person to another, the liability to pay that sum becomes a legal obligation that may be enforced in this country by an action of debt. Once the judgment is proved the burden lies upon the defendant to show why he should not perform the obligation: "The judgment of a court of competent jurisdiction over the defendant imposes a duty or obligation on him to pay the sum for which judgment is given, which the courts in this country are bound to enforce." [Schibsby v. Westenholz, L.R. 6 Q.B. 155, 159 (1870).] In other words, a new right has been vested in the creditor and a new obligation imposed upon the debtor at the instance of the foreign court.

Horace Emerson Read, Recognition and Enforcement of Foreign Judgments

62–63, 112–117 (Harvard University Press 1938)*

[I]t is untrue to say that the obligation imposed upon the defendant by the judgment is an absolute one, enforceable by the State alone. It is enforced through the machinery of the State and by its sanction, but only on behalf of and at the instance of the successful party. After a cause of action has been litigated there is left not only a person, the defendant against whom State force is demandable; there still is a person by whom State force is demandable, the successful plaintiff. In other words, there is still a person owing an obligation or duty to another person who has a correlative right to its performance. From the plaintiff's side of the transaction he has by the judgment not lost all right against the defendant. He has, indeed, acquired a new right; he has then not merely a procedural right, a right to avail himself of judicial machinery to have his original claim adjudicated, but a new substantive right to have the judgment satisfied or respect. Upon the defendant's side,... the judgment creates a fresh obligation, an obligation owed to the plaintiff to pay the amount of an award or respect a title or abide by a declaration of status as the case may be.... [T]he foreign judgment is treated as giving rise to a new and independent obligation which it is just and expedient to recognise and enforce. The law of the foreign district simply operates through its judicial process to create a new substantive right and duty.

The effect of a valid foreign judgment, then, is to create a new right and a new duty, and,... it is essentially that right and its correlative duty that is recognized and enforced,... not the foreign judgment, the state-sanctioned procedural device, itself. That this is true is obvious from the fact that procedurally... enforcement is not carried out by direct execution... but can be effected if at all only by a new action brought according to the ordinary procedure in which the foreign judgment if duly exemplified is admitted as evidence of the existence and extent of the rights claimed.

Comments and Questions

1. How does the legal obligation theory differ from comity, and is it, as Professor Geoffrey Cheshire suggests, "far more defensible"? Not all were convinced:

> What is meant by the term "legal obligation" in the connexion in which it is used? Undoubtedly we talk of the obligation to which a contract gives rise; but a "legal obligation" imports a sanction, and is inseparably connected with it. After action brought and judgment given, the so-called obligation of the contract merges into the legal obligation with which is has been clothed by the Courts. It has disappeared into one of a higher order, and is thenceforward of no practical utility. Its place has been taken by a real obligation to which a sanction is attached; and this sanction, or liability to evil, is enforceable by the State alone. It is obvious that it is enforceable only by the State in which it has been called into being.
>
> Is this brief outline of argument too Austinian for the present day? I cannot think so. Wrong decisions are too often arrived at by a careless misuse of terms of art; and it is difficult in this case to admit as a serious proposition of jurisprudence that foreign judgments are enforced here because the parties against whom they are pronounced are bound in duty to satisfy them.... "By civil laws," Hobbes said in his Leviathan, "I understand the laws that men are bound to observe, because they are members, not of this or that commonwealth in particular, but of a commonwealth." The Courts know of no such laws; nor is there any such general principle that our Courts enforce obligations unfulfilled in other States. But introduce the comity of nations into the argument and the matter becomes plain. Comity can be the only reason why our Courts should take pains to enforce a legal obligation which has arisen in another State; an obligation existing under the protection of its laws and procedure, but which, in the circumstances, that State is powerless to enforce.
>
> Francis Piggott, Foreign Judgments pt. I, at 13 (3d ed. 1908).

Do you agree?

2. The legal obligation theory is an excellent example of procedure animating substance. Assumpsit, that is, an action of debt, was the only conceivable form of action for enforcing a money judgment under the rigid procedures of the antiquated common law courts. And to shoehorn a foreign judgment into the available writ judges created the fiction that there was an implied contract to pay the amount of the foreign judgment. Hence the terms "judgment debtor" and "judgment creditor." But is a judgment like a contract debt?

3. One of the maxims of equity is that Equality is Equity. What does that mean or suggest in the context of recognizing foreign judgments?

4. Res Judicata

Willis L. M. Reese, The Policies Underlying Judgment Recognition

50 Colum. L. Rev. 783, 783–786 (1950)

... [Many] courts have held ... that the judgment of foreign nations, subject to only a few exceptions, are not open to reexamination on the merits when placed in issue before a local court. In explaining this result, the courts have usually resorted to one of two doctrines or modes of expression: that of "comity" and that of the "legal obligation of foreign judgments." ... There is no need to enter into a detailed discussion and comparison of these two phrases except to make clear that both merely state but do not explain the arrived-at result. Comity, a word of loose and uncertain meaning at best, has little significance in this context other than as a statement of the conflict of laws rules of the forum. And the same must be said of the legal obligation doctrine, which assumes that a valid judgment for a sum certain imposes upon the defendant a "legal obligation" to pay, which will be enforced by the forum. But this formulation does not explain why a foreign judgment results in a "legal obligation," nor why this "obligation" is enforced by the forum. Finally, neither doctrine affords any explanation for the existence of exceptions to the normal practice of enforcement.

The professed explanations being inadequate, we must therefore look beyond the usual reasoning of the courts to discover the real basis for their decisions. This, it seems clear, is none other than the doctrine of res judicata that "[p]ublic policy dictates that there be an end of litigation; that those who have contested an issue shall be bound by the result of the contest, and that matters once tried shall be considered forever settled as between the parties." This conclusion follows because the policy behind res judicata certainly applies to all judgments, whether local or foreign; furthermore, the doctrine constitutes so fundamental a tenet of the common law that it must inevitably have influenced the minds of the judges when faced with the problem of the foreign judgment; and, quite simply, there is no other satisfactory explanation for the fact that such judgments are usually enforced.

Res judicata is the policy favoring the enforcement and recognition of judgments of foreign nations; other policies have in rare instances led the courts to an opposite result.... Perhaps the most important of these... policies is that of reciprocity, or, stated in more explicit form, the desire that judgments rendered in this country should be held conclusive on the merits throughout the world, coupled with the thought that the best way to attain this end is to grant the judgment of a particular nation no more effect than the courts of that nation accord to [the judgments of the recognition state]. A second consideration which on occasion may outweigh that of res judicata is the desire to deal justly with the individual litigants.... Utterances of this type indicate a realization on the part of the judges that the world is composed of nations with widely divergent judicial systems, together with an unwillingness on their part to enforce a judgment which violates their basic conceptions of what is right and wrong. A third policy, largely complementary of the second, is the natural desire of a nation to protect its citizens and preserve its institutions. [C]ourts... do not make a practice of discriminating in favor of their nationals and against foreign litigants. But they would hardly enforce without question a judgment where there was substantial reason to believe that one of their nationals had been the victim of serious prejudice at the hands of the foreign court. And a similar fate might well befall a judgment rendered either in contemptuous disregard of the forum's law or contrary to its public policy.

Thus, this third policy is also grounded to some extent in the diversities presently existing between the laws and judicial systems of the various nations of the world....

Hans Smit, International Res Judicata and Collateral Estoppel
9 UCLA L. Rev. 44, 45–56 (1962)

...In the absence of statutory directives, most judicial pronouncements concerning the effect of foreign judgments often make only perfunctory, and never fully satisfactory, attempts to define the policy motivating whatever recognition is given. The commentators have been more articulate, but precise analysis of pertinent policy is generally wanting. More detailed discussion of policies and principles advanced would therefore seem appropriate.

1. Comity.

The term comity is chameleonic as its legal uses are varied. Because of its convenient vagueness it has been invoked rather frequently when an explanation for recognition of foreign judgments was deemed desirable, but even in that context its meaning has not always been clear.... It says in fact only that recognition will be given when it will be given. The decreasing reference to comity as the sole explicatory rationale in more recent cases concerning the effect of foreign judgments may be an indication of judicial awareness of the term's intrinsic uselessness.

2. Legal Obligation.

[Another doctrine insists] that a foreign judgment creates an obligation that the local courts will enforce as any other obligation created under foreign law.... More searching analysis of the doctrine exposes it as an unsound legal construction for a preconceived conclusion. The doctrine presupposes that a foreign judgment creates a legal obligation under the applicable foreign law without making any investigation as to what that foreign law provides. Nevertheless, an obligation created by the foreign judgment can be enforced locally only if it is indeed a legal obligation.... [T]he doctrine fails to explain why such an obligation should be enforced domestically. Finally, the obligation theory does not explain why the purported obligation is not enforced when one of the disqualifying elements, such as lack of jurisdiction, is present. It is clear that as an explanation for the recognition given to foreign judgments is completely wanting in soundness.

3. Res judicata.

Initially only incidentally referred to, but having since gained considerably in prominence, is the view that the principles underlying the doctrine of res judicata provide the only logical and satisfactory explanation for recognition of foreign judgments. This view seems the only correct one. While none of the other doctrines advanced can even purport to provide a satisfactory rationale, the maxims generally associated with the doctrine of res judicata—that there must be an end to litigation and that nobody should be allowed to vex his opponent twice—are clearly applicable when foreign judgments are concerned....

Comments and Questions

1. What does the doctrine of recognition of foreign judgments gain or lose if res judicata is the (only) real basis for recognizing foreign judgments? How does res judicata differ, in operation, from the comity and legal obligation theories?

2. According to Professor Reese, the policy of ending litigation has both a public and a private aspect. Articulate these public and private interests.

3. Of course, one might fairly question whether putting an end to litigation is the only (or even the dominant) policy basis of res judicata. In a purely domestic context, res judicata not only precludes relitigation; it also fosters stability and harmony within an integrated system of courts. Moreover, in a purely domestic context, a constitutional provision (such as the Full Faith and Credit Clause in the United States) orders a regime respecting finality. No binding international law requires such stability and collaboration among international actors.

4. Does the persuasiveness of the res judicata rationale differ if one considers foreign recognition from the perspective of a plaintiff successful in the foreign court seeking local enforcement, as opposed to a successful foreign defendant using a foreign judgment in his or her favor locally?

5. In the following excerpt, Professors von Mehren and Trautman suggest that we move beyond treating recognition problems as an aspect of res judicata. They instead propose that courts confront the policy bases for problems involving the recognition of foreign judgments.

5. Policy Considerations

von Mehren & Trautman, Recognition of Foreign Adjudications

81 Harv. L. Rev. 1601, 1603–1605 (1968)

...The ultimate justification for according some degree of recognition is that if in our highly complex and interrelated world each community exhausted every possibility of insisting on its parochial interests, injustice would result and the normal patterns of life would be disrupted. Can the relevant policies be stated more precisely at least when judgments emanate from legal systems with well-established legal institutions and traditions? It is the purpose of this article to state such policies and to examine the impact they should have on thinking about recognition problems.

We believe that at least five policies are important: a desire to avoid the duplication of effort and consequent waste involved in reconsidering a matter that has already been litigated; a related concern to protect the successful litigant, whether plaintiff or defendant, from harassing or evasive tactics on the part of his previously unsuccessful opponent; a policy against making the availability of local enforcement the decisive element, as a practical matter, in the plaintiff's choice of forum; an interest in fostering stability and unity in an international order in which many aspects of life are not confined to any single jurisdiction; and, in certain classes of cases, a belief that the rendering jurisdiction is a more appropriate forum than the recognizing jurisdiction, either because the former was more convenient or because as the predominantly concerned jurisdiction or for some other reason its views as to the merits should prevail.

The weight which a recognizing jurisdiction will give to each of these policies will depend in part upon attitudes it holds on related questions. To illustrate, the policy against duplication of effort should presumably be measured against a system's domestic procedural thinking about "splitting" a controversy that could conveniently be handled as a single matter. Procedural thinking in the United States tends toward enlarging the dimensions of a lawsuit: consider especially the broad notion of "cause of action" and the federal rules respecting compulsory counterclaims. Many countries, for example, Germany and France—are prepared to allow the parties, if they desire, to fragment a controversy that could be handled as a single matter. A jurisdiction like those in the United States presumably puts a fairly high general value on avoiding duplication of effort while jurisdictions like France and Germany assign a lower value. The former group's recognition practice will to this extent accord broader preclusive effects than the latter's.

Views diverge on the weight to be assigned to international order and stability and to the appropriateness or concerns of the rendering forum. Again, relevant information is to be found in the recognizing jurisdiction's general thinking underlying problems of choice of law and jurisdiction to adjudicate. Does that thinking attempt to contribute to the growth of international order? And does it attach substantial value to social and economic ties that transcend the traditional national political units? At the least, the recognizing jurisdiction can be expected to be consistent—in the sense that the views of general policy underlying the rules and principles in those two areas are compatible with those underlying the recognition of foreign adjudications.

Finally, the significance of the basic policies just discussed should be assessed in the context of the total situation relating the recognizing jurisdiction to the underlying litigation. For example, recognition may be made to depend upon whether the defendant is a member of the rendering community or of the community asked to recognize. Again, an adjudication that applies the same rules of decision as would have been applied by the recognizing community involves fewer difficulties than an adjudication in which a different regulating rule has been applied....

Comments and Questions

1. How do the first two categories differ from the interests that Professors Reese and Smit defined as res judicata?

2. How do the third, fourth, and fifth von Mehren/Trautman factors differ from each other?

3. A multifactor balancing test premised on policy considerations has intuitive appeal. But exactly how would courts apply such a test? Is this theory's dependence on individual judges and the consequent uncertainty a fatal flaw? The virtues and vices of certainty and predictability are explored in the following excerpt by Professor von Mehren.

Arthur T. von Mehren, Correctness and Repose Recognition and Enforcement of Foreign Judgments, Academie de Droit International

167 Recueil des Cours 20–24 (1981)

I. The Proper Accommodation of the Principles of Correctness and Repose: Prior Local and Prior Foreign Judgments Compared

A. Introduction

...[Q]uestions...respecting the significance to be accorded prior adjudication, involve the tension that is present in all areas of law between ideal and practical justice. What constitutes in given circumstances ideal justice, on the one hand, and practical justice, on the other, may be a matter of disagreement and debate. Considerable agreement presumably exists, however, respecting the nature of the distinction between the two conceptions. Ideal justice seeks rules and principles that are correct in some ultimate philosophical or ethical sense; adjudication must be based on as full an understanding and evaluation of all relevant facts as is possible, and in applying rules and principles the values and purposes that inform them must always be kept firmly in mind.

Practical justice is, in view of such advantages as greater ease in administration or reduced transaction costs, prepared to adopt rules and principles that are philosophically or ethically inferior to other possible rules or principles. In the administration of justice, practical justice is willing to accept solutions that are based on incomplete or misapprehended facts or involve logical or methodological mistakes because of the great costs and burdens of ensuring that adjudications do not suffer from such deficiencies.

Practical justice is accordingly prepared to accept in a certain percentage of cases results that are not ideally just in order to secure such advantages for the general run of cases as reduced costs or enhanced legal security.

In order to understand and assess the various positions that can be taken respecting the significance of prior adjudication where the recognition and enforcement of foreign judgments are in question, two themes must be pursued: (1) what considerations explain the significance given the fact of prior adjudication in the administration of justice in the case of local adjudication? (2) In what respects does the fact that a foreign adjudication is involved require or justify according different significance to the fact of prior adjudication? In considering the first theme, one explores the theoretical and practical considerations that determine the significance accorded the fact of prior adjudication when the administration of justice is entirely local. In discussing the second theme, the similarities and differences between an entirely local administration of justice and administration of justice that is partially foreign (the judgment is foreign) and partially local (the recognition of enforcement is local) must be developed. Against this background whether and why prior adjudication should have a different significance when it occurs in a foreign rather than a domestic adjudication can be considered.

B. The Significance of Prior Local Adjudication

1. In general

The significance accorded the fact of prior adjudication where the administration of justice is entirely local expresses the legal order's views respecting the proper accommodation of the conflicting principles of correctness and repose.

The principle of correctness expresses the concern that legal justice, as understood by the society in both substantive and procedural terms, be done; the principle of repose accepts the inherent imperfection of human knowledge and institutions and the need to put to rest quarrels and disputes that have arisen so that the energies of individuals and the resources of society can be devoted to more constructive tasks. The claim of each principle to respect is clear. However, embracing one to the complete exclusion of the other would be intolerable. Assigning an absolute value to correctness would create an enormous social and economic burden, unduly reward the disputatious, and undermine the security of transactions and relations that is essential if economic and social life are to go forward. On the other hand, giving full scope to the principle of repose would require that full and absolute finality be given to every determination made by an adjudicator of first instance. But the experience of failure of justice in individual cases is universal; a system of justice that, in the name of repose, denied in every case a second chance would be perceived as fundamentally unjust.

No universal or final solution can be provided to the question of the proper accommodation between the principles of correctness and repose. The values ultimately at stake—those of ideal justice and of practical justice—are incommensurable; in the absence of a superior principle in terms of which accommodation can be effected, a tension persists between the two principles and no solution can ever be entirely stable nor demonstrably correct.

2. The Relative Strength of the Principles of Correctness and Repose

The repose principle's claim to prevail over the correctness principles is strengthened by: (a) initiation of, or participation in, the process from which the prior adjudication resulted by the party who now invokes the latter principle; (b) the availability to that party (especially when utilized) of prior opportunities to challenge that adjudication; (c) the fact that no forum from which review might be sought has institutional qualities—skill, experience, numbers, and the like—significantly superior to those of the instance whose adjudication is challenged; (d) the fact that the other party is not in some special sense—e.g., through his fraud—responsible for the alleged miscarriage of justice; (e) the view that the issue adjudicated is not one of exceptional importance to the challenging party or to society; (f) the fact or likelihood of reliance, especially if reasonable, on the challenged adjudication by the other party or by third parties; (g) the cost to the parties and society of each additional step or procedure designed to vindicate the principle of correctness. Of course, the accommodation of the two principles will be affected by the kind of judgment that is in question. Thus, repose will be accorded, in principle, a higher value with respect to a civil judgment for money damages than to a criminal conviction....

The accommodation between the claims of the principles of correctness and of repose can be seen, therefore, as a function of seven variables: the extent to which the prior proceedings were contested; the opportunity that the party asserting the former principle has already had to vindicate it and the extent to which the probability of error being established has—or could have—been thereby reduced; the availability of a reviewing instance with institutional characteristics superior to those of the instance whose adjudication is challenged; the degree to which the asserted error is allegedly due to the other party's misconduct; the likelihood of reliance upon the adjudication; the costs of further proceedings to correct error especially as measured against the probability that error can be established; and the special significance of the alleged error from the perspective of the challenging party or of society.

The value assigned to repose is thus presumptively relatively low when, as in the case of a default judgment, the challenged adjudication was obtained without the participation of the challenging party. (On the other hand, the defaulting party's failure to avail himself of prior opportunities to challenge the adjudication or reliance—because of the passage of time or for other reasons—by the other party, or third parties, strengthens the claim of the repose principle.) The repose principle's claim is also diminished by the existence of a forum with superior institutional qualities. Here again, however, largely because of the likelihood of reasonable reliance on the adjudication by the other party or by third parties, the correctness principle loses force unless the challenge is made reasonably promptly. Thus, one or two instances of appellate review are generally available, but such review must be promptly initiated....

C. The Significance of Prior Foreign Adjudication

The principle of coherence or consistency, basic to so much of our thinking about law, would require that prior foreign adjudications be accorded the same effects as prior local adjudications where the same considerations bear upon the accommodation of the principles of correctness and repose. More generally, the same basic philosophy should inform a legal system's overall approach to the problem of the significance of prior adjudication taking into account, of course, the fact that the adjudication is, in one case, a local product while, in the other, it is imported. It is necessary, therefore to consider in what ways the problems of the effects to be accorded prior adjudication is affected by the foreignness of the adjudication in question....

The general analysis of how the principles of correctness and repose should be accommodated that was developed for local adjudications can also be applied to foreign adjudications. However, the fact that the prior adjudication is foreign requires that competing principles be accommodated in a significantly different context.

The fundamental differences between the two situations derive from the fact that a foreign—unlike a local—adjudication is not the product of the legal system to which the adjudicator who faces the problems of accommodating the competing principles belongs. It follows that the arguments advanced to justify appellate review of local adjudications support by analogy the review of foreign adjudications. The local system of administering justice, which is potentially available for further review of the matter, has institutional characteristics—for example, the availability or unavailability of discovery and the use or non-use of the jury—that presumably differ in significant respects from those of the system that handed down the foreign adjudication. Accordingly, there is an institutional basis for assuming that relitigation might well produce a different result. To this extent, the claim of the principle of repose is weaker than in the case of a comparable prior local judgment for which appellate review is no longer available.

The adjudication's foreignness also interjects a complex issue respecting the effect on legal security of according significance to such adjudications. Where the prior adjudication is local, giving effect to the principle of repose does not create any significant degree of uncertainty respecting the rules under which the legal order regulates situations or transactions of the general type in question. Precisely such uncertainty can be created, however, by according preclusive effects to a foreign judgment. According such effects is, in a sense, equivalent to establishing for the recognizing State a second set of courts with rules respecting adjudicatory jurisdiction, choice of law, procedure, and substance that may differ significantly from those utilized by the courts that would handle the controversy were it to be litigated locally. The effect is to make differing solutions available locally depending upon whether the original litigation takes place locally or abroad. As a result, legal security is reduced since often parties cannot know in advance the law that will ultimately govern their situation or transaction.

The foreignness of the adjudication also affects considerations relating to the cost to the parties and to society of each additional step designed to vindicate the principle of correctness. From the parties' perspective, denying preclusive effects to a foreign judgment may well result in costs considerably higher than those that would result from denying preclusive effects to a comparable local judgment. In particular, denying preclusive effects to a foreign judgment produces a significantly greater likehood [sic] than does the denial of such effects to a local adjudication that the entire matter will be fully relitigated. Moreover, as further proceedings will presumably occur in the forum in which the recognition problem has arisen, typically less reliance can be placed on what was done in the first proceedings than would be the case had these procedures eventuated in a local judgment; as a consequence, the litigation costs generated by denying preclusive effects to foreign judgments are likely to be significantly greater than those resulting from the denial of such effects to a local judgment.

From the perspective of the given society as a whole, however, the foreignness of the prior adjudication can be seen as reducing the cost arguments in favour of repose. In the case of a foreign judgment the legal order that will bear the institutional costs of further litigation has not previously incurred such costs. From its point of view, the situation can be assimilated to that presented when litigation is initiated for the first time. This posture changes, of course, if the litigation costs incurred by the legal order from which the foreign judgment emanated are taken into account. However, at least in fully international situations, each legal order may well view the cost problem from its own rather than from a broader perspective.

In one final point, the adjudication's foreignness can affect the accommodation of the principles of correctness and repose. In the case of a foreign judgment, the controversy may well have been resolved under rules and principles that ignore private rights and obligations or social policies that the legal order now facing the problem whether to accord preclusive effects to the judgment considers of great importance. The State addressed may consider the rules and principles applied by the foreign adjudicator unwise or unjust; in the case of a local adjudication, on the other hand, the adjudicator must ordinarily accept his own system's rules and principles as just and wise....

Comments and Questions

1. Where does the desire for "uniformity" fall within the dialectical relation between correctness and repose? How would you establish the hierarchy among these three competing norms?

2. We want to clarify some terminology before continuing further. In the context of interjurisdictional preclusion, "recognition" and "enforcement" are often understood as distinct concepts. Typically, a foreign-country judgment is "recognized" when a court determines that the judgment of a foreign state is valid, and that because a certain matter was addressed in the foreign-country judgment, it should not be litigated again. Thus if the foreign judgment is being asserted as part of a res judicata affirmative defense, it need only be "recognized" by the court. By contrast, a party is seeking "enforcement" of a foreign judgment if she is seeking affirmative relief based on the foreign judgment. Thus if the foreign judgment is being asserted as part of an action to collect on a judgment, mere recognition of the foreign judgment by the court would not suffice. Does it make sense to you that a court might be willing to recognize a judgment yet unwilling to enforce it? (Note that the converse situation could not occur. Recognition of a foreign judgment is a sine qua non to enforcement.)

C. National Practice

1. United States

The United States is among the countries in the world most receptive to the recognition and enforcement of foreign judgments. That status is particularly remarkable in light of the fact that the United States is not a party to any comprehensive bilateral or multilateral treaty concerning the recognition or enforcement of foreign judgments. Nor has the United States enacted any federal legislation on the recognition and enforcement of foreign judgments. Instead, efforts to promote uniformity and harmony in recognition and enforcement practice have led to a coordinated effort among the states to adopt a common analytical framework. To that end, a majority of states have adopted some version of the Uniform Foreign Money Judgments Recognition Act. However, because not all states have adopted the Uniform Act, and because the Uniform Act is limited to money judgments, a second analytical framework also serves an important function in the recognition and enforcement practice in the United States. The Restatement (Third) of Foreign Relations Law, adopted and promulgated by the American Law Institute in 1986, summarizes the prevailing common and statutory law of the States of the United States.

We begin this part with excerpts from the Restatement and then reprint several opinions that rely on the Uniform Act and/or the Restatement. The substantive content of the Uniform Act and the Restatement are substantially similar; accordingly, we reprint in detail only the latter.

Restatement (Third) of Foreign Relations Law
(1987)

§ 481. Recognition and Enforcement of Foreign Judgment.

Except as provided in § 482, a final judgment of a court of a foreign state granting or denying recovery of a sum of money, establishing or confirming the status of a person, or determining interests in property, is conclusive between the parties, and is entitled to recognition in courts in the United States....

Comment:
...c. Effect of foreign judgment. A foreign judgment is generally entitled to recognition by courts in the United States to the same extent as a judgment of a court of one State in the courts of another State. As in the case of a sister-State judgment, a judgment of a foreign country ordinarily has no greater effect in the United States than in the country where the judgment was rendered....

d. Reciprocity in enforcement of foreign judgments. A judgment otherwise entitled to recognition will not be denied recognition or enforcement because courts in the rendering state might not enforce a judgment of a court in the United States if the circumstances were reversed. Hilton v. Guyot, 159 U.S. 113 (1895), declared a limited reciprocity requirement applicable when the judgment creditor is a national of the state in which the judgment creditor is a national of the state in which the judgment was rendered and the judgment debtor is a national of the United States. Though that holding has not been formally overruled, it is no longer followed in the great majority of State and federal courts in the United States....

g. Proceedings to enforce foreign judgments in the United States. In many States, including those that have adopted the Uniform Foreign Money Judgments

Recognition Act,...an action to enforce a foreign money judgment may be initiated through expedited procedures, such as a motion for summary judgment in lieu of a complaint. Enforcement of a foreign judgment may also be pursued by counterclaim, cross-claim, or affirmative defense.

§ 482 Grounds for Nonrecognition of Foreign Judgments.

(1) A court in the United States may not recognize a judgment of the court of a foreign state if:
  (a) the judgment was rendered under a judicial system that does not provide impartial tribunals or procedures compatible with due process of law; or
  (b) the court that rendered the judgment did not have [personal] jurisdiction over the defendant...

(2) A court in the United States need not recognize a judgment of the court of a foreign state if:
  (a) the court that rendered the judgment did not have jurisdiction of the subject matter of the action;
  (b) the defendant did not receive notice of the proceedings in sufficient time to enable him to defend;
  (c) the judgment was obtained by fraud;
  (d) the cause of action on which the judgment was based, or the judgment itself, is repugnant to the public policy of the United States or of the State where recognition is sought;
  (e) the judgment conflicts with another final judgment that is entitled to recognition;
  (f) the proceeding in the foreign court was contrary to an agreement between the parties to submit the controversy on which the judgment is based to another forum.

Comments and Questions

1. By equating foreign judgments to sister State judgments, the statement in § 481 cmt. c establishes a strong policy in favor of recognizing and enforcing foreign judgments. Article IV Section 1 of the United States Constitution requires that "Full Faith and Credit shall be given in each State to the public Acts, Records, and judicial Proceedings of every other State." See also 28 U.S.C. § 1738 (implementing the constitutional mandate).

2. Note that if one of the defenses listed in Paragraph (1) of Section 482 is established, the court where recognition is sought is required to deny recognition. If one of the defenses listed in Paragraph (2) is established, the court has the discretion to deny recognition

3. Neither the Restatement nor the Uniform Act contemplates the enforcement of foreign penal or tax judgments.

Society of Lloyd's v. Ashenden
233 F.3d 473 (7th Cir. 2000)

POSNER, CIRCUIT JUDGE

These are diversity suits brought in the federal district court in Chicago by Lloyd's, a foreign corporation, against American members ("names") of insurance syndicates that Lloyd's manages. Lloyd's wanted to use the Illinois Uniform Foreign Money-Judgments Recognition Act to collect money judgments, each for several hundred thousand dollars, that it had obtained against the defendants in an English court after the names' repeated efforts in earlier litigation to knock out the forum-selection clause in their contracts with Lloyd's had failed. Pursuant to this strategy, Lloyd's filed the judgments in the district court and then issued "citations" pursuant to the Illinois procedure for executing a judgment. The filing of the judgments inaugurated this federal-court proceeding to collect them; and state law, in this case the Illinois citations statute, 735 ILCS 5/2-1402, supplies the procedure for executing a federal-court judgment. Fed. R. Civ. P. 69(a). The statute allows the holder of a judgment to depose the judgment debtor respecting the existence, amount, and whereabouts of assets that can be seized to satisfy the judgment; to impose a lien on those assets; and to command the debtor to turn over to the judgment creditor as many of the seizable assets as may be necessary to satisfy the judgment.

The defendants ignored the citations and instead asked the district court not to recognize the English judgments as being enforceable in Illinois. They argued that those judgments had denied them due process of law and therefore were not enforceable under the foreign money-judgments recognition act, which makes a judgment rendered by a court outside the United States unenforceable in Illinois if

> the judgment was rendered under a system which does not provide impartial tribunals or procedures compatible with the requirements of due process of law.

735 ILCS 5/12-621 (emphasis added). The district court rejected the argument and granted summary judgment for Lloyd's, declaring the judgments enforceable and so the issuance of citations proper.

We have italicized the word that defeats the defendants' argument. The judgments about which they complain were rendered by the Queen's Bench Division of England's High Court, which corresponds to our federal district courts; they were affirmed by the Court of Appeal, which corresponds to the federal courts of appeals; and the Appellate Committee of the House of Lords, which corresponds to the U.S. Supreme Court, denied the defendants' petition for review. Any suggestion that this system of courts "does not provide impartial tribunals or procedures compatible with the requirements of due process of law" borders on the risible. The courts of England are fair and neutral forums. The origins of our concept of due process of law are English, and the English courts, especially the Supreme Court of Judicature (composed of the High Court and the Court of Appeal) and the Appellate Committee of the House of Lords, the tribunals involved in the judgments challenged here, are highly regarded for impartiality, professionalism, and scrupulous regard for procedural rights. The English judicial system... is the very fount from which our system developed; a system which has procedures and goals which closely parallel our own. United States courts which have inherited major portions of their judicial traditions and procedure from the United Kingdom are hardly in a position to call the Queen's Bench a kangaroo court.

Not that the English concept of fair procedure is identical to ours; but we cannot believe that the Illinois statute is intended to bar the enforcement of all judgments of any foreign legal system that does not conform its procedural doctrines to the latest twist and turn of our courts regarding, for example, the circumstances under which due process requires an opportunity for a hearing in advance of the deprivation of a substantive right rather than afterwards. It is a fair guess that no foreign nation has decided to incorporate our due process doctrines into its own procedural law; and so we interpret "due process" in the Illinois statute (which, remember, is a uniform act, not one intended to reflect the idiosyncratic jurisprudence of a particular state) to refer to a concept of fair procedure simple and basic enough to describe the judicial processes of civilized nations, our peers. The statute requires only that the foreign procedure be "compatible with the requirements of due process of law," and we have interpreted this to mean that the foreign procedures are "fundamentally fair" and do not offend against "basic fairness." Ingersoll Milling Machine Co. v. Granger, 833 F.2d 680, 687–88 (7th Cir. 1987); see also Hilton v. Guyot, 159 U.S. 113, 202–03 (1895)....

It is true that no evidence was presented in the district court on whether England has a civilized legal system, but that is because the question is not open to doubt. We need not consider what kind of evidence would suffice to show that a foreign legal system "does not provide impartial tribunals or procedures compatible with the requirements of due process of law" if the challenged judgment had been rendered by Cuba, North Korea, Iran, Iraq, Congo, or some other nation whose adherence to the rule of law and commitment to the norm of due process are open to serious question, see, e.g., Bank Melli Iran v. Pahlavi, 58 F.3d 1406, 1411–12 (9th Cir. 1995); Choi v. Kim, 50 F.3d 244, 249–250 (3rd Cir. 1995)..., as England's are not. It is anyway not a question of fact. It is not, strictly speaking, a question of law either, but it is a question about the law of a foreign nation, and in answering such questions a federal court is not limited to the consideration of evidence that would be admissible under the Federal Rules of Evidence; any relevant material or source may be consulted. Fed. R. Civ. P. 44.1.

Rather than trying to impugn the English legal system en gross, the defendants argue that the Illinois statute requires us to determine whether the particular judgments that they are challenging were issued in proceedings that conform to the requirements of due process of law as it has come to be understood in the case law of Illinois and other American jurisdictions. The statute, with its reference to "system," does not support such a retail approach, which would moreover be inconsistent with providing a streamlined, expeditious method for collecting money judgments rendered by courts in other jurisdictions—which would in effect give the judgment creditor a further appeal on the merits. The process of collecting a judgment is not meant to require a second lawsuit, thus converting every successful multinational suit for damages into two suits.... But that is the implication of the defendants' argument. They claim to be free to object in the collection phase of the case to the procedures employed at the merits phase, even though they were free to challenge those procedures at that phase and indeed did so.

Comments and Questions

1. Judge Posner suggests that procedural systems should be viewed as a whole, because weakness in one aspect of "due process" may well be offset by strength in another (or by overall strength). But aren't some threshold concepts of our system of due process, in a sense, non-negotiable? Jury trials? The right to cross-examine a witness? Notice and the right to be heard in person? Discovery? The right to employ legal counsel? A written decision with explanation? Appeals? If there are some processes that cannot be compromised, how does a court identify and protect them if not by using a "retail approach"?

2. What sources will determine whether a nation has a commitment to the rule of law and to the norm of due process? Should the State Department maintain a definitive list for such purposes?

3. The generally favorable attitude of American courts toward judgments of other countries should not be equated to a "rubber stamp" approach to enforcement, however. The following cases show that United States courts are not hesitant to refuse enforcement of foreign judgments under certain circumstances.

Bridgeway Corporation v. Citibank

201 F.3d 134 (2nd Cir. 2000)

Calabresi, Circuit Judge

Bridgeway Corp. ("Bridgeway"), a Liberian corporation seeking to enforce a final judgment rendered by the Supreme Court of Liberia, appeals from the district court's decision denying Bridgeway's motion for summary judgment and granting, sua sponte, summary judgment in favor of the nonmoving party, Citibank. The district court held, first, that Citibank was not judicially estopped from challenging the fairness of the Liberian judicial system simply because it had participated voluntarily in litigation in Liberia and, second, that the evidence in the record established, as a matter of law, that the Liberian judicial system was not "a system that...provide[s] impartial tribunals or procedures compatible with the requirements of due process." We affirm.

I. Background

A. Overview of Liberian History

This appeal derives from an action by Bridgeway to enforce a money judgment against Citibank entered by the Supreme Court of Liberia on July 28, 1995. Because the merits of this case turn on the events surrounding the Liberian civil war during the first half of the 1990s, it is helpful to provide a brief overview of those circumstances before proceeding to discuss the case. The following facts are drawn from the district court's thoughtful opinion and are not traversed in the record before us.

Liberia was founded in 1817 to resettle freed American slaves, and in 1847 it became an independent republic. The original 1847 Constitution, amended in 1976 and again in 1986, established a government modeled on that of the United States. Under the 1986 Constitution, for example, the judicial powers of the Liberian government are vested in a Supreme Court and such subordinate courts as the Legislature may establish. The Supreme Court is composed of one chief justice and four associate justices. Justices and judges are nominated by the President and confirmed by the Senate and have life tenure unless impeached.

From 1980 to 1989, Samuel Kanyon Doe headed a Liberian government marked by corruption and human rights abuses, as well as by rampant inflation. In 1989, a group of dissidents seized power and, in 1990, executed Doe. Doe's death marked the beginning of a violent seven-year civil war. By 1991, Liberia was in effect ruled by two governments: one controlled Monrovia, the capital, while the other controlled the remainder of the country. Following several short-lived cease fires, a formal peace accord was signed in August 1995. After another outbreak of violence in 1996, elections were held in July 1997. In August 1997, Charles Taylor was inaugurated and the 1986 Constitution was reinstated.

Throughout the period of civil war, Liberia's judicial system was in a state of disarray and the provisions of the Constitution concerning the judiciary were no longer followed. Instead, under an agreement worked out among the warring parties in 1992, the Supreme Court was reorganized, with various factions each unilaterally appointing a specified number of justices. The U.S. State Department Country Reports for Liberia during this period paint a bleak picture of the Liberian judiciary. The 1994 Report observed that "corruption and incompetent handling of cases remained a recurrent problem." The 1996 Report stated that, "the judicial system, already hampered by inefficiency and corruption, collapsed for six months following the outbreak of fighting in April."

In 1997, before elections were held, the leaders of the various factions acknowledged that the integrity of the Supreme Court had been compromised by factional loyalties since 1992 and agreed that the Court would have to be reconstituted so that it might gain the legitimacy that would enable it to resolve successfully disputes that might arise concerning the elections. The members of the Court were therefore dismissed and new members were appointed based on the recommendations of the Liberian National Bar Association.

B. This Case

Plaintiff-appellant Bridgeway is a Liberian corporation with its principal place of business in Monrovia, Liberia. Defendant-appellee, Citibank, is a U.S. banking corporation with its principal place of business in New York. For many years Citibank maintained a branch in Monrovia, but it closed that branch in January 1992 and completely withdrew from Liberia by 1995. As required by Liberian law, Citibank, before withdrawing, formulated a plan of liquidation, which was approved by the National Bank of Liberia. According to this plan, funds were to be remitted by Citibank to Meridian Bank Liberia Ltd., in order to meet Citibank's obligations to depositors. Citibank alerted its customers to its plans so that they could withdraw their funds. On April 21, 1995, the National Bank of Liberia indicated by letter that Citibank had satisfactorily completed the liquidation plan and was no longer licensed to do business in Liberia.

Bridgeway had an account at Citibank's Liberian branch with a balance of $189,376.66. In November 1992, Bridgeway brought suit in Liberia against Citibank, seeking a declaration that Citibank was obligated to pay Bridgeway its balance in U.S. (rather than Liberian) dollars. In August 1993, the trial court ruled in favor of Citibank. The court found that, under Liberian law, a person may not refuse to accept Liberian dollars for the discharge of an obligation unless there is an express agreement to the contrary and that Liberian law gives the Liberian dollar a par value equal to the value of the U.S. dollar. The trial court also found that under Bridgeway's contract with Citibank, the latter had the right to decide the currency in which a withdrawal would be paid. Bridgeway appealed to the Liberian Supreme Court, which reversed the lower court's decision and entered judgment for Bridgeway.

Bridgeway filed suit in New York state court to enforce the Liberian Supreme Court judgment, and Citibank removed the case to the federal district court. When it became apparent that Citibank was going to defend itself by challenging the legitimacy of the Liberian judicial system, Bridgeway moved for summary judgment—arguing that Citibank was estopped from questioning the fairness of the Liberian judiciary. But the district court denied that motion and, sua sponte, granted summary judgment for Citibank. Specifically, the court found that, as a matter of law, Liberia's courts did not constitute "a system of jurisprudence likely to secure an impartial administration of justice" and that, as a result, the Liberian judgment was unenforceable in the United States. Bridgeway now appeals.

II. Discussion

...[A]. Judicial Estoppel

Bridgeway...argues that because Citibank voluntarily participated in litigation in Liberian courts, it was judicially estopped from raising any question as to the impartiality of those courts in the instant case. Bridgeway observes that Citibank has taken part in at least a dozen civil cases in Liberia since 1992. And in several of those cases, Citibank appeared as a plaintiff. Having availed itself of Liberia's courts without there raising any objections to the fairness of Liberian justice, Citibank should now be estopped, Bridgeway argues, from calling into question the validity of Liberian judgments. Citibank responds by arguing that its participation in Liberian litigation did not amount to an admission of the fairness of

Liberian courts. Moreover, it argues that it could not have raised its objections to Liberia's judicial system in Liberia, because Liberian courts routinely sanction lawyers who question the Liberian judicial system. The district court agreed with Citibank.

Judicial estoppel "prevents a party from asserting a factual position in a legal proceeding that is contrary to a position previously taken by [the party] in a prior legal proceeding." In this Circuit, "[a] party invoking judicial estoppel must show that (1) the party against whom the estoppel is asserted took an inconsistent position in a prior proceeding and (2) that position was adopted by the first tribunal in some manner." We have described the type of inconsistency required as a "clear inconsistency between [the party's] present and former positions."

In order for Bridgeway to prevail, we must conclude that voluntarily participating in litigation in a foreign tribunal is fundamentally inconsistent with the belief that the tribunal is unlikely to provide an impartial forum or one that comports with notions of due process. Such a position is without merit. Defending a suit where one has been haled into court, and suing where jurisdiction and venue readily exist do not constitute assertions that the relevant courts are fair and impartial. Accordingly, we do not view Citibank's voluntary participation in Liberian litigation, even as a plaintiff, as clearly contradictory to its present position.

[B]. Fairness of Liberian Courts[1]

i. Burden

The parties strenuously dispute who bears the ultimate burden of proof with respect to the fairness of the Liberian judicial system. Although there are cases in which the question of the burden might be significant, it does not ultimately matter here. Accordingly, we express no opinion on it. Even if Citibank were to bear both the burden of production and that of persuasion, it has come forward with sufficiently powerful and uncontradicted documentary evidence describing the chaos within the Liberian judicial system during the period of interest to this case to have met those burdens and to be entitled to judgment as a matter of law. Thus, the U.S. State Department Country Reports presented by Citibank indicate that the Liberian judicial system was in a state of disarray, as do, more subtly, the affidavits by Citibank's Liberian counsel, H. Varney G. Sherman.

The only evidence Bridgeway has introduced in support of its position are three statements by Liberian attorneys: (1) an affidavit of James E. Pierre, Esq., a member of the Liberian Bar, stating that the procedural rules of Liberia are modeled on those of New York State courts; (2) an affidavit introduced by Citibank, in which H. Varney G. Sherman, Citibank's Liberian counsel, states that "the

[1] In granting summary judgment, the district court reflexively applied New York law. Citibank argues that federal law should apply. Because of the similarity of the New York and federal standards concerning the enforcement of foreign judgments, however, the district court's application of New York law did not affect the outcome.... We therefore express no view on whether the district court was correct.

Liberian Government is patterned after the state governments of the United States of America;" and (3) an affidavit of N. Oswald Tweh, former Vice President of the Liberian National Bar Association, that "Liberia's judicial system was and is structured and administered to afford party-litigants therein impartial justice." The first statement concerns the design of the Liberian judicial system, but says nothing about its practice during the period in question.[2] The second, in addition to suffering from the same defect as the first, does not even discuss the Liberian judicial system directly. And the third is purely conclusory.

ii. Evidence

Summary judgment cannot be granted on the basis of inadmissible evidence. See Fed. R. Civ. P. 56(e). And Bridgeway raises many objections to the evidence relied upon by the district court in determining that Liberia's courts were, as a matter of law, unlikely to render impartial justice. Although the parties argue over a variety of different pieces of evidence, in the absence of any proof supporting Bridgeway's position, we need only consider whether Citibank adduced admissible evidence in sufficient amount to make the district court's decision regarding the performance of the Liberian judiciary during the civil war be supportable as well as uncontroverted. In fact, all of the district court's conclusions concerning this issue can be derived from just two sources: the affidavits of H. Varney G. Sherman ("Sherman affidavits") and the U.S. State Department Country Reports for Liberia for the years 1994–1997 ("Country Reports" or "Reports").

Bridgeway does not object to the admissibility of the Sherman affidavits (except on the ground that they support an argument that Bridgeway alleges Citibank is estopped from making). Indeed, in its brief, Bridgeway cites statements derived from these very affidavits in support of its own position. We will therefore assume that the Sherman material was properly relied upon by the district court.[3]

The district court also relied quite heavily on the Country Reports. Bridgeway argues that these Reports constitute excludable hearsay. Citibank replies that the Reports are admissible under Fed. R. Evid. 803(8)(C), which allows the admission

---

[2] Evidence concerning the design of a judicial system might be sufficient, in the absence of countervailing evidence. But where a party presents evidence concerning the actual practice of a judicial system, evidence about design is not likely to create a genuine issue of material fact.

[3] Sherman's affidavits contain much of the information on the basis of which the district court made its decision and wrote its opinion: the history of the Liberian governmental system, the history of the civil war, and some of the effects of the civil war on the Liberian judicial system. Although Sherman was somewhat restrained in his description, he did indicate that during the civil war the constitutional provisions governing the appointment of Supreme Court justices were not followed, members of the Supreme Court served at the "will and pleasure of the appointing powers," and, when elections were finally called, the parties acknowledged that "membership on the Supreme Court had been based on factional appointment and with factional loyalties." Cf. Restatement (Third) of Foreign Relations § 482 cmt. b. (1987) ("Evidence that the judiciary was dominated by the political branches of government... would support a conclusion that the legal system was one whose judgments are not entitled to recognition."). He concluded that "between July, 1990 and August, 1997, the Supreme Court was not organized in keeping with the 1986 Constitution."

of "factual findings resulting from an investigation made pursuant to authority granted by law, unless the sources of information or other circumstances indicate lack of trustworthiness."

Rule 803(8) "is based upon the assumption that public officers will perform their duties, that they lack motive to falsify, and that public inspection to which many such records are subject will disclose inaccuracies." 31 Michael H. Graham, Federal Practice and Procedure § 6759, at 663–64 (Interim ed.1992). "'Factual finding' includes not only what happened, but how it happened, why it happened, and who caused it to happen." Id. at 689. The rule therefore renders presumptively admissible "not merely... factual determinations in the narrow sense, but also... conclusions or opinions that are based upon a factual investigation." Gentile v. County of Suffolk, 926 F.2d 142, 148 (2d Cir. 1991).

In order to fit within the purview of Rule 803(8)(C), the evidence must (1) contain factual findings, and (2) be based upon an investigation made pursuant to legal authority. Once a party has shown that a set of factual findings satisfies the minimum requirements of Rule 803(8)(C), the admissibility of such factual findings is presumed. The burden to show "a lack of trustworthiness" then shifts to the party opposing admission. See Ariza v. City of New York, 139 F.3d 132, 134 (2d Cir. 1998).

In this case, there is little doubt that the Country Reports constitute "factual findings." Moreover, the Reports are certainly gathered pursuant to legal authority: federal law requires that the State Department submit the Reports annually to Congress, see 22 U.S.C. §§ 2151n(d), 2304(b) (1994 & Supp. 1999). They are therefore presumptively admissible.

Bridgeway attempts to rebut this presumption by arguing that the Reports are untrustworthy, and it points to language in the State Department's description of their preparation. The State Department says that "[w]e have given particular attention to attaining a high standard of consistency despite the multiplicity of sources and the obvious problems related to varying degrees of access to information, structural differences in political and social systems, and trends in world opinion regarding human rights practices in specific countries." Although this constitutes a frank recognition of the shortcomings intrinsic in any historical investigation, it does not amount (as Bridgeway argues) to an admission of the lack of trustworthiness required to reject the admissibility of these documents.

When evaluating the trustworthiness of a factual report, we look to (a) the timeliness of the investigation, (b) the special skills or experience of the official, (c) whether a hearing was held and the level at which it was conducted, and (d) possible motivation problems. See Fed. R. Evid. 803(8)(C) advisory committee's note. With the exception of (c), which is not determinative by itself, cf. id. ([T]he rule... assumes admissibility in the first instance but with ample provision for escape if sufficient negative factors are present. (emphasis added)), nothing about the Reports calls into question their reliability with respect to these factors. The Reports are submitted annually, and are therefore investigated in a timely manner. They are prepared by area specialists at the State Department. And nothing in the record or in Bridgeway's briefs indicates any motive for misrepresenting the facts concerning Liberia's civil war or its effect on the judicial system there.[4] See Bank Melli Iran v. Pahlavi, 58 F.3d 1406, 1411 (9th Cir. 1995) (relying on Country Reports in granting summary judgment on the issue of the fairness of Iranian courts).

In addition to its reliance on the Sherman affidavits and the Country Reports, the district court took judicial notice of historical facts drawn from a variety of sources. Bridgeway objects to this. Even if we agreed with Bridgeway's objection, we would affirm the district court's decision because the facts of which the district court took judicial notice were merely background history and of no moment to the ultimate determination of the fairness of Liberia's courts during the period of the civil war. The information in the district court's opinion concerning the functioning of the Liberian courts during the war is drawn (or could easily be drawn) entirely from the Sherman affidavits and the Country Reports, both of which were clearly admissible.

Having found all of Bridgeway's contentions to be without merit, we affirm the judgment of the district court.

Comments and Questions

1. Why wasn't Citibank's prior voluntary participation (as a plaintiff) in the judicial system of Liberia sufficient to demonstrate that system's fundamental impartiality and fairness?

2. In Liberia, Citibank prevailed at the trial court but lost on appeal. Does this make it harder or easier for Citibank to argue that it was denied meaningful process?

3. On consideration of whether to enforce the Liberian judgment, should the American court review the procedural protections of the Liberian appellate process, the trial process or both?

4. After Bridgeway, are all Liberian judgments (during the relevant time period) unenforceable? In other words, is Liberia now one of the countries that, like Cuba, North Korea, Iran, Iraq, and Congo, Judge Posner described as lacking a commitment to the rule of law and to the norm of due process? Or might it vary on a case-by-case basis? (But vary based on what?)

5. The previous two cases have focused on the inquiry whether the judgment was rendered under a judicial system that does not provide impartial tribunals or procedures compatible with due process of law. The next case examines another ground for denying recognition and enforcement. If the foreign court lacked personal jurisdiction, the local court is required to deny recognition and enforcement.

---

[4] One could certainly imagine situations in which motivational problems might plausibly be present (e.g., a country report on an avowed enemy or a significant ally of the United States), but Bridgeway has raised no such doubts here. Accordingly, we express no views on the admissibility of country reports in those circumstances.

Siedler v. Jacobson

383 N.Y.S.2d 833 (App. 1st 1976)

Per Curiam

While on a week's holiday in Vienna, defendant and his companion purchased an antique porcelain figure from plaintiff dealer, but subsequently refused to honor payment on the ground that plaintiff had misrepresented the article's age and value. Two years later, defendant was served in New York with process (in German) issued out of the Austrian Superior court, based upon that nation's counterpart to New York's "long-arm" statute (CPLR 302). Upon defendant's default, plaintiff instituted this action pursuant to Article 53 of the CPLR to enforce the foreign judgment.

We agree with Special Term's conclusion that the judgment should not be enforceable in New York for lack of jurisdiction over the defendant. Analysis of the legislative history of Article 53 makes clear that it was not within the intendment of that statute to adopt the broad definition of "transacting any business" applicable under CPLR section 302 as the criterion for extending recognition to foreign country judgments themselves bottomed upon correspondingly liberal bases of jurisdiction (CPLR 5305[a]5; 13 N.Y. Judicial conference Report, p. 223 [1968]; 6 Weinstein Korn & Miller, § 5305.02). While we are cognizant of the desirability of affording recognition to foreign country judgments so that judgments obtained in our own courts will receive reciprocally favorable treatment abroad, the nature of defendant's solitary act in this case was so casual and incidental to the foreign forum that it could not possibly serve as a jurisdictional predicate sufficient to grant conclusive effect to the default judgment sued upon.

Comments and Questions

1. Does it make sense that the New York court would impose a threshold for the Austrian court to establish personal jurisdiction over the defendant that is higher than its own standard (i.e., claims arising from the transaction of business)? Notwithstanding this case, it is generally thought that a foreign judgment based on jurisdictional grounds consistent with the United States jurisdictional standards would be enforced. See, for example, Bank of Montreal v. Kough, 430 F. Supp. 1243 (N.D. Cal. 1977) (enforcing a Canadian judgment rendered against a defendant who had breached a contract of guarantee with Canadian bank, where defendant was engaged in business in British Columbia, was a director and shareholder of a company operating there, and had signed a contract in British Columbia specifically related to dealings there), aff'd, 612 F. 2d 467 (9th Cir. 1980).

2. The next case examines one of the discretionary bases for denying enforcement. The issue presented is whether the action on which the judgment was based is repugnant to the public policy of the United States or of the State where recognition is sought.

Southwest Livestock and Trucking Co., Inc. v. Ramon

169 F.3d 317 (5th Cir. 1999)

Emilio M. Garza, Circuit Judge

Defendant-Appellant, Reginaldo Ramon, appeals the district court's grant of summary judgment in favor of Plaintiffs-Appellees, Southwest Livestock & Trucking Co., Inc., Darrel Hargrove and Mary Jane Hargrove. Ramon contends that the district court erred by not recognizing a Mexican judgment, that if recognized would preclude summary judgment against him. We vacate the district court's summary judgment and remand.

I

Darrel and Mary Jane Hargrove (the "Hargroves") are citizens of the United States and officers of Southwest Livestock & Trucking Co., Inc. ("Southwest Livestock"), a Texas corporation involved in the buying and selling of livestock. In 1990, Southwest Livestock entered into a loan arrangement with Reginaldo Ramon ("Ramon"), a citizen of the Republic of Mexico. Southwest Livestock borrowed $400,000 from Ramon. To accomplish the loan, Southwest Livestock executed a "pagare"—a Mexican promissory note—payable to Ramon with interest within thirty days. Each month, Southwest Livestock executed a new pagare to cover the outstanding principal and paid the accrued interest. Over a period of four years, Southwest Livestock made payments towards the principal, but also borrowed additional money from Ramon. In October of 1994, Southwest Livestock defaulted on the loan. With the exception of the last pagare executed by Southwest Livestock, none of the pagares contained a stated interest rate. Ramon, however, charged Southwest Livestock interest at a rate of approximately fifty-two percent. The last pagare stated an interest rate of forty-eight percent, and under its terms, interest continues to accrue until Southwest Livestock pays the outstanding balance in full.

After Southwest Livestock defaulted, Ramon filed a lawsuit in Mexico to collect on the last pagare. The Mexican court granted judgment in favor of Ramon, and ordered Southwest Livestock to satisfy its debt and to pay interest at forty-eight percent. Southwest Livestock appealed, claiming that Ramon had failed to effect proper service of process, and therefore, the Mexican court lacked personal jurisdiction. The Mexican appellate court rejected this argument and affirmed the judgment in favor of Ramon.

After Ramon filed suit in Mexico, but prior to the entry of the Mexican judgment, Southwest Livestock brought suit in United States District Court, alleging that the loan arrangement violated Texas usury laws. Southwest Livestock then filed a motion for partial summary judgment, claiming that the undisputed facts established that Ramon charged, received and collected usurious interest in violation of Texas law. Ramon also filed a motion for summary judgment. By then the Mexican court had entered its judgment, and Ramon sought recognition of that judgment. He claimed that, under principles of collateral estoppel and res judicata, the Mexican judgment barred Southwest Livestock's suit. The district court judge referred both motions to a magistrate judge.

The magistrate judge recommended that the district court grant Southwest Livestock's motion for summary judgment as to liability under Texas usury law, and recommended that it hold a trial to determine damages. In reaching her decision, the magistrate judge first addressed whether the Texas Uniform Foreign Country Money-Judgment Recognition Act (the "Texas Recognition Act") required the district court to recognize the Mexican judgment. See Tex. Civ. Prac. & Rem. Code Ann. § 36.001 et seq. (West 1998). As the magistrate judge observed, a judgment "that is not refused recognition... is conclusive between the parties to the extent that it grants or denies recovery of a sum of money." Tex. Civ. Prac. & Rem. Code Ann. § 36.004 (West 1998). The magistrate judge concluded that, contrary to Southwest Livestock's position, the Mexican court properly acquired personal jurisdiction over Southwest Livestock, and therefore, lack of jurisdiction could not constitute a basis for nonrecognition. Nonetheless, according to the magistrate judge, "the district court would be well within its discretion in not recognizing the Mexican judgment on the grounds that it violates the public policy of the state of Texas." Thus, the magistrate judge decided that the Mexican judgment did not bar Southwest Livestock's suit. The magistrate judge then addressed whether the district court should apply Texas or Mexican law to its resolution of Southwest Livestock's usury claim. The magistrate judge concluded that, under Texas choice of law rules, the district court should apply Texas law. Under Texas law, Ramon undisputably charged usurious interest.

The district court adopted the magistrate judge's recommendation, granting Southwest Livestock's motion for summary judgment as to liability under Texas usury law, and denying Ramon's motion for summary judgment. The district court agreed that the Mexican judgment violated Texas public policy, and that Texas law applied. The district court then heard evidence on the question of damages and granted $5,766,356.93 to Southwest Livestock. The district court also ordered that amount to "increase by $1,677.00 for every day after November 17, 1997, until the date this Judgment is signed," and awarded Southwest Livestock post-judgment interest and attorneys' fees. Ramon appealed.

Ramon asks us to reverse the district court's grant of summary judgment in favor of Southwest Livestock. He contends that the district court erred by failing to recognize the Mexican judgment. He also argues that the district court erred by applying Texas law. According to Ramon, the district court should have applied Mexican law because the pagares executed by Southwest Livestock designated Mexico as the place of payment, and Mexico has the most significant relationship to the loan transaction. Ramon also objects to the district court's continuing charge for usury. Finally, Ramon contends that the district court erred by using a Texas, rather than federal, post-judgment interest rate.

Southwest Livestock asks us to affirm the district court. It concedes that the district court should have used a federal post-judgment interest rate, but refutes

Ramon's other arguments. It contends that the district court properly withheld recognition of the Mexican judgment and properly applied Texas law. Additionally, as an alternative ground for upholding the district court's decision not to recognize the Mexican judgment, Southwest Livestock argues that Ramon failed to serve it with proper service of process, and therefore, the Mexican court lacked personal jurisdiction.

II

We must determine first whether the district court properly refused to recognize the Mexican judgment. Our jurisdiction is based on diversity of citizenship. Hence, we must apply Texas law regarding the recognition of foreign country money-judgments. See Erie R.R. Co. v. Tompkins, 304 U.S. 64 (1938) (holding that in a diversity action, a federal court must apply the law of the forum state); Success Motivation Inst. of Japan, Ltd. v. Success Motivation Inst. Inc., 966 F.2d 1007, 1009–10 (5th Cir. 1992) ("Erie applies even though some courts have found that these suits necessarily involve relations between the U.S. and foreign governments, and even though some commentators have argued that the enforceability of these judgments in the courts of the United States should be governed by reference to a general rule of federal law.").

Under the Texas Recognition Act, a court must recognize a foreign country judgment assessing money damages unless the judgment debtor establishes one of ten specific grounds for nonrecognition. See Tex. Civ. Prac. & Rem. Code Ann. § 36.005 (West 1998);[2] Dart v. Balaam, 953 S.W.2d 478, 480 (Tex. App.—Fort Worth 1997, no writ) (noting that "[t]he party seeking to avoid recognition has the burden of proving a ground for nonrecognition"). Southwest Livestock contends that it established a ground for nonrecognition. It notes that the Texas Constitution

---

[2] Tex. Civ. Prac. & Rem. Code Ann. § 36.005 (West 1998) provides:

(a) A foreign country judgment is not conclusive if:
  (1) the judgment was rendered under a system that does not provide an impartial tribunal or procedures compatible with the requirements of due process of law;
  (2) the foreign country court did not have personal jurisdiction over the defendant; or
  (3) the foreign country court did not have jurisdiction over the subject matter.

(b) A foreign country judgment need not be recognized if:
  (1) the defendant in the proceedings in the foreign country court did not receive notice of the proceedings in sufficient time to defend;
  (2) the judgment was obtained by fraud;
  (3) the cause of action on which the judgment is based is repugnant to the public policy of this state;
  (4) the judgment conflicts with another final and conclusive judgment;
  (5) the proceeding in the foreign country court was contrary to an agreement between the parties under which the dispute in question was to be settled otherwise than by proceedings in that court;
  (6) in the case of jurisdiction based only on personal service, the foreign country court was a seriously inconvenient forum for the trial of the action; or
  (7) it is established that the foreign country in which the judgment was rendered does not recognize judgments rendered in this state that, but for the fact that they are rendered in this state, conform to the definition of "foreign country judgment."

places a six percent interest rate limit on contracts that do not contain a stated interest rate. See Tex. Const. art. XVI, § 11. It also points to a Texas statute that states that usury is against Texas public policy. See Vernon's Tex. Civ. Stat., art. 5069-1C.001 ("All contracts for usury are contrary to public policy"). Thus, according to Southwest Livestock, the Mexican judgment violates Texas public policy, and the district court properly withheld recognition of the judgment.

We review the district court's grant of summary judgment de novo. In reviewing the district court's decision, we note that the level of contravention of Texas law has "to be high before recognition [can] be denied on public policy grounds." The narrowness of the public policy exception reflects a compromise between two axioms—res judicata and fairness to litigants—that underlie our law of recognition of foreign country judgments.

To decide whether the district court erred in refusing to recognize the Mexican judgment on public policy grounds, we consider the plain language of the Texas Recognition Act. Section 36.005(b)(3) of the Texas Recognition Act permits the district court not to recognize a foreign country judgment if "the cause of action on which the judgment is based is repugnant to the public policy" of Texas. This subsection of the Texas Recognition Act does not refer to the judgment itself, but specifically to the "cause of action on which the judgment is based." Thus, the fact that a judgment offends Texas public policy does not, in and of itself, permit the district court to refuse recognition of that judgment. See Norkan Lodge Co. Ltd. v. Gillum, 587 F. Supp. 1457, 1461 (ND. Tex. 1984) (noting that a "judgment may only be attacked in the event that 'the cause of action [on] which the judgment is based is repugnant to the public policy of this state,' not the judgment itself").

In this case, the Mexican judgment was based on an action for collection of a promissory note. This cause of action is not repugnant to Texas public policy. Under the Texas Recognition Act, it is irrelevant that the Mexican judgment itself contravened Texas's public policy against usury. Thus, the plain language of the Texas Recognition Act suggests that the district court erred in refusing to recognize the Mexican judgment.

Southwest Livestock, however, argues that we should not interpret the Texas Recognition Act according to its plain language. Southwest Livestock contends that Texas courts will not enforce rights existing under laws of other jurisdictions when to do so would violate Texas public policy. It believes that the reasoning of the Texas Supreme Court in DeSantis v. Wackenhut Corp., 793 S.W.2d 670 (Tex. 1990), requires us to affirm the district court's decision not to recognize the Mexican judgment. In DeSantis, the Court refused to apply Florida law to enforce a noncompetition agreement, even though the agreement contained an express choice of Florida law provision, and Florida had a substantial interest in the transaction. The Court concluded that "the law governing enforcement of noncompetition agreements is fundamental policy in Texas, and that to apply the law of another state to determine the enforceability of such an agreement in the circumstances of a case like this would be contrary to that policy." Id. At 681. Southwest Livestock argues similarly that the law governing usury constitutes a fundamental policy in Texas, and that to recognize the Mexican judgment would transgress that policy.

We find that, contrary to Southwest Livestock's argument, DeSantis does not support the district court's grant of summary judgment. First, in DeSantis the Court refused to enforce an agreement violative of Texas public policy; it did not refuse to recognize a foreign judgment. Recognition and enforcement of a judgment involve separate and distinct inquiries. See Guinness v. Ward, 955 F.2d 875, 889 (4th Cir. 1992) (noting the difference between recognizing and enforcing a foreign judgment); see also Restatement (Third) of Foreign Relations Law § 481 cmt. B (1986) (distinguishing between the recognition and enforcement of judgments). Second, unlike in DeSantis where the plaintiff sought to use foreign law offensively to enforce the noncompetition agreement, in this case, Ramon seeks recognition of the Mexican judgment as an affirmative defense to Southwest Livestock's usury claim. Different considerations apply when a party seeks recognition of a foreign judgment for defensive purposes. As Justice Brandeis once stated:

> [T]he company is in a position different from that of a plaintiff who seeks to enforce a cause of action conferred by the laws of another state. The right which it claims should be given effect is set up by way of defense to an asserted liability; and to a defense different considerations apply. A state may, on occasion, decline to enforce a foreign cause of action. In so doing, it merely denies a remedy leaving unimpaired the plaintiff's substantive right, so that he is free to enforce it elsewhere. But to refuse to give effect to a substantive defense under the applicable law of another state, as under the circumstances here presented, subjects the defendant to irremediable liability. This may not be done.
>
> Bradford Elec. Light Co. v. Clapper, 286 U.S. 145, 160 (1932); cf. Resource Sav. Assoc. v. Neary, 782 S.W.2d 897, 900 (Tex. App.—Dallas 1989, writ denied) (noting that because a party sought recognition of a foreign judgment for defensive purposes different considerations applied, but refusing to recognize the foreign judgment nonetheless).

Third, DeSantis involved a noncompetition agreement, and as we have explained elsewhere, "noncompetition agreements implicate an arguably stronger Texas public policy than usurious contracts." Admiral Ins. Co. v. Brinkcraft Dev., 921 F.2d 591, 594 (5th Cir. 1991).

We find our decision in Woods-Tucker Leasing Corp. v. Hutcheson-Ingram Dev. Co., 642 F.2d 744 (5th Cir. 1981), more helpful than DeSantis.[4] In Woods-Tucker we considered "whether a bankruptcy court sitting in Texas should honor a party contractual choice of Mississippi law in determining whether to apply the Texas or Mississippi usury statute to a transaction... between a Texas partnership and a Mississippi-headquartered corporate subsidiary of a Georgia corporation." Id. at 745. In deciding to honor the parties' choice of Mississippi

---

[4] We acknowledge that Woods-Tucker involves a sister state judgment, which distinguishes it from this case. Nevertheless, we find the decision in Woods-Tucker informative.

law, we noted that applying Mississippi law did not offend any Texas fundamental public policy:

> To be sure, it is the underlying policy of each state's usury laws to protect necessitous borrowers within its borders. Yet, as we have noted, we have found no Texas cases that have invalidated a party choice of law on grounds that the application of a foreign usury statute would violate public policy.

Id. at 753 n.13. We also relied on the Supreme Court's decision in Seeman v. Phila. Warehouse Co., 274 U.S. 403 (1927).

In Seeman, the Supreme Court emphasized its policy of "upholding contractual obligations assumed in good faith." It stated that, although parties may not willfully evade otherwise applicable usury laws by "entering into [a] contract... [that] has no normal relation to the transaction," if the rate of interest "allowed by the laws of the place of performance is higher than that permitted at the place of the contract," the parties may contract for a higher rate of interest without incurring the penalties of usury. Id. at 407–08. Woods-Tucker, and its reliance on Seeman, indicates that, although Texas has a strong public policy against usury, this policy is not inviolable.

We are especially reluctant to conclude that recognizing the Mexican judgment offends Texas public policy under the circumstances of this case. The purpose behind Texas usury laws is to protect unsophisticated borrowers from unscrupulous lenders. See Woods-Tucker, 642 F.2d at 753 n.13 ("[I]t is the underlying policy of each state's usury laws to protect necessitous borrowers within its borders"); see also Moore v. Lambert, 272 Ark. 324 (1981) ("As far as we know, usury laws exist in all states. Such laws are based upon a universally recognized public policy that protects necessitous borrowers from the exaction of exorbitant interest from unscrupulous lenders."). This case, however, does not involve the victimizing of a naive consumer. Southwest Livestock is managed by sophisticated and knowledgeable people with experience in business. Additionally, the evidence in the record does not suggest that Ramon misled or deceived Southwest Livestock. Southwest Livestock and Ramon negotiated the loan in good faith and at arms length. In short, both parties fully appreciated the nature of the loan transaction and their respective contractual obligations.

Accordingly, in light of the plain language of the Texas Recognition Act, and after consideration of our decision in Woods-Tucker and the purpose behind Texas public policy against usury, we hold that Texas's public policy does not justify withholding recognition of the Mexican judgment. The district court erred in deciding otherwise.

III

For the foregoing reasons, we VACATE the district court's summary judgment, and REMAND for further proceedings.

Comments and Questions

1. In this case, the foreign judgment was asserted as part of a res judicata affirmative defense. What would have been the result if Ramon were suing in Texas to enforce the foreign judgment? (You may wish to revisit the distinction between recognition and enforcement.)

2. An erroneous application of law or choice of law rules ordinarily will not alone suffice to trigger the public policy exception. Arguments to invoke the exception are most compelling when important interests or values are compromised. Consider the applicability of this exception in the context of the sample problem that opened this chapter.

Note on Treaties

We conclude our discussion of recognition and enforcement practice in the United States with a brief discussion of treaties. As stated previously, unlike most countries, the United States is not a party to any comprehensive bilateral or multilateral treaty concerning the recognition or enforcement of foreign judgments. There are three caveats to that assertion.

First, the United States is a party to some very specialized tax and "friendship, commerce, and navigation" treaties that require the recognition of judgments under certain circumstances. See Russell J. Weintraub, How Substantial is Our Need for a Judgments-Recognition Convention and What Should We Bargain Away to Get It?, 24 Brook. J. Int'l L. 167 (1998).

Second, the United States has ratified and implemented the United Nations Convention on the Recognition and Enforcement of Foreign Arbitral Awards. See 9 U.S.C. §§ 201–208 (Federal Arbitration Act). The Convention, often referred to as the New York Convention, is the primary legal basis for enforcing international commercial arbitration awards. We will discuss the enforcement of those awards in the next chapter.

Third, on the horizon for U.S. practitioners is the Hague Convention on Choice of Court Agreements, discussed in Chapter 5 (and elsewhere). At the time of publication of this text, however, only Mexico had ratified the treaty. We will return to this Hague Convention later in this chapter.

2. China

The recognition and enforcement of foreign judgments in China is governed by a provision of the Civil Procedure Law that was enacted in 1991. Article 268 provides:

> Having received an application or a request for recognition and enforcement of a legally effective judgment or ruling of a foreign court, a People's Court shall review such judgment or ruling pursuant to international treaties concluded or acceded to by the People's Republic of China or in accordance with the principles of reciprocity. If, on such review, the People's Court considers that such judgment or ruling neither contradicts the basic principles of the law of the People's Republic of China nor violates state sovereignty, security or the public interest, it shall rule to recognize its effectiveness. If enforcement is necessary, it shall issue an order of execution,

> which must be implemented in accordance with relevant provisions of this Law. If such judgment or ruling contradicts the basic principles of the law of the People's Republic of China or violates state sovereignty, security or the public interest, the People's Court shall refuse to recognize and execute the judgment or ruling.

The statute suggests a certain receptiveness to enforcement, but the country is not yet a party to any treaty dealing with the recognition and enforcement of foreign judgments. Moreover, the reciprocity requirement deters the development of a more robust recognition and enforcement practice. The following article describes one example of an effort to enforce a foreign judgment in China.

Jingzhou Tao, Enforcing Judgments in the People's Republic of China

Int'l Execution Against Judgment Debtors CHI-17–18 (2007)

Gomi Akira petitioned Dalian Municipal Intermediate People's Court (the "Dalian Court") over a loan dispute with Sino-Japanese Property Co., Ltd. of Japan (legal representative, Usa Kunio) for recognition of the legal effect and enforcement within China of a ruling made by the Odawara branch of Yokohama magistracy and of writs of debt attachment and debt transfer issued by the Tamana branch of Kumamoto magistracy.

Although the Odawara branch of Yokohama magistracy had ordered Usa Kunio and his company to repay a loan of Yen 140-million to creditor Gomi Akira, the court was told that Usa Kunio was incapable of paying back such a loan in his country. Furthermore, the Taman branch of Kumamoto magistracy had issued writs of debt attachment and debt transfer to include Usa Kunio's Sino-Japanese joint venture in Dalian, i.e., Fa Ri Seafood Co., Ltd., as a third party. The ruling stipulated that Fa Ri Seafood Co. Ltd. was to detain Usa Kunio's investment of Renminbi 4.85-million and transfer the money to Gomi Aira.

On learning of the ruling through the Chinese Ministry of Justice, Fa Ri Seafood Co., Ltd., refused to transfer the money on the grounds that the ruling was not legally binding on a Chinese legal person. Gomi Akira responded by submitting a petition to the Dalian Court for recognition and enforcement of the ruling.

In the ruling of 5 November 1994, the Dalian Court held that China had not concluded or acceded to any international treaty with Japan on reciprocal recognition and enforcement of court judgments or rulings, nor had it established a corresponding relationship of reciprocity with Japan. In accordance with article 268 of the new Civil Procedure Law, the Dalian Court rejected Gomi Akira's claim, and he was ordered to pay the expenses involved in the case, which amounted to Renminbi 200.

The Supreme People's Court concurred with this opinion and, on 26 June 1995, reiterated that China should not recognize or enforce the Japanese ruling in accordance with the provisions of article 268 of the new Civil Procedure Law.

Comments and Questions

1. Adoption of a reciprocity requirement indicates that a country is open to enforcing the judgments from other countries that are willing to do the same in return. But it also forces the "other" country to act first—to establish a record

of enforcing the judgments of the country that has the reciprocity requirement. If both (or all) countries have a reciprocity requirement, who acts first? Is there another more effective yet equally cautious method of demonstrating a receptiveness to enforcing foreign judgments provided the same courtesy is returned?

2. The Civil Procedure Law imposes a statute of limitations on enforcement actions—the statutory period is one year if one or both of the parties are individuals, and six months if both are legal persons. Understand that it may take considerable time for you to determine that the defendant (i) is not going to satisfy the foreign judgment voluntarily; (ii) does not have recoverable assets in the jurisdiction that rendered the judgment, and (iii) has assets in China. Why, then, such a short statute of limitations period?

3. Ecuador

Eduardo Carmigniani, Enforcing Judgments in Ecuador

Int'l Execution Against Judgment Debtors ECU-8-9 (1999)

There are two main cases relevant in Ecuador to the recognition and enforcement of foreign judgments, and those are discussed below.

I.

In General Cocoa Company v. Jose Jorgge Arevalo, [Supreme Court Judgment, June 27, 1972], the First Tribunal of the Supreme Court ruled that:

> Our Civil Procedural Law, takes into consideration the need of all jurisdictions to provide a system of law which governs the relations of men. In achieving this, the courts are prepared to enforce judgments issued abroad, when the requirements specified in article [424] of the Code of Civil Procedures are met. This procedure will be carried out even where the original court, which issued the summons, is of a different code or law to the Ecuadorian legal system. Once all the requirements have been met, it is the judge's obligation to order enforcement of the foreign judgment.

II.

In Marie K. Viteri v. Jose Viteri, [Supreme Court Judgment, September 19, 1975], one of the Tribunals of the Supreme court of Justice resolved the petition for the enforcement of a foreign judgment, which proclaimed that Mr. and Mrs. Viteri were divorced. After recognizing the foreign judgment and having it enforced, the Supreme Court fixed a fee of Sucres 2,000 for the plaintiff's lawyer.

This Tribunal ruled under the following headings:

a. Enforcement of Foreign Judgments

According to article [424] of the Code of Civil Procedure, judgments issued in a foreign country should be enforced in Ecuador, in accordance with treaties in force, if they do not contravene judicial national law or public order. In the relevant case, the divorce sentence between the spouses, Marie K. Viteri and Jose Viteri, had been issued for reasons of maltreatment. Custody of the minor, Dawn Elizabeth Viteri, was given to the mother. The authentication of the judgment and all documents annexed to the complaint constitute proof that, in the United States, the litigants who contracted marriage under the laws of that country have experienced a divorce trial and that the defendant was duly cited.

b. Ecuadorian Civil Procedure Code

The provisions of the Sanchez de Bustamente Code, upon which the courts of the first and second instance based their judgment, are irrelevant. This is due to the fact that even though the United States attended the Private International Law Convention agreed on by the sixth Pan-American Conference in La Havana, which in 1928 approved the Sanchez de Bustamente Code, it did not sign the declaration. However, the Civil Procedures Code must be followed, which states that where the foreign judgment is sufficiently clear and explicit, the Ecuadorian judge must enforce the ruling.

Furthermore, under the Civil Procedure Code, the Ecuadorian court also must examine its own law in order to determine the validity of the American judgment.

The court gave consideration to the following:

1. Article 142, Inc. 6, of the Constitution, which proclaims the defense of physical, mental, and moral health during infancy and the child's right to an education and home life;
2. Article 91 of the Civil Code, which establishes that a marriage celebrated in a foreign nation, in conformity with the laws of that nation or with Ecuadorian laws, will have the same civil effects in Ecuador as if it had been celebrated on Ecuadorian soil. In relation to divorce, it adds that if the competent authority has declared the nullity of a marriage celebrated in a foreign nation, the effects of that declaration will be respected. It appears that Marie de Viteri and Jose Viteri contracted marriage under North American Law and according to it they were also divorced. The Civil Code recognizes the validity of the declaration of divorce and therefore all its effects, among which is the assignation of the children to one of the parents;
3. The first rule of article 107 of the Civil Code, which prescribes that it is the mother's responsibility, if divorced or separated from her husband, to take care of preadolescent boys and girls of any age. The foreign judge's resolution is in complete conformity with the national legislation on that subject; and
4. The Minor's Code, which states that the nation is under an obligation to guarantee assistance, nourishment, and health to the minor until they have reached maturity. This should be carried out in an atmosphere of moral and physical security by people legally obliged to fulfill these duties; ensuring that they are not separated from their families, except in circumstances where the child's security is threatened. These regulations appear under sections b) and h) of the first article of the cited body of laws.

c. Examination of Procedure and Authority

Luis Felipe Borja states that:

> When a foreign judgment is presented, as an exception to res judicata,, demanding that it be declared an executive title, the judge or tribunal must examine many circumstances to decide if the judgment is effective or not. We find it correct to define judgment effectiveness as a whole of all the necessary requisites so that it may have extraterritorial effect. There should be a distinction between the form of the judgment and the resolution. It is necessary that the judgment be written according to the law or practices of the nation where it was issued. If the sentence is legalized, compliance is presumed, or if the other party affirms the contrary, the judge will grant a short period to show proof of the incident. After the judge has ensured the judgment is lex fori with regard to the fixed procedure, he examines if it has res judicata authority, and on this point lex fori is also applicable. The party that presents the judgment could also adjoin an authentic certificate stating that it has res judicata authority because it was proclaimed in last resort or because the terms in which they could interpose the resources the law concedes, has expired. When the judge examines the intrinsic requisites of the judgment, it is of prime importance that he investigate if it is contrary to international law or the public law of the state where it will be enforced.
>
> Luis Felipe Borja, Studies on the Chilean Civil Code, vol. I, article 47a.

d. Judgment of the Ecuadorian Court

The court found in favor of the American judgment for the following reasons:

1. All proceedings in the United States court had been translated into Spanish and, on this basis, the court decided that the judgment was both fair and rigorous and both parties were afforded every opportunity to argue their case; and
2. The foreign judgment was in agreement with Ecuadorian law.

Comments and Questions

1. In most civil law countries, enforcement of a foreign judgment is sought through a special petition to a court that has exclusive jurisdiction over recognition proceedings. The procedure (and the writ) is often called exequatur, and the court is usually an appellate court and often the highest court of appeal. If issued, the exequatur gives res judicata effect to the foreign judgment. This differs conceptually from the common law approach where courts will issue another judgment of their own to "enforce" the foreign judgment.

2. Many Latin American countries are parties to a number of treaties on enforcement. These multilateral approaches will be discussed later in this chapter.

4. Germany

In Germany, the basic rules regarding recognition and enforcement practice are set forth in the ZivilprozeBordnung (ZPO). Sections 722 and 723 establish a default that foreign judgments will be enforced without reexamining the merits of that dispute. The ZPO then excepts five categories:

(1) where the foreign court has no jurisdiction under German law;
(2) where insufficient service prejudiced the defendant's ability to proffer a defense;
(3) where the judgment is inconsistent with a German proceeding or another foreign judgment;
(4) where recognition would be manifestly incompatible with fundamental principles of German law;
(5) where there is no guarantee of reciprocity.

Joachim Zekoll, A Landmark Decision by the German Federal Court of Justice

30 Colum. J. Transnat'l L. 641 (1992)

I. Background of the Decision

... A recent decision of the German Federal Court of Justice ("Bundesgerichtshof" or "BGH"),[7] ... involves the recognition and enforcement[9] in Germany of an American damage award rendered against a defendant with dual American and German citizenship. The defendant had earlier been found guilty on criminal charges of sexual misconduct, and was sentenced to a long prison term in California. He avoided the criminal sentence by moving to Germany, but prior to his departure, the plaintiff-victim served a civil summons and complaint on the defendant in an action filed with the San Joaquin County Superior Court in California.[10] The defendant failed to appear at trial, and judgment was entered in favor of the plaintiff in the amount of $750,260, of which $150,260 was for past and future medical expenses, $200,000 for anxiety, pain, and suffering, and $400,000 as punitive damages. The American court also ordered that the plaintiff's attorney receive forty percent of the entire damage award as attorney's fees.

In an unpublished decision, the German court of first instance (Landgericht Düsseldorf), held that the American judgment was fully enforceable in Germany. The appellate court (Oberlandesgericht Düsseldorf) upheld the portion of the judgment awarding damages for past and future medical expenses, but limited the award for pain and suffering to $70,000, holding that the $200,000 amount exceeded what German public policy would tolerate. In addition, the $400,000 punitive damage award was limited to $55,065. This amount represented, in the

---

[7] Judgment of June 4, 1992, BGH Sen. Z., reprinted in 1992 Zeitschrift Für Wirtschaftsrecht Und Insolvenzpraxis [hereinafter ZIP] 1256 (F.R.G.).

[9] The recognition of a foreign decision in Germany creates a res judicata effect against a subsequent action in a German court involving identical parties and claims. Ordinarily, however, recognition does not attain independent importance; it merely serves a prerequisite for enforcement. *See* Joachim Zekoll, *Recognition and Enforcement of American Products Liability Awards in the Federal Republic of Germany*, 37 Am. J. Comp. L. 301, 303 n.8 (1989). This paper therefore uses the terms "recognition" and "enforcement" interchangeably.

[10] *John Doe v. Eckhard Schmitz*, No. 168-588, (Cal. Super. Ct. Apr. 24, 1985).

opinion of the court, acceptable attorney's fees awarded in the guise of punitive damages. The court denied enforcement of the balance of the damage award on the grounds that it would be incompatible with German public policy constraints.

The German Federal Court of Justice agreed only with the first finding of the appellate court, thus confirming the enforceability of the award for medical costs. The Court reversed the remaining portions of the appellate decision, holding that the award for pain and suffering was fully enforceable, but that the entire punitive damage award conflicted with overriding German public policy concerns, and therefore should not be enforced....

II. Public Policy Considerations

A. The Principle

Under § 723 of the ZivilprozeBordnung ("ZPO"), the German Code of Civil Procedure, a German court faced with an action for enforcement of a final foreign judgment may not reexamine the judgment on its merits. One exception to this principle is set forth in ZPO § 328(1) No. 4. Recognition will be denied if, particularly in view of basic constitutional rights, it would lead to a result that would be clearly incompatible with fundamental principles of German law. This public policy clause has been interpreted as a solution of last resort which only applies in extreme cases. Thus, even if a foreign court relies on rules which deviate from German law, this clause would not necessarily preclude the recognition of the foreign judgment. Although little discussion has been devoted in Germany to the rationales underlying this lenient approach, it is clearly warranted by the statutory mandate of ZPO § 723 for a German court not to revaluate the merits of the foreign decision.

It is the practical application of the public policy exception embodied in ZPO § 328(1) No. 4 that is at the heart of the controversy over the enforcement of American money judgments. Naturally, the defendant in this case advocated a wide interpretation of the exception, claiming that enforcement of the American court's decision would violate several indispensable principles of both procedural and substantive German law.

B. German Procedural Public Policy

...[1.] Discovery

The defendant's... objection on public policy grounds went to the fact-finding procedure underlying the original decision of the American court. The defendant had failed to comply with the plaintiff's discovery request, and the American court penalized his default by accepting as true the facts that led to the defendant's conviction in the criminal proceedings. The Court of Justice found no problem with this conclusion, especially since the defendant had never disputed the veracity of the facts established during the course of the criminal trial.

Rather than resting with this holding, however, the Court then addressed in dictum the larger question of whether full-fledged discovery under the American procedural system fundamentally conflicts with the German approach of tightly controlled judicial fact-finding. Those who argue against the recognition of American judgments on these grounds contend that the breadth and intrusiveness of American discovery is incompatible with fundamental tenets of German civil procedure.[26]

Others who favor a more lenient approach note that mere deviations from German legal mandates do not necessarily offend German public policy so as to warrant automatic rejection of the original decision. The Federal Court of Justice, recognizing the high level of tolerance accorded foreign judgments under ZPO § 328(1) No. 4, as well as the longstanding requirement that German courts evaluate the foreign law as it was applied in the particular case, ruled out a blanket rejection of cases involving full-fledged discovery.

Most important for future cases is the Court's view that an evaluation of American discovery methods must not be limited to a comparison with the rather narrow rules of fact-finding under German procedural law. The Court also noted that the inquiry must take into account both the duty to disclose facts under German substantive law,[29] which may operate as functional equivalent to American discovery rules, and the importance of particular evidence established through the American fact-finding process, such as defendant misconduct.

Although the Court did not further elaborate on the compatibility of the American discovery process with German public policy, the decision does display a generally favorable view towards enforceability in this respect. Not only does it dismiss the argument for a global rejection of American discovery, it also indicates a high level of tolerance in cases involving discovery that goes beyond German procedural limits.

[2.] Cost Allocation

The Court similarly rejected the defendant's contention that the judgment should be denied enforcement on the grounds that the American rule of costs is incompatible with German public policy mandates. Under German law, the losing party is liable not only for its own attorney fees and court costs, but also for the legal expenses of the prevailing party. Compared with this cost allocation, the American rule, which limits the losing party's risk to its own legal fees and costs, occasionally has been perceived as providing an incentive for speculative suits.[34]

---

[26] *See, e.g.*, Reinhard Greger, *Discovery am Amtsgericht?*, 1988 Zeitschrift Für Rechtspolitik [hereinafter ZRP] 164, 166; Rolf A. Schütze, *Probleme der Anerkennung US-Amerikanischer Zivilurteile in der Bundesrepublik Deutschland*, 1979 Wertpapiermitteilungen [hereinafter WM] 1174, 1175–1176; Rolf A. Schütze, *Die Anerkennung und Vollstreckbarerklärung US-amerikanischer Schadensersatzurteile in Produkthaftungssachen in der Bundesrepublik Deutschland*, in Festschrift Für Heinrich Nagel 392, 401 (1987) [hereinafter Schütze, Die Anerkennung]; *see also Re the Enforcement of a U.S. Judgment*, 3 Int'l Litig. Proc. 430 (1992).

[29] For example, a plaintiff in (or even prior to the filing of) a medical malpractice suit may gain access to medical records pursuant to Bürgerliches Gesetzbuch [hereinafter BGB] § 810 (F.R.G.). *See, e.g.*, Judgment of Nov. 23, 1982, BGH Sen. Z., 85 BGHZ 327, 329–338 (F.R.G.).

[34] *See, e.g.*, Rolf A. Schütze, *Conceptual Differences and Areas of Potential Collision Between the United States and 'Civil Law' Procedure from the German Perspective*, in Litigation of Business Matters in the United States and International Legal Assistance (Roger Zäch ed.) 21, 39–41 (1984).

The Court rejected the defendant's argument, acknowledging instead the legitimacy of the policy underlying the American rule of costs which, in conjunction with contingent fee arrangements, enables indigent parties to press meritorious claims. In evaluating the American solution, the Court again took a functional approach and found that this cost allocation serves as a quasi-substitute for what is accomplished through a German statute designed to provide government-funded legal aid for low income groups. Finally, as a basic fairness consideration, the Court observed that an application of the German rule of cost allocation would have resulted in an even greater financial burden for the defendant.

C. German Substantive Public Policy

1. Medical Expenses

Both American and German rules allow for the recovery of medical expenses which a plaintiff has sustained as a result of a tortfeasor's conduct. Contrary to American practice, however, a plaintiff under German law is not entitled to damages for future medical expenses when it is uncertain whether that plaintiff actually will undergo treatment. Since the American court had awarded such "fictitious" damages in the amount of $150,000,[39] the question arose whether this portion of the original judgment would satisfy German public policy standards. The Court of Justice answered in the affirmative and, in so doing, removed what has been perhaps the biggest obstacle to the enforcement of foreign tort judgments in Germany. Until this decision, it was unclear whether a narrow conflict of laws provision, Article 38 of the Einführungsgesetz zum Bürgerlichen Gesetzbuch ("EGBGB"),[40] could be raised as a defense in enforcement proceedings.

According to EGBGB art. 38, liability for a tort committed by a German national abroad in a case adjudicated by a German court applying foreign substantive law must not exceed liability limits prescribed by German law. Technically, the provision establishes rigid public policy limitations for the applicability of foreign laws in German courts. Nevertheless, it has been argued that the concept of German public policy is indivisible, and that therefore the clause also bars the enforcement of foreign court decisions granting relief beyond German bounds.

Although the Court previously held[42] that this unique protection for German tortfeasors does not apply to the enforcement of judgments rendered within

[39] This amount comprised $100,000 for future psychological treatment and $50,000 for hospitalization associated with that treatment. Judgment of June 4, 1992, 1992 ZIP at 1257.

[40] *See* EINFÜHRUNGSGESETZ ZUM BÜRGERLICHEN GESETZBUCH [Introductory Law to the German Civil Code] [hereinafter EGBGB] art. 38 (F.R.G.). The EGBGB codifies German private international law.

[42] Judgment of June 22, 1984, BGH Sen. Z., 88 BGHZ 17, 24–26 (F.R.G.). In this case, the plaintiff had first obtained a favorable judgment from an Italian court in an action for injuries which had been sustained in a car accident. The Italian court had ordered the German defendant to pay damages in excess of German limits for such actions and the German Federal Court of Justice, relying solely on the permissive policy standards expressed in the Brussels Convention, granted enforcement of the Italian decision. These standards are virtually identical with those enunciated in ZPO § 328(1) No. 4 applicable to foreign judgments that fall outside the jurisdiction of the Brussels Convention.

the jurisdiction of the Brussels Convention considerable doubt remained as to whether this favorable approach would be extended to "non- European" decisions. The Court ruled that it would indeed, holding that the provisions governing enforcement represent a conclusive statutory scheme that operates independently from constraints imposed on the application of foreign law by German courts pursuant to EGBGB art. 38.

The Court further noted that though the award for future medical expenses in this case would not have been available if German substantive law applied, the recognition and enforcement of this portion of the judgment would not serve to thwart the defendant's basic rights, and therefore did not come within the scope of ZPO § 328(1) No. 4. The reasoning underlying this result significantly improves the position of future tort judgment creditors, as it effectively prevents defendants in enforcement proceedings from relying on the rigid limitations prescribed by EGBGB art. 38.

2. Pain and Suffering

Like medical expenses, damages for pain and suffering are also recoverable under German tort rules. The controversy over the enforceability of American pain and suffering awards emanates from the size of these awards, which regularly exceed by a large amount those that a German court would grant for identical injuries. For example, had this case originally been adjudicated under German law, the plaintiff would have at best received $20,000, one tenth of the amount granted by the American court.

The Court nevertheless upheld the award, resting its conclusion primarily on the argument that the facts lacked sufficient contacts to the German forum to jeopardize German interests. The Court emphasized that the American decision settled a dispute between two individuals with American citizenship, and that the defendant committed the tort in the United States at a time when he maintained his permanent residence in that country. In the view of the Court, the defendant's dual German-American citizenship did not itself establish a significant link with Germany. The Court held that given these attenuated contacts to the German forum, the defendant's fundamental right and, thus, German public policy would not be offended by the pain and suffering award.[47] . . .

3. Contingent Fees

What is commonplace for most American plaintiff's attorneys is deemed unethical for their German counterparts; agreements that make the reimbursement for legal services contingent on the outcome of the litigation are void as violative of German bonos mores. Nevertheless, the Court of Justice rejected the defendant's challenge to the American court's forty percent contingent fee award, holding that foreign rules of professional responsibility ordinarily cannot be a concern of

---

[47] *Id.* at 1270. This approach marks a significant departure from the traditional public policy test of ZPO § 328(1) No. 4.

German public policy. The Court then addressed the defendant's contention that the American court had inflated the damage award to ensure that the plaintiff be fully compensated for his damages even after legal expenses had been deducted. This argument was not successful for the reasons the Court advanced to approve of the cost allocation prevailing in the American system; if, indeed, the American court tacitly included attorney fees, its decision to do so would fall squarely within the German rule which entitles the prevailing party to recoup all legal expenses from its opponent.

Although the Court concluded that an award which overcompensates the plaintiff for attorney's fees should prevent enforcement, it found that the fees were not excessive in this case. The Court observed that the amount of the contingent fees reflected the financial risks of losing the case, and that the various complications involved in the litigation had imposed particular burdens on the American attorney who had provided legal services for several years without payment. Thus, while the rule remains that excessive attorney's fees will not be enforced, it appears that the Court's reasoning will significantly narrow the category of cases in which this rule is successfully invoked in the future.

4. Punitive Damages

Although unavailable under German law, punitive damages have long been a topic of considerable interest in Germany. The interest has grown over the past two decades, as German exporters increasingly became exposed to punitive damage claims in American courts. Perhaps not surprisingly, most German commentators have spoken out against the enforceability of such awards.[62] Some even argue that punitive damages do not involve a civil or commercial matter at all,[63] and therefore do not meet the threshold requirement for enforcement. Others are inclined to accept such awards to the extent they provide compensation for litigation expenses and other losses which, though ordinarily unavailable in the American system, can be recovered under German rules.[64] The decision of the American court ordering the defendant to pay $400,000 in punitive damages provided the first opportunity for a German court to pass judgment on this type of award, since until now most punitive damages cases involved German parties with sufficient assets in the United States to cover the judgment.

Even though it stated that a private action involving punitive damages is a "civil and commercial matter," the Court of Justice rejected enforcement, holding that it would be incompatible with the German principle of proportionality. This holding, based on a comprehensive and thorough discussion on the nature of

---

[62] *See, e.g.*, Peter Hoechst, *Zur Versicherbarkeit von Punitive Damages*, 1983 VERSR 13, 16–17; Zekoll, supra note 1, at 323–330.

[63] *See, e.g.*, Schütze, *Die Anerkennung, supra* note 26, at 395–397; Hermann H. Hollmann, *Auslandszustellung in US-amerikanischen Zivil- und Verwaltungssachen*, 1982 RIW 784, 786.

[64] *See, e.g.*, Dieter Martiny, Handbuch Des Internationalen Zivilverfahrensrechts No. 507 (1984); Friedrich Graf von Westphalen, "Punitive Damages" in US-Amerikanischen Produkthaftungsklagen und der Vorbehalt des Art. 12 EGBGB, 1981 RIW 141, 147–149.

punitive damages, settles most of the uncertainty about the status of such damages in German enforcement proceedings.

After examining the various purposes they serve in American litigation, the Court identified punishment and deterrence as the prevailing forces behind the imposition of punitive damages.[66] This emphasis, indeed, is diametrically opposed to the very nature of German civil damage awards, which focus on the compensation of the injured party.[67] By contrast, the imposition in Germany of sanctions involving deterrence and punishment is ordinarily a matter of state criminal proceedings. These sanctions require adherence to strict standards, such as a high burden of proof and predictable sanctions, as prescribed by the German Strafgesetzbuch StGB Penal Code , the StrafprozeBordnung StPO Code of Criminal Procedure and German constitutional law.

Comments and Questions

1. The approach of the German Federal Court of Justice, although generally receptive to recognition and enforcement, nevertheless introduces considerable uncertainty in the analysis. The opinion seems to suggest that a defendant with less of a presence in the United States would have had a stronger public policy defense in resisting enforcement. Is this conflation of the analytical frameworks for jurisdiction and preclusion a new test? Or is it simply a more transparent and forthcoming explanation of the more traditional test?

2. Is partial enforcement of a foreign judgment logically defensible? Should jurisdictions undertake a "retail approach" to enforcement? Or should a judgment be accepted or rejected en masse?

3. For accounts of similar cases (and results) from Spain and Italy, see Scott R. Jablonski, Translation and Comment: Enforcing U.S. Punitive Damages Awards in Foreign Courts—A Recent Case in the Supreme Court of Spain, 24 J. L. & Com. 225 (2005); Lucia Ostoni, Italian Rejection of Punitive Damages in a U.S. Judgment, 24 J. L. & Com. 245 (2005).

---

[66] Judgment of June 4, 1992, BGH Sen. Z., reprinted in 1992 ZIP 1256, 1266–68 (F.R.G.). As in other parts of the opinion, the Court did not limit itself to German sources in support of its conclusion, but also examined numerous American publications, such as John G. Fleming, The American Tort Process (1988) and The American Law Institute, Enterprise Responsibility for Personal Injury (1991). This approach is unusual and underscores the significance which the Court attributed to this case.

[67] The Court explicitly rejected the proposition that damages for pain and suffering (Schmerzensgeld) awarded under German law serve similar functions as American punitive damages awards. Judgment of June 4, 1992, BGH Sen. Z., reprinted in 1992 ZIP 1256, 1267 (F.R.G.). This holding is in line with previous decisions in which the Court determined the size of Schmerzensgeld primarily in accordance with "the magnitude, severity, and duration of the pain, suffering and disfigurement," thereby emphasizing its compensatory function. See Judgment of July 6, 1955, BGH Gr. Sen. Z., 18 BGHZ 149, 154 (F.R.G.). By contrast, the element of retribution which is based on the nature of the misconduct and the defendant's financial condition may, but need not, constitute an additional factor for the computation of Schmerzensgeld. *See, e.g.*, Zekoll, *supra* note 1, at 327–329.

5. Denmark, Sweden, and Finland

Denmark, Sweden, and Finland have each adopted a rather extreme position regarding the enforcement of foreign judgments: unless there is an applicable treaty or convention to which the country is a party, judgments rendered by foreign courts are not enforced. Obviously, then, familiarity with the relevant bilateral and multilateral treaties and conventions is essential. For EU Member States, the Brussels Regulation is the backbone of recognition and enforcement practice. We will discuss this and other multilateral conventions later in this chapter.

Comments and Questions

1. Remember the difference between recognition and enforcement of foreign judgments. Why might a country have different policies with regard to recognition and enforcement, respectively?

2. A country could simply enforce another's judgments without negotiating or participating in a treaty or convention. Bilateral and multilateral treaties provide rather definite assurance of reciprocity; are there other benefits?

6. England

English courts recognize and enforce foreign money judgments in the absence of fraud or some other overriding consideration of public policy, provided that the foreign court had jurisdiction over the defendant. For some time, the English courts refused to enforce default judgments; the fact that a judgment was obtained by default remains a factor in the analysis. With regard to the jurisdictional prerequisite, the foreign court must have exercised personal jurisdiction in a manner that would have been consistent with English law.

Judgments are recognized and enforced provided they are for a debt or for a definite sum of money. An order of specific performance would typically be incapable of enforcement. Sums payable for taxes or penalties would also not be enforced. If a foreign judgment imposed a compensatory award in addition to criminal liability, the damages portion would be enforced while the penalty would not.

Adams v. Cape Industries, Plc.

Court of Appeal 1990 Eng. Ch. 433

SLADE, L.J.:

[Cape Industries, Plc. ("Cape"), an English company, presided over a group of subsidiary companies engaged in the mining in South Africa, and marketing, of asbestos. Hundreds of American plaintiffs filed several products liability actions in Texas against many defendants, including Cape and another English company Capasco Ltd. ("Capasco"). Cape and Capasco appeared and defended in the earlier actions (the Tyler I actions); these cases ultimately settled in 1978 for (US) $20 million, with Cape, Capasco, and its subsidiaries footing $5 million of that bill.

When a second round of actions were filed thereafter (the Tyler II actions), Cape and Capasco chose not to appear; a default judgment was entered in the amount of (US) $15,654,000.]

The presence issue

[In this section of the opinion, the Court held that an overseas trading corporation was likely to be treated by the English court as present within the jurisdiction of the courts of another country only where such a corporation had established and maintained at its own expense in that other country a fixed place of business and had carried on from there its business for more than a minimal period of time either through its servants or agents or through a representative; that in either of those instances presence could only be established where the overseas corporation's business, whether together with the representative's own business or not, had been transacted at or from the fixed place and, in order to ascertain whether the representative had carried on the corporation's business or his own, it would be necessary to investigate his functions and his relationship with the overseas corporation.] . . .

The natural justice issue

The assumptions upon which we consider this defence are that our decision on the presence issue is wrong and that the assumed presence of Cape/Capasco in Illinois at the commencement of the Tyler 2 proceedings rendered them subject to the jurisdiction of the Tyler court in those proceedings for the purpose of our law of enforcement of foreign judgments. . . .

The law applied by Scott J.

In the view of Scott J. the fundamental criterion for the success of a natural justice objection to the enforcement of a foreign judgment was to be found in the judgment of Lindley M.R. in Pemberton v. Hughes [1899] 1 Ch. 781, 790, where he said:

> If a judgment is pronounced by a foreign court over persons within its jurisdiction and in a matter with which it is competent to deal, English courts never investigate the propriety of the proceedings in the foreign court, unless they offend against English views of substantial justice. Where no substantial justice, according to English notions, is offended, all that English courts look to is the finality of the judgment and the jurisdiction of the court, in this sense and to this extent—namely, its competence to entertain the sort of case which it did deal with, and its competence to require the defendant to appear before it. If the court had jurisdiction in this sense and to this extent, the courts of this country never inquire whether the jurisdiction has been properly or improperly exercised, provided always that no substantial injustice, according to English notions, has been committed.

Thus in the opinion of Scott J. if the natural justice objection were to succeed, the proceedings in the foreign court must "offend against English views of substantial justice:" ante, p. 497F-G. With reference to that broad criterion he considered the procedure which led to the default judgment of 12 September 1983. The route which led him to his conclusion on this issue was very briefly as follows: (i) Cape/Capasco were in default and had forfeited any entitlement to a hearing save on the issue of damages. There was no injustice in that. (ii) Cape/Capasco were given sufficient notice of the application for the default judgment but the application for relief of which notice was given was for a judicial assessment of damages at a judicial hearing. (iii) The effect of the notice given to Cape/Capasco could not be divorced from the context of the Federal Rules for default judgments. Having regard to that context a defendant in default in an action for unliquidated damages in the Tyler court was entitled to expect that his liability to the plaintiff would be assessed by the judge in the light of evidence which the judge had considered and which, in the judge's opinion, justified the award which was made:

(iv) "The requirements of substantial justice in a particular case cannot...be divorced from the legitimate expectation of both the plaintiff and the defendant in the context of the procedural rules applicable to the case."

(v) Since there was no judicial assessment of the damages the proceedings offended our principles of substantial justice.

(vi) The fact that the default judgment might have been set aside on application to the judge, or an appeal, because of the breaches of local rules of procedure, did not as a matter of principle make the judgment enforceable notwithstanding the breach of natural justice....

The plaintiffs' submissions on natural justice

Mr. Falconer's submissions for the plaintiffs may be summarised as follows.

1. The natural justice defence has been limited by authority binding upon this court to lack of notice and denial of proper opportunity to be heard: see Jacobson v. Frachon (1928) 138 L.T. 386. The underlying basis or reason for. this limitation is that our law requires only that the judgment debtor be afforded by the foreign court a fair trial or the opportunity for a fair trial if the defendant chooses to take it. If the defendant is shown to have been deprived irremediably of a fair trial then the judgment is unenforceable here.
2. The defendant will be held to have been irremediably deprived of a fair trial by reason of defective procedure in two cases: (i) if the rules of procedure of the foreign court are themselves by our standards unfair, because, in that case, there can be no prospect of the foreign court correcting what has been done under its rules; and, (ii) if the rules of procedure of the foreign court are by our standards fair; and the defective procedure was caused by departure from those rules, but it is impossible or impracticable for the defect to have been corrected within the foreign system: e.g. because the defendant

only learned of the judgment too late to advance an effective appeal or procedure for setting the judgment aside.

3. If the procedural defect was reasonably capable of remedy within the procedure of the foreign court, whether by application to set aside the judgment, or by appeal, the defendant is not released from the obligation to obey the judgment by reason of the procedural defect because, being subject to the jurisdiction of the foreign court, he may properly be required to have resort to the remedies provided by the foreign system.
4. The basis and substance of those submissions for the plaintiffs were said to be in accordance with justice, with practicality and with the principles of our law in that (i) our law recognises that all courts make procedural mistakes: the fact that a mistake is made, for which the foreign court's procedure provides a remedy, should not release the defendant who chooses not to avail himself of the remedy; (ii) the argument is based upon the connection between the foreign court and the defendant created by the voluntary act of the defendant in being present within the foreign jurisdiction, or by submission thereto, etc.; (iii) it is desirable that our courts should not be required to act as a court of error for the examination and assessment of procedural defects within the foreign system for which that system provides an effective remedy; (iv) the submissions provide a framework of reasonable certainty and clarity for the decision of pleas of breach of natural justice. By contrast, the "broad criterion" applied by the judge, is too wide and too uncertain a test.
5. The reliance placed by Scott J. on "legitimate expectation" was unjustified. There had been no actual expectation on the part of Cape/Capasco nor any reliance upon any expected form of procedure. Nothing to that effect had been pleaded or proved. This concept of legitimate expectation amounted, it was said, to no more than the assertion that a defendant is entitled to expect that, in the conduct of the proceedings in the foreign court, that court will correctly apply its own procedure and that, if it does not, a sufficient breach of natural justice is demonstrated. (We will refer to the submissions summarised in this paragraph as "the legitimate expectation point.")
6. Upon the evidence and upon the findings of Scott J. the procedural rules applicable in the Tyler court were fair and just. The defendants could have applied to set aside the judgment on the grounds that the procedure for the assessment of damages was irregular under the relevant rules and such application would have been allowed if made in due time. Further, an appeal to the Circuit Court was open to Cape/Capasco. Since they took no step to correct the procedural defect, and the consequences of it, they cannot rely upon it as a defence in these proceedings.

The defendants' submissions on natural justice

To these submissions Mr. Playford for Cape/Capasco replied by contending that Scott J. was right in his conclusion for the reasons which he gave. Further, if it should appear to this court that the defendants could not impeach the judgment on the ground of a procedural defect which was capable of remedy within the system of the federal courts, then it was said that the defendants did not know in time of the procedural defects and could not reasonably be required or expected to have sought such remedy there.

The decision in Jacobson v. Frachon

A number of decisions were cited to us in the context of the natural justice issue. However, the most important of them was Jacobson v. Frachon, 138 L.T. 386, because it was said on behalf of the plaintiffs to establish legal principles which are binding on this court and render the natural justice defence unsustainable on the present facts by limiting that defence to lack of notice and denial of proper opportunity to be heard. Furthermore, it was common ground that this is the only case in which the Court of Appeal has considered points relevant to the questions raised in this case under the heading of the natural justice issue.

In Jacobson v. Frachon, this court applied rigorously the principle that our courts will not impeach the judgment of a foreign court having competent jurisdiction on its merits. However, the crucial passage in that case particularly relied upon by Mr. Falconer was a statement of Atkin L.J., who, after referring to the judgment of Lindley M.R. in Pemberton v. Hughes [1899] 1 ch. 781, 790, said, at p. 392, that a judgment could be impeached "if the proceedings, the method by which the court comes to a final decision" are contrary to English views of substantial justice, and continued:

"The Master of the Rolls seems to prefer, and I can quite understand the use of the expression, 'contrary to the principles of natural justice;' the principles it is not always easy to define or to invite everybody to agree about, whereas with our own principles of justice we are familiar. Those principles seem to me to involve this, first of all that the court being a court of competent jurisdiction, has given notice to the litigant that they are about to proceed to determine the rights between him and the other litigant; the other is that having given him that notice, it does afford him an opportunity of substantially presenting his case before the court. Both those considerations appear to be essential if they are to be in accordance with natural justice." (Emphasis added.)

We have had the benefit of very careful and detailed analyses in argument of the judgments in Jacobson v. Frachon. We intend no disrespect to such arguments if we do not prolong an already very long judgment (in which we have already decided that the defendants succeed on the presence issue) by recapitulating these analyses. We will summarise our conclusions in relation to Jacobson v. Frachon, 138 L.T. 386, as follows.

(1) Atkin L.J. in his judgment was not attempting to make an exclusive or comprehensive statement of the circumstances in which our courts will treat the procedure adopted by a foreign court in reaching its decision as offending against the principles of natural justice.

(2) Lord Hanworth M.R. was clearly of the view, at p. 390, which we share, that the requirements of due notice and proper opportunity to be heard will, in the majority of cases which can be expected to arise, sufficiently comprise the concept of natural justice in a procedural context, but he prudently qualified his statement by saying that they "almost, if not entirely" comprise it.
(3) We therefore reject the contention that the decision of this court in Jacobson v. Frachon restricted the defence of breach of procedural natural justice to the requirements of due notice and opportunity to put a case. Scott J. was entitled, in our view, to direct himself by reference to the test stated by Lindley M.R. in Pemberton v. Hughes [1899] 1 ch. 781, 790, and to consider whether the procedural defect alleged by Cape was such as to constitute a breach of an English court's views of substantial justice. The point was not concluded against the defendants merely because they had been given proper notice of the application for default judgment and would, if they had attended, have been allowed full opportunity to put their case.
(4) However, this court in Jacobson v. Frachon, 138 L.T. 386, was not required to consider the relevance, if any, of any remedy which might have been available to Jacobson under the French legal system, whether by way of appeal or by application for the judgment to be set aside, if the hearing in the French court had itself constituted a breach of natural justice.

"No judicial assessment of damages"

The next question is whether, as Scott J. considered, the "method by which the Tyler court came to its final decision," to use Atkin L.J.'s words, was contrary to our views of substantial justice on the grounds that there had been no judicial assessment of damages.

We have found this to be a matter of difficulty.... We recognize...that the federal courts have been required to determine, and to develop methods for the effective control and management of, civil litigation in product liability cases in which large numbers of plaintiffs have made claims against numerous defendants arising out of similar classes of injury and having broadly similar consequences but with differing degrees of severity....

[B]ut, as Scott J. observed, while damages calculated on an average per plaintiff basis may make very good sense for the purposes of a settlement, because defendants are not concerned with how the total will be divided up, a judicial award so calculated is the antithesis of an award based upon the individual entitlements of the respective plaintiffs....

[W]e find it impossible to say that, because the defendants did not apply to set the default judgment aside, they could not rely upon the substantial injustice in the proceedings constituted by the failure of the court to assess the damages judicially upon the evidence. They did not wish to dispute the amount of the damages award by presenting a case to the Tyler court. We cannot have regard, as an excuse available to them, to the reason why they chose not to appear, namely their unwillingness to submit to the jurisdiction of the Tyler court. However, it cannot, in our view, be required of them that they should have applied to the Tyler court to contest the amount of damages awarded when they were necessarily content to leave the amount of the damages to be assessed by the court. The only complaint which the defendants could thereafter make would be as to procedural irregularity. As to that, as we have stated, they had at the time of service of the judgment no knowledge. The defendants were not told before the application for the default judgment that plaintiffs' counsel intended to invite Judge Steger to accept the view of plaintiffs' counsel as to the total value of the claim, based upon an average of $120,000 per plaintiff, and that the plaintiffs would accept in substitution for the assessment of the damages by the judge, such counter- proposal based upon an average sum per plaintiff as the judge might be minded to make, from his general knowledge of the proceedings and of the settlement in the Tyler 2 proceedings to that date and from his knowledge of national average settlement figures in asbestosis cases.

The fact that information as to the procedural defect would probably have emerged if Cape had made an application to set the default judgment aside on other grounds, seems to us to be of no relevance. Cape are not to be treated as having information which they did not have because, if they had made an application which they had no reason to make, they could have obtained that information.

A harsh but accurate summary of what happened is, in our judgment, that those acting for the plaintiffs failed to give prior notice to the defendants of the unusual course which they intended to pursue; they chose not to try to prevent Judge Steger from adopting that method of assessment; and they drew up and served a form of judgment which did not reveal what had taken place. That was all done in good faith. There was no dishonest purpose. But the effect upon the defendants was, in our view, that they had at no material time knowledge of any basis for seeking relief from the Tyler court in respect of the defect which Scott J. rightly held to have been demonstrated by them to have occurred in the proceedings in the Tyler court.

The only basis for attributing to the defendants constructive knowledge of the defect, upon which they could reasonably be required to have used any available remedy in the Tyler court, would be that a defendant who has been given notice of the proceedings will be fixed with knowledge of everything which he would have learned if he had attended those proceedings. That, in our judgment, is not an acceptable basis for considering proof of procedural injustice. Plaintiffs can, we think fairly be left to avoid such procedural errors as will prevent enforcement of a judgment in this country.

Accordingly, on the natural justice issue, although for somewhat different reasons, we would uphold the decision of Scott J....

Comments and Questions

1. Three common reasons for suing a foreign parent company rather than the local operating company are: (1) multinational corporations are often organized in such a way that the local subsidiaries are insolvent and/or underinsured;

(2) the claimants have no meaningful access to justice in their home courts; and (3) workers' compensation schemes in the local jurisdiction preclude claims against an employer. Which of these situations prompted the Adams plaintiffs to seek enforcement of this judgment against Cape's assets in the United Kingdom?

2. The Court of Appeal seems to acknowledge that Cape was aware of its potential future liability with respect to these asbestosis claims and that Cape deliberately engineered the restructuring to reduce if not eliminate the appearance of any involvement by Cape. Why, then, didn't the Court enforce the judgment?

3. Why are neither thin capitalization nor control of the subsidiary by the parent corporation sufficient to lift the corporate veil?

4. Now suppose that the roles of the two court systems were reversed. Would the Restatement (and Uniform Act) have permitted enforcement?

D. Multilateral Approaches

1. Regional

One example of a regional approach to simplifying the recognition and enforcement of foreign judgments is the Brussels Convention of 1968, which we first discussed in Chapter 3. The Brussels Convention was called a "double" convention because it addressed both personal jurisdiction and the enforcement of judgments. But it was the harmonization and stabilization of the domestic law on the enforcement of judgments within the EU that was the primary aim. Uniform principles allowed the free circulation of judgments, promoting trade and inspiring confidence. "As a result of the safeguards granted to the defendant [with regard to where they could be sued,] the Convention is very liberal on the question of recognition, and enforcement."* The content of the Brussels Convention is now codified in the Brussels I Regulation.

You will recall that, for purposes of personal jurisdiction, the Brussels Regulation contemplated different analyses for defendants domiciled in EU Member States, on one hand, and non-EU domiciliaries on the other. The "exorbitant bases" for the exercise of jurisdiction were eliminated for the former, and retained for the latter. For purposes of enforcement, however, this duality is removed: all judgments emanating from EU Member State courts are entitled to recognition and enforcement by all other EU Member State courts. Appreciate the significance of that combination: if one EU Member State court asserts personal jurisdiction under an exorbitant basis (over a non-EU domiciliary), the courts of other EU Member States must recognize and enforce that judgment.

The rules on recognition and enforcement of one member state's judgment in another contracting state are found in Articles 32 through 56 of the Brussels Regulation. The rules on recognition and enforcement are brief and rather

---

* Report by Mr. P. Jenard on the Convention of 27 September 1968 on Jurisdiction and the Enforcement of Judgments in Civil and Commercial Matters, EC 22 O.J. C. 59/1 (5 March 1979).

straightforward. Provided that the member state's court proceedings from which the judgment emanated fall within the definition of civil and commercial matters, there are few exceptions to the general proposition that the judgment of another contracting state must be recognized or enforced. According to Article 34 of the Regulation, a judgment shall not be recognized:

1. if such recognition is manifestly contrary to public policy in the Member State in which recognition is sought;
2. where it was given in default of appearance, if the defendant was not served with the document which instituted the proceedings or with an equivalent document in sufficient time and in such a way as to enable him to arrange for his defence, unless the defendant failed to commence proceedings to challenge the judgment when it was possible for him to do so;
3. if it is irreconcilable with a judgment given in a dispute between the same parties in the Member State in which recognition is sought;
4. if it is irreconcilable with an earlier judgment given in another Member State or in a third State involving the same cause of action and between the same parties, provided that the earlier judgment fulfils the conditions necessary for its recognition in the Member State addressed.

On an initial application for recognition, the court must sua sponte examine whether any of these grounds for refusal exist. Moreover, when any of these grounds is present, the court lacks the discretion to recognize; it must refuse to recognize the judgment in question.

According to the first of these exceptions, a Member State's judgment shall not be recognized if such recognition is manifestly contrary to public policy in the Member State in which recognition is sought. It is noteworthy that the italicized adverb was not in the text of the Brussels Convention; it was added to the Brussels I Regulation to restrict the applicability of this exception. Even under the Convention, however, this was "a narrow exception, applicable only in extreme situations, and certainly not just because the enforcement State's courts would have applied a different law or reached a different result, (e.g.) because an Italian court set aside a disclaimer or arbitration clause which a German court could not."*

The third and fourth exceptions are seldom applicable because they contemplate parallel litigation by the same parties, a phenomenon that the Brussels schema often avoids. Moreover, the exceptions can be invoked only if the two judgments are irreconcilable, which has been interpreted to mean that enforcement of both judgments would result in legal consequences that are mutually exclusive. See Case-145/86 Hoffmann v. Krieg [1988] ECR 645 (referring to identical provision of the Brussels Convention).

The second of these codified exceptions is the subject of the Debaecker case below. The ECJ is reviewing the Brussels Convention rather than the Brussels I Regulation, but the applicable text is substantially similar.

---

* Joseph Lookofsky & Ketilbjorn Hertz, Transnational Litigation and Commercial Arbitration 703 (Juris 2d ed. 2003)

Debaecker v. Bouwman

Case 49/84, 1985 E.C.R. 1779

The Opinion of Advocate General VerLoren van Themaat, delivered 12 February 1985*

1. Introduction

The Hoge Raad der Nederlanden [Supreme Court of the Netherlands] has referred to the Court a number of questions concerning Article 27(2) of the convention of 27 September 1968 on Jurisdiction and the Enforcement of Judgments in civil and commercial Matters [hereinafter referred to as "the Convention"].

Article 27 provides as follows:

> "A judgment shall not be recognized:
> (1) if such recognition is contrary to public policy in the State in which recognition is sought;
> (2) where it was given in default of appearance, if the defendant was not duly served with the document which instituted the proceedings in sufficient time to enable him to arrange for his defence;..."

This case concerns in particular the rule laid down in that article that the defendant should receive service in sufficient time to ensure, as the Court stated in it judgment of 15 July 1982 in Case 228/81 Pendy Plastic v. Pluspunkt [1982] ECR 2723, at p. 2736, "that the defendant's rights are effectively protected" where recognition is sought in a State other than the State in which it was given. The Hoge Raad summarized the various questions in the following terms:

> "May facts which occurred later—that is to say, after the service of the document which instituted the proceedings—compel the plaintiff to take further steps to inform the defendant of the impending action, so that if such steps are not taken the time required by Article 27(2) does not begin to run?"

The facts of the case

...Mr. Bouwman, a Dutch national, signed a lease with Mr. Debaecker and his wife Berta Plouview, both of Belgian nationality, by which he agreed from 15 October 1980 to rent business premises situated at 18 Frankrijklei, Antwerp, where he intended to run an art gallery. On Monday, 21 September 1981, Mr. Bouwman left without giving notice or leaving a forwarding address. On Thursday, 24 September 1981, the Debaeckers' lawyer, Mr. Debaecker, who according to the Commission is their son, applied to the Vrederechter [Cantonal Judge], Antwerp, for leave to serve a writ on Mr. Bouwman at reduced notice, alleging inter alia that Mr. Bouwman had left, taking with him all his movable property, "like a thief in the night." The Vrederechter granted leave for Mr. Bouwman to be summoned to appear at the

* The original language of Advocate General VerLoren van Themaat's opinion was Dutch.

sitting on Thursday, 1 October 1981, and a writ dated 24 September 1981 was served on the Politiecommissariaat, Antwerp, in accordance with Article 37 of the Gerechtelijk Wetboek [Belgian Judicial Code]. That course was followed because at the time of service the lawyer was not aware of Mr. Bouwman's whereabouts. However, he assumed that Mr. Bouwman still resided in Antwerp because he was registered there. The writ could not be served at his home address, 18 Frankrijklei, because neither he nor any member of his household was there.

On 25 September 1981 Mr. Bouwman sent to the Debaeckers' lawyer a registered letter, in which he repudiated the lease, returned the keys and gave notice that he was to be reached "through post office box number 24, 2190 Essen" (likewise in Belgium). That letter reached the Debaeckers' lawyer on 28 September 1981. He, however, took no action and therefore left Mr. Bouwman unaware that a writ had been served on him at the Politiecommissariaat requiring him to appear before the Vrederechter on 1 October. On 1 October the Vrederechter gave judgment in default against Mr. Bouwman, terminating the lease and awarding Mr. and Mrs. Debaecker compensation of BFR 1 072 900.

The Commission informed the Court that that judgment was itself served in the same way: as Mr. Bouwman was not at his official place of residence in Frankrijklei, it was served at the Politiecommissariaat.

On 18 November the Registrar of the Vredegerecht, Antwerp, established that no appeal had been lodged against the judgment in default. On the same day Mr. and Mrs. Debaecker lodged an application with the President of the Arrondissementsrechtbank [District Court] in Breda (the Netherlands) for an order freezing Mr. Bouwman's bank account in Breda. It was presumably at about that time that Mr. Bouwman discovered that proceedings had been brought against him.

On 30 November the President of the Arrondissementsrechtbank, Breda, authorized the enforcement of the judgment of the Vrederechter. Mr. Bouwman appealed against that decision to the Arrondissementsrechtbank, Breda, on 6 January 1982. On 12 October 1982 that court held that the appeal was well founded and dismissed the application for the issue of an order for enforcement.

Mr. Bouwman based his appeal inter alia on Articles 20 and 27 of the Convention. The Arrondissementsrechtbank found that the claim based on Article 20 could not succeed because that article covered the situation in which a defendant residing in one Contracting State was sued in a court of another Contracting State. In this case, however, Mr. Bouwman was sued before a court in the same State and city as that in which he had his residence under Belgian law and the writ did not even have to leave the City of Antwerp in order to be validly served.

As regards Article 27(2), the Arrondissementsrechtbank found that it was not disputed that the document which instituted the proceedings had been duly served in accordance with Belgian law. However, Mr. Bouwman contended that, in order to satisfy the requirement that service should be effected in sufficient time, it would have been necessary not only to effect formal service in the prescribed manner but, in addition, to serve the writ requiring him to appear before the Vrederechter on 1 October 1981 through his post office box number, which was known to the Debaeckers' lawyer from 28 September 1981.

In that connection, in accordance with the judgment of the Court in Case 166/80 (Klomps v. Michel [1981] ECR 1593, at pp. 1608 and 1609), the Arrondissementsrechtbank considered "whether, in this particular case, there are exceptional circumstances which warrant the conclusion that, although service was duly effected, it was, however, inadequate for the purpose of causing the time needed for the defence to begin to run."

On that question the Arrondissementsrechtbank considered:

> "Although the applicant must himself be regarded as responsible for the fact that throughout the course of these proceedings he has retained as his official residence an address at premises of which he no longer even has the keys, and he will in principle have to bear the consequences, the question whether the summons to appear before the Vrederechter on 1 October 1981 gave the applicant sufficient time to arrange for his defence must be determined according to the particular circumstances obtaining at that time. The court considers that service exclusively on the Politiecommissariaat, when the applicant was not found at his official residence, which he was known to have left, such service not being followed by notice of a different kind when before the sitting on 1 October 1981 the respondents became aware of how the applicant could be reached, was insufficient to cause the time for the defence to begin to run. It was in fact impossible for the applicant to enter any kind of defence. The judgment in default given by the Vrederechter, Antwerp, therefore cannot be recognized in the Netherlands."

Mr. and Mrs. Debaecker appealed against that judgment to the Hoge Raad, on two grounds which may be summarized as follows. In the first place they claimed that Article 27(2) was not applicable in this situation since service "was effected in accordance with a period specified by the adjudicating court and the defendant's sole residence was within the jurisdiction of that court or in the same country as that court." Second, they argued that facts which occurred later—that is to say, after service of the document which instituted the proceedings—did not compel the plaintiff to take further steps to inform the defendants of the impending action, so that if steps were not taken the time required by Article 27(2) did not begin to run....

Judgment of the Court (Fourth Chamber), entered 11 June 1985*

...[5] Mr. and Mrs. Debaecker appealed to the Hoge Raad, which stayed the proceedings and referred to the Court the following questions for a preliminary ruling:

1. Is the requirement, laid down in Article 27(2) of the Convention on Jurisdiction and the Enforcement of Judgments in Civil and Commercial

---

* The original language of the case was Dutch.

Matters, that service of the document which instituted the proceedings should have been effected in sufficient time inapplicable if service was effected within a period prescribed by the Court of the State in which the judgment was given and/or the defendant resided, exclusive or otherwise, within the jurisdiction of that court or in the same country as that court?

If Question 1 is answered in the negative:

2. (a) In relation to the question whether, in a particular case, there are exceptional circumstances which warrant the conclusion that, although due service was effected, as provided for in Article 27(2), it was none the less inadequate for the purpose of causing the time required in that provision to begin to run, is account to be taken only of circumstances which existed at the time of service and which the plaintiff could take into consideration at that time?

If Question 2(a) is answered in the negative:

2. (b) Can the plaintiff be required as a result of circumstances which arose after service was effected, in particular notification to the plaintiff of the defendant's address, to take further steps to inform the defendant of the impending action, so that if such steps are not taken the time required by Article 27(2) does not begin to run?

If Question 2(b) is answered in the affirmative:

2. (c) What criterion must be applied in that regard? In particular, does the fact that the defendant was responsible for the failure of the duly served document to reach him prevent the court, where, for example, the plaintiff was aware that the defendant had left the address stated to be his place of residence, from considering that further steps as referred to above were required?

[6] Written observations were submitted by the parties to the main proceedings, the Government of the Federal Republic of Germany, the United Kingdom and the Commission of the European Communities.

[7] In Question 1 the Hoge Raad asks whether the requirement, laid down in Article 27(2) of the Convention, that service of the document which instituted the proceedings should have been effected in sufficient time is inapplicable if service was effected within a period prescribed by the court of the State in which the judgment was given and/or the defendant resided in that State....

[10] First of all, it should be stated that there is nothing in the wording of Article 27(2)—which does not lay down any condition as regards the defendant's place of residence—to suggest that the question asked by the Hoge Raad should be answered in the affirmative. Although the convention is, as is clear from the preamble, intended to "secure the simplification of formalities governing the reciprocal recognition and enforcement of judgments of courts or tribunals", that aim cannot, according to a series of decisions of the Court, be attained by undermining in any way the right to a fair hearing.

[11] It follows from the wording of Article 27 that the courts of a Contracting State may refuse to recognize a judgment only on one of the grounds expressly

mentioned in that provision. One of those grounds is that laid down in Paragraph (2), in order to ensure the adequate protection of the rights of a defendant against whom judgment is given in default of appearance abroad. Article 27(2) provides that a judgment shall not be recognized '...if the defendant was not duly served with the document which instituted the proceedings in sufficient time to enable him to arrange for his defence.' That provision takes account of the fact that certain Contracting States make provision for the fictitious service of process where the defendant has no known place of residence. The effects that are deemed to follow from such fictitious service vary and the probability of the defendant's actually being informed of service, so as to give him sufficient time to prepare his defence, may vary considerably, depending on the type of fictitious service provided for in each legal system.

[12] For that reason Article 27(2) must be interpreted as being intended to protect the right of a defendant to defend himself when recognition of a judgment given in default in another Contracting State is sought, even if the rules on service laid down in that Contracting State were complied with.

[13] The answer to the first question must therefore be that the requirement, laid down in Article 27(2) of the Convention, that service of the document which instituted the proceedings should have been effected in sufficient time is applicable even where service was effected within a period prescribed by the court of the State in which judgment was given or where the defendant resided, exclusively or otherwise, within the jurisdiction of that court or in the same country as that court.

[14] In Question 2(a) the Hoge Raad asks whether, in assessing whether there are exceptional circumstances which warrant the conclusion that, although due service was effected as provided for in Article 27(2), it was none the less inadequate for the purpose of causing the time required in that provision to begin to run, account is to be taken only of circumstances which existed at the time of service and which the plaintiff could take into consideration at that time....

[19] With regard to this question, it should be pointed out first that, if the circumstances to be taken into account were confined to those which were known at the time of service, there would be a danger of interpreting the requirement of service in sufficient time in such a restrictive and formalistic manner that it would in fact coincide with the requirement of due service, thus negating one of the safeguards laid down by the Convention for the protection of the defendant.

[20] Accordingly, in order to ascertain whether the requirement of service in sufficient time was fulfilled—that requirement being laid down precisely in order to ensure that the defendant's rights are effectively protected—regard must be had to facts which, although occurring after service was effected, may none the less have had the effect that service did not in fact enable the defendant to arrange for his defence.

[21] That view finds further support in Klomps v. Michel, where the Court ruled that, in ascertaining whether service was effected in sufficient time, a court might take account "of all the circumstances of the case in point, including the means employed for effecting service, the relations between the plaintiff and the

defendant or the nature of the steps which had to be taken in order to prevent judgment from being given in default." An appraisal of the steps which had to be taken in order to prevent judgment from being given in default is bound to concern factors arising after service was effected.

[22] The answer to question 2(a) must therefore be that the Court in which enforcement is sought may, in examining whether service was effected in sufficient time, take account of exceptional circumstances which arose after service was duly affected.

[23] In Question 2(b) the Hoge Raad asks whether the plaintiff can be required, as a result of circumstances which arose after service was effected, to take further steps to inform the defendant of the impending action, so that if such steps are not taken the time required by Article 27(2) does not begin to run. Question 2(c) asks whether the fact that the defendant was responsible for the failure of the duly served document to reach him prevents the court, where, for example, the plaintiff was aware that the defendant had left the address stated to be his place of residence, from considering that further steps as referred to in Question 2(b) should have been taken.

[24] With regard to Question 2(b), the plaintiffs in the main proceedings observe that no such obligation is provided for in the applicable national law or in the Convention itself and consider that a rule of that kind would impair legal certainty in the field of procedural law. In addition, they argue that there is no uniform practice in the legal systems of the Contracting States, some of which are more formalistic than others and thus less inclined to require any steps to be taken which are not prescribed by the law or the Convention. In any event, say the plaintiffs, although it may be expected that a lawyer might notify the opposite party or request an adjournment in a case such as this, a lawyer cannot be reproached for failing to do so.

[25] The Commission also considers that such an obligation would seriously jeopardize legal certainty. In its view, no consequence under procedural law should flow from the fact that the plaintiff does not notify the defendant when he learns after service that the defendant may be contacted at another address.

[26] The defendant in the main proceedings, the Federal Republic of Germany and the United Kingdom, on the other hand, propose an affirmative answer, stressing inter alia that the purpose of Article 27(2) is to guarantee not merely formal service but the right to be heard and thus the opportunity of pressing a defence. They therefore consider that every effort must be made to prevent judgment from being given against a defendant without his having had an opportunity of defending himself.

[27] On that point it must be borne in mind that the question whether service was effected in sufficient time is a question of fact and therefore cannot be determined on the basis of the domestic law of the adjudicating court or on the basis of the domestic law of the court in which enforcement is sought. However, the Convention does not impose on the plaintiff any obligation to take steps such as those referred to in Question 2(b). The failure to take such steps is in reality merely

a factor which must be taken into account in order to establish whether service was effected in sufficient time.

[28] Seen in that light, the fact that the plaintiff, after service, learns of the defendant's new address does not compel him to take any further steps, but renders his subsequent behavior important for the purpose of determining whether service was effected in sufficient time. By notifying the defendant at his new address, the plaintiff ensures that the court in which enforcement is sought cannot decide that the defendant's change of address is an exceptional circumstance which prevents the service effected at his former address from being regarded as having been effected in sufficient time.

[29] As regards Question 2(c), the plaintiffs in the main proceedings consider that, even if the plaintiff is bound to take further steps to notify the defendant, failure to do so does not necessarily result in the refusal of recognition or enforcement of the judgment if it is the defendant's fault that the plaintiff was unaware at the time of service of the address at which the defendant could have been contacted. They argue that it is not enough for the defendant to give a post office box number. The commission shares that view and considers that, if the defendant is responsible for the fact that he did not receive the document which was duly served, the plaintiff is under no obligation to take further steps, even if he subsequently discovers the defendant's new address.

[30] The defendant in the main proceedings, the Federal Republic of Germany and the United Kingdom consider that the defendant's behaviour is one of the circumstances which the court in which enforcement is sought may take into account in assessing whether service was effected in sufficient time, and its effect must be evaluated by that court in the light of the requirement that the defendant's rights should be effectively protected.

[31] In view of the fact that Article 27(2), as has already been stated, seeks to enable a defendant to defend himself effectively, the defendant's behavior may not be used as a basis for considering that service was effected in sufficient time even though the plaintiff subsequently became aware that the defendant could be reached at a new address. To admit such a proposition would be tantamount to acknowledging the existence of a presumption that service was effected in sufficient time. Although it may rightly be presumed that service was effected in sufficient time where the plaintiff did not know where to reach the defendant, such a presumption would clearly be contrary to the principle that the defendant's rights should be protected if, after service, the plaintiff learned where the defendant could be reached.

[32] Thus the defendant's behaviour cannot automatically rule out the possibility of taking into account exceptional circumstances which warrant the conclusion that service was not effected in sufficient time. Instead, such behavior may be assessed by the court in which enforcement is sought, as one of the matters in the light of which it determines whether service was effected in sufficient time. It will therefore be for that court to assess, in a case such as the present, to what extent the defendant's behavior is capable of outweighing the fact that the plaintiff was apprised after service of the defendant's new address.

[33] In view of the foregoing considerations, the answer to questions 2(b) and 2(c) must be that the fact that the plaintiff was apprised of the defendant's new address, after service was effected, and the fact that the defendant was responsible for the failure of the duly served document to reach him are matters which the court in which enforcement is sought may take into account in assessing whether service was effected in sufficient time.

On those grounds, the Court (Fourth Chamber), in answer to the questions submitted to it by the Hoge Raad der Nederlanden by judgment of 17 February 1984, hereby rules:

> (1) The requirement, laid down in Article 27(2) of the Convention on Jurisdiction and the Enforcement of Judgments in Civil and Commercial Matters, that service of the document which instituted the proceedings should have been effected in sufficient time is applicable where service was effected within a period prescribed by the court of the State in which the judgment was given or where the defendant resided, exclusively or otherwise, within the jurisdiction of that court or in the same country as that court.
>
> (2) In examining whether service was effected in sufficient time, the court in which enforcement is sought may take account of exceptional circumstances which arose after service was duly effected.
>
> (3) The fact that the plaintiff was apprised of the defendant's new address, after service was effected, and the fact that the defendant was responsible for the failure of the duly served document to reach him are matters which the court in which enforcement is sought may take into account in assessing whether service was effected in sufficient time.

Comments and Questions

1. The judgment reads that the aim of the free movement of judgments "cannot...be attained by undermining in any way the right to a fair hearing." Is that an equitable balance of the interests of judgment creditors and judgment debtors? What's the alternative?

2. The reference to "due" service has been omitted from Article 34(2) of the Brussels I Regulation. Under the new legislation, the document that institutes the proceedings must merely be "served," inter alia, "in such a way as to enable [the defendant] to arrange for his defence." This seems to codify, perhaps even expand the European Court of Justice's judgment in Debaecker. This may seem more equitable and fair, but at what cost to certainty and predictability?

3. Many Latin American countries are parties to a number of treaties on enforcement. The Bustamante Code, known more fully as the 1928 Pan American Code of Private International Law, is subscribed to by the following countries: Bolivia, Brazil, Chile, Costa Rica, Cuba, Dominican Republic, Ecuador, El Salvador, Guatemala, Haiti, Honduras, Nicaragua, Panama, Peru, and Venezuela. It provides that a judgment rendered in one contracting state would have force in

another if:

1. The rendering court was competent;
2. The parties were served;
3. The judgment does not conflict with public policy of the enforcing state;
4. The judgment is officially translated; and
5. The judgment is authentic in the State in which it was rendered (i.e. was published, etc.).

This Code was criticized for its unusual deference to the local interests of the enforcing state. Consequently, in 1979, a number of Latin countries ratified the Montevideo Convention. Its criteria for enforcement are:

1. The foreign judgment must be authentic where rendered;
2. The judgment must be translated;
3. The judgment must be duly legalized in accordance with the law of the State addressed;
4. The judge or tribunal rendering the judgment must be competent in the international sphere to try the matter and to pass judgment on it in accordance with the law of the state addressed;
5. The defending parties had notice and opportunity to be heard;
6. The judgment is final and has the force of res judicata in the State of origin; and
7. The judgment is not manifestly contrary to the principles and laws of the public policy of the State addressed.

See, generally, Matthew H. Adler, Enforcement in a New Age: Judgments in the United States and Mexico, 5 U.S.-Mex. L.J. 149 (1997). See also Amado, Recognition and Enforcement of Foreign Judgments in Latin American Countries: An Overview and Update, 31 Va. J. Int'l L. 99 (1990).

2. Global

Ronald A. Brand & Scott R. Jablonski, The Global Search for a Convention on Jurisdiction and Judgments

Forum Non Conveniens 142–148 (Oxford 2007)

[I.] The Hague Conference Process

In May of 1992, Edwin Williamson, then Legal Adviser at the U.S. Department of State, wrote to the Secretary General of the Hague Conference on Private International Law proposing that the Conference take up the negotiation of a multilateral convention on the recognition and enforcement of foreign judgments. The matter was considered by a Working Group at The Hague in October of 1992, which "unanimously recognized the desirability of attempting to negotiate multilaterally through the Hague Conference a convention on recognition and enforcement of judgments."...

From the beginning of the discussions, the United States took the position that the product of the Hague Conference Special Commission should be a "mixed" convention.... Single (sometimes referred to as "simple") conventions on the recognition of judgments deal only with indirect jurisdiction and apply only to the decision of the court asked to enforce a foreign a judgment. Thus the recognizing court considers the jurisdiction of the court issuing a judgment in deciding whether to recognize the judgment of the originating court.[*] Double conventions like the Brussels [Regulation], not only deal with recognition, but also provided rules for direct jurisdiction applicable in the court in which the case is first brought—thus addressing the matter from the outset and preempting the need for substantial indirect consideration of the issuing court's jurisdiction by the court asked to recognize the resulting judgment. The mixed convention is a variation on the double convention, providing rules for both jurisdiction and the recognition of judgments, but not purporting to be exhaustive in its list of required and prohibited bases of jurisdiction. It does not cover the entire field, but rather leaves some bases of jurisdiction available under national law, although these bases are not subject to the convention's rules on recognition and enforcement of any resulting judgment.

Under the mixed convention approach, there would exist a list of required bases of jurisdiction and a list of prohibited bases of jurisdiction. Judgments founded on required bases of jurisdiction would be entitled to recognition under the convention. Courts could not exercise jurisdiction founded only on bases on the prohibited list. For a few other situations, some exceptions to recognition would apply. Any jurisdictional basis not included on one of the two lists would be permitted, but a resulting judgment would not be entitled to recognition under the convention. Instead, such judgments would be subject to review in the recognizing court in the manner applicable in the absence of a treaty.

A clear focus on a mixed convention would have allowed the Hague Conference to build up a convention from the existing status quo, and would not have required agreement on a comprehensive set of jurisdictional rules that cover and connect the entire field of possibilities. It also would have allowed the use of a consensus process likely to produce a convention acceptable to the largest number of states. Such a convention would have allowed some areas of disagreement and experimentation to continue while at the same time locking in progress that could be achieved. A mixed convention also would have allowed certain issues that are unresolved in any single national legal system to remain outside the convention and subject to later conventions or protocols should an acceptable approach be developed.

In October of 1996, the Hague Conference decided to include the subject of a jurisdiction and judgments convention on the Agenda of its Nineteenth Session. Special Commission meetings from 1997 to 1999 led to a Preliminary Draft Convention text....

While the negotiating process had begun with discussion of a mixed convention, it was not until June of 1999 that the Special Commission voted specifically to adopt the mixed convention model. The intervening seven-year ambivalence of focus resulted in the primary development of double convention language. Thus even in the 2001 Interim Text of the Proposed Hague Convention on Jurisdiction and Recognition of

* *Eds.' Note:* For an example of this methodology, *see* Restatement (Third) of Foreign Relations Law § 482(1)(b), reprinted earlier in this chapter.

Judgments, which purports to follow a mixed convention approach, the words generally are those of a double convention. Given that the negotiations prior to June 2001 were conducted by a majority vote, and that (at that time) fifteen of the Hague Member States voting on specific articles during the process were also Member States of the European Union (and others were states planning and eager to become Member States of the EU), it is not surprising that the language of both the October 1999 Preliminary Draft...and the 2001 Hague Interim Text resembled that of the Brussels and Lugano Conventions in force in the EU states. It also is not surprising that the EU states would prefer a convention that looks as much as possible like the sets of rules they customarily apply in similar cases within their regional system....

Because the Hague negotiations had been channeled into a double convention model...resolving such differences was fundamental to the question of how to proceed at the end of 2001. The more modest alternative of a mixed convention...could have moved the law in all contracting states beyond the status quo in areas where that would be possible, while leaving the difficult areas for future evolution as legal developments permit. Such an approach was not taken, however, resulting in resort to an even more modest alternative: a Hague Convention on Choice of Court Agreements.

On April 24, 2002, Commission I of the Nineteenth Session of the Hague Conference acted to establish an informal working group to consider drafting a convention based on the jurisdictional provisions on which substantial consensus existed, beginning with jurisdiction based on agreement of the parties to the litigation....The final Hague Convention on Choice of Court Agreements was completed at a Diplomatic Conference in June of 2005.

2005 Hague Convention on Choice of Court Agreements

44 I.L.M. 1294

Article 1: Scope

1. This Convention shall apply in international cases to exclusive choice of court agreements concluded in civil or commercial matters.
2. For the purposes of Chapter II, a case is international unless the parties are resident in the same Contracting State and the relationship of the parties and all other elements relevant to the dispute, regardless of the location of the chosen court, are connected only with that State.
3. For the purposes of Chapter III, a case is international where recognition or enforcement of a foreign judgment is sought.

Article 2: Exclusions from scope

1. This Convention shall not apply to exclusive choice of court agreements—
   a) to which a natural person acting primarily for personal, family or household purposes (a consumer) is a party;
   b) relating to contracts of employment, including collective agreements.

2. This Convention shall not apply to the following matters -
   a) the status and legal capacity of natural persons;
   b) maintenance obligations;
   c) other family law matters, including matrimonial property regimes and other rights or obligations arising out of marriage or similar relationships;
   d) wills and succession;
   e) insolvency, composition and analogous matters;
   f) the carriage of passengers and goods;
   g) marine pollution, limitation of liability for maritime claims, general average, and emergency towage and salvage;
   h) anti-trust (competition) matters;
   i) liability for nuclear damage;
   j) claims for personal injury brought by or on behalf of natural persons;
   k) tort or delict claims for damage to tangible property that do not arise from a contractual relationship;
   l) rights in rem in immovable property, and tenancies of immovable property;
   m) the validity, nullity, or dissolution of legal persons, and the validity of decisions of their organs;
   n) the validity of intellectual property rights other than copyright and related rights;
   o) infringement of intellectual property rights other than copyright and related rights, except where infringement proceedings are brought for breach of a contract between the parties relating to such rights, or could have been brought for breach of that contract;
   p) the validity of entries in public registers.
3. Notwithstanding paragraph 2, proceedings are not excluded from the scope of this Convention where a matter excluded under that paragraph arises merely as a preliminary question and not as an object of the proceedings. In particular, the mere fact that a matter excluded under paragraph 2 arises by way of defence does not exclude proceedings from the Convention, if that matter is not an object of the proceedings.
4. This Convention shall not apply to arbitration and related proceedings.
5. Proceedings are not excluded from the scope of this Convention by the mere fact that a State, including a government, a governmental agency or any person acting for a State, is a party thereto.
6. Nothing in this Convention shall affect privileges and immunities of States or of international organisations, in respect of themselves and of their property.

Article 3: Exclusive choice of court agreements

For the purposes of this Convention—

a) "exclusive choice of court agreement" means an agreement concluded by two or more parties that meets the requirements of paragraph c) and designates, for the purpose of deciding disputes which have arisen or may arise in connection with a particular legal relationship, the courts of one Contracting State or one or more specific courts of one Contracting State to the exclusion of the jurisdiction of any other courts;

b) a choice of court agreement which designates the courts of one Contracting State or one or more specific courts of one Contracting State shall be deemed to be exclusive unless the parties have expressly provided otherwise;

c) an exclusive choice of court agreement must be concluded or documented—

   i) in writing; or

   ii) by any other means of communication which renders information accessible so as to be usable for subsequent reference;

d) an exclusive choice of court agreement that forms part of a contract shall be treated as an agreement independent of the other terms of the contract. The validity of the exclusive choice of court agreement cannot be contested solely on the ground that the contract is not valid.

Article 5: Jurisdiction of the chosen court

1. The court or courts of a Contracting State designated in an exclusive choice of court agreement shall have jurisdiction to decide a dispute to which the agreement applies, unless the agreement is null and void under the law of that State.
2. A court that has jurisdiction under paragraph 1 shall not decline to exercise jurisdiction on the ground that the dispute should be decided in a court of another State.
3. The preceding paragraphs shall not affect rules -
   a) on jurisdiction related to subject matter or to the value of the claim;
   b) on the internal allocation of jurisdiction among the courts of a Contracting State. However, where the chosen court has discretion as to whether to transfer a case, due consideration should be given to the choice of the parties.

Article 6: Obligations of a court not chosen

A court of a Contracting State other than that of the chosen court shall suspend or dismiss proceedings to which an exclusive choice of court agreement applies unless—

a) the agreement is null and void under the law of the State of the chosen court;

b) a party lacked the capacity to conclude the agreement under the law of the State of the court seised;

c) giving effect to the agreement would lead to a manifest injustice or would be manifestly contrary to the public policy of the State of the court seised;

d) for exceptional reasons beyond the control of the parties, the agreement cannot reasonably be performed; or
e) the chosen court has decided not to hear the case.

Article 8: Recognition and enforcement

1. A judgment given by a court of a Contracting State designated in an exclusive choice of court agreement shall be recognised and enforced in other Contracting States in accordance with this Chapter. Recognition or enforcement may be refused only on the grounds specified in this Convention.
2. Without prejudice to such review as is necessary for the application of the provisions of this Chapter, there shall be no review of the merits of the judgment given by the court of origin. The court addressed shall be bound by the findings of fact on which the court of origin based its jurisdiction, unless the judgment was given by default.
3. A judgment shall be recognised only if it has effect in the State of origin, and shall be enforced only if it is enforceable in the State of origin.
4. Recognition or enforcement may be postponed or refused if the judgment is the subject of review in the State of origin or if the time limit for seeking ordinary review has not expired. A refusal does not prevent a subsequent application for recognition or enforcement of the judgment.
5. This Article shall also apply to a judgment given by a court of a Contracting State pursuant to a transfer of the case from the chosen court in that Contracting State as permitted by Article 5, paragraph 3. However, where the chosen court had discretion as to whether to transfer the case to another court, recognition or enforcement of the judgment may be refused against a party who objected to the transfer in a timely manner in the State of origin.

Article 9: Refusal of recognition or enforcement

Recognition or enforcement may be refused if—

a) the agreement was null and void under the law of the State of the chosen court, unless the chosen court has determined that the agreement is valid;
b) a party lacked the capacity to conclude the agreement under the law of the requested State;
c) the document which instituted the proceedings or an equivalent document, including the essential elements of the claim,
    i) was not notified to the defendant in sufficient time and in such a way as to enable him to arrange for his defence, unless the defendant entered an appearance and presented his case without contesting notification in the court of origin, provided that the law of the State of origin permitted notification to be contested; or

ii) was notified to the defendant in the requested State in a manner that is incompatible with fundamental principles of the requested State concerning service of documents;

d) the judgment was obtained by fraud in connection with a matter of procedure;

e) recognition or enforcement would be manifestly incompatible with the public policy of the requested State, including situations where the specific proceedings leading to the judgment were incompatible with fundamental principles of procedural fairness of that State;

f) the judgment is inconsistent with a judgment given in the requested State in a dispute between the same parties; or

g) the judgment is inconsistent with an earlier judgment given in another State between the same parties on the same cause of action, provided that the earlier judgment fulfils the conditions necessary for its recognition in the requested State.

Article 11: Damages

1. Recognition or enforcement of a judgment may be refused if, and to the extent that, the judgment awards damages, including exemplary or punitive damages, that do not compensate a party for actual loss or harm suffered.
2. The court addressed shall take into account whether and to what extent the damages awarded by the court of origin serve to cover costs and expenses relating to the proceedings.

Article 19: Declarations limiting jurisdiction

A State may declare that its courts may refuse to determine disputes to which an exclusive choice of court agreement applies if, except for the location of the chosen court, there is no connection between that State and the parties or the dispute.

Article 20: Declarations limiting recognition and enforcement

A State may declare that its courts may refuse to recognise or enforce a judgment given by a court of another Contracting State if the parties were resident in the requested State, and the relationship of the parties and all other elements relevant to the dispute, other than the location of the chosen court, were connected only with the requested State.

Article 21: Declarations with respect to specific matters

1. Where a State has a strong interest in not applying this Convention to a specific matter, that State may declare that it will not apply the Convention to that matter. The State making such a declaration shall ensure that the declaration

is no broader than necessary and that the specific matter excluded is clearly and precisely defined.

2. With regard to that matter, the Convention shall not apply—
   a) in the Contracting State that made the declaration;
   b) in other Contracting States, where an exclusive choice of court agreement designates the courts, or one or more specific courts, of the State that made the declaration.

Article 22: Reciprocal declarations on non-exclusive choice of court agreements

1. A Contracting State may declare that its courts will recognise and enforce judgments given by courts of other Contracting States designated in a choice of court agreement concluded by two or more parties that meets the requirements of Article 3, paragraph c), and designates, for the purpose of deciding disputes which have arisen or may arise in connection with a particular legal relationship, a court or courts of one or more Contracting States (a non-exclusive choice of court agreement).
2. Where recognition or enforcement of a judgment given in a Contracting State that has made such a declaration is sought in another Contracting State that has made such a declaration, the judgment shall be recognised and enforced under this Convention, if—
   a) the court of origin was designated in a non-exclusive choice of court agreement;
   b) there exists neither a judgment given by any other court before which proceedings could be brought in accordance with the non-exclusive choice of court agreement, nor a proceeding pending between the same parties in any other such court on the same cause of action; and
   c) the court of origin was the court first seised.

Comments and Questions

1. "A choice of court agreement chooses a court, which is a public institution created by the governmental organs of a particular state, to perform certain judicial functions, subject to limitations imposed by the law and policy of that state. There is a strong tradition in many legal systems, and a rigid rule in some states, that public institutions must subordinate private choices to the law and policy of the sovereign that created the institution.... Concerns about sovereign function place limitations on what can be asked of national courts dealing with choice of court agreements and the resulting judgments." Ronald A. Brand & Paul M. Herrup, The 2005 Hague Convention on Choice of Court Agreements 23 (Cambridge 2008). Which demands more respect: party autonomy or state interest?

2. "There is a pervasive tension between the need for specific rules in the Convention and the need for flexibility. Benefits from having specific rules include (1) an arguable increase in the ex ante certainty about when the Convention will

apply; (2) uniformity of rules at the level of international law; and (3) a more effective and efficient international regime. These benefits must be balanced against the costs of specific rules of substance, including (1) greater difficulty in garnering acceptance by all states of a specific international rule that will replace national rules (no state in the negotitations was wiling to accept a wholesale abandonment of national rules and practices that give effect to national norms and policies); (2) a natural limit to the acceptable scope of prescriptive rules that impinge on specific state interests; and (3) the inherent lack of uniformity presented by national application of international rules." Brand & Herrup, supra, at 24. Would you characterize the Hague Convention as relying primarily on one paradigm or the other? If instead the Hague Convention is a combination, does it draw on the best of both paradigms, or the worst?

3. Do you believe there is a need for a universal treaty on the recognition and enforcement of judgments? Which constituencies would benefit and which would suffer?

4. Remember that, as of this writing (November 2008), only Mexico has ratified the Hague Convention on Choice of Court Agreements. However, the U.S. Secretary of State has authorized signature, and the Commission of the European Union has recommended that the European Union join as well. Thus we expect the treaty will find traction.

Concluding Comments and Questions

1. The Internet is a palpable example of the increasing internationalization of the economy. Does an efficient global economy require an interdependence that includes an unqualified respect for foreign adjudications?

2. Should respect for the foreign judgment turn on whether the foreign court would respect a judgment if the roles were reversed? If lack of reciprocity were the only basis for denying recognition and enforcement on these facts, what is gained and what is lost by relitigation?

3. The Yahoo! hypothetical that opened this chapter is a useful platform for exploring the recognition and enforcement practices of different countries. By changing the names of one or both of the countries in that hypothetical, you can consider myriad applications.

(a) Would another EU country enforce the French judgment pursuant to the Brussels Regulation?

(b) Would Germany enforce such a judgment if the United States were the rendering court? What about courts in Ecuador or Sweden?

(c) If a court in the People's Republic of China were contemplating enforcement of the French judgment, what factors would you emphasize in your argument? How would your argument differ if you were instead seeking enforcement before a trial court in Ecuador?

4. Imagine that all of the countries' recognition practices are plotted on a continuum between minimal and universal enforcement. Which countries occupy the

extreme positions? Articulate a general characterization of national practice that applies to all—or at least to most—countries. Upon reflection of the various applications, how would you characterize national attitudes toward foreign judgments?

E. Bibliography of Additional Resources

Adrian Briggs, AGREEMENTS ON JURISDICTION AND CHOICE OF LAW (Oxford 2008)

Charles Platto & William G. Horton, (eds.), ENFORCEMENT OF FOREIGN JUDGMENTS WORLDWIDE, SECOND EDITION (Graham & Trotman 1993)

Daniel J. Smith, Invalidity of Judgment of Court of Foreign Country, 9 AM. JUR. PROOF OF FACTS 3D 687 (1990 & Supp. 2007)

Dennis Campbell (ed.), Center for International Legal Studies, 1-3 INTERNATIONAL EXECUTION AGAINST JUDGMENT DEBTORS (Ocean Publications, Inc. 2003)

Donald J. Lange, THE DOCTRINE OF RES JUDICATA IN CANADA (Butterworths 2000)

Jay M. Zitter, Annotation, Construction and Application of Uniform Foreign Money-Judgments Recognition Act, 88 ALR 5th 545 (2001)

Justin Newton, THE UNIFORM INTERPRETATION OF THE BRUSSELS AND LUGANO CONVENTIONS (Hart Publishing 2002)

Paul J. Omar (ed.), PROCEDURES TO ENFORCE FOREIGN JUDGMENTS (Ashgate Publishing Ltd. 2002) (ISBN 0-7546-2010-7)

Richard H. Kreindler & Judith L. Holdsworth (eds.), TRANSNATIONAL LITIGATION: A PRACTITIONER'S GUIDE (Oceana 1997 & Supp. 2007)

Richard H. Kreindler, TRANSNATIONAL LITIGATION: A BASIC PRIMER (Oceana 1998)

Robert C. Casad, CIVIL JUDGMENT RECOGNITION AND THE INTEGRATION OF MULTIPLE-STATE ASSOCIATIONS: CENTRAL AMERICA, THE UNITED STATES OF AMERICA, AND THE EUROPEAN ECONOMIC COMMUNITY (Kansas 1981)

Robert E. Lutz, A LAWYER'S HANDBOOK FOR ENFORCING FOREIGN JUDGMENTS IN THE UNITED STATES AND ABROAD (Cambridge 2007)

Sheldon R. Shapiro, Annotation, Valid Judgment of Court of Foreign Country as Entitled to Extraterritorial Effect in Federal District Court, 13 A.L.R. FED. 208 (1972)

Tanya J. Monestier, Foreign Judgments at Common Law: Rethinking the Enforcement Rules, 28 DALHOUSIE L.J. 163 (2005)

Wanda Ellen Wakefield, Annotation, Judgment of Court of Foreign Country as Entitled to Enforcement or Extraterritorial Effect in State Court, 13 A.L.R. 4th 1109 (1982)

CHAPTER 12

Recognition and Enforcement of Arbitral Awards

A. Introduction

Arbitration can provide a neutral and effective forum for the resolution of transnational disputes. At the conclusion of such a proceeding, arbitrators typically enter an award declaring a victor and describing the appropriate relief. Losing parties who have been ordered by arbitrators to pay some amount or to perform or discontinue some act, might voluntarily comply at that time. But when these parties fail to perform promptly, arbitrators lack the vast authority of courts to enforce their awards. So prevailing parties—and, in a sense, the whole enterprise of arbitration—turn to courts for help.

This chapter thus raises many of the issues introduced in the previous chapter. As with the recognition and enforcement of foreign judgments, each country must calibrate its jurisprudence to strike a balance between, on the one hand, lending the imprimatur of its judiciary to enforce an award rendered in a proceeding that it did not host and pursuant to procedures that are not its own and that may have applied substantive law that the courts would not have applied, and, on the other hand, undermining the efficiency gains by relitigating the matter at the enforcement stage.

Consider, first, the enforcement of arbitral awards relative to the enforcement of foreign judgments. Would you expect countries to have more, less, or the same receptivity toward enforcing arbitral awards? Are court judgments and arbitral awards fundamentally the same thing? Arbitral proceedings typically are the product of an agreement by the parties to submit the matter thereto, while the exercise of jurisdiction by a foreign court may or may not have been pursuant to a forum selection clause signed by the parties; should that influence our enforcement policies? Should the award of an arbitrator deserve the same presumption of legitimacy and correctness accorded the judicial judgments of a fellow sovereign? If foreign judgments and foreign arbitral awards are thought to fundamentally similar, then a state could simply apply the jurisprudence of the former to the latter. But if arbitral awards are different than court judgments, then that jurisprudence must be tailored accordingly.

Much of the justification for the recognition and enforcement of foreign judgments is reciprocity, to-wit: while there is little to be gained when a Mexican court seizes the assets of one of its own citizens to enforce a French judgment that favors a French plaintiff, the gain is realized later when the French courts perform likewise and enforce the Mexican judgment. Is there an analogue to reciprocity in the context of enforcing arbitral awards?

The Problem: Court-Less Sell Phones*

Telenor AS, a Norwegian telecommunications company, and Storm LLC, a company organized under the laws of Ukraine, were partners in a Ukrainian telecommunications venture to establish Kyivstar G.S.M., a cell phone provider in Ukraine. The venture ran smoothly for about a year before friction developed. Telenor claimed that Storm was failing to satisfy its obligations under the agreement and, though other ventures, was competing with Kyivstar. Telenor eventually invoked an arbitration clause in the agreement, which provided that "[a]ny and all disputes and controversies arising under, relating to or in connection with" the agreement would be resolved in arbitration. After nine months of intermittent hearings, the panel of three arbitrators unanimously found in favor of Telenor. The tribunal awarded Telenor a modest amount of damages and required Storm to take numerous steps regarding the governance of the joint venture—including amending the charter, reconstituting the board of directors, and transferring the ownership of certain shares. Storm refuses to pay the award or to make the required changes.

Storm challenges the validity of the arbitrators' award. Three months after Telenor initiated the arbitral proceeding, Storm filed a petition with a Ukrainian court, seeking a declaration that the arbitration clause was unenforceable. Under Ukrainian law, the proceedings in the Ukrainian courts did not require Telenor's participation, and in fact Telenor was not notified. One month later, on review of the shareholder agreement and after hearing from Storm's representatives, the court issued an injunction prohibiting the arbitration. At that time, Storm withdrew from the arbitral proceedings. Thus Storm did not present a defense during the final four months of hearings before the arbitrators.

Telenor seeks judicial enforcement of the arbitral award in a court outside of Ukraine.

(1) Do you think the court should enforce this award? If yes, what effect are you giving the Ukrainian law that prohibits arbitration of this matter—a law intended to protect Ukrainian citizens (like Storm) and involving a joint business venture that is taking place in the Ukraine? If no, what if the

* This hypothetical is based on *Telenor Mobile Communications AS v. Storm LLC*, 524 F.Supp.2d 332 (S.D.N.Y. 2007).

arbitrators took scrupulous care to safeguard Storm's rights and defenses after they withdrew?

(2) Should it matter, for the purpose of enforcement elsewhere, where this arbitration took place? (Ukraine, Norway, Paris, New York?)

(3) Should it matter how the arbitral panel was constituted, what they allowed by way of pleadings, pretrial motions, and discovery, which evidentiary rules they applied, whether they allowed expert witnesses, or that they conducted all hearings on a written record (i.e., without oral testimony or argument)? If you answered yes to any of these questions, are you suggesting that there is some absolute or "right" procedures that arbitral panels must offer? (What is the source of those procedures?) And if you answered no, should it matter whether the arbitral panel followed its own procedural rules?

(4) Should the court inquire into the details of the arbitral proceedings to determine whether the arbitrators made any errors of law or any factual findings that were not supported by the evidence? If yes, how carefully must they investigate? (And what if there is no transcript of the arbitral proceedings?) If no, is this because it doesn't matter if the court applies the law incorrectly or finds facts that aren't supported by evidence?

(5) Should it matter where (outside of Ukraine) the enforcing court is located? Does this enforcing court need personal jurisdiction over Storm?

B. The New York Convention

The recognition and enforcement of arbitral awards is governed principally by a 1958 treaty usually referred to as the New York Convention. Unlike virtually every other topic explored in this course, the New York Convention is applicable almost universally. Indeed, as of July 2008, 142 states were parties, including the United States, Japan, Germany, China, the United Kingdom, France, Canada, Russia, and nearly all other commercial states from Afghanistan to Zimbabwe. Naturally, then, we begin with the text of the most pertinent articles of the so-called New York Convention. Although the materials in this chapter focus primarily on American case law, the same can be said of most national court decisions in other "developed jurisdictions."*

Convention on the Recognition and Enforcement of Foreign Arbitral Awards

Opened for signature June 10, 1958

21 U.S.T. 2517, T.I.A.S. No. 6997, 330 U.N.T.S. 3

Article I

1. This Convention shall apply to the recognition and enforcement of arbitral awards made in the territory of a State other than the State where the

* Born, International Commercial Arbitration 824–830 (2d ed. 2001).

recognition and enforcement of such awards are sought, and arising out of differences between persons, whether physical or legal. It shall also apply to arbitral awards not considered as domestic awards in the State where their recognition and enforcement are sought.

2. The term "arbitral awards" shall include not only awards made by arbitrators appointed for each case but also those made by permanent arbitral bodies to which the parties have submitted.
3. When signing, ratifying or acceding to this Convention, or notifying extension under article X hereof, any State may on the basis of reciprocity declare that it will apply the Convention to the recognition and enforcement of awards made only in the territory of another Contracting State. It may also declare that it will apply the Convention only to differences arising out of legal relationships, whether contractual or not, which are considered as commercial under the national law of the State making such declaration.

Article II

1. Each Contracting State shall recognize an agreement in writing under which the parties undertake to submit to arbitration all or any differences which have arisen or which may arise between them in respect of a defined legal relationship, whether contractual or not, concerning a subject matter capable of settlement by arbitration.
2. The term "agreement in writing" shall include an arbitral clause in a contract or an arbitration agreement, signed by the parties or contained in an exchange of letters or telegrams.
3. The court of a Contracting State, when seized of an action in a matter in respect of which the parties have made an agreement within the meaning of this article, shall, at the request of one of the parties, refer the parties to arbitration, unless it finds that the said agreement is null and void, inoperative or incapable of being performed.

Article III

Each Contracting State shall recognize arbitral awards as binding and enforce them in accordance with the rules of procedure of the territory where the award is relied upon, under the conditions laid down in the following articles. There shall not be imposed substantially more onerous conditions or higher fees or charges on the recognition or enforcement of arbitral awards to which this Convention applies than are imposed on the recognition or enforcement of domestic arbitral awards.

Article IV

1. To obtain the recognition and enforcement mentioned in the preceding article, the party applying for recognition and enforcement shall, at the time of

the application, supply:

(a) The duly authenticated original award or a duly certified copy thereof;

(b) The original agreement referred to in article II or a duly certified copy thereof.

2. If the said award or agreement is not made in an official language of the country in which the award is relied upon, the party applying for recognition and enforcement of the award shall produce a translation of these documents into such language. The translation shall be certified by an official or sworn translator or by a diplomatic or consular agent.

Article V

1. Recognition and enforcement of the award may be refused, at the request of the party against whom it is invoked, only if that party furnishes to the competent authority where the recognition and enforcement is sought, proof that:

(a) The parties to the agreement referred to in article II were, under the law applicable to them, under some incapacity, or the said agreement is not valid under the law to which the parties have subjected it or, failing any indication thereon, under the law of the country where the award was made; or

(b) The party against whom the award is invoked was not given proper notice of the appointment of the arbitrator or of the arbitration proceedings or was otherwise unable to present his case; or

(c) The award deals with a difference not contemplated by or not falling within the terms of the submission to arbitration, or it contains decisions on matters beyond the scope of the submission to arbitration, provided that, if the decisions on matters submitted to arbitration can be separated from those not so submitted, that part of the award which contains decisions on matters submitted to arbitration may be recognized and enforced; or

(d) The composition of the arbitral authority or the arbitral procedure was not in accordance with the agreement of the parties, or, failing such agreement, was not in accordance with the law of the country where the arbitration took place; or

(e) The award has not yet become binding on the parties, or has been set aside or suspended by a competent authority of the country in which, or under the law of which, that award was made.

2. Recognition and enforcement of an arbitral award may also be refused if the competent authority in the country where recognition and enforcement is sought finds that:

(a) The subject matter of the difference is not capable of settlement by arbitration under the law of that country; or

(b) The recognition or enforcement of the award would be contrary to the public policy of that country....

Article VII

1. The provisions of the present Convention shall not affect the validity of multilateral or bilateral agreements concerning the recognition and enforcement of arbitral awards entered into by the contracting States nor deprive any interested party of any right he may have to avail himself of an arbitral award in the manner and to the extent allowed by the law or the treaties of the country where such award is sought to be relied upon.
2. The Geneva protocol on Arbitration Clauses of 1923 and the Geneva Convention on the Execution of Foreign Arbitral Awards of 1927 shall cease to have effect between Contracting States on their becoming bound and, to the extent that they become bound, by this Convention....

Article X

1. Any State may, at the time of signature, ratification or accession, declare that this Convention shall extend to all or any of the territories for the international relations of which it is responsible. Such a declaration shall take effect when the Convention enters into force for the State concerned
2. At any time thereafter any such extension shall be made by notification addressed to the Secretary-General of the United Nations and shall take effect as from the ninetieth day after the day of receipt by the Secretary-General of the United Nations of this notification, or as from the date of entry into force of the Convention for the State concerned, whichever is the later
3. With respect to those territories to which this Convention is not extended at the time of signature, ratification or accession, each State concerned shall consider the possibility of taking the necessary steps in order to extend the application of this Convention to such territories, subject, where necessary for constitutional reasons, to the consent of the Governments of such territories.

Comments and Questions

1. The Convention pursues three fundamental objectives: First, Article II(1) requires national courts to recognize the validity of certain arbitration agreements. Second, Article II(3) requires national courts to refer parties to arbitration when they have entered into an enforceable agreement. And, third, Articles III and V require national courts to recognize and enforce certain arbitral awards.

2. The scope of the Convention is limited to the enforcement of "foreign" arbitral awards, to-wit: either the seat of the arbitration is another State or the local award is not "domestic." The latter is subject to varying interpretations. In France, for example, an arbitration between two French nationals that takes place in France may be nondomestic if the underlying transaction had some significant international component. At the other extreme, prior to the 1996 Arbitration Act, English arbitral awards were nondomestic only if none of the litigants was British.

3. Under the terms of the Convention, what is the currency of an arbitral award that is entered on default—where, for example, one of the parties fails to appear or withdraws from the proceeding after it is underway?

4. Understand the terminology and triggers of enforcement. Assume that P and D were parties to an arbitration that took place in Country A, and the enforcement by P against D is now sought in Country E. Must P and/or D be domiciled in or organized under the laws of a contracting state? Must Country A and/or Country E be contracting states?

Most of the contracting states have made the declaration contemplated in Article I(3) demanding reciprocity. A country-by-country listing of this and other declarations for this treaty (and others) is available at http://www.uncitral.org.

5. Another declaration contemplated by Article I(3) permits contracting states to limit the scope of the Convention to differences arising out of legal relationships that are considered "commercial" under their national law. A few dozen states, including the United States and China (but not including Japan, the United Kingdom, France, Germany, or Russia), have exercised this option.

6. In most jurisdictions, the New York Convention, a treaty, must be implemented through national legislation. In the United States, that legislation is the second chapter of the Federal Arbitration Act, 9 U.S.C. §§ 201–210. Implementing legislation can impose additional requirements and introduce significant variations in actual practice regarding the relationship between the courts and arbitration.

7. The Convention requires recognition and enforcement of virtually any award rendered on the basis of fair arbitral proceedings and a binding agreement to arbitrate an arbitrable dispute. Article V outlines the seven basic exceptions to enforcement:

- a party's incapacity or the agreement's invalidity, Art. V(1)(a)
- insufficient notice, Art. V(1)(b)
- an award beyond the scope of the arbitration agreement, Art. V(1)(c)
- unauthorized or illegal arbitral procedures, Art. V(1)(d)
- a non-binding award, Art. V(1)(e)
- a non-arbitrable subject matter, Art. V(2)(a)
- an award contrary to public policy, Art. V(2)(b)

Notice that the Convention does not authorize judicial review of the merits, including under the guise of "public policy" review.

8. Both parts of Article V begin with the words "Recognition and enforcement . . . may be refused" (emphasis added). Does this mean that there is no violation of the Convention even if a court chooses to enforce an award that satisfies one of the exceptions?

9. Many attribute the great success of the Convention to the pro-enforcement bias that Article V enjoys in most courts around the world. Parsons & Whittemore is one of the leading cases in this regard (and appears in most European texts, for example), and the opinion addresses the applicability of several of the exceptions.

Parsons & Whittemore Overseas Co., Inc. v. Societe Generale de L'Industrie du Papier (Rakta)

508 F.2d 969 (2nd Cir. 1974)

J. Joseph Smith, Circuit Judge:

Parsons & Whittemore Overseas Co., Inc., (Overseas), an American corporation, appeals from the entry of summary judgment on February 25, 1974, by Judge Lloyd F. MacMahon of the Southern District of New York on the counter-claim by Societe Generale de L'Industrie du Papier (RAKTA), an Egyptian corporation, to confirm a foreign arbitral award holding Overseas liable to RAKTA for breach of contract.... Jurisdiction is based on 9 U.S.C. § 203, which empowers federal district courts to hear cases to recognize and enforce foreign arbitral awards, and 9 U.S.C. § 205, which authorizes the removal of such cases from state courts, as was accomplished in this instance. We affirm the district court's confirmation of the foreign award....

In November 1962, Overseas consented by written agreement with RAKTA to construct, start up and, for one year, manage and supervise a paperboard mill in Alexandria, Egypt. The Agency for International Development (AID), a branch of the United States State Department, would finance the project by supplying RAKTA with funds with which to purchase letters of credit in Overseas' favor. Among the contract's terms was an arbitration clause, which provided a means to settle differences arising in the course of performance, and a "force majeure" clause, which excused delay in performance due to causes beyond Overseas' reasonable capacity to control.

Work proceeded as planned until May, 1967. Then, with the Arab-Israeli Six Day War on the horizon, recurrent expressions of Egyptian hostility to Americans-nationals of the principal ally of the Israeli enemy- caused the majority of the Overseas work crew to leave Egypt. On June 6, the Egyptian government broke diplomatic ties with the United States and ordered all Americans expelled from Egypt except those who would apply and qualify for a special visa.

Having abandoned the project for the present with the construction phase near completion, Overseas notified RAKTA that it regarded this postponement as excused by the force majeure clause. RAKTA disagreed and sought damages for breach of contract. Overseas refused to settle and RAKTA, already at work on completing the performance promised by Overseas, invoked the arbitration clause. Overseas responded by calling into play the clause's option to bring a dispute directly to a three-man arbitral board governed by the rules of the International Chamber of Commerce. After several sessions in 1970, the tribunal issued a preliminary award, which recognized Overseas' force majeure defense as good only during the period from May 28 to June 30, 1967. In so limiting Overseas' defense, the arbitration court emphasized that Overseas had made no more than a perfunctory effort to secure special visas and that AID's notification that it was withdrawing financial backing did not justify Overseas' unilateral decision to abandon the project. After further hearings in 1972, the tribunal made its final award in March,

1973: Overseas was held liable to RAKTA for $312,507.45 in damages for breach of contract and $30,000 for RAKTA's costs; additionally, the arbitrators' compensation was set at $49,000, with Overseas responsible for three-fourths of the sum.

Subsequent to the final award, Overseas in the action here under review sought a declaratory judgment to prevent RAKTA from collecting the award out of a letter of credit issued in RAKTA's favor by Bank of America at Overseas' request. The letter was drawn to satisfy any "penalties" which an arbitral tribunal might assess against Overseas in the future for breach of contract. RAKTA contended that the arbitral award for damages met the letter's requirement of "penalties" and counterclaimed to confirm and enter judgment upon the foreign arbitral award. Overseas' defenses to this counterclaim, all rejected by the district court, form the principal issues for review on this appeal. Four of these defenses are derived from the express language of the applicable United Nations Convention on the Recognition and Enforcement of Foreign Arbitral Awards (Convention), 330 U.N. Treaty Ser. 38, and a fifth is arguably implicit in the Convention. These include: enforcement of the award would violate the public policy of the United States, the award represents an arbitration of matters not appropriately decided by arbitration; the tribunal denied Overseas an adequate opportunity to present its case; the award is predicated upon a resolution of issues outside the scope of contractual agreement to submit to arbitration; and the award is in manifest disregard of law....

In 1958 the Convention was adopted by 26 of the 45 states participating in the United Nations Conference on Commercial Arbitration held in New York. For the signatory state, the New York Convention superseded the Geneva Convention of 1927, 92 League of Nations Treaty Ser. 302. The 1958 Convention's basic thrust was to liberalize procedures for enforcing foreign arbitral awards: While the Geneva Convention placed the burden of proof on the party seeking enforcement of a foreign arbitral award and did not circumscribe the range of available defenses to those enumerated in the convention, the 1958 Convention clearly shifted the burden of proof to the party defending against enforcement and limited his defenses to seven set forth in Article V. See Contini, International Commercial Arbitration, 8 Am. J. Comp. L. 283, 299 (1959). Not a signatory to any prior multilateral agreement on enforcement of arbitral awards, the United States declined to sign the 1958 Convention at the outset. The United States ultimately acceded to the Convention, however, in 1970, (1970) 3 U.S.T. 2517, T.I.A.S. No. 6997, and implemented its accession with 9 U.S.C. 201–208. Under 9 U.S.C. § 208, the existing Federal Arbitration Act, 9 U.S.C. §§ 1–14, applies to the enforcement of foreign awards except to the extent to which the latter may conflict with the Convention.

A. Public Policy

Article V(2)(b) of the Convention allows the court in which enforcement of a foreign arbitral award is sought to refuse enforcement, on the defendant's motion or sua sponte, if "enforcement of the award would be contrary to the public policy of (the forum) country." The legislative history of the provision offers no certain guidelines to its construction. Its precursors in the Geneva Convention and the 1958 Convention's ad hoc committee draft extended the public policy exception to, respectively, awards contrary to "principles of the law" and awards violative of "fundamental principles of the law." In one commentator's view, the Convention's failure to include similar language signifies a narrowing of the defense. Contini, supra, 8 Am. J. Comp. L. 283 at 304. On the other hand, another noted authority in the field has seized upon this omission as indicative of an intention to broaden the defense. Quigley, Accession by the United States to the United Nations Convention on the Recognition and Enforcement of Foreign Arbitral Awards, 70 Yale L.J. 1049, 1070–71 (1961).

Perhaps more probative, however, are the inferences to be drawn from the history of the Convention as a whole. The general pro-enforcement bias informing the Convention and explaining its supersession of the Geneva Convention points toward a narrow reading of the public policy defense. An expansive construction of this defense would vitiate the Convention's basic effort to remove preexisting obstacles to enforcement. See Straus, Arbitration of Disputes between Multinational Corporations, in New Strategies for Peaceful Resolution of International Business Disputes 114–15 (1971); Digest of Proceedings of International Business Disputes Conference, April 14, 1971, in id. at 191 (remarks of Professor W. Reese). Additionally, considerations of reciprocity—considerations given express recognition in the Convention itself[4]—counsel courts to invoke the public policy defense with caution lest foreign courts frequently accept it as a defense to enforcement of arbitral awards rendered in the United States.

We conclude, therefore, that the Convention's public policy defense should be construed narrowly. Enforcement of foreign arbitral awards may be denied on this basis only where enforcement would violate the forum state's most basic notions of morality and justice. Cf. 1 Restatement Second of the Conflict of Laws 117, comment c, at 340 (1971); Loucks v. Standard Oil Co., 224 N.Y. 99, 111 (1918).

Under this view of the public policy provision in the Convention, Overseas' public policy defense may easily be dismissed. Overseas argues that various actions by United States officials subsequent to the severance of American-Egyptian relations—most particularly, AID's withdrawal of financial support for the Overseas-RAKTA contract—required Overseas, as a loyal American citizen, to abandon the project. Enforcement of an award predicated on the feasibility of Overseas' returning to work in defiance of these expressions of national policy would therefore allegedly contravene United States public policy. In equating "national" policy with United States "public" policy, the appellant quite plainly misses the mark. To read the public policy defense as a parochial device protective of national political interests would seriously undermine the Convention's utility. This provision was not meant to enshrine the vagaries of international politics under the rubric of "public policy." Rather, a circumscribed public policy doctrine was contemplated by the Convention's framers and every indication is that the United States, in acceding to the Convention, meant to subscribe to this supranational emphasis. Cf. Scherk v. Alberto-Culver Co., 417 U.S. 506 (1974).

---

[4] A Contracting State shall not be entitled to avail itself of the present Convention against other Contracting States except to the extent that it is itself bound to apply the Convention.

To deny enforcement of this award largely because of the United States' falling out with Egypt in recent years would mean converting a defense intended to be of narrow scope into a major loophole in the Convention's mechanism for enforcement. We have little hesitation, therefore, in disallowing Overseas' proposed public policy defense.

B. Non-Arbitrability

Article V(2)(a) authorizes a court to deny enforcement, on a defendant's or its own motion, of a foreign arbitral award when "the subject matter of the difference is not capable of settlement by arbitration under the law of that (the forum) country." Under this provision, a court sitting in the United States might, for example, be expected to decline enforcement of an award involving arbitration of an antitrust claim in view of domestic arbitration cases which have held that antitrust matters are entrusted to the exclusive competence of the judiciary. See, e.g., American Safety Equipment Corp. v. J.P. Maguire & Co., 391 F.2d 821 (2d Cir. 1968). On the other hand, it may well be that the special considerations and policies underlying a "truly international agreement," Scherk v. Alberto-Culver Co., supra, 417 U.S. 506 at 515, call for a narrower view of non-arbitrability in the international than the domestic context. Compare id. with Wilko v. Swan, 346 U.S. 427 (1953) (enforcement of international but not domestic, agreement to arbitrate claim based on alleged Securities Act violations.)

Resolution of Overseas' non-arbitrability argument, however, does not require us to reach such difficult distinctions between domestic and foreign awards. For Overseas' argument, that "United States foreign policy issues can hardly be placed at the mercy of foreign arbitrators 'who are charged with the execution of no public trust' and whose loyalties are to foreign interests," Brief for Appellant at 23, plainly fails to raise so substantial an issue of arbitrability. The mere fact that an issue of national interest may incidentally figure into the resolution of a breach of contract claim does not make the dispute not arbitrable. Rather, certain categories of claims may be non-arbitrable because of the special national interest vested in their resolution. Cf. American Safety Equipment Corp., supra, 391 F.2d 821 at 826–827. Furthermore, even were the test for non-arbitrability of an ad hoc nature, Overseas' situation would almost certainly not meet the standard, for Overseas grossly exaggerates the magnitude of the national interest involved in the resolution of its particular claim. Simply because acts of the United States are somehow implicated in a case one cannot conclude that the United States is vitally interested in its outcome. Finally, the Supreme Court's decision in favor of arbitrability in a case far more prominently displaying public features than the instant one, Scherk v. Alberto-Culver Co., supra, compels by analogy the conclusion that the foreign award against Overseas dealt with a subject arbitrable under United States law.

The court below was correct in denying relief to Overseas under the Convention's non-arbitrability defense to enforcement of foreign arbitral awards. There is no special national interest in judicial, rather than arbitral, resolution of the breach of contract claim underlying the award in this case.

C. Inadequate Opportunity to Present Defense

Under Article V(1)(b) of the Convention, enforcement of a foreign arbitral award may be denied if the defendant can prove that he was 'not given proper notice...or was otherwise unable to present his case.' This provision essentially sanctions the application of the forum state's standards of due process....

Overseas seeks relief under this provision for the arbitration court's refusal to delay proceedings in order to accommodate the speaking schedule of one of Overseas' witnesses, David Nes, the United States Charge d'Affairs in Egypt at the time of the Six Day War. This attempt to state a due process claim fails for several reasons. First, inability to produce one's witnesses before an arbitral tribunal is a risk inherent in an agreement to submit to arbitration. By agreeing to submit disputes to arbitration, a party relinquishes his courtroom rights—including that to subpoena witnesses—in favor of arbitration "with all of its well known advantages and drawbacks." Washington-Baltimore Newspaper Guild, Local 35 v. The Washington Post Co., 143 U.S.App.D.C. 210, 442 F.2d 1234, 1238 (1971). Secondly, the logistical problems of scheduling hearing dates convenient to parties, counsel and arbitrators scattered about the globe argues against deviating from an initially mutually agreeable time plan unless a scheduling change is truly unavoidable. In this instance, Overseas' allegedly key witness was kept from attending the hearing due to a prior commitment to lecture at an American university—hardly the type of obstacle to his presence which would require the arbitral tribunal to postpone the hearing as a matter of fundamental fairness to Overseas. Finally, Overseas cannot complain that the tribunal decided the case without considering evidence critical to its defense and within only Mr. Nes' ability to produce. In fact, the tribunal did have before it an affidavit by Mr. Nes in which he furnished, by his own account, "a good deal of the information to which I would have testified." Appendix to Brief of Appellant at 184a. Moreover, had Mr. Nes wished to furnish all the information to which he would have testified, there is every reason to believe that the arbitration tribunal would have considered that as well.

The arbitration tribunal acted within its discretion in declining to reschedule a hearing for the convenience of an Overseas witness. Overseas' due process rights under American law, rights entitled to full force under the Convention as a defense to enforcement, were in no way infringed by the tribunal's decision.

D. Arbitration in Excess of Jurisdiction

Under Article V(1)(c), one defending against enforcement of an arbitral award may prevail by proving that:

> The award deals with a difference not contemplated by or not falling within the terms of the submission to arbitration, or it contains decisions on matters beyond the scope of the submission to arbitration....

This provision tracks in more detailed form 10(d) of the Federal Arbitration Act, 9 U.S.C. 10(d), which authorizes vacating an award 'where the arbitrators exceeded their powers.' Both provisions basically allow a party to attack an award predicated upon arbitration of a subject matter not within the agreement to submit to arbitration. This defense to enforcement of a foreign award, like the others already discussed, should be construed narrowly. Once again a narrow construction would comport with the enforcement-facilitating thrust of the Convention. In addition, the case law under the similar provision of the Federal Arbitration Act strongly supports a strict reading.

In making this defense as to three components of the award, Overseas must therefore overcome a powerful presumption that the arbitral body acted within its powers. Overseas principally directs its challenge at the $185,000 awarded for loss of production. Its jurisdictional claim focuses on the provision of the contract reciting that "neither party shall have any liability for loss of production." The tribunal cannot properly be charged, however, with simply ignoring this alleged limitation on the subject matter over which its decision-making powers extended. Rather, the arbitration court interpreted the provision not to preclude jurisdiction on this matter. As in United Steelworkers of America v. Enterprise Wheel & Car Corp., supra, the court may be satisfied that the arbitrator premised the award on a construction of the contract and that it is "not apparent," 363 U.S. 593 at 598, that the scope of the submission to arbitration has been exceeded.

The appellant's attack on the $60,000 awarded for start-up expenses and $30,000 in costs cannot withstand the most cursory scrutiny. In characterizing the $60,000 as 'consequential damages' (and thus proscribed by the arbitration agreement), Overseas is again attempting to secure a reconstruction in this court of the contract- an activity wholly inconsistent with the deference due arbitral decisions on law and fact. The $30,000 in costs is equally unassailable, for the appellant's contention that this portion of the award is inconsistent with guidelines set by the International Chamber of Commerce is twice removed from reality. First of all, contrary to Overseas' representations, these guidelines (contained in the Guide to ICC Arbitration and reproduced in relevant part in Appendix to Brief of Appellant at 408a) do not require, as a pre-condition to an award of expenses, express authority for such an award in the arbitration clause. The arbitration agreement's silence on this matter, therefore, is not determinative in the case under review. Secondly, since the parties in fact complied with the Guide's advice to reach agreement on this matter prior to arbitration—i.e., the request by each for such an award for expenses amounts to tacit agreement on this point—any claim of fatal deviation from the Guide is disingenuous to say the least.

Although the Convention recognizes that an award may not be enforced where predicated on a subject matter outside the arbitrator's jurisdiction, it does not sanction second-guessing the arbitrator's construction of the parties' agreement. The appellant's attempt to invoke this defense, however, calls upon the court to ignore this limitation on its decision-making powers and usurp the arbitrator's role. The district court took a proper view of its own jurisdiction in refusing to grant relief on this ground.

E. Award in "Manifest Disregard" of Law

Both the legislative history of Article V, see supra, and the statute enacted to implement the United States' accession to the Convention[6] are strong authority for treating as exclusive the bases set forth in the Convention for vacating an award. On the other hand, the Federal Arbitration Act, specifically 9 U.S.C. § 10, has been read to include an implied defense to enforcement where the award is in "manifest disregard" of the law. Wilko v. Swan, 346 U.S. 427, 436 (1953); Saxis Steamship Co. v. Multifacs International Traders, Inc., 375 F.2d 577, 582 (2d Cir. 1967); Amicizia Societa Navegazione v. Chilean Nitrate and Iodine Sales Corp., 274 F.2d 805, 808 (2d Cir. 1960).

This case does not require us to decide, however, whether this defense stemming from dictum in Wilko, supra, obtains in the international arbitration context. For even assuming that the "manifest disregard" defense applies under the Convention, we would have no difficulty rejecting the appellant's contention that such 'manifest disregard' is in evidence here. Overseas in effect asks this court to read this defense as a license to review the record of arbitral proceedings for errors of fact or law—a role which we have emphatically declined to assume in the past and reject once again. "Extensive judicial review frustrates the basic purpose of arbitration, which is to dispose of disputes quickly and avoid the expense and delay of extended court proceedings." Saxis Steamship Co., supra, 375 F.2d 577 at 582. See also, Amicizia Societa Navegazione, supra, 274 F.2d 805 at 808.

Insofar as this defense to enforcement of awards in "manifest disregard" of law may be cognizable under the Convention, it, like the other defenses raised by the appellant, fails to provide a sound basis for vacating the foreign arbitral award. We therefore affirm the district court's confirmation of award.

Comments and Questions

1. The court appears to agree that Overseas acted in accord with U.S. national policy in withdrawing from the project. Yet Overseas' public policy defense fails. Does the court enforce the award because enforcement is not contrary to public policy or because it is exercising its discretion to enforce an arbitral award even though it is contrary to public policy? If you were authoring the court's opinion, which of those two approaches would be easier to write?

The court reads the public policy exception very narrowly. What is included among the "most basic notions of morality and justice"? Based on what set of norms is a court supposed to determine this? Think of one such notion that might arise in the context of a commercial arbitration.

2. The court also rejects the nonarbitrability challenge. Overseas argued that "United States foreign policy issues can hardly be placed at the mercy of foreign arbitrators," but the court sees this case as one involving the "breach of a

---

[6] The court shall confirm the award unless it finds one of the grounds for refusal or deferral of recognition or enforcement specified in the said Convention. 9 U.S.C. § 207.

construction contract." Are only certain causes of action nonarbitrable (e.g., antitrust à la Mitsubishi, securities à la Scherk, see Chapter 5 or are certain factual scenarios nonarbitrable even if the formal cause of action is ordinary?

3. Furthermore, the court rejects the challenge regarding Overseas' ability to make a defense. Overseas argued that the tribunal did not reschedule a hearing to accommodate one of Overseas' witnesses. The court points out that this charge hardly rises to the level of denial of due process, such as is contemplated in Article V(1)(b). What if there had been a pattern of the tribunal accommodating the scheduling requests of RAKTA and denying Overseas? What if there is reason to believe that the tribunal chose the hearing date with knowledge that Overseas' key witness would be unavailable? Are these circumstances among those "well-known advantages and drawbacks" of arbitration to which the court refers?

4. The court tells us that the arbitrators awarded damages for loss of production, yet we know that the contract provided that "[n]either party shall have any liability for loss of production." Why, then, wasn't the arbitrators' award in excess of its jurisdiction, triggering Art. V(1)(c)?

5. Overseas argued that the arbitrators' award reflected a manifest disregard of law. But this defense does not appear in the New York Convention. Nor does it appear expressly in the Federal Arbitration Act, though it has been inferred into the latter. The availability of a manifest disregard exception to foreign cases under the Convention is debated. Although 9 U.S.C. § 207 states that the grounds for refusal or deferral of recognition or enforcement specified in the Convention are exclusive, some courts (like the Second Circuit here) are reluctant to say that manifest disregard of the law can never be raised to prevent the enforcement of a foreign arbitral award.

Even if it applies, expect the manifest disregard standard to be construed very narrowly. A party seeking to establish manifest disregard of the law sufficient to warrant setting aside an arbitral award must demonstrate that the arbitrators appreciated the existence and applicability of a controlling legal rule but intentionally decided not to apply it. Understand that it is not enough that the arbitrators made an error of law in reaching their award. Rather, they must know what the law is and consciously refuse to apply it. Moreover, some courts add that that (disregarded) law must be "well defined, explicit, and clearly applicable to the case." Bear Stearns & Co. v. 1109580 Ontario, Inc., 409 F.3d 87, 90 (2d Cir. 2005).

6. The routine enforcement of arbitral awards that are the product of inadequate factfinding and/or errors of law might discourage contracting parties from choosing arbitration in the first place. Some parties have sought greater certainty by inserting language into their contracts that would permit (or require) a much more expansive review by courts. A recent decision of the U.S. Supreme Court regarding the scope of the Federal Arbitration Act, however, suggests that such language is unlikely to work as intended. See Hall Street Associates, LLC v. Mattel, Inc., 128 S. Ct. 1396 (2008) (rejecting the contractual invitation for expanded review and finding the grounds stated in the Federal Arbitration Act the exclusive bases). How would you expect the parties who prefer arbitration but also demand greater

certainty (regarding the proper application of law to fact) to respond? How might the alternative dispute resolution industry respond?

C. Judicial Review at Arbitral Seat

In the previous section, we focused on the New York Convention and the enforcement of foreign arbitral awards. Now we consider the extent to which courts in the arbitral seat can prevent foreign enforcement of that award elsewhere. In Chromalloy, a U.S. court is being asked to enforce a foreign award that has been set aside by the court in the state where it was entered. The question involves an apparent conflict between Articles V and VII of the New York Convention.

Chromalloy Aeroservices, Inc. v. Arab Republic of Egypt

939 F. Supp. 907 (D.D.C. 1996)

JUNE L. GREEN, DISTRICT JUDGE:

I. Introduction

This matter is before the Court on the Petition of Chromalloy Aeroservices, Inc., ("CAS") to Confirm an Arbitral Award, and a Motion to Dismiss that Petition filed by the Arab Republic of Egypt ("Egypt"), the defendant in the arbitration. This is a case of first impression. The Court grants Chromalloy Aeroservices' Petition to Recognize and Enforce the Arbitral Award, and denies Egypt's Motion to Dismiss, because the arbitral award in question is valid, and because Egypt's arguments against enforcement are insufficient to allow this Court to disturb the award.

II. Background

This case involves a military procurement contract between a U.S. corporation, Chromalloy Aeroservices, Inc., and the Air Force of the Arab Republic of Egypt.

On June 16, 1988, Egypt and CAS entered into a contract under which CAS agreed to provide parts, maintenance, and repair for helicopters belonging to the Egyptian Air Force. On December 2, 1991, Egypt terminated the contract by notifying CAS representatives in Egypt. On December 4, 1991, Egypt notified CAS headquarters in Texas of the termination. On December 15, 1991, CAS notified Egypt that it rejected the cancellation of the contract "and commenced arbitration proceedings on the basis of the arbitration clause contained in Article XII and Appendix E of the Contract." Egypt then drew down CAS' letters of guarantee in an amount totaling some $11,475,968.

On February 23, 1992, the parties began appointing arbitrators, and shortly thereafter, commenced a lengthy arbitration. On August 24, 1994, the arbitral panel ordered Egypt to pay to CAS the sums of $272,900 plus 5 percent interest from July 15, 1991, (interest accruing until the date of payment), and $16,940,958 plus 5 percent interest from December 15, 1991, (interest accruing until the date of payment). The panel also ordered CAS to pay to Egypt the sum of 606,920 pounds sterling [approx. (US) $185,000], plus 5 percent interest from December 15, 1991, (interest accruing until the date of payment).

On October 28, 1994, CAS applied to this Court for enforcement of the award. On November 13, 1994, Egypt filed an appeal with the Egyptian Court of Appeal, seeking nullification of the award. On March 1, 1995, Egypt filed a motion with this Court to adjourn CAS's Petition to enforce the award. On April 4, 1995, the Egyptian Court of Appeal suspended the award, and on May 5, 1995, Egypt filed a Motion in this Court to Dismiss CAS's petition to enforce the award. On December 5, 1995, Egypt's Court of Appeal at Cairo issued an order nullifying the award. (Decision of Egyptian Court of Appeal ("Egypt Ct.") at 11.) This Court held a hearing in the matter on December 12, 1995.

Egypt argues that this Court should deny CAS' Petition to Recognize and Enforce the Arbitral Award out of deference to its court. CAS argues that this Court should confirm the award because Egypt "does not present any serious argument that its court's nullification decision is consistent with the New York Convention or United States arbitration law."

III. Discussion

A. Jurisdiction

This Court has original jurisdiction under the Foreign Sovereign Immunities Act, 28 U.S.C. § 1330, et. seq. (1976), which provides in relevant part that:

> The district courts shall have original jurisdiction without regard to amount in controversy of any non-jury civil action against a foreign state as defined in section 1603(a) of this title as to any claim for relief in personam with respect to which the foreign state is not entitled to immunity... under sections 1605-1607 of this title.
>
> 28 U.S.C. § 1330(a). Both the Arab Republic of Egypt and the Egyptian Air Force are foreign states under 28 U.S.C. § 1603(a) & (b).

See Republic of Argentina v. Weltover, 504 U.S. 607, 612, n. 1 (1992).

> (a) A foreign state shall not be immune from the jurisdiction of courts of the United States... in any case—
>
> ...(6) in which the action is brought, either to enforce an agreement made by the foreign state with or for the benefit of a private party to submit to arbitration all or any differences which have arisen or which may arise between the parties with respect to a defined legal relationship, whether contractual or not, concerning a subject matter capable of settlement by arbitration under the laws of the United States, or to confirm an award made pursuant to such an agreement, if
>
> ...(B) the agreement or award is... governed by a treaty or other international agreement in force for the United States calling for the recognition and enforcement of arbitral awards.
>
> 28 U.S.C. § 1605(a) & (a)(6) & (a)(6)(B) (emphasis added).

CAS brings this action to confirm an arbitral award made pursuant to an agreement to arbitrate any and all disputes arising under a contract between itself and Egypt, a foreign state, concerning a subject matter capable of settlement by arbitration under U.S. law. See 9 U.S.C. §§ 1–14. Enforcement of the award falls under the Convention on Recognition and Enforcement of Foreign Arbitral Awards, ("Convention"), 9 U.S.C. § 202, which grants "[t]he district courts of the United States... original jurisdiction over such an action or proceeding, regardless of the amount in controversy." 9 U.S.C. § 203.

B. Chromalloy's Petition for Enforcement

A party seeking enforcement of a foreign arbitral award must apply for an order confirming the award within three years after the award is made. 9 U.S.C. § 207. The award in question was made on August 14, 1994. CAS filed a Petition to confirm the award with this Court on October 28, 1994, less than three months after the arbitral panel made the award. CAS's Petition includes a "duly certified copy" of the original award as required by Article IV(1)(a) of the Convention, translated by a duly sworn translator, as required by Article IV(2) of the Convention, as well as a duly certified copy of the original contract and arbitration clause, as required by Article IV(1)(b) of the Convention. 9 U.S.C. § 201 note. CAS's Petition is properly before this Court.

1. The Standard under the Convention

This Court must grant CAS's Petition to Recognize and Enforce the arbitral "award unless it finds one of the grounds for refusal... of recognition or enforcement of the award specified in the... Convention." 9 U.S.C. § 207. Under the Convention, "Recognition and enforcement of the award may be refused" if Egypt furnishes to this Court "proof that... [t]he award has... been set aside... by a competent authority of the country in which, or under the law of which, that award was made." Convention, Article V(1) & V(1)(e) (emphasis added), 9 U.S.C. § 201 note. In the present case, the award was made in Egypt, under the laws of Egypt, and has been nullified by the court designated by Egypt to review arbitral awards. Thus, the Court may, at its discretion, decline to enforce the award.[2]

While Article V provides a discretionary standard, Article VII of the Convention requires that, "The provisions of the present Convention shall not... deprive any interested party of any right he may have to avail himself of an arbitral award in the manner and to the extent allowed by the law... of the count[r]y where such award is sought to be relied upon." 9 U.S.C. § 201 note (emphasis added). In other words, under the Convention, CAS maintains all rights to the enforcement of this Arbitral Award that it would have in the absence of the Convention. Accordingly,

[2] The French language version of the Convention, (which the Court notes is not the version codified by Congress), emphasizes the extraordinary nature of a refusal to recognize an award: "Recognition and enforcement of the award *will not be refused* ... unless.... " (Response to Petitioner's Post-Hearing Brief, at 3) (emphasis in the original).

the Court finds that, if the Convention did not exist, the Federal Arbitration Act ("FAA") would provide CAS with a legitimate claim to enforcement of this arbitral award....

2. Examination of the Award under 9 U.S.C. § 10

Under the laws of the United States, arbitration awards are presumed to be binding, and may only be vacated by a court under very limited circumstances:

> (a) In any of the following cases the United States court in and for the district wherein the award was made may make an order vacating the award upon the application of any party to the arbitration—
> (1) Where the award was procured by corruption, fraud, or undue means.
> (2) Where there was evident partiality or corruption in the arbitrators, or either of them.
> (3) Where the arbitrators were guilty of misconduct in refusing to postpone the hearing, upon sufficient cause shown, or in refusing to hear evidence pertinent and material to the controversy; or of any other misbehavior by which the rights of any party have been prejudiced.
> (4) Where the arbitrators exceeded their powers, or so imperfectly executed them that a mutual, final, and definite award upon the subject matter submitted was not made.
>
> 9 U.S.C. § 10.[3]

An arbitral award will also be set aside if the award was made in "'manifest disregard' of the law." First Options of Chicago v. Kaplan, 514 U.S. 938, ----, 115 S.Ct. 1920, 1923 (1995). "Manifest disregard of the law may be found if [the] arbitrator[s] understood and correctly stated the law but proceeded to ignore it." Kanuth v. Prescott, Ball, & Turben, Inc., 949 F.2d 1175, 1179 (D.C. Cir. 1991).

> Plainly, this non-statutory theory of vacatur cannot empower a District Court to conduct the same de novo review of questions of law that an appellate court exercises over lower court decisions. Indeed, we have in the past held that it is clear that [manifest disregard] means more than error or misunderstanding with respect to the law.
>
> Al-Harbi v. Citibank, 85 F.3d 680, 683 (D.C. Cir. 1996) (internal citations omitted).

In Al-Harbi, "The submission agreement under which the arbitrator decided the controversy mandated that the arbitrator apply 'the procedural and substantive laws of the Southern District of New York, U.S.A.'" Id. at 684. The arbitrator in Al-Harbi ruled that a court applying the laws of New York would dismiss the case on forum non conveniens grounds. Id. Appellant argued on appeal that the arbitrator had manifestly disregarded the substantive laws of New York by disposing

[3] The Court has reviewed the voluminous submissions of the parties and finds no evidence that corruption, fraud, or undue means was used in procuring the award, or that the arbitrators exceeded their powers in any way.

of the case on procedural grounds. Id. The D.C. Circuit emphatically rejected this argument, stating that:

> Appellant's argument then depends upon the proposition that where a tribunal is to render [a] decision based on procedural and substantive law that tribunal has not only erred, but acted in manifest disregard of the law if it finds that procedural factors are dispositive of the case without then going on to consider substantive law rendered apparently moot by that procedural decision. To state that proposition is to reject it. We find no basis for vacatur. (Id.)

In the present case, the language of the arbitral award that Egypt complains of reads:

> The Arbitral tribunal considers that it does not need to decide the legal nature of the contract. It appears that the Parties rely principally for their claims and defences, on the interpretation of the contract itself and on the facts presented. Furthermore, the Arbitral tribunal holds that the legal issues in dispute are not affected by the characterization of the contract.

Like the arbitrator in Al-Harbi, the arbitrators in the present case made a procedural decision that allegedly led to a misapplication of substantive law. After considering Egypt's arguments that Egyptian administrative law should govern the contract, the majority of the arbitral panel held that it did not matter which substantive law they applied-civil or administrative. Id. At worst, this decision constitutes a mistake of law, and thus is not subject to review by this Court. See Al-Harbi, 85 F.3d at 684.

In the United States, "[W]e are well past the time when judicial suspicion of the desirability of arbitration and of the competence of arbitral tribunals inhibited the development of arbitration as an alternative means of dispute resolution." Mitsubishi Motors Corp. v. Soler Chrysler-Plymouth, Inc., 473 U.S. 614, 626–27 (1985). In Egypt, however, "[I]t is established that arbitration is an exceptional means for resolving disputes, requiring departure from the normal means of litigation before the courts, and the guarantees they afford." (Nullification Decision at 8.) Egypt's complaint that, "[T]he Arbitral Award is null under Arbitration Law,...because it is not properly 'grounded' under Egyptian law," reflects this suspicious view of arbitration, and is precisely the type of technical argument that U.S. courts are not to entertain when reviewing an arbitral award....

The Court's analysis thus far has addressed the arbitral award, and, as a matter of U.S. law, the award is proper....The Court now considers the question of whether the decision of the Egyptian court should be recognized as a valid foreign judgment.

As the Court stated earlier, this is a case of first impression. There are no reported cases in which a court of the United States has faced a situation, under the Convention, in which the court of a foreign nation has nullified an otherwise valid arbitral award. This does not mean, however, that the Court is without guidance in this case. To the contrary, more than twenty years ago, in a case involving the enforcement of an arbitration clause under the FAA, the Supreme Court held that:

> An agreement to arbitrate before a specified tribunal is, in effect, a specialized kind of forum-selection clause.... The invalidation of such an agreement... would not only allow the respondent to repudiate its solemn promise but would, as well, reflect a parochial concept that all disputes must be resolved under our laws and in our courts.
>
> Scherk v. Alberto-Culver Co., 417 U.S. 506, 519 (1974) (reh. den., 419 U.S. 885 (1974)) (citations omitted).

In Scherk, the Court forced a U.S. corporation to arbitrate a dispute arising under an international contract containing an arbitration clause. Id. 417 U.S. at 518. In so doing, the Court relied upon the FAA, but took the opportunity to comment upon the purposes of the newly acceded-to Convention:

> The delegates to the Convention voiced frequent concern that courts of signatory countries in which an agreement to arbitrate is sought to be enforced should not be permitted to decline enforcement of such agreements on the basis of parochial views of their desirability or in a manner that would diminish the mutually binding nature of the agreements.... [W]e think that this country's adoption and ratification of the Convention and the passage of Chapter 2 of the United States Arbitration Act provide strongly persuasive evidence of congressional policy consistent with the decision we reach today.
>
> Id. at n. 15.

The Court finds this argument equally persuasive in the present case, where Egypt seeks to repudiate its solemn promise to abide by the results of the arbitration.[4]

C. The Decision of Egypt's Court of Appeal

1. The Contract

...Article XII of the contract requires that the parties arbitrate all disputes that arise between them under the contract. Appendix E, which defines the terms of any arbitration, forms an integral part of the contract. The contract is unitary. Appendix E to the contract defines the "Applicable Law Court of Arbitration." The clause reads, in relevant part:

> It is... understood that both parties have irrevocably agreed to apply Egypt (sic) Laws and to choose Cairo as seat of the court of arbitration.... The decision of the said court shall be final and binding and cannot be made subject to any appeal or other recourse.

This Court may not assume that the parties intended these two sentences to contradict one another, and must preserve the meaning of both if possible.... Egypt argues that the first quoted sentence supersedes the second, and allows an appeal to

---

[4] The fact that this case concerns the enforcement of an arbitral award, rather than the enforcement of an agreement to arbitrate, makes no difference, because without the knowledge that judgment will be entered upon an award, the term "binding arbitration" becomes meaningless.

an Egyptian court. Such an interpretation, however, would vitiate the second sentence, and would ignore the plain language on the face of the contract. The Court concludes that the first sentence defines choice of law and choice of forum for the hearings of the arbitral panel. The Court further concludes that the second quoted sentence indicates the clear intent of the parties that any arbitration of a dispute arising under the contract is not to be appealed to any court. This interpretation, unlike that offered by Egypt, preserves the meaning of both sentences in a manner that is consistent with the plain language of the contract. The position of the latter sentence as the seventh and final paragraph, just before the signatures, lends credence to the view that this sentence is the final word on the arbitration question. In other words, the parties agreed to apply Egyptian Law to the arbitration, but, more important, they agreed that the arbitration ends with the decision of the arbitral panel.

2. The Decision of the Egyptian Court of Appeal

The Court has already found that the arbitral award is proper as a matter of U.S. law, and that the arbitration agreement between Egypt and CAS precluded an appeal in Egyptian courts. The Egyptian court has acted, however, and Egypt asks this Court to grant res judicata effect to that action.

The "requirements for enforcement of a foreign judgment...are that there be 'due citation' [i.e., proper service of process] and that the original claim not violate U.S. public policy." Tahan v. Hodgson, 662 F.2d 862, 864 (D.C. Cir. 1981) (citing Hilton v. Guyot, 159 U.S. 113, 202 (1895)).... The U.S. public policy in favor of final and binding arbitration of commercial disputes is unmistakable, and supported by treaty, by statute, and by case law. The Federal Arbitration Act "and the implementation of the Convention in the same year by amendment of the Federal Arbitration Act," demonstrate that there is an "emphatic federal policy in favor of arbitral dispute resolution," particularly "in the field of international commerce." Mitsubishi v. Soler Chrysler-Plymouth, 473 U.S. 614, 631 (1985) (internal citation omitted). A decision by this Court to recognize the decision of the Egyptian court would violate this clear U.S. public policy.

3. International Comity

"No nation is under an unremitting obligation to enforce foreign interests which are fundamentally prejudicial to those of the domestic forum." Laker Airways Ltd. v. Sabena, Belgian World Airlines, 731 F.2d 909, 937 (D.C. Cir. 1984). "[C]omity never obligates a national forum to ignore 'the rights of its own citizens or of other persons who are under the protection of its laws.'" Id. at 942 (quoting Hilton v. Guyot, 159 U.S. 113, 164 (1895). Egypt alleges that, "Comity is the chief doctrine of international law requiring U.S. courts to respect the decisions of competent foreign tribunals." However, comity does not and may not have the preclusive effect upon U.S. law that Egypt wishes this Court to create for it.

The Supreme Court's unanimous opinion in W.S. Kirkpatrick & Co., Inc. v. Environmental Tectonics Corp., Int'l, 493 U.S. 400, 408 (1990), defines the proper limitations of the "act of state doctrine" and, by implication, judicial comity as well. Kirkpatrick arose out of a dispute between two U.S. companies over a government construction project in Nigeria. Kirkpatrick, the losing bidder, sued Environmental Techtonics, ("ETC"), the winning bidder, alleging that ETC acquired the contract by bribing Nigerian officials in violation of U.S. law. Id. ETC argued that the act of state doctrine precluded U.S. courts from hearing the case because to do so "would impugn or question the nobility of a foreign nation's motivations," and would "result in embarrassment to the sovereign or constitute interference in the conduct of [the] foreign policy of the United States." Id. at 408, 110 S.Ct. at 706. The Supreme Court rejected this argument:

> The short of the matter is this: Courts in the United States have the power, and ordinarily the obligation, to decide cases and controversies properly presented to them. The act of state doctrine does not establish an exception for cases and controversies that may embarrass foreign governments, but merely requires that, in the process of deciding, the acts of foreign sovereigns taken within their own jurisdictions shall be deemed valid. That doctrine has no application to the present case because the validity of no foreign sovereign act is at issue.
>
> Id. at 409 (emphasis added).

Similarly, in the present case, the question is whether this Court should give res judicata effect to the decision of the Egyptian Court of Appeal, not whether that court properly decided the matter under Egyptian law.[6] Since the "act of state doctrine," as a whole, does not require U.S. courts to defer to a foreign sovereign on these facts, comity, which is but one of several "policies" that underlie the act of state "doctrine," id. at 409, does not require such deference either.

4. Choice of Law

Egypt argues that by choosing Egyptian law, and by choosing Cairo as the sight of the arbitration, CAS has for all time signed away its rights under the Convention and U.S. law. This argument is specious. When CAS agreed to the choice of law and choice of forum provisions, it waived its right to sue Egypt for breach of contract in the courts of the United States in favor of final and binding arbitration of such a dispute under the Convention. Having prevailed in the chosen forum, under the chosen law, CAS comes to this Court seeking recognition and enforcement of the award. The Convention was created for just this purpose. It is untenable to argue that by choosing arbitration under the Convention, CAS has waived rights specifically guaranteed by that same Convention.

5. Conflict between the Convention & the FAA

As a final matter, Egypt argues that, "Chromalloy's use of [A]rticle VII [to invoke the Federal Arbitration Act] contradicts the clear language of the Convention and would create an impermissible conflict under 9 U.S.C. § 208," by eliminating all consideration of Article V of the Convention. See Vimar Seguros y Reaseguros, S.A. v. M/V Sky Reefer, 515 U.S. 528, ----, 115 S.Ct. 2322, 2325 (1995) (holding

---

[6] Indeed, the Court assumes that the decision of the Court of Appeal at Cairo is proper under applicable Egyptian law.

that, "[W]hen two statutes are capable of coexistence... it is the duty of the courts, absent a clearly expressed congressional intention to the contrary, to regard each as effective"). As the Court has explained, however, Article V provides a permissive standard, under which this Court may refuse to enforce an award. Article VII, on the other hand, mandates that this Court must consider CAS' claims under applicable U.S. law.

Article VII of the Convention provides that:

> The provisions of the present Convention shall not... deprive any interested party of any right he may have to avail himself of an arbitral award in the manner and to the extent allowed by the law... of the count[r]y where such award is sought to be relied upon.
>
> 9 U.S.C. § 201 note.

Article VII does not eliminate all consideration of Article V; it merely requires that this Court protect any rights that CAS has under the domestic laws of the United States. There is no conflict between CAS' use of Article VII to invoke the FAA and the language of the Convention.

IV. Conclusion

The Court concludes that the award of the arbitral panel is valid as a matter of U.S. law. The Court further concludes that it need not grant res judicata effect to the decision of the Egyptian Court of Appeal at Cairo. Accordingly, the Court grants Chromalloy Aeroservices' Petition to Recognize and Enforce the Arbitral Award, and denies Egypt's Motion to Dismiss that Petition.

Comments and Questions

1. Does the use of the word "may" in the introductory paragraph of Article V(1) of the New York Convention really mean that the court has discretion whether or not to enforce? Do courts have discretion to enforce an award even if one of the parties received no notice? (Art. V(1)(B))

Professor Pieter Sanders, one of the principal drafters of the New York Convention as head of the Netherlands delegation to the U.N. Conference, wrote:

> The word "may" stems from the original Dutch Proposal. At the 1958 New York Conference, "may" was not discussed at all. It certainly would have provoked an interesting debate if one of the delegates had observed that "may" grants discretionary power to the enforcement judge. In my understanding "may" points to the requirement that the party against whom enforcement is sought must first have proven that one of the following grounds exists, but one or more of these grounds are proven, refusal of enforcement will follow.*

* Pieter Sanders, *Quo Vadis Arbitration: Sixty Years of Arbitration Practice* 77–78 (1999).

Earlier drafts of the Convention, however, indicated that "[r]ecognition and enforcement... shall be refused..."^ Which reading makes more sense?

One commentator has written that "[b]y limiting the ability of courts in the countries of origin to thwart enforcement abroad through the use of their nullification powers, the court's decision sends a message to business, governments, and arbitrators that they can rely on international arbitration for final and binding resolution of the merits of disputes."* But what message does it send to courts?

Jan Paulsson, a prominent practitioner, has written approvingly of the Chromalloy decision:

> It surely must be preferable to use the Article VII approach ("our law requires us to enforce this award even though your courts annulled it") rather than the Article V(1)(e) approach ("we exercise our discretion to enforce an award which your court annulled....").
>
> I propose here to demonstrate that the leading commentator on the New York Convention, Prof. van den Berg, is wrong when he contends that Article V(1)(e) of the New York Convention precludes the enforcement of an award set aside in its country of origin. The fact is that courts of a State bound by the Convention cannot violate it by enforcing a foreign award. Rather, a violation would occur if such a court were to refuse enforcement in the absence of one of the limited exceptions defined in Article V(1).
>
> This brings us to a core objective of the New York Convention: to free the international arbitral process from the domination of the law of the place of arbitration.**

If not by setting aside awards as the court of Egypt did here, how is the substantive law of Egypt to apply when arbitrators act in violation of national law? Is that domination?

2. Is Judge Green suggesting that there was something inappropriate about the Egyptian court's decision setting aside the award? If no, then what is she suggesting? If yes, on what evidence should (or was) such a determination based?

3. Judge Green also suggests that if the Convention did not exist, the Federal Arbitration Act would entitle Chromalloy to enforcement of the award. The Convention is irrelevant because it prohibits nonenforcement except for specified reasons; it does not prohibit enforcement. Is that right?

4. Six months after the decision in the Chromalloy case in the United States District Court, the Court of Appeal of Paris upheld enforcement of the same award in France. La Republique Arabe d'Egypte v. Chromalloy Aero Services, Cour d'Appel de Paris, Jan. 14, 1997, 12 Mealey's Int'l Arb. Rep. (April 1997) at B-1. Thereafter,

^ *See, e.g.*, Gary H. Sampliner, *Enforcement of Nullified Foreign Arbitral Awards*, 14 J. Int'l Arbitration No. 3, p. 141 at 147–149 (1997).

* Sampliner, *Enforcement of Foreign Arbitral Awards After Annulment in Their Country of Origin*, 11-9 Measley's Int'l Arb. Rep. 22, 28 (1996).

** Jan Paulsson, Rediscovering the New York Convention: Further Reflections on *Chromalloy*." Mealey's International Arbitration Reports No. 4 p. 20, 24 (April 1997).

the Egyptian government paid the award in full, and Judge Green's decision did not come before an appeals court in the United States.

Concluding Comments and Questions

Return to the problem that opened this chapter. Should that award be enforced? Will it be enforced?

D. Bibliography of Additional Resources

A. Tweeddale & K. Tweeddale, ARBITRATION OF COMMERCIAL DISPUTES, INTERNATIONAL AND ENGLISH LAW AND PRACTICE (Oxford 2005)

Adam Samuel, JURISDICTIONAL PROBLEMS IN INTERNATIONAL COMMERCIAL ARBITRATION: A STUDY OF BELGIAN, DUTCH, ENGLISH, FRENCH, SWEDISH, SWISS, US AND WEST GERMAN LAW (Zurich 1989)

Hans Smit, INTERNATIONAL COMMERCIAL ARBITRATION AND THE COURTS (4th ed. JurisNet 2004)

Henri C. Alvarez, David Rivkin & Neil Kaplan, MODEL LAW DECISIONS: CASES APPLYING THE UNCITRAL MODEL LAW ON INTERNATIONAL COMMERCIAL ARBITRATION (Kluwer 2003)

J.W. Rowley, ARBITRATION WORLD: JURISDICTIONAL COMPARISONS (2d ed. European Lawyer Limited 2006)

Jean-Francois Poudret & Sebastien Besson, COMPARATIVE LAW OF INTERNATIONAL ARBITRATION, SECOND EDITION (Thomson 2007)

John A. Spanogle, The Enforcement of Foreign Arbitral Awards in the U.S.—A Matter of Federal Law, 13 U.S.-MEX. L.J. 97 (2005)

Mark Wakim, Public Policy Concerns Regarding Enforcement of Foreign International Arbitral Awards in the Middle East, 21 N.Y. INT'L L. REV. 1 (2008)

Molly Steele & Michael Heinlen, Challenges to Enforcing Arbitral Awards Against Foreign States in the United States, 42 INT'L L. 87 (2008)

Robert Kovacs, Challenges to International Arbitral Awards—the French Approach, 1 VINDOBONA J. INT'L COMML. L. & ARB. 159 (2007)

Stephen M. Schwebel, INTERNATIONAL ARBITRATION: THREE SALIENT PROBLEMS (Cambridge 1987)

William W. Park, ARBITRATION OF INTERNATIONAL DISPUTES (Oxford 2006)

William W. Park, The International Currency of Arbitral Awards, 777 PRACTISING LAW INSTIT. 359 (2008)

TABLE OF CASES

INDEX